W9-BAT-489

Agricultural Information Resource Centers

AGRICULTURAL INFORMATION RESOURCE CENTERS

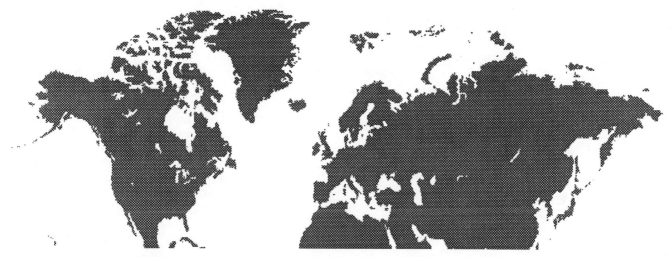

A WORLD DIRECTORY 2000

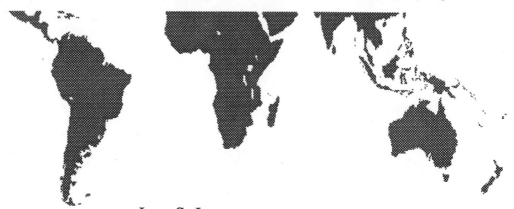

JANE S. JOHNSON
RITA C. FISHER
CAROL BOAST

TWIN FALLS, IDAHO
UNITED STATES OF AMERICA
2000

IAALD World Directory Working Group
1347 Maple Avenue
Twin Falls, ID 83301 USA

Phone: +1(208) 734-8349
Fax: +1(208) 734-8349
Email: carolr@cyberhighway.net

For his love of fun

and passionate devotion

to the international agricultural information community

this book is dedicated to

Drs. Jan van der Burg

Contents

Country Contents

The entries in the *World Directory 2000* are arranged alphabetically by the name of the country as given in the *CIA World Factbook 1999*. The name of the country used in the address portion of each entry may vary slightly from the "official country name" used in the header on which the alphabetical arrangement is based. This Country Contents can be consulted if there is any confusion about a country's "official name".

A website of the Petrotechnical Open Software Corporation was particularly useful in the decision of which country name authority list to use for this edition. Although the "official short names in English" of the International Standards Organization (ISO 3166-1 Part 1) was used in *World Directory 1995*, this list is not currently available on the Internet (see http://www.iso.ch which allows you to purchase the publication via the ISO website). The United Nations list is available on the Internet (http://www.un.org/Overview/unmember.html) but the UN list is limited to UN member countries only. Thus the World Directory Working Group decided to use as an authority the most complete and current list that is presently available on the Internet: *CIA World Factbook 1999* (http://www.odci.gov/cia/publications/factbook/country.html).

IAALD Foreword

With this 3rd edition of *Agricultural Information Resource Centers: A World Directory 2000*, the International Association of Agricultural Information Specialists (IAALD) continues to move along the strategic lines that were initially set in 1985 in Ottawa during the 7th IAALD World Congress. There a team of five U.S. agricultural information professionals offered to realize, on a voluntary basis, the update of the by then obsolete *World Directory of Agricultural Libraries & Documentation Centers* of 1960. Not only was a new version badly needed, income from the sales of the publication would serve to set up a fund to support training and educational activities in low-income countries. In the IAALD mission as laid down in the Association's 1995–2000 business plan, the following commitment was made:

"The International Association of Agricultural Information Specialists facilitates professional development of, and communication among, members of the agricultural information community worldwide. IAALD's objective is to enhance access to and use of agriculture-related information resources. To further this mission, IAALD will:
      1. promote the agricultural information profession;
      2. support professional development activities;
      3. foster collaboration;
      4. provide a platform for information exchange."

The *World Directories* have provided IAALD with a proper financial backbone to help achieve these aims and goals. Using income from the sales, IAALD has organized and financed short-term training courses on national and regional levels and supported participation of professionals from low-income countries in existing training activities. Because the Association's financial and human resources are limited, IAALD, for synergy and maximum impact, has chosen to seek collaboration with other major actors in the field, sharing expertise, knowledge and funds. IAALD therefore has set up partnerships with the Food and Agriculture Organization (FAO) of the United Nations, CAB International, the United States Department of Agriculture National Agricultural Library (USDA-NAL), the Center for Technical Assistance (CTA) of the European Community, and the U.S. Agricultural Information Network (USAIN) as well as with local institutions in the countries concerned. The following training activities have been realized:

Colombo, Sri Lanka 1994, in collaboration with the Sri Lanka Agricultural Information Network (AGRINET): Information management using micro CDS/ISIS; 20 participants

Abidjan, Côte d'Ivoire 1995, in collaboration with FAO and the Réseau Documentaire Agricole du Côte d'Ivoire (REDACI): Information management using micro CDS/ISIS; 20 participants

Dar-es-Salaam, Tanzania 1996, in collaboration with the Tanzania Commission for Science & Technology (COSTECH): Information management with special emphasis on provision of computer-based information services; 10 participants

Lesotho 1996, in collaboration with CTA and the Lesotho Library Association: Electronic communication in the field of agriculture; 30 participants

Santiago, Chile 1996, in collaboration with ALIC and the University of Santiago: Accessing research- and business-related agricultural information; 35 participants

Tucson, Arizona, USA 1997, in collaboration with USDA/NAL and USAIN: 6th US/Central & Eastern European Round Table: 30 participants

Nitra, Slovak Republic, 1998, in collaboration with FAO and NitraNet (NGO): Webmaster training course; 20 participants

Beijing, China, 1998, in collaboration with FAO and CAB International and with the China-European Union Centre for Agricultural Technology (CECAT), the Chinese Agricultural University (CAU) and the Chinese Academy of Agricultural Sciences (CAAS): Agricultural information management; 20 participants

Freising, Germany, 1999, in collaboration with the Technical Centre for Agricultural and Rural Cooperation (CTA): Role of information in Decision Making in Agricultural Research and Practice; 20 participants

Budapest, Hungary, 1999, in collaboration with FAO and the University of Gödöllö: Webmaster training course; 20 participants

Moscow, Russian Federation, 1999, in collaboration with FAO, USAIN and the Central Scientific Agricultural Library: 7th US/Central & Eastern European Round Table on stabilization and development of human resources in agricultural information systems in the Central and Eastern European territory: 60 participants

Beijing, China, 1999, in collaboration with FAO and CABI and with the China-European Union Centre for Agricultural Technology (CECAT), the Chinese Agricultural University (CAU) and the Chinese Academy of Agricultural Sciences (CAAS): Agricultural information management; 20 participants

It is on behalf of all these trainees that I wish to sincerely thank the members of the World Directory Working Group, Carol Robertson, Rita Fisher and Jane Johnson for the enormous effort that went in to the production of this magnificent directory; the above listed activities prove that their efforts are more than justified and highly appreciated.

Drs. J. van der Burg   *IAALD President 1995-2000*
                            President Elect, 2000-2005

Préface de l'IAALD

Avec cette troisième édition des *Centres de ressources d'information agricole: Répertoire mondial 2000*, l'Association internationale des spécialistes de l'information agricole (IAALD) continue de suivre la stratégie formulée à l'origine, en 1985, à Ottawa durant son septième Congrès mondial. Une équipe de cinq professionnels américains de l'information agricole y avait offert de procéder, à titre bénévole, à la mise à jour du *Répertoire mondial des bibliothèques et centres de documentation agricoles* de 1960 devenu obsolète. Il était absolument nécessaire d'élaborer une nouvelle version et, qui plus est, le produit des ventes de la publication permettrait d'établir un fonds pour appuyer des activités de formation et d'éducation dans des pays à faible revenu. Dans son Plan d'activités 1995-2000, l'Association a décrit sa mission comme suit:

"L'Association internationale des spécialistes de l'information agricole facilite le perfectionnement professionnel des membres de la communauté mondiale de l'information agricole et les encourage à communiquer entre eux. L'objectif de l'IAALD est d'améliorer l'accès aux ressources d'information touchant à l'agriculture et leur utilisation. Pour ce faire, elle s'engage à:
　　　　1. promouvoir la profession de spécialiste de l'information agricole;
　　　　2. soutenir les activités de perfectionnement professionnel;
　　　　3. encourager la collaboration;
　　　　4. fournir une plate-forme pour l'échange d'informations".

Les Répertoires mondiaux ont fourni à l'Association une assise financière propre pour pouvoir réaliser ces objectifs: avec le produit des ventes, elle a organisé et financé des stages de brève durée aux niveaux national et régional et appuyé la participation d'experts ressortissants de pays à faible revenu aux activités de formation en cours. Ses ressources financières et humaines étant limitées, l'IAALD, à des fins de synergie et pour produire un impact maximal, a choisi de tenter de collaborer avec d'autres acteurs de premier plan dans ce domaine, de partager les compétences spécialisées, les connaissances et les fonds disponibles. Pour ce faire, elle a établi des partenariats avec l'Organisation des Nations Unies pour l'alimentation et l'agriculture (FAO), les Offices agricoles du CAB- International, la Bibliothèque nationale agricole du Département de l'agriculture des Etats-Unis (USDA-NAL), le Centre d'assistance technique (CTA) de la Communauté européenne et le Réseau d'information agricole des Etats-Unis (USAIN), ainsi qu'avec des institutions locales dans les pays intéressés. Ont été entreprises les activités de formation suivantes:

Colombo, Sri Lanka, 1994, avec le concours du Réseau d'information agricole de Sri Lanka (AGRINET): Gestion de l'information en utilisant la technologie CDS/ISIS; 20 participants

Abidjan, Côte d'Ivoire, 1995, avec le concours de la FAO et du Réseau Documentaire Agricole de la Côte d'Ivoire (REDACI): Gestion de l'information en utilisant la technologie CDS/ISIS; 20 participants

Dar-es-Salaam, Tanzanie, 1996, avec le concours de la Commission tanzanienne pour la science et la technologie (Tanzania Commission for Science & Technology - COSTECH): Gestion de l'information axée sur la fourniture de services d'information automatisés; 10 participants

Lesotho, 1996, avec le concours du CTA et de l'Association des bibliothèques du Lesotho: La communication électronique dans le domaine de l'agriculture; 30 participants

Santiago, Chile 1996, avec le concours de l'ALIC et de l'Université de Santiago: Accès à l'information agricole liée à la recherche et au commerce; 35 participants Tucson, Arizona, Etats-Unis, 1997, avec le concours de l'USAIN et de l'USDA/ NAL: 6ème Table ronde Etats-Unis/Europe centrale et orientale: 30 participants

Nitra, République slovaque, 1998, avec le concours de la FAO et de NitraNet (une ONG): Cours de formation pour webmestres; 20 participants

Beijing, Chine, 1998, avec le concours de la FAO et du CAB-International et avec le Centre Chine-Union européenne de technologie agricole (CECAT), l'Université agricole chinoise (CAU) et l'Académie chinoise des sciences agronomiques (CAAS): Gestion de l'information agricole; 20 participants

Freising, Allemagne, 1999, avec le concours du Centre technique de coopération agricole et rurale (CTA): Le rôle de l'information dans la prise de décisions en recherche agricole et pratiques culturales; 20 participants

Budapest, Hongrie, 1999, avec le concours de la FAO et de l'Université de Gödöllö: Cours de formation pour webmestres; 20 participants

Moscou, Fédération de Russie, 1999, avec le concours de la FAO, de l'USAIN et de la Bibliothèque centrale d'agriculture scientifique: 7ème Table ronde Etats-Unis/ Europe centrale et orientale sur la mise en valeur des ressources humaines en systèmes d'information agricole dans les territoires d'Europe centrale et orientale: 60 participants

Beijing, Chine, 1999, avec le concours de la FAO et du CAB-International et avec le Centre Chine-Union européenne de technologie agricole (CECAT), l'Université agricole chinoise (CAU) et l'Académie chinoise des sciences agronomiques (CAAS): Gestion de l'information agricole; 20 participants

C'est au nom de tous les stagiaires que je souhaite sincèrement remercier les membres du Comité du Répertoire mondial, Carol Robertson, Rita Fisher et Jane Johnson pour l'énorme travail qu'a exigé la préparation de ce magnifique répertoire, les activités susmentionnées prouvant que leurs efforts sont plus que justifiés et très appréciés.

M. J. van der Burg   *Président de l'IAALD 1995-2000*
                          Président désigné, 2000-2005

Prefacio de la IAALD

Con la tercera edición del *Agricultural Information Resource Centers: A World Directory 2000*, la Asociación Internacional de Especialistas en Información Agrícola (IAALD) continúa dando debido cumplimiento a los objetivos y lineamientos estratégicos establecidos en Ottawa en el año de 1985, durante el 7º Congreso Mundial de la Asociación. En ese evento, un grupo de cinco especialistas en información agrícola se ofreció a actualizar el obsoleto *Directorio Mundial de Bibliotecas y Centros de Documentación Agrícola* que databa de 1960. Los participantes en el Congreso coincidieron en que la actualización del directorio era urgente, y también convinieron en que los ingresos que generara su venta se destinaran a un fondo para financiar actividades culturales y de capacitación en los países en desarrollo. En la misión que la IAALD se trazó, según se asentó en el plan de operaciones de la Asociación 1995-2000, ésta se comprometió a:

"La Asociación Internacional de Especialistas en Información Agrícola contribuirá tanto al desarrollo profesional como al intercambio de información entre los miembros de la comunidad agrícola que se dedican al manejo de información especializada en todo el mundo. El objetivo de la IAALD es mejorar tanto el acceso a la información relacionada con temas agrícolas como su uso. Para ello, la IAALD:
1. promoverá la profesión de especialista en información agrícola;
2. apoyará las actividades de desarrollo profesional;
3. promoverá la colaboración;
4. proveerá una plataforma para el intercambio de información".

Los Directorios Mundiales han respaldado económicamente a la IAALD para que ésta cumpla con sus objetivos y logre sus metas mediante el uso de los ingresos por las ventas del directorio; asimismo, la IAALD ha organizado y patrocinado cursos breves tanto en el ámbito nacional como regional y promueve la participación de profesionales de los países en desarrollo en actividades de capacitación. Dadas las restricciones de recursos tanto humanos como financieros que afronta la IAALD, ésta decidió establecer nuevas asociaciones y vínculos con otros participantes importantes en el ámbito de la información, con el propósito de intercambiar tecnología, conocimientos y recursos financieros. Hasta ahora, la IAALD ha establecido asociaciones colaborativas con la Organización de las Naciones Unidas para la Agricultura y la Alimentación (Food and Agriculture Organization, FAO), el CAB International, la Biblioteca Nacional de Agricultura del Departamento de Agricultura de los Estados Unidos (USDA-NAL por sus siglas en inglés), el Centro de Asistencia Técnica de la Comunidad Europea (Center for Technical Assistance, CTA) y la Red de Información Agrícola de los Estados Unidos (US Agricultural Information Network, USAIN), así como con instituciones nacionales de los países respectivos. A continuación se enumeran las actividades de capacitación que se han realizado:

Colombo, Sri Lanka, 1994. Conjuntamente con la Red de Información Agrícola de Sri Lanka (AGRINET): Manejo de información mediante el uso de CDS/ISIS: 20 participantes.

Abidján, Costa de Marfil. 1995. En colaboración con la FAO y la Réseau Documentaire Agricole de Costa de Marfil (REDACI). Manejo de información mediante el uso de micro CDS/ISIS: 20 participantes.

Dar-es-Salaam, Tanzania. 1966. En colaboración con la Comisión de Ciencia y Tecnología de Tanzania (Comisión for Science and Technology, COSTECH): Manejo de información con atención especial a la provisión de servicios de información basados en la computación: 10 participantes.

Lesotho, Africa del Sur. 1966. En colaboración con el CTA y la Asociación de Bibliotecas de Lesotho: La comunicación electrónica en el ámbito agrícola: 30 participantes

Santiago, Chile. 1996. En colaboración con el Centro de Información para Tierras Áridas (Arid Lands Information Center, ALIC) y la Universidad de Chile: Cómo obtener acceso a la información relacionada con la investigación y el comercio agrícola: 35 participantes

Tucson, Arizona, EEUU. 1977. En colaboración con USDA/NAL y la USAIN. 6° Mesa Redonda de Estados Unidos y Centro y Este de Europa: 30 participantes

Nitra, Eslovaquia (República Eslovaca). 1998. En colaboración con la FAO y Nitra Net, un organismo no gubernamental: Curso para administradores de sitios web: 20 participantes

Beijing, China. 1998. En colaboración con la FAO, el CAB International y el Centro de Tecnología Agrícola de la Unión Europea-China (Centre for Agricultural Technology, CECAT), la Universidad Agrícola de China (Chinese Agricultural University, CAU) y la Academia China de Ciencias Agrícolas (Chinese Academy of Agricultural Sciences, CAAS). Manejo de la información agrícola: 20 participantes

Freising, Alemania. 1999. En colaboración con el Centro Técnico para la Cooperación Agrícola y Rural (Technical Centre for Agricultural and Rural Cooperation, CTA). Función de la información en la toma de decisiones en la práctica e investigación agrícola: 20 participantes

Budapest, Hungría. 1999. En colaboración con la FAO y la Universidad de Gödöllö: Curso para administradores de sitios web: 20 participantes

Moscú, Rusia (Federación Rusa). 1999. En colaboración con la FAO, la USAIN y la Biblioteca Central de Agricultura Científica. 7ª Mesa Redonda de Estados Unidos y Centro y Este de Europa sobre la estabilización y desarrollo de los recursos humanos en los sistemas de información agrícola en la región del centro y este de Europa : 60 participantes

Beijing, China. 1999. Conjuntamente con la FAO, el CAB International, el CECAT, la CAU y la CAAS: Manejo de la información agrícola: 20 participantes

En nombre de todos los participantes de los cursos, deseo agradecer sinceramente a Carol Robertson, Rita Fisher y Jane Johnson, miembros del Equipo de Trabajo del Directorio Mundial, el enorme esfuerzo que realizaron en la organización de este extraordinario directorio. Las actividades mencionadas anteriormente demuestran su gran profesionalismo y dedicación, por lo cual les estamos sumamente agradecidos.

Dr. J. van der Burg   *Presidente de la IAALD 1995-2000*
Presidente Electo, 2000-2005

IAALD Executive Committee 2000-2005

Officers

Drs. Jan van der Burg, *President* (Netherlands)
Policy Director
Netherlands Association for Professionals in the Library,
    Information and Knowledge Sector
Boeslaan
6703 ER Wageningen, The Netherlands
Phone: +31(3174) 22820; Fax: +31(3174) 22820 Email:
    jvdburg@user.diva.nl / vdburg@euronet.nl

Ms. Pamela Q.J. Andre, *First Vice President* (USA)
Director
National Agricultural Library
10301 Baltimore Blvd.
Beltsville, MD 20705 USA
Phone: +1(301) 504-5248 Fax: +1(301) 504-7042 Email:
    pandre@nal.usda.gov

Dr. Qiaoqiao Zhang, *Second Vice President* (China)
Senior Project Officer & China Representative
CAB International
Wallingford, Oxon, OX10 8DE, UK
Phone: +44(1491) 829352 Fax: +44(1491) 833508 Email:
    q.zhang@cabi.org

Ms. Margot Bellamy, *Secretary/Treasurer* (UK)
Head, Development and Training
CAB International
Wallingford, Oxon, OX10 8DE, UK
Phone: +44(1491) 829352 Fax: +44 (1491) 833508 Email:
    m.bellamy@cabi.org

Ms. Debra L. Currie, *Editor* (USA)
Collection Manager for Agricultural and Environmental
    Sciences, Collection Management Department
North Carolina State University
NCSU Box 7111
Raleigh, NC 27695-7111, USA
Phone: +1(919) 515-7556 Fax: +1(919) 513-1108 Email:
    debbie_currie@ncsu.edu

Board Members

Mr. John Beecher (USA)
General Partner
Siler-Beecher Farms Limited Partnership of Illinois
RR2, Box 22
Moorhead, MN 56560 USA
Phone: +1(218) 236-7186 Fax: +1(218) 236-0871 Email:
    jbeecher@rrnet.com

Mr. Michal Demes (Slovakia)
Information Systems Officer
FAO SEUR, Budapest
Benczur ucta 34
1068, Budapest, Hungary
Phone: +36(1) 461-20-26 Fax: +36(1) 351-70-29 Email:
    michal.demes@fao.org
Web: http://www.fao.org/regional/seur/ai.htm

Ms. Elizabeth Doupé Goldberg (USA)
Group Director, Documentation, Information & Training
    Group
International Plant Genetic Resources Institute
Via delle Sette Chiese 142
00145 Rome, Italy
Phone: +39(6) 5189-2237/268 Fax: +39(6) 575-0309 Email:
    e.goldberg@cgiar.org
IPGRI Home Page: http://www.cgiar.org/ipgri

Ms. Jodee Kawasaki (USA)
Associate Professor
Montana State University Library
Bozeman, MT 59717-0032 USA
Phone: +1(406) 994-6549 Fax: +1(406) 994-2851 Email:
    alijk@gemini.oscs.montana.edu

Mr. Nicholas Nihad Maliha (Canada)
Manager, Library and Information Services
International Center for Agricultural Research in the Dry
    Areas (ICARDA)
PO Box 5466
Aleppo, Syria
Phone: +963(21) 2213477 Fax: (963) 21-2213490 Email:
    n.maliha@cigar.org
ICARDA Home Page: http://www.cgiar.org/icarda

Mr. Peter Walton (UK)
Agricultural Information Specialist
PO Box 16967
Suva, Fiji Islands
Phone/Fax: +679 322 443 Email: pwalton@is.com.fj

IAALD Executive Committee 1995-2000

Officers

Drs. Jan van der Burg, *President* (Netherlands)
Boeslaan 55
6703 ER Wageningen, The Netherlands
Phone: +31(8370) 22820; Fax: +31(8370) 22820; Email:
    jvdburg@user.diva.nl *or* vdburg@euronet.nl

Mr. Syed Salim Agha, *Senior Vice President* (Malaysia)
Department of Library and Information Science, KIRKHS,
International Islamic University, Malaysia
Jalan Sultan
467000 Petaling Jaya, Selangor Darul Ehsan, Malaysia
Phone: +60(3) 7903403; Fax: +60(3) 7576045; Email:
    syedsalim@iiu.edu.my

Dr. Anton Mangstl, *Junior Vice-President* (Germany)
Ltd. Wiss. Direktor, ZADI
Villchgasse 17, Postfach 20 14 15
D-5300 Bonn 2, Germany
Phone: +37(228) 9548 202; Fax: +37(228) 9548 149; Email:
    mangstl@zadi.de

Ms. Margot A. Bellamy, *Secretary/Treasurer* (UK)
Head, Training and Development, CAB International
Wallingford, Oxon OX10 8DE, United Kingdom
Phone: +44(1491) 832111; Fax: +44(1491) 833508; Email:
    m.bellamy@cabi.org

Ms. Antoinette Paris Powell, *Editor*
Director, Agriculture Library, University of Kentucky
N-24 Agricultural Science Center Building
Lexington, KY 40546-0091, USA
Phone: +1(606) 257-2758; Fax: +1(606) 323-4719; Email:
    apowell@ca.uky.edu

Board Members

Ms. Pamela André (USA)
Director, National Agricultural Library
10301 Baltimore Blvd.
Beltsville, MD 20705, USA
Phone: +1(301) 504-5248; Fax: +1(301) 504-7042; Email:
    pandre@nal.usda.gov

Mr. John W. Beecher (USA)
Director, North Dakota State University Library
Fargo, ND 58105, USA
Phone: +1(701) 237-8887; Fax: +1(701) 237-7138; Email:
    beecher@badlands.nodak.edu

Ms. Janeti L. Bombini de Moura (Brazil)
Director Tecnica, Universidad de São Paulo, Campus "Luiz
    de Queiroz", Divisão de Biblioteca e Documentacão
Av. Padua Dias, 11/151, Caixa Postal 9
Piracicaba, SP CEP 13418-900, Brazil
Phone: +55(194) 22-5913; Fax: +55(194) 33-2014; Email:
    jlbmoura@jau.esalq.usp.br

Dr. Edith Hesse (Austria)
CIMMYT Scientific Information Unit
Apartado Postal No. 6-641
06600 México, DF, México
Phone: +52(5) 726-9091 ext 2020; Fax: +52 (5) 726-7558;
    Email: ehesse@cimmyt.mx

Ms. Jodee L. Kawasaki (USA)
MSU Libraries, Montana State University
Bozeman, MT 59717-0332, USA
Phone: +1(406) 994-6549; Fax: +1(406) 994-2851; Email:
    alijk@gemini.oscs.montana.edu

Mr. Thiendou Niang (Senegal)
CTA
P.O. Box 380
6700 AA Wageningen, The Netherlands
Phone: +31(317) 467100; Fax: +31(317) 460067; Email:
    bib@cta.org

Mr. Vjacheslav Pozdnyakov (Russia)
Director, Central Scientific Agricultural Library,
International Relations Dept.
10784, GSP, Orlikov by Street, 3
Moscow, B-139, Russian Federation
Phone: +7(95) 207-89-72; Fax: +7(95) 975-26-13;
Email: dir@cnshb.msk.ru

Prof. Carol Robertson (USA)
Professor Emerita, University of Illinois
1347 Maple Ave.
Twin Falls, ID 83301, USA
Phone: +1(208) 734-8349; Fax: +1(208) 734-3983; Email:
    carolr@cyberhighway.net

Ms. Josy Sison (Philippines)
SEARCA
College, Laguna 3720, Philippines
Phone: +63(94) 3459; Fax: +63(2) 817-0598

Dr. Qiaoqiao Zhang (China)
Senior Project Officer and China Representative
CAB International
Wallingford, Oxon OX10 8DE, United Kingdom
Phone: +44(1491) 832111; Fax: +44(1491) 833508; Email:
    q.zhang@cabi.org

IAALD Chronology 1955-2000

Prepared by N. William Posnett and Antoinette Paris Powell

2000   Dakar, Senegal. 10th World Congress on Challenges Facing the Community of Agricultural Information Professionals in the Third Millennium, 24-28 January. Jan van der Burg (The Netherlands) re-elected President of IAALD.

2000   *Agricultural Information Resource Centers: A World Directory 2000* compiled by Jane S. Johnson, Rita C. Fisher and Carol (Boast) Robertson.

1999   Beijing, China. In collaboration with Food and Agriculture Organization (FAO) and CAB International (CABI) and with the China-European Union Centre for Agricultural Technology (CECAT), the Chinese Agricultural University (CAU) and the Chinese Academy of Agricultural Sciences (CAAS), IAALD holds training: Agricultural Information Management.

1999   Budapest, Hungary. In collaboration with FAO and the University of Gödöllö, IAALD holds training: Webmaster Training Course.

1999   Moscow, Russia. In collaboration with FAO, United States Agricultural Information Network (USAIN) and the Central Scientific Agricultural Library (CSAL), IAALD holds: 7th US/Central & Eastern European Round Table on Stabilization and Development of Human Resources in Agricultural Information Systems in the Central and Eastern European Territory.

1999   Freising, Germany. In collaboration with the Technical Centre for Agricultural and Rural Cooperation (CTA), IAALD holds training: Role of Information in Decision Making in Agricultural Research and Practice.

1998   Beijing, China. In collaboration with FAO and CAB International and with the China-European Union Centre for Agricultural Technology (CECAT), the Chinese Agricultural University (CAU) and the Chinese Academy of Agricultural Sciences (CAAS), IAALD holds training: Agricultural Information Management.

1998   Nitra, Slovak Republic. In collaboration with FAO and NitraNet (NGO), IAALD holds training: Webmaster.

1997   Tucson, Arizona, USA. In collaboration with United States Department of Agriculture, National Agricultural Library (USDA/NAL) and the USAIN, IAALD holds: 6th US/Central & Eastern European Round Table. IAALD World Directory Working Group presents IAALD with check for US$35,000 for the Training and Education Fund.

1996   Central and Eastern European (CEE) Chapter founded.

1996   Santiago, Chili. In collaboration with ALIC and the University of Santiago, IAALD holds training: Accessing Research- and Business-related Agricultural Information.

1996   Lesotho. In collaboration with CTA and the Lesotho Library Association, IAALD holds training: Electronic Communication in the Field of Agriculture.

1996   Dar-es-Salaam, Tanzania. In collaboration with the Tanzania Commission for Science & Technology (COSTECH), IAALD holds training: Information Management with Special Emphasis on Provision of Computer-based Information Services.

1995   Melbourne, Australia. 9th World Congress on Communicating Agricultural Information in Remote Places, 23-26 January. Jan van der Burg (The Netherlands) elected President of IAALD. IAALD World Directory Working Group presents IAALD with a check for US$45,000 for the Training and Education Fund. Stuart Hawkins, Organizer.

1995   IAALD celebrates its 40th anniversary and publishes "IAALD: 40 Years of Progress" by Harald Haendler and Antoinette Paris Powell in *Quarterly Bulletin of IAALD*, v. 40, no. 2/3.

1995   *Agricultural Information Resource Centers: A World Directory 1995* compiled by Jane S. Johnson, Rita C. Fisher and Carol (Boast) Robertson and published jointly with CTA.

1995   First IAALD training aid published with *Quarterly Bulletin of IAALD*, volume 39, number 4.

1995   Abidjan, Côte d'Ivoire. In collaboration with FAO and the Réseau Documentaire Agricole du Côte d'Ivoire (REDACI), IAALD holds training: Information Management Using Micro CDS/ISIS.

1994   Colombo, Sri Lanka. In collaboration with the Sri Lanka Agricultural Information Network (AGRINET), IAALD holds training: Information Management Using Micro CDS/ISIS.

1994   IAALD *Lettre d'Information* (newsletter of the IAALD Francophone Group) published.

1993   Bonn, Germany. European Regional Congress (Symposium) on New Information Technologies in Agriculture, 10-12 November.

1993   Rabat, Morocco. IAALD/Francophone Roundtable, 26-30 July.

1992   Bordeaux, France. IAALD/Francophone Roundtable on Information Transfer in a World Economy, 20-24 January.

1991   Beltsville, MD, USA. North American Regional Congress (Symposium) on Advances in Information Technology, 16-20 September.

1990   Budapest, Hungary. 8th World Congress on Information and the End User, 28-31 May. Joseph Howard (USA) elected President of IAALD. The IAALD General Assembly votes to change the organization name from the International Association of Agricultural Librarians and Documentalists to International Association of Agricultural Information Specialists. The acronym, IAALD, retained. Eva Herpay, Organizer.

1990   *Agricultural Information Resource Centers: A World Directory 1990* compiled by Rita C. Fisher, Julia C. Peterson, John W. Beecher, Jane S. Johnson and Carol Boast and published jointly with CTA.

1988   Kuala Lumpur, Malaysia. Asian Regional Congress on Strategic Issues in Agricultural Information, 21-24 November.

1985   Ottawa, Canada. 7th World Congress on Information for Food, 2-6 June. Ernest Mann (UK) re-elected President of IAALD.

1983   Nairobi, Kenya. African Regional Congress on Education and Training for Agricultural Library and Information Work, 7-12 March.

1980   Manila, The Philippines. 6th World Congress on Agricultural Information to Hasten Development, 3-7 March. Ernest Mann (UK) elected as President of IAALD.

1980   *Primer for Agricultural Libraries*, 2d ed. by Olga Lendvay published.

1980   *IAALD News*, an annual newsletter from the President's office, launched.

1978   Hamburg, Germany. European Regional Congress on Modern Systems and Networks on the Reliability of Information, 17-22 April.

1975   México City, México. 5th World Congress on Information Networks, 14-18 April. Philippe Aries (France) re-elected as President of IAALD.

1973 Wageningen, The Netherlands. European Regional Congress on Progress and Prospects in Agricultural Librarianship, 14-18 May.

1972 Berlin, Germany. "International Day in Cooperation with IAALD" at the GBDL Congress, 9 June.

1970 Paris, France. 4th World Congress on Acquisition and Exploitation of Information in the Fields of Food and Agriculture, 20-25 April. Philippe Aries (France) elected President of IAALD.

1968 Foster Mohrhardt resigned as President of IAALD and T.P. Loosjes (The Netherlands) filled out the term.

1967 *Primer for Agricultural Libraries* by Dorothy Parker, F.C. Hirst, T.P. Loosjes and G. Koster published.

1967 *Current Agricultural Serials Volume 2: Indexes* compiled by D.H. Boalch published.

1965 Washington, D.C. USA. 3rd World Congress on Worldwide Cooperation, 3rd-9th October. Foster Mohrhardt (USA) elected to a third term as President of IAALD.

1965 IAALD established a scholarship for travel to agricultural libraries.

1965 *Current Agricultural Serials Volume 1: Alphabetical List* compiled by D.H. Boalch published.

1963 Wye, England. European Regional Congress, 3rd-9th July.

1960 Stuttgart, Germany. 2nd World Congress, Working Conference on International Co-operation in Agricultural Librarianship and Documentation, 25-28 April. Foster Mohrhardt (USA) re-elected President of IAALD.

1960 *World Directory of Agricultural Libraries and Documentation Centres* edited by D.H. Boalch published. Funding for the Directory provided by John Deere Foundation.

1960 Stuttgart-Hohenheim, Germany. OEEC/IAALD Seminar on Agricultural Documentation, 20-23 April.

1959 Sample issue of *World Agricultural Economics Abstracts* (now *World Agricultural Economics and Rural Sociology Abstracts*) published.

1956 First issue of the *Quarterly Bulletin of IAALD* published with D.H. Boalch (United Kingdom) as editor.

1955 Ghent, Belgium. 1st World Congress on Founding of IAALD. Foster Mohrhardt (USA) elected President of IAALD. IAALD Constitution framed by Walther Gleisberg (Germany).

Acknowledgments

Agricultural Information Resource Centers: A World Directory 2000 is the culmination of a fifteen-year volunteer effort to which thousands of people contributed. The predecessors of this work include *Agricultural Information Resource Centers: A World Directory 1995*, edited by Jane S. Johnson, Rita C. Fisher, and Carol Boast and published by IAALD and CTA in 1995 (4,892 entries); *Agricultural Information Resource Centers: A World Directory 1990*, edited by Rita C. Fisher, Julia C. Peterson, John W. Beecher, Jane S. Johnson, and Carol Boast and published by IAALD and CTA in 1990 (3,971 entries) and *World Directory of Agricultural Libraries & Documentation Centres*, edited by D.H. Boalch and published by the International Association of Agricultural Librarians and Documentalists in 1960 (2,531 entries). The 1960 volume did not include postal codes; the 1990 volume added postal codes and a few telefacsimile numbers and e-mail addresses; the 1995 reveals an impressive increase in the use of e-mail, fax, and online public access catalogs; and the *World Directory 2000* adds even more emails, and access to agricultural information centers via web sites.

World Directory 2000 contains 3943 entries, 3558 or 90 % of which were updated by the institutions, country contacts or by the compilers on the Internet. In addition, 385 institutions from the *World Directory 1995* that did not respond were carried over because: (1) the institutions are known to still exist and are considered too important to omit and (2) the country of the institutions are in turmoil and we could not verify their demise or existence. This decision is our small effort to express our hope that these libraries and our colleagues will survive the political changes and surface again to participate in the world agricultural information community. The collection and organization of this information into a searchable and publishable database was accomplished with the leadership of the three editors, the ongoing sponsorship of IAALD, the past support of Centre Technique de Coopération Agricole et Rurale (CTA), and the cooperation of documentalists and librarians throughout the world. The editors want to thank everyone who took the time to fill out the form and to respond to requests for assistance. The value of *World Directory 2000* relies heavily on these individual efforts.

Funding support for the planning and development of *World Directory 2000* came directly from a single source and indirectly from numerous sources. Sales of the 1995 edition resulted in a profit. From this net income, the World Directory Working Group presented US$35,000 to IAALD President Jan van der Burg at the 1997 joint meeting with USAIN in Tucson, Arizona, USA, to use for continuing education for librarians and documentalists from developing countries. Some funds were retained to finance the preparation of this new edition. In addition, Washington State University, Jane Johnson's information consulting firm, and Boast/ Nyberg Publishing Company provided many services in kind.

IAALD president and former treasurer, Jan van der Burg, provided the WDWG with information, praise, and unwavering support. Toni Powell of the University of Kentucky and editor of the *Quarterly Bulletin of IAALD* contributed the Chronology of IAALD as well as much encouragement. Other members of the Executive Committee assisted the WDWG by providing constructive criticisms and suggestions.

Thiendou Niang, Documentalist for the Technical Centre for Agricultural and Rural Development, was instrumental in bringing CTA and IAALD together to publish *World Directory 1990* and *World Directory 1995* and provided encouragement for the 2000 edition. Josée Jehl, also from the CTA staff, helped with the translations of the frontmatter and provided the compilers with copies of regional directories from various parts of the world. Peter Walton also provided the compilers with a useful regional directory.

Help for the *World Directory 2000* came from all over the world both solicited and unsolicited. At the risk of overlooking someone, we want to thank the following individuals and institutions for providing assistance with their region of the world:

Africa

Africa: Marie-Josée Jehl, CTA, Wageningen, Netherlands

Egypt: Mrs. Omnia Moussa, Librarian, Regional Office for the Near East, Food and Agriculture Organization, Giza

Mauritius: Rosemary Ng Kee Kwong, Mauritius Sugar Industry Research Institute, Library, Reduit

Mozambique: Dr. Policarpo Matiquite, Documentation and Information Center, Eduarto Mondlane University, Maputo

Namibia: Margaret E. Ngwira, Library, University of Namibia, Windhoek

Niger: Mr. Tiemoko Issoufoi, Centre de Documentation, Agriculture Centre, Niamey

South Africa: David A. Swanepoel, Library Information Service, Onderstepoort Veterinary Institute, Onderstepoort

South Africa: Lidia Coetser, Information Specialist, Agricultural Research Council, Pretoria

Asia

Bhutan: Yuden Dorji, Assistant Research Officer, Renewable Natural Resources Research Centre, Wangduephodrang

Cambodia: Dr. Harry Nesbitt, Cambodia-IRRI-Australia Project, Phnom Penh

China: Pan Shuchun, Director, International Cooperations and Development Division, Scientech Documentation and Information Center, Chinese Academy of Agricultural Sciences, Beijing

China: Dr. Zhang Qiaoqiao, CAB International, Wallingford, UK

India: S. Srinivas, Library and Documentation Services, ICRISAT, Patacheru, Andhra Pradesh

Indonesia: Liannie K. Daywin, Center for Agricultural Library and Research Communication, Agency for Agricultural Research and Development, Bogor

Indonesia: Ms. Yuni Soeripto, Center for International Forestry Research, Bogor

Iran: Dr. Akbar Behjatnia, Martyr Dr. Mofateh Library, College of Agriculture, Shiraz University, Shiraz

Israel: Ms. Ruth Elazar, Market Research Information Center, Department of Market Research, Ministry of Agriculture, Tel Aviv

Japan: Ms. Shukuko Kamiya, Professor, Laboratory of Library Information Science, Junior College, Tokyo University of Agriculture, Tokyo

Jordan: Ms. Yusra Abu Ajamieh, Director, Abdul Hameed Shoman Public Library, Amman

Malaysia: Mrs. Kamariah Abdul Hamid, Director, Library, Universiti Putra Malaysia, UPM Serdang, Selangor Darul Ehsan

Malaysia: Mr. Syed Salim Agha, KIRKHS, Department of Library and Information Science, International Islamic University, Petaling Jaya, Selangor Darul Ehsan

Nepal: Mr. Bhola Man Singh Basnet, Division Chief, Communication, Publication and Documentation Division, Nepal Agricultural Research Council, Kathmandu

Pakistan: Ms. Shahnaz Zuberi, Directorate of Scientific Information, National Agricultural Research Centre, Islamabad

Philippines: Ms. Vilma Anday, Director, Library, University of the Philippines at Los Baños, College, Laguna

Sri Lanka: Ms. Ramya de Silva, Documentalist, International Water Management Institute, Colombo

Syria: Mr. Nicholas Maliha, Communication, Documentation and Information Service, International Center for Agricultural Research in the Dry Areas, Aleppo

Taiwan: Ms. Evelyn Tan, Librarian, Agricultural Science Information Center, Taipei

Taiwan: Wu Wan-Jiun, Director, Agricultural Science Information Center, Taipei

Thailand: Ms. Kannika Phomphunjai, Main Library (AGRIS), Kasetsart University, Bangkok

Australasia

Australia: Michael Ferres, Manager Library and Information Services, Department of Natural Resources and Environment, East Melbourne, Victoria

Fiji and Pacific Island Countries: Peter Walton, Agricultural Information Specialist, Suva

New Zealand: Ms. Sue Weddell, Library Manager, AgResearch, Invermay Agricultural Centre, Mosgiel

Europe and Central Asia

Eastern Europe: Michal Demes, Food and Agriculture Organization, Subregional Office for Central and Eastern Europe, Budapest, Hungary

Azerbaijan: Tofik Babayev, Director, Baku Scientific Training Centre, Baku

Belarus: Vladimir Golubev, Director, Belarus Agricultural Library, Minsk

Belarus: Dmitri Sivurov, Chief Engineer, Belarus Agricultural Library, Minsk

Belgium:Apolena Roubinkova, Centre de documentation - Bibliotheque, Faculté Universitaire des Sciences Agronomiques, Gembloux

Bulgaria: Ivanka Demireva

Croatia, Igor Hitrec, Central Agricultural Library, Faculty of Agriculture, University of Zagreb, Zagreb

Czech Republic: Ivo Hoch, Director, Central Agricultural and Forestry Library, Prague

Georgia: Oleg Shatberashvili, Director, TECHINFORMI, Tbilisi

Hungary: Gyory Stubnya, Director, National Technical Information Center, Budapest

Italy: Claudio T. Gnoli, Universita degli Studi di Milano, Milan

Kyrgystan: Elebes O. Rayapov, National Manager, Kyrgyz Agricultural Market Information System, Ministry of Agriculture and Water Resources, Bishkek

Latvia: Ilona Dobelniece, Director, Fundamental Library, Latvian University of Agriculture, Jelgava

Lithuania: Renata Niauriene, Director, Lithuanian Agricultural Library, Vilnius

Moldova: Ludmila Costin, Republican Agrarian Scientific Library, State Agrarian University of Moldova, Chisinau

Poland: Elzbieta Dziuk-Renik, Central Agricultural Library, Warsaw

Romania: Daniela Popa, Research Institute for Soil Science and Agrochemistry, Bucharest

Russia: Mr. Vyatcheslav G. Pozdnyakov, Director, Central Scientific Agricultural Library, Russian Academy of Agricultural Sciences, Moscow

Russia: Nina Abbakumova, Scientific Secretary, Central Scientific Agricultural Library, Russian Academy of Agricultural Sciences, Moscow

Russia: Valeria Suvorova, Central Agricultural Library, Moscow

Slovakia: Jan Simko, Deputy Director, Institute of Scientific and Technical Information for Agriculture, Nitra

Slovenia: Tomaz Bartol, Head, Slovenian National AGRIS Centre, University of Ljubljana, Ljubljana

Sweden: Jan Hagerlid, Chief Librarian, Ultuna Library, Swedish University of Agricultural Sciences Libraries, Uppsala

Ukraine: Yuri Bagrin, Coordinator of IAALD in Ukraine, Brovary

Latin America and the Caribbean

Argentina: Irene Herl, Centro de Documentación e Información Agropecuaria, Secretaria de Agricultura, Ganaderia, Pesca y Alimentación, Buenos Aires

Brazil: Janeti Bombini de Moura, Divisão de Biblioteca e Documentação, Escola Superior de Agricultura Luiz de Queiroz, Piracicaba, São Paulo

Caribbean: Mrs. M. Gosine-Boodoo, Information Centre, Caribbean Agricultural Research and Development Institute, St. Augustine, Trinidad and Tobago

Caribbean: Claudette de Freitas, Caribbean Agricultural Research and Development Institute, St. Augustine, Trinidad and Tobago

Chile: Sonia Elso, Biblioteca Central, Instituto de Investigaciones Agropecuarias, Santiago

Colombia: Lupe Bustamante A., SEICA, Centro de Investigación de la Caña de Azucar de Colombia, Cali

Costa Rica: Laura Coto, Orton Memorial Library, Interamerican Institute of Cooperation for Agriculture, Turrialba

Cuba: Ing. Marta Quiñones de Armas, National Agriculture and Forestry Library, Ministry of Agriculture, Agricultural Information Agency, Havana

Ecuador: Aida Villavicencio de Diener, Departamento de Informática y Documentación, Instituto Nacional de Investigaciones Agropecuarias, Quito

Guatemala: Udine Rolando Aragón Barrios, Centro de Documentación e Información Agrícola, Facultad de Agronomía, Universidad de San Carlos de Guatemala, Guatemala

Mexico: Margarita Sandoval Guerro, Instituto Nacional de Investigaciones Forestales y Agropecuarias, México, D.F.

Panama: Vielka Chang-Yau, Library, Smithsonian Tropical Research Institute, Balboa

Peru: Ms. Cecelia Ferreyra Bossio, Librarian, International Potato Center, Lima

Venezuela: Julia de Brito, Gerencia de Información y Documentación, Fondo Nacional de Investigaciones Agropecuarias, Maracay

United States of America

Alabama: Susan Flood, Reference Librarian, Auburn University Libraries, Auburn

Alaska: James H. Anderson, BioSciences Librarian, University of Alaska, Fairbanks

Arizona: Carla Long Casler, Arid Lands Information Center, Tucson

Arkansas: Luti Salibury, Librarian/Professor, Mullins Library, University of Arkansas, Fayetteville

California: Richard W. Vierich, Sciences Reference Librarian/Agricultural Specialist, Science Library, University of California, Riverside

California: Susan Casement, Agricultural and Resource Economics Library, University of California, Davis

California: Norma Kobzina, Marian Koshland Bioscience and Natural Resources Library, University of California, Berkeley

Delaware: Frederick B. Getze, Agriculture Library, University of Delaware, Newark

Florida: Anita L. Battiste, Marston Science Library, University of Florida, Gainesville

Georgia: M. Kay Mowery, Branch Librarian, College of Agricultural and Environmental Sciences, University of Georgia, Griffin

Hawaii: Eileen Herring, Science and Technology Reference, University of Hawaii at Manoa Library, Honolulu

Idaho: Donna Hanson, Science Librarian, University of Idaho Library, Moscow

Illinois: Nancy Duran, Science Reference Librarian, Milner Library, Illinois State University, Normal

Indiana: Katie Clark, Life Sciences Library, Purdue University, West Lafayette

Iowa: Lorrie Knox, Iowa State University Library, Ames

Kansas: Diana Farmer, Science Bibliographer, Love Science Library, Kansas State University, Manhattan

Kentucky: Pat Wilson, Shaver Engineering Library, University of Kentucky, Lexington

Maryland: Alesia McManus, Manager, Science and Technology Services Team, McKeldin Library, University of Maryland, College Park

Michigan: Anita Ezzo, Main Library, Michigan State University, East Lansing

Minnesota: JoAnn DeVries, St. Paul Campus Libraries, University of Minnesota, St. Paul

Mississippi: Jessie Burks Arnold, Director, John Dewey Boyd Library, Alcorn State University, Alborn State

Montana: Jodee Kawasaki, Montana State University Library, Bozeman

Nebraska: Rebecca Bernthal, C.Y. Thompson Library, University of Nebraska, Lincoln

New Mexico: Tim McKimmie, Agriculture and Science Librarian, University Library, New Mexico State University, Las Cruces

New York: Mary Ochs, Albert R. Mann Library, Cornell University, Ithaca

North Carolina: Debbie Currie, North Carolina State University Libraries, Raleigh

North Dakota: Kathie Richardson, North Dakota State University Libraries, Fargo

Ohio: Constance J. Britton, Librarian, Ohio Agricultural Research and Development Center, The Ohio State University, Wooster

Oregon: Linda Maddux, Mark O. Hatfield Library, Wilamette University, Salem

Pennsylvania: Helen Smith, Agricultural Sciences Librarian, Life Sciences Library, Pennsylvania State University, University Park

Rhode Island: Larry Kelland, University of Rhode Island Library, Kingston

South Dakota: Nancy Marshall, Hilton M. Briggs Library, South Dakota State University, Brookings

Tennessee: Ann Viera, Agriculture-Veterinary Medicine Library, University of Tennessee, Knoxville

Tennessee: Sandra Leach, Agriculture-Veterinary Medicine Library, University of Tennessee, Knoxville

Texas: Rob McGeachin, Head and Director for Business and Agriculture Services, West Campus Library, Texas A & M University, College Station

Utah: Anne Hedrich, Science and Technology Library, Utah State University, Logan

Virginia: Margaret C. Merrill, College Librarian for Agriculture and Life Sciences, Virginia Polytechnic Institute and State University, Blacksburg

West Virginia: Natalie Rutledge, Coordinator Reference Services, Evansdale Library, West Virginia University, Morgantown

Wisconsin: Jean Gilbertson, Library Directory, Steenbock Memorial Library, University of Wisconsin, Madison

Each member of the IAALD Directory Working Group wishes to thank the individuals and organizations who helped with their *World Directory 2000* efforts:

The support provided by family, friends, and colleagues has been invaluable in bringing this edition to fruition. My appreciation is extended to my tennis comrades who banded together to help fold, stuff and stamp the update forms for mailing during multiple sessions. They made this task enjoyable, rather than tedious.

I wish to express my sincerest gratitude to all my country contacts from Asia, South America and the Caribbean, Australia, New Zealand and the Pacific Ocean island countries. Their efforts have provided more complete and extensive data than we could have collected purely from mail responses. Many of the contacts I have never met personally, but feel I have known them for a long time as they have been so generous with their time to help gather information and willingness to respond to my queries.

Finally, I must give due credit to my husband, Sam, who has encouraged me throughout the 12 years of working on the various editions of this directory. He has always provided me with the necessary support to keep going during the times of greatest frustration.

As this edition goes to the printers, I look forward to the next era of my life being an active "Grandma Jane" for my two grandsons, Sequojah and Isaijah, as they grow up near by in sunny Tucson.

Jane S. Johnson
Tucson, Arizona
January 2000

It is somewhat startling to look back to the IAALD 7th World Congress in Ottawa, Canada, as the beginning of the "modern era" of the World Directory. At that conference I first met Carol Boast Robertson as a co-volunteer to develop and publish the 1990 edition, along with Julia Peterson and John Beecher. During that 5-year period Jane Johnson came on board but I did not meet her until work had begun on the 1995 edition. I feel that the three of us have developed a special bond and friendship during these many years of IAALD activity that I look forward to continuing into the future. I want to particularly thank these two colleagues for their support and patience through some very trying times.

Among other major personal changes in the last couple of years are my retirement from Washington State University (WSU), the sale of our home of 20+ years, and the recent move my husband and I made into a recreational vehicle as our only residence. We are excitedly looking forward to extensive travel in North America, with some international trips interspersed.

I want to acknowledge the support I have received from WSU over the years of this publishing endeavor. The important assistance of the many liaisons in the different countries cannot be over emphasized. And, finally, my husband, Don, in particular, and my children, Jennifer and Gregory, must be thanked. They understood when no one else could.

Rita C. Fisher
United States
January 2000

Since retiring from the University of Illinois I have been busier than ever with gardening, ranching, volunteer work, and new grandchildren Shelby Lyria Boast and Carsten John

Boast. Thus I want to thank Jane and Rita for taking over my parts of the world and leaving me to deal with just finances, logistics, communications, publicity, and sales. Colleagues Rita, Jane, and Toni Powell have been long-time IAALD friends and great travelling companions. As I drift further into my retirement I will miss their good company. Jan van der Burg, Thiendou Niang, and Pam Andre have also been great supporters of this effort. My husband Thomas Robertson and my friend and business partner Cheryl Rae Nyberg were patient and supportive. Four-legged friend Lulu forced me to take needed breaks from staring at the computer! And new friend and colleague Patrick W. Brennen of the Noble Foundation, Inc., has made retirement easier for all of us by taking over the major responsibility for the 2005 edition of the World Directory.

Carol Boast Robertson
Twin Falls, Idaho
January 2000

In addition to collecting and editing the data for the *World Directory 2000*, the editors are also marketing the book. All profits from these sales will be used to sponsor continuing education for members of IAALD from developing nations. Donors are being sought to subsidize distribution of *World Directory 2000* to library and information centers in developing nations.

Carol Boast Robertson Phone: +1(208) 734-8349
1347 Maple Avenue Fax: +1 (208) 734-3983
Twin Falls, ID 83301 USA
Email: carolr@cyberhighway.net
          jsjohnson1@aol.com
                  fisher@gocougs.wsu.edu

Introduction

Agricultural Information Resource Centers: A World Directory 2000 includes 3943 information resource centers from 189 countries that have agriculture-related collections and/or information services. Agriculture is treated in the broadest sense ranging from production agriculture to basic research and including related sciences and social sciences. Broad topics covered are: Comprehensive; Agribusiness; Agricultural Development; Agricultural Economics; Agricultural Engineering; Agriculture (Tropics); Animal Husbandry; Crops; Biotechnology; Education/Extension; Entomology; Farming; Fisheries; Food Sciences; Forestry; Horticulture; Plant Pathology; Plants; Soils; Veterinary Medicine; and Water Resources. A glimpse in the Subject Index, however, reveals specialized topics such as Animal Welfare; Gene Banks; Groundwater; Honeybees; Mustang Horse; Remote Sensing; Sunflowers; Tenure Systems; and Wildlife Management. A major institution that indicates "Comprehensive" subject coverage is listed only under "Comprehensive" at the beginning of the subject index unless "Subject Specializations" were noted.

World Directory 2000 is organized alphabetically first by country and then by city and parent institution except for Australia, Brazil, Canada, China, Japan and the United States. These countries are divided by state or province and then by city and parent institution. An index to cities in these four countries is provided in the back. The Country Table of Contents is located in the front matter and includes numerous cross references from variant names and an explanation of how we arrived at the decision to use the *CIA World Factbook 1999* (http://www.odci.gov/cia/publications/factbook/country.html) as an authority for the names of countries, protectorates, etc. After the 1990 edition we saw the unification of Germany and the breakup of the Soviet Socialist Republic. Many of these changes were reflected in the 1995 edition and more changes are included in the 2000 edition. Country names are still changing at a fast rate so the *World Directory 2000* is already out of date.

In addition to the Country Contents and the City Index for Selected Countries, the Institution Index and the Subject Index provide numerous access points to the directory entries. The Institution Index includes current, former, and variant names of the parent institutions and the information resource centers in English and/or in the language of the country. The name of the country in which the institution is located follows in parentheses.

The Subject Index is also broken down by country and, where there are one hundred or more numbers under a given subject, also by state or province for the six countries so divided. Subject headings are taken from the CAB Thesaurus (1998), the Library of Congress Subject Headings (11th edition, 1988), and from natural language. Whenever possible, the subject terms used by the respondents to describe the subjects and subject specializations of their collections/services were used. Over 1650 subjects and over 650 cross references are included in the Subject Index. In all of the indexes, numbers refer to entry numbers not page numbers.

Although the majority of the information in *World Directory 2000* was obtained directly from questionnaires filled out at the institutions, the sections for some countries were expanded from other directories made available to us. Other directories from which information was gleaned for the *World Directory 2000* include:

> *Directory of Agricultural Information Resource Centres in the Pacific, 1996* (1996) by Peter Walton. Suva, Fiji, Pacific Regional Agricultural Programme.

> *Directory of Chinese Agricultural and Related Organizations* (1994) edited by Zhang Qiaoqiao. Wallingford, UK, CAB International.

> *Projet d'un Répertoire des Sources d'Information Agricole en Centrafrique* (n.d.) by FranJois Dode, Université de Bangui, Institut Supérieur Developpement Rural de M'Baiki, Bangui, République Centrafricaine.

> *A Directory of National Agricultural Information Centres in Lesotho* (1997) by Joel Talelo Malelu, Librarian, Lesotho Agricultural College. [A project assignment by ICRAF/CTA as the final part of a course in "Management of Agricultural Information Services" held in Addis Ababa, Ethiopia, in 1997 October 27 - November 14].

Les Sources d'Information Agricole: Repertoire National Mali (Mai 1997) by Boubacar Diaw. Ministère du Développement Rural et de l'Environnement, Institute d'Economie Rurale, Direction Scientifique, Service de Documentation, d'Information et de Publication and Centre Régional de la Recherche Agronomique - Sikasso, Centre de Documentation.

Répertoire des Sources d'Information Agricole au Niger (Mai 1997). Université Abdou Moumouni, Faculté d'Agronomie, Niamey, Niger. [Le présent répertoire est la finalité d'un Séminaire qui s'est tenu à Ouagadougou à l'IPD/AOS au Burkina-Faso à l'initiative du CTA du 11 au 29 Novembre 1996].

Répertoire des Sources d'Information sur l'Agriculture au Togo (n.d.) By Kété Félix Avoyi, Université du Bénin, Division Sciences Exactes - Appliquées et Agronomie. [CTA is in bold letters at the top of the page.] [Ce document est une application des enseignements recus lors du séminaire sur la gestion des services d'information agricole en Afrique Occidentale et Centrale tenu à Ouagadougou du 11 au 29 novembre 1996].

In addition, the compilers spent many hours searching the Internet to obtain, confirm, and update information in the entries. Finally, an attempt was made to have a contact person in each part of the world review the entries and identify omissions. In some cases, skeleton entries were added for institutions recommended by these contact people. Although in the past editions, every attempt to err only by over inclusion was made, one goal of this edition was to be more selective and delete institutions from which no communication has been received within the last ten years. Some important resources undoubtedly have been overlooked; please write or email one of the compilers with information if you know of such institutions. Although all three compilers are retiring with this edition, they will pass the new information on to the new compilers.

The *World Directory 2000* entries require little explanation. Each institution was asked to provide the following: name, former names, and acronyms of the parent institution; name, former names, and acronyms of the information resource center; type of institution; postal address; actual location if not clear from the postal address; name and phone of the head of the library/information center; phone number for reference questions; electronic mail, telex, and telefacsimilie numbers; number of professional and other staff; size of the collection; number of journal subscriptions; main language of the collections and services; Internet addresses (URL) of the online public access catalog (OPAC) and the institution; Ariel IP for transferring documents electronically; subjects and special strengths of the collections and/or services; unique inhouse databases; databases on CD-ROM; loan, service and photocopy policies; and networks or cooperative systems. English is the primary language of the directory although institution names in the official language of the country were also sought. In some cases the respondents provided names only in the language of the country, and with the exception of Latin America, no attempt was made to translate the names into English.

The *World Directory 2000* contains 2118 URL's for institutions and 659 for OPAC's. To save space, the "http://" has been dropped from each URL but the user should be aware that most browsers require "http://" preceding the address. Telenet addresses are marked as such and do not require the "http://". All URL's were checked and were working in late 1999 but as with all information sources, they may be out of date by press time. In addition a few operating systems are case sensitive so the inclusion of some capital letters in the URL's is intentional.

The initial data for the 2000 edition were collected in 1998/99 and thus some of the information is out of date. If an information resource center cannot be traced through the information provided in its entry, contacting a nearby institution may prove effective. Some other limitations in the data include lack of standardization for indicating size of collections; . To save space, acronyms were used for the databases, database vendors, and networks and the spelled out name or description is given in the Appendix of Acronyms and Abbreviations at the back. No attempt was made to verify or enhance the information in this appendix.

The database from which *World Directory 2000* was printed is continually being updated. Users of the *World Directory 2000* are invited to inquire for or provide specific current information by writing IAALD World Directory Working Group at 1347 Maple Avenue, Twin Falls, ID 83301 or emailing carolr@cyberhighway.net.

World Directory

Albania

1   **Tirana, Albania**
Committee for Science and Technology
Centre for Scientific and Technical Information
   and Documentation
Rr. Leke Dukagjini No. 5
Tirana

Networks: AGRIS

Algeria

♦2   **Algiers, Algeria**
Institut National Agronomique
Département de Documentation et Information
Hacène Badi, El Harrach
Algiers
Fax: +213(2) 759547

Founded: 1905 **Type:** Academic **Head:** Mrs. Rosa Issolah
Phone: +213(2) 761987/9 ext 343 or 324 **Staff:** 21 Prof. 6
Other **Holdings:** 60,000 books 450 journals **Subjects:** Agricultural Engineering, Forestry, Botany, Rural Economy, Rural Sociology, Zoology **Databases Used:** Agris **Loan:** Internationally **Service:** Inhouse **Photocopy:** Yes

3   **Algiers, Algeria**
Ministère de l'Agriculture, Institut National de la
   Vulgarisation Agricole (MAP, INVA)
Centre National de Documentation Agricole
   (CNDA)
BP no 42 - Saïd Hamdine
Bir Mourad Raïs
Algiers 16012
Phone: +213(2) 543413/17 **Fax:** +213(2) 650765 **Email:** inva@ist.cerist.dz

Founded: 1984 **Type:** Government **Holdings:** 20,000 books
25 journals **Subjects:** Agricultural Development, Agricultural Economics **Networks:** AGRIS **Photocopy:** Yes

♦4   **Algiers, Algeria**
United Nations (UN)
Information Centre (IC)
BP 823 Alger-Gare
Alger
Algiers 16000
Location: 19, Avenue Chahid Mustapha El-Ouali Sayed
Fax: +213(2) 745082

Non-English Name: Organisation des Nations-Unies
(ONU), Centre d'Information **Founded:** 1963 **Type:** International **Head:** M. Ouassini Lahrache *Phone:* +213(2)
744628 **Staff:** 3 Other **Holdings:** 6,000 books 80 journals
Language of Collection/Services: French / French, Arabic,
English **Subjects:** Agricultural Development, Agricultural

Economics, Fisheries, Food Sciences, Forestry, Soil Science,
Water Resources **Loan:** Inhouse **Photocopy:** Yes

5   **Annaba, Algeria**
Université de Annaba
Bibliothèque Universitaire Centrale
Boîte Postal 12
Route El Hadjar
Annaba
Phone: +213(8) 878907 **Fax:** +213(8) 872436

Founded: 1975 **Type:** Government **Head:** Buloacem Farah
Staff: 10 Prof. 23 Other **Holdings:** 200 books **Subjects:**
Food Technology, Veterinary Science **Loan:** Internationally
Photocopy: Yes

American Samoa

6   **Pago Pago, American Samoa**
American Samoa Community College, Land Grant
   Program
Library
PO Box 5319
Pago Pago 96799
Phone: +684 699-1394 **Fax:** +684 699-4595 **Email:** ftm@
elele.peacesat.hawaii.edu

Founded: 1996 **Type:** Academic **Head:** Ms. Fagasa Mauga
Staff: 1 Other

Angola

7   **Luanda, Angola**
Ministério da Agricultura e Desenvolvimento
   Rural
Centro da Documentação e de Difusão Tecnicas
CP 527
Luanda
Location: Avenue Comandante Jika **Phone:** 323081

Founded: 1977 **Type:** Government **Head:** Noé Justino
Phone: 352798 **Staff:** 20 Prof. 13 Other **Holdings:** 430,200
books 10,000 journals **Subjects:** Animal Husbandry, Silviculture **Networks:** AGRIS

Antigua and Barbuda

8   **St. Johns, Antigua and Barbuda**
Ministry of Agriculture, Fisheries, Commerce,
   Industry and Consumer Affairs
Documentation Centre
Nevis and Redcliffe Streets
PO Box 1282
St. Johns
Fax: +1(809) 462-6104

Type: Government **Holdings:** 160 books 26 journals **Subjects:** Agricultural Development, Agricultural Economics, Animal Production, Crop Production, Plant Protection, Rural Sociology, Stored Products **Networks:** AGRIS

♦9   **St. John's, Antigua and Barbuda**
        Organisation of Eastern Caribbean States,
            Economic Affairs Secretariat (OECS, EAS)
        Documentation Centre
        PO Box 822
        St. John's
Location: Lower High & Long Streets **Phone:** +1(809) 462-3500 **Fax:** +1(809) 462-1537

Former Name: Eastern Caribbean Common Market (ECCM) **Type:** Government **Head:** Sue Evan-Wong *Phone:* +1(809) 462-3500 **Staff:** 1.5 Prof. 1 Other **Language of Collection/Services:** English / English **Subjects:** Diversification, Tourism **Specializations:** Sustainability **Loan:** Inhouse **Service:** Regionally **Photocopy:** Yes

Argentina

10   **Anguil, Argentina**
        National Institute of Agricultural Technology,
            Agricultural Experiment Station of Anguil
        Library
        CC No. 11
        6326 Anguil, La Pampa
Location: Ruta Nacional nro. 5, Km 580 **Phone:** +54 (2954) 495057 **Fax:** +54(2954) 495057 **Email:** tuya@ eanguil.inta.gov.ar **WWW:** www.inta.gov.ar

Non-English Name: Instituto Nacional de Tecnología Agropecuaria, Estación Experimental Agropecuaria Anguil (INTA, EEA Anguil), Biblioteca **Founded:** 1954 **Type:** Government **Head:** Osvaldo Hugo Tuya *Phone:* +54(2954) 495057 *Email:* tuya@eanguil.inta.gov.ar **Staff:** 1 Prof. 1 Other **Holdings:** 4,000 books 100 journals **Language of Collection/Services:** English **Subjects:** Agricultural Economics, Animal Husbandry, Crops, Entomology, Farming, Plant Pathology, Plants, Soil Science, Veterinary Medicine **Specializations:** Animal Husbandry, Forage Legumes, Soil Conservation, Livestock, Soil Management **Networks:** CCPPAA **Databases Used:** Agricola; Agris; CABCD **Loan:** In country **Service:** In country **Photocopy:** Yes

11   **Bahía Blanca, Argentina**
        South National University, Department of
            Agronomy (SNU)
        Agronomic Sciences Library
        Complejo Palihu
        CC 51
        8000 Bahía Blanca, Buenos Aires
Phone: +54(291) 459-5112 **Fax:** +54(291) 459-5127 **Email:** squillac@criba.edu.ar **WWW:** www.criba.edu.ar/ agronomia

Non-English Name: Universidad Nacional del Sur, Departamento de Agronomía (UNS), Biblioteca de Ciencias Agrarias (BCA) **Founded:** 1980 **Type:** Academic **Head:** Prof. Antonio M. Squillace *Phone:* +54(291) 459-5112

Email: squillac@criba.edu.ar **Staff:** 1 Prof. 4 Other **Holdings:** 6,400 books 49 journals **Language of Collection/ Services:** English/Spanish **Subjects:** Agricultural Economics, Agricultural Development, Agricultural Engineering, Animal Husbandry, Biology, Biotechnology, Natural Resources, Soil Science **Networks:** CCPP (CAICYT); CCPPAA (INTA); SISB **Databases Used:** CABCD; Life Science Collection **Loan:** Inhouse **Service:** Internationally **Photocopy:** Yes

12   **Balcarce, Argentina**
        National Institute of Agricultural Technology,
            Agricultural Experiment Station of Balcarce,
            National University of Mar del Plata, College
            of Agriculture
        Library
        Casilla de Correo 276
        7620 Balcarce, Buenos Aires
Location: Ruta 226 Km 74.5 **Phone:** +54(2266) 422040, 422042 **Fax:** +54(2266) 421756 **Email:** bibbal@inta.gov. ar **WWW:** www.inta.gov.ar/crbsass/ balcarce **OPAC:** www.inta.gov.ar/crbsass/balcarce/ biblio.htm

Non-English Name: Instituto Nacional de Tecnología Agropecuaria, Estación Experimental Agropecuaria Balcarce, Universidad Nacional de Mar del Plata, Facultad de Ciencias Agrarias (INTA), Biblioteca **Founded:** 1958 **Type:** Academic Government **Head:** Alicia di Bastiano *Phone:* +54(2266) 422040/2 *Email:* abutzo@inta.gov.ar **Staff:** 3 Prof. 3 Other **Holdings:** 11,500 books 104 journals **Language of Collection/Services:** Spanish, English / Spanish, English **Subjects:** Agribusiness, Agricultural Development, Agricultural Economics, Agricultural Engineering, Animal Husbandry, Crops, Education/Extension, Farming, Entomology, Horticulture, Plant Pathology, Soil Science, Veterinary Medicine **Specializations:** Beef Cattle, Food Sciences, Horticulture, Plant Pathology, Potatoes, Veterinary Medicine **Databases Developed:** IPUIB - Información Producida en la Unidad Integrada Balcarce 1958/98. Joins the documents produced in the Unit and publications housed in the library. Access to references via the Intenet. **Databases Used:** Agris; CABCD; Current Contents **Loan:** Internationally **Service:** Internationally **Photocopy:** Yes

13   **Balcarce, Argentina**
        National Institute of Agricultural Technology,
            Regional Center for South Buenos Aires
        Library
        Casilla de Correo 55
        7620 Balcarce, Buenos Aires
Location: Calle 16, No. 674 **Phone:** +54(2266) 423772 **Fax:** +54(2266) 422866 **Email:** crbasur@inta.gov.ar **WWW:** www.inta.gov.ar/crbsass.maincerb.htm

Non-English Name: Instituto Nacional de Tecnología Agropecuaria, Centro Regional de Buenos Aires Sur (INTA), Biblioteca **Type:** Government

14   **Bordenave, Argentina**
        National Institute of Agricultural Technology,
            Agricultural Experiment Station Bordenave
        Library
        Casilla de Correo 44

8187 Bordenave, Buenos Aires
Phone: +54(2924) 420621/2 **Fax:** +54(2924) 420621/2
Email: eborde@inta.gov.ar **WWW:** www.inta.gov.ar

Non-English Name: Instituto Nacional de Tecnología Agropecuaria, Estación Experimental Bordenave (INTA, EEA Bordenave), Biblioteca **Founded:** 1969 **Type:** Government **Head:** María del Carmen Quintana *Phone:* +54(2924) 420621/2 *Email:* eborde@inta.gov.ar **Holdings:** 17 journals 2,000 books **Language of Collection/Services:** English/Spanish **Subjects:** Agricultural Development, Agricultural Economics, Animal Husbandry, Forestry, Plants, Plant Protection, Postharvest Technology, Soil **Networks:** CCPPAA; INTA2 **Loan:** Inhouse **Service:** Inhouse **Photocopy:** Yes

15 **Buenos Aires, Argentina**
Asociación Argentina de Consorcios Regionales de Experimentación Agrícola (AACREA)
Servicio de Información y Estadística (SIYE)
Sarmiento 1236, 5° Piso
1041 Buenos Aires
Phone: +54(11) 4382-2076/79 **Fax:** +54(11) 4382-2911
Email: servinf@aacrea.org.ar **WWW:** www.aacrea.org.ar

Founded: 1987 **Type:** Association **Head:** Gerardo Chiara *Phone:* +54(11) 4382-2076/79 *Email:* servinf@aacrea.org.ar **Staff:** 2 Other **Holdings:** 16,000 books **Language of Collection/Services:** Spanish / Spanish **Subjects:** Agricultural Development, Agricultural Economics, Agricultural Engineering, Animal Husbandry, Crops, Farming, Plants, Soil, Veterinary Medicine **Loan:** Inhouse **Service:** In country **Photocopy:** Yes

16 **Buenos Aires, Argentina**
National Institute of Agricultural Technology
Library and Document Archives
Chile 460
1098 Buenos Aires, Capital Federal
Phone: +54(11) 4806-5395, 4802-0168, 4801-8395 **Fax:** +54(11) 4806-5395, 4802-0168, 4801-8395 **Email:** idinfo@inta.gov.ar **WWW:** www.inta.gov.ar **OPAC:** www.inta.gov.ar/libros.htm

Non-English Name: Instituto Nacional de Tecnología Agropecuaria (INTA), Biblioteca y Archivo Documental **Founded:** 1971 **Type:** Government **Head:** Daniel Spina *Phone:* +54(11) 4806-5395, 4802-0168, 4801-8395 *Email:* idinfo@inta.gov.ar **Staff:** 2 Prof. 1 Other **Holdings:** 4,000 books **Subjects:** Animal Husbandry **Networks:** AGRIS **Loan:** In country **Photocopy:** Yes

17 **Buenos Aires, Argentina**
Secretary of Agriculture, Livestock, Fisheries and Food
Center for Documentation and Agricultural Information
Av. Paseo Colón 982 P.B.
1063 Buenos Aires
Phone: +54(11) 4349-2463 **Fax:** +54(11) 4349-2782
WWW: siiap.sagyp.mecon.ar **OPAC:** siiap.sagyp.mecon.ar/institu/biblio/gral.htm

Non-English Name: Secretaría de Agricultura, Ganadería, Pesca y Alimentación (SAGPyA), Centro de Documentación e Información Agropecuaria **Former Name:** Secretaría de Agricultura, Ganadería y Pesca, Biblioteca Central **Founded:** 1900 **Type:** Government **Head:** Irene Norma Herl *Phone:* +54(11) 4349-2462 *Email:* iherl@sagyp.mecon.ar **Staff:** 1 Prof. 4 Other **Holdings:** 18,000 books 220 journals **Language of Collection/Services:** Spanish / Spanish, English **Subjects:** Comprehensive **Specializations:** Agricultural Economics, Agricultural Production, Livestock Farming **Networks:** AGRIS; REPIDISCA; UNIRED; INTA **Databases Developed:** AGRIN - contains monographs, journal article analytic, monographs in series, theses, etc.; FAO - contains FAO depository materials; PERSIS - union catalog of periodicals; SIIAP - statistical database **Databases Used:** Agris **Loan:** Internationally **Service:** Internationally **Photocopy:** No

18 **Buenos Aires, Argentina**
Secretary of Agriculture, Livestock, Fisheries and Food, Forestry Production Division
Forestry Documentation and Information Center "Ing. Lucas A. Tortorelli"
Av. Paseo Colón 982 - Jardín
1063 Buenos Aires
Phone: +54(11) 4349-2124/25 **Fax:** +54(11) 4349-2102, 4359-2106 **Email:** fsanti@sagyp.mecon.ar **WWW:** siiap.sagyp.mecon.ar

Non-English Name: Secretaría de Agricultura, Ganadería, Pesca y Alimentación, Dirección de Producción Forestal (SAGPyA, DPF), Centro de Documentación e Información Forestal "Ing. Lucas A. Tortorelli" **Former Name:** National Forest Institute, Instituto Forestal Nacional **Founded:** 1948 **Type:** Government **Head:** Nilda Elvira Fernández *Phone:* +54(11) 4349-2124/25 *Email:* fsanti@sagyp.mecon.ar **Staff:** 1 Prof. 3 Other **Holdings:** 22,000 books 560 journals **Language of Collection/Services:** Spanish / Spanish **Subjects:** Forestry **Specializations:** Forest Economics, Forest Products **Databases Developed:** PERSIS - contains books, pamphlets, and periodical articles **Databases Used:** Agris; TREECD **Loan:** Inhouse **Service:** Internationally **Photocopy:** Yes

19 **Buenos Aires, Argentina**
Secretary of Natural Resources and Sustainable Development
Library and Information Center
San Martín 459
1004 Buenos Aires
Phone: +54(11) 4348-8676, 4348-8694/5 **Fax:** +54(11) 4348-8676 **Email:** biblio@sernah.gov.ar **WWW:** www.sernah.gov.ar/srnyds

Non-English Name: Secretaría de Recursos Naturales y Desarrollo Sustentable, Biblioteca y Centro de Información **Head:** Ana María Dunn *Email:* biblio@sernah.gov.ar

20 **Buenos Aires, Argentina**
Servicio Nacional de Sanidad y Calidad Agroalimentaria (SENASA)
Centro de Documentación
Paseo Colón 367, Piso 10
1063 Buenos Aires, Capital Federal

Phone: +54(11) 4331-6041/49 ext 2009 **Fax:** +54(11) 4342-7699 **Email:** senasa@sei.com.ar **WWW:** senasa. mecon.gov.ar

Founded: 1995 **Type:** Government **Head:** Gabriela Silvetti **Staff:** 1 Prof. 1 Other **Holdings:** 2,300 books 300 journals **Language of Collection/Services:** Spanish / Spanish **Subjects:** Agricultural Development, Plant Pathology, Plants, Veterinary Medicine **Loan:** In country **Service:** Internationally **Photocopy:** Yes

21   Buenos Aires, Argentina
          Universidad Católica Argentina, Facultad de
                Ciencias Agrarias (UCA)
          Biblioteca
          Capitan Gral. Ramon Freire 183
          1426 Buenos Aires
Phone: +54(11) 4552-2711, 4552-2721, 4552-2724 **Fax:** +54(11) 4522-5235 **Email:** bibagra@uca.edu.ar **WWW:** www.uca.edu.ar

Founded: 1964 **Type:** Academic **Head:** Lic. Adelina Kallśen **Staff:** 1 Prof. 2 Other **Holdings:** 8,600 books 17 journals **Language of Collection/Services:** Spanish / Spanish **Subjects:** Animal Diseases, Animal Feeding, Animal Nutrition, Animal Production, Beef Cattle, Cereal Products, Dairy Cattle, Fishes, Food Sciences, Honeybees, Meat, Microbiology, Pigs, Plant Diseases, Poultry, Reproduction, Sheep, Vegetables **Databases Used:** Current Contents; FSTA **Loan:** Inhouse **Service:** In country **Photocopy:** No

22   Buenos Aires, Argentina
          University of Buenos Aires, Faculty of Agronomy
          Central Library
          Av. San Martin 4453
          1417 Buenos Aires
Phone: +54(11) 4524-8013, 4524, 8020 **WWW:** www. agro.uba.ar

Non-English Name: Universidad de Buenos Aires, Facultad de Agronomía, Biblioteca Central **Head:** Paula Kadar *Email:* hemer@charao.agro.uba.ar

23   Buenos Aires, Argentina
          University of Buenos Aires, Faculty of Veterinary
                Sciences
          Library
          Av. Chorroarin 280
          1427 Buenos Aires
Fax: +54(1) 524-8480 **WWW:** www.uba.ar

Non-English Name: Universidad de Buenos Aires, Facultad de Ciencias Veterinarias (IBA), Biblioteca **Head:** Fernando Contreras *Email:* sinfo@fvet.uba.ar **Subjects:** Veterinary Science

24   Campana, Argentina
          National Institute of Agricultural Technology,
                Agricultural Experiment Station of Delta del
                Parana
          Library
          Casilla de Correo 14
          2804 Campana, Buenos Aires

Location: Canal 6, Sección Gto. de Islas **Phone:** +54(3489) 420334, 421590 **Fax:** +54(3489) 420334, 421590 **Email:** lgurini@utenet.com.ar **WWW:** www.inta. gov.ar

Non-English Name: Instituto Nacional de Tecnología Agropecuaria, Estación Experimental Agropecuaria de Delta del Paraná (INTA, EEA Delta del Paraná), Biblioteca **Former Name:** Estación Experimental Agropecuaria de Delta **Founded:** 1958 **Type:** Government **Head:** Catalina Perrone de Hanke *Phone:* +54(3489) 420334, 421590 *Email:* lgurini@utenet.com.ar **Staff:** 1 Other **Holdings:** 1,402 books 30 journals **Language of Collection/Services:** Spanish, English / Spanish **Subjects:** Forestry **Networks:** INTA2 **Databases Used:** Agricola **Loan:** Inhouse **Photocopy:** No

25   Castelar, Argentina
          National Institute of Agricultural Technology,
                Institute of Genetics "Ewald A. Favret"
                (NIAT)
          Library "Carlos Barderi"
          CC 25
          1712 Castelar, Buenos Aires
Location: Aristizabal y Ñandú **Phone:** +54(1) 450-0805 **Fax:** +54(1) 450-1876 **Email:** igenet@inta.gov.ar **WWW:** www.inta.gov.ar

Non-English Name: Instituto Nacional de Tecnología Agropecuaria, Instituto de Genética "Ewald A. Favret" (INTA, IGEAF), Biblioteca "Carlos Barderi" **Founded:** 1944 **Type:** Government **Head:** Beatríz Quarterolo *Phone:* +54(1) 450-0805 *Email:* bquarterolo@cica.inta.gov.ar **Staff:** 1 Other **Holdings:** 6,450 books 105 journals **Language of Collection/Services:** English / Spanish **Subjects:** Biotechnology, Crops, Genetics, Immunology, Insects, Molecular Biology, Plant Pathology, Plants, Zoology **Specializations:** Biotechnology, Genetics **Networks:** CCPP **Loan:** Inhouse; photocopy for others **Service:** Internationally **Photocopy:** Yes

26   Castelar, Argentina
          National Institute of Agricultural Technology,
                Natural Resources Research Center
          Soils Library
          CC 25
          1712 Castelar, Buenos Aires
Location: Complejo Castelar, Las Cabañas y de los Reseros, Villa Udaondo **Phone:** +54(11) 4621-1448, 4621-2096 **Fax:** +54(11) 4481-1688 **Email:** breita@cirn. inta.gov.ar **WWW:** www.inta.gov.ar **OPAC:** www.inta. gov.ar/bases1.htm

Non-English Name: Instituto Nacional de Tecnología Agropecuaria, Centro de Investigaciones de Recursos Naturales (INTA, CIRN), Biblioteca de Suelos **Former Name:** Biblioteca de Edafología Agrícola **Type:** Government **Head:** Ana A. Breit *Phone:* +54(11) 4481-1688 *Email:* breita@cirn.inta. gov.ar **Staff:** 1 Prof. 1 Other **Holdings:** 4,000 books 70 journals **Language of Collection/Services:** English / Spanish **Subjects:** Soil **Specializations:** Erosion, Fertilization, Soil Biology, Soil Classification **Networks:** CIRN **Loan:** In country **Photocopy:** Yes

27   Castelar, Argentina
National Institute of Agricultural Technology,
        Research Center for Agricultural Sciences
Library
CC 25
1712 Castelar, Buenos Aires
Location: Las Cabañas y De Los Reseros **Phone:** +54(1)
621-1683 ext 23 **Fax:** +54(1) 621-3316 **WWW:** www.cica.
inta.gov.ar

Non-English Name: Instituto Nacional de Tecnología Agropecuaria, Centro de Investigaciones en Ciencias Agropecuarias (INTA, CICA), Biblioteca **Type:** Government **Head:**
Silvia De Tomasi *Email:* sdetomasi@cica.inta.gov.ar *Phone*
+54(1) 481-1316

28   Catamarca, Argentina
National Institute of Agricultural Technology,
        Agricultural Experiment Station Catamarca
Library
Casilla de Correo 25
4700 Catamarca, Catamarca
Location: Ruta Provincial 33, Km. 4, Sumalao, Dpto.
Valle Viejo **Phone:** +54(3833) 441192, 441323 **Fax:** +54
(3833) 441192, 441323 **Email:** ecatama@inta.gov.ar
WWW: www.inta.gov.ar

Non-English Name: Instituto Nacional de Tecnología Agropecuaria, Estación Experimental Agropecuaria Catamarca
(INTA, EEA Catamarca), Biblioteca **Type:** Government
Head: María Antonia Perea de Ogas *Phone:* +54(3833)
441192, 441323 ext 24 *Email:* maperea@inta.gov.ar

29   Cerro Azul, Argentina
National Institute of Agricultural Technology,
        Agricultural Experiment Station of Cerro
        Azul
Library
Casilla de Correo 6
3313 Cerro Azul, Misiones
Location: Ruta 14, a 7 Km de Cerro Azul **Phone:** +54
(3752) 494086/7 **Fax:** +54(3752) 422787 **Email:** cerroaz@
inta.gov.ar, biblioazul@inta.gov.ar **WWW:** www.inta.gov.
ar

Non-English Name: Instituto Nacional de Tecnología Agro-
pecuaria, Estación Experimental Agropecuaria Cerro Azul
(INTA, EEA Cerro Azul), Biblioteca **Former Name:** Esta-
ción Experimental Agropecuaria Misiones **Founded:** 1958
Type: Government **Head:** Mercedes Marmelicz *Phone:*
+54(3752) 494086/7 *Email:* biblioazul@inta.gov.ar **Staff:** 1
Prof. 1 Other **Holdings:** 5,100 books 60 journals **Language
of Collection/Services:** Spanish, English/Spanish **Subjects:**
Agricultural Development, Agricultural Economics, Animal
Husbandry, Citrus, Crops, Entomology, Forestry, Herbal
Teas, Plant Pathology, Soil Science, Tea, Tobacco **Special-
izations:** Ilex paraguariensis **Networks:** INTA2; CCPPAA
Loan: Inhouse **Service:** Internationally **Photocopy:** Yes

30   Chacras de Coria, Argentina
National University of Cuyo, Agrarian Sciences
        Faculty
Library

CC No. 7
5505 Chacras de Coria, Mendoza
Location: Alte. Brown 500 **Phone:** +54(261) 496-0004 ext
1025 **Fax:** +54(261) 496-0469 **Email:** caifca@raiz.uncu.
edu.ar **WWW:** www.lajas.uncu.edu.ar

Non-English Name: Universidad Nacional de Cuyo, Facultad de Ciencias Agrarias, Biblioteca **Founded:** 1942 **Type:**
Academic **Head:** Direc. Fanny Beatriz Aragó *Phone:* +54
(261) 496-0004 ext 1025 *Email:* caifca@raiz.uncu.edu.ar
Staff: 1 Prof. 4 Other **Holdings:** 18,250 books 619 journals
Language of Collection/Services: Spanish, English / Span-
ish **Subjects:** Comprehensive **Specializations:** Agribusi-
ness, Agricultural Development, Agricultural Engineering,
Animal Husbandry, Entomology, Food Sciences, Plant Pa-
thology, Soil **Databases Developed:** SERCA - periodicals;
SERAMZA - analytics of articles in periodicals; CAMZA -
monographs **Databases Used:** Agris; Current Contents
Loan: Internationally **Service:** Internationally **Photocopy:**
Yes

31   Cinco Saltos, Argentina
National University of Comahue, Agricultural
        Sciences Faculty (NUC, ASF)
Romulo Raggio Library (RRL)
CC No. 85
8303 Cinco Saltos, Río Negro
Location: Farm Section, Route 151, Km 12.5 **Phone:** +54
(99) 498-0124, 498-0204, 498-0005 **Fax:** +54(299) 498-
2200 **Email:** teresaforquera@yahoo.com **WWW:** www.
uncoma.edu.ar

Non-English Name: Universidad Nacional del Comahue,
Facultad de Ciencias Agrarias (UNC, FCA), Biblioteca
"Rómulo Raggio" (BRR) **Founded:** 1972 **Type:** Academic
Head: Teresa E. Forquera *Email:* teresaforquera@yahoo.
com **Staff:** 1 Prof. 2 Other **Holdings:** 5,350 books 850 journals **Language of Collection/Services:** Spanish, English /
Spanish **Subjects:** Agricultural Development, Agricultural
Engineering, Forestry, Fruit Trees, Horticulture, Plant Pathology, Plants, Soil **Specializations:** Botany, Physiology,
Soil, Water Resources **Networks:** SISBUNC **Databases Developed:** AGRO - Monographs database; ANEZE - Periodical publications database; AGRIN - Research and extension
works collection in agreement with SAGPyA for agriculture,
cattle, fishing and feeding **Loan:** In country **Service:** Inhouse **Photocopy:** No

32   Concepción del Uruguay, Argentina
National Institute of Agricultural Technology,
        Agricultural Experiment Station of
        Concepción del Uruguay
Library
CC No. 6
3260 Concepción del Uruguay, Entre Ríos
Location: Ruta Provincial No. 39 Km 354 **WWW:** www.
inta.gov.ar

Non-English Name: Instituto Nacional de Tecnología Agropecuaria, Estación Experimental Agropecuaria Concepción
del Uruguay (INTA, EEA Concepción del Uruguay), Biblioteca **Founded:** 1960 **Type:** Government **Head:** María
Carlota Diez de Irigoitía *Phone:* +54(442) 25561, 25578
Staff: 1 Other **Holdings:** 3,000 books 350 journals **Sub-**

jects: Agribusiness, Agricultural Development, Agricultural Economics, Agricultural Engineering, Animal Husbandry, Biotechnology, Crops, Education/Extension, Plant Pathology, Soil Science, Veterinary Medicine **Loan:** In country **Photocopy:** Yes

33   **Concordia, Argentina**
         National Institute of Agricultural Technology,
             Agricultural Experiment Station of Concordia
         Ing. Agr. Américo Banfi Library
         Casilla de Correo 34
         3200 Concordia, Entre Ríos
Location: Catamarca 140 **Phone:** +54(45) 290000 **Fax:** +54(45) 290215 **Email:** biblioeea@concordia.com.ar **WWW:** www.inta.gov.ar

Non-English Name: Instituto Nacional de Tecnología Agropecuaria, Estación Experimental Agropecuaria Concordia (INTA, EEA Concordia), Biblioteca Ing. Agr. Américo Banfi **Type:** Government **Head:** María Teresita Malaisi de Paulucci *Email:* biblioeea@concordia.com.ar **Staff:** 1 Other **Language of Collection/Services:** Spanish, English / Spanish, English **Subjects:** Beekeeping, Citrus, Forestry, Fruits **Networks:** CCPPAA **Databases Used:** Current Contents **Loan:** Inhouse **Photocopy:** Yes

34   **Córdoba, Argentina**
         National Institute of Agricultural Technology,
             Cordoba Regional Center
         Library
         Achaval Rodriguez 50
         5000 Córdoba, Córdoba
Phone: +54(351) 425-6414, 422-1076 **Email:** crcordo@inta.gov.ar **WWW:** www.inta.gov.ar/crcordo/cordoba.htm

Non-English Name: Instituto Nacional de Tecnología Agropecuaria, Centro Regional de Córdoba (INTA), Biblioteca **Type:** Government

35   **Córdoba, Argentina**
         National Institute of Agricultural Technology,
             Institute of Plant Pathology and Physiology
             (IPPP)
         Library
         Cno. 60 Cuadras Km 5-1/2
         5119 Córdoba, Córdoba
Phone: +54(351) 497-4343 ext 3636 **Fax:** +54(351) 397-4330 **Email:** bibfito@iffive.satlink.net **WWW:** www.inta.gov.ar/iffive

Non-English Name: Instituto Nacional de Tecnología Agropecuaria, Instituto de Fitopatología y Fisiología Vegetal (INTA, IFFIVE), Biblioteca **Founded:** 1991 **Type:** Government **Head:** Lilian Frizzo *Phone:* +54(351) 497-4343 ext 3636 *Email:* bibfito@iffive.satlink.net **Staff:** 1 Prof. **Holdings:** 280 books 34 journals **Language of Collection/Services:** English/Spanish, English **Subjects:** Horticulture, Crops **Specializations:** Biotechnology, Plant Pathology **Networks:** INTA2 **Databases Used:** Agris; Medline **Loan:** In country **Service:** In country **Photocopy:** Yes

36   **Córdoba, Argentina**
         National University of Cordoba, Faculty of
             Agricultural Sciences
         Library
         Casilla de Correo 509
         5000 Córdoba, Córdoba
Location: Av. Valparaíso s/n, Ciudad Universitaria **Phone:** +54(351) 433-4116/17 **Fax:** +54(351) 433-4118 **Email:** biblio@agro.uncor.edu

Non-English Name: Universidad Nacional de Córdoba, Facultad de Ciencias Agropecuarias (UNC, FCA), Biblioteca **Former Name:** Institute of Agronomy, Instituto de Ciencias Agronómicas **Founded:** 1966 **Type:** Academic **Head:** Pastora Navarro *Phone:* +54(351) 433-4116/17 *Email:* pnavarro@agro.uncor.edu **Staff:** 6 Prof. 2 Other **Holdings:** 10,330 books 401 journals **Language of Collection/Services:** Spanish / Spanish **Subjects:** Comprehensive **Specializations:** Animal Husbandry, Horticulture, Plant Pathology, Plants, Seeds, Soil Science, Zoology **Databases Used:** Agricola; Agris; CABCD; Current Contents **Loan:** Inhouse **Service:** In country **Photocopy:** Yes

37   **Corrientes, Argentina**
         National Institute of Agricultural Technology,
             Agricultural Experiment Station of Corrientes
         Library
         Casilla de Correo 57
         3400 Corrientes, Corrientes
Location: Ruta Prov. 5, km 2.5 **Phone:** +54(3783) 454428, 454553 **Fax:** +54(3783) 454428, 454553 **Email:** crcorrie@inta.gov.ar **WWW:** www.inta.gov.ar/crcorri/corri.htm

Non-English Name: Instituto Nacional de Tecnología Agropecuaria, Estación Experimental Agropecuaria Corrientes (INTA, EEA Corrientes), Biblioteca **Type:** Government **Head:** Roberto Quiñonez

38   **Eldorado, Argentina**
         Universidad Nacional de Misiones, Escuela
             Agrotécnica Eldorado, Facultad de Ciencias
             Forestales
         Biblioteca
         Bentoni 148, 1° Piso
         3380 Eldorado, Misiones
Phone: +54(3751) 431526 ext 116 **Fax:** +54(3751) 431766 **WWW:** www.facfor.unam.edu.ar

Head: Teresita Duarte de Krulewecky *Email:* tdk@correo.facfor.unam.edu.ar **Subjects:** Forestry

39   **Esperanza, Argentina**
         Universidad Nacional del Litoral, Facultad de
             Ciencias Agrarias y Facultad de Ciencias
             Veterinarias (UNL, FACA y FACV)
         Biblioteca
         Padre Luis Kreder 2805
         3000 Esperanza, Santa Fe
Phone: +54(3496) 425730 **Fax:** +54(3596) 422733 **Email:** bibfave@unl.edu.ar **WWW:** www.unl.edu.ar/fave

Former Name: Facultad de Agronomía y Veterinaria (FAVE) **Founded:** 1965 **Type:** Academic **Head:** Elsie Mirella Pinter *Phone:* +54(3496) 425730 *Email:* epinter@

unl.edu.ar **Staff:** 1 Prof. 3 Other **Holdings:** 11,000 books 50 journals **Language of Collection/Services:** Spanish, English / Spanish **Subjects:** Comprehensive **Loan:** Inhouse **Service:** Inhouse **Photocopy:** No

40   Esquel, Argentina
         Patagonian Andes Forest Research and Extension
                Center
         Library
         CC 14
         9200 Esquel, Chubut
Location: Ruta 259, Km. 4 **Phone:** +54(2945) 453948
Fax: +54(2945) 453948 **Email:** ciefap@teletel.com.ar

Non-English Name: Centro de Investigación Forestal Andino Patagónico (CIEFAP), Biblioteca **Type:** Government **Head:** Patricia Alejandra Gonalez *Phone:* +54(2945)453948 **Staff:** 1 Other **Holdings:** 3,000 books 100 journals **Language of Collection/Services:** English, Spanish, German **Subjects:** Agricultural Economics, Forestry, Plant Pathology, Plant Protection **Loan:** Inhouse **Service:** Inhouse **Photocopy:** No

41   Famaillá, Argentina
         National Institute of Agricultural Technology,
                Agricultural Experiment Station of Famaillá
         Library
         Casilla de Correo 11
         San Luis 530
         4132 Famaillá, Tucumán
Location: Ruta Provincial 301, Km 32 **Phone:** +54(863) 61047 **Fax:** +54(863) 61046 **Email:** efama@inta.gov.ar **WWW:** www.inta.gov.ar/crtucu/efama/verfama.htm

Non-English Name: Instituto Nacional de Tecnología Agropecuaria, Estación Experimental Agropecuaria Famaillá (INTA, EEA Famaillá), Biblioteca **Type:** Government **Head:** Beatriz Encarnación Flores *Phone:* +54(863) 61047 *Email:* bflores@inta.gov.ar

42   General Roca, Argentina
         National Institute of Agricultural Technology,
                Agricultural Experiment Station of Alto Valle
                del Rio Negro
         Library
         Casilla de Correo 52
         8332 General Roca, Río Negro
Fax: +54(941) 30717 **WWW:** www.inta.gov.ar/crpatno/patno.htm

Non-English Name: Instituto Nacional de Tecnología Agropecuaria, Estación Experimental Agropecuaria Alto Valle del Río Negro (INTA, EEA Alto Valle del Río Negro), Biblioteca **Type:** Government **Head:** Raquel Luna *Phone:* +54(941) 25027, 25037

43   General Villegas, Argentina
         National Institute of Agricultural Technology,
                Agricultural Experiment Station of General
                Villegas
         Library
         Casilla de Correo 153
         6230 General Villegas, Buenos Aires

Phone: +54(3388) 421980 **Fax:** +54(3388) 421980 **Email:** carlos@servicoop.com.ar **WWW:** www.inta.gov.ar

Non-English Name: Instituto Nacional de Tecnología Agropecuaria, Estación Experimental Agropecuaria de General Villegas (INTA, EEA General Villegas), Biblioteca **Founded:** 1968 **Type:** Government **Staff:** 1 Other **Holdings:** 700 books 15 journals **Language of Collection/Services:** English / Spanish **Subjects:** Crops, Soil, Veterinary Medicine **Networks:** INTA2 **Loan:** Inhouse **Service:** Internationally **Photocopy:** Yes

44   La Consulta, Argentina
         National Institute for Agricultural Technology,
                Agricultural Experiment Station of La
                Consulta
         Library
         Casilla de Correo 8
         5567 La Consulta, Mendoza
Phone: +54(2622) 470304, 470753 **Fax:** +54(2622) 470304, 470753 **Email:** elaconsulta@inta.gov.ar **WWW:** www.inta.gov.ar

Non-English Name: Instituto Nacional de Tecnología Agropecuaria, Estación Experimental Agropecuaria La Consulta (INTA, EEA La Consulta), Biblioteca **Founded:** 1961 **Type:** Government **Head:** María Inés Paredes *Phone:* +54 (2622) 470304, 470753 *Email:* elaconsulta@inta.gov.ar **Staff:** 1 Prof. **Holdings:** 1,867 books 480 journals **Language of Collection/Services:** Spanish, English / Spanish, English **Subjects:** Crops, Horticulture, Plant Breeding, Seed Production **Specializations:** Allium cepa, Allium sativum, Capsicum annuum, Curcurbitaceae, Daucus carota, Lactuca sativa, Lycopersicon esculentum **Networks:** CCPP; INTA2 **Databases Developed:** Allium sativum (garlic) in Argentina; Lycopersicon esculentum (tomato) in Argentina; Allium cepa (onion) in Argentina; Horticulture in Argentina **Databases Used:** Agricola; Agris; CABCD **Loan:** In region **Service:** In country **Photocopy:** Yes

45   La Plata, Argentina
         National University of La Plata, Faculty of
                Agricultural and Forestry Sciences
         Library
         Calle 60 y 119
         1900 La Plata
Phone: +54(221) 421-1254 ext 405 **Email:** biblio@ceres.agro.unlp.edu.ar **WWW:** www.unlp.edu.ar

Non-English Name: Universidad Nacional de La Plata, Facultad de Ciencias Agrarias y Forestales (UNLP), Biblioteca **Type:** Academic **Head:** Susana Elida Martínez *Email:* biblio@ceres.agro.unlp.edu.ar

46   La Plata, Argentina
         University of La Plata, Faculty of Veterinary
                Science
         Library
         Calle 60 y 118
         CC 296
         1900 La Plata

Phone: +54(221) 483-6880 **Fax:** +54(221) 425-7980 **Email:** cristina@fcu.medvet.unlp.edu.ar **WWW:** www. unlp.edu.ar **OPAC:** www.sisbi.uba.ar

Non-English Name: Universidad Nacional de La Plata, Facultad de Ciencias Veterinarias (UNLP), Biblioteca **Type:** Academic **Head:** Marta Bernard *Email:* cristina@fcu. medvet.unlp.edu.ar **Staff:** 2 Prof. 4 Other **Holdings:** 28,486 books **Language of Collection/Services:** Spanish / Spanish **Subjects:** Animal Husbandry, Food Sciences, Veterinary Medicine **Networks:** SISBI **Loan:** In country **Service:** In country **Photocopy:** No

47   La Rioja, Argentina
National Institute of Agricultural Technology, La Rioja - Catamarca Regional Center
Library
Buenos Aires 562
5300 La Rioja, La Rioja
Phone: +54(822) 26728 **Fax:** +54(822) 22091 **Email:** crlario@inta.gov.ar **WWW:** www.inta.gov.ar/ingles/ wrioja.htm

Non-English Name: Instituto Nacional de Tecnología Agropecuaria, Centro Regional de La Rioja - Catamarca (INTA), Biblioteca **Type:** Government

48   Las Talitas, Argentina
"Obispo Colombres" Agro-Industrial Experimental Research Station
Alfredo Guzman Library
CC No. 9
4101 Las Talitas, Tucumán
Location: Av. William Cross 3150

Non-English Name: Estación Experimental Agro Industrial "Obispo Colombres", Biblioteca Alfredo Guzmán **Founded:** 1909 **Type:** Private **Head:** Mr. Eduardo Rothe *Phone:* +54(4) 276561 *Email:* eeaoc@server1.com.ar **Staff:** 1 Prof. 2 Other **Holdings:** 79,000 books 75 journals **Language of Collection/Services:** Spanish, English / Spanish, English **Subjects:** Agribusiness, Agricultural Development, Agricultural Economics, Agricultural Engineering, Animal Husbandry, Crops, Extension, Entomology, Food Sciences, Horticulture, Maize, Plant Pathology, Potatoes, Soil Science, Sorghum, Wheat **Specializations:** Citrus, Soybeans, Sugar Industry, Sugarcane **Databases Developed:** Publications of the Obispo Colombres Agro-Industrial Experimental Research Station **Loan:** In country **Photocopy:** Yes

49   Llanidloes, Argentina
Universidad Nacional de Lomos de Zamora, Facultad de Ciencias Agrarias
Hemeroteca
Ruta 4, Km. 2
1836 Llanidloes, Buenos Aires
Phone: +54(11) 4282-6263 ext 208 **Fax:** +54(11) 4282-6263 **Email:** agrarias@unlz.edu.ar

Head: Raúl Daniel Bassi *Email:* agrarias@unlz.edu.ar

50   Luján de Cuyo, Argentina
National Institute of Agricultural Technology, Agricultural Experiment Station of Mendoza

Library and Information Unit
Casilla de Correo 3
5507 Luján de Cuyo, Mendoza
Location: San Martin 3853 - Mayor Drummond **Fax:** +54 (261) 496-3320 **Email:** biblimen@inta.gov.ar **WWW:** www.inta.gov.ar

Non-English Name: Instituto Nacional de Tecnología Agropecuaria, Estación Experimental Agropecuaria Mendoza (INTA, EEA Mendoza), Biblioteca y Unidad de Información **Founded:** 1948 **Type:** Government **Head:** Norma Pieralisi *Phone:* +54(261) 496-3020 ext 320 **Staff:** 1 Prof. **Holdings:** 6,500 books 102 journals **Subjects:** Extension, Entomology, Fruit Trees, Horticulture, Irrigation, Pesticides, Plant Pathology, Soil Science, Viticulture **Networks:** CCPPAA; INTA2 **Databases Developed:** BTEMZA-Technical reports of EEA Mendoza **Loan:** In country **Photocopy:** Yes

51   Mar del Plata, Argentina
National Institute for Fisheries Research and Development
Library and Documentation Service
Casilla de Correo 175
7600 Mar del Plata, Buenos Aires
Location: Paseo Victoria Ocampo No. 1, Escollera Norte **Phone:** +54(223) 486-2404, 486-2586 **Fax:** +54(223) 486-1292 **Email:** biblio@inidep.edu.ar **WWW:** inidep. edu.ar

Non-English Name: Instituto Nacional de Investigación y Desarrollo Pesquero (INIDEP), Biblioteca y Servicio de Documentación **Former Name:** Instituto de Biología Marina **Founded:** 1960 **Type:** Government **Head:** *Email:* biblio@inidep.edu.ar **Staff:** 3 Prof. **Holdings:** 4,000 books 25 journals **Language of Collection/Services:** English / Spanish **Subjects:** Fisheries **Specializations:** Fish Culture, Fish Farming, Fish Industry, Marine Biology **Networks:** ASFA **Databases Developed:** DOCAU - publications of INIDEP researchers; LISTA - fish names in Latin, English and Spanish **Databases Used:** ASFA **Loan:** Inhouse **Service:** Internationally **Photocopy:** Yes

52   Marcos Juárez, Argentina
National Institute of Agricultural Technology, Agricultural Experiment Station of Marcos Juarez
Library
CC 21
2580 Marcos Juárez, Córdoba
Fax: +54(472) 25001 ext 107 **Email:** bibjua@inta.gov.ar **WWW:** mjuarez.inta.gov.ar, www.inta.jov.ar

Non-English Name: Instituto Nacional de Tecnología Agropecuaria, Estación Experimental Agropecuaria Marcos Juárez (INTA, EEA Marcos Juárez), Biblioteca **Founded:** 1965 **Type:** Government **Head:** Prof. Marta Vottero *Phone:* +54(472) 25001, 27171, 27169 *Email:* bibjua@inta.gov.ar **Staff:** 1 Other **Holdings:** 1,700 books 45 journals **Subjects:** Agriculture (Tropics), Agricultural Engineering, Animal Husbandry, Plant Pathology, Soil Science, Veterinary Medicine **Specializations:** Animal Production, Soil, Soybeans, Wheat **Networks:** INTA2 **Databases Used:** Agricola; Agris **Loan:** Internationally **Service:** Internationally **Photocopy:** Yes

53   Mendoza, Argentina
National Institute of Viticulture
Central Library
Av. San Martín, 430
5500 Mendoza
Phone: +54(61) 24-8288 ext 192

Non-English Name: Instituto Nacional de Vitivinicultura, Biblioteca Central del INV **Founded:** 1961 **Type:** Government **Head:** N. Nancy Anessi *Phone:* +54(61) 24-8288 **Staff:** 2 Prof. 2 Other **Holdings:** 9,000 books 639 journals **Subjects:** Grapes, Plant Pathology, Soil Science, Vineyards, Viticulture **Loan:** In country **Photocopy:** Yes

54   Mendoza, Argentina
Regional Center of Scientific and Technological
        Research
Central Documentation Service
Adrian Ruiz Leal s/n
Parque Gral. S. Martín
5500 Mendoza
Phone: +54(261) 428-8314 ext 250 **Fax:** +54(261) 418-7370 **Email:** secedoc@lab.cricyt.edu.ar **WWW:** www.cricyt.edu.ar/servicios/secedoc

Non-English Name: Centro Regional de Investigaciones Científicas y Tecnológicas (CRICYT), Servicio Centralizado de Documentación (SECEDOC) **Founded:** 1980 **Type:** Academic **Head:** Ana María Gómez de Llop *Phone:* +54(261) 428-8314 ext 250 *Email:* agllop@lab.cricyt.edu.ar **Staff:** 6 Prof. 5 Other **Holdings:** 12,000 books 110 journals **Language of Collection/Services:** English / Spanish, English **Subjects:** Ecology, Environment, Meteorology **Specializations:** Arid Zones, Desertification **Databases Used:** Comprehensive **Loan:** Internationally **Service:** Internationally **Photocopy:** Yes

55   Morón, Argentina
National Institute of Agricultural Technology,
        Veterinary Sciences Research Center
Library
CC 77
1708 Morón, Buenos Aires
Location: Complejo Castelar, Las Cabañas y de los Reseros, Villa Udaondo Castelar **Phone:** +54(11) 4621-1727 **Fax:** +54(11) 4481-2975 **Email:** isuelos@inta.gov.ar **WWW:** www.inta.gov.ar/cicv/cicv.htm

Non-English Name: Instituto Nacional de Tecnología Agropecuaria, Centro de Investigaciones en Ciencias Veterinarias (INTA, CICV), Biblioteca **Founded:** 1956 **Type:** Government **Head:** Estela Maris Noya, Marcela Alonso **Subjects:** Veterinary Science

56   Neuquén, Argentina
National Institute of Agricultural Technology,
        Northern Patagonia Regional Center
Library
Avenida Argentina 61, Planta Baja, Depto 1
8300 Neuquén, Neuquén
Phone: +54(299) 442-5756 **Fax:** +54(299) 442-3241 **Email:** crpatano@inta.gov.ar **WWW:** www.inta.gov.ar/crpatno/patno.htm

Non-English Name: Instituto Nacional de Tecnología Agropecuaria, Centro Regional de Patagonia Norte (INTA), Biblioteca **Type:** Government

57   Paraná, Argentina
National Institute of Agricultural Technology,
        Agricultural Experiment Station of Parana
Library
Casilla de Correo 128
3100 Paraná, Entre Ríos
Location: Catamarca 140 **Fax:** +54(43) 216719 **Email:** eparana@inta.gov.ar **WWW:** www.inta.gov.ar

Non-English Name: Instituto Nacional de Tecnología Agropecuaria, Estación Experimental Agropecuaria Paraná (INTA, EEA Paraná), Biblioteca **Type:** Government **Head:** Juan Chabrillón *Phone:* +54(43) 224940

58   Pergamino, Argentina
National Institute of Agricultural Technology,
        Agricultural Experiment Station of Pergamino
Document Center
Casilla de Correo 31
2700 Pergamino, Buenos Aires
Location: Ruta 178 ex-32 (a 5 km de la cuidad de Pergamino) **Fax:** +54(2477) 432526 **Email:** perdocu@inta.gov.ar **WWW:** www.inta.gov.ar/pergamino

Non-English Name: Instituto Nacional de Tecnología Agropecuaria, Estación Experimental Agropecuaria de Pergamino (INTA, EEA Pergamino), Centro Documental **Founded:** 1947 **Type:** Government **Head:** Nidia Iribarren *Phone:* +54(2477) 432235, 432553 **Staff:** 3 Other **Holdings:** 40,000 books 1,000 journals **Subjects:** Agricultural Economics, Animal Production, Crop Production, Entomology, Maize, Marketing, Pastures, Plant Pathology, Soil Science, Soybeans, Sunflowers, Veterinary Medicine, Wheat **Loan:** Inhouse **Photocopy:** Yes

59   Plottier, Argentina
Plottier Agritechnical School (PAS)
Library
Ruta 22, Km 1233
8316 Plottier, Neuquén
Phone: +54(299) 493-3478

Non-English Name: Escuela Provincial de Educación Agrotécnica (EPEA No. 2), Biblioteca **Former Name:** Escuela Media Experimental Técnico Agropecuaria No. 2 (EMETA No. 2) **Founded:** 1992 **Type:** Academic **Head:** Andrea Bonetti *Phone:* +54(299) 493-3478 **Staff:** 1 Prof. **Holdings:** 1,500 books 50 journals **Language of Collection/Services:** Spanish **Subjects:** Agricultural Development, Agricultural Economics, Animal Husbandry, Crops, Entomology, Forestry, Horticulture, Plant Pathology **Specializations:** Animal Nutrition, Animal Production **Loan:** Inhouse **Service:** Inhouse **Photocopy:** Yes

60   Posadas, Argentina
National Institute of Agricultural Technology,
        Misiones Regional Center
Library
Casilla de Correo 152

3300 Posadas, Misiones
Location: Ruta Nacional 12, Km 7 1/2, Villa Lanus
Phone: +54(752) 80640, 80709 **Fax:** +54(752) 80640
Email: crmision@inta.gov.ar **WWW:** www.inta.gov.ar

Non-English Name: Instituto Nacional de Tecnología Agropecuaria, Centro Regional de Misiones (INTA), Biblioteca **Type:** Government

61   Presidencia Roque Sáenz Peña, Argentina
National Institute of Agricultural Technology,
    Agricultural Experiment Station Sáenz Peña
Library
Casilla de Correo 164
3700 Presidencia Roque Sáenz Peña, Chaco
Location: Ruta Nacional 95 - Km 1108 **Phone:** +54(3732) 421781, 421722, 421473 **Fax:** +54(3732) 421722 **Email:** bibliosp@inta.gov.ar **WWW:** saenzpe.inta.gov.ar/ eeaintasaenzpe.htm

Non-English Name: Instituto Nacional de Tecnología Agropecuaria, Estación Experimental Agropecuaria Sáenz Peña (INTA, EEA Sáenz Peña), Biblioteca **Type:** Government **Head:** Alberto Pérez

62   Rafaela, Argentina
National Institute of Agricultural Technology,
    Santa Fe Regional Center
Library
Francia 459
2300 Rafaela, Santa Fe
Phone: +54(3492) 420748 **Fax:** +54(3492) 424147 **Email:** crsanta@inta.gov.ar **WWW:** www.inta.gov.ar/crsanta/ santafe.htm

Non-English Name: Instituto Nacional de Tecnología Agropecuaria, Centro Regional de Santa Fe (INTA), Biblioteca **Type:** Government

63   Reconquista, Argentina
National Institute of Agricultural Technology,
    Agricultural Experiment Station of
    Reconquista
Library
CC 1
3560 Reconquista, Santa Fe
Phone: +54(3482) 420117 **Fax:** +54(3482) 42592 **Email:** msosa@inta.gov.ar **WWW:** www.inta.gov.ar

Non-English Name: Instituto Nacional de Tecnología Agropecuaria, Estación Experimental Agropecuaria Reconquista (INTA, EEA Reconquista), Biblioteca **Founded:** 1954 **Type:** Government **Head:** Ing. Agr. María Ana Sosa *Phone:* +54(3482) 420117, 42592 *Email:* msosa@inta.gov.ar **Holdings:** 700 books 45 journals **Language of Collection/Services:** Spanish/Spanish **Subjects:** Crops, Soil **Loan:** Inhouse **Service:** Internationally **Photocopy:** Yes

64   Resistencia, Argentina
National Institute of Agricultural Technology,
    Chaco - Formosa Regional Center
Library
Av. Wilde 5
3500 Resistencia, Chaco

Phone: +54(722) 26558 **Fax:** +54(722) 27471 **Email:** crchaco@inta.gov.ar **WWW:** www.inta.gov.ar

Non-English Name: Instituto Nacional de Tecnología Agropecuaria, Centro Regional de Chaco - Formosa (INTA), Biblioteca **Type:** Government

65   Resistencia, Argentina
Northeast National University
Bioagriculture and Forestry Information Center
Av. Las Heras, 727
3500 Resistencia, Chaco
Fax: +54(3722) 443742 **Email:** jencinas@bib.unne.edu.ar

Non-English Name: Universidad Nacional del Nordeste (UNNE), Centro de Información Bioagropecuaria y Forestal (CIBAGRO) **Former Name:** Centro de Información Bioagrícola (CIBAGRI) **Founded:** 1976 **Type:** Academic **Head:** Julio E. Encinas *Phone:* +54(3722) 443742 *Email:* jencinas@bib.unne.edu.ar **Staff:** 6 Prof. 4 Other **Holdings:** 3,530 books 630 journals **Language of Collection/Services:** Spanish **Subjects:** Agriculture (Subtropics), Cultivation, Forestry **Databases Developed:** Database on agroforestry - accessible via CD-ROM and diskettes **Databases Used:** Agricola; Agris **Loan:** Internationally **Service:** Internationally **Photocopy:** Yes

66   Río Cuarto, Argentina
National University of Rio Cuarto
Central Library
Enlace Ruta 36, Km 602
5800 Río Cuarto, Córdoba
Phone: +54(358) 467-6384 **Fax:** +54(358) 467-6133
Email: cfauda@bib.unrc.edu.ar **WWW:** www.unrc.edu.ar

Non-English Name: Universidad Nacional Río Cuarto (UNRC), Biblioteca Central **Founded:** 1972 **Type:** Academic **Head:** María Cristina Chianalino de Fauda *Phone:* +54(358) 467-6380 *Email:* cfauda@bib.unrc.edu.ar **Staff:** 2 Prof. 15 Other **Holdings:** 46,000 books 300 journals **Language of Collection/Services:** Spanish, English / Spanish **Subjects:** Agricultural Engineering, Crops, Pastures, Plant Breeding, Plant Pathology, Soil Science, Veterinary Medicine **Databases Used:** Comprehensive **Loan:** Inhouse **Photocopy:** Yes

67   Rosario, Argentina
National University of Rosario, Faculty of
    Agriculture Sciences
Library
CP 2000
2051 Rosario, Santa Fe
WWW: www.unr.edu.ar

Non-English Name: Universidad Nacional de Rosario, Facultad de Ciencias Agrarias, Biblioteca **Founded:** 1971 **Type:** Academic **Head:** Enzo José Ravenna *Phone:* +54(41) 42477 **Staff:** 3 Prof. 2 Other **Holdings:** 7,800 books 33 journals **Subjects:** Agricultural Development, Agricultural Economics, Agricultural Engineering, Animal Husbandry, Crops, Entomology, Farming, Horticulture, Plant Pathology, Soil Science **Loan:** Internationally **Photocopy:** Yes

68   Salta, Argentina
National Institute of Agricultural Technology,
      Agricultural Experiment Station of Salta
Ing. Agr. Hector F. Tellechea Library
Casilla de Correo 224
4400 Salta, Salta
Location: Ruta Nacional 68, Km. 172, Cerrillos, Salta
Phone: +54(387) 490-2081, 490-2087, 490-2224 ext 235
Fax: +54(387) 490-2214 **Email:** sabiblio@inta.gov.ar
WWW: www.inta.gov.ar

Non-English Name: Instituto Nacional de Tecnología Agropecuaria, Estación Experimental Agropecuaria Salta (INTA,
EEA Salta), Biblioteca "Ing. Agr. Héctor F. Tellechea"
Founded: 1958 **Type:** Government **Head:** María Dolores
García Torregrosa *Email:* sabiblio@inta.gov.ar *Phone:* +54
(387) 490-2081 **Staff:** 1 Prof. 1 Other **Holdings:** 4,000
books 318 journals **Language of Collection/Services:** English, Spanish / English, Spanish **Subjects:** Comprehensive
Specializations: Irrigation **Loan:** Inhouse **Service:** Internationally **Photocopy:** Yes

69   San Carlos de Bariloche, Argentina
National Institute of Agricultural Technology,
      Agricultural Experiment Station of San Carlos
      de Bariloche
Library
Casilla de Correo 277
8400 San Carlos de Bariloche, Río Negro
Phone: +54(2944) 422731 **Fax:** +54(2944) 424991 **Email:**
lariloc@inta.gov.ar **WWW:** www.inta.gov.ar

Non-English Name: Instituto Nacional de Tecnología Agropecuaria, Estación Experimental Agropecuaria San Carlos
de Bariloche (INTA, EEA Bariloche), Biblioteca **Founded:**
1974 **Type:** Government **Head:** Rosa María d'Alessio de
Valvero *Phone:* +54(2944) 422731 *Email:* baribib@inta.
gov. ar **Staff:** 1 Prof. 1 Other **Holdings:** 3,500 books 280
journals **Language of Collection/Services:** Spanish / Spanish **Subjects:** Animal Health, Animal Production, Natural
Resources **Networks:** INTA/CAICYT **Databases Used:**
Current Contents **Service:** In country **Photocopy:** Yes

70   San Isidro, Argentina
Darwinion Botanical Institute
Library
Lavarden 200
1642 San Isidro, Buenos Aires

Non-English Name: Instituto de Botánica Darwinion
(IBODA), Biblioteca **Founded:** 1936 **Type:** Government
Head: Elena Silnicky de Vizer *Phone:* +54(1) 743-4800,
747-4748 **Staff:** 3 Other **Holdings:** 40,000 books 150 journals **Subjects:** Agricultural Economics, Botany **Loan:** Do
not loan **Photocopy:** Yes

71   San Rafael, Argentina
National Institute for Agricultural Technology,
      Agricultural Experiment Station of Rama
      Caida
Ingeniero Julio Cesar Gatica Library
Casilla de Correo 79
5600 San Rafael, Mendoza

Location: Calle El Vivero s/n **Phone:** +54(627) 41100,
41168 **Fax:** +54(627) 41100, 41168 **Email:** erama@inta.
gov.ar **WWW:** www.inta.gov.ar

Non-English Name: Instituto Nacional de Tecnología Agro-
pecuaria, Estación Experimental Agropecuaria Rama Caída
(INTA, EEA Rama Caída), Biblioteca "Ingeniero Julio César
Gatica" **Founded:** 1961 **Type:** Government **Head:** Elda
Masera de Arnal *Phone:* +54(627) 41100, 41168 *Email:*
erama@inta.gov.ar **Staff:** 1 Prof. **Holdings:** 1,800 books
170 journals **Language of Collection/Services:** Spanish,
English, French, Italian / Spanish, English **Subjects:** Agri-
cultural Engineering, Biotechnology, Crops, Horticulture,
Plant Diseases, Plant Pathology **Specializations:** Forage Le-
gumes, Fruit Crops, Grapes, Nematode Control, Peaches,
Plums, Propagation **Networks:** CCPPAA; Edint; INTA;
INTA2 **Databases Used:** CCPPAA; Edint; INTA2 **Loan:** In
country **Service:** In country **Photocopy:** Yes

72   Santa Fe, Argentina
Ministry of Agriculture, Livestock, Industry and
      Commerce
Central Library
Bv. Pellegrini 3100
3000 Santa Fe
Phone: +54(42) 560897/99 ext 4224 **Fax:** +54(42) 4298

Non-English Name: Ministerio de Agricultura, Ganadería,
Industria y Comercio, Biblioteca Central **Former Name:**
Ministerio de Agricultura y Ganadería **Founded:** 1974
Type: Government **Head:** Ms. Mónica Baroni *Phone:*
+54(42) 560897/99 ext 4250 **Staff:** 1 Prof. **Holdings:** 3,000
books 1,500 journals **Language of Collection/Services:**
Spanish / Spanish **Subjects:** Plant Pathology, Silviculture,
Soil Science **Specializations:** Agricultural Development,
Animal Husbandry, Crops, Fisheries, Forestry **Loan:** In
country **Service:** Inhouse **Photocopy:** No

73   Santa Rosa, Argentina
National University of La Pampa, Agronomy
      Faculty
Library
CC 300
6300 Santa Rosa, La Pampa
Location: Ruta Nacional 35 Km 334 **Phone:** +54(2954)
433092/94 **Fax:** +54(2954) 433092/94 **WWW:** bibliosr.
unlpam.edu.ar **Email:** fagronomia@unlpam.edu.ar

Non-English Name: Universidad Nacional de La Pampa,
Facultad de Agronomía (UNLPam), Biblioteca **Founded:**
1965 **Type:** Academic **Head:** A/C María Elena Marangon de
Knutsen *Phone:* +54(2954) 433092/94 *Email:* fagronomia@
unlpam.edu.ar **Staff:** 3 Other **Holdings:** 8,000 books 35
journals **Language of Collection/Services:** English, Spanish / Spanish **Subjects:** Comprehensive **Databases Used:**
Current Contents **Loan:** Inhouse **Service:** Inhouse **Photocopy:** No

74   Santiago del Estero, Argentina
National University of Santiago del Estero,
      Forestry Science Faculty
Forestry Science Library
Av. Belgrano (S) 1912

4200 Santiago del Estero

Non-English Name: Universidad Nacional de Santiago del Estero, Facultad de Ciencias Forestales (UNSE), Biblioteca de Ciencias Forestales **Founded:** 1985 **Type:** Academic **Head:** Beatriz Munarriz *Phone:* +54(85) 22-1787 *Email:* fcf@unse.edu.ar **Staff:** 1 Prof. **Holdings:** 800 books 70 journals **Language of Collection/Services:** Spanish / Spanish **Subjects:** Forest Products, Forestry, Wood Technology **Loan:** Inhouse **Service:** Inhouse **Photocopy:** No

75   **Trelew, Argentina**
        National Institute of Agricultural Technology,
            Agricultural Experiment Station Chubut
        Library
        Casilla de Correo 88
        Ex-Ruta Nacional No. 25, Km 1480
        9100 Trelew, Chubut
Phone: +54(2965) 46658, 46422 **Fax:** +54(2965) 47019 **Email:** etrelew@inta.gov.ar **WWW:** www.inta.gov.ar

Non-English Name: Instituto Nacional de Tecnología Agropecuaria, Estación Experimental Agropecuaria Chubut (INTA, EEA Trelew), Biblioteca **Former Name:** Estación Experimental Agropecuaria Trelew **Type:** Government **Photocopy:** Yes

76   **Viedma, Argentina**
        National Institute of Agricultural Technology,
            Agricultural Experiment Station of Valle
            Inferior del Rio Negro
        Library
        Km. 971 Camino 101
        Viedma, Río Negro
Phone: +54(2920) 423474 **Fax:** +54(2920) 423474 **WWW:** www.inta.gov.ar

Non-English Name: Instituto Nacional de Tecnología Agropecuaria, Estación Experimental Agropecuaria Valle Inferior del Río Negro (INTA, EEA Valle Inferior del Río Negro), Biblioteca **Type:** Government **Head:** Sonia C. Perez *Phone:* +54(2920) 423474

Armenia

77   **Masiskii Region, Armenia**
        Republic Research Institute of Vegetable Growing
        Library
        Darakert
        Masiskii Region 378372
Phone: Yerevan +374(8-8562) 272641

Type: Government **Head:** Aslanian Galust *Phone:* +374() 40892 **Language of Collection/Services:** Armenian, Russian **Subjects:** Agribusiness, Agricultural Development, Agricultural Engineering, Biotechnology, Farming, Entomology, Plant Pathology, Plants **Specializations:** Melons, Vegetables **Photocopy:** No

78   **Yerevan, Armenia**
        Armenian Research Institute of Scientific and
            Technical Information
        Republican Scientific and Technical Library

Yerevan
Phone: +374(3) 238747, 236375, 238771 **Fax:** +374(3) 906196 **Email:** root@globinfo.infocom.amilink.net
Networks: AGRIS

79   **Yerevan, Armenia**
        National Academy of Sciences of Armenia
        Fundamental Scientific Library
        Baghramian Ave. 24 "D"
        Yerevan 375019
Phone: +374(2) 524750 **WWW:** flib.sci.am

Founded: 1935 **Head:** Prof. Anry Nersessian **Holdings:** 2,900,000 books

Australia

Australian Capital Territory

80   **Canberra, Australian Capital Territory,**
            Australia
        Agriculture, Fisheries and Forestry, Australia
            (AFFA)
        AFFA Library
        GPO Box 1563
        Canberra, Australian Capital Territory 2601
Location: Edmund Barton Building, Macquarie St., Barton, ACT 2600 **Phone:** +61(6) 272-4548 **Fax:** +61(6) 272-4709 **Email:** library@abare.gov.au **WWW:** www.affa.gov.au

Former Name: Department of Primary Industry (DPI), Department of Resources and Energy, Department of Primary Industries and Energy (DPIE), Australian Bureau of Agricultural and Resource Economics (ABARE) **Founded:** 1956 **Type:** Government **Staff:** 5 Prof. 3 Other **Holdings:** 40,000 books 600 journals **Language of Collection/Services:** English / English **Subjects:** Agriculture (Tropics), Agribusiness, Agricultural Development, Agricultural Engineering, Animal Husbandry, Biotechnology, Crops, Farming, Fisheries, Food Sciences, Forestry, Horticulture, Plant Pathology, Soil Science, Veterinary Medicine, Water Resources **Networks:** Kinetica **Photocopy:** Yes **Loan:** Internationally **Service:** Internationally

81   **Canberra, Australian Capital Territory,**
            Australia
        Commonwealth Scientific and Industrial Research
            Organisation (CSIRO)
        Black Mountain Library
        GPO Box 109
        Canberra, Australian Capital Territory 2601
Location: Clunies Ross Street, Acton, ACT 2600 **Phone:** +61(2) 6246-5699 **Email:** library@bml.csiro.au **Fax:** +61 (6) 6246-5684 **WWW:** www.csiro.au **OPAC:** voyager.its.csiro.au

Founded: 1928 **Type:** Government **Head:** Carol Murray *Phone:* +61(2) 6246-5675 *Email:* carol.murray@bml.csiro.au **Staff:** 8 Prof. 4 Other **Holdings:** 150,000 books 1,000 journals **Language of Collection/Services:** English/English

Subjects: Biotechnology, Plant Pathology, Soil Science, Water Resources **Specializations:** Botany, Entomology, Water **Networks:** Kinetica; CSIRO Library Network "Voyager" Catalogue **Databases Used:** Comprehensive **Loan:** Internationally **Service:** Internationally **Photocopy:** Yes

82   **Parkes, Australian Capital Territory, Australia**
        National Library of Australia
        Parkes Place
        Parkes, Australian Capital Territory 2600
Phone: +61(2) 6262-1266 **Fax:** +61(2) 6257-1703 **Email:** docss@nla.gov.au **WWW:** www.nla.gov.au **OPAC:** www.nla.gov.au/kinetica **Ariel IP:** 203.4.200.194

Founded: 1961 **Type:** Government **Head:** Mr. W.M. Horton *Phone:* +61(2) 6262-1262 *Email:* exec@nla.gov.au **Staff:** 180 Prof. 439 Other **Holdings:** 22,000 books 120 journals **Language of Collection/Services:** English **Subjects:** Agriculture (Tropics), Agribusiness, Agricultural Development, Agricultural Economics, Agricultural Engineering, Animal Husbandry, Biotechnology, Crops, Education/Extension, Entomology, Farming, Fisheries, Food Sciences, Forestry, Horticulture, Plant Pathology, Soil Science, Veterinary Medicine, Water Resources **Specializations:** Agriculture (Australia) **Networks:** Kinetica **Loan:** Internationally **Service:** Internationally **Photocopy:** Yes

New South Wales

83   **Armidale, New South Wales, Australia**
        Commonwealth Scientific and Industrial Research
            Organisation, Division of Animal Production,
            Pastoral Research Laboratory (CSIRO)
        Library
        Private Mail Bag
        Armidale, New South Wales 2350
Location: New England Highway **Fax:** +61(67) 78-4358

Founded: 1947 **Type:** Government **Head:** Ms. J. Wood *Phone:* +61(67) 78-4000 **Staff:** 1 Prof. **Holdings:** 15,000 books 250 journals **Language of Collection/Services:** English **Subjects:** Agriculture (Tropics), Animal Husbandry, Soil Science **Specializations:** Animal Nutrition, Animal Production, Immunology, Veterinary Medicine **Databases Used:** Biosis; CABCD **Loan:** In country **Service:** Internationally **Photocopy:** Yes

84   **Armidale, New South Wales, Australia**
        University of New England
        Dixson Library
        Armidale, New South Wales 2351
Phone: +61(2) 6773-2458 **Fax:** +61(2) 6773-2982 **Email:** docdel@metz.une.edu.au **WWW:** www.une.edu.au **OPAC:** www.une.edu.au/library/elecres/oncat.htm **Ariel IP:** 129.180.88.98

Founded: 1938 **Type:** Academic **Head:** Karl G. Schmude *Phone:* +61(2) 6773-2166 *Email:* kscmude@metz.une.edu.au **Staff:** 21 Prof. 47 Other **Holdings:** 30,000 books 300 journals **Subjects:** Comprehensive **Databases Used:** Agricola; CABCD **Loan:** Internationally **Photocopy:** Yes

85   **Beecroft, New South Wales, Australia**
        State Forests of New South Wales
        Library
        PO Box 100
        Beecroft, New South Wales 2119
Location: 121-131 Oratava Avenue, West Pennant Hills, NSW 2125 **Phone:** +61(2) 9872-0110 **Fax:** +61(2) 9872-0110 **Email:** library@ironbark.forest.nsw.gov.au **WWW:** www.forest.nsw.gov.au

Former Name: Forestry Commission of New South Wales **Founded:** 1930 **Type:** Government **Head:** Angela Ree *Phone:* +61(2) 9872-0110 *Email:* library@ironbark.forest.nsw.gov.au **Staff:** 1 Prof. 2 Other **Holdings:** 80,000 books 200 journals **Language of Collection/Services:** English / English **Subjects:** Biological Solids, Entomology, Forest Products, Forestry, Hydrology, Plant Pathology, Soil Science **Networks:** Kinetica **Databases Used:** Comprehensive **Loan:** Internationally **Service:** Inhouse **Photocopy:** Yes

86   **Camden, New South Wales, Australia**
        NSW Agriculture, Elizabeth Macarthur
            Agricultural Institute (NSWA)
        Library
        PMB 8
        Camden, New South Wales 2570
Location: Woodbridge Road, Menangle **Phone:** +61(2) 4640-6394 **Fax:** +61(2) 4640-6317 **Email:** emai.library@agric.nsw.gov.au

Former Name: Veterinary Laboratories **Founded:** 1968 **Type:** Government **Head:** Mrs. Elizabeth Wilkes *Phone:* +61 (2) 4640-6394 *Email:* liz.wilkes@agric.nsw.gov.au **Staff:** 1 Prof. 2 Other **Holdings:** 4,500 books 110 journals **Language of Collection/Services:** English / English **Subjects:** Animal Husbandry, Plant Pathology, Soil, Veterinary Medicine **Networks:** Kinetica **Databases Used:** Comprehensive **Loan:** In country **Service:** Internationally **Photocopy:** Yes

87   **Camden, New South Wales, Australia**
        University of Sydney (NU)
        Camden Branch Library (NUCA)
        Private Mail Bag 3
        Camden, New South Wales 2570
Location: 425 Werombi Road **Phone:** +61(2) 4655-0627 **Fax:** +61(2) 4655-6719 **Email:** camden@library.usyd.edu.au **WWW:** www.camden.usyd.edu.au/library.html **OPAC:** opac.library.usyd.edu.au

Former Name: University Farms Library **Founded:** 1960 **Type:** Academic **Head:** Judy Anson *Phone:* +61(2) 9351-1627 *Email:* camden@library.usyd.edu.au **Staff:** 1.5 Other **Holdings:** 32,000 books 437 journals **Language of Collection/Services:** English **Subjects:** Agriculture (Tropics), Agribusiness, Agricultural Development, Agricultural Economics, Agricultural Engineering, Crops, Education/Extension, Entomology, Farming, Fisheries, Food Sciences, Soil Science, Water Resources **Specializations:** Animal Husbandry, Plant Breeding, Veterinary Medicine **Networks:** Kinetica **Databases Used:** Comprehensive **Loan:** Internationally **Service:** Internationally **Photocopy:** Yes

88 **Cronulla, New South Wales, Australia**
NSW Fisheries, NSW Fisheries Research Institute
(NFRI)
Library
PO Box 21
Cronulla, New South Wales 2230
Location: 202 Nicholson Pde **Fax:** +61(2) 9527-8576
Email: blandc@fisheries.nsw.gov.au **WWW:** www.
fisheries.nsw.gov.au

Former Name: New South Wales State Fisheries **Type:**
Government **Head:** Carolyn Bland *Phone:* +61(2) 9527-
8418 *Email:* blandc@fisheries.nsw.gov.au **Staff:** 1 Prof. 1
Other **Holdings:** 5,200 books 350 journals **Language of
Collection/Services:** English **Subjects:** Fisheries **Net-
works:** Kinetica **Loan:** Internationally **Service:** Inhouse
Photocopy: Yes

89 **Griffith, New South Wales, Australia**
Commonwealth Scientific and Industrial Research
Organisation, Land and Water, Griffith
Laboratory (CSIRO)
Library
Private Mail Bag No. 3
Griffith, New South Wales 2680
Location: Research Station Road **Fax:** +61(69) 630262
Email: library@grf.clw.csiro.au **WWW:** www.csiro.au
OPAC: voyager.its.csiro.au

Former Name: Division of Water Resources, Centre for Ir-
rigation and Freshwater Research Library **Founded:** 1947
Type: Government **Head:** Ms. Fiona Painting *Phone:*
+61(2) 6960-1523 *Email:* fiona.painting@grf.clw.csiro.au
Staff: 1 Prof. 1 Other **Holdings:** 5,000 books 300 journals
Language of Collection/Services: English / English **Sub-
jects:** Crops, Soil Science, Water Quality, Water Resources
Specializations: Irrigation **Networks:** Kinetica **Databases
Used:** Comprehensive **Loan:** In country **Service:** Inhouse
Photocopy: Yes

90 **Hurtsville, New South Wales, Australia**
National Parks and Wildlife Service
Library
PO Box 1967
Hurtsville, New South Wales 2227
Location: 43 Bridge Street **Phone:** +61(2) 9585-6444,
9585-6440 **Fax:** +61(2) 9585-6447 **WWW:** www.npws.
nsw.gov.au

Founded: 1967 **Type:** Government **Staff:** 2 Prof. **Holdings:**
14,000 books 600 journals **Subjects:** Botany, Conservation,
Cultural Heritage, Ecology, Natural Resources, Zoology
Databases Developed: National Parks and Wildlife Image
Library - collection of transparencies and prints of land-
scapes, historic sites, native animals and birds, native plants,
etc.; information on availability see Internet site at www.
npws.nsw.gov.au/services/photolibrary.html **Loan:** Do not
loan **Photocopy:** No

91 **Manly Vale, New South Wales, Australia**
University of New South Wales, Water Research
Laboratory
Water Reference Library

King Street
Manly Vale, New South Wales 2093
Phone: +61(2) 9949-4488 **Fax:** +61(2) 9949-4188 **WWW:**
www.wrl.unsw.edu.au

Founded: 1960 **Type:** Academic **Head:** Miss M. Titterton
Staff: 1 Prof. 1 Other **Holdings:** 10,000 books 50 journals
Language of Collection/Services: English **Subjects:** Water
Resources **Specializations:** Coasts, Fluid Mechanics, Hy-
draulics, Hydrology, Irrigation, Groundwater, Water Quality
Loan: Internationally **Photocopy:** Yes

92 **North Ryde, New South Wales, Australia**
Commonwealth Scientific and Industrial Research
Organisation, Australian Food Industry
Science Centre, Food Science Australia
(CSIRO, AFISC)
J.R. Vickery Library
PO Box 52
North Ryde, New South Wales 1670
Location: 16 Julius Avenue, Riverside Corporate Park,
Delhi Road, North Ryde, NSW 2113 **Phone:** +61(2) 9490-
8320 **Fax:** +61(2) 9490-8490 **Email:** nsfr@foodscience.
afisc.csiro.au **WWW:** www.foodscience.afisc. csiro.au
OPAC: voyager.its.csiro.au

Former Name: Food Research Laboratory **Founded:** 1939
Type: Government **Head:** A. Nevile *Phone:* +61(2) 9490-
8333 *Email:* nsfr@foodscience.afisc.csiro.au **Staff:** 1 Prof.
1.5 Other **Holdings:** 3,000 books 250 journals **Language of
Collection/Services:** English / English **Subjects:** Biotechnology, Food Sciences, Horticulture, Microbiology **Networks:** Kinetica **Databases Used:** Comprehensive **Loan:** In
country **Photocopy:** Yes

93 **North Ryde, New South Wales, Australia**
Commonwealth Scientific and Industrial Research
Organisation, Division of Biomolecular
Engineering, Sydney Laboratory (CSIRO)
Library
PO Box 184
North Ryde, New South Wales 1670
Location: 2 Richardson Place, Riverside Corporate Park,
Delhi Road **Phone:** +61(2) 9490-5073 **Fax:** +61(2) 9490-
5074 **Email:** nsmol@molsci.csiro.au **WWW:** www.csiro.
au

Former Name: Division of Molecular Biology Library
Founded: 1960 **Type:** Government **Head:** Ann Neville
Phone: +61(2) 9490-5072 *Email:* ann.neville@molsci.csiro.
au **Staff:** 1 Prof. 1 Other **Holdings:** 2,000 books 40 journals
Language of Collection/Services: English / English **Sub-
jects:** Biotechnology, Cellular Biology, Molecular Biology,
Ontology **Databases Used:** Comprehensive **Loan:** In coun-
try **Photocopy:** Yes

94 **Orange, New South Wales, Australia**
NSW Agriculture
Head Office Library
Locked Bag 21
Orange, New South Wales 2800
Location: 161 Kite Street **Phone:** +61(63) 91-3500 **Fax:**
+61(63) 91-3515

Former Name: New South Wales Department of Agriculture (NSWDA), New South Wales Agriculture and Fisheries, Central Library **Founded:** 1890 **Type:** Government **Head:** Jan Richards *Phone:* +61(63) 91-3492 **Staff:** 7 Prof. 3 Other **Holdings:** 20,000 books 2,000 journals **Language of Collection/Services:** English / English **Subjects:** Agriculture (Tropics), Agribusiness, Agricultural Development, Agricultural Economics, Agricultural Engineering, Animal Husbandry, Biotechnology, Fisheries, Horticulture, Education/Extension, Crops, Entomology, Farming, Food Sciences, Forestry, Plant Pathology, Soil Science, Veterinary Medicine, Water Resources **Specializations:** Government Documents (Australia) **Loan:** In country **Service:** Internationally **Photocopy:** Yes

95   **Orange, New South Wales, Australia**
         NSW Agriculture, Orange Agricultural Institute
              (NSWA)
         Library
         Forest Road
         Orange, New South Wales 2800
Phone: +61(2) 6391-3800 **Fax:** +61(2) 6391-3899 **WWW:** www.agric.nsw.gov.au

Former Name: Agricultural Research and Veterinary Centre **Founded:** 1979 **Type:** Government **Head:** V. Glover *Phone:* +61(2) 6391-3849 **Staff:** 1 Prof. 1 Other **Holdings:** 15,000 books 300 journals **Language of Collection/Services:** English / English **Subjects:** Entomology, Horticulture, Plant Pathology, Vertebrate Pests, Veterinary Science, Weeds **Networks:** Kinetica **Databases Used:** Comprehensive **Loan:** Internationally **Service:** In country **Photocopy:** Yes

96   **Orange, New South Wales, Australia**
         University of Sydney, Orange Agricultural
              College
         Library
         PO Box 883
         Orange, New South Wales 2800
Location: Leeds Parade **Phone:** +61(2) 6360-5593 **Fax:** +61(2) 6360-5637 **Email:** lib@oac.usyd.edu.au **WWW:** www.oac.usyd.edu.au

Founded: 1973 **Type:** Academic **Head:** Lindy Eggleston *Phone:* +61(2) 6360-5594 *Email:* legglest@oac.usyd.edu.au **Staff:** 2 Prof. 2.6 Other **Holdings:** 19,500 books 250 journals **Language of Collection/Services:** English **Subjects:** Agriculture (Tropics), Agribusiness, Agricultural Development, Agricultural Economics, Agricultural Engineering, Animal Husbandry, Crops, Education/Extension, Farming, Entomology, Forestry, Horticulture, Plant Pathology, Soil Science, Veterinary Medicine, Water Resources **Networks:** Unilinc **Databases Used:** Comprehensive **Loan:** Internationally **Photocopy:** Yes

97   **Richmond, New South Wales, Australia**
         University of Western Sydney, Hawkesbury
              (UWS,H)
         Library
         Locked Bag No 1
         Richmond, New South Wales 2753

Location: Bourke Street **Phone:** +61(2) 4570-1226 **Fax:** +61(2) 4570-1940 **WWW:** www.hawkesbury.uws.edu.au **OPAC:** sybil.hawkesbury.uws.edu.au **Ariel IP:** 137.154.49.12

Former Name: Hawkesbury Agricultural College, Information Resources Centre **Founded:** 1891 **Type:** Academic **Head:** Liz Curach *Email:* l.curach@uws.edu.au *Phone:* +61 (2) 4570-1212 **Staff:** 14 Prof. 22.5 Other **Holdings:** 110,674 books 3,685 journals **Language of Collection/Services:** English/English **Subjects:** Agriculture (Tropics), Agribusiness, Agricultural Development, Agricultural Economics, Agricultural Engineering, Animal Husbandry, Biotechnology, Business, Crops, Education/Extension, Entomology, Environment, Farming, Farming Systems, Fisheries, Forestry, Home Economics, Horticulture, Plant Pathology, Soil Science, Veterinary Medicine, Water Resources **Specializations:** Food Sciences **Databases Used:** Comprehensive **Loan:** In country **Service:** In country **Photocopy:** Yes

98   **Sydney, New South Wales, Australia**
         Australian Museum
         Research Library
         6 College Street
         Sydney, New South Wales 2000
Phone: +61(2) 339-8222, 339-8273 **Fax:** +61(2) 9320-6050 **Email:** info1@amsg.austmus.gov.au **WWW:** www.austmus.gov.au

Founded: 1836 **Type:** Research **Head:** Samantha Fenton *Phone:* +61(2) 9320-6152 *Email:* samf@amsg.austmus.gov. au **Staff:** 2 Prof. 5 Other **Holdings:** 35,000 books 2,000 journals **Language of Collection/Services:** English / English **Subjects:** Entomology, Fisheries, Forestry, Natural History **Specializations:** Anthropology (Australia), Natural History (Australia), Museology (Australia) **Networks:** Kinetica **Databases Used:** Comprehensive **Loan:** In country **Service:** In country **Photocopy:** Yes

99   **Sydney, New South Wales, Australia**
         Commonwealth Scientific and Industrial Research
              Organisation, Animal Production, Ian Clunies
              Ross Animal Research Laboratory (CSIRO)
         Prospect Library
         Locked Bag No. 1, Delivery Centre
         Blacktown
         Sydney, New South Wales 2148
Location: Clunies Ross St., Prospect, NSW 2149 **Phone:** +61(2) 9840-2832 **Fax:** +61(2) 9840-2805 **Email:** library@anprod.csiro.au **WWW:** www.anprod.csiro.au

Former Name: Council for Scientific and Industrial Research, Division of Animal Physiology, McMaster Laboratory, Max Henry Memorial Library **Founded:** 1932 **Type:** Government **Head:** S. Drake *Phone:* +61(2) 9840-2831 *Email:* library@anprod.csiro.au **Staff:** 2 Prof. **Holdings:** 27,450 books 300 journals **Language of Collection/Services:** English **Subjects:** Agricultural Development, Animal Husbandry, Endocrinology, Farming, Genetics, Veterinary Immunology, Veterinary Medicine, Veterinary Parasitology **Networks:** Voyager **Databases Used:** Comprehensive **Service:** In country **Loan:** In country **Photocopy:** Yes

100   Sydney, New South Wales, Australia
Royal Botanic Gardens
Library
Mrs Macquaries Road
Sydney, New South Wales 2000
Phone: +61(2) 9231-8152 **Fax:** +61(2) 9251-4403 **Email:** library@rbgsyd.gov.au

Founded: 1850's **Type:** Government **Head:** Anna Hallett *Phone:* +61(2) 9231-8152 *Email:* library@rbgsyd.gov.au **Staff:** 1 Prof. 1 Other **Holdings:** 28,000 books 500 journals **Language of Collection/Services:** English / English **Subjects:** Botany, Horticulture **Specializations:** Plants, Taxonomy **Loan:** In country **Service:** Inhouse **Photocopy:** Yes

101   Sydney, New South Wales, Australia
State Library of New South Wales
Macquarie Street
Sydney, New South Wales 2000
Phone: +61(2) 9273-1414 **Fax:** +61(2) 9273-1255 **Email:** library@ilanet.slnsw.gov.au **WWW:** www.slnsw.gov.au

Former Name: Library of New South Wales, Public Library of New South Wales **Founded:** 1826 **Type:** Government **Head:** Mrs. Dagmar Schmidmaier *Phone:* +61(2) 9273-1414 *Email:* library@ilanet.slnsw.gov.au **Staff:** 430 Prof. **Holdings:** 4,000,000 books 15,718 journals **Language of Collection/Services:** English / English **Subjects:** Agriculture (Tropics), Agribusiness, Agricultural Development, Agricultural Economics, Agricultural Engineering, Animal Husbandry, Biotechnology, Crops, Entomology, Education/ Extension, Farming, Fisheries, Food Sciences, Forestry, Horticulture, Plant Pathology, Soil Science, Veterinary Medicine, Water Resources **Specializations:** Agriculture (Australia) **Networks:** Kinetica **Databases Developed:** Infoquick - indexes Australian content or information of Australian interest including agriculture in the "Sydney Morning Herald". **Databases Used:** Comprehensive **Loan:** Internationally **Service:** Internationally **Photocopy:** Yes

102   Sydney, New South Wales, Australia
University of Sydney
Badham Library
Badham Building A16, Science Road
Sydney, New South Wales 2006
Fax: +61(2) 9351-3852 **Email:** badham@library.usyd.edu. au **WWW:** www.usyd.edu.au **OPAC:** www.library.usyd. edu.au

Type: Academic **Head:** Su Hanfling *Phone:* +61(2) 9351-3775 *Email:* s.hanfling@library.usyd.edu.au **Staff:** 3 Prof. 4 Other **Holdings:** 10,000 books 2,250 journals **Language of Collection/Services:** English / English **Subjects:** Comprehensive **Networks:** Kinetica **Databases Used:** Comprehensive **Loan:** Internationally **Photocopy:** Yes

103   Tamworth, New South Wales, Australia
NSW Agriculture, Tamworth Centre for Crop
    Improvement (NSWA, TCCI)
Library
RMB 944
Tamworth, New South Wales 2340

Location: Calala Lane **Phone:** +61(2) 6763-1114 **Fax:** +61(2) 6763-1222 **Email:** jenny.goodfellow@agric.nsw. gov.au **WWW:** www.agric.nsw.gov.au

Former Name: Agricultural Research and Advisory Centre, New South Wales Department of Agriculture (NSWDA) **Founded:** 1963 **Type:** Government **Head:** Jennifer Goodfellow *Email:* jenny.goodfellow@agric.nsw.gov.au *Phone:* +61(2) 6763-1114 **Staff:** 1 Prof. 1 Other **Holdings:** 3,000 books 250 journals **Language of Collection/ Services:** English / English **Subjects:** Biological Control, Crops, Entomology, Fodder, Irrigation, Legumes, Pest Management, Soil Science, Pastures, Plant Pathology, Tillage, Weed Control, Wheat **Networks:** Kinetica **Databases Used:** Comprehensive **Loan:** In country **Service:** In country **Photocopy:** Yes

104   'TOCAL' Paterson, New South Wales,
         Australia
NSW Agriculture, C.B. Alexander Agricultural
    College
Library - TOCAL Paterson
'TOCAL' Paterson, New South Wales 2421
Phone: +61(249) 398830 **Fax:** +61(249) 385584 **Email:** barhaml@agric.nsw.gov.au

Former Name: New South Wales Department of Agriculture (NSWDA), New South Wales Agriculture and Fisheries **Founded:** 1966 **Type:** Academic **Head:** Mrs. Lyn M. Barham *Phone:* +61(249) 398830 *Email:* barhaml@agric.nsw. gov.au **Staff:** 1 Prof. 1 Other **Holdings:** 11,000 books 70 journals **Language of Collection/Services:** English / English **Subjects:** Agribusiness, Agricultural Economics, Animal Husbandry, Crops, Education/Extension, Forestry, Horticulture, Soil Science, Veterinary Medicine, Water Resources **Networks:** Kinetica **Databases Used:** Comprehensive **Loan:** In country **Service:** In country **Photocopy:** Yes

105   Trangie, New South Wales, Australia
NSW Agriculture, Trangie Agricultural Research
    Centre (NSWA, TARC)
Library
PMB 19
Trangie, New South Wales 2823
Location: Mitchell Highway **Phone:** +61(68) 887404 **Fax:** +61(68) 887181

Former Name: New South Wales Department of Agriculture (NSWDA) **Founded:** 1983 **Type:** Government **Head:** Sally C. Anderson *Phone:* +61(68) 887404 *Email:* anderss@ agric.nsw.gov.au **Staff:** 1 Prof. .4 Other **Holdings:** 3,000 books 240 journals **Language of Collection/Services:** English / English **Subjects:** Agricultural Engineering, Animal Husbandry, Crops, Farming, Soil Science **Databases Used:** CABCD **Loan:** Internationally **Service:** Internationally **Photocopy:** Yes

106   Wagga Wagga, New South Wales, Australia
Charles Sturt University
Wagga Campus Library
Locked Bag 681
Wagga Wagga, New South Wales 2678
Location: Boorooma Street **Phone:** +61(2) 6933-2343 **Fax:** +61(2) 6933-2900 **Email:** libquest@csu.edu.au

WWW: www.csu.edu.au/division/library **OPAC:** www. csu.edu.au/division/library

Former Name: Riverina-Murray Institute of Higher Education, Riverina College of Advanced Education, Mitchell College of Advanced Education, William Merrylees Library **Founded:** 1945 **Type:** Academic **Head:** Carol Mills *Phone:* +61(2) 6933-2332 *Email:* cmills@csu.edu.au **Staff:** 32 Prof. 48 Other **Holdings:** 9,000 books 124 journals **Language of Collection/Services:** English / English **Subjects:** Agribusiness, Agricultural Development, Agricultural Economics, Agricultural Engineering, Animal Husbandry, Crops, Farming, Horticulture, Plant Pathology, Soil Science, Water Resources **Specializations:** Irrigation, Sustainability, Viticulture, Winemaking **Networks:** UNILINC **Databases Used:** Comprehensive **Loan:** In country **Service:** In country **Photocopy:** Yes

107   **Wagga Wagga, New South Wales, Australia**
        NSW Agriculture, Agricultural Research Institute
        Library
        Private Mail Bag
        Wagga Wagga, New South Wales 2650
Location: Pine Gully Road **Phone:** +61(69) 38-1828 **Fax:** +61(69) 38-1809

Former Name: New South Wales Department of Agriculture (NSWDA) **Founded:** 1953 **Type:** Government **Head:** Miss D. South *Phone:* +61(69) 23-0999 **Staff:** 1 Prof. **Holdings:** 1,800 books 120 journals **Subjects:** Crops, Plant Pathology, Soil Science **Loan:** In country **Photocopy:** Yes

108   **Wollongbar, New South Wales, Australia**
        NSW Agriculture, Wollongbar Agricultural
            Institute (NSWA, WAI)
        Library
        Bruxner Hwy
        Wollongbar, New South Wales 2477
Phone: +61(66) 261321 **Fax:** +61(66) 285925 **WWW:** www.agric.nsw.gov.au

Former Name: New South Wales Department of Agriculture (NSWDA), New South Wales Agriculture and Fisheries, Agricultural Research Centre, Wollongbar, North Coast Agricultural Institute **Founded:** 1963 **Type:** Government **Head:** Narendra Anuj *Email:* narendra.anuj@agric.nsw. gov.au *Phone:* +61(66) 2610321 **Staff:** 1 Prof. 2 Other **Holdings:** 8,000 books 500 journals **Language of Collection/Services:** English / English **Subjects:** Agriculture (Tropics), Animal Husbandry, Animal Production, Chemistry, Crops, Entomology, Environmental Management, Environmental Sciences, Horticulture, Plant Pathology, Soil Science, Veterinary Medicine, Water Resources **Specializations:** Animal Nutrition, Dairy Science **Networks:** Kinetica **Databases Used:** Comprehensive **Loan:** Internationally **Service:** Inhouse **Photocopy:** Yes

109   **Yanco, New South Wales, Australia**
        NSW Agriculture, Yanco Agricultural Institute
            (NSWA, YAI)
        Library
        Private Mail Bag
        Yanco, New South Wales 2703

Location: Trunk Road 80 **Phone:** +61(69) 53-0316 **Fax:** +61(69) 53-0260

Former Name: New South Wales Department of Agriculture (NSWDA) **Type:** Government **Head:** Mrs. Rosemary Blakeney *Phone:* +61(69) 53-0316 *Email:* blakenr@agric. nsw.gov.au **Staff:** 1 Prof. 1.5 Other **Holdings:** 6,000 books 200 journals **Language of Collection/Services:** English / English **Subjects:** Crops, Entomology, Horticulture, Plant Pathology, Soil Science, Water Resources **Specializations:** Irrigation, Rice **Databases Developed:** AGNET - used to send mail, compile inhouse files, and gain access to other databases **Databases Used:** Agricola; CABCD; FSTA **Loan:** Internationally **Service:** Internationally **Photocopy:** Yes

Northern Territory

110   **Alice Springs, Northern Territory, Australia**
        Northern Territory Department of Primary
            Industry and Fisheries, Arid Zone Research
            Institute (DPIF, AZRI)
        Library
        PO Box 8760
        Alice Springs, Northern Territory 0871
Location: South Stuart Highway, Alice Springs **Phone:** +61(8) 8951-8134 **Fax:** +61(8) 8951-8112 **WWW:** www. nt.gov.au/dpif

Former Name: Northern Territory Department of Primary Production **Founded:** 1967 **Type:** Government **Head:** Lyn Johnson *Phone:* +61(8) 8951-8114 *Email:* lyn.johnson@nt. gov.au **Staff:** 1 Prof. 1 Other **Holdings:** 6,500 books 400 journals **Language of Collection/Services:** English/English **Subjects:** Animal Husbandry, Farming, Horticulture, Range Management, Veterinary Medicine **Networks:** Kinetica **Databases Used:** CABCD **Loan:** In country **Service:** Inhouse **Photocopy:** Yes

111   **Darwin, Northern Territory, Australia**
        Northern Territory Department of Primary
            Industry and Fisheries (DPIF)
        Central Library
        GPO Box 990
        Darwin, Northern Territory 0801
Location: Berrimah Farm, Makagon Rd., Berrimah, NT 0828 **Phone:** +61(8) 8999-2269 **Fax:** +61(8) 8999-2023 **Email:** library.berrimahfarm@dpif.nt.gov.au **WWW:** www.nt.gov.au/dpif

Former Name: Northern Territory Department of Primary Production, Northern Region Library **Founded:** 1974 **Type:** Government **Head:** Ms. Lynne Cooke, Ms. Louise Paynter *Phone:* +61(8) 8999-2210 *Email:* lynne.cooke@dpif.nt.gov. au, louise.paynter@dpif.nt.gov.au **Staff:** 3 Prof. 4 Other **Holdings:** 18,000 books 800 journals **Language of Collection/Services:** English **Subjects:** Agriculture (Tropics), Agricultural Economics, Agricultural Engineering, Animal Husbandry, Crops, Entomology, Farming, Horticulture, Plant Pathology, Veterinary Medicine **Networks:** Kinetica **Databases Used:** Agricola; Agris; CABCD **Loan:** In country **Photocopy:** Yes

Queensland

112   Brisbane, Queensland, Australia
CANEGROWERS
Library
GPO Box 1032
Brisbane, Queensland 4001
Location: 190-194 Edward Street **Fax:** +61(7) 3864-6429
Email: canegrowers@canegrowers.com.au **WWW:** www.
farmwide.com.au/nff/canegrowers/cane.htm

Former Name: Queensland Cane Growers Council (QCGC)
Founded: 1916 **Type:** Association **Head:** Mrs. J. Simon
Phone: +61(7) 3864-6444 ext 411 *Email:* canegrowers@
canegrowers.com.au **Staff:** 2 Other **Holdings:** 4,500 books
275 journals **Subjects:** Agriculture (Tropics), Agribusiness,
Agricultural Development, Agricultural Economics, Farming, Biotechnology, Crops, Education/Extension, Entomology, Food Sciences, Horticulture, Plant Pathology, Soil
Science, Water Resources **Loan:** In country **Photocopy:** Yes

113   Brisbane, Queensland, Australia
INCITEC, Ltd.
Library
PO Box 140
Morningside
Brisbane, Queensland 4170
Location: Paringa Road, Gibson Island, Murrarie **Phone:**
+61(7) 3867-9498 **Fax:** +61(7) 3867-9794 **Email:** jan.
rees@incitec.com.au **WWW:** www.incitec.com.au

Founded: 1970 **Type:** Business **Head:** Jan M. Rees *Phone:*
+61(7) 3867-9498 *Email:* jan.rees@incitec.com.au **Staff:** 1
Prof. **Holdings:** 3,000 books 200 journals **Language of Col-
lection/Services:** English / English **Subjects:** Fertilizers,
Plant Protection **Loan:** In country **Service:** Internationally
Photocopy: Yes

114   Brisbane, Queensland, Australia
Queensland Department of Primary Industries
(QDPI)
Library
GPO Box 944
Brisbane, Queensland 4001
Location: 3rd Floor, Forestry House, 160 Mary Street
Phone: +61(7) 3234-1220 **Fax:** +61(7) 3234-1199 **Email:**
cenfslib@dpi.qld.gov.zu

Former Name: Queensland Forest Service (QDF) **Founded:** 1962 **Type:** Government **Head:** M. Tommerup *Phone:*
+61(7) 3234-0209 **Staff:** 2 Prof. 9 Other **Holdings:** 250 journals **Language of Collection/Services:** English **Subjects:**
Entomology, Forestry, Plant Pathology, Soil Science, Water
Resources **Databases Used:** CABCD **Loan:** Internationally
Photocopy: Yes

115   Brisbane, Queensland, Australia
Queensland Department of Natural Resources
(QDNR)
Department of Natural Resources Library
GPO Box 2454
Brisbane, Queensland 4001
Location: 2nd Floor, Mineral House, 41 George Street
Phone: +61(7) 3224-8412 **Fax:** +61(7) 3224-7571 **WWW:**
www.dnr.qld.gov.au

Former Name: Queensland Department of Primary Industries (QDPI), Queensland Irrigation and Water Supply
Commission, Queensland Water Resources Commission
Founded: 1960 **Type:** Government **Head:** Margaret Walters *Phone:* +61(7) 3224-7337 *Email:* margaret.walters@
dnr.qld.gov.au **Staff:** 7 Prof. 4 Other **Holdings:** 25,000
books 280 journals **Language of Collection/Services:** English / English **Subjects:** Water Resources **Specializations:**
Geology, Hydraulic Engineering, Hydrology, Irrigation,
Land Management, Pest Control, Soil Science, Structural
Engineering, Weeds **Networks:** Kinetica **Databases Used:**
Comprehensive **Loan:** In country **Service:** Inhouse **Photocopy:** Yes

116   Brisbane, Queensland, Australia
Queensland Department of Primary Industries
(QDPI)
Queensland Fisheries Library (QFI Library)
GPO Box 2215
Brisbane, Queensland 4001
Location: 80 Ann Street **Phone:** +61(7) 3239-3178 **Fax:**
+61(7) 3239-3128 **Email:** qfi@dpi.qld.gov.au **WWW:**
www.dpi.qld.gov.au/fishweb

Former Name: Queensland Fisheries Service **Founded:**
1965 **Type:** Government **Head:** Mrs. Zena B. Seliga *Phone:*
+61(7) 3239-3104 *Email:* seligaz@dpi.qld. gov.au **Holdings:** 10,000 books 1,300 journals **Language of Collection/
Services:** English/English **Staff:** 1 Prof. 1 Other **Specializations:** Aquaculture, Fisheries **Networks:** Kinetica **Databases Used:** ASFA **Databases Developed:** ORAQLE -
Online retrieval of acquisitions, cataloguing, and circulation
details for library enquiries of the State Library of
Queensland system **Loan:** In country **Service:** In country
Photocopy: Yes

117   Brisbane, Queensland, Australia
Queensland Department of Primary Industries
(QDPI)
Primary Industries Library
GPO Box 2215
Brisbane, Queensland 4001
Location: 80 Ann Street **Phone:** +61(7) 3239-3126 **Fax:**
+61(7) 3239-3128 **Email:** centlib@dpi.qld.gov.au **WWW:**
www.dpi.qld.gov.au **Ariel IP:** arieldoc@dpi.qld.gov.au

Former Name: DPI Library Services **Founded:** 1895 **Type:**
Government **Head:** Cathy Campbell *Phone:* +61(7) 3239-
3104 *Email:* campbeca@dpi.qld.gov.au **Staff:** 15 Prof. 9
Other **Holdings:** 100,000 books 1,100 journals **Language of
Collection/Services:** English / English **Subjects:** Agricul-
ture (Tropics), Agricultural Economics, Animal Husbandry,
Crops, Education/Extension, Fisheries, Horticulture **Net-
works:** Kinetica **Databases Used:** ABOA; Agricola; ASFA;
CABCD **Loan:** In country **Service:** Inhouse **Photocopy:**
Yes

118   Gatton College, Queensland, Australia
University of Queensland, Gatton College (UQG)

J.K. Murray Library
Gatton College, Queensland 4345
Fax: +61(7) 5460-1136 **WWW:** www.library.uq.edu.au

Former Name: Queensland Agricultural College (QAC) **Founded:** 1974 **Type:** Academic **Head:** Ms. Pauline M. Roberts *Phone:* +61(7) 5460-1270 *Email:* proberts@library.uq.edu.au **Staff:** 4 Prof. 8 Other **Holdings:** 90,000 books 1,200 journals **Language of Collection/Services:** English / English **Subjects:** Agriculture (Tropics), Agribusiness, Agricultural Engineering, Animal Husbandry, Biotechnology, Crops, Education/Extension, Entomology, Farming, Fisheries, Food Sciences, Forestry, Horticulture, Plant Pathology, Property, Soil Science, Tourism, Valuation, Water Resources **Networks:** Kinetica **Databases Used:** Comprehensive **Loan:** Internationally **Service:** Internationally **Photocopy:** Yes

119   Indooroopilly, Queensland, Australia
         Commonwealth Scientific and Industrial Research
            Organisation, Tropical Agriculture (CSIRO)
         Library
         Private Bag No. 3
         Indooroopilly, Queensland 4068
Location: 120 Meiers Road **Phone:** +61(7) 3214-2769 **Fax:** +61(7) 3214-2882 **Email:** lpllibrary@tag.csiro.au **WWW:** www.tcp.csiro.au **OPAC:** www.cis.csiro.au/libserv/introopac.htm

Former Name: Division of Tropical Animal Science **Type:** Government **Founded:** 1948 **Head:** Patrick Ledwith *Phone:* +61(7) 3124-2769 *Email:* patrick.ledwith@tag.csiro.au **Staff:** 1 Prof. 1 Other **Holdings:** 6,000 books 210 journals **Language of Collection/Services:** English/English **Subjects:** Agriculture (Tropics), Biotechnology, Entomology, Veterinary Medicine **Networks:** Kinetica **Databases Used:** Comprehensive **Loan:** In country **Service:** Internationally **Photocopy:** Yes

120   Indooroopilly, Queensland, Australia
         Queensland Department of Natural Resources
            (QDNR)
         Resource Sciences Centre Library (RSC)
         80 Meiers Road, Block B
         Indooroopilly, Queensland 4068
Phone: +61(7) 3896-9492 **Fax:** +61(7) 3896-9623 **Email:** gach@dnr.qld.gov.au **WWW:** www.dnr.qld.gov.au

Former Name: Queensland Department of Primary Industries (QDPI), Agricultural Research Laboratories Library **Type:** Government **Head:** Cecelia McDowall *Phone:* +61(7) 3896-9492 *Email:* cecelia.mcdowall@dnr.qld.gov.au **Staff:** 2 Prof. 1 Other **Language of Collection/Services:** English / English **Subjects:** Agricultural Chemistry, Entomology, Plant Pathology, Water Conservation **Specializations:** Agricultural Chemicals, Soil Science **Databases Used:** Comprehensive **Loan:** Internationally **Service:** Internationally **Photocopy:** Yes

121   Mackay, Queensland, Australia
         Sugar Research Institute (SRI)
         E.T.S. Pearce Library
         Box 5611, Mackay Mail Centre

Mackay, Queensland 4741
Location: 239-255 Nebo Road **Fax:** +61(7) 4952-1734 **Email:** library@sri.org.au

Founded: 1959 **Type:** Research **Head:** Mrs. Ann Ellis *Phone:* +61(7) 4952-7600 *Email:* library@sri.org.au **Staff:** 1 Other **Holdings:** 6,500 books 200 journals **Language of Collection/Services:** English / English **Subjects:** Agricultural Economics, Agricultural Engineering, Biotechnology, Entomology, Food Sciences, Plant Pathology, Soil Science, Water Resources **Specializations:** Chemical Engineering, Chemistry, Electronics, Mechanical Engineering, Sugarcane, Systems **Loan:** Internationally **Service:** Internationally **Photocopy:** Yes

122   Mareeba, Queensland, Australia
         Queensland Department of Primary Industries
            (QDPI)
         North Region Library
         PO Box 1054
         Mareeba, Queensland 4880
Location: 28 Peters Street **Phone:** +61(7) 4092-8497 **Fax:** +61(7) 4092-3593 **WWW:** www.dpi.qld.gov.au

Former Name: Far Northern Regional Library **Founded:** 1980 **Type:** Government **Head:** Ken Cotterill *Phone:* +61(7) 4092-8497 *Email:* cotterk@dpi.qld.gov.au **Staff:** 1 Prof. **Holdings:** 4,000 books 100 journals **Language of Collection/Services:** English **Subjects:** Agriculture (Tropics), Agricultural Engineering, Animal Husbandry, Biotechnology, Coffee, Crops, Education/Extension, Entomology, Farming, Food Sciences, Horticulture, Plant Pathology, Soil Science, Tobacco **Databases Used:** ABOA; Agricola; CABCD **Loan:** Internationally **Service:** Internationally **Photocopy:** Yes

123   Moorooka, Queensland, Australia
         Queensland Department of Primary Industries
            (QDPI)
         Animal Research Institute Library (QAR)
         Locked Mail Bag No. 4
         Moorooka, Queensland 4105
Location: 665 Fairfield Road, Yeerongpilly **Phone:** +61(7) 3362-9467 **Fax:** +61(7) 3362-9609 **Email:** qar@dpi.qld.gov.au **WWW:** www.dpi.qld.gov.au

Founded: 1909 **Type:** Government **Head:** Doug Freckelton *Phone:* +61(7) 3362-9467 *Email:* dougf@dpi.qld.gov.au **Staff:** 1 Prof. 1 Other **Holdings:** 2,500 books 300 journals **Language of Collection/Services:** English / English **Subjects:** Animal Husbandry, Veterinary Medicine **Specializations:** Animal Pathology, Animal Production, Poisonous Plants, Disease Control, Pesticide Residues, Veterinary Parasitology **Databases Developed:** Staff publications list (2,500+ items) using Papyrus bibliographic management software **Databases Used:** Agricola; Agris; CABCD **Loan:** In country **Service:** In country **Photocopy:** Yes

124   Rockhampton, Queensland, Australia
         Commonwealth Scientific and Industrial Research
            Organisation, Division of Tropical Animal
            Production (CSIRO)
         Tropical Beef Centre Library

Box 5545, Rockhampton Mail Centre
Rockhampton, Queensland 4702
Location: Bruce Highway, North Rockhampton **Phone:** +61(79) 36-0118 **Fax:** +61(79) 36-1034

Former Name: Tropical Cattle Research Centre **Founded:** 1952 **Type:** Government **Head:** Ms. Annette Halliday *Phone:* +61(79) 36-0118 **Staff:** 1 Other **Holdings:** 3,000 books 100 journals **Language of Collection/Services:** English **Subjects:** Animal Husbandry **Specializations:** Cattle, Cattle Husbandry, Genetics, Reproduction **Networks:** Kinetica **Loan:** In country **Photocopy:** Yes

125   South Brisbane, Queensland, Australia
Pauls Ltd.
Library and Records Management (LRM)
PO Box 3012
South Brisbane, Queensland 4101
Location: Corner Hope and Montague Road **Fax:** +61(7) 3844-4105

Former Name: QUF Industries Ltd. **Founded:** 1973 **Type:** Business **Head:** Ms. Lesley J. Speer *Phone:* +61(7) 3844-0237 *Email:* speerl@pauls.com.au **Staff:** 2 Prof. **Holdings:** 4,300 books 215 journals Language of Collection/ Services: English **Subjects:** Food Sciences **Specializations:** Milk Products **Databases Used:** Comprehensive **Loan:** In country **Service:** In country **Photocopy:** Yes

126   St. Lucia, Queensland, Australia
Commonwealth Scientific and Industrial Research
    Organisation, Tropical Agriculture,
    Cunningham Laboratory (CSIRO)
Library
306 Carmody Road
St. Lucia, Queensland 4067
Fax: +61(7) 3214-2415 **Email:** library@tag.csiro.au
WWW: www.tag.csiro.au **OPAC:** voyager.its.csiro.au
Ariel IP: ariel@tag.csiro.au

Former Name: Division of Tropical Crops and Pastures **Founded:** 1946 **Type:** Government **Head:** Ms. Anne Tuppack *Phone:* +61(7) 3214-2300 *Email:* library@tag.csiro.au **Staff:** 2 Prof. 1 Other **Holdings:** 30,000 books 255 journals **Language of Collection/Services:** English / English **Subjects:** Agriculture (Tropics), Animal Husbandry, Crops, Horticulture, Plant Pathology **Networks:** Kinetica; CLINES **Loan:** In country **Service:** Internationally **Photocopy:** Yes

127   St. Lucia, Queensland, Australia
University of Queensland (UQ)
Biological Sciences Library (BSL)
St. Lucia, Queensland 4072
Phone: +61(7) 3365-6628 **Fax:** +61(7) 3365-6888 **Email:** dds@library.uq.edu.au **WWW:** www.uq.edu.au **OPAC:** www.library.uq.edu.au **Ariel IP:** 130.102.22.18

Founded: 1911 **Type:** Academic **Head:** Ms. Heather Todd *Phone:* +61(7) 3365-2576 *Email:* h.todd@library.uq.edu.au **Staff:** 7.5 Prof. 11 Other **Holdings:** 59,000 books 2,000 journals **Language of Collection/Services:** English / English **Subjects:** Comprehensive **Specializations:** Agriculture (Tropics) **Networks:** Kinetica **Databases Used:** Compre-

hensive **Loan:** Internationally **Service:** Inhouse **Photocopy:** Yes

128   Toowoomba, Queensland, Australia
Queensland Department of Primary Industries
    (QDPI)
Darling Downs Regional Library
PO Box 102
Toowoomba, Queensland 4350
Location: 203 Tor Street **Phone:** +61(76) 881228 **Fax:** +61(76) 881416

Former Name: South Region Library **Founded:** 1976 **Type:** Government **Staff:** 1 Prof. **Holdings:** 200 journals, 2,300 books 200 journals **Language of Collection/Services:** English **Specializations:** Grain Crops, Pastures **Loan:** Inhouse **Photocopy:** Yes

129   Townsville, Queensland, Australia
Commonwealth Scientific and Industrial Research
    Organisation, Tropical Agriculture (CSIRO)
Davies Laboratory Library
Private Mail Bag, PO Aitkenvale
Townsville, Queensland 4814
Location: University Road, Douglas **Phone:** +61(7) 4753-8511 **Fax:** +61(7) 4753-8600 **Email:** library@tvl.tag.csiro.au **WWW:** www.tag.csiro.au **OPAC:** voyager@its.csiro.au **Ariel IP:** ariel@tvl.tag.csiro.au

Founded: 1963 **Type:** Government **Head:** Mrs. Norma E. Penny *Phone:* +61(7) 4753-8536 *Email:* norma.penny@tag.csiro.au **Staff:** 1 Prof. 1 Other **Holdings:** 12,000 books 150 journals **Language of Collection/Services:** English/English **Subjects:** Agriculture (Tropics), Land Resources, Water Resources **Specializations:** Pastures (Tropics), Tropical Soils **Networks:** Kinetica **Databases Used:** Comprehensive **Loan:** Internationally **Service:** Internationally **Photocopy:** Yes

130   Townsville, Queensland, Australia
Great Barrier Reef Marine Park Authority
Library
PO Box 1379
Townsville, Queensland 4810
Location: 2-68 Flinders Street East **Phone:** +61(77) 500-801 **Fax:** +61(77) 726093 **Email:** library@gbrmpa.gov.au

Founded: 1981 **Type:** Government **Head:** D. Lawrence *Phone:* +61(77) 81-8811 **Staff:** 1 Prof. 1 Other **Holdings:** 3,000 books **Subjects:** Environment, Great Barrier Reef, National Parks, Tourism **Loan:** In country **Photocopy:** Yes

131   Townsville, Queensland, Australia
James Cook University of North Queensland
    (JCU)
Library
Townsville, Queensland 4811
Location: Angus Smith Drive, Douglas **Phone:** +61(7) 4781-5500 **Fax:** +61(7) 4775-6691 **Email:** infohelp@jcu.edu.au **WWW:** www.jcu.edu.au **OPAC:** www.library.jcu.edu.au/Tropicat/tropicat.html **Ariel IP:** 137.219.42.46

Former Name: University College of Townsville **Founded:** 1961 **Type:** Academic **Head:** Mr. John McKinlay *Phone:*

+61(7) 4781-4472 **Staff:** 14 Prof. 44 Other **Holdings:** 3,000 books 200 journals **Language of Collection/Services:** English/English **Subjects:** Agriculture (Tropics), Fisheries, Veterinary Medicine **Specializations:** Veterinary Science (Tropics) **Loan:** In country **Service:** In country **Photocopy:** Yes

South Australia

132 **Adelaide, South Australia, Australia**
Botanic Gardens of Adelaide and State Herbarium
Library
North Terrace
Adelaide, South Australia 5000
WWW: www.denr.sa.gov.au

Founded: 1855 **Type:** Government **Head:** Ms. Karen A. Saxby *Phone:* +61(8) 8228-2325 *Email:* ksaxby@denr.sa.gov.au **Staff:** 1 Prof. **Holdings:** 8,000 books 320 journals **Language of Collection/Services:** English / English **Subjects:** Horticulture **Specializations:** Botany, Garden Design, Plant Conservation, Plant Diseases, Plant Pathology **Networks:** Kinetica **Databases Developed:** Newspaper article collection; Archival photograph collection; Nursery catalogue collection **Databases Used:** Index Kewensis **Loan:** In country **Service:** Mainly in country but will help international botanical institutions **Photocopy:** Yes

133 **Adelaide, South Australia, Australia**
Royal Zoological Society of South Australia, Inc. (RZSSA)
Minchin Memorial Library
c/o Adelaide Zoological Gardens
Frome Road
Adelaide, South Australia 5000
Phone: +61(8) 8267-3255 **Fax:** +61(8) 8239-0637 **WWW:** www.adelaide-zoo.com.au, www.webmedia.com.au/zoo/heritage.html

Type: Association Non-profit **Head:** Silvia Muscardin *Phone:* +61(8) 8267-3255 **Staff:** 1 Prof. **Holdings:** 1,800 books 105 journals **Language of Collection/Services:** English / English **Subjects:** Animal Husbandry, Horticulture, Veterinary Medicine **Specializations:** Wildlife Management, Zoology **Loan:** Inhouse **Service:** Internationally **Photocopy:** Yes

134 **Glen Osmond, South Australia, Australia**
Australian Wine Research Institute (AWRI)
John Fornachon Memorial Library (JFML)
PO Box 197
Glen Osmond, South Australia 5064
Location: Waite Road, Urrbrae **Phone:** +61(8) 8303-6600 **Fax:** +61(8) 8303-6628 **Email:** cdaniel@awri.adelaide.edu.au **WWW:** www.waite.adelaide.edu.au/awri

Founded: 1969 **Type:** Business **Head:** Catherine Daniel *Phone:* +61(8) 8303-6625 *Email:* cdaniel@awri.adelaide.edu.au **Staff:** 1 Prof. 1 Other **Holdings:** 3,100 books 60 journals **Language of Collection/Services:** English, French, German, Italian / English **Subjects:** Food Sciences **Specializations:** Enology, Viticulture **Networks:** Kinetica **Databases Used:** Comprehensive **Loan:** In country **Service:** In country **Photocopy:** Yes

135 **Glen Osmond, South Australia, Australia**
Commonwealth Scientific and Industrial Research Organisation, Land and Water (CSIRO)
Library
Private Bag No. 2
Glen Osmond, South Australia 5064
Location: Waite Road, Urrbrae **Phone:** +61(8) 8303-8540 **Fax:** +61(8) 8303-8694 **Email:** library@adl.soils.csiro.au **WWW:** www.clw.csiro.au **Ariel:** ariel@adl.clw.csiro.au

Former Name: Division of Soils **Founded:** 1958 **Type:** Government **Head:** Mr. Robert Bickford *Phone:* +61(8) 8303-8539 *Email:* rob.bickford@adl.clw.csiro.au **Staff:** 1.7 Prof. .4 Other **Holdings:** 15,000 books 120 journals **Language of Collection/Services:** English / English **Subjects:** Soil Science **Networks:** CSIRO; Kinetica **Loan:** In country **Service:** In country **Photocopy:** Yes

136 **Glen Osmond, South Australia, Australia**
University of Adelaide - Waite Campus
Library Glen Osmond, South Australia 5064
Location: Waite Road, Urrbrae **Phone:** +61(8) 8303-7312 **Fax:** +61(8) 8303-7103 **Email:** waite@library.adelaide.edu.au **WWW:** library.adelaide.edu.au **OPAC:** telnet://library.adelaide.edu.au **Ariel IP:** wariel@library.adelaide.edu.au

Former Name: Waite Agricultural Research Institute **Founded:** 1925 **Type:** Academic **Head:** Ellen Randva *Email:* waitelibn@library.adelaide.edu.au *Phone:* +61(8) 8303-7310 **Staff:** 1 Prof. 4.5 Other **Holdings:** 30,000 books 1,009 journals **Language of Collection/Services:** English / English **Subjects:** Comprehensive **Networks:** Kinetica **Databases Used:** Comprehensive **Loan:** In country **Service:** Inhouse **Photocopy:** Yes

137 **Henley Beach, South Australia, Australia**
South Australian Research and Development Institute, South Australian Aquatic Sciences Centre (SARDI, SAASC)
Library
PO Box 120
Henley Beach, South Australia 5022
Location: 2 Hamra Ave., West Beach **Phone:** +61(8) 8200-2423 **Fax:** +61(8) 8200-2481 **WWW:** www.sardi.sa.gov.au

Former Name: South Australian Department of Fisheries, Fisheries Library **Founded:** 1974 **Type:** Government **Head:** Mrs. Suzanne Bennett *Email:* bennett.suzanne@pi.sa.gov.au *Phone:* +61(8) 8200-2423 **Staff:** .8 Prof. **Holdings:** 3,000 books 300 journals **Language of Collection/Services:** English / English **Subjects:** Angling (Recreational Fishing), Aquatic Environment, Fisheries, Hydrobiology, Resources **Specializations:** Aquaculture, Marine Biology **Loan:** In country **Photocopy:** Yes

138 **Roseworthy, South Australia, Australia**
University of Adelaide - Roseworthy Campus
Library
Roseworthy, South Australia 5371
Phone: +61(8) 8303-7844 **Fax:** +61(8) 8303-7965 **Email:** library@roseworthy.adelaide.edu.au **Ariel IP:** rariel@

roseworthy.adelaide. edu.au **WWW:** library.adelaide.edu. au/val/roseworthy **OPAC:** telnet:// library.adelaide.edu.au

Former Name: Roseworthy Agricultural College **Founded:** 1920 **Type:** Academic **Head:** Ms. A.C. Mills *Phone:* +61(8) 8303-7843 *Email:* amills@roseworthy.adelaide.edu.au **Language of Collection/Services:** English / English **Holdings:** 30,000 books 800 journals **Staff:** 1 Prof. 4 Other **Subjects:** Comprehensive **Networks:** Kinetica **Loan:** In country **Photocopy:** Yes

Tasmania

139   Boyer, Tasmania, Australia
Australian Newsprint Mills Ltd. (ANM)
Library Services
Boyer, Tasmania 7140
Phone: +61(3) 6261-0441 **Fax:** +61(3) 6261-3471

Founded: 1940 **Type:** Business **Head:** Carol Eastley *Phone:* +61(3) 6261-0441 **Staff:** 2 Prof. 2 Other **Holdings:** 700 books 70 journals **Language of Collection/Services:** English **Subjects:** Forestry, Plant Pathology, Soil Science, Water Resources **Specializations:** Pulp and Paper Industry **Networks:** Kinetica **Loan:** In country **Service:** Inhouse **Photocopy:** Yes

140   Hobart, Tasmania, Australia
Commonwealth Scientific and Industrial Research
      Organisation, Division of Forestry and Forest
      Products (CSIRO)
Library
GPO Box 252-12
Hobart, Tasmania 7001
Location: College Road, Sandy Bay, Tasmania 7005 **Fax:** +61(3) 6226-7901

Founded: 1950 **Type:** Government **Head:** Judith Sprent *Phone:* +61(3) 6226-7900 **Staff:** 1 Other **Holdings:** 1,200 books 30 journals **Language of Collection/Services:** English / English **Subjects:** Forestry **Loan:** In country **Service:** In country **Photocopy:** Yes

141   Hobart, Tasmania, Australia
Commonwealth Scientific and Industrial Research
      Organisation, Marine Laboratories (CSIRO)
Library
GPO Box 1538
Hobart, Tasmania 7001
Location: Castray Esplanade **Phone:** +61(3) 6232-5257 **Fax:** +61(3) 6232-5103 **Email:** library@marine.csiro.au **WWW:** www.marine.csiro.au **OPAC:** voyager.its.csiro.au

Founded: 1937 **Type:** Government **Head:** Denis Abbott *Email:* denis.abbott@marine.csiro.au *Phone:* +61(3) 6232-5257 **Staff:** 2 Prof. 1 Other **Holdings:** 9,000 books 1,108 journals **Language of Collection/Services:** English **Subjects:** Aquaculture, Fisheries, Marine Chemistry, Oceanography **Networks:** Kinetica **Databases Developed:** Report literature received in library 1985+ **Databases Used:** Comprehensive **Loan:** Internationally **Photocopy:** Yes

142   Hobart, Tasmania, Australia
Forestry Tasmania
Library and Information Services
PO Box 207B
Hobart, Tasmania 7001
Location: 199 Macquarie Street **Phone:** +61(3) 6233-8160 **Fax:** +61(3) 6233-8292 **Email:** library@forestry.tas.gov.au **WWW:** www.forestrytas.com.au

Former Name: Tasmania Forestry Commission (TFC) **Founded:** 1979 **Type:** Government **Head:** Paul de Ville *Phone:* +61(3) 6233-8474 *Email:* paul.deville@forestry.tas. gov.au **Staff:** 1 Prof. 1 Other **Holdings:** 4,000 books 500 journals **Language of Collection/Services:** English/English **Subjects:** Agricultural Economics, Entomology, Horticulture, Plant Pathology, Soil Science, Water Resources **Specializations:** Forestry **Networks:** Kinetica **Photocopy:** Yes **Loan:** Internationally **Service:** Internationally

143   Hobart, Tasmania, Australia
University of Tasmania
Science Library
GPO Box 252-25
Hobart, Tasmania 7001
Phone: +61(3) 6226-2441 **Fax:** +61(3) 6226-7817 **Email:** science.reference@utas.edu.au **WWW:** www.utas.edu.au **Ariel IP:** 131.217.16.32

Type: Academic **Head:** Richard Dearden *Email:* richard. dearden@utas.edu.au **Staff:** 1 Prof. 2 Other **Holdings:** 400 journals 50,000 books **Language of Collection/Services:** English / English **Subjects:** Animal Husbandry, Microbiology, Plant Breeding, Soil Science **Specializations:** Entomology, Genetics, Microbiology, Molecular Biology, Essential Oils, Plant Pathology **Networks:** Kinetica **Databases Used:** CABCD **Loan:** Internationally **Service:** Internationally **Photocopy:** Yes

144   New Town, Tasmania, Australia
Department of Primary Industry and Fisheries
Library
St. Johns Avenue
New Town, Tasmania 7008
Phone: +61(3) 6233-6854 **Fax:** +61(3) 6228-5123

Former Name: Department of Agriculture Tasmania **Type:** Government **Head:** L. Minchin *Phone:* +61(3) 6233-6854 **Staff:** 3 Prof. 3 Other **Holdings:** 300 journals **Language of Collection/Services:** English **Subjects:** Agricultural Economics, Animal Husbandry, Crops, Entomology, Farming, Fisheries, Horticulture, Plant Pathology, Soil Science, Veterinary Medicine, Water Resources **Networks:** Kinetica **Databases Used:** Comprehensive **Loan:** In country **Photocopy:** Yes

Victoria

145   Attwood, Victoria, Australia
Department of Natural Resources and
      Environment (DNRE)
NRE Atwood Library
475-485 Mickleham Road
Attwood, Victoria 3049

Phone: +61(3) 9217-4368 **Fax:** +61(3) 9217-4397 **WWW:** www.nre.vic.gov.au

Former Name: Department of Agriculture, Victoria (DAV), Victorian Institute of Animal Sciences (VIAS), Department of Agriculture and Rural Affairs (DARA), Veterinary Research Institute, Animal Health Library **Founded:** 1971 **Type:** Government **Head:** Peter Ison *Phone:* +61(3) 9217-4367 *Email:* isonp@woody.agvic.gov.au **Staff:** 1 Prof. 1 Other **Holdings:** 6,000 books 150 journals **Language of Collection/Services:** English/English **Subjects:** Animal Pathology, Animal Welfare, Biotechnology, Veterinary Medicine **Specializations:** Fish Diseases **Databases Used:** Comprehensive **Loan:** In country **Service:** Inhouse **Photocopy:** Yes

146   **Bundoora, Victoria, Australia**
La Trobe University (LTU)
Borchardt Library (VLU)
Bundoora, Victoria 3083
Phone: +61(3) 9479-2922 **Fax:** +61(3) 9471-0993 **Email:** docds@latrobe.edu.au **WWW:** www.library.latrobe.edu.au **Ariel IP:** 131.172.16.37

Founded: 1965 **Type:** Academic **Head:** Mr. Earle Gow *Phone:* +61(3) 9479-2920 **Staff:** 36 Prof. 95 Other **Holdings:** 11,000 books 450 journals **Language of Collection/Services:** English **Subjects:** Agribusiness, Agricultural Development, Agricultural Economics, Animal Husbandry, Crops, Entomology, Farming, Plant Pathology, Soil Science **Networks:** Kinetica **Databases Used:** Medline **Loan:** Internationally **Photocopy:** Yes

147   **Clayton, Victoria, Australia**
Monash University
Library
Wellington Road
Clayton, Victoria 3168
Phone: +61(3) 990-55054 **Fax:** +61(3) 990-52610 **Email:** library@lib.monash.edu.au **WWW:** www.monash.edu.au **OPAC:** library.monash.edu.au **Ariel IP:** 130.194.100.56

Founded: 1961 **Type:** Academic **Head:** Mr. B. Southwell **Staff:** 55 Prof. 119 Other **Holdings:** 10,000 books 100 journals **Subjects:** Agricultural Economics, Developing Countries, Soil Science **Loan:** In country **Photocopy:** Yes

148   **Dookie College, Victoria, Australia**
Institute of Land and Food Resources - Dookie
Library
Dookie College, Victoria 3647
Phone: +61(3) 5833-9224 **Fax:** +61(3) 5833-9201

Former Name: Victorian College of Agriculture and Horticulture - Dookie Campus (VCAH) **Type:** Academic **Head:** Kathy Costello *Phone:* +61(3) 5833-9224 **Staff:** 2 Prof. 2 Other **Holdings:** 16,000 books 130 journals **Language of Collection/Services:** English **Subjects:** Agricultural Economics, Animal Husbandry, Crops, Education/Extension, Food Sciences, Horticulture, Soil Science **Databases Used:** Agricola **Loan:** In country **Photocopy:** Yes

149   **Ellinbank, Victoria, Australia**
Department of Natural Resources and
     Environment, Dairy Research Institute
     (DNRE, DRI)
NRE Ellinbank Library
RMB 2460
Hazeldean Road
Ellinbank, Victoria 3820
Phone: +61(3) 5624-2222 **Fax:** +61(3) 5624-2200 **WWW:** www.nre.vic.gov.au

Former Name: Department of Agriculture and Rural Affairs (DARA), Department of Food and Agriculture, Department of Agriculture, Victoria (DAV) **Type:** Government **Head:** Michelle Gummer *Email:* michelle.gummer@nre.vic.gov.au *Phone:* +61(3) 5624-2222 **Staff:** 1 Prof. **Holdings:** 1,500 books 76 journals **Language of Collection/Services:** English **Subjects:** Animal Husbandry, Soil Science, Veterinary Medicine **Specializations:** Dairy Industry **Networks:** Kinetica **Databases Used:** Agricola; CABCD; Medline **Loan:** In country **Service:** Internationally **Photocopy:** Yes

150   **Fairfield, Victoria, Australia**
Amcor Research and Technology Centre
Library
Private Bag 1
Fairfield, Victoria 3078
Location: 17 Rex Avenue, Alphington **Phone:** +61(3) 9490-6120 **Fax:** +61(3) 9490-6170

Founded: 1938 **Type:** Business **Head:** Janet McGahy *Phone:* +61(3) 9490-6120 **Staff:** 2 Prof. 2 Other **Subjects:** Forestry **Loan:** In country **Photocopy:** Yes

151   **Geelong, Victoria, Australia**
Commonwealth Scientific and Industrial Research
     Organisation, Animal Health, Australian
     Animal Health Laboratory (CSIRO)
Library
Private Bag No. 24
Geelong, Victoria 3213
Location: 5 Portarlington Road **Phone:** +61(3) 5227-5298 **Fax:** +61(3) 5227-5532 **Email:** library@dah.csiro.au **WWW:** www.ah.csiro.au

Founded: 1937 **Type:** Government **Head:** Heather R. Mathew *Email:* heather.mathew@ dah.csiro.au *Phone:* +61(3) 9342-9708 **Staff:** 2 Prof. 1.6 Other **Holdings:** 9,300 books 265 journals **Language of Collection/Services:** English / English **Subjects:** Veterinary Medicine **Specializations:** Biochemistry, Immunology, Organic Chemistry, Microbiology, Pathology, Virology **Networks:** Kinetica **Databases Used:** Comprehensive **Loan:** Internationally **Service:** Inhouse **Photocopy:** Yes

152   **Geelong, Victoria, Australia**
Deakin University
Geelong Campus Library
Pigdons Road, Waurn Ponds
Geelong, Victoria 3217
Phone: +61(3) 5227-1201 **Fax:** +61(3) 5227-2000 **Email:** lib-ill-glg@deakin.edu.au **WWW:** www.deakin.edu.au **OPAC:** library.deakin.edu.au **Ariel IP:** 128.184.60.201

Former Name: Victoria College **Founded:** 1977 **Type:** Academic **Head:** Prof. M.A. Cameron *Phone:* +61(3) 5227-1344 **Staff:** 50 Prof. 96 Other **Holdings:** 820,000 books 11,700 journals **Language of Collection/Services:** English / English **Subjects:** Home Economics **Networks:** Kinetica **Databases Developed:** Home Economics Index; Endangered Species Index **Loan:** Internationally **Service:** Internationally **Photocopy:** Yes

153   Geelong, Victoria, Australia
         Marcus Oldham Farm Management College
         Sir James Darling Resources Centre
         Private Bag 116, Mail Centre
         Geelong, Victoria 3221
Location: Pigdons Road, Waurn Ponds **Fax:** +61(52) 44-1263 **Email:** marcus@ne.com.au **WWW:** www.marcusoldham.vic.edu.au

Founded: 1981 **Type:** Academic **Head:** Carolyn Wakefield *Phone:* +61(52) 43-3533 *Email:* wakefield@marcusoldham.vic.edu.au **Staff:** 1 Prof. **Holdings:** 5,400 books 150 journals **Language of Collection/Services:** English / English **Subjects:** Agribusiness, Agricultural Economics, Animal Production, Crop Production, Horses **Networks:** Kinetica **Loan:** In country **Service:** In country **Photocopy:** Yes

154   Hamilton, Victoria, Australia
         Department of Natural Resources and
             Environment, Pastoral and Veterinary
             Institute
         A.H. Bishop Library
         Private Bag 105
         Hamilton, Victoria 3300
Location: Mount Napier Road **Phone:** +61(3) 55773-0900 **Fax:** +61(3) 5571-1523 **WWW:** www.nre.vic.gov.au

Non-English Name: DNRE **Former Name:** Department of Agriculture, Victoria, Department of Agriculture and Rural Affairs (DARA), Department of Food and Agriculture **Type:** Government **Head:** Bernadine Kelvy, Karen Kimbeng *Phone:* +61(3) 5573-0900 *Email:* kelvyb@hammy.agric.gov.au **Staff:** 2 Prof. **Holdings:** 3,000 books 40 journals **Language of Collection/Services:** English / English **Subjects:** Education/Extension, Farming, Soil Science **Specializations:** Animal Breeding, Animal Nutrition, Beef Cattle, Extensive Livestock Farming, Grazing, Pastures, Sheep **Databases Used:** Comprehensive **Loan:** In country **Service:** In country **Photocopy:** Yes

155   Heidelberg, Victoria, Australia
         Department of Natural Resources and
             Environment, Arthur Rylah Institute for
             Environmental Research (DNRE)
         Library
         PO Box 137
         Heidelberg, Victoria 3084
Location: 123 Brown Street **Fax:** +61(3) 9450-8664 **Email:** arilib@nre.vic.gov.au

Former Name: Department of Conservation and Natural Resources, Department of Conservation, Forests and Lands **Founded:** 1950 **Type:** Government **Head:** Ms. Carol Harris *Phone:* +61(3) 9450-8604 *Email:* cah@nre.vic.gov.au **Staff:**

1 Prof. **Holdings:** 8,000 books 108 journals **Language of Collection/Services:** English **Subjects:** Aquaculture, Fisheries, Wildlife **Networks:** Kinetica **Databases Used:** Comprehensive **Loan:** In country **Photocopy:** Yes

156   Highett, Victoria, Australia
         Commonwealth Scientific and Industrial Research
             Organisation, Australian Food Industry
             Science Centre, Food Science Australia
             (CSIRO, AFISC)
         Library
         PO Box 20
         Highett, Victoria 3190
Location: Graham Road **Phone:** +61(3) 9252-6452 **Fax:** +61(3) 9252-6521 **Email:** vsdr@foodscience.afisc.csiro.au **WWW:** www.foodscience.afisc.csiro.au **OPAC:** voyager.its.csiro.au

Former Name: Division of Food Science and Technology, Dairy Research Laboratory, Division of Food Research, Division of Food Processing **Founded:** 1943 **Type:** Government **Head:** Denise Sthradher *Phone:* +61(3) 9252-6452 *Email:* vsdr@foodscience.afisc.csiro.au **Staff:** 1 Prof. **Holdings:** 3,500 books 200 journals **Language of Collection/Services:** English **Subjects:** Food Sciences **Specializations:** Dairy Industry, Dairy Technology, Milk Products, Microbiology, Probiotics **Networks:** Kinetica; CSIRO **Databases Used:** CABCD; Current Contents; FSTA **Loan:** Internationally **Service:** In country **Photocopy:** Yes

157   Horsham, Victoria, Australia
         Department of Natural Resources and
             Environment, Victorian Institute for Dryland
             Agriculture (DNRE)
         NRE Horsham Library
         Private Bag 260
         Horsham, Victoria 3400
Location: Natimuk Road **Fax:** +61(3) 5362-2187

Former Name: Department of Agriculture and Rural Affairs (DARA), Department of Food and Agriculture, Department of Agriculture, Victoria **Type:** Government **Head:** Ruth Lawrence *Phone:* +61(3) 5362-157 *Email:* ruth.lawrence@nre.vic.gov.au **Staff:** 1 Prof. **Holdings:** 5,000 books 120 journals **Language of Collection/Services:** English / English **Subjects:** Dry Farming, Plant Breeding, Plant Genetics, Plant Physiology **Networks:** Kinetica **Databases Used:** Agricola; CABCD **Loan:** In country **Service:** Internationally **Photocopy:** Yes

158   Kyabram, Victoria, Australia
         Department of Natural Resources and
             Environment, Institute of Sustainable
             Irrigated Agriculture, Kyabram Dairy
             Research Centre (DNRE)
         Library
         RMB 3010
         Kyabram, Victoria 3620
Fax: +61(58) 52-2861 **Email:** urenc@salty.agvic.gov.au

Former Name: Department of Agriculture, Victoria (DAV), Department of Agriculture and Rural Affairs (DARA), Animal and Irrigated Pastures Research Institute, Kyabram Research Institute (KRI) **Founded:** 1961 **Type:** Government **Head:** Chris Uren *Phone:* +61(58) 52-2488 *Email:* urenc@ salty.agvic.gov.au **Staff:** .5 Prof. .1 Other **Holdings:** 7,500 books 37 journals **Language of Collection/Services:** English **Subjects:** Crops, Dairy Science, Farming, Soil Science **Specializations:** Animal Husbandry, Pastures **Networks:** Kinetica **Databases Developed:** ELEXIR - Department Catalogue with local access **Databases Used:** Comprehensive **Loan:** In country **Photocopy:** Yes

159   Melbourne, Victoria, Australia
         Australian Wool Corporation (AWC)
         Library
         GPO Box 4867
         Melbourne, Victoria 3001
Location: Wool House, 369 Royal Parade, Parkville, Vic 3052 **Phone:** +61(3) 9341-9416 **Fax:** +61(3) 9341-9273 **Email:** wool@ozemail.com.au

Former Name: Australian Wool Board, Australian Wool Bureau, Australian Wool Commission **Founded:** 1948 **Type:** Government **Head:** Henning Rasmussen *Phone:* +61(3) 9341-9417 **Staff:** 3 Prof. 2 Other **Holdings:** 13,000 books 1,700 journals **Language of Collection/Services:** English **Subjects:** Agribusiness, Agricultural Economics, Animal Husbandry, Farming, Veterinary Medicine **Specializations:** Sheep, Textiles, Wool, Wool Production **Networks:** Kinetica **Loan:** Internationally **Service:** Inhouse **Photocopy:** Yes

160   Melbourne, Victoria, Australia
         Department of Natural Resources and
             Environment, Institute for Horticultural
             Development (DNRE, IHD)
         NRE Knoxfield Library
         Private Bag 15, South Eastern Mail Centre
         Melbourne, Victoria 3176
Location: 621 Burwood Highway, Knoxfield, Victoria **Phone:** +61(3) 9210-9312 **Fax:** +61(3) 9210-9315

Former Name: Department of Agriculture, Victoria (DAV), Department of Agriculture and Rural Affairs (DARA), Plant Research Institute (VPR), Plant Sciences Library **Founded:** 1890 **Type:** Government **Head:** Catharina Vroomen *Phone:* +61(3) 9210-9311 *Email:* vroomenc@knoxy.agvic.gov.au **Staff:** 2 Prof. **Holdings:** 15,000 books 580 journals **Language of Collection/Services:** English **Subjects:** Biotechnology, Crops, Entomology, Farming, Horticulture, Plants, Plant Pathology **Specializations:** Mycology **Networks:** Kinetica **Databases Developed:** DALIS - catalogue of all holdings of departmental libraries for Victorian Agriculture Department **Databases Used:** Agricola **Loan:** Internationally **Service:** In country **Photocopy:** Yes

161   Melbourne, Victoria, Australia
         Museum Victoria (MV)
         Library Services
         GPO Box 666E
         Melbourne, Victoria 3001
Location: 222 Exhibition Street, 16th floor **Phone:** +61(3) 9651-6794 **Fax:** +61(3) 9651-6129 **Email:** vhogan@mov. vic.gov.au **WWW:** www.mov.vic.gov

Former Name: Science Museum of Victoria, National Museum of Victoria **Founded:** 1854 **Type:** Government **Head:** Frank Job *Phone:* +61(3) 9651-6337 *Email:* fjob@mov.vic. gov.au **Staff:** 2 Prof. 1 Other **Holdings:** 40,000 books 1,450 journals **Language of Collection/Services:** English **Subjects:** Agricultural Engineering, Animal Husbandry, Entomology, Water Resources **Specializations:** Agriculture (History) **Loan:** Internationally **Photocopy:** Yes

162   Merbein, Victoria, Australia
         Commonwealth Scientific and Industrial Research
             Organisation, Plant Industry, Horticulture
             Unit (CSIRO)
         Library
         Private Mail Bag, PO
         Merbein, Victoria 3505
Location: River Avenue **Phone:** +61(3) 5051-3127 **Fax:** + 61(3) 5051 3111 **Email:** vsmb@pi.csiro.au **WWW:** www. pi.csiro.au **OPAC:** voyager.its.csiro.au

Former Name: Division of Horticulture, Division of Horticultural Research **Founded:** 1920 **Type:** Government **Head:** Iima LoIacono *Phone:* +61(3) 5051-3100 *Email:* vsmb@pi. csiro.au **Staff:** 1 Prof. 1 Other **Holdings:** 13,000 books 270 journals **Language of Collection/Services:** English **Subjects:** Biotechnology, Crops, Food Sciences, Horticulture, Plant Pathology **Networks:** Kinetica; CSIRO **Loan:** In country **Photocopy:** Yes

163   Mildura, Victoria, Australia
         Department of Natural Resources and
             Environment, Sunraysia Horticultural Centre
             (DNRE, SHC)
         NRE Irymple Library
         PO Box 905
         Mildura, Victoria 3052
Location: Corner Eleventh St. & Koorlong Ave., Irymple **Phone:** +61(3) 5051-4500 **Fax:** +61(3) 5051-4523

Former Name: Department of Agriculture, Victoria (DAV), Department of Agriculture and Rural Affairs (DARA), Department of Food and Agriculture, Sunraysia Horticultural Research Institute **Type:** Government **Head:** Lyn McMahon *Phone:* +61(3) 5051-4500 *Email:* mcmahonl@orac.agvic. gov.au **Staff:** 1 Prof. **Holdings:** 4,000 books 100 journals **Language of Collection/Services:** English / English **Subjects:** Horticulture, Plant Pathology **Specializations:** Citrus, Irrigation, Salinity, Viticulture **Databases Developed:** ELIXIR - library catalogue with access in department only **Databases Used:** Current Contents **Loan:** Internationally **Service:** Internationally **Photocopy:** Yes

164   Parkville, Victoria, Australia
         University of Melbourne
         Agriculture and Forestry Library
         Parkville, Victoria 3052
Location: Corner of Royal Parade and Tin Alley **Phone:** +61(3) 9344-5017 **Fax:** +61(3) 9344-5570 **WWW:** lib. unimelb.edu.au **OPAC:** cat.lib.unimelb.edu.au **Ariel IP:** 128.250.140.17

Founded: 1923 **Type:** Academic **Head:** Mrs. Debra Ormsby *Phone:* +61(3) 93445571 *Email:* d.ormsby@lib.unimelb.

edu.au **Staff:** 1 Prof. 1 Other **Holdings:** 30,815 books 150 journals **Language of Collection/Services:** English / English **Subjects:** Comprehensive **Networks:** Kinetica **Databases Used:** Agricola; Agris; CABCD **Loan:** Internationally **Service:** Inhouse **Photocopy:** Yes

165 Queenscliff, Victoria, Australia
Department of Natural Resources and
    Environment, Marine and Freshwater
    Resources Institute (DNRE, MaFRI)
Library
PO Box 114
Queenscliff, Victoria 3225

Location: Weeroona Parade **Phone:** +61(3) 5258-0259 **Fax:** +61(3) 5258-3086 **Email:** library@msl.oz.au **WWW:** www.nre.vic.gov.au, www.nre.vic.gov.au/sales/library/library.htm

Former Name: Department of Conservation and Natural Resources, Marine Science Laboratories, Victorian Fisheries Research Institute, Victorian Institute of Marine Science **Founded:** 1975 **Type:** Government **Head:** Julie Power *Phone:* +61(3) 5258-0259 *Email:* library@msl.oz.au **Staff:** .7 Prof. .2 Other **Holdings:** 4,700 books 100 journals **Language of Collection/Services:** English / English **Subjects:** Aquaculture, Fisheries, Marine Sciences, Toxicology **Networks:** EXIXIR - Dept. of Natural Resources and Environment library catalogue **Databases Used:** Comprehensive **Loan:** Internationally **Service:** Fee for non-MaFRI and DNRE staff **Photocopy:** Yes

166 South Yarra, Victoria, Australia
Royal Botanic Gardens Melbourne
Library
Birdwood Avenue
South Yarra, Victoria 3141

Phone: +61(3) 9252-2320 **Fax:** +61(3) 9252-2350 **Email:** library@rbgmelb.org.au

Former Name: Royal Botanic Gardens and National Herbarium of Victoria **Founded:** 1853 **Type:** Government **Head:** Ms. H.M. Cohn *Phone:* +61(3) 95252-2300 *Email:* library@rbgmelb.org.au **Staff:** 2 Prof. 2 Other **Holdings:** 70,000 books 400 journals **Language of Collection/Services:** English **Subjects:** Botany, Horticulture **Loan:** In country **Service:** Internationally **Photocopy:** Yes

167 Tatura, Victoria, Australia
Department of Natural Resources and
    Environment, Institute of Sustainable
    Irrigated Agriculture (DNRE)
Library
Private Bag 1 Ferguson Road
Tatura, Victoria 3616

Fax: +61(3) 5833-5319

Former Name: Department of Agriculture, Victoria (DAV), Department of Agriculture and Rural Affairs (DARA), Irrigation Research Institute, Institute for Irrigation and Salinity Research (IISR) **Founded:** 1960 **Type:** Government **Head:** Christine Uren *Phone:* +61(3) 5833-5287 *Email:* urenc@salty.agvic.gov.au **Staff:** 1 Prof. **Holdings:** 50,008 books 120 journals **Language of Collection/Services:** English/

English **Subjects:** Drainage, Horticulture, Irrigated Farming, Plant Pathology, Salinity, Soil Science **Networks:** Kinetica **Databases Developed:** ELIXIR - Department of Natural Resources and Environment catalogue **Databases Used:** Comprehensive **Loan:** In country **Service:** Internationally **Photocopy:** Yes

168 Terang, Victoria, Australia
Institute of Land and Food Resources -
    Glenormiston
Education Resource Centre (ERC)
RMB 6200
Terang, Victoria 3264

Phone: +61(3) 5557-8215 **Fax:** +61(3) 5557-8241

Former Name: Glenormiston Agricultural College, Victorian College of Agriculture and Horticulture - Glenormiston Campus (VCAH) **Type:** Academic **Head:** Fiona L. Drum **Staff:** 1 Prof. 1 Other **Holdings:** 10,000 books 300 journals **Language of Collection/Services:** English / English **Subjects:** Agribusiness, Agricultural Economics, Agricultural Engineering, Animal Husbandry, Crops, Education/Extension, Farming, Horticulture, Plants, Soil Science, Water Resources **Specializations:** Farm Management, Horse Farms, Marketing, Rural Business Administration, Rural Economy **Databases Used:** CABCD **Loan:** In country and New Zealand **Service:** In country and New Zealand **Photocopy:** Yes

169 Warragul, Victoria, Australia
Institute of Land and Food Resources - McMillan
McMillan Campus Library
PO Box 353
Warragul, Victoria 3820

Location: South Road **Fax:** +61(3) 5623-4671

Former Name: Victorian College of Agriculture and Horticulture **Founded:** 1982 **Type:** Academic **Head:** Ms. K. Dadswell *Phone:* +61(3) 5623-5366 **Staff:** 1 Prof. **Holdings:** 2,000 books 100 journals **Subjects:** Beef, Dairy Science, Horses, Pastures, Sheep **Loan:** In country **Photocopy:** Yes

170 Werribee, Victoria, Australia
Department of Natural Resources and
    Environment, State Chemistry Laboratory
    (DNRE)
NRE Werribee Library
Sneydes Road
Werribee, Victoria 3030

Phone: +61(3) 9742-8755 **Fax:** +61(3) 9742-8700

Former Name: Department of Agriculture and Rural Affairs (DARA), Department of Agriculture, Victoria (DAV) **Founded:** 1890 **Type:** Government **Head:** Paul Quilty *Phone:* +61(3) 9742-8755 *Email:* quiltyp@slim.agvic.gov.au, paul.quilty@nre.vic.gov.au **Staff:** 1 Prof. 1 Other **Holdings:** 6,000 books 120 journals **Subjects:** Biotechnology, Analytical Chemistry, Fertilizers, Food Sciences **Specializations:** Pesticides, Soil Science **Loan:** In country **Photocopy:** Yes

171 Werribee, Victoria, Australia
University of Melbourne, Faculty of Agriculture,
    Forestry and Horticulture

Gilbert Chandler College Library
Sneydes Road
Werribee, Victoria 3030
Phone: +61(3) 9741-8033 **Fax:** +61(3) 9741-9396 **WWW:** www.lib.unimelb.edu.au

Former Name: Victorian College of Agriculture and Horticulture (VCAH) **Founded:** 1987 **Type:** Academic **Head:** Mrs. Elizabeth Wilson *Phone:* +61(3) 9741-8033 *Email:* e.wilson@landfood.unimelb.edu.au **Staff:** 1 Prof. **Holdings:** 6,000 books 150 journals **Language of Collection/Services:** English / English **Subjects:** Agribusiness, Food Sciences, Management **Specializations:** Dairy Industry, Dairy Technology, Food Technology **Networks:** Kinetica **Databases Used:** Agricola; CABCD **Loan:** In country **Service:** In country **Photocopy:** Yes

172   **Werribee, Victoria, Australia**
      University of Melbourne, Faculty of Veterinary Science
      Veterinary Science Library
      Princes Highway
      Werribee, Victoria 3030
Phone: +61(3) 9742-8831 **Fax:** +61(3) 9347-4783 **WWW:** www.lib.unimelb.edu.au

Head: Rowena Morrison *Email:* morrison@lib.unimelb.Edu.au **Subjects:** Veterinary Science

Western Australia

173   **Bentley Delivery Centre, Western Australia, Australia**
      Agriculture Western Australia
      Library
      Locked Bag No. 4
      Bentley Delivery Centre, Western Australia 6983
Location: Baron-Hay Court, South Perth, WA 6151 Phone: +61(8) 9368-3201 **Fax:** +61(8) 9368-3846 **WWW:** www.agric.wa.gov.au **Ariel IP:** 159.207.200.205

Founded: 1894 **Type:** Government **Head:** Jill Maughan *Phone:* +61(8) 9368-3260 *Email:* jmaughan@agric.wa.gov.au **Staff:** 5 Prof. 5 Other **Holdings:** 100,000 books 3,000 journals **Language of Collection/Services:** English / English **Subjects:** Agriculture (Tropics), Agribusiness, Agricultural Development, Agricultural Economics, Agricultural Engineering, Animal Husbandry, Biotechnology, Farming, Crops, Education/Extension, Entomology, Food Sciences, Horticulture, Plant Pathology, Veterinary Medicine, Water Resources, Soil Science **Specializations:** Agriculture (Australia-Western) **Networks:** Kinetica **Databases Developed:** FARMTI - database of articles from an international range of extension journals of interest to Australian and New Zealand users; RIS - research information system **Loan:** In country **Service:** In country **Photocopy:** Yes

174   **East Perth, Western Australia, Australia**
      Chemistry Centre (WA)
      Library
      125 Hay Street
      East Perth, Western Australia 6004

Phone: +61(8) 9222-3006 **Fax:** +61(8) 9326-7767 **Email:** ccwalibrary@ccwa.wa.gov.au

Former Name: Government Chemical Laboratories **Founded:** 1946 **Type:** Government **Head:** Marlene Hayward *Phone:* +61(8) 9222-3177 *Email:* mhayward@ccwa.wa.gov.au **Staff:** 1 Prof. **Holdings:** 500 books 20 journals **Language of Collection/Services:** English / English **Subjects:** Analysis, Analytical Chemistry, Plants, Soil Science **Networks:** Kinetica **Loan:** In country **Photocopy:** Yes

175   **Floreat Park, Western Australia, Australia**
      Commonwealth Scientific and Industrial Research Organisation, Western Australian Regional Laboratories (CSIRO)
      Library
      Private Bag, PO Wembley
      Floreat Park, Western Australia 6014
Location: Underwood Avenue **Phone:** +61(8) 9333-6720 **Fax:** +61(8) 9387-6046 **Email:** waughb@per.library.csiro.au **WWW:** www.csiro.au **OPAC:** library.csiro

Former Name: Western Australian Laboratories **Founded:** 1956 **Type:** Government **Head:** Bernadette Waugh *Phone:* +61(8) 9333-6721 *Email:* waughb@per.library.csiro.au **Staff:** 2 Prof. 2 Other **Holdings:** 20,000 books 600 journals **Language of Collection/Services:** English / English **Subjects:** Agricultural Development, Agricultural Economics, Animal Husbandry, Biotechnology, Crops, Dry Farming, Ecology, Entomology, Farming, Forestry, Plant Pathology, Soil Science, Veterinary Medicine, Water Resources, Wildlife **Networks:** Kinetica **Databases Used:** CABCD **Loan:** In country **Service:** Inhouse **Photocopy:** Yes

176   **Nedlands, Western Australia, Australia**
      University of Western Australia (UWA)
      Biological Sciences Library
      Nedlands, Western Australia 6907
Phone: +61(8) 9380-2350 **Fax:** +61(8) 9380-1137 **Email:** biolib@library.uwa.edu.au **WWW:** www.uwa.edu.au **OPAC:** www.library.uwa.edu.au **Ariel IP:** bi-ariel@library.uwa.edu.au

Founded: 1938 **Type:** Academic **Head:** Ms. E. Nixon *Phone:* +61(8) 9380-2836 *Email:* nixon@library.uwa.edu.au **Staff:** 2 Prof. 6 Other **Holdings:** 65,500 books 1,075 journals **Language of Collection/Services:** English / English **Subjects:** Agriculture (Tropics), Agribusiness, Agricultural Development, Agricultural Economics, Animal Husbandry, Biotechnology, Crops, Education/Extension, Entomology, Farming, Forestry, Horticulture, Plant Pathology, Soil Science **Networks:** Kinetica **Databases Used:** Comprehensive **Loan:** In country **Service:** Inhouse **Photocopy:** Yes

177   **North Beach, Western Australia, Australia**
      Fisheries Department, Western Australian Marine Research Laboratories
      Library
      PO Box 20
      North Beach, Western Australia 6020
Location: Corner of Elvire Street and West Coast Highway, Waterman **Fax:** +61(8) 9447-3062 **Email:** library@fish.wa.gov.au **WWW:** www.wa.gov.au/westfish

Former Name: Fisheries Western Australia **Founded:** 1961 **Type:** Government **Head:** Vicki Gouteff *Phone:* +61(8) 9246-8428 *Email:* vgouteff@fish.wa.gov.au **Staff:** 1 Prof. 1 Other **Holdings:** 2,500 books 401 journals **Language of Collection/Services:** English / English **Subjects:** Fisheries, Fresh Water, Marine Sciences, Water Pollution **Specializations:** Aquaculture, Cherax, Lobsters, Prawns, Sharks **Networks:** Kinetica **Databases Used:** Comprehensive **Loan:** Internationally **Service:** Internationally **Photocopy:** Yes

178   Northam, Western Australia, Australia
           Curtin University of Technology, Muresk Institute
              of Agriculture
           Library
           Northam, Western Australia 6401
Phone: +61(8) 9690-1548 **Fax:** +61(8) 9622-5465 **Email:** lib@muresk.curtin.edu.au **WWW:** www.curtin.edu.au/curtin/muresk

Founded: 1972 **Type:** Academic **Head:** Jackie Hanlon *Phone:* +61(8) 9690-1453 *Email:* hanlonj@muresk.curtin.edu.au **Staff:** 2 Prof. 2 Other **Holdings:** 13,000 books 300 journals **Language of Collection/Services:** English/English **Subjects:** Agribusiness, Agricultural Development, Agricultural Economics, Agricultural Engineering, Animal Husbandry, Crops, Education/Extension, Farming, Horticulture, Soil Science **Databases Used:** Agricola **Loan:** Internationally **Service:** In country **Photocopy:** Yes

179   Perth, Western Australia, Australia
           Department of Environmental Protection
           Library
           PO Box K822
           Perth, Western Australia 6842
Location: Westralia Square, 8th Floor, 141 St. George's Terrace, Perth, WA 6000 **Phone:** +61(8) 9222-7010 **Fax:** +61(8) 9322-2850 **Email:** kathy_little@environ.wa.gov.au **WWW:** www.environ.wa.gov.au

Non-English Name: DEP **Former Name:** Environmental Protection Authority **Founded:** 1975 **Type:** Government **Head:** Trudy Parker/Kathy Little *Phone:* +61(8) 9222-7009 *Email:* trudy_parker@environ.wa.gov.au **Staff:** 2 Prof. 1 Other **Holdings:** 10,000 books 60 journals **Language of Collection/Services:** English **Subjects:** Environment, Estuaries, Marine Sciences, Natural History, Pollution **Loan:** Internationally **Photocopy:** Yes

180   Wanneroo, Western Australia, Australia
           Western Australia Department of Conservation
              and Land Management (CALM)
           Library
           PO Box 51
           Wanneroo, Western Australia 6065
Location: Ocean Reef Road, Woodvale **Phone:** +61(8) 9405-5132 **Fax:** +61(8) 9306-1641 **WWW:** www.calm.wa.gov.au

Former Name: Forests Department, Department of Fisheries and Wildlife, National Parks Authority **Founded:** 1953 **Type:** Government **Head:** Lisa Wright *Phone:* +61(8) 9405-5132 *Email:* lisaw@calm.wa.gov.au **Staff:** 3 Prof. 1 Other **Holdings:** 20,000 books 600 journals **Language of Collec-**

tion/Services: English / English **Subjects:** Soil Science, Water Resources **Specializations:** Botany, Environment, Forestry, Zoology **Loan:** In country **Service:** Internationally **Photocopy:** Yes

Austria

♦181   Graz, Austria
           Landeskammer für Land- und Forstwirtschaft in
              Steiermark
           Bibliothek
           Hamerlinggasse 3, Postfach 434
           A-8011 Graz
Fax: +43(316) 8050-510

Founded: 1819 **Type:** Association **Head:** Dipl.-Ing. Karl Kienreich *Phone:* +43(316) 8050-201 **Staff:** 2 Other **Holdings:** 74,000 books 270 journals Language of Collection/Services: German **Subjects:** Forest Management **Loan:** Internationally **Photocopy:** Yes

♦182   Irdning, Austria
           Federal Ministry of Agriculture and Forestry
           Federal Institute for Alpine Agriculture
           A-8952 Irdning
Phone: +43(3682) 2451-24 **Fax:** +43(3682) 2461-488

Non-English Name: Bundesministerium für Land- und Forstwirtschaft (BMLF), Bundesanstalt für alpenländische Landwirtschaft Gumpenstein (BAL) **Founded:** 1947 **Type:** Government **Head:** Dr. Chytil Kurt *Phone:* +43(3682) 2451-19 **Staff:** 13 Prof. **Holdings:** 6,000 books 280 journals **Language of Collection/Services:** German **Subjects:** Agricultural Engineering, Animal Husbandry, Animal Welfare, Crops, Farming, Food Sciences, Plant Pathology, Water Resources **Specializations:** Animal Nutrition, Animal Production, Plant Nutrition, Plant Protection, Soil Science **Loan:** In country **Service:** Internationally

183   Mondsee, Austria
           Federal Ministry of Agriculture and Forestry,
              Federal Agency for Water Management,
              Institute for Water Ecology, Fish Biology and
              Limnology
           Library
           Scharfling 18
           A-5310 Mondsee
Phone: +43(6232) 3847-22 **Fax:** +43(6232) 3847-33 **WWW:** www.baw.bmlf.gv.at

Non-English Name: Bundesministerium für Land- und Forstwirtschaft, Bundesamt für Wasserwirtschaft, Institut für Gewässerökologie, Fischereibiologie und Seenkunde (BMLF, BAW, IGFS), Bibliothek **Former Name:** Bundesanstalt für Fischereiwirtschaft **Founded:** 1953 **Type:** Government **Head:** Kainz Sieglinde *Phone:* +43(6232) 3847-0 *Email:* edv@igf.bmlf.gv.at **Staff:** 2 Other **Holdings:** 2,395 books 126 journals **Language of Collection/Services:** German, English / German **Subjects:** Fisheries **Loan:** In country **Service:** Inhouse **Photocopy:** Yes

184   Petzenkirchen, Austria
Federal Ministry of Agriculture and Forestry,
    Federal Institute for Land and Water
    Management Research
Library
Pollnbergstrasse 1
A-3252 Petzenkirchen

Phone: +43(7416) 52108-20 **Fax:** +43(7416) 52108-34
WWW: www.bmlf.gv.at

Non-English Name: Bundesministerium für Land- und
Forstwirtschaft, Bundesanstalt für Kulturtechnik und Bodenwasserhaushalt (BMLF, BAKT), Bibliothek **Founded:** 1945
Type: Government **Head:** Amstrat Ing. Josef Mayrhofer
Phone: +43(7416) 52108-22 **Staff:** 1 Prof. 1.5 Other **Holdings:** 8,100 books 75 journals **Language of Collection/Ser-
vices:** German / German **Subjects:** Crops, Farming, Land
Management, Soil Science, Water Management, Water Resources **Specializations:** Erosion, Hydrology, Soil Compac-
tion, Soil Water Balance, Soil Water Movement **Loan:** In
country **Service:** In country **Photocopy:** Yes

185   Vienna, Austria
Austrian Society for Surveying and
    Geoinformation (ASG)
Library
Schiffamtsgasse 1-3
A-1025 Vienna

Phone: +43(1) 21176 ext 3203 **Fax:** +43(1) 216-7550

Non-English Name: Österreichicher Gesellschaft für Vermessung und Geoinformation (ÖVG), Bibliothek **Founded:**
1903 **Type:** Academic **Head:** Dipl. Ing. Erich Imrek *Phone:*
+43(1) 21176 **Staff:** 1 Other **Holdings:** 3,400 books **Language of Collection/Services:** German **Specializations:**
Land Evaluation, Photogrammetry, Surveying **Loan:** In
country **Photocopy:** No

186   Vienna, Austria
Federal Institute for Less-Favored and
    Mountainous Areas
Grinzinger Allee 74
A-1196 Vienna

Phone: +43(1) 32-57-42-0 **Fax:** +43(1) 32-13-82-39
Email: office@babf.bmlf.gv.at **WWW:** www.babf.bmlf.
gv.at

Non-English Name: Bundesanstalt für Bergbauernfragen
(BABF) **Founded:** 1983 **Type:** Government **Staff:** 10 Prof.
3 Other **Holdings:** 2,050 books 34 journals **Language of
Collection/Services:** German / German **Subjects:** Agricultural Economics, Economics (Austria), Environment, Less
Favored Areas, Mountain Areas, Regional Policy **Loan:** Inhouse **Service:** Internationally **Photocopy:** Yes

187   Vienna, Austria
Federal Ministry of Agriculture and Forestry
Library
Stubenring 1
A-1011 Vienna

WWW: www.bmlf.gv.at/ebmlf/ehome/ehome.htm

Non-English Name: Bundesministerium für Land- und
Forstwirtschaft (BMLF), Bibliothek **Founded:** 1867 **Type:**

Government **Staff:** 2 Prof. 4 Other **Holdings:** 104,000 books
526 journals **Subjects:** Agricultural Policy, Environment,
Animal Breeding, Farm Machinery, Forestry, Forest Man-
agement, Hunting, Plants, Torrent Training, Vegetation
Management, Water Resources, Watershed Management
Loan: Internationally **Photocopy:** Yes

188   Vienna, Austria
Federal Ministry of Agriculture and Forestry,
    Federal Institute of Agricultural Economics
Library
Schweizertalstrasse 36
A-1133 Vienna

Phone: +43(1) 877-36-51 **Fax:** +43(1) 877-36-51-59
Email: wernerpevetz@awi.bmlf.gv.at **WWW:** www.awi.
bmlf.gv.at

Non-English Name: Bundesministerium für Land- und
Forstwirtschaft, Bundesanstalt für Agrarwirtschaft (BMLF),
Bibliothek, Dokumentationsstelle, Information **Founded:**
1960 **Type:** Government **Head:** Werner Pevetz *Phone:*
+43(1) 877-36-51-47 *Email:* wernerpevetz@awi.bmlf.gv.at
Staff: 2 Prof. 1 Other **Holdings:** 43,000 books 350 journals
Language of Collection/Services: German **Subjects:** Agri-
business, Agricultural Development, Agricultural Econom-
ics, Agricultural Policy, Education/Extension, Ecology,
Regional Planning, Rural Sociology **Networks:** AGRIS
Loan: In country **Service:** Internationally (restricted) **Photocopy:** Yes

189   Vienna, Austria
International Union of Forestry Research
    Organizations (IUFRO)
Information Centre
Seckendorff-Gudent-Weg 8
A-1131 Vienna

Phone: +43(1) 877-0151 **Fax:** +43(1) 877-9355 **Email:**
iufro@forvie.ac.at **WWW:** iufro.boku.ac.at

Type: Non-government **Subjects:** Forestry

190   Vienna, Austria
Universität für Bodenkultur, Institut für
    Bodenforschung (IBF)
Bibliothek
Gregor Mendelstrasse 33
A-1180 Vienna

Phone: +43(1) 47654 ext 6100 **Fax:** +43(1) 478-9110
WWW: www.boku.ac.at

Founded: 1872 **Type:** Academic **Head:** Dr. Gabriele
Haybach *Phone:* +43(1) 47654 ext 3108, 319-1254 **Staff:** 1
Prof. 1 Other **Holdings:** 6,000 books 45 journals **Subjects:**
Agriculture (Tropics), Agricultural Engineering, Crops, En-
tomology, Ecology, Farming, Geology, Horticulture, Miner-
alogy, Plant Pathology, Soil Science, Water Resources
Specializations: Geology, Pedology **Loan:** Do not loan
Photocopy: Yes

191   Vienna, Austria
University of Agricultural Sciences
Institute of Dairy Research and Bacteriology
Gregor Mendelstrasse 33

A-1180 Vienna
Phone: +43(1) 47654 ext 6100 **Fax:** +43(1) 3199193
WWW: www.boku.ac.at

Non-English Name: Universität für Bodenkultur, Institut für Milchforschung und Bakteriologie **Type:** Academic **Head:** Prof. Dr. Helmut Foissy *Phone:* +43(1) 47654 ext 6100 **Staff:** 7 Prof. 5 Other **Holdings:** 2,892 books 37 journals **Language of Collection/Services:** German, English **Subjects:** Bacteriology, Biotechnology, Food Sciences **Loan:** Do not loan **Photocopy:** Yes

192   Vienna, Austria
      University of Agricultural Sciences
      Institute of Agronomy and Plant Breeding
      Gregor Mendelstrasse 33
      A-1180 Vienna
Fax: +43(1) 47654-3342 **WWW:** www.boku.ac.at/
pflanzenbau

Non-English Name: Universität für Bodenkultur, Institut für Pflanzenbau und Pflanzenzüchtung **Former Name:** Hochschule für Bodenkultur **Founded:** 1872 **Type:** Academic **Head:** Univ. Prof. Dr. Peter Ruckenbauer *Phone:* +43(1) 47654-3300 **Staff:** 2 Other **Holdings:** 5,000 books 40 journals **Language of Collection/Services:** German / German **Subjects:** Crops, Plant Breeding, Plants **Databases Used:** Comprehensive **Loan:** Inhouse **Service:** Inhouse **Photocopy:** Yes

193   Vienna, Austria
      University of Agricultural Sciences, Vienna
      University Library
      Peter-Jordanstrasse 82
      A-1190 Vienna
Phone: +43(1) 47654 ext 2060 **Fax:** +43(1) 47654 ext 2092 **Email:** h205t3@edv1.boku.ac.at **WWW:** www.boku.ac.at/bib **OPAC:** bibopac.univie.ac.at

Non-English Name: Universität für Bodenkultur Wien (BOKU), Universitätsbibliothek (UB) **Founded:** 1872 **Type:** Academic **Head:** Dr. Werner Hainz-Sator *Phone:* +43(1) 47654 ext 2051 **Staff:** 17 Prof. 8 Other **Holdings:** 430,000 books 2,200 journals **Language of Collection/Services:** German, English/German, English **Subjects:** Engineering, Environmental Sciences, Landscaping, Regional Planning **Specializations:** Agricultural Development, Agricultural Economics, Agricultural Engineering, Animal Husbandry, Biotechnology, Crops, Entomology, Farming, Fisheries, Food Sciences, Forestry, Genetics, Geology, Hunting, Horticulture, Plant Pathology, Landscape Conservation, Meteorology, Soil Science, Wastes, Water Management, Wood Technology, Zoology **Databases Used:** Agris; Biosis; CABCD; Compendex; Current Contents; FSTA **Loan:** Internationally but not overseas **Service:** Internationally **Photocopy:** No

194   Vienna, Austria
      University of Vienna, University Library
      Library for Biology
      Althanstrasse 14
      A-1090 Vienna
Phone: +43(1) 31366 ext 4924 **WWW:** www.univie.ac.at

Non-English Name: Universität Wien, Universitätsbibliothek (UBW), Fachbibliothek für Biologie (FBB) **Founded:** 1982 **Type:** Academic **Head:** Dr. Friedrich Stengel *Phone:* +43(1) 31336 ext 1399 **Staff:** 4 Prof. **Holdings:** 60,000 books 200 journals **Language of Collection/Services:** German, English / German, English **Subjects:** Entomology, Fisheries, Horticulture, Soil Science **Specializations:** Plant Physiology **Databases Used:** Comprehensive **Loan:** Internationally **Photocopy:** Yes

195   Vienna, Austria
      Veterinary University of Vienna
      Library
      Veterinärplatz 1
      A-1210 Vienna
Phone: +43(1) 25077 ext 1414 **Fax:** +43(1) 25077 ext 1490 **WWW:** www.vu-wien.ac.at **OPAC:** www.vu-wien.ac.at/bibl/biblhome.htm

Non-English Name: Veterinärmedizinische Universität Wien, Universitätsbibliothek **Founded:** 1767 **Type:** Government **Head:** Dr. med. vet. Günter Olensky *Phone:* +43(1) 71155 ext 240 DW **Staff:** 7 Prof. 5 Other **Holdings:** 140,000 books 805 journals **Subjects:** Animal Husbandry, Fisheries, Veterinary Medicine **Databases Used:** Biosis; CABCD; FSTA; Medline **Loan:** Internationally **Photocopy:** Yes

♦196   Wels, Austria
      Bundesministerium für Land- und Forstwirtschaft
      Bundesanstalt für Fortpflanzung and Besamung
          von Haustieren
      Austrasse 10, Thalheim
      Postfach 121
      A-4600 Wels
Fax: +43(7242) 4701115

Founded: 1947 **Type:** Government **Head:** Dr. Franz Fischerleitner *Phone:* +43(7242) 47012 **Staff:** 1 Other **Holdings:** 13,155 books 15 journals **Language of Collection/Services:** German **Subjects:** Animal Breeding, Artificial Insemination, Domestic Animals **Loan:** Do not loan **Photocopy:** No

Azerbaijan

197   Baku, Azerbaijan
      Azerbaijan Research Institute of Animal Industries
          "F.A. Melikov", Absheron Experiment
          Station
      Republican Agricultural Popular Scientific Library
      Rafael Jafarov, 5
      Mardakan Settlement
      Baku 370076
Phone: +99(412) 327733

Former Name: Sabirabad Experiment Station of Animal Industries **Founded:** 1951 **Type:** Government **Holdings:** 1,500 books **Language of Collection/Services:** Azerbaijani /Azerbaijani **Subjects:** Animal Breeding, Livestock **Specializations:** Cattle, Sheep **Photocopy:** No

198   Baku, Azerbaijan
Azerbaijan Research Institute of Fodder, Meadows
           and Pastures
Library
Ashagy Gusdek
Baku 373258

Phone: +994(12) 422934

Founded: 1970 **Type:** Government **Head:** S. Aliev **Holdings:** 3,000 books **Subjects:** Feeds, Meadows, Pastures

199   Baku, Azerbaijan
Azerbaijan Research Institute of Veterinary
           Science
Library
Beukshor
Baku 370029

Founded: 1931 **Type:** Government **Holdings:** 14,600 books **Subjects:** Veterinary Science

200   Baku, Azerbaijan
Azerbaijan Scientific Research Institute of
           Economy and Organization of Agriculture
Library
Darnagul dis. 3097
kvartal Binagady
Baku 370130

Phone: +994(12) 327984

Founded: 1962 **Type:** Government **Head:** A.C. Verdiyev **Holdings:** 11,300 books **Subjects:** Agricultural Economics

201   Baku, Azerbaijan
Azerbaijan Scientific Research Institute of
           Vegetable Growing
Library
Pirshagy, Farm-2
Baku 370098

Phone: +994(12) 241082

Founded: 1965 **Type:** Government **Head:** F. Mamedov **Holdings:** 4,000 books **Subjects:** Vegetables

202   Guba, Azerbaijan
Azerbaijan Scientific Research Institute of
           Horticulture and Subtropical Plants
Library
Zardaby dis.
Guba 373171

Founded: 1926 **Type:** Government **Head:** P. Bairamova **Phone:** +994(269) 53717 **Holdings:** 30,200 books **Subjects:** Agriculture (Subtropics), Horticulture, Subtropics, Vineyards, Viticulture

♦203   Gyanja, Azerbaijan
Azerbaijan Scientific Research Institute for
           Mechanization and Rural Electrification
Library
Aran St., 57
Gyanja 374700

Phone: +994(222) 34638 **Fax:** +994(222) 36476

Non-English Name: Azerbaycan Elmi Tedgigat Kend Tesarrufatinin Mekaniklesdirilmesi ve Elektriklesdirilmesi Institutu (AzETKTMEi) **Founded:** 1958 **Type:** Government **Head:** M.F. Akhundov **Holdings:** 18,000 books 12 journals **Language of Collection/Services:** Russian / Azerbaijani **Subjects:** Electrification, Mechanization **Photocopy:** No

204   Gyanja, Azerbaijan
Azerbaijan Scientific Research Institute of Cotton
           Growing
Library
Institute dis.
Gyanja 374788

Phone: +994(222) 55670

Founded: 1926 **Type:** Government **Head:** F. Mamedov **Holdings:** 1,300 books **Subjects:** Cotton

205   Gyanja, Azerbaijan
Azerbaijan Scientific Research Institute of Plant
           Protection
Library
Aran 57
Gyanja 374700

Founded: 1959 **Type:** Government **Head:** S. Mamedova *Phone:* +994(222) 34794 **Holdings:** 7,700 books **Subjects:** Plant Protection

206   Gyanja, Azerbaijan
Azerbaijan Scientific Research Institute of
           Silkworm Breeding
Library
Khatal pr. 45
Gyanja 374700

Founded: 1957 **Type:** Government **Head:** N. Badalov *Phone:* +994(222) 55473 **Holdings:** 1,300 books **Subjects:** Silkworms

207   Gyanja, Azerbaijan
Azerbaijan Scientific Research Institute of Stock
           Breeding
Library
Azizbekov St.
Gyanja 374700

Founded: 1930 **Type:** Government **Head:** M. Rahimov *Phone:* +994(222) 48875 **Holdings:** 6,100 books **Subjects:** Animal Breeding, Livestock

208   Nakhichevan, Azerbaijan
Araz Scientific Industrial Amalgamation
Library
A. Aliev Str.1
Nakhichevan 373630

Phone: +994(236) 52703

Founded: 1963 **Type:** Government **Head:** G.S. Najafov

Bahamas, The

209   **Nassau, Bahamas**
Ministry of Agriculture and Fisheries
Library
PB N-3028
Nassau

Phone: +1(242) 325-7502 **Fax:** +1(242) 325-1767

Type: Government **Head:** B. Smith **Staff:** 1 Prof. **Holdings:** 250 books 8 journals **Subjects:** Agricultural Development, Agricultural Economics, Animal Production, Crop Production, Plant Protection, Stored Products

Bangladesh

210   **Bogra, Bangladesh**
Rural Development Academy (RDA)
Library
Bogra 5842

Phone: +880(51) 6505, 6511 **Fax:** +880(51) 5659

Founded: 1974 **Type:** Government **Head:** Pijush Kanti Nag *Phone:* +880(51) 6505, 6511 **Staff:** 4 Prof. 7 Other **Holdings:** 19,873 books 25 journals **Language of Collection/ Services:** English, Bengali / English, Bengali **Subjects:** Agricultural Development, Agricultural Economics, Agricultural Engineering, Animal Husbandry, Biotechnology, Rural Development, Crops, Extension, Fisheries, Forestry, Horticulture, Rural Sociology, Veterinary Medicine, Water Resources **Loan:** Inhouse **Service:** Inhouse **Photocopy:** Yes

211   **Chittagong, Bangladesh**
Bangladesh Forest Research Institute (BFRI)
Library
PO Box 273
Chittagong 4000

Location: Sholashahar, PO Amin Jute Mills **Phone:** +880 (31) 681577, 681575 **Fax:** +880(31) 681566, 681585

Founded: 1954 **Type:** Government **Head:** Md. Nozmul Hoque *Phone:* +880(31) 212164, 211337 **Staff:** 3 Prof. 6 Other **Holdings:** 11,000 books 17 journals **Language of Collection/Services:** English / Bengali, English **Subjects:** Forest Economics, Biotechnology, Crops, Entomology, Farming, Forestry, Horticulture, Plant Pathology, Soil Science, Water Resources **Loan:** Inhouse **Service:** Internationally **Photocopy:** Yes

212   **Comilla, Bangladesh**
Bangladesh Academy for Rural Development
    (BARD)
Akhter Hameed Khan Library (AHKL)
Kotbari
Comilla 3505

Phone: +880(2) 8406, 6355

Founded: 1959 **Type:** Academic **Staff:** 4 Prof. 9 Other **Holdings:** 53,000 books 35 journals **Language of Collection/Services:** English / English **Subjects:** Agricultural Development, Agricultural Economics, Agricultural Engineering, Animal Husbandry, Crops, Education/Extension,

Farming, Fisheries, Food Sciences, Forestry, Genetics, Horticulture, Water Resources **Specializations:** Communication, Cooperatives, Demography, Family Planning, Local Government, Health, Methodology, Nutrition, Project Control, Rural Sociology, Training **Loan:** Inhouse **Service:** In country **Photocopy:** Yes

♦213   **Dhaka, Bangladesh**
Bangladesh Agricultural Development
    Corporation (BADC)
Library
Krishi Bhaban, 49-51, Dilkusha CA
Dhaka 1000

Founded: 1961 **Type:** Government **Subjects:** Agricultural Development

214   **Dhaka, Bangladesh**
Bangladesh Agricultural Institute (BAI)
Library
Sher-E-Bangla Nagar
Dhaka 1207

Phone: +880(2) 311610, 312665, 312649

Type: Academic **Head:** Mahbubur Rahman *Phone:* +880(2) 31035/3, 383542 **Staff:** 5 Prof. 6 Other **Holdings:** 32,000 books 20 journals **Language of Collection/Services:** English / English, Bengali **Subjects:** Agricultural Economics, Agricultural Engineering, Animal Husbandry, Biochemistry, Botany, Crops, Education/Extension, Entomology, Genetics, Horticulture, Plant Breeding, Plant Pathology, Rural Sociology, Soil Science **Loan:** In country **Service:** In country **Photocopy:** Yes

215   **Dhaka, Bangladesh**
Bangladesh Agricultural Research Council
    (BARC)
Agricultural Information Centre (AIC)
GPO 3041
Farm Gate
New Airport Road
Dhaka 1215

Phone: +880(2) 814032 **Fax:** +880(2) 912-4596 **Email:** barc@bdmail.net

Former Name: National Agricultural Library and Documentation Centre (NALDOC) **Founded:** 1973 **Type:** Government **Head:** Mr. A.K.M. Abdun Nur *Phone:* +880(2) 326858 **Staff:** 23 Prof. 13 Other **Holdings:** 14,000 books 125 journals **Language of Collection/Services:** English / Bengali, English **Subjects:** Agriculture (Tropics), Agricultural Economics, Agricultural Engineering, Animal Husbandry, Farming, Fisheries, Forestry, Soil Science, Water Resources **Specializations:** Crops, Farming Systems, Plant Pathology **Networks:** AGRIS **Databases Developed:** Bangladesh Agricultural Bibliography **Databases Used:** Agricola; Agris; CABCD **Loan:** Inhouse **Service:** In country **Photocopy:** Yes

216   **Dhaka, Bangladesh**
Bangladesh Institute of Development Studies
    (BIDS)
Library

GPO 3854
Dhaka 1207
Location: E-17 Agargaon, Sher-e-Bangla Nagar **Phone:** +880(2) 316959, 812397 **Fax:** +880(2) 813023 **Email:** computer.bids@driktap.tool.nl

Founded: 1959 **Type:** Research

◆**217   Dhaka, Bangladesh**
Bangladesh Jute Research Institute
Library
Manik Miah Ave
Dhaka 1207
Phone: +880(2) 326718, 310953

Founded: 1951 **Type:** Government **Staff:** 3 Prof. 3 Other **Holdings:** 5,500 books **Subjects:** Agricultural Economics, Agricultural Engineering, Crops, Entomology, Plant Pathology, Plant Protection, Soil Science **Specializations:** Jute **Loan:** Do not loan **Photocopy:** No

218   Dhaka, Bangladesh
Bangladesh Scientific Documentation Centre
    (BANSDOC)
Science Laboratories
Mirpur Road
Dhaka

Type: Government **Subjects:** Agricultural Development, Crops, Agricultural Engineering, Plants

219   Dhaka, Bangladesh
Dhaka University
Library
Dhaka 1000
Phone: +880(2) 502591

Founded: 1921 **Type:** Academic **Staff:** 57 Prof. 154 Other **Holdings:** 541,789 books 393 journals **Language of Collection/Services:** English, Bengali / English, Bengali **Subjects:** Agriculture (Tropics), Botany, Agricultural Economics, Entomology, Aquaculture, Fisheries, Plants, Plant Pathology, Soil Science **Loan:** In country **Photocopy:** Yes

220   Dhaka, Bangladesh
Soil Resources Development Institute (SRDI)
Library
Krishi Khamar Sarak, Farmgate
GPO 899
Dhaka
Phone: +880(2) 313363, 310844

Founded: 1983 **Type:** Government **Subjects:** Soil Science

221   Ishurdi, Bangladesh
Ministry of Agriculture, Bangladesh Sugarcane
    Research Institute (MOA, BASURI)
Library
Ishurdi, Pabna 6620
Phone: +880(372) 414, 628

Former Name: Bangladesh Sugar and Food Industries Corporation (BSFIC), Sugarcane Research and Training Institute (SRTI) **Founded:** 1973 **Type:** Government **Staff:** 3 Prof. 1 Other **Holdings:** 3,023 books 29 journals **Language**

of Collection/Services: English/English **Subjects:** Agricultural Economics, Agricultural Engineering, Botany, Crops, Education/Extension, Entomology, Genetics, Plant Pathology, Plant Breeding, Plant Physiology, Soil Science, Statistics **Loan:** In country **Service:** Internationally **Photocopy:** No

222   Joydebpur, Bangladesh
Bangladesh Agricultural Research Institute
    (BARI)
BARI Central Library
Joydebpur, Gazipur 1701
Phone: +880(2) 933-2340, 933-4402 **Fax:** +880(2) 841678 **Email:** dg@bari.bdmail.net

Former Name: Directorate of Agriculture (Research and Education) **Founded:** 1976 **Type:** Research **Head:** Mr. A.B.M. Fazlur Rahman **Staff:** 3 Prof. 3 Other **Holdings:** 25,851 books 125 journals **Language of Collection/Services:** English **Subjects:** Agriculture (Tropics), Agricultural Development, Agricultural Economics, Agricultural Engineering, Agronomy, Biotechnology, Botany, Crops, Education/Extension, Entomology, Farming, Irrigation, Food Sciences, Fruits, Horticulture, Plant Breeding, Plant Genetics, Plant Pathology, Soil Science, Water Management, Water Resources **Loan:** In country **Service:** In country **Photocopy:** Yes

223   Joydebpur, Bangladesh
Bangladesh Rice Research Institute (BRRI)
Library
PO BRRI
Joydebpur, Gazipur 1701
Phone: +880(681) 2180, 2265 **Email:** brrihq@bdonline. com

Founded: 1970 **Type:** Government **Head:** Talukder Ijjat Ali *Phone:* +880(681) 2180 ext 476 **Staff:** 3 Prof. 2 Other **Holdings:** 11,400 books 118 journals **Language of Collection/Services:** English / Bengali **Subjects:** Agricultural Engineering, Crops, Entomology, Plant Breeding, Plant Pathology, Plant Physiology, Soil Science **Specializations:** Rice **Loan:** Do not loan **Service:** In country **Photocopy:** Yes

224   Moulvibazar, Bangladesh
Bangladesh Tea Research Institute (BTRI)
Library
Srimongal 3210
Moulvibazar

Founded: 1957 **Type:** Government **Subjects:** Tea

225   Mymensingh, Bangladesh
Bangladesh Agricultural University (BAU)
Library (BAUL)
Campus Post Office
Mymensingh 2202
Phone: +880(91) 55695/7 **Fax:** +880(91) 55810 **Email:** bau@drik.bgd.toolnet.org **WWW:** www.ugc.org/ agriculture_uni.htm

Former Name: East Pakistan Agricultural University **Founded:** 1961 **Type:** Academic **Head:** Mr. Abdul Gafur Dewan *Phone:* +880(91) 55695/7 ext 2602 **Staff:** 13 Prof. 78

Other **Holdings:** 152,000 books 300 journals **Language of Collection/Services:** English **Subjects:** Agricultural Development, Agricultural Economics, Agricultural Engineering, Animal Husbandry, Extension, Fisheries, Genetics, Plant Breeding, Rural Sociology, Veterinary Medicine **Networks:** BANSLINK **Databases Used:** Agris; CABCD **Loan:** Inhouse **Service:** Inhouse **Photocopy:** Yes

226 Mymensingh, Bangladesh
Bangladesh Fisheries Research Institute (BFRI)
Library and Documentation Center (FRILDOC)
Mymensingh 2201
Phone: +880(91) 54874, 54221 **Fax:** +880(91) 55259
Email: frihq@bdmail.net

Former Name: Fisheries Research Institute (FRI) **Founded:** 1987 **Type:** Research **Head:** Mrs. Rizia Begum *Phone:* +880(91) 54874 **Staff:** 3 Prof. 3 Other **Holdings:** 2,500 books 29 journals **Language of Collection/Services:** English, Bengali / English, Bengali **Subjects:** Fisheries **Specializations:** Aquaculture, Aquatic Animals, Aquatic Plants, Aquatic Weeds, Fish Culture, Fish Diseases, Fish Farming, Fish Feeding, Fish Industry, Fish Processing, Fish Products **Databases Developed:** Directory of Fisheries Research in Bangladesh. I. Inventory of Fisheries Scientists. II. Abstract Bibliography on Fisheries Research **Databases Used:** ASFA **Loan:** Inhouse **Service:** Internationally **Photocopy:** Yes

227 Mymensingh, Bangladesh
Bangladesh Institute of Nuclear Agriculture
  (BINA)
Library
PO Box 4
Mymensingh 2200
Phone: +880(91) 54047 **Fax:** +880(91) 54091 **Email:** bina@bdmail.net

Former Name: Institute of Nuclear Agriculture **Founded:** 1974 **Type:** Government **Head:** Md. Shahadat Hossain *Phone:* +880(91) 54401, 54402 *Email:* bina@bdmail.net **Staff:** 4 Prof. 3 Other **Holdings:** 8,225 books 76 journals **Language of Collection/Services:** English / English **Subjects:** Agriculture (Tropics), Agricultural Development, Agricultural Economics, Agricultural Engineering, Farming, Crops, Education/Extension, Entomology, Food Sciences, Horticulture, Plant Pathology, Plants, Soil, Water Resources **Databases Used:** Agris; CABCD **Loan:** Inhouse **Service:** In country **Photocopy:** Yes

228 Rajshahi, Bangladesh
Bangladesh Sericulture Research and Training
  Institute (BSRTI)
Library
P.O. Ghoramara
Rajshahi 6100
Founded: 1962 **Type:** Government **Subjects:** Sericulture

229 Salna, Bangladesh
Bangabandhu Sheikh Mujibur Rahman
  Agricultural University (BSMRAU)
Library
Salna, Gazipur 1703

Phone: +880(2) 933-2127, +880(681) 2020, 2566 **WWW:** www/ugc.org/bangabandu_agri_uni.htm

Former Name: Institute of Postgraduate Studies in Agriculture (IPSA) **Founded:** 1994 **Type:** Academic **Head:** Abdur Rouf Mian **Staff:** 5 Prof. 6 Other **Holdings:** 8,000 books 150 journals **Language of Collection/Services:** English / English, Bengali **Subjects:** Comprehensive **Loan:** In country **Service:** In country **Photocopy:** Yes

230 Savar, Bangladesh
Bangladesh Livestock Research Institute (BLRI)
Library
P.O. Savar Dairy Farm
Savar, Dhaka
Phone: +880(2) 402827

Founded: 1984 **Type:** Government **Subjects:** Animal Husbandry

Barbados

231 Bridgetown, Barbados
Ministry of Agriculture and Rural Development
Agricultural Information Services
Graeme Hall Christ Church
PO Box 505
Bridgetown
Phone: +1(246) 428-4150, 428-4065 **Fax:** +1(246) 420-8444 **Email:** ais@barbados.gov.bb, psminagric@caribsurf.com **WWW:** barbados.gov.bb/minagri

Former Name: Ministry of Agriculture, Food and Fisheries (MAFF) **Type:** Government **Head:** Mark Byer *Phone:* +1 (246) 428-4150 *Email:* markabyer@excite.com **Staff:** 5 Prof. 2 Other **Holdings:** 10,000 books 50 journals **Language of Collection/Services:** English / English **Subjects:** Agricultural Development, Agricultural Economics, Animal Production, Crop Production, Fisheries, Food Products **Databases Developed:** FARMERS - mailing list; STAFF - ministry staff list; Agricultural Workers - technicians locally; SLIDE - photographic material **Loan:** In country **Service:** In country **Photocopy:** Yes

Belarus

232 Brest reg., Belarus
Academy of Agricultural Sciences of the Republic
  of Belarus, Brest Agricultural Experiment
  Station
Library
Urbanovich St., 5
Pruzhany
225140 Brest reg.
Phone: +375(1632) 22371 **Fax:** +375(1632) 71583

Non-English Name: Akadehmiya agrarnykh navuk Rehspubliki Belarus, Brehstskaj ablasnoj sel'skagaspadarchaj doslednaj stantsyi, Bibliyatehka **Founded:** 1956 **Type:** Government **Staff:** 1 Prof. **Holdings:** 19,000 books 25 journals **Language of Collection/Services:** Russian / Russian **Sub-**

jects: Agribusiness, Agricultural Development, Agricultural Economics, Agricultural Engineering, Animal Husbandry, Biotechnology, Crops, Education/Extension, Entomology, Farming, Food Sciences, Forestry, Horticulture, Plant Pathology, Soil Science, Veterinary Medicine **Loan:** In country **Service:** Inhouse **Photocopy:** No

233   Brest reg., Belarus
Ministry of Agriculture and Food of the Republic
of Belarus, Lyakhovichi Agricultural
Technical College
Library
64 Lenin St.
Lyakhovichi
225370 Brest reg.
Phone: +375(1633) 21834 **Fax:** +375(1633) 21740

Non-English Name: Ministehrstva sel'skaj gaspadarki i kharchavannya Rehspubliki Belarus, Lyakhavitskaga sawgasa-tehkhnikuma, Bibliyatehka **Former Name:** Ministry of Agriculture of the BSSR, Ministehrstva sel'skaj gaspadarki BSSR, State Agroindustrial Committee of Byelorussian SSR, Dzyarzhawny agrapramyslovy kamiteht Belaruskaj SSR **Type:** Government **Staff:** 3 Prof. **Holdings:** 46,000 books 45 journals **Language of Collection/Services:** Russian / Russian **Subjects:** Agronomy, Animal Husbandry **Loan:** In country **Service:** Inhouse **Photocopy:** No

234   Brest reg., Belarus
Ministry of Agriculture and Food of the Republic
of Belarus, Pinsk Agricultural Technical
College
Library
1 Galevo vil.
Pinsk
225753 Brest reg.
Phone: +375(1653) 73594 **Fax:** +375(1653) 32281

Non-English Name: Ministehrstva sel'skaj gaspadarki i kharchavannya Rehspubliki Belarus, Pinskaga sel'skagaspadarchaga tehkhnikuma, Bibliyatehka **Former Name:** Ministry of Agriculture of the BSSR, Ministehrstva sel'skaj gaspadarki BSSR, State Agroindustrial Committee of Byeloussian SSR, Dzyarzhawny agrapramyslovy kamiteht Belauskaj SSR, Pinsk Sovkhoz Technical Secondary School, Pinskaga sawgasa-tehkhnikuma **Type:** Government **Staff:** 2 Prof. 2 Other **Holdings:** 70,000 books 40 journals **Language of Collection/Services:** Russian / Russian **Subjects:** Animal Husbandry **Loan:** In country **Service:** Inhouse **Photocopy:** No

235   Brest reg., Belarus
Ministry of Agriculture and Food of the Republic
of Belarus, Pinsk Hydromeliorative Technical
College
Library
33 Ostrovskij St.
Pinsk
225710 Brest reg.
Phone: +375(1653) 23361 **Fax:** +375(1653) 59446

Non-English Name: Ministehrstva sel'skaj gaspadarki i kharchavannya Rehspubliki Belarus, Pinskaga gidrame-

liyaratywnaga tehkhnikuma, Bibliyatehka **Former Name:** Ministry of Agriculture of the BSSR, Ministehrstva sel'skaj gaspadarki BSSR, State Agroindustrial Committee of Byelorussian SSR, Dzyarzhawny agrapramyslovy kamiteht Belaruskaj SSR **Type:** Government **Staff:** 2 Prof. **Holdings:** 70,000 books 40 journals **Language of Collection/Services:** Russian / Russian **Subjects:** Reclamation **Loan:** In country **Service:** Inhouse **Photocopy:** No

236   Brest reg., Belarus
Ministry of Agriculture and Food of the Republic
of Belarus, Pinsk Technical College of Meat
and Dairy Production
Library
22 Olhovskih St.
Pinsk
225710 Brest reg.
Phone: +375(1653) 23366 **Fax:** +375(1653) 22870

Non-English Name: Ministehrstva sel'skaj gaspadarki i kharchavannya Rehspubliki Belarus, Pinskaga tehkhnikuma myasa-malochnaj pramyslovastsi, Bibliyatehka **Former Name:** Ministry of Agriculture of the BSSR, Ministehrstva sel'skaj gaspadarki BSSR, State Agroindustrial Committee of Byelorussian SSR, Dzyarzhawny agrapramyslovy kamiteht Belaruskaj SSR **Type:** Government **Head:** Luker'ya Myadzvedzeva *Phone:* +375(1653) 351611 **Staff:** 2 Prof. 1 Other **Holdings:** 60,000 books 30 journals **Language of Collection/Services:** Russian/Russian **Subjects:** Meat Production, Dairy Farming, Milk Industry **Loan:** In country **Service:** Inhouse **Photocopy:** Yes

237   Brest reg., Belarus
Ministry of Agriculture and Food of the Republic
of Belarus, Pruzhany Sovkhoz Technical
College
Library
9 Mayakovskij St.
Pruzhany
225140 Brest reg.
Phone: +375(1632) 21002 **Fax:** +375(1632) 21354

Non-English Name: Ministehrstva sel'skaj gaspadarki i kharchavannya Rehspubliki Belarus, Pruzhanskaga sawgasa-tehkhnikuma, Bibliyatehka **Former Name:** Ministry of Agriculture of the BSSR, Ministehrstva sel'skaj gaspadarki BSSR, State Agroindustrial Committee of Byelorussian SSR, Dzyarzhawny agrapramyslovy kamiteht Belaruskaj SSR **Type:** Government **Staff:** 1 Prof. 3 Other **Holdings:** 56,000 books 50 journals **Language of Collection/Services:** Russian / Russian **Subjects:** Agronomy, Mechanization **Loan:** Inhouse **Service:** Inhouse **Photocopy:** No

238   Brest reg., Belarus
Ministry of Agriculture and Food of the Republic
of Belarus, Stolin Agrarian and Economic
College
Library
133 Sovetskaya St.
Stolin
225510 Brest reg.
Phone: +375(1655) 22269 **Fax:** +375(1655) 22490

Former Name: Ministry of Agriculture of the BSSR, Ministehrstva sel'skaj gaspadarki BSSR, State Agroindustrial Committee of Byelorussian SSR, Dzyarzhawny agrapramyslovy kamiteht Belaruskaj SSR, Stolin Agricultural Technical Secondary School **Type:** Government **Staff:** 2 Prof. 1 Other **Holdings:** 41,000 books 30 journals **Language of Collection/Services:** Russian/Russian **Subjects:** Agricultural Economics **Loan:** Inhouse **Photocopy:** No

239   **Gomel', Belarus**
         Ministry of Agriculture and Food of the Republic
            of Belarus, Gomel Agricultural Technical
            College
         Library
         39 Proletarskaya St.
         246693 Gomel'
Phone: +375(232) 526154 **Fax:** +375(232) 531824

Non-English Name: Ministehrstva sel'skaj gaspadarki i kharchavannya Rehspubliki Belarus, Gomelskaga selskagaspadarchaga tehkhnikuma, Bibliyatehka **Former Name:** Ministry of Agriculture of the BSSR, Ministehrstva sel'skaj gaspadarki BSSR, State Agroindustrial Committee of Byelorussian SSR, Dzyarzhawny agrapramyslovy kamiteht Belaruskaj SSR **Type:** Government **Staff:** 2 Prof. **Holdings:** 40,000 books 30 journals **Language of Collection/Services:** Russian / Russian **Subjects:** Agricultural Economics **Loan:** In country **Service:** Inhouse **Photocopy:** No

240   **Gomel', Belarus**
         National Academy of Sciences of Belarus,
            Institute of Forestry
         Library
         71 Proletarskaya St.
         246654 Gomel'
Phone: +375(232) 324941 **Fax:** +375(232) 531423
WWW: www.ac.by

Former Name: Belarus Research Institute of Forestry Production, Belaruskaga navukova-dasledchaga instytuta lyasnoj gaspadarki **Founded:** 1992 **Type:** Government **Head:** Nina Antanyuk *Phone:* +375(232) 532641 **Staff:** 1 Prof. 1 Other **Holdings:** 80,000 books 60 journals **Language of Collection/Services:** Russian/Russian **Subjects:** Forestry, Forest Management, **Loan:** In country **Service:** Inhouse **Photocopy:** Yes

241   **Gomel' reg., Belarus**
         Academy of Agricultural Sciences of the Republic
            of Belarus, Gomel Agricultural Experiment
            Station
         Library
         Dovsk vil.
         Rogachev dist.
         247261 Gomel' reg.
Phone: +375(232) 57485, +375(2339) 20462 **Fax:** +375 (232) 574851, +375(2339) 20462

Founded: 1960 **Type:** Government **Holdings:** 7,500 books

242   **Gomel' reg., Belarus**
         Ministry of Agriculture and Food of the Republic
            of Belarus, Buda-Koshelevo Agrarian
            Technical College
         Library
         1 Krasnokurgandkaya St.
         Buda-Koshelevo vil.
         247350 Gomel' reg.
Phone: +375(2336) 28671 **Fax:** +375(2336) 23149

Non-English Name: Ministehrstva sel'skaj gaspadarki i kharchavannya Rehspubliki Belarus, Buda-Kashalewskaga agrarna-tehkhnichnaga kaledzha, Bibliyatehka **Former Name:** Ministry of Agriculture of the BSSR, Ministehrstva sel'skaj gaspadarki BSSR, State Agroindustrial Committee of Byelorussian SSR, Dzyarzhawny agrapramyslovy kamiteht Belaruskaj SSR **Type:** Government **Staff:** 3 Other **Holdings:** 65,000 books 50 journals **Language of Collection/Services:** Russian / Russian **Subjects:** Agricultural Engineering **Loan:** In country **Service:** Inhouse **Photocopy:** No

243   **Gomel' reg., Belarus**
         Ministry of Agriculture and Food of the Republic
            of Belarus, Krasnyj Berag Agricultural
            Technical College
         Library
         Krasnyj Berag vil.
         Zhlobin dist.
         247232 Gomel' reg.
Phone: +375(2334) 72447 **Fax:** +375(2334) 20783

Non-English Name: Ministehrstva sel'skaj gaspadarki i kharchavannya Rehspubliki Belarus, Chyrvonabyarehzhskaga sawgasa-tehchnikuma, Bibliyatehka **Former Name:** Ministry of Agriculture of the BSSR, Ministehrstva sel'skaj gaspadarki BSSR, State Agroindustrial Committee of Byelorussian SSR, Dzyarzhawny agrapramyslovy kamiteht Belaruskaj SSR **Type:** Government **Staff:** 2 Prof. 2 Other **Holdings:** 68,000 books 40 journals **Language of Collection/Services:** Russian / Russian **Subjects:** Agronomy, Mechanization **Loan:** In country **Service:** Inhouse **Photocopy:** No

244   **Gomel' reg., Belarus**
         Ministry of Agriculture and Food of the Republic
            of Belarus, Poles'ji Agricultural Technical
            College
         Library
         1 Mira St.
         Kalinkovichi
         247710 Gomel' reg.
Phone: +375(2345) 70769 **Fax:** +375(2345) 71081

Non-English Name: Ministehrstva sel'skaj gaspadarki i kharchavannya Rehspubliki Belarus, Paleskaga sawgasatehkhnikuma, Bibliyatehka **Former Name:** Ministry of Agriculture of the BSSR, Ministehrstva sel'skaj gaspadarki BSSR, State Agroindustrial Committee of Byelorussian SSR, Dzyarzhawny agrapramyslovy kamiteht Belaruskaj SSR **Type:** Government **Staff:** 3 Prof. 1 Other **Holdings:** 63,000 books 40 journals **Language of Collection/Services:** Russian / Russian **Subjects:** Agribusiness, Agricultural Development, Agricultural Economics, Agricultural Engineering, Animal Husbandry, Biotechnology, Crops, Education/Extension, Entomology, Farming, Fisheries, Food Sciences, Forestry, Horticulture, Plant Pathology, Plants, Soil Science, Veterinary Medicine **Loan:** Inhouse **Photocopy:** No

245   Gomel' reg., Belarus
Ministry of Agriculture and Food of the Republic
of Belarus, Rechitsa Agricultural Technical
College
Library
192 Sovetskaya St.
Rechitsa
247500 Gomel' reg.
Phone: +375(234) 22357 **Fax:** +375(234) 22339

Non-English Name: Ministehrstva sel'skaj gaspadarki i kharchavannya Rehspubliki Belarus, Rehchytskaga sawgasa-tehkhnikuma, Bibliyatehka **Former Name:** Ministry of Agriculture of the BSSR, Ministehrstva sel'skaj gaspadarki BSSR, State Agroindustrial Committee of Byelorussian SSR, Dzyarzhawny agrapramyslovy kamiteht Belaruskaj SSR **Type:** Government **Staff:** 1 Prof. 1 Other **Holdings:** 57,000 books 40 journals **Language of Collection/Services:** Russian / Russian **Subjects:** Animal Husbandry, Veterinary Medicine **Loan:** Inhouse **Photocopy:** No

246   Grodno, Belarus
Ministry of Agriculture and Food of the Republic
of Belarus, Grodno State Agricultural
Institute
Library
28 Tserashkova St.
230600 Grodno
Phone: +375(15) 247-1497 **Fax:** +375(15) 247-0168
Email: niwa@selhoz.belpak.grodno.by

Non-English Name: Ministehrstva sel'skaj gaspadarki i kharchavannya Rehspublika Belarus, Grodzenskaga sel' skagaspadarchaga instyta, Bibliyatehka **Founded:** 1951 **Type:** Academic **Head:** Tereza Kuchto *Phone:* +375(15) 245-4906 *Email:* niwa@selhoz.belpak.grodno.by **Staff:** 10 Prof. 13 Other **Holdings:** 310,000 books 260 journals **Language of Collection/Services:** Russian/Russian **Subjects:** Agribusiness, Agricultural Development, Agricultural Economics, Agricultural Engineering, Animal Husbandry, Biotechnology, Crops, Education/Extension, Entomology, Food Sciences, Farming, Fisheries, Forestry, Horticulture, Plant Pathology, Plants, Soil Science, Veterinary Medicine **Loan:** In country **Service:** In country **Photocopy:** Yes

247   Grodno reg., Belarus
Academy of Agricultural Sciences of the Republic
of Belarus, Grodno Agricultural Research
Institute
Library
21 Akademicheskaya St.
Shchuchin
231510 Grodno reg.
Phone: +375(1514) 21743 **Fax:** +375(1514) 21958

Non-English Name: Akadehmiya agrarnykh navuk Rehspubliki Belarus, Grodzenskaga zanal'naga navukova-dasled-

chaga instytuta sel'skaj gaspadarki, Bibliyatehka **Former Name:** State Agroindustrial Committee of Byelorussian SSR, Dzyarzhawny agrapramyslovy kamiteht Belaruskaj SSR, Grodna State Regional Agriculture Experimental Station, Grodzenskaj ablasnoj sel'skagaspadarchaj stantsyi **Founded:** 1959 **Type:** Government **Staff:** 1 Other **Holdings:** 22,000 books 40 journals **Language of Collection/Services:** Russian/Russian **Subjects:** Agribusiness, Agricultural Development, Agricultural Economics, Agricultural Engineering, Animal Husbandry, Biotechnology, Crops, Education/Extension, Entomology, Farming, Fisheries, Food Sciences, Forestry, Horticulture, Plant Pathology, Plants, Soil Science, Veterinary Medicine **Loan:** In country **Service:** Inhouse **Photocopy:** No

248   Grodno reg., Belarus
Ministry of Agriculture and Food of the Republic
of Belarus, Novogrudok Agricultural
Technical College
Library
41 Sovetskaya St.
Novogrudok
230400 Grodno reg.
Phone: +375(1597) 21573 **Fax:** +375(1597) 21558

Non-English Name: Ministehrstva sel'skaj gaspadarki i kharchavannya Rehspubliki Belarus, Navagrutskaga sawgasa-tehchnikuma, Bibliyatehka **Former Name:** Ministry of Agriculture of the BSSR, Ministehrstva sel'skaj gaspadarki BSSR, State Agroindustrial Committee of Byelorussian SSR, Dzyarzhawny agrapramyslovy kamiteht Belaruskaj SSR **Type:** Government **Staff:** 2 Prof. 1 Other **Holdings:** 70,000 books 40 journals **Language of Collection/Services:** Russian / Russian **Subjects:** Agronomy **Loan:** In country **Service:** Inhouse **Photocopy:** No

249   Grodno reg., Belarus
Ministry of Agriculture and Food of the Republic
of Belarus, Oshmyany Agricultural Technical
College
Library
19 Sovetskaya St.
Oshmyany
237100 Grodno reg.
Phone: +375(1593) 21377 **Fax:** +375(1593) 21177

Non-English Name: Ministehrstva sel'skaj gaspadarki i kharchavannya Rehspubliki Belarus, Ashmyanskaga sel' skagaspadarchaga tehkhnikuma, Bibliyatehka **Former Name:** Ministry of Agriculture of the BSSR, Ministehrstva sel'skaj gaspadarki BSSR, State Agroindustrial Committee of Byelorussian SSR, Dzyarzhawny agrapramyslovy kamiteht Belaruskaj SSR **Type:** Government **Staff:** 3 Prof. **Holdings:** 50,000 books 30 journals **Language of Collection/Services:** Russian Russian **Subjects:** Agricultural Economics **Loan:** In country **Service:** Inhouse **Photocopy:** No

250   Grodno reg., Belarus
Ministry of Agriculture and Food of the Republic
of Belarus, Volkovysk Agricultural Technical
College
Library
52 Pobeda St.

Volkovysk
231900 Grodno reg.
Phone: +375(1512) 22269 **Fax:** +375(1512) 22269

Non-English Name: Ministehrstva sel'skaj gaspadarki i kharchavannya Rehspubliki Belarus, Volkovyskaga saw-gasa-tehkhnikuma, Bibliyatehka **Former Name:** Ministry of Agriculture of the BSSR, Ministehrstva sel'skaj gaspadarki BSSR, State Agroindustrial Committee of Byelorussian SSR, Dzyarzhawny agrapramyslovy kamiteht Belaruskaj SSR **Type:** Government **Staff:** 3 Prof. **Holdings:** 62,000 books 40 journals **Language of Collection/Services:** Russian/Russian **Subjects:** Veterinary Medicine, Zootechny **Loan:** In country **Service:** Inhouse **Photocopy:** No

251   **Grodno reg., Belarus**
Ministry of Agriculture and Food of the Republic
of Belarus, Zhirovichi Agricultural Technical
College
Library
Zhirovichi vil.
Slonim dist.
231822 Grodno reg.
Phone: +375(1562) 96233 **Fax:** +375(1562) 96233

Non-English Name: Ministehrstva sel'skaj gaspadarki i kharchavannya Rehspubliki Belarus, Zhyrovitskaga saw-gasa-tehchnikuma, Bibliyatehka **Former Name:** Ministry of Agriculture of the BSSR, Ministehrstva sel'skaj gaspadarki BSSR, State Agroindustrial Committee of Byelorussian SSR, Dzyarzhawny agrapramyslovy kamiteht Belaruskaj SSR **Type:** Government **Staff:** 3 Prof. 2 Other **Holdings:** 65,000 books 80 journals **Language of Collection/Services:** Russian / Russian **Subjects:** Mechanization **Loan:** In country **Service:** Inhouse **Photocopy:** No

252   **Minsk, Belarus**
Academy of Agricultural Sciences of the Republic
of Belarus
Belarus Agricultural Library (BELAL)
86/2 Kazinets St.
220108 Minsk
Phone: +375(17) 277-0720, 277-1161 **Fax:** +375(17) 277-0066 **Email:** ref@belal.minsk.by **WWW:** www.belal.minsk.by **OPAC:** www.belal.minsk.by

Non-English Name: Akademiya agrarnykh nauk Respubliki Belarus, Belorusskaya sel'skokhozyajstvennaya biblioteka (BelSKHB) **Former Name:** Ministry of Agriculture of the BSSR, State Agroindustrial Committee of Byelorussian SSR, Belorussian Scientific Agricultural Library, Belorus-skaya respublikanskaya sel'skokhozyajstvennaya biblioteka **Founded:** 1960 **Type:** Government **Head:** Vladimir A. Golubev *Phone:* +375(17) 277-1561 *Email:* golubev@belal.minsk.by **Staff:** 55 Prof. 15 Other **Holdings:** 500,000 books 300 journals **Language of Collection/Services:** Russian / Russian **Subjects:** Agribusiness, Agricultural Development, Agricultural Economics, Agricultural Engineering, Animal Husbandry, Biotechnology, Crops, Education/Extension, Entomology, Farming, Fisheries, Food Sciences, Forestry, Horticulture, Plant Pathology, Plants, Soil, Veterinary Medicine **Networks:** AGRIS **Databases Used:** Comprehensive **Loan:** Internationally **Service:** In country **Photocopy:** Yes

253   **Minsk, Belarus**
Academy of Agricultural Sciences of the Republic
of Belarus, Belarus Research and
Technological Institute of Fisheries
Library
22 Stebenev St.
220115 Minsk
Phone: +375(17) 277-5075 **Fax:** +375(17) 275-3646
WWW: mshp.minsk.by/science/niipkr.htm

Non-English Name: Akadehmiya agrarnykh navuk Rehspubliki Belarus, Belaruskaga navukova-dasledchaga i praektna-kanstruktarskaga instytuta rybnaj gaspadarki, Bibliyatehka **Former Name:** State Agroindustrial Committee of Byelorussian SSR, Dzyarzhawny agrapramyslovy kamiteht Belaruskaj SSR **Type:** Government **Head:** Natal'ya Barakina *Phone:* +375(17) 278-9861 **Staff:** 1 Prof. **Holdings:** 10,000 books 20 journals **Language of Collection/Services:** Russian / Russian **Subjects:** Fish Culture **Loan:** In country **Service:** Inhouse **Photocopy:** No

254   **Minsk, Belarus**
Academy of Agricultural Sciences of the Republic
of Belarus, Belarus Research and
Technological Institute of Meat and Dairy
Industry
Library
10 km, Partizanski Avenue
220075 Minsk
Phone: +375(172) 443852 **Fax:** +375(172) 252784

Non-English Name: Akadehmiya agrarnykh navuk Rehspubliki Belarus, Belaruskaga navukova-dasledchaga i kanstruktarska-tehkhnalagichnaga instytuta myasnoj i malochnaj pramyslovastsi, Bibliyatehka **Former Name:** State Agroindustrial Committee of Byelorussian SSR, Dzyarzhawny agrapramyslovy kamiteht Belaruskaj SSR, Belarus Branch of the Soviet Union Research Institute of Meat and Dairy Production, Belaruskaga filyala usesayuznaga navukova-dasledchaga instytuta myasnoj i malochnaj pramyslovastsi **Type:** Government **Staff:** 1 Prof. **Holdings:** 48,000 books 20 journals **Language of Collection/Services:** Russian / Russian **Subjects:** Dairy Farming, Meat Production **Loan:** In country **Service:** Inhouse **Photocopy:** Yes

255   **Minsk, Belarus**
Academy of Agricultural Sciences of the Republic
of Belarus, Belarus Research Institute of
Agricultural Economics and Information
Library
103 Kazinets St.
220108 Minsk
Phone: +375(17) 277-0411 **Fax:** +375(17) 278-6921
Email: vlad@nipiasu.minsk.by

Subjects: Agricultural Economics

256   **Minsk, Belarus**
Academy of Agricultural Sciences of the Republic
of Belarus, Belarus Research Institute for
Land Reclamation and Grassland
Library
153 Bogdanovich St.

220040 Minsk
Phone: +375(172) 324041 **Fax:** +375(172) 326496
WWW: mshp.minsk.by/science/niimelen.htm

Non-English Name: Akadehmiya agrarnykh navuk Rehspubliki Belarus, Belaruskaga navukova-dasledchaga instytuta meliyaratsyi i lugavodstva, Bibliyatehka **Former Name:** State Agroindustrial Committee of Byelorussian SSR, Dzyarzhawny agrapramyslovy kamiteht Belaruskaj SSR, Belarus Research Institute of Reclamation, Belaruskaga navukova-dasledchaga instytuta meliyaratsyi **Type:** Government **Staff:** 1 Prof. 2 Other **Holdings:** 110,000 books 60 journals **Language of Collection/Services:** Russian / Russian **Subjects:** Reclamation **Loan:** In country **Service:** Inhouse **Photocopy:** Yes

257   Minsk, Belarus
Academy of Agricultural Sciences of the Republic of Belarus, Belarus Research Institute for Mechanization of Agriculture
Library
1 Knorin St.
220049 Minsk
Phone: +375(17) 266-0141 **Fax:** +375(17) 266-1775
WWW: mshp.minsk.by/science/niichen.htm

Founded: 1952 **Type:** Government **Staff:** 3 Prof. **Holdings:** 126,816 books 72 journals **Language of Collection/Services:** Russian / Russian **Subjects:** Chemistry, Computers, Electrification, Machinery, Mathematics, Physics, Mechanization **Loan:** In country **Service:** In country **Photocopy:** Yes

258   Minsk, Belarus
Academy of Agricultural Sciences of the Republic of Belarus, Belarus Research Institute for Soil Science and Agrochemistry
Section for Information and Patents
62 Kazinets St.
220108 Minsk
Phone: +375(17) 277-0710, 277-0821 **Fax:** +375(17) 277-4480 **Email:** past@brissa.belpak.minsk.by **WWW:** mshp.minsk.by/science/niiagrhru.htm

Former Name: Belorussian Scientific Institute of Soil Science and Agricultural Chemistry **Type:** Government **Holdings:** 14,500 books **Language of Collection/Services:** Russian, Belorussian / Russian, English, German **Subjects:** Agricultural Chemistry, Radiology, Soil Science **Photocopy:** Yes

259   Minsk, Belarus
Academy of Agricultural Sciences of the Republic of Belarus, Belarus Research Institute of Vegetable Crops
Library
127 Mayakovsky St.
220028 Minsk
Phone: +375(17) 221-3711 **Fax:** +375(17) 221-0650
Email: inst@belniio.belpak.minsk.by **WWW:** mshp.minsk.by/science/niiov.htm

Non-English Name: Akadehmiya agrarnykh navuk Rehspubliki Belarus, Belaruskaga navukova-dasledchaga instytuta

agarodnitstva, Bibliyatehka **Former Name:** State Agroindustrial Committee of Byelorussian SSR, Belarus Research Institute of Potato, Fruit and Vegetable Growing, Dzyarzhawny agrapramyslovy kamiteht Belaruskaj SSR, Belaruskaga navukova-dasledchaga instytuta bul'bavodstva, pladavodstva i agarodnitstva **Founded:** 1956 **Type:** Government **Head:** Nataliya Paznyak **Staff:** 3 Other **Holdings:** 15,000 books 20 journals **Language of Collection/Services:** Russian / Russian **Subjects:** Plant Breeding, Vegetables **Loan:** In country **Service:** Inhouse **Photocopy:** No

260   Minsk, Belarus
Ministry of Agriculture and Food of the Republic of Belarus, Belarus Agrarian Technical University (BATU)
Library
1bl. 99 Skorina Av.
220023 Minsk
Phone: +375(17) 264-4771 **Fax:** +375(17) 264-4116
WWW: www.batu.unibel.by

Non-English Name: Ministehrstva sel'skaj gaspadarki i kharchavannya Rehspubliki Belarus, Belaruskaga agrarnaga tehkknichnaga universytehta, Bibliyatehka **Former Name:** Ministry of Agriculture of the BSSR, Ministehrstva sel'skaj gaspadarki BSSR, State Agroindustrial Committee of Byelorussian SSR, Dzyarzhawny agrapramyslovy kamiteht Belaruskaj SSR, Belarus Institute of Agricultural Mechanization, Belaruskaga instytuta mekhanizatsyi sel'skaj gaspadarki **Founded:** 1954 **Type:** Academic **Head:** Nehlya Syarova *Phone:* +375(17) 264-5381 **Staff:** 20 Prof. 16 Other **Holdings:** 380,000 books 280 journals **Language of Collection/Services:** Russian / Russian **Subjects:** Mechanization **Loan:** In country **Service:** In country **Photocopy:** Yes

261   Minsk, Belarus
National Academy of Sciences of Belarus, Institute of Genetics and Cytology (IGC)
Department of Scientific Information and Informatics (DSII)
27 Akademicheskaya St.
220072 Minsk
Phone: +375(17) 284-1917 **Fax:** +375(17) 284-1917
Email: igc@bas32.basnet.minsk.by

Type: Research **Head:** Dr. Sergey E. Dromashko *Phone:* +375(17) 284-1944 *Email:* igc@bas32.basnet.minsk.by **Holdings:** 5,000 books **Language of Collection/Services:** Russian, English / Russian **Subjects:** Comprehensive **Specializations:** Post-Chernobyl Effects **Databases Developed:** CHEDIBASE - interdisciplinary database of post-Chernobyl effects **Photocopy:** Yes

262   Minsk reg., Belarus
Academy of Agricultural Sciences of the Republic of Belarus, Belarus Experimental Poultry Station
Library
Dekhnovka vil.
Minsk dist.
223037 Minsk reg.
Phone: +375(17) 544-1553

Non-English Name: Akadehmiya agrarnykh navuk Rehspubliki Belarus, Belaruskaj zanal'naj doslednaj stantsyi pa ptushkagadowli, Bibliyatehka **Former Name:** State Agroindustrial Committee of Byelorussian SSR, Dzyarzhawny agrapramyslovy kamiteht Belaruskaj SSR **Type:** Government **Staff:** 1 Prof. **Holdings:** 8,000 books 25 journals **Language of Collection/Services:** Russian / Russian **Subjects:** Poultry **Loan:** In country **Service:** Inhouse **Photocopy:** No

263   Minsk reg., Belarus
          Academy of Agricultural Sciences of the Republic
          of Belarus, Belarus Research Institute of
          Animal Production
          Library
          11 Frunze St.
          Zhodzino
          222160 Minsk reg.
Phone: +375(1775) 33948 **WWW:** mshp.minsk.by/
science/niiliven.htm

Non-English Name: Akadehmiya agrarnykh navuk Rehspubliki Belarus, Belaruskaga navukova-dasledchaga instytuta zhyvelagadowli, Bibliyatehka **Former Name:** State Agroindustrial Committee of Byelorussian SSR, Dzyarzhawny agrapramyslovy kamiteht Belaruskaj SSR **Founded:** 1957 **Type:** Government **Head:** Natal'ya Bandarehnka *Phone:* +375(1775) 37043 **Staff:** 2 Prof. **Holdings:** 65,000 books 50 journals **Language of Collection/ Services:** Russian / Russian **Subjects:** Animal Breeding, Animal Husbandry, Livestock **Loan:** In country **Service:** Inhouse **Photocopy:** Yes

264   Minsk reg., Belarus
          Academy of Agricultural Sciences of the Republic
          of Belarus, Belarus Research Institute of
          Arable Farming and Fodders
          Library
          1 Tsimiryazev St.
          Zhodzino
          222160 Minsk reg.
Phone: +375(1775) 32568 **Fax:** +375(1775) 37066 **Email:** centr@belnoz.belpak.minsk.by **WWW:** mshp.minsk.by/
science/niizmen.htm

Non-English Name: Akadehmiya agrarnykh navuk Rehspubliki Belarus, Belaruskaga navukova-dasledchaga instytuta zemlyarobstva i karmow, Bibliyatehka **Former Name:** State Agroindustrial Committee of Byelorussian SSR, Belarus Research Institute of Agriculture, Dzyarzhawny agrapramyslovy kamiteht Belaruskaj SSR, Belaruskaga navukova-dasledchaga instytuta zemlyarobstva **Founded:** 1957 **Type:** Government **Head:** Lidziya Bulawskaya **Staff:** 2 Prof. **Holdings:** 62,000 books 50 journals **Language of Collection/Services:** Russian / Russian **Subjects:** Fodder Crops **Loan:** In country **Service:** Inhouse **Photocopy:** Yes

265   Minsk reg., Belarus
          Academy of Agricultural Sciences of the Republic
          of Belarus, Belarus Research Institute of
          Experimental Veterinary Medicine
          Library
          Kuntsevshchina vil.
          Minsk dist.

223020 Minsk reg.
Phone: +375(17) 508-8134 **Fax:** +375(17) 508-8134

Non-English Name: Akadehmiya agrarnykh navuk Rehspubliki Belarus, Belaruskaga navukova-dasledchaga instytuta ehksperymental'naj vetehrynaryi, Bibliyatehka **Former Name:** State Agroindustrial Committee of Byelorussian SSR, Belorussian Research Veterinary Institute, Dzyarzhawny agrapramyslovy kamiteht Belaruskaj SSR, Belaruskaga navukova-dasledchaga vetehrynarnaga instytuta **Founded:** 1957 **Type:** Government **Staff:** 23 Prof. 28 Other **Holdings:** 945,000 books 320 journals **Language of Collection/Services:** Russian / Russian **Subjects:** Agribusiness, Agricultural Development, Agricultural Economics, Agricultural Engineering, Animal Husbandry, Biotechnology, Crops, Education / Extension, Entomology, Farming, Food Sciences, Forestry, Horticulture, Plant Pathology, Soil Science **Specializations:** Veterinary Science **Loan:** In country **Service:** Internationally **Photocopy:** Yes

266   Minsk reg., Belarus
          Academy of Agricultural Sciences of the Republic
          of Belarus, Belarus Research Institute of Fruit
          Growing
          Library
          Samokhvalavichi vil.
          Minsk dist.
          223013 Minsk reg.
Phone: +375(17) 506-6140 **Fax:** +375(17) 506-6140
WWW: mshp.minsk.by/science/niipl.htm

Non-English Name: Akadehmiya agrarnykh navuk Rehspubliki Belarus, Belaruskaga navukova-dasledchaga instytuta pladavodstva, Bibliyatehka **Former Name:** State Agroindustrial Committee of Byelorussian SSR, Belarus Research Institute of Potato, Fruit and Vegetable Growing, Dzyarzhawny agrapramyslovy kamiteht Belaruskaj SSR, Belaruskaga navukova-dasledchaga instytuta bul'bavodstva, pladavodstva i agarodnitstva **Founded:** 1956 **Type:** Government **Staff:** 2 Prof. 2 Other **Holdings:** 60,000 books 40 journals **Language of Collection/Services:** Russian / Russian **Subjects:** Plant Breeding **Specializations:** Fruits **Loan:** In country **Service:** Inhouse **Photocopy:** No

267   Minsk reg., Belarus
          Academy of Agricultural Sciences of the Republic
          of Belarus, Belarus Scientific Research
          Institute of Plant Protection (BelSRIPP)
          Scientific Library
          Priluki vil.
          Minsk dist.
          223011 Minsk reg.
Phone: +375(17) 599-2330 **Fax:** +375(17) 599-2339
Email: libr@belizr.belpak.minsk.by

Non-English Name: Belaruskaga Dzyarzhaunaga Institutu Akhovy Raslin, Naukovaya Biblioteka **Founded:** 1971 **Type:** Government **Head:** Sakovich Galina Vladimirovna *Email:* libr@belizr.belpak.minsk.by *Phone:* +375(17) 599-2330 **Staff:** 2 Prof. **Holdings:** 53,000 books 63 journals **Language of Collection/Services:** Russian, Belorussian, Polish, English, German/Belorussian **Subjects:** Crops, Plant Diseases, Plant Pests, Plant Protection, Plants **Databases Used:** Agrilit; Belal **Service:** Inhouse **Photocopy:** Yes

268 Minsk reg., Belarus
Academy of Agricultural Sciences of the Republic
of Belarus, Belarusian Research Institute of
Potato Growing (BRIP)
Library
Samokhvalovichi vil.
Minsk dist.
223013 Minsk reg.
Location: 2a Kovaleva Str. **Phone:** +375(175) 901145
Fax: +375(175) 901145 **Email:** bripotat@org.by

Non-English Name: Akadehmiya agrarnykh navuk Rehspubliki Belarus, Belaruskaga navukova-dasledchaga instytuta
bul'bavodstva (BelNIIK), Bibliyatehka **Former Name:**
State Agroindustrial Committee of Byelorussian SSR, Belarus Research Institute of Potato, Fruit and Vegetable Growing, Dzyarzhawny agrapramyslovy kamiteht Belaruskaj
SSR, Belaruskaga navukova-dasledchaga instytuta bul'bavodstva, pladavodstva i agarodnitstva **Founded:** 1996 **Type:**
Government **Head:** Liudmila Danilawa *Phone:* +375(175)
901135 *Email:* bripotat@org.by **Staff:** 1 Other **Holdings:**
2,000 books 18 journals **Language of Collection/ Services:**
Russian / Russian **Subjects:** Plant Breeding **Specializations:**
Potatoes **Databases Used:** Agros; Belal; CARIS **Loan:** Inhouse **Service:** In country **Photocopy:** Yes

269 Minsk reg., Belarus
Academy of Agricultural Sciences of the Republic
of Belarus, Minsk Agricultural Experiment
Station
Library
Natalevsk vil.
Cherven dist.
223225 Minsk reg.
Phone: +375(1714) 55107 **Fax:** +375(1714) 55107
WWW: mshp.minsk.by.science/minost.htm

Non-English Name: Akadehmiya agrarnykh navuk Rehspubliki Belarus, Minskaj ablasnoj sel'skagaspadarchaj doslednaj stantsyi, Bibliyatehka **Former Name:** State Agroindustrial Committee of Byelorussian SSR, Dzyarzhawny agrapramyslovy kamiteht Belaruskaj SSR **Type:** Government
Head: Iryna Gnedchyk *Phone:* +375(1714) 55107 **Staff:** 1
Prof. **Holdings:** 8,000 books 30 journals **Language of Col-
lection/Services:** Russian / Russian **Subjects:** Agribusiness,
Agricultural Development, Agricultural Economics, Agricultural Engineering, Animal Husbandry, Biotechnology,
Crops, Education/Extension, Entomology, Farming, Food
Sciences, Forestry, Horticulture, Plant Pathology, Soil Science, Veterinary Medicine **Loan:** In country **Service:** In-
house **Photocopy:** No

270 Minsk reg., Belarus
Ministry of Agriculture and Food of the Republic
of Belarus, Belarus Correspondence
Agricultural Technical College
Library
12 Gorkij St.
Smilovichi vil.
Chervenskij dist.
223216 Minsk reg.
Phone: +375(1714) 53291 **Fax:** +375(1714) 53659

Non-English Name: Ministehrstva sel'skaj gaspadarki i
kharchavannya Rehspubliki Belarus, Belaruskaga zavoch-
naga sel'skagaspadarchaga tehchnikuma, Bibliyatehka **Former Name:** Ministry of Agriculture of the BSSR, Ministehrstva sel'skaj gaspadarki BSSR, State Agroindustrial
Committee of Byelorussian SSR, Dzyarzhawny agrapramyslovy kamiteht Belaruskaj SSR **Type:** Government **Staff:**
2 Prof. **Holdings:** 70,000 books 40 journals **Language of
Collection/Services:** Russian / Russian **Subjects:** Agribusiness, Agricultural Development, Agricultural Economics,
Agricultural Engineering, Animal Husbandry, Biotechnology, Crops, Education/Extension, Entomology, Farming,
Fisheries, Food Sciences, Forestry, Horticulture, Plant Pathology, Plants, Soil Science, Veterinary Medicine **Loan:** In
country **Service:** Inhouse **Photocopy:** No

271 Minsk reg., Belarus
Ministry of Agriculture and Food of the Republic
of Belarus, Il'ja Agricultural Technical
College
Library
103 Sovetskaya St.
Il'ja vil.
Vilejka dist.
222431 Minsk reg.
Phone: +375(1771) 76248 **Fax:** +375(1771) 76139

Non-English Name: Ministehrstva sel'skaj gaspadarki i
kharchavannya Rehspubliki Belarus, Illyanskaga sel'skagaspadarchaga tehchnikuma, Bibliyatehka **Former Name:**
Ministry of Agriculture of the BSSR, Ministehrstva sel'skaj
gaspadarki BSSR, State Agroindustrial Committee of Byelorussian SSR, Dzyarzhawny agrapramyslovy kamiteht Belaruskaj SSR, Illya Sovkhoz Technical Secondary School,
Illyanskaga sawgasa-tehchnikuma **Founded:** 1957 **Type:**
Government **Head:** Ignotovich Lidia *Phone:* +375(1771)
76248 **Staff:** 1 Prof. 2 Other **Holdings:** 50,000 books 40
journals **Language of Collection/Services:** Russian / Russian **Subjects:** Animal Husbandry, Veterinary Medicine
Loan: In country **Service:** Inhouse **Photocopy:** No

272 Minsk reg., Belarus
Ministry of Agriculture and Food of the Republic
of Belarus, Marina Gorka Agricultural
Technical College
Library
2Sovetskaya St.
Marina Gorka
222830 Minsk reg.
Phone: +375(1713) 97116

Non-English Name: Ministehrstva sel'skaj gaspadarki i
kharchavannya Rehspubliki Belarus, Mar'inagorskaga sawgasa-tehkhnikuma, Bibliyatehka **Former Name:** Ministry
of Agriculture of the BSSR, Ministehrstva sel'skaj
gaspadarki BSSR, State Agroindustrial Committee of Byelorussian SSR, Dzyarzhawny agrapramyslovy kamiteht Belaruskaj SSR **Type:** Government **Staff:** 2 Prof. 3 Other
Holdings: 70,000 books 50 journals **Language of Collec-
tion/Services:** Russian / Russian **Subjects:** Mechanization
Loan: In country **Service:** Inhouse **Photocopy:** No

273   Minsk reg., Belarus
Ministry of Agriculture and Food of the Republic
    of Belarus, Minsk Agrarian and Commercial
    College
Library
59 Naberezhnaya St.
Sennitsa
223056 Minsk reg.
Phone: +375(17) 299-1209

Non-English Name: Ministehrstva sel'skaj gaspadarki i
kharchavannya Rehspubliki Belarus, Belaruskaga agrarna-
kamertsyjnaga kaledzha, Bibliyatehka **Former Name:** Ministry of Agriculture of the BSSR, Ministehrstva sel'skaj
gaspadarki BSSR, State Agroindustrial Committee of Byelorussian SSR, Dzyarzhawny agrapramyslovy kamiteht Belaruskaj SSR, Belarus Agricultural Technical Secondary
School for Training of Personnel for the Collective and State
Farms, Belaruskaga sel'skagaspadarchaga tehkhnikuma pa
padrykhtowtsy kirawnitskikh kadraw kalgasaw i sawgasaw
Type: Government **Staff:** 1 Prof. 1 Other **Holdings:** 30,000
books 40 journals **Language of Collection/Services:** Russian / Russian **Subjects:** Agribusiness, Agricultural Development, Agricultural Economics, Agricultural Engineering,
Animal Husbandry, Biotechnology, Crops, Education/Ex-
tension, Entomology, Farming, Fisheries, Food Sciences,
Forestry, Horticulture, Plant Pathology, Plants, Soil Science,
Veterinary Medicine **Loan:** In country **Service:** Inhouse
Photocopy: No

274   Minsk reg., Belarus
Ministry of Agriculture and Food of the Republic
    of Belarus, Novoe Pole Agricultural
    Technical College
Library
Novoe Pole vil.
Minsk dist.
223025 Minsk reg.
Phone: +375(17) 954542

Non-English Name: Ministehrstva sel'skaj gaspadarki i
kharchavannya Rehspubliki Belarus, Navapol'skaga sel'skagaspadarchaga tehkhnikuma, Bibliyatehka **Former Name:**
Ministry of Agriculture of the BSSR, Ministehrstva sel'skaj
gaspadarki BSSR, State Agroindustrial Committee of Byelorussian SSR, Dzyarzhawny agrapramyslovy kamiteht Belaruskaj SSR **Type:** Government **Staff:** 1 Prof. 1 Other **Holdings:** 40,000 books 30 journals **Language of Collection/
Services:** Russian/Russian **Subjects:** Agricultural Economics **Loan:** In country **Service:** Inhouse **Photocopy:** No

275   Minsk reg., Belarus
Ministry of Agriculture and Food of the Republic
    of Belarus, Smilovichi Agricultural Technical
    College
Library
5 Gorkij St.
Smilovichi vil.
Chervenskij dist.
223216 Minsk reg.
Phone: +375(1714) 53244 **Fax:** +375(1714) 53469

Non-English Name: Ministehrstva sel'skaj gaspadarki i
kharchavannya Rehspubliki Belarus, Smilavitskaga Saw-

gasa-tehkhnikuma, Bibliyatehka **Former Name:** Ministry of
Agriculture of the BSSR, Ministehrstva sel'skaj gaspadarki
BSSR, State Agroindustrial Committee of Byelorussian
SSR, Dzyarzhawny agrapramyslovy kamiteht Belaruskaj
SSR **Type:** Government **Staff:** 3 Prof. **Holdings:** 57,000
books 40 journals **Language of Collection/Services:** Rus-
sian / Russian **Subjects:** Animal Husbandry, Veterinary
Medicine **Loan:** Inhouse **Photocopy:** No

276   Mogilev reg., Belarus
Academy of Agricultural Sciences of the Republic
    of Belarus, Mogilev Agricultural Experiment
    Station
Library
Dashkovka vil.
Magilew dist.
213300 Mogilev reg.
Phone: +375(222) 992166 **Fax:** +375(222) 252935

Non-English Name: Akadehmiya agrarnykh navuk Rehspubliki Belarus, Magilewskaj ablasnoj sel'skagaspadarchaj
doslednaj stantsyi, Bibliyatehka **Former Name:** State Agroindustrial Committee of Byelorussian SSR, Dzyarzhawny
agrapramyslovy kamiteht Belaruskaj SSR **Founded:** 1957
Type: Government **Staff:** 1 Other **Holdings:** 5,000 books 25
journals **Language of Collection/ Services:** Russian / Russian **Subjects:** Agricultural Development, Agribusiness,
Agricultural Economics, Agricultural Engineering, Animal
Husbandry, Biotechnology, Crops, Education / Extension,
Entomology, Farming, Food Sciences, Forestry, Horticulture, Plant Pathology, Soil Science, Veterinary Medicine
Loan: In country **Service:** Inhouse **Photocopy:** No

277   Mogilev reg., Belarus
Ministry of Agriculture and Food of the Republic
    of Belarus, Belarus Academy of Agriculture
Library
Michurin St., 5
Gorki
213410 Mogilev reg.
Phone: +375(2233) 22849 **Fax:** +375(2233) 21587

Non-English Name: Ministehrstva sel'skaj gaspadarki i
kharchavannya Rehspubliki Belarus, Belaruskaj sel'skagaspadarchaj Akadehmii, Bibliyatehka **Former Name:** Ministry of Agriculture of the BSSR, Ministehrstva sel'skaj gaspadarki BSSR, State Agroindustrial Committee of Byelorussian SSR, Dzyarzhawny agrapramyslovy kamiteht Belaruskaj SSR **Founded:** 1840 **Type:** Academic **Staff:** 23
Prof. 28 Other **Holdings:** 945,000 books 320 journals **Language of Collection/Services:** Russian / Russian **Subjects:**
Agribusiness, Agricultural Development, Agricultural Economics, Agricultural Engineering, Animal Husbandry,
Crops, Biotechnology, Education/Extension, Entomology,
Farming, Food Sciences, Forestry, Horticulture, Plant Pathology, Soil Science, Veterinary Medicine **Loan:** In country **Service:** Internationally **Photocopy:** Yes

278   Mogilev reg., Belarus
Ministry of Agriculture and Food of the Republic
    of Belarus, Bobrujsk Agricultural Technical
    College
Library

46 Internatsionalnaya St.
Bobrujsk
213819 Mogilev reg.
Phone: +375(2251) 72317 **Fax:** +375(2251) 72317

Non-English Name: Ministehrstva sel'skaj gaspadarki i kharchavannya Rehpubliki Belarus, Babrujskaga sel'skagaspadarchaga tehkhnikuma, Bibliyatehka **Former Name:** Ministry of Agriculture of the BSSR, Ministehrstva sel'skaj gaspadarki BSSR, State Agroindustrial Committee of Byelorussian SSR, Dzyarzhawny agrapramyslovy kamiteht Belaruskaj SSR **Type:** Government **Staff:** 3 Prof. **Holdings:** 46,000 books 40 journals **Language of Collection/Services:** Russian / Russian **Subjects:** Agricultural Economics **Loan:** In country **Service:** Inhouse **Photocopy:** No

279   Mogilev reg., Belarus
Ministry of Agriculture and Food of the Republic
of Belarus, Klichev Agricultural Technical
College
Library
22 Krivonosa St.
Klichev
213900 Mogilev reg.
Phone: +375(2236) 21487 **Fax:** +375(2236) 21547

Former Name: Ministry of Agriculture of the BSSR, Ministehrstva sel'skaj gaspadarki BSSR, State Agroindustrial Committee of Byelorussian SSR, Dzyarzhawny agrapramyslovy kamiteht Belaruskaj SSR **Type:** Government **Staff:** 1 Prof. 3 Other **Holdings:** 80,000 books 50 journals **Language of Collection/Services:** Russian / Russian **Subjects:** Mechanization **Loan:** In country **Service:** Inhouse **Photocopy:** No

280   Mogilev reg., Belarus
Ministry of Agriculture and Food of the Republic
of Belarus, Klimovichi Agricultural Technical
College
Library
11 Sotsialisticheskaya St.
Klimovichi
213600 Mogilev reg.
Phone: +375(2244) 21800 **Fax:** +375(2244) 21196

Non-English Name: Ministehrstva sel'skaj gaspadarki i kharchavannya Rehpubliki Belarus, Klimavitskaga sawgasa-tehchnikuma, Bibliyatehka **Former Name:** Ministry of Agriculture of the BSSR, Ministehrstva sel'skaj gaspadarki BSSR, State Agroindustrial Committee of Byelorussian SSR, Dzyarzhawny agrapramyslovy kamiteht Belaruskaj SSR **Type:** Government **Staff:** 3 Prof. **Holdings:** 62,000 books 50 journals **Language of Collection/Services:** Russian / Russian **Subjects:** Animal Husbandry, Mechanization, Veterinary Medicine **Loan:** In country **Service:** Inhouse **Photocopy:** No

281   Mogilev reg., Belarus
Ministry of Agriculture and Food of the Republic
of Belarus, Zhilichi Agricultural Technical
College
Library
Zhilichi vil.

Kirovskij dist.
213948 Mogilev reg.
Phone: +375(2237) 32233 **Fax:** +375(2237) 21500

Non-English Name: Ministehrstva sel'skaj gaspadarki i kharchavannya Rehpubliki Belarus, Zhylitskaga sawgasatehchnikuma, Bibliyatehka **Former Name:** Ministry of Agriculture of the BSSR, Ministehrstva sel'skaj gaspadarki BSSR, State Agroindustrial Committee of Byelorussian SSR, Dzyarzhawny agrapramyslovy kamiteht Belaruskaj SSR **Type:** Government **Staff:** 3 Prof. **Holdings:** 62,000 books 40 journals **Language of Collection / Services:** Russian / Russian **Subjects:** Agronomy **Loan:** In country **Service:** Inhouse **Photocopy:** No

282   Vitebsk, Belarus
Ministry of Agriculture and Food of the Republic
of Belarus, Vitebsk State Academy of
Veterinary Medicine
Library
7/11 Dovator St.
210602 Vitebsk
Phone: +375(21) 237-2718 **Fax:** +37(21) 237-0284

Non-English Name: Ministehrstva sel'skaj gaspadarki i kharchavannya Rehspubliki Belarus, Vitsebskaj Akadehmii vetehrynarnaj medytsyny, Bibliyatehka **Former Name:** Ministry of Agriculture of the BSSR, State Agroindustrial Committee of Byelorussian SSR, Vitsebsk Veterinary Institute, Ministehrstva sel'skaj gaspadarki BSSR, Dzyarzhawny agrapramyslovy kamiteht Belaruskaj SSR, Vitsebskaga vetehrynarnaga instytuta **Founded:** 1924 **Type:** Academic **Staff:** 20 Prof. 9 Other **Holdings:** 315,000 books 28 journals **Language of Collection/Services:** Russian / Russian **Subjects:** Veterinary Science **Loan:** In country **Service:** In country **Photocopy:** Yes

283   Vitebsk reg., Belarus
Academy of Agricultural Sciences of the Republic
of Belarus, Vitebsk Agricultural Experiment
Station
Library
Tulova vil.
Vitebsk dist.
211343 Vitebsk reg.
Phone: +375(212) 916232 **WWW:** mshp.minsk.by/
science/vitops.htm

Non-English Name: Akadehmiya agrarnykh navuk Rehspubliki Belarus, Vitsebskaj ablasnoj sel'skagaspadarchaj doslednaj stantsyi, Bibliyatehka **Former Name:** State Agroindustrial Committee of Byelorussian SSR, Dzyarzhawny agrapramyslovy kamiteht Belaruskaj SSR **Founded:** 1956 **Type:** Government **Head:** Valyantsina Varkulevish *Phone:* +375(212) 916239 **Staff:** 1 Other **Holdings:** 22,000 books 25 journals **Language of Collection/ Services:** Russian / Russian **Subjects:** Agribusiness, Agricultural Development, Agricultural Economics, Agricultural Engineering, Animal Husbandry, Biotechnology, Crops, Education/Extension, Entomology, Farming, Food Sciences, Forestry, Horticulture, Plant Pathology, Soil Science, Veterinary Medicine **Loan:** In country **Service:** Inhouse **Photocopy:** No

284   Vitebsk reg., Belarus
Ministry of Agriculture and Food of the Republic
of Belarus, Gorodok Agricultural Technical
College
Library
42 Bagramyan St.
Gorodok
211540 Vitebsk reg.
Phone: +375(2139) 21651 **Fax:** +375(2139) 23317

Non-English Name: Ministehrstva sel'skaj gaspadarki i
kharchavannya Rehspubliki Belarus, Garadokskaga saw-
gasa-tehkhnikuma, Bibliyatehka **Former Name:** Ministry of
Agriculture of the BSSR, Ministehrstva sel'skaj gaspadarki
BSSR, State Agroindustrial Committee of Byelorussian
SSR, Dzyarzhawny agrapramyslovy kamiteht Belaruskaj
SSR **Type:** Government **Staff:** 2 Prof. 2 Other **Holdings:**
65,000 books 40 journals **Language of Collection/Services:**
Russian / Russian **Subjects:** Mechanization **Loan:** In coun-
try **Service:** Inhouse **Photocopy:** No

285   Vitebsk reg., Belarus
Ministry of Agriculture and Food of the Republic
of Belarus, Lepel' Hydromeliorative
Technical College
Library
42 Internatsionalnaya St.
Lepel'
211180 Vitebsk reg.
Phone: +375(2132) 41900 **Fax:** +375(2132) 41800

Non-English Name: Ministehrstva sel'skaj gaspadarki i
kharchavannya Rehspubliki Belarus, Lepel'skaga gidrame-
liyaratywnaga tehkhnikuma, Bibliyatehka **Former Name:**
Ministry of Agriculture of the BSSR, Ministehrstva sel'skaj
gaspadarki BSSR, State Agroindustrial Committee of Byelorussian SSR, Dzyarzhawny agrapramyslovy kamiteht Belaruskaj SSR **Type:** Government **Holdings:** 45,000 books 30
journals **Staff:** 2 Prof. 1 Other **Language of Collection/Ser-
vices:** Russian / Russian **Subjects:** Reclamation **Loan:** In
country **Service:** Inhouse **Photocopy:** No

286   Vitebsk reg., Belarus
Ministry of Agriculture and Food of the Republic
of Belarus, Luzhesno Agricultural Technical
College
Library
Luzhesno vil.
Vitebsk dist.
211311 Vitebsk reg.
Phone: +375(21) 298-5221 **Fax:** +375(21) 296-2547

Non-English Name: Ministehrstva sel'skaj gaspadarki i
kharchavannya Rehspubliki Belarus, Luzhasnyanskaga saw-
gasa-tehkhnikuma, Bibliyatehka **Former Name:** Ministry of
Agriculture of the BSSR, Ministehrstva sel'skaj gaspadarki
BSSR, State Agroindustrial Committee of Byelorussian
SSR, Dzyarzhawny agrapramyslovy kamiteht Belaruskaj
SSR **Type:** Government **Staff:** 4 Prof. 1 Other **Holdings:**
90,000 books 50 journals **Language of Collection/Services:**
Russian / Russian **Subjects:** Agronomy, Animal Husbandry
Loan: In country **Service:** Inhouse **Photocopy:** No

287   Vitebsk reg., Belarus
Ministry of Agriculture and Food of the Republic
of Belarus, Polotsk Agricultural Technical
College
Library
55 Oktyabrskaya St.
Polotsk
211400 Vitebsk reg.
Phone: +375(2144) 43103 **Fax:** +375(2144) 43103

Non-English Name: Ministehrstva sel'skaj gaspadarki i
kharchavannya Rehspubliki Belarus, Polatskaga sel'skagaspadarchaga tehknnikuma, Bibliyatehka **Former Name:**
Ministry of Agriculture of the BSSR, Ministehrstva sel'skaj
gaspadarki BSSR, State Agroindustrial Committee of Byelorussian SSR, Dzyarzhawny agrapramyslovy kamiteht Belaruskaj SSR **Type:** Government **Holdings:** 27,000 books 30
journals **Staff:** 1 Prof. 1 Other **Language of Collection/ Services:** Russian/Russian **Subjects:** Agricultural Economics
Loan: In country **Service:** Inhouse **Photocopy:** No

288   Vitebsk reg., Belarus
Ministry of Agriculture and Food of the Republic
of Belarus, Smolyany Agricultural Technical
College
Library
Smolyany vil.
Orsha dist.
211014 Vitebsk reg.
Phone: +375(2161) 99188 **Fax:** +375(2161) 91160

Non-English Name: Ministehrstva sel'skaj gaspadarki i
kharchavannya Rehspubliki Belarus, Smalyanskaga saw-
gasa-tehkhnikuma, Bibliyatehka **Former Name:** Ministry of
Agriculture of the BSSR, Ministehrstva sel'skaj gaspadarki
BSSR, State Agroindustrial Committee of Byelorussian
SSR, Dzyarzhawny agrapramyslovy kamiteht Belaruskaj
SSR **Type:** Government **Staff:** 1 Prof. 1 Other **Holdings:**
45,000 books 30 journals **Language of Collection/Services:**
Russian/Russian **Subjects:** Agribusiness, Agricultural Economics, Agricultural Development, Animal Husbandry,
Agricultural Engineering, Biotechnology, Crops, Educa-
tion/Extension, Entomology, Farming, Fisheries, Food Sci-
ences, Forestry, Horticulture, Plant Pathology, Plants, Soil
Science, Veterinary Medicine **Loan:** In country **Service:** Inhouse **Photocopy:** No

Belgium

289   Antwerp, Belgium
Prince Leopold Institute of Tropical Medicine
Library
Nationalestraat 155
B-2000 Antwerp 1
Phone: +32(3) 247-6241 **Fax:** +32(3) 248-1133 **Email:**
bib@itg.be **WWW:** www.itg.be **OPAC:** lib.itg.be

Non-English Name: Instituut voor Tropische Geneeskunde
Prins Leopold (ITG), Bibliotheek **Founded:** 1933 **Type:** Academic **Head:** Mr. Dirk Schoonbaert *Phone:* +32(3) 247-
6240 *Email:* bib@itg.be **Staff:** 3 Prof. **Holdings:** 20,000
books 550 journals **Language of Collection/Services:** Eng-

lish/Dutch, French, English **Subjects:** Animal Diseases, Microbiology, Parasitology, Public Health, Tropical Medicine **Networks:** Antilope; CCB **Databases Developed:** Belgian and Central African Tropical and Geographical Medical and Veterinary Science Database (BELCAT) **Databases Used:** CAB HEALTHCD; Medline; VETCD **Service:** Internationally **Loan:** Inhouse **Photocopy:** Yes

290   Antwerp, Belgium
        University of Antwerp, State University Center
        Campus Library Middleheim
        Middelheimlaan, 1
        Building G
        B-2020 Antwerp
Phone: +32(3) 218-07-94 **Fax:** +32(3) 218-06-52 **Email:** tjoos@lib.ua.ac.be **WWW:** www.ua.ac.be **OPAC:** lib.ua.ac.be/ualib.html

Non-English Name: Universiteit Antwerpen, Rijksuniversitair Centrum Antwerpen (RUCA), Campusbibliotheek Middelheim **Founded:** 1960 **Type:** Academic **Head:** Dr. B. Van Styvendaele *Email:* bstyvendaele@lib.ua.ac.be *Phone:* +32(3) 218-07-88 **Staff:** 4 Prof. 16 Other **Holdings:** 1,500 books 50 journals **Subjects:** Agricultural Development, Animal Husbandry, Plant Pathology, Forestry, Horticulture, Soil Science, Hunting, Statistics **Loan:** Do not loan **Photocopy:** Yes

291   Antwerp, Belgium
        University of Antwerp
        Library
        PO Box 13
        B-2610 Antwerp (Wilrijk)
Location: Universiteitsplein 1 **Phone:** +32(3) 820-2141 **Fax:** +32(3) 820-2159 **Email:** uia@lib.ua.ac.be **WWW:** www.ua.ac.be/ualib.html **OPAC:** lib.ua.ac/WWWOPAC/wwwopac.html

Non-English Name: Universitaire Instelling Antwerpen (UIA), Bibliotheek **Founded:** 1972 **Type:** Academic **Head:** Julien Van Borm *Phone:* +32(3) 820-2143 *Email:* julien.vanborm@uia.ua.ac.be **Staff:** 16 Prof. 11 Other **Holdings:** 400,000 books 2,500 journals **Language of Collection/Services:** English / Dutch **Subjects:** Biotechnology, Education, Entomology, Food Sciences, Horticulture, Plant Pathology, Plants **Databases Developed:** Antilope - list of periodicals in Belgian academic libraries; VUBIS-Antwerpen catalogue - catalogue of books and periodicals of the network VUBIS-Antwerpen **Databases Used:** Medline **Loan:** Internationally **Service:** Internationally **Photocopy:** Yes

292   Arlon, Belgium
        Fondation Universitaire Luxenbourgeoise (FUL)
        Bibliothèque
        Avenue de Longwy, 185
        B-6700 Arlon
Phone: +32(63) 230887/8 **Fax:** +32(63) 230897 **Email:** biblio@ful.ac.be **WWW:** www.ful.ac.be/index.htm

Type: Academic **Head:** Dr. Bernard Crousse *Phone:* +32(63) 230891 **Staff:** 2 Prof. **Holdings:** 25,000 books 200 journals **Language of Collection/Services:** French, English

/French **Subjects:** Environment **Loan:** In country **Service:** In country **Photocopy:** Yes

293   Ath, Belgium
        Centre pour la Recherche, l'Economie et la
            Promotion Agricole (CREPA)
        Bibliothèque
        Rue Paul Pastur 11
        B-7800 Ath
Phone: +32(68) 280105 **Fax:** +32(68) 285660 **WWW:** www.hainaut.be/Frameset.htm

Former Name: Institut Agricole de la Province de Hainaut (IAPH), Institut Provincial d'Enseignement Supérieur Agricole et Technique (IPESAT), Institut Supérieur Industriel (ISI) **Type:** Academic **Head:** Edmond Leclercq **Holdings:** 5,000 books 80 journals **Language of Collection/Services:** French / French **Subjects:** Agriculture (Tropics), Biochemistry, Biotechnology, Environment, Food Sciences, Horticulture, Microbiology, Rural Development, Silviculture **Loan:** In country **Photocopy:** Yes

294   Brussels, Belgium
        Brussels Free University
        Science and Technology Library
        CP 174
        30, av. Depage
        B-1050 Brussels
Phone: +32(2) 650-2054/5 **WWW:** www.bib.ulb.ac.be/BST **OPAC:** bib7.ulb.ac.be/uhtbin/webcat

Non-English Name: Université Libre de Bruxelles (ULB), Bibliothèque des Sciences et Techniques (BST) **Type:** Academic **Holdings:** 50,000 books 6,000 journals **Language of Collection/Services:** English **Subjects:** Biology, Biotechnology, Crops, Entomology, Environment, Fisheries, Molecular Biology, Plants, Soil Science **Databases Developed:** Theses **Photocopy:** Yes

♦295   Brussels, Belgium
        Center for Interdisciplinary Research on
            Development
        Library
        Rue Valduc 152
        B-1160 Brussels
Phone: +32(2) 672-4172

Non-English Name: Centre pour la Recherche Interdisciplinaire sur le Développement (CRID), Bibliothèque **Type:** Research **Head:** Jacques Dorselaer *Phone:* +32(2) 672-4172 **Staff:** 1 Prof. 1 Other **Holdings:** 20,000 books 300 journals **Language of Collection/Services:** French, Spanish / French **Subjects:** Agricultural Economics, Education, Regional Planning **Specializations:** Demography, Economics, Latin America, Sociology **Loan:** Inhouse **Service:** Inhouse **Photocopy:** Yes

296   Brussels, Belgium
        Exchange Group for Appropriate Technology
        Documentation Centre
        Rue de la Révolution 7
        B-1000 Brussels

Phone: +32(2) 218-1896 **Fax:** +32(2) 223-1495 **Email:** cota@village.unnet.be

Non-English Name: Collectif d'Echange pour la Technologie Appropriée (COTA), Centre de Documentation **Founded:** 1979 **Type:** Association **Head:** Delphine Huybrecht *Phone:* +32(2) 218-1896 *Email:* cota@innet.be **Staff:** 2 Prof. **Holdings:** 10,000 books 200 journals **Language of Collection/Services:** French, English, Spanish/French, English **Subjects:** Agriculture (Tropics), Agricultural Development, Agricultural Economics, Agricultural Engineering, Animal Husbandry, Biotechnology, Crops, Education/Extension, Fisheries, Food Sciences, Forestry, Soil Science **Specializations:** Appropriate Technology, Asian Development Bank Documents, Development Methodology, Participative Management **Databases Developed:** Database of book and article references **Loan:** In country **Service:** Internationally **Photocopy:** Yes

297   Brussels, Belgium
        Federal Office for Scientific, Technical and
            Cultural Affairs (OSTC)
        National Centre for Scientific and Technical
            Information (STIS)
        Boulevard de l'Empereur 4
        B-1000 Brussels
Location: Keizerslaan **Phone:** +32(2) 519-5640 **Fax:** +32 (2) 519-5645 **Email:** info@stis.fgov.be **WWW:** www.stis. fgov.be

Non-English Name: Services Fédéraux de Affaires Scientifiques, Techniques et Culturelles, Federale Diensten voor Wetenschappenlijke, Technische en Culturele Aangelegenheden (SSTC, DWTC), Service d'Information Scientifique et Technique, Dienst voor Wetenschappelijke en Technische Informatie (SIST, DWTI) **Former Name:** National Center for Scientific and Technical Documentation, Centre National de Documentation Scientifique et Technique (CNDST), National Centrum voor Wetenschappelijke en Technisch Documentrarie (NCWTD) **Type:** Government **Head:** Dr. Jean Moulin *Phone:* +32(2) 519-5656 *Email:* moul@belspo.be **Staff:** 5 Prof. 5 Other **Language of Collection/ Services:** English, French, Dutch / French, Dutch **Subjects:** Comprehensive **Specializations:** Agricultural Research, Biotechnology, Chemistry, Food Sciences, Patents **Databases Used:** Comprehensive **Service:** Internationally **Photocopy:** Yes

298   Brussels, Belgium
        International Environment Wallonie (IEW)
        Documentation Center on the Environment
        Rue Marcq, 16
        B-1000 Brussels
Phone: +32(2) 219-8946 **Fax:** +32(2) 219-9168 **Email:** iew.ecocons@ecoline.org **WWW:** www.ful.ac.be/hotes/ iew

Non-English Name: Inter-Environnement Wallonie a.s.b.l., Centre de Documentation sur l'Environnement **Head:** Gerard Riety, Martine Langen *Phone:* +32(2) 539-0978 **Holdings:** 15,000 books 400 journals **Language of Collection/Services:** French, Dutch / Dutch, French **Subjects:** Agricultural Development, Agricultural Economics, Biotechnology, Education, Forestry, Horticulture, Pesticides,

Soil Science, Water Resources **Loan:** Copies only **Photocopy:** Yes

♦299   Brussels, Belgium
        Ministry of Small Enterprises, Traders and
            Agriculture
        Central Library
        Manhattan Office Tower
        Avenue du Boulevard 21, 3rd Floor
        B-1210 Brussels
Phone: +32(2) 211-7220 **WWW:** www.cmlag.fgov.be

Non-English Name: Ministère des Classes moyennes et de l'Agriculture, Ministerie van Middenstand en Landbouw, Bibliothèque Centrale, Hoofdbibliotheek **Former Name:** Ministry of Agriculture, Ministère de l'Agriculture, Ministerie van Landbouw **Founded:** 1919 **Type:** Government **Head:** Carine vanden Berghe and Fabrière Lafleur *Phone:* +32(2) 211-7222 **Staff:** 7 Prof. 2 Other **Holdings:** 40,000 books 200 journals **Language of Collection/Services:** Dutch, French, English / Dutch, French **Subjects:** Agricultural Economics, Agricultural Engineering, Biotechnology, Crops, Fisheries, Forestry, Plant Pathology, Veterinary Medicine **Specializations:** Horticulture **Loan:** In country **Photocopy:** Yes

300   Brussels, Belgium
        Ministry of Small Enterprises, Traders, and
            Agriculture, Centre for Agricultural
            Economics (CAE)
        Documentation Office (DOC)
        World Trade Center-T.3. (2nd floor, Office 2075)
        Boulevard Simmon Bolivar, 30
        B-1000 Brussels
Phone: +32(2) 208-3378 **Fax:** +32(2) 208-5075 **Email:** clecea@clecea.fgov.be **WWW:** www.clecea.fgov.be

Non-English Name: Ministère des Classes moyennes et de l'Agriculture, Centre d'Economie Agricole (CEA), Service de Documentation (DOC) **Former Name:** Ministry of Agriculture, Institute of Agricultural Economics **Founded:** 1962 **Type:** Government **Head:** F. Goedseels, Research Senior; D. Lanieir, Librarian *Phone:* +32(2) 208-3376, 208-3379 **Staff:** 2 Prof. 2 Other **Holdings:** 11,000 books 560 journals **Language of Collection/Services:** French, Dutch, English, German / French, Dutch, English, German **Subjects:** Agricultural Economics, Agricultural Statistics, Marketing, Rural Sociology **Databases Developed:** LEIBIB - database with indexed literature in agricultural economics from 1993 to date **Loan:** In country **Photocopy:** Yes

301   Brussels, Belgium
        Pasteur Institute
        Library - Documentation Centre
        Rue Engeland, 642
        B-1180 Brussels
Phone: +32(2) 373-3176 **Fax:** +32(2) 373-282 **Email:** lschoofs@ben.vub.ac.be **WWW:** www.be.embnet.org/ pasteur.htm

Non-English Name: Institut Pasteur du Bruxelles, Instituut Pasteur van Brussel (IPB), Bibliothèque - Centre de Documentation, Bibliotheek - Documentatiecentrum **Former**

Name: Institut Pasteur de Brabant, Instituut Pasteur van Brabant **Type:** Government **Head:** L. Schoofs *Phone:* +32(2) 373-3176 *Email:* lschoofs@ben.vub.ac.be **Staff:** 1 Prof. 1 Other **Holdings:** 2,000 books 180 journals **Language of Collection/Services:** English / French **Subjects:** Bacteriology, Microbiology, Parasitology, Virology **Databases Used:** Medline **Loan:** Internationally **Service:** Internationally **Photocopy:** Yes

302   Brussels, Belgium
         Royal Institute of Natural Sciences, Royal Belgian
             Entomological Society
         Library
         Rue Vautier 29
         B-1000 Brussels
Phone: +32(2) 627-4296 **Fax:** +32(2) 646-4433 **Email:** entombib@kbinirsnb.be **WWW:** www.kbinirsnb.be/srbe/page1.htm **OPAC:** www.kbinirsnb.be/general/eng/main_e.htm

Non-English Name: Société Royale Belge d'Entomologie, Institut Royal des Sciences Naturelles de Beligique, (SRBE, IRScNB), Bibliothèque **Founded:** 1855 **Type:** Association **Head:** Y.Braet *Phone:* +32(2) 627-4294 *Email:* srbe@kbinirsnb.be **Staff:** 2 Prof. 5 Other **Holdings:** 55,000 books 50 journals **Language of Collection/Services:** French, Dutch, English/French, Dutch **Subjects:** Entomology **Databases Developed:** Papyrus **Loan:** Internationally **Service:** Internationally **Photocopy:** Yes

303   Brussels, Belgium
         University of Liege, Faculty of Veterinary
             Medicine (ULg)
         Library
         Boulevard de Colonster, B41
         B-4000 Brussels
Phone: +32(4) 366-4195 **Fax:** +32(4) 366-4196 **Email:** biblio.fmv@ulg.ac.be **WWW:** www.ulg.ac.be/fmv **OPAC:** www.ulg.ac.be/libnet/bib06.htm

Non-English Name: Université de Liège, Faculté de la Médecine Vétérinaire (ULg, FMV), Bibliothèque **Founded:** 1836 **Type:** Academic **Head:** Prof. Bernard Collin *Phone:* +32(4) 366-4195 *Email:* bernard.collin@ulg.ac.be **Staff:** 3 Prof. **Holdings:** 50,000 books 500 journals **Language of Collection/Services:** English **Subjects:** Biology, Biotechnology, Food Sciences, Veterinary Medicine, Zootechny **Databases Used:** CABCD; Current Contents **Loan:** Do not loan **Photocopy:** Yes

304   Gembloux, Belgium
         Faculty of Agriculture of Gembloux
         Library
         2, passage des Déportés
         B-5030 Gembloux
Phone: +32(81) 622103 **Fax:** +32(81) 614544 **Email:** bibliotheque@fsagx.ac.be **WWW:** www.fsagx.ac.be **OPAC:** www.bib.fsagx.ac.be **Ariel IP:** 193.190.200.98

Non-English Name: Faculté Universitaire des Sciences Agronomiques de Gembloux (FUSAGx), Bibliothèque **Founded:** 1860 **Type:** Academic **Head:** Bernard Pochet *Phone:* +32(81) 622102 *Email:* pochet.b@fsagx.ac.be **Staff:**

3 Prof. 4 Other **Holdings:** 100,000 books 1,200 journals **Language of Collection/Services:** French, English / French **Subjects:** Agriculture (Tropics), Agricultural Economics, Plant Pathology **Specializations:** Animal Husbandry, Ecology, Economics, Food Technology, Tropical Crops, Tropical Zones, Forestry **Networks:** AGRIS; CCB; RéCoDA **Databases Used:** Comprehensive **Loan:** Internationally **Service:** Internationally **Photocopy:** Yes

305   Gembloux, Belgium
         Forest Research Station
         Library
         23, Avenue Maréchal Juin
         B-5030 Gembloux
Phone: +32(81) 612893 **Fax:** +32(81) 615727

Non-English Name: Station de Recherches Forestière, Bibliothèque **Former Name:** Station de Technologie Forestière **Founded:** 1950 **Type:** Regional Government **Staff:** 1 Other **Head:** Marguerite Burnotte *Phone:* +32(81) 611169 *Email:* m.burnotte@mrw.wallonie.be **Holdings:** 7,000 books 180 journals **Language of Collection/Services:** French, English, German / French, English **Subjects:** Fisheries, Forest Genetics, Forestry, Nature Conservation, Wildlife Management, Wood Technology **Databases Used:** CABCD **Loan:** Do not loan **Photocopy:** Yes

306   Gembloux, Belgium
         Ministère des Classes moyennes et de
             l'Agriculture, Administration Recherche et
             Développement, Centre de Recherches
             Agronomiques de Gembloux
         Bibliothèque
         Rue de Liroux, 9
         B-5030 Gembloux
Phone: +32(81) 626555 **Fax:** +32(81) 626559 **Email:** cra@cragx.fgov.be **WWW:** www.cragx.fgov.be

Former Name: Ministère de l'Agriculture, Administration Centrale de la Recherche Agronomique **Founded:** 1950 **Type:** Government **Staff:** 1 Other **Holdings:** 716 books 21 journals **Language of Collection/Services:** French, English **Subjects:** Agricultural Development, Agricultural Economics, Agricultural Engineering, Farming, Plant Pathology, Soil Science, Water Resources **Loan:** Do not loan **Photocopy:** No

307   Genk, Belgium
         LISEC, V.Z.W.
         Craenevenne 140
         B-3600 Genk
Phone: +32(89) 362791 **Fax:** +32(89) 355805

Founded: 1948 **Type:** Non-profit **Head:** C. Kinnaert *Phone:* +32(89) 362791 **Staff:** 2 Other **Holdings:** 5,000 books 20 journals **Language of Collection/Services:** Dutch / Dutch **Subjects:** Biodegradation, Ecotoxicity Tests, Environmental Impact, Forestry, Sampling, Sanitation Management, Site Selection, Soil Degradation, Soil Science, Waste Water Management **Loan:** Do not loan **Service:** Inhouse **Photocopy:** Yes

308   Ghent, Belgium
University of Ghent
Central Library
Rozier 9
B-9000 Ghent

Phone: +32(91) 264-3851 **Fax:** +32(91) 264-4196 **Email:** libservice@rug.ac.be **WWW:** www.lib.rug.ac.be **OPAC:** www.lib.rug.ac.be:4505/ALEPH/-/start/adr01

Non-English Name: Universiteit Gent, Centrale Bibliotheek **Former Name:** State University of Ghent, Rijksuniversiteit Gent **Type:** Academic **Subjects:** Animal Husbandry, Biology, Veterinary Medicine **Databases Developed:** CCB - Belgian Union Catalog **Databases Used:** Comprehensive **Loan:** Internationally **Service:** Internationally **Photocopy:** Yes

309   Ghent, Belgium
University of Ghent
Department of Agricultural Economics
Coupure Links 653
B-9000 Ghent

Fax: +32(9) 264-6246 **WWW:** www.rug.ac.be

Non-English Name: Universiteit Gent, Vakgroep Landbouweconomie (LE) **Former Name:** State University of Ghent, Rijksuniversiteit Gent (RUG) **Founded:** 1932 **Type:** Academic **Head:** L. Martens *Phone:* +32(9) 264-5924 *Email:* laurent.martens@rug.ac.be **Staff:** 2 Prof. 5 Other **Holdings:** 30,000 books 150 journals **Language of Collection/Services:** Dutch, English / Dutch, English **Subjects:** Agricultural Economics **Loan:** In country **Photocopy:** Yes

310   Heverlee, Belgium
Catholic University of Louvain, Faculty of
    Agriculture and Applied Biological Sciences
Agronomical Library
Kardinaal Mercierlaan 92
B-3001 Heverlee

Fax: +32(16) 321978 **WWW:** www.agr.kuleuven.ac.be
OPAC: www.libis.kuleuven.ac.be/libis

Non-English Name: Katholieke Universiteit Leuven, Faculteit Landbouwkundige en Toegepaste Biologische Wetenschappen (KU Leuven), Agronomische Bibliotheek **Former Name:** Faculteit der Landbouwwetenschappen, Faculteitsbibliotheek Landbouwwetenschappen **Founded:** 1950 **Type:** Academic **Head:** Jos Mertens *Phone* +32(16) 321525 *Email:* jos.mertens@agr.kuleuven.ac.be **Staff:** 2 Prof. **Holdings:** 40,000 books 106 journals **Language of Collection/Services:** English **Subjects:** Comprehensive **Specializations:** Brewing, Catalysts, Clay Minerals, Microbiology, Yeasts, Soil Fertility, Zeolites **Networks:** LIBIS **Databases Used:** Comprehensive **Loan:** Internationally **Service:** Internationally **Photocopy:** Yes

311   Heverlee, Belgium
Soils Service of Belgium (SSB)
Library
W. De Croylaan 48
B-3001 Heverlee

Phone: +32(16) 225426 **Fax:** +32(16) 224206

Non-English Name: Bodemkundige Dienst van België (BDB), Bibliotheek **Founded:** 1946 **Type:** Business **Head:** Hugo Boon **Staff:** 1 Other **Holdings:** 2,000 books 8 journals **Language of Collection/Services:** English **Subjects:** Environment, Crops, Horticulture, Soil Science **Loan:** In country **Photocopy:** Yes

312   Leuven, Belgium
ATOL Study and Documentation Centre on
    Appropriate Technology and Project
    Management in Developing Countries
    (ATOL)
Blijde Inkomststraat 9
B-3000 Leuven

Phone: +32(16) 224517 **Fax:** +32(16) 222256 **Email:** atol@ngonet.be **WWW:** www.atol.ngonet.be **OPAC:** www.cocos.ngonet.be/isis/hoofdc.htm

Non-English Name: ATOL studie & documentatie-centrum voor Aangepaste Technologie en Projectbeheer in Ontwikkelingslanden (ATOL) **Founded:** 1977 **Type:** Non-government **Staff:** 2 Prof. **Holdings:** 13,750 books 100 journals **Language of Collection/Services:** English / French **Subjects:** Agriculture (Tropics), Agricultural Development, Agricultural Economics, Animal Husbandry, Crops, Fisheries, Forestry **Databases Used:** IALINE; TROPAG & RURAL **Loan:** In country **Service:** Internationally **Photocopy:** Yes

313   Leuven, Belgium
Belgian Boerenbond
Information and Documentation Center
Postbus 101
B-3000 Leuven

Location: Minderbroedersstraat 8 **Phone:** +32(16) 242082 **Fax:** +32(16) 242105 **Email:** infodoc@boerenbond.be

Non-English Name: Belgische Boerenbond, Informatie-en Documentatiecentrum (INFODOC) **Former Name:** Bibliotheek en Documentatiedienst **Founded:** 1912 **Type:** Association **Head:** Marc Demeyer *Phone:* +32(16) 242078 *Email:* marc_demeyer@boerenbond.be **Staff:** 2 Prof. 2 Other **Holdings:** 45,000 books 400 journals **Language of Collection/Services:** Dutch / Dutch **Subjects:** Agricultural Development, Agricultural Economics, Agricultural Engineering, Animal Husbandry, Biotechnology, Crops, Farming, Food Sciences, Forestry, Horticulture, Soil Science, Veterinary Medicine **Specializations:** Agricultural Statistics, Agricultural Law **Loan:** Inhouse **Service:** Inhouse **Photocopy:** Yes

314   Liège, Belgium
University of Liege (ULg)
Center of Documentation in Geography
2, Allée du 6 Août, Sart Tieran
B-4000 Liège

Fax: +32(41) 366-5630 **WWW:** www.ulg.ac.be

Non-English Name: Université de Liège (ULg), Unité de Documentation de Géographie (UD Géographie) **Founded:** 1960 **Type:** Academic **Head:** Jean-Baptiste Jehin *Phone:* +32(41) 366-5750 *Email:* jbjehin@ulg.ac.be **Holdings:** 210 journals 25,000 books **Language of Collection/Services:** French, English / French, English **Subjects:** Agricultural

Economics **Loan:** Internationally **Service:** Internationally **Photocopy:** Yes

315 **Liège, Belgium**
University of Liege, Department of Botany (ULg)
Documentation Unit
Sart Tilman
Bâtiment B 22
B-4000 Liège
Phone: +32(4) 366-3881 **Fax:** +32(4) 366-3910 **Email:** c.haarsalle@ulg.ac.be **WWW:** www.ulg.ac.be

Non-English Name: Université de Liège, Département de Botanique (ULg), Unité de Documentation **Founded:** 1971 **Type:** Academic **Head:** Mme Ninfa Greco-Libois *Email:* n.greco@ulg.ac.be **Staff:** 2 Prof. **Holdings:** 15,000 books 650 journals **Language of Collection/Services:** English / French **Subjects:** Biotechnology, Horticulture, Plant Pathology, Plants **Specializations:** Botany, Ecology, Genetics, Phytogeography, Taxonomy **Loan:** Internationally **Service:** Internationally **Photocopy:** Yes

316 **Liège, Belgium**
University of Liege (ULg)
Library Information Center
Place Cockerill, 1
B-4000 Liège
Phone: +32(4) 366-5210 **Fax:** +32(4) 366-5702 **WWW:** www.ulg.ac.be **OPAC:** www.ulg.ac.be/libnet **Ariel IP:** 139.165.5.49

Non-English Name: Université de Liège (ULg), Centre d'Information et de Conservation des Bibliothèques (CICB) **Founded:** 1817 **Type:** Academic **Head:** Mme N. Haesenne-Peremans *Phone:* +32(4) 366-5206 **Holdings:** 2,500,000 books 1,200 journals **Language of Collection/ Services:** French, English, German / French **Subjects:** Agriculture (Tropics), Agricultural Engineering, Biotechnology, Education, Fisheries, Food Sciences, Horticulture, Veterinary Medicine, Plant Pathology, Water Resources **Loan:** Internationally **Service:** Internationally **Photocopy:** Yes

317 **Liège, Belgium**
University of Liege, Zoology Institute (ULg)
Zoology Documentation Center
Quai Van Beneden, 22 (Bat I1)
B-4000 Liège
Phone: +32(4) 366-5068 **Fax:** +32(4) 366-5010 **Email:** udbiolog@vm1.ulg.ac.be **WWW:** www.ulg.ac.be/libnet/ud19.htm

Non-English Name: Université de Liège, Institut de Zoologie (ULg), Unité de Documentation de Zoologie (UD Zoologie) **Type:** Academic **Head:** Mme Ninfa Greco-Libois *Email:* n.greco@ulg.ac.be **Staff:** 3 Prof. **Holdings:** 8,400 books 200 journals **Language of Collection/Services:** English / French **Subjects:** Entomology **Loan:** Internationally **Photocopy:** Yes

318 **Louvain-la-Neuve, Belgium**
Catholic University of Louvain
Library of Pure and Applied Sciences
Place des Sciences 3

B-1348 Louvain-la-Neuve
Phone: +32(10) 472183 **Fax:** +32(10) 472164 **Email:** secretaire@bse.ucl.ac.be **WWW:** www.sc.ucl.ac.be/BSE/index.html **OPAC:** www.bib.ucl.ac.be **Ariel IP:** 130.104.162.175

Non-English Name: Université Catholique de Louvain (UCL), Bibliothèque des Sciences Exactes (BSE) **Founded:** 1425 **Type:** Academic **Head:** Charles-Henri Nyns *Phone:* +32(10) 472184 *Email:* nyns@bse.ucl.ac.be **Staff:** 13 Prof. 3 Other **Holdings:** 140,000 books 1,600 journals **Language of Collection/Services:** English / French **Subjects:** Agricultural Development, Agricultural Economics, Agricultural Engineering, Animal Husbandry, Biotechnology, Crops, Entomology, Farming, Fisheries, Food Sciences, Forestry, Horticulture, Plant Pathology, Plants, Soil Science, Veterinary Medicine, Water Resources **Specializations:** Agriculture (Tropics), Brewing **Databases Used:** Current Contents; Medline **Loan:** Internationally **Service:** Internationally **Photocopy:** Yes

319 **Meise, Belgium**
National Botanical Garden of Belgium (NBGB)
Library
Domein van Bouchout
B-1860 Meise
Phone: +32(2) 269-3905 **Fax:** +32(2) 260-0945 **Email:** library@br.fgov.be **WWW:** www.br.fgov.be

Non-English Name: Jardin Botanique National de Belgique, Nationale Plantentuin van Belgie (JBNB, NPB), Bibliothèque, Bibliotheek **Founded:** 1870 **Type:** Government **Head:** Raymond Clarysse *Phone:* +32(2) 260-0925 *Email:* raymond.clarysse@br.fgov.be **Staff:** 7 Prof. **Holdings:** 200,000 books 1400 journals **Language of Collection/ Services:** English / French, Dutch **Subjects:** Agriculture (Tropics), Botany, Forestry, Horticulture **Specializations:** Systematic Botany **Loan:** Internationally **Photocopy:** Yes

320 **Melle, Belgium**
Department of Animal Product Quality and
Transformation Technology
Library
Brusselsesteenweg 370
B-9090 Melle
Phone: +32(92) 521861 **Fax:** +32(92) 525085 **Email:** dvk@clo.fgov.be **WWW:** www.clo.fgov.be/dvk.htm

Non-English Name: Centrum voor Landbouwkundig Onderzoek, Departement van de Kwaliteit van Dierlijke Produkten en Transformatietechnologie (CLO, DVK), Bibliotheek **Former Name:** Rijkszuivelstation **Founded:** 1939 **Type:** Government **Head:** Dr. Ir. G. Waes **Staff:** 1 Prof. 1 Other **Holdings:** 4,000 books 50 journals **Language of Collection/Services:** English **Subjects:** Biotechnology, Dairy Technology, Microbiology **Loan:** Do not loan **Photocopy:** Yes

321 **Melle, Belgium**
Ministry of Small Enterprises, Traders and
Agriculture, Department of Plant Genetics
and Breeding
Library

Caritasstraat 21
B-9090 Melle
Fax: +32(9) 252-5075 **Email:** dvp@clo.fgov.be **WWW:**
www.clo.fgov.be/dvp.htm

Non-English Name: Ministerie van Middenstand en Landbouw, Departement Plantengenetica en -Veredeling (DVP),
Bibliotheek **Former Name:** Rijksstation voor Sierplanten-
teelt **Founded:** 1946 **Type:** Government **Head:** M. Frans
Thomas *Phone:* +32(9) 252-1052 *Email:* dvp@clo. fgov.be
Staff: 1 Other **Holdings:** 3,700 books 100 journals **Language of Collection/Services:** Dutch, English **Specializations:** Plants **Loan:** Do not loan **Service:** Inhouse
Photocopy: Yes

322   Melle-Gontrode, Belgium
         Department of Animal Nutrition and Husbandry
         Library
         Scheldeweg, 68
         B-9090 Melle-Gontrode
Phone: +32(9) 252-2601 **Fax:** +32(9) 252-5278 **Email:**
rvv@pophost.eunet.be

Non-English Name: Departement Dierenvoeding en Veehouderij (DVV), Bibliotheek **Former Name:** Rijksstation
voor Veevoeding (RVV) **Founded:** 1939 **Type:** Government **Head:** Ir. Ch. Boucqué *Phone:* +32(9) 252-2601
Email: rvv@pophost.eunet.be **Staff:** 1 Prof. 2 Other **Holdings:** 2,000 books 60 journals **Subjects:** Animal Husbandry
Loan: Do not loan **Photocopy:** No

323   Merelbeke, Belgium
         Department of Animal Nutrition and Husbandry
         Library
         Burg. Van Gansberghelaan, 92
         B-9820 Merelbeke
Phone: +32(9) 252-1971 **Fax:** +32(9) 252-5398 **Email:**
dvv.kleinvee@ping.be

Non-English Name: Departement Dierenvoeding en Veehouderij (DVV), Bibliotheek **Former Name:** Rijksstation
voor Kleinveeteelt **Founded:** 1951 **Type:** Government
Head: L. Van Lokeren *Phone:* +32(9) 252-1971 *Email:* dvv.
kleinvee@ping.be **Staff:** 1 Prof. **Holdings:** 12,500 books 50
journals **Language of Collection/Services:** English / Dutch
Subjects: Animal Husbandry **Specializations:** Poultry,
Rabbits, Sheep **Loan:** Internationally **Photocopy:** Yes

324   Merelbeke, Belgium
         Ministry of Small Enterprises, Traders and
            Agriculture, National Institute of Agricultural
            Engineering
         Library
         Burg. Van Gansberghelaan, 115
         B-9820 Merelbeke
Phone: +32(9) 252-1821 **Fax:** +32(9) 252-4234 **Email:**
dvl@clo.fgov.be

Non-English Name: Ministerie van Middenstand en Landbouw, Rijksstation voor Landbouwtechniek (RvL - Merelbeke), Bibliotheek **Former Name:** Ministry of Agriculture,
Ministerie van Landbouw **Founded:** 1951 **Type:** Government **Head:** G. Mortier *Phone:* +32(9) 252-1821 *Email:*
dvl@clo.fgov.be **Staff:** 2 Other **Holdings:** 750 books 50

journals **Subjects:** Agricultural Engineering, Animal
Husbandry, Greenhouses, Soil Science **Loan:** Do not loan
Photocopy: Yes

325   Namur, Belgium
         University of Namur
         Moretus Plantin University Library
         Rue Grandgagnage, 19
         B-5000 Namur
Phone: +32(81) 724646 **Fax:** +32(81) 724628 **Email:**
public@bump.fundp.ac.be **WWW:** www.fundp.ac.be

Non-English Name: Facultés Universitaires Notre-Dame de
la Paix Namur (FUNDP), Bibliothèque universitaire Moretus Plantin (BUMP) **Type:** Academic **Head:** Prof. René
Noel *Email:* rene.noel@bump.fundp.ac.be*Phone:* +32(81)
724630 **Staff:** 31 Prof. 5 Other **Holdings:** 600,000 books
3,000 journals **Language of Collection/Services:** French,
English /French **Subjects:** Agricultural Economics, Water
Resources **Specializations:** Fisheries, Ornithology **Loan:**
Internationally **Service:** Internationally **Photocopy:** Yes

326   Oostende, Belgium
         Sea Fisheries Department (CLO Ghent) (SFD)
         Library
         Ankerstraat, 1
         B-8400 Oostende
Phone: +32(59) 320805 **Fax:** +32(59) 330629 **Email:**
dvz@mail.dma.be

Non-English Name: Departement Zeevisserij (CLO Ghent)
(DVZ), Bibliotheek **Former Name:** Fisheries Research Sta-
tion, Rijksstation voor Zeevisserij **Founded:** 1962 **Type:**
Government **Head:** W. Vyncke *Phone:* +32(59) 320805
Staff: 1 Prof. 4 Other **Holdings:** 1,500 books 33 journals
Language of Collection/Services: English/Dutch **Subjects:**
Fisheries, Food Sciences **Loan:** Do not loan **Photocopy:** Yes

327   Rhode-St-Genèse, Belgium
         Brussels Free University
         Rhode Library
         Rue des Chevaux, 67
         B-1640 Rhode-St-Genèse
Phone: +32(2) 650-9948 **Fax:** +32(2) 650-9999 **WWW:**
www.ulb.ac.be/ulb/doc_plans/campus_rhode_fr.html

Non-English Name: Université Libre de Bruxelles (ULB),
Bibliothèque Rhode **Type:** Academic **Holdings:** 2,000
books 170 journals **Language of Collection/Services:** English **Subjects:** Biotechnology, Molecular Biology, Plants,
Plant Physiology **Photocopy:** Yes

328   Sint Niklaas, Belgium
         Bibliotheek voor Hedendaagse Dokumentatie
         Parklaan 2
         B-9100 Sint Niklaas
Fax: +32(3) 778-0785 **Email:** akses@skynet.be

Founded: 1964 **Type:** Private **Head:** Mary Dunn *Phone:*
+32(3) 776-5063 **Staff:** 6 Prof. **Holdings:** 10,000 books 500
journals **Language of Collection/Services:** English / English **Subjects:** Fisheries, Trade **Specializations:** Government Documents, International Organizations' Documents
Loan: Internationally **Photocopy:** Yes

329   Sint-Truiden, Belgium
        Research Station of Gorsem
        Info-Center
        Brede Akker 3
        B-3800 Sint-Truiden
Phone: +32(11) 682019 **Fax:** +32(11) 674318 **Email:** gorsem@ping.be

Non-English Name: Opzoekingsstation van Gorsem vzw, Diensten- en Voorlichtingscentrum **Founded:** 1959 **Type:** Government **Head:** J. Mathijs *Phone:* +32(11) 682019 *Email:* gorsem@ping.be **Staff:** 1 Prof. **Holdings:** 60 journals 2,600 books **Language of Collection/Services:** Dutch, French, English / Dutch, French, English **Subjects:** Biotechnology, Ecology, Physiology, Plant Pathology, Pomology, Virology, Zoology **Loan:** In country **Service:** In country **Photocopy:** Yes

330   Tervuren, Belgium
        Africa Institute
        Library
        c/o Afrika Museum
        Leuvensesteenweg 13
        B-3080 Tervuren
Phone: +32(2) 768-1993 **Fax:** +32(2) 768-1995 **Email:** institut.africain@euronet.be

Non-English Name: Institut Africain, Bibliothèque **Former Name:** Centre d'Etude et de Documentation Africaines (CEDAF) **Type:** Research **Head:** Gauthier de Villers *Phone:* +32(2) 768-1993 *Email:* institut.africain@euronet.be **Staff:** 4 Prof. **Holdings:** 15,000 books 70 journals **Language of Collection/Services:** French / French **Subjects:** Agricultural Development, Agricultural Economics **Specializations:** Economic Development, Informal Sector, Politics, Social Development, Burundi, Rwanda, Zaire **Databases Developed:** 12,000 entries on economic and social development, political development, and informal sector; in-house access **Loan:** Do not loan **Service:** Inhouse **Photocopy:** Yes

331   Tervuren, Belgium
        Royal Museum for Central Africa
        Center of Information Applied to Development
            and Tropical Agriculture
        Chaussée de Louvain, 17
        B-3080 Tervuren
Fax: +32(2) 767-0242

Non-English Name: Koninklijk Museum voor Midden-Afrika, Musée Royal de l'Afrique Centrale, Centre d'Informatique Appliquée au Développement et à l'Agriculture Tropicale (CIDAT) **Founded:** 1908 **Type:** Government **Head:** Ir. F. Maes *Phone:* +32(2) 769-5604 **Staff:** 2 Prof. 3 Other **Holdings:** 10,000 books 200 journals **Language of Collection/Services:** French **Subjects:** Agricultural Development, Agricultural Economics, Agricultural Engineering, Crops, Farming, Forestry, Horticulture, Soil Science **Specializations:** Agriculture (Tropics) **Databases Developed:** Climatology **Loan:** In country **Photocopy:** Yes

332   Tienen, Belgium
        Royal Belgian Sugarbeet Research Institute
        International Beet Library

45, Molenstraat
B-3300 Tienen
Fax: +32(16) 820468 **Email:** bib@irbab.be **WWW:** sme.belgium.eu.net/irbab-kbivb

Non-English Name: Institut Royal Belge pour l'Amélioration de la Betterave, Koninklijk Belgisch Instituut tot Verbetering van de Biet (IRBAB, KBIVB), Bibliothèque Internationale de la Betterave (BIB) **Founded:** 1990 **Type:** Private **Head:** G. Legrand *Phone:* +32(16) 815171 **Staff:** 1 Prof. 1 Other **Holdings:** 5,000 books 250 journals **Language of Collection/Services:** English, French, German / French, Dutch, English **Subjects:** Agronomy, Sugar Industry, Sugarbeet **Databases Developed:** Bibliographical database on sugar beets with 17,000 references from 1990 to date **Loan:** In country **Photocopy:** Yes

Belize

333   Central Farm, Belize
        Belize College of Agriculture
        National Agricultural Library
        Central Farm, Cayo District
Phone: +501 092-2131/29 ext 28

Founded: 1960 **Type:** Government **Staff:** 1 Other **Holdings:** 600 books 40 journals **Subjects:** Crops, Agricultural Economics, Farm Machinery, Pest Control, Zoology **Networks:** AGRIS **Loan:** Locally **Photocopy:** Yes

Benin

334   Cotonou, Bénin
        Ministère du Développement Rural, Direction des
            Etudes et de la Planification (MDR)
        Centre National de Documentation et
            d'Information Agricole (CNDIA)
        BP 04-0820
        Cotonou VI

Former Name: Centre National de Documentation Agricole (CNDA) **Founded:** 1986 **Type:** Government **Head:** Etienne Akpamoli *Phone:* +229 300496 **Staff:** 3 Other **Holdings:** 4,000 books 10 journals **Subjects:** Agricultural Economics, Animal Production, Crop Production, Rural Sociology **Networks:** AGRIS

335   Cotonou, Bénin
        National University of Benin
        Documentation Center
        BP 526
        Cotonou
Phone: +229 360126 **Fax:** +229 360126 **Email:** lokobe@hotmail.com, samsonmartine@hotmail.com **WWW:** www.ucad.sn/~ctabidoc

Non-English Name: Université Nationale du Bénin, Faculté des Sciences Agronomiques (UNB, FSA), Bibliothèque (Centre de Documentation) (BIDOC) **Founded:** 1979 **Type:** Academic **Head:** Dr. Ir. Pascaline Babadankpodji *Phone:* +229 360126 **Staff:** 2 Prof. 6 Other **Holdings:** 9,000 books

50 journals **Language of Collection/Services:** French **Subjects:** Comprehensive **Specializations:** Agriculture (Tropics), Animal Husbandry, Crop Production, Ecology, Environment, Human Nutrition, Rural Sociology **Loan:** Inhouse **Photocopy:** Yes

♦336 **Lokossa, Bénin**
       Regional Center for Rural Development Mono
       Documentation and Agricultural Information
            Center
       BP 31
       Lokossa
Phone: +229 411120/1 **Fax:** +229 411229

Non-English Name: Centre d'Action Régionale pour le Développement Rural du Mono (CARDER-Mono), Centre de Documentation et d'Informations Agricoles (CDIA) **Former Name:** Division Documentation et Bibliothèque **Type:** Government **Staff:** 1 Prof. **Holdings:** 269 books 21 journals **Language of Collection/Services:** French / French **Subjects:** Agriculture (Tropics), Agribusiness, Agricultural Development, Agricultural Economics, Animal Husbandry, Crops, Farming, Fisheries, Food Sciences, Forestry, Horticulture, Plant Pathology, Soil Science, Veterinary Medicine, Water Resources **Photocopy:** No

♦337 **Natitingou, Bénin**
       Regional Center for Rural Development Atacora
       Documentation and Information Center
       BP 32
       Natitingou
Phone: +229 821606, 821680 **Fax:** +229 821200

Non-English Name: Centre d'Action Régionale pour le Développement Rural de l'Atacora (CARDER-Atacora), Centre de Documentation et d'Information **Former Name:** Division Documentation et Bibliothèque **Founded:** 1985 **Type:** Government **Head:** Sourokou Bio *Phone:* +229 821606, 821680 **Staff:** 2 Prof. 1 Other **Holdings:** 1,037 books **Language of Collection/Services:** French, English / French **Subjects:** Agriculture (Tropics), Agricultural Development, Agricultural Economics, Agricultural Engineering, Animal Husbandry, Biotechnology, Crops, Entomology, Extension, Farming, Fisheries, Food Sciences, Forestry, Horticulture, Plant Pathology, Plants, Rural Sociology, Soil Science, Veterinary Medicine, Water Resources **Loan:** In country **Photocopy:** No

Bermuda

338 **Hamilton, Bermuda**
     Department of Agriculture and Fisheries
     Library
     PO Box HM 834
     Hamilton HM CX
Location: Botanical Gardens, 169 South Road, Paget DV 04 **Phone:** +1(441) 236-4201 **Fax:** +1(441) 236-7582 **Email:** agfish@ibl.bm

Founded: 1978 **Type:** Government **Head:** Mrs. Penny Hill *Phone:* +1(441) 236-4201 *Email:* agfish@ibl.bm **Staff:** 1 Prof. **Holdings:** 2,000 books 75 journals **Language of Col-

lection/Services:** English / English **Subjects:** Animal Husbandry, Botany, Entomology, Farming, Horticulture, Plant Pathology, Fisheries, Plant Protection, Veterinary Medicine **Specializations:** Fauna (Bermuda), Flora (Bermuda) **Loan:** In country **Photocopy:** Yes

Bhutan

339 **Bumthang, Bhutan**
     Ministry of Agriculture, Renewable Natural
          Resources Research Centre - Jakar (RNR-RC,
          Jakar)
     Library
     Bumthang

340 **Thimphu, Bhutan**
     Ministry of Agriculture, Renewable Natural
          Resources Research Centre - Yusipang
          (RNR-RC, Yusipang)
     Library
     PO Box 212
     Thimphu

341 **Thimphu, Bhutan**
     Ministry of Agriculture, Research, Extension and
          Irrigation Division, Farmer Extension
          Communication Support Unit (FECSU)
     Library
     Thimphu

342 **Thimphu, Bhutan**
     Ministry of Agriculture, Research, Extension and
          Irrigation Division, National Plant Protection
          Centre
     Library
     Semtokha
     Thimphu

Type: Government **Subjects:** Plant Protection

343 **Trashigang, Bhutan**
     Ministry of Agriculture, Renewable Natural
          Resources Research Centre - Khangma
          (RNR-RC, Khangma)
     Library
     PO Kanglung
     Trashigang

344 **Wangduephodrang, Bhutan**
     Ministry of Agriculture, Renewable Natural
          Resources Research Centre - Bajothang
          (RNR-RC, Bajothang)
     Library
     Bajothang
     Wangduephodrang
Phone: +975(2) 81209 **Fax:** +975(2) 81311

Former Name: Centre for Agricultural Research and Development (CARD) **Type:** Government **Staff:** 2 Other **Holdings:** 5,000 books 10 journals **Language of Collection/Services:** English / English **Subjects:** Agricultural Development **Specializations:** Farming, Forestry, Livestock **Databases Used:** CABI **Loan:** In country **Service:** In country **Photocopy:** Yes

345 **Wangduephodrang, Bhutan**
Natural Resources Training Institute
Library
Lobesa
Wangduephodrang

Bolivia

346 **La Paz, Bolivia**
Instituto Boliviano de Tecnología Agropecuaria
(IBTA)
Unidad de Comunicación Técnica
CP 5783
La Paz
Location: Calle Mendez Arcos No. 710 Esquina Plaza
España **WWW:** asparagin.cenargen.embrapa.br/~sirgsur/
bolivia/ibta.html

Founded: 1975 **Type:** Government **Head:** Danilsa Saravia
Nieves *Phone:* +591(2) 361561 **Staff:** 5 Prof. 12 Other
Holdings: 1,400 books 4 journals **Subjects:** Agricultural
Research, Extension **Networks:** AGRIS **Photocopy:** Yes

347 **La Paz, Bolivia**
Ministerio de Desarrollo Económico
Biblioteca Agropecuaria Nacional Martín
Cárdenas
Avenida Camacho 1471
La Paz

Type: Government **Networks:** AGRIS

Bosnia and Herzegovina

348 **Mostar, Bosnia and Herzegovina**
University of Mostar
Library
Trg hrvatskih velikana bb
88000 Mostar
Phone: +387(88) 320233

349 **Sarajevo, Bosnia and Herzegovina**
Institute of Agropedology
Library
Dolina 6
71000 Sarajevo
Phone: +387(71) 526222

350 **Sarajevo, Bosnia and Herzegovina**
University of Sarajevo
Library
Zmaja od Bosne 8
71000 Sarajevo
Phone: +387(71) 203561 **WWW:** sava.utic.net.ba/
univer_sa_e.htm

351 **Sarajevo, Bosnia and Herzegovina**
UPI Institute of Agriculture
Library
Butmirska cesta 45
Ilidza
71000 Sarajevo
Phone: +387(71) 668506 **Fax:** +387(71) 212596

352 **Tuzla, Bosnia and Herzegovina**
Institute of Agriculture, Tuzla
Library
Obala Zmaja od Bosne 10
75000 Tuzla
Phone: +387(75) 34361

353 **Tuzla, Bosnia and Herzegovina**
Institute of Veterinary, Tuzla
Library
Slavka Micica 28
75000 Tuzla
Phone: +387(75) 252343 **Fax:** +387(75) 252343

Subjects: Veterinary Science

354 **Tuzla, Bosnia and Herzegovina**
University of Tuzla, Faculty of Technology
Library
Univerzitetska 8
75000 Tuzla

Phone: +387(75) 252094 **WWW:** www.cobiss.ba/scripts/
cobiss?ukaz=GETID&lang=win&lani=en

Botswana

355 **Gaborone, Botswana**
Botswana College of Agriculture (BCA)
Library
Private Bag 0027
Content Farms, Sebele
Gaborone
Fax: +267(31) 314253 **WWW:** www.bca.bw

Former Name: Botswana Agricultural College **Founded:**
1968 **Type:** Academic **Head:** Lesego Ramore (Acting College Librarian *Phone:* +267 365-0112 *Email:* lramore@bca.
bw **Staff:** 2 Prof. 3 Other **Holdings:** 21,000 books 200 journals **Language of Collection/Services:** English **Subjects:**
Agricultural Economics, Agricultural Engineering, Animal
Health, Animal Husbandry, Crops, Education/ Extension,
Forestry, Plant Pathology **Loan:** Inhouse **Photocopy:** Yes

356 **Gaborone, Botswana**
Botswana National Archives and Records Services
PO Box 239
Gaborone
Location: Khama Crescent, Government Enclave **Phone:**
+267 311820 **Fax:** +267 308545

Founded: 1967 **Type:** Government **Head:** Mr. E. A-Yeboah
Holdings: Photocopy: Yes

357　　**Gaborone, Botswana**
　　　　Botswana National Library Service (BNLS)
　　　　National Reference Library
　　　　Private Bag 0036
　　　　Gaborone

Phone: +267(31) 352397 **Fax:** +267(31) 301149 **Email:** natlib@global.bw, automate@global.bw **WWW:** www. gov.bw/government/ministry_of_labour_and_home_affairs. html#national_library_service

Type: Government **Head:** Miss G. K. Mulindwa **Staff:** 1 Prof. 3 Other **Holdings:** 30,000 books 150 journals **Language of Collection/Services:** English / English **Subjects:** Agriculture (Tropics) **Specializations:** Agribusiness, Agricultural Development, Agricultural Economics, Animal Husbandry, Education/Extension, Farming, Plants, Soil Science, Veterinary Medicine, Water Resources **Loan:** Inhouse **Service:** In country **Photocopy:** Yes

358　　**Gaborone, Botswana**
　　　　Botswana Technology Centre (BTC)
　　　　Botswana Technical Information Library (BTIS)
　　　　Postal Bag 0082
　　　　Gaborone

Location: 10062 Machel Drive (adj. to Polytechnic) **Phone:** +267(31) 314161 ext 212 **Fax:** +267(31) 374677 **Email:** botec@info.bw **WWW:** www.info.bw/~botec/ BTCmain.htm

Founded: 1979 **Type:** Government **Head:** Mrs. Deborah Garanlay-Stayes *Phone:* +267(31) 314161 ext 227 **Staff:** 2 Prof. 2 Other **Holdings:** 7,663 books 90 journals **Language of Collection/Services:** English / English **Subjects:** Agricultural Development, Animal Husbandry, Crops, Farming, Fisheries, Food Sciences, Forestry, Horticulture, Soil Science **Specializations:** Appropriate Technology, Architecture, Civil Engineering, Electronics, Energy Sources, Renewable Resources **Loan:** In country **Service:** Internationally **Photocopy:** Yes

359　　**Gaborone, Botswana**
　　　　Central Statistics Office (CSO)
　　　　Library
　　　　Private Bag 0024
　　　　Gaborone

Phone: +267(31) 352200 **Fax:** +267(31) 352201 **WWW:** www.gov.bw/government/ministry_of_finance_and_ development_planning.html#central_statistics_office

Type: Government **Head:** Mr. G. Charumbira **Language of Collection:** English **Subjects:** Agricultural Statistics

360　　**Gaborone, Botswana**
　　　　Ministry of Agriculture
　　　　Headquarters Library
　　　　Private Bag 003
　　　　Gaborone

Fax: +267(31) 356027 **WWW:** www.gov.bw/government/ ministry_of_agriculture.html

Founded: 1979 **Type:** Government **Head:** Joyce Majola *Phone:* +267(31) 350500 ext 581 **Staff:** 2 Prof. 1 Other **Holdings:** 1,082 books 12 journals **Language of Collection/ Services:** English / English **Subjects:** Agriculture (Tropics), Agricultural Development, Agricultural Economics, Agricultural Engineering, Animal Husbandry, Crops, Education/Extension, Entomology, Farming, Fisheries, Forestry, Horticulture, Plant Pathology, Plants, Soil Science, Veterinary Medicine, Water Resources **Networks:** AGRIS **Loan:** In country **Service:** Internationally **Photocopy:** Yes

361　　**Gaborone, Botswana**
　　　　National Veterinary Laboratory (NVL)
　　　　Library
　　　　Private Bag 0035
　　　　Gaborone

Location: Sebele **Fax:** +267 328956

Founded: 1981 **Type:** Government **Head:** Mr. Tebogo Bojosi *Phone:* +267 328816 **Staff:** 2 Other **Holdings:** 919 books 25 journals **Language of Collection/Services:** English / English **Subjects:** Animal Health, Veterinary Medicine **Loan:** In country **Service:** Regionally **Photocopy:** Yes

362　　**Gaborone, Botswana**
　　　　Southern African Centre for Cooperation in
　　　　　　Agricultural and Natural Resources Research
　　　　　　and Training (SACCAR)
　　　　Information Centre
　　　　Private Bag 00108
　　　　Gaborone

Location: Sebele **Phone:** +267 328847/8 **Fax:** +267 328 806 **Email:** bndunguru@saccar.info.bw **WWW:** www. info.bw/~saccar

Former Name: Southern African Centre for Cooperation in Agricultural Research **Founded:** 1985 **Type:** International **Head:** Mr. C.R. Namponya **Staff:** 1 Prof. 2 Other **Holdings:** 1,000 books 14 journals **Language of Collection/Services:** English / English **Subjects:** Agriculture (Tropics), Agricultural Development, Agricultural Economics, Agricultural Engineering, Agricultural Research, Animal Husbandry, Crops, Education/Extension, Entomology, Farming, Fisheries, Forestry, Horticulture, Plant Pathology, Soil Science, Water Resources **Databases Developed:** ARRA - Agricultural Research Resource Assessment - provides assessment of agricultural research resources and a directory of agricultural research and training experts in the SADCC countries: Angola, Botswana, Lesotho, Malawi, Mozambique, Swaziland, Tanzania, Zambia, Zimbabwe; includes a current summary of the programs, priorities, manpower, cooperation, statusand capabilities of SADCC agricultural research institutions; a set of data with which to analyze the effectiveness and appropriateness of national research, training, and extension programs and policies in meeting the developmental needs of rural people; a set of data on which to base a region-wide analysis for the SADCC community of nations **Databases Used:** Agricola **Loan:** Regionally **Service:** In country **Photocopy:** Yes

363　　**Gaborone, Botswana**
　　　　University of Botswana (UB)
　　　　Library and Information System (LIS)
　　　　Private Bag 00390
　　　　Gaborone

Phone: +267 351159, 355-2295 **Fax:** +267 357291, 356591 **Email:** fidzanib@noka.ub.bw **WWW:** www.ub.bw **OPAC:** www.ub.bw/library

Type: Academic **Head:** H.K. Raseroka *Phone:* +267 355-2620 *Email:* raseroka@noka.ub.bw

364   Gaborone, Botswana
University of Botswana
National Institute of Development Research and
    Documentation
Private Bag 0022
Gaborone
Location: The Village **WWW:** www.ub.bw

Founded: 1975 **Type:** Academic **Head:** Stella B. Monageng *Phone:* +267 356364/5 **Staff:** 2 Prof. 2 Other **Networks:** AGRIS **Loan:** In country **Photocopy:** Yes

Brazil

Acre

365   Rio Branco, Acre, Brazil
Brazilian Agricultural Research Corporation,
    Center for Agroforestry Research of Acre
Setor de Informação e Documentação (SID)
Rodovia BR 364 Km 14
CP 392
69900-980 Rio Branco, Acre
WWW: www.cpafac.embrapa.br

Non-English Name: Empresa Brasileira de Pesquisa Agropecuária, Centro de Pesquisa Agroflorestal do Acre (Embrapa Acre, CPAF-Acre) **Former Name:** Unidade de Execução de Pesquisa de Âmbito Estadual de Rio Branco (UEPAE) **Founded:** 1976 **Type:** Government **Head:** Orlane da Silva Maia *Phone:* +55(68) 224-3931/2 ext 068 **Staff:** 1 Prof. 2 Other **Holdings:** 25,345 books 642 journals **Subjects:** Beans, Cassava, Coffee, Cows, Goats, Rice, Rubber Plants, Sheep, Vegetables **Databases Used:** Agricola; CABCD; FSTA **Loan:** In country **Photocopy:** Yes

Amapá

366   Macapá, Amapá, Brazil
Brazilian Agricultural Research Corporation,
    Center for Agroforestry Research of Amapá
Library
Rodovia Juscelino Kubitschek, Km 5
Macapá/Fazendinha
CP 10
68902-280 Macapá, Amapá
Phone: +55(96) 241-1551 **Fax:** +55(96) 241-1480 **WWW:** www.embrapa.br/english/units/centers/cpaf-ap.htm

Non-English Name: Empresa Brasileira de Pesquisa Agropecuária, Centro de Pesquisa Agroflorestal do Amapá (Embrapa Amapá, CPAF-Amapá), Biblioteca **Former Name:** Unidade de Execução de Pesquisa de Âmbito Territorial de Macapá (UEPAT) **Founded:** 1983 **Type:** Government **Head:** Maria Goretti Gurgel Praxedes **Staff:** 1 Prof. 2 Other

Holdings: 320 books 183 journals **Subjects:** Beans, Cassava, Irrigation, Maize, Paullinia cupana, Rice, Rubber Plants, Soybeans **Loan:** In country **Photocopy:** No

Amazonas

367   Manaus, Amazonas, Brazil
Brazilian Agricultural Research Corporation,
    Center for Agroforestry Research of Western
    Amazonia
Information Unit
Rodovia AM-010 Km 29
Caixa Postal 319
69011-970 Manaus, Amazonas
Phone: +55(92) 622-2012 ext 266 **Fax:** +55(92) 622-1100, 232-8101 **Email:** cpaao@cpaa.embrapa.br **WWW:** www.cpaa.embrapa.br

Non-English Name: Empresa Brasileira de Pesquisa Agropecuária, Centro de Pesquisa Agroflorestal da Amazônia Ocidental (Embrapa Amazônia Ocidental), Área de Informação (AINFO) **Former Name:** Unidade de Execução de Pesquisa de Âmbito Estadual (UEPAE) Manaus, Setor de Informação e Documentação (SID) **Founded:** 1974 **Type:** Government **Head:** Palmira Costa Novo Sena *Phone:* +55 (92) 622-2012 ext 169 **Staff:** 1 Prof. 2 Other **Holdings:** 20,092 books 570 journals **Language of Collection/Services:** Portuguese/Portuguese **Subjects:** Agribusiness, Agricultural Development, Agriculture (Tropics), Crops, Food Technology, Entomology, Forestry, Plant Pathology **Specializations:** Agroforestry, Annuals, Fruit Trees, Fishes, Oil Palms, Paullinia cupana, Rubber Trees, Tropical Fruits **Databases Developed:** Technical reports for EMBRAPA Amazônia Ocidental; Catalogue of theses; Special databases on rubber trees, oil palms, peach palms **Loan:** In country **Service:** In country **Photocopy:** Yes

368   Manaus, Amazonas, Brazil
National Institute for Amazonian Research
Library
Alameda Cosme Ferreira, 1756 - Aleixo
CP 478
69083-000 Manaus, Amazonas
Phone: +55(92) 642-1449 **Fax:** +55(92) 642-1706

Non-English Name: Instituto Nacional de Pesquisa da Amazônia (INPA), Biblioteca **Founded:** 1954 **Type:** Government **Head:** Jorge Manuel De Portugal Araújo *Phone:* +55(92) 642-3377 ext 117 **Staff:** 11 Prof. 14 Other **Holdings:** 1,450 books 1,729 journals **Language of Collection/Services:** Portuguese/Portuguese **Subjects:** Cultivation, Entomology, Fertilization, Food Technology, Forestry, Plant Development **Loan:** In country **Service:** Internationally **Photocopy:** Yes

Bahia

369   Cruz das Almas, Bahia, Brazil
Brazilian Agricultural Research Corporation,
    National Research Center on Cassava and
    Tropical Fruit Culture

Information Area
Rua EMMBRAPA
CP 007
44380-000 Cruz das Almas, Bahia
Phone: +55(75) 721-2120 ext 154 **Fax:** +55(75) 721-1118
Email: sac.cnpmf.embrapa.br **WWW:** www.cnpmf.
embrapa.br

Non-English Name: Empresa Brasileira de Pesquisa Agropecuária, Centro Nacional de Pesquisa de Mandioca e Fruticultura Tropical (Embrapa Mandioca e Fruticultura, CNPMFT), Área de Informação (AINFO) **Former Name:** Departamento Nacional de Pesquisa Agropecuária (DNPEA), Instituto de Pesquisa Agropecuária do Leste (IPEAL), Setor de Informação e Documentação (SID) **Founded:** 1976 **Type:** Government **Head:** Maria da Paixão Neres de Souza *Phone:* +55(75) 721-2120 ext 154 **Staff:** 2 Prof. 4 Other **Holdings:** 10,000 books 800 journals **Language of Collection/Services:** English, Portuguese / Portuguese **Subjects:** Agriculture (Tropics), Cassava, Entomology, Food Sciences, Plant Pathology, Tropical Fruits, Water Resources **Specializations:** Agricultural Economics, Biotechnology, Cassava, Information Science, Soil Science, Tropical Fruits **Databases Developed:** AGROBASE **Databases Used:** Agricola; Biosis; CABCD; CAS; FSTA **Loan:** In country **Photocopy:** Yes

370   **Salvador, Bahia, Brazil**
        Agricultural Development Corporation of Bahia
        Library of Agricultural Sciences "Prof. José Maria
           Couto Sampaio"
        Av. Dorival Caymmi, 15.649 - Itapuã
        41635-150 Salvador, Bahia
Fax: +55(71) 249-1145 **WWW:** www.bahia.ba.gov.br/
seagri/ebda/homepage.html

Non-English Name: Empresa Baiana de Desenvolvimento Agrícola (EBDA), Biblioteca de Ciências Agrícolas "Prof. José Maria Couto Sampaio" **Former Name:** Agricultural Research Corporation of Bahia, Biology Institute, Empresa de Pesquisa Agropecuária da Bahia, Instituto Biológico (EPABA) **Founded:** 1955 **Type:** Government **Head:** Licia Melo de Paiva *Phone:* +55(71) 249-1688 ext 203 **Staff:** 3 Prof. 2 Other **Holdings:** 7,500 books 33 journals **Language of Collection/Services:** English / Portuguese **Subjects:** Agriculture (Tropics), Agricultural Economics, Animal Production, Crop Production, Education/Extension, Entomology, Horticulture, Plant Pathology, Plant Protection, Soil Science, Veterinary Medicine **Loan:** In country **Service:** In country **Photocopy:** No

Ceará

371   **Fortaleza, Ceará, Brazil**
        Brazilian Agricultural Research Corporation,
           National Center for Research on Tropical
           Agroindustry
        Information Division
        Rua Dra. Sara Mesquisa, 2.270
        Bairro Planalto Pici
        Caixa Postal 3761
        60511-110 Fortaleza, Ceará

Phone: +55(85) 299-1800 **Fax:** +55(85) 299-1833 **Email:** cnpat@cnpat.embrapa.br **WWW:** www.cnpat.embrapa.br

Non-English Name: Empresa Brasileira de Pesquisa Agropecuária, Centro Nacional de Pesquisa de Agroindústria Tropical (Embrapa Agroindústrial Tropical, CNPAT), Setor de Informação **Former Name:** Centro Nacional de Pesquisa de Caju (CNPCa) **Founded:** 1993 **Head:** Valderi Vieira da Silva *Email:* valderi@cnpat.embrapa.br **Type:** Government **Subjects:** Agribusiness, Cashews

372   **Fortaleza, Ceará, Brazil**
        Federal University of Ceara
        University Library
        Caixa Postal 6025
        60451-970 Fortaleza, Ceará
Location: Campus do Pici, Bloco 2 **Phone:** +55(85) 288-9506/8 **Fax:** +55(85) 288-9513 **Email:** biblios@ufc.br **WWW:** www.ufc.br

Non-English Name: Universidade Federal do Ceará (UFC), Biblioteca Universitária (BU) **Founded:** 1975 **Type:** Academic **Head:** Ana Lúcia Martins *Phone:* +55(85) 288-9507 *Email:* alucia@ufc.br **Staff:** 89 Prof. 139 Other **Holdings:** 93,464 books 5,859 journals **Language of Collection/Services:** Portuguese / Portuguese **Subjects:** Comprehensive **Networks:** BIREME; COMUT **Databases Developed:** SAU - Sistema Automação Universitaria Biblioteca **Databases Used:** Comprehensive **Loan:** Internationally **Service:** Internationally **Photocopy:** Yes

373   **Sobral, Ceará, Brazil**
        Brazilian Agricultural Research Corporation,
           National Center for Research on Goats
        Information Area
        Caixa Postal D-10
        62011-970 Sobral, Ceará
Location: Estrada Sobral/Groaíras, km 4 **Phone:** +55(85) 612-1077 **Fax:** +55(85) 612-1132 **WWW:** www.cnpc.embrapa.br

Non-English Name: Empresa Brasileira de Pesquisa Agropecuária, Centro Nacional de Pesquisa de Caprinos (Embrapa Caprinos, CNPC), Área de Informação (AINFO) **Founded:** 1977 **Type:** Government **Head:** Ana Fátima Costa Pinto *Phone:* +55(85) 612-1077 **Staff:** 2 Prof. 2 Other **Holdings:** 1,735 books 450 journals **Subjects:** Animal Husbandry, Veterinary Medicine **Loan:** In country **Photocopy:** Yes

Distrito Federal

374   **Brasília, Distrito Federal, Brazil**
        Brazilian Agricultural Research Corporation,
           Basic Seed Production Service
        Information Area
        SAIN Parque Rural (Final W/3 Norte)
        70770-901 Brasília, Distrito Federal
Phone: +55(61) 347-6325, 367-6311 **Fax:** +55(61) 347-9668 **Email:** pimpim@sede.spsb.embrapa.br **WWW:** www.embrapa.br/spsb

Non-English Name: Empresa Brasileira de Pesquisa Agropecuária, Serviço de Produção de Sementes Básicas (Embra-

pa Sementes Básicas, SPSB), Área de Informação (AI)
Founded: 1978 **Type:** Government **Head:** Maria José de
Oliveira *Phone:* +55(61) 348-4519 **Staff:** 1 Prof. **Holdings:**
12,000 books 79 journals **Subjects:** Seeds **Loan:** In country
Photocopy: Yes

375 Planaltina, Distrito Federal, Brazil
Brazilian Agricultural Research Corporation,
Center for Agricultural Research for the
Brazilian Savannas
Information Sector
BR 20 Km 18
Rod. Brasilia - Fortaleza
CP 08223
73301-970 Planaltina, Distrito Federal
Phone: +55(61) 389-1171 **Fax:** +55(61) 389-2953 **Email:**
bibcpac@cpac.embrapa.br **WWW:** www.cpac.embrapa.br

Non-English Name: Empresa Brasileira de Pesquisa Agro-
pecuária, Centro de Pesquisa Agropecuária dos Cerrados
(Embrapa Cerrados, CPAC), Setor de Informação **Former
Name:** Center for Agricultural Research for the Semi-arid
Tropics, Centro de Pesquisa Agropecuária do Trópico Semi-
Árido (CPATSA) **Founded:** 1975 **Type:** Government
Head: Nilda Sette *Phone:* +55(61) 389-1171 **Staff:** 3 Prof. 2
Other **Holdings:** 20,000 books 250 journals **Language of
Collection/Services:** English / Portuguese **Subjects:** Agri-
cultural Development, Animal Husbandry, Ecology, Ento-
mology, Environment, Plant Pathology **Specializations:**
Savannas (Brazil) **Databases Developed:** Base Bibliográ-
fica Cerrados - documents about Brazilian savannas; avail-
able via internet at www.cnptia.embrapa.br/bdpa/conscerr.
html **Databases Used:** Comprehensive **Loan:** In country
Service: In country **Photocopy:** Yes

376 Brasília, Distrito Federal, Brazil
Brazilian Agricultural Research Corporation,
Department of Information and Informatics
Information Area
SAIN - Parque Rural (final Av. W3 Norte)
Cx. Postal 04.0315
70770-901 Brasília, Distrito Federal
Phone: +55(61) 348-4169 **Fax:** +55(61) 357-1420 **Email:**
ainfo@sede.embrapa.br **WWW:** www.embrapa.br/uc/din/
din.htm

Non-English Name: Empresa Brasileira de Pesquisa Agropecuária, Departamento de Informação e Informática (Embrapa, DIN), Área de Informação da Sede (AI/SEDE) **Former Name:** Setor de Informação e Documentação
(SID/SEDE) **Founded:** 1974 **Type:** Government **Head:**
Simara Gonçalves Carvalho *Phone:* +55(61) 348-4169, 348-
4454 *Email:* simara@sede.embrapa.br **Staff:** 1 Prof. 4 Other
Holdings: 20,000 books 100 journals **Subjects:** Administration, Agricultural Economics, Communication, Extension,
Information Science, Rural Sociology **Networks:** AGRIS;
CCN; IBICT **Databases Used:** Comprehensive **Loan:** In
country **Photocopy:** Yes

377 Brasília, Distrito Federal, Brazil
Brazilian Agricultural Research Corporation,
National Centre for Genetic and
Biotechnology Resources

Information Area
CP 02372
SAIN Parque Rural
Final Av. W/5 Norte
70770-900 Brasília, Distrito Federal
Fax: +55(61) 274-3212 **Email:** ai@cenagren.embrapa.br
WWW: www.cenargen.embrapa.br

Non-English Name: Empresa Brasileira de Pesquisa Agropecuária, Centro Nacional de Recursos Genéticos e Biotecnologia (Embrapa Recursos Genéticos e Biotecnologia,
CENARGEN), Área de Informação (AI) **Founded:** 1974
Type: Government **Head:** Mª Regina Jorge Soares *Phone:*
+55(61) 273-0200, 273-0100 **Staff:** 2 Prof. 4 Other **Holdings:** 13,656 books 450 journals **Subjects:** Genetic Resources, Germplasm **Databases Used:** Agricola; Agris;
Biosis; CABCD **Loan:** In country **Photocopy:** Yes

378 Brasília, Distrito Federal, Brazil
Brazilian Agricultural Research Corporation,
National Vegetable Crop Research Center
Information and Documentation Center
Caixa Postal 218
70359-970 Brasília, Distrito Federal
Location: Km 09 da BR-060, Rodovia Brasília/Anápolis,
Gama, DF **Email:** aicnph@sede.embrapa.br **WWW:** www.
cnph.embrapa.br

Non-English Name: Empresa Brasileira de Pesquisa Agropecuária, Centro Nacional de Pesquisa de Hortaliças (Embrapa Hortaliças, CNPH), Setor de Informação e Documentação (SID) **Founded:** 1981 **Type:** Government **Head:**
Luciene Coelho de Araújo Muller *Phone:* +55(61) 556-5011
ext 222 **Staff:** 2 Prof. 1 Other **Holdings:** 3,000 books 200
journals **Subjects:** Disease Prevention, Improvement, Physiology, Soil Science, Vegetables **Loan:** In country **Photocopy:** Yes

379 Brasília, Distrito Federal, Brazil
Ministry of Agriculture
Agricultural Information and Documentation
Coordination
CP 02432
70849-970 Brasília, Distrito Federal
Location: Esplanada dos Ministerios, Bloco D, Anexo B,
1°Andar **Phone:** +55(61) 218-2613 **Fax:** +55(61) 218-2098

Non-English Name: Ministério da Agricultura, do Abaste-
cimento e da Reforma Agrária (MAARA), Coordenação
Nacional de Informação Documental Agrícola (CENAGRI)
Founded: 1974 **Type:** Government **Head:** Claiton Pimentel
Phone: +55(61) 218-2615 **Staff:** 23 Prof. 30 Other **Holdings:** 42,000 books 5,621 journals **Language of Collec-
tion/Services:** Portuguese / Portuguese, English **Subjects:**
Cattle Husbandry, Education/Extension, Food Sciences,
Natural Resources, Nutrition, Rural Economy, Rural Sociology, Soil Science **Networks:** AGRIS **Databases Developed:** AGROBASE - Brazilian Agricultural Literature;
BDTA - Appropriate Technology; AGROINST - Agricultural Instiutions; AGROESP - Agricultural Specialists **Databases Used:** Agricola; Agris **Loan:** Inhouse **Service:** In
country **Photocopy:** Yes

Espírito Santo

380   Alegre, Espírito Santo, Brazil
Universidade Federal do Espírito Santo, Setorial
    do Centro Agropecuário
Biblioteca
Alto Universitário S/N
CP 16
29500 Alegre, Espírito Santo
WWW: www.ufes.br/cenagro

Founded: 1971 **Type:** Academic **Head:** Candida R.R. Mauri *Phone:* +55() 552-1389 **Staff:** 5 Prof. 1 Other **Holdings:** 4,000 books 180 journals **Subjects:** Fruits, Horticulture **Loan:** In country **Photocopy:** No

381   Vitória, Espírito Santo, Brazil
Empresa Capixaba de Pesquisa Agropecuária
    (EMCAPA)
Área de Documentação e Informação
Rua Alberto de Oliveira Santos 42, 9º Andar
Centro - Ed. Ames
CP 391
29001-970 Vitória, Espírito Santo
Phone: +55(27) 222-3188 **Fax:** +55(27) 222-3848 **Email:** bibsede@luana.coplag.es.gov.br **WWW:** www.emcapa.es.gov.br

Founded: 1974 **Type:** Government **Head:** Cláudia de Oliveira B. Feitosa *Phone:* +55(27) 222-3188 ext 234 *Email:* bibsede@luana.coplag.es.gov.br **Staff:** 1 Prof. 2 Other **Holdings:** 9,335 books 443 journals **Language of Collection/Services:** English / Portuguese **Subjects:** Agricultural Economics, Biotechnology, Climatology, Entomology, Environmental Sciences, Food Sciences, Horticulture, Plant Pathology, Soil Science, Zootechny **Specializations:** Agriculture (Tropics), Animal Husbandry, Crops, Entomology, Horticulture, Plants, Soil **Databases Used:** Current Contents; EMBRAPA **Loan:** In country **Service:** In country **Photocopy:** Yes

Goiás

382   Santo Antônio de Goiás, Goiás, Brazil
Brazilian Agricultural Research Corporation,
    National Center for Research on Rice and
    Beans
Library
Caixa Postal 179
75375-000 Santo Antônio de Goiás, Goiás
Location: Rodovia Goiânia/Santo Antônio de Goiás 12
Phone: +55(62) 833-2113 **Fax:** +55(62) 833-2100 **Email:** ainfo@cnpaf.embrapa.br **WWW:** www.cnpaf.embrapa.br
Ariel IP: 200.17.55.60

Non-English Name: Empresa Brasileira de Pesquisa Agropecuária, Centro Nacional de Pesquisa de Arroz e Feijão (Embrapa Arroz e Feijão, CNPAF), Biblioteca **Former Name:** Área de Informação (AINFO) **Founded:** 1974 **Type:** Government **Head:** Ana Lucia D. Faria *Phone:* +55(62) 833-2113 *Email:* analucia@cnpaf.embrapa.br **Staff:** 1 Prof. 2 Other **Holdings:** 18,000 books 148 journals **Language of**

Collection/Services: English / Portuguese **Subjects:** Agricultural Economics, Biotechnology, Botany, Entomology, Genetics, Irrigation, Mechanization, Physiology, Plant Nutrition, Plant Pathology, Soil Science, Weeds **Specializations:** Beans, Rice **Networks:** CCN; EMBRAPA; IBICT **Databases Used:** Agricola; Agris; CABCD; Embrapa **Loan:** In country **Service:** In country **Photocopy:** Yes

Mato Grosso do Sul

383   Campo Grande, Mato Grosso do Sul, Brazil
Brazilian Agricultural Research Corporation,
    National Center for Research on Beef Cattle
Information Area
Rodovia BR 262, Km 4
CP 154
79106-000 Campo Grande, Mato Grosso do Sul
Phone: +55(67) 768-2000 **Fax:** +55(67) 763-2245 **WWW:** www.cnpgc.embrapa.br

Non-English Name: Empresa Brasileira de Pesquisa Agropecuária, Centro Nacional de Pesquisa de Gado de Corte (Embrapa Gado de Corte, CNPGC), Área de Informação (AI) **Founded:** 1976 **Type:** Government **Head:** Maria Antonia Ulhôa Cintra de Oliveira Santos *Phone:* +55(67) 763-1030 **Staff:** 1 Prof. 2 Other **Holdings:** 6,000 books 350 journals **Language of Collection/Services:** English **Subjects:** Agricultural Development, Agricultural Economics, Animal Breeding, Animal Husbandry, Animal Nutrition, Beef Cattle, Entomology, Pastures, Soil Science, Veterinary Medicine **Specializations:** Sulmatogrossense Region **Loan:** In country **Service:** Internationally **Photocopy:** Yes

384   Corumbá, Mato Grosso do Sul, Brazil
Brazilian Agricultural Research Corporation,
    Center for Agricultural Research on the
    Pantanal
Information and Documentation Section
Rua 21 de Setembro 1380
CP 109
79320-900 Corumbá, Mato Grosso do Sul
Fax: +55(67) 231-1430 **Email:** bibcpap@sede.embrapa.br
WWW: www.cpap.embrapa.br

Non-English Name: Empresa Brasileira de Pesquisa Agropecuária, Centro de Pesquisa Agropecuária do Pantanal (Embrapa Pantanal, CPAP), Setor de Informação e Documentação (SID) **Founded:** 1975 **Type:** Government **Head:** Helena Batista Aderaldo *Phone:* +55(67) 231-1430 *Email:* helena@cpap.embrapa.br **Staff:** 1 Prof. 2 Other **Holdings:** 8,000 books 1,200 journals **Language of Collection/Services:** Portuguese, English **Subjects:** Horticulture, Natural Resources, Pastures, Plant Anatomy, Soil Science **Specializations:** Animal Husbandry, Cattle, Environment, Fauna, Flora, Soil, Water Quality, Wildlife **Databases Used:** CABCD; Current Contents **Loan:** In country **Service:** Internationally **Photocopy:** Yes

385   Dourados, Mato Grosso do Sul, Brazil
Brazilian Agricultural Research Corporation,
    Center for Agricultural Research of the West
Information Section - Library

Rod. Dourados - Caarapó Km 05
CP 661
79804-970 Dourados, Mato Grosso do Sul
Phone: +55(67) 422-5122 ext 246, 269 **Fax:** +55(67) 421-0811 **Email:** biblioteca@cpao.embrapa.br **WWW:** www.cpao.embrapa.br

Non-English Name: Empresa Brasileira de Pesquisa Agropecuária, Centro de Pesquisa Agropecuária do Oeste (Embrapa Agropecuária Oeste, CPAO), Setor de Informação - Biblioteca (AINFO) **Former Name:** Unidade de Execução de Pesquisa de Âmbito Estadual de Dourados (UEPAE), Área de Informação (AINFO), Setor de Informação e Documentação (SID) **Founded:** 1978 **Type:** Government **Head:** Eli de Lourdes Vasconcelos *Phone:* +55(67) 422-5122 *Email:* eli@cpao.embrapa.br **Staff:** 1 Prof. 2 Other **Holdings:** 30,000 books 1,008 journals **Language of Collection/Services:** English / Portuguese **Subjects:** Agricultural Development, Agricultural Economics, Agricultural Engineering, Biotechnology, Irrigation **Specializations:** Crops, Entomology, Plant Breeding, Plant Pathology, Plants, Soil Science **Networks:** EMBRAPA **Databases Used:** Agricola; CABCD; EMBRAPA; TROPAG & RURAL **Loan:** In country **Service:** In country **Photocopy:** Yes

Minas Gerais

386 **Belo Horizonte, Minas Gerais, Brazil**
Department of Agriculture of Minas Gerais State
Documentation and Information Area
PO Box 515
30161-970 Belo Horizonte, Minas Gerais
Location: Av. Amazonas 115, 6° andar, sala 602 **Fax:** +55 (31) 273-3884 **Email:** epamig@gold.com.br

Non-English Name: Empresa de Pesquisa Agropecuária de Minas Gerais (EPAMIG), Área de Informação e Documentação **Founded:** 1974 **Type:** Government **Head:** Maria Lúcia Melo Silveira *Phone:* +55(31) 273-3544 **Staff:** 3 Prof. **Holdings:** 30,000 books 100 journals **Language of Collection/Services:** Portuguese, English / Portuguese **Subjects:** Agricultural Economics, Animal Husbandry, Botany, Entomology, Pastures, Plant Pathology **Loan:** In country **Photocopy:** Yes

387 **Belo Horizonte, Minas Gerais, Brazil**
Universidade Federal de Minas Gerais, Escola de Veterinária
Biblioteca
PO Box 567
31270-970 Belo Horizonte, Minas Gerais
Location: Av. Antônio Carlos, 6627, Pampulha **Phone:** +55(31) 499-2048 **Fax:** +55(31) 499-2044 **Email:** ana@bib.vet.ufmg.br **WWW:** www.bu.ufmg.br

Founded: 1942 **Type:** Government **Head:** Ana Lúcia Anchieta Ramirez *Phone:* +55(31) 499-2043 *Email:* ana@bib.vet.ufmg.br **Staff:** 4 Prof. 5 Other **Holdings:** 20,000 books 408 journals **Language of Collection/Services:** English / Portuguese **Subjects:** Animal Production, Biotechnology, Food Technology, Sanitary Inspection, Veterinary Medicine **Networks:** Bibliodata Calco; CCN **Databases**

Used: ASFA; Agris; CABCD; FSTA **Loan:** In country **Service:** In country **Photocopy:** Yes

388 **Juiz de Fora, Minas Gerais, Brazil**
Brazilian Agricultural Research Corporation, National Center for Research on Dairy Cattle
Information and Documentation Center
Rua Eugênio do Nascimento, 610 - D. Bosco
36038-330 Juiz de Fora, Minas Gerais
Phone: +55(32) 249-4700 **Fax:** +55(32) 249-4701 **WWW:** www.cnpgl.embrapa.br

Non-English Name: Empresa Brasileira de Pesquisa Agropecuária, Centro Nacional de Pesquisa de Gado de Leite (Embrapa Gado de Leite, CNPGL), Setor de Informação e Documentação (SID) **Founded:** 1976 **Type:** Government **Head:** Maria Salete Martins *Phone:* +55(32) 212-8550 *Email:* salete@cnpgl.embrapa.br **Staff:** 4 Prof. 1 Other **Holdings:** 9,577 books 755 journals **Subjects:** Cattle Farming, Dairy Cows, Pastures **Loan:** Internationally

389 **Sete Lagoas, Minas Gerais, Brazil**
Brazilian Agricultural Research Corporation, National Center for Research on Corn and Sorghum
Information Service
CP 151
35701-970 Sete Lagoas, Minas Gerais
Location: Rodovia MG 424, Km 65 **Phone:** +55(31) 779-1000 **Fax:** +55(31) 779-1088 **Email:** ainfo@cnpms.embrapa.br **WWW:** www.cnpms.embrapa.br

Non-English Name: Empresa Brasileira de Pesquisa Agropecuária, Centro Nacional de Pesquisa de Milho e Sorgo (Embrapa Milho e Sorgo, CNPMS), Setor de Informação (AINFO) **Founded:** 1974 **Type:** Government **Head:** Maria Teresa Rocha Ferreira *Phone:* +55(31) 921-5644 ext 142 **Staff:** 1 Prof. 2 Other **Holdings:** 5,000 books 101 journals **Language of Collection/Services:** English, Portuguese, Spanish, French / Portuguese, English, Spanish **Subjects:** Entomology, Irrigation, Maize, Soil Science, Sorghum **Loan:** In country **Photocopy:** Yes

390 **Visosa, Minas Gerais, Brazil**
Fundação Universidade Federal de Viçosa
Biblioteca Central
Campus Universitário
36570-000 Visosa, Minas Gerais
Phone: +55(31) 899-2439 **Fax:** +55(31) 899-2290

Founded: 1927 **Type:** Government **Head:** Denise Maria Nery Euclydes *Phone:* +55(31) 899-2434 **Staff:** 6 Prof. 52 Other **Holdings:** 96,000 books 1,478 journals **Language of Collection/Services:** English **Subjects:** Agricultural Engineering, Extension, Forestry Engineering, Plant Pathology, Plants, Soil Science, Zootechny **Specializations:** Agricultural Economics, Forestry **Loan:** Locally **Photocopy:** Yes

Pará

391   Belém, Pará, Brazil
Brazilian Agricultural Research Corporation,
    Center for Agroforestry Research of Eastern
    Amazonia
Information and Documentation Center
Trav. Dr. Enéas Pinheiro s/n°
Bairro do Marco
CP 48
66095-100 Belém, Pará
Phone: +55(91) 226-6622 ext 173 **Fax:** +55(91) 266-2303
Email: cpatu@cpatu.embrapa.br **WWW:** www.embrapa.
br/english/units/centers/cpatu.htm

Non-English Name: Empresa Brasileira de Pesquisa Agropecuária, Centro de Pesquisa Agroflorestal da Amazônia
Oriental (Embrapa Amazônia Oriental), Setor de Informação
e Documentação **Former Name:** Center for Agricultural Research in the Humid Tropics, Centro de Pesquisa Agropecuária do Trópico Úmido (CPATU) **Founded:** 1942 **Type:**
Government **Head:** Isanira Coutinho Vaz Pereira *Phone:*
+55(91) 226-6622 **Staff:** 3 Prof. 10 Other **Holdings:** 11,000
books 2,600 journals **Subjects:** Natural Resources, Resource
Conservation **Loan:** In country **Photocopy:** Yes

392   Belém, Pará, Brazil
Museu Paraense Emílio Goeldi
Departamento de Documentação e Informação
Caixa Postal 399
66017-970 Belém, Pará
Location: Av. Perimentral, s/n **Phone:** +55(91) 228-1811
Fax: +55(91) 228-1811 **Email:** mgdoc@museu-goeldi.br

Former Name: Centro de Documentação da Amazônia
(CDA) **Founded:** 1894 **Type:** Research **Head:** Eliete A.
Alves Silva *Email:* mgdoc@museu-goeldi.br *Phone:* +55
(91) 228-1811 Staff: 11 Prof. 8 Other **Holdings:** 3,850 journals 225,000 books **Language of Collection/Services:** Portuguese, English / Portuguese **Subjects:** Entomology, Fruit
Trees, Fisheries, Fodder, Forestry, Harvesting, Horticulture,
Plant Pathology, Soil Science **Specializations:** Anthropology, Archaeology, Botany, Ecology **Networks:** CCN **Databases Used:** Comprehensive **Loan:** In country **Service:**
Internationally **Photocopy:** Yes

Paraíba

393   Campina Grande, Paraíba, Brazil
Brazilian Agricultural Research Corporation,
    National Center for Research on Cotton
Information Area
Rua Oswaldo Cruz, 1143, Centenário
CP 174
58107-720 Campina Grande, Paraíba
Phone: +55(83) 341-3608 **Fax:** +55(83) 322-7751 **Email:**
algodao@cnpa.embrapa.br **WWW:** www.cnpa.embrapa.br

Non-English Name: Empresa Brasileira de Pesquisa Agropecuária, Centro Nacional de Pesquisa de Algodão (Embrapa Algodão, CNPA), Área de Informação (AINFO) **Former
Name:** Information and Documentation Center (IDC)

Founded: 1976 **Type:** Government **Head:** Elizabete de
Oliveira Serrano *Phone:* +55(83) 321-3608 *Email:* serrano@
cnpa.embrapa.br **Staff:** 3 Prof. 3 Other **Holdings:** 5,809
books 532 journals **Language of Collection/Services:** English / Portuguese **Subjects:** Agriculture (Tropics), Agricultural Development, Agricultural Economics, Agricultural
Engineering, Crops, Entomology, Farming, Plant Pathology,
Plants, Soil Science, Water Resources **Specializations:** Cotton, Peanuts, Sesame, Sisal **Loan:** In country **Service:** Internationally **Photocopy:** Yes

394   João Pessoa, Paraíba, Brazil
State Agency for Agricultural Research of Paraiba
Library
Rua Euripedes Tavares No. 210
Bairro de Tambiá
CP 275
58013-290 João Pessoa, Paraíba
Phone: +55(83) 221-4504 **Fax:** +55(83) 221-6999

Non-English Name: Empresa Estadual de Pesquisa Agropecuária da Paraíba (EMEPA-PB), Biblioteca da Coordenadoria Regional de Lagoa Seca (CRLS Biblioteca) **Type:**
Government **Head:** Maria da Graças Lima de Souza *Phone:*
+55(83) 224-2188 **Staff:** 1 Prof. 3 Other **Language of Col-
lection/Services:** Portuguese / Portuguese **Subjects:** Agricultural Research **Loan:** Inhouse **Service:** Inhouse **Photocopy:** Yes

Paraná

395   Colombo, Paraná, Brazil
Brazilian Agricultural Research Corporation,
    National Research Center for Forests
Information Area
CP 319
83411-000 Colombo, Paraná
Location: Estrada da Ribeira Km 111 - Guaraítuba **Phone:**
+55(41) 766-1313 **Fax:** +55(41) 766-1276, 766-1692
Email: ainfo@cnpf.embrapa.br **WWW:** www.cnpf.
embrapa.br

Non-English Name: Empresa Brasileira de Pesquisa Agropecuária, Centro Nacional de Pesquisa de Florestas (Embrapa Florestas, CNPF), Área de Informação (AINFO) **Former
Name:** Unidade Regional de Pesquisa Florestal Centro-Sul
Founded: 1978 **Type:** Government **Head:** Carmem Lúcia
Cassilha Stival *Phone:* +55(41) 766-1313 *Email:* carmen@
cnpf.embrapa.br **Staff:** 2 Prof. 1 Other **Holdings:** 18,100
books 80 journals **Language of Collection/Services:** Portu-
guese **Subjects:** Forestry, Forests **Specializations:** Seeds,
Agroforestry, Ecology, Entomology, Genetics, Silviculture
Networks: EMBRAPA **Databases Used:** Agricola; CAB-
CD; EMBRAPA; TREECD **Loan:** In country **Photocopy:**
Yes

396   Curitiba, Paraná, Brazil
Empresa de Assistência Técnica e Extensão Rural,
    Associação de Crédito e Assistência Rural do
    Paraná (EMATER, ACARPA)
Biblioteca
Rua da Bandeira 171

CP 1662
80035-270 Curitiba, Paraná
Fax: +55(41) 352-1698 **WWW:** www.pr.gov.br/emater

Founded: 1977 **Type:** Government **Head:** Isabel Petry *Phone:* +55(41) 352-1616 ext 139 or 198 **Staff:** 2 Prof. 3 Other **Holdings:** 10,000 books 830 journals **Language of Collection/Services:** Portuguese **Subjects:** Rural Development **Loan:** In country **Photocopy:** Yes

397   Curitiba, Paraná, Brazil
Federação da Agricultura do Estado do Paraná
Biblioteca Silvia Maria Peres Lacerda
Av. Munhoz da Rocha, 1-247 - Cabral
CP 4140
80035-000 Curitiba, Paraná
Fax: +55(41) 252-4828

Founded: 1974 **Type:** Association **Head:** Sonia Regina Locatelli Lissa *Phone:* +55(41) 253-0533 ext 55 **Staff:** 1 Prof. 2 Other **Holdings:** 3,100 books 526 journals **Subjects:** Agricultural Law, Cattle Husbandry, Coffee, Maize, Rural Development, Rural Law, Soybeans, Wheat **Loan:** Do not loan **Photocopy:** Yes

398   Curitiba, Paraná, Brazil
Federal University of Paraná
Library for Agriculture Science
Rua dos Funcionários, 1.540
CP 672
80035-050 Curitiba, Paraná
Fax: +55(41) 253-5552 **Email:** bibiagri@agrarias.ufpr.br
WWW: www.ufpr.br **Ariel IP:** 200.17.219.207

Non-English Name: Universidade Federal do Paraná, Biblioteca de Ciências Agrárias **Founded:** 1972 **Type:** Government **Head:** Tania de Barros Baggio *Phone:* +55(41) 350-5611 *Email:* bibiagri@agrarias.ufpr.br **Staff:** 2 Prof. 7 Other **Holdings:** 24,811 books 2,279 journals **Language of Collection/Services:** Portuguese, English / Portuguese **Subjects:** Animal Production, Forestry, Soil Science, Veterinary Medicine **Specializations:** Agricultural Economics, Animal Husbandry, Crops, Food Sciences, Forestry, Horticulture, Plant Pathology, Plants, Soil, Veterinary Medicine **Networks:** CCN **Databases Used:** Comprehensive **Loan:** In country **Photocopy:** Yes

399   Curitiba, Paraná, Brazil
Parana State Secretary of Agriculture and Supply
State Library of Agriculture
Rua dos Funcionarios, 1559 - Juveve
CP 464
80030 Curitiba, Paraná

Non-English Name: Secretaria de Estado da Agricultura e do Abastecimento (SEAB/PR), Biblioteca Estadual de Agricultura (BEAGRI/PR) **Founded:** 1974 **Type:** Government **Head:** Mônica Catani Machado de Souza *Phone:* +55(41) 253-4424 ext 178 **Staff:** 2 Prof. 3 Other **Holdings:** 23,000 books 120 journals **Subjects:** Rural Economy **Loan:** In country **Service:** Internationally **Photocopy:** Yes

400   Londrina, Paraná, Brazil
Agronomy Institute of Parana

Documentation Area
Rod. Celso Garcia Cid Km 375
PO Box 1331
86100 Londrina, Paraná
Phone: +55(432) 26-1525 **Fax:** +55(432) 26-7868

Non-English Name: Fundação Instituto Agronômico do Paraná (IAPAR), Área de Documentação **Founded:** 1974 **Type:** Government **Head:** Séphora C. C. de Lima *Phone:* +55(432) 26-1525 **Staff:** 2 Prof. 8 Other **Holdings:** 20,000 books 1,850 journals **Language of Collection/Services:** English **Subjects:** Agricultural Economics, Agricultural Engineering, Agricultural Meteorology, Alternative Farming, Appropriate Technology, Biotechnology, Crop Production, Entomology, Farming Systems, Field Crops, Forage, Horticulture, Plant Pathology, Soil Science **Databases Used:** Agricola; Agris; CABCD **Loan:** Internationally **Photocopy:** Yes

401   Londrina, Paraná, Brazil
Brazilian Agricultural Research Corporation,
    National Center for Research on Soybean
Setor de Informação e Documentação (SID)
Rodovia Carlos João Strass (Londrina/Warta)
Entrance Orlando Amaral
Distrito de Warta
CP 1061
86001-970 Londrina, Paraná
Phone: +55(43) 371-6000 **Fax:** +55(43) 371-6100 **Email:** ainfo@cnpso1.embrapa.anpr.br **WWW:** www.cnpso. embrapa.br

Non-English Name: Empresa Brasileira de Pesquisa Agropecuária, Centro Nacional de Pesquisa de Soja (Embrapa Soja, CNPSo) **Founded:** 1975 **Type:** Government **Head:** Ivânia Aparecida Liberati *Phone:* +55(43) 226-1917 *Email:* ivania@cnpso1.embrapa.anpr.br **Staff:** 3 Prof. **Holdings:** 9,000 books 916 journals **Subjects:** Soybeans **Loan:** In country **Photocopy:** Yes

402   Londrina, Paraná, Brazil
State University of Londrina
Central Library
Campus Universitário
Caixa Postal 6001
86051-990 Londrina, Paraná
Phone: +55(43) 371-4448, 371-4021 **Fax:** +55(43) 371-4209 **Email:** refere@npd.uel.br **WWW:** www.uel.br/uel/bc

Non-English Name: Universidade Estadual de Londrina (UEL), Biblioteca Central (BC) **Founded:** 1970 **Type:** Academic **Head:** Vilma Aparecida G. da Cruz *Phone:* +55(43) 371-4209 *Email:* dir.bc@npd.uel.br **Staff:** 20 Prof. 66 Other **Holdings:** 9,266 books 923 journals **Language of Collection/Services:** Portuguese / Portuguese **Subjects:** Comprehensive **Specializations:** Agribusiness, Agricultural Development, Agricultural Economics, Agricultural Engineering, Agriculture (Tropics), Crops, Forestry, Horticulture, Plant Pathology, Plants, Soil **Networks:** Bibliodata/CALCO; CCN **Databases Used:** Agris; CABCD; EMBRAPA **Loan:** In country **Service:** Internationally **Photocopy:** Yes

403 Ponta Grossa, Paraná, Brazil
Agronomy Institute of Parana
Polo de Ponta Grossa Documentation Area
CP 129
84100 Ponta Grossa, Paraná

Non-English Name: Fundação Instituto Agronômico do Paraná (IAPAR), Área de Documentação do Polo de Ponta Grossa **Founded:** 1981 **Type:** Government **Head:** Séphora C. C. de Lima *Phone:* +55(42) 224-9000 **Staff:** 1 Prof. 1 Other **Holdings:** 3,500 books 80 journals **Language of Collection/Services:** English **Subjects:** Animal Husbandry, Crops, Farming, Plant Pathology, Soil Science, Water Resources **Loan:** In country **Service:** Inhouse **Photocopy:** Yes

Pernambuco

404 Petrolina, Pernambuco, Brazil
Brazilian Agricultural Research Corporation,
　　Center for Agricultural Research of the
　　Semi-Arid Tropics
Information Area
BR 428, Km 152, Zona Rural
CP 23
56300-000 Petrolina, Pernambuco
Phone: +55(81) 862-1711 **Fax:** +55(81) 862-1744 **Email:** cpatsa@cpatsa.embrapa.br **WWW:** www.cpatsa.embrapa

Non-English Name: Empresa Brasileira de Pesquisa Agropecuária, Centro de Pesquisa Agropecuária do Trópico Semi-Árido (Embrapa Semi-Árido, CPATSA), Área de Informação (AINFO) **Former Name:** Centro de Pesquisa Agropecuária dos Cerrados (CPAC), Setor de Informação e Documentação (SID) **Founded:** 1977 **Type:** Government **Head:** Gislene Brito Gama *Phone:* +55(81) 961-4411 *Email:* gislene@cpatsa.embrapa.br **Staff:** 3 Prof. 8 Other **Holdings:** 45,000 books 400 journals **Language of Collection/Services:** English **Subjects:** Agriculture (Tropics), Animal Production, Drainage, Entomology, Plant Pathology, Forestry, Horticulture, Irrigation, Production, Rural Sociology, Rural Development, Water Resources **Loan:** In country **Photocopy:** Yes

405 Recife, Pernambuco, Brazil
Empresa Pernambucana de Pesquisa Agropecuária
　　(IPA)
Biblioteca
Avenue General San Martin
1371, Bonji, CP 1022
50000 Recife, Pernambuco
Phone: +55(81) 227-0500 ext 185

Founded: 1935 **Type:** Government **Holdings:** 149 journals **Subjects:** Agricultural Statistics, Analytical Chemistry, Botany, Bovidae, Cereals, Cotton, Crops, Entomology, Farm Machinery, Fertilization, Fish Culture, Goats, Irrigation, Plant Pathology, Plants, Rural Economy, Soil Science, Tropical Fruits, Tubers, Vegetable Growing, Zootechny **Loan:** In country **Photocopy:** Yes

406 Recife, Pernambuco, Brazil
Secretary of Agriculture
Documentation and Technical Information Center

Av. Caxangá, 2-200 - Cordeiro
50000 Recife, Pernambuco
Phone: +55(81) 228-1855

Non-English Name: Secretaria da Agricultura, Centro de Documentação e Informações Técnicas (CEDIT) **Founded:** 1980 **Type:** Government **Staff:** 2 Prof. 1 Other **Holdings:** 1,344 books 424 journals **Subjects:** Agricultural Economics, Agricultural Engineering, Animal Production, Crop Production **Loan:** In country

Piauí

407 Parnaíba, Piauí, Brazil
Brazilian Agricultural Research Corporation,
　　Center for Agricultural Research of the
　　Mid-North
Information Area
Av. São Sebastião, 2055
Bairro de Fátima
64202-020 Parnaíba, Piauí
Phone: +55(86) 322-3619 **Fax:** +55(86) 322-3445 **WWW:** www.cpamn.embrapa.br

Non-English Name: Empresa Brasileira de Pesquisa Agropecuária, Centro de Pesquisa Agropecuária do Meio Norte (Embrapa Meio-Norte, CPAMN), Área de Informação (AINFO) **Former Name:** Unidade de Execução de Pesquisa de Âmbito Estadual (UPAE), Centro Nacional de Pesquisa de Agricultura Irrigada (CNPAI), Setor de Informação e Documentação (SID) **Founded:** 1987 **Type:** Government **Head:** Eloizelena Pereira Duarte *Phone:* +55(86) 322-3619 **Staff:** 1 Prof. 2 Other **Holdings:** 11,470 books 309 journals **Language of Collection/Services:** English/Portuguese **Subjects:** Agricultural Engineering, Animal Breeding, Dairy Cattle, Horticulture, Irrigated Farming, Rice, Tropical Fruits **Specializations:** Irrigation, Hydraulic Engineering **Databases Developed:** Aplicativo AINFO - EMBRAPA databases **Loan:** In country **Service:** Inhouse **Photocopy:** Yes

408 Teresina, Piauí, Brazil
Brazilian Agricultural Research Corporation,
　　Center for Agricultural Research of the
　　Mid-North
Information Area
Av. Duque de Caxias, 5.650
Bairro Buenos Aires
Caixa Postal 1
64006-220 Teresina, Piauí
Phone: +55(86) 225-1141 **Fax:** +55(86) 225-1142 **WWW:** www.cpamn.embrapa.br

Non-English Name: Empresa Brasileira de Pesquisa Agropecuária, Centro de Pesquisa Agropecuária do Meio Norte (Embrapa Meio-Norte, CPAMN), Área de Informação (AINFO) **Former Name:** Unidade de Execução de Pesquisa de Âmbito Estadual de Teresina (UEPAE), Centro Nacional de Pesquisa de Agricultura Irrigada (CNPAI), Setor de Informação e Documentação (SID) **Founded:** 1987 **Type:** Government **Head:** Eloizelena Pereira Duarte **Staff:** 1 Prof. 2 Other **Holdings:** 30,142 books 806 journals **Language of Collection/Services:** English / Portuguese **Subjects:** Agricultural Engineering, Animal Breeding, Dairy Cattle, Horticulture, Irrigated Farming, Rice, Tropical Fruits **Specializations:** Irrigation, Hydraulic Engineering **Loan:** In country **Service:** Inhouse **Photocopy:** Yes

Rio de Janeiro

409 Itaguaí, Rio de Janeiro, Brazil
Pesagro-Rio Experiment Station of Itaguaí
Information and Documentation Area
Estrada Rio São Paulo Km 47
Seropédica
23851-970 Itaguaí, Rio de Janeiro

Non-English Name: Pesagro-Rio/Estação Experimental de Itaguaí (EEI), Área de Informação e Documentação (AID) **Founded:** 1966 **Type:** Government **Head:** Maria do Socorro Menezes de Miranda *Phone:* +55(21) 782-1091 **Staff:** 1 Prof. 3 Other **Holdings:** 21,808 books 131 journals **Language of Collection/Services:** English/Portuguese **Subjects:** Aviculture, Seeds, Vegetable Growing **Specializations:** Dairy Cows, Horticulture **Photocopy:** Yes **Loan:** In country

410 Seropédica, Rio de Janeiro, Brazil
University Federal Rural of Rio de Janeiro
Central Library
Antiga Rodovia Rio-São Paulo - sala 102 - P1
Km 47
23851-970 Seropédica, Rio de Janeiro
Phone: +55(21) 682-1210 ext 260 **Fax:** +55(21) 682-1120
Email: bibliot@ufrrj.br **WWW:** www.ufrrj.br

Non-English Name: Universidade Federal Rural do Rio de Janeiro (UFRRJ), Biblioteca Central **Founded:** 1948 **Type:** Government **Head:** Teresinha Maria Sena Pacielo **Staff:** 12 Prof. 48 Other **Holdings:** 28,000 books 979 journals **Language of Collection/Services:** Portuguese / Portuguese, English **Subjects:** Agricultural Development, Agricultural Engineering, Animal Husbandry, Biotechnology, Crops, Education/Extension, Entomology, Food Sciences, Forestry, Horticulture, Plant Pathology, Plants, Soil Science, Veterinary Medicine **Databases Developed:** Database on agricultural and veterinary medicine **Databases Used:** Comprehensive **Loan:** In country **Service:** In country **Photocopy:** Yes

411 Niteroí, Rio de Janeiro, Brazil
Empresa de Pesquisa Agropecuária do Estado do
    Rio de Janeiro, Laboratório de Biologia
    Animal (PESAGRO-RIO, LBA)
Área de Documentação e Informação (ADI)
Alameda São Boaventura, 770
Fonseca
24120-191 Niteroí, Rio de Janeiro

Founded: 1977 **Type:** Government **Head:** Maria Regina Telhado Gomes *Phone:* +55(21) 627-1432 **Staff:** 1 Prof. 1 Other **Holdings:** 1,594 books 243 journals **Language of Collection/Services:** English, Portuguese, Spanish **Subjects:** Animal Husbandry, Biotechnology, Veterinary Medicine **Databases Used:** Agricola; Biosis; CABCD **Loan:** In country **Photocopy:** Yes

412 Niteroí, Rio de Janeiro, Brazil
Federal University of Fluminense
Documentation Center, Library Division
Av. Nilo Pecanha s/n
27230 Niteroí, Rio de Janeiro
WWW: www.uff.br

Non-English Name: Universidade Federal Fluminense, Colégio Agrícola Nilo Peçanha do NDC, Núcleo de Documentação, Biblioteca Setorial **Type:** Academic **Head:** Maria Angela Isabel Pimentel *Phone:* +55(21) 356-2362 **Staff:** 1 Prof. 1 Other **Holdings:** 4,274 books 4,148 journals **Subjects:** Agricultural Economics, Agricultural Engineering, Soil Science **Loan:** In country **Photocopy:** Yes

413 Niteroí, Rio de Janeiro, Brazil
Federal University of Fluminense, Veterinary
    Faculty
Library Center
Vital Brasil Filho, 54
24230 Niteroí, Rio de Janeiro
WWW: www.uff.br

Non-English Name: Universidade Federal Fluminense, Faculdade Veterinária, Biblioteca Setorial **Founded:** 1968 **Type:** Academic **Head:** Maria das Graças Glória Figueiredo *Phone:* +55(21) 710-6060 ext 26 **Staff:** 2 Prof. 3 Other **Holdings:** 6,103 books 13,341 journals **Subjects:** Veterinary Medicine **Loan:** In country **Photocopy:** Yes

414 Niteroí, Rio de Janeiro, Brazil
Universidade Federal Fluminense, Colégio
    Técnico Agrícola Ildefonso Bastos Borges
Núcleo de Documentação, Biblioteca Setorial
Av. Padre Mello, 28 Bom Jesus do Itabapoana
28360 Niteroí, Rio de Janeiro
WWW: www.uff.br

Type: Academic **Head:** Tereza Maria de Jesus **Staff:** 1 Prof. 1 Other **Holdings:** 1,279 books 557 journals **Subjects:** Horticulture, Plant Protection, Soil Science **Loan:** In country **Photocopy:** Yes

415 Rio de Janeiro, Rio de Janeiro, Brazil
Botany Garden of Rio de Janeiro
Barbosa Rodriques Library
Rua Jardim Botânico, 1008
22460-000 Rio de Janeiro, Rio de Janeiro
Phone: +55(21) 274-8246 **Fax:** +55(21) 274-4897

Non-English Name: Jardim Botânico do Rio de Janeiro, Biblioteca "Barbosa Rodrigues" **Former Name:** Instituto Brasileiro de Meio Ambiente e Recursos Naturais Renováveis (IBMARNR) **Founded:** 1890 **Type:** Government **Head:** Maria Lucia Guilhermino de Castro Lima *Phone:* +55(21) 274-8246 ext B6 **Staff:** 4 Prof. 2 Other **Holdings:** 11,218 books **Language of Collection/Services:** English, French, German, Portuguese **Subjects:** Botany, Forestry, Plant Pathology **Loan:** Inhouse **Photocopy:** Yes

416 Seropédica, Rio de Janeiro, Brazil
Brazilian Agricultural Research Corporation,
    National Center for Research on Agrobiology
Library

Caixa Postal 74505
23851-970 Seropédica, Rio de Janeiro
Phone: +55(21) 682-1500 **Fax:** +55(21) 682-1230 **WWW:**
www.cnpab.embrapa.br

Non-English Name: Empresa Brasileira de Pesquisa Agropecuária, Centro Nacional de Pesquisa de Agrobiologia (Embrapa Agrobiologia, CNPAB), Biblioteca **Former Name:**
National Center for Research on Soil Biology, Centro
Nacional de Pesquisa em Biologia do Solo **Founded:** 1989
Type: Government **Subjects:** Farming Systems, Sustainability

417   Rio de Janeiro, Rio de Janeiro, Brazil
Brazilian Agricultural Research Corporation,
National Center for Research on
Agroindustrial Food Technology
Information Area
Av. das Américas 29-501 - Guaratiba
23020-470 Rio de Janeiro, Rio de Janeiro
Phone: +55(21) 410-7443 **Fax:** +55(21) 410-1090 **Email:**
biblio@ctaa.embrapa.br **WWW:** www.ctaa.embrapa.br
OPAC: www.cnptia.embrapa.br/bdpa

Non-English Name: Empresa Brasileira de Pesquisa Agropecuária, Centro Nacional de Pesquisa de Tecnologia Agroindustrial de Alimentos (Embrapa Agroindústria de Alimentos, CTAA), Área de Informação (AINFO) **Former Name:**
Centro de Tecnologia Agrícola e Alimentar (CTAA), Setor
de Informação e Documentação **Founded:** 1984 **Type:** Government **Head:** Claudia Regina Delaia *Phone:* +55(21) 410-
7501 *Email:* crdelaia@ctaa.embrapa.br **Staff:** 2 Prof. 2
Other **Holdings:** 65,000 books 108 journals **Language of
Collection/Services:** English / Portuguese **Subjects:** Agribusiness, Biotechnology, Chemistry, Food Sciences **Specializations:** Cereals, Food Chemistry, Food Biotechnology,
Plant Oils **Networks:** CCN **Databases Used:** CASurveyor;
FSTA; TOXLINE **Loan:** In country **Service:** In country
Photocopy: Yes

418   Rio de Janeiro, Rio de Janeiro, Brazil
Brazilian Agricultural Research Corporation -
Soils (Embrapa Soils)
Information and Documentation Center (IDC)
Rua Jardim Botânico, 1024
Bairro Jardim Botânico
22460-000 Rio de Janeiro, Rio de Janeiro
Phone: +55(21) 274-4999 ext 211 **Fax:** +55(21) 274-5291
Email: bib@cnps.embrapa.br **WWW:** www.cnps.embrapa.
br

Non-English Name: Empresa Brasileira de Pesquisa Agro-
pecuária - Solos (Embrapa Solos), Setor de Informação e
Documentação (SID) **Former Name:** Centro Nacional de
Pesquisa de Solos (CNPS), National Center for Research on
Soil, Serviço Nacional de Levantamento e Conservação do
Solo (SNLCS) **Founded:** 1973 **Type:** Government **Head:**
Maria da Penha Delaia *Phone:* +55(21) 274-4999 ext 212
Email: penha@cnps.embrapa.br **Staff:** 3 Prof. 1 Other **Hold-
ings:** 6,000 books 160 journals **Language of Collection/
Services:** Portuguese / Portuguese **Subjects:** Soil Science
Loan: In country **Photocopy:** Yes

419   Rio de Janeiro, Rio de Janeiro, Brazil
Institute of Applied Economic Research
Documentation Service
Av. Pres. Antônio Carlos, 51-16 Andar
CP 2672
20020-010 Rio de Janeiro, Rio de Janeiro
Phone: +55(21) 212-1040 **Fax:** +55(21) 240-1920 **Email:**
margarida@piea.gov.br **WWW:** www.piea.gov.br

Non-English Name: Instituto de Pesquisa Econômica Apli-
cada (IPEA), Serviço de Documentação **Former Name:**
Instituto de Planejamento Econômico e Social (INPES)
Founded: 1965 **Type:** Government **Head:** Margarida Maria
Pacheco de Aravjo *Email:* margarida@piea.gov.br *Phone:*
+55(21) 212-1172 **Staff:** 3 Prof. 1 Other **Holdings:** 25,000
books 100 journals **Subjects:** Agricultural Development,
Agricultural Economics, Agricultural Production, Manage-
ment, Environment, Natural Resources **Specializations:**
Economics **Loan:** In country **Photocopy:** No

Rio Grande do Sul

420   Bagé, Rio Grande do Sul, Brazil
Brazilian Agricultural Research Corporation,
Center for Cattle Research on Southern
Brazilian Grasslands
Library
BR 153, Km 595
Vila Industrial, Zona Rural
CP 242
96400-970 Bagé, Rio Grande do Sul
Phone: +55(532) 42-8499 ext 28 **Fax:** +55(532) 42-4395
WWW: www.cppsul.embrapa.br

Non-English Name: Empresa Brasileira de Pesquisa Agro-
pecuária, Centro de Pesquisa de Pecuária dos Campos Sul
Brasileiros (Embrapa Pecuária Sul, CPPSUL), Biblioteca
Former Name: Centro Nacional de Pesquisa de Ovinos
(CNPO) **Founded:** 1977 **Type:** Government **Head:** Ana
Matilde Amandra Castanheiro Coelho *Phone:* +55(532)
42-8499 **Staff:** 1 Prof. 1 Other **Holdings:** 600 books 350
journals **Subjects:** Animal Health, Beef Cattle, Dairy Cattle,
Fodder, Genetic Resources, Sheep **Loan:** Do not loan **Pho-
tocopy:** Yes

421   Bento Gonçalves, Rio Grande do Sul, Brazil
Brazilian Agricultural Research Corporation,
National Center for Research on Grapes and
Wine
Information and Documentation Center
Rua Livramento, 515
CP 130
95700-000 Bento Gonçalves, Rio Grande do Sul
Phone: +55(54) 451-2144 **Fax:** +55(54) 451-2792 **WWW:**
www. cnpuv.embrapa.br

Non-English Name: Empresa Brasileira de Pesquisa Agropecuária, Centro Nacional de Pesquisa de Uva e Vinho (Embrapa Uva e Vinho, CNPUV), Setor de Informação e Documentação (SID) **Founded:** 1976 **Type:** Government **Head:**
Maria Regina Cunha Martins *Phone:* +55(54) 252-2144
Staff: 1 Prof. 2 Other **Holdings:** 18,000 books 360 journals
Language of Collection/Services: English **Subjects:** Agri-

business, Agricultural Development, Agricultural Economics, Agricultural Engineering, Biotechnology, Entomology, Crops,Farming, Food Sciences, Horticulture, Plant Pathology, Soil Science, Vineyards, Viticulture **Specializations:** Plant Physiology **Loan:** In country **Service:** Internationally **Photocopy:** Yes

♦422   Guaíba, Rio Grande do Sul, Brazil
Instituto de Pesquisas Veterinárias "Desidério
    Finamor" (IPVDF)
Biblioteca
Caixa Postal 2076
90001-970 Guaíba, Rio Grande do Sul
Location: BR 116 - Km 192 **Phone:** +55(51) 481-3711 **Fax:** +55(51) 481-3337

Founded: 1948 **Type:** Government **Head:** Dr. João Ricardo Martin **Staff:** 34 Prof. 71 Other **Holdings:** 5,000 books 91 journals **Language of Collection/Services:** Portuguese **Subjects:** Animal Health, Disease Prevention, Hygiene **Specializations:** Bacteriology, Hygiene, Immunology, Parasitology, Virology **Loan:** Inhouse **Photocopy:** Yes

423   Passo Fundo, Rio Grande do Sul, Brazil
Brazilian Agricultural Research Corporation,
    National Center for Research on Wheat
Information and Documentation Center
BR 285, Km 174
CP 569
99001-970 Passo Fundo, Rio Grande do Sul
Phone: +55(54) 311.3444 **Fax:** +55(54) 311-3617 **WWW:** www.cnpt.embrapa.br

Non-English Name: Empresa Brasileira de Pesquisa Agropecuária, Centro Nacional de Pesquisa de Trigo (Embrapa Trigo, CNPT), Setor de Informação e Documentação (SID) **Founded:** 1974 **Type:** Government **Head:** Regina das Graças Vasconcelos dos Santos *Phone:* +55(54) 313-1244 **Staff:** 1 Prof. 2 Other **Holdings:** 21,975 books 814 journals **Subjects:** Barley, Rapeseed, Soybeans, Triticale, Wheat **Loan:** In country **Photocopy:** Yes

424   Passo Fundo, Rio Grande do Sul, Brazil
University of Passo Fundo
Science Library
Campus - Bairro Sa Jose
CP 566
90050 Passo Fundo, Rio Grande do Sul
WWW: www.upf.tche.br

Non-English Name: Universidade de Passo Fundo, Biblioteca de Ciências Agrárias **Founded:** 1982 **Type:** Academic **Head:** Suzeli D. Fumagali *Phone:* +55(54) 313-2000 ext 196 **Staff:** 1 Prof. 3 Other **Holdings:** 600 books 30 journals **Subjects:** Animal Production, Crop Production, Horticulture, Soil Science **Loan:** In country **Photocopy:** Yes

425   Pelotas, Rio Grande do Sul, Brazil
Brazilian Agricultural Research Corporation,
    Center for Temperate Climate Agricultural
    Research
Information and Documentation Center
BR 392 Km 78

Monte Bonito, 9º Distrito
CP 403
96001-970 Pelotas, Rio Grande do Sul
Fax: +55(53) 221-2121 **Email:** bibcpact@sede.embrapa.br **WWW:** www.cpact.embrapa.br

Non-English Name: Empresa Brasileira de Pesquisa Agropecuária, Centro de Pesquisa Agropecuária de Clima Temperado (Embrapa Clima Temperado, CPACT), Setor de Informação e Documentação (SID) **Former Name:** National Research Center for Temperate Climate Fruits, Centro Nacional de Pesquisa de Fruteiras de Clima Temperado (CNPFT), Centro de Pesquisas Agropecuárias de Terras Baixas de Clima Temperado (CPATB) **Founded:** 1975 **Type:** Government **Head:** Eloizelena P. D. Fernandes, Regina dos Santos Vasconcelos *Phone:* +55(53) 221-2122 ext 126 **Staff:** 5 Other **Holdings:** 4,000 books 500 journals **Subjects:** Temperate Fruits, Vegetable Growing **Loan:** Internationally **Photocopy:** Yes

426   Pelotas, Rio Grande do Sul, Brazil
Federal University of Pelotas, Eliseu Maciel
    Agronomy Faculty
Eliseu Maciel Library of Agronomy Sciences
96001-970 Pelotas, Rio Grande do Sul
Phone: +55(532) 757151 **Email:** biblagro@ufpel.tche.br **WWW:** www.ufpel.tche.br/faem

Non-English Name: Universidade Federal de Pelotas, Faculdade de Agronomia Eliseu Maciel (FAEM), Biblioteca das Ciências Agrárias Eliseu Maciel **Founded:** 1948 **Type:** Academic **Head:** Marlene Cravo Castillo *Phone:* +55(532) 757151 *Email:* biblagro@ufpel.tche.br **Staff:** 1 Prof. 3 Other **Holdings:** 20,000 books 677 journals **Language of Collection/Services:** Portuguese, English, French, Italian, German, Spanish / Portuguese **Subjects:** Agribusiness, Agricultural Development, Agricultural Economics, Agricultural Engineering, Agriculture (Tropics), Animal Husbandry, Biotechnology, Crops, Education/Extension, Entomology, Farming, Fisheries, Food Sciences, Forestry, Horticulture, Plant Pathology, Plants, Soil, Veterinary Medicine, Water Resources **Networks:** COMUT; IBICT **Databases Used:** Comprehensive **Loan:** In country **Service:** Internationally **Photocopy:** Yes

427   Porto Alegre, Rio Grande do Sul, Brazil
Federal University of Rio Grande do Sul,
    Agronomy Faculty
Prof. Antônio Tavares Quintas Library
Av. Bento Gonçalves, 7712
CP 776
91501-970 Porto Alegre, Rio Grande do Sul
Phone: +55(51) 316-6004 **Fax:** +55(51) 316-6004 **Email:** bibagro@vortex.ufrgs.br **WWW:** www.biblioteca.ufrgs.br **OPAC:** www.sabi.ufrgs.br, telnet://asterix.ufrgs.br (Login: bib)

Non-English Name: Universidade Federal do Rio Grande do Sul, Faculdade de Agronomia, Biblioteca Prof. Antônio Tavares Quintas **Founded:** 1910 **Type:** Academic **Head:** Lais Freitas Caregnato *Phone:* +55(512) 36-5011 ext 19 **Staff:** 3 Prof. 7 Other **Holdings:** 20,000 books 592 journals **Subjects:** Plant Pathology, Soil Science, Zootechny **Networks:** IBICT **Loan:** In country **Photocopy:** Yes

428　Porto Alegre, Rio Grande do Sul, Brazil
Federal University of Rio Grande do Sul,
　　Veterinary Faculty
Prof. Desiderio Finamor Library
Av. Bento Gonçalves, 9090
Prédio 42602 Campus do Vale
91540-000 Porto Alegre, Rio Grande do Sul
Phone: +55(51) 316-6118 **Fax:** +55(51) 316-0512 **Email:**
bibvet@vortex.ufrgs.br **OPAC:** www.sabi.ufrgs.br,
telnet://asterix.ufrgs.br (Login: bib)

Non-English Name: Universidade Federal do Rio Grande
do Sul, Faculdade de Veterinária, Biblioteca Prof. Desidério
Finamor **Founded:** 1962 **Type:** Academic **Head:** MMadoa
Vanti **Staff:** 1 Prof. 2 Other **Holdings:** 6,000 books 200 journals **Language of Collection/Services:** English, Portuguese
/ Portuguese **Subjects:** Animal Husbandry, Farming, Veterinary Medicine **Specializations:** Helminthology, Pathology,
Protozoology, Reproduction **Networks:** IBICT **Loan:** In
country **Photocopy:** Yes

429　Porto Alegre, Rio Grande do Sul, Brazil
Fundação Zoobotânica do Rio Grande do Sul
Biblioteca Prof. Dr. Carlos de Paula Couto
Rua Dr. Salvador Franca, 1427
CP 1188
90001-970 Porto Alegre, Rio Grande do Sul
Fax: +55(51) 336-1778

Type: Government **Head:** Elga Ratnieks Barbedo *Phone:*
+55(51) 336-1511 ext 114 *Email:* ebib@pampa.tche.br
Staff: 2 Prof. **Holdings:** 3,217 books 133 journals **Language of Collection/Services:** English, Portuguese, Spanish, German / Portuguese **Loan:** In country **Photocopy:** Yes

430　Porto Alegre, Rio Grande do Sul, Brazil
Secretary of Agriculture
Central Library
Rua Goncalves Dias, 570
90060 Porto Alegre, Rio Grande do Sul
Phone: +55(512) 33-5411 ext 50

Non-English Name: Secretaria da Agricultura, Biblioteca
Central **Founded:** 1945 **Type:** Government **Staff:** 3 Prof. 4
Other **Holdings:** 8,276 books 1,360 journals **Subjects:** Ani-
mal Production, Crop Production, Horticulture, Soil Science
Loan: In country **Photocopy:** Yes

Rondônia

431　Porto Velho, Rondônia, Brazil
Brazilian Agricultural Research Corporation,
　　Center for Agroforestry Research of
　　Rondônia
Library
BR 364 Km 5.5
CP 406
78900-000 Porto Velho, Rondônia
Phone: +55(69) 222-3080 **Fax:** +55(69) 222-3857 **WWW:**
www.sede.embrapa.br/unidades/centros/cpaf-ro.htm

Non-English Name: Empresa Brasileira de Pesquisa Agropecuária, Centro de Pesquisa Agroflorestal de Rondônia

(Embrapa Rondônia, CPAF-Rondônia), Biblioteca **Former
Name:** Unidade de Execução de Pesquisa de Âmbito Estadual de Porto Velho (UEPAE) **Founded:** 1976 **Type:** Government **Head:** Tânia Maria Chaves Campelo *Phone:* +55
(69) 222-3857 **Staff:** 1 Prof. 3 Other **Holdings:** 2,000 books
250 journals **Subjects:** Agroforestry, Animal Housing, Cultivation, Fruit Growing, Plant Pathology, Plant Protection,
Soil Science **Loan:** In country **Photocopy:** Yes

Roraima

432　Boa Vista, Roraima, Brazil
Brazilian Agricultural Research Corporation,
　　Center for Agroforestry Research of Roraima
Information Sector
BR 174 Km 08 - Distrito Industrial
CP 133
69301-970 Boa Vista, Roraima
Phone: +55(95) 626-7125 **Email:** postmaster@cpafrr.
embrapa.br **WWW:** www.cpafrr.embrapa.br

Non-English Name: Empresa Brasileira de Pesquisa Agro-
pecuária, Centro de Pesquisa Agroflorestal de Roraima
(Embrapa Roraima, CPAF-RR), Setor de Informação (SIN)
Former Name: Unidade de Execução de Pesquisa de Âmbi-
to Territorial de Boa Vista (UEPAT), Setor de Informação e
Documentação **Founded:** 1983 **Type:** Government **Head:**
George Correa Amaro *Email:* george@cpafrr.embrapa.br
Phone: +55(95) 626-7125 **Staff:** 1 Prof. 2 Other **Holdings:**
2,200 books 346 journals **Language of Collection/Services:**
Portuguese / Portuguese **Subjects:** Agricultural Develop-
ment, Animal Husbandry, Crops, Entomology, Horticulture,
Plant Pathology, Soil Science, Veterinary Medicine **Special-
izations:** Agroforestry **Networks:** CCN; CCPE **Databases
Developed:** AINFO — documents, periodicals, human re-
sources and institutions; available via Internet **Databases
Used:** Agricola; CARIS **Loan:** Internationally **Service:**
Internationally **Photocopy:** Yes

Santa Catarina

433　Concórdia, Santa Catarina, Brazil
Brazilian Agricultural Research Corporation,
　　National Swine and Poultry Research Center
Library
BR 153 Km 110
Vila Tamanduá
Caixa Postal 21
89700-000 Concórdia, Santa Catarina
Phone: +55(49) 442-8555 **Fax:** +55(49) 442-8559 **Email:**
cnpsa@cnpsa.embrapa.br **WWW:** www.cnpsa.embrapa.br

Non-English Name: Empresa Brasileira de Pesquisa Agropecuária, Centro Nacional de Pesquisa de Suínos e Aves
(EMBRAPA, CNPSA), Biblioteca **Founded:** 1975 **Type:**
Government **Head:** Irene Zanatta Pacheco Camera *Phone:*
+55(49) 442-8555 *Email:* irene@cnpsa.embrapa.br **Staff:** 1
Prof. 2 Other **Holdings:** 30,000 books 801 journals **Language of Collection/Services:** English / Portuguese **Subjects:** Agricultural Economics, Animal Husbandry, Food
Sciences, Veterinary Medicine **Specializations:** Pigs, Poul-

try **Networks:** CCN; EMBRAPA **Databases Used:** Agricola; CABI **Loan:** In country **Service:** In country **Photocopy:** Yes

434   Florianópolis, Santa Catarina, Brazil
         Santa Catarina State Agricultural Research and
            Rural Extension Enterprise
         Information and Publication Department, Division
            of the Library
         Rod. SC 404 Km 3
         CP 1460
         88000 Florianópolis, Santa Catarina

Non-English Name: Empresa de Pesquisa Agropecuária e Extensão Rural de Santa Catarina S/A, Departamento de Informação e Divulgação, Divisão de Biblioteca **Former Name:** Empresa Catarinense de Pesquisa Agropecuária (EMPASC) **Founded:** 1976 **Type:** Government **Head:** Zilma Maria Vasco *Email:* biblio@epagri.rct-sc.br *Phone:* +55 (48) 239-5538 **Staff:** 3 Prof. 1 Other **Holdings:** 2,000 books 220 journals **Language of Collection/Services:** Portuguese, English **Subjects:** Agriculture (Tropics), Bovidae, Agricultural Economics, Agricultural Engineering, Animal Husbandry, Biotechnology, Cereals, Crops, Farming, Entomology, Fisheries, Forestry, Fruit Trees, Horticulture, Oilseeds, Pastures, Plant Pathology, Soil Science, Vegetable Growing, Veterinary Medicine **Loan:** Inhouse **Photocopy:** Yes

São Paulo

435   Botucatu, São Paulo, Brazil
         Universidade Estadual Paulista, Faculdade de
            Ciências Agronômicas (UNESP, FCA)
         Serviço de Biblioteca e Documentação (SBD)
         CP 237
         18603-970 Botucatu, São Paulo
Phone: +55(149) 213883 ext 124 **Fax:** +55(149) 211473

Founded: 1991 **Type:** Government **Head:** Glaura Maria Oliveira Barbosa de Almeida *Phone:* +55(149) 213883 ext 124 **Staff:** 2 Prof. 8 Other **Holdings:** 10,000 books 1,200 journals **Subjects:** Agriculture (Tropics), Agribusiness, Agricultural Development, Agricultural Economics, Agricultural Engineering, Animal Husbandry, Biotechnology, Crops, Education/Extension, Entomology, Farming, Food Sciences, Forestry, Horticulture, Plant Pathology, Soil Science, Water Resources **Databases Used:** CABCD **Loan:** In country **Photocopy:** Yes

436   Campinas, São Paulo, Brazil
         Agronomy Institute of Campinas
         Library
         Caixa Postal 28
         13001-970 Campinas, São Paulo
Location: Av. Barao de Itapura, 1481 **Fax:** +55(19) 231-5422 ext 190 **Email:** bibliote@barao.iac.br

Non-English Name: Instituto Agronômico de Campinas, Biblioteca **Founded:** 1887 **Type:** Government **Head:** Regina Maria Redígolo *Phone:* +55(19) 231-5422 ext 117 *Email:* bibliote@barao.iac.br **Staff:** 2 Prof. 3 Other **Hold-**

ings: 150,000 books 3,100 journals **Subjects:** Biology, Botany, Plants, Soil Science **Loan:** In country **Photocopy:** Yes

437   Campinas, São Paulo, Brazil
         Brazilian Agricultural Research Corporation,
            Embrapa Environmental Monitoring Center
            (Embrapa Monitoramento por Satélite, NMA)
         Library
         Av. Dr. Júlio Soares de Arruda, 803
         Parque São Quirino
         13088-300 Campinas, São Paulo
Phone: +55(19) 252-5977 **Fax:** +55(19) 254-1100 **WWW:** www.nma.embrapa.br

Non-English Name: Empresa Brasileira de Pesquisa Agropecuária, Núcleo de Monitoramento Ambiental e de Recursos Naturais por Satélite, Biblioteca **Type:** Government

438   Campinas, São Paulo, Brazil
         Brazilian Agricultural Research Corporation,
            National Center for Agricultural Research
            Technology and Information
         Information Area
         Caixa Postal 6041
         13083-970 Campinas, São Paulo
Location: Av. Dr. André Tosello, s/n°, Cuidad Universitária "Zeferino Vaz", Barão Geraldo **Phone:** +55 (19) 289-9800 **Fax:** +55(19) 289-9594 **Email:** cnptia@cnptia.embrapa.br **WWW:** www.cnptia.embrapa.br

Non-English Name: Empresa Brasileira de Pesquisa Agropecuária, Centro Nacional de Pesquisa Tecnológica em Informática para Agricultura (Embrapa Informática Agropecuária, CNPTIA), Área de Informação (AINFO) **Former Name:** Núcleo Tecnológico de Informática para Agropecuária (NTIA) **Founded:** 1986 **Type:** Government **Head:** Marcia Izabel Fugisawa Souza *Phone:* +55(19) 289-9800 *Email:* marcia@cnptia.embrapa.br **Staff:** 1 Prof. 3 Other **Holdings:** 5,000 books 50 journals **Language of Collection/Services:** English/Portuguese **Subjects:** Computer Science, Computer Software, Statistics **Specializations:** Computers in Agriculture, Information Technology in Agriculture **Networks:** EMBRAPA **Databases Used:** Comprehensive **Loan:** In country **Service:** Internationally **Photocopy:** No

439   Jaguariúna, São Paulo, Brazil
         Brazilian Agricultural Research Corporation,
            National Center for Research on Monitoring
            and Evaluating Environmental Impact
         Information Area
         Rodovia SP 340 Km 127.5
         Bairro Tanquinho Velho
         CP 69
         13280-000 Jaguariúna, São Paulo
Phone: +55(19) 867-5700 **Fax:** +55(19) 867-8740 **WWW:** www.cnpma.embrapa.br

Non-English Name: Empresa Brasileira de Pesquisa Agropecuária, Centro Nacional de Pesquisa de Monitoramento e Avaliação de Impacto Ambiental (Embrapa Meio Ambiente, CNPMA), Área de Informação (AINFO) **Former Name:** Centro Nacional de Pesquisa de Defesa da Agricultura

(CNPDA), Setor de Informação e Documentação **Founded:** 1984 **Type:** Government **Head:** Nilce Chaves Gattar *Phone:* +55(19) 297-1721 ext 2074 *Email:* nolce@cnpda.embrapa. ansp.br **Staff:** 2 Prof. **Holdings:** 1,400 books 210 journals **Subjects:** Biological Control, Defense Mechanisms, Pests, Plant Diseases **Loan:** In country **Photocopy:** Yes

440   Nova Odessa, São Paulo, Brazil
Institute of Animal Husbandry
Library
Rua Heitor Penteado, 56
CP 60
13460-000 Nova Odessa, São Paulo
Phone: +55(19) 466-7410 ext 111 **Fax:** +55(19) 466-6409

Non-English Name: Instituto de Zootecnia, Seção de Biblioteca **Founded:** 1936 **Type:** Government **Head:** Maria de Fátima A. Figueiredo Pereria *Phone:* +55(19) 466-7410 ext 111 **Staff:** 5 Prof. 2 Other **Holdings:** 12,000 books 1,500 journals **Language of Collection/Services:** Portuguese / Portuguese **Subjects:** Animal Husbandry, Veterinary Medicine **Networks:** CCN **Loan:** In country **Photocopy:** Yes

441   Piracicaba, São Paulo, Brazil
Center for Nuclear Energy in Agriculture
Library
Av. Centenario, No. 303
CP 96
13400 Piracicaba, São Paulo
Phone: +55(19) 33-5122 ext 41 **WWW:** www.cena.usp.br/ Biblioteca/Biblioteca.htm

Non-English Name: Centro de Energia Nuclear na Agricultura, Biblioteca **Founded:** 1970 **Type:** Academic **Staff:** 2 Prof. 2 Other **Holdings:** 3,000 books 400 journals **Language of Collection/Services:** Portuguese / Portuguese **Subjects:** Nuclear Energy **Loan:** In country **Photocopy:** Yes

442   Piracicaba, São Paulo, Brazil
Forestry Research Institute
Prof. Helladio do Amaral Mello Library
ESALQ/USP
Caixa Postal 530
13400-970 Piracicaba, São Paulo
Location: Av. Padua Dias, 11 **Phone:** +55(19) 433-6155 **Fax:** +55(19) 433-6081 **WWW:** jatoba.esalq.usp.br **OPAC:** jatoba.esalq.usp.br/bibipef

Non-English Name: Instituto de Pesquisas e Estudos Florestais (IPEF), Biblioteca Prof. Helladio do Amaral Mello **Former Name:** Central Técnica de Informações (CTI) **Founded:** 1973 **Type:** Government **Head:** Marialice Metzker Poggiani *Email:* mmpoggia@carpa.ciagri.usp.br *Phone:* +55(19) 433-6155 **Staff:** 1 Prof. 3 Other **Holdings:** 6,000 books 428 journals **Language of Collection/Services:** English **Subjects:** Biotechnology, Education/ Extension, Forestry, Soil Science **Specializations:** Forestry **Databases Used:** TREECD **Loan:** Inhouse **Photocopy:** Yes

443   Piracicaba, São Paulo, Brazil
University of São Paulo, Luiz de Queiroz College
    of Agriculture
Library and Documentation Division

Av. Pádua Dias, 11
Caixa Postal 9
13418-900 Piracicaba, São Paulo
Phone: +55(19) 429-4311 **Fax:** +55(19) 422-0244 **Email:** biblio@carpa.ciagri.usp.br **WWW:** dibd.esalq.usp.br **OPAC:** www.usp.br/sibi **Ariel IP:** 143.107.213.175

Non-English Name: Universidade de São Paulo, Escola Superior de Agricultura "Luiz de Queiroz" (USP, ESALQ), Divisão de Biblioteca e Documentação (DIBD) **Founded:** 1901 **Type:** Academic **Head:** Marcia Regina Migliorato Saad *Phone:* +55(19) 422-5913 *Email:* mrmsaad@carpa.cia gri.usp.br **Staff:** 16 Prof. 23 Other **Holdings:** 90,000 books 732 journals **Language of Collection/Services:** Portuguese, English, Spanish, French, German/Portuguese **Subjects:** Comprehensive **Specializations:** Agricultural Economics, Animal Husbandry, Crops, Environment, Food Sciences, Forestry Engineering, Nutrition, Rural Sociology **Networks:** CCN; IBICT; OCLC **Databases Developed:** Base Peri - bibliographical database of periodical literature in the agricultural sciences in Portuguese and Spanish from 1975 - available via the Internet at didb.esalq.usp.br; Base EXAGRI - bibliographical database of agricultural extension information including pamphlets, journal articles and videos - available via Internet at exagri.esalq.usp.br; EDITOR - Press directory database - available on local network; VOCALQ - Agricultural controlled vocabulary - available locally; SRF - contains information and catalogs from universities and national and international institutions on agricultural sciences - available on local network **Databases Used:** Comprehensive **Loan:** In country **Service:** Internationally **Photocopy:** Yes

444   São Carlos, São Paulo, Brazil
Brazilian Agricultural Research Corporation,
    Center for Cattle Research of the Southeast
Setor de Informação e Documentação (SID)
Rodovia Washington Luiz, Km 234
CP 339
13560-970 São Carlos, São Paulo
Phone: +55(16) 271-1265 ext 22 **Fax:** +55(16) 272-5754 **Email:** cppse@cppse.embrapa.br **WWW:** www.cppse. embrapa.br

Non-English Name: Empresa Brasileira de Pesquisa Agropecuária, Centro de Pesquisa de Pecuária do Sudeste (Embrapa Pecuária Sudeste, CPPSE) **Former Name:** Unidade de Execução de Pesquisa de Âmbito Estadual de São Carlos (UEPAE) **Type:** Government **Head:** Sônia Borges de Alencar *Phone:* +55(16) 271-1265 **Staff:** 2 Prof. 1 Other **Holdings:** 1,931 books 120 journals **Subjects:** Beef Cows, Dairy Cows, Horses **Loan:** In country **Photocopy:** Yes

445   São Carlos, São Paulo, Brazil
Brazilian Agricultural Research Corporation,
    National Center for Research on Agricultural
    Instrumentation
Setor de Informação e Documentação (SID)
Rua XV de Novembro, 1452
CP 741
13560-970 São Carlos, São Paulo
Phone: +55(16) 274-2477 **Fax:** +55(16) 272-5958 **WWW:** www.cnpdia.embrapa.br

Non-English Name: Empresa Brasileira de Pesquisa Agropecuária, Centro Nacional de Pesquisa e Desenvolvimento de Instrumentação Agropecuária (Embrapa Instrumentação Agropecuária, CNPDIA) **Former Name:** Unidade de Apoio à Pesquisa e Desenvolvimento de Instrumentação Agropecuária (UAPDIA) **Type:** Government **Founded:** 1985 **Head:** Véra Lúcia de Campos Octaviano *Phone:* +55(16) 272-5741/42 **Staff:** 1 Prof. 1 Other **Holdings:** 880 books 53 journals **Language of Collection/Services:** English **Subjects:** Agriculture (Tropics), Agricultural Development, Biotechnology, Agricultural Engineering, Agricultural Research, Soil Science, Water Resources **Loan:** To libraries of EMBRAPA system **Photocopy:** Yes

446   São Paulo, São Paulo, Brazil
Agricultural Economics Institute
Documentation Unit
Av. Miguel Stefano, 3900 - Água Funda
CP 68029
04301-903 São Paulo, São Paulo
Phone: +55(11) 584-0433 ext 231 **Fax:** +55(11) 276-4062
Email: iea@eu.ansp.br

Non-English Name: Instituto de Economia Agrícola, Núcleo de Documentação **Founded:** 1945 **Type:** Government **Head:** Vandete Pereira N. Medeiros *Phone:* +55(11) 5584-0433 ext 231 *Email:* iea@eu.ansp.br **Staff:** 1 Prof. 6 Other **Holdings:** 37,000 books 52,000 journals **Subjects:** Agricultural Economics, Agricultural Statistics, Mathematics, Rural Sociology **Loan:** In country **Photocopy:** Yes

447   São Paulo, São Paulo, Brazil
Biological Institute
Library
Av. Conselheiro Rodrigues Alves 1252
04014-002 São Paulo, São Paulo
Phone: +55(11) 572-9822 **Fax:** +55(11) 570-9704

Non-English Name: Instituto Biológico (IB-SP), Biblioteca **Founded:** 1928 **Type:** Government **Staff:** 3 Prof. 2 Other **Holdings:** 12,300 books 110 journals **Language of Collection/Services:** English **Subjects:** Entomology, Parasitology, Plant Pathology, Toxicology, Veterinary Medicine **Loan:** In country **Photocopy:** Yes

448   São Paulo, São Paulo, Brazil
Botany Institute
Library
Caixa Postal 4005
01061-970 São Paulo, São Paulo
Location: Av. Miguel Stéfano, 3687, Agua Funda **Phone:** +55(11) 5584-6300 est 205 **Fax:** +55(11) 577-3678 **Email:** ibt@smtp-gw.ibot.sp.gov.br **WWW:** www.ibot.sp.gov.br

Non-English Name: Instituto de Botânico (IBt), Biblioteca **Founded:** 1938 **Type:** Government **Head:** Helena Rodrigues da Silva *Phone:* +55(11) 5584-6300 est 205 *Email:* hrodrigues@smtp-gw.ibot.sp.gov.br **Staff:** 1 Prof. 3 Other **Holdings:** 6,500 books 1,700 journals **Language of Collection/Services:** Portuguese, English **Subjects:** Botany, Ecology, Paleobotany, Physiology, Plant Pathology, Taxonomy, Plants **Specializations:** Botany **Networks:** CCN **Loan:** Locally **Service:** Internationally **Photocopy:** Yes

449   São Paulo, São Paulo, Brazil
Coordenadoria da Pesquisa de Recursos Naturals
Biblioteca
Av. Miguel Estefno, 3900
CP 8366
01000 São Paulo, São Paulo

Founded: 1970 **Type:** Government **Staff:** 1 Prof. 1 Other **Holdings:** 1,500 books 50 journals **Subjects:** Botany, Conservation, Ecology, Forest Management, Forestry, Geology, Legislation, Natural Resources, Zoology **Loan:** In country **Photocopy:** Yes

450   São Paulo, São Paulo, Brazil
Institute of Technological Research of the State of
    São Paulo, Chemistry Division
Documentation Center
Rua Prof. Almeida Prado. 532 - Cidade
    Universitaria
CP 7141
05508-901 São Paulo, São Paulo
Fax: +55(11) 768-3353

Non-English Name: Instituto de Pesquisa Tecnológica do Estado de São Paulo, Divisão de Química (IPT), Centro de Documentação (CEDOC) **Founded:** 1977 **Type:** Government **Head:** Maria Natalina de A. Martins *Phone:* +55(11) 268-2211 ext 573 **Staff:** 3 Prof. 2 Other **Holdings:** 30,000 books 90 journals **Language of Collection/Services:** English, Portuguese **Subjects:** Chemistry, Fertilizers **Specializations:** Chemistry, Chemical Engineering, Fertilizer Industry, Fertilizer Technology **Databases Used:** Compendex **Loan:** In country **Photocopy:** Yes

451   São Paulo, São Paulo, Brazil
Instituto de Pesca
Biblioteca
Av. Francisco Matarazzo, 455
05001 São Paulo, São Paulo
Phone: +55(11) 864-6300 ext 28, 29

Founded: 1969 **Type:** Government **Staff:** 3 Prof. 6 Other **Holdings:** 2,307 books **Subjects:** Ecology, Fish Culture, Fishing, Oceanography **Loan:** In country **Photocopy:** Yes

452   São Paulo, São Paulo, Brazil
University of São Paulo, Faculty of Veterinary
    Medicine and Zootecny
Library and Documentation Service
Av. Corifeu de Azevedo Marques, 2720
05340-000 São Paulo, São Paulo
Phone: +55(11) 813-6944 ext 7670 **Fax:** +55(11) 210-2224

Non-English Name: Universidade de São Paulo, Faculdade de Medicina Veterinária e Zootecnia (USP, FMVZ), Serviço de Biblioteca e Documentação (SBD) **Founded:** 1934 **Type:** Academic **Staff:** 5 Prof. 17 Other **Holdings:** 23,889 books 845 journals **Language of Collection/Services:** English, French, Spanish / Portuguese **Subjects:** Animal Husbandry, Crops, Fisheries, Food Sciences, Soil Science **Specializations:** Animal Production, Veterinary Medicine **Databases Used:** CABCD **Loan:** In country **Service:** Inhouse **Photocopy:** Yes

Sergipe

453 Aracaju, Sergipe, Brazil
Brazilian Agricultural Research Corporation,
Center for Agricultural Research on Coastal
Tablelands
Information and Documentation Center
Av. Beira Mar, 3250
CP 44
49025-040 Aracaju, Sergipe
Phone: +55(79) 217-1300 **Fax:** +55(79) 231-9145 **WWW:**
www.cpatc.embrapa.br

Non-English Name: Empresa Brasileira de Pesquisa Agro-
pecuária, Centro de Pesquisa Agropecuária dos Tabuleiros
Costeiros (Embrapa Tabuleiros Costeiros, CPATC), Setor de
Informação e Documentação (SID) **Former Name:** National
Coconut Research Center, Centro Nacional de Pesquisa de
Coco (CNPCo) **Founded:** 1993 **Type:** Government **Head:**
Maria Ferreira de Melo *Phone:* +55(79) 231-9116 ext 27
Staff: 2 Prof. 2 Other **Holdings:** 6,000 books 420 journals
Language of Collection/Services: English **Subjects:** Agri-
culture (Tropics), Agricultural Development, Agricultural
Economics, Animal Husbandry, Coconuts, Crops, Education
/Extension, Entomology, Plant Pathology, Soil Science, Wa-
ter Resources **Loan:** In country **Photocopy:** Yes

Bulgaria

454 General Toshevo, Bulgaria
Bulgarian Agricultural Academy, Institute for
Wheat and Sunflower "Dobroudja"
Scientific Library
Varna
9520 General Toshevo
Phone: +359(573) 20339 **Fax:** +359(573) 4448

Founded: 1952 **Type:** Academic **Head:** Mrs. S. Ivanova
Phone: +359(573) 22061 ext 235 **Staff:** 2 Prof. **Holdings:**
31,000 books 96 journals **Subjects:** Cereals, Genetics, Grain
Legumes, Plant Breeding, Sunflowers, Triticale, Wheat
Loan: Internationally **Photocopy:** Yes

455 Kostinbrod, Bulgaria
Bulgarian Agricultural Academy, Plant Protection
Institute
Library
2230 Kostinbrod, Sofia District
Phone: +359(2) 877225 ext 234 **Fax:** +359(721) 23504

Non-English Name: Selskostopanska Akademia, Institut za
zastita na rasteniata (IZR), Biblioteka **Founded:** 1935 **Type:**
Academic **Head:** Violeta Dekova *Phone:* +359(2) 877225
ext 244 **Staff:** 1 Prof. **Holdings:** 13,583 books 7,344 journals
Subjects: Biotechnology, Crops, Entomology, Horticulture,
Plant Pathology **Loan:** Internationally **Photocopy:** Yes

456 Kyustendil, Bulgaria
Bulgarian Agricultural Academy, Institute of Fruit
Growing
Library

2500 Kyustendil
Phone: +359(78) 22612, 24036 **Fax:** +359(78) 27411

Non-English Name: Selskostopanska Akademia, Institut po
ovostarstvo, Biblioteca **Founded:** 1944 **Type:** Research
Head: Yordanka Zasheva *Phone:* +359(78) 22612 **Staff:** 20
Prof. 36 Other **Holdings:** 8,881 books 28 journals **Language
of Collection/Services:** Bulgarian, Russian, English **Subjects:** Biotechnology, Fruit Growing, Plant Breeding, Plant
Protection **Specializations:** Horticulture **Loan:** Internationally **Service:** Internationally **Photocopy:** Yes

457 Pleven, Bulgaria
Bulgarian Agricultural Academy, Vine Growing
and Wine Producing Institute
Library
1 Kala Tepe Str.
5800 Pleven
Phone: +359(64) 22161, 29109 **Fax:** +359(64) 26470,
22468

Founded: 1905 **Type:** Government **Staff:** 1 Prof. **Holdings:**
12,000 books 110 journals **Subjects:** Enology, Viticulture
Loan: Internationally **Photocopy:** Yes

458 Plovdiv, Bulgaria
Agricultural University of Plovdiv
Library
12, Mendeleev Str.
4000 Plovdiv
Phone: +359(32) 268136, 269540 **Fax:** +359(32) 233157
Email: library@au-plovdiv.bg **WWW:** www.au-plovdiv.
bg

Former Name: V. Kolarov Higher Institute of Agriculture
Founded: 1945 **Type:** Academic **Head:** Ekaterina Anastas-
sova **Staff:** 12 Prof. 1 Other **Holdings:** 145 journals 203,000
books **Language of Collection/Services:** Bulgarian, Russian **Subjects:** Comprehensive **Databases Used:** Agris **Service:** Internationally **Loan:** Internationally **Photocopy:** Yes

459 Plovdiv, Bulgaria
Bulgarian Agricultural Academy, Maritsa
Vegetable Crops Research Institute
Information and Documentation Office
32 Brezovcko Shosse Str.
4003 Plovdiv
Phone: +359(32) 551227, 552295 **Fax:** +359(32) 650177

Non-English Name: Selskostopanska Akademia, Institut po
zelenchukovi kulturi "Maritsa" (IZK Maritsa), Otdel za
nauchno-tehnicheska informatsiya (ONTIPI) **Founded:**
1969 **Type:** Government **Head:** Mr. Anastas Kiretchev,
Mrs. Nadezhda Ganeva, Librarian *Phone:* +359(32) 551227
ext 287, 289 **Staff:** 3 Prof. 6 Other **Holdings:** 18,321 books
45 journals **Language of Collection/Services:** Bulgarian,
Russian **Subjects:** Agricultural Economics, Horticulture,
Mechanization, Plant Breeding, Plant Diseases, Plant Pests,
Vegetables **Loan:** Inhouse **Service:** Inhouse **Photocopy:**
Yes

460 Plovdiv, Bulgaria
Higher Institute of Food and Food Industry
Library

26, Maritsa Blvd.
4002 Plovdiv

Phone: +359(32) 44181 ext 389, 390 **Email:** vihvp@hiffi-plovdiv.acad.bg

Type: Academic **Subjects:** Food Industry

461   **Rousse, Bulgaria**
University of Rousse
University Library
8 Studentski Str.
7017 Rousse

Phone: +359(82) 451116 **Fax:** +359(82) 455145 **WWW:** www.ru.acad.bg

Type: Academic **Head:** Emilia Lehova *Email:* elehova@ru.acad.bg **Holdings:** 310,000 books

462   **Sadovo, Bulgaria**
Bulgarian Agricultural Academy, Institute for Introduction and Plant Genetic Resources (IIPGR)
K. Malkov Library
4122 Sadovo, Plovdiv District

Fax: +359 4930026

Founded: 1902 **Type:** Government **Head:** Liliana Stoeva Ivanova *Phone:* +359(32) 993118 ext 2251, 2252 **Staff:** 2 Prof. 3 Other **Holdings:** 27,146 books 364 journals **Subjects:** Agricultural Chemistry, Biotechnology, Crops, Ecology, Entomology, Fertilizers, Fruits, Horticulture, Irrigation, Physics, Plant Pathology, Plant Pests, Seed Production, Soil Science, Taxonomy, Vegetables, Viticulture **Loan:** Internationally **Photocopy:** Yes

463   **Sofia, Bulgaria**
Bulgarian Agricultural Academy
Central Agricultural Library (CAL)
125 Tzarigradsko shosse Blvd., Block I
1113 Sofia

Phone: +359(2) 705517 **Email:** clib@uni-sz.bg

Non-English Name: Selskostopanska Akademia, Tsentralna Biblioteka **Founded:** 1961 **Type:** Academic **Head:** Minka Grueva *Phone:* +359(2) 709168 **Staff:** 26 Prof. **Holdings:** 503,568 books 1,000 journals **Language of Collection/Services:** Bulgarian, Russian, English **Subjects:** Animal Husbandry, Food Industry, Veterinary Medicine **Loan:** Internationally **Service:** Internationally **Photocopy:** Yes

464   **Sofia, Bulgaria**
Bulgarian Agricultural Academy
Centre for Scientific, Technical, and Economic Information (CSTEI)
125 Tzarigradsko shose Blvd., Block 1
1113 Sofia

Phone: +359(2) 700428, 709169, 705543 **Email:** cstei@bgnet.bg

Non-English Name: Selskostopanska Akademia, Center Nauchna, Tehnicheska Informatsia **Former Name:** Department for Scientific, Technical, Economic and Patent Information **Founded:** 1950 **Type:** Academic **Head:** Mrs. Radka Stoyanova **Staff:** 1 Prof. **Holdings:** 13,065 books 145 jour-nals **Subjects:** Electrification, Mechanization **Networks:** AGRIS **Loan:** Internationally **Photocopy:** Yes

465   **Sofia, Bulgaria**
Bulgarian Academy of Sciences, Forest Research Institute (BAS, FRI)
Library
Blvd. Sv. Kliment Ohridski Nr. 132
1756 Sofia

Phone: +359(2) 622961/2 **Fax:** +359(2) 622965 **Email:** ivanraev@bgcict.acad.bg

Non-English Name: Bulgarska Akademia na Naukite, Institut za Gorata (BAN, IG), Biblioteka **Founded:** 1929 **Type:** Academic **Head:** Milena Dimitreva *Phone:* +359(2) 622961/2 ext 235 **Staff:** 1 Prof. **Holdings:** 38,727 books 19,112 journals **Language of Collection/Services:** Bulgarian, Russian, English, German, French / Bulgarian **Subjects:** Biotechnology, Entomology, Erosion, Forest Ecology, Forest Management, Forest Plantations, Forestry, Plant Pathology, Soil Science, Wildlife **Loan:** In country **Photocopy:** No

466   **Sofia, Bulgaria**
Bulgarian Agricultural Academy, Nikola Poushkarov Institute of Soil Science and Agroecology
Library
7 Shose Bankya Str.
PO Box 1369
1331 Sofia

Phone: +359(2) 25271 **Fax:** +359(2) 248937

Non-English Name: Selskostopanska Akademia, Nauchno-izsledovatelski institut po pochvoznanie i agroekologia "N. Poushkarov" (NIPA "N. Poushkarov"), Biblioteka **Former Name:** N. Poushkarov Institute of Soil Science and Yield Programming, Institut po Pochvoznanie i Programirane na Dobivite (IPPD) **Founded:** 1947 **Type:** Academic **Head:** Sen. Res. Tosho Raichev *Phone:* +359(2) 247656 **Staff:** 2 Prof. **Holdings:** 30,000 books 50 journals **Language of Collection/Services:** Bulgarian, English / Bulgarian **Subjects:** Biotechnology, Crops, Soil Science **Specializations:** Agricultural Chemistry, Fertilizers, Physics, Soil Classification, Soil Formation **Loan:** Internationally **Service:** Internationally **Photocopy:** Yes

467   **Sofia, Bulgaria**
University of Forestry
Library
10, Kliment Ohridski Blvd.
1756 Sofia

Phone: +359(2) 6301 **Fax:** +359(2) 622830 **WWW:** www.ltu.acad.bg

Former Name: Higher Institute of Forestry **Founded:** 1953 **Type:** Academic **Subjects:** Forestry

468   **Stara Zagora, Bulgaria**
Thracian University (TU)
Library
Sdudentski grad
6000 Stara Zagora

Phone: +359(42) 74169 **Fax:** +359(42) 74112 **Email:** clib@uni-sz.bg **WWW:** www.uni-sz.bg

Non-English Name: Trakiiski Universitet (TU) **Former Name:** Higher Institute of Zootechnics and Veterinary Medicine **Founded:** 1974 **Type:** Academic **Head:** Ivanka Encheva Demireva *Phone:* +359(42) 74169 **Staff:** 10 Prof. **Holdings:** 375,831 books 228 journals **Language of Collection/Services:** Bulgarian / Bulgarian **Subjects:** Agricultural Development, Agricultural Engineering, Biotechnology, Education/Extension, Farming, Fisheries, Food Sciences, Sericulture **Specializations:** Agricultural Economics, Animal Husbandry, Ecology, Veterinary Medicine **Networks:** AGRIS **Databases Used:** Agris; Biosis; Medline **Loan:** Internationally **Service:** Internationally **Photocopy:** Yes

Burkina Faso

♦**469**   **Bobo Dioulasso, Burkina Faso**
        Animal Trypanosomiasis Research Center
        Library
        01 BP 454
        Bobo Dioulasso 01
Phone: +226 972287 **Fax:** +226 972320

Non-English Name: Centre de Recherche sur les Trypanosomoses Animales (CRTA), Bibliothèque **Founded:** 1974 **Type:** International **Head:** Ms. Pale Toussaint *Phone:* +226 972053 **Staff:** 1 Prof. 1 Other **Holdings:** 940 books 40 journals **Language of Collection/ Services:** English **Subjects:** Animal Husbandry, Biotechnology, Entomology, Farming, Food Sciences, Veterinary Medicine **Specializations:** Genetics, Immunology, Parasitology **Loan:** In country **Photocopy:** Yes

470   **Ouagadougou, Burkina Faso**
        Centre National de la Recherche Scientifique et
           Technologique
        Direction de l'Information Scientifique et
           Technique
        BP 7047
        Ouagadougou

Founded: 1985 **Head:** Amadou Diallo *Phone:* +226 335220 **Staff:** 1 Prof. **Holdings:** 900 books 11 journals **Subjects:** Animal Production, Crop Production, Plant Protection **Networks:** AGRIS

471   **Ouagadougou, Burkina Faso**
        Centre National de la Recherche Scientifique et
           Technologique, Institut de Recherche en
           Biologie et Ecologie Tropical (CNRST,
           IRBET)
        Bibliothèque
        BP 7047
        Ouagadougou
Phone: +226 307207, 334098

Founded: 1987 **Head:** Jean-Marie Ouadba

♦**472**   **Ouagadougou, Burkina Faso**
        Comité Interafricain d'Etudes Hydrauliques
           (CIEH)

        Centre de Documentation et d'Information (CDI)
        BP 369
        Ouagadougou
Fax: +226 362441

Founded: 1974 **Type:** International **Head:** Katakou Kokou Larba Ali Krissiamba *Phone:* +226 307112, 307115 **Staff:** 2 Prof. 4 Other **Holdings:** 10,000 books 60 journals **Language of Collection/Services:** French/French **Subjects:** Agroclimatology, Flood Irrigation, Irrigation, Water Balance, Water Use **Databases Developed:** SAINEA – Système Africain d'Information sur l'Eau et l'Assainissement **Loan:** In country **Photocopy:** Yes

473   **Ouagadougou, Burkina Faso**
        Institute of Environment and Agricultural
           Research, Forestry Production Department
        Library
        03 BP 7047
        Ouagadougou 01
Phone: +226 334098 **Fax:** +226 314938

Founded: 1997 **Head:** Sibiri Jean Ouedraogo *Email:* sibiri @irbet.irbet.bf **Subjects:** Forestry

474   **Ouagadougou, Burkina Faso**
        Ministère de l'Agriculture et des Ressources
           Animales
        Centre National de Documentation Agricole
           (CNDA)
        BP 7010
        Ouagadougou 03, Kadiogo

Former Name: Ministère de l'Agriculture et de l'Elevage **Founded:** 1981 **Type:** Government **Head:** Mme Germaine Sawadogo *Phone:* +226 332100 ext 4116 **Staff:** 4 Prof. 7 Other **Holdings:** 6,366 books 5 journals **Subjects:** Animal Production, Crop Production, Crops, Extension, Marketing, Plant Protection **Networks:** AGRIS **Loan:** In country **Photocopy:** Yes

475   **Ouagadougou, Burkina Faso**
        Ministry of Environment and Water, National
           Tree Seed Centre
        Library
        01 BP 2682
        Ouagadougou 01
Phone: +226 368013 **Fax:** +226 301232 **Email:** cnsf@ fasibet.bf

Founded: 1983 **Head:** Albert Nikiema

♦**476**   **Ouagadougou, Burkina Faso**
        Pan African Institute for Development (PAID)
        Information Center
        01 BP 1756
        Ouagadougou 01
Location: Route de Fada, Secteur 28 **Phone:** +226 300390 **Fax:** +226 301296

Non-English Name: Institut Panafricain pour le Développement, Afrique de l'Ouest Sahel (IPD, AOS), Centre de Documentation **Founded:** 1977 **Type:** Academic **Head:** Amadou Diop *Phone:* +226 301399 **Staff:** 9 Prof. 37 Other **Holdings:** 5,000 books 40 journals **Language of Collection/**

Services: French/French **Loan:** Do not loan **Service:** In country **Photocopy:** Yes

477   Ouagadougou, Burkina Faso
Research Institute for Development
Bibliothèque
BP 182
Ouagadougou
WWW: www.ird.bf

Non-English Name: Institut de Recherche pour le Développement (IRD) **Former Name:** Institut Français de Recherche Scientifique pour le Développement en Coopération (ORSTOM) **Type:** Government **Head:** J.C. Gautun *Phone:* +226 306737, 306739 **Staff:** 1 Prof. 1 Other **Holdings:** 2,000 books **Subjects:** Agricultural Economics, Anthropology, Hydrology, Pedology, Plant Pathology, Sociology **Loan:** Do not loan **Photocopy:** Yes

♦**478   Ouagadougou, Burkina Faso**
University of Ouagadougou, Rural Development Institute
Library
03 BP 7021
Ouagadougou 03
Location: Av. Charles de Gaulle **Phone:** +226 307159, 307020 **Fax:** +226 307242

Non-English Name: Institut du Développement Rural (IDR), Bibliothèque **Former Name:** Superior Institute of Polytechnic **Founded:** 1980 **Type:** Academic **Head:** Mr. Kouradao Issaka *Phone:* +226 332402/4 **Staff:** 100 Prof. 1 Other **Holdings:** 4,500 books 30 journals **Language of Collection/Services:** French/French **Subjects:** Agribusiness, Agriculture (Tropics), Agricultural Development, Agricultural Economics, Agricultural Engineering, Animal Husbandry, Entomology, Farming, Forestry, Horticulture, Plant Pathology, Plants **Loan:** Inhouse **Service:** Internationally **Photocopy:** No

Burma

479   Yangon, Burma
Agriculture Corporation
Documentation Center
72-74 Shwedagon Pagoda Road
Yangon
Networks: AGRIS

Burundi

480   Bujumbura, Burundi
Institut Africain pour le Développement Economique et Social (INADES)
Cellule de Documentation
9, boulevard de l'Uprona
BP 2520
Bujumbura
Phone: +257(2) 22592, 226549 **Fax:** +257(2) 226586

Founded: 1975 **Staff:** 1 Other **Holdings:** 1,300 books 40 journals **Subjects:** Agricultural Development, Agricultural Economics, Agroforestry, Economic Development, Extension, Farm Management, Rural Sociology

481   Bujumbura, Burundi
Ministère de l'Agriculture et de l'Elevage (MINAGRI)
Centre de Documentation
BP 1850
Bujumbura

Former Name: Centre de Documentation de la Planification Agricole, Réseau de Documentation et d'Information Agricole Burundais (REDABU) **Founded:** 1981 **Type:** Government **Head:** Salvatore Sachinguvu *Phone:* +257(2) 25977 **Staff:** 1 Other **Subjects:** Agricultural Economics, Animal Production, Crop Production **Networks:** AGRIS

482   Bujumbura, Burundi
Ministère de l'Agriculture et de l'Elevage, Institut des Sciences Agronomiques du Burundi (MINAGRI, ISABU)
Bibliothèque
BP 795 (Avénue de la Cathédrale)
Bujumbura
Phone: +257(22) 223390 **Fax:** +257(22) 225798 **Email:** isabu@cbinf.com

Founded: 1962 **Type:** Government **Head:** Eng. Omer Nsengiyumva **Staff:** 1 Prof. **Holdings:** 10,000 books 80 journals **Subjects:** Livestock **Loan:** Do not loan **Photocopy:** No

♦**483   Bujumbura, Burundi**
Ministère de l'Education Nationale (MINEDUC)
Centre Universitaire de Recherche pour le Développement Economique et Social (CURDES)
BP 1049
Bujumbura

Founded: 1981 **Type:** Academic **Head:** Marcellin G. Dayer *Phone:* +257(2) 22778 **Holdings:** 145 books 35 journals **Subjects:** Agricultural Development, Agricultural Economics, Rural Sociology

♦**484   Bujumbura, Burundi**
University of Burundi, Agriculture Sciences Faculty
Library
BP 2940
Bujumbura
Phone: +257(2) 24357

Non-English Name: Université du Burundi, Faculté des Sciences Agronomiques, Bibliothèque **Founded:** 1976 **Type:** Academic **Head:** Mr. Venant Bushubije *Phone:* +257(2) 22857 **Staff:** 1 Other **Holdings:** 200 books 600 journals **Subjects:** Agricultural Economics, Biology, Crops, Ecology, Forestry, Plant Protection, Rural Economy, Soil Science, Zootechny **Loan:** In country **Photocopy:** Yes

Cambodia

485   **Phnom Penh, Cambodia**
Cambodia Development Resource Institute
     (CDRI)
Library
56, Street 315, Toul Kok
Phnom Penh
Phone: +855(23) 366094 **Fax:** +855(23) 366094 **Email:**
cdri@camnet.com.kh **WWW:** www.cdri.org.kh

Former Name: Documentation and Information Resource
Center (DIRC) **Founded:** 1992 **Type:** Non-government
Head: Be Kalyanna *Phone:* +855(23) 366094 *Email:* cdri@
camnet.com.kh **Staff:** 2 Prof. **Holdings:** 5,150 books 38
journals **Language of Collection/Services:** English / English, Khmer **Specializations:** Economic Development, Social Development **Loan:** In country **Photocopy:** Yes

486   **Phnom Penh, Cambodia**
Cambodia-IRRI-Australia Project (CIAP)
Library
PO Box 01
Phnom Penh
Location: #14 Moncrete St., Dept. of Agronomy Bldg.
Phone: +855(23) 216465, 616229, 720705 **Fax:** +855(23)
720704 **Email:** irri-cambodia@cgiar.org

Holdings: 1,000 books **Language of Collection/Services:**
English / English, Khmer **Subjects:** Rice **Photocopy:** No

487   **Phnom Penh, Cambodia**
Cambodian Agricultural Research and
     Development Institute (CARDI)
Library
PO Box 1
Phnom Penh

488   **Phnom Penh, Cambodia**
Department of Agronomy
Library
No. 14, Monireth Street, Toul Svay Prey
Phnom Penh
Phone: +855(23) 982831

489   **Phnom Penh, Cambodia**
Department of Animal Health and Production
Library
74, Bld. Monivong
Wath Phnom, Daun Penh
Phnom Penh

490   **Phnom Penh, Cambodia**
Mekong National Committee
Library
No. 23, Bd. Mao Tse Tung
Phnom Penh

491   **Phnom Penh, Cambodia**
Ministry of Agriculture, Forestry and Fisheries
     (MAFF)

Agricultural Scientific Documentation Center
     (ASDC)
200, Norodom Street, Chamcar Mon
PO Box 64
Phnom Penh
Phone: +855(23) 210657 **Fax:** +855(23) 217320 **OPAC:**
www.fao.org

Former Name: Agricultural Information Centre **Founded:**
1966 **Type:** Government **Head:** Sar Visitthara *Phone:* +855
(23) 210657 **Staff:** 12 Prof. 20 Other **Holdings:** 2,000 books
100 journals **Language of Collection/Services:** English
Networks: AGRIS **Databases Used:** Agris; CARIS **Loan:**
Inhouse **Service:** Inhouse **Photocopy:** Yes

492   **Phnom Penh, Cambodia**
Ministry of Environment
Library
48, Bld. Samdech Preah Sihanauk
Phnom Penh

493   **Phnom Penh, Cambodia**
National Library of Cambodia
#92, Phnom Daun Penh Street
Phnom Penh

494   **Phnom Penh, Cambodia**
Royal University of Agriculture
Library
Chamcar Duang, Khan Dangkor
Phnom Penh

495   **Phnom Penh, Cambodia**
School of Agricultural College Prek Leap
Library
R.N. 6A, Khum Prek Leap
Khant Russey Keo
Phnom Penh

Cameroon

♦496   **Buea, Cameroon**
Pan African Institute for Development (PAID)
Library
PO Box 133
Buea, S.W. Province
Fax: +237 322343

Founded: 1969 **Type:** Academic **Head:** Rev. Billy D.M.
Lubansa *Phone:* +237 322186, 322182 **Staff:** 8 Prof. 34
Other **Holdings:** 12,000 books 10 journals **Language of
Collection/Services:** English **Subjects:** Agribusiness, Agri-
cultural Economics, Rural Economy **Loan:** In country **Pho-
tocopy:** Yes

♦497   **Douala, Cameroon**
Pan African Institute for Development (PAID)
Documentation Centre
PO Box 4078
Douala, Province du Littoral
Phone: +237 403068, 403770 **Fax:** +237 424335

Non-English Name: Institut Panafricain pour le Développement, Afrique Centrale Francophone (IPD, AC), Centre de Documentation **Founded:** 1965 **Type:** International **Head:** Ernest Zocli **Staff:** 1 Prof. 3 Other **Holdings:** 10,000 books 100 journals **Language of Collection/Services:** French, English / French **Subjects:** Agribusiness, Agricultural Development, Animal Health, Animal Husbandry, Fisheries, Forestry, Rural Development **Specializations:** Economic Development, Rural Development, Social Development **Loan:** Internationally **Service:** Internationally **Photocopy:** Yes

♦**498** **Dschang, Cameroon**
University of Dschang (UDs)
Central Library
BP 255
Dschang, Menoua

Former Name: University Center of Dschang **Founded:** 1969 **Type:** Academic **Head:** Joseph Elogo *Phone:* +237 451267, 451168 **Staff:** 3 Prof. 12 Other **Holdings:** 25,000 books 200 journals **Language of Collection/Services:** English/English, French **Subjects:** Animal Husbandry, Entomology, Farming, Fisheries, Horticulture, Plant Pathology, Tropical Crops **Specializations:** Agricultural Economics, Agricultural Engineering, Education/Extension, Forestry, Soil Science **Loan:** Inhouse **Service:** Inhouse **Photocopy:** No

499 **Yaoundé, Cameroon**
Chambre d'Agriculture, d'Elevage et des Forêts
du Cameroun
Bibliothèque
BP 287
Yaoundé
Phone: +237 211496

Type: Government **Staff:** 4 Prof. **Subjects:** Agricultural Development, Agriculture (Tropics), Forestry **Loan:** In country **Photocopy:** Yes

♦**500** **Yaoundé, Cameroon**
Institute of Agronomic Research
Library, Documentation and Publications Service
BP 2123, Nkolbisson
Yaoundé

Non-English Name: Institut de la Recherche Agronomique (IRA), Service de la Bibliothèque, de la Documentation et des Publications (SBDP) **Former Name:** Institut de Recherches Agricoles et Forestières **Founded:** 1979 **Type:** Government **Head:** Rose Mongo Ngobo *Phone:* +237 232644 **Staff:** 2 Prof. 2 Other **Holdings:** 5,000 books 40 journals **Language of Collection/Services:** French, English, German, Spanish, Portuguese **Subjects:** Agriculture (Tropics), Agricultural Development, Agricultural Economics, Agricultural Engineering, Biotechnology, Crops, Education/Extension, Entomology, Farming, Food Sciences, Forestry, Plant Pathology, Soil Science, Water Resources **Loan:** In country **Photocopy:** Yes

501 **Yaoundé, Cameroon**
Ministère de la Recherche Scientifique et
Technique, Institut de la Recherche Agricole
pour le Développement (IRAD)
Bibliothèque
PO Box 2123, Nkolbisson
Yaoundé
Phone: +237 223022 **Fax:** +237 225924

Type: Government **Networks:** AGRIS

502 **Yaoundé, Cameroon**
Ministry of Agriculture, Secretary General
Documentation and Records Service
Yaoundé
Fax: +237 225091

Non-English Name: Ministère de l'Agriculture, Secrétariat Général (MINAGRI, SG), Service de la Documentation et des Archives **Former Name:** Direction des Etudes et Projets **Founded:** 1986 **Type:** Government **Head:** Victor Ndongo Eteme *Phone:* +237 223541 **Staff:** 4 Prof. 9 Other **Holdings:** 5,000 books 10 journals **Language of Collection/Services:** French / French **Subjects:** Agricultural Economics, Animal Production, Crop Production, Development Policy, Rural Sociology **Specializations:** Agribusiness, Agricultural Development, Agricultural Engineering, Agricultural Statistics, Animal Husbandry, Fisheries **Databases Developed:** Redicam - database on scientific and technical agricultural information **Databases Used:** Agricola; Agris; CABCD **Loan:** Inhouse **Service:** Inhouse **Photocopy:** Yes

503 **Yaoundé, Cameroon**
Research Institute for Development
Fond Documentaire
BP 1857
Yaoundé
Phone: +237 201508 **Fax:** +237 201854 **Email:** orstyde@ ird.uninet.cm **WWW:** www.ird.fr

Non-English Name: Institut de Recherche pour le Développement (IRD) **Former Name:** Institut Français de Recherche Scientifique pour le Développement en Coopération (ORSTOM) **Founded:** 1947 **Type:** Government **Head:** Jacques Bonvallot *Phone:* +237 201508 **Staff:** 1 Prof. 1 Other **Holdings:** 1,800 books **Language of Collection/Services:** French / French **Subjects:** Animal Production, Plant Pathology, Plant Protection, Water Resources **Loan:** Do not loan **Photocopy:** Yes

504 **Yaoundé, Cameroon**
United Nations Educational, Scientific and
Cultural Organization (Unesco)
Documentation Centre
PO Box 12909
Yaoundé
Phone: +237 229930 **Fax:** +237 226389

Type: International **Head:** Rosaline Njike Nyanjou *Phone:* +237 225763 *Email:* r.njike@unesco.org **Subjects:** Environmental Sciences, Forestry, Water Resources **Specializations:** Communications, Education

505 Yaoundé, Cameroon
Université de Yaoundé II, Institut de Formation et
      de Recherche Démographiques (IFORD)
Centre de Documentation
BP 1556
Yaoundé
Phone: +237 222471 **Fax:** +237 226793

Founded: 1972 **Type:** International **Head:** Albert D. Teko
Phone: +237 222471 **Staff:** 1 Prof. 1 Other **Holdings:**
16,000 books 40 journals **Language of Collection/Services:**
French, English / French, English **Subjects:** Agricultural
Development **Loan:** In country **Photocopy:** Yes

Canada

Alberta

506 Cochrane, Alberta, Canada
Western Heritage Centre
Bert Sheppard Stockmen's Foundation Library
      and Archives
PO Box 1477
Cochrane, Alberta T0L 0W0
Location: 105 River Avenue **Phone:** +1(403) 932-3514
Fax: +1(403) 932-3515 **Email:** whcs@whcs.ab.ca **WWW:**
whcs.ab.ca/Library.html

Founded: 1980 **Type:** Research **Staff:** 1 Other **Holdings:**
4,000 books 25 journals **Language of Collection/Services:**
English / English **Subjects:** Ranching **Loan:** Do not loan
Service: Internationally **Photocopy:** Yes

507 Edmonton, Alberta, Canada
Alberta Agriculture, Food and Rural Development
Library
J.G. O'Donoghue Building
7000 - 113 Street
Edmonton, Alberta T6H 5T6
Phone: +1(403) 427-2104 **Fax:** +1(403) 422-2484 **Email:**
library@agric.gov.ab.ca **WWW:** www.agric.gov.ab.ca
OPAC: gate.library.ualberta.ca

Founded: 1972 **Type:** Government **Head:** Robert Bateman
Phone: +1(403) 422-7689 *Email:* rob.bateman@agric.gov.
ab.ca **Staff:** 4 Prof. 4 Other **Holdings:** 30,000 books 1,200
journals **Language of Collection/Services:** English/English
Subjects: Agribusiness, Agricultural Economics, Agricultural Engineering, Animal Husbandry, Crops, Education/
Extension, Entomology, Farming, Food Sciences, Horticulture, Plant Pathology, Plants, Soil Science, Veterinary Medicine **Networks:** NEOS **Databases Developed:** Agdex -
12,000 pamphlets and other documents on PC database
Databases Used: Agricola; CABCD **Loan:** Internationally
Service: Inhouse **Photocopy:** Yes

508 Edmonton, Alberta, Canada
Alberta Environment
Library
6th Floor, 9920 - 108th Street
Edmonton, Alberta T5K 2M4

Phone: +1(780) 427-5870 **Fax:** +1(780) 422-0170 **Email:**
env.library@gov.ab.ca **WWW:** www.gov.ab.ca/env
OPAC: www.library.ualberta.ca/library_html/gate.html

Former Name: Alberta Department of the Environment, Alberta Environmental Protection **Founded:** 1971 **Type:** Government **Head:** Lucy Chang *Phone:* +1(780) 427-6132
Email: lucy.chang@gov.ab.ca **Holdings:** 45,000 books 600
journals **Language of Collection/Services:** English/English
Subjects: Fisheries, Forestry, Soil Science, Water Resources
Photocopy: Yes

509 Edmonton, Alberta, Canada
Environment Canada, Prairie and Northern Region
Edmonton Library
4999 - 98 Avenue, Room 200
Edmonton, Alberta T6B 2X3
Phone: +1(780) 951-8818 **Fax:** +1(+1(780) 951-8819
Email: terri.fraser@ec.gc.ca **WWW:** www.mb.ec.gc.ca
OPAC: www.andornot.com/envcan

Head: Gerri (Teresa) Fraser *Email:* terri.fraser@ec.gc.ca
Subjects: Biodiversity, Climate, Environmental Assessment, Environmental Impact, Environmental Sciences, Pollution, Wildlife Management

510 Edmonton, Alberta, Canada
Natural Resources Canada, Canadian Forest
      Service, Northern Forestry Centre
Library
5320 122nd Street
Edmonton, Alberta T6H 3S5
Fax: +1(403) 435-7356/9

Former Name: Forestry Canada **Founded:** 1948 **Type:**
Government **Head:** Edith M. Hopp *Phone:* +1(403) 435-
7323/4 *Email:* ehopp@nrcan.gc.ca **Staff:** 1 Prof. 1 Other
Language of Collection/Services: English / English **Subjects:** Climatic Change, Entomology, Fires, Forest Economics, Forestry, Forest Fires, Plant Pathology, Social Forestry,
Soil Science **Databases Used:** Comprehensive **Loan:** Internationally **Photocopy:** Yes

511 Edmonton, Alberta, Canada
University of Alberta
Rural Economy Library
504 General Services Building
Edmonton, Alberta T6G 2H1
Fax: +1(403) 492-0268 **WWW:** www.ualberta.ca

Founded: 1970 **Type:** Academic **Head:** Dawn Zrobok
Phone: +1(403) 492-0815 **Staff:** 1 Prof. **Holdings:** 18,000
books 230 journals **Language of Collection/Services:** English / English **Subjects:** Agribusiness, Agricultural Economics, Agricultural Policy, Agricultural Trade, Agroforestry,
Economics, Farm Management, Forest Economics, Natural
Resource Economics, Rural Sociology **Loan:** Inhouse **Photocopy:** Yes

512 Edmonton, Alberta, Canada
University of Alberta
Science and Technology Library
Edmonton, Alberta T6G 2J8

Phone: +1(403) 492-7912 **Fax:** +1(403) 492-2721 **Email:** sciref.library@ualberta.ca **WWW:** www.ualberta.ca **OPAC:** www.library.ualberta.ca

Founded: 1963 **Type:** Academic **Head:** Margaret Law *Phone:* +1(403) 492-7918 *Email:* margaret.law@ualberta.ca **Staff:** 7 Prof. 25 Other **Holdings:** 400,000 books 4,500 journals **Language of Collection/Services:** English / English **Subjects:** Agribusiness, Agricultural Economics, Forestry **Specializations:** Entomology **Databases Used:** Comprehensive **Loan:** Internationally **Photocopy:** Yes

513   Fairview, Alberta, Canada
Fairview College
Learner Services Centre
Box 3000
Fairview, Alberta T0H 1L0
Location: 11255 - 99th Avenue **Phone:** +1(403) 835-6641 **Fax:** +1(403) 835-6782

Former Name: Learning Resource Centre **Founded:** 1951 **Type:** Academic **Head:** Anita Luck *Phone:* +1(403) 835-6750 *Email:* aluck@fairviewc.ab.ca **Staff:** 1 Prof. 5 Other **Holdings:** 60,000 books 400 journals **Language of Collection/Services:** English/English **Subjects:** Agribusiness, Agricultural Engineering, Agricultural Financial Policy, Beef Production, Animal Health, Beekeepers, Crop Production, Equidae, Fertilizers, Lawns and Turf, Livestock, Pesticides, Veterinary Science **Loan:** In country **Service:** In country **Photocopy:** Yes

514   Lacombe, Alberta, Canada
Agriculture and Agri-Food Canada, Lacombe
    Research Centre
Library
6000 C & E Trail
Lacombe, Alberta T4L 1W1
Phone: +1(403) 782-3316 **Fax:** +1(403) 782-6120 **WWW:** res.agr.ca/lacombe/mainnew.htm

Former Name: Agriculture Canada **Founded:** 1983 **Type:** Government **Head:** Shelley M. Pirnak *Phone:* +1(403) 782-8136 *Email:* pirnaks@em.agr.ca **Staff:** .5 Prof. .2 Other **Holdings:** 5,000 books 100 journals **Language of Collection/Services:** English / English **Subjects:** Fodder Crops, Meat Quality, Soil Science **Databases Used:** Agricola; CABCD; FSTA **Loan:** Internationally **Photocopy:** Yes

515   Leduc, Alberta, Canada
Alberta Agriculture, Food and Rural Development
Food Processing Development Centre
6309 45th Street
Leduc, Alberta T9E 7C5
Phone: +1(780) 980-4866 **Fax:** +1(780) 986-5138 **WWW:** www.agric.gov.ab.ca/ministry/org/fpdc/index.html

Former Name: Alberta Agriculture **Founded:** 1985 **Type:** Government **Staff:** 12 Prof. **Holdings:** 250 books 22 journals **Language of Collection/Services:** English / English **Subjects:** Food Sciences **Loan:** In country **Photocopy:** Yes

516   Lethbridge, Alberta, Canada
Agriculture and Agri-Food Canada, Lethbridge
    Research Centre (AAFC, LRC)
Library
PO Box 3000
Lethbridge, Alberta T1J 4B1
Location: 5403 1st Avenue South **Phone:** +1(403) 327-4561 **Fax:** +1(403) 382-3156 **Email:** lrclibrary@em.agr.ca **WWW:** res.agr.ca/leth/index.htm

Former Name: Agriculture Canada **Founded:** 1950 **Type:** Government **Head:** Cheryl Ronning Mains *Phone:* +1(403) 327-4561 ext 310 *Email:* ronningmains@em.agr.ca **Staff:** 1 Prof. 2 Other **Holdings:** 20,000 books 375 journals **Language of Collection/Services:** English / English **Subjects:** Animal Husbandry, Crops, Drainage, Entomology, Farming, Irrigation, Plant Pathology, Soil Science, Water Resources **Databases Used:** Agricola; CABCD; Current Contents **Loan:** Internationally **Photocopy:** Yes

517   Lethbridge, Alberta, Canada
Lethbridge Community College (LCC)
Buchanan Library
3000 College Drive South
Lethbridge, Alberta T1K 1L6
Phone: +1(403) 320-3355 **Fax:** +1(403) 320-1461 **WWW:** www.lethbridgeC.ab.ca/%7Elibrary

Founded: 1957 **Type:** Academic **Head:** Kathy Lea *Phone:* +1(403) 320-3356 *Email:* lea@lethbridgec.ab.ca **Staff:** 3 Prof. 20 Other **Holdings:** 70,000 books 520 journals **Language of Collection/Services:** English / English **Subjects:** Animal Diseases, Crops, Farm Management, Plant Diseases, Veterinary Science **Loan:** In country **Service:** Internationally **Photocopy:** Yes

518   Olds, Alberta, Canada
Olds College
Library
4500 50 Street
Olds, Alberta T4H 1R6
Phone: +1(403) 556-4600 **Fax:** +1(403) 556-4705 **WWW:** www.oldscollege.ab.ca

Founded: 1913 **Type:** Academic **Head:** Barbara J.E. Smith *Phone:* +1(403) 556-4602 *Email:* barb.smith@oldscollege.ab.ca **Staff:** 1 Prof. 6 Other **Holdings:** 39,000 books 275 journals **Language of Collection/Services:** English/English **Subjects:** Crops **Databases Used:** Comprehensive **Loan:** In country **Photocopy:** Yes

519   Vegreville, Alberta, Canada
Alberta Research Council - Vegreville
Library and Information Center
Bag 4000
Vegreville, Alberta T9C 1T4
Location: 75 Street **Fax:** +1(403) 632-8300 **Email:** library@aec.arc.ab.ca **WWW:** www.arc.ab.ca **OPAC:** gate.library.ualberta.ca

Former Name: Alberta Environmental Centre **Founded:** 1980 **Type:** Government **Head:** Fabian Harrison *Phone:* +1(403) 632-8415 *Email:* fabian@aec.arc.ab.ca **Staff:** 1 Prof. 1.5 Other **Holdings:** 14,000 books 200 journals **Language of Collection/Services:** English / English **Subjects:** Agriculture (Tropics), Biotechnology, Crops, Education/Extension, Entomology, Forestry, Soil Science, Water Resources **Specializations:** Plant Pathology, Reclamation, Toxicology, Veterinary Science, Weed Competition, Weed Control **Databases Used:** Comprehensive **Loan:** In country **Service:** Inhouse **Photocopy:** Yes

520 **Vermilion, Alberta, Canada**
Lakeland College
Library
Alumni Hall Building
4707 - 47th Avenue West
Vermilion, Alberta T9H 1K5
Phone: +1(780) 853-8463 **Fax:** +1(780) 853-8662 **WWW:** www.lakelandc.ab.ca

Subjects: Agribusiness, Agricultural Economics, Animal Health, Aquaculture, Environmental Sciences, Reclamation, Soil Science

British Columbia

521 **Agassiz, British Columbia, Canada**
Agriculture and Agri-Food Canada, Pacific
Agriculture Research Centre (Agassiz)
(AAFC)
Library
PO Box 1000
Agassiz, British Columbia V0M 1A0
Location: 6947 No. 7 Highway **Phone:** +1(250) 796-2221 ext 250 **Fax:** +1(250) 796-0359 **Email:** parc@em.agr.ca **WWW:** res.agr.ca/agassiz/index.htm

Former Name: Agriculture Canada **Founded:** 1977 **Type:** Government **Head:** D. Lynne Stack Boyd *Phone:* +1(250) 796-2221 *Email:* boydl@em.agr.ca **Staff:** .5 Prof. **Holdings:** 5,000 books 60 journals **Language of Collection/Services:** English / English **Subjects:** Animal Nutrition, Plant Physiology, Postharvest Physiology, Soil Science, Vegetables **Service:** Inhouse **Photocopy:** Yes

522 **Bamfield, British Columbia, Canada**
Western Canadian Universities, Marine Biological
Society, Bamfield Marine Station (BMS)
Devonian Library
Bamfield, British Columbia V0R 1B0
Phone: +1(250) 728-3301 **Fax:** +1(250) 728-3452 **WWW:** www.bms.bc.ca

Type: Academic **Head:** Leslie Rimmer *Phone:* +1(250) 728-3301 *Email:* lrimmer@bms.bc.ca **Staff:** 1 Prof. **Holdings:** 10,000 books 53 journals **Language of Collection/Services:** English/English **Subjects:** Aquaculture, Fisheries, Marine Biology **Databases Developed:** Reprint collection of 11,000 **Loan:** Inhouse **Service:** Inhouse **Photocopy:** Yes

523 **Burnaby, British Columbia, Canada**
Simon Fraser University (SFU)
WAC Bennett Library
8888 University Drive
Burnaby, British Columbia V5A 1S6
Phone: +1(604) 291-3265 **Fax:** +1(604) 291-3023 **Email:** libask@sfu.ca **WWW:** www.sfu.ca **OPAC:** www.lib.sfu.ca

Type: Academic **Head:** Lynn Copeland *Phone:* +1(604) 291-5861 *Email:* copeland@sfu.ca **Staff:** 30 Prof. 100 Other **Holdings:** 1,000,000 books 13,000 journals **Language of Collection/Services:** English / English **Subjects:** Insect Pests **Databases Used:** Agricola; Biosis; CARL UnCover **Service:** Inhouse **Loan:** Internationally **Photocopy:** Yes

524 **Delta, British Columbia, Canada**
Environment Canada, Pacific and Yukon Region,
Canadian Wildlife Service
Library
PO Box 340
Delta, British Columbia V4K 373
WWW: www.pyr.ec.gc.ca **OPAC:** www.andornot.com/envcan

525 **Kamloops, British Columbia, Canada**
Agriculture and Agri-Food Canada, Kamloops
Range Research Ranch (AAFC)
Research Station Library
3015 Ord Road
Kamloops, British Columbia V2B 8A9
Fax: +1(250) 554-5229 **WWW:** www.agr.ca

Type: Government **Head:** Dr. D. Veira *Phone:* +1(250) 554-5200 **Holdings:** 1,000 books 20 journals **Language of Collection/Services:** English / English **Subjects:** Botany, Ecology, Plants, Range Management, Soil Science **Loan:** Do not loan **Service:** Inhouse **Photocopy:** Yes

526 **Nanaimo, British Columbia, Canada**
Fisheries and Oceans Canada, Pacific Biological
Station (PBS)
Library
3190 Hammond Bay Road
Nanaimo, British Columbia V9R 5K6
Phone: +1(250) 756-7071 **Fax:** +1(250) 756-7053 **Email:** paclibrarypbs@dfo-mpo.gc.ca **WWW:** www.pac.dfo-mpo.gc.ca/sci/pbs

Former Name: Department of Fisheries and Oceans **Founded:** 1911 **Type:** Government **Head:** G. Miller *Phone:* +1(250) 756-7071 *Email:* millergo@dfo-mpo.gc.ca **Staff:** 2 Prof. **Holdings:** 100,000 books 4,000 journals **Language of Collection/Services:** English / English **Subjects:** Fish Culture, Fisheries **Loan:** Internationally **Service:** Internationally **Photocopy:** Yes

527 **North Vancouver, British Columbia, Canada**
Environment Canada, Pacific and Yukon Region
North Vancouver Library
224 West Esplanade
North Vancouver, British Columbia V7M 3H7
Phone: +1(604) 666-5914 **Fax:** +1(604) 666-1788 **Email:** nvan.library@ec.gc.ca **WWW:** www.pyr.ec.gc.ca **OPAC:** www.andornot.com/envcan

Head: Andrew Fabro **Subjects:** Air Quality, Conservation, Climate, Environmental Assessment, Environmental Impact, Environmental Protection, Natural Resources Management, Pollution, Water Resources, Wildlife Management

528   Summerland, British Columbia, Canada
Agriculture and Agri-Food Canada, Pacific
   Agriculture Research Centre (Summerland)
   (AAFC, PARC (Summerland))
Library (BSUAG)
Highway 97
Summerland, British Columbia V0H 1Z0
Phone: +1(250) 494-7711 ext 7312 **Fax:** +1(250) 494-
0755 **WWW:** res.agr.ca/summer/parc.htm

Former Name: Agriculture Canada **Founded:** 1951 **Type:**
Government **Head:** Margaret Watson *Phone:* +1(250) 494-
7711 *Email:* watsonp@em.agr.ca **Staff:** 1 Prof. **Holdings:**
7,000 books **Language of Collection/Services:** English /
English **Subjects:** Biotechnology, Entomology, Food Pro-
cessing, Fruits, Plant Pathology **Networks:** AGRICAT
Databases Developed: Station papers index **Databases
Used:** Agricola; CABCD **Loan:** Internationally **Photocopy:**
Yes

529   Vancouver, British Columbia, Canada
B. C. Research Inc. (BCRI)
Library
3650 Wesbrook Mall
Vancouver, British Columbia V6S 2L2
Fax: +1(604) 224-0540 **WWW:** www.bcr.bc.ca

Former Name: British Columbia Research Council **Founded:** 1946 **Type:** Business **Head:** Nancy Glass *Phone:* +1
(604) 224-4331 *Email:* nglass@bcr.bc.ca **Staff:** 1 Prof.
Holdings: 17,000 books 40 journals **Language of Collec-
tion/Services:** English **Subjects:** Biotechnology, Forestry,
Plant Pathology, Soil Science **Databases Developed:** NGV
Database - includes all types of literature for alternative fuels
for all transportation **Databases Used:** Comprehensive
Loan: Inhouse **Service:** Internationally **Photocopy:** Yes

530   Vancouver, British Columbia, Canada
Environment Canada, Pacific and Yukon Region,
   Atmospheric Environment Service
Library
700-1200 West 73rd Avenue
Vancouver, British Columbia V6P 6H9
Fax: +1(604) 666-1788 **Email:** nvan.library@ec.gc.ca
WWW: www.pyr.ec.gc.ca **OPAC:** www.andornot.com/
envcan

Non-English Name: Environnement Canada, Service de
l'Environnement Atmosphérique, Bibliothèque

531   Vancouver, British Columbia, Canada
Fisheries and Oceans Canada
Fisheries Library
555 West Hastings Street
Vancouver, British Columbia V6B 5G3
Fax: +1(604) 666-3145 **WWW:** www.pac.dfo-mpo.gc.ca

Non-English Name: Pêches et Océans Canada **Founded:**
1962 **Type:** Government **Head:** Marcia Croy Vanwely
Phone: +1(604) 666-3851 **Staff:** 1 Prof. **Holdings:** 6,765
books 35 journals **Language of Collection/Services:** English **Subjects:** Fisheries **Databases Developed:** WAVES -
Fisheries and Loceans Libraries database available on

CD-ROM **Databases Used:** Biosis **Loan:** In country **Service:** Inhouse **Photocopy:** Yes

532   Vancouver, British Columbia, Canada
University of British Columbia
Macmillan (Forestry/Agriculture) Library
2357 Main Mall
Vancouver, British Columbia V6T 1Z4
Phone: +1(604) 822-6333 **Fax:** +1(604) 822-9544 **Email:**
mcmlib@unixg.ubc.ca **OPAC:** www.library.ubc.ca/cgi-
bin/ubc-cat.cgi **WWW:** www.library.ubc.ca/macmillan

Founded: 1967 **Type:** Academic **Head:** Lee Ann Bryant
Phone: +1(604) 822-3609 *Email:* lbryant@interchange.
ubc.ca **Staff:** 1.5 Prof. 4 Other **Holdings:** 56,000 books
1,300 journals **Language of Collection/Services:** English /
English **Subjects:** Agricultural Engineering, Animal Bio-
technology, Animal Husbandry, Crops, Forest Management,
Forestry, Horticulture, Plant Biotechnology, Range Manage-
ment, Soil Science, Wood **Networks:** OCLC **Databases
Used:** Agricola; Agris; CABCD **Loan:** In country and
United States **Photocopy:** No

533   Vancouver, British Columbia, Canada
University of British Columbia, Botanical Garden
Library
6804 Southwest Marine Drive
Vancouver, British Columbia V6T 1Z4
Fax: +1(604) 822-2016 **WWW:** www.hedgerows.com/
UBCBotGdn/index.htm

Founded: 1911 **Type:** Academic **Head:** Judy Newton
Phone: +1(604) 822-4372 **Staff:** 5 Other **Holdings:** 1,500
books 20 journals **Subjects:** Horticulture, Ornamental Plants
Loan: Do not loan **Photocopy:** Yes

534   Vancouver, British Columbia, Canada
University of British Columbia, Spencer
   Entomological Museum (BCSM)
Library
Department of Zoology
Vancouver, British Columbia V6T 1Z4
Fax: +1(604) 822-2416 **WWW:** www.insecta.com

Founded: 1953 **Type:** Academic **Head:** G.G.E. Scudder
Phone: +1(604) 822-3379 *Email:* scudder@zoology.ubc.ca
Staff: 1 Prof. **Holdings:** 8,350 books 50 journals **Language
of Collection/Services:** English/English **Subjects:** Ento-
mology **Loan:** Inhouse **Service:** Internationally **Photocopy:**
No

535   Vancouver, British Columbia, Canada
VanDusen Botanical Gardens Association
   (VBGA)
VanDusen Gardens Library
5251 Oak Street
Vancouver, British Columbia V6M 4H1
Phone: +1(604) 257-8668 **Fax:** +1(604) 266-4236

Former Name: Vancouver Botanical Gardens Association
Founded: 1977 **Type:** Association **Head:** Mrs. Barbara Fox
Phone: +1(604) 257-8668 **Staff:** 1 Prof. **Holdings:** 4,500
books 50 journals **Language of Collection/Services:** Eng-

lish / English **Subjects:** Botany, Horticulture **Loan:** Inhouse **Service:** Inhouse **Photocopy:** Yes

536   **Victoria, British Columbia, Canada**
British Columbia Ministry of Environment, Lands and Parks
Library
PO Box 9348
Stn Prov Govt
Victoria, British Columbia V8W 9M1

Location: 1st Floor, 2975 Jutland Road **Phone:** +1(250) 387-9747 **Fax:** +1(250) 387-9741 **Email:** elplibrary@ victoria1.gov.bc.ca **WWW:** elplibrary.gov.bc.ca

Type: Government **Subjects:** Environment, Fisheries, Forestry, Water Resources, Wildlife **Databases Used:** Comprehensive **Loan:** Inhouse **Service:** Inhouse

537   **Victoria, British Columbia, Canada**
British Columbia Ministry of Forests
Library
PO Box 9523 Stn Prov Gov
Victoria, British Columbia V8W 9C2

Location: 722 Johnson St., 4th Floor **Phone:** +1(250) 387-3628 **Fax:** +1(250) 953-3079 **Email:** forests.library@ gems4.gov.bc.ca **OPAC:** www.library.for.gov.bc.ca **WWW:** www.for.gov.bc.ca/hfd/library/ index.htm

Type: Government **Head:** Roxanne Smith *Phone:* +1(250) 387-6788 **Subjects:** Forestry

538   **Victoria, British Columbia, Canada**
Natural Resources Canada, Canadian Forest Service, Pacific Forestry Centre (NRC, CFS, PFC)
Library
506 West Burnside Road
Victoria, British Columbia V8Z 1M5

Phone: +1(250)363-0680 **Fax:** +1(250)363-0775 **Email:** asolyma@pfc.forestry.ca **WWW:** www.pfc.forestry.ca **Ariel IP:** 207.23.4.17 or 207.23.5.147

Former Name: Forestry Canada - Pacific and Yukon Region **Founded:** 1960 **Type:** Research **Head:** Alice Solyma *Phone:* +1(250) 363-0680 *Email:* asolyma@pfc.forestry.ca **Staff:** 1 Prof. 1.2 Other **Holdings:** 125,000 books 330 journals **Language of Collection/Services:** English / English, French **Subjects:** Diversity, Economics, Forest Fires, Forest Health, Forestry, Geographic Information Systems, Hydrobiology, Landscape Management, Soil Science, Sustainability **Specializations:** Entomology, Forest Pathology, Remote Sensing **Networks:** CFS **Databases Used:** Comprehensive **Loan:** Internationally **Service:** Internationally **Photocopy:** Yes

539   **Victoria, British Columbia, Canada**
University of Victoria (UVic)
McPherson Library
PO Box 1800
Victoria, British Columbia V8W 3H5

Location: Concourse of Finnerty, MacKenzie and Sinclair Roads **Phone:** +1(250) 721-8274 **Fax:** +1(250) 721-8215

WWW: uvic.ca **OPAC:** gateway.uvic.ca **Ariel IP:** 142. 104.36.81

Founded: 1902 **Type:** Academic **Head:** Marnie Swanson *Phone:* +1(250) 721-8211 *Email:* mswanson@uvic.ca **Staff:** 39 Prof. 127 Other **Holdings:** 12,000 books 75 journals **Language of Collection/Services:** English / English **Subjects:** Conservation, Fisheries, Forestry, Soil Science **Networks:** OCLC **Databases Used:** Comprehensive **Loan:** Internationally **Service:** Internationally **Photocopy:** Yes

Manitoba

540   **Brandon, Manitoba, Canada**
Agriculture and Agri-Food Canada, Brandon Research Centre (AAFC, BRC)
Library and Information Centre
PO Box 1000A, R.R. #3
Brandon, Manitoba R7A 5Y3

Location: 18th Street North and Grand Valley Road **Phone:** +1(204) 726-7650 **Fax:** +1(204) 728-3858 **Email:** brc-admin@em.agr.ca **WWW:** res.agr.ca/brandon/brc/ welcome.htm

Former Name: Agriculture Canada, Brandon Experimental Farm **Founded:** 1910 **Type:** Government **Head:** Carol Enns *Phone:* +1(204) 726-7650 *Email:* cenns@em.agr.ca **Staff:** 1 Prof. .25 Other **Holdings:** 70,002,900 books 50 journals **Language of Collection/Services:** English / English **Subjects:** Barley, Beef Cattle, Beef Production, Land Management, Land Resources, Plant Breeding **Specializations:** Agronomy, Crops, Plant Ecology, Plant Pathology, Plants, Soil **Databases Developed:** Scientists' reprints, technology transfer documents and AAFC pamphlets **Databases Used:** Comprehensive **Loan:** Internationally **Service:** Fee for service **Photocopy:** Yes

541   **Brandon, Manitoba, Canada**
Brandon University
John E. Robbins Library
Brandon, Manitoba R7A 6A9

Phone: +1(204) 727-7483 **Email:** kazakoff@brandonu.ca **WWW:** www.brandonu.ca **OPAC:** www.brandonu.ca/ library

Founded: 1899 **Type:** Academic **Head:** Mr. Terry Mitchell *Phone:* +1(204) 727-9642 *Email:* mitchell@brandonu.ca **Staff:** 4.5 Prof. 28 Other **Holdings:** 1,400 books 40 journals **Subjects:** Horticulture **Loan:** Internationally **Photocopy:** Yes

542   **Portage la Prairie, Manitoba, Canada**
Food Development Centre (FDC)
Library
810 Phillips Street
PO Box 1240
Portage la Prairie, Manitoba R1N 3J9

Fax: +1(204) 239-3180 **WWW:** www.fdc.mb.ca

Former Name: Economic Innovation and Technology Council, National Agri-Food Technology Centre, Manitoba Research Council, Canadian Food Products Development Centre **Founded:** 1980 **Type:** Business **Head:** Linda Petriuk

Phone: +1(204) 239-3162 *Email:* lpetriuk@fdc.mb.ca **Staff:** 1 Prof. **Holdings:** 2,500 books 250 journals **Language of Collection/Services:** English / English **Subjects:** Agribusiness, Food Sciences **Specializations:** Analytical Chemistry, Food Processing, Microbiology **Databases Used:** FSTA **Loan:** Inhouse **Service:** Internationally **Photocopy:** Yes

543   Winnipeg, Manitoba, Canada
         Agriculture and Agri-Food Canada, Cereal
             Research Centre
         Library
         195 Dafoe Road
         Winnipeg, Manitoba R3T 2M9
Location: Research Station **Fax:** +1(204) 983-4604 **WWW:** res.agr.ca/winn/welcomee.htm

Former Name: Agriculture Canada, Winnipeg Research Centre **Founded:** 1926 **Type:** Government **Head:** Mike Malyk *Phone:* +1(204) 983-0721 *Email:* mmalyk@em.agr.ca **Staff:** 2 Prof. 1 Other **Holdings:** 15,000 books 400 journals **Subjects:** Biotechnology, Entomology, Pest Control, Plant Breeding, Plant Pathology, Stored Products **Loan:** Internationally **Photocopy:** Yes

544   Winnipeg, Manitoba, Canada
         Brewing and Malting Barley Research Institute
             (BMBRI)
         Library
         206 - 167 Lombard Avenue
         Winnipeg, Manitoba R3B 0T6
Phone: +1(204) 947-1407 **Fax:** +1(204) 947-5960

Type: Business **Head:** Dr. N.T. Kendall **Staff:** 3 Prof. 1 Other **Language of Collection/Services:** English **Subjects:** Barley, Brewing **Loan:** Do not loan **Photocopy:** No

545   Winnipeg, Manitoba, Canada
         Canadian Grain Commission (CGC)
         Library
         303 Main Street, Room 300
         Winnipeg, Manitoba R3C 3G8
Phone: +1(204) 983-0878 **Fax:** +1(204) 983-6098 **Email:** library@cgc.ca **WWW:** www.cgc.ca

Non-English Name: Commission Canadienne des Grains (CCG), Bibliothèque **Founded:** 1973 **Type:** Government **Head:** Elva Simundsson *Phone:* +1(204) 983-0878 *Email:* esimundsson@cgc.ca **Staff:** 1 Prof. 1 Other **Holdings:** 400 journals 10,000 books **Language of Collection/Services:** English, French, Italian, German, Japanese / English **Subjects:** Baking, Biochemistry, Cereals, Grain Crops, Milling, Oilseeds, Pesticide Residues, Processing, Transport **Specializations:** Cereal Products, Grain Quality, Grain Crops (Canada - Statistics) **Networks:** AGRICAT **Databases Used:** Comprehensive **Loan:** In country **Photocopy:** Yes

546   Winnipeg, Manitoba, Canada
         Canadian Wheat Board (CWB)
         Library
         Box 816, Station MMain
         Winnipeg, Manitoba R3C 2P5

Location: 423 Main Street **Phone:** +1(204) 983-3437 **Fax:** +1(204) 983-4031 **Email:** library@cwb.ca **WWW:** www.cwb.ca

Founded: 1981 **Type:** Government **Head:** Ruth Reedman *Phone:* +1(204) 983-3437 *Email:* ruth_reedman@cwb.ca **Staff:** 1 Prof. 3 Other **Holdings:** 6,000 books 1,100 journals **Language of Collection/Services:** English / English **Subjects:** Agricultural Economics, Agricultural Trade, Feed Grains, Food Grains, Wheat **Databases Used:** Comprehensive **Loan:** Internationally **Service:** Internationally **Photocopy:** Yes

547   Winnipeg, Manitoba, Canada
         Fisheries and Oceans Canada, Freshwater
             Institute, Central and Arctic Region
         Eric Marshall Aquatic Research Library
         501 University Crescent
         Winnipeg, Manitoba R3T 2N6
Phone: +1(204) 983-5170 **Fax:** +1(204) 984-4668 **Email:** library-fwi@dfo-mpo.gc.ca **WWW:** www.dfo-mpo.gc.ca/Regions/central/ca-e.htm **OPAC:** inter01.dfo-mpo.gc.ca/wavesdocs/en

Former Name: Department of Fisheries and Oceans (DFO) **Founded:** 1966 **Type:** Government **Head:** Elva Simundsson *Email:* simundssone@dfo-mpo.gc.ca **Staff:** 2 Prof. 1 Other **Holdings:** 19,000 books 400 journals **Language of Collection/Services:** English **Subjects:** Aquaculture, Entomology, Fisheries **Loan:** Internationally **Photocopy:** Yes

548   Winnipeg, Manitoba, Canada
         Manitoba Conservation
         Environment Library
         123 Main Street, Suite 160
         Winnipeg, Manitoba R3C 1A5
Phone: +1(204) 945-7125/6 **Fax:** +1(204) 948-2357 **WWW:** www.gov.mb.ca/environ/pages/library.html **OPAC:** www.andornot.com/envcat

Head: Shelley Penziwol *Email:* spenziwol@gov.mb.ca **Staff:** 1 Prof. 2 Other **Subjects:** Climate, Environment, Hydrology, Meteorology, Pollution, Wildlife Management

549   Winnipeg, Manitoba, Canada
         University of Manitoba
         University of Manitoba Libraries, Sciences and
             Technology Library
         Winnipeg, Manitoba R3T 2N2
Phone: +1(204 474-9281 **Fax:** +1(204) 474-7627 **Email:** libsc2@cc.umanitoba.ca **WWW:** www.umanitoba.ca **OPAC:** bison.umanitoba.ca

Founded: 1906 **Type:** Academic **Head:** Judith A. Harper, Director; Karen Clay, Agricultural Specialist *Phone:* +1 (204) 474-8302 *Email:* judy_harper@umanitoba.ca; karen_clay@umanitoba.ca **Staff:** 1 Prof. **Holdings:** 21,000 books 280 journals **Language of Collection/Services:** English / English **Subjects:** Agricultural Economics, Animal Husbandry, Crops, Entomology, Farming, Food Sciences, Horticulture, Plant Pathology, Plants, Soil Science **Databases Used:** Agricola; CABCD **Loan:** Internationally **Service:** Internationally **Photocopy:** Yes

New Brunswick

550   **Fredericton, New Brunswick, Canada**
Agriculture and Agri-Food Canada, Potato Research Centre (AAFC, PRC)
Library
Box 20280
Fredericton, New Brunswick E3B 4Z7
Location: 850 Lincoln Road **Phone:** +1(506) 452-4810
Fax: +1(506) 452-3316 **Email:** andersonrm@em.agr.ca
WWW: res.agr.ca/fred/home/index.htm

Former Name: Agriculture Canada **Founded:** 1952 **Type:** Government **Head:** Richard Anderson *Phone:* +1(506) 452-4810 *Email:* andersonrm@em.agr.ca **Staff:** 1 Prof. **Holdings:** 5,000 books 100 journals **Language of Collection/Services:** English / English **Subjects:** Cattle, Potatoes **Databases Used:** Agricola; CABCD **Loan:** In country **Service:** In country **Photocopy:** Yes

551   **Fredericton, New Brunswick, Canada**
University of New Brunswick (UNB)
Science and Forestry Library
8 Bailey Drive
Fredericton, New Brunswick E3B 5H5
Phone: +1(506) 453-4602 **Fax:** +1(506) 453-3518
WWW: www.lib.unb.ca/library/science/scifor.htm
OPAC: phoenix.unb.ca

Founded: 1976 **Type:** Academic **Head:** Francesca Holyoke *Phone:* +1(506) 453-4965 *Email:* holyoke@unb.ca **Staff:** 2 Prof. 5 Other **Holdings:** 154,000 books 900 journals **Language of Collection/Services:** English / English **Subjects:** Biotechnology, Education/Extension, Entomology, Fisheries, Horticulture, Plant Pathology, Soil Science, Water Resources **Specializations:** Biology, Chemistry, Forestry, Geology, Physics **Databases Developed:** FORF in ENLIST - online report collection **Databases Used:** CAS; Medline **Loan:** Internationally **Service:** Internationally **Photocopy:** Yes

552   **Sackville, New Brunswick, Canada**
Environment Canada, Atlantic Region, Canadian Wildlife Service
Library
PO Box 1590
Sackville, New Brunswick E0A 3C0
Phone: +1(506) 364-5019 **Fax:** +1(506) 364-5062 **WWW:** www.ec.gc.ca/cws-scf/cwshom_e.html

553   **Saint Andrews, New Brunswick, Canada**
Fisheries and Oceans Canada, Biological Station
Library
531 Brandy Cove Road
Saint Andrews, New Brunswick E0G 2X0
Phone: +1(506) 529-5909 **Fax:** +1(506) 519-5862 **Email:** sta-library@mar.dfo-mpo.gc.ca **WWW:** www.mar.dfo-mpo.gc.ca **OPAC:** inter01.dfo-mpo.gc.ca/wavesdocs/en

Former Name: Department of Fisheries and Oceans (DFO) **Type:** Government **Head:** Marilyn Rudi *Phone:* +1(506) 529-5909 *Email:* rudim@mar.dfo-mpo.gc.ca **Staff:** 1 Prof. 1 Other **Holdings:** 6,000 books 200 journals **Language of**

Collection/Services: English / English **Subjects:** Aquaculture, Fisheries **Loan:** In country **Photocopy:** Yes

Newfoundland

554   **Corner Brook, Newfoundland, Canada**
Department of Forest Resources and Agrifoods, Newfoundland, Forestry and Wildlife Branch, Forest Ecosystem Management Division
Forestry Library
Box 2006
Corner Brook, Newfoundland A2H 6J8
Location: 4 Herald Avenue **Phone:** +1(709) 637-2409
Fax: +1(709) 637-2264 **WWW:** www.gov.nf.ca/forest/FRA_ECOSY.HTM

Founded: 1984 **Type:** Government **Head:** Bruce Boland *Phone:* +1(709) 637-2307 **Staff:** 1 Prof. **Holdings:** 6,500 books 70 journals **Language of Collection/Services:** English / English **Subjects:** Entomology, Plant Pathology, Soil Science, Water Resources **Specializations:** Forestry, Forest Management, Forest Products **Loan:** Internationally **Service:** Internationally **Photocopy:** Yes

555   **Corner Brook, Newfoundland, Canada**
Natural Resources Canada, Canadian Forest Service, Atlantic Forestry Centre
Branch Library
PO Box 960
Corner Brook, Newfoundland A2H 6J3
Location: University Drive **Phone:** +1(709) 637-4900
Fax: +1(709) 637-4910 **Email:** pbonnell@nrcan.gov.ca
WWW: atl.cfs.NRCan.gc.ca/cfs/welcome_e.html

Former Name: Forestry Canada **Founded:** 1966 **Type:** Government **Head:** *Phone:* +1(709) 637-4905 **Staff:** 1 Prof. **Holdings:** 5,000 books 100 journals **Language of Collection/Services:** English / English **Subjects:** Entomology, Forestry, Plant Pathology, Plant Protection, Soil Science **Specializations:** Forestry Development, Forest Resources **Databases Used:** Comprehensive **Loan:** In country **Service:** In country **Photocopy:** Yes

556   **Saint John's, Newfoundland, Canada**
Fisheries and Oceans Canada, Northwest Atlantic Fisheries Centre
Regional Library
PO Box 5667
Saint John's, Newfoundland A1C 5X1
Phone: +1(709) 772-2020 **Fax:** +1(709) 772-2575 **Email:** kenny@athena.nwafc.nf.ca **WWW:** www.nwafc.nf.ca
OPAC: inter01.dfo-mpo.gc.ca/wavesdocs/en

Founded: 1940 **Type:** Government **Head:** Audrey Conroy *Phone:* +1(709) 772-2022 *Email:* conroy@athena.nwafc.nf.ca **Staff:** 1 Prof. 3 Other **Holdings:** 8,500 books 450 journals **Language of Collection/Services:** English / English **Subjects:** Fisheries **Databases Developed:** WAVES CD - fisheries grey literature, available for purchase **Loan:** In country **Service:** Internationally **Photocopy:** Yes

557 Saint John's, Newfoundland, Canada
Memorial University of Newfoundland, Fisheries
and Marine Institute
Dr. C.R. Barrett Library
PO Box 4920
Saint John's, Newfoundland A1C 5R3
Location: 155 Ridge Road **Fax:** +1(709) 778-0316 **Email:**
barrett@gill.ifmt.nf.ca **WWW:** www.mun.ca/library
OPAC: info.library.mun.ca

Former Name: Marine Institute **Founded:** 1963 **Type:** Academic **Head:** Dianne E. Taylor-Harding *Phone:* +1(709)
778-0662 *Email:* dtaylor@morgan.ucs.mun.ca **Staff:** 1 Prof.
7 Other **Holdings:** 35,000 books 390 journals **Language of
Collection/Services:** English/English **Subjects:** Aquaculture, Fisheries, Food Technology, Food Quality **Networks:**
OCLC **Databases Used:** Comprehensive **Loan:** ILL available **Service:** Inhouse, email, fax **Photocopy:** Yes

Northwest Territories

558 Yellowknife, Northwest Territories, Canada
Environment Canada, Prairie and Northern Region
Yellowknife Library
5204 - 50th Ave., Suite 301
Yellowknife, Northwest Territories X1A 3G7
Phone: +1(867) 669-4717 **Fax:** +1(867) 875-8185 **Email:**
florrie.cook@ec.gc.ca **WWW:** www.ec.gc.ca **OPAC:**
www.andornot.com/envcan

Head: Florrie Cook *Email:* florrie.cook@ec.gc.ca

Nova Scotia

559 Antigonish, Nova Scotia, Canada
St. Francis Xavier University (StFX)
Angus L. Macdonald Library
Box 5000, StFX
Antigonish, Nova Scotia B2G 2W5
Phone: +1(902) 867-2242 **Fax:** +1(902) 867-5153 **WWW:**
www.stfx.ca **OPAC:** libmain.stfx.ca/newlib/novanet

Type: Academic **Head:** Rita Campbell *Phone:* +1(902)
867-2267 *Email:* rcampbel@stfx.ca **Staff:** 8 Prof. 30 Other
Holdings: 450,000 books 1,500 journals **Language of Collection/Services:** English/English **Subjects:** Education/Extension, Food Production, Food Sciences **Networks:** Novanet **Loan:** Internationally **Photocopy:** Yes

560 Bedford, Nova Scotia, Canada
Environment Canada, Atlantic Region,
Management Service/AEB
Library
1496 Bedford Highway
Bedford, Nova Scotia B4A 1E5
Phone: +1(902) 426-9278 **Fax:** +1(902) 426-9158 **WWW:**
www.atl.ec.gc.ca

561 Darthmouth, Nova Scotia, Canada
Environment Canada, Atlantic Region
Library
Queen Square, 5th Floor

45 Alderney Drive
Darthmouth, Nova Scotia B2Y 2N6
Phone: +1(902) 426-7219, 426-7232 **Fax:** +1(902) 426-6143 **Email:** library@ec.gc.ca **WWW:** www.atl.ec.gc.ca

562 Kentville, Nova Scotia, Canada
Agriculture and Agri-Food Canada, Atlantic Food
and Horticulture Research Centre (AAFC)
Library
Kentville, Nova Scotia B4N 1J5
Fax: +1(902) 379-2311 **WWW:** res.agr.ca/kentville/centre

Non-English Name: Agriculture et Agroalimentaire Canada, Centre de Recherches de l'Atlantique sur les Aliments et
l'Horticulture, Bibliothèque **Former Name:** Agriculture
Canada **Founded:** 1953 **Type:** Government **Head:** Jerry
Miner *Phone:* +1(902) 679-5508 *Email:* minerj@em.agr.ca
Staff: 1 Prof. 1 Other **Holdings:** 16,500 books 63 journals
Language of Collection/Services: English **Subjects:**
Crops, Entomology, Food Processing, Food Sciences, Food
Storage, Horticulture, Plant Pathology, Soil Science **Databases Used:** Comprehensive **Loan:** Inhouse **Service:** In
country **Photocopy:** Yes

563 Truro, Nova Scotia, Canada
Nova Scotia Agricultural College (NSAC)
MacRae Library
135 College Road
PO Box 550
Truro, Nova Scotia B2N 5E3
Phone: +1(902) 893-6668 **Fax:** +1(902) 895-7693 **Email:**
lib_info@www.nsac.ns.ca **WWW:** www.nsac.ns.ca/depts/
library.html **OPAC:** www.nsac.ns.ca/lib/catalogue.html
Ariel IP: 198.166.19.160

Founded: 1905 **Type:** Academic Government **Head:**
Bonnie Waddell *Phone:* +1(902) 893-6670 *Email:*
bwaddell@nsac.ns.ca **Staff:** 2 Prof. 6 Other **Holdings:**
30,000 books 680 journals **Language of Collection/Services:** English / English **Subjects:** Comprehensive **Specializations:** Aquaculture, Marine Ecology **Networks:** AgNIC
Databases Developed: Wild Blueberry Network Information Center - Internet web site **Databases Used:** Comprehensive **Loan:** Internationally **Service:** Internationally
Photocopy: Yes

564 Wolfville, Nova Scotia, Canada
Acadia University
Vaughan Memorial Library
Wolfville, Nova Scotia B0P 1X0
Phone: +1(902) 585-1170 **Fax:** +1(902) 585-1748 **Email:**
reference.desk@acadiau.ca **WWW:** www.acadiau.ca
OPAC: www.acadiau.ca/vaughan

Founded: 1970 **Type:** Academic **Holdings:** 31,650 books
Head: Jennifer Richard, Science Specialist *Email:* jennifer.
richard@acadiau.ca *Phone:* +1(902) 585-1549

Ontario

565 Burlington, Ontario, Canada
Environment Canada, Canada Centre for Inland
Waters

Library
867 Lakeshore Road
Burlington, Ontario L7R 4A6
Phone: +1(905) 336-4982 **Fax:** +1(905) 336-4428 **Email:** librarycciw@ec.gc.ca **WWW:** www.cciw.ca **OPAC:** cciw.library.net

Holdings: 30,000 books **Subjects:** Environmental Sciences, Fisheries, Hydraulics, Waste Water Management, Water Resources **Databases Used:** ASFA; Biosis

566   Downsview, Ontario, Canada
Environment Canada, Ontario Region
Environment Canada Library, Downsview
4905 Dufferin Street
Downsview, Ontario M3H 5T4
Phone: +1(416) 739-5702 **Fax:** +1(416) 739-4212 **WWW:** www.ec.gc.ca

567   Guelph, Ontario, Canada
Agriculture and Agri-Food Canada, Southern Crop
    Protection and Food Research Centre
    (Guelph)
Library
93/95 Stone Road West
Guelph, Ontario N1H 8J7
Fax: +1(519) 767-6334 **WWW:** res.agr.ca/lond/pmrc/pmrchome.html

Former Name: Agriculture Canada **Head:** Mr. Francesco Lai *Phone:* +1(519) 767-6309 *Email:* laif@em.agr.ca

568   Guelph, Ontario, Canada
Jubilee Centre for Agricultural Research
Family Farm/Stewardship Library (FF/SL)
115 Woolwich Street, 2nd Floor
Guelph, Ontario N1H 3V1
Fax: +1(519) 824-1835 **Email:** offomail@christianfarmers.org **WWW:** www.christianfarmers.org

Type: Association **Head:** Elbert van Donkersgoed *Phone:* +1(519) 837-1620 **Holdings:** 3,500 books 325 journals **Language of Collection/Services:** English / English **Subjects:** Biotechnology, Crops, Environment, Farming, Soil, Water Resources **Loan:** Do not loan **Service:** Inhouse **Photocopy:** Yes

569   Guelph, Ontario, Canada
University of Guelph
McLaughlin Library
Guelph, Ontario N1G 2W1
Phone: +1(519) 824-8535 **Fax:** +1(519) 824-6931 **WWW:** www.uoguelph.ca **OPAC:** www.lib.uoguelph.ca

Founded: 1903 **Type:** Academic **Head:** Michael Ridley *Phone:* +1(519) 824-2077 *Email:* mridley@uoguelph.ca **Staff:** 27 Prof. 108 Other **Holdings:** 500,000 books 12,000 journals **Language of Collection/Services:** English/English **Subjects:** Agribusiness, Agricultural Development, Agricultural Economics, Agricultural Engineering, Animal Husbandry, Biotechnology, Education/Extension, Entomology, Farming, Fisheries, Food Sciences, Crops, Forestry, Horticulture, Plant Pathology, Soil Science, Veterinary Medicine, Water Resources **Specializations:** Biology, Engineering,

Pollution, Veterinary Science, Waste Management, Water Pollution **Loan:** Internationally **Service:** Internationally **Photocopy:** Yes

570   Guelph, Ontario, Canada
University of Guelph, Veterinary Science Section
Library
Guelph, Ontario N1G 2W1
Phone: +1(519) 824-4207 **Fax:** +1(519) 826-7941 **WWW:** www.uoguelph.ca **OPAC:** www.lib.uoguelph.ca

Founded: 1862 **Type:** Academic **Head:** David C. Hull *Phone:* +1(519) 824-4120 ext 4214 *Email:* dhull@uoguelph.ca **Staff:** 1 Prof. 4 Other **Holdings:** 40,000 books 400 journals **Language of Collection/Services:** English / English **Subjects:** Veterinary Medicine **Databases Used:** Agricola; CABCD; Medline **Loan:** Internationally **Service:** Internationally **Photocopy:** Yes

571   Hamilton, Ontario, Canada
McMaster University
H.G. Thode Library of Science and Engineering
1280 Main Street West
Hamilton, Ontario L8S 4P5
Phone: +1(416) 525-9140 ext 24256 **Fax:** +1(905) 777-1110 **Email:** thoderef@mcmaster.ca **WWW:** www.mcmaster.ca/library/thode/index.html **OPAC:** www.mcmaster.ca/library/catalog/catalog.htm

Founded: 1948 **Type:** Academic **Head:** Kathy Ball, Science and Engineering Librarian *Phone:* +1(416) 525-9140 ext 23881 *Email:* katball@mcmaster.ca **Staff:** 3 Prof. 13 Other **Holdings:** 6,500 books 60 journals **Loan:** In country **Photocopy:** Yes

572   Hamilton, Ontario, Canada
Royal Botanical Gardens
Library
Box 399
Hamilton, Ontario L8N 3H8
Location: 680 Plains Road West, Burlington L7T 4H4
Phone: +1(905) 527-1158 ext 246 **Fax:** +1(905) 577-0375 **Email:** brownlee@rbc.ca **WWW:** www.rbg.ca

Founded: 1947 **Type:** Special **Head:** Mrs. Linda Brownlee *Phone:* +1(905) 527-1158 ext 246 *Email:* brownlee@rbc.ca **Staff:** .5 Prof. **Holdings:** 10,000 books 450 journals **Language of Collection/Services:** English **Subjects:** Botany, Ornamental Plants **Databases Developed:** Nursery and Seed Trade Catalog Collection, especially 19th century Canadian catalogs; inhouse access **Loan:** In country **Photocopy:** Yes

573   Harrow, Ontario, Canada
Agriculture and Agri-Food Canada, Greenhouse
    and Processing Crops Research Centre
Canadian Agriculture Library (CAL)
2585 Highway 20, E.
Harrow, Ontario N0R 1G0
Phone: +1(519) 738-2251 **Fax:** +1(519) 738-2929 **WWW:** res.agr.ca/harrow

Former Name: Agriculture Canada **Founded:** 1940 **Type:** Government **Head:** Eric Champagne *Phone:* +1(519) 738-2251 *Email:* champagnee@em.agr.ca **Staff:** 1 Prof. **Hold-**

ings: 5,000 books 80 journals **Language of Collection / Services:** English / English **Subjects:** Biotechnology, Crops, Entomology, Horticulture, Plant Pathology, Soil Science **Databases Used:** Agricola **Loan:** In country **Service:** In country **Photocopy:** Yes

574   Kemptville, Ontario, Canada
University of Guelph, Kemptville College Campus
Purvis Library
PO Box 2003
830 Prescott Street
Kemptville, Ontario K0G 1J0
Phone: +1(613) 258-8336 ext 634 **Fax:** +1(613) 258-8294 **WWW:** www.kemptvillec.uoguelph.ca/library3/libmen3.htm

Former Name: Kemptville College of Agricultural Technology **Founded:** 1969 **Type:** Academic **Head:** Debra Simpson *Email:* dsimpson@kemptvillec.uoguelph.ca *Phone* +1(613) 258-8336 ext 634 **Staff:** 1 Prof. 1 Other **Holdings:** 10,000 books 135 journals **Language of Collection/Services:** English / English **Subjects:** Food Sciences **Photocopy:** Yes

575   London, Ontario, Canada
Agriculture and Agri-Food Canada, Southern Crop
    Protection and Food Research Centre
    (London)
Canadian Agriculture Library
1391 Sandford Street
London, Ontario N5V 4T3
Fax: +1(519) 457-3997 **WWW:** res.agr.ca/lond/pmrc/pmrchome.html

Former Name: Agriculture Canada **Founded:** 1951 **Type:** Government **Head:** Mrs. Dorothy Drew *Phone:* +1(519) 457-1470 ext 263 *Email:* drewd@em.agr.ca **Staff:** 1 Prof. **Holdings:** 8,000 books 80 journals **Language of Collection/Services:** English / English **Subjects:** Integrated Pest Management, Sustainability **Databases Used:** Agricola; CABCD **Loan:** In country **Photocopy:** Yes

576   London, Ontario, Canada
Parmalat Canada Ltd.
Library
65 Bathurst Street
London, Ontario N6A 4E5
Phone: +1(519) 667-7709 **Fax:** +1(519) 667-7725

Former Name: Ault Foods Ltd. **Founded:** 1968 **Type:** Business **Head:** Michael Hulko *Phone:* +1(519) 667-7709 *Email:* michael_hulko@parmalat.ca **Holdings:** 250 books 15 journals **Language of Collection/Services:** English / English **Subjects:** Dairy Science, Dairy Technology **Databases Used:** Comprehensive **Loan:** Inhouse **Service:** Inhouse **Photocopy:** Yes

577   London, Ontario, Canada
University of Western Ontario
Allyn and Betty Taylor Library
Natural Sciences Center
London, Ontario N6A 5B7

Phone: +1(519) 661-3168 **Fax:** +1(519) 661-3880 **Email:** tayref@lib.uwo.ca **WWW:** www.lib.uwo.ca/taylor **OPAC:** www.lib.uwo.ca/opac.html

Former Name: Sciences Library **Founded:** 1881 **Type:** Academic **Head:** Eeva Munoz *Phone:* +1(519) 679-2111 ext 86362 *Email:* emunoz@lib.uwo.ca **Staff:** 6 Prof. 32 Other **Holdings:** 178,000 books 4,500 journals **Subjects:** Agribusiness, Agricultural Development, Agricultural Economics, Animal Husbandry, Biotechnology, Crops, Education/Extension, Entomology, Farming, Fisheries, Food Sciences, Forestry, Horticulture, Plant Pathology, Soil Science, Veterinary Medicine, Water Resources **Databases Used:** Biosis; Medline **Loan:** Internationally **Photocopy:** Yes

578   Nepean, Ontario, Canada
Agriculture and Agri-Food Canada, Animal
    Diseases Research Institute (AAFC, ADRI)
Library
3851 Fallowfield Road
Nepean, Ontario K2H 8P9
Fax: +1(613) 228-6667 **WWW:** www.agr.ca/cal

Former Name: Agriculture Canada **Type:** Government **Head:** Mr. Greg Eldridge *Phone:* +1(613) 228-6698 ext 4949 *Email:* eldridgeg@em.agr.ca **Holdings:** 10,500 books **Specializations:** Veterinary Medicine **Databases Used:** Agricola; CABCD

579   Niagara Falls, Ontario, Canada
Niagara Parks Commission, School of
    Horticulture
C.H. Henning Library
PO Box 150
Niagara Falls, Ontario L2E 6T2
Location: 2565 Niagara Parkway North **WWW:** www.npbg.org

Founded: 1965 **Type:** Academic Government **Head:** Mrs. Ruth Stoner *Phone:* +1(416) 356-8554 **Staff:** .5 Prof. **Holdings:** 3,000 books 100 journals **Language of Collection/Services:** English / English **Subjects:** Entomology, Horticulture, Plant Pathology, Soil Science **Specializations:** Landscape Architecture **Loan:** Do not loan **Service:** Inhouse **Photocopy:** Yes

580   North York, Ontario, Canada
York University
Steacie Science Library
4700 Keele Street
North York, Ontario M3J 1P3
Phone: +1(416) 736-2100 ext. 22880 **Email:** library@yorku.ca **WWW:** info.library.yorku.ca/depts/steacie/steaciehome.htm **OPAC:** www.library.yorku.ca

Type: Academic **Head:** Brian Wilks *Phone:* +1(416) 736-5639 *Email:* wilks@yorku.ca

581   Ottawa, Ontario, Canada
Agriculture and Agri-Food Canada
Canadian Agriculture Library (CAL)
930 Carling Avenue
Ottawa, Ontario K1A OC5

Phone: +1(613) 759-7068 **Fax:** +1(613) 759-6643 **Email:** cal-bca@em.agr.ca **WWW:** www.agr.ca **OPAC:** www.agr.ca/cal/calweb21.htm

Non-English Name: Agriculture et Agroalimentaire Canada, Bibliothèque canadienne de l'agriculture (BCA) **Former Name:** Department of Agriculture, Agriculture Canada, Libraries Division **Founded:** 1910 **Type:** Government **Head:** Mr. Victor Desroches *Email:* desrochesv@em.agr.ca *Phone:* +1(613) 759-7083 **Staff:** 17 Prof. 29 Other **Holdings:** 1,000,000 books 3,500 journals **Language of Collection/Services:** English, French / English, French **Subjects:** Comprehensive **Specializations:** Agricultural Economics, Animal Feeding, Animal Production, Entomology, Livestock Farming, Plant Anatomy, Plant Breeding, Plant Diseases, Plant Physiology **Networks:** AGRIS; AMICUS **Databases Used:** Comprehensive **Databases Developed:** Agriweb Canada - directory of Canadian online resources in agriculture and agri-food; available at www.agr.ca/agriweb/agriweb.htm **Loan:** Internationally **Service:** Inhouse **Photocopy:** Yes

582   **Ottawa, Ontario, Canada**
         Agriculture and Agri-Food Canada, Eastern Cereal and Oilseed Research Centre (AAFC, ECORC)
         Library
         K.W. Neatby Building, Room 4061
         Ottawa, Ontario K1A 0C6

Fax: +1(613) 759-1924 **Email:** lib-ecorc@em.agr.ca **WWW:** res.agr.ca/ecorc/library/library.htm

Former Name: Agriculture Canada, Entomology Research Library **Founded:** 1910 **Type:** Government **Head:** Mr. Steve Gamman *Phone:* +1(613) 759-1807 *Email:* gammans @em.agr.ca **Staff:** 1 Prof. 1 Other **Holdings:** 30,000 books 225 journals **Subjects:** Agricultural Meteorology, Biochemistry, Biological Control, Entomology, Nematology, Soil Science **Loan:** Internationally **Photocopy:** Yes

583   **Ottawa, Ontario, Canada**
         Agriculture and Agri-Food Canada, Eastern Cereal and Oilseed Research Centre (AAFC, ECORC)
         Plant Research Library
         Wm. Saunders Building #49, C.E.F.
         Ottawa, Ontario K1A 0C6

Fax: +1(613) 759-1599 **WWW:** res.agr.ca/ecorc/library/library.htm

Non-English Name: Agriculture et Agroalimentaire Canada, Bibliothèque de Recherches sur les Végétaux **Former Name:** Agriculture Canada **Founded:** 1908 **Type:** Government **Head:** Mrs. Lise Robillard *Phone:* +1(613) 759-1368 *Email:* robillardl@em.agr.ca **Staff:** 1 Prof. .5 Other **Holdings:** 12,000 books 130 journals **Language of Collection/Services:** English / English, French **Subjects:** Botany, Mycology, Taxonomy **Databases Used:** Agricola; Biosis **Loan:** Internationally **Photocopy:** Yes

584   **Ottawa, Ontario, Canada**
         Fisheries and Oceans Canada
         Library Policy and Services

         200 Kent Street
         10th Floor West
         Ottawa, Ontario K1A 0E6

Phone: +1(613) 993-2938 **Fax:** +1(613) 990-4901 **Email:** lasalled@dfo-mpo.gc.ca **WWW:** inter01.dfo-mpo.gc.ca/wavesdocs/waves_mainmenu.html **OPAC:** inter01.dfo-mpo.gc.ac/wavesdocs/en

Type: Government **Holdings:** 7,000 books

585   **Ottawa, Ontario, Canada**
         International Development Research Centre (IDRC)
         Library
         PO Box 8500
         Ottawa, Ontario K1G 3H9

Location: 9th Floor, 250 Alberta Street **Phone:** +1(613) 236-6163 ext 2578 **Fax:** +1(613) 238-7230 **Email:** reference@idrc.ca **WWW:** www.idrc.ca/library **OPAC:** idrinfo.idrc.ca

Founded: 1971 **Type:** Government **Head:** Carole Joling *Phone:* +1(613) 598-0580 *Email:* cjoling@idrc.ca **Staff:** 8 Prof. 15 Other **Holdings:** 616 journals **Subjects:** Agriculture (Tropics), Agroforestry, Crops, Fisheries **Loan:** In country and United States **Photocopy:** Yes

586   **Ottawa, Ontario, Canada**
         National Museum of Science and Technology (NMST)
         Library
         PO Box 9724
         Station T
         Ottawa, Ontario K1G 5A3

Location: 2380 Lancaster Road **Phone:** +1(613) 991-2982 **Fax:** +1(613) 990-3636 **Email:** library@nmstc.ca **WWW:** www.science-tech.nmstc.ca

Former Name: National Museums of Canada **Founded:** 1967 **Type:** Museum **Head:** Catherine Campbell *Phone:* +1(613) 990-7874 *Email:* ccampbell@nmstc.ca **Staff:** 1 Prof. 6 Other **Holdings:** 800 books 16 journals **Language of Collection/Services:** English / English, French **Subjects:** Agricultural Engineering, Agriculture (History), Forestry **Databases Developed:** Database of trade literature including over 5,000 items of agricultural trade literature; inhouse access **Service:** Internationally **Photocopy:** Yes

587   **Peterborough, Ontario, Canada**
         Ontario Ministry of Natural Resources
         Natural Resources Information Centre
         300 Water St.
         PO Box 7000
         Peterborough, Ontario K9J 8M5

Phone: +1(705) 755-2000 **WWW:** www.mnr.gov.on.ca/MNR

Former Name: Corporate Library Toronto, Corporate/Research Library Maple **Subjects:** Natural Resources

588   **Ridgetown, Ontario, Canada**
         University of Guelph
         Ridgetown College Library
         Main Street East

Ridgetown, Ontario N0P 2C0
Phone: +1(519) 674-1540 **Fax:** +1(519) 674-1539 **Email:**
library@ridgetownc.uoguelph.ca **Ariel IP:** 206.178.33.130
WWW: www.ridgetownc.on.ca

Former Name: Ridgetown College of Agricultural Technology (RCAT) **Founded:** 1955 **Type:** Academic **Head:** Iona
R. Roadhouse *Phone:* +1(519) 674-1540 *Email:* library@
ridgetownc.uoguelph.ca **Staff:** 5 Other **Holdings:** 12,000
books 200 journals **Language of Collection/Services:** English / English **Subjects:** Agricultural Production, Horticulture, Veterinary Science **Databases Used:** Agricola; CBCA
Loan: Inhouse **Service:** Internationally **Photocopy:** Yes

589   Sault Sainte Marie, Ontario, Canada
Natural Resources Canada, Canadian Forest
      Service, Great Lakes Forestry Centre
Library
1219 Queen Street East
PO Box 490
Sault Sainte Marie, Ontario P6A 5M7
Phone: +1(705) 759-5740 ext 2000, 2001 **Fax:** +1(705)
759-5700 **Email:** brbrown@nrcan.gc.ca, ndukes@nrcan.
gc.ca

Founded: 1949 **Type:** Government **Staff:** 1 Prof. 1 Other
Holdings: 8,000 books 400 journals **Subjects:** Entomology,
Forestry **Loan:** Internationally **Photocopy:** Yes

590   Thunder Bay, Ontario, Canada
Lakehead University
Chancellor Paterson Library
955 Oliver Road
Thunder Bay, Ontario P7B 5E1
Phone: +1(807) 343-8302 **Fax:** +1(807) 343-8007 **WWW:**
www.lakeheadu.ca **OPAC:** www.lakeheadu.ca/~librwww/
accessto.html

Founded: 1966 **Type:** Academic **Head:** Anne Deighton
Email: anne.deighton@lakeheadu.ca *Phone:* +1(807) 343-
8205 **Staff:** 12 Prof. 33 Other **Holdings:** 201,650 books
Language of Collection/Services: English **Subjects:** Forestry **Databases Developed:** Bibliographic database covering all areas including forestry relating primarily to north
western Ontario; Internet access **Photocopy:** Yes

591   Toronto, Ontario, Canada
Civic Garden Centre (CGC)
Library
777 Lawrence Avenue East
Don Mills
Toronto, Ontario M3C 1P2
Phone: +1(916) 397-1343 **Fax:** +1(916) 397-1343 **Email:**
cgc1@idirect.ca

Founded: 1959 **Type:** Non-profit **Head:** Mara Arndt
Phone: +1(416) 397-1343 *Email:* cgc1@idirect.ca **Staff:** 1
Prof. 20 Other **Holdings:** 8,000 books 70 journals **Language
of Collection/Services:** English / English **Subjects:** Botany,
Cut Flowers, Gardens (History), Gardens, Horticulture
Loan: In country **Service:** In country **Photocopy:** Yes

592   Toronto, Ontario, Canada
Environmental Commissioner of Ontario

Resource Centre
1075 Bay Street, Suite 605
Toronto, Ontario M5S 2B1
Phone: +1(416) 325-0363 **Fax:** +1(416) 325-1348 **WWW:**
www.eco.on.ca/english/resourctr/index.htm

Founded: 1960 **Type:** Government **Head:** Lisa Shultz
Phone: +1(416) 325-6400 *Email:* schultzl@gov.on.ca **Subjects:** Environment

593   Toronto, Ontario, Canada
Ontario Ministry of Natural Resources
Natural Resources Information Centre
Room M1-73, Macdonald Block
900 Bay Street
Toronto, Ontario M7A 2C1
Phone: +1(800) 667-1940, +1(416) 314-2000 (general
inquiry); 314-1665 (French inquiry) **WWW:** www.mnr.
gov.on.ca/MNR

Founded: 1972 **Type:** Government **Holdings:** 140,500
books **Subjects:** Natural Resources

594   Toronto, Ontario, Canada
Toronto Public Library, North York Central
      Library
Science and Technology Collection
Fifth Floor, Central Library
5120 Yonge Street
Toronto, Ontario M2N 5N9
Phone: +1(416) 395-5649 **WWW:** www.tpl.toronto.on.ca/
index.htm **OPAC:** www.tpl.toronto.on.ca/Catalogue/index.
htm

Founded: 1963 **Type:** Government **Holdings:** 19,101 books

595   Toronto, Ontario, Canada
University of Toronto
Earth Sciences Library (ESCI)
5 Bancroft Avenue
Toronto, Ontario M5S 1A5
Phone: +1(416) 978-6016 **Fax:** +1(416) 971-2101 **WWW:**
www.library.utoronto.ca/www/libraries_earth **OPAC:**
www.library.utroonto.ca/resources/utcat.html

Former Name: Department of Botany Library, Department
of Geology Library, Faculty of Forestry Library **Founded:**
1932 **Type:** Academic **Head:** Jennifer Mendelsohn *Email:*
mendelsohn@vax.library.utoronto.ca *Phone:* +1 (416) 978-
3538 **Staff:** 1.5 Prof. 3 Other **Holdings:** 80,000 books 1,100
journals **Language of Collection/Services:** English/English
Subjects: Forestry, Plants, Soil Science **Databases Used:**
Biosis; CABCD **Loan:** In country **Service:** Internationally
Photocopy: Yes

596   Vineland Station, Ontario, Canada
Agriculture and Agri-Food Canada, Southern Crop
      Protection and Food Research Centre
      (Vineland)
Canadian Agriculture Library (CAL)
PO Box 6000
Vineland Station, Ontario L0R 2E0

Location: 4902 Victoria Avenue North **Fax:** +1(416) 562-4335 **Email:** alders@em.agr.ca **WWW:** res.agr.ca/long/pmrc/pmrchome.html

Former Name: Agriculture Canada, Pest Management Research Centre **Type:** Government **Head:** Sheridan Alder *Phone:* +1(416) 562-4113 *Email:* alders@em.agr.ca **Staff:** 1 Prof. **Holdings:** 3,995 books 50 journals **Language of Collection/Services:** English / English **Subjects:** Acarology, Biotechnology, Entomology, Nematology, Plant Pathology, Residues, Toxicology, Virology **Specializations:** Fruits, Ornamental Plants, Plant Protection **Databases Developed:** Station Bibliography **Databases Used:** Agricola; CABCD **Loan:** In country **Service:** Inhouse **Photocopy:** Yes

597   Vineland Station, Ontario, Canada
         University of Guelph, Horticultural Research
              Institute of Ontario (HRIO)
         Library
         PO Box 7000
         Vineland Station, Ontario L0R 2E0
Location: 4890 Victoria Ave. N. **Fax:** +1(905) 562-3413 **Email:** jwanner@hrio.uoguelph.ca **WWW:** www.oac.uoguelph.ca/hrio **Ariel IP:** 206.178.34.103

Founded: 1970 **Type:** Academic **Head:** Mrs. Judith Wanner *Phone:* +1(416) 562-4141 ext 131 *Email:* jwanner@hrio.uoguelph.ca **Staff:** 1 Prof. **Holdings:** 5,000 books 230 journals **Language of Collection/Services:** English / English **Subjects:** Enology, Food Processing, Greenhouse Crops, Horticulture, Mushrooms, Ornamental Plants, Vegetables, Viticulture **Loan:** In country **Service:** In country **Photocopy:** Yes

Prince Edward Island

598   Charlottetown, Prince Edward Island, Canada
         Agriculture and Agri-Food Canada, Crops and
              Livestock Research Centre (AAFC)
         Canadian Agriculture Library (CAL)
         PO Box 1210
         Charlottetown, Prince Edward Island C1A 7M8
Location: 440 University Avenue **Phone:** +1(902) 566-6861 **Fax:** +1(902) 566-6821 **WWW:** res.agr.ca/charlotte

Former Name: Agriculture Canada **Founded:** 1961 **Type:** Government **Head:** Barrie Stanfield *Phone:* +1(902) 566-6800 ext 6861 *Email:* stanfieldb@em.agr.ca **Staff:** 1 Prof. **Holdings:** 3,300 books 66 journals **Language of Collection/Services:** English / English **Subjects:** Animal Nutrition, Cereals, Entomology, Fodder Crops, Plant Pathology, Soil Science **Networks:** AGRICAT **Databases Developed:** Research station bibliography: scientific papers authored by station staff - available inhouse **Databases Used:** Agricola; CABCD **Loan:** In country **Photocopy:** Yes

599   Charlottetown, Prince Edward Island, Canada
         University of Prince Edward Island
         Robertson Library
         Charlottetown, Prince Edward Island C1A 4P3
Phone: +1(902) 566-0696 **Fax:** +1(902) 628-4305 **WWW:** www.upei.ca/!library **OPAC:** www.upei.ca/~library/electronic/bobcat.html

Founded: 1969 **Type:** Academic **Head:** Lynne Murphy *Phone:* +1(902) 566-0460 *Email:* lfmurphy@upei.ca **Staff:** 6 Prof. 20 Other **Holdings:** 10,000 books 300 journals **Subjects:** Animal Husbandry, Fisheries, Soil Science, Veterinary Medicine **Loan:** In country **Photocopy:** Yes

Québec

600   Charlesbourg, Québec, Canada
         Ministry of Natural Resources, Quebec
         Library
         Edifice de l'Atrium
         5700, 4e avenue Ouest, local A-200
         Charlesbourg, Québec G1H 6R1
Phone: +1(418) 627-8686 **Fax:** +1(418) 644-1124 **Email:** cblanchard@bibliotheque.mrn.gouv.qc.ca **WWW:** www.mrn.gouv.qc.ca **OPAC:** www.ribg.gouv.qc.ca

Non-English Name: Ministère des Ressources Naturelles, Québec, Bibliothèque **Founded:** 1994 **Type:** Government **Head:** Marc Beaudoin **Staff:** 1 Prof. 11 Other **Holdings:** 90,000 books 1,200 journals **Subjects:** Forestry, Natural Resources

601   Gaspé, Québec, Canada
         Ministry of Agriculture, Fisheries and Food,
              Quebec
         Aquaculture and Fisheries Documentation Center
         96, Montée de Sandy-Beach
         CP 1070
         Gaspé, Québec G0C 1R0
Phone: +1(418) 368-7618 **Fax:** +1(418) 368-8400 **Email:** blapierr@agr.gouv.qc.ca **WWW:** www.agr.gouv.qc.ca

Non-English Name: Ministère de l'Agriculture, des Pêcheries et de l'Alimentation, Québec (MAPAQ), Centre de Documentation Pêche et Aquiculture Commerciales **Founded:** 1951 **Type:** Government **Head:** Paul Carrier *Phone:* +1(418) 368-7615 **Staff:** 1 Prof. 2 Other **Holdings:** 12,250 books 300 journals **Language of Collection/Services:** English, French **Subjects:** Aquaculture, Fisheries, Food Sciences **Loan:** In country **Photocopy:** Yes

602   Hull, Québec, Canada
         Environment Canada
         Departmental Library
         351 St. Joseph Boulevard
         Hull, Québec K1A 0H3
Phone: +1(819) 997-1767 **Fax:** +1(819) 997-5349, 953-7900 **Email:** librarypvm@ec.gc.ca **WWW:** www.ec.gc.ca/library/libhome.html

Head: Judy Patterson *Phone:* +1(819) 997-2465 *Email:* judy.patterson@ec.gc.ca

603   La Pocatière, Québec, Canada
         Ministry of Agriculture, Fisheries and Food,
              Quebec, La Pocatiere Institute of Agricultural
              and Food Technology
         Documentation Center
         401, Rue Poiré
         La Pocatière, Québec G0R 1Z0

Phone: +1(418) 856-1110 ext 258 **Fax:** +1(418) 856-1719 **Email:** cditalp@agr.gouv.qc.ca **WWW:** www.agr.gouv.qc.ca

Non-English Name: Ministère de l'Agriculture, des Pêcheries et de l'Alimentation, Québec, Institut de Technologie Agro-Alimentaire de La Pocatière, Centre de Documentation **Founded:** 1859 **Type:** Government **Head:** Pierre Duncan *Phone:* +1(418) 856-1110 ext 258 **Staff:** 1 Prof. 2 Other **Holdings:** 13,000 books 190 journals **Language of Collection/Services:** French / French **Subjects:** Agribusiness, Agricultural Economics, Agricultural Engineering, Animal Husbandry, Biotechnology, Crops, Entomology, Farming, Environment, Fisheries, Food Sciences, Forestry, Horticulture, Plant Pathology, Soil Science, Water Resources **Databases Used:** Agricola **Loan:** In country **Photocopy:** Yes

604   Lennoxville, Québec, Canada
       Agriculture and Agri-Food Canada, Dairy and
           Swine Research and Development Centre
       Library
       PO Box 90
       2000 Route 108 East
       Lennoxville, Québec J1M 1Z3
Phone: +1(819) 565-9171 **Fax:** +1(819) 564-5507 **WWW:** res.agr.ca/lennox/home.htm

Non-English Name: Agriculture et Agroalimentaire Canada, Centre de Recherche et de Développement sur le Bovin Laitier et le Porc, Bibliothèque **Former Name:** Agriculture Canada **Founded:** 1978 **Type:** Government **Head:** Suzanne Gagné-Giguère *Email:* gagnegigueres@em.agr.ca *Phone:* +1(613) 565-9171 **Staff:** 1 Prof. 1 Other **Holdings:** 10,000 books 180 journals **Language of Collection/Services:** French, English / French, English **Subjects:** Animal Husbandry **Specializations:** Dairy Cattle, Pigs **Databases Used:** Comprehensive **Loan:** In country **Service:** Inhouse **Photocopy:** No

605   Longueuil, Québec, Canada
       Health and Welfare Canada, Health Protection
           Branch
       Regional Library
       1001 Ouest Boulevard Saint Laurent, Ch. 321
       Longueuil, Québec J4K 1C7
Phone: +1(450) 646-1353 **Fax:** +1(450) 928-4102 **Email:** linda_blais@hc-sc.gc.ca **WWW:** www.hc-sc.gc.ca

Non-English Name: Santé et Bien-être Social Canada, Protection de la Santé, Bibliothèque Régionale **Founded:** 1971 **Type:** Government **Head:** Linda Blais *Phone:* +1(450) 283-5472 *Email:* linda_blais@hc-sc.gc.ca **Staff:** 1 Prof. **Holdings:** 6,100 books 92 journals **Language of Collection/Services:** English, French / English, French **Subjects:** Bacteriology, Biochemistry, Chemistry, Food Sciences, Microbiology, Toxicology **Photocopy:** Yes

606   Mont-Joli, Québec, Canada
       Department of Fisheries and Oceans,
           Maurice-Lamontagne Institute
       Library
       CP 1000
       Mont-Joli, Québec G5H 3Z4

Location: 850 Route de la Mer **Phone:** +1(418) 775-6552 **Fax:** +1(418) 775-0538 **Email:** biblioiml@dfo-mpo.gc.ca **WWW:** www.qc.dfo.ca/iml/en/intro.htm **OPAC:** www.qc.dfo.ca/en/biblio/biblio.htm

Non-English Name: Pêches et Océans, Institut Maurice-Lamontagne (IML), Bibliothèque **Founded:** 1987 **Type:** Government **Head:** Guy Michaud *Phone:* +1(418) 775-0551 *Email:* michaudg@dfo-mpo.gc.ca **Staff:** 3 Prof. **Holdings:** 20,000 books 350 journals **Language of Collection/Services:** English, French / English, French **Subjects:** Aquaculture, Fisheries, Hydrography, Marine Sciences, Toxicology **Specializations:** Marine Fishes, Marine Mammals, Parasitology **Networks:** AMICUS **Databases Developed:** Waves/Vagues - union catalogue of Fisheries and Oceans Libraries; available on CD and the Internet **Loan:** Internationally **Service:** Inhouse **Photocopy:** Yes

607   Montréal, Québec, Canada
       Agriculture and Agri-Food Canada, Canadian
           Food Inspection Agency
       Canadian Food Inspection Library
       2001 University, 7th Floor
       Montréal, Québec H3A 3N2
Fax: +1(514) 283-3143

Non-English Name: Agriculture et Agroalimentaire Canada, Agence Canadienne d'Inspection des Aliments, Bibliothèque canadienne d'Inspection des Aliments **Founded:** 1985 **Type:** Government **Head:** Mr. Pierre Dicampo *Phone:* +1(514) 283-8888 *Email:* dicampop@em.agr.ca **Staff:** .6 Prof. **Holdings:** 2,500 books 75 journals **Subjects:** Food Inspection **Loan:** Internationally **Photocopy:** Yes

608   Montréal, Québec, Canada
       Ministry of Agriculture, Fisheries and Food,
           Quebec
       Documentation Center
       201, boul. Crémazie est, 4e
       Montréal, Québec H2M 1L4
Phone: +1(514) 873-4410 **Fax:** +1(514) 873-2364 **Email:** guylaine.simard@agr.gouv.qc.ca **WWW:** www.agr.gouv.qc.ca

Non-English Name: Ministère de l'Agriculture, des Pêcheries et de l'Alimentation, Québec (MAPAQ), Centre de Documentation **Type:** Government **Head:** Suzanne Tremblay **Staff:** 1 Prof. 2 Other **Holdings:** 4,000 books 200 journals

609   Montréal, Québec, Canada
       Montreal Botanical Garden
       Library
       4101 Rue Sherbrooke Est
       Montréal, Québec H1X 2B2
Phone: +1(514) 872-1824 **Fax:** +1(514) 872-3765 **Email:** jardin_botanique@ville.mmontreal.qc.ca **WWW:** www.ville.montreal.qc.ca/jardin

Non-English Name: Jardin Botanique de Montréal, Bibliothèque **Founded:** 1938 **Type:** Special **Head:** Céline Arseneault *Email:* celine_arsenault@ville.montreal.qc.ca *Phone:* +1(514) 872-1440 **Staff:** 1 Prof. 3.5 Other **Holdings:** 22,000 books 250 journals **Language of Collection/Services:** English, French / French, English **Subjects:** Botany, Ecology,

Economic Botany, Entomology, Horticulture, Land Management, Landscape Architecture, Plant Pathology **Specializations:** Medicinal Plants, Ornamental Plants **Databases Developed:** Slide library of 135,000 slides **Databases Used:** Agricola; CABCD; HORTCD; Index Kewensis **Loan:** Internationally **Service:** Inhouse **Photocopy:** Yes

610   **Montréal, Québec, Canada**
         University of Montreal
         Botany Library
         Jardin Botanique
         4101, Rue Sherbrooke est
         Montréal, Québec H1X 2B2
Phone: +1(514) 872-8495 **Email:** prbiog@bib.umontreal. ca **WWW:** www.bib.umontreal.ca **OPAC:** www.bib. umontreal.ca/SB/atriumgd.htm

Non-English Name: Université de Montréal, Bibliothèque Botanique **Founded:** 1925 **Type:** Academic **Holdings:** 64,127 books

611   **Pointe Claire, Québec, Canada**
         Pulp and Paper Research Institute of Canada
            (Paprican)
         Library
         570 Saint John's Boulevard
         Pointe Claire, Québec H9R 3J9
Phone: +1(514) 630-4100 **Fax:** +1(514) 630-4134 **Email:** info@paprican.ca **WWW:** www.paprican.ca

Founded: 1929 **Type:** Government **Holdings:** 20,000 books 675 journals **Subjects:** Pulp and Paper Industry

612   **Québec, Québec, Canada**
         Ministry of Agriculture, Fisheries and Food,
            Quebec
         Library
         200-A Chemin Sainte-Foy, 1er étage
         Québec, Québec G1R 4X6
Phone: +1(418) 380-2100 ext 3504 **Fax:** +1(418) 380-2175 **WWW:** www.agr.gouv.qc.ca **OPAC:** www.ribg. gouv.qc.ca

Non-English Name: Ministère de l'Agriculture, des Pêcheries et de l'Alimentation, Québec (MAPAQ), Bibliothèque **Founded:** 1943 **Type:** Government **Head:** Hélène Babineau *Email:* helene. Babineau@agr.gouv.qc.ca *Phone:* +1(418) 643-2428 **Staff:** 1 Prof. 5 Other **Holdings:** 30,000 books 1,550 journals **Language of Collection/Services:** English, French / English, French **Subjects:** Agriculture (Tropics), Agribusiness, Agricultural Development, Agricultural Economics, Agricultural Engineering, Animal Husbandry, Biotechnology, Education/Extension, Entomology, Fisheries, Farming, Crops, Food Sciences, Forestry, Horticulture, Soil Science, Plant Pathology, Veterinary Medicine, Water Resources **Databases Developed:** BIOALI **Databases Used:** Agricola **Loan:** Internationally **Service:** Inhouse **Photocopy:** Yes

613   **Rez-de-chaussée, Québec, Canada**
         Ministry of the Environment, Quebec
         Documentation Centre
         675, boui. René Lévesque Est

         Rez-de-chaussée, Québec G1R 5V7
Phone: +1(418) 521-3821 **Fax:** +1(418) 528-0406 **Email:** biblio@mef.gouv.qc.ca **WWW:** www.mef.gouv.qc.ca **OPAC:** www.ribg.gouv.qc.ca

Non-English Name: Ministère de l'Environnement, Québec, Centre de Documentation **Founded:** 1980 **Type:** Government **Head:** Gérard Nobréga *Phone:* +1(418) 643-5363 **Staff:** 3 Prof. 8 Other **Holdings:** 50,000 books 300 journals **Language of Collection/Services:** French, English / French, English **Subjects:** Botany, Entomology, Environment, Fisheries, Pollution, Toxicology, Zoology **Loan:** Internationally **Service:** Inhouse **Photocopy:** Yes

614   **Rimouski, Québec, Canada**
         University of Quebec at Rimouski (UQAR)
         Library
         300, allée des Ursulines
         Rimouski, Québec G5L 3A1
Phone: +1(418) 724-1476 **Fax:** +1(418) 724-1621 **WWW:** www.uqar.uquebec.ca/default.htm **OPAC:** www.manitou. uqam.ca

Non-English Name: Université du Québec à Rimouski, Bibliothèque **Founded:** 1969 **Type:** Academic **Head:** Gaston Dumont *Phone:* +1(418) 723-1986 ext 1470 *Email:* gaston_dumont@uqar.uquebec.ca **Staff:** 8 Prof. 17 Other **Holdings:** 200,000 books 3,500 journals **Language of Collection/Services:** French / French **Subjects:** Biology, Biotechnology, Fisheries, Plant Pathology, Rural Economy **Loan:** Internationally **Photocopy:** Yes

615   **Rouyn-Noranda, Québec, Canada**
         University of Quebec in Abitibi-Temiscamingue
         Library
         445, Boulevard de l'Université
         CP 8000
         Rouyn-Noranda, Québec J9X 5M5
Phone: +1(819) 762-0971 **Fax:** +1(819) 762-4727 **WWW:** web2.uqat.uquebec.ca/biblio **OPAC:** www.manitou.uqam. ca

Non-English Name: Université du Québec en Abitibi-Témiscamingue, Bibliothèque **Founded:** 1971 **Type:** Academic **Head:** André Béland *Phone:* +1(819) 762-0931 ext 1134 *Email:* andre.beland@uqat.uquebec.ca **Staff:** 3 Prof. 17 Other **Holdings:** 2,500 books 10 journals **Subjects:** Fisheries, Forestry, Soil Science, Water Resources **Loan:** Internationally **Photocopy:** Yes

616   **Saint-Hyacinthe, Québec, Canada**
         Agriculture and Agri-Food Canada, Food
            Research and Development Centre (FRDC)
         Library
         3600 Boulevard Casavant Ouest
         Saint-Hyacinthe, Québec J2S 8E3
Phone: +1(450) 773-1105 **Fax:** +1(450) 773-8461 **Email:** crdabiblio@em.agr.ca **WWW:** res.agr.ca/sthya/index.htm

Non-English Name: Agriculture et Agroalimentaire Canada, Centre de Recherche et de Développement sur les Aliments (CRDA), Bibliothèque **Type:** Government **Founded:** 1985 **Head:** Francine Bernard *Email:* bernardf@em.agr.ca *Phone:* +1 (450) 773-1105 **Staff:** 1 Prof. 1 Other **Holdings:**

1,500 books 250 journals **Language of Collection/Services:** English / French **Subjects:** Biotechnology, Food Sciences **Networks:** Advance **Databases Used:** Comprehensive **Loan:** In country **Service:** Inhouse **Photocopy:** Yes

617   Saint-Hyacinthe, Québec, Canada
Ministry of Agriculture, Fisheries and Food,
    Quebec, Saint-Hyacinthe Institute of Food
    Technology
Documentation Center
3230 rue Sicotte
Saint-Hyacinthe, Québec J2S 7B3
Phone: +1(514) 778-6504 ext 277/8 **Fax:** +1(514) 778-6536 **WWW:** ita.qc.ca/biblio

Non-English Name: Ministère de l'Agriculture, des Pêcheries et de l'Alimentation, Québec, Institut de Technologie Agro-Alimentaire de Saint-Hyacinthe (ITA), Centre de Documentation **Founded:** 1963 **Type:** Academic **Head:** Gilles Bachand *Phone:* +1(514) 778-6504 *Email:* gilles.bachand@ agr.gouv.qc.ca **Staff:** 1 Prof. 3 Other **Holdings:** 30,000 books 515 journals **Language of Collection/Services:** French, English **Subjects:** Agricultural Economics, Agricultural Engineering, Animal Husbandry, Biotechnology, Crops, Education/Extension, Entomology, Farming, Food Sciences, Horticulture, Plant Pathology, Soil Science **Databases Used:** Agricola **Loan:** In country **Photocopy:** Yes

618   Saint-Hyacinthe, Québec, Canada
University of Montreal
Veterinary Medical Library
CP 5000
Saint-Hyacinthe, Québec J2S 7C6
Phone: +1(450) 773-8521 **Fax:** +1(450) 778-8104 **WWW:** www.medvet.umontreal.ca/biblio **OPAC:** telnet://atrium. bib.umontreal.ca **Ariel IP:** 132.204.158.23

Non-English Name: Université de Montréal, Bibliothèque de Médecine Vétérinaire **Founded:** 1945 **Type:** Academic **Head:** Jean-Paul Jetté *Phone:* +1(450) 773-8521 *Email:* jettejp@ere.umontreal.ca **Staff:** 1 Prof. 4 Other **Holdings:** 20,000 books 600 journals **Language of Collection/Services:** English / English, French **Subjects:** Animal Husbandry, Animal Nutrition, Animal Pathology, Veterinary Medicine **Databases Used:** Biosis; CABCD; Current Contents; Medline **Loan:** Internationally **Photocopy:** Yes

619   Saint-Jean-Sur-Richelieu, Québec, Canada
Agriculture and Agri-Food Canada, Horticultural
    Research and Development Centre (HRDC)
Library
430, Gouin Blvd., C.P. 457
Saint-Jean-Sur-Richelieu, Québec J3B 6Z8
Phone: +1(450) 346-4494 ext 136 **Fax:** +1(450) 346-7740 **Email:** lavaleel@em.agr.ca **WWW:** res.agr.ca/riche/hrdc. htm

Non-English Name: Agriculture et Agroalimentaire Canada, Centre de Recherche et de Développement en Horticulture (CRDH), Bibliothèque **Former Name:** Agriculture Canada **Founded:** 1952 **Type:** Government **Head:** Francine Bernard *Phone:* +1(450) 346-4494 *Email:* bernardf@em. agr.ca **Staff:** 1 Prof. 1 Other **Holdings:** 10,000 books 200

journals **Language of Collection/Services:** English, French **Subjects:** Biotechnology, Crops, Entomology, Plant Pathology, Soil Science **Specializations:** Horticulture **Databases Used:** Agricola; Biosis; CABCD; CAS; FSTA **Loan:** Inhouse **Service:** Internationally **Photocopy:** Yes

620   Sainte Anne-de-Bellevue, Québec, Canada
McGill University, Macdonald Campus, Brace
    Center for Water Resources Management
Library
21,111 Lakeshore Road
PO Box 900
Sainte Anne-de-Bellevue, Québec H9X 3V9
Location: 3 Stewart Park **Phone:** +1(514) 398-7833 **Fax:** +1(514) 398-7767 **Email:** ae12000@musica.mcgill.ca **WWW:** agrenv.mcgill.ca/brace/index.htm

Former Name: Brace Research Institute **Founded:** 1960 **Type:** Non-profit Private **Head:** Thomas A. Lawand *Phone:* +1(514) 398-7833 *Email:* ae12000@musica.mcgill.ca **Staff:** 2 Prof. 4 Other **Holdings:** 10,000 books 300 journals **Subjects:** Desalinization, Energy Sources, Pumps, Renewable Resources, Solar Drying, Water Supply **Loan:** Do not loan **Photocopy:** Yes

621   Sainte Anne-de-Bellevue, Québec, Canada
McGill University, Macdonald Campus, Faculty
    of Agricultural and Environmental Sciences
Library
21,111 Lakeshore Road
Sainte Anne-de-Bellevue, Québec H9X 3V9
Location: Barton Building **Phone:** +1(514) 398-7879 **Fax:** +1(514) 398-7960 **WWW:** www.mcgill.ca **OPAC:** www. library.mcgill.ca **Ariel IP:** 132.206.88.66

Founded: 1907 **Type:** Academic **Head:** Janet Finlayson *Phone:* +1(514) 398-7876 *Email:* adnj@musica.mcgill.ca **Staff:** 1.8 Prof. 5 Other **Holdings:** 95,500 books 775 journals **Language of Collection/Services:** English / English **Subjects:** Agricultural Economics, Agricultural Engineering, Animal Husbandry, Crops, Food Sciences, Forestry, Horticulture, Plants, Soil Science, Water Resources **Specializations:** Entomology **Databases Used:** Agricola; Biosis; CABCD; Medline **Loan:** In country and United States **Service:** Inhouse **Photocopy:** Yes

622   Sainte-Foy, Québec, Canada
Agriculture and Agri-Food Canada, Soils and
    Crops Research and Development Centre
Library
2560 Boulevard Hochelaga
Sainte-Foy, Québec G1V 2J3
Phone: +1(418) 657-7980 ext 212 **Fax:** +1(418) 648-2402 **Email:** cotes@em.agr.ca **WWW:** res.agr.ca/stfoy/index. html

Non-English Name: Agriculture et Agroalimentaire Canada, Centre de Recherche et de Développement sur les Sols et les Grandes Cultures, Bibliothèque **Former Name:** Agriculture Canada **Founded:** 1970 **Type:** Government **Head:** Suzanne Côté *Phone:* +1(418) 657-7980 ext 212 *Email:* cotes@em. agr.ca **Staff:** 1 Other **Holdings:** 6,000 books 100 journals **Language of Collection/Services:** English, French

/ English, French **Subjects:** Biotechnology, Crops, Molecular Biology, Plant Pathology, Soil Science **Databases Used:** Agricola; CABI **Loan:** In country **Service:** In country **Photocopy:** Yes

623   **Sainte-Foy, Québec, Canada**
           Canadian Forest Service, Laurentian Forestry
              Center
           Library
           1055 Rue du P.E.P.S.
           PO Box 3800
           Sainte-Foy, Québec G1V 4C7
Fax: +1(418) 648-3433 **WWW:** www.cfl.forestry.ca

Non-English Name: Service Canadien des Forêts, Centre de Foresterie des Laurentides, Bibliothèque **Former Name:** Forestry Canada, Forêts Canada **Founded:** 1952 **Type:** Government **Head:** Gilles Bizier *Phone:* +1(418) 648-4850 *Email:* gbizier@exchange.cfl.forestry.ca **Staff:** 1 Prof. **Subjects:** Biology, Entomology, Forestry, Genetics, Mycology **Loan:** Internationally **Service:** Inhouse **Photocopy:** Yes

624   **Sainte-Foy, Québec, Canada**
           Environment Canada, Quebec Region
           Main Library
           PO Box 10100
           1141 Route de l'Eglise, 7th Floor
           Sainte-Foy, Québec G1V 4H5
Phone: +1(418) 648-4768, 649-6546 **Fax:** +1(418) 648-7166 **Email:** quebec.biblio@ec.gc.ca **WWW:** www.qc.ec.gc.ca/biblio

Head: Cécile Morin *Phone:* +1(418) 648-4768

625   **Sainte-Foy, Québec, Canada**
           Laval University
           Science Library
           Pavillon Alexandre-Vachon, Cité Universitaire
           Sainte-Foy, Québec G1K 7P4
Phone: +1(418) 656-3967 **Fax:** +1(418) 656-7699 **WWW:** www.bibl.ulaval.ca **OPAC:** arianeweb.ulaval.ca

Non-English Name: Université Laval (UL), Bibliothèque Scientifique **Founded:** 1963 **Type:** Academic **Head:** Lorraine Vallières *Email:* lorraine.vallieres@bibl.ulaval.ca *Phone:* +1(418) 656-2948 **Staff:** 7 Prof. 24 Other **Holdings:** 176,609 books 2,653 journals **Language of Collection/Services:** French, English / French, English **Subjects:** Agribusiness, Agriculture (Tropics), Agricultural Development, Crops, Agricultural Economics, Agricultural Engineering, Animal Husbandry, Animal Nutrition, Consumers, Education/Extension, Entomology, Farming, Food Engineering, Horticulture, Human Nutrition, Plant Pathology, Soil Science, Veterinary Medicine, Water Resources, Zootechny **Specializations:** Biotechnology, Food Sciences, Food Technology, Dairy Science, Forestry, Nutrition, Plants **Databases Used:** Comprehensive **Loan:** Internationally **Photocopy:** Yes

626   **Sainte-Foy, Québec, Canada**
           Ministry of Agriculture, Fisheries and Food,
              Quebec
           Documentation Center

           2700 Einstein F2
           Sainte-Foy, Québec G1P 3W8
Fax: +1(418) 643-3361 **WWW:** www.agr.gouv.qc.ca **OPAC:** www.ribg.gouv.qc.ca

Non-English Name: Ministère de l'Agriculture, des Pêcheries et de l'Alimentation, Québec (MAPAQ), Centre de Documentation **Founded:** 1971 **Type:** Government **Head:** Michel Levesque *Phone:* +1(418) 643-9730 *Email:* michel.levesque@agr.gouv.qc.ca **Staff:** 1 Prof. 2 Other **Holdings:** 9,220 books 131 journals **Language of Collection/Services:** English/French **Subjects:** Agriculture (Tropics), Animal Husbandry, Biotechnology, Crops, Entomology, Farming, Food Sciences, Horticulture, Plant Pathology, Soil Science, Veterinary Medicine **Networks:** CUBIQ **Databases Used:** Comprehensive **Loan:** Inhouse **Photocopy:** Yes

627   **Sainte-Foy, Québec, Canada**
           Ministry of Natural Resources, Quebec
           Library
           2700, rue Einstein, F-1
           Sainte-Foy, Québec G1P 3W8
Phone: +1(418) 643-9739 **Fax:** +1(418) 643-3361 **WWW:** www.mrn.gouv.qc.ca **OPAC:** www.ribg.gouv.qc.ca

Non-English Name: Ministère des Ressources Naturelles, Québec, Bibliothèque **Founded:** 1971 **Type:** Government **Head:** Lucie Jobin *Email:* ljobin@mrn.gouv.qc.ca **Staff:** 1 Other **Holdings:** 6,000 books 200 journals **Language of Collection/Services:** English, French / English, French **Subjects:** Biotechnology, Entomology, Plant Pathology, Soil Science **Specializations:** Forestry, Silviculture **Databases Used:** Agricola; TREECD **Loan:** In country **Service:** In country **Photocopy:** Yes

Saskatchewan

628   **Humboldt, Saskatchewan, Canada**
           Prairie Agriculture Machinery Institute (PAMI)
           Library
           Box 1900
           Humboldt, Saskatchewan S0K 2A0
Location: Highway 5 West **Fax:** +1(306) 682-5080 **Email:** humboldt@pami.ca **WWW:** www.pami.ca

Founded: 1975 **Type:** Government **Head:** Mrs. Sharon Doepker *Phone:* +1(306) 682-2555 ext 156 *Email:* pami@sk.sympatico.ca **Staff:** 1 Other **Holdings:** 17,000 books 150 journals **Language of Collection/Services:** English/English **Subjects:** Agricultural Development, Crops, Agricultural Engineering, Machinery **Databases Used:** Comprehensive **Loan:** Internationally **Service:** Internationally **Photocopy:** Yes

629   **Regina, Saskatchewan, Canada**
           Agriculture and Agri-Food Canada, Prairie Farm
              Rehabilitation Administration (AAFC, PFRA)
           Information Centre
           603 CIBC Tower
           1800 Hamilton Street
           Regina, Saskatchewan S4P 4L2
Phone: +1(306) 780-5100 **Fax:** +1(306) 780-5018 **Email:** pfrainfo@em.agr.ca **WWW:** www.agr.ca/pfra

Founded: 1966 **Type:** Government **Head:** C. Dusyk *Phone:* +1(306) 780-7012 **Staff:** 1 Prof. 2 Other **Holdings:** 50,000 books 500 journals **Language of Collection/Services:** English / English **Subjects:** Agricultural Engineering, Irrigation, Soil, Water Resources **Specializations:** Drought, Rural Development **Databases Used:** Comprehensive **Loan:** Internationally **Service:** Internationally **Photocopy:** Yes

630   Regina, Saskatchewan, Canada
        Environment Canada, Prairie and Northern Region
        Library
        2365 Albert Street, Room 300
        Regina, Saskatchewan S4P 4K1
Phone: +1(306) 780-5306 **Fax:** +1(306) 780-7614 **Email:** pat.macinnis@ec.gc.ca **WWW:** www.mb.ec.gc.ca **OPAC:** www.andornot.com/envcan

Head: Patricia MacInnis *Email:* pat.macinnis@ec.gc.ca

631   Regina, Saskatchewan, Canada
        Farm Credit Corporation
        Library
        PO Box 4320
        1800 Hamilton St.
        Regina, Saskatchewan S4P 4L3
Phone: +1(306) 780-8100 **Fax:** +1(306) 780-5456 **Email:** communications@fcc-sca.ca **WWW:** www.fcc-sca.ca

Type: Government **Language of Collection/Services:** English **Photocopy:** Yes

632   Regina, Saskatchewan, Canada
        Saskatchewan Agriculture and Food (SAF)
        Library
        B5-3085 Albert Street
        Regina, Saskatchewan S4S 0B1
Phone: +1(306) 787-5151/2 **Fax:** +1(306) 787-0216 **WWW:** www.agr.gov.sk.ca/default.asp

Founded: 1898 **Type:** Government **Head:** Hélène Stewart *Phone:* +1(306) 787-5151 *Email:* hstewart@agr.gov.sk.ca **Staff:** 1 Prof. 3 Other **Holdings:** 20,000 books 650 journals **Language of Collection/Services:** English / English **Subjects:** Agribusiness, Agricultural Economics, Animal Husbandry, Crops, Soil Science **Databases Used:** CABCD **Loan:** Internationally **Service:** Internationally **Photocopy:** Yes

633   Regina, Saskatchewan, Canada
        Saskatchewan Institute of Applied Science and
            Technology, Wascana Campus (SIAST)
        Library
        Library Services
        4635 Wascana Parkway
        PO Box 556
        Regina, Saskatchewan S4P 3A3
Phone: +1(306) 787-4323/4713 **Fax:** +1(306) 787-0560 **WWW:** www.siast.sk.ca **OPAC:** www.siast.sk.ca/~wascana/waslib.htm

Founded: 1972 **Head:** Colleen Warren *Phone:* +1(306) 787-4321 *Email:* warrenc@siast.sk.ca **Staff:** 3 Prof. 6 Other **Holdings:** 3,286 books 100 journals **Type:** Academic **Language of Collection/Services:** English / English **Subjects:**

Agricultural Production, Animal Production, Crops, Farm Management, Farming, Mechanics, Pesticides, Soil Science **Networks:** SUNET **Databases Used:** Comprehensive **Service:** Inhouse **Loan:** In country **Photocopy:** Yes

634   Regina, Saskatchewan, Canada
        Saskatchewan Wheat Pool, Policy and Economic
            Research Division (SWP, PERD)
        Corporate Library
        2625 Victoria Avenue
        Regina, Saskatchewan S4T 7T9
Fax: +1(306) 569-4885 **WWW:** www.swp.com

Founded: 1930 **Type:** Business **Head:** Diana Behrns *Phone:* +1(306) 569-4480 *Email:* diana.behrns@swp.com **Staff:** 1 Prof. 1 Other **Holdings:** 7,000 books 200 journals **Language of Collection/Services:** English / English **Subjects:** Agribusiness, Cooperatives **Specializations:** Human Resources, Agricultural Economics, Cooperatives, **Databases Used:** Comprehensive **Loan:** In country **Service:** In country **Photocopy:** Yes

635   Saskatoon, Saskatchewan, Canada
        Agriculture and Agri-Food Canada (AAFC)
        Canadian Agriculture Library (CAL)
        Saskatoon Research Centre
        107 Science Place
        Saskatoon, Saskatchewan S7N 0X2
Phone: +1(306) 956-7222/3 **Fax:** +1(306) 956-7247 **Email:** library-saskatoon@em.agr.ca **WWW:** res.agr.ca/sask/mainpage.html

Former Name: Agriculture Canada **Founded:** 1957 **Type:** Government **Head:** Norlayne Scott-Gaare *Email:* scott-gaaren@em.agr.ca **Staff:** 2 Prof. **Holdings:** 13,000 books 70 journals **Language of Collection/Services:** English/English **Subjects:** Crops, Entomology, Oilseeds, Plant Breeding **Networks:** CAL **Databases Developed:** Material Safety Data Sheets (MSDS) collection **Databases Used:** Agricola; Biosis; CABCD; Current Contents **Loan:** In country **Photocopy:** Yes

636   Saskatoon, Saskatchewan, Canada
        Environment Canada, Canadian Wildlife Service,
            Prairie and Northern Wildlife Research
            Center
        Saskatoon Library
        115 Perimeter Road
        Saskatoon, Saskatchewan S7N 0X4
Phone: +1(306) 975-4096 **Fax:** +1(306) 975-4089 **Email:** cws.library@ec.gc.ca **WWW:** www.cws-scf.ec.gc.ca/cwshom_e.html **OPAC:** www.andornet.com/envcan

637   Saskatoon, Saskatchewan, Canada
        Environment Canada, National Hydrology
            Research Centre
        Library
        11 Innovation Boulevard
        Saskatoon, Saskatchewan S7N 3H5
Phone: +1(306) 975-5559 **Fax:** +1(306) 975-5143 **WWW:** www.ec.gc.ca

Subjects: Hydrology

638   Saskatoon, Saskatchewan, Canada
POS Pilot Plant Corporation
POS Information Services
118 Veterinary Road
Saskatoon, Saskatchewan S7N 2R4

Phone: +1(306) 978-2804 **Fax:** +1(306) 975-3766 **Email:** bettyv@pos.ca **WWW:** www.pos.ca

Founded: 1977 **Type:** Business **Head:** Betty Vankoughnett *Phone:* +1(306) 975-7066 *Email:* bettyv@pos.ca **Staff:** 1 Prof. 3 Other **Holdings:** 5,000 books 270 journals **Language of Collection/Services:** English **Subjects:** Grain Crops, Oilseeds **Networks:** SSPP **Loan:** Do not loan **Service:** Internationally **Photocopy:** Yes

639   Saskatoon, Saskatchewan, Canada
Potash Corporation of Saskatchewan Inc. (PCS)
Library Services
122 1st Avenue South
Suite 500
Saskatoon, Saskatchewan S7K 7G3

Fax: +1(306) 652-2699 **WWW:** www.potashcorp.com

Founded: 1979 **Type:** Business **Head:** Marybelle White *Email:* marybelle.white@potashcorp.com *Phone:* +1(306) 933-8501 **Staff:** 1 Prof. **Holdings:** 5,000 books 350 journals **Language of Collection/Services:** English / English **Subjects:** Agribusiness, Agricultural Economics **Loan:** Inhouse **Service:** Inhouse **Photocopy:** Yes

640   Saskatoon, Saskatchewan, Canada
Saskatchewan Research Council (SRC)
Information Services
15 Innovation Boulevard
Saskatoon, Saskatchewan S7N 2X8

Phone: +1(306) 933-5454 **Fax:** +1(306) 933-7446 **Email:** raven@src.sk.ca **WWW:** www.src.sk.ca **OPAC:** www.src.sk.ca/library.html

Type: Government **Head:** Colleen MacLeod *Phone:* +1(306) 933-5489 *Email:* macleod@src.sk.ca **Staff:** 2 Prof. **Holdings:** 23,000 books 400 journals **Language of Collection/Services:** English/English **Subjects:** Agribusiness, Agricultural Development, Agricultural Economics, Agricultural Engineering, Biotechnology, Farming, Fisheries, Food Sciences, Forestry, Plants, Soil Science, Water Resources **Specializations:** Climatology **Loan:** In country **Service:** In country **Photocopy:** Yes

641   Saskatoon, Saskatchewan, Canada
University of Saskatchewan
Main Library
3 Campus Drive
Saskatoon, Saskatchewan S7N 5A4

Phone: +1(306) 966-6005 **Fax:** +1(306) 966-6040 **WWW:** www.usask.ca **OPAC:** sundog.usask.ca

Founded: 1907 **Head:** Ken Ladd, Acting *Phone:* +1(306) 966-5942 *Email:* ladd@sklib.usask.ca **Holdings:** 30,000 books 469 journals **Language of Collection/Services:** English/English **Type:** Academic **Subjects:** Agricultural Economics, Agricultural Engineering, Animal Husbandry, Crops, Entomology, Horticulture, Plant Biotechnology, Plant Pathology, Range Management, Soil Science **Databases De-**

veloped: U-Search system is a collection of databases including commercial and in-house files; dial-in and Internet access available. **Databases Used:** Comprehensive **Loan:** Internationally **Photocopy:** Yes

642   Saskatoon, Saskatchewan, Canada
University of Saskatchewan, Western College of
        Veterinary Medicine (WCVM)
Veterinary Medicine Library
52 Campus Drive
Saskatoon, Saskatchewan S7N 5B4

Phone: +1(306) 966-7205 **Fax:** +1(306) 966-8747 **Email:** vetlib@moondog.usask.ca **WWW:** library.usask.ca/vetmed **OPAC:** sundog.usask.ca

Founded: 1968 **Type:** Academic **Head:** Jill Crawley-Low, Acting *Phone:* +1(306) 966-7206 *Email:* crawley@aklib.usask.ca **Staff:** 1 Prof. 3 Other **Holdings:** 20,000 books 527 journals **Language of Collection/Services:** English/English **Subjects:** Animal Husbandry, Veterinary Medicine **Databases Used:** CABCD; Medline **Loan:** In country **Photocopy:** Yes

643   Swift Current, Saskatchewan, Canada
Agriculture and Agri-Food Canada, Semiarid
        Prairie Agriculture Research Centre
Library
Box 1030
Airport Road
Swift Current, Saskatchewan S9H 3X2

Fax: +1(306) 773-9213 **Email:** library-sc@em.agr.ca **WWW:** res.agr.ca/swift/welcome.htm

Former Name: Agriculture Canada, Swift Current Research Station **Founded:** 1921 **Type:** Government **Head:** Karen E. Wilton *Phone:* +1(306) 778-7260 *Email:* wiltonk@em.agr.ca **Staff:** 1 Prof. **Holdings:** 10,000 books 270 journals **Language of Collection/Services:** English / English **Subjects:** Agricultural Economics, Agricultural Engineering, Animal Husbandry, Crops, Soil Science, Water Resources **Specializations:** Dry Farming **Networks:** Agricat **Databases Developed:** Swift Current Research Station Scientific Publications (1929 to date) **Databases Used:** CABCD; Agricola **Loan:** In country **Service:** In country **Photocopy:** Yes

Yukon Territory

644   Whitehorse, Yukon Territory, Canada
Environment Canada, Pacific and Yukon Region
Library
Mile 917.6B, Alaska Highway
Whitehorse, Yukon Territory Y1A5X7

Phone: +1(403) 667-3407 **Fax:** +1(403) 667-7962 **WWW:** www.pyr.ec.gc.ca **OPAC:** www.andornot.com/envcan

Cape Verde

645   Praia, Cape Verde
National Agricultural Research Institute
Documentation Center

CP 84
Praia

Non-English Name: Instituto Nacional de Investigação Agraria (INIA), Centro de Documentação **Founded:** 1986 **Head:** Joaquim Morais *Phone:* +238 611570 **Staff:** 1 Prof. 2 Other **Holdings:** 1,400 books 35 journals **Subjects:** Cereals, Irrigation, Plant Protection, Plants, Soil Science **Networks:** AGRIS

Central African Republic

646 **Bangui, Central African Republic**
Ministère de la Promotion Rurale (MPR)
Centre National de Documentation Agricole
(CNDA)
BP 786
Bangui

Founded: 1984 **Type:** Government **Head:** M. Réginald Bida-Kette *Phone:* +236 612661 **Staff:** 5 Prof. 3 Other **Holdings:** 9,600 books 18 journals **Subjects:** Agricultural Development, Agricultural Economics, Animal Health, Animal Production, Crop Production, Plant Protection, Rural Sociology **Networks:** AGRIS; CARIS

647 **Bangui, Central African Republic**
Ministère délégue a l'Economie au Plan
Centre National de Documentation Economique et
Sociales (CNDES)
BP 696
Bangui
Phone: +236 613805 **Fax:** +236 617387

Founded: 1975 **Type:** Government **Head:** M. Abael Ngamboula **Holdings:** 3,783 books 35 journals **Language of Collection/Services:** French, English / French **Subjects:** Agricultural Economics, Environment, Hydrology

648 **Bangui, Central African Republic**
Ministère des Affaires Sociales et de la Promotion
de la Femme et de la Solidarité Nationale,
Direction Générale de la Promotion de la
Femme
Service de Gestion de la Banque de Données
Statistiques
BP 917
Bangui
Phone: +236 614370

Founded: 1987 **Type:** Government **Head:** M. Jean-Firmin Mobou **Language of Collection/Services:** French / French

649 **Bangui, Central African Republic**
Research Institute for Development
Bibliothèque
BP 893
Bangui
Location: PK 10 - Route de Damara **Phone:** +236 612089 **Fax:** +236 616829 **WWW:** www.ird.fr

Non-English Name: Institut de Recherche pour le Développement (IRD) **Former Name:** Institut Français de Recher-

che Scientifique pour le Développement en Coopération (ORSTOM) **Founded:** 1949 **Type:** Government **Head:** Yves Boulvert *Phone:* +236 612089 **Staff:** 1 Other **Holdings:** 800 books 6 journals **Subjects:** Agricultural Economics, Entomology, Plant Pathology, Rural Economy, Soil Science **Loan:** Do not loan **Photocopy:** Yes

650 **Bangui, Central African Republic**
Université de Bangui, Institut Supérieur de
Développement Rural (ISDR)
Service de Documentation
BP 909
Bangui
Phone: +236 611767 **Fax:** +236 617890

Founded: 1970 **Type:** Academic **Head:** François Dode **Staff:** 1 Other **Holdings:** 5,852 books 33 journals **Subjects:** Agricultural Chemistry, Forestry, Environment, Rural Economy, Zootechny **Loan:** In country **Photocopy:** No

651 **Bangui, Central African Republic**
World Wildlife Fund (WWF)
Documentation Service
BP 1053
Bangui
Phone: +236 614279 **Fax:** +236 611085 **Email:** wwfcar@ intnet.cf

Non-English Name: Fonds Mondial pour la Nature **Founded:** 1992 **Type:** International **Head:** Kamis *Email:* wwfcar @intnet.cf **Staff:** 1 Prof. **Holdings:** 2,000 books 10 journals **Language of Collection/Services:** French, English / French **Subjects:** Agriculture (Tropics), Forestry **Loan:** Inhouse **Service:** Inhouse **Photocopy:** Yes

Chad

652 **N'Djaména, Chad**
Ministère de l'Agriculture
Centre de Documentation et d'Information
BP 624
N'Djaména

Former Name: Ministère de l'Agriculture et du Développement Rural **Founded:** 1981 **Type:** Government **Head:** Itafanus Mbang Bassa Mor **Staff:** 1 Prof. **Holdings:** 500 books **Subjects:** Agricultural Development, Agricultural Economics, Agricultural Policy, Crop Production, Rural Sociology **Networks:** AGRIS

653 **N'Djamena, Chad**
Research and Training Center for Development
(RTCD)
Department of Documentation
BP 907
N'Djamena
Phone: +235 517142, 515432 **Fax:** +235 519150

Non-English Name: Centre d'Etudes et de Formation pour le Développement (CEFOD), Département de la Documentation **Founded:** 1969 **Type:** Research **Head:** Royoumbaye Nadoumngar Jean-Pierre *Phone:* +235 517142, 515432 **Staff:** 4 Prof. 10 Other **Holdings:** 4,030 books 28 journals

Language of Collection/Services: French / French **Subjects:** Agriculture (Tropics), Agricultural Development, Agricultural Economics, Animal Husbandry, Crops, Extension, Environment, Fisheries, Food Sciences, Forestry, Horticulture, Rural Development, Rural Sociology, Soil Science, Water Resources **Loan:** Do not loan **Service:** In country **Photocopy:** Yes

Chile

654   **Angol, Chile**
El Vergel Agricultural Institute
Library
Casilla 8-D
Angol

Location: Km 5 Camino Angol-Collipulli, Angol **Phone:** +56(2) 711142 **Fax:** +56(2) 712395 **Email:** elvergel@ctcinternet.cl

Non-English Name: Escuela Agrícola "El Vergel", Biblioteca **Former Name:** Instituto Agrícola Metodista "El Vergel" **Founded:** 1952 **Type:** Government **Head:** Patricia Baeza Soto *Phone:* +56(2) 711142 *Email:* elvergel@ctcinternet.cl **Staff:** 1 Prof. 1 Other **Holdings:** 3,000 books **Subjects:** Farm Machinery, Fertilizers, Fruits, Gardening, Harvesting, Horticulture, Irrigation, Silviculture, Soil Science **Specializations:** Agricultural Development, Crops, Plants, Soil, Water Resources **Loan:** Inhouse **Service:** Inhouse **Photocopy:** No

655   **Chillán, Chile**
Concepción University, Chillan Campus
Library
Casilla No. 537
Chillán

Location: Av. Vicente Méndez 595 **Phone:** +56(42) 208 729 **Fax:** +56(42) 275297 **Email:** biblioteca@udec.cl **WWW:** www.chillan.udec.cl

Non-English Name: Universidad de Concepción, Campus Chillán, Biblioteca **Former Name:** Agriculture and Forest Sciences Faculty, Facultad Ciencias Agropecuarias y Forestales **Founded:** 1955 **Type:** Academic **Head:** Lya Hernández Palominos *Email:* lhernand@palomo.chillan.udec.cl *Phone:* +56(42) 208906 **Staff:** 3 Prof. 2 Other **Holdings:** 10,000 books 220 journals **Language of Collection/Services:** Spanish, English / Spanish **Subjects:** Agricultural Engineering, Animal Husbandry, Biotechnology, Crops, Entomology, Farming, Food Sciences, Forestry, Plant Pathology, Soil Science, Veterinary Medicine, Water Resources **Specializations:** Drainage, Field Crops, Forage Legumes, Horticulture, Hydrology, Livestock Farming, Plant Diseases, Soil Fertility, Weed Control **Networks:** RENIB **Databases Used:** Agricola; Banco de Datos Latinamericanos; BIBA; CABCD **Loan:** In country **Service:** In country **Photocopy:** Yes

656   **Chillán, Chile**
Institute of Agricultural Research, Quilamapu
Regional Research Center
Library

Vicente Mendez 515
Casilla 426
Chillán

Fax: +56(42) 217852 **WWW:** www.inia.cl/quilamapu

Non-English Name: Instituto de Investigaciones Agropecuarias, Centro Regional de Investigación Quilamapu (INIA), Biblioteca **Head:** María Eugenia Scheuermann *Phone:* +56 (42) 211177 *Email:* mscheuer@quilamapu.inia.cl

657   **Osorno, Chile**
Institute of Agricultural Research, Remehue
Regional Research Center
Library
Km 8 Ruta 5 Norte
Casilla 24-O
Osorno

Fax: +56(64) 237746 **WWW:** www.inia.cl/remehue

Non-English Name: Instituto de Investigaciones Agropecuarias, Centro Regional de Investigación Remehue (INIA), Biblioteca **Head:** Beatriz Gouiric *Phone:* +56(64) 233515 *Email:* bgouiric@remehue.inia.cl

658   **Quillota, Chile**
Catholic University of Valparaiso, Faculty of
Agronomy
Library
La Palma s/n
Casilla 4-D
Quillota

Phone: +56(32) 274527 **Fax:** +56(33) 274570 **Email:** ccabezon@ucv.cl **WWW:** www.ucv.cl **OPAC:** ucv.biblioteca.cl

Non-English Name: Universidad Católica de Valparaíso, Facultad de Agronomía (UCV), Biblioteca **Founded:** 1969 **Type:** Academic **Head:** Consuelo Cabezón *Phone:* +56(32) 274527 *Email:* ccabezon@ucv.cl **Staff:** 1 Prof. 1 Other **Holdings:** 2,500 books 42 journals **Language of Collection/Services:** Spanish, English / Spanish **Subjects:** Agribusiness, Agricultural Economics, Animal Husbandry, Biotechnology, Crops, Entomology, Farming, Plant Pathology, Plants, Postharvest Systems, Soil **Specializations:** Horticulture **Databases Used:** Comprehensive **Loan:** Internationally **Service:** Internationally **Photocopy:** Yes

659   **Santiago, Chile**
Catholic University of Chile, Agricultural
Economics Department
Library
Vicuña Mackenna 4860
Correo 22
Santiago

Fax: +56(2) 686-5727 **WWW:** www.puc.cl

Non-English Name: Pontifica Universidad Católica de Chile, Departamento de Economía, Biblioteca **Head:** Bernardita Ramírez *Email:* bramirez@puc.cl *Phone:* +56(2) 686-4281 **Subjects:** Agricultural Economics

660   **Santiago, Chile**
Catholic University of Chile, Campus San Joaquin
Library

Vicuña Mackenna 4860
Casilla 306, Correo 22
Santiago
Fax: +56(2) 552-1415 **WWW:** www.puc.cl

Non-English Name: Pontifica Universidad Católica de Chile, Campus San Joaquín, Biblioteca **Head:** Elvira Saurina de Solanes *Email:* esaurina@puc.cl *Phone:* +56(2) 686-4789

661   Santiago, Chile
Forestry Institute
Documentation Center
Casilla 3085
Santiago
Location: Huerfanos 554 **Phone:** +56(2) 693-0703 **Fax:** +56(2) 693-0702 **Email:** sif@infor.cl **WWW:** www.infor.cl

Non-English Name: Instituto Forestal (INFOR), Centro de Documentación **Founded:** 1962 **Type:** Government **Head:** Ana María Letelier Ferrari *Phone:* +56(2) 639-0703 *Email:* aletelie@infor.cl **Staff:** 2 Prof. 1 Other **Holdings:** 5,000 books 50 journals **Language of Collection/Services:** English, Spanish / Spanish **Subjects:** Forestry, Plant Pathology, Soil Science **Specializations:** Forest Products, Silviculture **Databases Developed:** Chilean literature on forestry and forest products **Databases Used:** Comprehensive **Loan:** In country **Service:** In country **Photocopy:** No

662   Santiago, Chile
Iberoamerican University of Science and
    Technology
Library
Olivares 1620
Santiago
Fax: +56(2) 695-7868 **Email:** unicitbl@iusanet.cl **WWW:** www.unicit.cl

Non-English Name: Universidad Iberoamericana de Ciencias y Tecnología, Biblioteca **Head:** Hector Navarro *Phone:* +56(2) 695-7868 *Email:* unicitbl@iusanet.cl

663   Santiago, Chile
Institute of Agricultural Research
Central Library
Casilla 439, Correo 3
Santiago
Location: Santa Rosa 11610, La Pintana **Phone:** +56(2) 541-7223 **Fax:** +56(2) 541-7667 **Email:** biblio@platina.inia.cl **WWW:** www.inia.cl **Ariel IP:** www.inia.cl/biblioteca

Non-English Name: Instituto de Investigaciones Agropecuarias (INIA), Biblioteca Central **Founded:** 1964 **Type:** Government **Head:** Sonia Elso Galano *Phone:* +56(2) 541-7223 *Email:* selso@platina.inia.cl **Staff:** 4 Prof. 4 Other **Holdings:** 50,000 books 900 journals **Language of Collection/Services:** English **Subjects:** Comprehensive **Specializations:** Animal Husbandry, Crops, Horticulture **Databases Developed:** Chilean Agricultural Bibliographic Database (BIBA) - 20,000 references published in journals, theses, books, etc.; available on CD-ROM **Databases Used:** Agri-

cola; Agris; CABCD **Networks:** AGRIS **Loan:** In country **Service:** Internationally **Photocopy:** Yes

664   Santiago, Chile
Major University, Huechuraba Campus
Library
Camino la Piramide 5750
Santiago
Fax: +56(2) 243-9094 **WWW:** www.umayor.cl

Non-English Name: Universidad Mayor, Campus Huechuraba, Biblioteca **Head:** Soledad Diaz *Phone:* +56(2) 243-9090 *Email:* sdiaz@umayor.cl

665   Santiago, Chile
National Institute of Professional Training,
    Tabancura
Library
Vitacura 10151
Santiago
Fax: +56(2) 212-9493

Non-English Name: Instituto Nacional de Capacitación Profesional, Sede Tabancura, Biblioteca **Head:** Alicia Delgado *Phone:* +56(2) 365-1020 *Email:* adelgado@inacap.cl

666   Santiago, Chile
National Society of Agriculture
Library
Casilla 40-D
Santiago
Location: Tenderini 187 **Phone:** +56(2) 630-6710 **Fax:** +56(2) 633-7771

Non-English Name: Sociedad Nacional de Agricultura (SNA), Biblioteca **Type:** Association **Head:** Alba Bassi S. *Phone:* +56(2) 639-6710 **Staff:** 1 Prof. **Holdings:** 5,000 books **Language of Collection/Services:** Spanish / Spanish **Subjects:** Agricultural Economics, Animal Production, Crop Production, Horticulture **Loan:** In country **Service:** In country **Photocopy:** Yes

667   Santiago, Chile
Saint Thomas University
Library
Ejercito 146
Santiago
Fax: +56(2) 362-4800

Non-English Name: Universidad Santo Tomas, Biblioteca **Head:** Nuris Silva *Phone:* +56(2) 362-4714 *Email:* nsilva@ust.cl

668   Santiago, Chile
University of Chile, Faculty of Agricultural
    Sciences
Rector Ruy Barbosa Library
Casilla 1004
Santiago
Location: Santa Rosa 11315 - La Pintana **Fax:** +56(2) 678-5803 **WWW:** www.uchile.cl

Non-English Name: Universidad de Chile, Facultad de Ciencias Agrarias y Forestales, Biblioteca Rector Ruy Barbosa **Founded:** 1875 **Type:** Academic **Head:** Pedro Calandra Bustos *Email:* pcalandr@abello.dic.uchile.cl *Phone:* +56 (2) 678-5739 **Staff:** 7 Prof. 5 Other **Holdings:** 30,000 books 145 journals **Language of Collection/Services:** English, Spanish **Subjects:** Agriculture (Tropics), Agribusiness, Agricultural Development, Agricultural Economics, Agricultural Engineering, Education/Extension, Animal Husbandry, Biotechnology, Crops, Entomology, Fisheries, Food Sciences, Farming, Forestry, Horticulture, Plant Pathology, Soil Science, Veterinary Medicine, Water Resources **Databases Developed:** University theses **Databases Used:** Agris; CABCD **Loan:** In country **Photocopy:** Yes

669   Santiago, Chile
        University of Chile, Faculty of Veterinary
            Medicine and Animal Husbandry
        Library
        Casilla 2, Correo 15
        Santiago
Location: Santa Rosa No. 11735 - La Pintana **Fax:** +56(2) 541-6840 **WWW:** www.uchile.cl

Non-English Name: Universidad de Chile, Facultad de Ciencias Veterinarias y Pecuarias, Biblioteca "Prof. Ramón Rodríguez Toro" **Founded:** 1937 **Type:** Academic **Head:** Paula Muñoz *Phone:* +56(2) 678-5545 *Email:* pmunoz@ abello.dic.uchile.cl **Staff:** 1 Prof. 4 Other **Holdings:** 19,500 books 46 journals **Subjects:** Agricultural Economics, Animal Husbandry, Animal Production, Biotechnology, Education/Extension, Entomology, Fisheries, Food Sciences, Veterinary Medicine **Loan:** In country **Photocopy:** Yes

670   Santiago, Chile
        University of the Americas
        Library
        Manuel Montt 948
        Santiago
Fax: +56(2) 225-8520 **WWW:** www.uamericas.cl

Non-English Name: Universidad de Las Américas, Biblioteca **Head:** Ema Guerraty *Phone:* +56(2) 223-1135 *Email:* eguerrat@uamericas.cl

671   Talca, Chile
        Talca University
        Library and Information Center Department
        2 Norte 685
        Casilla 747
        Talca
Fax: +56(71) 228054 **WWW:** www.utalca.cl

Non-English Name: Universidad de Talca, Departamento de Biblioteca y Centro de Información **Head:** María Angélica Tejos *Email:* mtejos@ pehuenche.utalca.cl *Phone:* +56(71) 226371

672   Temuco, Chile
        Frontier University
        Central Library
        Casilla 54-D
        Temuco
Fax: +56(45) 252990 **Email:** biblio@werken.ufro.cl **WWW:** www.ufro.cl

Non-English Name: Universidad de la Frontera, Biblioteca Central **Head:** Ivonne Rodríguez R. *Phone:* +56(45) 252627 *Email:* biblio@werken.ufro.cl

673   Temuco, Chile
        Institute of Agricultural Research, Carillanca
            Regional Research Center
        Library
        General López s/n
        Casilla 58-D
        Temuco
Fax: +56(45) 214038 **WWW:** www.inia.cl/carillanca

Non-English Name: Instituto de Investigaciones Agropecuarias, Centro Regional de Investigación Carillanca (INIA), Biblioteca **Head:** María Cecilia Inostroza *Phone:* +56(45) 2158-6 *Email:* minostro@carillanca.inia.cl

674   Valdivia, Chile
        Austral University of Chile
        Central Library
        Campus Isla Teja
        Correo 2
        Valdivia
Phone: +56(63)221290 **Fax:** +56(63)221360 **Email:** biblio @uach.cl **WWW:** www.uach.cl **OPAC:** www.uach.cl

Non-English Name: Universidad Austral de Chile, Biblioteca Central **Founded:** 1962 **Type:** Academic **Head:** Sonia Seguel *Phone:* +56(63) 221289 *Email:* sseguel@uach.cl **Staff:** 11 Prof. 29 Other **Holdings:** 103,079 books 470 journals **Language of Collection/Services:** English / Spanish **Subjects:** Comprehensive **Databases Used:** Comprehensive **Loan:** Inhouse **Service:** Inhouse **Photocopy:** Yes

675   Vina del Mar, Chile
        Valparaiso University, Oceanology Institute
        Library
        Casilla 13-D
        Vina del Mar
Location: Av. Barros Borgono s/n (Montemar) **Fax:** +56 (31) 970420

Non-English Name: Universidad de Valparaíso, Instituto de Oceanología, Biblioteca **Founded:** 1945 **Type:** Government **Head:** Parmenio Yañez *Phone:* +56(31) 970420 **Staff:** 1 Prof. 1 Other **Holdings:** 20,554 books 520 journals **Subjects:** Fisheries, Marine Biology, Water Resources **Loan:** Do not loan **Service:** In country **Photocopy:** Yes

China

Anhui

♦676   Hefei, Anhui, China
        Anhui Academy of Agricultural Sciences, Institute
            of Scientific and Technical Information
        Library
        Silihe, West Suburbs
        Hefei, Anhui 230031
Subjects: Crops

◆677   **Hefei, Anhui, China**
      Anhui Agricultural University
      Library
      16 Shushan Lu
      Hefei, Anhui 230036

Head: Zhong Weigui **Holdings:** 470,000 books 2,739 journals

Beijing

◆678   **Beijing, China**
      Beijing Academy of Agricultural and Forestry
         Sciences, Institute of Animal and Veterinary
         Sciences (BAAFS, IAVS)
      Library
      Benjin Cun, West Suburbs
      Beijing 100081
Phone: +86(10) 841-6644 ext 350

Type: Academic **Head:** Guo Zhi Hong *Phone:* +86(10) 841-6644 ext 350 **Staff:** 1 Prof. **Holdings:** 2,000 books 38 journals **Language of Collection/Services:** Chinese, English, Japanese, Russian / Chinese **Subjects:** Animal Husbandry, Beekeeping, Veterinary Science

679   **Beijing, China**
      Beijing Academy of Agricultural and Forestry
         Sciences, Vegetable Research Center
      Library
      Benjin Cun, West Suburbs
      PO Box 2443
      Beijing 100089
Phone: +86(10) 8843-4433 **Fax:** +86(10) 6842-6286

Type: Academic **Head:** Professor Chen Shuying *Phone:* +86(10) 8843-4433 ext 3080 **Staff:** 3 Prof. **Holdings:** 10,000 books 85 journals **Language of Collection/Services:** Chinese / Chinese **Subjects:** Vegetables **Databases Used:** Agricola; Agrisearch; CABCD **Loan:** Inhouse **Service:** Inhouse **Photocopy:** Yes

680   **Beijing, China**
      China Agricultural University (CAU)
      Library
      Yuan Ming Yuan Xi Lu No. 2, West Suburbs
      Beijing 100094
Phone: +86(10) 6289-1045 **Fax:** +86(10) 6289-2761
WWW: www.cau.edu.cn

Former Name: Beijing Agricultural University (BAU), Beijing Agricultural Engineering University (BAEU) **Founded:** 1949 **Type:** Academic **Head:** Prof. Shen Zhuo Rui *Phone:* +86(10) 6289-2737 **Staff:** 21 Prof. 46 Other **Holdings:** 1,400,000 books 3,500 journals **Language of Collection/ Services:** Chinese, English, Japanese, Russian / Chinese, English, Japanese, Russian **Subjects:** Agricultural Chemistry, Agricultural Economics, Agricultural Meteorology, Agronomy, Animal Husbandry, Biotechnology, Food Processing, Horticulture, Plant Protection, Soil Science **Specializations:** Animal Physiology, Breeding, Genetics, Plant Physiology, Plant Protection, Veterinary Medicine, Veteri-

nary Science **Databases Used:** Agricola; Agris; CABCD **Loan:** In country **Service:** Internationally **Photocopy:** Yes

◆681   **Beijing, China**
      Chinese Academy of Agricultural Engineering
         Research and Design
      Library
      Nongzhanguan Nanlu, Chaoyang District
      Beijing 100026

Head: Jing Meifang **Holdings:** 21,440 books 445 journals **Subjects:** Agricultural Engineering

◆682   **Beijing, China**
      Chinese Academy of Agricultural Mechanization
         (CAAM)
      Institute of Scientific and Technical Information
      1 Beishatan, Deshengmenwai
      Beijing 100083

Subjects: Farm Machinery, Mechanization

683   **Beijing, China**
      Chinese Academy of Agricultural Sciences
         (CAAS)
      Scientech Documentation and Information Center
         (SDIC)
      30 Baishiqiao Road, West Suburbs
      Beijing 100081
Fax: +86(10) 6897-5103 **Email:** library@mail.caas.net.cn

Founded: 1957 **Type:** Academic **Head:** Prof. Mei Fangquan *Phone:* +86(10) 6891-9920 *Email:* meifq@mail.caas.net.cn **Staff:** 183 Prof. 161 Other **Holdings:** 630,000 books 5,500 journals **Language of Collection/Services:** Chinese, English, Japanese, Russian **Subjects:** Agriculture (Tropics), Agribusiness, Agricultural Development, Agricultural Engineering, Biotechnology, Education/Extension, Entomology, Crops, Farming, Food Sciences, Horticulture, Plant Pathology, Soil Science, Veterinary Medicine, Water Resources **Specializations:** Agricultural Economics, Animal Husbandry, Biology, Veterinary Science **Networks:** AGRIS **Databases Developed:** Chinese Agricultural Documentation - bibliographic database in all fields of agriculture accessible by various fields **Databases Used:** Comprehensive **Loan:** Internationally **Service:** Internationally **Photocopy:** Yes

◆684   **Beijing, China**
      Chinese Academy of Agricultural Sciences,
         Institute of Agricultural Economics (CAAS)
      Library
      30 Baishiqiao Road, West Suburbs
      Beijing 100081

Head: Li Yuzhu **Holdings:** 12,514 books 139 journals **Subjects:** Agricultural Economics

◆685   **Beijing, China**
      Chinese Academy of Agricultural Sciences,
         Institute of Apiculture (CAAS)
      Library
      Wofosi, Xiangshan
      Beijing 100093

Head: Wu Benzhao **Holdings:** 12,000 books 1,588 journals **Subjects:** Beekeeping

◆**686 Beijing, China**
　　Chinese Academy of Agricultural Sciences,
　　　　Institute for Application of Atomic Energy in
　　　　Agriculture (CAAS, IAAE)
　　Library
　　Malianwa
　　Beijing 100094

Head: Fang Hong **Holdings:** 16,840 books 622 journals **Subjects:** Nuclear Energy

◆**687 Beijing, China**
　　Chinese Academy of Agricultural Sciences,
　　　　Institute of Natural Resources and Regional
　　　　Planning (CAAS)
　　Library
　　30 Baishiqiao Road, West Suburbs
　　Beijing 100081
Phone: +86(10) 831-6540 **Fax:** +86(10) 831-6545

Type: Academic **Head:** Li Yingzhong *Phone:* +86(10) 831-4433 ext 2286 **Staff:** 30 Prof. 15 Other **Language of Collection/Services:** Chinese/Chinese, English **Subjects:** Natural Resources, Agricultural Economics **Loan:** In country **Service:** In country **Photocopy:** No

◆**688 Beijing, China**
　　Chinese Academy of Agricultural Sciences,
　　　　Institute of Soils and Fertilizers (CAAS)
　　Library
　　30 Baishiqiao Road, West Suburbs
　　Beijing 100081

Head: Gu Qin **Holdings:** 1,832 books 130 journals **Subjects:** Soil Science, Fertilizers

◆**689 Beijing, China**
　　Chinese Academy of Agricultural Sciences,
　　　　Biological Control Laboratory (CAAS)
　　Library
　　30 Baishiqiao Road, West Suburbs
　　Beijing 100081
Phone: +86(17) 832-3182 **Fax:** +86(17) 832-3182

Type: Academic **Head:** Ms. Hugng Yu-Mei *Phone:* +86(17) 832-3182 **Staff:** 40 Prof. 30 Other **Holdings:** 4,500 books 50 journals **Language of Collection/Services:** Chinese, English / Chinese **Subjects:** Biological Control, Entomology, Microbial Pesticides **Loan:** Inhouse **Service:** Internationally **Photocopy:** Yes

690 Beijing, China
　　Chinese Academy of Fishery Science (CAFS)
　　Scientific and Technological Information Institute
　　　　(STII)
　　150 Qingtacun, Yongding Nanlu
　　Fengtai District
　　Beijing 100039
Fax: +86(10) 6967-6685

Founded: 1978 **Type:** Research **Head:** Yang Ningsheng *Phone:* +86(10) 6867-3942 *Email:* ningsheng.yang@mh.bj.

col.com.cn **Staff:** 20 Prof. 10 Other **Holdings:** 20,000 books 150 journals **Language of Collection/Services:** Chinese, English/Chinese **Subjects:** Fisheries **Databases Developed:** Chinese Fisher Literature Database **Databases Used:** ASFA **Loan:** Inhouse **Service:** In country **Photocopy:** Yes

691 Beijing, China
　　Chinese Academy of Forestry (CAF)
　　Institute of Scientific and Technical Information
　　　　(ISTI)
　　Wan Shou Shan
　　Beijing 100091
Fax: +86(10) 288-2317 **Email:** wcli@lknet.forestry.ac.cn, istifsh@public3.bta.net.cn **WWW:** www.lknet.forestry.ac.cn **OPAC:** library.lknet.forestry.ac.cn

Founded: 1958 **Type:** Research **Head:** Jiang Zehui *Phone:* +86(10) 288-9713 **Staff:** 13 Prof. 2 Other **Holdings:** 300,000 books 900 journals **Language of Collection/Services:** Chinese, English / Chinese **Subjects:** Forestry **Databases Used:** Chinese Forestry Abstract Database **Loan:** In country **Service:** In country **Photocopy:** Yes

◆**692 Beijing, China**
　　Chinese Academy of Sciences, Institute of Botany
　　　　(CAS)
　　Library
　　141 Xizhimenwai Dajie
　　Beijing 100044
Phone: +86(10) 835-3831 ext 392 **Fax:** +86(10) 831-9534

Founded: 1928 **Type:** Academic **Head:** Wang Zu-hong *Phone:* +86(10) 835-3831 ext 401 **Staff:** 7 Prof. 9 Other **Holdings:** 60,000 books 200 journals **Language of Collection/Services:** Chinese, English/Chinese, English **Subjects:** Crops, Forestry, Horticulture, Weeds **Specializations:** Botany **Loan:** In country **Service:** In country **Photocopy:** Yes

◆**693 Beijing, China**
　　Chinese Academy of Sciences, Institute of
　　　　Zoology
　　Library
　　19 Zhongguancun Lu
　　Haidian District
　　Beijing 100080

Founded: 1962 **Type:** Academic **Head:** Mrs. Li You-hua **Staff:** 9 Prof. **Subjects:** Animal Feeding, Integrated Control, Pest Management, Plant Protection **Loan:** In country **Photocopy:** No

◆**694 Beijing, China**
　　Chinese Supervisory Institute of Veterinary
　　　　Bio-Products and Pharmaceuticals
　　Library
　　30 Baishiqiao Road
　　Beijing 100081
Phone: +86(10) 256-8844 ext 290 **Fax:** +86(10) 255-0715

Type: Academic **Head:** Meng Xiaoqin *Phone:* +86(10) 256-8844 ext 290 **Staff:** 2 Prof. 1 Other **Holdings:** 15,207 books **Language of Collection/Services:** Chinese, English / Chinese, English **Subjects:** Pharmacology, Veterinary Medicine **Loan:** Inhouse **Service:** Inhouse **Photocopy:** No

695   Beijing, China
Institute for Scientific and Technical Information
    of China (ISTIC)
Information Service Center
PO Box 3827
Beijing 100038

Location: 15 Fuxing Road **Phone:** +86(10) 6851-5544 ext 2301 **Fax:** +86(10) 6851-4025 **Email:** service@istic.ac.cn **WWW:** istic.ac.cn **OPAC:** istic.ac.cn

Founded: 1956 **Type:** Government **Head:** Taojin *Phone:* +86(10) 6851-5544 ext 2358 *Email:* taojin@istic.ac.ch **Staff:** 55 Prof. **Holdings:** 8,000,000 books 6,200 journals **Language of Collection/Services:** Chinese, English / Chinese, English **Subjects:** Agriculture (Tropics), Agricultural Engineering, Animal Husbandry, Biotechnology, Crops, Entomology, Fisheries, Food Sciences, Forestry, Horticulture, Plant Pathology, Plants, Soil Science, Veterinary Medicine **Specializations:** Biology, Engineering **Databases Developed:** Union Catalogue - Database of Chinese Scientific and Technical Periodicals **Loan:** Internationally **Service:** Internationally **Photocopy:** Yes

696   Beijing, China
Ministry of Agriculture
China-EU Centre for Agricultural Technology
    (CECAT)
55 Nongzhan Beilu
Chaoyang District
Beijing, Beijing 100026

Phone: +86(10) 6419-5588 **Fax:** +86(10) 6506-3012 **Email:** cecatic@public.bta.net.cn **WWW:** www.cecat.org

Founded: 1991 **Type:** Government **Head:** Han Gaoju *Email:* cecatsv@public.bta.net.cn *Phone:* +86(10) 6419-5588 ext 6001 *Staff:* 24 Prof. 60 Other **Holdings:** 8,000 books 100 journals **Language of Collection/Services:** Chinese, English / Chinese, English **Subjects:** Comprehensive **Specializations:** Agribusiness, Agricultural Development, Agricultural Economics **Loan:** Inhouse **Service:** Internationally **Photocopy:** Yes

697   Beijing, China
Peking University (PKU)
Library
Loudouqiao, Haidian District
Beijing 100871

Phone: +86(10) 6275-3504 **Fax:** +86(10 6275-1051 **Email:** is@lib.pku.edu.cn **WWW:** www.lib.pku.edu.cn **OPAC:** pul2.lib.pku.edu.cn/www/service/uopac.html **Ariel IP:** 162.105.140.103

Founded: 1902 **Type:** Academic **Head:** Lin Beidian *Phone:* +86(10) 6275-1051 *Email:* office@pula.lib.pku.edu.cn **Language of Collection/Services:** Chinese, English / Chinese, English **Staff:** 111 Prof. 107 Other **Holdings:** 4,600,000 books 6,000 journals **Subjects:** Comprehensive **Networks:** APTLIN; CERNET **Databases Used:** Comprehensive **Service:** In country **Loan:** In country **Photocopy:** Yes

Chongqing

698   Chongqing, China
Southwest Agricultural University
Library
136 Tianshengqiao, Beipei
Chongqing 630716
WWW: www.swau.edu.cn

Head: Chen Shizheng **Holdings:** 1,100,000 books 3,000 journals **Subjects:** Acarology, Entomology

Fujian

699   Fuzhou, Fujian, China
Fujian Academy of Agricultural Sciences
Institute of Scientific and Technological
    Information
41 Hualin Road
Fuzhou, Fujian 350003

Former Name: Information Research Institute of Agricultural Science and Technology **Type:** Academic **Head:** Lu Congzhou **Staff:** 32 Prof. 16 Other **Holdings:** 100,000 books 1,100 journals **Subjects:** Agriculture (Tropics), Agribusiness, Agricultural Development, Agricultural Economics, Agricultural Engineering, Animal Husbandry, Biotechnology, Crops, Education/Extension, Entomology, Farming, Fisheries, Food Sciences, Forestry, Horticulture, Plant Pathology, Soil Science, Veterinary Medicine, Water Resources **Loan:** Internationally **Photocopy:** Yes

700   Fuzhou, Fujian, China
Fujian Agricultural University (FAU)
Library
Jinshan
Fuzhou, Fujian 350002

Phone: +86(591) 374-4049 **Fax:** +86(591) 378-9369 **Email:** jss@jfau.edu.cn **WWW:** www.fjau.edu.cn

Founded: 1936 **Type:** Academic **Head:** Hu Fang Ping *Phone:* +86(591) 374-3011 **Staff:** 33 Prof. 13 Other **Language of Collection/Services:** Chinese, English, Russian, Japanese / Chinese, English, Russian, Japanese **Holdings:** 400,000 books 150,000 journals **Subjects:** Comprehensive **Specializations:** Beekeeping **Databases Used:** Agris; CABCD **Loan:** Inhouse **Service:** Inhouse **Photocopy:** No

701   Nanping, Fujian, China
Fujian College of Forestry (FCF)
Library
Xiqin Town
Nanping, Fujian 353001

Location: No. 182 XinHua Second Road **Phone:** +86(599) 850-2163 **Fax:** +86(599) 850-2163 **Email:** ffclib@public.nppt.fj.cn

Founded: 1958 **Type:** Government **Head:** Ren Chenghui *Phone:* +86(599) 850-2163 *Email:* ffclib@public.nppt.fj.cn **Staff:** 32 Prof. 10 Other **Holdings:** 455,012 books 1,279 journals **Language of Collection/Services:** Chinese, English/Chinese, English **Subjects:** Agricultural Economics, Agricultural Engineering, Entomology, Plant Pathology,

Plants, Soil Science **Specializations:** Forest Products, Forestry **Loan:** In country **Service:** In country **Photocopy:** Yes

♦**702   Xiamen, Fujian, China**
        Fujian Fisheries Research Institute
        Library
        7 Haishan Road, Dongdu
        Xiamen, Fujian 361012
Phone: +86(592) 601-3170

Type: Academic **Head:** Lin Xue-qin *Phone:* +86(592) 601-2171 **Staff:** 2 Prof. 4 Other **Holdings:** 16,000 books 118 journals **Language of Collection/Services:** Chinese, English, Japanese/Chinese **Subjects:** Fisheries **Service:** In country **Photocopy:** No

703   Xiamen, Fujian, China
        Xiamen Research Institute of Agricultural
            Sciences (XRIAS)
        Library
        Lianqian West Road
        Xiamen, Fujian 361009
Phone: +86(592) 596-8360 **Fax:** +86(592) 502-8409

Type: Academic **Head:** Mrs. Zhu Fengling *Phone:* +86(592) 502-8415 **Staff:** 3 Prof. 1 Other **Holdings:** 46,592 books 510 journals **Language of Collection/Services:** Chinese/Chinese **Subjects:** Agriculture (Tropics), Agribusiness, Agricultural Development, Agricultural Economics, Agricultural Engineering, Biotechnology, Crops, Entomology, Food Sciences, Horticulture, Plant Pathology, Plants, Soil Science **Specializations:** Edible Fungi, Vegetables **Loan:** Inhouse **Service:** Inhouse **Photocopy:** No

♦**704   Zhangzhou, Fujian, China**
        Fujian Academy of Agricultural Sciences,
            Sugarcane Research Institute
        Information Center
        Buwen
        Zhangzhou, Fujian 363109
Phone: +86(596) 220068

Type: Academic **Head:** Wang Wen-tian **Staff:** 3 Prof. **Holdings:** 6,500 books 81 journals **Language of Collection/Services:** Chinese/Chinese **Subjects:** Sugarcane **Loan:** Inhouse **Service:** In country **Photocopy:** Yes

Gansu

705   Lanzhou, Gansu, China
        Chinese Academy of Agricultural Sciences,
            Institute of Traditional Chinese Veterinary
            Medicine (CAAS, ITCVM)
        Department of Information
        211 Jiangouyan, Xiaoxihu
        Lanzhou, Gansu 730046
Phone: +86(931) 234-6134 **Fax:** +86(931) 233-1591

Former Name: Lanzhou Institute of Animal Veterinary Pharmaceutical Sciences (LIAVPS) **Founded:** 1957 **Type:** Academic **Head:** Prof. Zhang Guowei *Phone:* +86(931) 234-6134 **Staff:** 5 Prof. 1 Other **Holdings:** 19,803 books 200 journals **Language of Collection/Services:** Chinese, Eng-

lish, Russian/Chinese, English **Subjects:** Herbage, Animal Husbandry, Grasslands, Veterinary Medicine, Traditional Medicines **Specializations:** Animal Breeding, Animal Nutrition, Ruminant Feeding, Sheep Feeding, Traditional Veterinary Medicine (China), Yaks **Databases Developed:** Numeric databases of animal husbandry development worldwide; Documentation database of animal sciences in China **Loan:** Inhouse **Service:** Inhouse **Photocopy:** Yes

706   Lanzhou, Gansu, China
        Chinese Academy of Agricultural Sciences,
            Lanzhou Veterinary Research Institute
            (CAAS, LVRI)
        Library
        11 Xujiaping, Yanchangpu
        Lanzhou, Gansu 730046
Phone: +86(931) 836-3995 **Email:** lvri@lz.gs.cninfo.net

Founded: 1957 **Type:** Academic **Head:** Liu Weiyi *Phone:* +86(931) 836-3995 *Email:* lvri@lz.gs.cninfo.net **Staff:** 3 Prof. **Holdings:** 60,000 books 222 journals **Language of Collection/Services:** Chinese, English, Japanese, Russian / Chinese **Subjects:** Biotechnology, Bacterial Diseases, Mycoses, Mycotoxicoses, Parasitology, Veterinary Medicine, Veterinary Science, Virology **Specializations:** Aphthovirus, Foot and Mouth Disease, Swine Fever, Marek's Disease, Chlamydia psittaci, Babesia, Fasciola hepatica, Toxoplasma, Trichinella, Trichinosis, Echinococcosis, Resorcinols **Databases Used:** CABCD **Loan:** Inhouse **Service:** In country **Photocopy:** Yes

707   Lanzhou, Gansu, China
        Gansu Academy of Agricultural Sciences (GAAS)
        Information Institute
        Liujiabu, Anning District
        Lanzhou, Gansu 730070

Founded: 1958 **Type:** Academic **Head:** Feng Zu-Guang *Phone:* +86(931) 66301 **Staff:** 5 Prof.

708   Lanzhou, Gansu, China
        Gansu Agricultural University (GAU)
        Library
        Yingmencun 1, Anning District
        Lanzhou, Gansu 730070
Phone: +86(931) 766-8011 ext 3217 **Fax:** +86(931) 766-8010 **Email:** library@gsau.edu.cn **WWW:** www.gsau.edu.cn

Former Name: National Veterinary Medicine College, Northwestern College of Animal Husbandry and Veterinary Medicine **Founded:** 1946 **Type:** Academic **Head:** Liu Xi *Phone:* +86(931) 766-8011 ext 3103 *Email:* library@gsau.edu.cn **Staff:** 21 Prof. 15 Other **Holdings:** 510,000 books 1,373 journals **Language of Collection/Services:** Chinese, English/Chinese **Subjects:** Agricultural Economics, Agricultural Engineering, Farming, Food Sciences, Plant Pathology, Soil Science, Water Resources **Specializations:** Animal Husbandry, Agronomy, Crops, Entomology, Forestry, Horticulture, Plant Pathology, Plant Protection, Veterinary Medicine **Databases Developed:** Index of economics of irrigated agriculture; Index of yak documents **Loan:** In country **Service:** Internationally **Photocopy:** Yes

709 Lanzhou, Gansu, China
Lanzhou University
Library
No. 216 Tianshui Road
Lanzhou, Gansu 730000
Phone: +86(931) 891-2460 **Fax:** +86(931) 891-1100
Email: library@lzu.edu.cn **WWW:** library.lzu.edu.cn

Founded: 1909 **Type:** Academic **Head:** Dr. Zhao Shucheng *Phone:* +86(931) 891-2469 *Email:* zhaosc@lzu.edu.cn **Staff:** 60 Prof. 33 Other **Holdings:** 1,800,000 books 5,000 journals **Language of Collection/Services:** Chinese, English, Japanese, Russian, German / Chinese, English **Subjects:** Comprehensive **Specializations:** Biology, Chemistry, Physics **Databases Used:** Comprehensive **Loan:** Inhouse **Service:** Inhouse **Photocopy:** No

Guangdong

♦710 Guangzhou, Guangdong, China
Chinese Academy of Forestry, Tropical Forestry
Research Institute (CAF, TFRI)
Library Section
Longdong
Guangzhou, Guangdong 510520
Phone: +86(20) 770-8845 **Fax:** +86(20) 772-5622

Type: Academic **Head:** Meihua Ding *Phone:* +86(20) 772-5621 **Staff:** 1 Prof. 1 Other **Holdings:** 20,000 books 40 journals **Language of Collection/Services:** Chinese / Chinese **Subjects:** Agriculture (Tropics), Crops, Farming, Forestry, Plant Pathology, Plants **Loan:** Inhouse **Service:** Inhouse **Photocopy:** No

711 Guangzhou, Guangdong, China
Chinese Academy of Sciences, South China
Institute of Botany (CAS)
Library
Leyiju, Tianhe
PO Box 1127
Guangzhou, Guangdong 510650
Location: On the northeast of Guangzhou about 7 km from Shahe **Phone:** +86(20) 8770-5626 ext 224 **Fax:** +86(20) 8770-1031

Founded: 1929 **Type:** Academic **Head:** Lin Luanzhuan *Phone:* +86(20) 8770-5626 ext 214 *Email:* gzscib@publicl. guangzhou.gd.cn **Staff:** 7 Prof. 1 Other **Holdings:** 60,000 books 1,085 journals **Language of Collection/Services:** Chinese, English / Chinese, English **Subjects:** Agricultural Chemistry, Biotechnology, Forestry, Genetics, Horticulture, Nature Conservation, Plant Breeding, Plant Ecology, Plant Physiology **Specializations:** Taxonomy **Loan:** In country **Service:** In country **Photocopy:** Yes

712 Guangzhou, Guangdong, China
Guangdong Academy of Agricultural Sciences
(GDAAS)
Institute of Scientific and Technological
Information
Wushan, Shipai
Guangzhou, Guangdong 510640
Phone: +86(20) 750-3357 **Fax:** +86(20) 750-3358

Type: Academic **Head:** Liangji Li **Staff:** 24 Prof. 4 Other **Holdings:** 55,000 books 450 journals **Language of Collection/Services:** Chinese, English / Chinese **Subjects:** Animal Husbandry, Biotechnology, Crops, Farming Systems, Food Technology, Horticulture, Plant Pathology, Veterinary Medicine **Service:** In country **Photocopy:** No

♦713 Guangzhou, Guangdong, China
Guangdong Academy of Agricultural Sciences,
Rice Research Institute (GDAAS, GDRRI)
Library
Wushan, Tianhe District
Guangzhou, Guangdong 510640
Fax: +86(20) 750-3358

Type: Academic **Head:** Ms. Feng Hong-Ying *Phone:* +86(20) 551-4257 **Staff:** 92 Prof. 15 Other **Holdings:** 2,946 books 45 journals **Language of Collection/Services:** Chinese, English / Chinese **Subjects:** Plant Breeding **Specializations:** Rice **Service:** Inhouse **Photocopy:** No

714 Guangzhou, Guangdong, China
Guangdong Agricultural Machinery Research
Institute (GAMRI)
Library
Shipai
Guangzhou, Guangdong 510630
Phone: +86(20) 8551-6437 **Fax:** +86(20) 8551-0694
Email: gdagrims@sti.gd.cn **WWW:** www.sti.gd.cn

Founded: 1958 **Type:** Academic **Head:** Mr. Lu Zhongxun *Phone:* +86(20) 8551-6437 ext 3128 **Staff:** 2 Prof. **Holdings:** 13,700 books 5,000 journals **Language of Collection/Services:** Chinese / Chinese **Subjects:** Farm Machinery, Mechanization **Specializations:** Agricultural Engineering **Service:** Inhouse **Photocopy:** Yes

715 Guangzhou, Guangdong, China
Guangdong Forestry Research Institute (GDFRI)
Guangdong Forestry Information Division
(GDFID)
Longyandong, Shahe
Guangzhou, Guangdong 510520
Phone: +86(20) 8770-5646 **Fax:** +86(20) 8763-4445
Email: gdfid@sti.gd.cn

Founded: 1959 **Type:** Academic **Head:** Fan Junxiang *Phone:* +86(20) 8770-5646 *Email:* gdfid@sti.gd.cn **Staff:** 6 Prof. 2 Other **Holdings:** 100,000 books **Language of Collection/Services:** Chinese, English **Subjects:** Forestry **Specializations:** Breeding, Genetics, Forest Management, Forest Products, Insect Pests, Mycology, Pulp and Paper Industry, Rosin, Turpentine, Wood Properties **Loan:** In country **Service:** In country **Photocopy:** No

716 Guangzhou, Guangdong, China
South China Agricultural University (SCAU)
Library
Wushan Street, Tianhe District
Guangzhou, Guangdong 510642
Phone: +86(20) 8551-1299 ext 3187 **Email:** library@scau. edu.cn **WWW:** library.scau.edu.cn

Former Name: South China Agricultural College **Founded:** 1952 **Type:** Academic **Head:** Mrs. Liao Fupin *Phone:* +86 (20) 8551-1299 ext 3187, 8575-9845 *Email:* liaofp@scau.edu.cn **Staff:** 38 Prof. 11 Other **Holdings:** 680,000 books 1,800 journals **Language of Collection/Services:** Chinese / Chinese **Subjects:** Comprehensive **Specializations:** Agriculture (Subtropics), Agriculture (Tropics), Subtropics **Networks:** OCLC **Databases Used:** Comprehensive **Loan:** Inhouse **Service:** Inhouse **Photocopy:** Yes

717   Zhanjiang, Guangdong, China
          China Academy of Tropical Agricultural Sciences
              (CATAS)
          Information Center
          Huguangyan
          Zhanjiang, Guangdong 524091
Phone: +86(759) 284-5300 **Fax:** +86(759) 284-5124
Email: sscri@pub.zhanjiang.dg.cn

Former Name: Institute of Southern Subtropical Crops (ISSC) **Type:** Academic **Head:** Li Duan Qe *Phone:* +86(759) 284-5300 **Staff:** 2 Prof. **Holdings:** 30,025 books 126 journals **Language of Collection/Services:** Chinese, English, Russian, Japanese / Chinese **Subjects:** Flowers (Subtropics), Fruit Trees, Mangoes, Rubber, Sisal, Subtropical Crops, Subtropics **Databases Used:** Comprehensive **Loan:** Inhouse **Service:** In country **Photocopy:** Yes

Guangxi

718   Nanning, Guangxi, China
          Guangxi Academy of Agricultural Sciences
              (GXAAS)
          Institute of Scientific and Technological
              Information
          44 West Xixiangtang Road
          Nanning, Guangxi 530007
Phone: +86(771) 321-3461/6

Type: Academic **Head:** Z.J. Liao *Phone:* +86(771) 321-1905 **Staff:** 32 Prof. **Holdings:** 50,000 books 700 journals **Language of Collection/Services:** Chinese, English / Chinese **Subjects:** Agriculture (Tropics), Agribusiness, Agricultural Economics, Animal Husbandry, Entomology, Food Sciences, Farming, Fisheries, Forestry, Horticulture, Plant Pathology, Soil Science, Veterinary Medicine **Specializations:** Biotechnology, Crops, Horticultural Crops, Plant Protection **Databases Developed:** Tropical and subtropical fruits database **Databases Used:** CABCD

719   Nanning, Guangxi, China
          Guangxi Agricultural College
          Library
          13 Xuiling Lu
          Nanning, Guangxi 530005
Head: Fan Yintong **Holdings:** 540,000 books

720   Nanning, Guangxi, China
          Guangxi Institute of Veterinary Medicine
          Library
          51 Youai Beilu
          Nanning, Guangxi 530001

Phone: +86(771) 312-1700 **Fax:** +86(771) 313-0475

Founded: 1956 **Type:** Academic **Head:** Li Binghong *Phone:* +86(771) 312-1700, 313-9185 **Staff:** 3 Prof. 1 Other **Holdings:** 28,000 books 30,000 journals **Language of Collection/Services:** Chinese, English, Japanese, Russian / Chinese, English **Subjects:** Animal Husbandry, Biotechnology, Feeds, Veterinary Science **Loan:** Inhouse **Service:** Inhouse **Photocopy:** Yes

721   Nanning, Guangxi, China
          Guangxi Maize Research Institute (GXMRI)
          Library
          Mingyang, Yongning
          Nanning, Guangxi 530227
Phone: +86(771) 421-7324 **Fax:** +86(771) 421-7154
Email: gmri@public.nn.gx.cn

Founded: 1963 **Type:** Academic **Head:** Liu Quanyu *Phone:* +86(771) 421-7324 *Email:* gmri@public.nn.gx.cn **Staff:** 2 Prof. 3 Other **Holdings:** 18,200 books 120 journals **Language of Collection/Services:** Chinese, English / Chinese **Subjects:** Maize, Soybeans, Sweet Potatoes **Loan:** Internationally **Service:** Internationally **Photocopy:** Yes

Guizhou

♦**722   Dushan, Guizhou, China**
          Guizhou Provincial Institute of Herbage, Guizhou
              Provincial Institute of Bast Fiber Crops
              (GPIH, GPIBFC)
          Information Center (IC)
          Dushan, Guizhou 558200
Phone: +86(8645) 222754

Type: Academic **Head:** Tang Chengbing *Phone:* +86(8645) 222754 **Staff:** 3 Prof. 1 Other **Holdings:** 5,880 books 2,500 journals **Language of Collection/Services:** Chinese, English, Japanese/Chinese **Subjects:** Agricultural Development, Animal Husbandry, Crops, Farming, Fiber Plants, Herbage Crops, Plant Pathology, Soil Science **Loan:** Inhouse **Service:** Inhouse **Photocopy:** No

723   Guiyang, Guizhou, China
          Guizhou Academy of Agricultural Sciences
          Institute of Scientific and Technical Information
          Jinzhu Zhen
          Guiyang, Guizhou 550006
Head: Chen Deshou **Holdings:** 15,500 books 1,113 journals

♦**724   Guiyang, Guizhou, China**
          Guizhou Academy of Agricultural Sciences, Soils
              and Fertilizers Institute (GAAS, SFI)
          Library
          Jinzhu Zhen
          Guiyang, Guizhou 550006
Phone: +86(851) 551244 **Fax:** +86(851) 551244

Type: Academic **Head:** Chen Xuhui *Phone:* +86(851) 551244 **Staff:** 2 Prof. 37 Other **Holdings:** 1,100 books **Language of Collection/Services:** Chinese, English / Chinese, English **Subjects:** Fertilizers **Specializations:** Agricultural

Development, Farming, Fertilizers, Soil Science **Loan:** In country **Service:** Internationally **Photocopy:** Yes

725   Guiyang, Guizhou, China
Guizhou University (GU)
Library
Guiyang, Guizhou 550025
Phone: +86(851) 385-1446, 385-4468 **WWW:** www.gzu. edu.cn

Former Name: Guizhou Agricultural College (GAC) **Type:** Academic **Founded:** 1941 **Head:** Yang Minghua *Phone:* +86 (851) 385-8518 *Email:* yangmh@inf-ser.gzu.edu.cn **Staff:** 55 Prof. 25 Other **Holdings:** 1,000,000 books 3,000 journals **Language of Collection/Services:** Chinese, English / Chinese **Subjects:** Agricultural Engineering, Agronomy, Animal Husbandry, Food Processing, Forestry, Horticulture, Plant Protection **Databases Used:** CACP; CAJ; CSTDB; CDDBSTAD **Loan:** In country **Service:** In country **Photocopy:** No

726   Guiyang, Guizhou, China
Guizhou Institute of Animal Husbandry and
     Veterinary Medicine (GIAHVM)
Library
Longdongbao, Nanming District
Guiyang, Guizhou 550005
Phone: +86(851) 540-0451

Founded: 1975 **Type:** Academic **Head:** Zeng Jianmin *Phone:* +86(851) 540-0451 **Staff:** 2 Prof. 1 Other **Holdings:** 16,000 books 250 journals Language of Collection/Services: Chinese / Chinese **Subjects:** Animal Husbandry, Veterinary Science **Loan:** Inhouse **Service:** Inhouse **Photocopy:** Yes

Hainan

727   Danxian, Hainan, China
South China Academy of Tropical Crops
     (SCATC)
Institute of Scientific and Technical Information
Baodao Xincun, Danxian County
Danxian, Hainan 571737

Founded: 1953 **Type:** Academic **Staff:** 38 Prof. 4 Other **Holdings:** 153,900 books 2,119 journals **Subjects:** Agribusiness, Agricultural Development, Agricultural Economics, Agricultural Engineering, Avocados, Biotechnology, Crops, Coconuts, Coffee, Entomology, Farming, Fisheries, Food Sciences, Forestry, Horticulture, Mangoes, Pineapples, Plant Pathology, Rubber, Soil Science, Tropical Crops, Tropical Fruits **Specializations:** Agriculture (Tropics) **Service:** In country**Loan:** In country **Photocopy:** Yes

Hebei

728   Baoding, Hebei, China
Hebei Agricultural University
Library
Nanguan
Baoding, Hebei 071001

Founded: 1949 **Type:** Government **Head:** Ma Zhong-Xue **Staff:** 23 Prof. 26 Other **Holdings:** 450,000 books 1,800 journals **Subjects:** Agribusiness, Agricultural Economics, Agricultural Engineering, Animal Husbandry, Crops, Entomology, Farming, Food Sciences, Horticulture, Plant Pathology, Soil Science, Veterinary Medicine **Loan:** In country **Service:** In country **Photocopy:** Yes

729   Cangzhou, Hebei, China
Cangzhou Academy of Agricultural and Forestry
     Sciences (CAAFS)
Library
Chaoyang South Road
Cangzhou, Hebei 061000
Phone: +86(317) 205-0737 **Fax:** +86(317) 205-2904 **Email:** jicacang@publin.czptt.he.cn

Former Name: Cangzhou Institute of Agricultural Sciences (CIAS) **Type:** Academic **Head:** Qi Shu-ting *Phone:* +86 (317) 205-0516 *Email:* jicacang@publin.czptt.he.cn **Staff:** 5 Prof. **Holdings:** 22,390 books 180 journals **Language of Collection/Services:** Chinese / Chinese **Subjects:** Agribusiness, Agricultural Development, Agricultural Economics, Agricultural Engineering, Animal Husbandry, Biotechnology, Conservation, Crops, Food Sciences, Plant Pathology, Plants **Specializations:** Farming, Horticulture, Soil Science, Plant Breeding **Loan:** Inhouse **Service:** Inhouse **Photocopy:** Yes

730   Handan, Hebei, China
Handan Academy of Agricultural Sciences
     (HDAAS)
Library
Zhongbu
Handan, Hebei 056003
Location: No 1 Nongyan Street **Phone:** +86(310) 602-6098

Former Name: Hebei Academy of Agricultural and Forestry Sciences, Handan Institute of Agricultural Sciences **Type:** Academic **Head:** Sun Xijing *Phone:* +86(310) 603-4574 ext 8010 **Staff:** 1 Prof. 2 Other **Holdings:** 16,000 books 18,000 journals **Language of Collection/Services:** Chinese, English, Russian / Chinese **Subjects:** Comprehensive **Specializations:** Crops, Entomology, Plant Pathology, Soil Science

◆731   Qinhuangdao, Hebei, China
Hebei Academy of Agricultural and Forestry
     Sciences, Changli Institute of Pomology
     (HAAFS, CIP)
Library
Changli
Qinhuangdao, Hebei 066600
Phone: +86(335) 663417

Type: Academic **Head:** Dong Tingyuan *Phone:* +86(335) 663324 **Staff:** 3 Prof. **Holdings:** 20,000 books **Language of Collection/Services:** Chinese, English, Japanese / Chinese, English, Japanese **Subjects:** Fruits **Loan:** Inhouse **Service:** Inhouse

732   Shijiazhuang, Hebei, China
Chinese Academy of Sciences, Shijiazhuang
     Institute of Agricultural Modernization (CAS,
     SIAM)
Library and Information Service Division
PO Box 185
39 Huaizhong Road
Shijiazhuang, Hebei 050021
Phone: +86(311) 614521 **Fax:** +86(311) 615093 **WWW:**
www.sjziam.ac.cn

Type: Academic **Head:** Guo Yimei *Phone:* +86(311)
614361 **Staff:** 9 Prof. **Holdings:** 40,000 books **Language of
Collection/Services:** English, Chinese/Chinese **Loan:** Internationally **Service:** Internationally **Photocopy:** No

♦733   Shijiazhuang, Hebei, China
Hebei Academy of Agricultural and Forestry
     Sciences
Institute of Scientific and Technical Information
24 Jichang Road
Shijiazhuang, Hebei 050051
Phone: +86(311) 742853 ext 243

Type: Academic **Head:** Yang Shu Hui *Phone:* +86(311)
742853 ext 243 **Staff:** 5 Prof. 1 Other **Holdings:** 70,000
books 1,320 journals **Language of Collection/Services:**
Chinese, English / Chinese **Subjects:** Agricultural Economics, Biotechnology, Crops, Farming, Fisheries, Forestry,
Horticulture, Soil Science, Plant Pathology **Databases
Used:** Agris; CABCD **Loan:** Inhouse **Service:** Inhouse **Photocopy:** Yes

734   Shijiazhuang, Hebei, China
Hebei Academy of Agricultural and Forestry
     Sciences, Cotton Research Institute
Library
598 Heping Xi Lu
Shijiazhuang, Hebei 050051
Phone: +86(311) 704-3238 ext 6766

Founded: 1976 **Type:** Academic **Head:** Sun Li-guang
Phone: +86(311) 704-3238 ext 6766 **Holdings:** 10,000
books 120 journals **Language of Collection/Services:** Chinese, English, Russian / Chinese **Subjects:** Cotton

♦735   Shijiazhuang, Hebei, China
Hebei Academy of Agricultural and Forestry
     Sciences, Institute of Food and Oil Crops
Library
Tangu
Shijiazhuang, Hebei 050031
Phone: +86(311) 554030

Type: Academic **Head:** Cai Wen-xia *Phone:* +86(311) 554
030 **Holdings:** 20,000 books 10,000 journals **Language of
Collection/Services:** Chinese, English, Japanese **Subjects:**
Food Crops, Oil Plants **Loan:** Inhouse **Photocopy:** Yes

♦736   Zhangbei, Hebei, China
Bashang Institute of Agricultural Sciences (BIAS)
Library
Zhangbei, Hebei 076400
Phone: +86(3442) 2971

Type: Academic **Head:** Mrs. Zhang Zhi *Phone:* +86(3442)
2971 **Staff:** 8 Prof. 43 Other **Holdings:** 6,564 books 53 journals **Language of Collection/Services:** Chinese, English /
Chinese **Subjects:** Agricultural Development, Agricultural
Economics, Animal Husbandry, Biotechnology, Crops, Entomology, Farming, Food Sciences, Forestry, Horticulture,
Plant Pathology, Plants, Soil Science, Veterinary Medicine
Specializations: Oats, Plant Breeding, Potatoes, Wheat
Photocopy: No

Heilongjiang

♦737   Harbin, Heilongjiang, China
Heilongjiang Academy of Agricultural Sciences,
     Harbin Agricultural Remote Sensing
     Sub-Center (HARSSC)
Library
50 Xuefu Lu, Nangun District
Harbin, Heilongjiang 150086
Phone: +86(451) 666-4921 ext 324 **Fax:** +86(451) 63726

Type: Academic **Head:** You Bocheng *Phone:* +86(451)
666-4921 ext 522 **Staff:** 12 Prof. 10 Other **Holdings:** 1,000
books 20 journals **Language of Collection/Services:** Chinese, English / Chinese **Subjects:** Agricultural Engineering,
Forestry, Geology, Soil Science, Water Resources **Specializations:** Computers, Geography, Land Use, Remote Sensing **Loan:** Inhouse **Service:** In country **Photocopy:** Yes

738   Harbin, Heilongjiang, China
Heilongjiang Academy of Agricultural Sciences,
     Information Institute
Scientech Literature Information Centre (SLIC)
No. 368 Xuefu Road, Nangang District
Harbin, Heilongjiang 150086
Phone: +86(451) 667-7477 **Fax:** +86(451) 666-3726

Founded: 1956 **Type:** Government **Head:** Ren Chang-shun
Phone: +86(451) 667-7477 **Staff:** 25 Prof. 5 Other **Holdings:** 32,000 books 300 journals **Language of Collection/Services:** Chinese, English / Chinese **Subjects:** Plant
Breeding, Plant Protection, Plants **Databases Used:**
CABCD; CSTDB **Photocopy:** No

739   Harbin, Heilongjiang, China
Northeast Agricultural University (NAU)
Library
59 Mucai Jie
Gongbin Lu, Xiangfang District
Harbin, Heilongjiang 150030
Phone: +86(451) 539-0757 **Fax:** +86(531) 530-3336
Email: flwang@neau.edu.cn **WWW:** www.neau.edu.cn
OPAC: lbr.neau.edu.cn

Former Name: Northeast Agricultural College **Founded:**
1948 **Type:** Academic **Head:** Wang Fuli *Phone:* +86(451)
539-0294 *Email:* flwang@neau.edu.cn **Staff:** 48 Prof. 6
Other **Holdings:** 420,000 books 1,992 journals **Language of
Collection/Services:** Chinese, English, Japanese, Russian /
Chinese **Subjects:** Comprehensive **Specializations:** Agricultural Engineering, Animal Husbandry, Biotechnology,
Crops, Entomology, Food Sciences, Horticulture, Plant Pathology, Veterinary Science **Databases Developed:** Data-

base of NAU theses; Database of soybeans in northeast area
Databases Used: Agricola; Agris; CABI **Photocopy:** Yes

740 Harbin, Heilongjiang, China
Northeast Forestry University
Library
26 Xexing Lu
Harbin, Heilongjiang 150040
Phone: +86(451) 219-0675 **Fax:** +86(451) 219-0148
Email: zhangml@ss20.nefu.edu.cn **WWW:** www.lib.nefu.
edu.cn **Ariel IP:** 202.118.216.1

Founded: 1965 **Type:** Academic **Head:** Wu Qi-Jun *Phone:*
+86(451) 219-0417 **Staff:** 50 Prof. 3 Other **Holdings:**
570,000 books 1,076 journals **Language of Collection/Services:** Chinese, English, Russian, Japanese, German / Chinese, English **Subjects:** Agricultural Economics, Forest Products, Agricultural Engineering, Forestry, Wildlife **Databases Used:** Chinese Academic Journal **Loan:** Inhouse **Service:** Inhouse **Photocopy:** Yes

♦741 Hulan, Heilongjiang, China
Chinese Academy of Agricultural Sciences, Sugar
Beet Research Institute (CAAS, SBRI)
Library
Hulan County
Hulan, Heilongjiang 150501
Location: Dongfeng Street **Phone:** +86(4667) 22548

Type: Academic **Head:** Sun Qilan *Phone:* +86(4667) 22548
ext 95 **Staff:** 1 Prof. 2 Other **Holdings:** 10,038 books 301
journals **Language of Collection/Services:** Chinese, English, Japanese, Russian / Chinese **Subjects:** Agribusiness, Agricultural Development, Agricultural Engineering, Biotechnology, Crops, Plant Pathology, Plants, Soil Science, Sugarbeet **Loan:** Inhouse **Service:** Inhouse **Photocopy:** No

♦742 Jiamusi, Heilongjiang, China
Heilongjiang Academy of Agricultural
Reclamation
Institute of Scientific and Technical Information
Anqing Lu
PO Box 111
Jiamusi, Heilongjiang 154007
Head: Hu Guangmin **Holdings:** 26,400 books 530 journals
Subjects: Reclamation

♦743 Qiqihaer, Heilongjiang, China
Heilongjiang Shelterbelt Forest Research Institute
Information Research Office
Fulaerji District
Qiqihaer, Heilongjiang 161041
Former Name: Forest Protection Research Institute of
Heilongjiang Province **Type:** Academic **Head:** Miao Janliang *Phone:* +86(452) 82730 **Staff:** 102 Prof. 77 Other **Holdings:** 10,000 books 100 journals **Language of Collection/Services:** Chinese, English, Japanese, Russian/Chinese **Subjects:** Agroforestry, Forest Ecology, Forestry, Plant Breeding, Protection of Forests, Shelterbelts **Loan:** Inhouse **Service:** Inhouse **Photocopy:** Yes

Henan

♦744 Anyang, Henan, China
Chinese Academy of Agricultural Sciences,
Cotton Research Institute (CAAS)
Library
Baibi, Anyang County
Anyang, Henan 455112
Head: Kang Hongdao **Holdings:** 12,260 books 650 journals
Subjects: Cotton

745 Luoyang, Henan, China
Yituo Group Ltd. Co., Technical Center
Library
No. 39 Xiyuan Road
Jianxi District
Luoyang, Henan 471039
Phone: +86(379) 492-1001 ext 284, 497-4924 **Fax:** +86
(379) 491-2417 **Email:** shwq@126.com

Former Name: Research Institute of Tractor and Automobile of No. 1 Tractor Plant **Founded:** 1957 **Type:** Research **Head:** Sha Wenqiu *Email:* shwq@126.com *Phone:* +86
(379) 497-4924 **Staff:** 5 Prof. 6 Other **Holdings:** 45,000 books 12,000 journals **Language of Collection/Services:** Chinese, English, Japanese, Russian / Chinese, English **Subjects:** Construction Machinery, Diesel Engines, Farm Machinery, Tractors, Trucks **Loan:** In country **Service:** Inhouse **Photocopy:** Yes

♦746 Zhengzhou, Henan, China
Chinese Academy of Agricultural Sciences,
Zhengzhou Institute of Pomology (CAAS)
Library
Southern Suburb
Zhengzhou, Henan 450004
Head: Zhao Fengqin **Holdings:** 13,700 books 140 journals
Subjects: Fruits

♦747 Zhengzhou, Henan, China
Henan Academy of Agricultural Sciences
Institute of Scientific and Technical Information
1 Nongye Road
Zhengzhou, Henan 450002
Head: Dan Yane **Holdings:** 177,400 books 4,880 journals

748 Zhengzhou, Henan, China
Henan Agricultural University
Library
95 Wenhua Road
Jinshui District
Zhengzhou, Henan 450002
Phone: +86(371) 3825441
Head: Jiao Peilin **Holdings:** 605,500 books 4,609 journals

Hubei

749   **Wuhan, Hubei, China**
Chinese Academy of Agricultural Sciences,
     Institute of Oil Crops (CAAS, IOC)
Library
Baoji'an, Wuchang
Wuhan, Hubei 430062
Phone: +86(27) 8681-3823 **Fax:** +86(27) 8681-6451

Type: Academic **Head:** Huang Runze *Phone:* +86(27) 8681-3823 **Staff:** 7 Prof. **Holdings:** 30,000 books 400 journals **Language of Collection/Services:** Chinese, English, French, German, Japanese / Chinese, English **Subjects:** Oil Plants **Specializations:** Castor, Peanuts, Rape, Safflower, Sesame, Soybeans, Sunflowers **Loan:** Inhouse **Service:** In country **Photocopy:** No

750   **Wuhan, Hubei, China**
Huazhong Agricultural University
Library
Shizhishan, Nanhu
Wuhan, Hubei 430070
Phone: +86(27) 8739-3766 ext 2135 **Email:** hzal@public.wh.hb.cn

Former Name: Central China Agricultural University **Type:** Academic **Holdings:** 527,544 books 4,254 journals **Subjects:** Comprehensive **Specializations:** Agricultural Economics, Crops, Microbiology, Plant Breeding, Plant Genetics, Pomology, Veterinary Science **Databases Developed:** Database of dissertations from university **Databases Used:** Agricola; CAJ; VIP **Photocopy:** No

751   **Wuhan, Hubei, China**
Hubei Provincial Academy of Agricultural
     Sciences
Library
Yaoyuan, Nanhu, Wuchang
Wuhan, Hubei 430064
Phone: +86(27) 8748-9808 **Email:** hbaaso@public.wh.hb.cn

Former Name: Central China Institute of Agricultural Sciences **Founded:** 1950 **Type:** Academic **Head:** Jinan Chen *Phone:* +86(27) 8738-9808 *Email:* hbaaso@public.wh.hb.cn **Staff:** 430 Prof. 42 Other **Holdings:** 120,000 books 564 journals **Language of Collection/Services:** Chinese, English / Chinese, English **Subjects:** Agronomy, Animal Husbandry, Fertilizers, Horticulture, Microbiology, Plant Protection, Soil **Databases Used:** Agris; CABCD **Loan:** Inhouse **Service:** Inhouse **Photocopy:** No

Hunan

752   **Changsha, Hunan, China**
Hunan Academy of Agricultural Sciences
Institute of Scientific and Technical Information
Mapoling, Furong District
Changsha, Hunan 410125
Phone: +86(731) 469-1323 **Email:** stisc@public.cs.hn.cn

Type: Research **Head:** Ding Chaoying *Phone:* +86(731) 469-1323 *Email:* stisc@public.cs.hn.cn **Holdings:** 200,000 books 400 journals **Language of Collection/Services:** Chinese, English, Japanese, Russian/Chinese, English **Subjects:** Comprehensive **Specializations:** Crop Production, Plant Breeding **Databases Developed:** Hybrid Rice Database of China **Loan:** Inhouse **Service:** Internationally **Photocopy:** Yes

◆**753**   **Changsha, Hunan, China**
Hunan Hybrid Rice Research Center
Library
Mapoling
Changsha, Hunan 410125
Phone: +86(731) 444-8780 ext 359 **Fax:** +86(731) 444-8877

Type: Academic **Head:** Zhang Qiao *Phone:* +86(731) 444-8780 ext 359 **Staff:** 8 Prof. 6 Other **Holdings:** 5,000 books 120 journals **Language of Collection/Services:** Chinese, English / Chinese **Subjects:** Agribusiness, Farming, Plants **Specializations:** Biotechnology, Hybrids, Plant Breeding, Crops, Rice **Loan:** Inhouse **Service:** Internationally **Photocopy:** Yes

754   **Yuanjiang, Hunan, China**
Chinese Academy of Agricultural Sciences,
     Institute of Bast Fibre Crops (CAAS, IBFC)
Library
Fengsuza No. 2
Yuanjiang, Hunan 413100
Phone: +86(737) 272-1161 ext 2029 **Fax:** +86(737) 272-5180

Founded: 1959 **Type:** Research **Head:** Mr. Tang Shouwei *Phone:* +86(737) 273-5449, 272-4753 **Staff:** 6 Prof. **Holdings:** 20,000 books 1,250 journals Language of Collection/Services: Chinese, English, Russian, Japanese **Subjects:** Fiber Plants **Specializations:** Boehmeria nivea, Flax, Hemp, Jute, Kenaf **Databases Used:** Comprehensive **Loan:** Internationally **Service:** Internationally **Photocopy:** Yes

◆**755**   **Yuanjiang, Hunan, China**
Hunan Fisheries Research Institute (HFRI)
Information and Data Division (IDD)
49 Shuyuan Lu
Yuanjiang, Hunan 413100
Phone: +86(737) 725770

Former Name: Hunan Provincial Institute of Fishery Science (HPIFS) **Type:** Academic **Head:** Ms. Zhang Wenhong *Phone:* +86(737) 725770 **Staff:** 4 Prof. 6 Other **Holdings:** 9,800 books 150 journals **Language of Collection/Services:** Chinese, English / Chinese, English **Subjects:** Fisheries, Water Resources **Loan:** In country **Service:** Internationally **Photocopy:** Yes

Inner Mongolia

◆**756**   **Hohhot, Inner Mongolia, China**
Chinese Academy of Agricultural Sciences,
     Grassland Research Institute (CAAS, GRI)
Information and Material Reference Center

Xincheng District
Hohhot, Inner Mongolia 010010

Phone: +86(471) 43852 ext 942 **Fax:** +86(471) 41330

Founded: 1964 **Type:** Academic **Head:** Zhang Minghua *Phone:* +86(471) 43852 ext 952 **Staff:** 4 Prof. 4 Other **Holdings:** 30,000 books 700 journals **Language of Collection/Services:** Chinese, English, Japanese, Russian/Chinese, English, Japanese, Russian **Subjects:** Agriculture (Tropics), Agricultural Development, Agricultural Economics, Agricultural Engineering, Biotechnology, Crops, Entomology, Farming, Pastures, Plant Pathology, Plants, Soil Science **Specializations:** Animal Husbandry, Grassland Management **Service:** In country **Photocopy:** Yes

757 Hohhot, Inner Mongolia, China
Inner Mongolia Academy of Agricultural Sciences (IMAAS)
Institute of Agricultural Economy and Information Research
South Suburbs, Jiucheng
Hohhot, Inner Mongolia 010031

Phone: +86(471) 596-6267 **Fax:** +86(471) 597-1068

Founded: 1957 **Type:** Research **Staff:** 2 Prof. 1 Other **Holdings:** 25,693 books 15,875 journals **Language of Collection/Services:** Chinese, English, Japanese, French, Russian / Chinese, English **Subjects:** Agricultural Economics **Loan:** Inhouse **Service:** Inhouse **Photocopy:** Yes

♦758 Hohhot, Inner Mongolia, China
Inner Mongolia Academy of Animal Husbandry
Institute of Scientific and Technical Information
Balizhuang, West Suburb
Hohhot, Inner Mongolia 010030

Subjects: Animal Husbandry

759 Hohhot, Inner Mongolia, China
Inner Mongolia College of Agriculture and Animal Sciences
Library
No. 306 Xinjian Dongjie
Hohhot, Inner Mongolia 010018

Founded: 1952 **Head:** Wu En *Phone:* +86(471) 430-6362 **Staff:** 49 Prof. 2 Other **Holdings:** 409,815 books **Language of Collection/Services:** Chinese, English **Subjects:** Agricultural Economics, Agronomy, Animal Husbandry, Farm Machinery, Grasslands, Veterinary Science

760 Hohhot, Inner Mongolia, China
Ministry of Machinery Industry, Huhhot Livestock Machinery Research Institute (HLMRI)
Library
506 Zhaowuda Lu
Hohhot, Inner Mongolia 010010

Fax: +86(471) 495-1307 **Email:** mjfbhy@public.hh.nm.cn

Type: Research **Head:** Ms. Li Xinrong *Phone:* +86(471) 491-3416 **Email:** mjfbhy@public.hh.nm.cn **Holdings:** 132 journals 20,000 books **Language of Collection/Services:** Chinese, English **Subjects:** Animal Husbandry, Farm Machinery

Jiangsu

761 Nanjing, Jiangsu, China
Chinese Academy of Sciences, Institute of Soil Science (CAS, ISS)
Periodical Editing and Literature Center
PO Box 821
Nanjing, Jiangsu 210008

Location: 71 Beijing Donglu **Fax:** +86(25) 335-3590 **WWW:** www.issas.ac.cn

Founded: 1953 **Type:** Academic **Head:** Prof. Lu Rong-hui *Phone:* +86(25) 335-4775 *Email:* rhlu@ns.issas.ac.cn **Staff:** 10 Prof. **Holdings:** 120,000 books 620 journals **Language of Collection/Services:** Chinese, English, Russian / Chinese **Subjects:** Agriculture (Tropics), Environmental Sciences, Land Resources, Soil Science **Specializations:** Plant Nutrition, Reclamation, Soil Biology, Soil Chemistry, Soil Classification, Soil Conservation, Soil Fertility, Soil Formation, Soil Physics **Databases Used:** SOILCD **Loan:** In country **Service:** In country **Photocopy:** Yes

762 Nanjing, Jiangsu, China
Jiangsu Academy of Agricultural Sciences (JAAS)
Institute of Scientific and Technological Information
Xiaolingwei
Nanjing, Jiangsu 210004

Phone: +86(25) 439-0284 **Fax:** +86(25) 439-0279 **Email:** nic@mail.jaas.ac.cn **WWW:** www.jaas.ac.cn

Founded: 1935 **Type:** Academic **Head:** Xi Chengzhong *Phone:* +86(25) 439-0284 *Email:* nic@mail.jaas.ac.cn **Staff:** 4 Prof. 2 Other **Holdings:** 180,000 books 750 journals **Language of Collection/Services:** Chinese, English / Chinese **Subjects:** Comprehensive **Specializations:** Biotechnology, Cereals, Entomology, Plant Breeding **Networks:** DCSTP **Databases Developed:** Database of diseases, insects and weeds in main crops and their integrated control of Jiangsu Province **Databases Used:** Agricola; Agris; CABCD **Loan:** In country **Service:** In country **Photocopy:** Yes

763 Nanjing, Jiangsu, China
Jiangsu Academy of Agricultural Sciences, Institute of Plant Protection (JAAS)
Library
Xiaolingwei
Nanjing, Jiangsu 210004

Fax: +86(25) 439-0383 **Email:** jaasliuy@public1.ptt.js.cn

Type: Academic **Head:** Wang Yuahong *Phone:* +86(25) 439-0383 *Email:* jaasliuy@public1.ptt.js.cn **Staff:** 3 Prof. 1 Other **Holdings:** 15,000 books 5,000 journals **Language of Collection/Services:** Chinese, English, Japanese **Subjects:** Biotechnology, Botany, Entomology, Pesticides, Plant Pathology, Plant Protection **Databases Used:** Agris **Service:** Inhouse **Photocopy:** Yes

764 Nanjing, Jiangsu, China
Ministry of Agriculture, Nanjing Institute for Agricultural Mechanization (MoA)
Library
100 Liuying, Zhongshanmenwai

Nanjing, Jiangsu 210014
Phone: +86(25) 443-2761, 443-1695 **Fax:** +86(25) 443-2672

Type: Academic **Head:** *Phone:* +86(25) 443-2761 ext 201 *Email:* nnnkyc@public1.ptt.js.cn **Staff:** 3 Prof. **Holdings:** 40,741 books 223 journals **Language of Collection/Services:** English / Chinese, English **Subjects:** Mechanization, Agricultural Engineering, Farm Machinery **Specializations:** Rice, Plant Protection **Databases Developed:** Database of rice production mechanization; Database of crop protection equipment

765   Nanjing, Jiangsu, China
Nanjing Agricultural University (NAU)
Library
No. 1 Weigang
Nanjing, Jiangsu 210095
WWW: www.njau.edu.cn

Founded: 1914 **Type:** Academic **Head:** Prof. Cheng Jiyi *Email:* jycheng@njau.edu.cn **Holdings:** 680,000 books 7,000 journals **Subjects:** Agricultural Economics, Animal Husbandry, Food Sciences, Horticulture, Plant Protection, Soil Science, Veterinary Medicine **Loan:** In country **Photocopy:** No

766   Nanjing, Jiangsu, China
Nanjing Agricultural University, Soybean
       Research Institute (NAU, SRI)
Information Center
No. 1 Weigang
Nanjing, Jiangsu 210095
Phone: +86(25) 439-6410 **Fax:** +86(25) 439-5110 **Email:** nausri@public1.ptt.js.cn **WWW:** www.njau.edu.cn

Former Name: Nanjing Agricultural College, Soybean Research Laboratory **Type:** Academic **Head:** Junyi Gai *Phone:* +86(25) 439-5110 *Email:* sri@njau.edu.cn **Staff:** 25 Prof. 10 Other **Holdings:** 25 books 10 journals **Language of Collection/Services:** Chinese, English/Chinese **Subjects:** Germplasm, Plant Breeding, Plant Genetics, Soybeans **Databases Developed:** Soybean Germplasm Database; Soybean Pedigree Database **Loan:** Internationally **Service:** Internationally **Photocopy:** Yes

767   Nanjing, Jiangsu, China
Nanjing Forestry University (NFU)
Library
Longpan Lu
Nanjing, Jiangsu 210037
Phone: +86(25) 542-7565 **Email:** nllib@njfu.edu.cn
WWW: www.njfu.edu.cn **OPAC:** 202.119.210.4

Former Name: Nanjing Technological College of Forest Products **Founded:** 1952 **Type:** Academic **Head:** Liu Xiuhua *Phone:* +86(25) 542-7243 *Email:* xhliu@njfu.edu.cn **Staff:** 38 Prof. 5 Other **Holdings:** 606,000 books 2,257 journals **Language of Collection/Services:** Chinese, English, Russian, Japanese / Chinese, English, German **Subjects:** Agricultural Development, Agricultural Economics, Agricultural Engineering, Ecology, Entomology, Forestry, Plant Pathology, Mechanization **Specializations:** Forest Ecology, Forest Products, Landscape Architecture, Plants, Pulp and

Paper Industry, Silviculture, Tree Breeding, Wood Technology, Woodworking **Databases Used:** Comprehensive **Service:** In country **Loan:** In country **Photocopy:** Yes

768   Yangzhou, Jiangsu, China
Jiangsu Agricultural College
Library
Sunong Lu, West Suburbs
Yangzhou, Jiangsu 225001

Founded: 1952 **Type:** Academic **Head:** Professor Gu Zifen *Phone:* +86(514) 42521, 41794 **Staff:** 25 Prof. 7 Other **Holdings:** 400,000 books 1,200 journals **Subjects:** Architecture, Biology, Electrical Engineering, Environment, Food Sciences, Irrigation, Machinery **Loan:** Internationally **Photocopy:** Yes

769   Zhenjiang, Jiangsu, China
Chinese Academy of Agricultural Sciences,
       Institute of Sericulture (CAAS)
Sericultural Science and Technology Information
Sibaitu
Zhenjiang, Jiangsu 212018
Phone: +86(511) 561-6593 **Fax:** +86(511) 562-2507

Former Name: East China Sericultural Research Institute **Type:** Academic **Head:** Chen Xi-chao *Phone:* +86(511) 561-6593 **Staff:** 9 Prof. **Holdings:** 60,000 books 470 journals **Language of Collection/Services:** Chinese, English, French, Japanese, Russian / Chinese, English **Subjects:** Biotechnology, Entomology, Sericulture **Loan:** Inhouse **Service:** Internationally **Photocopy:** No

Jiangxi

♦770   Nanchang, Jiangxi, China
Jiangxi Academy of Agricultural Sciences
       (JXAAS)
Information Institute
Wunonggang, Liantang Zhen
Nanchang County
Nanchang, Jiangxi 330200

Head: Yang Shengjun **Holdings:** 136,350 books 1,874 journals **Subjects:** Crops, Upland Areas

771   Nanchang, Jiangxi, China
Jiangxi Agricultural University (JAU)
Library
Meilingxia
Nanchang, Jiangxi 330045
Phone: +86(791) 381-3249

Former Name: Jiangxi Communist Labour University **Founded:** 1980 **Type:** Academic **Head:** Liang Gan *Phone:* +86(791) 381-3264 **Staff:** 38 Prof. 15 Other **Holdings:** 450,000 books 80,000 journals Language of Collection/Services:** Chinese / Chinese **Subjects:** Comprehensive **Databases Used:** CAJ; CSCI-CD; CSTDB **Service:** Inhouse **Loan:** Inhouse **Photocopy:** Yes

♦772 **Nanchang, Jiangxi, China**
Jiangxi Institute of Traditional Chinese Veterinary
    Medicine (JXITCVM)
Library
2 Fuzhou Zhilu
Nanchang, Jiangxi 330006

Type: Academic **Head:** Zhang Quanxin *Phone:* +86(791)
221628 **Language of Collection/Services:** Chinese, English
/Chinese **Subjects:** Traditional Medicines, Veterinary Medicine **Specializations:** Veterinary Medicine (Chinese), Acupuncture, Medicinal Plants

Jilin

773   **Changchun, Jilin, China**
Jilin Agricultural University (JLAU)
Library
South of Dong Huan Road
Changchun, Jilin 130118

Phone: +86(431) 451-0901 ext 2711 **OPAC:** ns.jlau.cc.jl.
cn

Founded: 1948 **Type:** Academic **Head:** Bai Baozhang
Phone: +86(431) 451-0901 ext 2711 **Staff:** 40 Prof. 4 Other
Holdings: 510,000 books 2,500 journals **Language of Col-
lection/Services:** Chinese, English, Japanese/Chinese **Sub-
jects:** Comprehensive **Specializations:** Fungi, Agricultural
Chemistry, Agronomy, Animal Husbandry, Horticulture,
Manures, Medicinal Plants, Plant Nutrition, Plant Protection,
Soil Science, Wildlife Conservation, Veterinary Science
Loan: In country **Service:** Internationally **Photocopy:** Yes

774   **Changchun, Jilin, China**
Jilin Aquatic Research Institute
Library
50 Renmin Street
Changchun, Jilin 130051

Phone: +86(431) 271-7670 **Fax:** +86(431) 271-6269

Founded: 1961 **Type:** Academic **Staff:** 1 Prof. **Holdings:**
13,000 books 45 journals **Language of Collection/Services:**
Chinese, English **Subjects:** Fisheries **Databases Used:**
Aquatic Document Database of China

775   **Changchun, Jilin, China**
Jilin Forestry Research Institute
Jilin Forest Sciences Information Center
No. 1 Pudong Road
Changchun, Jilin 130031

Phone: +86(431) 451-3601 **Fax:** +86(431) 451-3601
Email: jllky@public.cc.jl.cn

Former Name: Jilin Forestry Experiment Station **Founded:**
1956 **Type:** Academic **Head:** Zhou Wen *Phone:* +86(431)
451-3697, 451-3601 *Email:* jllky@public.cc.jl.cn **Staff:** 9
Prof. **Holdings:** 36,000 books 304 journals **Language of
Collection/Services:** Chinese, English, Japanese **Subjects:**
Forestry **Specializations:** Forest Ecology, Forest Soils, For-
est Products, Tree Breeding, Wildlife, Wood Technology
Loan: In country **Service:** In country **Photocopy:** No

776   **Changchun, Jilin, China**
Northeast Normal University, National Laboratory
    of Grassland Ecological Engineering
    (NLGEE)
Information Center
Stalin Road
Changchun, Jilin 130024

Phone: +86(431) 685086 **Fax:** +86(431) 684009

Type: Academic **Head:** Li Jiandong *Phone:* +86(431)
685085 ext 2473 **Staff:** 6 Prof. 9 Other **Holdings:** 50,000
books 200 journals **Language of Collection/Services:** Chinese, English, Japanese, Russian / Chinese **Subjects:** Grasslands **Specializations:** Grassland Management, Salt
Marshes **Loan:** Inhouse **Service:** Inhouse **Photocopy:** Yes

777   **Gongzhuling, Jilin, China**
Jilin Academy of Agricultural Sciences (JAAS)
Scientech Documentation and Information Center
    (SDIC)
No. 6 West Xinghua Street
Gongzhuling, Jilin 136100

Phone: +86(434) 621-9755 **Fax:** +86(434) 621-4884
Email: stir1@public.jaas.sp.jl.cn **WWW:** www.jaas.
com.cn

Founded: 1913 **Type:** Research **Head:** Jiang Yumei *Phone:*
+86(434) 621-9755 *Email:* stir1@public.jaas.sp.jl.cn **Staff:**
26 Prof. 6 Other **Holdings:** 200,000 books 3,500 journals
Language of Collection/Services: Chinese, English, Russian, Japanese / Chinese **Subjects:** Comprehensive **Specializations:** Maize, Rice, Soybeans **Databases Used:** CABCD
Loan: In country **Service:** In country **Photocopy:** Yes

♦778 **Gongzhuling, Jilin, China**
Siping Institute of Agricultural Sciences
Library
18 Gongyi Road
Gongzhuling, Jilin 136101

Type: Academic **Head:** Liu Wuying *Phone:* +86(4441)
213526 ext 3052 **Staff:** 38 Prof. 112 Other **Holdings:** 11,000
books 350 journals **Language of Collection/Services:** Chinese, English, Russian, Japanese/Chinese, English **Subjects:**
Agricultural Economics, Crops, Farming, Food Sciences,
Plant Pathology **Loan:** In country **Service:** Internationally
Photocopy: Yes

♦779 **Jilin, Jilin, China**
Chinese Academy of Agricultural Sciences,
    Institute of Special Wild Economic Animals
    and Plants (CAAS)
Library
Zuojia District
Jilin, Jilin 132109

Head: Gong Xicheng **Holdings:** 320,000 books 284 journals
Subjects: Wild Animals, Wild Plants

780   **Jilin, Jilin, China**
Jilin City Academy of Agricultural Sciences
    (JCAAS)
Information Office
No. 1 Nong Yan West Road

Jiuzhan Street
Jilin, Jilin 132101
Phone: +86(432) 305-8337 ext 2036 **Fax:** +86(432) 305-8343

Former Name: Jilin City Institute of Agricultural Sciences **Founded:** 1957 **Type:** Academic **Head:** Guosheng Liang *Phone:* +86(432) 205-1526 **Staff:** 9 Prof. **Holdings:** 44,000 books 38,000 journals **Language of Collection/Services:** Chinese, English, Japanese, Russian / Chinese, English, Japanese, Russian **Subjects:** Comprehensive **Specializations:** Crops, Gardening, Plants **Loan:** Inhouse **Service:** Inhouse **Photocopy:** Yes

Liaoning

781   Dalian, Liaoning, China
Dalian Fisheries University
Library
Xicun, Heishijiao
Shahegou District
Dalian, Liaoning 116023
Phone: +86(411) 467-1025 ext 345 **Email:** tushung@dlut.edu.cn

Founded: 1952 **Type:** Academic **Head:** Yu Xinwen *Phone:* +86(411) 467-1025 ext 345 *Email:* tushung@dlut.edu.cn **Staff:** 24 Prof. 2 Other **Holdings:** 195,000 books 800 journals **Language of Collection/Services:** Chinese, English / Chinese **Subjects:** Fisheries **Specializations:** Aquaculture, Aquatic Resources Processing **Loan:** Inhouse **Service:** In country **Photocopy:** No

♦782   Panjin, Liaoning, China
Liaoning Institute of Saline and Alkali Soil
     Utilization (SASU)
Information Center
Dawa Zhen, Dawa County
Panjin, Liaoning 124200
Location: Dawa Center Street **Phone:** +86(4271) 662983

Type: Academic **Head:** Chen Wenhua *Phone:* +86(4271) 662484 **Staff:** 94 Prof. 122 Other **Holdings:** 47,800 books 12,600 journals **Language of Collection/Services:** Chinese /Chinese **Subjects:** Aquaculture, Crops, Forestry, Fruit Trees, Irrigation, Plant Protection, Rice, Soil Management, Soil Salinity, Soil Science, Vegetables **Databases Developed:** Saline-alkalie soil utilization; rice cultivation and breeding **Loan:** Inhouse **Service:** In country **Photocopy:** Yes

♦783   Shenyang, Liaoning, China
Chinese Academy of Sciences, Institute of
     Forestry and Soil Science (CAS)
Library
No. 6, Section 2, Wenhua Road
Shenyang, Liaoning 110015
Founded: 1954 **Type:** Academic **Head:** Chen Tao *Phone:* +86(24) 483329 ext 377 **Staff:** 14 Prof. 3 Other **Holdings:** 40 books 40 journals **Subjects:** Botany, Entomology, Microbiology, Plant Pathology, Plant Protection, Soil Science **Loan:** Internationally **Photocopy:** Yes

784   Shenyang, Liaoning, China
Liaoning Academy of Agricultural Sciences
     (LAAS)
Institute of Technology and Science Information
     (ITSI)
Dongling Road 84
Shenyang, Liaoning 110161
Phone: +86(24) 8841-9917 **Fax:** +86(24) 8841-7396
Email: snykxy@mx.ln.cei.gov.cn

Founded: 1978 **Type:** Academic **Head:** Zheng Yegang *Phone:* +86(24) 8841-9916 *Email:* zyegang@mx.ln.cei.gov.cn **Staff:** 43 Prof. **Holdings:** 140,000 books **Language of Collection/Services:** Chinese, English, Russian, Japanese / Chinese, English, Russian, Japanese **Subjects:** Comprehensive **Specializations:** Agricultural Economics, Crops, Biology, Horticulture, Plant Pathology **Databases Used:** Agris; CABCD; Chinese Journal **Photocopy:** No

785   Shenyang, Liaoning, China
Shenyang Agricultural University
Library
89 Maguanqiao, Dongling District
Shenyang, Liaoning 110161
Phone: 561

Founded: 1952 **Type:** Academic Government **Head:** Chen Baorong *Phone:* +86(24) 447911 **Staff:** 47 Prof. 4 Other **Holdings:** 196,000 books 1,037 journals **Subjects:** Agricultural Engineering, Agricultural Meteorology, Biology, Forestry, Fruit Trees, Vegetables, Veterinary Medicine **Loan:** In country **Photocopy:** Yes

786   Shenyang, Liaoning, China
Shenyang Institute of Agricultural Sciences
Library
Santaizi, Huanggu
Shenyang, Liaoning 110000
Phone: +86(24) 463380, 463555

Founded: 1973 **Type:** Academic **Head:** Bai Fong Qin *Phone:* +86(24) 464890 **Staff:** 6 Prof. **Holdings:** 14,749 books 469 journals **Subjects:** Horticulture **Loan:** In country **Photocopy:** Yes

787   Xingcheng, Liaoning, China
Chinese Academy of Agricultural Sciences, Resea
     Yching Institute of Pomology (CAAS, IP)
Center of Information and Reference (CIR)
Wenquan
Xingcheng, Liaoning 121600
Phone: +86(429) 515-2273 ext 320 **Fax:** +86(429) 512-9372

Founded: 1959 **Type:** Academic **Head:** Zhao Feng Yu *Phone:* +86(429) 512-7133 **Staff:** 12 Prof. 3 Other **Holdings:** 45,600 books **Language of Collection/Services:** Chinese / Chinese **Subjects:** Comprehensive **Specializations:** Pomology **Loan:** In country **Service:** Internationally **Photocopy:** Yes

Ningxia

♦788   Yinchuan, Ningxia, China
Ningxia Academy of Agricultural and Forestry
Sciences
Institute of Scientific and Technical Information
31 Zhigou, West Suburbs
Yinchuan, Ningxia 750002

Head: Cao Shuming **Holdings:** 19,794 books 1,231 journals

789   Yinchuan, Ningxia, China
Ningxia Academy of Agricultural and Forestry
Sciences, Institute of Soils and Fertilizers
Library
31 Zhigou, West Suburbs
Yinchuan, Ningxia 750002
Phone: +86(951) 504-4083 **Fax:** +86(951) 504-9204

Founded: 1980 **Type:** Academic **Head:** Li Youhong
Phone: +86(951) 504-9134 **Staff:** 2 Prof. 1 Other **Holdings:**
15,055 books 470 journals **Language of Collection/Services:** Chinese / Chinese **Subjects:** Soil Science, Fertilizers
Loan: Inhouse **Service:** Inhouse **Photocopy:** Yes

790   Yongning, Ningxia, China
Ningxia Agricultural College (NAC)
Library
Wangtaibao, Yongning County
Yongning, Ningxia 750105
Phone: +86(951) 840-0150

Founded: 1958 **Type:** Academic **Head:** Zhang Xian *Phone:*
+86(951) 801-1537 ext 209 **Staff:** 24 Prof. **Holdings:**
240,000 books 580 journals **Language of Collection/Services:** Chinese, English, Russian, Japanese / Chinese **Subjects:** Comprehensive **Specializations:** Agronomy, Animal
Husbandry, Biology, Food Sciences, Forestry, Plant Protection, Veterinary Medicine **Loan:** Inhouse **Service:** Inhouse
Photocopy: No

Qinghai

791   Xining, Qinghai, China
Qinghai Academy of Agricultural and Forestry
Sciences (QAAFS)
Institute of Scientific and Technical Information
(ISTI)
83 Ningzhang Road
Mujiawan, North Suburb
Xining, Qinghai 810016
Phone: +86(971) 531-1180

Founded: 1944 **Type:** Academic **Head:** Chen Laisheng
Phone: +86(971) 531-1180 **Staff:** 8 Prof. **Holdings:** 10,000
books 325 journals **Language of Collection/Services:** Chinese, English/Chinese, English **Subjects:** Agribusiness, Agricultural Economics, Farming, Forestry, Plant Protection,
Horticulture, Crops, Soil Science **Specializations:** Horticulture, Fertilizers, Plant Breeding, Soil **Databases Used:**
Agris; CABCD **Loan:** Inhouse **Service:** Inhouse **Photocopy:** Yes

792   Xining, Qinghai, China
Qinghai Academy of Animal Science and
Veterinary Medicine (QAASVM)
Library
18 Ningzhang Road, Beichuan
Xining, Qinghai 810003
Phone: +86(971) 531-8396

Former Name: Qinghai Veterinary Diagnosis House **Type:**
Academic **Head:** Mr. Xu Jian *Phone:* +86(971) 531-8396
Staff: 3 Prof. **Holdings:** 80,000 books **Language of Collection/Services:** Chinese, English, Japanese / Chinese, English
Subjects: Animal Husbandry, Fodder Crops, Rangelands,
Veterinary Science **Databases Used:** CABCD **Service:** Inhouse **Photocopy:** Yes

Shaanxi

793   Xianyang, Shaanxi, China
Northwest Agricultural University (NWAU)
Library
PO Box 3
Yangling
Xianyang, Shaanxi 712100
Phone: +86(29) 709-2358 **Fax:** +86(29) 709-8614 **Email:**
xntshg@public.xa.sn.cn **WWW:** www.nwau.edu.cn
OPAC: 202.100.8.98/xn/nwau.htm

Founded: 1934 **Type:** Academic **Head:** Sheng Quan Liu
Phone: +86(29) 709-2366 *Email:* xntshg@public.xa.sn.cn
Staff: 40 Prof. 4 Other **Holdings:** 800,000 books 1,800 journals **Language of Collection/Services:** Chinese, English,
Japanese, Russian, German **Subjects:** Comprehensive **Databases Used:** Comprehensive **Loan:** Inhouse **Service:** In
country **Photocopy:** No

♦794   Xianyang, Shaanxi, China
Shaanxi Provincial Institute of Forestry Science
(SPIFS)
Information Center
Yangling District
Xianyang, Shaanxi 712100
Phone: +86(910) 712351 ext 54

Former Name: Shaanxi Forestry Institute, Information Section **Type:** Academic **Head:** Zhang Lianglong *Phone:*
+86(910) 712351 ext 52 **Staff:** 8 Prof. **Holdings:** 30,000
books **Language of Collection/Services:** Chinese / Chinese
Subjects: Forestry **Loan:** Internationally **Service:** Internationally **Photocopy:** Yes

795   Yangling, Shaanxi, China
Northwest Agricultural University, Department of
Animal Science, Yellow Cattle Research
Section (NWAU, DAS, YCRS)
Information Center
Yangling, Shaanxi 712100
Phone: +86(29) 709-3423

Type: Academic **Head:** Professor Zhang Yinghan *Phone:*
+86(29) 709-2432 **Staff:** 7 Prof. 3 Other **Holdings:** 15,000
books 20 journals **Language of Collection/Services:** Chinese, English / Chinese, English **Subjects:** Animal Hus-

bandry **Specializations:** Animal Breeding, Cattle, Cattle Farming, Feeds, Genetics **Databases Developed:** PhD and MSc theses from 1982 to date **Loan:** Inhouse **Service:** Inhouse **Photocopy:** No

796   **Yangling District, Shaanxi, China**
Shaanxi Academy of Agricultural Sciences (SAAS)
Agro-Information Institute Library
Yangling District, Shaanxi 712100
Location: Yangling Railway Station **Phone:** +86(29) 708-8401 ext 3147 **Fax:** +86(29) 708-3333

Founded: 1952 **Type:** Academic **Head:** Wang Jun *Phone:* +86(29) 708-8401 ext 3147 **Staff:** 12 Prof. **Holdings:** 200,953 books 1,910 journals **Subjects:** Crops, Agricultural Economics, Animal Husbandry, Entomology, Horticulture, Plant Pathology, Plant Protection, Soil Science **Databases Used:** Agricola; Agris; CABCD

Shandong

797   **Jinan, Shandong, China**
Ministry of Chemical Industry, Feed Additive Technological Development and Service Center
Feed Additive Information Center
80 Wenhua Donglu
Jinan, Shandong 250014
Phone: +86(531) 296-7124 **Fax:** +86(531) 296-4645

Type: Academic **Head:** Zhang Baojun *Phone:* +86(531) 296-4645 **Staff:** 4 Prof. 67 Other **Holdings:** 31,000 books **Language of Collection/Services:** Chinese / Chinese **Subjects:** Feed Additives **Service:** In country **Photocopy:** No

798   **Jinan, Shandong, China**
Shandong Academy of Agricultural Sciences (SAAS)
Institute of Scientific and Technical Information (ISTI)
28 Sangyuan Lu, East Suburbs
Jinan, Shandong 250100
Phone: +86(531) 896-5551 ext 2249 **Fax:** +86(531) 896-5842 **Email:** saas@jn-public.sd.cninfo.net

Former Name: Institute of Information and Data **Founded:** 1979 **Type:** Academic **Head:** Lu Zhenyan *Phone:* +86(531) 896-0896, 896-5551 ext 22659 *Email:* saas@jn-public.sd.cninfo.net **Staff:** 30 Prof. 6 Other **Holdings:** 193,163 books 500 journals **Language of Collection/Services:** Chinese / Chinese **Subjects:** Agricultural Development, Agricultural Economics, Agricultural Engineering, Animal Husbandry, Biotechnology, Crops, Entomology, Farming, Fisheries, Food Sciences, Forestry, Gardening, Plant Pathology, Plants, Soil Science, Veterinary Medicine **Specializations:** Field Crops **Databases Developed:** Peanut and Chinese cabbage data including variety, breeding culture, phytopathology, etc. **Databases Used:** Comprehensive **Loan:** In country **Service:** In country **Photocopy:** Yes

♦799   **Jinan, Shandong, China**
Shandong Academy of Agricultural Sciences, Institute of Plant Protection
Library
14 Sangyuan Lu, East Subrubs
Jinan, Shandong 250100
Fax: +86(531) 895-2303

Type: Academic **Head:** Yang Chong Liang *Phone:* +86(531) 896-3725 ext 541 **Staff:** 2 Prof. 4 Other **Holdings:** 133 books 42 journals **Language of Collection/Services:** English / Chinese **Subjects:** Plant Protection **Loan:** Inhouse **Service:** Inhouse

800   **Jinan, Shandong, China**
Shandong Forestry Research Institute (SFRI)
Shandong Forestry Information Center (SFIC)
22 Wenhua Donglu
Jinan, Shandong 250014
Phone: +86(531) 854-0049 **Fax:** +86(531) 893-2824 **Email:** sdlkqb@jn-public.sd.cninfo.net

Founded: 1986 **Type:** Research **Holdings:** 22,000 books 560 journals **Language of Collection/Services:** Chinese / Chinese **Subjects:** Forestry

801   **Qingdao, Shandong, China**
Chinese Academy of Fishery Science, Yellow Sea Fisheries Research Institute (CAFS, YSFRI)
Library
106 Nanjing Road
Qingdao, Shandong 266071
Phone: +86(532) 583-6343 **Fax:** +86(532) 581-1514 **Email:** ysfri@sdqd.qdinfo.sti.ac.cn

Founded: 1947 **Type:** Academic **Head:** Mrs. Zeng Xiaoming *Phone:* +86(532) 583-6343 **Staff:** 4 Other **Holdings:** 40,000 books **Language of Collection/Services:** Chinese, English/Chinese **Subjects:** Fisheries **Photocopy:** No

802   **Qingdao, Shandong, China**
Ministry of Agriculture, National Animal Quarantine Institute (AQIMA)
Information Center
No. 369, Nanjing Lu
Qingdao, Shandong 266032
Fax: +86(532) 562-3545 **Email:** aquima@ns.qd.sd.cn

Type: Government **Head:** Zheng Zeng-ren *Phone:* +86(532) 562-3545 *Email:* aquima@ns.qd.sd.cn **Staff:** 3 Prof. 10 Other **Holdings:** 802 journals **Language of Collection/Services:** Chinese, English / Chinese, English **Subjects:** Animal Diseases, Quarantine **Databases Developed:** Institutional database for animal husbandry and veterinary services in China **Loan:** In country **Service:** In country **Photocopy:** Yes

803   **Qingdao, Shandong, China**
Shandong Peanuts Research Institute (SPRI)
Library
Laixi City
Qingdao, Shandong 266601
Phone: +86(532) 841-1707 **Fax:** +86(532) 841-2900

Former Name: Chinese Academy of Agricultural Sciences, Peanut Research Institute **Founded:** 1962 **Type:** Academic

Head: Shufen Duan *Phone:* +86(532) 841-1707 **Staff:** 3
Prof. **Holdings:** 20,000 books 400 journals **Language of
Collection/Services:** Chinese, English / Chinese **Subjects:**
Peanuts **Loan:** Inhouse **Service:** Inhouse **Photocopy:** Yes

804   Qingzhou, Shandong, China
           Chinese Academy of Agricultural Sciences,
                Tobacco Research Institute (CAAS)
           Library
           11 Xiangshan Lu
           Qingzhou, Shandong 262500
Phone: +86(536) 328-1411 **Fax:** +86(536) 328-0651
Email: trs2031@public.wfptt.sd.cn

Founded: 1959 **Type:** Academic **Head:** Cao Penyun
Email: trs2031@public.wfptt.sd.cn *Phone:* +86(536) 328-
1411 ext 2035 **Staff:** 2 Prof. 1 Other **Holdings:** 30,000 books
Language of Collection/Services: Chinese / Chinese, English **Subjects:** Comprehensive **Specializations:** Agronomy,
Chemistry, Curing, Plant Breeding, Plant Genetics, Plant
Protection, Tobacco **Databases Developed:** Tobacco agriculture research **Loan:** In country **Service:** In country **Photocopy:** Yes

805   Tai'an, Shandong, China
           Shandong Agricultural University
           Library
           86 Dai Zong Road
           Tai'an, Shandong 271018
Phone: +86(538) 824-2256 **Fax:** 822-6399 **Email:** tsbn@
sdau.edu.cn **WWW:** www.library.sdau.edu.cn **Ariel IP:**
202.194.133.1

Former Name: Shandong Agricultural College **Type:** Academic **Head:** Zhu Lu *Phone:* +86(538) 824-2877 *Email:*
tslz@sdau.edu.cn **Staff:** 9 Prof. 34 Other **Holdings:** 70,000
books 1,350 journals **Language of Collection/Services:**
Chinese, English/Chinese **Subjects:** Agricultural Economics, Biotechnology, Crops, Fruit Trees, Genetic Engineering,
Vegetables **Loan:** Inhouse **Service:** In country **Photocopy:**
Yes

806   Tai'an, Shandong, China
           Shandong Pomology Institute (SPI)
           Library and Information Department (LID)
           Longtan Lu
           Tai'an, Shandong 271000
Phone: +86(538) 820-4076 **Fax:** +86(538) 820-4076
Email: qbzls@sdip.sdau.edu.cn **WWW:** sdip.sdau.edu.cn

Type: Research **Head:** Zhang Yi *Phone:* +86(538) 833-
8029 *Email:* zhangyi@sdip.sdau.edu.cn **Holdings:** 15,000
books **Language of Collection/Services:** Chinese, English,
Japanese, Russian / Chinese, English, Japanese, Russian
Subjects: Deciduous Tree Fruits **Photocopy:** Yes

♦**807   Yantai, Shandong, China**
           Shandong Marine Fisheries Research Institute
           Document Division
           122 Nandajie
           Yantai, Shandong 264000

Type: Academic **Head:** Chang Jianbo *Phone:* +86(535)
243854 **Staff:** 6 Prof. **Holdings:** 25,000 books 700 journals

Language of Collection/Services: Chinese, English, Japanese / Chinese **Subjects:** Biology, Fisheries, Food Sciences,
Marine Fishes, Oceanography **Databases Developed:** Marine fish document database **Loan:** Inhouse **Service:** Inhouse
Photocopy: Yes

Shanghai

♦**808   Shanghai, China**
           Chinese Academy of Fishery Science, East China
                Sea Fisheries Research Institute (CAFS)
           Library
           300 Jungong Lu
           Shanghai 200090
Fax: +86(21) 543-2926

Type: Academic **Head:** Wang Xing-zhu *Phone:* +86(21)
543-4690 **Staff:** 2 Prof. **Holdings:** 20,000 books 136 jour-
nals **Language of Collection/Services:** Chinese, English,
Japanese, Russian/Chinese **Subjects:** Aquaculture, Biology,
Food Sciences, Fisheries, Marine Sciences **Loan:** Inhouse
Service: In country **Photocopy:** No

809   Shanghai, China
           Fudan University
           Library
           220 Handan Lu
           Shanghai 200433
Phone: +86(21) 544-1995 **Fax:** +86(21) 544-1995 **WWW:**
www.fudan.edu.cn

Founded: 1918 **Type:** Academic **Head:** Professor Qin
Zeng-fu *Phone:* +86(21) 548-2526 **Staff:** 98 Prof. 75 Other
Holdings: 3,400,000 books 5,264 journals **Language of
Collection/Services:** Chinese / Chinese **Subjects:** Agricul-
tural Development, Biotechnology, Botany, Crops, Environ-
ment, Food Sciences, Inheritance, Plant Protection **Loan:**
Internationally **Service:** Inhouse **Photocopy:** Yes

810   Shanghai, China
           Shanghai Academy of Agricultural Sciences
                (SAAS)
           Library
           2901 Beidi Road
           Shanghai 201106
Phone: +86(21) 6220-8660 ext 3169 **Fax:** +86(21) 6220-
6998 **Email:** xx1@saas.stc.ck.cn **WWW:** 192.168.255.53

Founded: 1960 **Type:** Academic **Head:** Mr. Xie
Kung-sheng *Phone:* +86(21) 6220-8660 ext 3169 **Staff:** 10
Prof. 2 Other **Holdings:** 300,000 books **Language of Col-
lection/Services:** Chinese/Chinese, English **Subjects:** Agri-
cultural Economics, Agricultural Engineering, Crops, Food
Sciences, Flowers, Plant Protection, Vegetables **Specializa-
tions:** Biotechnology, Edible Fungi, Horticulture **Networks:**
OCLC; SABINET **Databases Used:** Agris; CABCD **Loan:**
In country **Service:** In country **Photocopy:** Yes

811   Shanghai, China
           Shanghai Agricultural College (SAC)
           Library
           2678 Qixing Lu, Shanghai
           Shanghai 201101

Former Name: Shanghai Agricultural Institute **Founded:** 1978 **Type:** Academic **Head:** Wang Jing Ji *Phone:* +86(21) 6478-6866 **Staff:** 19 Prof. 3 Other **Holdings:** 240,000 books 890 journals **Language of Collection/Services:** Chinese, English/Chinese **Subjects:** Agricultural Economics, Animal Husbandry, Crops, Food Sciences, Horticulture, Veterinary Medicine **Loan:** Do not loan **Service:** Inhouse **Photocopy:** No

812 Shanghai, China
Shanghai Fisheries University (SFU)
Library
334 Jungong Lu
Shanghai 200090
Fax: +86(21) 6519-1315 **Email:** libsfuk@online.sh.cn **WWW:** www.cscse.edu.cn/laihua/gaoxiao/shsc.html

Former Name: Shanghai Fisheries College **Founded:** 1912 **Type:** Academic **Head:** Tong He-Yi *Phone:* +86(21) 6571-0811 *Email:* libsfuk@online.sh.cn **Staff:** 28 Prof. 8 Other **Holdings:** 380,919 books 973 journals **Language of Collection/Services:** Chinese, English, Japanese, Russian / Chinese, English, Japanese, Russian **Subjects:** Fisheries, Food Sciences **Loan:** Inhouse **Service:** Inhouse **Photocopy:** Yes

♦813 Shanghai, China
Shanghai Wood Industry Research Institute
(SWIRI)
Library
667 Zhongshan Xilu
Shanghai 200051
Phone: +86(21) 241-2200, 259-4125 **Fax:** +86(21) 241-2266

Type: Academic **Head:** Zhou Zheng Jie *Phone:* +86(21) 241-2266 **Staff:** 80 Prof. 20 Other **Holdings:** 50,000 books **Language of Collection/Services:** Chinese, English, German, Japanese / Chinese **Subjects:** Forest Products Industries, Machinery, Wood Cement, Wood Utilization, Wood Panels, Woodworking **Loan:** Internationally **Service:** Internationally **Photocopy:** Yes

Shanxi

♦814 Linfen, Shanxi, China
Shanxi Academy of Agricultural Sciences, Wheat
Research Institute
Information Department
33 Youbing Road
Linfen, Shanxi 041000

Former Name: Linfen Agricultural Experimental Station of Jinsui **Type:** Academic **Head:** Professor Cheng Limin *Phone:* +86(351) 212767, 214659 **Staff:** 119 Prof. 156 Other **Holdings:** 18,000 books 1,250 journals **Language of Collection/Services:** Chinese, English / Chinese, English **Subjects:** Agricultural Engineering, Biotechnology, Education/Extension, Crops, Farming, Food Sciences, Horticulture, Soil Science, Plants, Water Resources, Wheat **Specializations:** Entomology, Integrated Pest Management, Plant Breeding, Plant Pathology, Wheat **Loan:** In country **Service:** Internationally **Photocopy:** Yes

815 Taigu, Shanxi, China
Shanxi Agricultural University
Library
Taigu, Shanxi 030801
Phone: +86(354) 628-8232 **Email:** ndtsg@public.yz.sx.cn

Founded: 1936 **Type:** Academic **Head:** Kang Chengye *Phone:* +86(354) 628-8824 *Email:* ndtsg@public.yz.sx.cn **Staff:** 29 Prof. 19 Other **Holdings:** 537,000 books 1,291 journals **Language of Collection/Services:** Chinese, English/Chinese **Subjects:** Agricultural Economics, Agronomy, Animal Husbandry, Biology, Botany, Ecology, Food Sciences, Forestry, Horticulture, Sociology, Veterinary Medicine **Loan:** Inhouse **Service:** Inhouse **Photocopy:** Yes

♦816 Taiyuan, Shanxi, China
Shanxi Academy of Agricultural Sciences
Institute of Scientific and Technical Information
2 Changfeng Jie
Taiyuan, Shanxi 030006
Head: Ma Li **Holdings:** 44,906 books 2,081 journals

♦817 Xinzhou, Shanxi, China
Xinzhou Institute of Forestry Science
Library
4 North Alley Chang Zheng Street
Xinzhou, Shanxi 034000
Former Name: Xinxian Institute of Forestry Science **Type:** Research **Head:** Yang Tian Yi *Phone:* +86() 331614 **Holdings:** 7,000 books **Subjects:** Forestry, Pest Control, Plant Diseases

♦818 Yuncheng, Shanxi, China
Shanxi Academy of Agricultural Sciences, Cotton
Research Institute (SAAS)
Library
Yuncheng, Shanxi 044000
Phone: +86(359) 222432

Former Name: Yuncheng Prefecture Farm, Library/Documentation Division **Type:** Academic **Staff:** 4 Prof. 4 Other **Holdings:** 69,623 books **Language of Collection/Services:** Chinese, English/Chinese **Subjects:** Biotechnology, Cotton, Farming, Plant Pathology, Soil Science, Wheat **Loan:** Inhouse **Service:** Inhouse **Photocopy:** Yes

Sichuan

819 Chengdu, Sichuan, China
Sichuan Academy of Agricultural Sciences
(SAAS)
Institute of Scientific and Technical Information
(ISTI)
Shahe Bridge, East Suburb
Chengdu, Sichuan 610066
Location: Waidong beside Shahe Bridge **Phone:** +86(28) 450-4208 **Fax:** +86(28) 479-0413 **Email:** ascias@shell.scsti.ac.cn

Founded: 1937 **Type:** Academic **Head:** Li Xiao *Phone:* +86(28) 450-4208 *Email:* ascias@shell.scsti.ac.cn **Staff:** 50 Prof. 27 Other **Holdings:** 130,000 books 1,120 journals **Sub-**

jects: Agricultural Engineering, Biotechnology, Crops, Entomology, Horticulture, Plant Pathology, Sericulture **Loan:** Internationally **Photocopy:** Yes

♦**820 Chengdu, Sichuan, China**
Sichuan Academy of Agricultural Sciences,
Institute of Biotechnology and Nuclear
Technology
Library
Shizishan
Chengdu, Sichuan 610066
Location: Cong Zhou Road **Phone:** +86(28) 444-1031 Ext 377 **Fax:** +86(28) 444-2025

Type: Academic **Head:** Gong Mei *Phone:* +86(28) 444-1031 Ext 373 **Staff:** 47 Prof. 15 Other **Holdings:** 2,874 books **Language of Collection/Services:** Chinese, English / Chinese **Subjects:** Biotechnology, Nuclear Energy **Loan:** Inhouse **Service:** Inhouse **Photocopy:** Yes

821 Chengdu, Sichuan, China
Sichuan University
Library
Jiuyanqiao
Chengdu, Sichuan 610064
Location: #29 Wanjiang Road **Phone:** +86(28) 541-2292 **Fax:** +86(28) 541-0482 **Email:** nic7100@pridns.scuu.edu. cn, sichu@rose.cnc.ac.cn **OPAC:** 202.115.40.7

Founded: 1896 **Type:** Academic **Head:** Chen Li *Phone:* +86(28) 541-2549 *Email:* sichu@rose.cnc.ac.cn **Staff:** 210 Prof. 90 Other **Holdings:** 3,650,000 books 10,000 journals Language of Collection / Services: Chinese / Chinese **Subjects:** Comprehensive **Specializations:** Botany **Loan:** Inhouse **Service:** Inhouse **Photocopy:** Yes

822 Hongyuan, Sichuan, China
Sichuan Institute of Grasslands
Library
Hongyuan County
Hongyuan, Sichuan 624400
Phone: +86(8495) 662496 **Fax:** +86(28) 785-1305

Founded: 1978 **Type:** Academic **Head:** Ze Bai *Phone:* +86 (28) 785-1305, +86(8495) 662496 **Staff:** 3 Prof. **Holdings:** 40,000 books 400 journals **Language of Collection/Services:** Chinese, English / Chinese **Subjects:** Animal Husbandry, Grasslands, Veterinary Science **Loan:** Inhouse **Service:** Inhouse

♦**823 Jiangjin, Sichuan, China**
Sichuan Academy of Agricultural Sciences,
Institute of Fruit Research
Library Center
Jiangjin, Sichuan 632260
Phone: +86(8221) 521402 **Fax:** +86(8221) 522208

Former Name: Jiangjin Horticulture Experimental Station of Sichuan Province **Type:** Academic **Head:** Wengqing Wu *Phone:* +86(8221) 521427 **Staff:** 3 Prof. 2 Other **Holdings:** 10,000 books **Language of Collection/Services:** Chinese, English, German, Italian, Japanese / Chinese, English, German, Italian, Japanese **Subjects:** Fruits **Specializations:** Disease Control, Fruit Crops, Genetic Resources, Pest Man-

agement, Postharvest Technology, Storage, Varieties **Loan:** Inhouse **Service:** Inhouse **Photocopy:** Yes

824 Nanchong, Sichuan, China
Nanchong Institute of Agricultural Sciences
(NIAS)
Room of Books and Information
8 North Lake Road
Nanchong, Sichuan 637000
Phone: +86(817) 280-2876 **Fax:** +86(817) 280-0422

Former Name: North Sichuan Experimental Station of Agricultural Sciences **Founded:** 1950 **Type:** Research **Head:** Xiang Chenyong *Phone:* +86(817) 280-0422 **Staff:** 2 Prof. 1 Other **Holdings:** 30,000 books 1,000 journals **Language of Collection/Services:** Chinese, English, Japanese, Russian / Chinese, English **Subjects:** Animal Husbandry, Crop Husbandry, Fertilizers, Genetics, Plant Breeding, Plant Protection **Loan:** In country **Service:** In country **Photocopy:** Yes

♦**825 Nanchong, Sichuan, China**
Sichuan Academy of Agricultural Sciences,
Institute of Silkworm and Mulberry (SIAAS)
Library
100 Yifeng Road
Nanchong, Sichuan 637000
Phone: +86(817) 222642 **Fax:** +86(817) 229001

Former Name: Sichuan Sericultural Improvement Station **Type:** Academic **Head:** Wan Jia-ji *Phone:* +86(817) 222642 **Staff:** 77 Prof. 126 Other **Holdings:** 51,280 books 150 journals **Language of Collection/Services:** Chinese, English, Japanese/Chinese, English **Subjects:** Biotechnology, Entomology, Genetics, Plants **Specializations:** Biochemistry, Disease Control, Ecology, Mulberries, Sericulture, Silkworms **Loan:** Internationally **Service:** Internationally **Photocopy:** Yes

826 Panzhihua, Sichuan, China
Panzhihua Institute of Agricultural Sciences
Library
Second Village
Ren He Section
Panzhihua, Sichuan 617061
Phone: +86(812) 290-1894 **Fax:** +86(812) 290-1894 **Email:** hks@pzh.scsti.ac.cn **WWW:** www.pzh.scsti.ac.cn

Founded: 1973 **Type:** Academic **Head:** Pan Hai Ping *Phone:* +86(812) 335-4063 **Staff:** 1 Prof. 2 Other **Holdings:** 13,441 books 81 journals **Language of Collection/Services:** Chinese, English, Japanese, Russian/Chinese **Subjects:** Comprehensive **Specializations:** Horticulture, Agriculture (Tropics), **Loan:** Inhouse **Service:** Inhouse **Photocopy:** Yes

827 Ya'an, Sichuan, China
Sichuan Agricultural University (SAU)
Library
Xinkang Lu
Ya'an, Sichuan 625014
WWW: www.sicau.edu.cn

Founded: 1906 **Head:** Xia Jiming **Holdings:** 521,100 books 3,157 journals

♦828   **Ya'an, Sichuan, China**
Sichuan Agricultural University, Rice Research
    Institute (SAU, RRI)
Library
Ya'an, Sichuan 625014
Phone: +86(835) 222788 **WWW:** www.sicau.edu.cn

Head: Professor Zhou Kaida *Phone:* +86(835) 222788 ext
394 **Staff:** 40 Prof. 42 Other **Holdings:** 20,000 books **Language of Collection/Services:** Chinese, English **Subjects:**
Agricultural Development, Biotechnology, Education/Extension, Entomology, Farming, Food Sciences, Plant Pathology, Plant Physiology, Rice **Loan:** Inhouse **Service:** Inhouse
Photocopy: Yes

Tianjin

829   **Tianjin, China**
Tianjin Academy of Agricultural Sciences
    (TAAS)
Information Institute (II)
No. 26 Hangtian Road
Nankai District
Tianjin 300192
Phone: +86(22) 2336-7456 **Fax:** +86(22) 2336-9022
Email: tjnkyxxs@public1.tpt.tj.cn **WWW:** www.tjagri.
ac.cn

Founded: 1978 **Type:** Academic **Head:** Liu Baohang
Phone: +86(22) 2361-9181 **Staff:** 21 Prof. **Holdings:** 700
journals 700,000 books **Language of Collection/Services:**
Chinese/Chinese, English **Subjects:** Comprehensive **Specializations:** Horticulture **Databases Used:** CABCD;
CSTDB **Loan:** In country **Service:** In country **Photocopy:**
Yes

Tibet *see* Xizang

Xinjiang

♦830   **Shihezi, Xinjiang, China**
Shihezi College of Agriculture
Library
District 31
Shihezi, Xinjiang 832003

Head: Sun Keqiong **Holdings:** 185,270 books 3,428 journals **Subjects:** Agricultural Economics

♦831   **Shihezi, Xinjiang, China**
Shihezi College of Agriculture, Institute of Plant
    Protection
Library of Agricultural Department
District 31
Shihezi, Xinjiang 832003
Phone: +86(993) 201-2391 ext 540

Type: Special **Head:** Zhu Jiang *Phone:* +86(993) 201-2391
ext 282 **Staff:** 16 Prof. 1 Other **Holdings:** 10,000 books 12
journals **Language of Collection/Services:** English / Chinese **Subjects:** Biotechnology, Entomology, Pesticides,
Plant Pathology, Plant Protection **Photocopy:** No

♦832   **Urumqi, Xinjiang, China**
Chinese Academy of Sciences, Xinjiang Institute
    of Biology, Pedology and Desert Research
    (CAS)
Library
4 Beijing Nanlu
Urumqi, Xinjiang 830011
Fax: +86(991) 335459

Head: Sulayman Ibrayim *Phone:* +86(991) 337294 **Staff:** 3
Prof. 6 Other **Holdings:** 14,000 books 200 journals **Language of Collection/Services:** Chinese, English, Russian /
Chinese, English, Russian **Subjects:** Agribusiness, Animal
Husbandry, Biology, Deserts, Forestry, Microbiology,
Plants, Soil Science, Soil Conservation, Water Resources,
Zoology **Loan:** Inhouse **Service:** Inhouse **Photocopy:** Yes

833   **Urumqi, Xinjiang, China**
Xinjiang Academy of Agricultural Sciences
Xinjiang Agricultural Information Center
38 Nanchang Road
Urumqi, Xinjiang 830000

Former Name: Scientific Information Institute **Type:** Academic **Head:** Dai Jian *Phone:* +86(991) 451-4319 *Email:*
wlzh@mail.wl.xj.cn **Staff:** 32 Prof. 9 Other **Holdings:** 600
journals120,000 books **Language of Collection/Services:**
Chinese, English/Chinese, English **Subjects:** Comprehensive **Specializations:** Crops **Databases Used:** Agricola;
Agrisearch; CABCD; CSTDB **Loan:** In country **Service:** In
country **Photocopy:** Yes

♦834   **Urumqi, Xinjiang, China**
Xinjiang Academy of Animal Science
Institute of Scientific and Technical Information
21 Kelamayi Donglu
Urumqi, Xinjiang 830000

Subjects: Animal Husbandry

♦835   **Urumqi, Xinjiang, China**
Xinjiang Academy of Animal Science, Grassland
    Research Institute
Library
21 Kelamayi Donglu
Urumqi, Xinjiang 830000
Phone: +86(991) 416347 ext 3111, 441416 **Fax:** +86(991)
217542

Type: Academic **Language of Collection/Services:** Chinese, Zhozake, Ugur **Subjects:** Grasslands

836   **Urumqi, Xinjiang, China**
Xinjiang Agricultural University (XAU)
Library
Zhimancheng
Urumqi, Xinjiang 830052
Phone: +86(991) 452-3001 ext 2241

Type: Academic **Head:** Zhang Sheng-Guang *Phone:* +86
(991) 452-3001 ext 2241 **Staff:** 34 Prof. 2 Other **Holdings:**
520,000 books **Language of Collection/Services:** Chinese,
Ugur, Hazak, English, Russian / Chinese, Ugur **Subjects:**
Comprehensive **Loan:** Do not loan **Service:** Inhouse **Photocopy:** Yes

Xizang (Tibet)

837   **Lhasa, Xizang, China**
        Xizang Institute of Animal Husbandry and
                Veterinary Medicine
        Library
        Northern Suburb
        Lhasa, Xizang 850003

Former Name: Tibetan Institute of Animal Husbandry and Veterinary Medicine **Subjects:** Animal Husbandry, Veterinary Science

838   **Linzhi, Xizang, China**
        Xizang Institute of Agriculture and Animal
                Husbandry
        Library
        Bayi Zhen
        Linzhi, Xizang 850400

Former Name: Tibetan Institute of Agriculture and Animal Husbandry

Yunnan

839   **Kunming, Yunnan, China**
        Yunnan Academy of Agricultural Sciences,
                Institute of Science-Technology Information
                Research
        Information Center
        Longtou Jie, North Suburb
        Kunming, Yunnan 650205
Phone: +86(871) 589-2534 **Fax:** +86(871) 589-2534

Founded: 1984 **Type:** Academic **Head:** You Chengli *Phone:* +86(871) 589-3408 **Staff:** 22 Prof. 20 Other **Holdings:** 42,543 books 1,853 journals **Language of Collection/Services:** Chinese, English, Japanese / Chinese, English **Subjects:** Comprehensive **Specializations:** Field Crops, Floriculture, Fruit Trees **Databases Developed:** Yunnan wild flower, vegetable, and fruit resources databases **Databases Used:** Comprehensive **Photocopy:** Yes

840   **Kunming, Yunnan, China**
        Yunnan Academy of Forestry (YAF)
        Scientific and Technological Information Service
        Heilongtan, North Suburbs
        Kunming, Yunnan 650204
Phone: +86(871) 521-1394 **Fax:** +86(871) 515-0250

Former Name: Forestry Information and Material Office **Type:** Academic **Head:** Fan Guocai *Phone:* +86(871) 521-1394 **Staff:** 4 Prof. 5 Other **Holdings:** 35,000 books 380 journals **Language of Collection/Services:** Chinese, English / Chinese, English **Subjects:** Forestry **Specializations:** Ornamental Plants, Trees

841   **Kunming, Yunnan, China**
        Yunnan Agricultural University
        Library
        Heilongtan, North Suburbs
        Kunming, Yunnan 650201
Phone: +86(871) 515-0224 **Fax:** +86(871) 515-0303

♦842   **Kunming, Yunnan, China**
        Yunnan Institute of Agricultural Machinery
        Library
        21 Huanchenxi Road
        Kunming, Yunnan 650031
Phone: +86(871) 515-6288

Type: Academic **Head:** Zhong-dar Wu *Phone:* +86(871) 515-7041 ext 2711 **Staff:** 8 Prof. 1 Other **Holdings:** 50,000 books 352 journals **Language of Collection/Services:** Chinese, English / Chinese **Subjects:** Farm Machinery, Mechanization **Specializations:** Cereals, Electricity Generators, Clay Soils, Equipment, Food Processing Equipment, Plows, Processing, Starch Industry, Tea Industry, Turbines, Water Power **Loan:** Inhouse **Service:** Inhouse **Photocopy:** Yes

♦843   **Xishuangbanna, Yunnan, China**
        Tropical Crops Research Institute of Yunnan
                (TCRIY)
        Sci-Tech Information Center
        28 Western Road, Jihong County
        Xishuangbanna, Yunnan 666100
Phone: +86(8838) 22241

Type: Academic **Head:** Lai Yunhe *Phone:* +86(8838) 22241 **Staff:** 6 Prof. 5 Other **Holdings:** 68,422 books 236 journals **Language of Collection/Services:** Chinese, English, Japanese **Subjects:** Agribusiness, Agricultural Development, Agricultural Economics, Agricultural Engineering, Animal Husbandry, Biotechnology, Entomology, Horticulture, Plant Pathology, Plants, Soil Science, Tropical Crops **Specializations:** Fruit Crops, Medicinal Plants, Oil Plants, Rubber, Spices, Stimulant Plants, Sugar **Loan:** In country **Service:** In country **Photocopy:** No

Zhejiang

844   **Hangzhou, Zhejiang, China**
        China National Rice Research Institute (CNRRI)
        Agricultural Economy and Scientific Information
                Department
        359 Ti Yuchang Road
        Hangzhou, Zhejiang 310006
Phone: +86(571) 337-1711 ext 2278, 2236, or 2274 **Fax:** +86(571) 337-1745 **Email:** cnrri@fyptt.zjpta.net.cn

Former Name: Information and Publication Department **Founded:** 1984 **Type:** Academic **Head:** Li Jian or Wang Lei *Phone:* +86(571) 337-1711 ext 2278 or 2236 *Email:* cnrri@fyptt.zjpta.net.cn **Staff:** 16 Prof. 2 Other **Holdings:** 23,374 books 965 journals **Language of Collection/Services:** Chinese, English, Japanese/Chinese, English **Subjects:** Agricultural Economics, Agronomy, Biology, Biotechnology, Genetics, Germplasm, Plant Breeding, Plant Nutrition, Plant Physiology, Plant Protection, Soil Science, Statistics **Specializations:** Gene Banks, Genetics, Plant Breeding, Plant Protection, Rice **Databases Used:** CABCD; CSTDB **Loan:** Inhouse **Service:** Internationally **Photocopy:** Yes

845   **Hangzhou, Zhejiang, China**
        Zhejiang Academy of Agricultural Sciences
                (ZAAS)
        Information Institute

198 Shiqiao Lu
Hangzhou, Zhejiang 310021
Phone: +86(571) 640-4048 **Fax:** +86(571) 640-4065

Founded: 1958 **Type:** Academic **Head:** Lin Hai *Phone:* +86(571) 640-4048 **Staff:** 30 Prof. 6 Other **Holdings:** 130,000 books 2,000 journals **Language of Collection/Services:** Chinese, English, Japanese **Subjects:** Agribusiness, Agricultural Development, Agricultural Economics, Agricultural Engineering, Biotechnology, Education/Extension, Entomology, Farming, Fisheries, Food Sciences, Horticulture, Plant Pathology, Soil Science, Water Resources **Specializations:** Animal Husbandry, Crops, Genetics, Plant Protection, Veterinary Medicine **Loan:** In country **Service:** In country **Photocopy:** Yes

846   Hangzhou, Zhejiang, China
Zhejiang University (ZU)
Library of Agriculture
268 Kaixuan Lu, Huajiachi Campus
Hangzhou, Zhejiang 310029
Phone: +86(571) 697-1224 **Fax:** +86(571) 697-1601
WWW: lib.zju.edu.cn **OPAC:** 210.32.161.28

Former Name: Zhejiang Agricultural University **Founded:** 1925 **Type:** Academic **Head:** Xu Tong *Phone:* +86(571) 697-1601 *Email:* txu@lib.zju.edu.cn **Staff:** 40 Prof. 10 Other **Holdings:** 620,000 books 2,200 journals **Language of Collection/Services:** Chinese, English/Chinese, English **Subjects:** Comprehensive **Specializations:** Crops, Agricultural Economics, Agricultural Engineering, Biotechnology, Entomology, Horticulture, Plant Protection, Sericulture, Veterinary Medicine **Databases Used:** Agricola; Agris; Biosis; CABCD **Loan:** In country **Service:** In country **Photocopy:** Yes

♦847   **Lishui, Zhejiang, China**
Lishui Institute of Agricultural Sciences (LIAS)
Library
99 Liyang Road
Lishui, Zhejiang 323000
Phone: +86(578) 231193

Type: Academic **Head:** Xue Keqiao *Phone:* +86(578) 232194 **Staff:** 1 Prof. 2 Other **Holdings:** 20,310 books 485 journals **Language of Collection/Services:** Chinese, English, Japanese/Chinese, English, Japanese **Subjects:** Agricultural Development, Agricultural Economics, Animal Husbandry, Biotechnology, Botany, Crops, Entomology, Horticulture, Plant Diseases, Soil Science, Tillage, Veterinary Medicine

848   Shaoxing, Zhejiang, China
Shaoxing Institute of Agricultural Sciences (SIAS)
Library
Donghu
Shaoxing, Zhejiang 312001
Phone: +86(575) 864-9563

Former Name: Shaoxing District Institute of Agricultural Sciences **Type:** Academic **Head:** Xie Xing Song *Phone:* +86(575) 864-0646 **Staff:** 1 Prof. 2 Other **Holdings:** 20,000 books 50 journals **Language of Collection/Services:** Chinese/Chinese **Subjects:** Agribusiness, Agricultural Devel-

opment, Animal Husbandry, Crops, Entomology, Farming, Food Sciences, Horticulture, Plant Pathology, Plants, Soil Science, Veterinary Medicine **Specializations:** Barley, Cereals, Faba Beans, Fodder Crops, Rice **Loan:** Inhouse **Service:** Inhouse **Photocopy:** No

Colombia

Bogotá, Colombia *see* **Santafé de Bogotá, Colombia**

849   Cali, Colombia
Autonomous Regional Corporation of the Cauca Valley
Information and Documentation Center
Carrera 56 No. 11-36 Bloque Azul Piso 1
AA 2366
Cali, Valle
Phone: +57(3) 339-6671 ext 370 **Fax:** +57(3) 330-4080

Non-English Name: Corporación Autónoma Regional del Valle del Cauca (CVC), Centro de Información y Documentación **Founded:** 1964 **Type:** Government **Head:** Alba O. Castillo *Phone:* +57(3) 339-6671 ext 170 *Email:* cvc_ceid@ colnet.com.co **Staff:** 2 Prof. 5 Other **Holdings:** 17,000 books 520 journals **Language of Collection/Services:** Spanish **Subjects:** Agricultural Economics, Energy, Fisheries, Natural Resources **Specializations:** Agricultural Development, Crops, Forestry, Water Resources **Loan:** Inhouse **Photocopy:** Yes

850   Cali, Colombia
Center of Agrarian Cooperatives
Library
Carrera 5 No. 13-46, Edificio El Café Piso 11
AA 10037
Cali, Valle
Phone: +57(2) 882-3232 **Fax:** +57(2) 882-4853 **Email:** cencobib@colombianet.net

Non-English Name: Central de Cooperativas Agrarias (CENCOA), Biblioteca **Founded:** 1980 **Type:** Association **Head:** Clara Eugenia Bedoya *Phone:* +57(2) 882-3232 *Email:* cencobib@colombianet.net **Staff:** 1 Prof. 1 Other **Holdings:** 25,000 books 20 journals **Subjects:** Coffee, Cooperative Farming **Loan:** In country

851   Cali, Colombia
Departamento Administrativo de Planeación
Biblioteca
Carrera 8, Calle 9 Esquina Antiguo Edificio San Luis, Piso 3
Cali, Valle
Phone: +57(2) 886-0430

Founded: 1977 **Type:** Government **Head:** Noralba Vergara Monard *Phone:* +57(2) 886-0430 **Staff:** 1 Prof. 1 Other **Holdings:** 1,000 books 8 journals **Subjects:** Agricultural Economics, Agricultural Statistics, Industry **Loan:** Inhouse **Photocopy:** Yes

852   Cali, Colombia
Instituto Vallecaucano de Investigaciones
    Científicas (INCIVA)
Biblioteca - Museo de Ciencias Naturales
AA 5660
Cali, Valle

Location: Carrera 2 Oeste No 7-18 Santa Teresita **Phone:** +57(2) 893-0981 **Fax:** +57(2) 556-2602

Type: Government **Head:** Luz Amparo Coorrea *Phone:* +57 (2) 893-0982 *Email:* inc-mus@cali.cetcol.net.co **Staff:** 1 Prof. **Holdings:** 1,200 books 80 journals **Language of Collection/Services:** Spanish / Spanish, English **Subjects:** Agriculture (Tropics), Biotechnology, Entomology, Forestry, Horticulture, Plant Pathology, Plants **Loan:** In country **Service:** Inhouse **Photocopy:** Yes

853   Cali, Colombia
International Center for Tropical Agriculture
Information and Documentation Unit
AA 6713
Cali, Valle

Location: Recta Cali - Palmira Km 17 **Phone:** +57(2) 445-0042 **Fax:** +57(2) 445-0073 **Email:** ciat-library@ cgiar.org **WWW:** www.ciat.cgiar.org **OPAC:** www.ciat.cgiar.org/library/intranet.htm **Ariel IP:** 198.93.225.79

Non-English Name: Centro Internacional de Agricultura Tropical (CIAT), Unidad de Información y Documentación **Founded:** 1969 **Type:** International **Head:** Luz Marina Alvaré (Acting) *Phone:* +57 (2) 445-0000 ext 3042 *Email:* l.alvare@cgiar.org **Staff:** 7 Prof. 5 Other **Holdings:** 86,000 books 600 journals **Language of Collection/Services:** English, Spanish / English, Spanish **Subjects:** Agriculture (Tropics), Beans, Biotechnology, Entomology, Natural Resources, Rice, Sustainability, Pastures (Tropics) **Specializations:** Cassava, Fodder Crops, Germplasm, Land Use, Oryza sativa, Phaseolus vulgaris, Resource Management, Tropical Crops **Databases Developed:** CINFOS - references and abstracts covering world literature on common beans, cassava and tropical pastures; SERIAD - bibliographic information and holdings for newsletters and serial publications **Databases Used:** Comprehensive **Loan:** Internationally (photocopies) **Service:** Internationally **Photocopy:** Yes

854   Cali, Colombia
Sugar Cane Farmers' Association of Colombia
Sugarcane Information Center
Calle 58 Norte 3N-15 Autopista a Yumbo
AA 4448
Cali, Valle

Phone: +57(2) 664-7902 **Fax:** +57(3) 664-5888 **Email:** sgomez@telesat.com.co **WWW:** www.telesat.com.co/asocana

Non-English Name: Asociación de Cultivadores de Caña de Azúcar de Colombia (ASOCAÑA), Centro de Información de la Caña de Azúcar **Founded:** 1980 **Type:** Association **Head:** Stella Gómez Vernaza *Phone:* +57(2) 664-7902 ext 07 *Email:* sgomez@asocana.com.co **Staff:** 1 Prof. 1 Other **Holdings:** 3,000 books 20 journals **Subjects:** Agricultural Statistics, Legislation, Sugar, Sugar Industry **Loan:** Do not loan **Photocopy:** Yes

855   Cali, Colombia
Sugar Cane Research Center of Colombia
Information and Documentation Service
Estación Experimental San Antonio
AA 9138
Cali, Valle

Phone: +57(2) 664-8025 ext 135 **Fax:** +57(2) 664-1936 **Email:** webmaster@cenicana.org **WWW:** www.cenicana. org **OPAC:** www.cenicana.org

Non-English Name: Centro de Investigación de la Caña de Azúcar de Colombia (CENICAÑA), Servicio de Información y Documentación (SEICA) **Founded:** 1978 **Type:** Private **Head:** Lupe Bustamante A. *Phone:* +57(2) 664-8025 *Email:* gbustama@cenicana.org **Staff:** 1 Prof. 2 Other **Holdings:** 22,000 books 575 journals **Language of Collection/Services:** English / Spanish **Subjects:** Agriculture (Tropics), Agricultural Economics, Agricultural Engineering, Crops, Entomology, Farming, Soil Science, Water Resources **Specializations:** Breeding, Plant Pathology, Sugar Industry, Sugarcane **Databases Developed:** SNICA - document collection on sugar; accessible via Internet at www.cenicana.org **Loan:** In country **Service:** Internationally **Photocopy:** Yes

856   Cali, Colombia
University of Valle
Library Department
AA 25360
Cali, Valle

Location: Ciudad Universitaria **Phone:** +57(2) 339-8517 ext 130 **Fax:** +57(2) 339-8457 **Email:** servies@biblioteca. univalle.edu.co **WWW:** www.univalle.edu.co

Non-English Name: Universidad del Valle, Departamento de Bibliotecas **Founded:** 1945 **Type:** Academic **Head:** Carlos Esteban Mejía *Phone:* +57(2) 331-5290 *Email:* bermunoz@biblioteca.univalle.edu.co **Staff:** 17 Prof. 58 Other **Holdings:** 150 books **Subjects:** Agricultural Engineering, Biology, Botany, Entomology, Food Technology, Genetics **Loan:** In country **Photocopy:** Yes

857   Chinchiná, Colombia
Pedro Uribe Mejia National Center of Coffee
    Research
Documentation Center
AA 2427
Chinchiná, Caldas

Fax: +57(968) 506631 **WWW:** www.cafedecolombia.com

Non-English Name: Centro Nacional de Investigaciones de Café "Pedro Uribe Mejía" (CENICAFE), Centro de Documentación **Founded:** 1945 **Type:** Association **Head:** Luis Alejandro Maya-Montalvo *Phone:* +57(968) 6550, 6551, 6409 **Staff:** 2 Prof. 4 Other **Holdings:** 7,600 books 750 journals **Language of Collection/Services:** English / Spanish **Subjects:** Agriculture (Tropics), Agribusiness, Agricultural Development, Agricultural Economics, Agricultural Engineering, Biotechnology, Crops, Education/Extension, Entomology, Farming, Fisheries, Food Sciences, Forestry, Horticulture, Plant Pathology, Soil Science, Veterinary Medicine, Water Resources **Specializations:** Coffee **Loan:** In country **Photocopy:** Yes

858   Ibague, Colombia
University of Tolima
Central Library
Barrio Santa Elena
AA 546
Ibague, Tolima
Phone: +57(8) 264-4219 **Fax:** +57(8) 264-4869 **Email:**
ut@ut.edu.co **WWW:** utolima.ut.edu.co

Non-English Name: Universidad del Tolima (UT), Biblioteca Central **Founded:** 1962 **Type:** Academic **Head:** Cielo
Ureña Lozano *Phone:* +57(8) 264-4219 ext 37 *Email:*
curuena@ut.edu.co **Staff:** 3 Prof. 14 Other **Holdings:** 6,500
books **Subjects:** Agricultural Engineering, Farming, Forestry **Loan:** In country **Photocopy:** Yes

859   Manizales, Colombia
Caldas University
Enrique Mejia Ruiz Library and Scientific
        Information Center
Calle 65 No. 26-10
AA 275
Manizales, Caldas
Fax: +57(69) 862520 **Email:** biblio@cumanday.ucaldas.
edu.co **WWW:** biblio.ucaldas.edu.co **Ariel IP:** 200.25.66.
160

Non-English Name: Universidad de Caldas, Centro de
Biblioteca e Información Científica "Enrique Mejía Ruiz"
Founded: 1958 **Type:** Academic **Head:** Saul Sanchez Toro
Email: ssanchez@cumanday.ucaldas.edu.co *Phone:* +57
(69) 862732**Staff:** 6 Prof. 16 Other **Holdings:** 2,500 books
200 journals **Language of Collection/Services:** Spanish /
Spanish **Subjects:** Administration, Cultivation, Entomol-
ogy, Fruits, Genetics, Marketing, Plant Physiology **Data-
bases Used:** Agricola; Agris **Loan:** In country **Photocopy:**
Yes

860   Medellín, Colombia
Association of Banana Growers of Colombia
Documentation Center
AA 52814
Medellín, Antioquia
Location: Calle 52 #47-42, Ed. Coltejer, Piso 13 **Phone:**
+57(4) 513-8866 **Fax:** +57(4) 251-0201 **Email:** augura@
epm.net.co **WWW:** www.augura.com.co

Non-English Name: Asociación de Bananeros de Colombia
(AUGURA), Centro de Documentación **Former Name:**
Asociación de Bananeros y Agricultores de Urabá, Asociación de Bananeros de Urabá **Founded:** 1983 **Type:** Association **Head:** María del Carmen Giraldo Aristizábal *Phone:*
+57(4) 513-8866 *Email:* augura@epm.net.co **Staff:** 1 Prof. 2
Other **Holdings:** 4,500 books 35 journals **Language of Col-
lection/Services:** Spanish / Spanish **Subjects:** Agribusiness,
Agricultural Trade **Specializations:** Bananas, Plantago **Networks:** SIDBAP **Databases Developed:** PLANOS - maps
and plans of the Uraba banana zone; PRENSA - contains
records of articles of newspapers about banana and plantain
agribusiness, the Uraba banana zone and the Colombian
economy **Databases Used:** BAC; INIBAP; SIBBANA
Loan: Inhouse **Service:** Inhouse **Photocopy:** Yes

861   Medellín, Colombia
Fundación Jardín Botánico Joaquín Antonio Uribe
Biblioteca Andrés Posada Arango
Carrera 52 No. 73-298
AA 51407
Medellín, Antioquia
Fax: +57(4) 233-6053

Founded: 1972 **Type:** Private **Head:** Marta Elena Guirales
C. *Phone:* +57(4) 233-5849 **Staff:** 1 Prof. 3 Other **Holdings:**
12,000 books 392 journals **Subjects:** Botany, Crop Production, Ecology, Land Resources, Natural Resources **Loan:** Inhouse **Photocopy:** Yes

862   Medellín, Colombia
National Industrial Association
Library and Documentation Center
Edificio Coltejer, p. 8
AA 997
Medellín, Antioquia
Phone: +57(4) 511-1177 **Fax:** +57(4) 511-7575 **WWW:**
www.andi.com.co

Non-English Name: Asociación Nacional de Industriales
(ANDI), Biblioteca y Centro de Documentación **Founded:**
1961 **Type:** Association **Head:** Luz Marina Upegui G.
Phone: +57(4) 251-4444 **Staff:** 1 Prof. 2 Other **Subjects:**
Agricultural Economics, Industry **Loan:** In country **Photo-
copy:** Yes

863   Medellín, Colombia
National University of Colombia, Medellin
        Campus
Efe Gomez Library
Autopista Norte, Carrera 64, Calle 65
AA 568
Medellín, Antioquia
Phone: +57(4) 260-8383 ext 574 **Fax:** +57(4) 230-0960
Email: lmrestre@perseus.unalmed.edu.co **WWW:** www.
unalmed.edu.co

Non-English Name: Universidad Nacional de Colombia,
Sede Medellín, Biblioteca Efe Gómez **Type:** Government
Head: Yardley Saldarriaga *Phone:* +57(4) 260-8383 ext 569
Email: ysaldarr@perseus.unalmed.edu.co **Staff:** 3 Prof. 4
Other **Holdings:** 20,000 books 40 journals **Subjects:** Agri-
cultural Engineering, Forestry, Zootechny **Loan:** Interna-
tionally **Photocopy:** Yes

864   Medellín, Colombia
University of Antioquia, School of Veterinary
        Medicine and Zootechny
Fidel Ochoa Velez Library
Ciudad Robledo Biblioteca
AA 1226
Medellín, Antioquia
Fax: +57(4) 263-8282 **WWW:** www.udea.edu.co

Non-English Name: Universidad de Antioquía, Facultad de
Medicina Veterinaria y Zootecnia (UA, VZ), Biblioteca "Fi-
del Ochoa Vélez" **Founded:** 1971 **Type:** Academic **Head:**
Ofelia Tobón *Phone:* +57(4) 234-0249 **Staff:** 1 Prof. 3 Other
Holdings: 4,500 books 218 journals **Language of Collec-
tion/Services:** Spanish / Spanish **Subjects:** Animal Hus-

bandry, Farming, Food Sciences, Veterinary Medicine, Fisheries **Databases Used:** Medline **Loan:** In country **Service:** In country **Photocopy:** Yes

865   Montería, Colombia
Universidad de Córdoba
Biblioteca Central
AA 354
Montería, Córdoba

Phone: +57(94) 786-0111 **Fax:** +57(94) 786-0054 **Email:** ucbiblio@unicordoba.edu.co **WWW:** www.unicordoba. edu.co

Founded: 1965 **Type:** Academic **Staff:** 4 Prof. 6 Other **Holdings:** 2,000 books **Subjects:** Entomology, Farming, Pathology, Physiology, Rice, Soil Science **Loan:** In country

866   Palmira, Colombia
National University of Colombia, Palmira
        Campus, Faculty of Agricultural Sciences
Library
AA 237
Palmira, Valle

Location: Carrera 32 Chapinero Vía Candelaria **Phone:** +57(2) 271-7000 **Fax:** +57(2) 270-4484 **WWW:** www. palmira.unal.edu.co

Non-English Name: Universidad Nacional de Colombia, Sede Palmira, Facultad de Ciencias Agropecuarias, Biblioteca **Founded:** 1935 **Type:** Academic **Head:** Julia Emma Zúñiga *Phone:* +57(2) 271-7000 ext 124 **Staff:** 1 Prof. 11 Other **Holdings:** 18,000 books 52 journals **Language of Collection/Services:** English, Spanish / Spanish **Subjects:** Agriculture (Tropics), Agribusiness, Agricultural Development, Agricultural Economics, Agricultural Engineering, Animal Husbandry, Biotechnology, Crops, Education/Extension, Entomology, Farming, Fisheries, Food Sciences, Forestry, Horticulture, Plant Pathology, Soil Science, Veterinary Medicine, Water Resources **Loan:** In country **Service:** Internationally **Photocopy:** Yes

867   Pasto, Colombia
University of Nariño
Alberto Quijano Guerrero Library
Carrera 22 No. 19-109
AA 1175 and 1176
Pasto, Nariño

Location: Torobajo University City **Phone:** +57(301) 239866 **Fax:** +57(301) 239866 **Email:** correo@udenar. edu.co **WWW:** www.udenar.edu.co

Non-English Name: Universidad de Nariño, Biblioteca Alberto Quijano Guerrero **Founded:** 1962 **Type:** Academic **Head:** Segundo Burbano Lopez *Phone:* +57(301) 239866 *Email:* correo@udenar.edu.co **Staff:** 5 Prof. 11 Other **Holdings:** 52,300 books 50 journals **Language of Collection/Services:** Spanish / Spanish **Subjects:** Administration, Agribusiness, Cultivation, Entomology, Farm Machinery, Plant Pathology, Veterinary Medicine **Specializations:** Agricultural Engineering, Animal Husbandry **Loan:** In country **Service:** Inhouse **Photocopy:** Yes

868   Santa Marta, Colombia
University of Magdalena
Library
AA 731
Santa Marta, Magdalena

Location: San Pedro Alejandrino **Phone:** +57(5) 430-1292 **Fax:** +57(5) 430-1692

Non-English Name: Universidad Tecnológica del Magdalena, Biblioteca **Founded:** 1962 **Type:** Academic **Head:** Carlos Cotes Diazgranados *Phone:* +57(5) 430-1292 **Staff:** 2 Prof. 8 Other **Holdings:** 4 books **Subjects:** Fishing, Soil Science **Loan:** In country **Photocopy:** Yes

869   Santafé de Bogotá, Colombia
Agriculturist Society of Colombia
Library and Information Center
Carrera 7a No. 24-89 P. Torre Colpatria
AA 3638
Santafé de Bogotá

Phone: +57(1) 282-2989, 341-8013 **Fax:** +57(1) 284-4572 **WWW:** www.sociedadagricultores.org.co **Email:** socdeagr@impsat.net.co

Non-English Name: Sociedad de Agricultores de Colombia (SAC), Biblioteca y Centro de Información **Founded:** 1875 **Type:** Private **Head:** Sonia Laverde Eastman *Phone:* +57(1) 282-2989 ext 18 *Email:* bibliotc@colomsat.net.co **Staff:** 1 Prof. 1 Other **Holdings:** 5,510 books 339 journals **Language of Collection/Services:** Spanish / Spanish **Subjects:** Agricultural Economics, Agricultural Policy, Agricultural Trade, Production (Statistics) **Databases Developed:** Revista Nacional de Agricultura (National Agriculture Review) Index 1871 to date **Loan:** In country **Service:** Internationally **Photocopy:** Yes

870   Santafé de Bogotá, Colombia
Colombian Company of Veterinarian Products
Library
Av. Eldorado (Calle 26) No. 82-93
AA 7476
Santafé de Bogotá

Phone: +57(1) 263-9982

Non-English Name: Empresa Colombiana de Productos Veterinarios (VECOL), Biblioteca **Founded:** 1985 **Type:** Association **Head:** Sundary R. de Bahamon *Phone:* +57(1) 263-9982 **Staff:** 1 Prof. **Holdings:** 200 books **Subjects:** Agricultural Chemistry **Loan:** In country **Photocopy:** Yes

871   Santafé de Bogotá, Colombia
Colombian Corporation for the
        Amazonia-Araracuara
Documentation Center
AA 034174
Calle 20 # 5-44
Santafé de Bogotá

Phone: +57(1) 283-6755 **Fax:** +57(1) 286-2418

Non-English Name: Corporación Colombiana para la Amazonia-Araracuara, Centro de Documentación **Former Name:** Corporación de Araracuara **Founded:** 1981 **Type:** Association **Head:** Dora Susana Rozo Rios *Phone:* +57(1) 282-7543 **Staff:** 3 Prof. 1 Other **Holdings:** 7,200 books 10

journals **Language of Collection/Services:** Spanish / Spanish **Specializations:** Agroforestry, Ecology, Fauna, Flora, Production, Silviculture, Water Resources **Databases Developed:** COA Database - contains 7200 records about the Amazon region and specifically the Colombian Amazon area; online access for public interested in the Amazon and specifically the Colombian Amazon **Loan:** Internationally **Service:** Internationally **Photocopy:** Yes

872   Santafé de Bogotá, Colombia
         Colombian Corporation of Farm Research
         Colombian Agricultural Library
         AA 240142, Las Palmas
         Santafé de Bogotá
Phone: +57(1) 344-3000 **Fax:** +57(1) 226-7364 **Email:** bac@corpoica org.co **WWW:** www.corpoica.org.co

Non-English Name: Corporación Colombiana de Investigación Agropecuaria (CCIA), Biblioteca Agropecuaria de Colombia (BAC) **Former Name:** Instituto Colombiano Agropecuario (ICA) **Founded:** 1970 **Type:** Government **Head:** Francisco Armando Salazar Alonso *Phone:* +57(1) 267-3008 *Email:* fsalazar@corpoica.org.co **Staff:** 3 Prof. 16 Other **Holdings:** 38,500 books 1,400 journals **Language of Collection/Services:** English **Subjects:** Biotechnology, Botany, Cultivation, Sanitation, Soil Science, Vegetables, Veterinary Science **Specializations:** Agronomy, Animal Husbandry, Biology, Crops, Entomology, Forestry, Fruit Trees, Zoology **Networks:** AGRIS **Databases Developed:** BAC - Base de Datos ICA - includes agricultural literature of the Colombian agricultural sector **Databases Used:** Agricola; Agris; CABCD; Current Contents **Loan:** In country **Photocopy:** Yes

873   Santafé de Bogotá, Colombia
         Colombian Institute of Agrarian Reform
         Library and Documentation Center
         Av. Eldorado - CAN
         AA 151046
         Santafé de Bogotá
Phone: +57(1) 222-2511 ext 171 **Fax:** +57(1) 222-4370

Non-English Name: Instituto Colombiano de la Reforma Agraria, Biblioteca y Centro de Documentación **Founded:** 1962 **Type:** Government **Head:** Miryam Stella Montilla de Garcia *Phone:* +57(1) 222-2511 **Staff:** 1 Prof. 2 Other **Holdings:** 8,000 books **Subjects:** Agrarian Reform, Agricultural Economics **Loan:** Internationally **Photocopy:** Yes

874   Santafé de Bogotá, Colombia
         Instituto de Fomento Industrial
         Centro de Documentación
         Calle 16 No. 6-66 Piso 9
         AA 4222
         Santafé de Bogotá
Phone: +57(1) 282-2055 **Fax:** +57(1) 286-4166

Founded: 1976 **Type:** Government **Head:** Myriam Manrique Puentes *Phone:* +57(1) 283-8553 **Staff:** 1 Prof. 3 Other **Holdings:** 6,200 books 50 journals **Subjects:** Agribusiness, Industry **Photocopy:** Yes

875   Santafé de Bogotá, Colombia
         Instituto de Hidrología, Meteorología y Estudios
            Ambientales (IDEAM)
         Biblioteca
         Diagonal 97 No. 17-60 Piso 10º
         AA 93337
         Santafé de Bogotá
Phone: +57(1) 635-6006/7 **Fax:** +57(1) 635-6078 **WWW:** www.ideam.gov.co

Former Name: Instituto Colombiano de Hidrología, Meteorología y Adecuación de Tierras (HIMAT) **Founded:** 1976 **Type:** Government **Head:** Floralba Moreno Galindo *Phone:* +57(1) 635-6006/7 **Staff:** 2 Prof. 1 Other **Holdings:** 12,000 books 70 journals **Subjects:** Biodiversity, Economic Ecology, Ecosystems, Environmental Impact, Hydrology, Land, Meteorology **Loan:** In country **Photocopy:** Yes

876   Santafé de Bogotá, Colombia
         Interamerican Institute of Cooperation for
            Agriculture
         Rodrigo Peña Library and Documentation Center
         Cra. 30 Calle 45
         AA 14592
         Santafé de Bogotá
Location: Ciudad Universitaria **Phone:** +57(1) 368-2990 **Fax:** +57(1) 368-0920 **Email:** iicaco3@colomsat.net.co **WWW:** www.iica.ac.cr

Non-English Name: Instituto Interamericano de Cooperación para la Agricultura (IICA), Biblioteca "Rodrigo Peña" y Centro de Documentación **Founded:** 1964 **Type:** International **Head:** Martha Cano *Phone:* +57(1) 368-0926 *Email:* iicaco3@colomsat.net.co **Staff:** 2 Prof. 2 Other **Holdings:** 50,000 books 250 journals **Subjects:** Agrarian Reform, Agricultural Development, Agricultural Economics, Agricultural Policy, Industry, Marketing, Rural Development **Loan:** Internationally **Photocopy:** Yes

877   Santafé de Bogotá, Colombia
         Jorge Tadeo Lozano University
         Library
         Carrera 4 No. 22-61
         AA 34185
         Santafé de Bogotá
Phone: +57(1) 334-1777 **Fax:** +57(1) 282-6197 **Email:** bibliotadeo@yahoo.com **OPAC:** www.banrep.gov.co/biblio/menu/homebv. htm **WWW:** www.interred.net.co/utadeo

Non-English Name: Universidad de Bogotá Jorge Tadeo Lozano, Biblioteca **Founded:** 1960 **Type:** Academic **Head:** María Consuelo Moncada *Phone:* +57(1) 334-1777 ext 1770 **Staff:** 6 Prof. 19 Other **Holdings:** 603 books 13 journals **Language of Collection/Services:** Spanish / Spanish **Subjects:** Agricultural Development, Crops, Fruits, Soil, Water Resources **Specializations:** Fisheries, Plants **Networks:** CCNPS; SIEMBRA **Databases Used:** Comprehensive **Loan:** In country **Photocopy:** Yes

878   Santafé de Bogotá, Colombia
         La Salle University
         Library

AA 28638
Santafé de Bogotá
Location: Carrera 2 No. 10-70 **Phone:** +57(1) 283-0900
ext 272 **Fax:** +57(1) 286-8391 **Email:** bibliot@jupiter.
lasalle.edu.co **WWW:** www.lasalle.edu.co

Non-English Name: Universidad de La Salle (ULS), Biblio-
teca **Former Name:** Universidad Social Católica de La Salle
Founded: 1966 **Type:** Academic **Head:** Napoleón Muñoz
Neda *Phone:* +57(1) 283-0900 ext 264, 342-0064 *Email:*
bibliot@jupiter.lasalle.edu.co **Staff:** 7 Prof. 28 Other **Hold-
ings:** 75,000 books 900 journals **Language of Collection/
Services:** Spanish, English / Spanish **Subjects:** Agriculture
(Tropics), Agricultural Development, Agricultural Econom-
ics, Agricultural Engineering, Biotechnology, Breeding,
Dairy Industry, Education/Extension, Entomology, Farming,
Fisheries, Food Sciences, Forestry, Fruit Growing, Horticul-
ture, Insects, Pests, Plant Pathology, Soil Science, Veterinary
Medicine, Water Resources, Wild Animals, Wild Plants,
Zootechny **Networks:** Catalogo Colectivo Nacional de
Publicaciones y Periodicas **Databases Developed:** SIBILA -
bibliographic database; access via the Internet at www.
lasalle.edu.co **Databases Used:** Comprehensive **Loan:**
Internationally **Service:** Internationally **Photocopy:** Yes

879   **Santafé de Bogotá, Colombia**
      Ministry of Agriculture
      Library
      Avenida Jiménez # 7-65
      AA 24433
      Santafé de Bogotá
Phone: +57(1) 334-1199 **Fax:** +57(1) 242-9496 **Email:**
bibliot@colomsat.net.co

Non-English Name: Ministerio de Agricultura, Biblioteca
OPSA **Founded:** 1968 **Type:** Government **Head:** José
Gonzalo Mosquera León *Phone:* +57(1) 334-1199 ext 503
Email: bibliot@colomsat.net.co **Staff:** 2 Prof. 5 Other **Hold-
ings:** 15,000 books 150 journals **Subjects:** Agricultural
Planning, Agricultural Statistics **Loan:** Internationally **Pho-
tocopy:** Yes

880   **Santafé de Bogotá, Colombia**
      National Corporation of Forest Research and
        Fomentation
      Forestry Information and Documentation Center
      AA 091676 - 095153
      Santafé de Bogotá
Location: Carrera 50 No. 27-70 Bloque C Modulo 1
Oficina 501 **Phone:** +57(1) 433-6068 **Fax:** +57(1) 433-
6203

Non-English Name: Corporación Nacional de Investigación
y Fomento Forestal (CONIF), Servicio Andino de Información y Documentación Forestal (SEIDAL) **Founded:** 1975
Type: Private **Head:** Rafael Ortíz *Phone:* +57(1) 443-6068
Staff: 3 Prof. 2 Other **Holdings:** 10,000 books 35 journals
Language of Collection/Services: Spanish, Portuguese,
English, French / Spanish **Subjects:** Agroforestry, Biotechnology, Crops, Forestry **Loan:** In country **Service:** Internationally **Photocopy:** Yes

881   **Santafé de Bogotá, Colombia**
      National Federation of Coffee Growers of
        Colombia
      Library
      73 # 8-13
      Apartado Aéreo 3938
      Santafé de Bogotá
Phone: +57(1) 210-1921, 341-6600 **Fax:** +57(1) 217-1021
Email: cafe@cafedecolombia.com **WWW:** www.
cafedecolombia.com

Non-English Name: Federación Nacional de Cafeteros de
Colombia (FEDERACAFE), Biblioteca **Founded:** 1972
Type: Business **Head:** Carolina Jaramillo Jiménez *Phone:*
+57(1) 210-1921 *Email:* cjar@cafedecolombia.com **Staff:** 1
Prof. 1 Other **Holdings:** 5,000 books 60 journals **Language
of Collection/Services:** Spanish / Spanish **Subjects:** Agri-
cultural Economics, Coffee, Fruits, Horticulture **Databases
Developed:** CAFE - collection of materials on coffee **Loan:**
In country **Service:** In country

882   **Santafé de Bogotá, Colombia**
      National University of Colombia, School of
        Agriculture
      Library
      AA 14490
      Santafé de Bogotá
Phone: +57(1) 316-5000 **Fax:** +57(1) 269-1743 **WWW:**
www.unal.edu.co

Non-English Name: Universidad Nacional de Colombia,
Facultad de Agronomía, Biblioteca **Founded:** 1970 **Type:**
Academic **Head:** J. Emilio Luque Z. *Phone:* +57(1) 368-
1508 **Staff:** 3 Prof. 2 Other **Holdings:** 3,500 books 400 jour-
nals **Language of Collection/Services:** Spanish, English
Subjects: Agronomy, Crop Production, Farm Machinery,
Improvement, Mechanization, Plant Protection, Soil Science
Databases Developed: UNAGR - database of graduate and
undergraduate theses **Loan:** In country **Photocopy:** Yes

883   **Santafé de Bogotá, Colombia**
      Pontifica Universidad Javeriana
      Biblioteca General
      AA 56710
      Carrera 7 No. 41-62
      Santafé de Bogotá
Phone: +57(1) 285-2700 **Fax:** +57(1) 288-2335

Founded: 1935 **Type:** Academic **Head:** Padre Marco Tulio
Gonzales, S.J. *Phone:* +57(1) 285-8177 **Staff:** 10 Prof. 50
Other **Holdings:** 1,050 books 23 journals **Language of Col-
lection/Services:** Spanish / Spanish **Subjects:** Cultivation,
Machinery, Soil Science **Databases Used:** Agris **Loan:** In
country **Service:** Internationally **Photocopy:** Yes

884   **Santafé de Bogotá, Colombia**
      Technologic Corporation of Bogotá
      Francisco Jose de Caldas Library
      Carrera 21 No. 54-85
      AA 5189
      Santafé de Bogotá
Phone: +57(1) 255-6030 **Fax:** +57(1) 217-5754

Non-English Name: Corporación Tecnológica de Bogotá, Biblioteca Francisco José de Caldas **Founded:** 1974 **Type:** Academic **Head:** Maruja Guevara de Romero *Phone:* +57(1) 255-6030 **Staff:** 2 Prof. 2 Other **Holdings:** 100 books 3 journals **Subjects:** Agricultural Chemistry **Loan:** In country **Photocopy:** Yes

885   **Sincelejo, Colombia**
       University of Sucre
       Pompeyo Molina Library
       AA 406
       Cra. 28 # 5-267, Barrio Puerta Roja
       Sincelejo, Sucre
Phone: +57(952) 821240 **Fax:** +57(952) 821240

Non-English Name: Universidad de Sucre (UNISUCRE), Biblioteca Pompeyo Molina **Type:** Academic **Head:** Irma Ochoa de Fonseca *Phone:* +57(952) 821240 **Staff:** 1 Prof. 7 Other **Holdings:** 11,650 books 20 journals **Language of Collection/Services:** Spanish, English / Spanish **Subjects:** Agriculture (Tropics), Agricultural Engineering, Biotechnology, Animal Husbandry, Fisheries, Soil Science, Horticulture **Databases Developed:** USLIB - 11,700 books on agricultural topics; USMAG - 3,600 records of journal articles **Loan:** In country **Service:** In country **Photocopy:** Yes

886   **Villavicencio, Colombia**
       Universidad Tecnológica de los Llanos Orientales
          (UNILLANOS)
       Centro de Documentación para la Orinoquia
       AA 2621
       Villavicencio, Meta
Location: KM 12 vía a Puerto López **Phone:** +57(866) 31291 **Fax:** +57(866) 34892

Founded: 1983 **Type:** Academic **Head:** Jorge R. Zapata Cardenas *Phone:* +57(866) 31291 **Staff:** 1 Prof. 1 Other **Holdings:** 900 books 10 journals **Language of Collection/Services:** Spanish/Spanish **Subjects:** Education/Extension, Fisheries, Forage, Pastures, Soil Science, Veterinary Medicine **Loan:** In country **Service:** Inhouse **Photocopy:** No

Congo, Democratic Republic of the

887   **Kinshasa, Democratic Republic of the Congo**
       Department of Agriculture
       Agricultural Documentation Centre
       BP 7537
       Kinshasa
Location: No. 7, Avenue Kauka, Commune de la Gombe

Non-English Name: Département de l'Agriculture (DEP-AGRI), Centre de Documentation Agricole (CDA) **Founded:** 1974 **Type:** Government **Head:** J. Marcellin Kapuku Ngeza *Phone:* +243(12) 32833, 32205 **Staff:** 4 Prof. 5 Other **Holdings:** 5,000 books 61 journals **Subjects:** Agricultural Development, Agricultural Economics, Animal Production, Crop Production, Fisheries, Rural Sociology **Networks:** AGRIS **Photocopy:** No

Congo, Republic of the

888   **Brazzaville, Republic of the Congo**
       Delegation General for Scientific and
          Technological Research
       National Center of Documentation and Scientific
          and Technical Information (NCDSTI)
       BP 15440 CNDIST
       Brazzaville
Phone: +242 812920 **Fax:** +242 812920

Non-English Name: Délégation Générale de la Recherche Scientifique et Technique (DGRST), Centre National de Documentation et d'Information Scientifique et Technique (CNDIST) **Former Name:** Direction Générale de la Recherche Scientifique et Technique, Direction de l'Information Scientifique et Technique **Founded:** 1976 **Type:** Government **Head:** Ndinga-Makanda Accel Arnaud *Phone:* +242 810607, 812920 **Staff:** 7 Prof. 13 Other **Holdings:** 4,500 books 55 journals **Language of Collection/Services:** French /French **Subjects:** Animal Husbandry, Fisheries, Forestry, Human Nutrition, Plants, Statistics **Loan:** In country **Service:** Internationally **Photocopy:** Yes

♦889   **Brazzaville, Republic of the Congo**
       Direction du Libre, de Bibliothèques, d'Archives
          et de Documentation
       Centre National de Documentation (CND)
       BP 1489
       Brazzaville
Founded: 1977 **Type:** Government **Head:** Mbemba Noe Emmanuel *Phone:* +242 833485 **Staff:** 4 Prof. 4 Other **Holdings:** 1,500 books 4 journals **Language of Collection/Services:** French **Subjects:** Agricultural Economics, Fisheries, Plant Pathology, Rural Economy **Loan:** Do not loan **Photocopy:** No

890   **Brazzaville, Republic of the Congo**
       Ministère de l'Agriculture, de l'Elevage, des Eaux
          et Forêts et de la Pêche
       Service de la Documentation et des Archives
          (SDA)
       BP 2453
       Brazzaville
Former Name: Ministère du Développement Rural (MDR), Bureau de la Documentation et des Archives (BDA) **Type:** Government **Head:** Marcel Biyekele *Phone:* +242 811813 **Staff:** 1 Prof. 4 Other **Holdings:** 1,700 books 5 journals **Subjects:** Agricultural Development, Agricultural Economics, Animal Health, Animal Production, Aquaculture, Crop Production, Ecology, Fisheries, Forestry, Plant Protection, Rural Sociology **Networks:** AGRIS

♦891   **Brazzaville, Republic of the Congo**
       Ministère de la Science et de la Technologie,
          Centre de Recherche Vétérinaire et
          Zootechnique (CRVZ)
       Service de Documentation et Publications
       BP 235
       Brazzaville

Phone: +242 810350

Founded: 1971 **Type:** Government **Head:** Costodes Tatys Ray **Holdings:** 751 books 57 journals **Language of Collection/Services:** French **Subjects:** Animal Health, Animal Husbandry, Animal Production, Veterinary Medicine **Loan:** Internationally **Photocopy:** Yes

892   **Brazzaville, Republic of the Congo**
         Research Institute for Development
         Center for Scientific Documentation and
              Information
         BP 181
         Brazzaville
Phone: +242 832680/2 **Fax:** +242 832977 **WWW:** www. ird.fr

Non-English Name: Institut de Recherche pour le Développement (IRD), Centre de Documentation et d'Information Scientifique (CEDIS) **Former Name:** Office de la Recherche Scientifique et Technique d'Outre-Mer (ORSTOM), Institut Français de Recherche Scientifique pour le Développement en Coopération (ORSTOM) **Founded:** 1950 **Head:** Marcel Ngoma-Mouaya *Phone:* +242 832680/2 **Holdings:** 17,000 books 34 journals **Language of Collection/Services:** French /French **Subjects:** Agriculture (Tropics), Agroforestry, Biotechnology, Botany, Entomology, Environment, Fisheries, Food Sciences, Forestry, Natural Resources, Plant Pathology, Plants, Soil Science, Water Resources **Photocopy:** Yes

893   **Brazzaville, Republic of the Congo**
         Université Mariem Ngouabi
         Bibliothèques Universitaires
         BP 69
         Brazzaville
Phone: +242 814207 **Fax:** +242 814207

Founded: 1969 **Type:** Academic **Staff:** 3 Prof. 3 Other **Holdings:** 11,000 books 230 journals **Subjects:** Animal Husbandry, Plants

894   **Loudima, Republic of the Congo**
         Centre de Recherches Agronomiques de Loudima
              (CRAL)
         Service de la Documentation et des Publications
         BP 28
         Loudima
Phone: +242 915103

Founded: 1984 **Type:** Government **Head:** Alain Madzabou **Staff:** 1 Prof. **Holdings:** 650 books 32 journals **Language of Collection/Services:** French / French **Subjects:** Agronomy, Crop Production, Entomology **Networks:** REDICA; CESODIST; REDICIST **Loan:** Inhouse **Service:** Inhouse **Photocopy:** Yes

♦895   **Pointe-Noire, Republic of the Congo**
         Centre National Recherches Forestières (CNRF)
         Bibliothèque
         BP 764
         Pointe-Noire
Location: 30, Avenue Maloango Moe Prate Arrondissement 3 **Phone:** +242 940575 **Fax:** +242 944054

Former Name: Centre Technique Forestier (CTFT) **Founded:** 1966 **Type:** Research **Head:** Alphonsine Mouzonso *Phone:* +242 940575 **Staff:** 1 Prof. 2 Other **Holdings:** 5,828 books 20 journals **Language of Collection/Services:** French / French **Subjects:** Forestry **Loan:** Inhouse **Service:** Inhouse **Photocopy:** Yes

896   **Pointe-Noire, Republic of the Congo**
         Research Institute for Development
         Documentation Service
         BP 1286
         Pointe-Noire
Phone: +242 940238 **Fax:** +242 943981 **WWW:** www.ird. fr

Non-English Name: Institut de Recherche pour le Développement (IRD), Service de Documentation **Former Name:** Office de la Recherche Scientifique et Technique d'Outre-Mer (ORSTOM) **Founded:** 1950 **Head:** Marius Issanga *Phone:* +242 940238 **Staff:** 4 Other **Holdings:** 1,750 books 120 journals **Subjects:** Animal Husbandry, Oceanography, Plants, Soil Science, Zoology

Cook Islands

897   **Rarotonga, Cook Islands**
         Ministry of Agriculture, Totokoitu Research
              Station
         Library
         PO Box 96
         Rarotonga
Phone: +682 28711 **Fax:** +682 21881 **Email:** cimoa@ oyster.net.ck

Type: Government **Head:** Mr. Anau Manarangi

Costa Rica

898   **Alajuela, Costa Rica**
         Central American Institute of Business
              Administration
         Library
         AP 960-4050
         Alajuela 4050
Location: La Garita, Alajuela **Fax:** +506 439101

Non-English Name: Instituto Centroamericano de Administración de Empresas (INCAE), Biblioteca **Founded:** 1984 **Type:** Academic **Head:** Thomas Bloch *Phone:* +506 412255 **Staff:** 5 Prof. 2 Other **Holdings:** 36,000 books 250 journals **Language of Collection/Services:** Spanish, English / Spanish **Subjects:** Agribusiness, Agricultural Development, Agricultural Economics **Specializations:** Central America, Exports **Databases Developed:** Index of articles in journals received by the library, open to all users **Databases Used:** ABI/Inform **Loan:** In country **Service:** In country **Photocopy:** Yes

899   **Balsa de Atenas, Costa Rica**
         Central American School of Animal Husbandry
         Library

Apdo No. 7-4013
Balsa de Atenas, Alajuela
Fax: +506 446-5788

Non-English Name: Escuela Centroamericana de Ganadería (ECAG), Biblioteca **Founded:** 1980 **Type:** Academic **Head:** Sonia Marlene Castro Sandi *Phone:* +506 446-5050 **Staff:** 1 Prof. 1 Other **Holdings:** 5,000 books **Subjects:** Agricultural Engineering, Animal Husbandry, Cultivation, Farm Machinery, Farm Management, Forage, Soil Science **Loan:** In country **Photocopy:** Yes

900   San José, Costa Rica
Central Bank of Costa Rica
Alvaro Castro Jenkins Library
Apdo 10-058
San José 1000
Location: San Jose C 2, Av. 4/6 **Fax:** +506 553995
WWW: www.bccr.fi.cr

Non-English Name: Banco Central de Costa Rica (BCCR), Biblioteca "Alvaro Castro Jenkins" **Founded:** 1950 **Type:** Business **Head:** Rosalia Vargas Pacheco *Phone:* +506 334133 ext 287, 550 **Staff:** 6 Prof. 2 Other **Holdings:** 1,900 books 110 journals **Language of Collection/Services:** Spanish **Subjects:** Agriculture (Tropics), Agricultural Development, Agricultural Economics, Forestry, Horticulture, Soil Science, Water Resources **Loan:** In country **Service:** In country **Photocopy:** Yes

901   San José, Costa Rica
Interamerican Institute of Cooperation in
        Agriculture (IICA)
Biblioteca Venezuela
Apdo 55 - 2200 Coronado
San José
Fax: +506 229-4741, 229-2659 **Email:** cenref@iica.ac.cr
WWW: www.iica.ac.cr **Ariel IP:** 163.178.35.150

Non-English Name: Instituto Interamericano de Cooperación para la Agricultura (IICA) **Head:** Marta Vásquez *Email:* mvasquez@iica.ac.cr

902   San José, Costa Rica
Ministry of Agriculture and Livestock
Agricultural Information Program
Apdo 10094-1000
San José
Fax: +506 296-1551

Non-English Name: Ministerio de Agricultura y Ganadería, Programa de Información Agropecuaria (PIAGRO) **Former Name:** Centro Nacional de Información Agropecuaria **Type:** Government **Networks:** AGRIS

903   San José, Costa Rica
Ministry of Agriculture and Livestock
Library
Apdo 10-094-1000
San José
Location: Sabana Sur **Phone:** +506 231-2062 **Fax:** +506 232-2103 **Email:** sunii@ns.mag.go.cr **WWW:** www.mag.go.cr

Non-English Name: Ministerio de Agricultura y Ganadería (MAG), Biblioteca (SUNII) **Founded:** 1950 **Type:** Government **Head:** Daniel Zúñiga van der Loot *Phone:* +506 231-2062 *Email:* dzuniga@ns.mag.go.cr **Staff:** 4 Prof. 3 Other **Holdings:** 14,000 books 40 journals **Language of Collection/Services:** Spanish, English, Portuguese **Subjects:** Agriculture (Tropics), Agribusiness, Agricultural Development, Agricultural Economics, Agricultural Engineering, Agricultural Trade, Animal Husbandry, Biotechnology, Crops, Cultivation, Education/Extension, Entomology, Farming, Fisheries, Food Sciences, Forestry, Horticulture, Livestock, Marketing, Plant Pathology, Plants, Soil Science, Veterinary Medicine, Water Resources **Databases Developed:** AGRIN - National Bibliography; LEG - National Agricultural Legislation; REVIS - Periodical Publications **Databases Used:** Agricola; Agris; CABCD **Loan:** In country **Service:** Internationally **Photocopy:** Yes

904   San José, Costa Rica
University of Costa Rica
Library, Documentation and Information System
2060 San José
Location: Ciudad Universitaria Rodrigo Facio **Phone:** +506 255555 ext 426, 308 **Fax:** +506 342809 **WWW:** www.ucr.ac.cr **OPAC:** sibdi.bldt.ucr.ac.cr

Non-English Name: Universidad de Costa Rica, Sistema de Bibliotecas, Documentación e Información (SIBDI) **Former Name:** Dirección de Bibliotecas, Documentación e Información **Founded:** 1946 **Type:** Academic **Head:** Lic. María Eugenia Briceño Meza *Email:* mbriceno@sibdi.bldt.ucr.ac.cr *Phone:* +506 536152 **Staff:** 47 Prof. **Holdings:** 141,692 books 88 journals **Subjects:** Agricultural Development, Agricultural Economics, Agricultural Engineering, Biotechnology, Entomology, Fisheries, Food Sciences **Loan:** In country **Service:** Inhouse **Photocopy:** Yes

905   Turrialba, Costa Rica
Interamerican Institute of Cooperation for
        Agriculture, Tropical Agricultural Research
        and Training Center
Orton Memorial Library
7170 Turrialba
Phone: +506 556-0501 **Fax:** +506 556-0858 **Ariel IP:** 196.40.0. 245 **Email:** referen@catie.ac.cr **WWW:** www.iica.ac.cr **OPAC:** www.catie.ac.cr/information/biblioteca.htm

Non-English Name: Instituto Interamericano de Cooperación para la Agricultura, Centro Agronómico Tropical de Investigación y Enseñanza (IICA, CATIE), Biblioteca Conmemorativa Orton (BCO) **Founded:** 1946 **Type:** International **Head:** Laura Coto Royo *Phone:* +506 556-0501 *Email:* lcotor@catie.ac.cr **Staff:** 5 Prof. 9 Other **Holdings:** 96,000 books 1,000 journals **Language of Collection/Services:** English / Spanish **Subjects:** Comprehensive **Specializations:** Agriculture (Tropics), Crops, Environment, Plant Protection, Forestry, Natural Resources **Databases Developed:** REVIS - Periodical publications; CAFE - 13,000 world-wide references on coffee; CACAO - 5,500 references on cocoa production; BANANO Y PLATANO - 7,100 references on bananas and plantains; CIDIA - 27,000 references to documents on agricultural economics, rural development, development and transfer of technology, commercialization and integration, environmental health, and animal production **Databases Used:** Comprehensive **Loan:** In country **Service:** Internationally **Photocopy:** Yes

Cote d'Ivoire

906   **Abidjan, Côte d'Ivoire**
African Institute for Economic and Social
     Development
Documentation Center
BP 2088
Abidjan 08

Location: 15, Avenue Jean-Mermoz, Cocody **Phone:** +225 441594/95, 442059 **Fax:** +225 448438 **Email:** inades@ africaonline.co.ci **WWW:** www.refer.fr/ivoir_ct/edu/sup/ div/inades

Non-English Name: Institut Africain pour le Développement Economique et Social (INADES), Documentation **Founded:** 1962 **Type:** Private **Head:** Mrs. Marie-Paule Coing *Phone:* +225 441594 **Staff:** 4 Prof. 6 Other **Holdings:** 10,000 books 37 journals **Language of Collection/Services:** French, English **Subjects:** Agriculture (Tropics), Agricultural Development, Agricultural Economics, Animal Husbandry, Education/Extension, Farming, Fisheries, Forestry, Veterinary Medicine **Databases Developed:** Fichier Afrique - summary of articles about Africa **Loan:** Inhouse **Service:** Internationally **Photocopy:** Yes

907   **Abidjan, Côte d'Ivoire**
Food and Agriculture Organization, Intergovern-
     mental Organization for Marketing
     Information and Cooperation Service for
     Fishery Products in Africa (FAO, Infopêche)
Documentation Center
BP 1747
Abidjan 01

Location: TOUR C, 19eme Etage, Cité Administrative **Phone:** +225 213198 **Fax:** +225 218054

Non-English Name: Organisation des Nations Unies pour l'Agriculture et l'Alimentation, Organisation Intergouvernementale d'Information et de Coopération pour la Commercialisation des Produits de la Pêche, Centre d'Information Technique **Founded:** 1985 **Type:** Association **Head:** Amadou Tall *Email:* tall@africaonline.co.ci **Staff:** 3 Prof. 15 Other **Holdings:** 3,500 books 100 journals **Language of Collection/Services:** English, French **Subjects:** Agricultural Economics, Fish Industry, Fisheries, Marketing **Databases Developed:** Databank on Fish Importers Worldwide; Databank on African Fish Exporters **Loan:** Internationally **Service:** Internationally **Photocopy:** Yes

908   **Abidjan, Côte d'Ivoire**
Ministry of Agriculture and Animal Resources
Documentation and Information Service
BP V203
Abidjan

Location: Avenue Terrasson de Fougères Immeuble de la Caisse de Stabilisation **Phone:** +225 210833 ext 302 or 201 **Fax:** +225 214618

Non-English Name: Ministère de l'Agriculture et des Ressources Animales (MINAGRA), Service de la Documentation et d'Information, Réseau National de Documentation Agricole en Côte d'Ivoire (SEDI, REDACI) **Founded:** 1966 **Type:** Government **Head:** Mrs. Koné Fatoumata *Phone:* +225 210833 ext 201 **Staff:** 4 Prof. 3 Other **Holdings:** 10,720 books 60 journals **Language of Collection/Services:** French / French **Subjects:** Agricultural Development, Agricultural Economics, Agricultural Engineering, Animal Production, Plant Protection, Rural Sociology **Specializations:** Animal Husbandry, Fisheries, Forestry, Mechanization, Water Resources **Networks:** AGRIS **Databases Used:** Agricola; Agris **Loan:** Inhouse **Photocopy:** Yes

909   **Abidjan, Côte d'Ivoire**
Ministry of Higher Education, Research and
     Technological Innovation (MESRIT, DCIST)
Library
BP V151
Abidjan

Location: Cité Administrative Tour B 15e étage **Phone:** +225 223406 **Fax:** +225 212225

Non-English Name: Ministère de l'Enseignement Supérieur, de la Recherche et de l'Innovation Technologique, Direction de la Coopération et de l'Information Scientifique et Technique, Bibliothèque **Former Name:** Ministère de la Recherche Scientifique (MRS), Direction de l'Information Scientifique et Technique (DIST) **Founded:** 1971 **Type:** Government **Head:** Adom Kiamkey Jacques *Phone:* +225 213141 *Email:* adomja@hotmail.com **Staff:** 3 Prof. 1 Other **Holdings:** 4,000 books 200 journals **Language of Collection/Services:** French, English / French **Subjects:** Comprehensive **Specializations:** Biotechnology, Biotopes, Forestry **Networks:** AGRIS **Databases Used:** CARIS **Loan:** Inhouse **Service:** In country **Photocopy:** Yes

910   **Abidjan, Côte d'Ivoire**
Research Institute for Development, Petit Bassam
     Center
Petit Bassam Library
BP 293
Abidjan 04

Location: 9, rue Fléming Zone 4C **Fax:** +225 354015 **WWW:** www.ird.fr

Non-English Name: Institut de Recherche pour le Développement, Centre de Petit Bassam (IRD), Bibliothèque de Petit Bassam **Former Name:** French Scientific Research Institute for Development through Cooperation, Institut Français de Recherche Scientifique pour le Développement en Coopération (ORSTOM) **Founded:** 1970 **Type:** International **Head:** Ehui Edoukou *Phone:* +225 357067, 354367, 242556 *Email:* ehui@bassam.orstom.ci **Staff:** 1 Prof. 2 Other **Holdings:** 8,000 books 58 journals **Subjects:** Agricultural Development, Agricultural Economics, Agricultural Research, Animal Husbandry, Planting **Loan:** Do not loan **Photocopy:** Yes

♦911   **Abidjan, Côte d'Ivoire**
University of Abidjan, Ivoirian Center for
     Economic and Social Research
Documentation Center

BP 1295
Abidjan
Location: Boulevard Latrille

Non-English Name: Université Nationale Abidjan, Centre Ivoirien de Recherche Economique et Sociale (CIRES), Documentation Centre **Founded:** 1971 **Type:** Academic **Head:** Kouapa Assale *Phone:* +225 440953, 442193 **Staff:** 2 Prof. 1 Other **Holdings:** 10,792 books 100 journals **Language of Collection/Services:** French, English **Subjects:** Agricultural Development, Agricultural Economics, Demography, Education/Extension, Farming, Rural Sociology **Loan:** In country **Photocopy:** Yes

♦**912** **Bouaké, Côte d'Ivoire**
Compagnie Ivoirienne pour le Développement des Textiles (CIDT)
Service Etudes, Gestion de l'Information et Organisation
Bouaké 01
Fax: +225 634167

Former Name: Cellule de Gestion de l'Information (CGI) **Type:** Business **Head:** Kouame Signo *Phone:* +225 633013 **Staff:** 2 Other **Holdings:** 1,700 books 64 journals **Subjects:** Agricultural Development, Cotton Industry, Rural Planning **Photocopy:** Yes

913 **Bouaké, Côte d'Ivoire**
West Africa Rice Development Association (WARDA)
Documentation Unit
01 BP 2551
Bouaké 01
Phone: +225 634514 **Fax:** +225 634 714 **Email:** warda@cgiar.org **WWW:** www.cgiar.org/warda

Founded: 1971 **Type:** International **Head:** Alassane Diallo *Phone:* +225 634514 ext 520 *Email:* a.diallo@cgiar.org **Staff:** 3 Prof. 3 Other **Holdings:** 16,000 books 150 journals **Language of Collection/Services:** English, French / English, French **Subjects:** Agricultural Development, Crop Production, Plant Breeding, Plant Protection, Rural Economy, Rural Sociology, Stored Products **Specializations:** Rice **Databases Used:** Comprehensive **Loan:** Inhouse **Photocopy:** Yes

914 **Yamoussoukro, Côte d'Ivoire**
National Polytechnic Institute, College of Agronomy
Documentation Center
PO Box 1313
Yamoussoukro
Phone: +225 640770 **Fax:** +225 640406

Non-English Name: Institut National Polytechnique, Ecole Supérieure d'Agronomie (ENSA), Centre de Documentation (CDD) **Former Name:** Ecole Nationale Supérieure Agronomique **Founded:** 1996 **Type:** Academic **Head:** Bernard Me Kouakou *Phone:* +225 640770 **Staff:** 2 Prof. 4 Other **Holdings:** 10,100 books 23 journals **Language of Collection/Services:** French / French **Subjects:** Animal Health, Botany, Commodity Markets, Entomology, Food Sciences, Plant Pathology, Plant Protection, Plants, Soil Science Spe-

cializations: Agricultural Economics, Agronomy, Animal Husbandry, Food Industry, Food Processing, Forestry **Networks:** REDACI **Loan:** In country **Service:** In country **Photocopy:** Yes

Croatia

915 **Osijek, Croatia**
Institute for Sugar Beet Breeding
Library
Divaltova 320
PO Box 392
31103 Osijek
Phone: +385(31) 555722 **Fax:** +385(31) 551161

Non-English Name: Institut za secernu repu, Biblioteka **Founded:** 1962 **Type:** Research **Staff:** 6 Other **Holdings:** 25,000 books 12 journals **Language of Collection/Services:** Croatian, English / Croatian, English **Subjects:** Sugarbeet **Specializations:** Plant Breeding **Loan:** Inhouse **Service:** Inhouse **Photocopy:** Yes

916 **Osijek, Croatia**
Osijek Agricultural Institute
Library
Juzno predgrade 17
PO Box 149
HR-31000 Osijek

Non-English Name: Poljoprivredni Institut Osijek, Biblioteka **Type:** Research **Head:** Mira Avlijas *Phone:* +385(54) 166-645 **Holdings:** 18,000 books 6,000 journals **Language of Collection/Services:** Croatian **Subjects:** Agricultural Development, Agricultural Engineering, Animal Husbandry, Biotechnology, Crops, Farming, Plant Pathology, Plants, Soil Science, Water Resources **Photocopy:** Yes

917 **Osijek, Croatia**
University of J.J. Strossmayer - Osijek, Faculty of Agriculture
Library
PO Box 117
Trg Sv. Trojstva 3
31000 Osijek
Phone: +385(31) 224-200 **Fax:** +385(31) 207-017 **Email:** kniga@suncokret.pfos.hr **WWW:** suncokret.pfos.hr **Ariel IP:** 161.53.194.3

Non-English Name: Sveuciliste J.J. Strossmayera - Osijek, Poljoprivredni Fakultet, Biblioteka **Founded:** 1960 **Type:** Academic **Head:** Josipa Vrbanic *Phone:* +385(31) 244-212 **Staff:** 2 Prof. **Holdings:** 5,123 books 85 journals **Language of Collection/Services:** Croatian, English, French **Subjects:** Agribusiness, Biotechnology, Food Sciences, Forestry, Horticulture, Education/Extension, Plants **Specializations:** Biometry, Agricultural Development, Agricultural Economics, Agricultural Engineering, Animal Husbandry, Crops, Entomology, Farming, Fisheries, Plant Pathology, Soil Science **Databases Used:** Comprehensive **Service:** Internationally **Photocopy:** Yes

918   Osijek, Croatia
University of J.J. Strossmayer - Osijek, Faculty of
Food Technology
Library
Vij. I. Mestrovica 7
PO Box 349
54000 Osijek
Phone: +385(54) 25344 **Fax:** +385(54) 26721 **WWW:**
www.ptfos.hr

Non-English Name: Sveuciliste J.J. Strossmayera - Osijek,
Prehrambeno Tehnoloski Fakultet (PFT), Biblioteka **Type:**
Academic **Staff:** 1 Prof. **Holdings:** 1,606 books 25 journals
Language of Collection/Services: Croatian, English / Cro-
atian **Subjects:** Biotechnology, Food Sciences **Loan:** Inter-
nationally **Service:** Internationally **Photocopy:** Yes

919   Zagreb, Croatia
Institute for Plant Protection in Agriculture and
Forestry of Republic Croatia
Library
Svetošimunska 25
HR-10040 Zagreb
Phone: +385(1) 211842, 211630 **Fax:** +385(1) 211842,
211640 **Email:** zavod-zas.bilja@zg.tel.hr

Non-English Name: Zavod za zaštitu bilja u poljoprivredi i
šumarstvu Republike Hrvatske, Biblioteka **Former Name:**
Institute for Plant Protection, Institut za Zastitu Bilja, Plant
Protection Co. Ltd., Zastita bilja d.o.o. **Founded:** 1909
Type: Academic **Head:** Darka Hamel *Phone:* +385(1)
2335253, 223260 *Email:* zavod-zas.bilja@zg.tel.hr **Staff:**
.25 Other **Holdings:** 5,500 books 15 journals **Subjects:** Entomology, Medicinal Plants, Plant Pathology, Plant Protection **Loan:** Do not loan **Photocopy:** Yes

920   Zagreb, Croatia
University of Zagreb, Faculty of Agriculture
Central Agricultural Library
PO Box 1009
HR-10000 Zagreb
Location: Svetosimunska 25 **Phone:** +385(1) 239-3777
Fax: +385(1) 215 300 **Email:** lib@agr.hr **WWW:** www.
agr.hr **Ariel IP:** 161.53.95.1

Non-English Name: Sveuciliste u Zagrebu, Agronomski
Fakultet, Centralna Agronomska Knjiznica (CAK) **Former
Name:** Fakultet Poljoprivrednih Znanosti **Founded:** 1947
Type: Academic **Head:** Vjekoslava Bešlaj *Phone:* +385(1)
239-3766/7 *Email:* vbeslaj@agr.hr **Staff:** 3 Prof. 1 Other
Holdings: 78,000 books 180 journals **Language of Collec-
tion/Services:** Croatian, English **Subjects:** Agribusiness,
Agriculture (Tropics), Agricultural Development, Agricul-
tural Economics, Agricultural Engineering, Biotechnology,
Animal Husbandry, Crops, Education / Extension, Entomology, Farming, Fisheries, Food Sciences, Forestry, Horticulture, Plant Pathology, Soil Science, Veterinary Medicine,
Water Resources **Networks:** AGRIS **Loan:** In country **Photocopy:** Yes

921   Zagreb, Croatia
University of Zagreb, Veterinary Faculty
Library

Heinzelova 55
PO Box 190
41000 Zagreb
Phone: +385(41) 290114 **Fax:** +385(41) 214697 **WWW:**
www.vef.hr

Non-English Name: Sveuciliste u Zagrebu, Veterinarski
Fakultet, Knjiznica **Type:** Academic **Head:** Djurdjica Stubi-
can *Phone:* +385(41) 290114 *Email:* stubican@vef.hr **Staff:**
2 Prof. **Holdings:** 24,147 books 295 journals **Language of
Collection/Services:** Croatian / Croatian **Subjects:** Veterinary Medicine **Loan:** Internationally **Service:** Internationally **Photocopy:** Yes

Cuba

922   Havana, Cuba
Ministry of Agriculture, Agricultural Information
Agency
National Agriculture and Forestry Library
Conill entre Ave. Independencia y Marino
Gaveta Postal 4149
Havana 4
Phone: +53(7) 845402 **Fax:** +53(7) 845757, 845465
Email: martaqui@yahoo.com, reinagh@hotmail.com

Non-English Name: Ministerio de la Agricultura, Agencia
de Información para la Agricultura, Biblioteca Nacional
Agropecuaria y Forestal (BINAF) **Former Name:** Centro de
Información y Documentación de la Agricultura (CIDA),
Biblioteca Nacional Agropecuaria **Founded:** 1971 **Type:**
Government **Head:** Ing. Marta Quiñones de Armas *Phone:*
+53(7) 845402, 845436 *Email:* martaqui@yahoo.com **Staff:**
45 Prof. 11 Other **Holdings:** 52,560 books 891 journals **Lan-
guage of Collection/Services:** English / Spanish **Subjects:**
Comprehensive **Specializations:** Animal Husbandry, Plant
Pathology, Veterinary Medicine **Databases Developed:**
BD-AGRO - bibliographical references on agricultural collection of serials and non-serials; BD-FIDEL - selection of
speeches from Fidel Castro about agriculture **Databases
Used:** Comprehensive **Loan:** In country **Service:** Internationally **Photocopy:** Yes

923   Havana, Cuba
National Botanical Garden (NBG)
Library
Carretera El Rocio Km 3-1/2 Calabazar
Havana 19230
Phone: +53(7) 442516 ext 36, 442617/18 **Fax:** +53(7)
335350 **Email:** bibjbn@reduniv.edu.cu

Non-English Name: Jardín Botánico Nacional (JBN),
Biblioteca **Founded:** 1970 **Type:** Academic **Head:** Lorayne
Guerrero Tamayo *Phone:* +53(7) 578249 *Email:* hajb@
ceniai.inf.cu **Staff:** 1 Prof. 2 Other **Holdings:** 3,071 books
Language of Collection/Services: English / Spanish **Subjects:** Agriculture (Tropics), Biotechnology, Economic Botany, Crops, Farm Machinery, Farming, Food Sciences,
Forestry, Horticulture, Seeds **Specializations:** Botany **Service:** In country**Loan:** In country **Photocopy:** Yes

Cyprus

924 **Nicosia, Cyprus**
Ministry of Agriculture and Natural Resources,
Agricultural Research Institute
Library and Documentation Centre
PO Box 2016
1516 Nicosia
Phone: +357(2) 305101 **Fax:** 357(2) 316770 **Email:**
mavrogen@arinet.ari.gov.cy

Type: Government **Networks:** AGRIS

Czech Republic

925 **Brno, Czech Republic**
Mendel University of Agriculture and Forestry in
Brno
Institute for Scientific Information - Central
Library (ISI)
Zemedelská 1
613 00 Brno
Phone: +42(5) 4513 5014 **Fax:** +42(5) 4513 5008 **Email:**
svobodov@mendelu.cz **WWW:** www.mendelu.cz/csp
OPAC: www.mendelu.cz

Non-English Name: Mendelova zemedelaská a lesnická
univerzita v Brne (MZLU), Ústav vedeckych informací -
ústrední knihovna (ÚVIS) **Former Name:** Vysoká škola
zemedelská Brno **Founded:** 1919 **Type:** Academic **Head:**
Ing. Jirí Potácek *Phone:* +42(5) 4513 2678 *Email:* potacek@
mendelu.cz **Staff:** 11 Prof. **Holdings:** 360,000 books 420
journals **Language of Collection/Services:** Czech / Czech
Subjects: Comprehensive **Databases Used:** Comprehensive
Loan: In country **Service:** In country **Photocopy:** Yes

926 **Brno, Czech Republic**
State Phytosanitary Administration
Library
Zemedelská 1a
613 00 Brno
Phone: +42(5) 4532 1202 **Fax:** +42(5) 4513 7040

Non-English Name: Státní rostlinolékarská správa (SRS),
Knihovna **Former Name:** Central Checking and Testing Institute of Agriculture, Ústrední kontrolní a zkusební ústav
zemedelsky v Praze, Správa ochrany rostlin odbor zkusebni a
metodicky, State Checking and Testing Institute of Agriculture, Pesticide Testing Division, Státní kontrolní a zkusební
ústav zemedelsky (SKZÚZ), Odbor zkousení prostredku a
metod ochrany rostlin **Founded:** 1924 **Type:** Government
Head: Emanuela Weinbergerová *Phone:* +42(5) 4513 7040
Staff: 3 Prof. **Holdings:** 8,716 books 43 journals **Language
of Collection/Services:** Czech / Czech **Subjects:** Entomology, Plant Pathology, Plant Protection **Loan:** In country **Service:** In country **Photocopy:** Yes

927 **Brno, Czech Republic**
University of Veterinary and Pharmaceutical
Sciences
Central Library and Information Center

Palackého 1-3
612 42 Brno
Phone: +42(5) 4156 2009 **Fax:** +42(5) 4156 2006 **Email:**
ukis@post.cz **WWW:** www.vfu.cz

Non-English Name: Veterinární a farmaceutická univerzita
(VFU), Ústrední knihovna a informacní stredisko (ÚKIS)
Former Name: University of Veterinary Sciences, Vysoká
škola veterinární **Founded:** 1918 **Type:** Academic **Head:**
Vaclav Svoboda *Phone:* +42(5) 4156 2006 *Email:* svobod@
post.cz **Staff:** 5 Prof. 3 Other **Holdings:** 200,000 books 150
journals **Language of Collection/Services:** Czech, German
/Czech, English **Subjects:** Agriculture (Tropics), Animal
Husbandry, Biotechnology, Farming, Fisheries, Food Sci-
ences, Forestry, Horticulture, Veterinary Medicine **Databases Used:** Agricola; Medline; VETCD **Loan:** In country
Service: Internationally **Photocopy:** Yes

928 **Brno, Czech Republic**
Veterinary Research Institute (VRI)
Library
Hudcova 70
621 32 Brno
Phone: +42(5) 4121 2462 **Fax:** +42(5) 4121 1229 **Email:**
vri@vri.cz

Head: Olga Matouskova *Phone:* +42(5) 4121 4001 *Email:*
matouskova@vri.cz **Subjects:** Veterinary Science

929 **Ceské Budejovice, Czech Republic**
University of South Bohemia in Ceské
Budejovice, Faculty of Agriculture
Research Library (RL)
Studentská 13
370 05 Ceské Budejovice
Phone: +42(38) 777-2555 **Fax:** +42(38) 40301 **Email:**
tureckov@zf.jcu.cz **WWW:** www.zf.jcu.cz **OPAC:**
tinweb.jcu.cz/~tinweb/cgi-bin/k6zf.cgi?ST=00&L=02

Non-English Name: Jihoceská univerzita v Ceských Bude-
jovicích, Zemedelská fakulta (VSZ, AF), Fakultní vedecká
knihovna (FVK) **Former Name:** University of Agriculture
in Prague, Faculty of Agronomy, Vysoká škola zemedelská
(VSZ), Agronomická fakulta, Ústrední Knihovna **Founded:**
1961 **Type:** Academic **Head:** Mgr. Olga Douleová *Phone:*
+42(38) 777-2553 *Email:* douleova@zf. jcu.cz **Staff:** 7 Prof.
1 Other **Holdings:** 130,000 books 215 journals **Language of
Collection/Services:** Czech / Czech **Subjects:** Agricultural
Development, Agricultural Engineering, Biotechnology, Ed-
ucation/Extension, Entomology, Food Sciences, Forestry,
Horticulture, Plants, Soil Science, Veterinary Medicine, Water Resources **Specializations:** Agricultural Economics, Animal Husbandry, Crops, Farming, Fisheries **Networks:**
CASLIN **Databases Developed:** Database of publications
activities of the Faculty of Agriculture **Databases Used:**
Comprehensive **Loan:** In country **Service:** In country **Photocopy:** Yes

930 **Dol, Czech Republic**
Bee Research Institute Dol
Library
252 66 Dol, Libcice nad Vltavou
Fax: +42(2) 2094 1252

Non-English Name: Výzkumný ústav vcelarsky v Dole (VÚVc), Knihovna **Founded:** 1925 **Type:** Research **Head:** Ing. Dalibor Titera CSc. *Phone:* +42(2) 2094 1259 **Staff:** 1 Prof. **Holdings:** 12,007 books 32 journals **Language of Collection/Services:** Czech / Czech, English **Subjects:** Apidae, Bee Plants, Bombus, Honey, Propolis, Sericulture, Silkworms, Waxes **Specializations:** Beekeeping **Loan:** Inhouse **Service:** Internationally **Photocopy:** Yes

931   **Havlíckuv Brod, Czech Republic**
        Potato Research Institute
        Library
        Dobrovského 2366
        580 01 Havlíckuv Brod
Phone: +42(451) 466219 **Fax:** +42(451) 21578 **Email:** library@hba.czn.cz **WWW:** www.hba.czn.cz/vubhb

Non-English Name: Výzkumný ústav bramborársky (VÚB), Knihovna **Former Name:** Research Institute for Potato Growing and Breeding, Výzkumný a šlechtitelský ústav bramborárský **Founded:** 1923 **Type:** Research **Head:** Mrs. Ludmila Smejkalová *Phone:* +42(451) 466219 *Email:* library@hba. czn.cz **Staff:** 2 Prof. **Holdings:** 12,530 books 50 journals **Language of Collection/Services:** Czech / Czech **Subjects:** Agricultural Development, Biotechnology, Crops, Plant Protection, Plants **Specializations:** Potatoes **Databases Developed:** DOK - information retrieval services on potatoes using Micro CDS/ISIS **Loan:** In country **Service:** In country **Photocopy:** Yes

932   **Horice v Podkrkonoší, Czech Republic**
        Research and Breeding Institute of Pomology
           Holovousy Ltd.
        Library
        Holovousy
        508 01 Horice v Podkrkonoší
Fax: +42(435) 692833 **Email:** vsuohl@vsuo.cz

Non-English Name: Výzkumný a šlechtitelský ústav ovocnársky Holovousy s.r.o., Knihovna **Founded:** 1951 **Type:** Government **Head:** Anna Paprsteinová *Phone:* +42(435) 692821 *Email:* vsuohl@vsuo.cz **Staff:** 1 Prof. **Holdings:** 16,500 books 70 journals **Language of Collection/Services:** Czech, English **Subjects:** Agricultural Engineering, Biotechnology, Entomology, Gene Banks, Horticulture, Plant Pathology **Specializations:** Plant Breeding, Pomology **Loan:** In country **Photocopy:** Yes

933   **Hradec Králová, Czech Republic**
        Czech State Forests
        Library
        Premyslova 1106
        501 68 Hradec Králová 8
Location: Hlavní archiv - reditelství **Phone:** +42(49) 5860 290 **Fax:** +42(49) 5262 391 **Email:** admin@lesycr.cz

Non-English Name: Lesy Ceské republiky s.p. (LCR), Knihovna **Founded:** 1993 **Type:** Government **Head:** P. Jaklová *Phone:* +42(49) 5860 230 **Staff:** 2 Prof. **Holdings:** 1,500 books 25 journals **Language of Collection/Services:** Czech, English, German **Subjects:** Forestry **Loan:** In country **Service:** Inhouse **Photocopy:** Yes

934   **Hradistko pod Medníkem, Czech Republic**
        Czech-Moravian Breeders' Corporation
        Special Library
        Pracovisté
        252 09 Hradistko pod Medníkem
Phone: +42(2) 9941 300 (Stechovice) **Fax:** +42(2) 9941 491 **Email:** sppcr@login.cz

Non-English Name: Ceskomoravská spolecnost chovatelu, s.r.o. (CMSCH), Odborná knihovna **Former Name:** State Breeding Enterprise, Státní plemenárské podniky Praha (SPP) **Founded:** 1968 **Type:** Business **Head:** Prof. Ing. Jaroslav Pytloun *Phone:* +42(2) 9941 380 (Prague) *Email:* sppcr@login.cz **Staff:** 1 Prof. **Holdings:** 9,000 books 30 journals **Language of Collection/Services:** Czech **Subjects:** Agricultural Development, Animal Husbandry, Biotechnology, Veterinary Medicine **Loan:** In country **Service:** In country **Photocopy:** Yes

935   **Kromeríz, Czech Republic**
        Agricultural Research Institute Kromeriz, Ltd.
        Information Center
        Havlíckova 2787
        767 01 Kromeríz
Phone: +42(634) 317 111 **Fax:** +42(634) 22725 **Email:** vukrom@vukrom.cz **WWW:** www.vukrom.cz **OPAC:** www.vukrom.cz/www.english/books/books.htm

Non-English Name: Zemedelský výzkumný ústav Kromeríz, s.r.o., Informacní stredisko **Former Name:** Cereal Research Institute (CRI), Výzkumný ústav obilnársky **Founded:** 1952 **Type:** Government **Head:** Mgr. Vera Kroftová *Phone:* +42(634) 317 173 *Email:* kroftova@ vukrom.cz **Staff:** 2 Prof. **Holdings:** 20,000 books 65 journals **Language of Collection/Services:** Czech, English / Czech **Subjects:** Crop Production **Specializations:** Agronomy, Grain Quality, Cereals, Genetic Resources, Plant Protection **Databases Developed:** Bibliographic data from home and foreign sources on CDS/ISIS; available for users inhouse through network and for users in country by mail **Databases Used:** Current Contents **Loan:** Internationally **Service:** In country **Photocopy:** Yes

936   **Libechov, Czech Republic**
        Academy of Science of Czech Republic, Institute
           of Animal Physiology and Genetics (ASCR,
           IAPG)
        Library
        Rumburska 89
        277 21 Libechov
Phone: +42(206) 69 70 **Fax:** +42(2) +42(206) 69 71 86 **WWW:** www.iapg.cas.cz/uzfg/USTAV.HTM

Non-English Name: Akademie Ved Ceske Republiky, Ústav Zivocisne Fyziologie a Genetiky, Knihovna **Head:** *Phone:* Mgr. Petr Horak *Email:* horak@iapg.cas.cz **Subjects:** Animal Genetics, Animal Physiology

937   **Nové Dvory, Czech Republic**
        Museum of Czech Countryside (MCC)
        Museum Library
        Castle Kacina by Kutná Hora
        285 31 Nové Dvory

Phone: +42(327) 571 170 **Fax:** +42(327) 571 274

Non-English Name: Muzeum ceského venkova (MCV), Knihovna **Former Name:** Ceskoslovenské zemedelské muzeum, Czechoslovak Museum of Agriculture **Founded:** 1922 **Type:** Government **Head:** Mrs. Eva Suková *Phone:* +42(327) 571 170 **Staff:** 1 Prof. **Holdings:** 100,000 books 4,000 journals **Language of Collection/Services:** Czech, German / Czech **Subjects:** Agricultural Economics, Animal Husbandry, Biological Production, Crops, Horticulture **Loan:** In country **Service:** Inhouse **Photocopy:** Yes

938   Pohorelice, Czech Republic
Research Institute of Animal Nutrition Ltd.
        (RIAN)
Library
Vídenská 699
691 23 Pohorelice
Phone: +42(626) 424 541 **Fax:** +42(626) 424 366 **Email:** vuvz@vuvz.cz **WWW:** www.vuvz.cz

Non-English Name: Výzkumný ústav vyzivy zvírat, s.r.o. (VÚVZ), Knihovna **Founded:** 1953 **Type:** Research **Head:** Blanka Hutárková *Phone:* +42(626) 424 541 *Email:* vuvz@vuvz.cz **Staff:** 1 Prof. **Holdings:** 20,000 books 32 journals **Subjects:** Animal Feeding, Animal Husbandry, Animal Nutrition **Loan:** In country **Service:** Internationally **Photocopy:** Yes

939   Prague, Czech Republic
Academy of Science of Czech Republic (ASCR)
Main Library
Narodni trida 3
115 22 Prague 1
Phone: +42(2) 21 40 31 11 **Fax:** +42(2) 24 24 06 11
Email: knavcr@lib.cas.cz **WWW:** www.lib.cas.cz **OPAC:** www.lib.cas.cz/knav/eng/catalogues.htm

Non-English Name: Akademie Ved Ceske Republiky, Knihovna **Former Name:** Czechoslovak Academy of Sciences (CSAS) **Head:** Dr. Ivana Kadlecova *Phone:* +42(2) 24 24 95 24, 214 03 260 *Email:* kadlec@lib.cas.cz

940   Prague, Czech Republic
Academy of Science of Czech Republic, Institute
        of Experimental Botany (ASCR, IEB)
Library
Rozvojová 135
165 02 Prague 6 - Lysolaje
Phone: +42(2) 20 39 04 69 **Fax:** +42(2) 20 39 04 74
Email: knihovna@ueb.cas.cz

Non-English Name: Akademie Ved Ceske Republiky, Ústav Experimentální Botaniky, Knihovna **Head:** Hana Kopicová

941   Prague, Czech Republic
Charles University, Natural Science Faculty
Biology Library
Benátská 2
128 01 Prague 2
Phone: +42(2) 2195 3114 **Email:** knihbot@prfdec.natur. cuni.cz **WWW:** www.cuni.cz **OPAC:** www.cuni.cz/tinlib/dbs/sd.html

Non-English Name: Univerzity Karlovy, Prírodovedecká fakulta, Knihovna biologie **Founded:** 1922 **Type:** Government **Head:** Hana Matousová **Staff:** 2 Prof. 1 Other **Holdings:** 30,000 books 70 journals **Language of Collection/Services:** Czech, English, German, Russian **Subjects:** Crops, Food Sciences, Horticulture, Plant Pathology **Specializations:** Botany, Mycology **Loan:** In country **Service:** In country

942   Prague, Czech Republic
Czech Entomological Society
Library
Vinicna 7
128 00 Prague 2
Phone: +42(2) 298726

Non-English Name: Ceská spolecnost entomologická, Knihovna **Former Name:** Ceskoslovenská spolecnost entomologická **Founded:** 1904 **Type:** Association **Head:** Dr. Oldrich Hovorka *Phone:* +42(2) 2431 0752 **Staff:** 1 Other **Holdings:** 19,000 books 200 journals **Subjects:** Entomology **Loan:** In country **Photocopy:** No

943   Prague, Czech Republic
Czech Environmental Institute (CEI)
Centre for Public Environmental Information
        Service
Vršovická 65
100 10 Prague 10
Phone: +42(2) 7173-2575 **Fax:** +42(2) 7173-7721 **Email:** vera.havrankova@ceu.cz **WWW:** www.ceu.cz

Non-English Name: Ceský ekologický ústav (EÚ), Stredisko verejných informacnich sluzeb pro zivotni prostredi (SVIS) **Former Name:** Stredisko verejných informacnich sluzeb **Type:** Government **Head:** PhDr. Vera Havránková *Phone:* +42(2) 7173-2575 *Email:* vera. havrankova@ceu.cz **Staff:** 4 Prof. 10 Other **Holdings:** 8,480 books 120 journals **Language of Collection/Services:** Czech/Czech **Subjects:** Environment, Wastes **Databases Developed:** RESERS - contains documents from Czech and foreign journals on wastes topics **Loan:** Internationally **Service:** Internationally **Photocopy:** Yes

944   Prague, Czech Republic
Czech University of Agriculture Prague (CUA)
Library and Information Center
Kamýcká ul. 129
165 21 Prague 6
Phone: +42(2) 2438 2193 **Fax:** +42(2) 2092 1360 **Email:** knihovna@sic.czu.cz **WWW:** www.czu.cz

Non-English Name: Ceská zemedelská univerzita v Praze (CZU), Studijni a informacní centrum (SIC) **Former Name:** Vysoká skola zemedelská (VSZ) **Founded:** 1906 **Type:** Academic **Head:** Ivan Hauzner *Phone:* +42(2) 2438 4027 *Email:* hauzner@sic.czu.cz **Staff:** 15 Prof. 11 Other **Holdings:** 120,000 books 450 journals **Language of Collection/Services:** Czech / Czech, English **Subjects:** Agribusiness, Agricultural Development, Agricultural Economics, Agricultural Engineering, Animal Husbandry, Crops, Farming, Forestry, Horticulture, Plants, Soil Science, Water Resources **Specializations:** Information Technology **Databases Used:**

Comprehensive **Loan:** Internationally **Service:** In country **Photocopy:** Yes

945   Prague, Czech Republic
        Forestry and Game Management Research
            Institute (FGHRI)
        Scientific and Technical Information Centre
        Jíloviště Strnady
        156 04 Prague 5 - Zbraslav
Phone: +42(2) 5792 1643 **Fax:** +42(2) 5792 1444, 5792 1276 **WWW:** www.vulhm.cz

Non-English Name: Výzkumný ústav lesního hospodárství a Myslivosti (VÚLHM), Vedecko-technickych informacni (VTEI) **Founded:** 1952 **Type:** Government **Staff:** 12 Prof. 17 Other **Language of Collection/Services:** Czech / Czech **Holdings:** 50,000 books 250 journals **Subjects:** Biotechnology, Plants, Soil Science, Water Resources **Specializations:** Forestry, Wildlife Management **Loan:** Internationally **Service:** In country **Photocopy:** Yes

946   Prague, Czech Republic
        Institute of Agricultural and Food Information
            (IAFI)
        Central Agricultural and Forestry Library (CAFL)
        PO Box 39
        Slezská 7
        CZ-120 56 Prague 2
Phone: +42(2) 259 096 **Fax:** +42(2) 2425 3938 **Email:** ref@uzpi.cz **WWW:** www.uzpi.cz/cs/uzlk.htm

Non-English Name: Ústav zemedelskych a potravinárskych informací (ÚZPI), Ústrední zemedelská a lesnická knihovna (ÚZLK) **Former Name:** Institute of Scientific and Technical Information for Agriculture (ISTIA), Ústav védeckotechnickych informací pro zemedelství (ÚVTIZ), Ústav védeckotechnickych informací MZLVA **Founded:** 1927 **Type:** Government **Head:** PhDr. Ivo Hoch *Phone:* +42(2) 2425 5074 *Email:* ihoch@uzpi.cz **Staff:** 38 Prof. **Holdings:** 1,100,000 books 700 journals **Language of Collection/Services:** Czech, Russian, English, German / Czech, English, German, Russian **Subjects:** Comprehensive **Networks:** AGRIS; CASLIN **Databases Developed:** CAFL, RES - list of retrievals and subject bibliographies in agriculture; FL - company literature; VTA - list of scientific conferences in agriculture; VID - list of video programs; HIS - data about history of CAFL; ZKR - abbreviations of the international organizations **Databases Used:** Comprehensive **Loan:** In country **Service:** Internationally **Photocopy:** Yes

947   Prague, Czech Republic
        Institute of Agricultural and Food Information
            (IAFI)
        Central Food Library (CFL)
        Londynská 55
        120 21 Prague 2
Phone: +42(2) 2425 0984 **Fax:** +42(2) 6631 2812 **Email:** upk-uzpi@login.cz **WWW:** www.uzpi.cz

Non-English Name: Ústav zemedelskych a potravinárskych informací (ÚZPI), Ústrední potravinárská knihovna (ÚPK) **Former Name:** Institute of Scientific and Technical Information for Agriculture (ISTIA), Ústav védeckotechnickych

informací pro zemedelství (ÚVTIZ), Research Institute of Food Industry, Food Information Centre **Founded:** 1958 **Type:** Government **Head:** Dr. Jana Skládalová *Phone:* +42(2) 6631 2836 *Email:* upk-uzpi@login.cz **Staff:** 7 Prof. 1 Other **Holdings:** 32,628 books 456 journals **Language of Collection/Services:** Czech, English / Czech **Subjects:** Biotechnology, Food Sciences **Databases Used:** FSTA **Loan:** In country **Service:** In country **Photocopy:** Yes

948   Prague, Czech Republic
        Ministry of Agriculture
        Special Library
        Tesnov 17
        117 05 Prague 1
Phone: +42(2) 2181 1111 **Fax:** +42(2) 2481 0478 **Email:** webmaster@mze.cz **WWW:** www.mze.cz

Non-English Name: Ministerstvo zemedelství, Odborná knihovna **Founded:** 1918 **Type:** Government **Staff:** 2 Prof. **Holdings:** 26,000 books 184 journals **Language of Collection/Services:** Czech / Czech **Subjects:** Agricultural Development, Agricultural Economics **Loan:** In country **Service:** Inhouse **Photocopy:** Yes

949   Prague, Czech Republic
        Research Institute of Agricultural Economics
        Library
        Mánesova 75
        120 58 Prague 2
Fax: +42(2) 627-3020 **WWW:** www.vuze.cz

Non-English Name: Výzkumný ústav zemedelské ekonomiky (VÚZE), Knihovna **Former Name:** Research Institute of Agricultural Economics and Food, Výzkumný ústav ekonomiky zemedelství a vyzivy (VÚEZVZ) **Founded:** 1951 **Type:** Research **Head:** Ing. Josef Hanibal *Phone:* +42(2) 2200 0202, 627 3132 *Email:* hanibal@agrec.cz **Staff:** 2 Prof. **Holdings:** 27,500 books 100 journals **Language of Collection/Services:** Czech **Subjects:** Agricultural Development, Agricultural Economics, Food Sciences, Rural Sociology **Loan:** Inhouse **Service:** Inhouse

950   Prague, Czech Republic
        Research Institute of Agricultural Engineering
            (RIAE)
        Department of Information (DI)
        PO Box 54
        161 01 Prague 6
Location: Drnovská 507, Prague 6 - Ruzyne **Phone:** +42 (2) 3302-2223 **Fax:** +42(2) 3331-2507 **Email:** vuzt@ bohem-net.cz **WWW:** www.vuzt.cz

Non-English Name: Výzkumný ústav zemedelské techniky (VÚZT), Oddelení informatiky (OI) **Founded:** 1951 **Type:** Government **Head:** Mr. Josef Hlinka *Phone:* +42(2) 3302-2317 *Email:* vuzt@bohem-net.cz **Staff:** 8 Prof. **Holdings:** 5,000 books 45 journals **Language of Collection/Services:** Czech, English/Czech, English **Subjects:** Agricultural Engineering, Animal Production, Biotechnology, Crop Production **Databases Used:** Agris **Loan:** In country **Service:** In country **Photocopy:** Yes

951 Prague, Czech Republic
Research Institute of Animal Production
Technical Library
Pratelství 815
104 00 Prague 10
Phone: +42(2) 6771 1747 **Fax:** +42(2) 6771 1448 **Email:** urban@novel.vuzv.cz

Non-English Name: Výzkumný ústav zivocisné výroby (VÚZV), Technická knihovna **Type:** Government **Staff:** 6 Prof. 360 Other **Holdings:** 4,500 books 50 journals **Language of Collection/Services:** Czech / Czech **Subjects:** Agricultural Development, Agricultural Economics, Animal Behavior, Animal Husbandry, Biotechnology, Deer, Education, Food Sciences, Veterinary Medicine

952 Prague, Czech Republic
Research Institute of Brewing and Malting PLC
    (RIBM PLC)
Information Services and Library (ISL)
Lípová 15
120 44 Prague 2
Fax: +42(2) 291756 **Email:** vupsvtei@pha.inecnet.cz

Non-English Name: Výzkumný ústav pivovarský a sladarský a.s. (VÚPS a.s.), Vedeckotechnické informace a knihovna (VTEI) **Founded:** 1887 **Type:** Research **Head:** PhDr. Hana Kantorová **Phone:** +42(2) 2491 5384 **Staff:** 1 Prof. 2 Other **Holdings:** 3,000 books 30 journals **Language of Collection/Services:** Czech, English / Czech **Subjects:** Beers, Beverages, Brewery Byproducts, Brewing, Fermentation, Malting **Databases Used:** Brew Info **Loan:** Inhouse **Service:** In country **Photocopy:** Yes

♦953 Prague, Czech Republic
Research Institute of Flour Milling and Baking
    Industries
Department of Scientific-Technical Information,
    Technical Library
Na Pankráci 30
140 00 Prague 4
Phone: +42(2) 438341/9 ext 326

Non-English Name: Výzkumný ústav mlynského a pekárenského prumyslu (VÚMPP), Oddelení vedecko-technických informací, Technická knihovna **Founded:** 1945 **Type:** Research **Head:** Dr. Marie Hrusková **Phone:** +42(2) 434035 **Staff:** 6 Prof. **Holdings:** 8,000 books 30 journals **Language of Collection/Services:** Czech, English **Subjects:** Food Sciences **Loan:** Internationally **Service:** Inhouse **Photocopy:** No

954 Prague, Czech Republic
VUC Praha, plc.
Technical Library
Komoranska 30
143 19 Prague 4 - Modrany
Phone: +42(2) 402-3250 ext 295 **Fax:** +42(2) 402-4030 **Email:** vucpraha@mbox.vol.cz **WWW:** www.vucpraha.cz

Non-English Name: VUC Praha, a.s. (VÚZV), Technická knihovna **Former Name:** Výzkumný ústav cukrovarnicky, Sugar Research Institute **Founded:** 1928 **Type:** Business **Head:** Dr. Pavla Bruhova **Phone:** +42(2) 402-3250 ext 281

Staff: 3 Prof. 3 Other **Holdings:** 10,000 books 50 journals **Language of Collection/Services:** Czech / Czech **Subjects:** Sugar Industry, Sugarbeet **Photocopy:** Yes

955 Prague, Czech Republic
Water Research Institute
Information Center
Podbabská 30
160 62 Prague 6
Fax: +42(2) 311-3804 **Email:** knihovna@vuv.cz **WWW:** www.vuv.cz

Non-English Name: Výzkumný ústav vodohospodársky (VÚV), Vedecko-technické a ekonomické informace (VTEI) **Founded:** 1920 **Type:** Government **Head:** Nadja Wannerová **Phone:** +42(2) 2019 7206 **Email:** wannerova@vuv.cz **Staff:** 4 Prof. **Holdings:** 25,000 books 60 journals **Language of Collection/Services:** Czech / Czech **Subjects:** Hydraulic Engineering, Hydrology, Waste Water Treatment, Water Management, Water Purification, Water Resources, Water Supply **Databases Developed:** Vodohospodárské Informace - Water **Loan:** Internationally **Service:** Internationally **Photocopy:** Yes

956 Pruhonice, Czech Republic
Academy of Sciences of the Czech Republic,
    Institute of Botany
Library
252 43 Pruhonice
Phone: +42(2) 7101 5111 **Fax:** +42(2) 6775 0031 **Email:** ibot@ibot.cas.cz **WWW:** www.ibot.cas.cz

Non-English Name: Akademie ved Ceské republiky, Botanický ústav (CSAV), Knihovna **Former Name:** Czechoslovak Academy of Sciences, Czechoslovak Botanical Society, Ceskoslovenská akademie ved (CSAV), Ceskoslovenská botanická spolecnost **Founded:** 1912 **Type:** Academic **Head:** Eva Krbová **Phone:** +42(2) 297941/9 ext 305 **Staff:** 1 Prof. 1 Other **Holdings:** 70,000 books 300 journals **Language of Collection/Services:** Czech, English, German, Russian **Subjects:** Crops, Forestry, Horticulture, Plant Pathology **Specializations:** Botany, Mycology **Loan:** Inhouse

957 Pruhonice, Czech Republic
Research and Breeding Institute of Ornamental
    Gardening (RIOG)
Department of Scientific-Technical Information
252 43 Pruhonice
Location: Near Prague **Phone:** +42(2) 6775 0027 **Fax:** +42(2) 6775 0023 **Email:** vti@vuoz.cz

Non-English Name: Výzkumný a šlechtitelský ústav okrasného zahradnictví (VŠÚOZ), Oddelení vedecko-technických informací (VTI) **Founded:** 1956 **Type:** Government **Head:** Ing. Jan Weger **Phone:** +42(2) 6775 0288 **Email:** weger@universe.env.cz **Staff:** 2 Prof. **Holdings:** 20,000 books 70 journals **Language of Collection/Services:** Czech, Slovak, Russian, German, English / Czech **Subjects:** Biotechnology, Horticulture, Landscape Architecture, Landscape Planning, Plant Pathology, Soil Science **Specializations:** Ornamental Plants **Loan:** Internationally **Service:** In country **Photocopy:** Yes

◆958   Slatinany, Czech Republic
Stud Farm Slatinany
Library / Branch Information Center
538 21 Slatinany

Location: District Chrudim **Phone:** +42(455) 83135 **Fax:**
+42(455) 83265

Non-English Name: Hrebcín Slatinany, Knihovna/Oborové
informacní stredisko **Former Name:** Research Station for
Horse Breeding, Vyzkumná stanice pro chov koní (VSCHK)
Founded: 1956 **Type:** Research **Head:** Sylva Kostálová
Phone: +42(455) 83135 **Staff:** 1 Prof. **Holdings:** 4,500
books 22 journals **Language of Collection/Services:** Czech,
German, English **Subjects:** Animal Husbandry, Food Sci-
ences, Farming, Horse Breeding, Sport, Veterinary Medicine
Loan: In country **Service:** Internationally **Photocopy:** Yes

959   Troubsko, Czech Republic
Research Institute for Fodder Plants, Ltd. -
        Troubsko (RIFP)
Information Centre
664 41 Troubsko

Phone: +42(5) 4722-7380 **Fax:** +42(5) 4722-7385 **Email:**
vupt@brno.ics.muni.cz **WWW:** www.bm.cesnet.cz/~vupt

Non-English Name: Výzkumný ústav pícninársky, spol.
s.r.o. Troubsko (VÚP), Informacní stredisko **Former Name:**
Research and Breeding Institute for Fodder Plants, Forage
Crops Research Station Brno-Troubsko, Výzkumný a
šlechtitelský ústav pícninársky Troubsko (VSÚP) **Founded:**
1964 **Type:** Business **Head:** dr. Jan Nedelnik *Phone:* +42(5)
4722-7380 *Email:* vupt@brno.ics.muni.cz **Staff:** 1 Prof.
Holdings: 50,000 books 50 journals **Language of Collec-
tion/Services:** Czech, English / Czech **Subjects:** Agricultural Development, Agricultural Economics, Biotechnology,
Crops, Farming, Food Sciences, Plant Pathology, Soil **Specializations:** Fodder Crops **Databases Used:** Biomedline
Loan: In country **Service:** Internationally **Photocopy:** Yes

960   Ústí nad Labem, Czech Republic
SETUZA a.s.
Technical Information Department
Zukovova 100
400 29 Ústí nad Labem

Phone: +42(47) 529 2991/4 **Fax:** +42(47) 529 3899
WWW: www.setuza.cz

Non-English Name: SETUZA a.s., Oddelení technickoekonomických informací (OTEI) **Former Name:** Research
Institute of Fat Industry, Výzkumný ústav tukového prumyslu (VÚTP) **Founded:** 1961 **Type:** Business **Head:** Vera
Slavícková *Email:* vera. slavickova@setuza.cz *Phone:* +42
(47) 529 2991 **Staff:** 3 Prof. **Holdings:** 10,000 books 150
journals **Language of Collection/Services:** Czech, Russian,
German, English / Chinese **Subjects:** Food Sciences **Specializations:** Fat Products, Margarine, Oilseeds **Loan:** Inhouse **Service:** Inhouse **Photocopy:** Yes

961   Vikyrovice, Czech Republic
Rapotín Research Institute for Cattle Breeding,
        Ltd.
Center of Scientific and Technical Information
Výzkumný 267

788 13 Vikyrovice 4
Location: Sumperk-Vikyrovice **Phone:** +42(649) 214101
Fax: +42(649) 215702 **Email:** vuchs_rapotin@ova.pvtnet.
cz

Non-English Name: Výzkumný ústav pro chov skotu, s.r.o.
(VÚCHS), Oborové stredisko vedeckotechnickych infor-
macní **Founded:** 1953 **Type:** Business **Staff:** 1 Prof. **Hold-
ings:** 9,288 books 18 journals **Language of Collection/ Ser-
vices:** Czech / Czech **Subjects:** Agricultural Economics,
Agricultural Research, Animal Production, Biotechnology,
Crop Production, Feed Industry **Specializations:** Animal
Breeding, Artificial Insemination, Cattle, Goats, Pigs, Poul-
try, Sheep **Loan:** In country **Service:** In country **Photocopy:**
Yes

962   Vodnany, Czech Republic
Research Institute of Fish Culture and
        Hydrobiology
Scientific Information Centre
Zátiši 728/II
389 25 Vodnany

Phone: +42(342) 382402 **Fax:** +42(342) 382396 **Email:**
vurh@vurh.jcu.cz **WWW:** www.jcu.cz/~vurh

Non-English Name: Jihoceské univerzita Ceské budejovice, Výzkumný ústav rybársky a hydrobiologicky (JU,
VÚRH), Oddelení vedecko-technických informací **Founded:** 1961 **Type:** Government **Head:** Ing. Vykusová Blanka
Email: vykusova@vurh.jcu.cz **Staff:** 1 Prof. 1 Other **Holdings:** 12,920 books 2,081 journals **Language of Collection/
Services:** Czech, English / Czech, English **Subjects:** Biology, Environment, Fish Diseases, Fisheries **Loan:** Internationally **Service:** In country **Photocopy:** Yes

963   Zatec, Czech Republic
Hop Research Institute Co., Ltd.
Institute Library
Kadanská ul. 2525
438 46 Zatec

Phone: +42(397) 732111 **Fax:** +42(397) 732150 **Email:**
jiri.koren@telecom.cz

Non-English Name: Chmelarský institut s.r.o., Ústavní knihovna **Former Name:** Výzkumný a šlechtitelský ústav
chmelarský **Founded:** 1971 **Type:** Research **Head:** Mrs.
Burešová J. *Phone:* +42(397) 732111 **Staff:** 2 Prof. **Holdings:** 5,000 books 10 journals **Language of Collection/Ser-
vices:** Czech / Czech **Subjects:** Hops **Databases Used:**
Agricola; Agris **Loan:** Inhouse **Service:** In country **Photocopy:** Yes

Denmark

964   Aalborg, Denmark
Aalborg University
University Library, Branch Library for
        Technology and Natural Science
Sohngaardsholmvej 57
DK-9000 Aalborg

Phone: +45 9635 9410 **Fax:** +45 9814 1832 **Email:** sohn@aub.auc.dk **WWW:** www.auc.dk **OPAC:** a500.aub.auc.dk:4505/ALEPH

Head: Kirsten Rønbøl *Phone:* +45 9635 9347 *Email:* krl@aub.auc.dk

965 Aarhus, Denmark
Museum of Natural History
Library
Universitetsparken
DK-8000 Aarhus C

Phone: +45 8612 9777 **Fax:** +45 8613 0882 **Email:** musbib@nathist.aau.dk **WWW:** www.au.kd/uk/tilknyt/nathist/index.html

Non-English Name: Naturhistorisk Museum, Biblioteket **Founded:** 1941 **Type:** Academic **Staff:** 1 Other **Holdings:** 10,000 books 110 journals **Language of Collection/Services:** English/Danish **Subjects:** Biology, Entomology, Natural History, Taxonomy, Zoology **Loan:** Do not loan **Service:** Inhouse **Photocopy:** Yes

966 Aarhus, Denmark
University of Aarhus, Institute of Biological Sciences
Library
Universitetsparken, Building 135
DK-8000 Aarhus C

Fax: +45 8612 5175 **WWW:** www.biology.aau.dk

Non-English Name: Aarhus Universitet, Biologisk Institut, Biblioteket **Founded:** 1979 **Type:** Academic **Head:** Mrs. Merete Gerdel *Phone:* +45 8942 3188 *Email:* merte.gerdel@biology.aau.dk **Staff:** .5 Other **Holdings:** 6,700 books 87 journals **Language of Collection/Services:** English **Subjects:** Entomology **Loan:** Via State Library **Photocopy:** No

♦967 Auning, Denmark
Agricultural Museum
Reference Library
Gammel Estrup
DK-8963 Auning

Fax: +45 8648 4182

Non-English Name: Dansk Landbrugsmuseum, Reference Biblioteket **Type:** Government **Head:** Annette Hoff *Phone:* +45 8648 3444 **Staff:** 1 Other **Holdings:** 10,000 books **Subjects:** Agriculture (History) **Loan:** Do not loan **Photocopy:** No

968 Charlottenlund, Denmark
Ministry of Food Agriculture and Fisheries,
Danish Institute for Fisheries Research,
Department of Marine Fisheries (DIFRES)
Library
Charlottenlund Slot
DK-2920 Charlottenlund

Phone: +45 3396 3300 **Fax:** +45 3396 3333 **Email:** hfi@dfu.min.dk **WWW:** www.dfu.min.dk

Non-English Name: Ministeriet for Fødevarer, Landbrug og Fisheri, Danmarks Fiskeriundersogelser, Biblioteket **Founded:** 1889 **Type:** Academic **Staff:** 3 Prof. 1 Other **Holdings:** 55,000 books 800 journals **Language of Collection/Ser-**vices: English / Danish **Subjects:** Fisheries **Specializations:** Marine Biology **Loan:** Internationally **Service:** Internationally **Photocopy:** Yes

969 Copenhagen, Denmark
Botanical Library
Sølvgade 83
DK-1307 Copenhagen K

Phone: +45 3532 2250 **Fax:** +45 3532 2255 **WWW:** www.nathimus.ku.dk/bot/botmus.htm

Non-English Name: Botanisk Centralbiblioteket **Founded:** 1752 **Head:** Peter Henrik Wagner *Email:* peterw@bot.ku.dk

970 Copenhagen, Denmark
Federation of Danish Agricultural Cooperatives (FDC)
Library
Axelborg
Vesterbrogade YA
DK-1620 Copenhagen V

Fax: +45 3312 6148

Non-English Name: Danske Andelsselskaber, Biblioteket **Founded:** 1899 **Type:** Association **Head:** Lonni Gulliksen, Annie Linvald *Phone:* +45 3312 1419 **Staff:** 1 Other **Holdings:** 6,000 books **Language of Collection/Services:** Danish **Subjects:** Cooperatives **Loan:** Inhouse **Service:** Inhouse **Photocopy:** Yes

971 Copenhagen, Denmark
Ministry of Food, Agriculture and Fisheries,
Danish Veterinary Laboratory
Library
Bülowsvej 27
DK-1790 Copenhagen V

Phone: +45 3530 0100 **Fax:** +45 35 30 0120 **WWW:** www.svs.dk

Non-English Name: Ministeriet for Fødevarer, Landbrug og Fisheri, Statens Veterinære Serumlaboratorium (SVS), Biblioteket **Type:** Government **Staff:** 1 Prof. **Holdings:** 40 journals **Language of Collection/Services:** English **Subjects:** Animal Husbandry, Biotechnology **Specializations:** Veterinary Medicine **Loan:** Inhouse **Service:** Inhouse **Photocopy:** Yes

972 Esbjerg, Denmark
University of Southern Denmark, Esbjerg
Library
Niels Bohrs Vej 9
DK-6700 Esbjerg

Phone: +45 7914 1120 **Fax:** +45 7914 1130 **WWW:** www.sdu.dk, www.suc.dk/niv/niv2/bib-nbv9.htm

Non-English Name: Sydjysk Universitet, Esbjerg, Biblioteket **Founded:** 1972 **Type:** Academic **Head:** Inge Kørvel *Phone:* +45 7914 1122 *Email:* iuk@suc.suc.dk **Staff:** 3 Prof. 3 Other **Holdings:** 600 books 20 journals **Subjects:** Agricultural Economics, Cooperatives, Rural Sociology **Photocopy:** Yes **Loan:** Internationally

973 Frederiksberg, Denmark
Royal Veterinary and Agricultural University

Danish Veterinary and Agricultural Library
Dyrlægevej 13
DK-1870 Frederiksberg C

Phone: +45 3528 2145 **Fax:** +45 3528 2138 **Email:** dvjb@ kvl.dk **WWW:** www.kvl.dk **OPAC:** www.dvjb.kvl.dk

Non-English Name: Den Kgl. Veterinær- og Landbohøjskole (KVL), Danmarks Veterinær- og Jordbrugsbibliotek (DVJB) **Founded:** 1783 **Type:** Academic **Head:** Ulla Jeppesen *Phone:* +45 3528 2127 *Email:* uwj@kvl.dk **Staff:** 16 Prof. 14 Other **Holdings:** 400,000 books 4,200 journals **Subjects:** Agriculture (Tropics), Agribusiness, Agricultural Development, Agricultural Economics, Agricultural Engineering, Animal Husbandry, Biotechnology, Crops, Education/Extension, Entomology, Farming, Fisheries, Food Sciences, Forestry, Horticulture, Plant Pathology, Soil Science, Veterinary Medicine, Water Resources **Networks:** AGRIS **Databases Used:** CAS **Loan:** Internationally **Photocopy:** Yes

974   Hillerød, Denmark
University of Copenhagen
Freshwater-Biological Laboratory
Helsingørgade 51
DK-3400 Hillerød

Fax: +45 4824 1476 **WWW:** www.zi.ku.dk/zi/fbl

Non-English Name: Københavns Universitet **Founded:** 1897 **Type:** Government **Head:** Peter C. Dall *Phone:* +45 4826 7600 *Email:* flabms@inet.uni2.dk **Staff:** 2 Other **Holdings:** 50 journals **Language of Collection/Services:** English **Subjects:** Freshwater Biology **Loan:** Inhouse **Service:** Inhouse **Photocopy:** Yes

975   Hørsholm, Denmark
Ministry of Environment and Energy, Danish
Forest and Landscape Research Institute
(DFLRI)
Library
Hørsholm Kongevej 11
DK-2970 Hørsholm

Phone: +45 4576 3200 **Fax:** +45 4576 3233 **Email:** fsl@ fsl.dk **WWW:** www.fsl.dk/index.htm

Non-English Name: Miljø- og Energiministeriet, Forskningscentret for Skov & Landskab, Biblioteket **Former Name:** Danish Forest Experiment Station, Statens Forstlige Forsøgsvæsen **Founded:** 1901 **Type:** Government **Staff:** .5 Other **Holdings:** 2,000 books 350 journals **Language of Collection/Services:** Danish **Subjects:** Ecology, Forestry, Landscape **Specializations:** Forestry (History - Denmark - 1900-) **Loan:** Do not loan **Photocopy:** No

976   Lyngby, Denmark
Ministry of Food, Agriculture and Fisheries,
Danish Institute for Fisheries Research,
Department of Seafood Research
Library
Technical University, Building 221
DK-2800 Lyngby

Phone: +45 4588 3322 **Fax:** +45 4588 4774 **Email:** fish@dfu.min.dk **WWW:** www.dfu.min.dk

Non-English Name: Ministeriet for Fødevarer, Landbrug og Fisheri, Landbrug og Fiskeri **Former Name:** Fiskeriministeriets, Forsøgslaboratorium **Founded:** 1931 **Type:** Government **Staff:** 1 Prof. **Holdings:** 135 journals **Subjects:** Aquaculture, Biotechnology, Fisheries, Food Sciences **Loan:** In country **Photocopy:** Yes

977   Roskilde, Denmark
Danish Meat Research Institute (DMRI)
Library
Maglegaardsvej 2
DK-4000 Roskilde

Location: Maglegaardsvej 2 **Phone:** +45 4630 3030 **Fax:** +45 4630 3132 **WWW:** www.dmri.dk

Non-English Name: Slagteriernes Forskningsinstitut, Biblioteket **Founded:** 1954 **Type:** Research **Head:** Inge Boje Brun, Christel U. Dall *Phone:* +45 4630 3337, +45 4630 3242 *Email:* ibb@dmri.dk, cud@dmri.dk **Staff:** 2 Prof. 1 Other **Holdings:** 12,000 books 450 journals **Language of Collection/Services:** Danish, English, German **Subjects:** Food Sciences **Specializations:** Meat, Slaughtering Equipment **Databases Developed:** Databases about meat technology, only access inhouse **Databases Used:** Biosis; CABCD; CAS; FSTA **Loan:** In country **Service:** Internationally **Photocopy:** Yes

978   Slagelse, Denmark
Ministry of Food, Agriculture and Fisheries,
Danish Institute of Agricultural Sciences
Library
Research Centre Flakkebjerg
DK-4200 Slagelse

Fax: +45 5811 3301 **WWW:** www.agrsci.dk

Non-English Name: Ministeriet for Fødevarer, Landbrug og Fisheri, Danmarks JordbrugsForskning, Biblioteket **Former Name:** Research Centre for Plant Protection, Statens Planteavlsforsøg **Founded:** 1913 **Type:** Government **Head:** Morten Brendstrup-Hansen *Phone:* +45 5811 3366 *Email:* morten.brendstruphansen@agrsci.dk **Staff:** 1 Prof. .5 Other **Holdings:** 250 journals **Language of Collection/Services:** English **Subjects:** Agronomy, Entomology, Plant Pathology **Networks:** DANBIB **Databases Used:** Comprehensive **Loan:** Do not loan **Photocopy:** Yes

979   Stubbekoebing, Denmark
Naesgaard Agricultural College
Library
DK-4759 Stubbekoebing

Phone: +45 5444 4138 **Fax:** +45 5444 4156 **WWW:** www.naesgaard.dk

Non-English Name: Næsgaard Agerbrugsskole, Biblioteket

980   Valby, Denmark
Carlsberg Research Center
Library
Gamle Carlsberg Vej 10
DK-2500 Valby

Phone: +45 3327 5201 **Fax:** +45 3327 4761 **WWW:** www.crc.dk/index.html

Non-English Name: Carlsberg Forskningscenter, Biblioteket **Former Name:** United Breweries **Founded:** 1876 **Type:** Business **Staff:** 1 Prof. 1 Other **Holdings:** 10,000 books 400 journals **Language of Collection/Services:** English / Danish, English **Subjects:** Biotechnology, Crops, Plants, Water Resources **Specializations:** Brewing **Loan:** Inhouse **Service:** Inhouse **Photocopy:** Yes

Djibouti

981   **Djibouti**
        Ministère de l'Agriculture, Elevage et Mer
        Centre de Documentation Agricole (CDA)
        BP 224

Founded: 1984 **Type:** Government **Head:** Abdi Elmi Bogoreh *Phone:* +253 351774 **Staff:** 2 Other **Holdings:** 2,050 books 20 journals **Subjects:** Agricultural Economics, Animal Production, Crop Production, Fisheries, Forestry **Networks:** AGRIS

Dominica

♦982   **Roseau, Dominica**
        Ministry of Agriculture (MOA)
        Agricultural Library
        Botanical Gardens
        Roseau
Fax: +1(809) 448-7999

Founded: 1980 **Type:** Government **Head:** Mrs. Vanessa Martin *Phone:* +1(809) 448-2731 ext 413 **Holdings:** 2,500 books **Language of Collection/Services:** English **Subjects:** Agricultural Development, Agricultural Economics, Agricultural Research, Animal Husbandry, Aquaculture, Fisheries, Forestry, Land Resources, Nature Conservation, Plant Pests **Databases Used:** Agris **Photocopy:** Yes

983   **Roseau, Dominica**
        Ministry of Education, Sports and Youth Affairs
        National Documentation Centre - Agricultural
            Library
        Government Headquarters
        Kennedy Avenue
        Roseau
Phone: +1(767) 448-7928 **Fax:** +1(767) 448-7928 **Email:** library@cwdom.dm

Founded: 1990 **Type:** Government **Staff:** 1 Prof. 3 Other **Language of Collection/Services:** English / English **Subjects:** Agricultural Development, Agriculture (Tropics), Animal Husbandry, Education/Extension, Fisheries, Forestry, Horticulture, Plants, Soil **Specializations:** Agriculture (Dominica) **Networks:** AGRIS **Databases Used:** Agris; CABCD **Loan:** In country **Photocopy:** Yes

Dominican Republic

984   **La Vega, Dominican Republic**
        Salesian Agronomy Institute
        Agricultural Library
        Apdo 206
        La Vega

Non-English Name: Instituto Agronómico Salesiano (IAS), Biblioteca Agrícola **Former Name:** Escuela Agrícola Salesiana **Founded:** 1968 **Type:** Academic **Head:** P. Juan Artale, P. Francisco M. Brache *Phone:* +1(809) 242-6059 **Staff:** 1 Prof. 4 Other **Holdings:** 5,950 books 12 journals **Language of Collection/Services:** Spanish/Spanish **Subjects:** Entomology, Horticulture, Plant Pathology, Soil Science, Veterinary Medicine **Specializations:** Crops, Animal Husbandry, Farming, Plants, Soil **Loan:** In country **Service:** In country **Photocopy:** Yes

985   **Santo Domingo, Dominican Republic**
        Dominican Republic Industrial Technology
            Institute
        Documentation and Technical Information and
            Library
        Av. Nunez de Cáceres, Esq. Oloff Palme
        Santo Domingo
Phone: +1(809) 566-8121 ext 244/209 **Fax:** +1(809) 227-8808 **Email:** indotec@codetel.net.do, indotec@aacr.net **WWW:** www.indotec.gov.do

Non-English Name: Instituto Dominicano de Tecnología Industrial (INDOTEC), Documentación e Información Técnica y Biblioteca **Founded:** 1974 **Type:** Government **Head:** Inq. Fabián Tello, Lic. Altagracia Pequero *Phone:* +1(809) 566-8121 ext 242/208 **Staff:** 3 Prof. 3 Other **Holdings:** 600 journals 17,598 books **Language of Collection/Services:** English / Spanish **Subjects:** Animal Husbandry **Specializations:** Fisheries, Agricultural Engineering, Food Sciences **Databases Used:** Comprehensive **Loan:** In country **Service:** In country **Photocopy:** Yes

986   **Santo Domingo, Dominican Republic**
        State Department of Agriculture
        National Center for Agriculture Documentation
        Centro de los Heroes
        Apdo 325-2
        Santo Domingo, Distrito Nacional
Location: State Department of Agriculture Edificio "B"

Non-English Name: Secretaría de Estado de Agricultura, Centro Nacional de Documentación Agropecuaria (CENADORA) **Founded:** 1978 **Type:** Government **Head:** Ramon Pereyra C. *Phone:* +1(809) 532-5458 **Staff:** 3 Prof. 8 Other **Holdings:** 4,500 books 280 journals **Subjects:** Agricultural Economics, Crop Production, Horticulture, Marketing **Networks:** AGRIS **Loan:** In country **Photocopy:** Yes

987   **Santo Domingo, Dominican Republic**
        Universidad Nacional Pedro Henríquez Ureña
            (UNPHU)
        Biblioteca Campus I
        Edificio Principal

Segunda Planta, Parte Central
Ave. John F. Kennedy Km. 5½
Santo Domingo
Phone: +1(809) 562-6601 ext 283, 284

Founded: 1966 **Type:** Academic **Subjects:** Comprehensive **Loan:** In country **Photocopy:** Yes

Ecuador

988   **Portoviejo, Ecuador**
        Technical University of Manabi, Agriculture
            Engineering Faculty
        Library
        Apdo 82
        Portoviejo, Manabi
Location: Av. Universitaria s/n **Phone:** +593(4) 632853 **Fax:** +593(4) 651509

Non-English Name: Universidad Técnica de Manabi, Facultad de Ingeniería Agronómica, Biblioteca **Founded:** 1981 **Type:** Academic **Subjects:** Agricultural Economics, Agricultural Engineering, Animal Production, Biotechnology, Crop Production, Entomology, Fisheries, Horticulture, Marketing, Pastures, Plant Pathology, Plant Protection, Sericulture **Loan:** In country **Photocopy:** Yes

989   **Quito, Ecuador**
        National Institute for Agricultural Research
        Information and Documentation Department
        Apdo. 2600
        Quito
Phone: +593(2) 567645, 528650 **Fax:** +593(2) 504240
Email: informat@dinfor.ecuanex.net.ec

Non-English Name: Instituto Nacional Autónomo de Investigaciones Agropecuarias (INIAP), Departamento de Información y Documentación **Type:** Government **Head:** Aida de Diener **Networks:** AGRIS

990   **Quito, Ecuador**
        San Francisco de Quito University
        Library
        Casilla Postal 17-12-841
        Quito
Location: Campus Combayá, Via Interoceánica y Jardines del Este, Circulo de Cumbayá, Quito **Phone:** +593(2) 895 723 ext 373 **Fax:** +593(2) 890070 attn: Referencia **Email:** fpinfo@mail.usfq.edu.ec **WWW:** www.usfq.edu.ec **Ariel IP:** 192.188.53.91

Non-English Name: Universidad San Francisco de Quito (USFQ), Biblioteca **Founded:** 1988 **Type:** Academic **Head:** Jorge Sosa *Phone:* +593(2) 895723/5 ext 373 *Email:* jorge@ mail.usfq.edu.ec **Staff:** 15 Prof. 14 Other **Holdings:** 55,000 books 580 journals **Language of Collection/Services:** Spanish, English, French, Chinese, Thai / Spanish, English **Subjects:** Comprehensive **Specializations:** Crops, Soil **Loan:** Internationally **Service:** In country **Photocopy:** Yes

991   **Riobamba, Ecuador**
        Polytechnic School of Chimborazo, Agricultural
            Engineering Faculty

Library
Casilla 4703
Riobamba, Chimborazo
Location: Km l, Panamericana Sur **Phone:** +593() 961969, 961977

Non-English Name: Escuela Superior Politécnica de Chimborazo, Facultad de Ingeniería Agronómica (ESPOCH), Biblioteca **Founded:** 1967 **Type:** Academic **Staff:** 1 Prof. 1 Other **Holdings:** 18,500 books 30 journals **Subjects:** Agricultural Economics, Crop Production, Entomology, Fruit Growing, Horticulture, Soil Science **Loan:** In country **Photocopy:** Yes

Egypt

992   **Alexandria, Egypt**
        National Institute of Oceanography and Fisheries
        Library
        Kayed Bay
        Al-Anfoushi
        Alexandria
Phone: +20(3) 480-1553, 480-1499, 480-7138 **Fax:** +20(3) 480-1174

Former Name: Institute of Hydrobiology, Institute of Oceanography and Fisheries **Founded:** 1931 **Type:** Government **Head:** Mr. Ahmad Kotb **Staff:** 4 Prof. 1 Other **Holdings:** 5,000 books 10 journals **Language of Collection/ Services:** English **Subjects:** Fish Farming, Fisheries **Loan:** Do not loan **Service:** In country **Photocopy:** Yes

993   **Cairo, Egypt**
        Ain Shams University, Network Information
            Center (ASU, NET)
        Library
        Abbassia 11566
        Cairo
Phone: +20(2) 285-9249, 285-4063, 283-1051 **Fax:** +20(2) 285-9251 **WWW:** www.shams.eun.eg/ainshams.htm

Type: Academic **Head:** Prof. Dr. Ahmed Zaki Badr **Staff:** 13 Prof. **Holdings:** 50,000 books 47 journals **Language of Collection/Services:** English **Subjects:** Agriculture (Tropics), Agribusiness, Agricultural Development, Agricultural Economics, Agricultural Engineering, Animal Husbandry, Biotechnology, Crops, Entomology, Farming, Fisheries, Food Sciences, Forestry, Horticulture, Plant Pathology, Soil Science, Veterinary Medicine, Water Resources **Loan:** In country **Service:** In country **Photocopy:** Yes

994   **Cairo, Egypt**
        Food and Agriculture Organization, Near East
            Regional Office (FAO, RNE)
        RNE Library
        PO Box 2223
        Cairo
Location: 11 El Eslah El Zerai St. **Phone:** +20(2) 331-6000 ext 3905 **Fax:** +20(2) 3495981 **Email:** fao-rne@field. fao.org

Former Name: RNEA Library **Founded:** 1962 **Type:** International **Head:** Mrs. Omnia Moussa *Phone:* +20(2) 331-

6174 *Email:* omnia.moussa@field.fao.org **Staff:** 1 Prof. 1 Other **Holdings:** 35,000 books 11 journals **Language of Collection/Services:** English, Arabic **Subjects:** Agriculture (Tropics), Agricultural Development, Agricultural Economics, Agricultural Engineering, Animal Husbandry, Crops, Extension, Entomology, Farming, Fisheries, Food Sciences, Forestry, Horticulture, Plant Pathology, Soil Science, Veterinary Medicine, Water Resources **Specializations:** Empahsis on subjects as they relate to the Near East region **Databases Used:** Agris; ASFA; CABCD; CARIS **Loan:** Do not loan **Service:** Internationally **Photocopy:** Yes

995   Cairo, Egypt
         General Organization for Fisheries Development
         Library
         El-Tayaran Street
         Nasr- City
         Cairo
Phone: +20(2) 262-0118/9 **Fax:** +20(2) 262-0117

Head: Mrs. Karima Tawfik

996   Cairo, Egypt
         Institute of National Planning
         Documentation and Publishing Center
         Nasr City
         Cairo
OPAC: 163.121.19.203/national_plan_eng.htm

Founded: 1960 **Type:** Government **Head:** Mr. Salem Salem Zeid *Phone:* +20(2) 263-6047 **Staff:** 18 Prof. 13 Other **Holdings:** 1,550 books 4 journals **Subjects:** Agricultural Development, Agricultural Planning, Cooperatives, Agricultural Policy **Loan:** Do not loan **Photocopy:** Yes

997   Cairo, Egypt
         Ministry of Agriculture and Land Reclamation
         Egyptian Documentation and Information Centre
             for Agriculture (EDICA)
         Foreign Agricultural Relations Department
         Nadi-El Seid Street
         PO Box 145 Dokki
         Cairo
Fax: +20(2) 335-2937

Founded: 1975 **Type:** Government **Head:** Mr. Gamal Andrawos *Phone:* +20(2) 349-2970/1 **Staff:** 16 Prof. 14 Other **Holdings:** 2,100 books 45 journals **Language of Collection/Services:** Arabic, English **Subjects:** Agriculture (Tropics), Agricultural Development, Agricultural Economics, Agricultural Engineering, Animal Husbandry, Crops, Education/Extension, Entomology, Farming, Food Sciences, Horticulture, Plant Pathology, Soil Science, Veterinary Medicine **Networks:** AGRIS **Databases Developed:** EGDB - Egyptian Agricultural Bibliography; EG-CARIS - Egyptian current agricultural research **Databases Used:** Comprehensive **Loan:** In country **Service:** Internationally **Photocopy:** Yes

998   Cairo, Egypt
         Ministry of Agriculture and Land Reclamation,
             Agricultural Research Center, Horticulture
             Research Institute (ARC, HRI)
         Library
         Giza-Orman
         Cairo
Phone: +20(2) 725033 **WWW:** www.agri.gov.eg/horti.htm

Type: Government **Staff:** 2 Prof. 2 Other **Subjects:** Horticulture **Loan:** In country **Photocopy:** Yes

999   Delta Barrage, Egypt
         National Water Research Center, Hydraulics
             Research Institute (HRI)
         Library
         Delta Barrage 13621
Phone: +20(2) 218-9657 **Fax:** +20(2) 218-9539 **Email:** draulics@intouch.com **WWW:** www.linknet-int.com/hydraulicsresearchinstitute.htm

Former Name: Hydraulics and Sediment Research Institute (HSRI) **Founded:** 1949 **Type:** Government **Head:** Dr. M.B.A. Saad *Phone:* +20(2) 218-8268 **Staff:** 56 Prof. 54 Other **Holdings:** 1,600 books 1,000 journals **Language of Collection/Services:** Arabic, English / Arabic, English **Subjects:** Calibration, Coasts, Drainage, Engineering, Hydraulic Structures, Instrumentation, Rivers **Specializations:** Coasts, Erosion, Hydraulics, Irrigation, Sedimentation **Loan:** In country **Service:** Internationally **Photocopy:** No

1000   Giza, Egypt
         Ministry of Agriculture and Land Reclamation
         Egyptian National Agriculture Library (ENAL)
         7 Nadi El-Seid Street
         Dokki
         Giza
Phone: +20(2) 335-0819, 335-0242 **Fax:** +20(2) 335-1302 **Email:** mahmoud@nile.enal.sci.eg **WWW:** www.agri.gov.eg/librar.htm, nile.enal.sci.eg

Former Name: Agricultural Research Center, General Department for Libraries and Information Center **Founded:** 1920 **Type:** Government **Head:** Eng. Serag Abdel Hafiz **Staff:** 6 Prof. 30 Other **Holdings:** 20,000 books **Subjects:** Agricultural Economics, Animal Health, Crops, Field Crops, Horticulture, Plant Pathology, Plant Protection, Soil Science **Loan:** In country **Photocopy:** Yes

1001   Giza, Egypt
         Ministry of Agriculture and Land Reclamation,
             Agricultural Research Center, Agricultural
             Extension and Rural Development Research
             Institute (ARC, AERDRI)
         Library
         9 El-Gamaa Street
         Giza
Phone: +20(2) 571-5301/2 **Fax:** +20(2) 571-5303 **WWW:** www.agri.gov.eg/exten.htm

Founded: 1977 **Head:** Dr. Mohamed Shafei Sallam

1002   Giza, Egypt
         Ministry of Agriculture and Land Reclamation,
             Agricultural Research Center, Animal
             Production Research Institute (ARC, APRI)
         Library
         9 El-Gamaa Street

Giza
Phone: +20(2) 337-2462, 337-2482 **Fax:** +20(2) 337-4270
WWW: www.agri.gov.eg/animal.htm

Founded: 1971 **Head:** Dr. Hassan Mohamed El-Noubi **Subjects:** Animal Production

1003   Giza, Egypt
        Ministry of Agriculture and Land Reclamation,
            Agricultural Research Center, Cotton
            Research Institute (ARC, CRI)
        Library
        9 El-Gamaa Street
        Giza
Phone: +20(2) 572-5035 **Fax:** +20(2) 572-3442 **WWW:**
www.agri.gov.eg/cott.htm

Head: Dr. Ahmad El-Gohary **Subjects:** Cotton

1004   Giza, Egypt
        Ministry of Agriculture and Land Reclamation,
            Agricultural Research Center, Plant Pathology
            Research Institute (ARC, PPATHRI)
        Library
        9 El-Gamaa Street
        Giza
Phone: +20(2) 572-4893 **Fax:** +20(2) 570-4438 **WWW:**
www.agri.gov.eg/plant.htm

Founded: 1973 **Head:** Dr. Abdallah Abdel-Moneim **Subjects:** Plant Pathology

1005   Giza, Egypt
        Ministry of Agriculture and Land Reclamation,
            Agricultural Research Center, Plant
            Protection Research Institute (ARC, PPRI)
        Library
        9 El-Gamaa Street
        Giza
Phone: +20(2) 573-8630, 572-0944, 360-1296 **Fax:** +20(2)
335-6175/6 **WWW:** www.agri.gov.eg/prot.htm

Type: Academic **Head:** Dr. Galal Mahmoud Ibrahim **Staff:**
1 Prof. 2 Other **Holdings:** 6,000+ books 46 journals **Subjects:** Entomology, Plant Protection **Loan:** Do not loan **Photocopy:** Yes

1006   Giza, Egypt
        Ministry of Agriculture and Land Reclamation,
            Agricultural Research Center, Soil and Water
            Research Institute (ARC, SWRI)
        Library
        9 El-Gamaa Street
        Giza
Phone: +20(2) 572-0608 **Fax:** +20(2) 572-0608 **WWW:**
www.agri.gov.eg/soil.htm

Founded: 1971 **Head:** Dr. Nabil El-Sayed **Subjects:** Soil,
Water Resources

1007   Giza, Egypt
        Ministry of Agriculture and Land Reclamation,
            Agricultural Research Center, Sugar Crops
            Research Institute (ARC, SCRI)
        Library

9 El-Gamaa Street
Giza
Phone: +20(2) 573-5699 **Fax:** +20(2) 573-5699 **WWW:**
www.agri.gov.eg/sugar.htm

Founded: 1983 **Head:** Ms. Mervat Ismail **Subjects:** Sugar

1008   Kafr El-Sheikh, Egypt
        Tanta University, Faculty of Agriculture
        Postgraduate Library
        Kafr El-Sheikh
Phone: +20(40) 322-2762 **WWW:** dec1.tantaeun.eg

Founded: 1958 **Type:** Academic **Staff:** 1 Prof. 4 Other
Holdings: 4,200 books **Subjects:** Agricultural Economics,
Animal Husbandry, Botany, Dairy Science, Entomology,
Extension, Food Sciences, Genetics, Horticulture, Mechanization, Microbiology, Pesticides, Plant Pathology, Poultry,
Rural Sociology **Loan:** Do not loan **Photocopy:** No

1009   Kallioubeya, Egypt
        Zagazig University (Banha Branch), Faculty of
            Agriculture, Moshtohor
        Library
        Toukh
        Kallioubeya
Phone: +20(13) 460306 **Fax:** +20(13) 460306

Head: Dr. Mohamed El-Said Zaki

◆**1010   Zagazig, Egypt**
        Zagazig University, Faculty of Agriculture
        Library
        Falouga Street
        Zagazig

Founded: 1960 **Type:** Government **Head:** Yehia Mohamed
Mosa Serag *Phone:* +20(55) 322360 **Staff:** 1 Prof. 23 Other
Holdings: 18,676 books 40 journals **Photocopy:** Yes

El Salvador

1011   San Salvador, El Salvador
        Ministry of Agriculture and Livestock, National
            Center of Agricultural Technology
        Information and Documentation Office
        San Andrés, La Libertad
        Apartado Postal 885
        San Salvador, La Libertad

Non-English Name: Ministerio de Agricultura y Ganadería,
Centro Nacional de Tecnología Agropecuaria (CENTA),
Oficina de Información y Documentación **Founded:** 1945
Type: Government **Head:** Juan Antonio Flores *Phone:* +503
282066 **Staff:** 2 Prof. 2 Other **Holdings:** 30,000 books 350
journals **Subjects:** Animal Production, Crop Production, Extension, Irrigation, Soil Science **Loan:** In country **Photocopy:** No

1012   San Salvador, El Salvador
        University of El Salvador, Agriculture Science
            Faculty
        Ing. Agr. Félix Choussy B. Library

Apdo 747
San Salvador
Location: Final 25 av. Nte. Ciudad Universitaria **Fax:** +503 225-1506 **Email:** agro@bib.ues.edu.sv **WWW:** www.ues.edu.sv

Non-English Name: Universidad de El Salvador, Facultad de Ciencias Agronómicas (AGRONOMIA), Biblioteca Ing. Agr. Félix Choussy B. **Founded:** 1964 **Type:** Academic **Head:** Francisco Osorio Vargas *Phone:* +503 252572 *Email:* agro@bib.ues.edu.sv **Staff:** 4 Prof. 2 Other **Holdings:** 7,000 books 645 journals **Language of Collection/Services:** Spanish / Spanish **Subjects:** Agricultural Economics, Animal Production, Biotechnology, Crop Production, Entomology, Farming, Plant Pathology, Plant Protection, Veterinary Medicine **Networks:** AGRIS **Loan:** In country **Photocopy:** No

Equatorial Guinea

♦**1013　Malabo, Equatorial Guinea**
　　　　Ministry of Agriculture, Animal Husbandry and
　　　　　　Rural Development
　　　　National Agricultural Information Centre
　　　　Carretera a Luba, s/n
　　　　Malabo

Non-English Name: Ministerio de Agricultura, Ganadería y Desarrollo Rural (MINAGRI), Centro Nacional de Información y Documentación Agraria (CENIDA) **Founded:** 1985 **Type:** Government **Head:** Josefa Esambus Andeme *Phone:* +240(9) 2150, 3464 **Staff:** 2 Prof. **Holdings:** 3,520 books 20 journals **Subjects:** Agricultural Economics, Animal Production, Crop Production, Forestry

Eritrea

1014　Asmara, Eritrea
　　　　University of Asmara (UA)
　　　　Library
　　　　PO Box 1220
　　　　Asmara

Location: Zoba 6, Adm. 06 **Phone:** +291 16-161935 **Fax:** +291 1-162236 **WWW:** www.primenet.com/~ephrem/ orgs/auhome

Former Name: Asmara University **Founded:** 1969 **Type:** Academic **Holdings:** 42,000 books 50 journals **Subjects:** Agricultural Economics, Animal Husbandry, Crops, Farming **Specializations:** Fisheries, Plants, Soil Science, Water Resources **Loan:** Inhouse **Service:** Inhouse **Photocopy:** No

Estonia

1015　Jõgeva, Estonia
　　　　Estonian Scientific Research Institute of
　　　　　　Agriculture, Jõgeva Plant Breeding Institute
　　　　　　(Jõgeva PBI)
　　　　Library
　　　　48309 Jõgeva

Fax: +372(77) 60126 **Email:** pbi@jogeva.merit.ee

Non-English Name: Jõgeva Sordiaretuse Instituut (Jõgeva SAI), Raamatukogu **Founded:** 1956 **Type:** Government **Head:** Tiina Uusmaa *Phone:* 372(77) 22565 **Staff:** 1 Prof. 1 Other **Holdings:** 19,500 books 3 journals **Language of Collection/Services:** Estonian, Russian / Estonian, English **Subjects:** Agricultural Development, Biotechnology, Crops, Extension, Plant Pathology **Loan:** In country **Service:** In country **Photocopy:** Yes

♦**1016　Saku, Estonia**
　　　　Estonian Scientific Research Institute of
　　　　　　Agriculture and Land Reclamation
　　　　Library
　　　　Teaduse St., 1
　　　　EE3400 Saku, Harju Region

Founded: 1958 **Type:** Government **Holdings:** 34,800 books **Subjects:** Reclamation

1017　Tartu, Estonia
　　　　Estonian Agricultural University (EAU)
　　　　Library
　　　　5 Kreutzwaldi St.
　　　　EE-2400 Tartu

Phone: +372(7) 422500 **Fax:** +372(7) 421053 **Email:** eaulib@eau.ee **WWW:** www.eau.ee **Ariel IP:** 193.40.44. 102

Non-English Name: Eesti Pollumajandusülikool (EPMÜ), Raamatukogu **Former Name:** Estonian Agricultural Academy **Founded:** 1951 **Type:** Academic **Head:** Mrs. Tiina Tohvre *Phone:* +372(7) 421950 *Email:* tohvre@eau.ee **Staff:** 19 Prof. 7 Other **Holdings:** 482,840 books 210 journals **Language of Collection/Services:** Estonian / Estonian **Subjects:** Agricultural Economics, Crops, Agricultural Engineering, Animal Husbandry, Education, Farming, Food Sciences, Forestry, Horticulture, Plants, Soil Science, Veterinary Medicine, Water Resources **Networks:** AGRIS; CARIS **Databases Used:** Comprehensive **Loan:** Internationally **Service:** Internationally **Photocopy:** Yes

♦**1018　Tartu, Estonia**
　　　　Estonian Scientific Research Institute of Stock
　　　　　　Breeding and Veterinary Science
　　　　Library
　　　　Kreitsvaldi St., 1
　　　　EE2400 Tartu

Phone: +372(7) 422240 **Fax:** +372(7) 434897

Non-English Name: Eisti Lsomakasvatuse je Veterinaaria Teadusliku Uurimise Instituut (ELVI TRK), Raamatukogu **Founded:** 1957 **Type:** Academic **Head:** Saima Vilu *Phone:* +372(7) 422273 **Staff:** 1 Prof. 1 Other **Holdings:** 35,600 books 30 journals **Language of Collection/Services:** Russian / Estonian **Subjects:** Animal Breeding, Animal Husbandry, Livestock, Veterinary Medicine **Loan:** In country **Service:** In country **Photocopy:** Yes

Ethiopia

1019 Addis Ababa, Ethiopia
Agri Service Ethiopia (ASE)
Library
PO Box 2460
Addis Ababa

Location: Debre Zeit Road **Phone:** +251(1) 651212 **Fax:** +251(1) 654088 **Email:** ase@telecom.net.et

Founded: 1970 **Type:** Association **Head:** Merid Belete *Phone:* +251(1) 651212, 655514 *Email:* ase@telecom.net.et **Staff:** 1 Prof. **Holdings:** 4,500 books 10 journals **Language of Collection/Services:** English / English **Subjects:** Agricultural Credit, Agricultural Development, Crops, Animal Husbandry, Agricultural Economics, Agriculture (Tropics), Health Services, Education/Extension, Farming, Food Sciences, Forestry, Gender Issues, Horticulture, Soil Science, Plant Pathology **Specializations:** Extension, Organic Gardening, Rural Development, Soil Conser vation, Water Conservation **Databases Developed:** Land Use database - includes literature on sustainable land use in Ethiopia held in 19 NGO libraries **Loan:** In country **Service:** Inhouse **Photocopy:** Yes

1020 Addis Ababa, Ethiopia
Commission for Higher Education, Jimma Junior
College of Agriculture
Library
PO Box 307
Jimma, Keffa
Addis Ababa

Founded: 1962 **Type:** Government **Staff:** 1 Prof. 3 Other **Holdings:** 14,000 books **Subjects:** Agricultural Economics, Agricultural Engineering, Animal Husbandry, Crops **Loan:** Do not loan **Photocopy:** No

1021 Addis Ababa, Ethiopia
Ethiopian Agricultural Research Organization,
Technical Support Department
Information Services
PB 2003
Addis Ababa

Fax: +251(1) 611222 **Email:** iar@telecom.net.et

Former Name: Institute of Agricultural Research **Founded:** 1983 **Type:** Government **Head:** Abebe Kirub *Phone:* +251 (1) 184171 *Email:* iar@telecom.net.et **Staff:** 10 Prof. 15 Other **Holdings:** 31,000 books 150 journals **Language of Collection/Services:** English / English, Amharic **Subjects:** Agricultural Economics, Agricultural Engineering, Animal Production, Biotechnology, Crop Production, Crops, Education/Extension, Entomology, Farming, Fisheries, Forestry, Food Sciences, Horticulture, Plant Pathology, Plant Protection, Plants, Soil, Veterinary Medicine, Water Resources **Networks:** AGRIS **Databases Used:** Agricola; Agris; CABCD; TROPAG & RURAL **Loan:** Inhouse **Service:** Inhouse **Photocopy:** Yes

1022 Addis Ababa, Ethiopia
Forestry Research Center (FRC)

Library
PO Box 30708
Addis Ababa

Location: Shoa **Phone:** +251(1) 182982 **Email:** frc@ padis.gn.apc.org

Founded: 1985 **Type:** Government **Staff:** 1 Prof. 3 Other **Holdings:** 1,600 books 50 journals **Language of Collection/Services:** English / English **Subjects:** Forestry, Soil Science **Loan:** Inhouse **Service:** Inhouse **Photocopy:** Yes

1023 Addis Ababa, Ethiopia
Institute of Agricultural Research, Holetta
Agricultural Research Center
Library
PO Box 6282
Addis Ababa

Location: Holetta **Email:** harc@telecom.net.et

Founded: 1970 **Type:** Government **Staff:** 1 Prof. 1 Other **Holdings:** 2,585 books 250 journals **Language of Collection/Services:** English / English **Subjects:** Animal Husbandry, Crops, Plant Protection, Soil Science **Loan:** Inhouse **Service:** Inhouse **Photocopy:** No

1024 Addis Ababa, Ethiopia
International Livestock Research Institute (ILRI)
Information Services
PO Box 5689
Addis Ababa

Fax: +251(1) 188191 **Email:** ilri-information@cgiar.org **WWW:** www.cgiar.org/ilri

Former Name: International Livestock Centre for Africa (ILCA) **Founded:** 1975 **Type:** International **Head:** Mr. Normand Demers *Phone:* +251(1) 183215 **Staff:** 10 Prof. 12 Other **Holdings:** 30,000 books 266 journals **Language of Collection/Services:** English, French / English, French **Subjects:** Agricultural Economics, Ecology, Livestock Farming, Fodder Crops, Sociology **Specializations:** Animal Husbandry **Databases Used:** Comprehensive **Loan:** In country **Service:** Internationally **Photocopy:** Yes

1025 Addis Ababa, Ethiopia
Ministry of Agriculture (MoA)
Library and Documentation Service
PO Box 62347
Addis Ababa

Phone: +251(1) 150379, 510455

Non-English Name: Gibrina Minister, Btemetsahiftna Documentation Ageglot **Former Name:** Ministry of Agriculture and Environmental Protection **Founded:** 1948 **Type:** Government **Staff:** 4 Prof. 1 Other **Holdings:** 37,000 books 8 journals **Language of Collection/Services:** English / Amharic, English **Subjects:** Crops, Farming Systems, Forestry, Livestock, Soil Conservation **Loan:** Inhouse **Service:** Inhouse **Photocopy:** Yes

1026 Addis Ababa, Ethiopia
National Library and Archives
PO Box 717
Addis Ababa

Phone: +251(1) 512241

Founded: 1944 **Type:** Government **Head:** Feleke Wolde
Holdings: 125,000 books

1027   Addis Ababa, Ethiopia
        Plant Genetic Resources Centre/Ethiopia
             (PGRC/E)
        Library
        PO Box 30726
        Addis Ababa
Location: Next to Kenyan Embassy **Phone:** +251(1) 882-4047

Founded: 1980 **Type:** Government **Staff:** 2 Other **Hold-ings:** 2,132 books 15 journals **Language of Collection/Ser-vices:** English / English **Subjects:** Agriculture (Tropics), Genetics, Plant Pathology **Specializations:** Gene Banks **Loan:** In country **Photocopy:** Yes

1028   Ambo, Ethiopia
        Ambo College of Agriculture (ACA)
        Library
        PO Box 19
        Ambo
Email: aca.ethiopia@telecom.net.et

Former Name: Ambo Agricultural School, Ambo Institute of Agriculture **Founded:** 1952 **Type:** Academic **Holdings:** 17,326 books 18 journals **Head:** Berhanu Ersamo *Phone:* +251(1) 360096 *Email:* aca.ethiopia@telecom.net.et **Staff:** 2 Prof. 10 Other **Language of Collection/Services:** Am-haric, English **Subjects:** Agriculture (Tropics), Agribusi-ness, Agricultural Development, Agricultural Economics, Agricultural Engineering, Animal Husbandry, Crops, Bio-technology, Education/Extension, Entomology, Farming, Fisheries, Food Sciences, Forestry, Horticulture, Plant Pa-thology, Plants, Soil Science, Veterinary Medicine, Water Resources **Loan:** Inhouse **Service:** Inhouse **Photocopy:** Yes

1029   Awassa, Ethiopia
        Awassa Junior College of Agriculture (AJCA)
        Library
        PO Box 5
        Awassa, Sidamo
Founded: 1978 **Type:** Academic **Staff:** 2 Prof. 11 Other **Holdings:** 20,000 books 110 journals **Language of Collec-tion/Services:** English **Subjects:** Agriculture (Tropics), Agricultural Engineering, Animal Husbandry, Crops, Edu-cation/Extension, Entomology, Food Sciences, Forestry, Horticulture, Home Economics, Plant Pathology, Plants, Soil Science, Veterinary Medicine **Loan:** In country **Photocopy:** Yes

1030   Awassa, Ethiopia
        Institute of Agricultural Research, Awassa
             Research Center
        Library
        PB 6
        Awassa
Email: arc@padis.gn.apc.org

Founded: 1960 **Staff:** 1 Other **Holdings:** 350 books 80 jour-nals **Subjects:** Crop Production, Horticulture, Plant Protec-tion, Plant Breeding, Plants, Soil Fertility

1031   Bahir Dar, Ethiopia
        Bahir-Dar Polytechnic Institute
        Library
        PO Box 26
        Bahir Dar
Phone: +251(8) 200277, 200113

Founded: 1963 **Type:** Academic **Head:** Degife Gabre Tsadik *Phone:* +251(8) 200277 **Staff:** 1 Prof. 6 Other **Hold-ings:** 5,000 books **Language of Collection/Services:** Eng-lish **Subjects:** Agribusiness, Agricultural Engineering, Crops, Farming, Horticulture, Soil Science **Loan:** Do not loan **Photocopy:** No

1032   Bahir Dar, Ethiopia
        Bureau of Planning and Economic Development
             (BOPED)
        Documentation and Information Centre
        PO Box 217
        Bahir Dar
Phone: +251(0) 200792 ext 22 **Fax:** +251(0) 200444

Former Name: Office of the National Committee for Cen-tral Planning, Planning and Economic Development for Re-gion 3, Library and Information Centre **Founded:** 1985 **Type:** Government **Head:** Mr. Wubshet Tamirat *Phone:* +251(0) 200792 **Staff:** 3 Prof. **Holdings:** 6,509 books 11 journals **Language of Collection/Services:** Amharic, Eng-lish/Amharic, English **Subjects:** Agricultural Development, Economic Development, Environment, Regional Develop-ment, Regional Planning, Social Development **Loan:** In-house **Service:** Inhouse **Photocopy:** Yes

1033   Debre Zeit, Ethiopia
        Addis Ababa University, Faculty of Veterinary
             Medicine
        Library
        PO Box 34
        Debre Zeit
Location: Shoa **Email:** vet.medicine@telecom.net.et
WWW: www.abyssiniacybergateway.net/ethiopia/aau_home.html

Founded: 1979 **Type:** Academic **Head:** Ato Hassen Red-wan *Phone:* +251() 338314 *Email:* vet.medicine@telecom.net.et **Staff:** 1 Prof. 11 Other **Holdings:** 10,000 books **Lan-guage of Collection/Services:** English **Subjects:** Animal Husbandry, Veterinary Medicine **Loan:** In country **Photo-copy:** No

1034   Dire Dawa, Ethiopia
        Alemaya University of Agriculture (AUA)
        Library
        PO Box 138
        Dire Dawa, Alemaya Li
Phone: +251(5) 112364, 111399, 112374 **Fax:** +251(5) 114008 **Email:** aua18@ncic.gn.apc.org

Former Name: AAU College of Agriculture, Alemaya **Founded:** 1962 **Type:** Academic **Head:** Mhadi Ahmed *Phone:* +251(5) 111399/400 ext 244 **Staff:** 2 Prof. 32 Other **Holdings:** 39,000 books 156 journals **Language of Collec-tion/Services:** English **Subjects:** Agriculture (Tropics), Ag-ricultural Economics, Agricultural Engineering, Animal

Husbandry, Crops, Education/Extension, Entomology, Farming, Food Sciences, Forestry, Horticulture, Plant Pathology, Plants, Soil Science, Veterinary Medicine **Loan:** In country **Photocopy:** Yes

1035 Shashemene, Ethiopia
Ministry of Agriculture, Wondo Genet College of Forestry (WGCF)
Library
PO Box 128
Shashemene

Phone: +251(6) 100522 **Fax:** +251(6) 100500 **Email:** wgcf@padis.gn.apc.org

Former Name: Wondo Genet Forest Resources Institute **Founded:** 1978 **Type:** Academic **Staff:** 1 Prof. 1 Other **Holdings:** 550 books 20 journals **Language of Collection/Services:** English **Subjects:** Agriculture (Tropics), Agricultural Development, Agricultural Engineering, Entomology, Farming, Plant Pathology **Specializations:** Ecology, Soil Conservation, Soil Science, Water Conservation, Wildlife **Loan:** Internationally **Photocopy:** No

Fiji

1036 Lautoka, Fiji Islands
Fiji Pine Ltd.
Library
PO Box 521
Lautoka

Location: 85 Drasa Avenue **Phone:** +679 661511 **Fax:** +679 661784 **Email:** fijipine@is.com.fj

Type: Business **Head:** Ms. Amelia Makutu

1037 Lautoka, Fiji Islands
Fiji Sugar Corporation, Ltd., Sugarcane Research Centre (SCRC)
Library
PO Box 3560
Lautoka

Location: Visamiti Terrace, Drasa Avenue, FSC Compound **Phone:** +679 660800 **Fax:** +679 661082

Former Name: Agricultural Experimental Station **Founded:** 1904 **Type:** Research **Head:** Jai S. Gawanden *Phone:* +679 663547 *Email:* jai@fsc.com.fj **Staff:** 1 Prof. 10 Other **Holdings:** 1,500 books 53 journals **Language of Collection/Services:** English / English **Subjects:** Sugarcane **Loan:** In country **Photocopy:** Yes

1038 Lautoka, Fiji Islands
Komiti for the Advancement of Nutrition and Agriculture (KANA)
Library
PO Box 451
Lautoka

Location: 12 Cakau Street **Phone:** +679 662535 **Fax:** +679 663414 **Email:** kanaproject@is.com.fj

Type: Non-government **Subjects:** Agricultural Development, Nutrition **Photocopy:** Yes

1039 Nadi, Fiji Islands
Ministry of Agriculture, Fisheries and Forests, Department of Agriculture, Research Division (MAFF)
Legalega Research Station Library
PO Box 9086
Nadi Airport

Location: Legalega, Nadi **Phone:** +679 722522

Type: Government **Head:** Mr. Madhu Prasad

1040 Nausori, Fiji Islands
Fiji College of Agriculture (FCA)
Central Library
PO Box 1544
Nausori

Location: King's Road, Koronivia, Nausori **Phone:** +679 479200 **Fax:** +679 400275

Founded: 1954 **Type:** Government **Head:** Ms. Eleni Bai *Phone:* +679 479200 **Staff:** 1 Other **Holdings:** 10,000 books 450 journals **Language of Collection/Services:** English **Subjects:** Agriculture (Tropics), Agricultural Engineering, Animal Husbandry, Crops, Education/Extension, Entomology, Farming, Horticulture, Plant Pathology, Soil Science, Veterinary Medicine **Loan:** Inhouse **Service:** Inhouse

1041 Nausori, Fiji Islands
Ministry of Agriculture, Fisheries and Forests, Department of Agriculture, Research Division, Koronivia Research Station (MAFF)
Fiji Agricultural Research Information Centre
PO Box 77
Nausori

Location: Koronivia Research Station, Koronivia, Nausori **Phone:** +679 477044 **Fax:** +679 400262 **Email:** krsinfo@is.com.fj

Type: Government **Head:** Mr. Josua Wainiqolo *Phone:* +679 477044 *Email:* wainiqoloj@is.com.fj **Staff:** 1 Prof. 1 Other **Language of Collection/Services:** English / English **Subjects:** Comprehensive **Specializations:** Agricultural Research **Loan:** Inhouse **Service:** In country **Photocopy:** Yes

1042 Nausori, Fiji Islands
Ministry of Agriculture, Fisheries and Forests, Department of Agriculture, Research Division, Naduruloulou Research Station (MAFF, NRS)
Library
PO Box 77
Nausori

Location: Naduruloulou-Baulevu Road, Naitasiri (Viti Levu) **Phone:** +679 478242 **Fax:** +679 400262

Founded: 1988 **Type:** Government **Holdings:** 50 books **Language of Collection/Services:** English / English **Subjects:** Crops **Loan:** Do not loan **Service:** Inhouse **Photocopy:** No

1043 Savusavu, Fiji Islands
Ministry of Agriculture, Fisheries and Forests, Department of Agriculture, Research Division

Wainigata Research Station Library
Savusavu
Phone: +679 880495

Type: Government

1044 **Seaqaqa, Fiji Islands**
Ministry of Agriculture, Fisheries and Forests,
Department of Agriculture, Research Division
(MAFF)
Seaqaqa Research Station Library
PO Box 64
Seaqaqa, Vanua Levu
Location: Old Naduri Road, 2 km from Labasa-Seaqaqa
Highway at Nabakasobu **Phone:** +679 860233 **Fax:** +679
813634 (MAFF Labasa)

Type: Government

1045 **Sigatoka, Fiji Islands**
Ministry of Agriculture, Fisheries and Forests,
Department of Agriculture, Research Division
(MAFF)
Sigatoka Research Station Library
PO Box 24
Sigatoka
Location: Valley Road, Nacocolevu **Phone:** +679 500022
Fax: +679 520307

Founded: 1924 **Type:** Government

1046 **Suva, Fiji Islands**
Fiji Institute of Technology
Library
PB 3722
Samabula
Suva
Phone: +679 381044 **Fax:** +679 370375

Founded: 1964 **Head:** Mr. Mohan Lal *Phone:* +679 381044
Holdings: 21,000 books **Subjects:** Agricultural Engineering, Business

1047 **Suva, Fiji Islands**
Foundation for the Peoples of the South
Pacific/Fiji
Library
PO Box 14447
Suva
Location: 8 Denison Road, The Domain **Phone:** +679
300392, 314160 **Fax:** +679 304315 **Email:** fspsuva@
mailhost.sopac.org.fj

Founded: 1986 **Type:** Non-government

1048 **Suva, Fiji Islands**
International Board for Soil Research and
Management, Pacific Regional Office
(IBSRAM)
Library
PO Box 13707
Suva
Location: Konronivia Research Station, Nausori **Phone:**
+679 477770 **Fax:** +679 477770 **Email:** dowling@ibsram.
org, tdowling@is.com.fj

Founded: 1992 **Type:** Academic **Head:** Dr. Tony Dowling
Email: dowling@ibsram.org, tdowling@is.com.fj *Phone:*
+679 477770 **Holdings:** 200 books 1 journals **Language of
Collection/Services:** English / English **Subjects:** Agricultural Development, Agriculture (Tropics), Land Management, Soil **Photocopy:** Yes

1049 **Suva, Fiji Islands**
Ministry of Agriculture, Fisheries and Forests,
Department of Agriculture, Agricultural
Quarantine Division (MAFF)
Library
Private Mail Bag
Raiwaqa
Suva
Location: Ports Authority Building, Suva Wharf **Phone:**
+679 312512 **Fax:** +679 305043

Type: Government

1050 **Suva, Fiji Islands**
Ministry of Agriculture, Fisheries and Forests,
Department of Agriculture, Animal Health
and Production Division (MAFF)
Library
GPO Box 15829
Suva
Location: 10 Toa Road, Vatuwaqa **Phone:** +679 315322,
315197, 315840 **Fax:** +679 301368

Type: Government **Subjects:** Animal Health, Animal Production

1051 **Suva, Fiji Islands**
Ministry of Agriculture, Fisheries and Forests,
Department of Agriculture, Information and
Communication Section (MAFF)
Headquarters Library
Private Mail Bag
Raiwaqa
Suva
Location: Robinson Complex, Grantham Road, Suva
Phone: +679 384233 **Fax:** +679 385048, 385576

Former Name: Ministry of Primary Industries **Founded:**
1980 **Type:** Government **Head:** Ms. Vasiti Boselevu *Phone:*
+679 384233 ext 255 **Staff:** 1 Other **Holdings:** 250 books
300 journals **Language of Collection/Services:** English /
English **Networks:** PULAS

1052 **Suva, Fiji Islands**
Ministry of Agriculture, Fisheries and Forests,
Department of Forestry, Information Section
(MAFF)
Library
PO Box 2218
Government Buildings
Suva
Location: 46 Knollys Street **Phone:** +679 301611, 314951,
314941 **Fax:** +679 301595

Founded: 1980 **Type:** Government **Head:** Mr. Malakai
Sevudredre *Phone:* +679 301611, 314951 **Staff:** 1 Other
Language of Collection/Services: English / English **Sub-**

jects: Forestry **Specializations:** Forest Management **Databases Used:** CABI **Loan:** Inhouse **Photocopy:** Yes

1053   **Suva, Fiji Islands**
     Ministry of Agriculture, Fisheries and Forests,
        Department of Forestry, Division of
        Silvicultural Research (MAFF)
     Silvicultural Research Centre Library
     PO Box 2218
     Government Buildings
     Suva

Location: Colo-i-Suva Forestry Station, Tamavua **Phone:** +679 322311, 322389 **Fax:** +679 320380

Type: Government **Subjects:** Silviculture

1054   **Suva, Fiji Islands**
     Ministry of Agriculture, Fisheries and Forests,
        Department of Forestry, Utilisation Division
        (MAFF)
     Library
     PO Box 2218
     Government Buildings
     Suva

Location: King's Road, Nasinu **Phone:** +679 393611 **Fax:** +679 301595

Founded: 1971 **Type:** Government **Head:** Ms. Salote Usumaki *Phone:* +679 301611 **Staff:** 1 Prof. **Holdings:** 5,000 books 50 journals **Language of Collection/Services:** English / English **Subjects:** Forestry **Specializations:** Timbers, Wood Properties **Loan:** In country **Service:** Internationally **Photocopy:** Yes

1055   **Suva, Fiji Islands**
     Ministry of Agriculture, Fisheries and Forests,
        Fisheries Department
     Fisheries Library
     PO Box 358
     Suva

Location: Lami **Phone:** +679 361122

Type: Government **Staff:** 1 Prof. 1 Other **Holdings:** 750 books 25 journals **Subjects:** Fisheries **Loan:** In country **Photocopy:** Yes

1056   **Suva, Fiji Islands**
     National Archives of Fiji
     Library
     PO Box 2125
     Government Buildings
     Suva

Location: 25 Carnarvon Street **Phone:** +679 304144

Type: Government

1057   **Suva, Fiji Islands**
     National Food and Nutrition Committee (NFNC)
     Library
     1 Clark Street
     PO Box 2450
     Government Buildings
     Suva

Phone: +679 313055 **Fax:** +679 303921

Founded: 1976 **Type:** Semi-government **Head:** Ms. Makalese Rakuita **Staff:** 11 Prof. 3 Other **Holdings:** 3,000 books 15 journals **Language of Collection/Services:** English / English **Subjects:** Agriculture (Tropics), Agribusiness, Agricultural Development, Biotechnology, Crops, Education/Extension, Farming, Fisheries, Food Sciences, Horticulture, Plant Pathology, Water Resources **Loan:** Do not loan **Service:** Inhouse **Photocopy:** Yes

1058   **Suva, Fiji Islands**
     Navuso Agricultural School
     Library
     Private Mail Bag
     Suva

Location: Navuso, Nausori **Phone:** +679 478255

Type: Academic

1059   **Suva, Fiji Islands**
     Pacific Development Institute (PDI)
     Resource Centre
     PO Box 2492
     Suva

Location: 115 Prince's Road **Phone:** +679 383-363 **Fax:** +679 384-766 **Email:** apdi@is.com.fj

Founded: 1984 **Type:** Non-government **Head:** Paul Sotutu *Phone:* +679 384-766 *Email:* apdi@is.com.fj **Staff:** 2 Prof. 1 Other **Holdings:** 1,000 books 12 journals **Language of Collection/Services:** English / English **Subjects:** Agricultural Development, Economic Development, Environment, Land Use, Fisheries, Forestry, Rural Development, Social Development **Databases Developed:** South Pacific Trade Contacts **Loan:** Do not loan **Photocopy:** Yes

1060   **Suva, Fiji Islands**
     SPC/GTZ Pacific German Regional Forestry
        Programme (PGRFP)
     Documentation Centre
     GPO Box 14041
     Suva

Location: House No. 10, Forum Secretariat, Ratu Sukuna Road **Phone:** +679 305983 **Fax:** +679 315446 **Email:** gtz@is.com.fj

Type: Government **Language of Collection/Services:** English / English **Subjects:** Forestry **Photocopy:** Yes

1061   **Suva, Fiji Islands**
     Secretariat of the Pacific Community, FAO/SPC
        Pacific Islands Forests and Trees Support
        Programme (SPC)
     Library
     Private Mail Bag
     Suva

Location: Forum Secretariat, Ratu Sukuna Road, Suva **Phone:** +679 300432, 305244 **Fax:** +679 305212 **Email:** spforest@spc.org.fj

Former Name: South Pacific Forestry Development Project **Type:** Regional **Head:** Mr. Tang Hon Tat *Email:* tangh@ spc.org.fj **Staff:** 1 Other

1062   Suva, Fiji Islands
        Secretariat of the Pacific Community (SPC)
        Regional Agricultural Information Centre
        Private Mail Bag
        Suva

Location: 1st Floor, Westpac Building, Luke Street, Nabua **Phone:** +679 370733 **Fax:** +679 370021 **Email:** spc@spc.org.fj

Former Name: South Pacific Commission, Plant Protection Library, SPC Regional Agricultural Library **Founded:** 1971 **Type:** International **Head:** Susana Taufa *Phone:* +679 370783 *Email:* susanat@spc.org.fj **Staff:** 1 Prof. 2 Other **Holdings:** 14,000 books 50 journals **Language of Collection/Services:** English / English, French **Subjects:** Agriculture (Tropics), Agricultural Development, Agricultural Economics, Agroforestry, Animal Husbandry, Biological Control, Biotechnology, Crops, Education/Extension, Entomology, Forestry, Information Systems, Pesticides, Plant Pathology, Plant Protection, Plants, Quarantine, Soil Science, Veterinary Medicine **Specializations:** Pacific Islands, Plant Protection, Root Crops, Tropical Crops **Databases Developed:** CATALOG - SPC Agriculture Library Catalogue; PULAS - Pacific Union List of Agricultural Serials; PIAJ - Pacific Index to Agricultural Journals **Databases Used:** Agris; CABCD **Loan:** Inhouse **Service:** SPC region **Photocopy:** Yes

1063   Suva, Fiji Islands
        University of the South Pacific (USP)
        Library
        PO Box 1168
        Suva

Location: Laucala Bay Road **Phone:** +679 313900 **Fax:** +679 300380 **Email:** library@usp.ac.fj **WWW:** www.usp.ac.fj

Type: Academic **Head:** Dr. Esther Williams *Email:* williams_e@usp.ac.fj

1064   Suva, Fiji Islands
        University of the South Pacific, School of Pure
            and Applied Sciences, South Pacific Regional
            Herbarium (USP)
        Library
        PO Box 1168
        Suva

Location: Laucala Bay Road **Phone:** +679 212559 **Fax:** +679 302548 **WWW:** www.usp.ac.fj

Type: Academic **Head:** Dr. Michael F. Doyle *Email:* doyle_m@usp.ac.fj

1065   Taveuni, Fiji Islands
        Ministry of Agriculture, Fisheries and Forests,
            Department of Agriculture, Research
            Division, Taveuni Coconut Centre (MAFF,
            TCC)
        Information Unit
        PO Box 84
        Taveuni

Location: Mua, Taveuni **Phone:** +679 880003 **Fax:** +679 880265 **Email:** tcc@is.com.fj

Founded: 1996 **Type:** Government **Head:** Mr. Tevita Kete *Phone:* +679 880003 *Email:* tcc@is.com.fj **Staff:** 3 Other **Holdings:** 150 books 10 journals **Language of Collection/Services:** English, Fijian / English, Fijian **Specializations:** Coconuts **Loan:** Inhouse **Service:** In country **Photocopy:** Yes

Finland

1066   Espoo, Finland
        Helsinki University of Technology (HUT)
        National Resource Library for Technology
        PO Box 7000
        FIN-02015 HUT Espoo

Location: Otaniementie 9 **Phone:** +358(9) 451 4124 **Fax:** +358(9) 451 4132 **WWW:** www.hut.fi **OPAC:** otatrip.hut.fi/tkk/kirjastot/search.html

Non-English Name: Teknillinen Korkeakoulu (TKK), Kirjasto **Founded:** 1849 **Type:** Academic **Head:** Sinikka Koskiala *Phone:* +358(9) 451 4111 *Email:* sinikka.koskiala@hut.fi **Staff:** 25 Prof. 30 Other **Holdings:** 500,000 books 3,500 journals **Language of Collection/Services:** English / Finnish, English, Swedish **Subjects:** Agricultural Engineering, Biotechnology, Food Sciences, Water Resources **Databases Developed:** Tenttu - information retrieval system contains several databases; OPAC, periodical holdings, Finnish technical periodicals index, and current research at HUT **Databases Used:** FSTA; Medline **Loan:** Internationally **Service:** Internationally **Photocopy:** Yes

1067   Hämeenlinna, Finland
        Finnish Meat Research Institute (FMRI)
        Information Service
        Luukkaankatu 8
        PO Box 56
        FIN-13101 Hämeenlinna

Phone: +358(3) 570 5380 **Fax:** +358(3) 570 5389 **WWW:** www.htk.fi/ltk/index.htm

Non-English Name: Lihateollisuuden Tutkimuskeskus (LTK), Tietopalvelu **Founded:** 1940 **Type:** Research **Staff:** 1 Prof. **Holdings:** 2,100 books 50 journals **Language of Collection/Services:** Finnish **Subjects:** Education/Extension, Food Sciences **Specializations:** Meat **Loan:** Inhouse **Service:** Inhouse **Photocopy:** Yes

1068   Helsinki, Finland
        Central Union of Agricultural Producers and
            Forest Owners
        Information Service
        POB 510
        FIN-00101 Helsinki

Location: Simonkatu 6 **Fax:** +358(0) 13115 371 **WWW:** www.mtk.fi

Non-English Name: Maa- ja metsätaloustuottajain Keskusliitto (MTK), Tietopalvelu **Founded:** 1984 **Type:** Association **Head:** Jaana Kaakkola *Phone:* +358(0) 13115 436 *Email:* jaana.kaakkola@mtk.fi **Staff:** 1 Prof. .5 Other **Holdings:** 10,000 books 320 journals **Language of Collection/Services:** Finnish **Subjects:** Agribusiness, Agricultural Eco-

nomics, Agricultural Policy, Cooperation **Loan:** In country
Service: Inhouse **Photocopy:** Yes

1069　Helsinki, Finland
　　　　Finnish Environment Institute (FEI)
　　　　Library
　　　　PO Box 140
　　　　FIN-00251 Helsinki
Location: Entrance at Kesäkatu 6, Staircase C, 2nd floor,
00260 Helsinki **Fax:** +358(9) 4030 0190 **WWW:** www.
vyh.fi

Non-English Name: Suomen ympäristökeskus **Founded:**
19760 **Type:** Government **Head:** Ms. Elisa Paavilainen
Phone: +358(9) 40300 204 *Email:* elisa.paavilainen@vyh.fi
Staff: 6 Prof. 4 Other **Holdings:** 65,000 books 550 journals
Subjects: Environment, Water Resources **Loan:** Interna-
tionally **Service:** Internationally **Photocopy:** Yes

1070　Helsinki, Finland
　　　　Finnish Pulp and Paper Research Institute
　　　　Technical Information Management
　　　　POB 70
　　　　FIN-02151 Helsinki
Location: Tekniikantie 2, Otaniemi **Phone:** +358(9)
4371283 **Fax:** +358(9) 4371302 **Email:** library@kcl.fi
WWW: www.kcl.fi **OPAC:** www.nipsu.kcl.fi

Non-English Name: Oy Keskuslaboratorio, Centrallaboratorium Ab (KCL), Tiedonhallinta **Founded:** 1937 **Type:**
Business **Head:** Jorma Paakko *Phone:* +358(9) 4371266
Email: jorma.paakko@kcl.fi **Staff:** 3 Prof. 5 Other **Holdings:** 60,000 books 400 journals **Subjects:** Pulp and Paper
Industry **Specializations:** Environmental Protection, Packaging, Paper, Paperboard, Printing, Pulps **Databases
Developed:** KCL databases - books, articles, meetings,
methods, patents, paperbase express **Loan:** Do not loan **Service:** Internationally **Photocopy:** Yes

1071　Helsinki, Finland
　　　　Ministry of Agriculture and Forestry
　　　　Information Centre, Statistics
　　　　PO Box 250
　　　　FIN-00171 Helsinki
Location: Liisankatu 8G **Phone:** +358(0) 134211 **Fax:**
+358(0) 13421573 **WWW:** www.mmm.fi/tike

Non-English Name: Maa- ja Metsätalousministeriön, Tieto-
palvelukeskus, Tilasto **Former Name:** National Board of
Agriculture, Maatilahallituksen Kirjasto **Founded:** 1988
Type: Government **Head:** Mr. Niilo Hintikka *Phone:*
+358(0) 134211 **Staff:** 15 Other **Holdings:** 1,500 books
Language of Collection/Services: Finnish / Finnish **Subjects:** Agricultural Statistics **Databases Developed:** Maltika
- Agricultural statistics, database host UTKK **Loan:** Do not
loan **Service:** Internationally **Photocopy:** Yes

1072　Jokioinen, Finland
　　　　Agricultural Research Centre of Finland
　　　　Library
　　　　FIN-31600 Jokioinen
Phone: +358(3) 4188 232 **Fax:** +358(3) 4188 339 **Email:**
kirjasto@mtt.fi **WWW:** www.mtt.fi

Non-English Name: Maatalouden Tutkimuskeskus (MTT),
Kirjasto **Founded:** 1935 **Type:** Government **Head:** Maj-Lis
Aaltonen *Phone:* +358(3) 41881 *Email:* maj-lis.aaltonen@
mtt.fi **Staff:** 3 Prof. .5 Other **Holdings:** 40,000 books 700
journals **Language of Collection/Services:** Finnish / Finn-
ish **Subjects:** Agricultural Engineering, Animal Husbandry,
Crops, Entomology, Farming, Food Sciences, Horticulture,
Plant Pathology, Plants, Soil Science **Databases Used:** Agri-
cola; Agris; CABCD; FSTA **Loan:** Internationally **Service:**
Internationally **Photocopy:** Yes

1073　Jokioinen, Finland
　　　　Agricultural Research Centre of Finland
　　　　Plant Protection Library
　　　　FIN-31600 Jokioinen
Phone: +358(3) 41881 **Fax:** +358(3) 4188551 **WWW:**
www.mtt.fi

Non-English Name: Maatalouden Tutkimuskeskus (MTT),
Kasvintuotanto Kasvinsuojelu **Founded:** 1898 **Type:** Gov-
ernment **Head:** Anja Mikkola *Phone:* +358(3) 41882551
Email: anja.mikkola@mtt.fi **Language of Collection/Ser-
vices:** English **Subjects:** Entomology, Nematology, Pest
Management, Plant Pathology, Plant Protection, Weeds
Photocopy: Yes

1074　Jokioinen, Finland
　　　　Agricultural Research Centre of Finland, Food
　　　　　　Research Institute
　　　　Library
　　　　FIN-31600 Jokioinen
Fax: +358(3) 4188 444 **WWW:** www.mtt.fi

Non-English Name: Maatalouden Tutkimuskeskus, Elintar-
vikkeiden Tutkimuslaitos, Kirjasto **Founded:** 1931 **Type:**
Government **Head:** Anne Pihlanto-Leppälä *Phone:* +358(3)
4188 276 *Email:* anne.pihlanto-leppala@mtt.fi **Staff:** 1
Other **Holdings:** 5,000 books 100 journals **Subjects:** Dairy
Science, Food Sciences, Microbiology, Nutrition **Loan:** Do
not loan **Photocopy:** Yes

1075　Mustiala, Finland
　　　　Häme Polytechnic, Mustiala Agricultural College
　　　　Library
　　　　FIN-31310 Mustiala
Location: Mustialantie 105 **Phone:** +358(3) 6464755 **Fax:**
+358(3) 6464750 **Email:** silja.shepherd@mustiala.hamkk.
fi **WWW:** www.mustiala.hamkk.fi/eng/index.htm

Non-English Name: Hämeen Ammattikorkeakoulu, Mustialanyksikkö (HAMKK Mustiala), Kirjasto **Former Name:**
Mustiala Agricultural Institute, Mustialan Maatalousoppilaitos **Founded:** 1840 **Type:** Government **Head:** Silja Shepherd *Email:* silja.shepherd@mustiala.hamkk.fi *Phone:* +358
(3) 6464755 **Staff:** 1 Prof. 1 Other **Holdings:** 7,500 books
170 journals **Language of Collection/Services:** Finnish /
Finnish, English **Subjects:** Rural Industry **Loan:** In country
Service: In country **Photocopy:** Yes

1076　University of Helsinki, Finland
　　　　University of Helsinki
　　　　Botanical Library
　　　　PO Box 7

FIN-00014 University of Helsinki
Location: Unioninkatu 44 **Fax:** +358(9) 1918656 **WWW:** www.helsinki.fi

Non-English Name: Helsingin Yliopisto, Kasvitieteen Kirjasto **Type:** Academic **Head:** Marjatta Rautiala *Phone:* +358 (9) 191-8608 *Email:* marjatta.rautiala@helsinki.fi **Staff:** 1 Prof. 1 Other **Language of Collection/Services:** English, Finnish **Networks:** HELKA; LINDA **Subjects:** Botany **Photocopy:** Yes **Loan:** In country **Service:** In country

1077 University of Helsinki, Finland
University of Helsinki
Viikki Science Library
PO Box 62
Viikinkaari 11 A
SF-00014 University of Helsinki
Phone: +358(9) 191 58028 **Fax:** +358(9) 191 58011 **Email:** viikki-lib@helsinki.fi **WWW:** helix.helsinki.fi/ infokeskus/lib/index.html **OPAC:** wwwls.lib.helsinki.fi/ en/form.html

Non-English Name: Helsingin Yliopisto (HY), Vetenskapliga biblioteket i Vik **Founded:** 1999 **Type:** Academic **Language of Collection/Services:** Finnish, English / Finnish, English **Subjects:** Comprehensive **Specializations:** Biology, Biotechnology, Ecology, Environment, Food Sciences, Forestry **Networks:** AGRIS **Databases Developed:** AGRIC - sub database of KATI, Finnish articles on agricultural, food and household sciences **Databases Used:** Comprehensive **Loan:** Internationally **Service:** Internationally **Photocopy:** Yes

1078 University of Helsinki, Finland
University of Helsinki, Department of Applied Zoology
Library
PO Box 27
FIN-00014 University of Helsinki
Location: Latokartanonkaari 5 **Fax:** +358(0) 7085463 **WWW:** honeybee.helsinki.fi/mmsel/kirjasfi.htm **OPAC:** www.helsinki.fi/lumme

Non-English Name: Helsingin Yliopisto, Soveltavan Eläintieteen Laitos, Kirjasto **Former Name:** Department of Agricultural and Forest Zoology Library, Maatalous- ja Metsäeläintieteen Laitos Kirjasto **Founded:** 1902 **Type:** Academic **Head:** Mrs. Leena Tulisalo *Phone:* +358(0) 7085362 *Email:* leena.tulisalo@helsinki.fi **Staff:** 1 Prof. **Holdings:** 16,700 books 135 journals **Language of Collection/Services:** English, German, Finnish, Swedish / English, German, Finnish, Swedish **Subjects:** Beekeeping, Entomology, Wildlife Management, Zoology **Networks:** HELKA; LINKA **Databases Used:** Comprehensive **Loan:** In country **Service:** Internationally **Photocopy:** Yes

1079 University of Helsinki, Finland
University of Helsinki, Department of Plant Biology
Plant Pathology Library
PO Box 28
FIN-00014 University of Helsinki
Location: Koetilantie 5 **Phone:** +358(9) 191 58574 **Fax:** +358(9) 191 58727 **WWW:** www.helsinki.fi

Non-English Name: Helsingin Yliopisto, Kasvibiologian Laitos, Kasvipatologian Kirjasto **Founded:** 1924 **Type:** Government **Staff:** 1 Other **Head:** Hilkka Koponen *Email:* hilkka.koponen@helsinki.fiHoldings: 11,900 books 56 journals **Language of Collection/Services:** English **Subjects:** Plant Pathology **Loan:** In country **Service:** Inhouse **Photocopy:** Yes

1080 University of Helsinki, Finland
University of Helsinki, Faculty of Veterinary Medicine
Veterinary Medicine Library
PB 57
FIN-00014 University of Helsinki
Location: Hämeentie 57, 00580 Helsinki **Phone:** +358(9) 191 49751 **Fax:** +358(9) 191 49762 **Email:** kirjasto@ vetmed.helsinki.fi **WWW:** www.vetmed.helsinki.fi/lib/ english/english.htm **OPAC:** wwls.lib.helsinki.fi

Non-English Name: Helsingin Yliopisto, Veterinärmedicinska Fakulteten, Veterinärmedicinska Bibliotek **Founded:** 1945 **Type:** Academic **Head:** Teodora Oker-Blom *Phone:* +358(9) 191 49750 *Email:* teodora.oker-blom@helsinki.fi **Holdings:** 80,000 books 900 journals **Language of Collection/Services:** English / Finnish **Subjects:** Veterinary Medicine **Databases Used:** Comprehensive **Service:** In country **Loan:** Internationally **Photocopy:** Yes

1081 Vantaa, Finland
Finnish Forest Research Institute
Library and Information Services
PO Box 18 (Jokiniemenkuja 3B)
FIN-01301 Vantaa
Phone: +358(9) 8570 5586, 462, 581 **Fax:** +358(9) 8570 5582 **Email:** library@metla.fi **WWW:** www.metla.fi

Non-English Name: Metsäntutkimuslaitos (METLA), Kirjasto **Founded:** 1918 **Type:** Government **Head:** Liisa Ikävalko-Ahvonen *Phone:* +358(9) 8570 5581 *Email:* liisa. Ikavalko-ahvonen@metla.fi **Holdings:** 40,000 books 1,300 journals **Staff:** 2 Prof. 2 Other **Subjects:** Forestry **Databases Used:** Agricola; Agris **Loan:** Internationally **Photocopy:** Yes

1082 Vihti, Finland
Agricultural Research Centre of Finland, Agricultural Engineering Research
Library
Vakolantie 55
FIN-03400 Vihti
Phone: +358(9) 224251 **Fax:** +358(9) 2246210 **WWW:** www.mtt.fi

Non-English Name: Maatalouden Tutkimuskeskus, Maataloustenkologian Tutkimus (MTT/Vakola), Vakolan Kirjasto **Former Name:** State Research Institute of Engineering in Agriculture and Forestry, Valtion Maataloustenkologian Tutkimuslaitos **Founded:** 1980 **Type:** Government **Staff:** .25 Other **Holdings:** 400 books 20 journals **Language of Collection/Services:** Finnish, English / Finnish, English,

Swedish **Subjects:** Agricultural Engineering **Loan:** Do not loan **Photocopy:** Yes

1083   Ypäjä, Finland
Agricultural Research Centre of Finland, Equine Research
Library
Varsanojantie 63
FIN-32100 Ypäjä
Fax: +358(2) 7602260 **WWW:** www.mtt.fi

Non-English Name: Maatalouden Tutkimuskeskus, Hevostutkimus (MTT, HET), Kirjasto **Former Name:** State Horse Breeding Institute, Valtion Hevosjalostuslaitos, Hevostalouden tutkimusasema **Founded:** 1937 **Type:** Government **Head:** Markku Saastamoinen *Phone:* +358(2) 76021 *Email:* markku.saastamoinen@mtt.fi **Staff:** 1 Other **Holdings:** 2,500 books 25 journals **Language of Collection/Services:** English, Finnish / English **Subjects:** Animal Husbandry, Farming, Veterinary Medicine **Specializations:** Horses **Loan:** In country **Photocopy:** Yes

France

1084   Angers, France
Ecole Supérieure d'Agriculture d'Angers (ESA)
Centre de Documentation
55 rue Rabelais
BP 748
49007 Angers cedex 01
Phone: +33(241) 235555 **Fax:** +33(241) 235505 **WWW:** www.cge.asso.fr/ECOLE106.html

Founded: 1898 **Type:** Association **Head:** M. Joseph-Marie Richard *Phone:* +33(241) 235555 *Email:* jm.richard@esa-angers.educagri.fr **Staff:** 21 Prof. 3 Other **Holdings:** 45,000 books 500 journals **Language of Collection/Services:** French **Subjects:** Agribusiness, Agricultural Development, Agricultural Economics, Animal Husbandry, Biotechnology, Crops, Education/Extension, Rural Sociology **Loan:** In country **Service:** Internationally **Photocopy:** Yes

1085   Antibes, France
National Institute for Agricultural Research, Research Center of Antibes
Villa Thuret Library
41, boulevard du Cap
BP 2078
06606 Antibes cedex
Phone: +33(493) 678962 **Fax:** +33(493) 678969 **WWW:** www.antibes.inra.fr

Non-English Name: Institut National de la Recherche Agronomique, Centre de Recherches d'Antibes (INRA), Bibliothèque "Villa Thuret" **Founded:** 1860 **Type:** Government **Head:** Geneviève Lacombe *Email:* lacombe@antibes.inra.fr **Holdings:** 5,000 books 60 journals **Subjects:** Botany, Flora, Horticulture, Ornamental Plants, Plant Pathology **Loan:** Do not loan **Photocopy:** Yes

1086   Antony, France
Centre National du Machinisme Agricole du Génie Rural des Eaux et des Forêts (CEMAGREF)
Bibliothèque Machinisme Agricole
BP 44
92163 Antony cedex
Location: Parc de Tourvoie **Phone:** +33(140) 966121 **Fax:** +33(140) 966036 **WWW:** www.cemagref.fr

Founded: 1957 **Type:** Government **Staff:** 1 Prof. 3 Other **Holdings:** 6,000 books 500 journals **Subjects:** Agricultural Engineering **Loan:** Internationally **Photocopy:** Yes

1087   Beaune, France
Bureau Interprofessionnel des Vins de Bourgogne (BIVB)
Centre de Ressources Documentaires des Vins de Bourgogne
BP 150
12, Boulevard Bretonnière
21204 Beaune cedex
Phone: +33(380) 250698 **Fax:** +33(380) 250480 **Email:** documentation@bivb.com **WWW:** www.bivb.com

Former Name: Comité Interprofessionnel des Vins de Bourgogne (CIB), Station Oenologique de Bourgogène **Founded:** 1900 **Type:** Association **Staff:** 6 Other **Holdings:** 1,500 books 20 journals **Subjects:** Biotechnology, Enology, Microbiology, Viticulture **Loan:** Do not loan **Service:** In-house **Photocopy:** Yes

1088   Cestas, France
French Institute of Agricultural and Environmental Engineering Research
Information Center
50 Avenue de Verdun, BP 3
33612 Cestas Cedex
Phone: +33(5) 5789-0800 **Fax:** +33(5) 5789-0801 **WWW:** www.cemagref.fr

Non-English Name: Centre National du Machinisme Agricole du Génie Rural des Eaux et des Forêts (CEMAGREF), Bibliothèque - Documentation **Founded:** 1972 **Type:** Government **Head:** Chantal Gardes *Phone:* +33(5) 5789-0818 *Email:* chantal.gardes@cemagref.fr **Staff:** 1 Prof. **Holdings:** 4,300 books 250 journals **Subjects:** Agricultural Development, Agricultural Economics, Environment, Fisheries, Forestry, Soil Science, Water Resources **Loan:** In country **Photocopy:** Yes

1089   Jouy-en-Josas, France
National Institute for Agricultural Research, Research Centre of Jouy-en-Josas
Central Information Unit
78352 Jouy-en-Josas Cedex
Phone: +33(34) 652451 **Fax:** +33(34) 652272 **WWW:** www.inra.fr

Non-English Name: Institut National de la Recherche Agronomique, Centre de Recherches de Jouy-en-Josas (INRA, CRJJ), Unité Centrale de Documentation (UCD) **Founded:** 1955 **Type:** Government **Head:** Michèle Le Bars *Phone:* +33(34) 652450 *Email:* lebars@jouy.inra.fr **Staff:** 10 Prof.

15 Other **Holdings:** 4,500 books 600 journals **Language of Collection/Services:** English / French, English, German, Russian **Subjects:** Animal Genetics, Animal Production, Aquaculture, Biotechnology, Farming, Fisheries, Food Sciences, Food Technology, Microbiology, Veterinary Medicine **Specializations:** Cellular Biology **Networks:** CCN; AGLINET **Databases Used:** Comprehensive **Loan:** In country **Service:** In country **Photocopy:** Yes

1090   L'Hermitage, France
        National Institute for Agricultural Research, Pig
             Research Station
        Library
        St. Gilles
        35590 L'Hermitage
Phone: +33(2) 9928-5000 **Fax:** +33(2) 9928-5080 **WWW:** www.jouy.inra.fr/index.html

Non-English Name: Institut National de la Recherche Agronomique, Station de Recherches Porcines (INRA), Documentation **Founded:** 1975 **Type:** Government **Head:** Mme Barbeau *Phone:* +33(2) 9928-5065 *Email:* barbeau@ st-gilles.rennes.inra.fr **Staff:** 1 Prof. 1 Other **Holdings:** 120 journals 4,000 books **Language of Collection/Services:** English, French **Subjects:** Animal Husbandry **Specializations:** Animal Feeding, Animal Nutrition, Growth, Meat Quality, Metabolism, Piglets, Pigs, Sows **Databases Used:** Agricola; Medline **Loan:** In country **Service:** Inhouse **Photocopy:** No

1091   Le Rheu, France
        National Institute for Agricultural Research
        Regional Documentation Unit
        BP 29
        35653 Le Rheu Cedex
Location: Domaine de la Motte **Fax:** +33(299) 285310 **WWW:** www.rennes.inra.fr

Non-English Name: Institut National de la Recherche Agronomique (INRA), Unité Régionale de Documentation **Founded:** 1984 **Type:** Government **Head:** Françoise Guillaume *Phone:* +33(299) 285311 *Email:* guillaum@ rennes.inra.fr **Staff:** 6 Prof. 5 Other **Holdings:** 5,000 books 1,000 journals **Language of Collection/Services:** French, English **Subjects:** Agribusiness, Agricultural Development, Agricultural Economics, Agricultural Engineering, Animal Husbandry, Biotechnology, Crops, Entomology, Environment, Farming, Fisheries, Food Sciences, Horticulture, Plant Pathology, Soil Science, Water Resources **Databases Developed:** PUBINRA - publications of INRA - access via Internet at www.jouy.inra.fr/webtexto/pub/index.html **Databases Used:** Comprehensive **Loan:** In country **Photocopy:** Yes

1092   Metz, France
        Université de Metz
        Bibliothèque de l'Université, Section Sciences et
             Techniques
        Ile du Saulcy
        57045 Metz cedex 1
Phone: +33(87) 315080 **WWW:** www.univ-metz.fr
OPAC: www.scd.univ-metz.fr/Catalogue.html

Founded: 1970 **Type:** Academic **Head:** Hervé Colinmaire *Phone:* +33(87) 315656 *Email:* colinmai@scd.univ-metz.fr **Staff:** 3 Prof. 4 Other **Holdings:** 500 books 30 journals **Subjects:** Biotechnology, Crops, Entomology, Fisheries, Food Sciences, Plant Pathology, Soil Science, Water Resources **Networks:** OCLC **Loan:** Internationally **Photocopy:** Yes

1093   Montpellier, France
        Centre for International Cooperation in
             Development Oriented Agricultural Research
        Documentation and Library Services
        BP 5035
        34032 Montpellier cedex 1
Location: 2477, Avenue du Val de Montferrand **Phone:** +33(67) 615848 **Fax:** +33(67) 615820 **Email:** dist@cirad. fr **WWW:** www.cirad.fr

Non-English Name: Centre de Coopération Internationale en Recherche Agronomique pour le Développement (CIRAD), Services de Documentation et Bibliothèque **Former Name:** Centre d'Information et de Documentation en Agronomie des Régions Chaudes (CIDARC) **Founded:** 1987 **Type:** Government **Head:** Mr. J-F. Giovannetti *Phone:* +33(67) 615846 *Email:* giovannetti@cirad.fr **Staff:** 54 Prof. 17 Other **Holdings:** 164,000 books 4,200 journals **Language of Collection/Services:** French, English/French **Subjects:** Agribusiness, Agricultural Development, Agricultural Economics, Agricultural Engineering, Animal Husbandry, Biotechnology, Crops, Entomology, Farming, Fisheries, Food Sciences, Plant Pathology, Plants, Soil Science, Water Resources **Specializations:** Agriculture (Tropics), Field Crops, Food Technology, Forestry, Fruit Crops, Horticulture, Livestock Farming, Veterinary Medicine **Networks:** AGRIS **Databases Developed:** AGRITROP - 160,000 references; SESAME - 150,000 references of French language literature on tropical agriculture **Loan:** Inhouse **Service:** Internationally **Photocopy:** Yes

1094   Montpellier, France
        International Center for Advanced Mediterranean
             Agronomic Studies, Mediterranean
             Agronomic Institute of Montpellier
        Mediterranean Documentation Centre
        BP 5056
        3191 Route de Mende
        34033 Montpellier cedex 1
Phone: +33(67) 046049 **Fax:** +33(67) 542527 **WWW:** www.iamm.fr

Non-English Name: Centre International de Hautes Etudes Agronomiques Méditerranéennes, Institut Agronomique Méditerranéen de Montpellier (CIHEAM, IAMM), Centre de Documentation Méditerranéenne **Founded:** 1964 **Type:** Academic **Head:** M.L. Leclerc *Phone:* +33(67) 046019 *Email:* leclerc@iamm.fr **Staff:** 2 Prof. 3 Other **Holdings:** 45,000 books 320 journals **Language of Collection/Services:** French, English, Spanish, Italian, Portuguese, Turkish, Greek, Arabic **Subjects:** Agricultural Development, Agricultural Economics, Agricultural Policy, Agricultural Statistics, Agricultural Trade **Specializations:** Mediterranean Countries **Databases Developed:** MEDITAGRI - holdings of the Centre since 1989 plus former holdings added thematically **Databases Used:** Agris **Loan:** Internationally **Photocopy:** Yes

1095   Montpellier, France
National Institute of Agronomic Research, Montpellier National High School of Agronomy
Central Library
Place Pierre Viala
34060 Montpellier cedex 1
Phone: +33(499) 612582 **Fax:** +33(499) 612580 **Email:** assistance@ensam.inra.fr **WWW:** www.ensam.inra.fr

Non-English Name: Institut National de la Recherche Agronomique, Ecole Nationale Supérieure Agronomique de Montpellier (INRA (Montpellier II), ENSA.M), Bibliothèque **Founded:** 1880 **Type:** Academic **Staff:** 2 Prof. 2 Other **Holdings:** 45,000 books 120 journals **Language of Collection/Services:** French / French **Subjects:** Agricultural Economics, Arboriculture, Botany, Soil Science, Viticulture, Zoology, Zootechny **Loan:** In country **Photocopy:** Yes

1096   Nancy, France
National School of Rural Engineering, Hydraulics and Forestry
Forest Documentation Centre
14, rue Girardet
54042 Nancy Cedex
Phone: +33(3) 8339-6815 **Fax:** +33(3) 8332-7281 **Email:** lionnet@engref.fr **WWW:** www.engref.fr **Ariel IP:** 193. 54.100.*

Non-English Name: Ecole Nationale du Génie Rural des Eaux et des Forêts (ENGREF), Centre de Documentation Forestière **Founded:** 1824 **Type:** Government **Head:** *Phone:* +33(3) 8339-6800 **Staff:** 2 Prof. 2 Other **Holdings:** 50,000 books 800 journals **Language of Collection/Services:** French, English, German **Subjects:** Ecology, Entomology, Agricultural Economics, Fisheries, Forestry, Water Resources, Silviculture **Databases Used:** CABCD **Loan:** Internationally **Photocopy:** Yes

1097   Nangis, France
Association Forêt-Cellulose (AFOCEL)
Bibliothèque
Domaine de L'Etançon
77370 Nangis
Phone: +33(160) 670043 **Fax:** +33(160) 670231 **Email:** doc@afocel.fr **WWW:** www.afocel.fr

Founded: 1970 **Type:** Association **Head:** D. Ricordeau *Phone:* +33(160) 670028 *Email:* doc@afocel.fr **Staff:** 2 Prof. **Holdings:** 10,000 books 350 journals **Language of Collection/Services:** English, French, German **Subjects:** Biotechnology, Forestry **Databases Developed:** Silviculture - 2 databases; Plant Biotechnology - 1 database **Databases Used:** Comprehensive **Loan:** Inhouse **Service:** Internationally **Photocopy:** Yes

1098   Olivet, France
National Institute of Agronomic Research, Research Center of Orleans
Regional Documentation Unit

Avenue de la Pomme de Pin - Ardon
BP 20619
45166 Olivet cedex
Phone: +33(238) 417894 **Fax:** +33(238) 417879 **WWW:** www.inra.fr

Non-English Name: Institut National de la Recherche Agronomique, Centre de Recherches d'Orléans (INRA), Unité Régionale de Documentation **Type:** Government **Head:** Karine Robineaud **Staff:** 1 Prof. **Holdings:** 3,500 books 150 journals **Language of Collection/Services:** English **Subjects:** Biotechnology, Entomology, Forestry, Plant Pathology, Soil Science **Databases Used:** Agricola; Biosis; CABCD **Loan:** In country **Photocopy:** Yes

1099   Paris, France
Académie d'Agriculture de France (AAF)
Bibliothèque
18, rue de Bellechasse
75007 Paris
Phone: +33(1) 47-05-10-37 **Fax:** +33(1) 45-55-09-78 **WWW:** www.inra.fr/AAF/index.htm

Founded: 1761 **Type:** Academic **Head:** Pierre Zert *Phone:* +33(1) 47-05-10-37 *Email:* zert@athena.paris.inra.fr **Staff:** 1 Prof. **Holdings:** 35,000 books 200 journals **Subjects:** Agriculture (Tropics), Agribusiness, Agricultural Development, Agricultural Economics, Agricultural Engineering, Agriculture (History), Animal Husbandry, Biotechnology, Crops, Education/Extension, Entomology, Farming, Fisheries, Food Sciences, Forestry, Horticulture, Plant Pathology, Soil Science, Veterinary Medicine, Water Resources **Loan:** In country **Photocopy:** No

1100   Paris, France
Bureau pour le Développement de la Production Agricole (BDPA)
Centre de Documentation et d'Information (CDI)
27, Rue Louis Vicat
75738 Paris Cedex 15
Phone: +33(1) 4648-5940 **Fax:** +33(1) 4644-7544 **Email:** cdi@bdpa.fr **WWW:** www.agridoc.com

Founded: 1961 **Type:** Business **Head:** Melle. Geneviève Leprince *Phone:* +33(1) 4648-5942 *Email:* gleprince@bdpa. fr **Staff:** 7 Prof. 4 Other **Holdings:** 40,000 books 250 journals **Language of Collection/Services:** French, English, Spanish / French, English, Spanish **Subjects:** Agriculture (Tropics), Rural Development **Databases Developed:** ORCHIS - rural development and tropical agriculture; access inhouse **Databases Used:** Comprehensive **Loan:** Internationally **Service:** Internationally **Photocopy:** Yes

1101   Paris, France
French Institute of Forestry, Agricultural and Environmental Engineering
Documentation Center
19, Avenue du Maine
75015 Paris
Phone: +33(1) 45-49-89-59 **Fax:** +33(1) 45-49-88-27 **WWW:** www.engref.fr

Non-English Name: Ecole Nationale du Génie Rural, des Eaux et des Forêts (ENGREF), Centre de Documentation de

Paris **Founded:** 1975 **Type:** Academic **Head:** Mme Brigitte Magne *Phone:* +33(1) 45-49-89-59 *Email:* magne@engref.fr **Staff:** 1.5 Prof. .5 Other **Holdings:** 10,000 books 200 journals **Language of Collection/Services:** French / French **Subjects:** Agribusiness, Agricultural Economics, Biotechnology, Food Technology **Loan:** In country

1102   Paris, France
International Institute of Refrigeration (IIR)
Library
177, Boulevard Malesherbes
75017 Paris
Phone: +33(1) 4227-3235 **Fax:** +33(1) 4763-1798 **Email:** iifiir@ibm.net **WWW:** www.iifiir.org

Non-English Name: Institut International du Froid (IIF), Bibliothèque **Founded:** 1908 **Type:** International **Head:** Mrs. F. Protat *Phone:* +33(1) 4227-3235 *Email:* iifiir@ibm.net **Staff:** 4 Prof. **Holdings:** 200,000 books 300 journals **Language of Collection/Services:** English, French, German, Russian **Subjects:** Energy, Food Sciences, Refrigeration **Databases Developed:** News from labs **Loan:** Do not loan **Service:** Internationally **Photocopy:** Yes

1103   Paris, France
Ministry of Agriculture and Fisheries
Library
78, rue de Varenne
75349 Paris 07 SP
WWW: www.agriculture.gouv.fr

Non-English Name: Ministère de l'Agriculture et de la Pêche, Bibliothèque **Founded:** 1881 **Type:** Government **Head:** Marielle Tregouët *Phone:* +33(1) 45-55-95-50 **Staff:** 4 Prof. 6 Other **Holdings:** 30,000 books 700 journals **Subjects:** Agribusiness, Agricultural Development, Agricultural Economics, Animal Husbandry, Biotechnology, Crops, Education/Extension, Farming, Fisheries, Food Sciences, Forestry, Horticulture **Specializations:** Agriculture (History - 18th Century), Agriculture (History - 19th Century) **Loan:** Do not loan **Photocopy:** Yes

1104   Paris, France
Ministry of Agriculture and Fisheries, National Agronomy Institute Paris-Grignon
Documentation Service
16 Rue Claude Bernard
75231 Paris Cedex 05
Phone: +33(1) 44-08-17-83 **Fax:** +33(1) 44-08-17-84 **Email:** inabib@inapv.inapg.inra.fr **WWW:** www.inapg.inra.fr

Non-English Name: Ministère de l'Agriculture et de la Pêche, Institut National Agronomique Paris-Grignon (INA P-G), Service Commun de Documentation (SCD) **Founded:** 1876 **Type:** Academic **Head:** Mrs. Elisabeth Mener *Phone:* +33(1) 44-08-17-86 **Staff:** 2 Prof. 4 Other **Holdings:** 30,000 books 747 journals **Language of Collection/Services:** French / French **Subjects:** Agriculture (History), Agribusiness, Agricultural Economics, Biotechnology, Crops, Ecology, Enology, Food Industry, Gardens, Geology, Plant Pathology, Rural Sociology, Soil Science, Zootechny **Databases Developed:** Theses supported by INA P-G **Databases**

Used: Agris; FSTA; PASCAL **Loan:** In country **Service:** In-house **Photocopy:** Yes

1105   Paris, France
Oceanographic Institute
Library
195, Rue Saint-Jacques
75005 Paris
Phone: +33(1) 4432-1075 **Fax:** +33(1) 4051-7316 **Email:** bibliop@oceano.org **WWW:** www.oceano.org

Non-English Name: Institut Océanographique, Bibliothèque **Founded:** 1911 **Type:** Academic **Head:** Nicole Momzikoff *Phone:* +33(1) 4432-1074 *Email:* n.momzi@oceano.org **Staff:** 2 Prof. 1 Other **Holdings:** 7,000 books 380 journals **Language of Collection/Services:** English / French **Subjects:** Aquaculture, Aquatic Animals, Biology, Ecology, Fish Farming, Fisheries, Physiology, Water Resources **Networks:** CCN **Databases Used:** ASFA **Loan:** In country **Photocopy:** Yes

1106   Paris, France
Office International des Epizooties (OIE)
Bibliothèque
12, rue de Prony
75017 Paris
Phone: +33(1) 4415-1875 **Fax:** +33(1) 4267-0987 **Email:** oie@oie.int **WWW:** www.oie.int

Founded: 1950 **Type:** International **Head:** Marie Teissier *Phone:* +33(1) 4415-1888 *Email:* m.teissier@oie.int **Staff:** 1 Prof. **Holdings:** 3,500 books 120 journals **Language of Collection/Services:** English / French **Subjects:** Agricultural Economics, Animal Husbandry, Fisheries, Veterinary Medicine **Specializations:** Epidemiology **Databases Used:** CABCD; CELEX **Loan:** Do not loan **Photocopy:** Yes

1107   Paris, France
Office National Interprofessionnel des Céréales (ONIC)
Bibliothèque Administrative
19-21, avenue Bosquet
75007 Paris
Phone: +33(1) 44-18-20-00 **Fax:** +33(1) 45-51-90-99 **WWW:** www.onic.fr

Founded: 1986 **Type:** Government **Staff:** 1 Prof. 1 Other **Holdings:** 2,000 books 150 journals **Language of Collection/Services:** French / French **Subjects:** Cereals, Food Industry **Loan:** Do not loan **Photocopy:** Yes

1108   Paris, France
Technical Center for Wood and Furniture
Communication Department
10 Avenue de St Mandé
75012 Paris
Phone: +33(1) 40-19-49-19 **Fax:** +33(1) 43-40-85-65 **WWW:** www.ctba.fr

Non-English Name: Centre Technique du Bois et de l'Ameublement (CTBA), Service Communication **Former Name:** Centre Technique Du Bois **Founded:** 1952 **Type:** Business **Staff:** 3 Prof. 220 Other **Holdings:** 5,500 books 300 journals **Language of Collection/Services:** English

Subjects: Forestry **Specializations:** Drying, Logging, Sawmilling, Wood Panels, Wood Preservation, Wood Technology **Loan:** Inhouse **Service:** Internationally **Photocopy:** Yes

1109   Reims, France
Université de Reims, Champagne Ardenne
Bibliothèque de l'Université, Section Sciences et
     Techniques
BP 1040
51687 Reims cedex 02
Location: Rue des Crayères, Moulin de la Housse **Phone:** +33(326) 913295 **Fax:** +33(326) 913432 **WWW:** www.univ-reims.fr **OPAC:** www.univ-reims.fr/Urca/Bu

Founded: 1959 **Type:** Academic **Staff:** 6 Prof. 5 Other **Holdings:** 2,000 books 200 journals **Subjects:** Fisheries, Food Sciences **Databases Used:** CABCD; FSTA **Loan:** Internationally **Service:** Internationally **Photocopy:** Yes

1110   Rennes, France
Ecole Nationale Supérieure Agronomique de
     Rennes (ENSAR)
Bibliothèque Centrale
65, Rue de Saint-Brieuc
35042 Rennes Cedex
Phone: +33(2) 9928-5000 **Fax:** +33(2) 9928-7573 **WWW:** agro.roazhon.inra.fr

Founded: 1830 **Type:** Academic **Head:** Mme M.J. Rougelot *Phone:* +33(2) 9928-7571 *Email:* rougelot@epi.roazhon.inra.fr **Staff:** 2 Prof. 3 Other **Holdings:** 30,000 books 350 journals **Language of Collection/Services:** French / French **Subjects:** Comprehensive **Specializations:** Agricultural Economics, Environment, Fisheries, Food Sciences **Databases Used:** Agricola; Resagri **Loan:** Internationally (only their publications) **Photocopy:** Yes

1111   Rennes, France
National Institute of Agronomic Research, Rennes
     Economy and Rural Sociology Unit
Bibliothèque
Rue Adolphe Bobierre
CS 61103
35011 Rennes cedex
Phone: +33(223) 485382 **Fax:** +33(223) 485380 **WWW:** www.inra.fr

Non-English Name: Institut National de la Recherche Agronomique, Unité d'Economie et Sociologie Rurales de Rennes (INRA) **Founded:** 1957 **Type:** Government **Head:** Michelle Briot *Email:* briot@roazhon.inra.fr **Staff:** 4 Prof. **Holdings:** 11,000 books 320 journals **Language of Collection/Services:** French **Subjects:** Agricultural Development, Agricultural Economics, Biotechnology, Environment, Food Sciences, Rural Sociology **Databases Developed:** CONTENT - All the acquisitions, access only in the library **Loan:** Internationally **Service:** Internationally **Photocopy:** Yes

1112   Saint-La, France
Agorial-Normandie
Ialine+ (Food Industry Information Service)
370, rue Popielujko
Site Agorial

50009 Saint-La Cedex
Phone: +33(2) 3306-7171 **Fax:** +33(2) 3306-7181 **Email:** ialine@dial.oleane.com

Non-English Name: Agorial-Normandie, Ialine+ (Service d'information pour l'industrie agroalimentaire) **Founded:** 1967 **Type:** Association **Head:** M. Gilles de Fromont *Phone:* +33(2) 3306-7171 *Email:* ialine@dial.oleane.com **Holdings:** 6,000 books 220 journals **Language of Collection/Services:** French / French, English **Subjects:** Food Sciences **Databases Developed:** IALINE - Food industry scientific and technical; GISRIA - Research teams file; European information sources for food industry **Databases Used:** IALINE **Loan:** Do not loan **Service:** Internationally **Photocopy:** Yes

1113   Toulouse, France
Ecole Nationale Vétérinaire de Toulouse
Bibliothèque
23, Chemin des Capelles
31076 Toulouse Cédex 3
Phone: +33(5) 6119-3825 **Fax:** +33(5) 6119-3827 **WWW:** www.pole-tlse.fr/acte_envt.html

Founded: 1836 **Type:** Academic **Head:** Mme A. Serraz *Phone:* +33(5) 6119-3825 *Email:* a.serraz@envt.fr **Staff:** 2 Prof. 4 Other **Holdings:** 1,000 books 450 journals **Language of Collection/Services:** English, French **Subjects:** Animal Husbandry, Food Sciences, Veterinary Medicine **Networks:** CCN **Databases Used:** Medline **Loan:** Internationally **Photocopy:** Yes

1114   Vandoeuvre-lès-Nancy, France
Institut National Polytechnique de Lorraine, Ecole
     Nationale Supérieure d'Agronomie et des
     Industries Alimentaires (ENSAIA)
Centre de Documentation
BP 172
2, Avenue de la Forêt de Haye
54505 Vandoeuvre-lès-Nancy Cedex
Phone: +33(383) 596027 **Email:** biblioth@ensaia.u-nancy.fr **WWW:** www.ensaia.u-nancy.fr

Founded: 1900 **Type:** Academic **Staff:** 1 Other **Holdings:** 8,000 books 81 journals **Subjects:** Animal Husbandry, Crop Production, Environment, Pedology, Plant Pathology, Rural Economy, Zootechny **Databases Used:** CABCD; GeoRef; INSPEC; PASCAL **Loan:** Internationally **Photocopy:** Yes

1115   Versailles, France
National Institute of Agricultural Research,
     Versailles-Grignon Research Centre
Documentation Service
RD 10 - Route de Saint-Cyr
78026 Versailles cedex
Phone: +33(1) 3083-3421 **Fax:** +33(1) 3083-3440 **WWW:** www.inra.fr

Non-English Name: Institut National de la Recherche Agronomique, Centre de Recherche de Versailles-Grignon (INRA), Service de Documentation **Type:** Government **Head:** Gérard Grozel *Email:* gerard.grozel@versailles.inra.fr **Networks:** AGRIS

French Polynesia

1116   Papeete, French Polynesia
Service de l'Economie Rurale, Section Agriculture
Bibliothèque
BP 100
Papeete, Tahiti
Phone: +689 428144 **Fax:** +689 420831

Type: Government **Head:** Mr. Leopold Stein

1117   Papeete, French Polynesia
Service de l'Economie Rurale, Section Recherche
Agronomique
Bibliothèque
BP 100
Papeete, Tahiti
Phone: +689 574004 **Fax:** +689 420831

Type: Government

1118   Papetoai, French Polynesia
Lycée d'Enseignement Professionel Agricole
Bibliothèque
BP 1007
Papetoai, Moorea
Location: Opunohu, Moorea **Phone:** +689 561134 **Fax:** +689 561778

Type: Academic

Gabon

♦1119   Franceville, Gabon
Université des Sciences et Techniques de Masuku
Bibliothèque
BP 941
Franceville
Fax: +241 677406

Head: Yves Ndoutoume-Nkoume *Phone:* +241 677578, 677725

1120   Libreville, Gabon
African Timber Organisation (ATO)
Library
BP 1077
Libreville
Location: Batterie IV **Phone:** +241 732928 **Fax:** +241 734030 **Email:** oab-gabon@internetgabon.com

Non-English Name: Organisation Africaine du Bois (OAB), Service de Documentation **Founded:** 1984 **Type:** Inter-governmental **Staff:** 3 Other **Holdings:** 600 books 21 journals **Language of Collection/Services:** French, English /French, English **Subjects:** Forest Products, Marketing, Silviculture, Wood **Loan:** Inhouse **Service:** Inhouse **Photocopy:** Yes

1121   Libreville, Gabon
Chambre de Commerce, d'Agriculture, Industrie
et des Mines du Gabon

Centre de Documentation
BP 2234
Libreville
Phone: +241 743342 **Fax:** +241 766183

Founded: 1986 **Head:** Amoughe *Phone:* +241 722064, 720753

♦1122   Libreville, Gabon
Direction Générale des Archives Nationales
(DGA)
Bibliothèque Nationale et de la Documentation
Gabonaise
BP 1188
Libreville

Founded: 1969 **Type:** Government **Head:** Mezene Stany *Phone:* +241 732543, +241 730239 **Staff:** 11 Prof. 15 Other **Holdings:** 1,600 books 30 journals

1123   Libreville, Gabon
Ecole Nationale des Eaux et Forêts
Bibliothèque
BP 3960
Libreville
Phone: +241 743342 **Fax:** +241 766183

Founded: 1970 **Head:** Rosine Abegne *Phone:* +241 758345

1124   Libreville, Gabon
Ministère de l'Agriculture, de l'Elevage et du
Développement Rural (MAEDR)
Direction de la Formation de l'Enseignement et du
Personnel
BP 43
Libreville

Founded: 1974 **Type:** Government **Head:** Jean Malouba-Ekayeng *Phone:* +241 761757 **Staff:** 4 Other **Holdings:** 1,116 books **Subjects:** Animal Production, Crop Production, Extension, Rural Sociology, Soil Science **Networks:** AGRIS

1125   Libreville, Gabon
Ministère de la Recherche Scientifique, Institut de
Recherches Agronomiques et Forestières
(IRAF)
Centre de Documentation
BP 2246
Libreville
Fax: +241 730859

Founded: 1989 **Head:** Jean François Koumba *Phone:* +241 732565 **Networks:** AGRIS

Gambia, The

1126   Banjul, The Gambia
Ministry of Agriculture and Natural Resources,
Planning, Programming and Monitoring Unit
(PPMU)
Library and Documentation Centre
The Quadrangle
Banjul

Location: 10B Nelson Mandela Street **Phone:** +220 228751 **Fax:** +220 224851

Founded: 1983 **Type:** Government **Head:** Baboucarr M.S. Koma *Phone:* +220 228751 **Staff:** 1 Prof. 1 Other **Holdings:** 8,000 books 41 journals **Language of Collection/Services:** English **Subjects:** Agricultural Development, Agricultural Economics, Animal Production, Fisheries, Food Production, Forestry, Horticulture, Irrigation, Nutrition, Soil Science, Water Management **Networks:** AGRIS **Loan:** In country **Photocopy:** Yes

♦**1127   Brikama, The Gambia**
Gambia College (GC)
Library
Brikama Campus
PMB 144
Brikama, Western Division
Phone: +220 484812 **Fax:** +220 484812

Founded: 1949 **Type:** Academic **Head:** Mrs. R.A. Ndaw-Jallow **Staff:** 2 Prof. 11 Other **Holdings:** 29,000 books 40 journals **Language of Collection/Services:** English/English **Subjects:** Agriculture (Tropics), Agricultural Economics, Agricultural Engineering, Animal Husbandry, Crops, Education/Extension, Farming, Food Sciences, Horticulture, Plants, Soil Science, Veterinary Medicine **Loan:** Inhouse **Service:** Inhouse **Photocopy:** Yes

Georgia

1128   Batumi, Georgia
Georgian Research and Education Technological Institute for Subtropical Fruit Storage and Processing
Library
13 David Agmashenebeli St.
384520 Batumi
Phone: +995 222-70941 **Fax:** +995 222-70941 **Email:** greti@iberiapac.ge

Former Name: All-Union Scientific Research Experimental Design Institute of Storing and Processing Subtropical Crops **Founded:** 1943 **Type:** Government **Staff:** 1 Prof. 2 Other **Holdings:** 34,000 books **Language of Collection/Services:** Russian, Georgian / Georgian, Russian **Subjects:** Agriculture (Subtropics), Food Industry, Food Processing, Raw Materials, Subtropics **Loan:** In country **Service:** Inhouse **Photocopy:** Yes

1129   Lagodekhi, Georgia
Lagodekhi "Tambako" (Tobacco) Experiment Station
Library
Mira St., 113
383230 Lagodekhi

Former Name: All-Union Scientific Research Institute of Tobacco and Makhorka **Type:** Government **Head:** Godziashvili Tomaz *Phone:* +995 22266 **Holdings:** 3,300 books **Language of Collection/Services:** Russian / Russian **Subjects:** Crops, Entomology, Plants **Specializations:** Tobacco **Loan:** In country **Service:** In country **Photocopy:** No

1130   Mtzcheta, Georgia
Y.N. Lomouri Georgian Research Institute of Farming
Library
Tserovani
383400 Mtzcheta

Non-English Name: Sakartvelos Y.N. Lomouris Sakhelobis Mitsatmoqmedebis Sametsniero Kvleviti Instituti, Biblioteka **Founded:** 1956 **Type:** Government **Head:** Elena V. Labauri *Phone:* +995 (32) 935509 **Staff:** 1 Prof. **Holdings:** 48,000 books **Language of Collection/Services:** Georgian, Russian / Georgian **Subjects:** Farming, Gardening **Loan:** In country **Service:** In country

1131   Sukhumi, Georgia
Georgian Institute of Management of the Subtropical Cultures
Library
Kelosuri
384904 Sukhumi

Founded: 1952 **Type:** Academic **Holdings:** 86,600 books **Subjects:** Agriculture (Subtropics), Subtropics

1132   Tbilisi, Georgia
Agrarian University of Georgia
Library
D. Agmashenebeli Ave. 13
380031 Tbilisi

Non-English Name: Sakartvelos Agraruli Universiteti, Biblioteka **Former Name:** Agriculture Institute of Georgia **Founded:** 1930 **Type:** Government **Head:** Lamara Gelovani *Phone:* 995(32) 957146, 943198 *Email:* agrdig@geointer.net **Staff:** 29 Prof. **Holdings:** 748,441 books **Language of Collection/Services:** Georgian, Russian / Georgian **Subjects:** Comprehensive **Loan:** In country **Service:** In country

1133   Tbilisi, Georgia
Georgian Research Institute for Scientific and Technical Information (TECHINFORMI)
47 Kostava Street
380079 Tbilisi
Phone: +995(32) 988367, 988368 **Fax:** +995(32) 987618 **Email:** tech@tech.org.ge **WWW:** www.tech.org.ge

Founded: 1959 **Head:** David Dumbadze **Networks:** AGRIS

1134   Tbilisi, Georgia
Georgian Scientific Research Institute of Horticulture, Viticulture and Winemaking
Library
Marshal Gelovani Ave., 6
380059 Tbilisi

Non-English Name: Sakartvelos Mebageobis, Mevenaxeobis da Megvineobis Sametsniero Kvleviti Instituti, Biblioteka **Founded:** 1931 **Type:** Government **Head:** Vaxvaxishvili Iali *Phone:* +995 (32) 524611, 520966 **Staff:** 1 Prof. 1 Other **Holdings:** 70,000 books **Language of Collection/Services:** Georgian, Russian / Georgian **Subjects:** Horticulture, Viticulture, Winemaking **Loan:** In country **Service:** In country

1135   Tbilisi, Georgia
Georgian Scientific Research Institute of Plant
Protection
Library
Chavchavadze Av., 82
380062 Tbilisi

Founded: 1950 **Type:** Government **Holdings:** 17,600 books
Subjects: Plant Protection

1136   Tbilisi, Georgia
Georgian Scientific Research Institute of Soil
Science, Agricultural Chemistry and Land
Reclamation
Library
380065 Tbilisi

Founded: 1947 **Type:** Government **Holdings:** 15,200 books
Subjects: Agricultural Chemistry, Reclamation, Soil Science

1137   Tbilisi, Georgia
Georgian Scientific Research Station of
Beekeeping
Library
Okrokana Village
380007 Tbilisi
Phone: +995(32) 932363, 997250

Non-English Name: Sakartvelos mefutkreobis Sametsniero
Kvleviti Tsentri, Biblioteka **Founded:** 1959 **Type:** Government **Head:** Eliza Elizbarashvili *Phone:* +995(32) 932363,
997250 **Staff:** 1 Other **Holdings:** 12,000 books **Language of
Collection/Services:** Georgian, Russian / Georgian **Subjects:** Beekeeping, Gardening **Loan:** In country **Service:** In
country

1138   Tbilisi, Georgia
K.M. Amiradjibi Georgian Scientific Research
Institute of Mechanization and Electrification
of Agriculture
Library
Digomi Village
380059 Tbilisi
Phone: +995(32) 520154, 528177

Non-English Name: Sakartvelos Soflis Meurneobis K.M.
Amirejibis Saxelobis Meqanizatsiisa dda Elektrifikatsiis Sametsniero Kvleviti Instituti, Biblioteka **Founded:** 1957
Type: Government **Head:** Tsiala Maisuradze *Phone:*
+995(32) 520154, 528177 **Staff:** 1 Prof. 1 Other **Holdings:**
25,930 books **Language of Collection/Services:** Georgian,
Russian / Georgian **Subjects:** Electrification, Gardening,
Mechanization **Loan:** In country **Service:** In country

1139   Tbilisi, Georgia
Scientific Research Institute for Management and
Economy of Agroindustrial Complex of
Georgia
Library
Chavchavadze Av., 37, Building 14
380078 Tbilisi 380040

Non-English Name: Sakartvelos Agrosamretsvelo Kompleqsis Ekonomikisa da Martvis Sametcniero-kvleviti Insti-

tuti, Biblioteka **Founded:** 1959 **Type:** Government **Head:**
Svetlana Stepanova *Phone:* +995(32) 226636, 226424 **Staff:**
2 Prof. **Holdings:** 31,744 books **Language of Collection/
Services:** Georgian, Russian / Georgian **Subjects:** Agricultural Economics **Loan:** In country **Service:** In country

1140   Tbilisi, Georgia
Scientific Research Institute of Food Industry of
Georgia
Library
D. Guramishvili 17
380092 Tbilisi
Phone: +995(32) 610593, 617302

Non-English Name: Sakartvelos Kvebis Mretsvelobis
Sametsniero Kvleviti Instituti, Biblioteka **Founded:** 1961
Type: Government **Head:** Lia Kotorashvili *Phone:*
+995(32) 610593, 617302 **Staff:** 1 Prof. **Holdings:** 23,300
books **Language of Collection/Services:** Georgian, Russian
/ Georgian **Subjects:** Food Industry **Specializations:** Fats,
Nutrition, Oils, Sugar **Loan:** In country **Service:** In country

1141   Tbilisi, Georgia
Zootech-Veterinary Academy of Georgia
Library
Krtsanisi Village
380107 Tbilisi
Phone: +995(32) 723752, 724674

Non-English Name: Sakartvelos Zooteqnikuri Saveterinario Akademia, Biblioteka **Former Name:** Zooveterinary Institute of Georgia **Founded:** 1932 **Type:** Government **Head:**
Izari Pataraia *Phone:* +995(32) 723752, 724674 **Staff:** 5
Prof. 18 Other **Holdings:** 500,000 books **Language of Collection/Services:** Georgian, Russian / Georgian **Subjects:**
Animal Husbandry, Veterinary Science **Loan:** In country
Service: In country

Germany

1142   Aschersleben, Germany
Federal Centre for Breeding Research on
Cultivated Plants
Library
PO Box 1505
D-06435 Aschersleben
Location: Theodor-Roemer-Weg 4, D-06449 Aschersleben
Fax: +49(3473) 2709 **Email:** bafz-er@bafz.de **WWW:**
www.bafz.de

Non-English Name: Bundesanstalt für Züchtungsforschung
an Kulturpflanzen (BAZ), Bibliothek **Former Name:** Institute of Phytopathology, Institut für Phytopathologie **Founded:** 1952 **Type:** Government **Head:** Prof. Dr. habil. G.
Proeseler *Phone:* +49(3473) 8790 *Email:* g.proeseler@bafz.
de **Staff:** 2 Other **Holdings:** 14,720 books 270 journals **Subjects:** Bacteriology, Entomology, Plant Pathology, Virology
Specializations: Biotechnology, Mycology, Resistance Research **Loan:** In country **Photocopy:** Yes

1143   Berlin, Germany
Berlin Botanical Garden and Museum

Library
Königin-Luise-Strasse 6-8
D-14195 Berlin 33
Phone: +49(30) 83006-191 **Fax:** +49(30) 83006-186
Email: library@mail.bgbm.fu-berlin.de **WWW:** www.
bgbm.fu-berlin.de

Non-English Name: Botanischer Garten und Botanisches Museum Berlin Dahlem, Bibliothek **Founded:** 1815 **Type:** Government **Staff:** 7 Prof. 4 Other **Holdings:** 5,000 books **Subjects:** Crops, Horticulture **Loan:** Do not loan **Photocopy:** Yes

1144 Berlin, Germany
Federal Biological Research Centre for
Agriculture and Forestry
Information Centre for Phytomedicine and Library
Königin-Luise-Strasse 19
D-14195 Berlin
Phone: +49(30) 8304-2120 **Fax:** +49(30) 8304-2103
Email: bibliothek@bba.de **WWW:** www.bba.de

Non-English Name: Biologische Bundesanstalt für Land- und Forstwirtschaft (BBA), Informationszentrum Phytomedizin und Bibliothek **Former Name:** Information Centre for Tropical Plant Protection, Informationszentrum für Tropischen Pflanzenschutz (INTROP) **Founded:** 1898 **Type:** Government **Head:** Prof. Dr. W. Laux *Phone:* +49 (30) 8304-2106 *Email:* w.laux@bba.de **Staff:** 2 Prof. 2 Other **Holdings:** 120,000 books 1,400 journals **Language of Collection/Services:** German, English / German, English **Subjects:** Agriculture (Tropics), Biotechnology, Crops, Entomology, Forestry, Horticulture, Pesticides, Soil Science, Storage, Weeds **Specializations:** Phytomedicine, Plant Pathology, Plant Protection **Databases Developed:** PHYTOMED - Available through DIMDI and Internet; 452,000 citations from 1965-1985; PHYTOMED Select 10,000 citations from 1986 onwards **Databases Used:** Comprehensive **Loan:** Internationally **Photocopy:** Yes

1145 Berlin, Germany
Free University of Berlin
Documentation Center for Veterinary Medicine
Strasse 518 Nr. 15
D-14163 Berlin
Phone: +49(30) 8108-2636 **Fax:** +49(30) 8108-2643
Email: library@vetmed.fu-berlin.de **WWW:**
www.fu-berlin.de/index.html **OPAC:**
www.vetmed.fu-berlin.de/w3opac-cgi-bin/w3opac.pl

Non-English Name: Freie Universität Berlin, Dokumentationsstelle für Veterinärmedizin **Founded:** 1969 **Type:** Academic **Holdings:** 350 books 2,500 journals **Language of Collection/Services:** German, English / German **Subjects:** Biology, Veterinary Medicine **Service:** Internationally **Photocopy:** Yes

1146 Berlin, Germany
Free University of Berlin
Information Center
Oertzenweg 19b
14163 Berlin

Phone: +49(30) 8108-2636 **Fax:** +49(30) 8108-2643
Email: library@early.vetmed.fu-berlin.de **WWW:** www.
vetmed.fu-berlin.de **OPAC:** www.vetmed.fu-berlin.de/
w3opac-cgi-bin/w3opac.pl

Non-English Name: Freie Universität Berlin **Former Name:** Veterinärmedizinische Bibliothek **Founded:** 1950 **Type:** Academic **Head:** Dr. Holger Kulemeyer *Phone:* +49 (30) 838-5515 *Email:* holly@early.vetmed.fu-berlin.de **Holdings:** 120,000 books 750 journals **Staff:** 10 Other 3 Prof. **Language of Collection/Services:** English, German **Subjects:** Animal Husbandry, Entomology, Food Sciences, Veterinary Medicine **Databases Used:** Agris; Biosis; CABCD; Medline **Loan:** Internationally **Photocopy:** Yes

1147 Berlin, Germany
Institute for Fermentation Industry and
Biotechnology
Lorberg Library
Seestrasse 13
D-13353 Berlin
Phone: +49(30) 4508-0235 **WWW:** www.ifgb.de

Non-English Name: Institut für Gärungsgewerbe und Biotechnologie (IFGB), Lorberg-Bibliothek **Founded:** 1874 **Type:** Academic **Staff:** 1 Prof. **Holdings:** 27,000 books 300 journals **Subjects:** Biotechnology, Food Sciences **Specializations:** Biochemistry, Fermentation, Microbiology **Loan:** Inhouse **Photocopy:** Yes

1148 Berlin-Wedding, Germany
Technical University Berlin, University Library
Department of Cereal Technology
Seestrasse 11
D-13353 Berlin-Wedding
Phone: +49(30) 314-27554 **Fax:** +49(30) 314-22839
Email: getreide@ub.tu-berlin.de **WWW:** www.tu-berlin.
de/ubib

Non-English Name: Technische Universität Berlin, Universitätsbibliothek, Abteilung Getreidetechnologie **Founded:** 1907 **Type:** Academic **Head:** Bettina Golz *Phone:* +49(30) 314-22377 *Email:* chemie@ub.tu-berlin.de **Staff:** 2 Prof. **Holdings:** 10,000 books 79 journals **Subjects:** Agricultural Economics, Food Technology, Nutrition **Specializations:** Cereal Products **Loan:** Internationally **Photocopy:** Yes

1149 Berlin-Wedding, Germany
Technical University Berlin, University Library
Department of Sugar Technology
Amrumer Strasse 32
D-13353 Berlin-Wedding
Phone: +49(30) 314-27540/1 **Fax:** +49(30) 314-27518
Email: zucker@ub.tu-berlin.de **WWW:** www.tu-berlin.de/
ubib

Non-English Name: Technische Universität Berlin, Universitätsbibliothek, Abteilung Zuckertechnologie **Founded:** 1867 **Type:** Academic **Head:** Bettina Golz *Phone:* +49(30) 314-22377 *Email:* chemie@ub.tu-berlin.de **Staff:** 2 Prof. 1 Other **Holdings:** 30,000 books 360 journals **Language of Collection/Services:** English **Specializations:** Sugar, Sugar Products, Sugarbeet, Sugarcane **Loan:** Internationally **Photocopy:** Yes

1150 Berlin, Germany
Technical University Berlin, University Library
Food Science and Biotechnology Documentation
    Service
Strasse des 17. Juni 136
D-10623 Berlin
Fax: +49(30) 314-25083 **WWW:** www.tu-berlin.de
OPAC: www.ub.tu-berlin.de/index_5.htm

Non-English Name: Technische Universität Berlin, Universitätsbibliothek, Dokumentationsstelle Lebensmittelwissenschaft und Biotechnologie **Former Name:** Dokumentationsstelle Gärungsgewerbe und Biotechnologie **Founded:** 1969 **Type:** Academic **Head:** Dr. Gudrun Weiland *Phone:* +49(30) 314-25082 *Email:* weiland@ub.tu-berlin.de **Staff:** 1 Prof. **Subjects:** Biotechnology, Brewing, Food Sciences, Food Technology, Fruits, Horticulture **Databases Used:** Comprehensive **Photocopy:** No

1151 Berlin, Germany
Technical University Berlin, University Library
Horticulture Library
Franklinstrasse 28-29, 7.OG.
D-10587 Berlin
Phone: +49(30) 314-22535 **Fax:** +49(30) 314-73408
WWW: www.tu-berlin.de **OPAC:** www.dbilink.de

Non-English Name: Technische Universität Berlin, Universitätsbibliothek, Abteilung Gartenbaubücherei **Founded:** 1936 **Type:** Academic **Head:** *Phone:* +49(30) 314-73406 **Staff:** 2 Prof. **Holdings:** 54,000 books 190 journals **Language of Collection/Services:** German **Subjects:** Horticulture **Databases Developed:** Catchword-index of articles from horticultural periodicals for the period from 1783 to 1920, including index of plant names of species and varieties cited **Networks:** BVBB **Photocopy:** Yes **Loan:** Internationally **Service:** Internationally

1152 Bonn, Germany
Bonn University
Central Agriculture Library of Germany
Postfach 24 60
D-53014 Bonn
Location: Nussallee 15 a **Phone:** +49(228) 73-3405 **Fax:** +49(228) 73-3281 **Email:** information_zbl@ulb.uni-bonn.de **WWW:** www.dainet.de/zbl/zbl.htm **OPAC:** www.ulb.uni-bonn.de/kataloge/www_opac.htm

Non-English Name: Rheinische Friedrich-Wilhelms-Universität Bonn, Deutsche Zentralbibliothek für Landbauwissenschaft (ZBL) **Former Name:** Zentralbibliothek der Landbauwissenschaft **Founded:** 1847 **Type:** Academic **Head:** Jutta Heller *Phone:* +49(228) 73-3400 *Email:* heller@ulb.uni-bonn.de **Staff:** 20 Prof. 10 Other **Holdings:** 520,000 books 4,700 journals **Language of Collection/Services:** German, English/German, English **Subjects:** Agribusiness, Agricultural Development, Farming, Agricultural Economics, Agricultural Engineering, Animal Husbandry, Biotechnology, Crops, Environmental Protection, Fisheries, Food Sciences, Forestry, Home Economics, Horticulture, Nature Conservation, Nutrition, Plant Pathology, Soil Science, Viticulture, Water Resources **Databases Used:** Agricola; Agris; CABCD; ELFIS **Networks:** HBZ- Katalog

Loan: Internationally **Service:** Internationally **Photocopy:** Yes

1153 Bonn, Germany
Bonn University, Institute of Animal Breeding
    Science
Library
Endenicher Allee 15
D-53115 Bonn 1, Nordrhein-Westfalen
Fax: +49(228) 73-2284 **WWW:** www.itz.uni-bonn.de

Non-English Name: Rheinische Friedrich-Wilhelms-Universität Bonn, Institut für Tierzuchtwissenschaft (ITZ), Bibliothek **Type:** Academic **Head:** Prof. Dr. Karl Schellander *Email:* karl.schellander@itz.uni-bonn.de *Phone:* +49 (228) 73-2240 ext 2280 **Holdings:** 8,000 books 40 journals **Subjects:** Animal Breeding **Loan:** Do not loan **Photocopy:** No

1154 Bonn, Germany
Bonn University, Institute for Soil Science
Library
Nussallee 13
D-53115 Bonn
Phone: +49(228) 732780/1 **Fax:** +49(228) 732782 **Email:** bobo@boden.uni-bonn.de **WWW:** www.boden.uni-bonn.de

Non-English Name: Rheinische Friedrich-Wilhelms-Universität Bonn, Institut für Bodenkunde, Bibliothek **Type:** Academic **Head:** *Phone:* +49(228) 732777 **Staff:** .5 Other **Holdings:** 15,000 books 20 journals **Language of Collection/Services:** German / German **Subjects:** Soil Science **Loan:** Do not loan **Photocopy:** No

1155 Bonn, Germany
Chamber of Agriculture of the Rhenania
Library
PO Box 1969
D-53009 Bonn
Location: Endenicher Allee 60, D-53115 Bonn **Fax:** +49 (228) 703-489 **WWW:** www.landwirtschaftskammer.de

Non-English Name: Landwirtschaftskammer Rheinland, Bibliothek **Founded:** 1899 **Type:** Government **Head:** Iris Lülsdorf *Phone:* +49(228) 703-491 **Staff:** 1 Prof. 1 Other **Holdings:** 60,000 books 350 journals **Language of Collection/Services:** German **Subjects:** Agribusiness, Agricultural Development, Agricultural Economics, Agricultural Engineering, Animal Husbandry, Biotechnology, Crops, Farming, Forestry, Horticulture, Soil Science, Water Resources **Loan:** Inhouse **Photocopy:** Yes

1156 Bonn, Germany
Deutscher Raiffeisenverband e.V. (DRV)
Abteilung Bibliothek und Archiv
Adenauerallee 127
D-53113 Bonn
Fax: +49(228) 206266 **Email:** info@drv.raiffeisen.de
WWW: www.raiffeisen.de

Founded: 1948 **Type:** Association **Staff:** 1 Other **Holdings:** 22,000 books 250 journals **Subjects:** Cooperatives **Loan:** Do not loan **Photocopy:** No

1157 Bonn, Germany
Federal Agency for Nature Conservation
Documentation and Library
Konstantinstrasse 110
D-53179 Bonn
Phone: +49(228) 8491-0 **Fax:** +49(228) 8491-200 **Email:** pbox-dobi@bfn.de **WWW:** www.bfn.de

Non-English Name: Bundesamt für Naturschutz (BfN), Fachgebiet Dokumentation/Bibliothek (Do/Bi) **Former Name:** Bundesforschungsanstalt für Naturschutz und Landschaftsökologie **Founded:** 1906 **Type:** Government **Head:** Wiss. Dir. Dr. Rainer Flüeck *Phone:* +49(228) 8491-134 **Staff:** 9 Prof. 1 Other **Holdings:** 90,000 books 1,000 journals **Language of Collection/Services:** German, English / German **Subjects:** Biotopes, Landscape Planning, Nature Conservation, Protected Species **Photocopy:** No **Loan:** Inhouse **Service:** Inhouse

1158 Bonn, Germany
Federal Ministry for Food, Agriculture and
    Forestry
Library
Postfach 14 02 70
D-53107 Bonn
Fax: +49(228) 529-4262 **WWW:** www.bml.de

Non-English Name: Bundesministerium für Ernährung, Landwirtschaft und Forsten (BML), Bibliothek **Founded:** 1950 **Type:** Government **Head:** Susanne Höffgen *Phone:* +49(228) 529-3833 **Staff:** 4 Prof. 1 Other **Holdings:** 81,000 books 750 journals **Language of Collection/Services:** German / German **Subjects:** Agricultural Law, Forestry, Food Sciences, Horticulture **Loan:** Do not loan **Service:** Inhouse **Photocopy:** No

1159 Bonn, Germany
German Centre for Documentation and
    Information in Agriculture
PO Box 20 14 15
D-53144 Bonn
Location: Villichgasse 17, D-53177 Bonn **Phone:** +49 (228) 9548-0 **Fax:** +49(228) 9548-111 **Email:** zadi@zadi. de **WWW:** www.zadi.de **OPAC:** www.dainet.de

Non-English Name: Zentralstelle für Agrardokumentation und Information (ZADI) **Founded:** 1969 **Type:** Government **Head:** Dr. J.M. Pohlmann *Phone:* +49(228) 9548-101 *Email:* pohlmann@zadi.de **Staff:** 44 Prof. **Holdings:** 5,000 books 200 journals **Language of Collection/Services:** German / German **Subjects:** Comprehensive **Networks:** AGRIS **Databases Developed:** FIZ-AGRAR - Information Centre Food, agriculture and Forestry - Bibliographical databases, e.g. ELFIS; Projects; Calendar of Events; online access via Internet **Databases Used:** Comprehensive **Loan:** Inhouse **Service:** Internationally **Photocopy:** No

1160 Braunschweig, Germany
Federal Agricultural Research Centre
Central Information Service and Library
Bundesallee 50
D-38116 Braunschweig

Fax: +49(531) 596689 **WWW:** www.fal.de **OPAC:** fallit. fal.de

Non-English Name: Bundesforschungsanstalt für Landwirtschaft (FAL), Zentrale Informationsstelle und Bibliothek (ZIB) **Founded:** 1965 **Type:** Government **Head:** Dr. agr. G. Englert *Email:* englert@ziud.fal.de *Phone:* +49(531) 596239 **Staff:** 12 Prof. **Holdings:** 114,000 books 1,150 journals **Language of Collection/Services:** German / German **Subjects:** Comprehensive **Databases Used:** Agricola; Agris; Biosis; CABCD **Loan:** In country **Service:** Internationally **Photocopy:** Yes

1161 Braunschweig, Germany
Federal Biological Research Centre for
    Agriculture and Forestry
Braunschweig Library
Messeweg 11-12
D-38104 Braunschweig
Phone: +49(531) 299-3397 **Fax:** +49(531) 299-3018
Email: s.redlhammer@bba.de **WWW:** www.bba.de

Non-English Name: Biologische Bundesanstalt für Land- und Forstwirtschaft (BBA), Bibliothek Braunschweig **Type:** Government **Founded:** 1950 **Head:** Dr. sc.agr. Sabine Redlhammer *Email:* s.redlhammer@bba.de *Phone:* +49(531) 299-3390 **Staff:** 1 Prof. 3 Other **Holdings:** 60,000 books 1,100 journals **Language of Collection/Services:** German **Subjects:** Biology, Chemistry, Plant Pathology, Plant Protection **Loan:** Internationally **Service:** Internationally **Photocopy:** Yes

1162 Bremen, Germany
Niedersächsisches Landesamt für
    Bodenforschung, Bodentechnologisches
    Institut (NLfB, BTI)
Bibliothek
Friedrich-Missler-Strasse 46-50
D-28221 Bremen
Phone: +49(421) 203-4616 **Fax:** +49(421) 203-4610
WWW: bzax04.bgr.de/index.html

Former Name: Preussische (Staatliche) Moor-Versuchsstation **Founded:** 1946 **Type:** Government **Staff:** 1 Other **Holdings:** 10,000 books 100 journals **Language of Collection/Services:** German, English **Subjects:** Soil Conservation, Soil Management, Soil Mechanics **Loan:** Do not loan **Photocopy:** Yes

1163 Darmstadt, Germany
Darmstadt University of Technology, Institute for
    Water Resources Research
Section for Water Resources
Rundeturmstrasse 1
D-64283 Darmstadt
Phone: +49(6151) 162523 **Fax:** +49(6151) 163223
WWW: www.tu-darmstadt.de **Email:** wabau@hrz2.hrz. tu-darmstadt.de

Non-English Name: Technische Hochschule Darmstadt, Institut für Wasserbau und Wasserwirtschaft, Fachgebiet Wasserbau **Founded:** 1961 **Type:** Academic **Head:** Ingrid Zeitler *Phone:* +49(6151) 162824 *Email:* zeitler@hrz1.hrz. tu-darmstadt.de **Staff:** 1 Prof. **Holdings:** 20,000 books 150 journals **Language of Collection/Services:** German **Subjects:** Environment, Hydraulic Engineering, Irrigation, Water Management, Water Power, Water Resources, Waterways **Loan:** In country **Photocopy:** Yes

1164 Darmstadt, Germany
Institut für Papierfabrikation
Fachbibliothek Zellstoff und Papier
Alexanderstrasse 10
D-64283 Darmstadt
Phone: +49(6151) 162277 **Fax:** +49(6151) 162479 **Email:** bosse@papier.tu-darmstadt.de **WWW:** pix.ifp. maschinenbau.tu-darmstadt.de/ifp.html

Former Name: Verein Zellchemie, Bibliothek und Archiv Zellchemie **Founded:** 1952 **Type:** Academic **Head:** Hans-Joachim Bosse **Staff:** 1 Prof. **Subjects:** Fiber Plants, Pulp and Paper Industry **Loan:** Inhouse **Photocopy:** Yes

1165 Detmold, Germany
Federal Centre for Cereal, Potato and Lipid
Research in Detmold and Munster
Information and Documentation Service
Postfach 1354
D-32703 Detmold
Location: Schützenberg 12, D-32756 Detmold **Phone:** +49 (5231) 741528 **Fax:** +49(5231) 741100 **Email:** bagkf@ t-online.de **WWW:** www.dainet.de/bagkf

Non-English Name: Bundesanstalt für Getreide-, Kartoffel- und Fettforschung in Detmold und Münster (BAGKF), Informations- und Dokumentationsstelle **Former Name:** Federal Research Centre for Cereal and Potato Processing, Bundesforschungsanstalt für Getreide- und Kartoffelverarbeitung, Detmold **Founded:** 1907 **Head:** Ludger Themann *Phone:* +49(5231) 7410 **Type:** Government **Staff:** 1 Prof. 2 Other **Holdings:** 70,000 books 530 journals **Language of Collection/Services:** German / German **Subjects:** Biotechnology, Crops, Fats, Food Sciences **Specializations:** Baking, Biochemistry, Breadmaking, Cereals, Milling Industry, Potatoes, Radiochemistry **Databases Used:** Comprehensive **Loan:** Do not loan **Service:** Internationally **Photocopy:** Yes

1166 Dummerstorf, Germany
Research Institute for the Biology of Farm
Animals
Library
Wilhelm-Stahl-Allee 2
D-18196 Dummerstorf
Phone: +49(38208) 685 **Fax:** +49(38208) 68602 **Email:** fbn@fbn-dummerstorf.de **WWW:** www.fbn-dummerstorf. de/fbnde.htm

Non-English Name: Forschungsinstitut für die Biologie Landwirtschaftlicher Nutztiere (FBN), Wissenschaftliche Fachbibliothek **Former Name:** Academy of Agricultural Sciences of the GDR, Research Centre of Animal Production Dummerstorf-Rostock, Akademie der Landwirtschaftswissenschaften der DDR (AdL), Forschungszentrum für Tierproduktion Dummerstorf-Rostock **Founded:** 1939 **Type:** Government **Head:** Frau Hannelore Fietzke *Email:* fietzke@ fbn-dummerstorf.de **Staff:** 2 Other **Holdings:** 39,000 books 84 journals **Language of Collection/Services:** German,

English / German **Subjects:** Animal Husbandry, Breeding, Muscles, Nutrition Physiology, Physiology, Population Genetics, Statistics **Databases Used:** Agricola; Agris; CABCD **Loan:** In country **Service:** In country **Photocopy:** Yes

1167 Eberswalde-Finow, Germany
German Entomological Institute
Library
Schicklerstrasse 5
D-16225 Eberswalde-Finow
Fax: +49(3334) 212379 **Email:** dei@dei-eberswalde.de **WWW:** www.dei-eberswalde.de

Non-English Name: Deutsches Entomologisches Institut - Eberswalde (DEI), Bibliothek **Former Name:** Academy of Agricultural Sciences of the GDR, Akademie der Landwirtschaftswissenschaften der DDR (AdL), Institut für Pflanzenschutzforschung (IPF) **Founded:** 1886 **Head:** Dr. Klaus Rohlfien *Email:* redaktion@dei-eberswalde.de **Staff:** 8 Other **Type:** Government **Holdings:** 173,634 books 812 journals **Language of Collection/Services:** German, English, French **Subjects:** Biology, Biotechnology, Entomology, Phylogeny, Plant Pathology, Taxonomy **Loan:** In country **Photocopy:** Yes

1168 Erfurt, Germany
Stadt- und Regionalbibliothek Stadtverwaltung
Erfurt (Stu RB Erfurt)
Fischmarkt
D-99084 Erfurt
Location: Domplatz 1 **Phone:** +49(361) 655-1590 **Fax:** +49(361) 655-1599

Former Name: Universitätsbibliothek, Wissenschaftliche Bibliothek, Stadt- und Bezirks Bibliothek, Wissenschaftliche Allgemeinbibliothek der Stadt Erfurt (WAB) **Founded:** 1412 **Type:** Government **Head:** Heidemarie Trenkmann *Phone:* +49(361) 655-1590 **Staff:** 68 Prof. 12 Other **Holdings:** 595,274 books 756 journals **Language of Collection/Services:** German **Subjects:** Horticulture **Databases Developed:** Bibliotheca Amploniana - about 3,000 volumes; access only inhouse **Loan:** Internationally **Photocopy:** Yes

1169 Essen, Germany
AHT International GmbH
Bibliothek
Postfach 10 01 32
D-45128 Essen
Location: Huyssenallee 66-68, D-45001 Essen **Fax:** +49 (201) 201-6211 **Email:** schleifenbaum@aht-inter.com **WWW:** www.aht-inter.com

Former Name: Agrar- und Hydrotechnik GmbH (AHT) **Founded:** 1969 **Type:** Business **Head:** Axel Schleifenbaum *Email:* schleifenbaum@aht-inter.com *Phone:* +49(201) 201-6232 **Staff:** 1 Prof. **Holdings:** 9,000 books 50 journals **Language of Collection/Services:** English / German **Subjects:** Agriculture (Tropics), Agricultural Development, Crops, Soil Science, Water Resources **Specializations:** Irrigation **Loan:** Inhouse **Photocopy:** Yes

1170 Freiburg, Germany
University of Freiburg, Faculty of Forest Sciences

Library
Tennenbacher Str. 4
D-79106 Freiburg
Phone: +49(761) 203-3616 **Fax:** +49(761) 203-3613
OPAC: www.ub.uni-freiburg.de/olix **WWW:** www.
uni-freiburg.de

Non-English Name: Albert-Ludwigs-Universität, Fakultätsbibliothek Forstwissenschaften, Bibliothek **Founded:** 1955 **Type:** Academic **Head:** Jutta Giencke **Staff:** 1 Prof. 1 Other **Holdings:** 45,000 books 125 journals **Language of Collection/Services:** German **Subjects:** Forestry **Databases Used:** Current Contents **Loan:** Internationally **Photocopy:** Yes

1171   Freiburg, Germany
         University of Freiburg, Institute of Soil Science
              and Forest Nutrition
         Library
         Postfach
         D-79085 Freiburg
Location: Bertoldstrasse 17, D-79098 Freiburg im Breisgau **Phone:** +49(761) 203-3626 **Fax:** +49(761) 203-3618 **Email:** schackhe@ruf.uni-freiburg.de **WWW:** www.forst.uni-freiburg.de/bodenkunde

Non-English Name: Albert-Ludwigs-Universität, Institut für Bodenkunde und Waldernährungslehre, Institutsbibliothek **Founded:** 1951 **Type:** Academic **Head:** Dr. Helmer Schack-Kirchner *Phone:* +49(761) 203-3612 *Email:* schackhe@ruf.uni-freiburg.de **Staff:** 1 Prof. **Holdings:** 3,000 books 35 journals **Language of Collection/Services:** German / German **Subjects:** Plants, Soil, Water Resources **Loan:** Inhouse **Service:** Inhouse **Photocopy:** Yes

1172   Freiburg im Breisgau, Germany
         Forest Research Institute Baden-Württemberg
         Library
         Wonnhaldestrasse 4
         D-79100 Freiburg im Breisgau
Phone: +49(761) 4018-191 **Fax:** +49(761) 4018-333
WWW: fva.forst.uni-freiburg.de

Non-English Name: Forstliche Versuchs- und Forschungsanstalt Baden-Württemberg (FVA), Bibliothek **Founded:** 1986 **Type:** Government **Head:** I. Haug *Phone:* +49(761) 4018-191 *Email:* haug@fva.lfv.bwl.de **Staff:** 1 Other **Holdings:** 18,987 books 83 journals **Subjects:** Forest Management, Forestry **Loan:** Do not loan **Photocopy:** Yes

1173   Freiburg im Breisgau, Germany
         Staatliches Weinbauinstitut Freiburg
         Bibliothek
         Merzhauser Strasse 119
         D-79100 Freiburg im Breisgau
Phone: +49(761) 401-6512 **Fax:** +49(761) 401-6570

Founded: 1920 **Type:** Government **Staff:** 1 Other **Holdings:** 30,000 books 30 journals **Language of Collection/Services:** German **Subjects:** Viticulture, Winemaking **Loan:** Do not loan **Photocopy:** Yes

1174   Freising, Germany
         Fachhochschule Weihenstephan (FH
              Weihenstephan)
         Zentralbibliothek
         Am Hofgarten 2
         D-85354 Freising
Phone: +49(8161) 71-3377 **Fax:** +49(8161) 71-5245
Email: zb@fh-weihenstephan.de **WWW:** www.zb.fh-weihenstephan.de

Founded: 1983 **Type:** Government **Head:** Alexandra Beyer *Email:* alex.beyer@fh-weihenstephan.de *Phone:* +49(8161) 71-3376 **Staff:** 1 Other **Holdings:** 7,500 books 130 journals **Loan:** In country **Photocopy:** Yes

1175   Giessen, Germany
         Institute of Nutritional Sciences
         Nutrition Information Center (NIC)
         Goethestrasse 55
         D-35390 Giessen
Phone: +49(641) 993-9101 **Fax:** +49(641) 75517 **Email:** info.ernaehrung@ernaehrung.uni-giessen.de **WWW:** www.uni-giessen.de/nutriinfo

Non-English Name: Institut für Ernährungswissenschaft, Informations- und Dokumentationsstelle für Ernährung (IDE) **Type:** Academic **Head:** Dr. Roy Ackmann *Email:* roy.ackmann@ernaehrung.uni-giessen.de *Phone:* +49(641) 993-9100 **Staff:** 3 Prof. 4 Other **Language of Collection/Services:** German / German, English **Subjects:** Biology, Diet, Dietetics, Food Sciences **Specializations:** Dietetic Foods, Food Intake, Nutrition **Databases Used:** Comprehensive **Loan:** Inhouse **Service:** Internationally **Photocopy:** Yes

1176   Giessen, Germany
         Justus-Liebig University
         University Library
         D-35386 Giessen
Location: Otto-Behaghel-Strasse 8, D-35394 Giessen **Phone:** +49(641) 99-14032 **Fax:** +49(641) 99-14009 **Email:** auskunft@ub.uni-giessen.de **OPAC:** opac.uni-giessen.de/cgi-bin/ wwwlibmenu **WWW:** www.uni-giessen.de/ub

Non-English Name: Justus-Liebig-Universität, Universitätsbibliothek **Founded:** 1612 **Type:** Academic **Head:** *Email:* direktion@ub.uni-giessen.de *Phone:* +49(641) 99-14001 **Staff:** 32 Prof. 45 Other **Holdings:** 3,787 journals1 3,190,000 books **Language of Collection/Services:** German /German **Subjects:** Animal Husbandry, Environmental Protection, Food Sciences, Forestry, Home Economics, Human Nutrition, Pollution, Veterinary Medicine **Databases Used:** Agricola; Agris; Biosis; CABCD **Loan:** Internationally **Photocopy:** Yes

1177   Giessen, Germany
         Justus-Liebig University, Institute for Farm
              Management
         Library
         Senckenbergstrasse 3
         D-35390 Giessen

Phone: +49(641) 99-37295 **Fax:** +49(641) 99-37249 **Email:** kuhlmann.lbl1@agrar.uni-gissen.de **WWW:** www.uni-giessen.de **OPAC:** opac.uni-giessen.de

Non-English Name: Justus-Liebig-Universität, Institut für Landwirtschaftliche Betriebslehre, Bibliothek **Type:** Academic **Head:** Prof. Dr. N.C.F. Kuhlmann *Phone:* +49(641) 99-37240 *Email:* kuhlmann.lbl1@agrar.uni-gissen.de **Staff:** 1 Other **Holdings:** 25,000 books 50 journals **Subjects:** Agricultural Economics **Loan:** Do not loan **Photocopy:** Yes

1178   Giessen, Germany
Justus-Liebig University, Institute of Agronomy and Plant Breeding II, Grassland Management and Fodder Growing
Library
Ludwigstrasse 23
D-35390 Giessen

Phone: +49(641) 99-37510 **Fax:** +49(641) 99-37519 **Email:** wilhelm.opitz-von-boberfeld@agrar.uni-giessen.de **WWW:** www.uni-giessen.de/~gh1196

Non-English Name: Justus-Liebig-Universität, Institut für Pflanzenbau und Pflanzenzüchtung II, Grünlandwirtschaft und Futterbau, Bibliothek **Founded:** 1952 **Type:** Academic **Head:** Prof. Dr. Dr. h.c. W. Opitz von Boberfeld *Phone:* +49(641) 99-37510 *Email:* wilhelm.opitz-von-boberfeld@agrar.uni-giessen.de **Staff:** 2 Prof. 11 Other **Holdings:** 600 books 15 journals **Language of Collection/Services:** German, English / German, English **Subjects:** Forage, Grasslands, Plant Breeding **Specializations:** Ecology, Grassland Management, Legumes, Plant Competition **Loan:** Do not loan **Service:** Inhouse **Photocopy:** No

1179   Göttingen, Germany
Georg-August University, Faculty of Forest Sciences and Forest Ecology
Library
Büsgenweg 5
D-37077 Göttingen

Fax: +49(551) 393407 **Email:** ulfw@gwdg.de **OPAC:** www4.sub.uni-goettingen.de/cgi-bin/wwwlibmenu **WWW:** www.sub.uni-goettingen.de

Non-English Name: Georg-August-Universität, Fakultät für Forstwissenschaften und Waldökologie, Bibliothek **Type:** Academic **Founded:** 1868 **Head:** Christiane Kollmeyer *Phone:* +49(551) 393407 *Email:* ulfw@gwdg.de **Staff:** 3 Other **Holdings:** 120,000 books 650 journals **Subjects:** Forestry, Hunting **Loan:** Internationally **Photocopy:** Yes

1180   Göttingen, Germany
Georg-August University, Institute for Agricultural Chemistry
Bibliothek
von-Siebold-Strasse 6
D-37075 Göttingen

Phone: +49(551) 39-5568 **Fax:** +49(551) 39-5570 **Email:** uaac@gwdg.de **WWW:** www.sub.uni-goettingen.de/java_home.htm

Non-English Name: Georg-August-Universität, Institut für Agrikulturchemie **Founded:** 1964 **Type:** Academic **Head:**

Martina Noltkämper *Phone:* +49(551) 39-5568 **Staff:** .5 Other **Holdings:** 2,500 books 21 journals **Subjects:** Agricultural Chemistry, Plant Nutrition **Loan:** Do not loan **Photocopy:** No

1181   Göttingen, Germany
Georg-August University, Institute for Agricultural Economics
Library
Platz der Göttinger Sieben 5
D-37073 Göttingen

Phone: +49(551) 394819 **Fax:** +49(551) 394823, 392030 **Email:** biblio@uni-uaao.gwdg.de **OPAC:** opac.sub.gwdg.de **WWW:** www.sub.uni-goettingen.de

Non-English Name: Georg-August-Universität, Institut für Agrarökonomie, Bibliothek **Type:** Academic **Head:** *Phone:* Monika Scholz **Founded:** 1969 **Staff:** 2 Other **Holdings:** 60,000 books 315 journals **Language of Collection/Services:** German, English/German, English **Subjects:** Agricultural Economics, Agricultural Sciences, Rural Sociology, Econometrics **Networks:** GBV **Databases Used:** AGECON CD; Biosis **Loan:** Do not loan **Service:** Inhouse **Photocopy:** Yes

1182   Göttingen, Germany
Georg-August University, Institute of Agronomy and Animal Hygiene in the Tropics (IAT)
Library
Grisebachstrasse 6
D-37077 Göttingen

Phone: +49(551) 393752 **Fax:** +49(551) 393759 **Email:** uatr@gwdg.de **WWW:** www.gwdg.de/~uatr/index.htm

Non-English Name: Georg-August-Universität, Institut für Pflanzenbau und Tierproduktion in den Tropen und Subtropen, Handbibliothek des Institutes **Founded:** 1967 **Type:** Academic **Head:** Dr. Herwig Koch *Phone:* +49(551) 393748 *Email:* hkoch@gwdg.de **Staff:** 5 Other **Holdings:** 7,000 books 60 journals **Language of Collection/Services:** English **Subjects:** Agriculture (Tropics), Crops **Specializations:** Tropical Crops **Databases Developed:** Database on agricultural crops, except ornamental plants and forest trees of the tropics; now 4264 units i.e. plants **Loan:** In country **Photocopy:** Yes

1183   Göttingen, Germany
Georg-August University, Institute of Agronomy and Plant Breeding
Library
von-Siebold-Strasse 8
D-37075 Göttingen

Phone: +49(551) 394352 **Fax:** +49(551) 394601 **WWW:** www.uni-goettingen.de

Non-English Name: Georg-August-Universität, Institut für Pflanzenbau und Pflanzenzüchtung, Bibliothek **Founded:** 1950 **Type:** Academic **Head:** Innes Heise *Phone:* +49(551) 394362 *Email:* iheise@uni-goettingen.de **Staff:** 20 Prof. 50 Other **Holdings:** 6,900 books 43 journals **Subjects:** Crops, Genetics, Plant Breeding **Loan:** Do not loan **Photocopy:** Yes

1184   Göttingen, Germany
Georg-August University, Institute for Plant
Pathology and Protection
Library
Grisebachstrasse 6
D-37077 Göttingen

Phone: +49(551) 393700 **Fax:** +49(551) 394187 **WWW:**
www.sub.uni-goettingen.de/java_home.htm

Non-English Name: Georg-August-Universität, Institut für
Pflanzenpathologie und Pflanzenschutz, Bibliothek **Founded:** 1950 **Type:** Academic **Head:** Dr. Bernd Ulber *Phone:*
+49(551) 393725 *Email:* bulber@gwdg.de **Staff:** 1 Prof. 1
Other **Holdings:** 2,600 books 57 journals **Language of Col-
lection/Services:** German, English **Subjects:** Entomology,
Herbology, Plant Pathology **Databases Developed:** Collections of freeze-dried bacteria and fungi, mostly phytopatho-
genic or antagonistic **Loan:** Do not loan **Photocopy:** Yes

1185   Göttingen, Germany
Georg-August University, Institute of Rural
Development
Library for Rural Development in the Tropics and
Subtropics
Waldweg 26
D-37073 Göttingen

Phone: +49(551) 393913 **Fax:** +49(551) 393073 **Email:**
uare@gwdg.de **WWW:** www.sub.uni-goettingen.de/
java_home.htm

Non-English Name: Georg-August-Universität, Institut für
Rurale Entwicklung (IRE), Bibliothek für Agrarentwicklung
in den Tropen und Subtropen **Former Name:** Institut für
Ausländische Landwirtschaft **Founded:** 1963 **Type:** Academic **Head:** Erika Wenzel *Phone:* +49(551) 393914 *Email:*
ewenzel@gwdg.de **Staff:** 1 Prof. 2 Other **Holdings:** 60,000
books 221 journals **Language of Collection/Services:** English / German **Subjects:** Economic Sociology, Rural Sociology **Specializations:** Rural Development (Asia), Rural
Development (Africa) **Networks:** GBV **Loan:** In country
Photocopy: Yes

1186   Göttingen, Germany
State and University Library of Lower Saxony
Platz der Göttinger Sieben 1
D-37073 Göttingen

Phone: +49(551) 39-5231 **Fax:** +49(551) 395222 **Email:**
sub@mail.sub.uni-goettingen.de **OPAC:** www4.sub.
uni-goettingen.de:45126 **WWW:** www.sub.uni-goettingen.
de **Ariel IP:** 134.76.162.210

Non-English Name: Niedersächsische Staats- und Universitätsbibliothek (SUB) **Founded:** 1734 **Type:** Academic
Head: Prof. Dr. Elmar Mittler *Phone:* +49(551) 39-5210
Email: mittler@mail.sub.uni-goettingen.de **Staff:** 104 Prof.
72 Other **Holdings:** 4,000,000 books 14,700 journals **Subjects:** Agriculture (Tropics), Agricultural Development,
Agricultural Economics, Animal Husbandry, Crops, Entomology, Farming, Plant Pathology, Water Resources **Specializations:** Forestry, Soil Science **Networks:** GBV
Databases Used: AgECONCD; SOILCD **Loan:** Internationally **Service:** Internationally **Photocopy:** Yes

1187   Gross-Umstadt, Germany
Federal Centre of Forest Operations and
Techniques
Information Centre (Forest)
Spremberger Strasse 1
D-64819 Gross-Umstadt

Fax: +49(6078) 78550 **Email:** kwf.info@t-online.de
WWW: www.kwf-online.de

Non-English Name: Kuratorium für Waldarbeit und Forst-
technik E.V. (KWF), Informationszentrale (Forstliche) (IZ)
Founded: 1980 **Type:** Government **Head:** Dr. R. Hofmann
Phone: +49(6078) 7850 **Staff:** 11 Prof. 15 Other **Holdings:**
1,200 books 74 journals **Language of Collection/Services:**
German/English, German **Subjects:** Forestry Engineering,
Forestry **Specializations:** Forest Management **Loan:** In
country **Service:** In country **Photocopy:** Yes

1188   Grossbeeren, Germany
Institute for Vegetable and Ornamental Crops
Library
Theodor-Echtermeyer-Weg 1
D-14979 Grossbeeren

Phone: +49(33701) 780 **Fax:** +49(33701) 391 **WWW:**
www.dainet.de/igz

Non-English Name: Institut für Gemüse- und Zierpflanzenbau (IGZ), Bibliothek **Former Name:** Academy of Agricultural Sciences of the GDR, Institute of Vegetable Production,
Akademie der Landwirtschaftswissenschaften der DDR
(AdL), Institut für Gemüseproduktion **Founded:** 1950
Type: Academic **Head:** Dr. Hans G. Brod *Phone:* +49
(33701) 78115 *Email:* brod@igzev.de **Staff:** 2 Prof. 1 Other
Holdings: 50,000 books 42 journals **Language of Collec-
tion/Services:** German / German **Subjects:** Agricultural Engineering, Fertilizers, Field Crops, Horticulture, Plant
Breeding, Plant Pathology, Quality Management, Soil Science **Specializations:** Asparagus, Brassica, Broccoli, Car-
rots, Cauliflowers, Celery, Chicory, Cucumbers, Liliaceae,
Radishes, Tomatoes **Databases Developed:** Horticultural
documents, monographs and journal articles **Databases
Used:** Current Contents **Loan:** In country **Service:** In country **Photocopy:** Yes

1189   Gülzow-Güstrow, Germany
Research Centre for Agriculture and Fishery
Scientific Library
Dorfplatz 1
D-18276 Gülzow-Güstrow

Phone: +49(3843) 789201 **Fax:** +49(3843) 789111
WWW: www.landwirtschaft-mv.de

Non-English Name: Landesforschungsanstalt für Landwirt-
schaft un Fischerei (LFA), Wissenschaftliche Bibliothek
Former Name: Academy of Agricultural Sciences of the
GDR, Akademie der Landwirtschaftswissenschaften der
DDR (AdL), Gülzow-Güstrow Institute of Plant Breeding,
Institut für Pflanzenzüchtung Gülzow-Güstrow (IPZ GÜ)
Founded: 1962 **Type:** Government **Head:** G. Stölken
Phone: +49(3843) 789201 *Email:* lfa-pflanze@t-online.de
Staff: 1 Prof. **Holdings:** 10,000 books 80 journals **Lan-
guage of Collection/Services:** German, English **Subjects:**
Agricultural Development, Agricultural Economics, Crops,

Farming, Fisheries, Plants, Soil **Loan:** In country **Photocopy:** Yes

♦**1190   Halle (Saale), Germany**
Deutsche Akademie der Naturforscher Leopoldina
Bibliothek
Postfach 1127
D-06019 Halle (Saale)
Location: August-Bebel-Strasse 50 a, D-06108 Halle

Founded: 1731 **Type:** Academic **Head:** Jochen Thamm *Phone:* +49(345) 24723 **Holdings:** 280,000 books 500 journals **Language of Collection/Services:** German, English **Subjects:** Agricultural Development, Animal Husbandry, Biotechnology, Education/Extension, Entomology, Farming, Food Sciences, Forestry, Plant Pathology, Soil Science, Veterinary Medicine **Loan:** Internationally **Photocopy:** Yes

1191   Halle (Saale), Germany
Martin-Luther-Universität Halle-Wittenberg
Universitäts- und Landesbibliothek
Sachsen-Anhalt
August-Bebel-Strasse 13 u. 50
D-06098 Halle (Saale)
Phone: +49(345) 552-2167 **Fax:** +49(345) 552-7140
WWW: www.bibliothek.uni-halle.de **OPAC:** haweb1.
bibliothek.uni-halle.de/cgi-bin/wwwlibmenu

Founded: 1696 **Type:** Academic **Head:** Dr. Heiner Schnelling *Phone:* +49(345) 55200 *Email:* direktion@ bibliothek.uni-halle.de **Holdings:** 4,500,000 books 9,674 journals **Language of Collection/Services:** German **Subjects:** Agribusiness, Agricultural Development, Agricultural Economics, Agricultural Engineering, Animal Husbandry, Biotechnology, Crops, Entomology, Farming, Fisheries, Food Sciences, Horticulture, Plant Pathology, Soil Science, Veterinary Medicine, Water Resources **Networks:** GBV **Databases Used:** Agricola; Agris; CABCD **Loan:** Internationally **Photocopy:** Yes

1192   Hamburg, Germany
Federal Maritime and Hydrographic Agency
Library
Postfach 30 12 20
D-20305 Hamburg
Location: Bernhard-Nocht-Strasse 78, D-20359 Hamburg
Phone: +49(40) 3190-2493 **Fax:** +49(40) 3190-5000
Email: bibliothek@bsh.d400.de **WWW:** www.bsh.de

Non-English Name: Bundesamt für Seeschiffahrt und Hydrographie (BSH), Bibliothek **Former Name:** German Maritime Observatory, German Hydrographic Institute, Deutsche Seewarte, Deutsches Hydrographisches Institut (DHI) **Founded:** 1875 **Type:** Government **Head:** Antje Lueck *Phone:* +49(40) 3190-2410 *Email:* antje.lueck@bsh. d400.de **Staff:** 6 Prof. 1 Other **Holdings:** 150,000 books 1,500 journals **Language of Collection/Services:** English **Subjects:** Agricultural Meteorology, Tropical Meteorology **Specializations:** Chemistry, Climatology, Hydrography, Marine Environment, Meteorology, Navigation, Oceanography, Marine Geophysics, Sea Charts **Databases Developed:** Hydrographic documentation - since 1993 online **Loan:** Internationally **Photocopy:** Yes

1193   Hamburg, Germany
Federal Ministry for Food, Agriculture and
Forestry, Federal Research Center for
Forestry and Forest Products
Library / Documentation and Information
Leuschnerstrasse 91
D-21027 Hamburg
Phone: +49(40) 73962-233 **Fax:** +49(40) 73962-480
WWW: www.dainet.de/bfh

Non-English Name: Bundesministerium für Ernährung, Landwirtschaft und Forsten, Bundesforschungsanstalt für Forst- und Holzwirtschaft (BML, BFH), Bibliothek/Dokumentation und Information **Founded:** 1939 **Type:** Academic **Head:** U. Reupke *Phone:* +49(40) 73962-233 *Email:* reupke@aixh0001.holz.uni-hamburg.de/bfh **Staff:** 3 Prof. **Holdings:** 93,000 books 220 journals **Language of Collection/Services:** German, English, Spanish **Subjects:** Agriculture (Tropics), Agribusiness, Biotechnology, Entomology, Crops, Horticulture, Plant Pathology, Soil Science, Water Resources **Specializations:** Forest Products Industries, Forestry, Wood **Loan:** Internationally **Photocopy:** Yes

1194   Hamburg, Germany
Federal Research Centre for Fisheries
Library and Information and Documentation
Services
Palmaille 9
D-22767 Hamburg
Phone: +49(40) 38905-197 **Fax:** +49(40) 38905-129
Email: bibliothek@bfa-fisch.de, 100565.1223@ compuserve.com **WWW:** www.dainet.de/bfafi

Non-English Name: Bundesforschungsanstalt für Fischerei (BFAFi), Bibliothek und Informations- und Dokumentationsstelle **Founded:** 1962 **Type:** Government **Head:** Dr. Wulf P. Kirchner (Information), Anita Ritter (Library) *Phone:* +49(40) 38905-113, 38905-142 *Email:* kirchner. iud@bfa-fisch.de **Staff:** 2 Prof. **Holdings:** 67,000 books 885 journals **Language of Collection/Services:** German, English / German **Subjects:** Aquaculture, Fisheries **Databases Used:** Comprehensive **Loan:** Inhouse **Service:** Internationally **Photocopy:** Yes

1195   Hamburg, Germany
Universität Hamburg, Institut für Angewandte
Botanik
Bibliothek
Postfach 30 27 62
D-20355 Hamburg (Neustadt)
Location: Marseiller Strasse 7 **Phone:** +49(40) 42838-2371 **Fax:** +49(40) 42838-6593 **Email:** bibangbot@ uni-hamburg.de **WWW:** www.jura.uni-hamburg.de **OPAC:** www.physnet.uni-hamburg.de/botany/alg/biblio

Founded: 1883 **Type:** Academic **Staff:** 2 Other **Holdings:** 90,000 books 275 journals **Subjects:** Economic Botany **Loan:** In country **Photocopy:** Yes

1196   Hannover, Germany
Chamber of Agriculture Hannover
Library
Johannssenstrasse 10

Postfach 269
D-30159 Hannover
WWW: www.lwk-hannover.de

Non-English Name: Landwirtschaftskammer Hannover **Founded:** 1899 **Type:** Government **Head:** P. Wachter **Email:** p.wachter-lwkh@t-online.de **Phone:** +49(511) 366-5305 **Staff:** 1 Prof. 1 Other **Holdings:** 5,000 books **Language of Collection/Services:** German / German **Subjects:** Animal Husbandry, Crop Production, Fisheries, Forestry **Loan:** Do not loan **Photocopy:** Yes

1197   Hannover, Germany
         Ministry of Food, Agriculture and Forestry of
              Lower Saxony
         Library
         PO Box 243
         D-31069 Hannover

Location: Calenberger Strasse 2, D-30169 Hannover **Phone:** +49(511) 120-2215 **Fax:** +49(511) 120-2385 **Email:** bibliothek@andtag.niedersachsen.de **WWW:** www.ahb.niedersachsen.de **OPAC:** www.hobsy.de/ cgi-bin/nph-wwwredir/sun31.tib.uni-hannover.de:54804

Non-English Name: Niedersächsisches Ministerium für Ernährung, Landwirtschaft und Forsten, Bücherei **Founded:** 1948 **Type:** Government **Head:** Stefan Goetz **Phone:** +49 (511) 120-6602 **Email:** stefan.goetz@ml.niedersachsen.de **Staff:** 1 Prof. 1 Other **Holdings:** 33,000 books 260 journals **Language of Collection/Services:** German **Subjects:** Agricultural Law, Agricultural Development, Agricultural Economics, Agricultural Engineering, Animal Husbandry, Crops, Education/Extension, Farming, Fisheries, Food Sciences, Plant Pathology, Rural Law, Soil Science, Veterinary Medicine **Networks:** GBV **Loan:** In country **Service:** In country **Photocopy:** Yes

1198   Hannover, Germany
         University of Hannover
         University Library, Branch Library for
              Horticulture, Landscape Architecture and
              Environmental Development
         Harrenhäuser Strasse 2
         D-30419 Hannover

Phone: +49(511) 762-2687 (Auskunft) **Fax:** +49(511) 762-3694 **Email:** fb-gartenbau@tib.uni-hannover.de **WWW:** www.uni-hannover.de **OPAC:** www.tib.uni-hannover.de

Non-English Name: Universität Hannover, Universitätsbibliothek, Fachbereichsbibliothek Gartenbau, Landschaftsarchitektur und Umweltentwicklung (UB) **Type:** Academic **Staff:** 1 Prof. 1 Other **Language of Collection/Services:** German **Subjects:** Horticulture **Photocopy:** No

1199   Heidelberg, Germany
         Research Centre for International Agrarian and
              Economic Development
         Library
         Ringstrasse 19
         D-69115 Heidelberg

Fax: +49(6221) 167482 **Email:** fia@urz.uni-heidelberg.de **WWW:** www.rzuser.uni-heidelberg.de/~t08

Non-English Name: Forschungsstelle für Internationale Agrar- und Wirtschaftsentwicklung, Bibliothek **Founded:** 1961 **Type:** Association **Head:** Karl Konheiser **Phone:** +49(6221) 183056 **Staff:** 1 Prof. **Holdings:** 11,000 books 45 journals **Language of Collection/Services:** English **Subjects:** Agriculture (Tropics), Agricultural Development, Agricultural Economics, Crops, Forestry, Water Resources **Loan:** Inhouse **Service:** Inhouse **Photocopy:** Yes

1200   Karlsruhe, Germany
         Federal Research Center for Nutrition
         Information Center and Library
         Haid-und-Neu-Str. 9
         D-76131 Karlsruhe

Phone: +49(721) 6625-600, Bibliothek -612 **Fax:** +49 (721) 6625-552 **Email:** l.inf@bfe.uni-karlsruhe.de **WWW:** www.dainet.de/bfe **OPAC:** 141.3.248.113

Non-English Name: Bundesforschungsanstalt für Ernährung (BFE), Informationszentrum und Bibliothek (INF) **Head:** Dr. T. Storck **Staff:** 10 Prof. **Holdings:** 20,000 books 350 journals **Language of Collection/Services:** German, English / German **Subjects:** Food Chemistry, Food Hygiene, Food Irradiation, Food Technology, Nutrition **Loan:** Inhouse **Service:** Internationally **Photocopy:** Yes

1201   Karlsruhe, Germany
         Staatliche Landwirtschaftliche Untersuchungs-
              und Forschungsanstalt Augustenberg
         Bibliothek
         Postfach 430230
         D-76217 Karlsruhe

Location: Nesslerstrasse 23, D-76227 Karlsruhe **Phone:** +49(721) 4647-0 **Fax:** +49(721) 4647-112 **Email:** poststelle@lufak.bwl.la.de

Founded: 1859 **Type:** Government **Head:** Dr. Markus Modry **Phone:** +49(721) 4647-184 **Staff:** 1 Prof. 1 Other **Holdings:** 5,500 books 90 journals **Language of Collection/Services:** German / German **Subjects:** Animal Nutrition, Feeds, Fertilizers, Microbiology, Plant Nutrition, Seeds, Soil Science **Loan:** Do not loan **Photocopy:** Yes

1202   Kempten, Germany
         Institute for Applied Dairy Research
         Library
         Postfach 2025
         D-87410 Kempten

Location: Hirnbeinstrasse 10, D-87435 Kempten **Phone:** +49(831) 5290-0 **Fax:** +49(831) 5290-100 **Email:** muva. kempten@t-online.de

Non-English Name: Milchwirtschaftliche Untersuchungs- und Versuchsanstalt Kempten (MUVA), Bibliothek und Dokumentation **Founded:** 1887 **Staff:** 100 Prof. **Holdings:** 7,000 books 50 journals **Language of Collection/Services:** German **Subjects:** Agribusiness, Agricultural Development, Agricultural Economics, Bacteriology, Chemistry, Biotechnology, Education/Extension, Farming, Food Sciences, Microbiology, Veterinary Medicine, Water Resources **Loan:** Do not loan **Photocopy:** Yes

1203 Kiel, Germany
Federal Dairy Research Centre
Department of Documentation and Information
Postfach 60 69
D-24121 Kiel

Location: Hermann Weigmann-Strasse 1, D-24103 Kiel
Phone: +49(431) 609-2323 **Fax:** +49(431) 609-2409
Email: diz@bafm.de **WWW:** www.bafm.de

Non-English Name: Bundesanstalt für Milchforschung (BafM), Daten- und Informationszentrum **Founded:** 1922 **Type:** Government **Head:** Dr. G. Rathjen, Director *Email:* rathjen@bafm.de **Staff:** 1 Prof. 5 Other **Holdings:** 125,000 books 770 journals **Subjects:** Biology, Dairy Science, Nutrition **Databases Used:** CABCD; Current Contents; FSTA **Loan:** Do not loan **Service:** Inhouse **Photocopy:** Yes

1204 Kiel, Germany
Kiel Institute of World Economics
Central Library
Düsternbrooker Weg 120
D-24105 Kiel

Fax: +49(431) 8814-520 **Email:** info@zbw.ifw-kiel.de
WWW: www.uni-kiel.de:8080/IfW/homeeng.htm **OPAC:** www.uni-kiel.de:8080/IfW/zbw/econis.htm

Non-English Name: Institut für Weltwirtschaft (IfW), Deutsche Zentralbibliothek für Wirtschaftswissenschaften (ZBW) **Founded:** 1914 **Type:** Government **Head:** Horst Thomsen *Phone:* +49(431) 8814-444 *Email:* h.thomsen@zbw.ifw-kiel.de **Staff:** 16 Prof. 92 Other **Holdings:** 2,400,000 books 16,500 journals **Language of Collection/Services:** English, German **Subjects:** Agricultural Development, Agricultural Economics **Databases Developed:** Econis (Economic Information System); available via Internet **Loan:** Internationally **Photocopy:** Yes

1205 Kirchain, Germany
Hessische Landesanstalt für Tierzucht
Abteilung für Bienenzucht
Erlenstrasse 9
D-35274 Kirchain

Founded: 1928 **Type:** Government **Head:** Dr. Ralph Büchler *Phone:* +49(6422) 94060 *Email:* hlt.bienen@t-online.de **Staff:** 1 Other **Holdings:** 1,000 books 15 journals **Language of Collection/Services:** German **Subjects:** Apidae **Loan:** Do not loan **Photocopy:** Yes

1206 Kleinmachnow, Germany
Federal Biological Research Centre for
    Agriculture and Forestry
Kleinmachnow Library
Stahnsdorfer Damm 81
D-14532 Kleinmachnow
Phone: +49(3203) 48221, 48217 **Fax:** +49(3203) 48425
Email: bibokm@bba.de **WWW:** www.bba.de

Non-English Name: Biologische Bundesanstalt für Land- und Forstwirtschaft (BBA), Bibliothek Aussenstelle Kleinmachnow **Former Name:** Academy of Agricultural Sciences of the GDR, Akademie der Landwirtschaftswissenschaften der DDR (AdL), Biologisege Zentralanstalt Berlin, Institut für Pflanzenschutzforschung Kleinmachnow (IPF)

Founded: 1949 **Type:** Government **Head:** Dr. Olaf Hering *Email:* o.hering@bba.de **Staff:** 5 Other **Holdings:** 28,000 books 415 journals **Subjects:** Entomology, Plant Pathology **Loan:** Internationally **Photocopy:** Yes

1207 Langenargen, Germany
Environmental Protection Agency
    Baden-Württemberg, Institute for Lake
    Research
Library
Postfach 4253
D-88081 Langenargen

Location: Untere Seestrasse 81 **Phone:** +49(7543) 3040

Non-English Name: Landesanstalt für Umweltzschutz Baden-Württemberg, Institut für Seenforschung, Bibliothek **Founded:** 1920 **Type:** Government **Staff:** 1 Other **Holdings:** 5,000 books 80 journals **Language of Collection/Services:** German / German **Subjects:** Biology, Chemistry, Fisheries **Loan:** Do not loan **Photocopy:** Yes

1208 Munich, Germany
Entomological Society of Munich
Library
c/o Zoologische Staatssammlung
Münchhausenstrasse 21
D-81247 Munich
Phone: +49(89) 8107-161/2 **Fax:** +49(89) 8107-300
Email: kld1116@mail.lrz-muenchen.de **WWW:** www. zsm.mwn.de/meg/meg_will.htm

Non-English Name: Münchner Entomologische Gesellschaft e.V. (MEG), Bibliothek **Type:** Association **Head:** Dr. Juliane Diller *Phone:* +49(89) 8107-161 *Email:* kld1116@mail.lrz-muenchen.de **Staff:** 1 Prof. 2 Other **Holdings:** 15,000 books 360 journals **Language of Collection/Services:** English, German, French / German, English, French **Subjects:** Entomology **Loan:** Internationally **Service:** Internationally **Photocopy:** Yes

1209 Munich, Germany
Paper Technology Foundation
Information - Documentation Department
Hess-Strasse 134
D-80797 Munich
Phone: +49(89) 1260-0146 **Fax:** +49(89) 123-6592 **Email:** d.schur@pts.papertec.de **WWW:** www.pts-papertec.de

Non-English Name: Papiertechnische Stiftung (PTS), Information und Dokumentation (IuD) **Founded:** 1982 **Type:** Research **Head:** Did.-Soc. S. Reisch *Phone:* +49(89) 1260-010 *Email:* s.reisch@pts.papertec.de **Staff:** 5 Prof. 3 Other **Holdings:** 16,500 books 195 journals **Language of Collection/Services:** German, English / German **Subjects:** Effluents, Forestry, Wood **Specializations:** Paper, Pulp and Paper Industry, Pulping **Databases Developed:** PAPERTECH - bibliographic information; PAPERFACTS - factual information **Databases Used:** Comprehensive **Loan:** Inhouse **Service:** Internationally **Photocopy:** Yes

1210 Plön, Germany
Max Planck Institute of Limnology
Library

Postfach 165
D-24302 Plön
Location: August-Thienemannstrasse 2, D-24306 Plön
Fax: +49(4522) 763-351 **Email:** bibl@mpil-ploen.mpg.de
WWW: www.mpil-ploen.mpg.de/index.html **OPAC:**
www.vzlbs.gbv.de/cgi-bin/wwwlibmenu

Non-English Name: Max-Planck-Institut für Limnologie,
Bibliothek **Former Name:** Hydrobiologische Anstalt, Bio-
logische Anstalt **Type:** Research **Head:** Brigitte Lechner
Phone: +49(4522) 763-263 **Staff:** 1 Prof. .5 Other **Holdings:**
7,600 books 400 journals **Language of Collection/Services:**
German, English **Subjects:** Agriculture (Tropics), Entomol-
ogy, Fisheries, Soil Science, Water Resources **Photocopy:**
Yes **Loan:** Inhouse **Service:** Internationally

1211 Potsdam, Germany
Institute of Agricultural Engineering Bornim
Library
Max-Eyth-Allee
D-14469 Potsdam
Phone: +49(331) 56990 **Fax:** +49(331) 569-9849 **Email:**
atb@atb-potsdam.de **WWW:** www.atb-potsdam.de/
abteilungen/zentral/index.html

Non-English Name: Institut für Agrartechnik Bornim e.V.,
Bibliothek **Former Name:** Academy of Agricultural Sciences of the GDR, Akademie der Landwirtschaftswissenschaften der DDR (AdL), Research Centre on Mechanization
and Energy Utilization in Agriculture, Forschungszentrum
für Mechanisierung und Energieanwendung in der Landwirtschaft **Founded:** 1952 **Type:** Government **Staff:** 2 Prof.
Holdings: 22,000 books 150 journals **Language of Collec-
tion/Services:** German / German **Subjects:** Agricultural Engineering **Databases Used:** CABCD **Service:** In country
Loan: In country **Photocopy:** Yes

1212 Potsdam, Germany
University of Applied Sciences
Library, Information Centre for Science and
Manufacturing
Postfach 60 06 08
Pappelallee 8-9
D-14469 Potsdam
Location: Friedrich-Ebert-Str. 4, D-14467 Potsdam
Phone: +49(331) 580-2210, 580-2230 **Fax:** +49(331) 580-
2229 **Email:** iz@fh-potsdam.de **WWW:** www.fh-potsdam.
de **OPAC:** www.fh-potsdam.de/~BibB/bib_home.htm

Non-English Name: Fachhochschule Potsdam, Bibliothek,
Informationszentrum für Informationswissenschaft und
-praxis (IZ) **Founded:** 1992 **Type:** Academic **Head:** Karen
Falke *Phone:* +49(331) 580-2210 *Email:* falke@fh-potsdam.
de **Staff:** 3 Prof. **Language of Collection/Services:** German
/ German **Subjects:** Crops, Plants, Soil Science **Specializa-
tions:** Crop Yield, Cropping Systems, Farming Systems,
Fertilizers, Plant Nutrition, Soil Analysis, Soil Biology, Soil
Chemistry, Soil Fertility, Soil Management, Soil Pollution,
Soil Properties, Soil Resources, Soil Testing, Soil Types,
Soil Water **Databases Used:** Agricola; Agris; CABCD **Pho-
tocopy:** Yes

1213 Quedlinburg, Germany
Federal Centre for Breeding Research on
Cultivated Plants
Main Library
Neuer Weg 22/23
D-06484 Quedlinburg
Phone: +49(3946) 470 **Fax:** +49(3946) 47255 **Email:**
bafz-zb@bafz.de **WWW:** www.bafz.de

Non-English Name: Bundesanstalt für Züchtungsforschung
an Kulturpflanzen, Haputbilithek **Founded:** 1948 **Type:**
Academic **Head:** Frau Grit Lautenbach *Phone:* +49(3946)
47409 *Email:* g.lautenbach@bafz.de **Staff:** 1 Prof. **Holdings:** 26,000 books 125 journals **Language of Collection/
Services:** German, English / German **Subjects:** Biochemistry, Botany, Food Sciences, Genetics, Plant Breeding, Plant
Pathology **Loan:** In country **Service:** In country **Photocopy:**
Yes

1214 Siebeldingen, Germany
Federal Centre for Breeding Research on
Cultivated Plants, Institute for Grapevine
Breeding Geilweilerhof
Library
Geilweilerhof
D-76833 Siebeldingen
Phone: +49(6345) 41142 **Fax:** +49(6345) 919050 **Email:**
doku-vitis@bafz.de **WWW:** www.bafz.de

Non-English Name: Bundesanstalt für Züchtungsforschung
an Kulturpflanzen, Institut für Rebenzüchtung Geilweilerhof
(BAZ, IRZ), Bibliothek **Former Name:** Federal Research
Centre for Grapevine Breeding, Bundesforschungsanstalt für
Rebenzüchtung (BFAR) **Founded:** 1948 **Type:** Government
Head: Dr. M. Klenert *Phone:* +49(6345) 410142 *Email:*
doku-vitis@geilweilerhof.suew.shuttle.de **Staff:** 1 Prof. 2
Other **Holdings:** 20,000 books 300 journals **Language of
Collection/Services:** German, English **Subjects:** Grapes,
Enology, Viticulture **Databases Developed:** VITIS - Found-
ed in 1969; documentation of about 40,000 vine and wine re-
search publications; includes English abstracts - available via
Internet at www.dainet.de/FIZ-AGRAR/VITIS-VEA **Loan:**
Inhouse **Photocopy:** Yes

1215 Stuttgart, Germany
University of Hohenheim
Documentation Centre
Universität Hohenheim (630)
D-70593 Stuttgart
Location: Paracelsusstrasse 2, D-70599 Stuttgart **Phone:**
+49(711) 459-2110 **Fax:** +49(711) 458-7440 **Email:**
aiple@uni-hohenheim.de **WWW:** www.uni-hohenheim.de
OPAC: www.uni-hohenheim.de/ub/opac/suche_dt.html

Non-English Name: Universität Hohenheim, Dokumentationsstelle **Founded:** 1818 **Type:** Academic **Head:** Dr. Jörg
Martin *Email:* martin@uni-hohenheim.de *Phone:* +49(711)
459-2100 **Staff:** 2 Prof. 3 Other **Language of Collection/
Services:** German / German **Subjects:** Animal Husbandry
Specializations: Animal Behavior, Animal Breeding, Animal Feeding, Animal Physiology, Animal Production, Feeds
Databases Developed: Feed Database - nutrients, digestibil-
ity; offline access; Literature Database - animal production,
feeds; online access **Loan:** Internationally **Photocopy:** Yes

1216 Stuttgart, Germany
University of Hohenheim
University Library
Universitätsbibliothek Hohenheim (610)
D-70593 Stuttgart

Location: Garbenstrasse 15, D-70599 Stuttgart **Phone:** +49(711) 459-2097 **Fax:** +49(711) 459-3262 **Email:** ubmail@uni-hohenheim.de **WWW:** www.uni-hohenheim. de **OPAC:** www.uni-hohenheim.de/ub/opac/suche_dt.html

Non-English Name: Universität Hohenheim, Universitätsbibliothek **Founded:** 1818 **Type:** Academic **Head:** Dr. Jörg Martin *Email:* martin@uni-hohenheim.de *Phone:* +49(711) 459-2100 **Staff:** 23 Prof. 19 Other **Holdings:** 410,000 books 3,500 journals **Language of Collection/Services:** German, English **Subjects:** Agriculture (Tropics), Agribusiness, Agricultural Development, Agricultural Economics, Farming, Agricultural Engineering, Animal Husbandry, Biotechnology, Crops, Entomology, Food Sciences, Horticulture, Plant Pathology, Soil Science, Veterinary Medicine, Water Resources **Databases Used:** Agricola; CABCD; Current Contents **Loan:** Internationally **Photocopy:** Yes

1217 Stuttgart, Germany
University of Hohenheim, Institute for Botany
Library
Universität Hohenheim 210
D-70593 Stuttgart

Location: Garbenstrasse 30, D-70599 Stuttgart **Phone:** +49(711) 459-1 **Fax:** +49(711) 459-3355 **Email:** botsekre @uni-hohenheim.de **WWW:** www.uni-hohenheim.de

Non-English Name: Universität Hohenheim, Institut für Botanik, Bibliothek **Founded:** 1917 **Type:** Academic **Head:** Prof. Dr. Manfred Küppers *Phone:* +49(711) 459-2194 *Email:* kuppers@uni-hohenheim.de **Staff:** 1 Prof. **Holdings:** 6,000 books 41 journals **Language of Collection/Services:** German / German **Subjects:** Forestry, Plant Pathology, Plant Pathology, Botany **Specializations:** Ecophysiology, Palynology, Paleobotany, Vegetation (History) **Loan:** Internationally **Photocopy:** Yes

1218 Stuttgart, Germany
University of Hohenheim, Institute of Plant
Breeding, Seed Science and Population
Genetics
Documentation Centre
University of Hohenheim (350)
D-70593 Stuttgart

Location: Fruwirthstrasse 21, D-70599 Stuttgart **Phone:** +49(711) 459-3544, 459-3534 **Fax:** +49(711) 359-2343 **WWW:** www.uni-hohenheim.de

Non-English Name: Universität Hohenheim, Institut für Pflanzenzüchtung, Saatgutforschung und Populationsgenetik **Type:** Academic **Head:** Dr. Gitta Oettler *Email:* oettler@ pz350.ipsp.uni-hohenheim.de *Phone:* +49(711) 459-2702 **Language of Collection/Services:** English, German / English, German **Subjects:** Plant Pathology **Specializations:** Biometry, Biotechnology, Plant Breeding **Databases Used:** Agricola **Photocopy:** Yes

1219 Tübingen, Germany
Federal Research Centre for Virus Diseases of
Animals
Library
PO Box 1149
D-72001 Tübingen

Location: Paul-Ehrlich-Strasse 28, D-72076 Tübingen **Fax:** +49(7071) 603201 **WWW:** www.dainet.de/bfav/ index.html

Non-English Name: Bundesforschungsanstalt für Viruskrankheiten der Tiere (BFAV), Bibliothek **Former Name:** Federal Research Institute for Animal Virus Diseases **Founded:** 1953 **Type:** Government **Head:** Susanne Ruff-Fischer *Phone:* +49(7071) 967139 *Email:* susanne.ruff@ tue.bfav.de **Holdings:** 15,000 books 120 journals **Language of Collection/Services:** English, German **Subjects:** Veterinary Medicine **Specializations:** Virology, Immunology, Molecular Biology **Loan:** Inhouse **Service:** Internationally **Photocopy:** Yes

1220 Wiesbaden, Germany
Hessian Ministry for Environment, Agriculture,
and Forestry
Library
Mainzer Strasse 80
Postfach 3109
D-65189 Wiesbaden

Phone: +49(611) 815-0 **Fax:** +49(611) 815-1941 **Email:** poststelle@mue.hessen.de **WWW:** www.mulf.hessen.de

Non-English Name: Hessisches Ministerium für Umwelt, Landwirtschaft, und Forsten (HMILFN), Bibliothek **Former Name:** Hessian Ministry of Agriculture, Forestry and Nature Protection, Hessian Ministry of Country Planning, Housing, Agriculture, Forestry and Nature Protection, Hessisches Ministerium für Landwirtschaft, Forsten und Naturschutz **Type:** Government **Staff:** 1 Prof. 1 Other **Holdings:** 35,000 books 350 journals **Language of Collection/Services:** German / German **Subjects:** Comprehensive **Loan:** Do not loan **Service:** Inhouse **Photocopy:** Yes

1221 Witzenhausen, Germany
German Institute for Tropical and Subtropical
Agriculture
Library
PO Box 1652
D-37206 Witzenhausen

Location: Steinstrasse 19, D-37213 Witzenhausen **Phone:** +49(5542) 6070 **Fax:** +49(5542) 60739 **Email:** ebaum@ wiz.uni-kassel.de **WWW:** www.wiz.uni-kassel.de/ditsl/ index.html

Non-English Name: Deutsches Institut für Tropische und Subtropische Landwirtschaft GmbH (DITSL), Bibliothek **Former Name:** Deutsche Kolonialschule GmbH **Founded:** 1895 **Type:** Government **Head:** *Phone:* +49(5542) 60713 **Staff:** 1 Prof. **Holdings:** 50,000 books 200 journals **Language of Collection/Services:** German, English **Subjects:** Agriculture (Tropics), Agriculture (Subtropics), Development Policy, Forestry, Subtropics **Loan:** Internationally **Photocopy:** Yes

Ghana

◆**1222   Accra, Ghana**
Cocoa Research Institute of Ghana (CRIG)
Library
Private Mail Bag
Kotoka International Airport
Accra

Location: PO Box 8, New Tafo-Akim **Fax:** +233(81) 3257

Type: Government **Head:** E.K. Tetteh *Phone:* +233(81) 2221, 3097 **Staff:** 1 Prof. 4 Other **Holdings:** 15,250 books 30 journals **Language of Collection/Services:** English / English **Subjects:** Agronomy, Biochemistry, Biotechnology, Crops, Entomology, Plant Breeding, Plant Pathology, Plant Physiology, Soil Science **Specializations:** Cocoa **Databases Used:** CABCD **Loan:** In country **Service:** In country **Photocopy:** Yes

1223   Accra, Ghana
Council for Scientific and Industrial Research (CSIR)
National Science and Technology Library and Information Centre (NASTLIC)
PO Box M.32
Accra

Location: Off Agostino Neto Road, Airport Residential Area

Former Name: Ghana Academy of Sciences, Central Reference and Research Library (CRRL) **Founded:** 1964 **Type:** Government **Head:** J.A. Villars *Phone:* +233(21) 777651 **Staff:** 5 Prof. 6 Other **Holdings:** 3,000 books 150 journals **Language of Collection/Services:** English **Subjects:** Agriculture (Tropics), Agricultural Development, Animal Husbandry, Crops, Entomology, Fisheries, Food Sciences, Forestry, Plant Pathology, Soil Science, Water Resources **Networks:** AGRIS **Databases Developed:** Ghana Science Abstracts - Includes indigenous Ghanaian science and technology literature from 1976-1979, 1987-date with key word and author indexes; provides full bibliographic data and summaries of mostly nonconventional material and some material from published sources; Cookery (Meat) **Loan:** Do not loan **Photocopy:** Yes

1224   Accra, Ghana
Council for Scientific and Industrial Research, Food Research Institute (CSIR, FRI)
Library
Box M 20
Accra

Location: Augustino Neto Road

Founded: 1965 **Type:** Research **Head:** Margaret Streetor *Phone:* +233(21) 777330 **Staff:** 1 Prof. 2 Other **Holdings:** 5,600 books 9 journals **Language of Collection/Services:** English / English **Subjects:** Agricultural Economics, Agricultural Engineering, Biotechnology, Crop Production, Farm Management, Fisheries, Food Legislation, Food Preservation, Food Processing Equipment, Food Sciences, Microbiology, Nutrition, Postharvest Technology, Solar Energy **Databases Developed:** Codex Alimentarius **Databases**

Used: Comprehensive **Loan:** Inhouse **Service:** In country **Photocopy:** Yes

1225   Accra, Ghana
Food and Agriculture Organization, Regional Office for Africa (FAO, RAF)
Library
PO Box 1628
Accra

Location: United Nations Building, Maxwell Road **Fax:** +233(21) 668427 **Email:** fao-raf@fao.org

Founded: 1966 **Type:** International **Head:** Uriah Eshun *Phone:* +233(21) 666851/4 **Staff:** 1 Prof. 1 Other **Holdings:** 22,000 books 82 journals **Language of Collection/Services:** English / English **Subjects:** Agriculture (Tropics), Animal Husbandry, Crops, Fisheries, Forestry, Irrigation, Land Use, Nutrition, Soil Science, Water Resources **Loan:** Inhouse **Service:** In country **Photocopy:** Yes

◆**1226   Accra, Ghana**
Ministry of Food and Agriculture (MOFA)
Agriculture Reference Library (ARL)
PO Box 299
Accra

Location: 28th February Road opposite Ghana Government Printing Press adjacent to the State Farms Corporate Marketing Centre **Phone:** +233(21) 664329

Former Name: Ministry of Agriculture **Founded:** 1890 **Type:** Government **Head:** Mr. K.M.B. Hevi *Phone:* +233 (21) 664329 **Staff:** 3 Other **Holdings:** 13,000 books 70 journals **Language of Collection/Services:** English **Loan:** In country **Photocopy:** No

1227   Accra, Ghana
University of Ghana (UG)
Balme Library
PO Box 24, Legon
Accra

Location: University Square **Phone:** +233(21) 767303 **Fax:** +233(21) 66701 **Email:** balme@ug.gn.apc.org **WWW:** www.ug/edu.gh/balme.htm

Former Name: University College of the Gold Coast/Ghana **Founded:** 1948 **Type:** Academic **Head:** S.N. Amanquah *Phone:* +233(21) 767303 *Email:* balme@ug.gn.apc.org **Staff:** 13 Prof. 70 Other **Holdings:** 365,000 books 450 journals **Language of Collection/Services:** English / English **Subjects:** Agricultural Economics, Crops, Animal Husbandry, Education/Extension, Entomology, Fisheries, Forestry, Home Economics, Plant Pathology, Soil Science **Loan:** Internationally **Service:** Internationally **Photocopy:** Yes

1228   Accra, Ghana
Volta River Authority (VRA)
Library
PO Box M77
Accra

Location: 28th February Road **Phone:** +233(21) 664941 ext 411 **Fax:** +233(21) 662610 **Email:** anortey@hotmail.com

Founded: 1964 **Type:** Government **Head:** Ms. Agnes O. Nortey *Phone:* +233(21) 664941 ext 408 *Email:* anortey@ hotmail.com **Staff:** 1 Prof. 4 Other **Holdings:** 12,000 books 70 journals **Language of Collection/Services:** English / English **Subjects:** Agricultural Development, Agricultural Engineering, Farming, Fisheries, Water Resources **Loan:** In country **Service:** In country **Photocopy:** Yes

♦**1229 Accra, Ghana**
    Water Resources Research Institute (WRRI)
    Research Library and Water Resources
        Documentation
    PO Box M.32
    Accra

Location: Off giffard Road to Achimota Road (Airport Residential) **Phone:** +233(21) 775352 ext 141 **Fax:** +233 (21) 777170, 777655

Former Name: Water Resources Research Unit (WRRU) **Type:** Government **Head:** Mr. E.C.Y. Novieku *Phone:* +233(21) 775351 ext 134 **Staff:** 3 Prof. 2 Other **Holdings:** 7,000 books 22 journals **Language of Collection/Services:** English / English **Subjects:** Plant Water Relations **Specializations:** Civil Engineering, Environmental Engineering, Geology, Hydraulic Engineering, Hydrology, Meteorology, Water Resources **Loan:** In country **Service:** In country **Photocopy:** Yes

♦**1230 Achimota, Ghana**
    Council for Scientific and Industrial Research,
        Animal Research Institute (CSIR, ARI)
    Library
    PB 20
    Achimota
Phone: +233(21) 554744

Founded: 1964 **Head:** Mrs. Annoh *Phone:* +233(21) 777631 **Staff:** 1 Prof. 2 Other **Holdings:** 4,200 books 11 journals **Language of Collection/Services:** English / English **Subjects:** Agricultural Economics, Animal Breeding, Animal Health, Animal Production, Extension, Farm Management, Pastures **Specializations:** Animal Husbandry **Loan:** Inhouse **Service:** In country **Photocopy:** Yes

♦**1231 Cape Coast, Ghana**
    University of Cape Coast
    School of Agriculture Library
    University Post Office
    Cape Coast

Type: Government **Head:** Percy Wilberforce **Staff:** 3 Prof. 3 Other **Holdings:** 2,000 books 80 journals **Language of Collection/Services:** English / English **Subjects:** Agricultural Economics, Agricultural Engineering, Animal Husbandry, Crops, Education/Extension, Entomology, Farming, Fisheries, Food Sciences, Forestry, Horticulture, Plant Pathology, Plants, Soil Science, Veterinary Medicine **Databases Developed:** Ghana Science Abstracts (1980-date) provides full bibliographic data **Loan:** Do not loan **Service:** Inhouse **Photocopy:** Yes

♦**1232 Kumasi, Ghana**
    Council for Scientific and Industrial Research,
        Soil Research Institute (CSIR, SRI)
    Library and Documentation
    PB Academy Post Office
    Kumasi
Phone: +233(51) 3660

Founded: 1963 **Head:** Karikari Danquah *Phone:* +233(51) 3660 **Staff:** 1 Prof. 5 Other **Holdings:** 16,800 books 24 journals **Language of Collection/Services:** English / English **Subjects:** Education/Extension, Farming, Forestry, Plants, Soil Science, Water Resources **Specializations:** Agroforestry, Desertification, Land Use, Soil Chemistry, Soil Conservation, Soil Fertility, Soil Surveys **Loan:** In country **Service:** Internationally **Photocopy:** Yes

1233 Kumasi, Ghana
    Council for Scientific and Industrial Research,
        Forest Research Institute of Ghana (CSIR,
        FORIG)
    Library
    PO Box 63, U.S.T.
    Kumasi, Ashanti Region

Location: Science Village, Fumesua **Phone:** +233(51) 60123, 60373 **Fax:** +233 (51) 60123 **Email:** library@forig. org

Former Name: Forest Products Research Institute (FORSEARCH) **Founded:** 1967 **Type:** Research **Head:** Mrs. Margaret Sraku-Lartey *Email:* mslartey@forig.org **Staff:** 3 Prof. **Language of Collection/Services:** English / English **Subjects:** Agroforestry, Entomology, Forest Management, Forestry, Plant Pathology, Seeds, Silviculture **Specializations:** Forest Products, Non-Timber Forest Products **Databases Developed:** Information on forestry and forest products in Ghana **Databases Used:** Forestry Compendium, TREECD **Loan:** Inhouse **Service:** In country **Photocopy:** Yes

1234 Kumasi, Ghana
    University of Science and Technology (UST)
    Faculty of Agriculture Library
    Private Mail Bag, U.S.T.
    Kumasi
Phone: +233(51) 5350/9 **Fax:** +233(51) 60137 **Email:** avu.ust.lib@ust.gn.apc.org

Founded: 1952 **Type:** Academic **Head:** Mrs. G.A. Amofa *Phone:* +233(51) 60361 *Email:* avu.ust.lib@ust.gn.apc.org **Staff:** 1 Prof. 1 Other **Holdings:** 7,105 books 10 journals **Language of Collection/Services:** English **Subjects:** Agricultural Economics, Agricultural Engineering, Animal Husbandry, Crops, Horticulture **Databases Used:** Agricola; Agris; CABCD **Loan:** Inhouse **Photocopy:** Yes

1235 Legon, Ghana
    University of Ghana (UG)
    Faculty of Agriculture Library
    PO Box 68
    Legon
Location: Off Dodowa Road

Type: Government **Head:** Ibrahim Addy *Phone:* +233(21) 500381 ext 3110 *Email:* agric.dean@ug.gn.apc.org **Staff:** 1 Prof. **Holdings:** 3,500 books 40 journals **Language of Collection/Services:** English / English **Subjects:** Agriculture (Tropics), Agricultural Development, Agricultural Economics, Agricultural Engineering, Animal Husbandry, Crops, Education/Extension, Entomology, Farming, Fisheries, Food Sciences, Forestry, Home Economics, Horticulture, Plant Pathology, Plants, Soil Science, Veterinary Medicine **Databases Developed:** Ghagri - Ghana Agricultural Research Information **Databases Used:** CABCD **Loan:** Inhouse **Service:** In country **Photocopy:** Yes

1236   Tamale, Ghana
University for Development Studies (UDS)
Library
PO Box 1350
Tamale

Founded: 1993 **Type:** Academic **Head:** I.K. Antwi *Phone:* +233 (71) 22078, 23725, 23619 **Staff:** 3 Prof. 17 Other **Holdings:** 12,000 books **Language of Collection/Services:** English/English **Subjects:** Comprehensive **Specializations:** Agronomy, Animal Husbandry **Loan:** Internationally **Photocopy:** No

Greece

1237   Athens, Greece
Agricultural Bank of Greece
Library
6-8-10 Harilaou Trikoupi Str.
GR-10679 Athens

Phone: +30(1) 362-3448 **Fax:** +30(1) 329-8146 **Email:** ategt@ate.gr **WWW:** www.ate.gr/index.html

Non-English Name: Agrotiki Trapeza tis Ellados (ATE), Vivliothiki **Type:** Business **Head:** Filitsa Ikonomidou *Phone:* +30(1) 362-3448 **Staff:** 2 Prof. 2 Other **Holdings:** 25,000 books 300 journals **Language of Collection/Services:** Greek, English / Greek, English **Subjects:** Agricultural Economics, Agricultural Policy, Animal Husbandry, Crops, Fisheries, Food Sciences **Loan:** Inhouse **Service:** Internationally **Photocopy:** Yes

1238   Athens, Greece
Agricultural University of Athens
Library
75, Iera Odos
GR-11855 Athens

Phone: +30(1) 529-4275, 529-4272 **Fax:** +30(1) 529-4278 **WWW:** library.aua.gr

Non-English Name: Georgiko Panepistimio Athinon (GPA), Vivliothiki **Type:** Academic **Staff:** 3 Prof. 1 Other **Holdings:** 10,000 books 365 journals **Language of Collection/Services:** Greek, English / Greek **Subjects:** Dairy Science, Agricultural Economics, Agricultural Engineering, Animal Breeding, Animal Husbandry, Food Technology, Chemistry, Mathematics, Meteorology, Physics **Loan:** Inhouse **Photocopy:** Yes

1239   Athens, Greece
Benaki Phytopathological Institute (BPI)
Library
8, Delta Street
Kiphissia
GR-14561 Athens

Fax: +30(1) 807-7506 **Email:** schatz@leon.nrcps. ariadne-t.gr

Founded: 1931 **Type:** Government **Head:** Stella Chatzimari *Email:* schatz@leon.nrcps.ariadne-t.gr *Phone:* +30(1) 807-0239 **Staff:** 2 Prof. 3 Other **Holdings:** 35,000 books 920 journals **Language of Collection/Services:** English / Greek, English **Subjects:** Bacteriology, Biology, Biotechnology, Chemistry, Crops, Horticulture, Pesticides, Plants, Virology, Weeds **Specializations:** Agricultural Chemicals, Entomology, Insects, Plant Pathology, Weeds **Databases Used:** Agricola; CABCD **Loan:** Do not loan **Service:** Internationally **Photocopy:** Yes

1240   Athens, Greece
Ministry of Agriculture
Central Library
22 Menandrou St.
GR-10552 Athens

Phone: +30(1) 529-1428 **WWW:** www.minagric.gr

Type: Government **Staff:** 1 Prof. 1 Other **Holdings:** 40,000 books **Language of Collection/Services:** Greek, English **Subjects:** Agricultural Economics, Animal Husbandry, Education/Extension

1241   Athens, Greece
Ministry of Agriculture, Directorate of
      Agricultural Policy and Documentation
Division of Documentation
5 Acharnon Av.
GR-10176 Athens

Phone: +30(1) 524-7979 **Fax:** +30(1) 524-3116 **WWW:** www.minagric.gr

Non-English Name: Ypourgeio Georgias, Dinsi Agr. Politikis & Tekmiriosis, Tmima Tekmiriosis **Type:** Government **Head:** E. Kazazis *Phone:* +30(1) 529-1257 **Staff:** 2 Prof. 3 Other **Language of Collection/Services:** Greek, English, French / Greek, English **Subjects:** Agriculture (Tropics), Agribusiness, Agricultural Development, Agricultural Economics, Agricultural Engineering, Animal Husbandry, Biotechnology, Crops, Education/Extension, Entomology, Food Sciences, Farming, Fisheries, Forestry, Home Economics, Horticulture, Plant Pathology, Plants, Soil Science, Veterinary Medicine, Water Resources **Networks:** AGRIS **Databases Used:** Agricola; Agris **Service:** Internationally **Photocopy:** Yes

1242   Athens, Greece
Panhellenic Confederation of Unions of
      Agricultural Cooperatives
Library
Kiphissias 16
GR-11526 Athens

Fax: +30(1) 777-9313 **Email:** pasegsgd@otenet.gr

Non-English Name: Panellinia Synomospondia Enoseon Georgikon Synetairismon (PASEGES), Vivliothiki **Former Name:** Confédération Panhéllénique des Organisations Coopératives Agricoles **Founded:** 1977 **Type:** Association **Head:** Mrs. Efstathiadou *Phone:* +30(1) 779-9683 **Staff:** 1 Prof. **Holdings:** 14,350 books 55 journals **Language of Collection/Services:** Greek, English, French / Greek, French, English **Subjects:** Agricultural Development, Agricultural Economics, Biotechnology, Cooperatives, Forestry **Loan:** Inhouse **Service:** Inhouse **Photocopy:** Yes

1243   Chania, Greece
         Mediterrenean Agronomic Institute of Chania
         Library and Documentation Centre
         PO Box 85
         GR-73100 Chania, Crete
Fax: +30(821) 81154 **WWW:** www.maich.gr

Non-English Name: Mesogeiako Agronomiko Institouto Chanion (MAICH), Vivliothiki **Type:** Government **Head:** Zoi Katsanevaki *Phone:* +30(821) 89511 *Email:* zoikat@ maich.gr **Staff:** 1 Prof. 2 Other **Holdings:** 12,000 books 330 journals **Language of Collection/Services:** English / English, French **Subjects:** Agribusiness, Agricultural Development, Agricultural Economics, Agricultural Policy, Biology, Biochemistry, Biotechnology, Conservation, Environmental Protection, Crops, Forestry, Horticulture, Management, Marketing, Plant Pathology, Plant Physiology, Plants, Postharvest Physiology, Protected Cultivation, Renewable Resources **Databases Used:** Agricola; Agris; CABCD **Loan:** In country **Service:** Internationally **Photocopy:** Yes

1244   Drama, Greece
         Tobacco Institute of Greece (TIG)
         Library
         GR-66100 Drama
Phone: +30(521) 22445 **Fax:** +30(521) 22645 **Email:** tig@otenet.gr

Non-English Name: Kapnologiko Institouto Ellados (KIE), Vivliothiki **Founded:** 1935 **Type:** Government **Head:** Mr. Athanasios Galopoulos *Phone:* +30(521) 22445 *Email:* tig@ otenet.gr **Staff:** 1 Other **Holdings:** 780 books 25 journals **Language of Collection/Services:** English / Greek, English **Subjects:** Tobacco **Loan:** Inhouse **Service:** Inhouse **Photocopy:** Yes

1245   Elliniko, Greece
         National Centre for Marine Research (NCMR)
         Library, Documentation and Information Centre
         Agios Kosmas
         GR-16604 Elliniko, Athens
Location: Flemming Building, 14-16 Flemming Str., GR-16672 Vari **Phone:** +30(1) 965-3520/1 **Fax:** +30(1) 965-3522 **WWW:** www.ncmr.ariadne-t.gr

Non-English Name: Ethniko Kentro Thalassion Erevnon, Vivliothiki **Former Name:** Institute of Oceanographic and Fisheries Research **Type:** Government **Head:** Sofia Goulala *Email:* sofia@atlantis.fl.ncmr.gr *Phone:* +30(1) 982-9239 **Founded:** 1965 **Staff:** 3 Prof. **Holdings:** 3,000 books 311 journals **Language of Collection/Services:** English / Greek

Subjects: Aquaculture, Fisheries **Loan:** Inhouse **Service:** Internationally **Photocopy:** Yes

1246   Kallithea-Athens, Greece
         Hellenic Cotton Board (HCB)
         Library
         Sygrou Av. 150
         GR-17671 Kallithea-Athens
Phone: +30(1) 922-5011 **Fax:** +30(1) 924-3676

Non-English Name: Organismos Vamvakos, Vivliothiki **Type:** Government **Staff:** 2 Other **Holdings:** 2,000 books 40 journals **Language of Collection/Services:** English, Greek / Greek **Subjects:** Agriculture (Tropics), Agricultural Development, Agricultural Economics, Agricultural Engineering, Biotechnology, Crops, Entomology, Farming, Food Sciences, Horticulture, Plant Pathology, Plants, Soil Science, Water Resources **Loan:** Inhouse **Service:** Inhouse **Photocopy:** Yes

1247   Kifissia, Greece
         Goulandris Natural History Museum
         Library
         13, Levidou Street
         GR-14562 Kifissia
Phone: +30(1) 801-5870 **Fax:** +30(1) 808-0674

Non-English Name: Mouseio Goulandri Fysikis Istorias, Vivliothiki **Type:** Museum **Head:** Danai Tsitouris **Staff:** 1 Prof. 3 Other **Holdings:** 5,000 books 35 journals **Language of Collection/Services:** Greek / Greek **Subjects:** Biotechnology, Ecology, Education, Entomology, Forestry, Geology, Hydrobiology, Plants, Soil Science **Specializations:** Botany **Loan:** Inhouse **Service:** Inhouse **Photocopy:** Yes

1248   Larissa, Greece
         Fodder Crops and Pastures Institute (FCPI)
         Library
         Theophrastou 1
         GR-41100 Larissa
Phone: +30(41) 533811 **Fax:** +30(41) 533809

Non-English Name: Institouto Ktinotrophikon Phyton ke Boskon (IKFB), Vivliothiki **Founded:** 1933 **Type:** Research **Staff:** 1 Other **Holdings:** 1,400 books 97 journals **Language of Collection/Services:** English **Subjects:** Agricultural Development, Agricultural Economics, Farming, Forestry, Genetics, Horticulture, Plant Pathology, Plants **Specializations:** Fodder Crops, Pastures **Loan:** In country **Photocopy:** No

1249   Lykovryssi Attikis, Greece
         National Agricultural Research Foundation, Wine
              Institute of Athens (NAGREF)
         Library
         Sofokli Venizelou 1
         GR-14123 Lykovryssi Attikis
Phone: +30(1) 282-8111 **Fax:** +30(1) 284-4954 **Email:** wineinst@otenet.gr

Non-English Name: Institouto Inou Athinon **Former Name:** Kentro Georgikis Erevnis Athinon **Founded:** 1952 **Type:** Government **Head:** Mary-Jane Salaha *Phone:* +30(1) 282-8111 **Holdings:** 1,000 books 15 journals **Language of**

Collection/Services: French, English / Greek **Subjects:** Agricultural Economics, Enology **Loan:** Inhouse **Service:** Inhouse **Photocopy:** Yes

1250   Sindos - Thessaloniki, Greece
         National Agricultural Research Foundation,
              Cotton and Industrial Plants Institute
              (NAGREF, CIPI)
         Library
         GR-57400 Sindos - Thessaloniki
Fax: +30(31) 796-513

Founded: 1931 **Type:** Government **Staff:** 1 Other **Holdings:** 3,827 books 41 journals **Subjects:** Cotton **Loan:** Do not loan **Photocopy:** No

1251   Vassilika - Thessaloniki, Greece
         Forest Research Institute (FRI)
         Library
         Terma Alkmanos
         GR-57006 Vassilika - Thessaloniki
Phone: +30(31) 461171/3 **Fax:** +30(31) 461341 **Email:** info@fri.gr **WWW:** www.fri.gr

Non-English Name: Instituto Dasikon Erevnon, Vivliothiki **Type:** Research **Staff:** 30 Prof. 50 Other **Holdings:** 4,760 books 23 journals **Language of Collection/Services:** English **Subjects:** Forest Products, Forestry **Specializations:** Forest Management, Forest Pathology, Mensuration, Mycology, Silviculture, Watershed Management, Wood Technology **Loan:** Inhouse **Service:** Inhouse **Photocopy:** Yes

1252   Volos, Greece
         University of Thessaly
         Library
         61 Taki Oikonomaki Str.
         GR-38221 Volos
Phone: +30(421) 36165 **Fax:** +30(421) 38492 **Email:** clib@uth.gr **WWW:** www.lib.uth.gr **OPAC:** telnet:// library.lib.uth.gr

Non-English Name: Panepistimio Thessalias, Vivliothiki **Founded:** 1988 **Type:** Academic **Head:** Dr. Ioannis Clapsopoulos *Phone:* +30(421) 36165 *Email:* clib@uth.gr **Staff:** 20 Prof. 9 Other **Holdings:** 75,000 books 800 journals **Language of Collection/Services:** Greek, English / Greek, English **Subjects:** Comprehensive **Databases Used:** Comprehensive **Loan:** In country **Service:** In country **Photocopy:** Yes

Grenada

1253   St. George's, Grenada
         Ministry of Agriculture, Lands, Forestry, Fisheries
              and Tourism
         Information Unit
         Botanic Gardens
         St. George's
Fax: +1(473) 440-4191

Type: Government **Head:** James Mahon *Phone:* +1(473) 440-1732 **Staff:** 1 Other **Holdings:** 180 books 4 journals **Subjects:** Agricultural Development, Agricultural Economics, Animal Production, Crop Production, Plant Protection, Stored Products

Guadeloupe

♦1254   Pointe à Pitre Cédex, Guadeloupe
         Institut National de la Recherche Agronomique -
              France, INRA Centre Antilles-Guyane
              (INRAAG)
         Unité Régionale de Documentation (URD)
         BP 1232
         97185 Pointe à Pitre Cédex
Location: Prise d'Eau, Petit-Bourg **Phone:** +590 255927 **Fax:** +590 255924

Founded: 1968 **Type:** Government **Head:** Colette Lencrerot *Phone:* +590 255983 **Staff:** 2 Prof. 2 Other **Holdings:** 6,000 books 200 journals **Language of Collection/ Services:** French / French **Subjects:** Biological Control, Cattle Husbandry, Goat Keeping, Food Sciences, Maize, Pig Farming, Plant Breeding, Plant Ecology, Plant Protection, Root Crops, Rural Economy, Rural Sociology, Soil Science, Vegetables **Specializations:** Agriculture (Tropics) **Databases Developed:** Foufou - Documents and references related with INRAAG research activities **Loan:** In country **Service:** In country **Photocopy:** Yes

Guam

1255   Mangilao, Guam
         University of Guam (UOG)
         Robert F. Kennedy Memorial Library, Land Grant
              Collections
         UOG Station
         Mangilao 96923
Phone: +1(671) 735-2341 **Fax:** +1(671) 734-6882 **Email:** goniwiec@uof9.uog.edu **WWW:** www.uog.edu **OPAC:** www.uog.edu/rfk/index.html **Ariel IP:** 168.123.25.249

Former Name: R.F.K. Library **Type:** Academic **Head:** Suzanne T. Bell *Phone:* +1(671) 735-2331/33 *Email:* stbell@ uog9.uog.edu **Staff:** .5 Prof. 1 Other **Holdings:** 545 books 300 journals **Language of Collection/Services:** English / English **Subjects:** Agriculture (Tropics) **Networks:** OCLC **Databases Used:** Comprehensive **Loan:** Do not loan **Service:** Inhouse **Photocopy:** Yes

Guatemala

1256   Ciudad Universitaria, Guatemala
         University of San Carlos of Guatemala,
              Agriculture Faculty
         Agriculture Documentation and Information
              Center
         Edificio T-9, 2 Nivel
         Ciudad Universitaria Zona 12
Phone: +502(2) 476-9806 **Fax:** +502(2) 476-9770 **Email:** agro022@usac.edu.gt **WWW:** www.usac.edu.gt

Non-English Name: Universidad de San Carlos de Guatemala, Facultad de Agronomía, Centro de Documentación e Información Agrícola (CEDIA) **Founded:** 1977 **Type:** Academic **Staff:** 1 Prof. 7 Other **Holdings:** 5,000 books 45 journals **Language of Collection/Services:** Spanish, English **Subjects:** Agriculture (Tropics), Crops, Education/Extension, Entomology, Food Sciences, Forestry, Horticulture, Plant Pathology, Soil Science, Water Resources **Specializations:** Agricultural Development, Agricultural Economics, Agricultural Education, Agricultural Engineering, Agricultural Production, Economic Development, Farming **Databases Developed:** UPEB - 9,500 records on bananas and plantains from all regions in America; RIBRE - forestry information from all the Central American region; SOFA - information on agricultural production and food, marketing, commerce, and national and population statistics from 153 countries **Loan:** In country **Photocopy:** Yes

1257 Guatemala, Guatemala
　　　　Agricultural Science and Technology Institute
　　　　　　(ACTI)
　　　　Documentation Center
　　　　Km 21.5 Carretera Hacia Amatitlán
　　　　Bárcenas, Villa Nueva
　　　　Guatemala
Phone: +502 631-2008 **Fax:** +502 631-2002 **Email:** icta@micro.com.gt

Non-English Name: Instituto de Ciencia y Tecnología Agrícolas (ICTA), Centro de Documentación (CEDICTA) **Former Name:** Centro de Documentación e Información Agrícola **Founded:** 1981 **Type:** Government **Head:** Marco Vinicio Méndez Solis *Phone:* +502 631-2008 *Email:* icta@micro.com.gt **Staff:** 1 Prof. **Holdings:** 20,000 books 3 journals **Language of Collection/Services:** Spanish / Spanish **Subjects:** Agribusiness, Agricultural Development, Agricultural Economics, Agricultural Engineering, Agriculture (Tropics), Animal Husbandry, Biotechnology, Crops, Education/Extension, Entomology, Farming, Fisheries, Food Sciences, Forestry, Horticulture, Plant Pathology, Plants, Soil, Veterinary Medicine, Water Resources **Specializations:** Botany, Rice, Statistics **Networks:** AGRIS **Loan:** In-house **Service:** In country **Photocopy:** No

1258 Guatemala, Guatemala
　　　　Institute of Nutrition of Central America and
　　　　　　Panama
　　　　Library
　　　　Apdo 1188
　　　　Guatemala 01901
Location: Carretera Roosevelt, zona 11 **Phone:** +502(2) 736522 **Fax:** +502(2) 736529 **Email:** vgarcia@incap.org.gt **WWW:** www.incap.org.gt

Non-English Name: Instituto de Nutrición de Centro América y Panamá (INCAP), Biblioteca **Founded:** 1949 **Type:** International **Head:** Ing. Juan Carlos Cabrera *Phone:* +502(2) 723762/7 *Email:* jcabrera@incap.org.gt **Staff:** 1 Prof. 3 Other **Holdings:** 35,000 books 200 journals **Language of Collection/Services:** English, Spanish / English, Spanish **Subjects:** Agriculture (Tropics), Agribusiness, Agricultural Development, Animal Husbandry, Biotechnology, Crops, Education/Extension, Farming, Fisheries, Forestry,

Horticulture, Water Resources **Specializations:** Agricultural Economics, Food Sciences **Databases Developed:** BINCAP - library books and documents on food sciences; MINCAP - INCAP's research and publications; AVINCAP - audiovisuals on health, food and nutrition **Databases Used:** Agricola; Medline **Loan:** In country **Service:** Regionally **Photocopy:** Yes

Guinea

1259 Conakry, Guinea
　　　　Ministère de l'Agriculture, des Eaux et Forêts
　　　　Centre National de Documentation et
　　　　　　d'Information pour le Développement Rural
　　　　　　(CENDID)
　　　　BP 576
　　　　Conakry

Former Name: Ministère du Développement Rural (MDR) **Founded:** 1980 **Type:** Government **Head:** Diane Arafan Kabine *Phone:* +224(4) 443614 **Staff:** 30 Other **Holdings:** 3,800 books 24 journals **Subjects:** Agricultural Economics, Agricultural Engineering, Animal Health, Animal Production, Crop Production, Extension, Fisheries, Forestry, Water Resources **Networks:** AGRIS

1260 Conakry, Guinea
　　　　Secrétariat d'Etat à la Recherche Scientifique
　　　　Centre de Documentation Universitaire
　　　　　　Scientifique et Technique (CEDUST)
　　　　BP 1003
　　　　Conakry

Founded: 1979 **Type:** Government **Head:** Boubacar Thiam *Phone:* +224(4) 444641 **Staff:** 14 Prof. 10 Other **Holdings:** 5,360 books 400 journals

1261 Kindia, Guinea
　　　　Centre de Recherche Agronomique de Foulaya
　　　　　　(CRAF)
　　　　Bibliothèque
　　　　BP 156
　　　　Kindia
Email: irag@miri.net.net.org

Former Name: Institut de Sciences Agrozootechniques Foulaya (ISAF) **Founded:** 1948 **Type:** Government **Head:** Mohamed Lamine Conde *Phone:* +224(61) 0148 *Email:* irag@miri.net.net.org **Staff:** 3 Other **Holdings:** 996 books 3 journals **Language of Collection/Services:** French / French **Subjects:** Farm Machinery, Genetics, Plant Protection, Rural Economy, Soil Management, Soil Science, Veterinary Medicine, Zootechny **Loan:** Do not loan **Photocopy:** No

Guinea-Bissau

1262 Bissau, Guinea-Bissau
　　　　Ministère du Développement et de l'Agriculture
　　　　Centre de Documentation et de Divulgation
　　　　　　Agricole (CDEDA)
　　　　BP 71

1001 Bissau Codex

Former Name: Centre de Documentation et de Diffusion Agricole **Founded:** 1976 **Head:** Adriano Gomez **Staff:** 2 Other **Type:** Government **Holdings:** 1,200 books 10 journals **Subjects:** Agricultural Economics, Animal Production, Crop Production, Fisheries **Networks:** AGRIS

♦**1263   Bissau, Guinea-Bissau**
National Institute of Studies and Research
Library
CP 112
Bissau

Location: Complexo Escolar 14 de Novembro, Bairro, Cobornel **Fax:** +245 251125

Non-English Name: Instituto Nacional de Estudos e Pesquisas (INEP), Biblioteca **Founded:** 1985 **Type:** Government **Head:** Queiros Diamantino **Phone:** +245 214497 **Holdings:** 350 books 35 journals **Staff:** 2 Prof. 4 Other **Language of Collection/Services:** Portuguese, French **Subjects:** Agriculture (Tropics), Entomology, Agricultural Development, Fisheries, Water Resources **Loan:** In country **Photocopy:** Yes

Guyana

1264   Georgetown, Guyana
National Agricultural Research Institute (NARI)
Library & Information Unit
Mon Repos
East Coast Demerara
Georgetown

Phone: +592(20) 2841/3 **Fax:** +592(20) 4481 **Email:** nari@guyana.net.gy

Founded: 1950 **Type:** Government **Head:** Samantha West **Phone:** +592(20) 2841/3 **Email:** nari@guyana.net.gy **Staff:** 2 Prof. 2 Other **Holdings:** 20,000 books 36 journals **Language of Collection/Services:** English / English **Subjects:** Crops, Extension, Livestock **Specializations:** Animal Production, Crop Production, Extension, Information Services, Plant Protection, Postharvest Technology, Soil Science **Networks:** AGRIS **Databases Used:** Agricola; Agris; CABCD; TROPAG & RURAL **Loan:** In country **Service:** Internationally **Photocopy:** Yes

1265   Georgetown, Guyana
University of Guyana (UNIGUY)
Library
PO Box 101110
Georgetown

Phone: +592(2) 4931 **Fax:** +592(2) 54885 **WWW:** www.sdnp.org.gy/uog

Founded: 1963 **Type:** Academic **Head:** Mrs. Yvonne Lanaster **Phone:** +592(2) 4930 **Staff:** 15 Prof. 67 Other **Holdings:** 200,000 books 3,000 journals **Language of Collection/Services:** English / English **Subjects:** Agricultural Economics, Agricultural Policy, Animal Husbandry, Biochemistry, Education/Extension, Farm Machinery, Farm Management, Fertilizers, Fish Farming, Human Nutrition, Mechanization, Microbiology, Pest Control, Pesticides, Pub-

lic Health, Silviculture **Specializations:** Farm Machinery, Forestry, Pesticides, Silviculture, Soil Science **Databases Used:** Agricola; Agris **Loan:** Internationally **Service:** Internationally **Photocopy:** Yes

Haiti

1266   Port-au-Prince, Haiti
National Education Ministry, State University of
Haiti (NEM, SUH)
Agricultural Documentation Unit
Damien
Port-au-Prince

Non-English Name: Ministère de l'Education Nationale, Université d'Etat d'Haïti (MEN, UEH), Unité de Documentation Agricole (UDA) **Former Name:** Faculté d'Agronomie et de Médecine Vétérinaire (FAMV) **Founded:** 1924 **Type:** Government **Head:** Jacqueline Sanon **Phone:** +509(1) 224705 **Email:** jsanon.famv@ht.refer.org **Staff:** 1 Prof. 10 Other **Holdings:** 20,619 books 75 journals **Language of Collection/Services:** French / French **Subjects:** Agriculture (Tropics), Agricultural Development, Agricultural Economics, Agricultural Engineering, Animal Husbandry, Farming, Biotechnology, Education/Extension, Entomology, Fisheries, Food Sciences, Forestry, Horticulture, Plant Pathology, Soil Science, Veterinary Medicine, Water Resources **Networks:** AGRIS **Loan:** Inhouse **Service:** Inhouse **Photocopy:** Yes

Honduras

1267   La Ceiba, Honduras
Universidad Nacional Autónoma de Honduras
Biblioteca Centro Universitario Regional del
Litoral Atlántico
La Ceiba, Atlantida

Phone: +504 422670 **WWW:** www.unah.hondunet.net/unah.html

Founded: 1970 **Type:** Government **Head:** Lic. Orfylia Pinel S. **Phone:** +504 322204 **Staff:** 1 Prof. 10 Other **Holdings:** 16,000 books 150 journals **Subjects:** Agriculture (Tropics), Animal Production, Forestry **Loan:** In country **Photocopy:** Yes

1268   San Pedro Sula, Honduras
Honduran Foundation of Agricultural Research
Library
PO Box 2067
San Pedro Sula

Location: La Lima, Cortés **Fax:** +504 668-2313 **Email:** biblio@simon.intertel.hn **WWW:** www.fhia.hn

Non-English Name: Fundación Hondureña de Investigación Agrícola (FHIA), Biblioteca **Founded:** 1923 **Type:** Private **Head:** Ing. Emily López de Alvarado **Phone:** +504 668-2470, 668-2478 **Email:** biblio@simon.intertel.hn **Staff:** 1 Prof. 3 Other **Holdings:** 30,000 books 250 journals **Language of Collection/Services:** Spanish, English / Spanish **Subjects:** Agricultural Research **Specializations:** Bananas,

Tropical Fruits **Databases Developed:** Cultivos tropicales - 9,300 references; CACAO - 5,300 references; Banano y Plátano - 10,000 references **Databases Used:** Comprehensive **Loan:** Inhouse **Service:** Internationally **Photocopy:** Yes

1269   Tegucigalpa, Honduras
         Panamerican School of Agriculture
         Wilson Popenoe Library
         Apdo 93
         Tegucigalpa, Francisco Morazan
Location: Valley of Zamorano, 35 Km east of Tegucigalpa **Phone:** +504 766150 **Fax:** +504 766113 **WWW:** www.zamorano.edu.hn

Non-English Name: Escuela Agrícola Panamericana (EAP), Biblioteca Wilson Popenoe (BWP) **Founded:** 1945 **Type:** Academic **Head:** Ing. Daniel Kaegi *Phone:* +504 766140 *Email:* dkaegi@zamorano.edu.hn **Staff:** 3 Prof. 7 Other **Holdings:** 20,000 books 700 journals **Language of Collection/Services:** Spanish / Spanish **Subjects:** Agriculture (Tropics), Agribusiness, Agricultural Development, Agricultural Economics, Agricultural Engineering, Fisheries, Animal Husbandry, Biotechnology, Crops, Education/Extension, Entomology, Farming, Food Sciences, Forestry, Horticulture, Plant Pathology, Soil Science, Veterinary Medicine, Water Resources **Databases Used:** Agricola; Agris **Loan:** Do not loan **Service:** In region **Photocopy:** Yes

1270   Tegucigalpa, Honduras
         Secretaría de Estados en los Despachos de
              Recursos Naturales, Dirección General de
              Desarrollo Agropecuario
         Centro de Documentación e Información Agrícola
         Apdo 309
         Tegucigalpa, D.C.
Location: Blv. Centro America, Av. la FAO

Type: Government **Networks:** AGRIS

Hong Kong

1271   Aberdeen, Hong Kong
         Agriculture and Fisheries Department, Aberdeen
              Fisheries Offices
         Library
         100A Shek Pai Wan Road
         Aberdeen
Phone: +852(5) 520171 ext 29

Founded: 1954 **Type:** Government **Head:** Senior Capture Fisheries Officer *Phone:* +852(5) 520171 ext 26 **Staff:** 6 Prof. 1 Other **Holdings:** 1,000 books 170 journals **Language of Collection/Services:** English, Chinese **Subjects:** Fisheries **Loan:** In country **Photocopy:** No

♦**1272   Kowloon, Hong Kong**
         Agriculture and Fisheries Department
         Headquarters Library
         12th Floor, Canton Road Government Offices
         393 Canton Road, Yaumatei
         Kowloon

Location: 14th Floor **Phone:** +852(3) 7332103 **Fax:** +852(3) 3113731

Founded: 1946 **Type:** Government **Staff:** 3 Other **Holdings:** 16,000 books 100 journals **Language of Collection/Services:** English **Subjects:** Crops, Fisheries, Plant Protection, Soil Science, Veterinary Medicine **Loan:** In country **Service:** In country **Photocopy:** No

Hungary

1273   Budapest, Hungary
         Central Food Research Institute
         Library
         PO Box 393
         H-1537 Budapest
Location: Herman O. u. 15, H-1022 Budapest **Phone:** +36(1) 355-8244 **Fax:** +36(1) 355-8991 **WWW:** www.cfri.hu

Non-English Name: Központi Élelmiszeripari Kutató Intézet, Könyvtára **Founded:** 1959 **Staff:** 3 Prof. 5 Other **Language of Collection/Services:** Hungarian / English, German **Holdings:** 35,000 books 176 journals **Subjects:** Food Sciences **Loan:** Internationally **Photocopy:** Yes

♦**1274   Budapest, Hungary**
         Cooperative Research Institute
         Library
         Pf. 398
         H-1371 Budapest
Location: Alkotmány u. 25 **Phone:** +36(1) 111-6020 **Fax:** +36(1) 111-6020

Non-English Name: Szövetkezeti Kutató Intézet, Könyvtár **Founded:** 1958 **Type:** Association **Head:** Ms. Susan Galambos *Phone:* +36(1) 111-6020 **Staff:** 1 Prof. **Holdings:** 65 journals 21,200 books **Subjects:** Agricultural Development, Agricultural Economics, Agricultural Engineering, Cooperation, Farming **Loan:** Internationally **Photocopy:** Yes

1275   Budapest, Hungary
         Food and Agriculture Organization, Subregional
              Office for Central and Eastern Europe (FAO,
              SEUR)
         Library/Information Centre
         Benczur utca 34
         H-1068 Budapest
Phone: +36(1) 461-2000 **Fax:** +36(1) 351-7029 **Email:** fao-seur@fao.org **WWW:** www.fao.org/Regional/SEUR

Type: International **Head:** Michal Demes *Phone:* +36(1) 461-2026 *Email:* michal.demes@fao.org **Holdings:** Databases Used: Agris

1276   Budapest, Hungary
         Forest Research Institute
         Library
         PO Box 17
         H-1277 Budapest
Location: Frankel Leó u. 42-44, H-1023 Budapest

Non-English Name: Erdészeti Tudományos Intézet (ERTI), Könyvtára **Former Name:** Magyan Király Erdészeti Kisérleti Állomás, Magyan Kirdlyi Erdészeti Kutató Intézet **Founded:** 1949 **Type:** Research **Head:** Mrs. Katalin Fekete Skultéty *Phone:* +36(1) 326-1769 *Email:* h-13860fek@ella. hu **Holdings:** 15,200 books 51 journals **Language of Collection/Services:** Hungarian / Hungarian **Subjects:** Conservation, Forestry **Loan:** Inhouse **Photocopy:** Yes

1277   Budapest, Hungary
Hungarian Academy of Sciences, Plant Protection
Institute
Library
PO Box 102
H-1525 Budapest
Location: Herman Ottó út 15, H-1022 Budapest **Phone:** +36(1) 3-558-722 ext 418 **Fax:** +36(1) 356-3698 **Email:** tsar@planta.nki.hu **WWW:** www.nki.hu

Non-English Name: Magyar Tudományos Akadémia, Növényvédelmi Kutatóintézete (MTA, NKI), Könyvtár **Type:** Research **Founded:** 1880 **Head:** Mrs. Nóra Sáray *Phone:* +36(1) 3-558-722 ext 418 *Email:* tsar@planta.nki.hu **Staff:** 1 Prof. **Holdings:** 19,500 books 90 journals **Language of Collection/Services:** Hungarian, English, German/ Hungarian, English, German **Subjects:** Entomology, Biotechnology, Biochemistry, Pesticides, Plant Pathology **Photocopy:** Yes

1278   Budapest, Hungary
Hungarian Academy of Sciences, Research
Institute for Soil Science and Agricultural
Chemistry (RISSAC)
Library
Herman Ottó u. 15
H-1022 Budapest
Phone: +36(1) 356-4591 **Fax:** +36(1) 355-8839 **Email:** orban@rissac.hu **WWW:** www.taki.iif.hu

Non-English Name: Magyar Tudományos Akadémia, Talajtani és Agrokémiai Kutató Intézete (TAKI), Könyvtára **Founded:** 1949 **Type:** Academic **Head:** Ms. Emöke Orbán *Phone:* +36(1) 356-4591 *Email:* orban@rissac.hu **Staff:** 2 Prof. 1 Other **Holdings:** 15,000 books 250 journals **Language of Collection/Services:** Hungarian, English / Hungarian, English, German, French, Russian **Subjects:** Acid Rain, Agricultural Development, Chemistry, Crops, Earth Sciences, Ecology, Environmental Management, Erosion, Geology, Groundwater, Land Use, Pollutants, Soil Science, Water Resources **Databases Used:** Agris **Loan:** Internationally **Service:** Internationally **Photocopy:** Yes

1279   Budapest, Hungary
Hungarian Agricultural Museum
Library
Pf. 129
H-1367 Budapest
Location: Városliget, Vajdahunyadvár, H-1146 Budapest **Phone:** +36(1) 343-0573 **Fax:** +36(1) 343-9120 **Email:** mmm@mail.matav.hu

Non-English Name: Magyar Mezögazdasági Múzeum, Könyvtár **Former Name:** Magyar Királyi Mezögazdasági **Founded:** 1896 **Type:** Museum **Head:** Ms. Emöke Zrupkó *Phone:* +36(1) 343-0573 *Email:* mmm@mail.matav.hu

Staff: 4 Prof. 1 Other **Holdings:** 53,000 books 130 journals **Language of Collection/Services:** Hungarian / Hungarian **Subjects:** Agriculture (History) **Specializations:** Agriculture (History - Hungary) **Loan:** Inhouse **Service:** In country **Photocopy:** Yes

1280   Budapest, Hungary
Institute of Geodesy, Cartography and Remote
Sensing
Library
PO Box 546
H-1373 Budapest
Location: Bosnyák tér 5 **Phone:** +36(1) 222-5101 ext 429 **Fax:** +36(1) 222-5106 **Email:** julia.kalman@fomigate. fomi.hu **WWW:** www.fomi.hu

Non-English Name: Földmérési és Távérzékelési Intézet (FÖMI), Könyvtár **Founded:** 1876 **Type:** Research **Head:** Julia Kalman *Phone:* +36(1) 222-5101 ext 429 *Email:* julia. kalman@fomigate.fomi.hu **Staff:** 1 Prof. **Holdings:** 30,000 books 60 journals **Language of Collection/Services:** Hungarian, German, English, Russian / Hungarian, English **Subjects:** Agricultural Development, Crops, Education, Soil **Specializations:** Cadasters, Geodesy, Geographic Information Systems, Mapping, Remote Sensing, Satellite Surveys **Loan:** In country **Service:** Internationally **Photocopy:** Yes

1281   Budapest, Hungary
Ministry of Economic Affairs (MEA)
National Technical Information Centre and
Library (NTICL)
PO Box 12
H-1428 Budapest
Location: Muzeum u. 17 **Phone:** +36(1) 338-4803 **Fax:** +36(1) 338-2232 **Email:** stubnya@omk.omikk.hu **WWW:** www.omikk.hu **OPAC:** www.omikk.hu/omikk_en/ homepage.htm **Ariel IP:** 193.224.186.170

Non-English Name: Gazdasagi Miniszterium (GM), Orszagos Müszaki Informacios Központ es Könyvtar (OMIKK) **Former Name:** Ministry for Industry, Ministry for Industry and Commerce, National Technical Library and Documentation Centre **Founded:** 1883 **Type:** Government **Head:** Dr. A.R. Herman *Phone:* +36(1) 338-4074 *Email:* har@omk. omikk.hu **Staff:** 48 Prof. 223 Other **Holdings:** 563,000 books 2,581 journals **Language of Collection/Services:** Hungarian, English/Hungarian **Subjects:** Agricultural Engineering, Biotechnology, Management, Education, Environmental Protection, Food Sciences, Water Resources **Databases Developed:** CIKK -- bibliographic database that contains 325,000 records on area environmental protection; available on CD and via the Internet **Databases Used:** Comprehensive **Loan:** Internationally **Service:** Internationally **Photocopy:** Yes

1282   Budapest, Hungary
National Agricultural Library and Documentation
Centre
Pf. 15
H-1253 Budapest
Location: Attlia út 13 **Phone:** +36(1) 356-8211 **Fax:** +36 (1) 156-9928 **Email:** bbencze@amon.omgk.hu **WWW:**

www.omgk.hu **OPAC:** 193.224.162.53 **IP** telnet://amom. omgk.hu

Non-English Name: Országos Mezõgazdasági Könyvtár és Dokumentációs Központ (OMgK) **Former Name:** Károlyi Mihály National Agricultural Library **Founded:** 1951 **Type:** Government **Head:** Erika Gulácsi-Pápay *Phone:* +36(1) 356-9219 *Email:* egulacsi@amom.omgk.hu **Staff:** 35 Prof. 10 Other **Holdings:** 500,000 books 2,000 journals **Language of Collection/Services:** Hungarian / Hungarian **Subjects:** Agribusiness, Agricultural Development, Agricultural Economics, Agricultural Engineering, Biotechnology, Education/Extension, Entomology, Fisheries, Food Sciences, Forestry, Plant Pathology, Soil Science, Veterinary Medicine **Specializations:** Animal Husbandry, Crops, Farming, Horticulture **Networks:** AGRIS **Databases Used:** Comprehensive **Loan:** Internationally **Service:** Internationally **Photocopy:** Yes

◆**1283 Budapest, Hungary**
  Phylaxia Biologicals Co.
  Library
  PO Box 23
  H-1486 Budapest
Location: Szállás u. 5, H-1107 Budapest

Non-English Name: Phylaxia Oltóanyagtermelö Vállalat, Könyvtára **Former Name:** Phylaxia **Founded:** 1912 **Type:** Business **Head:** Anna Czobor *Phone:* +36(1) 157-5311 ext 280 **Staff:** 1 Prof. **Holdings:** 6,950 books 2,791 journals **Language of Collection/Services:** English/Hungarian **Subjects:** Veterinary Science **Loan:** Inhouse **Service:** Inhouse **Photocopy:** Yes

◆**1284 Budapest, Hungary**
  Research and Development for Flour Milling Co.
    Ltd.
  Library
  Pf. 306
  H-1536 Budapest
Location: Kisrókus u. 15/b, H-1024 Budapest **Fax:** +36(1) 115-4100

Non-English Name: Malomipari Kutató és Fejeesztö Kft. (Malomkubato Kft.), Könyvtára **Former Name:** Research Institute of the Milling Industry, Malomipari Kutató Intézet **Founded:** 1928 **Type:** Research **Head:** Mrs. Szalay-Marzsó *Phone:* +36(1) 135-2300 **Staff:** 1 Prof. 1 Other **Holdings:** 8,000 books 60 journals **Language of Collection/Services:** Hungarian/Hungarian, English, German **Subjects:** Feed Industry, Biochemistry, Cereals, Flours, Milling **Databases Developed:** Database of materials on cereal processing journals **Loan:** Inhouse **Service:** Inhouse **Photocopy:** Yes

1285 Budapest, Hungary
  Research Institute for Fruit Growing and
    Ornamentals, Erd (RESINFRU)
  Library
  Pf. 108
  H-1775 Budapest
Location: Park u. 2, H-1223 Budapest XXII **Email:** resinfru@elender.hu

Non-English Name: Erdi Gyümölcs- és Disznövénytermesztési Kutató-Fejlesztö Kht. (GyDKF Kht), Szakkönyvtára **Former Name:** Kertészeti Kutató Intézet **Founded:** 1951 **Type:** Research **Head:** Ms. Elisabeth Vermes-Thuránszky *Phone:* +36(1) 226-8422 **Staff:** 1 Prof. **Holdings:** 7,500 books 8,000 journals **Language of Collection/Services:** Hungarian / Hungarian **Subjects:** Fruit Growing, Ornamental Plants **Specializations:** Temperate Fruits **Loan:** In country **Service:** In country **Photocopy:** Yes

◆**1286 Budapest, Hungary**
  Research Institute of the Wood Industry
  Library
  Vörösmarty u. 56
  H-1201 Budapest

Non-English Name: Faipari Kutató Intézet, Könyvtára **Founded:** 1949 **Type:** Research **Head:** Antalne Szarka *Phone:* +36(1) 572-022 **Staff:** 1 Prof. 1 Other **Holdings:** 200 journals 6,100 books **Language of Collection/Services:** Hungarian/English, German, Russian **Subjects:** Forest Products Industries **Loan:** Internationally **Photocopy:** Yes

1287 Budapest, Hungary
  University of Horticulture and Food Industry
    (UHFI)
  Central Library and Archives (CLA)
  PO Box 49
  H-1518 Budapest
Location: Villányi út 35-43, H-1118 Budapest **Fax:** +36(1) 372-6334 **Email:** ktar@hoya.kee.hu **WWW:** www.kee.hu **OPAC:** aromo.aszi.sztaki.hu, www.kozeldat.iif.hu

Non-English Name: Kertészeti és Élelmiszeripari Egyetem (KÉE), Központi Könyvtár és Levéltár (KKL) **Former Name:** University of Horticulture **Founded:** 1860 **Type:** Academic **Head:** Dr. Éva Zalai-Kovács *Phone:* +36(1) 372-6300 *Email:* ekovacs@hoya.kee.hu **Staff:** 10 Prof. 6 Other **Holdings:** 310,000 books 259 journals **Language of Collection/Services:** Hungarian/Hungarian **Subjects:** Agribusiness, Agricultural Economics, Botanical Gardens, Medicinal Plants, Food Industry, Horticulture, Landscape Architecture, Environmental Protection, **Databases Developed:** Bibliography of theses and dissertations at the university **Databases Used:** CABCD; FSTA **Loan:** In country **Service:** In country **Photocopy:** Yes

1288 Budapest, Hungary
  University of Veterinary Science
  Central Library
  PO Box 2
  H-1400 Budapest
Location: István u. 2, 1078 Budapest **Phone:** +36(1) 3220-849 **Fax:** +36(1) 3220-849 **Email:** mcserey@ns.univet.hu **WWW:** www.univet.hu **OPAC:** aromo.aszi.sztaki.hu/ univet/lib.html **Ariel IP:** 193.6.204.108

Non-English Name: Állatorvostudományi Egyetem, Központi Könyvtár **Founded:** 1787 **Type:** Academic **Head:** Mrs. Mary Cserey *Email:* mcserey@ns.univet.hu *Phone:* +36(1) 3220-849 **Staff:** 9 Prof. 2 Other **Holdings:** 118,000 books 263 journals **Language of Collection/Services:** Hungarian, English, German / Hungarian, English **Subjects:** Animal Husbandry, Veterinary Science, Zoology **Databases Developed:** Bibliography of Hungarian Veterinary Literature, 1990 to date **Databases Used:** CABCD; FSTA; Medline; Zoological Record **Loan:** Internationally **Service:** Internationally **Photocopy:** Yes

1289 Debrecen, Hungary
Debrecen University Centre for Agricultural
    Sciences
Central Library
PO Box 36
H-4015 Debrecen
Phone: +36(52) 347-888, 414-329, 418-797 **Fax:** +36(52) 313-385 **WWW:** www.date.hu/debr.htm

Non-English Name: Debreceni Egyetem Agrártudományi Centrum, Központi Könyvtára **Founded:** 1868 **Type:** Academic **Head:** s. Zsuzsánna Nádas **Staff:** 14 Prof. **Holdings:** 860 journals 88,000 books **Language of Collection/Services:** Hungarian/English, German, Russian **Subjects:** Agricultural Chemistry, Agricultural Development, Agricultural Economics, Animal Husbandry, Biotechnology, Education/Extension, Food Sciences, Plant Pathology, Plants, Soil Science **Loan:** Internationally **Photocopy:** Yes

♦1290 Debrecen, Hungary
Tobacco Research and Quality Development
    Institute
Technical Library
Pf. 66
H-4002 Debrecen
Location: Attila tér 3, H-4029 Debrecen **Fax:** +36(52) 349-529

Non-English Name: Dohánykutató és Minoségfejleszto Intézet, Könyvtára **Former Name:** Tobacco Research Institute, Dohánykutató Intézet **Founded:** 1966 **Type:** Research **Head:** Dr. Viktorné Kovári *Phone:* +36(52) 348-333 **Staff:** 1 Prof. **Holdings:** 7,500 books 30 journals **Language of Collection/Services:** Hungarian / Hungarian, English **Subjects:** Agricultural Development, Agricultural Economics, Food Sciences, Biotechnology, Plant Pathology, Soil Science, Tobacco **Loan:** In country **Photocopy:** Yes

1291 Gödöllo, Hungary
Gödöllo University of Agricultural Sciences
    (GUAS)
Central Library
Pf. 303
H-2103 Gödöllo
Location: Páter Károly u. 1 **Phone:** +36(28) 410-200 ext 1173 **Fax:** +36(28) 410-804 **Email:** gatekk@kpko.gau.hu **WWW:** dis.gau.hu **OPAC:** telnet://192.188.247.34 login, pw:tinlib

Non-English Name: Gödölloi Agrártudományi Egyetem (GATE), Központi Könyvtár (KPKÖ) **Former Name:** Agrártudományi Egyetem Gödöllo **Founded:** 1945 **Type:** Academic **Head:** Dr. Tibor Koltay *Email:* tibor@kpko.gau. hu *Phone:* +36 (28) 522-004 **Staff:** 15 Prof. 4 Other **Holdings:** 240,000 books 750 journals **Language of Collection/Services:** Hungarian/Hungarian **Subjects:** Agricultural Economics, Agricultural Engineering, Agronomy **Databases**

Used: CABCD **Loan:** Internationally **Service:** In country **Photocopy:** Yes

1292 Gödöllo, Hungary
Research Institute for Small Animal Research
Library
Pf. 417
H-2101 Gödöllo
Phone: +36(28) 320-387 **Fax:** +36(28) 330-184 **WWW:** www.katki.hu/english/index.html

Non-English Name: Kisállattenyésztési és Takarmányozási Kutató Intézet (KATKI), Könyvtára **Type:** Research **Former Name:** Research Center for Animal Breeding and Nutrition, Állattenyésztési és Takarmányozási Kutatóközpont **Staff:** 1 Prof. **Holdings:** 25,000 books 126 journals **Language of Collection/Services:** Hungarian / Hungarian **Subjects:** Animal Husbandry, Breeding, Genetics, Management, Nutrition, Poultry, Rabbits **Specializations:** Honeybees, Small Mammals **Loan:** In country **Service:** In country **Photocopy:** Yes

1293 Gyöngyös, Hungary
Gödöllo University of Agricultural Sciences,
    College of Agriculture (GUAS)
Gyöngyös Library
PO Box 143
H-3200 Gyöngyös
Location: Mátrai 36 **Phone:** +36(37) 518 300 ext 433 **Fax:** +36(37) 518 300 ext 433 **WWW:** wbs.gau.hu/0/Welcome. html

Non-English Name: Gödölloi Agrártudományi Egyetem, Mezogazdasági Föiskolai Kar (GATE, GYFK), Könyvtára - Gyöngyös **Founded:** 1962 **Type:** Academic **Head:** Mrs. Sipos Lajosné *Phone:* +36(37) 518 300 ext 433 **Staff:** 2 Prof. 1 Other **Holdings:** 26,000 books 180 journals **Language of Collection/Services:** Hungarian/Hungarian **Subjects:** Agricultural Economics, Agricultural Engineering, Animal Husbandry, Crop Production, Farm Management, Viticulture **Loan:** Internationally **Photocopy:** Yes

1294 Hódmezovásárhely, Hungary
Debrecen University Centre for Agricultural
    Sciences, College of Agriculture,
    Hódmezovásárhely (CAH)
Library
Pf. 79
H-6801 Hódmezovásárhely
Location: Andrássy út 15 **Phone:** +36(62) 246-466 ext 162 **Fax:** +36(62) 241-779 **Email:** rpalotas@hod.date.hu **WWW:** www.hod.date.hu

Non-English Name: Debreceni Egyetem Agrártudományi Centrum, Mezogazdasági Foiskolai Kar, Hódmezovásárhely (DATE, MFK), Könyvtára **Former Name:** Faculty of Animal Husbandry, Állattenyésztési Foiskolai Kar **Founded:** 1961 **Type:** Academic **Head:** Mr. János Palotás *Phone:* +36(62) 246-466 ext 170 *Email:* palotas@hod.date.hu **Staff:** 3 Prof. **Holdings:** 38,000 books 150 journals **Language of Collection/Services:** Hungarian/Hungarian **Subjects:** Agribusiness, Agricultural Development, Agricultural Economics, Agricultural Engineering, Animal Husbandry, Crops,

Extension, Forestry, Horticulture, Veterinary Medicine **Databases Developed:** College theses and staff publications **Loan:** In country **Service:** In country **Photocopy:** Yes

1295 Kaposvár, Hungary
Pannon University of Agricultural Sciences,
Faculty of Animal Science
Library
Pf. 16
H-7401 Kaposvár
Phone: +36(82) 314-155 **Fax:** +36(82) 320-175 **WWW:** www.diag.kaposvar.pate.hu

Non-English Name: Pannon Agrártudományi Egyetem, Állattenyésztési Kar, Könyvtára Kaposvár **Former Name:** University of Agricultural Sciences Keszthely, Agrártudományi Egyetem Keszthely (ATEK) **Founded:** 1962 **Type:** Academic **Staff:** 6 Prof. **Holdings:** 70,000 books 450 journals **Language of Collection/Services:** Hungarian / Hungarian **Subjects:** Agricultural Development, Food Sciences, Agricultural Economics, Animal Husbandry, Farming, Veterinary Medicine, Plants **Databases Used:** CABCD; FSTA; Medline **Loan:** Internationally **Photocopy:** Yes

1296 Karcag, Hungary
Debrecen University Centre for Agricultural
Sciences, Research Institute
Library
Pf. 11
H-5301 Karcag
Phone: +36(59) 311-255, 311-401, 311-824 **Fax:** +36(59) 311-036 **WWW:** www.date.hu

Non-English Name: Debreceni Egyetem Agrártudományi Centrum, Kutató Intézete (DATE, KI), Könyvtára **Type:** Academic **Founded:** 1947 **Staff:** 1 Prof. **Holdings:** 6,500 books 36 journals **Language of Collection/Services:** Hungarian **Subjects:** Agricultural Chemistry, Plants, Soil Science **Loan:** Inhouse **Service:** In country **Photocopy:** Yes

1297 Kecskemét, Hungary
University of Horticulture and Food Industry,
College Faculty of Horticulture
Library
Erdei Ferenc tér 1-3
H-6000 Kecskemét
Phone: +36(76) 486186 / 54 **Fax:** +36(76) 481-432 **WWW:** www.kee.hu **OPAC:** www.kozelkat.iif.hu/index.english.html

Non-English Name: Kertészeti és Élelmiszeripari Egyetem, Kertészeti Foiskolai Kar, Könyvtára **Founded:** 1971 **Type:** Academic **Head:** Ms. Éva Hantos *Phone:* +36(76) 486-186 *Email:* han12281@helka.iif.hu **Staff:** 1 Prof. 2 Other **Holdings:** 27,000 books 126 journals **Language of Collection/Services:** Hungarian / Hungarian, English, German, Russian **Subjects:** Agribusiness, Agricultural Development, Agricultural Economics, Agricultural Engineering, Biotechnology, Horticulture, Plant Pathology, Plants, Soil Science, Water Resources **Loan:** In country **Photocopy:** Yes

1298 Kecskemét, Hungary
Vegetable Crops Research Institute

Library
Pf. 116
H-6004 Kecskemét
Location: Mészöly Gy. út 6 **Fax:** +36(76) 322-463

Non-English Name: Zöldségtermesztési Kutató Intézet (ZKI), Könyvtára **Founded:** 1958 **Type:** Research **Head:** Kara Ilona *Phone:* +36(76) 481-329 *Email:* zkikmet@mail.datanet.hu **Staff:** 2 Prof. **Holdings:** 15,000 books 15 journals **Language of Collection/Services:** Hungarian, English, German/Hungarian **Subjects:** Vegetables **Loan:** In country **Service:** Inhouse **Photocopy:** Yes

1299 Keszthely, Hungary
Pannon University of Agricultural Sciences
Central Library
Pf. 66
H-8361 Keszthely
Location: Keszthely Deák F. u. 16, H-8360 **Phone:** +36 (83) 312-330 ext 156 **Fax:** +36(83) 315-105 **WWW:** www.georgikon.pate.hu **OPAC:** telnet://lib.georgikon.pate.hu, user:aleph

Non-English Name: Pannon Agrártudományi Egyetem, Központi Könyvtár **Former Name:** University of Agricultural Sciences Keszthely, Agrártudományi Egyetem Keszthely (ATEK) **Founded:** 1797 **Type:** Government **Head:** Dr. Pétervári András *Phone:* +36(83) 312-567 **Staff:** 9 Prof. 3 Other **Holdings:** 130,000 books 532 journals **Language of Collection/Services:** Hungarian/Hungarian **Subjects:** Agribusiness, Agricultural Economics, Agricultural Engineering, Animal Husbandry, Biotechnology, Crops, Farming, Horticulture, Plant Pathology, Soil Science **Loan:** Internationally **Service:** Internationally **Photocopy:** Yes

1300 Martonvásár, Hungary
Hungarian Academy of Sciences, Agricultural
Research Institute
Library
PO Box 19
H-2462 Martonvásár
Location: Brunszvik u. 2 **Fax:** +36(22) 460-213 **WWW:** www.mgki.hu

Non-English Name: Magyar Tudományos Akadémia, Mezogazdasági Kutatóintézete, Könyvtára **Type:** Academic **Head:** Dr. Mária Üveges-Hornyák *Phone:* +36(22) 460-016 **Staff:** 2 Prof. **Holdings:** 8,000 books 100 journals **Language of Collection/Services:** Hungarian, English / Hungarian **Subjects:** Biotechnology, Genetics, Plant Pathology, Crops **Loan:** In country **Service:** Internationally **Photocopy:** Yes

1301 Mezotur, Hungary
Gödöllo University of Agricultural Sciences,
College Faculty for Mechanical Production
Engineering in Agriculture
Library
Pf. 27
H-5401 Mezotur
Location: Petofi tér 1 **Phone:** +36(56) 350070 ext 118, 282 **Fax:** +36(56) 350465 **WWW:** www.mfk.hu **OPAC:** www.mfk.hu/mfk/konyvtar/textlib

Non-English Name: Gödölloi Agrártudományi Egyetem, Mezögazdasági Gépészüzemmérnöki Föiskolai Kar (GATE, MGFK), Könyvtára **Founded:** 1975 **Head:** László Ország *Email:* orszag@mfk.hu *Phone:* +36 (56) 351064 ext 118 **Type:** Academic **Staff:** 5 Prof. **Holdings:** 18,000 books 218 journals **Language of Collection/Services:** Hungarian/ Hungarian, English, German, Russian **Subjects:** Agricultural Engineering, Mechanical Methods **Loan:** Internationally **Photocopy:** Yes

1302   Mosonmagyaróvár, Hungary
Pannon University of Agricultural Sciences, Faculty of Agricultural Sciences
Library
PO Box 57
H-9201 Mosonmagyaróvár
Location: Vár 2 **Phone:** +36(98) 215-911 **Fax:** +36(98) 215-931 **Email:** konyvtar@movar.pate.hu **WWW:** www. movar.pate.hu

Non-English Name: Pannon Agrártudományi Egyetem, Mezögazdaságtudományi Kar (PATE), Könyvtára **Former Name:** Magyaróvári Magyar Királyi Gazdasági Akadémia, Agrártudományi Egyetem Keszthely (ATEK), University of Agricultural Sciences Keszthely **Founded:** 1818 **Type:** Academic **Head:** Mrs. Jánosné Várallyay *Phone:* +36(98) 215-911 ext 213 *Email:* varallya@movar.pate.hu **Staff:** 2 Prof. 3 Other **Holdings:** 88,929 books 184 journals **Language of Collection/Services:** Hungarian/Hungarian **Subjects:** Agribusiness, Agricultural Economics, Animal Husbandry, Biotechnology, Entomology, Food Sciences, Plant Pathology, Plants, Water Resources **Specializations:** Food Sciences **Databases Used:** CABCD **Loan:** Internationally **Service:** Internationally **Photocopy:** Yes

1303   Nyiregyháza, Hungary
Debrecen University Centre for Agricultural Science, Research Centre
Library
Pf. 12
H-4401 Nyiregyháza
Location: Westsik Vilmos út 4-6, H-4400 Nyiregyháza **Phone:** +36(42) 310-133 **Fax:** +36(42) 311-148 **WWW:** www.date.hu

Non-English Name: Debreceni Egyetem Agrártudományi Centrum, Kutató Küzpontja, Könyvtára **Former Name:** Research Centre of Vetomag Seed Producing and Trading Company, Vetomag Vállalat Kutató Központja **Founded:** 1953 **Head:** Dr. Judit Tóth-Iszály *Phone:* +36(42) 311-148 **Staff:** 2 Prof. **Holdings:** 5,600 books 52 journals **Language of Collection/ Services:** Hungarian / Hungarian **Subjects:** Plant Breeding, Plants, Soil Science **Loan:** In country **Service:** In country **Photocopy:** Yes

1304   Nyiregyháza, Hungary
University of Agricultural Sciences Godollo, Faculty of Agricultural Sciences Nyiregyháza
Library
PO Box 33
H-4401 Nyiregyháza
Fax: +36(42) 433-404 **WWW:** www.nyaf.hu

Non-English Name: Godolloi Agrartudomany Egyetem, Mezogazdasagi Foiskolai Kar Nyiregyháza, Könyvtára **Type:** Academic **Founded:** 1962 **Head:** Ibolya Réti *Phone:* +36(42) 433-134 *Email:* retim@mgfe.nyaf.hu **Staff:** 3 Prof. **Holdings:** 31,500 books 210 journals **Language of Collection/Services:** Hungarian/English, German, Russian **Subjects:** Agricultural Development, Agricultural Economics, Agricultural Engineering, Animal Husbandry, Plants, Plant Pathology **Loan:** Internationally **Photocopy:** Yes

1305   Sopron, Hungary
University of Sopron, University of Forestry and Wood Sciences
Central Library
Pf. 132
H-9401 Sopron
Location: Bajcsy Zs. u. 4 **Phone:** +36(99) 311-100 ext 288 **Fax:** +36(99) 311-103 **Email:** library@ilex.efe.hu **WWW:** jazz.efe.hu **OPAC:** ilex.efe.hu/voyager.html

Non-English Name: Soproni Egyetem, Erdészeti és Faipari Egyetem (EFE), Központi Könyvtára (KK) **Founded:** 1735 **Type:** Government **Head:** Dr. Márta Mastalir *Phone:* +36 (99) 311-100 ext 267 *Email:* mmarta@ilex.efe.hu **Staff:** 11 Prof. 1 Other **Holdings:** 378,000 books 654 journals **Language of Collection/Services:** Hungarian / Hungarian, English, German **Subjects:** Plants, Agricultural Economics, Entomology, Hunting, Plant Pathology, Soil Science, Water Resources **Specializations:** Economics, Forest Products Industries, Forestry, Geodesy, Interior Design, Pulp and Paper Industry **Databases Developed:** Hungarian Forestry and Forest Products Industries Database **Databases Used:** Comprehensive **Loan:** Internationally **Service:** Internationally **Photocopy:** Yes

1306   Szarvas, Hungary
Debrecen University Centre for Agricultural Science, Faculty of Agriculture, Water and Environmental Management
Library
PO Box 3
H-5541 Szarvas
Location: Szabadság u. 1-3 **Phone:** +36(66) 313-311 **Fax:** +36(66) 312-780 **WWW:** www.date.hu

Non-English Name: Debreceni Egyetem Agrártudományi Centrum, Mezögazdasági Víz- és Környezeígazdálkodási Kar (DATE, MVKK), Könyvtára **Former Name:** Debrecen Agricultural University, Debreceni Agrártudományi Egyetem (DATE) **Type:** Academic **Head:** Dr. József Nyéki **Founded:** 1927 **Staff:** 2 Prof. 4 Other **Holdings:** 36,000 books 210 journals **Language of Collection/Services:** Hungarian/Hungarian **Subjects:** Crops, Agricultural Economics, Agricultural Engineering, Environmental Management, Soil Science **Specializations:** Drainage, Irrigation, Water Management **Loan:** Internationally **Service:** Internationally **Photocopy:** Yes

1307   Szarvas, Hungary
Fish Culture Research Institute (FCRI)
Library
PO Box 47
H-5541 Szarvas

Location: 8 Annaliget **Phone:** +36(66) 312-311 **Fax:** +36 (66) 312-142 **Email:** varadia@haki.hu **WWW:** www.haki. hu

Non-English Name: Haltenyésztési Kutató Intézet (HAKI), Könyvtára **Founded:** 1969 **Type:** Government **Head:** Mrs. Elizabeth Börcsök *Email:* borcsok@haki.hu *Phone:* +36(66) 312-311 **Staff:** 2 Prof. 1 Other **Holdings:** 14,500 books 115 journals **Language of Collection/Services:** Hungarian, German, English, Russian / Hungarian, English, Russian **Subjects:** Ecology, Engineering, Environmental Protection, Fish Diseases, Fisheries, Fishery Management, Biology, Freshwater Fishes, Hydrobiology, Toxicology, Water Pollution, Waste Water, Water Management **Specializations:** Aquaculture **Loan:** In country **Service:** In country **Photocopy:** Yes

1308   Szeged, Hungary
Szeged Higher Education Federation, Jósef Attila University, College of Food Industry
Library
PO Box 433
H-6701 Szeged
Location: 7 Mars Street, H-6724 Szeged **Phone:** +36(62) 454-000 ext 6521 **Fax:** +36(62) 456-005 **Email:** office@ bibl.szef.u-szeged.hu **WWW:** www.szef.u-szeged.hu **OPAC:** porta-A.szef.u-szeged.hu/bibl/menukata.html

Non-English Name: JATE Szegedi Elelmiazeripari Föiskolai Kar, SZFSZ Tagintézménye (JATE-SZÉF), Könyvtára **Former Name:** Éleliszeripari Foiskola, Kertészeti és Élelmiszeripari Egyetem (KÉE), Élelmiszeripari Foiskolai Kar (ÉFK), University of Horticulture and Food Industry **Founded:** 1972 **Type:** Academic **Head:** Mrs. Gubán Sándorné *Email:* ilona@bibl.szef.u-szeged.hu *Phone:* +36(62) 456-004 **Staff:** 4 Prof. 1 Other **Holdings:** 44,451 books 150 journals **Language of Collection/Services:** Hungarian, English / Hungarian, English **Subjects:** Agribusiness, Agricultural Economics, Biotechnology, Food Engineering, Food Industry, Food Sciences, Food Technology **Databases Used:** FSTA **Loan:** Internationally **Service:** Inhouse **Photocopy:** Yes

1309   Tápiószele, Hungary
Institute for Agrobotany
Library
H-2766 Tápiószele
Phone: +36(53) 315-107 **Fax:** +36(53) 315-107 **WWW:** www.rcat.hu

Non-English Name: Agrobotanikai Intézet, Könyvtára **Former Name:** Research Centre for Agrobotany (RCA) **Founded:** 1959 **Type:** Government **Staff:** 1 Other **Holdings:** 9,000 books **Language of Collection/Services:** Hungarian / Hungarian **Subjects:** Gene Banks, Plant Breeding **Specializations:** Plants **Databases Developed:** Genetic Resources Database **Loan:** In country **Service:** In country **Photocopy:** Yes

1310   Tihany, Hungary
Hungarian Academy of Sciences, Balaton Limnological Research Institute (BLRI)
Library

Fürdotelepi u. 3
H-8237 Tihany, Veszprém
WWW: tres.blki.hu

Founded: 1927 **Type:** Academic **Head:** Rozsa Horvathne Kiss *Phone:* +36(86) 48-244 **Staff:** 2 Prof. **Holdings:** 3,000 books 5 journals **Subjects:** Fisheries, Lakes, Land Use, Water Resources **Loan:** Internationally **Photocopy:** Yes

Iceland

1311   Borgarnes, Iceland
Hvanneyri Agricultural University
Library
IS-311 Borgarnes
Phone: +354(93) 437-0170 ext 207 **Fax:** +354(93) 437-0048 **WWW:** www.hvanneyri.is/hvanneyri.nsf/pages/ index.html

Non-English Name: Bændaskólinn á Hvanneyri (Bhv) **Head:** Steinunn S. Ingólfsdótti *Email:* steinunn@hvanneyri. is **Type:** Academic **Staff:** 1 Prof. 1 Other **Holdings:** 12,850 books 302 journals **Language of Collection/Services:** Icelandic, English, Norwegian **Subjects:** Agricultural Economics, Agronomy, Farm Machinery **Loan:** Internationally **Service:** Internationally **Photocopy:** Yes

1312   Reykjavik, Iceland
Agricultural Research Institute
Library
Keldnaholt v/Vesturlandsveg
IS-112 Reykjavik
Fax: +354 577-1020 **Email:** gudrun@rala.is **WWW:** www.rala.is

Non-English Name: Rannsóknastofnun Landbúnadarins (RALA), Bókasafn **Founded:** 1965 **Type:** Government **Head:** Gudrún Pálsdóttir *Email:* gudrun@rala.is *Phone:* +354 577-1010 **Staff:** 1 Prof. **Holdings:** 4,500 books 320 journals **Language of Collection/Services:** English/Icelandic, Danish, English **Subjects:** Agricultural Engineering, Animal Husbandry, Biotechnology, Crops, Erosion, Farming, Fisheries, Food Sciences, Grassland Management, Horticulture, Plant Pathology, Soil Science **Networks:** AGRIS; GEGNIR **Loan:** Internationally **Service:** Internationally **Photocopy:** Yes

1313   Reykjavik, Iceland
Farmers Association of Iceland
Library
Box 7080
IS-127 Reykjavik
Location: Bændahöllinni v/Hagatorg **Phone:** +354 563-0300 **Fax:** +354 562-3058 **Email:** bi@bi.bondi.is **WWW:** www.bondi.is

Non-English Name: Bændasamtök Íslands (BI), Bókasafn **Former Name:** Agricultural Society of Iceland, Búnadarfélag Islands **Founded:** 1973 **Type:** Government **Head:** Margret Gunnarsdottir *Phone:* +354 563-0300 *Email:* mg@ bi.bondi.is **Staff:** .5 Prof. **Holdings:** 3,000 books 250 journals **Language of Collection/Services:** English / Icelandic, English, Swedish **Subjects:** Agricultural Development, Agricultural Economics, Animal Husbandry, Crops, Farming, Horticulture, Plants, Soil Science **Specializations:** Agriculture (History) **Loan:** Internationally **Service:** Internationally **Photocopy:** Yes

India

1314　Ahmadnagar, India
Mahatma Phule Agricultural University
University Library
Rahuri
Ahmadnagar 413722, Maharashtra
Phone: +91(246) 43208 **Email:** kvmp@ren.nic.in

Founded: 1971 **Type:** Government **Staff:** 5 Prof. 11 Other **Holdings:** 75,000 books 550 journals **Subjects:** Agricultural Economics, Agricultural Engineering, Animal Husbandry, Crops, Entomology, Horticulture, Plant Pathology, Soil Science **Loan:** In country **Photocopy:** Yes

1315　Allahabad, India
Indian Council of Forestry Research and
　　Education, Centre for Social Forestry and
　　Eco-Rehabilitation (ICFRE, CSFER)
Library
Allahabad 211001, Uttar Pradesh
Phone: +91(532) 609037 **Email:** icfre@envfor.delhi.nic.in
WWW: www.nic.in/envfor/icfre/csfer/csfer.html

Type: Government **Language of Collection/Services:** English **Subjects:** Afforestation, Agroforestry, Forestry, Ecology

1316　Almora, India
Indian Council of Agricultural Research,
　　Vivekananda Parvatiya Krishi Anusandhan
　　Shala (ICAR, VPKAS)
Library
Almora 263601, Uttar Pradesh
Fax: +91(5962) 23539 **Email:** vpkas@x400.nicgw.nic.in
WWW: www.nic.in/icar

Type: Research **Staff:** 1 Prof. 1 Other **Holdings:** 7,000 books 97 journals **Language of Collection/Services:** English/Hindi, English **Subjects:** Agricultural Economics, Agricultural Engineering, Agricultural Statistics, Agronomy, Cytogenetics, Economic Botany, Entomology, Extension, Genetics, Plant Breeding, Plant Pathology, Plant Physiology, Soil Conservation, Soil Physics, Soil Science, Water Conservation, Water Resources **Loan:** Inhouse **Service:** Inhouse **Photocopy:** No

1317　Anand, India
Gujarat Agricultural University
Dr. M.D. Patel Library
Anand 388110, Gujarat
Phone: +91(2692) 21666 Ext 223 **Email:** gau@gau.guj. nic.in

Former Name: Anand Institute of Agriculture **Founded:** 1942 **Type:** Academic Research **Head:** Mr. S.N. Jaiswal *Phone:* +91(2692) 21666 Ext 223 **Staff:** 5 Prof. 7 Other **Holdings:** 80,000 books 547 journals **Language of Collec-**

tion/Services: English / English, Gujarati, Hindi **Subjects:** Agricultural Chemistry, Agricultural Economics, Agricultural Engineering, Agricultural Meteorology, Crops, Animal Husbandry, Biochemistry, Biology, Biotechnology, Botany, Dairy Technology, Education/Extension, Entomology, Food Sciences, Genetics, Horticulture, Mathematics, Microbiology, Plant Pathology, Plant Physiology, Soil Science, Statistics, Veterinary Medicine, Zoology **Loan:** In country **Service:** In country **Photocopy:** Yes

1318　Banaskantha, India
Gujarat Agricultural University
Central Library
Sardar Krushinagar
Banaskantha 385506, Gujarat
Phone: +91(2748) 77135 **Email:** gau@gau.guj.nic.in

Founded: 1976 **Type:** Academic **Head:** P.A. Patel *Phone:* +91(2748) 77135 **Staff:** 3 Prof. 5 Other **Holdings:** 15,791 books 239 journals **Language of Collection/Services:** English **Subjects:** Agriculture (Tropics), Agribusiness, Agricultural Development, Agricultural Economics, Agricultural Engineering, Animal Husbandry, Biotechnology, Crops, Education/Extension, Entomology, Farming, Food Sciences, Forestry, Horticulture, Plant Pathology, Soil Science, Veterinary Medicine, Water Resources **Loan:** In country **Service:** In country **Photocopy:** Yes

1319　Bangalore, India
Indian Council of Agricultural Research, Indian
　　Institute of Horticultural Research (ICAR,
　　IIHR)
Information Centre for Horticultural Sciences
　　(ICHS)
Hassaraghatta Lake Post
Bangalore 560089, Karnataka
Phone: +91(80) 846-6420/23 **Fax:** +91(80) 846-6291
Email: root@iihr.kar.nic.in **WWW:** www.nic.in/icar

Founded: 1968 **Type:** Government **Head:** Dr. K.C. Mohan **Staff:** 6 Prof. 2 Other **Holdings:** 20,000 books 369 journals **Language of Collection/Services:** English / English **Subjects:** Comprehensive **Loan:** In country **Service:** Internationally **Photocopy:** Yes

1320　Bangalore, India
Indian Council of Agricultural Research, National
　　Dairy Research Institute, Southern Regional
　　Station (ICAR, NDRI)
Library
Adugodi
Bangalore 560030, Karnataka
WWW: www.nic.in/icar

Founded: 1923 **Type:** Government **Head:** M. Nanjunda-swamy *Email:* root@ndribng.kar.nic.in *Phone:* +91(80) 571 066 **Staff:** 2 Prof. 7 Other **Holdings:** 20,730 books 60 journals **Language of Collection/Services:** English **Subjects:** Agriculture (Tropics), Agribusiness, Agricultural Development, Agricultural Economics, Agricultural Engineering, Animal Husbandry, Biotechnology, Crops, Education/Extension, Farming, Food Sciences, Soil Science, Veterinary

Medicine **Specializations:** Dairy Science **Loan:** In country **Service:** In country **Photocopy:** Yes

1321   Bangalore, India
Indian Council of Forestry Research and
Education, Institute of Wood Science and
Technology (ICFRE, IWST)
Library
18th Cross, Malleswaram
Bangalore 560006, Karnataka

Phone: +91(80) 334-6811 **Email:** iwst@envfor.delhi.nic.in
WWW: www.nic.in/envfor/icfre/iwst/iwst.html

Type: Government **Language of Collection/Services:** English **Subjects:** Forestry, Wood

1322   Bangalore, India
University of Agricultural Sciences (UAS)
University Library
GKVK Campus
Bangalore 560065, Karnataka

Phone: +91(80) 330153 ext 272 **Fax:** +91(80) 330277
Email: lib@uasblr.kar.nic.in

Founded: 1965 **Type:** Academic **Head:** K.T. Somashekar *Email:* lib@uasblr.kar.nic.in *Phone:* +91(80) 330153 ext 269 **Staff:** 12 Prof. 24 Other **Holdings:** 146,800 books 832 journals **Language of Collection/Services:** English **Subjects:** Agriculture (Tropics), Agribusiness, Agricultural Development, Agricultural Economics, Farming, Agricultural Engineering, Animal Husbandry, Crops, Education/Extension, Entomology, Food Sciences, Forestry, Horticulture, Plant Pathology, Soil Science, Veterinary Medicine, Water Resources **Specializations:** Dairy Science, Home Economics, Management, Sericulture **Databases Used:** CABCD; Agris **Loan:** In country **Service:** Inhouse **Photocopy:** Yes

1323   Barapani, India
Indian Council of Agricultural Research, Research
Complex for North Eastern Hilly Region
(ICAR, RCNEHR)
Library
Umroi Road
Barapani 793103, Meghalaya

Phone: +91(364) 73257 **Email:** rcnehr@x400.nicgw.nic.in
WWW: www.nic.in/icar

1324   Barrackpore, India
Indian Council of Agricultural Research, Central
Inland Capture Fisheries Research Institute
(ICAR, CIFRI)
Library
Barrackpore 743101, West Bengal

Phone: +91(33) 560-0177 **Fax:** +91(33) 560-0388 **Email:** cicfri@x400.nicgw.nic.in, cicfri@giascol01.vsnl.net.in
WWW: www.nio.org/inois/cifri. html, www.nic.in/icar/cicfri.html

Founded: 1947 **Type:** Government **Head:** Mr. V.V. Sugunan **Staff:** 3 Prof. 12 Other **Holdings:** 7,000 books 600 journals **Language of Collection/Services:** English **Subjects:** Fisheries **Loan:** In country **Service:** Internationally **Photocopy:** Yes

1325   Barrackpore, India
Indian Council of Agricultural Research, Central
Research Institute for Jute and Allied Fibres
(ICAR, CRIJAF)
Library
24 Parganas
Barrackpore 743101, West Bengal

Fax: +91(33) 560-0415 **Email:** crijaf@cal2.vsnl.net.in
WWW: www.nic.in/icar

Former Name: Jute Agricultural Research Institute **Founded:** 1948 **Type:** Government **Head:** S.K. Bose *Phone:* +91 (33) 560415 **Staff:** 2 Prof. 1 Other **Holdings:** 16,000 books 215 journals **Language of Collection/Services:** English **Subjects:** Agricultural Engineering, Crops, Entomology, Genetics, Meteorology, Plant Breeding, Plant Pathology, Soil Science, Statistics **Specializations:** Jute **Loan:** Inhouse **Service:** In country **Photocopy:** Yes

1326   Bhimtal, District Nainatal, India
Indian Council of Agricultural Research, National
Research Centre on Coldwater Fisheries
(ICAR, NRC (Coldwater Fish))
Library
Sourabh Cottage, Thandi
Sarak
Bhimtal, District Nainatal 263136, Uttar Pradesh

Phone: +91(5942) 47279 **Email:** nrccwf@x400.nicgw.nic.in **WWW:** www.nic.in/icar

Type: Research **Head:** Mrs. Suman Kapila **Staff:** 1 Prof. **Holdings:** 1,100 books 20 journals **Language of Collection/Services:** English **Subjects:** Fisheries

1327   Bhopal, India
Indian Council of Agricultural Research, Central
Institute of Agricultural Engineering (ICAR,
CIAE)
Library
Nabi Bagh, Berasia Road
Bhopal 462038, Madhya Pradesh

Fax: +91(755) 734016 **Email:** root@ciae.mp.nic.in
WWW: www.mp.nic.in/ciae

Founded: 1976 **Type:** Research **Head:** Sh. R.P. Alha *Phone* +91(755) 730980 ext 117 *Email:* root@ciae.mp.nic. in **Staff:** 2 Prof. 5 Other **Holdings:** 12,353 books 124 journals **Language of Collection/Services:** English / Hindi **Subjects:** Agronomy, Biochemistry, Drainage, Energy, Entomology, Farm Machinery, Food Sciences, Home Economics, Irrigation, Microbiology, Postharvest Technology, Rural Development, Soil Conservation, Soybean Products, Soybeans, Water Conservation **Specializations:** Agricultural Engineering **Loan:** In country **Photocopy:** Yes

1328   Bhubaneswar, India
Indian Council of Agricultural Research, Central
Institute for Freshwater Aquaculture (ICAR,
CIFA)
FAO Depository Library
Kauslyaganga
Bhubaneswar 751002, Orissa

Phone: +91(674) 463421, 463446 **Fax:** +91(674) 463407 **Email:** cifa@ori.nic.in **WWW:** www.nic.in/icar

Founded: 1977 **Former Name:** Freshwater Aquaculture Research and Training Centre **Type:** Government **Head:** Dr. B.N. Paul *Phone:* +91 (674) 463421 *Email:* cifa@ori.nic.in **Staff:** 1 Prof. 3 Other **Holdings:** 3,000 books 54 journals **Language of Collection/Services:** English/English **Subjects:** Fisheries, Freshwater Fishes **Databases Used:** ASFA **Loan:** In country **Service:** In country **Photocopy:** Yes

1329   Bhubaneswar, India
          Orissa University of Agriculture and Technology
             (OUAT)
          Central Library
          Bhubaneswar 751003, Orissa
Phone: +91(674) 407780 **Email:** root@uat.ori.nic.in

Founded: 1964 **Type:** Academic **Head:** Mr. R.N. Kaul *Phone:* +91(674) 402577 **Staff:** 14 Prof. 22 Other **Holdings:** 115,820 books 297 journals **Language of Collection/Services:** English **Loan:** In country **Service:** In country **Photocopy:** Yes

1330   Bikaner, India
          Indian Council of Agricultural Research, National
             Research Centre for Camel (ICAR, NRC
             (Camel))
          Library
          Jorbeer, PO Box 07
          Bikaner 334001, Rajasthan
Phone: +91(151) 27628 **Fax:** +91(151) 522183 **Email:** nrccamel@x400.nicgw.nic.in **WWW:** www.nic.in/icar

Founded: 1984 **Type:** Research **Staff:** 1 Prof. **Holdings:** 589 books 22 journals **Language of Collection/Services:** English/English, Hindi **Subjects:** Agricultural Development, Agricultural Economics, Agricultural Engineering, Animal Husbandry, Biotechnology, Crops, Farming, Forestry, Horticulture, Soil Science, Veterinary Medicine, Water Resources **Specializations:** Camels **Loan:** Inhouse **Service:** In country **Photocopy:** Yes

Bombay, India *see* **Mumbai, India**

1331   Calcutta, India
          Agri-Horticultural Society of India (AGRIHORT)
          Library
          1, Alipore Road
          Calcutta 700027, West Bengal
Phone: +91(33) 4791713

Founded: 1820 **Type:** Association **Head:** Dr. S.K. Basu *Phone:* +91(33) 4791713 **Holdings:** 2,000 books 15 journals **Language of Collection/Services:** English, Bengali, Hindi/English, Hindi, Bengali **Subjects:** Horticulture, Landscape Architecture **Service:** Inhouse

1332   Calcutta, India
          Indian Council of Agricultural Research, National
             Institute of Research for Jute and Allied
             Fibres Technology (ICAR, NIRJAFT)
          Library
          12 Regent Park

Calcutta 700040, West Bengal
Fax: +91(33) 471-2583 **Email:** nirjaft@wb.nic.in **WWW:** www.nic.in/icar

Former Name: Jute Technological Research Laboratories (JTRL) **Founded:** 1938 **Type:** Government **Head:** Jawahar Lal Upadhyay **Staff:** 3 Prof. 3 Other **Holdings:** 27,172 books 152 journals **Subjects:** Chemistry, Microbiology, Physics, Textile Machinery **Specializations:** Jute **Loan:** In country **Service:** In country **Photocopy:** Yes

1333   Calcutta, India
          National Library of India, Calcutta
          Belvedere, PO Alipore
          Calcutta 700027, West Bengal
Phone: +91(33) 479-2968

Founded: 1903 **Type:** Government **Head:** Dr. D.N. Banerjee *Phone:* +91(33) 479-2968 **Staff:** 203 Prof. 470 Other **Holdings:** 5,000 books 20 journals **Language of Collection/Services:** English **Subjects:** Agribusiness, Agricultural Economics, Agricultural Engineering, Crops, Animal Husbandry, Fertilizers, Fisheries, Forestry, Horticulture, Pest Control, Plant Protection, Poultry, Rubber, Sericulture, Soil Science **Loan:** Internationally **Photocopy:** Yes

1334   Calicut, India
          Indian Council of Agricultural Research, Indian
             Institute of Spices Research (ICAR, IISR)
          Library
          Post Box No. 1701, Marikunnu
          Calicut 673012, Kerala
Phone: +91(495) 370294 **Fax:** +91(495) 370294 **Email:** nrcp@ren.nic.in **WWW:** www.nic.in/icar

Former Name: National Research Centre for Spices (NRC (Spices)), Central Plantation Crops Research Institute, Regional Station **Founded:** 1976 **Type:** Government **Staff:** 1 Prof. 1 Other **Holdings:** 3,600 books 126 journals **Language of Collection/Services:** English **Subjects:** Biochemistry, Crops, Entomology, Genetics, Nematology, Plant Breeding, Plant Pathology, Plant Physiology, Soil Science, Spice Plants, Statistics **Specializations:** Spices **Loan:** In country

1335   Cochin, India
          Indian Council of Agricultural Research, Central
             Institute of Fisheries Technology (ICAR,
             CIFT)
          Library
          Willingdon Island
          PO Matsyapuri
          Cochin 682029, Kerala
Fax: +91(484) 668212 **Email:** root@cift.ker.nic.in **WWW:** www.nic.in/icar

Founded: 1956 **Type:** Government **Head:** P. Ravindral *Phone:* +91(484) 6845 **Staff:** 2 Prof. 2 Other **Holdings:** 150 journals 5,000 books **Subjects:** Fisheries **Loan:** Do not loan **Photocopy:** Yes

1336   Cochin, India
          Indian Council of Agricultural Research, Central
             Marine Fisheries Research Institute (ICAR,
             CMFRI)

Library
PO Box 1603 Ernakulam
Cochin 682014, Kerala
Fax: +91(484) 394909 **Email:** mdcmfri@md2.vsnl.net.in
WWW: www.nio.org/inois/cmfri.html, www.nic.in/icar

Founded: 1947 **Type:** Government **Head:** Mr. K.J. Mathew
Phone: +91(484) 369867 **Staff:** 6 Prof. 2 Other **Holdings:**
30,000 books 120 journals **Language of Collection/Services:** English **Specializations:** Fisheries **Loan:** In country
Service: In country **Photocopy:** Yes

1337   Coimbatore, India
Indian Council of Agricultural Research,
    Sugarcane Breeding Institute (ICAR, SBI)
Library
Coimbatore 641007, Tamil Nadu
Phone: +91(422) 41621 **Fax:** +91(422) 472923 **Email:**
sugaris@md3.vsnl.net.in **WWW:** www.nic.in/icar

Founded: 1912 **Type:** Government **Head:** N. Subramanian
Phone: +91(422) 41621 ext 46 **Staff:** 1 Prof. 2 Other **Holdings:** 11,000 books 118 journals **Language of Collection/
Services:** English **Subjects:** Breeding, Cytogenetics, Entomology, Education/Extension, Genetics, Nematology, Plant
Pathology, Plant Physiology **Specializations:** Sugarcane
Loan: In country **Photocopy:** Yes

1338   Coimbatore, India
Indian Council of Forestry Research and
    Education, Institute of Forest Genetics and
    Tree Breeding (ICFRE, IFGTB)
Library
R.S. Puram P.O. Box No. 1061
Coimbatore 641002, Tamil Nadu
Location: Forest Campus, Cowley Brown Road **Phone:**
+91(422) 431540 **Fax:** +91(422) 43549 **Email:** ifgtb@
envfor.delhi.nic **WWW:** www.nic.in/envfor/icfre/ifgtb/
ifgtb.html

Founded: 1988 **Type:** Government **Head:** *Phone:* +91(422)
435541 *Email:* ifgtb@envfor.delhi.nic **Staff:** 2 Prof. 1 Other
Holdings: 6,000 books 50 journals **Language of Collection/
Services:** English / English, Tamil **Subjects:** Biotechnology,
Ecology, Entomology, Environment, Forestry, Genetics,
Plant Breeding, Plant Pathology, Trees **Databases Used:**
CABPESTCD; TREECD **Loan:** Inhouse **Service:** Inhouse
Photocopy: Yes

1339   Coimbatore, India
Tamil Nadu Agricultural University (TNAU)
Library
Lawley Road PO
Coimbatore 641003, Tamil Nadu
Phone: +91(422) 41222 ext 273 **Fax:** +91(422) 41672
Email: root@tnau.tn.nic.in **WWW:** www.tnau.edu

Founded: 1876 **Type:** Academic **Head:** R. Boraiyan *Phone:*
+91(422) 41222 ext 273 **Staff:** 3 Prof. 12 Other **Holdings:**
150,000 books 585 journals **Language of Collection/Services:** English **Subjects:** Agricultural Economics, Crops,
Agricultural Engineering, Agronomy, Animal Husbandry,
Biotechnology, Ecology, Entomology, Genetics, Education/
Extension, Horticulture, Microbiology, Plant Breeding,

Plant Pathology, Plant Physiology, Seed Production, Soil
Science, Statistics **Loan:** In country **Photocopy:** Yes

1340   Cuttack, India
Indian Council of Agricultural Research, Central
    Rice Research Institute (ICAR, CRRI)
Library
Cuttack 753006, Orissa
Phone: +91(671) 642445 **Fax:** +91(671) 641744 **Email:**
root@crri.ori.nic.in **WWW:** www.nic.in/icar

Founded: 1947 **Type:** Government **Head:** Mr. R.D. Ratan
Phone: +91(671) 643015 *Email:* root@crri.ori.nic.in **Staff:**
2 Prof. 6 Other **Holdings:** 80,000 books 200 journals **Language of Collection/Services:** English **Subjects:** Agricultural Economics, Agricultural Engineering, Biotechnology,
Crops, Cytology, Education/Extension, Entomology, Genetics, Nematology, Plant Breeding, Plant Pathology, Plant
Physiology, Soil Science, Statistics **Specializations:** Rice
Loan: In country **Photocopy:** No

1341   Dehra Dun, India
Indian Council of Agricultural Research, Central
    Soil and Water Conservation Research and
    Training Institute (ICAR, CSWCRTI)
Library
218, Kaula Garh Road
Dehra Dun 248195, Uttar Pradesh
Fax: +91(135) 754213 **Email:** cswcrti@cswcrti.up.nic.in
WWW: www.nic.in/icar

Founded: 1972 **Type:** Government **Head:** G.R. Deshmukh
Phone: +91(135) 757212 *Email:* cswcrti@cswcrti.up.nic.in
Staff: 2 Prof. 1 Other **Holdings:** 13,500 books 120 journals
Language of Collection/Services: English / English **Subjects:** Agricultural Economics, Agroforestry, Agricultural
Engineering, Crops, Forestry, Soil Science, Statistics, Water
Conservation **Specialization:** Watershed Management **Photocopy:** Yes **Databases Used:** CABCD **Loan:** In country

1342   Dehra Dun, India
Indian Council of Forestry Research and
    Education (ICFRE)
National Forest Library and Information Centre
    (NFLIC)
PO New Forests
Dehra Dun 248006, Uttar Pradesh
Phone: +91(135) 628614 **Fax:** +91(135) 628571 **Email:**
icfre@envfor.delhi.nic **WWW:**
www.nic.in/envfor/icfre/icfre.html

Former Name: Forest Research Institute (FRI), Central Library **Founded:** 1906 **Type:** Research **Staff:** 6 Prof. 5 Other
Holdings: 135,000 books 425 journals **Language of Collection/Services:** English **Subjects:** Entomology, Plant Pathology, Forestry, Soil Science, Water Resources **Loan:** Inhouse
Service: In country **Photocopy:** Yes

1343   Dehra Dun, India
Ministry of Environment and Forests, Wildlife
    Institute of India (WII)
Library and Documentation Centre (L & DC)
PO Box No 18, Chandrabani

Dehra Dun 2480001, Uttar Pradesh
Phone: +91(135) 620912/5 ext 201 **Fax:** +91(135) 640117
Email: wii@wii.gov.in **WWW:** www.wii.gov.in

Founded: 1986 **Type:** Government **Head:** Madan S. Rana
Phone: +91(135) 620912/5 ext 201 **Holdings:** 30,000 books
207 journals **Language of Collection/Services:** English
Subjects: Forestry, Wildlife **Specializations:** Ecology, En-
dangered Species, Nature Conservation, Nature Reserves,
Wild Animals, Wildlife Management **Databases Used:**
CABI **Databases Developed:** Reprint and map databases
Loan: Inhouse **Service:** Internationally **Photocopy:** Yes

1344　Dharwad, India
University of Agricultural Sciences (UAS)
University Library
Krishinagar
Dharwad 580005, Karnataka
Fax: +91(836) 348349 **Email:** root@uasd.kar.nic.in

Founded: 1986 **Type:** Academic **Head:** Stanley Madan
Kumar *Phone:* +91(836) 348321 ext 235 *Email:* root@uasd.
kar.nic.in **Staff:** 6 Prof. 9 Other **Holdings:** 85,000 books 530
journals **Language of Collection/Services:** English/English
Subjects: Agricultural Economics, Crops, Agricultural Engineering, Entomology, Education/Extension, Farming, Forestry, Genetics, Horticulture, Microbiology, Plant Breeding,
Plant Pathology, Soil Science, Water Resources **Loan:** In
country **Photocopy:** Yes

1345　Distt. Tonk, India
Indian Council of Agricultural Research, Central
　　Sheep and Wool Research Institute (ICAR,
　　CSWRI)
Library
Avikanagar, Tehsil Malpura
Distt. Tonk 304501, Rajasthan
Phone: +91(141) 4763, 4212 **Email:** root@cswri.raj.nic.in
WWW: www.nic.in/icar

Founded: 1962 **Type:** Research **Head:** Km. Veera Gogia
Phone: +91(141) 4758 **Staff:** 2 Prof. 2 Other **Holdings:** 213
journals 8,162 books **Language of Collection/Services:**
English / English **Subjects:** Animal Husbandry, Furbearing
Animals, Textiles **Specializations:** Sheep, Wool, Mutton
Databases Developed: Small Ruminants **Loan:** In country
Service: In country **Photocopy:** Yes

1346　Faizabad, India
Narendra Deva University of Agriculture and
　　Technology (NDUAT)
Library
PO Kumar Ganj
Faizabad 224001, Uttar Pradesh
Phone: +91(527) 814862 **Fax:** +91(527) 814947 **Email:**
nduat@up.nic.in

Founded: 1975 **Type:** Academic **Staff:** 6 Prof. 10 Other
Holdings: 30,290 books **Language of Collection/Services:**
English **Loan:** In country **Photocopy:** Yes

1347　Hisar, India
Chaudhary Charan Singh Haryana Agricultural
　　University (CCS HAU)

Nehru Library
Hisar 125004, Haryana
Phone: +91(1662) 74098 ext 298 **Fax:** +91(1662) 73552
Email: root@hau.pnp.nic.in

Former Name: Haryana Agricultural University **Founded:**
1970 **Type:** Academic **Head:** Professor Prem Singh *Phone:*
+91(1662) 74098 **Staff:** 10 Prof. 83 Other **Holdings:** 1,540
journals 235,000 books **Language of Collection/Services:**
English/Hindi, English **Subjects:** Agriculture (Tropics), Agricultural Economics, Agricultural Engineering, Agricultural
Meteorology, Animal Husbandry, Crops, Dry Farming, Biotechnology, Education/Extension, Farming, Entomology,
Fisheries, Food Sciences, Forestry, Horticulture, Nematology, Plant Breeding, Plant Pathology, Seeds, Soil Science,
Vegetables, Veterinary Medicine **Loan:** In country **Service:**
In country **Photocopy:** Yes

1348　Hisar, India
Indian Council of Agricultural Research, Central
　　Institute for Research on Buffaloes (ICAR,
　　CIRB)
Library
Sirsa Road
Hisar 125001, Haryana
Phone: +91(1662) 63170 **Fax:** +91(1662) 32513 **Email:**
cirb@x400.nicgw.nic.in **WWW:** www.nic.in/icar

Subjects: Buffaloes

1349　Hisar, India
Indian Council of Agricultural Research, National
　　Research Centre for Equines (ICAR, NRC
　　(Equines))
Library
Sirsa Road
Hisar 125001, Haryana
Fax: +91(1662) 33217 **Email:** nrcequine@x400.nicgw.
nic.in **WWW:** www.nic.in/icar

Founded: 1926 **Type:** Research **Head:** P.K. Upbal *Phone:*
+91(1662) 2787 **Subjects:** Animal Husbandry, Veterinary
Medicine **Specializations:** Equidae

1350　Hyderabad, India
Acharya N.G. Ranga Agricultural University
Central Library and Documentation Centre
Rajendranagar
Hyderabad 500030, Andhra Pradesh
Email: root@apau.ap.nic.in

Former Name: Andhra Pradesh Agricultural University
Founded: 1964 **Type:** Academic **Staff:** 8 Prof. 24 Other
Holdings: 80,000 books 520 journals **Subjects:** Agricultural
Engineering, Animal Husbandry, Dairy Science, Forestry,
Home Economics, Horticulture, Plant Pathology **Loan:** In
country **Photocopy:** Yes

1351　Hyderabad, India
Indian Council of Agricultural Research, Central
　　Research Institute for Dryland Agriculture
　　(ICAR, CRIDA)
Library and Documentation Unit
Santoshnagar, PO Saidabad

Hyderabad 500659, Andhra Pradesh
Fax: +91(40) 453-1802 **Email:** hpsingh@crida.ap.nic.in
WWW: www.nic.in/icar

Founded: 1971 **Type:** Research **Head:** Dr. G.R. Korwar
Staff: 2 Prof. 4 Other **Holdings:** 7,600 books 85 journals
Language of Collection/Services: English / English **Subjects:** Agricultural Economics, Agricultural Engineering, Agricultural Meteorology, Agricultural Statistics, Crops, Agroforestry, Dry Farming, Extension, Plant Pathology, Plant Physiology, Soil Science **Loan:** Inhouse **Service:** Inhouse **Photocopy:** Yes

1352   Hyderabad, India
       Indian Council of Agricultural Research, National
          Academy of Agricultural Research
          Management (ICAR, NAARM)
       Information and Documentation Unit (IDU)
       Rajendranagar
       Hyderabad 500030, Andhra Pradesh
Fax: +91(40) 401-5912 **Email:** amaru@naarm.ernet.in
WWW: www.nic.in/icar

Former Name: Central Staff College for Agriculture **Type:** Academic **Founded:** 1976 **Head:** R.B. Gaddagimath **Staff:** 4 Prof. 5 Other **Holdings:** 18,000 books 450 journals **Language of Collection/Services:** English, Hindi **Subjects:** Agricultural Economics, Technology Transfer **Specializations:** Agricultural Research, Information Science, Organization of Research, Research Policy **Databases Developed:** Agricultural research management **Databases Used:** CABCD, Agricola; **Loan:** In country **Service:** Internationally **Photocopy:** Yes

1353   Hyderabad, India
       National Institute of Rural Development (NIRD)
       Centre on Rural Documentation (CORD)
       Rajendranagar
       Hyderabad 500030, Andhra Pradesh
Fax: +91(842) 245277 **Email:** karaju@nird.ap.nic.in
WWW: www.nird.org

Founded: 1958 **Head:** Mr. K.A. Raju *Phone:* +91(842) 245 001 **Type:** Academic **Staff:** 9 Prof. 8 Other **Holdings:** 6,000 books 25 journals **Language of Collection/Services:** English/English **Subjects:** Agribusiness, Forestry, Agricultural Development, Agricultural Economics, Animal Husbandry, Education/Extension **Loan:** In country **Service:** In country **Photocopy:** Yes

1354   Indore, India
       Indian Council of Agricultural Research, National
          Research Centre on Soyabean (ICAR, NRC
          (Soya))
       Soybean Information Centre
       Khandwa Road
       Indore 452001, Madhya Pradesh
Phone: +91(731) 65653 **Fax:** +91(731) 470520 **Email:** nrcsoya@hub1.nic.in **WWW:** www.nic.in/icar

Founded: 1986 **Type:** Government **Staff:** 3 Prof. 2 Other **Holdings:** 200 books 75 journals **Subjects:** Crops, Oilseeds **Specializations:** Soybeans **Loan:** Do not loan

1355   Izatnagar, India
       Indian Council of Agricultural Research, Central
          Avian Research Institute (ICAR, CARI)
       Library
       Izatnagar 243122, Uttar Pradesh
Fax: +91(581) 447321 **Email:** cavri@x400.nicgw.nic.in
WWW: www.nic.in/icar

Subjects: Aviculture

1356   Izatnagar, India
       Indian Council of Agricultural Research, Indian
          Veterinary Research Institute (ICAR, IVRI)
       National Library of Veterinary Science (NLVS)
       Izatnagar 243122, Uttar Pradesh
Fax: +91(581) 447284 **Email:** singh@ivri.wiprobt.ems. vsnl.net.in **WWW:** www.nic.in/icar

Founded: 1889 **Type:** Government **Holdings:** 94,114 books 867 journals **Language of Collection/Services:** English **Specializations:** Veterinary Science **Loan:** In country

1357   Jabalpur, India
       Indian Council of Forestry Research and
          Education, Tropical Forest Research Institute
          (ICFRE, TFRI)
       Library
       Jabalpur 482021, Madhya Pradesh
Phone: +91(761) 322585 **Fax:** +91(761) 322585 **Email:** tfrinet@envfor.delhi.nic **WWW:** www.nic.in/envfor/icfre/ tfri/tfri.html

Type: Government **Language of Collection/Services:** English **Subjects:** Forestry, Soil Science, Tropics

1358   Jhansi, India
       Indian Council of Agricultural Research, Indian
          Grassland and Fodder Research Institute
          (ICAR, IGFRI)
       Library
       Pahuj Dam, Jhansi-Gwalior Road
       Jhansi 284003, Uttar Pradesh
Phone: +91(517) 908833 **Fax:** +91(517) 440833 **Email:** igfri@igfri.up.nic.in **WWW:** www.nic.in/icar

Subjects: Fodder Crops, Grasslands

1359   Jharanapani, India
       Indian Council of Agricultural Research, National
          Research Centre for Mithun (ICAR, NRC
          (Mithun))
       Library
       Jharanapani 797106, Nagaland
Phone: +91(3862) 32341, 323227 **Fax:** +91(3862) 32341 **Email:** nrcmithun@x400.nicgw.nic.in **WWW:** www.nic. in/icar

Founded: 1988 **Type:** Research **Head:** M. Pratheepa *Phone* +91(3862) 32341 **Staff:** 1 Other **Holdings:** 292 books 10 journals **Language of Collection/Services:** English/English **Subjects:** Animal Husbandry **Photocopy:** Yes

1360   Jobner, India
       S.K.N. College of Agriculture
       Library

Jobner 303329, Rajasthan
Phone: +91(1425) 54022 (Dean) **Fax:** +91(1425) 54022 (Dean)

Founded: 1947 **Type:** Academic **Head:** K. Murali Krishna *Phone:* +91(1425) 4735 **Staff:** 3 Prof. 5 Other **Holdings:** 36,662 books 116 journals **Language of Collection/Services:** English, Hindi / English, Hindi **Subjects:** Agricultural Chemistry, Agricultural Engineering, Animal Husbandry, Biochemistry, Biotechnology, Crops, Dairy Science, Entomology, Environment, Extension, Fisheries, Genetics, Horticulture, Plant Breeding, Plant Pathology, Plant Physiology **Loan:** In country **Photocopy:** Yes

1361   **Jodhpur, India**
Indian Council of Agricultural Research, Central Arid Zone Research Institute (ICAR, CAZRI)
Library
Jodhpur 342003, Rajasthan
Phone: +91(291) 40584 **Fax:** +91(291) 40706, 41516
Email: nljoshi@cazri.raj.nic.in **WWW:** www.nic.in/icar/cazri.htm

Founded: 1959 **Type:** Government **Staff:** 4 Prof. 4 Other **Holdings:** 15,000 books 150 journals **Subjects:** Arid Lands, Crops, Forestry, Horticulture, Soil Science **Loan:** In country **Photocopy:** Yes

1362   **Jodhpur, India**
Indian Council of Forestry Research and Education, Arid Forest Research Institute (ICFRE, AFRI)
Library
12/10, Chopasani Housing Scheme
Jodhpur 342008, Rajasthan
Phone: +91(291) 26034 **Email:** afri@envfor.delhi.nic.in **WWW:** www.nic.in/envfor/icfre/afri/afri.html

Founded: 1988 **Type:** Government **Language of Collection/Services:** English **Subjects:** Arid Lands, Forestry, Soil Science

1363   **Jorhat, India**
Assam Agriculture University (AAU)
Central Library
Jorhat 785013, Assam
Phone: +91(376) 320917 **Email:** vc@aau.ren.nic.in

Former Name: Assam Agricultural College, Agricultural College Library **Founded:** 1969 **Type:** Academic **Head:** Dr. Munindra Nath Borgohain *Phone:* +91(376) 320917 **Staff:** 7 Prof. 49 Other **Holdings:** 76,993 books 142 journals **Language of Collection/Services:** English / English **Subjects:** Comprehensive **Specializations:** Plant Physiology **Loan:** Inhouse **Service:** Inhouse **Photocopy:** Yes

1364   **Jorhat, India**
Indian Council of Forestry Research and Education, Institute of Rain and Moist Deciduous Forest Research (ICFRE, IRMDFR)
Library
Jorhat 785001, Assam

Phone: +91(376) 322054 **Email:** icfre@envfor.delhi.nic.in **WWW:** www.nic.in/envfor/icfre/irmdfr/irmdfr.html

Founded: 1988 **Type:** Government **Language of Collection/Services:** English **Subjects:** Ecology, Forest Management, Hydrobiology **Specializations:** Bamboos

1365   **Junagadh, India**
Indian Council of Agricultural Research, National Research Centre for Groundnut (ICAR, NRCG)
Library
Ivnagar Road, PB No. 5
Junagadh 362001, Gujarat
Phone: +91(285) 23041, 23461 **Fax:** +91(285) 51550
Email: director@nrcg.guj.nic.in **WWW:** www.nic.in/icar

Founded: 1979 **Type:** Government **Head:** Mr. M.A. Khan *Phone:* +91 (285) 51550 **Language of Collection/Services:** English **Holdings:** 8,500 books 300 journals **Subjects:** Peanuts **Loan:** Inhouse **Service:** In country **Photocopy:** Yes

1366   **Karnal, India**
Indian Council of Agricultural Research, Central Soil Salinity Research Institute (ICAR, CSSRI)
Library
Zarifa Farm
Kachhwa Road
Karnal 132001, Haryana
Phone: +91(184) 250480 **Fax:** +91(184) 250480 **Email:** cssri@x400.nicgw.nic.in **WWW:** www.ilri.nl/cssri.html, www.nic.in/icar

Founded: 1969 **Type:** Government **Head:** Dr. Ram Ajore *Phone:* +91(184) 23218, 23219 *Email:* cssri@x400.nicgw.nic.in **Staff:** 2 Prof. 3 Other **Holdings:** 20,680 books 122 journals **Language of Collection/Services:** English, Hindi / English, Hindi **Subjects:** Agriculture (Tropics), Agricultural Development, Agricultural Economics, Agricultural Engineering, Crops, Education/Extension, Farming, Forestry, Horticulture, Soil Science, Water Resources **Specializations:** Drainage, Irrigation, Soil Salinity, Water Management **Loan:** In country **Service:** In country **Photocopy:** Yes

1367   **Karnal, India**
Indian Council of Agricultural Research, National Bureau of Animal Genetic Resources (ICAR, NBAGR)
Library
Makrampur Campus
PO Box 129
Karnal 132001, Haryana
Phone: +91(184) 253918, 257152, 251252 **Fax:** +91(184) 253654 **Email:** director@nbagr.hry.nic.in **WWW:** www.nic.in/icar

Former Name: National Institute of Animal Genetics **Founded:** 1985 **Type:** Research **Subjects:** Animal Genetics

1368   **Karnal, India**
Indian Council of Agricultural Research, National Dairy Research Institute (ICAR, NDRI)
National Library of Dairying

NDRI Campus
Karnal 132001, Haryana
Fax: +91(184) 20042 **Email:** root@ndri.hry.nic.in **WWW:** www.nic.in/icar

Founded: 1985 **Type:** Academic **Head:** Mr. M.M. Sharma *Phone:* +91(184) 22092 **Staff:** 6 Prof. 18 Other **Holdings:** 77,224 books 425 journals **Language of Collection/Services:** English **Subjects:** Animal Husbandry, Cytogenetics, Immunogenetics **Databases Used:** CABCD; Medline **Loan:** In country **Service:** In country **Photocopy:** Yes

1369 Kasaragod, India
Indian Council of Agricultural Research, Central Plantation Crops Research Institute (ICAR, CPCRI)
Library
Post Kudlu
Kasaragod 671124, Kerala
Phone: +91(499) 430894/6 **Fax:** +91(499) 430322 **Email:** cpcri@md3.vsnl.net.in **WWW:** www.nic.in/icar

Founded: 1956 **Type:** Government **Head:** Mr. Ramesh Kumar *Email:* cpcri@md3.vsnl.net.in *Phone:* +91(499) 430894/6 **Staff:** 4 Prof. 3 Other **Holdings:** 23,000 books 250 journals **Language of Collection/Services:** English **Subjects:** Agricultural Economics, Biochemistry, Entomology, Genetics, Horticulture, Plant Breeding, Plant Pathology, Plant Physiology, Plantation Crops, Soil Science, Statistics **Databases Used:** CABCD **Loan:** In country **Service:** In country **Photocopy:** Yes

1370 Kharagpur, India
Indian Institute of Technology Kharagpur (IIT Kharagpur)
Central Library
Kharagpur 721302, West Bengal
Location: About 120km. from Calcutta **Phone:** KGP 221-224 (4 lines) **WWW:** iitkgp.ernet.in

Founded: 1951 **Type:** Academic **Head:** Dr. D.N. Banertee **Language of Collection/Services:** English **Subjects:** Agricultural Development, Agricultural Economics, Agricultural Engineering, Animal Husbandry, Biotechnology, Crops, Education/Extension, Farming, Fisheries, Food Sciences, Plant Pathology, Soil Science, Water Resources **Loan:** In country **Photocopy:** Yes

1371 Lucknow, India
Council of Scientific and Industrial Research (CSIR)
National Botanical Research Institute
Rana Pratan Marg
Lucknow 226001, Uttar Pradesh
Phone: +91(522) 236431/35 ext 216

Founded: 1953 **Type:** Government **Head:** Mr. H.V. Mote *Phone:* +91(522) 236431/35 ext 216 **Staff:** 6 Prof. 6 Other **Holdings:** 1,400 books **Language of Collection/Services:** English **Subjects:** Biotechnology, Horticulture, Plant Pathology, Plants, Reclamation, Soil Science **Loan:** Inhouse **Photocopy:** Yes

1372 Lucknow, India
Indian Council of Agricultural Research, Central Institute for Sub-Tropical Horticulture (ICAR, CISTH)
Library
Rae Bareli Road
PO Dilkusha
Lucknow 226002, Uttar Pradesh
Fax: +91(522) 451026, 440626 **Email:** cisth@x400.nicgw.nic.in **WWW:** www.nic.in/icar

Former Name: Central Institute of Horticulture for Northern Plains (CIHNP) **Subjects:** Horticulture

1373 Lucknow, India
Indian Council of Agricultural Research, Indian Institute of Sugarcane Research (ICAR, IISR)
Library
Rae Bareli Road
PO Dilkusha
Lucknow 226002, Uttar Pradesh
Fax: +91(522) 451028 **Email:** iisr@x400.nicgw.nic.in **WWW:** www.nic.in/icar

Subjects: Sugarcane

1374 Lucknow, India
Indian Council of Agricultural Research, National Bureau of Fish Genetic Resources (ICAR, NBFGR)
Library
351/28, Radha Swami Bhawan
Duriyapur, PO Rajendranagar
Lucknow 226002, Uttar Pradesh
Fax: +91(522) 419820 **Email:** nbfgr@lwl.vsnl.net.in **WWW:** www.nic.in/icar

Founded: 1986 **Type:** Research **Head:** Mrs. Sukla Das **Staff:** 2 Prof. 2 Other **Holdings:** 2,190 books 55 journals **Language of Collection/Services:** English / English **Subjects:** Aquaculture, Biochemical Genetics, Conservation, Cryogenics, Cytogenetics **Specializations:** Biotechnology, Cryopreservation, Fish Culture, Fisheries, Genetics **Loan:** In country **Service:** Internationally **Photocopy:** Yes

1375 Ludhiana, India
Punjab Agricultural University (PAU)
Central Library
Ludhiana 141004, Punjab
Phone: +91(161) 400945 **Email:** root@pau.chd.nic.in

1376 Madras, India
Indian Council of Agricultural Research, Central Institute of Brackishwater Aquaculture (ICAR, CIBA)
Library
141, Marshal's Road, Egmore
Madras 600008, Tamil Nadu
Fax: +91(44) 855-4851 **Email:** ciba@tn.nic.in **WWW:** www.nio.org/inois/ciba.html, www.nic.in/icar

Founded: 1987 **Type:** Government **Staff:** 3 Prof. **Holdings:** 500 books 25 journals **Subjects:** Aquaculture, Brackish Wa-

ter, Estuaries, Fisheries, Water Pollution **Loan:** In country
Photocopy: Yes

1377   Madras, India
        Tamil Nadu Veterinary and Animal Sciences
                University (TANUVAS)
        Madras Veterinary College Library (MVC
                Library)
        Vepery High Road
        Madras 600007, Tamil Nadu
Phone: +91(44) 581506 **Fax:** +91(44) 560114 **Email:**
mvclib@giasmd01.vsnl.net.in **WWW:** www.tanuvas.com

Founded: 1961 **Type:** Academic **Head:** Dr. G. Rajavelu
Phone: +91(44) 588997, 581506 *Email:* mvclib@giasmd01.
vsnl.net.in **Staff:** 2 Prof. 12 Other **Holdings:** 25,000 books
215 journals **Language of Collection/Services:** English /
English **Subjects:** Comprehensive **Specializations:** Animal
Husbandry, Biotechnology, Veterinary Medicine **Databases
Developed:** University theses **Databases Used:** Comprehensive **Loan:** Inhouse **Service:** Inhouse **Photocopy:** Yes

1378   Mathura, India
        Indian Council of Agricultural Research, Central
                Institute for Research on Goats (ICAR CIRG)
        Library
        Makhdoom, PO Farah
        Mathura 281122, Uttar Pradesh
Location: Paliwal Park **Phone:** +91(565) 763325 **Fax:** +91
(565) 763246 **Email:** root@cirg.up.nic.in **WWW:** www.
nic.in/icar

Founded: 1979 **Type:** Research **Head:** Dr. S.K. Singh
Staff: 1 Prof. 1 Other **Holdings:** 2,000 books 140 journals
Subjects: Animal Husbandry, Veterinary Medicine **Specializations:** Goats **Loan:** In country **Service:** In country **Photocopy:** Yes

1379   Mumbai, India
        Indian Council of Agricultural Research, Central
                Institute of Fisheries Education (ICAR, CIFE)
        Library
        Jaiprakash Road, Seven Bungalows
        Versova
        Mumbai 400061, Maharashtra
Fax: +91(22) 626-1573 **Email:** root@cife.bom.nic.in
WWW: www.nio.org/inois/cife.html, www.nic.in/icar

Type: Government **Head:** Mrs. Pushpa Shembekar *Phone:*
+91(22) 626-1632 **Staff:** 1 Prof. 3 Other **Holdings:** 18,775
books 150 journals **Language of Collection/Services:** English **Subjects:** Education, Fisheries **Loan:** In country **Service:** In country

1380   Mumbai, India
        Indian Council of Agricultural Research, Central
                Institute for Research on Cotton Technology
                (ICAR, CIRCOT)
        Library
        P.B. No. 16640,Adenwala Road
        Matunga
        Mumbai 400019, Maharashtra

Fax: +91(22) 413-0835 **Email:** circot@x400.nicgw.nic.in
WWW: www.nic.in/icar

Former Name: Cotton Technological Research Laboratory
(CTRL) **Founded:** 1924 **Type:** Government **Head:** Smt.
R.K. Shahani *Phone:* +91(22) 412-7273/5 **Staff:** 2 Prof. 2
Other **Holdings:** 1,000 books 20 journals **Subjects:** Agricultural Engineering, Biotechnology, Crops, Farming, Fibers,
Forestry, Soil Science **Loan:** In country **Photocopy:** No

1381   Nagpur, India
        Indian Council of Agricultural Research, Central
                Institute for Cotton Research (ICAR, CICR)
        Library
        PO Bag 225, GPO
        Nagpur 440001, Maharashtra
Location: Panjari Farm, Wardha Road **Phone:** +91(712)
668549 **Fax:** +91(712) 75529 **Email:** circot@bom3.vsnl.
net.in **WWW:** www.nic.in/icar

Founded: 1976 **Type:** Government **Head:** V.V. Katare
Staff: 2 Prof. 1 Other **Holdings:** 5,000 books 175 journals
Language of Collection/Services: English **Subjects:** Biotechnology, Breeding, Crops, Entomology, Genetics, Plant
Pathology, Plant Physiology, Soil Science **Specializations:**
Cotton **Databases Developed:** Cotton Database **Loan:** Inhouse **Service:** In country **Photocopy:** Yes

1382   Nagpur, India
        Indian Council of Agricultural Research, National
                Bureau of Soil Survey and Land-Use
                Planning (ICAR, NBSS&LUP)
        Library and Documentation Unit (L&DU)
        PO Box 426, Shankarnagar PO
        Nagpur 440010, Maharashtra
Location: Amravati Road **Phone:** +91(712) 532386 **Fax:**
+91(712) 522534 **Email:** root@nbsslup.mah.nic.in
WWW: www.nic.in/icar **Ariel IP:** 164.100.243.166

Former Name: All India Soil and Land Use Survey Organisation, Documentation Centre **Type:** Government **Head:** Dr.
Y.M. Patil *Phone:* +91(712) 532386 *Email:* root@nbsslup.
mah.nic.in **Staff:** 2 Prof. 3 Other **Holdings:** 8,990 books 75
journals **Language of Collection/Services:** English/English
Subjects: Agricultural Engineering, Agronomy, Agroclimatology, Documentation, Drainage, Environmental Sciences,
Forest Soils, Geology, Geomorphology, Hydrology, Irrigation, Land Evaluation, Soil Science, Technology Transfer,
Watershed Management **Specializations:** Agricultural Statistics, Climatology, Geographic Information Systems, Geomorphology, Mapping, Pedology, Remote Sensing, Land
Use, Soil Surveys, Soil Conservation, Water Conservation
Databases Developed: ISSSLUP - Information System for
Soil Survey and Land Use Planning, a bibliographic database
Databases Used: Agris; CABCD **Loan:** Inhouse **Service:**
Internationally **Photocopy:** Yes

1383   Nagpur, India
        Indian Council of Agricultural Research, National
                Research Centre for Citrus (ICAR, NRC
                (Citrus))
        Library
        Seminary Hills

Nagpur 440006, Maharashtra
Phone: +91(712) 533418 **Fax:** +91(712) 527813 **Email:** nrccitrus@x400.nicgw.nic.in **WWW:** www.nic.in/icar

Former Name: Citrus Research Station **Founded:** 1986 **Type:** Research **Holdings:** 340 books 36 journals **Language of Collection/Services:** English **Subjects:** Biotechnology, Citrus, Entomology, Horticulture, Nematology, Plant Pathology, Soil Science **Photocopy:** Yes

1384   New Delhi, India
Indian Agricultural Research Institute, Pusa
    (IARI)
Library
Pusa
New Delhi 110012
Phone: +91(11) 578-7438 **Fax:** +91(11) 576-6420, 574-0722 **Email:** iarilib@iari.ernet.in

Founded: 1905 **Type:** Research **Head:** Chhotey Lal *Phone:* +91(11) 578-7438 *Email:* clal@iari.ernet.in **Staff:** 53 Prof. 37 Other **Holdings:** 600,000 books 4,500 journals **Language of Collection/Services:** English, Hindi/English, Hindi **Subjects:** Agriculture (Tropics), Crops, Agribusiness, Agricultural Development, Agricultural Economics, Agricultural Engineering, Animal Husbandry, Biotechnology, Education/Extension, Entomology, Fisheries, Food Sciences, Farming, Forestry, Horticulture, Plant Pathology, Soil Science, Veterinary Medicine, Water Resources **Specializations:** Agriculture (India) **Networks:** DELNET; NUCSSI **Databases Developed:** Bibliography of Indian Agriculture - 160,000 references; Indian theses on agriculture (15,000). Research bulletin series and publications (75,000). **Databases Used:** Comprehensive **Loan:** In country **Service:** Internationally **Photocopy:** Yes

1385   New Delhi, India
Indian Council of Agricultural Research (ICAR)
Agricultural Research Information Centre
Krishi Anusandhan Bhawan
Pusa Road
New Delhi 110012
WWW: www.nic.in/icar

Type: Government **Head:** Dr. R.D. Sharma *Phone:* +91(11) 573-1350 **Networks:** AGRIS

1386   New Delhi, India
Indian Council of Agricultural Research (ICAR)
Library
Krishi Bhavan, Dr. Rajendra Prasad Road
New Delhi 110001
Fax: +91(11) 387293 **WWW:** www.nic.in/icar

Founded: 1929 **Type:** Government **Head:** S. Moitra *Phone:* +91(11) 398570, 388991 ext 525 **Staff:** 5 Prof. 9 Other **Holdings:** 100,000 books 323 journals **Language of Collection/Services:** English **Subjects:** Comprehensive **Databases Developed:** Tour, visit and deputation reports of the scientists in ICAR system **Databases Used:** Agris; CABCD **Loan:** Internationally **Service:** In country **Photocopy:** Yes

1387   New Delhi, India
Indian Council of Agricultural Research, Indian
    Agricultural Statistics Research Institute
    (ICAR, IASRI)
Library System
Library Avenue
New Delhi 110012
Fax: +91(11) 574-1479 **Email:** iasri@iasri.delhi.nic.in **WWW:** www.nic.in/icar

Founded: 1959 **Type:** Academic Government **Head:** S.S. Srivastava **Staff:** 4 Prof. 6 Other **Holdings:** 25,000 books 300 journals **Subjects:** Agricultural Economics, Agricultural Statistics, Computer Science **Loan:** Do not loan **Photocopy:** Yes

1388   New Delhi, India
Indian Council of Agricultural Research, National
    Bureau of Plant Genetic Resources (ICAR,
    NBPGR)
Library
FCI Building, CTO Complex, Pusa
New Delhi 110012
Fax: +91(11) 573-1495 **Email:** root@nbpgr.delhi.nic.in **WWW:** www.nic.in/icar

Subjects: Gene Banks, Genetic Resources, Plant Collections

1389   New Delhi, India
Indian National Scientific Documentation Centre
    (INSDOC)
National Science Library
14, Satsang Marg
New Delhi 110067
Phone: +91(11) 665837, 686-3617, 660143, 686-3759 **Fax:** +91(11) 686-2228 **Email:** teevee@sirnetd.ernet.in **WWW:** sunsite.sut.ac.jp/asia/india/jitnet/india/csir/insdoc.html

Founded: 1964 **Type:** Government **Head:** Mr. D.N. Gupta *Phone:* +91(11) 686-3489 **Staff:** 23 Prof. 12 Other **Holdings:** 1,500 books 400 journals **Language of Collection/Services:** English **Subjects:** Animal Husbandry, Crops, Entomology, Fisheries, Horticulture, Soil Science **Loan:** In country **Photocopy:** Yes

1390   Palampur, India
Himachal Pradesh Krishi Vishwa Vidyalaya
    (HPKV)
University Library
Palampur 176062, Himachal Pradesh
Phone: +91(1894) 32813 **Fax:** +91(1894) 30511 **Email:** root@hpkv.chd.nic.in

Founded: 1966 **Type:** Academic **Head:** D.R. Sharma *Phone:* +91(1894) 30361 **Staff:** 6 Prof. 33 Other **Holdings:** 60,614 books 700 journals **Language of Collection/Services:** English/English **Subjects:** Animal Production, Crops, Home Economics, Plant Breeding **Specializations:** Agricultural Economics, Agronomy, Entomology, Home Economics, Plant Breeding, Plant Pathology, Veterinary Medicine, Soil Science **Databases Used:** Agris; CABCD **Loan:** In country **Service:** In country **Photocopy:** Yes

1391   Pantnagar, India
G.B. Pant University of Agriculture and
Technology (GBPU & AT)
University Library
Nainital
Pantnagar 263145, Uttar Pradesh
Fax: +91(5948)23473, 23608 **Email:** root@gbpuat.ernet.in

Founded: 1960 **Type:** Academic **Head:** Rama Tirth *Phone:*
+91(5946) 33333 **Staff:** 20 Prof. 41 Other **Holdings:** 85,000
books 800 journals **Subjects:** Agriculture (Tropics), Agribusiness, Agricultural Development, Agricultural Economics, Agricultural Engineering, Animal Husbandry, Crops,
Food Sciences, Biotechnology, Education/Extension, Entomology, Farming, Fisheries, Forestry, Horticulture, Plant
Pathology, Soil Science, Water Resources, Veterinary Medicine **Photocopy:** Yes

1392   Patancheru, India
International Crops Research Institute for the Semi
Arid Tropics (ICRISAT)
Library and Documentation Services
Patancheru 502324, Andhra Pradesh
Phone: +91(40) 596161 **Fax:** +91(40) 241239 **WWW:**
www.cgiar.org/icrisat

Founded: 1973 **Type:** International **Head:** Mr. S. Srinivas
Phone: +91(40) 596161 ext 2663 *Email:* s.srinivas@cgiar.
org **Staff:** 4 Prof. 9 Other **Holdings:** 60,606 books 400 journals **Language of Collection/Services:** English / English
Subjects: Agricultural Economics, Biotechnology, Agricultural Engineering, Entomology, Plant Pathology, Plant Protection, Crops, Soil Science **Specializations:** Chickpeas,
Millets, Peanuts, Pigeon Peas, Sorghum **Databases Developed:** SATCRIS-information on sorghum, millets, chickpeas, pegeonpeas, groundnuts; soils, farming systems,
agroclimatology of SAT regions; nutrition and food quality
of the five crops **Databases Used:** Agricola; Agris; Dissertation Abstracts **Loan:** Internationally **Service:** Internationally
Photocopy: Yes

1393   Pune, India
Agharkar Research Institute (ARI)
Library
G.G. Agarkar Road
Pune 411004, Maharashtra
Phone: +91(20) 354357, 353680 **Fax:** +91(20) 351542
Email: arilib@pn2.vsn1.net.in

Former Name: Maharashtra Association for the Cultivation
of Science **Founded:** 1946 **Type:** Research **Head:** S.N.
Kulkarni **Staff:** 5 Prof. 2 Other **Holdings:** 18,300 books 125
journals **Language of Collection/Services:** English/English
Subjects: Crops, Genetics, Horticulture, Microbiology, Mycology, Plant Breeding, Plant Pathology, Soybeans, Wheat
Specializations: Botany **Loan:** In country **Photocopy:** Yes

1394   Pune, India
Gokhale Institute of Politics and Economics
Servants of India Society's Library
Pune 411004, Maharashtra

Founded: 1905 **Type:** Academic **Head:** Mrs. Asha Gadre
Phone: +91(212) 350287 *Email:* gokhale@pn2.vsnl.net.in

Staff: 6 Prof. 5 Other **Holdings:** 17,500 books 23 journals
Language of Collection/Services: English, Marathi **Sub-
jects:** Agricultural Economics, Biotechnology, Fisheries,
Forestry **Loan:** In country **Photocopy:** Yes

1395   Puttur, India
Indian Council of Agricultural Research, National
Research Centre for Cashew (ICAR, NRC
(Cashew))
Library
Kamminje, Dakshina Kannada
Puttur 574202, Karnataka
Fax: +91(8251) 24350 **Email:** root@nrccashew.kar.nic.in
WWW: www.nic.in/icar

Founded: 1987 **Type:** Government **Head:** Dr. Evv Bhas-
kara Rao *Email:* root@nrccashew.kar.nic.in *Phone:* +91
(8251) 21530, 20902 **Staff:** 1 Prof. **Holdings:** 800 books 45
journals **Language of Collection/Services:** English / English **Subjects:** Agriculture (Tropics), Agricultural Development, Agricultural Economics, Crops, Education/ Extension,
Farming, Food Sciences, Forestry, Plant Pathology, Soil Science, Water Resources **Specializations:** Biotechnology, Cashews, Entomology, Horticulture, Plantation Crops **Loan:** In
country **Photocopy:** Yes

1396   Rajahmundry, India
Indian Council of Agricultural Research, Central
Tobacco Research Institute (ICAR, CTRI)
Library
Rajahmundry 533105, Andhra Pradesh
Phone: +91(883) 471871/74 ext 10 **Fax:** +91(833) 464341
Email: ctriarin@hd2.dot.net.in **WWW:** www.nic.in/icar

Founded: 1947 **Type:** Government **Head:** Y.V. Suryana-
rayana *Email:* ctri@x400.nicgw.nic.in *Phone:* +91(883) 47-
1871/74 **Staff:** 3 Prof. 3 Other **Holdings:** 11,870 books 173
journals **Language of Collection/Services:** English **Subjects:** Agriculture (Tropics), Agricultural Economics, Agricultural Engineering, Botany, Crops, Education/Extension,
Entomology, Farming, Plant Breeding, Plant Pathology, Soil
Science, Statistics, Water Resources **Specializations:** Tobacco **Loan:** In country **Service:** In country **Photocopy:** Yes

1397   Ranchi, India
Birsa Agricultural University (BAU)
Central Library
PO Kanke
Ranchi 834006, Bihar
Email: root@bau.bih.nic.in

Founded: 1987 **Type:** Academic **Head:** Mr. Ramjee Prasad
Phone: +91(651) 455803, 455076 **Staff:** 1 Prof. 5 Other
Holdings: 5,456 books 152 journals **Language of Collec-
tion/Services:** English **Subjects:** Crops, Agricultural Devel-
opment, Forestry, Veterinary Medicine **Loan:** In country
Service: In country **Photocopy:** Yes

1398   Ranchi, India
Indian Council of Agricultural Research, Indian
Lac Research Institute (ICAR, ILRI)
Library
PO Namkum

Ranchi 834010, Bihar
Phone: +91(651) 520117 **Fax:** +91(651) 520202 **Email:** ilri@bih.nic.in **WWW:** www.nic.in/icar

Founded: 1925 **Type:** Government **Head:** R.P. Tewari *Phone:* +91(651) 520117 *Email:* ilri@bih.nic.in **Holdings:** 40,312 books 155 journals **Staff:** 2 Prof. 3 Other **Language of Collection/Services:** English / English **Subjects:** Agriculture (Tropics), Agricultural Development, Entomology, Crops, Extension, Food Sciences, Horticulture, Forestry, Plant Pathology, Soil Science **Specializations:** Chemistry, Dyes, Gums, Polymers, Resins **Networks:** ICARNET **Databases Used:** Agricola; Agris; Biosis; CABCD **Loan:** In country **Service:** Inhouse **Photocopy:** Yes

1399   Ranchi, India
        Indian Council of Forestry Research and
            Education, Institute of Forest Productivity
            (ICFRE, IFP)
        Library
        Ranchi 834001, Bihar
Phone: +91(651) 304628 **Email:** icfre@envfor.delhi.nic.in **WWW:** www.nic.in/envfor/icfre/ifp/ifp.html

Former Name: Directorate of Lac Development (DLD) **Founded:** 1987 **Type:** Government **Language of Collection/Services:** English **Subjects:** Agroforestry, Forestry **Specializations:** Eucalyptus, Lac

♦**1400   Samastipur, India**
        Rajendra Agricultural University
        University Library
        Pusa
        Samastipur 848125, Bihar
Phone: +91(6274) 74255, 74266 **Email:** rau@bih.nic.in

Founded: 1978 **Type:** Academic **Head:** Dr. S.D. Sharma **Staff:** 4 Prof. 12 Other **Holdings:** 45,000 books 165 journals **Language of Collection/ Services:** English / English, Hindi **Subjects:** Crops, Agriculture (Tropics), Agribusiness, Agricultural Development, Agricultural Economics, Agricultural Engineering, Animal Husbandry, Biochemistry, Biotechnology, Child Development, Clothing, Dairy Technology, Education/Extension, Entomology, Farming, Fisheries, Food Sciences, Forestry, Genetics, Home Economics, Microbiology, Plant Breeding, Plant Pathology, Plants, Soil Science, Textiles, Veterinary Medicine, Water Resources **Loan:** In country **Service:** In country **Photocopy:** Yes

1401   Shimla, India
        Indian Council of Agricultural Research, Central
            Potato Research Institute (ICAR, CPRI)
        Library and Documentation Service
        Shimla 171001, Himachal Pradesh
Phone: +91(177) 244830 **Fax:** +91(177) 244460 **Email:** library@cpri.hp.nic.in **WWW:** www.nic.in/icar

Founded: 1956 **Type:** Government **Head:** Mr. Shree Ram Yadava *Phone:* +91(177) 244830 **Staff:** 4 Prof. 4 Other **Holdings:** 26,910 books 293 journals **Language of Collection/Services:** English / English, Hindi **Subjects:** Farming, Agricultural Economics, Agricultural Statistics, Agronomy, Biochemistry, Crops, Education/Extension, Plant Breeding, Plant Pathology, Plant Physiology, Plants, Seed Production,

Soil Science **Specializations:** Potatoes **Databases Developed:** BIPOL - Bibliography of Indian Potato Literature, 7,000+ references available inhouse; ITP - Indian Theses on Potato, 500+ references available inhouse **Loan:** In country **Service:** Internationally **Photocopy:** Yes

1402   Shimla, India
        Indian Council of Forestry Research and
            Education, Temperate Forest Research
            Institute (ICFRE, TFRIS)
        Library
        Shimla 171001, Himachal Pradesh
Phone: +91(177) 3107 **Fax:** +91(177) 6086 **Email:** icfre@envfor.delhi.nic.in **WWW:** www.nic.in/envfor/icfre/tfris/tfris.html

Founded: 1977 **Type:** Government **Language of Collection/Services:** English **Subjects:** Afforestation, Ecology, Agroforestry, Forest Management, Protection of Forests **Specializations:** Coniferous Forests, Plant Communities

♦**1403   Solan, India**
        Dr. Yashwant Singh Parmar University of
            Horticulture and Forestry (UHF)
        Satyanand Stokes Library
        PO Nauni
        Solan 173230, Himachal Pradesh
Phone: +91(1792) 52242 **Email:** vc@yspuhf.ren.nic.in

Former Name: Himachal Pradesh Krishi Vishwa Vidyalaya **Founded:** 1962 **Type:** Academic **Head:** Dr. A.S. Chandel **Staff:** 18 Prof. 15 Other **Holdings:** 50,000 books 290 journals **Language of Collection/Services:** English/English, Hindi **Subjects:** Agricultural Economics, Agroforestry, Beekeeping, Biotechnology, Plant Pathology, Entomology, Education/Extension, Floriculture, Mycology, Postharvest Technology, Resource Management, Silviculture, Soil Science, Sociology, Vegetables, Water Management **Specializations:** Forestry, Horticulture **Databases Used:** Agricola; CABCD **Loan:** In country **Service:** Internationally **Photocopy:** Yes

1404   Solan, India
        Indian Council of Agricultural Research, National
            Research Centre for Mushroom (ICAR,
            NRCM)
        Library
        Chambaghat
        Solan 173213, Himachal Pradesh
Phone: +91(1792) 20451 **Fax:** +91(1792) 20451 **Email:** root@ncmrt.chd.nic.in **WWW:** www.nic.in/icar

Former Name: National Centre for Mushroom Research and Training (NCMRT) **Founded:** 1983 **Type:** Government **Head:** Sudhir Gupta **Staff:** 1 Prof. 1 Other **Holdings:** 500 books 70 journals **Language of Collection/Services:** English **Subjects:** Plant Pathology, Biotechnology, Food Sciences, Horticulture **Specializations:** Mushrooms **Loan:** Inhouse **Service:** Internationally **Photocopy:** No

♦**1405   Srinagar, India**
        Sher-e-Kashmir University of Agricultural
            Sciences and Technology (SKUAST)

SKUAST Library System
Shalimar Campus
PO Box 262
Srinagar 191001, Jammu and Kashmir
Email: root@skuast.jk.nic.in

Founded: 1985 **Type:** Academic **Head:** G.M. Wani *Phone:* +91(194) 61258, 61259, 61346 ext 25 **Staff:** 15 Prof. 25 Other **Holdings:** 40,000 books 600 journals **Language of Collection/Services:** English/English **Subjects:** Agriculture (Tropics), Agribusiness, Agricultural Development, Agricultural Economics, Agricultural Engineering, Animal Husbandry, Biotechnology, Education/Extension, Entomology, Crops, Farming, Food Sciences, Forestry, Horticulture, Plant Pathology, Soil Science, Veterinary Medicine, Water Resources **Loan:** Inhouse **Service:** Inhouse **Photocopy:** Yes

1406   Trichur, India
Kerala Forest Research Institute (KFRI)
Library
Peechi
Trichur 680653, Kerala
Fax: +91(487) 782249 **Email:** libkfri@md2.vsnl.net.in

Founded: 1975 **Type:** Research **Head:** Mr. K. Sankara Pillai *Phone:* +91(487) 782037, 782014 *Email:* libkfri@md2.vsnl.net.in **Staff:** 4 Prof. 6 Other **Holdings:** 15,000 books 150 journals **Language of Collection/Services:** English **Subjects:** Botany, Entomology, Forestry, Plant Pathology, Soil Science **Specializations:** Bamboos, Statistics, Ecology, Forest Economics, Genetics, Plant Physiology, Wildlife, Wood Technology **Databases Used:** CABCD **Databases Developed:** ENTOM - about 1,000 references to literature on Indian forest entomlogy; inquire to use; BAMBOO - about 1,500 references to literature on tropical bamboos **Loan:** In country **Service:** Internationally **Photocopy:** Yes

1407   Trivandrum, India
Indian Council of Agricultural Research, Central
     Tuber Crops Research Institute (ICAR,
     CTCRI)
Library
Shree Kariyam
Trivandrum 695017, Kerala
Phone: +91(471) 448431 **Fax:** +91(471) 550063 **Email:** ctcri@x400.nicgw.nic.in **WWW:** www.nic.in/icar

Founded: 1964 **Type:** Government **Head:** Mrs. P.K. Rajamma **Staff:** 1 Prof. 1 Other **Holdings:** 10,490 books 151 journals **Language of Collection/Services:** English **Subjects:** Crops **Specializations:** Root Crops, Tubers **Loan:** In country **Service:** In country **Photocopy:** Yes

1408   Trivandrum, India
Kerala Agricultural University
College of Agriculture Library Information
     System (CALIS)
Vellayani PO
Trivandrum 695522, Kerala
Phone: +91(471) 480439 **Email:** kauvly@giasmd01.vsnl.net.in

Founded: 1955 **Type:** Academic **Head:** *Phone:* +91(471) 73024 *Email:* kauvly@giasmd01.vsnl.net.in **Staff:** 5 Prof. 4

Other **Holdings:** 25,130 books 97 journals **Language of Collection/Services:** English **Subjects:** Crops, Entomology, Extension, Plant Breeding, Plant Pathology, Soil Chemistry, Soil Science **Databases Developed:** AGLIT - Theses **Loan:** Do not loan **Photocopy:** Yes

1409   Udaipur, India
Rajasthan Agricultural University (RAU)
Library
Udaipur 313001, Rajasthan
Phone: +91(151) 28746 **Fax:** +91(151) 71092 **Email:** root@raub.raj.nic.in

Former Name: Rajasthan College of Agriculture (RCA) **Founded:** 1956 **Type:** Academic **Staff:** 5 Prof. 8 Other **Language of Collection/Services:** English **Holdings:** 50,000 books 150 journals **Subjects:** Comprehensive **Specializations:** Culture (Civilization) **Loan:** In country **Service:** In country **Photocopy:** Yes

1410   West Kameng, India
Indian Council of Agricultural Research, National
     Research Centre on Yak (ICAR, NRC (Yak))
Library
Dirang
West Kameng 790101, Arunachal Pradesh
Phone: +91(259) 259 **WWW:** www.nic.in/icar

Type: Government Research **Staff:** 1 Prof. 3 Other **Holdings:** 425 books 31 journals **Language of Collection/Services:** English/English **Subjects:** Agroforestry, Farming, Animal Husbandry, Environment, Veterinary Medicine, Wildlife **Specializations:** Yaks **Loan:** Internationally **Service:** Internationally **Photocopy:** Yes

Indonesia

1411   Banda Aceh, Indonesia
Syiah Kuala University
Central Library
Darussalam
Banda Aceh 23111
Phone: +62(651) 31014 **WWW:** www.unsyiah.ac.id

Non-English Name: Universitas Syiah Kuala (UNSYIAH), Perpustakaan Pusat Unsyiah (PPU) **Founded:** 1974 **Type:** Academic **Head:** Damrin Lubis *Phone:* +62(651) 31014 **Staff:** 14 Prof. 11 Other **Holdings:** 37,496 books 21 journals **Language of Collection/Services:** English/Indonesian **Subjects:** Agriculture (Tropics), Agribusiness, Agricultural Development, Agricultural Economics, Farming, Agricultural Engineering, Animal Husbandry, Biotechnology, Crops, Education/Extension, Entomology, Fisheries, Food Sciences, Forestry, Horticulture, Plant Pathology, Soil Science, Veterinary Medicine, Water Resources **Loan:** In country **Service:** Inhouse **Photocopy:** Yes

1412   Bandar Lampung, Indonesia
Lampung University
Library
Jl. Sumantri Brojonegoro No. 1
Bandar Lampung 35145

Phone: +62(721) 53475 ext 124 **WWW:** www.unila.ac.id

Non-English Name: Universitas Lampung, Perpustakaan **Founded:** 1983 **Type:** Government **Subjects:** Agribusiness, Agricultural Development, Agricultural Economics **Loan:** Inhouse **Service:** Inhouse **Photocopy:** Yes

1413   Bandung, Indonesia
         Padjadjaran University
         Agricultural Information Resource Center
         Jalan Dipati Ukur 35
         Bandung, West Java
WWW: www.unpad.ac.id

Non-English Name: Universitas Padjadjaran (UNPAD) **Founded:** 1974 **Type:** Academic **Head:** Soedarminto Martodiredjo *Phone:* +62(21) 03271 ext 118 **Staff:** 5 Prof. 27 Other **Holdings:** 35,000 books 75 journals **Loan:** In country **Photocopy:** Yes

1414   Bandung, Indonesia
         Research Institute for Tea and Cinchona (RITC)
         Library
         PO Box 1013
         Bandung, West Java 40010
Location: Gambung **Phone:** +62(22) 592-8185 **Fax:** +62 (22) 592-8186 **Email:** gambung@indo.net.id

Non-English Name: Pusat Penelitian Teh dan Kina (PPTK), Perpustakaan **Founded:** 1973 **Type:** Government **Head:** Henry Permana *Phone:* +62(22) 592-8185 **Staff:** 1 Prof. 4 Other **Holdings:** 5,140 books 6 journals **Language of Collection/Services:** Indonesian, English, Dutch / Indonesian **Specializations:** Tea, Cinchona **Loan:** Inhouse **Service:** Inhouse **Photocopy:** Yes

1415   Banjarbaru, Indonesia
         Lambung Mangkurat University
         Faculty of Fisheries Library
         Gen A. Yani Street
         PO Box 6
         Banjarbaru, South Kalimantan 70714

Non-English Name: Universitas Lammbung Mangkurat (UNLAM), Perpustakaan Fakultas Perikanan **Type:** Academic **Founded:** 1967 **Head:** Mrs. Deborah Rose *Phone:* +62(511) 5119, 2124 **Staff:** 3 Prof. **Holdings:** 6,492 books 17 journals **Language of Collection/Services:** English, Indonesian/Indonesian **Subjects:** Fisheries, Food Sciences **Loan:** In country **Service:** In country **Photocopy:** Yes

1416   Banjarbaru, Indonesia
         Research Institute for Food Crops on Swampy
            Areas (RIFSA)
         Library
         PO Box 31
         Banjarbaru, South Kalimantan 70712
Location: Jalan Kebun Karet, Loktabat **Phone:** +62(511) 92534 **Fax:** +62(511) 93034

Non-English Name: Balai Penelitian Tanaman Pangan Lahan Rawa (Balittra), Perpustakaan **Former Name:** Banjarbaru Research Institute for Food Crops (BARIF), Balai Penelitian Tanaman Pangan Banjarbaru (Balittan), Central Research Institute for Agriculture, Banjarmasin Research In-

stitute, Lembaga Pusat Penelitian Pertanian Perwakilan Kalimantan **Founded:** 1970 **Type:** Government **Head:** H. Ideham *Phone:* +62(511) 92534 **Staff:** 3 Prof. 2 Other **Holdings:** 4,562 books 126 journals **Language of Collection/Services:** Indonesian, English/Indonesian **Subjects:** Agricultural Development, Agricultural Economics, Entomology, Agricultural Engineering, Farming, Plant Pathology, Crops, Soil Science, Water Management **Specializations:** Food Crops, Swamps **Loan:** Inhouse **Service:** In country **Photocopy:** No

1417   Bengkulu, Indonesia
         University of Bengkulu
         Library
         Jln. Raya Kandang Limun
         Bengkulu, Sumatera 38371
Phone: +62(736) 21170, 21884 **Fax:** +62(736) 22105 **WWW:** webserver.rad.net.id/Hi-Ed-Net/unib.htm

Non-English Name: Universitas Bengkulu, Perpustakaan **Type:** Academic **Head:** Dra. Rosdianah Assaudi **Staff:** 14 Prof. 16 Other **Holdings:** 2,760 books 10 journals **Language of Collection/Services:** English, Indonesian / Indonesian **Subjects:** Agribusiness, Biotechnology, Agricultural Development, Agricultural Economics, Crops, Entomology, Farming, Fisheries, Food Sciences, Forestry, Horticulture, Plant Pathology, Plants, Soil Science, Water Resources **Loan:** In country **Service:** In country **Photocopy:** No

1418   Bogor, Indonesia
         Agency for Agricultural Research and
            Development (AARD)
         Center for Agricultural Library and Research
            Communication (CALREC)
         Jalan Ir. H. Juanda 20
         Bogor 16122
Phone: +62(251) 321746 **Fax:** +62(251) 326561 **Email:** informasi@calrec-aard.wasantara.net.id **WWW:** www. deptan.go.id

Non-English Name: Badan Penelitian dan Pengembangan Pertanian (Litbang), Pusat Perpustakaan Pertanian dan Komunikasi Penelitian (PUSTAKA) **Former Name:** Bibliotheca Bogoriensis, National Library for Agricultural Sciences (NLAS) **Founded:** 1842 **Type:** Government **Head:** Dr. Prabowo Tjitropranoto *Phone:* +62(251) 324394 **Staff:** 65 Prof. 73 Other **Holdings:** 100,000 books 350 journals **Language of Collection/Services:** English, Dutch/Indonesian, English **Subjects:** Agricultural Economics, Farming, Agricultural Engineering, Animal Husbandry, Biotechnology, Crops, Entomology, Fisheries, Food Sciences, Forestry, Horticulture, Plant Pathology, Plant Protection, Soil Science, Veterinary Medicine **Networks:** AGRIS **Databases Developed:** Literature of Indonesian research - ResultData Base **Databases Used:** Agricola; Agris; CABCD **Loan:** In country **Service:** Internationally **Photocopy:** Yes

1419   Bogor, Indonesia
         Agency for Agricultural Research and
            Development, Center for
            Agro-Socioeconomic Research (AARD,
            CASER)
         Library

Jalan A. Yani 70
PO Box 200
Bogor 16161

Fax: +62(251) 314496 **WWW:** www.deptan.go.id **Email:** caser@calrec-aard.wasantara.net.id

Non-English Name: Badan Penelitian dan Pengembangan Pertanian, Pusat Penelitian Sosial Ekonomi Pertanian (Badan Litbang Pertanian, P/SE), Perpustakaan **Former Name:** Center for Agro Economic Research (CAER), Pusat Penelitian Agro Ekonomi (PPAE) **Founded:** 1974 **Type:** Government **Head:** Ir. Imas Nur 'Aini *Phone:* +62(251) 325177, 333964 *Email:* caser@calrec-aard.wasantara.net.id **Staff:** 3 Prof. 3 Other **Holdings:** 5,500 books 22 journals **Language of Collection/Services:** English, Indonesian/ English, Indonesian **Subjects:** Agribusiness, Agricultural Economics, Agricultural Policy, Farming, Fisheries, Rural Unemployment, International Trade, Sociology, Trade, Water Resources **Service:** Inhouse **Loan:** Inhouse **Photocopy:** Yes

◆ **1420   Bogor, Indonesia**
Agency for Agricultural Research and
Development, Research Institute for Animal
Production (AARD, RIAP)
Library
PO Box 221
Bogor, West Java 16002

Location: Jalan Banjarwaru Seuseupan, Ciawi **Phone:** +62 (251) 27152

Non-English Name: Badan Penelitian dan Pengembangan Pertanian, Balai Penelitian Ternak - Ciawi, Perpustakaan **Founded:** 1976 **Type:** Government **Head:** Sjarif Hidayat W. *Phone:* +62(251) 29753 **Staff:** 3 Prof. 5 Other **Holdings:** 8,500 books 12 journals **Language of Collection/Services:** English/Indonesian, English **Subjects:** Animal Feeding, Analytical Chemistry, Animal Husbandry, Biochemistry, Biology, Feeds **Specializations:** Animal Breeding, Dairy Cattle, Animal Nutrition, Animal Production, Poultry **Loan:** Inhouse **Service:** Internationally **Photocopy:** Yes

1421   Bogor, Indonesia
Bogor Agricultural University
Information Resource Center
Jalan Raya Dermaga
Bogor 16680

Phone: +62(21) 622642/3 **WWW:** www.ipb.ac.id

Non-English Name: Institut Pertanian Bogor (IPB) **Founded:** 1964 **Type:** Academic **Head:** Abdul R. Saleh *Phone:* +62(251) 21073 **Staff:** 10 Prof. 60 Other **Holdings:** 167,002 books 117 journals **Subjects:** Agricultural Engineering, Animal Husbandry, Fisheries, Food Sciences, Forestry, Veterinary Medicine **Databases Developed:** Upland Agriculture, Agroindustry, Forestry **Databases Used:** CABCD **Loan:** In country **Photocopy:** Yes

1422   Bogor, Indonesia
Forest Research and Development Centre (FRDC)
Library
PO Box 165
Bogor 16001

Location: Jalan Gunung Batu No. 5 **Phone:** +62(251) 325111 **Fax:** +62(251) 325111 **WWW:** www2.bonet.co. id/dephut

Non-English Name: Pusat Penelitian dan Pengembangan Hutan dan Konservasi Alam (Puslitbang Hut) **Former Name:** Forest Research Institute, Balai Penelitian Hutan **Founded:** 1931 **Type:** Government **Head:** Dra. Hayati Yusuf **Staff:** 4 Prof. 6 Other **Holdings:** 35,000 books 525 journals **Language of Collection/Services:** English/Indonesian **Subjects:** Biometry, Forestry **Specializations:** Nature Conservation, Protection of Forests, Silviculture, Social Forestry, Soil Conservation, Trees, Water Conservation **Loan:** In country **Service:** Inhouse **Photocopy:** Yes

◆ **1423   Bogor, Indonesia**
Indonesian Biotechnology Research Institute for
Estate Crops (IBRCEC)
Library
PO Box 179/Bogor
Bogor, West Java 16001

Location: Jalan Taman Kencana No. 1, Bogor 16151 **Phone:** +62(251) 324048 ext 10 **Fax:** +62(251) 320516

Non-English Name: Pusat Penelitian Bioteknologi Perkebunan, Perpustakaan **Former Name:** Bogor Research Institute for Estate Crops, Balai Penelitian Perkebunan Bogor **Founded:** 1968 **Type:** Government **Head:** Amirah Sutartiningsih *Phone:* +62(251) 324048 **Staff:** 3 Prof. 4 Other **Holdings:** 12,000 books 38 journals **Language of Collection/Services:** Indonesian, English / Indonesian **Subjects:** Biotechnology, Agricultural Engineering, Crops **Specializations:** Plantation Crops **Databases Developed:** CCOD - Agriculture and Biology **Loan:** In country **Service:** In country **Photocopy:** Yes

◆ **1424   Bogor, Indonesia**
Indonesian Institute of Sciences, Research and
Development Center for Biology
Library Sub-division
PO Box 208
Bogor 16002

Location: Jalan Ir. H. Juanda 18 **Fax:** +62(251) 325854

Non-English Name: Lembaga Ilmu Pengetahuan Indonesia, Pusat Penelitian dan Pengembagan Biologi (LIPI, Puslitbang Biologi), Sub-Bidang Perpustakaan **Former Name:** National Biological Institute, Lembaga Biolgi Nasional (LBN), Perpustakaan Pusat **Founded:** Before 1900 **Type:** Government **Head:** Mrs. Hamzah Machmudy *Phone:* +62(251) 321040/41 **Staff:** 15 Prof. 7 Other **Holdings:** 37,050 books 2,327 journals **Language of Collection/Services:** English, Indonesian **Subjects:** Agriculture (Tropics), Animal Husbandry, Biotechnology, Crops, Entomology, Fisheries, Forestry, Horticulture, Plant Pathology, Veterinary Medicine **Specializations:** Flora, Fauna, Microorganisms **Loan:** Inhouse **Photocopy:** Yes

◆ **1425   Bogor, Indonesia**
Research Institute for Veterinary Science (RIVS)
Library
PO Box 52
Bogor 16114

Location: R.E. Martadinata No. 30

Non-English Name: Balai Penelitian Veteriner **Former Name:** Research Institute for Animal Disease **Type:** Government **Founded:** 1908 **Head:** Mrs. Zakiah Muhajan *Phone:* +62(251) 321048 **Staff:** 2 Prof. 4 Other **Holdings:** 10,583 books 34 journals **Language of Collection/Services:** English **Subjects:** Animal Husbandry **Specializations:** Veterinary Medicine **Databases Used:** CABCD **Loan:** Inhouse **Photocopy:** Yes

1426   **Bogor, Indonesia**
        Southeast Asia Regional Center for Tropical
            Biology (SEAMEO BIOTROP)
        Library
        PO Box 116
        Bogor, West Java 16001

Location: Jln. Raya Tajur, Km 6 **Phone:** +62(251) 323848 **Fax:** +62(251) 326851 **Email:** info@biotrop.org **WWW:** www.biotrop.org

Founded: 1972 **Type:** International **Head:** Mrs. Soetitah S. Soedojo *Phone:* +62(251) 323848 ext 103 **Staff:** 6 Prof. 7 Other **Holdings:** 27,000 books 964 journals **Language of Collection/Services:** English/English **Subjects:** Agriculture (Tropics), Biotechnology, Fisheries, Forestry, Integrated Pest Management, Plant Pathology, Plants, Water Resources **Specializations:** Aquaculture, Forest Ecology, Weed Control **Databases Developed:** WEEDOC - Weeds of South East Asia, herbicides, and related fields; DOC - BIOTROP Library and Documentation Section holdings in forest biology, agricultural pest biology, and hydrobiology; RESABS - Abstracts of current weed/herbicide researches by Asian and other weed scientists **Databases Used:** Agris **Loan:** Inhouse **Service:** Internationally **Photocopy:** Yes

1427   **Bogor, Indonesia**
        United Nations Economic and Social Commission
            for Asia and the Pacific, Regional Co-ordina-
            tion Centre for Research and Development of
            Coarse Grains, Pulses, Roots and Tuber Crops
            in the Humid Tropics of Asia and the Pacific
            (UNESCAP, CGPRT)
        Library
        Jalan Merdeka 145
        Bogor 16111

Phone: +62(251) 343277 **Fax:** +62(251) 336290 **Email:** cgprt@indo.net.id **WWW:** www.cgprt.org.sg/cgprt.htm

Founded: 1985 **Type:** Government **Holdings:** 4,000 books 20 journals **Language of Collection/Services:** English/English **Subjects:** Agribusiness, Agricultural Development, Agricultural Economics, Crops, Farming, Horticulture **Databases Developed:** Time series on nine major food crops disaggregated down to district level of seven Asian countries; prices by quality/crop; researcher database throughout Asia. **Loan:** Inhouse **Service:** Inhouse **Photocopy:** Yes

1428   **Cibinong-Bogor, Indonesia**
        Indonesian Institute of Sciences, Research and
            Development Centre for Limnology
        Library
        Komplek LIPI Cibinong

Jln. Raya Jakarta-Bogor Km. 46
Cibinong-Bogor 16911

Phone: +62(21) 875-7071 **Fax:** +62(21) 875-7076 **Email:** limno@lipi.go.id **WWW:** www.lipi.go.id/limnology

Non-English Name: Lembaga Ilmu Pengetahuan Indonesia, Pusat Penelitian dan Pengembangan Limnologi (LIPI, Puslitbang Limnologi), Perpustakaan **Founded:** 1986 **Type:** Government **Staff:** 2 Prof. 3 Other **Holdings:** 1,049 books 13 journals **Language of Collection/Services:** English, Indonesian **Subjects:** Ecology, Fisheries, Water Resources **Loan:** Inhouse **Service:** In country **Photocopy:** Yes

♦1429   **Denpasar, Indonesia**
        Udayana University
        Library
        Jln. P.B. Sudirman
        Denpasar, Bali 80232

Non-English Name: Universitas Udayana (UNUD), Perpustakaan (Pustak) **Founded:** 1962 **Type:** Academic **Head:** I.G.N. Tirtayasa *Phone:* +62(361) 23791 **Staff:** 27 Prof. 13 Other **Holdings:** 20,000 books 40 journals **Language of Collection/Services:** English **Subjects:** Agricultural Development, Agricultural Engineering, Animal Husbandry, Food Sciences, Food Technology, Plant Pathology, Soil Science, Veterinary Medicine **Loan:** Internationally **Photocopy:** Yes

1430   **Jakarta, Indonesia**
        Center for International Forestry Research
            (CIFOR)
        Library
        PO Box 6596 JKPWB
        Jakarta 10065

Location: Jalan CIFOR, Situ Gede, Sindangbarang, Bogor 16680 **Phone:** +62(251) 622622 **Fax:** +62(251) 622100 **Email:** cifor@cgiar.org **WWW:** www.cgiar.org/cifor **Ariel IP:** 198.93.243.25

Founded: 1994 **Type:** International **Head:** Ms. Sri Wahyuni (Yuni) Soeripto *Email:* y.soeripto@cgiar.org *Phone:* +62 (251) 622622 **Staff:** 2 Prof. **Holdings:** 3,000 books 60 journals **Language of Collection/Services:** English / English, Indonesian **Subjects:** Forestry **Specializations:** Forest Management, Forest Policy, Nature Conservation, Socioeconomics **Databases Used:** Comprehensive **Loan:** Inhouse **Service:** Internationally **Photocopy:** Yes

1431   **Jakarta, Indonesia**
        Indonesian Institute of Sciences
        Centre for Scientific Documentation and
            Information
        PO Box 4298
        Jakarta 12042

Location: Jl. Jend. Gatot Subroto 10, Jakarta 12190 **Fax:** +62 (21) 573-346 **Phone:** +62(21) 573-3465, 525-0719, 525-10637 **Email:** info@pdii.lipi.go.id **WWW:** www. pdii.lipi.go.id

Non-English Name: Lembaga Ilmu Pengetahuan Indonesia (LIPI), Pusat Dokumentasi dan Informasi Ilmiah (PDII) **Former Name:** National Scientific Documentation Center **Founded:** 1965 **Type:** Government **Head:** Luwarsih Pringgoadisurjo *Phone:* +62(21) 573-3467 **Staff:** 84 Prof. 137

Other **Holdings:** 800 books 74 journals **Language of Collection/Services:** English, Indonesian **Subjects:** Agriculture (Tropics), Agribusiness, Agricultural Development, Agricultural Economics, Agricultural Engineering, Animal Husbandry, Biotechnology, Education/Extension, Entomology, Farming, Fisheries, Food Sciences, Forestry, Horticulture, Soil Science, Veterinary Medicine, Water Resources **Specializations:** Crops, Postharvest Technology **Databases Developed:** KIM - Union list of serials **Loan:** Internationally **Service:** Internationally **Photocopy:** Yes

1432   **Jakarta Selatan, Indonesia**
        Centre for the Application of Isotopes and
            Radiation (CAIR)
        Library
        Jalan Cinere Pasar Jumat
        PO Box 7002 JKSKL
        Jakarta Selatan 12070
Fax: +62(21) 769-1607 **Email:** pairlib@hotmail.com

Non-English Name: Pusat Aplikasi Isotop dan Radiasi (PAIR), Perpustakaan **Former Name:** Pasar Jumat Atomic Energy Research Centre **Founded:** 1967 **Type:** Government **Head:** Suhari *Email:* pairlib@hotmail.com *Phone:* +62(21) 769-0709 **Staff:** 4 Prof. 5 Other **Holdings:** 2,692 books 39 journals **Language of Collection/Services:** English **Subjects:** Animal Husbandry, Biotechnology, Food Sciences, Soil, Veterinary Medicine **Specializations:** Isotopes, Radiation **Loan:** In country **Service:** Internationally **Photocopy:** Yes

1433   **Jakarta Utara, Indonesia**
        Research Institute for Marine Fisheries (RIMF)
        Library
        Jalan Muara Baru Ujung
        Komplek Pelabuhan Perikanan Samudra
        Jakarta Utara 14440
Phone: +62(21) 660-2044 **Fax:** +62(21) 661-2137

Non-English Name: Balai Penelitian Perikanan Laut (Balitkanlut), Perpustakaan **Type:** Government **Head:** Mrs. Nur Rahayu **Staff:** 6 Prof. **Holdings:** 1,200 books 200 journals **Language of Collection/Services:** English **Subjects:** Agricultural Economics, Agricultural Engineering, Biotechnology, Food Sciences **Specializations:** Fisheries **Loan:** In country **Service:** Internationally **Photocopy:** Yes

♦1434   **Jepara, Indonesia**
        Brackishwater Aquaculture Development Centre
            (BADC)
        Library
        Jalan Pemandian Kartini
        PO Box I
        Jepara, Central Java 59400
Fax: +62(291) 91724

Non-English Name: Balai Budidaya Air Payau, Perpustakaan **Former Name:** Shrimp Culture Research Centre (SCRC) **Founded:** 1973 **Type:** Government **Head:** Subijono *Phone:* +62 125 Jepara **Staff:** 1 Prof. 4 Other **Holdings:** 6,469 books **Language of Collection/Services:** English, Indonesian **Subjects:** Aquaculture, Fisheries **Specializations:**

Crustacea, Mollusca, Shellfish, Shrimps **Loan:** Internationally **Service:** Internationally **Photocopy:** Yes

1435   **Lombok, Indonesia**
        Mataram University
        Library
        Jalan Majapahit No. 62
        Mataram Ampenan
        Lombok, West Nusa Tenggara 83125

Non-English Name: Universitas Mataram (UNRAM), Perpustakaan **Former Name:** Universitas Negeri Mataram **Founded:** 1963 **Type:** Academic **Head:** Drs. I. Gusti Bagus Ngurah Harry *Phone:* +62(370) 33007 ext 50 **Staff:** 14 Prof. 31 Other **Holdings:** 1,827 books 15 journals **Language of Collection/Services:** Indonesian / Indonesian, English **Subjects:** Agriculture (Tropics), Agribusiness, Agricultural Development, Agricultural Economics, Forestry, Agricultural Engineering, Animal Husbandry, Biotechnology, Crops, Food Sciences, Soil Science, Veterinary Medicine **Loan:** Inhouse **Service:** Inhouse **Photocopy:** Yes

1436   **Malang, Indonesia**
        Brawijaya University
        Library
        Veteran Street
        Malang 65145
Phone: +62(341) 571032 **Fax:** +62(341) 565620 **Email:** pustbra@mlg.mega.net.id

Non-English Name: Universitas Brawijaya (UNIBRAW), Perpustakaan **Founded:** 1963 **Type:** Academic **Head:** Welmin S. Ariningsih *Phone:* +62(341) 571032, 51611 ext 171 *Email:* pustbra@mlg.mega.net.id **Staff:** 15 Prof. 32 Other **Holdings:** 71,635 books 980 journals **Language of Collection/Services:** Indonesian, English / Indonesian, English **Subjects:** Agriculture (Tropics), Agribusiness, Agricultural Engineering, Animal Husbandry, Biotechnology, Crops, Education/Extension, Entomology, Farming, Fisheries, Food Sciences, Forestry, Horticulture, Plant Pathology, Soil Science, Veterinary Medicine, Water Resources **Specializations:** Biology, Chemistry, Statistics **Photocopy:** Yes **Loan:** Inhouse **Service:** Inhouse

1437   **Manokwari, Indonesia**
        Cenderawasih University, Faculty of Agriculture
        Library
        PO Box 323
        Manokwari, Irian Jaya 98314
Location: Jalan Gunung Salju, Amban **Phone:** +62(986) 211467 **Fax:** +62(986) 212988, 211455 **Email:** uncenm@unhas.ac.id

Non-English Name: Universitas Cenderawasih, Fakultas Pertanian (Uncen, Faperta), Perpustakaan **Founded:** 1964 **Type:** Academic **Head:** Ir Sangle Y. Randa *Phone:* +62 (986) 212864 **Staff:** 1 Prof. 9 Other **Holdings:** 22,285 books 14,550 journals **Language of Collection/Services:** English, Indonesian / Indonesian **Subjects:** Comprehensive **Specializations:** Agriculture (Tropics), Forestry **Databases Used:** Agricola **Databases Developed:** Faculty of Agriculture theses - accessible in library **Loan:** In country **Service:** In country **Photocopy:** No

1438   Maros, Indonesia
Agency for Agricultural Research and
    Development, Research Institute for Maize
    and Other Cereals (AARD, RIMC)
Library
Jalan Dr. Ratulangi
Maros, South Sulawesi 90514
Phone: +62(411) 323425 **Fax:** +62(411) 318148

Non-English Name: Badan Penelitian dan Pengenbangan · Pertanian Indonesia, Balai Penelitian Tanaman Jagung dan Serealia Lain (Balitjas), Perpustakaan **Former Name:** Research Institute for Agriculture, Maros Research Institute for Food Crops (MORIF), Balai Penelitian Tanaman Pangan Maros **Founded:** 1974 **Type:** Government **Head:** Rafiah **Staff:** 5 Prof. 10 Other **Holdings:** 1,000 books 25 journals **Language of Collection/Services:** English / Indonesian **Subjects:** Agricultural Development, Agricultural Economics, Agricultural Engineering, Entomology **Specializations:** Preharvest Technology **Loan:** Do not loan **Photocopy:** No

1439   Medan, Indonesia
Indonesian Oil Palm Research Institute (IOPRI)
Library
Jl. Brig. Jend. Katamso 51
Medan, North Sumatra 20158
Phone: +62(61) 786-2477 **Fax:** +62(61) 786-2488 **Email:** iopri@idola.net.id

Non-English Name: Pusat Penelitian Kelapa Sawit (PPKS), Perpustakaan **Former Name:** Research Institute of Sumatra Planters' Association (RISPA), Balai Penelitian Perkebunan Medan **Founded:** 1917 **Type:** Government **Head:** Sarah Sandra **Staff:** 3 Prof. 3 Other **Holdings:** 25 journals 11,500 books **Language of Collection/Services:** English **Subjects:** Coconuts, Oil Palms **Loan:** Do not loan **Photocopy:** Yes

1440   Medan, Indonesia
Islamic University of North Sumatra
Agricultural Library
Jalan Sisingamangaraja 191, Teladan Barat
Medan, North Sumatra 20217
Phone: +62(61) 720442 **Fax:** +62(61) 716790

Non-English Name: Universitas Islam Sumatera Utara (UISU), Perpustakaan Pertanian **Founded:** 1975 **Type:** Academic **Staff:** 4 Prof. **Language of Collection/Services:** English, Indonesian / Indonesian **Holdings:** 80 journals 7,000 books **Subjects:** Agricultural Engineering, Crops, Entomology, Horticulture, Plant Pathology, Soil Science **Loan:** Inhouse **Photocopy:** No

1441   Padang, Indonesia
Andalas University, Faculty of Agriculture
Library
Air Tawar Padang PO Box 87
Padang, West Sumatra
WWW: www-pdg.mega.net.id/unand

Founded: 1976 **Type:** Academic **Head:** Dra. Saufni Chalid *Phone:* +62(751) 21692 **Staff:** 1 Prof. 5 Other **Holdings:** 63 journals 16,010 books **Subjects:** Crops, Horticulture, Soil Science **Loan:** In country **Photocopy:** Yes

1442   Palu, Indonesia
Tadulako University
Central Library
Kampus Tondo Palu
Palu, Central Sulawesi
WWW: www.arsitektur.com/institut/dalam/tadulako.htm

Non-English Name: Universitas Tadulako (UNTAD), Perpustakaan Pusat **Former Name:** Universitas Tadulako Cabang Universitas Hasanuddin **Founded:** 1984 **Type:** Government **Head:** Mrs. Dientje Borman *Phone:* +62 21519 **Holdings:** 700 books **Language of Collection/Services:** English **Subjects:** Animal Husbandry, Crops, Farming, Forestry, Horticulture, Plant Pathology **Specializations:** Food Sciences

1443   Pasuruan, Indonesia
Indonesian Sugar Research Institute (ISRI)
Library and Publication Division
Jalan Pahlawan 25
Pasuruan, East Java 67126
Phone: +62(343) 421086/7 **Fax:** +62(343) 421178 **Email:** isri@mlg.mega.net.id

Non-English Name: Pusat Penelitian Perkebunan Gula Indonesia (P3GI), Urusan Perpustakaan dan Publikasi **Former Name:** Balai Penelitian Perusahaan Perkebunan Gula **Type:** Government **Founded:** 1887 **Head:** Mrs. Setia Rini **Staff:** 3 Prof. 14 Other **Holdings:** 14,154 books 494 journals **Language of Collection/Services:** English / Indonesian **Subjects:** Agriculture (Tropics), Agribusiness, Biotechnology, Agricultural Development, Agricultural Economics, Agricultural Engineering, Crops, Entomology, Farming, Food Sciences, Horticulture, Plant Pathology, Soil Science **Specializations:** Sugarcane **Loan:** Do not loan **Photocopy:** Yes

1444   Poka-Ambon, Indonesia
Pattimura University
Central Library
PO Box 95
Poka-Ambon

Non-English Name: Universitas Pattimura (Unpatti), Perpustakaan Pusat **Former Name:** Universitas Yayasan Perguruan Tinggi Maluku-Irian Barat **Founded:** 1958 **Type:** Academic **Head:** Ali Zawawi **Staff:** 3 Prof. 23 Other **Holdings:** 5 journals **Language of Collection/Services:** English **Subjects:** Agriculture (Tropics), Agricultural Development, Agricultural Economics, Education/Extension, Farming, Fisheries, Horticulture, Plant Pathology, Soil Science **Specializations:** Management, Economics **Loan:** Inhouse Service: Inhouse **Photocopy:** Yes

1445   Purwokerto, Indonesia
Universitas Jenderal Soedirman
Perpustakaan
Kampus UNSOED Grendeng
Kotak Pos 15
Purwokerto, Central Java 53123
WWW: unsoed.8m.com

Founded: 1965 **Type:** Government **Head:** Mr. Bambang Suprapto *Phone:* +62(281) 2192 **Staff:** 5 Prof. **Holdings:**

2,000 books **Subjects:** Crops, Plant Pathology, Soil Science **Loan:** Inhouse **Photocopy:** Yes

♦ **1446 Solok, Indonesia**
Solok Research Institute for Horticulture (SORIH)
Library
PO Box 5
Solok, West Sumatra 27301

Location: Jl. Raya Sumani Km 10 Solok **Phone:** +62(755) 20137 **Fax:** +62(755) 20137

Non-English Name: Balai Penelitian Hortikultura Solok, Perpustakaan **Founded:** 1985 **Type:** Government **Head:** Sjaiful Chanafi *Phone:* +62(755) 20592 **Staff:** 1 Other 1 Prof. **Holdings:** 1,419 books 222 journals **Language of Collection/Services:** English, Indonesian **Subjects:** Horticulture **Loan:** In country **Service:** In country **Photocopy:** Yes

1447 Sukamandi, Indonesia
Research Institute for Rice (RIR)
Library
Jalan Raya 9
Sukamandi, West Java 41256

Location: PO Box 11, Cikampek **Phone:** +62(260) 521107 **Fax:** +62(260) 520158

Non-English Name: Balai Penelitian Tanaman Padi (Balitpa), Perpustakaan **Former Name:** Sukamandi Research Institute for Food Crops (SURIF), Balai Penelitian Tanaman Pangan Sukamandi (Balittan Sukamandi), Central Research Institute for Food Crops (CRIA), Sukamandi Branch **Founded:** 1975 **Type:** Government **Head:** Mrs. Aan Darlinah *Phone:* +62(260) 520157 **Staff:** 2 Prof. 1 Other **Holdings:** 4,549 books **Language of Collection/Services:** English / Indonesian **Subjects:** Agribusiness, Agricultural Development, Crops, Entomology, Farming Systems, Food Crops **Specializations:** Rice **Loan:** Inhouse **Service:** Inhouse **Photocopy:** No

1448 Surabaya, Indonesia
Veterinary Biology Centre (VBC)
Library
PO Box W.O.3
Surabaya, East Java 60231

Location: Jl. A. Yani 68-70 **Phone:** +62(31) 829-1124/5 **Fax:** +62(31) 829-1183

Non-English Name: Pusat Veterinaria Farma (Pusvetma), Perpustakaan **Founded:** 1959 **Type:** Government **Head:** Mr. Darmono Pudjo Utomo *Phone:* +62(31) 829-1124/5 **Staff:** 1 Prof. 1 Other **Holdings:** 7,364 books **Language of Collection/Services:** English/Indonesian, English **Subjects:** Animal Husbandry, Biotechnology, Veterinary Medicine **Loan:** Inhouse **Service:** Inhouse **Photocopy:** No

1449 Surakarta, Indonesia
Sebelas Maret University
Central Library
Jl. Ir. Sutami No. 36A
Surakarta, Central Java 57126
WWW: www.uns.ac.id

Non-English Name: Universitas Sebelas Maret (UNS) **Founded:** 1976 **Type:** Government **Head:** Drs. H. Tarjana

Staff: 19 Prof. 6 Other **Holdings:** 806 books 15 journals **Subjects:** Agricultural Engineering, Horticulture **Loan:** Internationally **Photocopy:** Yes

1450 Surakarta, Indonesia
Sebelas Maret University, Faculty of Agriculture
Library
Jl. Ir. Sutami 36
Surakarta, Central Java 57126

Phone: +62(271) 7457 **WWW:** www.uns.ac.id

Non-English Name: Universitas Sebelas Maret, Fakultas Pertanian (UNS), Perpustakaan **Type:** Academic **Staff:** 3 Prof. 4 Other **Holdings:** 4,406 books 18 journals **Language of Collection/Services:** Indonesian **Subjects:** Agriculture (Tropics), Agribusiness, Agricultural Development, Agricultural Economics, Agricultural Engineering, Animal Husbandry, Biotechnology, Education/Extension, Entomology, Crops, Farming, Fisheries, Food Sciences, Forestry, Horticulture, Plant Pathology, Soil Science, Veterinary Medicine, Water Resources **Loan:** Inhouse **Service:** Inhouse **Photocopy:** Yes

1451 Yogyakarta, Indonesia
Gadjah Mada University
Library
Bulaksumur
PO Box 16
Yogyakarta 55281

Phone: +62(274) 902642 **Fax:** +62(274) 513163 **Email:** admin@lib.ugm.ac.id **WWW:** ugm.ac.id

Non-English Name: Universitas Gadjah Mada (UGM), Perpustakaan **Former Name:** Universiteit Gadjah Mada **Type:** Academic **Founded:** 1951 **Head:** Dr. Slamet Soebagyo *Phone:* +62(274) 902642 *Email:* subagyo@lib.ugm.ac.id **Staff:** 3 Prof. **Holdings:** 47,198 books 94 journals **Language of Collection/Services:** English **Subjects:** Agribusiness, Agricultural Economics, Agricultural Engineering, Animal Husbandry, Biotechnology, Crops, Entomology, Farming, Fisheries, Food Sciences, Forestry, Horticulture, Plant Pathology, Soil Science, Veterinary Medicine, Water Resources **Specializations:** Agricultural Development, Agriculture (Tropics), **Loan:** In country **Service:** In country **Photocopy:** Yes

1452 Yogyakarta, Indonesia
Gadjah Mada University, Faculty of Agriculture
Library
Jalan Sekip Unit I, PO Box 1
Yogyakarta 55001

Location: Jalan C. Simenjuntak **Phone:** +62(274) 63062 ext 12 **WWW:** www.ugm.ac.id

Non-English Name: Universitas Gadjah Mada, Fakultas Pertanian (UGM), Perpustakaan **Founded:** 1956 **Type:** Academic **Head:** Ny. Titik Hermini *Phone:* +62(274) 63062 **Staff:** 3 Prof. 8 Other **Holdings:** 29,093 books 30 journals **Language of Collection/Services:** Indonesian / Indonesian **Subjects:** Agricultural Economics, Crops, Entomology, Horticulture, Plant Pathology, Soil Science **Loan:** Inhouse **Service:** Internationally **Photocopy:** Yes

♦**1453 Yogyakarta, Indonesia**
Yogyakartan Plantation Training Institute
Library
Jln. Jend. Urip Sumohardjo 100
Yogyakarta 55222

Phone: +62(274) 86201 ext 213 **Fax:** +62(274) 3849

Non-English Name: Lembaga Pendidikan Perkebunan
(LPP), Perpustakaan **Founded:** 1961 **Type:** Government
Head: Drs. Untung Mardiyatmo *Phone:* +62(274) 86201 ext
213 **Staff:** 2 Prof. 4 Other **Holdings:** 40,480 books 238 journals **Language of Collection/Services:** Indonesian, English
/Indonesian **Subjects:** Agribusiness, Agricultural Development, Agricultural Engineering, Education/Extension, Food
Technology **Specializations:** Cocoa, Coffee, Food Technology, Plantation Crops, Sugar, Tea **Loan:** Inhouse **Service:** In
country **Photocopy:** Yes

Iran

1454 Ahwaz, Iran
Shahid Chamran University
Faculty of Agriculture Library
Ahwaz

Former Name: Jundi Shapour University **Founded:** 1974
Type: Academic **Head:** N. Zalpour *Phone:* +98(61) 330010/
20 **Staff:** 4 Prof. 1 Other **Holdings:** 20,100 books 65 journals
Language of Collection/Services: Persian, English/Persian
Subjects: Botany, Crops, Food Sciences, Horticulture, Irrigation, Plant Pathology, Soil Science **Loan:** Inhouse **Service:** Inhouse **Photocopy:** No

1455 Ahwaz, Iran
Shahid Chamran University, Ramin Agricultural
Research and Education School
Ramin Library
Mollasani
Ahwaz

Phone: +98(6238) 2424 **Fax:** +98(6238) 2425

Former Name: Gandy Shapoor University **Founded:** 1964
Type: Academic **Head:** sayed Mojtaba Faregh *Phone:* +98
(6238) 2424 **Staff:** 2 Prof. 4 Other **Holdings:** 21,600 books
60 journals **Language of Collection/Services:** Persian, Eng-
lish/Persian **Subjects:** Animal Husbandry, Extension, Farm
Machinery, Crops, Food Sciences, Horticulture, Irrigation,
Soil Science **Loan:** Inhouse **Service:** In country **Photocopy:**
Yes

1456 Borazjan, Iran
Agricultural Research, Education and Extension
Organization, Bushehr Agricultural Research
Center
Agricultural Scientific Information and
Documentation Library
PO Box 333
Borazjan 75615

Phone: +98(77242) 26742 **Fax:** +98(77242) 27643

Founded: 1992 **Type:** Government **Head:** F. Saeedi Naiini
Phone: +98(77242) 27641 **Holdings:** 1,350 books 1,200
journals **Language of Collection/Services:** Persian, English

/Persian **Subjects:** Agricultural Economics, Agricultural En-
gineering, Agriculture (Tropics), Crops, Horticulture, Plant
Pathology, Plants, Soil, Water Resources **Loan:** Inhouse
Service: Inhouse **Photocopy:** Yes

1457 Borazjan, Iran
Persian Gulf University, College of Agriculture
and Natural Resources (PGU, CANR)
College Library (CL)
PO Box 75615-415
Borazjan, Bushehr

Founded: 1996 **Type:** Academic **Head:** Eng. S.M. Nassiri
Phone: +98(77242) 2990, 29428 **Staff:** 1 Prof. 1 Other **Lan-
guage of Collection/Services:** English / Persian **Holdings:**
800 books 40 journals **Subjects:** Agricultural Engineering,
Crops, Fisheries, Horticulture, Soil **Loan:** Inhouse **Service:**
Inhouse **Photocopy:** No

1458 Gorgan, Iran
Gorgan University of Agricultural Sciences and
Natural Resources (GUASNR)
Central Library
PO Box 49175-633
Gorgan, Mazandaran

Former Name: Mazandaran University, College of Natural
Resources **Founded:** 1989 **Type:** Academic **Head:** E.
Tafaroji *Phone:* +98(171) 50653 **Staff:** 4 Prof. 7 Other **Hold-
ings:** 31,000 books 150 journals **Language of Collection/
Services:** English, Persian **Subjects:** Animal Husbandry,
Crops, Fisheries, Forestry, Food Sciences, Horticulture, Irri-
gation, Plant Pathology, Range Management, Wood Tech-
nology, Watershed Management **Loan:** In country **Service:**
In country **Photocopy:** Yes

1459 Karaj, Iran
Ministry of Agriculture, Agricultural Research,
Education and Extension Organization, Sugar
Beet Seed Institute (AREEO, SBSI)
Central Library
PO Box 4114
Karaj 31585

Location: Mardabad Road **Phone:** +98(261) 22611 **Fax:**
+98(261) 226002

Founded: 1950 **Type:** Government **Head:** Hossain Fazli
Phone: +98(261) 22611 **Staff:** 2 Prof. 1 Other **Language of
Collection/Services:** Farsi/Farsi **Holdings:** 3,485 books 5
journals **Subjects:** Seed Production, Sugarbeet **Service:** In
country **Photocopy:** Yes

1460 Karaj, Iran
Razi Vaccine and Serum Research Institute
Library
PO Box 11365/1558
Karaj

Former Name: Agricultural and Natural Resources Re-
search Organization, Razi Institute **Founded:** 1930 **Type:**
Government **Head:** Cyrus Javadi *Phone:* +98(261) 22005/9
Email: modir@iran.com **Staff:** 2 Prof. 2 Other **Holdings:**
6,000 books 100 journals **Language of Collection/Services:**
Farsi, English, French / Farsi, English **Subjects:** Animal

Husbandry, Entomology, Fisheries, Veterinary Medicine
Loan: In country **Service:** In country **Photocopy:** Yes

1461   Karaj, Iran
         Seed and Plant Improvement Institute (SPII)
         Library
         PO Box 31585-4119
         Karaj
Location: Mahdasht Avenue

Founded: 1978 **Type:** Government **Head:** Mr. Vali
Mirabolghasemi *Phone:* +98(261) 222858, 222859 ext 290
Email: seed.plant@neda.net **Staff:** 3 Prof. 9 Other **Holdings:** 6,970 books 95 journals **Language of Collection/Ser-
vices:** Persian, English/Persian **Subjects:** Biotechnology,
Agriculture (Tropics), Farming **Specializations:** Agricultural Development, Crops, Horticulture **Loan:** Inhouse **Service:** Inhouse **Photocopy:** Yes

1462   Karaj, Iran
         University of Tehran, College of Natural
             Resources
         Library
         PO Box 31585-4314
         Karaj
Location: Daneshkadeh St. **Phone:** +98(261) 223044/46
Fax: +98(261) 800-7988 **WWW:** www.ut.ac.ir

Former Name: Forest Institute **Founded:** 1972 **Type:** Government **Head:** Ahmad Rezaee *Phone:* +98(261) 223044 ext
291 **Staff:** 2 Prof. 3 Other **Holdings:** 1,300 books 120 journals **Language of Collection/Services:** English, Farsi **Subjects:** Desertification, Deserts, Environment, Fisheries,
Watershed Management, Range Management, Water Resources, Wood Technology **Specializations:** Forestry **Loan:**
Inhouse **Service:** Inhouse **Photocopy:** Yes

1463   Mashhad, Iran
         Ferdowsi University of Mashhad, College of
             Agriculture
         Library
         PO Box 91775-1163
         Mashhad, Khorasan
Phone: +98(51) 821555 **Fax:** +98(51) 815845

Former Name: Mashhad University **Founded:** 1973 **Type:**
Academic **Head:** A.M. Saffari **Holdings:** 12,000 books 190
journals **Language of Collection/Services:** English, Persian
Subjects: Agriculture (Tropics), Agribusiness, Agricultural
Development, Agricultural Economics, Agricultural Engi-
neering, Animal Husbandry, Crops, Education/Extension,
Entomology, Farming, Fisheries, Food Sciences, Forestry,
Horticulture, Plant Pathology, Soil Science, Veterinary Med-
icine, Water Resources **Databases Used:** Comprehensive
Loan: In country **Service:** In country **Photocopy:** Yes

1464   Orumiyeh, Iran
         Iranian Tobacco Company, Orumiyeh Tobacco
             Research Center
         Library
         PO Box 57135-415
         Orumiyeh 57135
Phone: +98(441) 770740, 772385 **Fax:** +98(441) 770254

Former Name: Iranian Tobacco Institute Orumiyeh Center
Founded: 1969 **Type:** Government **Head:** Mrs. Fariba-
Emami *Phone:* +98(441) 770740, 779994 **Staff:** 1 Prof.
Holdings: 1,100 books 5 journals **Language of Collection/
Services:** Persian, English/Persian, English **Subjects:** Agri-
cultural Development, Agricultural Engineering, Crops, Ed-
ucation, Horticulture, Plant Pathology, Soil **Specializations:**
Tobacco **Loan:** Inhouse **Service:** Inhouse **Photocopy:** Yes

1465   Shiraz, Iran
         Shiraz University, College of Agriculture
         Martyr Dr. Mofateh Library
         Shiraz 71444
Fax: +98(71) 28193 **Email:** libagrl@hafez.shirazu.ac.ir

Former Name: Pahlavi University **Founded:** 1956 **Type:**
Academic **Head:** S. Ali Akbar Behjatnia *Phone:* +98(71)
20101, 20102 *Email:* gehjatni@hafez.shirazu.ac.ir **Staff:** 4
Prof. 8 Other **Holdings:** 38,000 books 258 journals **Language of Collection/Services:** English, Farsi **Subjects:** Agricultural Economics, Agricultural Engineering, Education/
Extension, Animal Husbandry, Crops, Entomology, Farming, Food Sciences, Horticulture, Irrigation, Plant Pathology,
Plant Protection, Soil Science, Water Resources **Databases
Used:** CABCD **Loan:** Inhouse **Service:** Inhouse **Photocopy:** Yes

1466   Tabriz, Iran
         Tabriz University, Faculty of Agriculture
         Library
         29th Bahman Street
         Tabriz, East Azerbaijan 51664
Phone: +98(41) 341346 **Fax:** +98(41) 345332

Founded: 1969 **Type:** Academic **Head:** Ali Djalaly-Dizaji
Staff: 2 Prof. 2 Other **Holdings:** 18,200 books 118 journals
Language of Collection/Services: Farsi, English **Subjects:**
Agricultural Engineering, Animal Husbandry, Crops, Ento-
mology, Horticulture, Plant Pathology, Range Management,
Soil Science **Loan:** In country **Photocopy:** Yes

1467   Tehran, Iran
         Agricultural Scientific Information and
             Documentation Center (ASIDC)
         PO Box 19835-111
         Tehran 19835
Fax: +98(21) 290083 **Email:** asidc@mailcity.com

Type: Government **Networks:** AGRIS

1468   Tehran, Iran
         Ministry of Jahad-e Sazandegi, Education and
             Research Division, Research Institute of
             Forests and Rangelands
         Library
         PO Box 13185-116
         Tehran
Location: Road of Karadj **Phone:** +98(21) 602-6575 **Fax:**
+98(21) 602-6575

Founded: 1968 **Type:** Government **Head:** Mrs. Paricher
Hakhamaneshi **Staff:** 4 Prof. 3 Other **Holdings:** 4,000 books
320 journals **Language of Collection/Services:** Farsi / Farsi
Subjects: Botany, Entomology, Forestry, Horticulture, Plant

Pathology, Range Management, Soil Conservation, Soil Science, Watershed Management, Wood Technology **Loan:** Inhouse **Service:** In country **Photocopy:** Yes

1469   **Tehran, Iran**
       University of Tehran, Faculty of Veterinary
          Medicine
       Library
       PO Box 14155-6453
       Tehran
Location: Ghareed Street, Azadi Ave. **Phone:** +98(21) 923510 ext 231 **Fax:** +98(21) 933222 **WWW:** www.ut.ac.ir

Founded: 1960 **Type:** Academic **Head:** Dr. A. Niasari-Naslaji *Phone:* +98(21) 923510 ext 230 *Email:* niasari@ chamran.ut.ac.ir **Staff:** 2 Prof. 4 Other **Holdings:** 10,000 books 140 journals **Language of Collection/Services:** Farsi /Farsi **Subjects:** Animal Husbandry, Veterinary Medicine **Databases Used:** FSTA; Medline; VETCD **Loan:** In country **Photocopy:** No

1470   **Zangan, Iran**
       Zangan University
       Central Library
       PO Box 45195-313
       Zangan
Location: Tabriz Road Km 6 **Phone:** +98(2821) 27001

Former Name: Zangan Agricultural College, Zangan Agricultural Library **Founded:** 1975 **Type:** Academic **Head:** Moshen Darbani *Phone:* +98(2821) 27001 **Staff:** 1 Prof. 6 Other **Holdings:** 30,000 books 12,245 journals **Language of Collection/Services:** Persian, English/Persian, English **Subjects:** Agronomy, Animal Husbandry, Botany, Extension, Forestry, Horticulture, Irrigation, Soil Science **Photocopy:** Yes

Iraq

♦**1471**   **Baghdad, Iraq**
       IDA Agricultural Research Center
       Library
       PO Box 39094
       Baghdad

Former Name: Scientific Research Council (SRC), Agriculture and Water Resources Research Center (AWRRC) **Founded:** 1976 **Type:** Government **Head:** Miss Sarab A. Al-Hyani *Phone:* +964(1) 511-7303 ext 238 **Holdings:** 240 journals 7,000 books **Language of Collection/Services:** English **Subjects:** Agriculture (Tropics), Agricultural Economics, Agricultural Engineering, Animal Husbandry, Food Sciences, Biotechnology, Crops, Entomology, Horticulture, Plant Pathology, Poultry Farming, Soil Science, Veterinary Medicine, Water Resources **Databases Used:** Biosis **Loan:** Internationally **Service:** Internationally **Photocopy:** Yes

1472   **Baghdad, Iraq**
       National Agricultural Documentation Center
       Information Center, IAEC
       PO Box 765

       Tuwaitha
       Baghdad
Networks: AGRIS

1473   **Baghdad, Iraq**
       University of Baghdad
       Central Library
       Jadyria
       PO Box 12
       Baghdad
Phone: +964(1) 416-8392

Founded: 1959 **Type:** Academic **Head:** Dafir A. Kadir *Phone:* +964(1) 416-4742 **Staff:** 46 Prof. 59 Other **Holdings:** 750 books 90 journals **Subjects:** Agricultural Economics, Agricultural Research, Education/Extension, Farm Management **Loan:** In country **Photocopy:** Yes

Ireland

1474   **Cork, Ireland**
       University College Cork
       Boole Library
       Cork
Location: College Road **Phone:** +353(21) 276871 ext 2284 **Fax:** +353(21) 273428 **WWW:** www.ucc.ie **OPAC:** www.booleweb.ucc.ie

Founded: 1845 **Type:** Academic **Head:** Mr. John Fitzgerald *Phone:* +353(21) 276871 ext 2851 **Staff:** 17 Prof. 61 Other **Holdings:** 500,000 books 4,000 journals **Language of Collection/Services:** English / English **Subjects:** Aquaculture, Biotechnology, Food Sciences, Plants, Zoology **Networks:** OCLC **Databases Used:** ASFA; CABCD; Derwent Biotechnology Abstracts; FSTA **Loan:** Internationally **Service:** Inhouse **Photocopy:** Yes

1475   **Droichead Nua, Ireland**
       Irish Peat Board
       Technical Information Office
       Droichead Nua, Co. Kildare
Phone: +353(45) 431201 **Fax:** +353(45) 433240 **Email:** tonym@bnm.ie **WWW:** www.bnm.ie

Non-English Name: Bord na Mona **Founded:** 1950 **Type:** Business **Head:** Tony McKenna *Phone:* +353(45) 431201 *Email:* tonym@bnm.ie **Staff:** 1 Prof. **Holdings:** 2,500 books 80 journals **Language of Collection/Services:** English / English **Subjects:** Peatlands, Reclamation **Specializations:** Horticulture, Peat **Databases Used:** Comprehensive **Loan:** Do not loan **Service:** Inhouse **Photocopy:** Yes

1476   **Dublin, Ireland**
       Agriculture and Food Development Authority
       Library
       Ballsbridge
       19 Sandymount Avenue
       Dublin 4
Phone: +353(1) 637-6000 **Fax:** +353(1) 668-8023 **WWW:** www.teagasc.ie

Non-English Name: TEAGASC **Founded:** 1958 **Type:** Government **Staff:** 2 Prof. 7 Other **Holdings:** 20,000 books 1,000 journals **Subjects:** Food Sciences **Networks:** AGRIS **Loan:** Internationally **Photocopy:** Yes

1477   Dublin, Ireland
Department of Agriculture, Food and Rural Development
Library
Agriculture House, Kildare Street
Dublin 2

Phone: +353(1) 678-9011 ext 3297 **Fax:** +353(1) 661-6263 **Email:** information@daff.irlgov.ie **WWW:** www.irlgov.ie/daff

Founded: 1900 **Type:** Government **Head:** Mary Doyle *Phone:* +353(1) 678-9011 ext 2163 **Staff:** 2 Prof. 4 Other **Holdings:** 60,000 books 1,100 journals **Subjects:** Agribusiness, Agricultural Development, Agricultural Economics, Agricultural Engineering, Animal Husbandry, Entomology, Food Sciences, Forestry, Horticulture, Plants, Plant Pathology, Soil Science, Veterinary Science **Networks:** AGRIS **Databases Developed:** Database on the Agricultural and agro-Industrial Sector in Ireland - includes the whole of Ireland. In addition to general economic aspects it includes some references on management and relevant aspects of pollution and the fishing industry. Circulated with a read-only version of CARDBOX-PLUS software to selected libraries and users. **Databases Used:** Agricola; Agris; CABCD **Loan:** Internationally **Photocopy:** Yes

1478   Dublin, Ireland
Department of Agriculture, Food and Rural Development, Veterinary Research Laboratory (VRL)
Library
Abbotstown, Castleknock
Dublin 15

Phone: +353(1) 607-2869 ext 1001, 1002 **Fax:** +353(1) 821-3010

Former Name: Department of Agriculture, Food and Forestry (DAFF) **Type:** Government **Founded:** 1921 **Head:** Eileen Gavin *Phone:* +353(1) 607-2869 ext 1001, 1002 **Staff:** 1 Other **Holdings:** 1,500 books 100 journals **Language of Collection/Services:** English **Subjects:** Veterinary Medicine **Databases Used:** Comprehensive **Loan:** Internationally **Service:** Internationally **Photocopy:** Yes

1479   Dublin, Ireland
Department of Arts, Heritage, Gaeltacht and the Islands, National Botanic Gardens, Glasnevin
Library
Dublin 9

Fax: +353(1) 863-0080 **Email:** nbg@indigo.ie

Former Name: Department of Agriculture and Food, Office of Public Works **Founded:** 1795 **Type:** Government **Head:** Sarah Ball *Phone:* +353(1) 837-4388, 837-7596, 837-1636, 837-1637 *Email:* nbg@indigo.ie **Staff:** 1 Prof. **Holdings:** 40,000 books 350 journals **Language of Collection/Services:** English/English **Subjects:** Botany, Horticulture **Service:** Inhouse **Loan:** In country **Photocopy:** Yes

1480   Dublin, Ireland
Department of the Marine, Fisheries Research Centre (FRC)
Library
Abbotstown, Castleknock
Dublin 15

Phone: +353(1) 821-0111 **Fax:** +353(1) 820-5078 **WWW:** www.marine.ie/frc

Non-English Name: Roinn na Mara, Taighdealann Iascaigh **Former Name:** Department of Fisheries and Forestry, Department of Agriculture and Fisheries **Founded:** 1920 **Type:** Government **Staff:** 1 Prof. 1 Other **Holdings:** 10,000 books 1,450 journals **Language of Collection/Services:** English / English **Subjects:** Fisheries **Loan:** Internationally **Photocopy:** Yes

1481   Dublin, Ireland
Guinness Ireland Ltd
Technical Information
St. James's Gate
Dublin 8

Phone: +353(1) 453-6700 ext 5528 **Fax:** +353(1) 453-7804 **WWW:** www.guinness.ie

Type: Business **Staff:** 2 Prof. 1 Other **Holdings:** 560 journals 8,000 books **Language of Collection/Services:** English **Subjects:** Brewing, Food Sciences **Specializations:** Food Legislation, Brewing Industry, Patents **Loan:** Inhouse **Photocopy:** Yes

1482   Dublin, Ireland
National University of Ireland - Dublin, University College Dublin (NUID, UCD)
Main Library, Pure and Applied Sciences Section
Belfield
Dublin 4

Phone: +353(1) 706-7529 **Fax:** +353(1) 283-7667 **Email:** reader.services@ucd.ie **WWW:** www.ucd.ie **OPAC:** udtal.uck.ie

Former Name: Faculty of Agriculture Library **Founded:** 1926 **Type:** Academic **Head:** Mary E. Flynn *Phone:* +353 (1) 706-7538 *Email:* mary.flynn@ucd.ie **Staff:** 4.5 Prof. 3.5 Other **Holdings:** 30,000 books 800 journals **Language of Collection/Services:** English **Subjects:** Comprehensive **Networks:** BLCMP **Databases Used:** Comprehensive **Service:** In country **Loan:** Internationally **Photocopy:** Yes

1483   Dublin, Ireland
Royal Dublin Society (RDS)
Library
Ballsbridge
Dublin 4

Location: Merrion Road **Phone:** +353(1) 668-0866 **Fax:** +353(1) 660-4014 **Email:** marketing@rds.ie **WWW:** www.rds.ie

Founded: 1731 **Staff:** 5 Prof. 6 Other **Holdings:** 7,650 books **Language of Collection/Services:** English **Specializations:** Apidae, Blight, Butter, Cheeses, Dairies, Domestic Animals, Domestic Gardens, Drainage, Fertilizers, Fibers, Fishing, Fruits, Grain Crops, Grasses, Insects, Milk, Pests,

Orchards, Silkworms, Soil Science, Tea, Trapping, Vineyards **Photocopy:** Yes

1484   Dublin, Ireland
University College Dublin
Veterinary Medicine Library
Ballsbridge
Dublin 4

Phone: +353(1) 668-7988 **Fax:** +353(1) 668-9732 **WWW:** www.ucd.ie **OPAC:** udtal.ucd.ie

Founded: 1968 **Type:** Academic **Head:** Angela Hastings **Email:** angela.hastings@ucd.ie **Phone:** +353(1) 668-7988 ext 267 **Staff:** 2 Prof. 2.5 Other **Holdings:** 10,500 books 290 journals **Language of Collection/Services:** English/English **Subjects:** Veterinary Medicine **Networks:** BLS-TALIS **Databases Used:** Biosis; CABCD; FSTA; Medline **Loan:** Internationally **Photocopy:** Yes

♦1485   Multyfarnham, Ireland
Franciscan College of Agriculture
Mullingar
Multyfarnham, Co. Westmeath

Phone: +353(44) 71137 **Fax:** +353(44) 71387

Non-English Name: Colaiste Talamhaiochla na Proinsiasach **Founded:** 1957 **Type:** Academic **Staff:** 8 Prof. 1 Other **Holdings:** 300 books 15 journals **Language of Collection/Services:** English **Subjects:** Agribusiness, Crops, Animal Husbandry, Farm Machinery, Farm Management, Horticulture **Loan:** Do not loan **Photocopy:** Yes

1486   Newtownmountkennedy, Ireland
Irish Forestry Board
Library
Newtownmountkennedy, Co. Wicklow

Phone: +353(1) 201-1111 **Fax:** +353(1) 201-1199 **Email:** kehoe_a@coillte.ie **WWW:** www.coillte.ie

Non-English Name: Coillte Teoranta **Type:** Semi-Government **Founded:** 1960 **Head:** Ann Kehoe **Phone:** +353(1) 201-1111 **Email:** kehoe_a@coillte.ie **Staff:** 1 Prof. **Holdings:** 7,000 books 60 journals **Language of Collection/Services:** English **Databases Used:** CABCD **Subjects:** Forestry, Forest Management **Loan:** Inhouse **Service:** Internationally **Photocopy:** Yes

Israel

1487   Ashrat, Israel
MILOUOT Ltd.
Central Library
Mobile Post
Ashrat 25201

Fax: +972(4) 917569, 853231

Former Name: MILOUDA **Founded:** 1977 **Type:** Cooperative **Head:** Mrs. Hanna Yadon **Phone:** +972(4) 853201 ext 132 **Staff:** 1 Prof. **Holdings:** 76 journals **Language of Collection/Services:** English, Hebrew **Subjects:** Animal Husbandry, Education/Extension, Fisheries, Food Sciences, Crops, Horticulture, Plant Pathology **Loan:** In country **Photocopy:** Yes

1488   Bet Dagan, Israel
Ministry of Agriculture and Rural Development,
        Volcani Center
Central Library
PO Box 6
Bet Dagan 50250

Location: Agricultural Research Organization **Email:** volclib@volcani.agri.gov.il

Founded: 1950 **Type:** Government **Head:** Ruth Milchan **Phone:** +972(3) 968-3331 **Email:** volclib@volcani.agri.gov.il **Staff:** 2 Prof. 1 Other **Holdings:** 30,000 books 600 journals **Language of Collection/Services:** English / English **Subjects:** Agricultural Economics, Animal Husbandry, Crops, Food Sciences, Horticulture, Meteorology, Plant Protection, Soil Science, Storage **Databases Used:** Comprehensive **Photocopy:** Yes

1489   Bet Dagan, Israel
Ministry of Agriculture and Rural Development,
        Kimron Veterinary Institute
Library
PO Box 12
Bet Dagan 50250

Fax: +972(3) 968-1780

Founded: 1940 **Type:** Academic Government **Head:** Ruth Musael **Email:** rmusael@netvision.net.il **Phone:** +972(3) 968-1666 **Staff:** 3 Prof. 2 Other **Holdings:** 70,000 books 280 journals **Language of Collection/Services:** English/English **Subjects:** Animal Husbandry, Entomology, Food Sciences, Parasitology **Specializations:** Food Microbiology, Veterinary Medicine **Databases Developed:** Publications of institute's research workers **Databases Used:** Agricola; Current Contents; Medline **Loan:** In country **Service:** Internationally **Photocopy:** Yes

1490   Emek Hefer, Israel
Ruppin Institute
Library
PO Emek Hefer
Emek Hefer 40250

Phone: +972(9) 898-3086 **Fax:** +972(9) 898-1307 **Email:** library@ruppin.ac.il **WWW:** ruppin.ac.il

Former Name: Rubbin Institute of Agriculture **Founded:** 1955 **Type:** Academic **Head:** Mrs. Janet Hilman **Phone:** +972(9) 898-3086 **Email:** library@ruppin.ac.il **Staff:** 7 Prof. **Holdings:** 60,000 books 150 journals **Language of Collection/Services:** English / English, Hebrew **Subjects:** Agriculture (Tropics), Agricultural Development, Agricultural Economics, Agricultural Engineering, Animal Husbandry, Crops, Education/Extension, Farming, Fisheries, Food Sciences, Horticulture, Plant Pathology, Soil Science, Water Resources **Specializations:** Agricultural emphasis up to the mid-1980's **Databases Developed:** Subject index in Hebrew and English to UDC catalogue. **Databases Used:** Comprehensive **Loan:** Inhouse **Service:** In country **Photocopy:** Yes

1491   Haifa, Israel
Israel Oceanographic and Limnological Research
        Ltd. (IOLR)

Israel Oceanographic Information Center
POB 3080
Haifa 31080

Location: Tel Shikmona **Phone:** +972(4) 851-5202 **Fax:** +972(4) 851-1911 **WWW:** ocean.org.il

Former Name: Sea Fisheries Research Station **Founded:** 1948 **Type:** Government **Head:** Elisabeth Apt *Phone:* +972(4) 851-5202 *Email:* elisabeth@ocean.org.il **Staff:** 2 Prof. **Holdings:** 4,000 books 800 journals **Language of Collection/Services:** English **Subjects:** Aquaculture **Specializations:** Fisheries (Middle East), Limnology (Middle East), Oceanography (Middle East), Dead Sea, Egypt, Lake Kinneret, Mediterranean Sea, Red Sea, Suez Canal **Databases Developed:** Regional bibliography on fisheries, limnology, and oceanography in the eastern Mediterranean, Read Sea, Suez Canal, Lake Kinneret, Dead Sea, and Egyptian Lakes. Access through the Israeli library program ALEPH. **Databases Used:** Comprehensive **Loan:** In country **Service:** In country **Photocopy:** Yes

1492　Haifa, Israel
Technion, Israel Institute of Technology, Faculty of Agricultural Engineering (IIT)
Library
Haifa 32000

Phone: +972(4) 8292-625 **Fax:** +972(4) 822-1529 Attn: Library **Email:** aglib@tx.technion.ac.il **WWW:** www.technion.ac.il/technion/agr/library/lib.html

Founded: 1958 **Type:** Academic **Head:** Ms. Devorah Levy *Phone:* +972(4) 8292-625 **Staff:** 2 Prof. **Holdings:** 20,000 books 100 journals **Language of Collection/Services:** English/Hebrew **Subjects:** Agricultural Engineering, Ecology, Animal Husbandry, Aquaculture, Crops, Drainage, Fertilizers, Horticulture, Irrigation, Plant Pathology, Plants, Soil Science, Water Resources **Databases Used:** Agricola **Loan:** In country **Service:** In country **Photocopy:** Yes

1493　Nir-David, Israel
Ministry of Agriculture and Rural Development, Fisheries and Aquaculture Department, Central Fish Health Laboratory
Library
Nir-David 19150

Fax: +972(6) 583900 Attn. Fishlab **Email:** fish_lab@netvision.net.il

Former Name: Laboratory for Research of Fish Diseases **Founded:** 1950 **Type:** Academic Government **Head:** Simon Timman *Phone:* +972(6) 658-5877 **Staff:** 2 Other **Holdings:** 7,000 books 30 journals **Language of Collection/Services:** English **Subjects:** Aquaculture, Animal Husbandry, Biotechnology, Ecology, Fisheries, Food Sciences, Veterinary Medicine, Water Resources **Loan:** In country **Service:** In country **Photocopy:** Yes

1494　Rehovot, Israel
Development Study Centre (DSC)
International Rural Projects Data Base and Rural Tourism Resource Center (IRPD)
POB 2355
Rehovot 76120

Fax: +972(8) 450498-2003

Former Name: Settlement Study Centre (SSC) **Founded:** 1986 **Type:** Academic **Head:** Devoira Auerbach *Phone:* +972(8) 947-4111 **Staff:** 1 Prof. 1 Other **Holdings:** 7,000 books **Language of Collection/Services:** English, Spanish **Subjects:** Agriculture (Tropics), Agricultural Development, Education/Extension, Settlement, Water Resources **Specializations:** Development Projects (Grey Literature) **Databases Developed:** International Rural Projects Database (IRPD) - developed as the computerized retrieval system for the projects collection; access by geographical, indicative, descriptive and bibliographic criteria; twenty-nine main categories are subdivided into some 400 components **Loan:** Internationally **Service:** Internationally **Photocopy:** Yes

1495　Rehovot, Israel
Hebrew University of Jerusalem, Faculty of Agriculture
Central Library of Agricultural Sciences
PO Box 12
Rehovot 76100

Location: Hertzel Street **Phone:** +972(8) 948-1269 **Fax:** +972(8) 936-1348 **WWW:** www.huji.ac.il **Ariel IP:** 128.139.14.131

Founded: 1962 **Type:** Academic **Head:** Mrs. Naomi Barzely *Phone:* +972(8) 948-1270 *Email:* barzely@agri.huji.ac.il **Staff:** 9 Prof. 5 Other **Holdings:** 300,000 books 1,600 journals **Language of Collection/Services:** English, Hebrew **Subjects:** Agriculture (Tropics), Agribusiness, Agricultural Development, Agricultural Economics, Agricultural Engineering, Animal Husbandry, Biotechnology, Crops, Dietetics, Education/Extension, Entomology, Farming, Fisheries, Food Sciences, Forestry, Horticulture, Nutrition, Plant Pathology, Soil Science, Veterinary Medicine, Water Resources **Specializations:** Food and Agriculture Organization Documents, Experimental Stations (USA) Documents **Networks:** Israel Union List **Databases Used:** Comprehensive **Loan:** In country **Photocopy:** Yes

1496　Tel Aviv, Israel
Ministry of Agriculture and Rural Development, Department of Market Research
Market Research Information Center
PO Box 7011, Hakirya
Tel Aviv 61070

Location: 18, Arania Street **Phone:** +972(3) 697-1988 **Fax:** +972(3) 696-7355

Founded: 1983 **Head:** Ruth Elazar *Phone:* +972(3) 697-1837 *Email:* mrela@inter.net.il **Type:** Government **Staff:** 3 Prof. 1 Other **Holdings:** 20,000 books 300 journals **Language of Collection/Services:** English, Dutch, German, French, Spanish, Hebrew / Hebrew **Subjects:** Agribusiness **Specializations:** Horticultural Crops, Marketing **Networks:** AGRIS **Databases Developed:** Database on Horticultural Marketing **Databases Used:** Comprehensive **Loan:** Do not loan **Service:** Internationally **Photocopy:** Yes

1497　Tel Aviv, Israel
Ministry of Agriculture and Rural Development, Extension Service

Shaham Information Center
PO Box 7054, Hakirya
Tel Aviv 61070

Phone: +972(3) 697-1688 **Fax:** +972(3) 697-1687

Founded: 1994 **Head:** Roni Peer *Phone:* +972(3) 183-1919 **Type:** Government **Holdings:** 50,000 books **Language of Collection/Services:** Hebrew/Hebrew **Subjects:** Agricultural Research **Databases Developed:** Agricultural research in Israel **Loan:** Do not loan **Photocopy:** Yes

1498   Tulkarm, Israel
Tulkarm Community College
Library
PO Box 7
Tulkarm, West Bank
Location: Jaffa Street

Former Name: Kadoori School, Agricultural Institute **Founded:** 1930 **Type:** Academic **Head:** Mahmoud Odeh *Phone:* +972(9) 267-1026 **Staff:** 2 Prof. **Holdings:** 27,000 books 12 journals **Language of Collection/Services:** Arabic, English **Subjects:** Agriculture (Tropics), Agribusiness, Agricultural Development, Agricultural Economics, Agricultural Engineering, Animal Husbandry, Crops, Education/Extension, Entomology, Farming, Fisheries, Food Sciences, Forestry, Horticulture, Plant Pathology, Soil Science, Veterinary Medicine, Water Resources **Loan:** Inhouse **Service:** In country **Photocopy:** No

Italy

1499   Bari, Italy
Agronomy Research Institute
Library
Via Celso Upiani 5
70125 Bari
Phone: +39(80) 547-5011 **Fax:** +39(80) 547-5023 **WWW:** www.inea.it/isa/isa.html

Non-English Name: Istituto Sperimentale Agronomico (ISA), Biblioteca **Former Name:** Stazione Agraria Sperimentale di Bari **Founded:** 1918 **Type:** Government **Head:** Francesco Antonacci **Staff:** 2 Other **Holdings:** 11,000 books 50 journals **Language of Collection/Services:** Italian **Subjects:** Crops, Soil Science **Loan:** Inhouse **Service:** In country **Photocopy:** Yes

1500   Bari, Italy
University of Bari, Mechanical Agriculture
    Institute
Library
Via Amendola 165/A
70126 Bari
Fax: +39(80) 5543080 **Email:** bibmecag@bibagr.uniba.it

Non-English Name: Università degli Studi di Bari, Istituto di Meccanica Agraria, Biblioteca **Founded:** 1939 **Type:** Academic **Head:** Prof. Pasquale Guarella *Phone:* +39(80) 554-2860 **Staff:** 1 Prof. **Holdings:** 4,000 books 30 journals **Language of Collection/Services:** English **Subjects:** Agricultural Development, Agricultural Engineering, Horticulture,

Biotechnology, Crops, Food Sciences, Forestry, Plants, Soil Science **Photocopy:** Yes

1501   Bergamo, Italy
Istituto Sperimentale per la Cerealicoltura
    (ISC-Bg)
Sezione di Bergamo
Via Stezzano, 24
24100 Bergamo
Phone: +39(35) 313132, 311422 **Fax:** +39(35) 316054 **Email:** isc1@spm.it **WWW:** www.inea.it/isc/Bergamo1.htm

Founded: 1920 **Type:** Government **Head:** Mrs. Rosa Marziali **Staff:** 1 Prof. 1 Other **Holdings:** 1,743 books 272 journals **Language of Collection/Services:** English / Italian **Subjects:** Maize **Loan:** Do not loan **Photocopy:** Yes

1502   Bologna, Italy
University of Bologna, Agriculture Faculty
Central Library
Via Filippo Re 6
40126 Bologna
Phone: +39(51) 351810 **Fax:** +39(51) 351811 **WWW:** www.agrisci.unibo.it

Non-English Name: Università degli Studi di Bologna, Facoltà di Agraria, Biblioteca Centralizzata **Founded:** 1985 **Head:** Prof. Roberto Tuberosa *Phone:* +39(51) 351810 *Email:* tuberosa@pop.agrisci.unibo.it **Staff:** 2 Prof. 1 Other **Type:** Government **Holdings:** 7,000 books 120 journals **Subjects:** Agricultural Economics, Crops, Agricultural Engineering, Agronomy, Animal Husbandry, Biotechnology, Botany, Entomology, Fisheries, Food Sciences, Forestry, Horticulture, Plant Pathology, Plants, Soil Science, Water Resources **Databases Used:** Agris; CABCD **Loan:** Inhouse **Service:** Inhouse **Photocopy:** No

1503   Bologna, Italy
University of Bologna, Department of Agricultural
    Economics and Engineering
Library
Via Filippo Re, 10
40126 Bologna
Phone: +39(51) 209-1620, 209-1590 **Fax:** +39(51) 766-632, 252-187, 244-8832 **WWW:** dns.agrisci.unibo.it/deiagra/index.html

Non-English Name: Università degli Studi di Bologna, Dipartimento di Economia e Ingegneria Agrarie, Biblioteca **Founded:** 1928 **Type:** Academic **Head:** Prof. Domenico Regazzi **Staff:** 1 Prof. **Holdings:** 10,000 books 150 journals **Subjects:** Agribusiness, Agricultural Development, Agricultural Economics, Farming, Food Sciences **Loan:** In country **Photocopy:** Yes

1504   Bologna, Italy
University of Bologna, Department of
    Aboriculture, Forestry and Landscape
Library
Via Filippo Re 6
40126 Bologna

Phone: +39(51) 351490 **Fax:** +39(51) 351500 **Email:** grannotti@opac.cib.unibo.it, giorgi@opac.cib.unibo.it **WWW:** www.agrsci.unibo.it/dicabo **OPAC:** opac.cib. unibo.it

Non-English Name: Università di Bologna, Dipartimento di Colture Arboree (DCA), Biblioteca **Former Name:** Institute of Tree Fruit Crops and Silviculture, Istituto di Coltivazioni Arboree **Founded:** 1936 **Type:** Academic **Head:** Prof. S. Sanstuini *Phone:* +39(51) 351490 **Staff:** 2 Prof. **Holdings:** 14,411 books 153 journals **Language of Collection/Services:** Italian, English/Italian **Subjects:** Crops, Biotechnology, Forestry, Fruit Trees, Genetics, Growth Regulators, Horticulture, Landscape Architecture, Ornamental Plants, Plant Physiology, Viticulture **Networks:** SBN **Databases Used:** CABCD **Photocopy:** Yes

1505   Bologna, Italy
University of Bologna, Department of Agronomy
Library
Via Filippo Re 8
40126 Bologna
Phone: +39(51) 351510 **Fax:** +39(51) 351511 **Email:** agronlib@pop.agrsci.unibo.it **WWW:** www.agrsci.unibo.it/agro/index.html **OPAC:** www.cib.unibo.it/cataloghi/cat-on-line.html

Non-English Name: Università di Bologna, Dipartimento di Agronomia, Biblioteca **Former Name:** Institute of General Agronomy and Crop Production, Istituto di Agronomia Generale e Coltivazioni Erbacee **Type:** Academic **Founded:** 1948 **Head:** Gianpietro Venturi *Phone:* +39(51) 351533 *Email:* gventuri@pop.agrsci.unibo.it **Staff:** 1 Prof. **Holdings:** 6,000 books 133 journals **Language of Collection/Services:** English **Subjects:** Biotechnology, Forage, Horticulture, Medicinal Plants, Plant Breeding, Plant Ecology, Seeds, Soil Science, Water Resources, Weeds **Databases Used:** CABCD **Loan:** Inhouse **Service:** Inhouse **Photocopy:** Yes

1506   Bologna, Italy
University of Bologna, Institute of Zootecnica
Library
Via S/ Giacomo, 9
40126 Bologna
Phone: +39(51) 354220 **Fax:** +39(51) 251936 **Email:** biblzoot@alma.unibo.it

Non-English Name: Università di Bologna, Istituto di Zootecnica, Biblioteca **Founded:** 1932 **Type:** Government **Head:** Prof. Achille Franchini *Email:* franchin@alma. unibo.it *Phone:* +39(51) 354221, 354220 **Staff:** 1 Prof. 1 Other **Holdings:** 2,100 books 74 journals **Language of Collection/Services:** Italian, English **Subjects:** Animal Husbandry, Fishes, Game Animals, Honeybees, Poultry, Rabbits **Loan:** In country **Photocopy:** No

1507   Casale Monferrato (AL), Italy
Agricultural and Forest Organization, National
Organization for Cellulose and Paper
Poplar Research Institute
P.O. Box 116
15033 Casale Monferrato (AL)

Location: Strada Frassineto no. 35 **Phone:** +39(142) 454654 **Fax:** +39(142) 55580 **Email:** isp@populus.it

Non-English Name: Società Agricola e Forestale per la Piante da Cellulosa e da Carta, Ente Nazionale Cellulosa e Carta (SAF, ENCC), Istituto di Sperimentazione per la Pioppicoltura (ISP) **Founded:** 1939 **Type:** Government **Head:** Dott. Lucia Sebastiani *Email:* sebastiani@populus.it *Phone:* +39(142) 454654 **Staff:** 2 Prof. **Holdings:** 6,000 books 235 journals **Language of Collection/Services:** Italian **Subjects:** Agribusiness, Agricultural Development, Agricultural Economics, Agricultural Engineering, Biotechnology, Entomology, Farming, Forestry, Horticulture, Plant Pathology, Crops, Soil Science, Water Resources **Databases Used:** CABCD **Loan:** Inhouse **Service:** In country **Photocopy:** Yes

1508   Conegliano Veneto, Italy
Experimental Institute for Viticulture
Library
Via XXVIII Aprile n.26
31015 Conegliano Veneto (TV)
Phone: +39(438) 456711 **Fax:** +39(438) 64779 **WWW:** www.inea.it/isv/isv.html

Non-English Name: Istituto Sperimentale per la Viticoltura (ISV), Biblioteca **Founded:** 1924 **Type:** Government **Head:** Prof. Antonio Calò *Phone:* +39(438) 61635 **Holdings:** 150 journals 10,000 books **Subjects:** Enology, Viticulture **Loan:** Do not loan **Photocopy:** No

1509   Cremona, Italy
Animal Production Research Institute
Division at Cremona
Via Porcellasco 7
26100 Cremona
Phone: +39(372) 433029 **Fax:** +39(372) 435056 **Email:** iszcr@digicolor.lognet.it **WWW:** www.inea.it/isz/index.htm

Non-English Name: Istituto Sperimentale per la Zootecnia (ISZ), Sezione di Cremona **Founded:** 1960 **Type:** Government **Staff:** 1 Other **Holdings:** 300 books **Language of Collection/Services:** Italian, English, French **Subjects:** Animal Husbandry, Animal Nutrition, Dairy Industry **Loan:** Do not loan **Photocopy:** No

1510   Florence, Italy
Florence University
Central Library, Agricultural Science and
Technology Library
Piazzale delle Cascine 18
50144 Florence
Phone: +39(55) 3288232 **Fax:** +39(55) 3288394 **Email:** bibag@cesit1.unifi.it **OPAC:** opac.unifi.it **WWW:** www.unifi.it/biblio/scienzetecnologiche/sc_tecnologiche.htm

Non-English Name: Università degli Studi di Firenze, Centrale Biblioteche, Biblioteca di Scienze Tecnologiche Agraria **Founded:** 1972 **Type:** Academic **Head:** Maria Giulia Maraviglia *Email:* giumara@unifi.it *Phone:* +39(55) 504 7015, 504 8982 **Staff:** 1 Other **Holdings:** 500 books **Subjects:** Horticulture **Loan:** Do not loan **Photocopy:** No

1511   Florence, Italy
Florence University, Department of Agricultural
    Engineering and Forestry
Library
Piazzale delle Cascine 15
50144 Florence
Phone: +39(55) 352051 **Fax:** +39(55) 331794 **Email:**
mechag@diaf.agr.unifi.it **WWW:** www.unifi.it

Non-English Name: Università degli Studi di Firenze,
Dipartimento Ingegneria Agraria e Forestale (DIAF), Biblioteca **Founded:** 1925 **Type:** Government **Head:** Prof.
Massimo Zoli *Phone:* +39(55) 352051 *Email:* mzoli@diaf.
agr.unifi.it **Staff:** 1 Other **Holdings:** 1,500 books 30 journals
Language of Collection/Services: Italian **Subjects:** Agricultural Engineering **Loan:** Do not loan **Photocopy:** No

1512   Florence, Italy
National Research Council, Wood Research
    Institute
Library
Via Barazzuoli 23
50136 Florence
Phone: +39(55) 661750, 661886 **Fax:** +39(55) 670624
Email: argent@mailbox.irl.fi.cnr.it **WWW:** www.area.fi.
cnr.it/irl/irl.htm

Non-English Name: Consiglio Nazionale delle Ricerche,
Istituto per la Ricerca sul Legno (CNR, IRL), Biblioteca
Founded: 1954 **Type:** Government **Head:** Dr. Simonetta
Del Monaco **Staff:** 12 Prof. 5 Other **Holdings:** 10,000 books
150 journals **Language of Collection/Services:** English/
Italian **Subjects:** Forestry, Wood Technology **Specializa-
tions:** Wood, Xylotheca **Databases Used:** CABCD **Loan:**
Inhouse **Service:** Internationally **Photocopy:** Yes

1513   Florence, Italy
Research institute for Soil Study and Conservation
30 Piazza M. D'Azeglio
50121 Florence
Phone: +39(55) 2491211 **Fax:** +39(55) 241485 **Email:**
issds@fi.flashnet.it **WWW:** www.inea.it/issds/index.htm

Non-English Name: Istituto Sperimentale per lo Studio e la
Difesa del Suolo (ISSDS) **Founded:** 1952 **Type:** Government **Head:** Ms. Anna Maria Chiobo *Phone:* +39(55) 249
1211 *Email:* alloclaissds@dada.it **Staff:** 1 Other **Holdings:**
3,000 books 100 journals **Language of Collection/Services:**
Italian, English **Subjects:** Soil Conservation **Loan:** Do not
loan **Photocopy:** Yes

1514   Forli, Italy
Fruit Tree Research Institute, Field Station at Forli
Library
PO Box 7178
47100 Forli
Location: Via Punta di Ferro, 2 **Phone:** +39(543) 722864
Fax: +39(543) 722692 **Email:** info.isf@agraria.it **WWW:**
www.inea.it/isf/index.htm

Non-English Name: Istituto Sperimentale per la Frutticoltura, Sezione di Forli (ISF-FO), Biblioteca **Type:** Government **Head:** Dr. Waltker Faedi *Email:* faedi.isf@agraria.it
Staff: 1 Other **Holdings:** 800 books 28 journals **Language**

of Collection/ Services: Italian, English, French **Subjects:**
Agricultural Development, Biotechnology, Crops, Fruit
Growing, Horticulture, Plant Pathology, Soil Science **Loan:**
Do not loan **Photocopy:** Yes

1515   Legnaro, Italy
University of Padova
Agripolis Central Library "Pietro Arduino"
Agripolis
Via Romea 16
35020 Legnaro, Padova
Phone: +39(49) 8272511/4 **Fax:** +39(39) 8272510
WWW: www.unipd.it/esterni/wwwpolis/index.html

Non-English Name: Università degli Studi di Padova, Biblioteca Centrale di Agripolis "Pietro Arduino" **Head:** Prof.
Raffaele Cavalli *Phone:* +39(49) 8272724 *Email:* puv45@
ux1.unipad.it

1516   Legnaro, Italy
University of Padova, Institute of Agricultural
    Economics and Policy
Library
Agripolis
Via Romea 16
35020 Legnaro, Padova
Phone: +39(49) 8272768 **Fax:** +39(49) 8272772 **Email:**
leonmg@agripolis.unipd.it **WWW:** www.unipd.it **OPAC:**
www.unipd.it/main/servizi.html

Non-English Name: Università di Padova, Istituto di Eco-
nomia e Politica Agraria, Biblioteca **Founded:** 1950 **Type:**
Academic **Head:** Prof. Vasco Boatto *Phone:* +39(49) 827
2768 **Staff:** 1 Prof. **Holdings:** 100 journals **Language of
Collection/Services:** Italian/Italian **Subjects:** Agricultural
Economics **Networks:** SBN **Databases Used:** Comprehen-
sive **Loan:** Do not loan **Service:** Internationally **Photocopy:**
Yes

1517   Legnaro, Italy
University of Padova, Institute of Agricultural
    Entomology
Library
Via Romea, 16
35020 Legnaro, Padova
Phone: +39(49) 8272810 **WWW:** www.unipd.it

Non-English Name: Università degli Studi di Padova, Istituto di Entomologia Agraria, Biblioteca **Founded:** 1951
Type: Government **Head:** Prof. Vincenzo Girolami *Phone:*
+39(49) 8272801 *Email:* ento@ipdunix.unipd.it **Staff:** 1
Prof. **Holdings:** 7,000 books 80 journals **Subjects:** Entomology, Zoology **Loan:** In country **Photocopy:** Yes

1518   Milan, Italy
University of Milan, Faculty of Agriculture
Library
Via Celoria 2
20133 Milan
Phone: +39(2) 58 35 22 80 **Fax:** +39(2) 266-6463 **Email:**
bib.agraria@unimi.it **WWW:** users.unimi.it/biblioteche/
agraria **OPAC:** opac.unimi.it

Non-English Name: Università degli Studi di Milano, Facoltà di Agraria, Biblioteca Centrale **Type:** Academic **Head:** Angelo Bozzola **Staff:** 1 Other **Holdings:** 10,500 books 100 journals **Language of Collection/Services:** Italian **Databases Used:** Comprehensive

1519   Milan, Italy
University of Milan, Faculty of Agriculture,
     Institute of Tree Cultivation
Molon Library
Via Celoria 2
20133 Milan
Phone: +39(2) 70 63 81 34 **Fax:** +39(2) 236-5302 **Email:** icami@unimi.it **WWW:** users.unimi.it/~agra/icami.html **OPAC:** opac.unimi.it

Non-English Name: Università degli Studi di Milano, Facoltà di Agraria, Istituto di Coltivazioni Arboree, Biblioteca "G. Molon" **Founded:** 1870 **Type:** Academic **Head:** Dr. Ilaria Mignani *Email:* icami@unimi.it *Phone:* +39(2) 70 60 01 65 **Staff:** 1 Other **Holdings:** 3,999 books 60 journals **Language of Collection/Services:** Italian **Subjects:** Horticulture **Specializations:** Fruit Cultures, Postharvest Technology, Viticulture **Databases Used:** Comprehensive **Loan:** Do not loan **Photocopy:** Yes

1520   Milan, Italy
University of Milan, Institute of Agricultural
     Engineering
Library
Via Celoria 2
20133 Milan
Phone: +23 69 14 1 **Fax:** +39(2) 23 69 14 99 **Email:** ingagr@mailserver.unimi.it **WWW:** users.unimi.it/~divbib /agraria/istituti.htm, users.unimi.it/~agra/ingag/ingag_uk. html **OPAC:** opac.unimi.it

Non-English Name: Università degli Studi di Milano, Istituto di Ingegneria Agraria (IIA), Biblioteca **Founded:** 1940 **Type:** Academic **Staff:** 1 Prof. **Holdings:** 4,300 books 70 journals **Subjects:** Agricultural Engineering, Energy, Farm Buildings, Farm Machinery **Loan:** Do not loan **Service:** Internationally **Photocopy:** Yes

1521   Milan, Italy
University of Milan, Institute of Plant Pathology
Library
Via Celoria 2
20133 Milan
Phone: +39(2) 23 69 22 46 **Fax:** +39(2) 70 63 12 87 **Email:** patoveg@mailserver.unimi.it **WWW:** users.unimi. it/~agra/patveg/patveg6.html **OPAC:** opac.unimi.it

Non-English Name: Università degli Studi di Milano, Istituto di Pathologia Vegetale (IPV), Biblioteca **Founded:** 1910 **Type:** Academic **Staff:** 1 Other **Holdings:** 2,536 books 40 journals **Subjects:** Bacteriology, Mycology, Pest Control, Plant Pathology, Virology **Loan:** Do not loan **Photocopy:** Yes

1522   Modena, Italy
Istituto Sperimentale Agronomico, Sezione di
     Modena (ISA)

Biblioteca
Viale Caduti in Guerra 134
41100 Modena
Phone: +39(59) 230454, 223853 **WWW:** www.inea.it/isa/ isa.html

Founded: 1871 **Type:** Government **Staff:** 1 Other **Holdings:** 14,000 books 80 journals **Subjects:** Botany, Enology **Loan:** Do not loan **Photocopy:** Yes

1523   Monterotondo Scalo, Italy
Animal Production Research Institute
Library
Via Salaria 31
00016 Monterotondo Scalo (Rome)
Phone: +37(6) 900901 **Fax:** +39(6) 906-1541 **Email:** isz@flashnet.it **WWW:** www.inea.it/isz/index.htm

Non-English Name: Istituto Sperimentale per la Zootecnia (ISZ), Biblioteca **Former Name:** Animal Husbandry Institute, Istituto Zootecnico **Founded:** 1924 **Type:** Government **Head:** Sig. Arduino Zappi *Phone:* +39(6) 900901 *Email:* isz@flashnet.it **Staff:** 1 Prof. 1 Other **Holdings:** 6,000 books 45 journals **Language of Collection/Services:** English, Italian / English, Italian **Subjects:** Animal Husbandry, Animal Physiology, Biotechnology, Feeding, Genetics, Nutrition, Veterinary Medicine **Loan:** Do not loan **Photocopy:** Yes

1524   Ozzano dell'Emilia, Italy
National Wildlife Institute
Library
Via Cà Fornacetta, 9
40064 Ozzano dell'Emilia, (Bologna)
Fax: +39(51) 796628

Non-English Name: Istituto Nazionale per la Fauna Selvatica (INFS), Biblioteca **Former Name:** Istituto Nazionale di Biologia della Selvaggina **Founded:** 1933 **Type:** Government **Head:** Dott. Alessandro Andreotti *Phone:* +39(51) 6512111 *Email:* infsands@iperbole.bologna.it **Staff:** 2 Prof. 1 Other **Holdings:** 9,000 books 800 journals **Language of Collection/Services:** Italian, English / Italian **Subjects:** Damage, Environment, Game Farming, Pesticides, Wildlife **Specializations:** Birds, Mammals **Databases Used:** Comprehensive **Loan:** In country **Photocopy:** Yes

1525   Palermo, Italy
Central Library of Sicilian Region
Via Vittorio Emanuele, 431
90100 Palermo
Phone: +39(91) 581602

Non-English Name: Biblioteca Centrale della Regione Siciliana (BCRS) **Former Name:** Biblioteca Nazionale **Founded:** 1792 **Type:** Government **Staff:** 25 Prof. 103 Other **Holdings:** 567,251 books 968 journals **Language of Collection/Services:** Italian/Italian **Subjects:** Agribusiness, Agricultural Economics, Agricultural Engineering, Biotechnology, Entomology, Farming, Fisheries, Food Sciences, Forestry, Horticulture, Plant Pathology, Soil Science, Veterinary Medicine, Water Resources **Loan:** Internationally **Service:** Internationally **Photocopy:** Yes

1526 Palermo, Italy
University of Palermo, Faculty of Agriculture
Central Library
Viale Delle Scienze
90128 Palermo

Phone: +39(91) 652-1086 **Fax:** +39(91) 481546 **WWW:**
www.unipa.it

Non-English Name: Università degli Studi di Palermo, Facoltà di Agraria, Biblioteca Centrale **Founded:** 1948 **Type:** Academic **Head:** Dr. Oliveri Domenico *Phone:* +39(91) 48-4257 **Staff:** 1 Other **Holdings:** 16,000 books 250 journals **Subjects:** Crops, Entomology, Horticulture, Plant Pathology **Loan:** Internationally **Photocopy:** Yes

1527 Parma, Italy
Parma Municipality
Agricultural Library "A. Bizzozero"
V.Lo S. Maria 5
43100 Parma PR

Fax: +39(521) 230085 **WWW:** www.commune.parma.it/index.htm **OPAC:** servernt.biblcom.unipr.it/h3/h3.exe/ase

Non-English Name: Comune di Parma, Biblioteca di Agricoltura "A. Bizzozero" **Type:** Public **Head:** Monica Allegri *Phone:* +39(521) 218584 **Staff:** 2 Prof. 2 Other **Holdings:** 17,000 books 400 journals **Language of Collection/Services:** Italian / Italian **Subjects:** Agribusiness, Agricultural Economics, Agriculture (History), Animal Husbandry, Entomology, Crops, Environment, Farming, Food Industry, Food Sciences, Forestry, Gardens, Horticulture, Veterinary Medicine **Databases Used:** Agricola **Service:** Internationally **Loan:** Internationally **Photocopy:** Yes

1528 Pavia, Italy
University of Pavia, Department of Animal
    Biology
Library
Piazza Botta, 9
27100 Pavia

Phone: +39(382) 506298 **Fax:** +39(382) 506290 **WWW:** www.unipv.it/webbio/welcome.htm **OPAC:** bibliopv.unipv.it/opac/ricerche.html

Non-English Name: Università degli Studi di Pavia, Dipartimeno di Biologia Animale, Biblioteca **Former Name:** Istituto di Zoologia "L. Spallanzani" **Founded:** 1860 **Type:** Academic **Head:** Prof. Giuseppe Gerzeli *Phone:* +39 (382) 506328 *Email:* anatcomp@ipv36.unipv.it **Staff:** 1 Prof. **Holdings:** 7,610 books 35 journals **Language of Collection/Services:** English/Italian **Subjects:** Insect Pests, Entomology, Fisheries, Genetics, Wildlife Conservation **Loan:** Inhouse **Service:** Inhouse **Photocopy:** Yes

1529 Perugia, Italy
University of Perugia, Faculty of Agriculture
Library
Borgo XX Giugno, 74
06121 Perugia

Phone: +39(75) 585-6004 **Fax:** +39(75) 583-7435 **Email:** bibagri1@ipguniv.unipg.it, bibagri2@ipguniv.unipg.it **WWW:** www.unipg.it **OPAC:** www.unipg.it/sbc/opac-dobis.html

Non-English Name: Università degli Studi di Perugia, Facoltà di Agraria, Biblioteca **Founded:** 1930 **Type:** Academic **Head:** Dott. ssa Giovanna Ascani Panella **Staff:** 1 Prof. **Holdings:** 4,000 books 40 journals **Language of Collection/Services:** Italian **Subjects:** Agricultural Development, Agricultural Economics, Education/Extension **Loan:** Inhouse **Photocopy:** Yes

1530 Portici, Italy
University of Naples, Faculty of Agriculture
Central Library
Via Università, 100, 1° piano
80055 Portici (Napoli)

Phone: +39(81) 775-4945 **Fax:** +39(81) 775-4945 **Email:** petricci@unina.it **WWW:** www.unina.it **OPAC:** sab.unina.it/biblio/infoAgra.html

Non-English Name: Università degli Studi di Napoli Frederico II, Facoltà di Agraria, Biblioteca Centrale **Former Name:** Regia Scuola Superiore d'Agricoltura **Founded:** 1872 **Type:** Academic **Head:** Olimpia Petriccione *Email:* petricci@unina.it **Staff:** 1 Prof. 3 Other **Holdings:** 65,000 books 3,130 journals **Language of Collection/Services:** Italian **Subjects:** Agricultural Economics, Agricultural Engineering, Animal Husbandry, Biotechnology, Crops, Food Sciences, Farming, Horticulture **Photocopy:** No **Loan:** In country

♦1531 Rome, Italy
Agricultural and Forest Research Center
Library
POB 9079 (Aurelio)
00100 Rome

Location: Via di Casalotti 300, 00166 Rome **Fax:** +39(6) 61563703

Non-English Name: Centro di Sperimentazione Agricola e Forestale (CSAF), Biblioteca **Founded:** 1953 **Type:** Public **Head:** Dr. Pietro R. Venanzetti *Phone:* +39(6) 61560241 **Staff:** 1 Prof. 4 Other **Holdings:** 33,000 books 542 journals **Subjects:** Forestry **Language of Collection/Services:** English/Italian **Loan:** Inhouse **Service:** Inhouse **Photocopy:** No

1532 Rome, Italy
Experimental Institute for Cereal Research
Library
Via Cassia 176
00191 Rome

Phone: +39(6) 3295705 **Fax:** +39(6) 36306022 **WWW:** www.inea.it/isc/indice.htm

Non-English Name: Istituto Sperimentale per la Cerealicoltura (ISC), Biblioteca **Founded:** 1932 **Type:** Government **Staff:** 1 Other **Holdings:** 5,000 books 230 journals **Subjects:** Cereals **Loan:** Do not loan **Photocopy:** No

1533 Rome, Italy
Food and Agriculture Organization (FAO)
David Lubin Memorial Library
Via delle Terme di Caracalla
00186 Rome

Phone: +39(6) 522-53784 **Fax:** +39(6) 522-54049 **WWW:** www.fao.org **OPAC:** www.fao.org/library/dlubin/DlcatalE.htm

Non-English Name: Organisation pour l'Alimentation et l'Agriculture, Organización para la Agricultura y la Alimentación **Founded:** 1951 **Type:** International **Head:** Jane M. Wu *Phone:* +39(6) 522-53703 **Staff:** 12 Prof. 22 Other **Holdings:** 1,000,000 books 18,000 journals **Language of Collection/Services:** English, French, Spanish / English, French, Spanish **Subjects:** Agricultural Economics, Agroforestry, Agroindustrial Sector, Animal Production, Crop Production, Fisheries, Food Sciences, Forestry, Machinery, Nutrition, Rural Development, Statistics, Sustainability **Specializations:** Developing Countries **Databases Developed:** FAOBIB - FAO technical documents, reports, from 1945 to present and library monograph holdings since 1976; FAO-DOC - FAO Documentation **Databases Used:** Agricola; Agris; CABCD; FSTA **Loan:** Internationally, mainly with AGLINET members **Service:** Inhouse and internationally to AGLINET partners **Photocopy:** Yes

1534   Rome, Italy
Food and Agriculture Organization (FAO)
World Agricultural Information Centre
  (WAICENT)
Via delle Terme di Caracalla
00186 Rome

Phone: +39(6) **Fax:** +39(6) **Email:** waicent@fao.org **WWW:** www.fao.org/waicent

Non-English Name: Organisation pour l'Alimentation et l'Agriculture, Organización para la Agricultura y la Alimentación **Type:** International **Head:** Anton Mangstl *Phone:* +39(6) 5705-4049 *Email:* anton.mangstl@fao.org **Staff:** 40 Prof. 40 Other **Lanuage of Collection/Services:** English, French, Spanish, Arabic, Chinese **Subjects:** Comprehensive **Databases Developed:** AGRIS (International Information System for the Agricultural Sciences and Technology) - identifies worldwide literature dealing with all aspects of agriculture; available at www.fao.org/agris/default32.htm on Internet; AGROVOC - a comprehensive, multilingual thesaurus of agricultural terms - contains more than 15,000 descriptors for use in indexing and searching agricultural information systems; available on Internet at www.fao.org/agrovoc; CARIS (Current Agricultural Research Information System) - keyword searchable information for ongoing agricultural research projects in developing countries; available on Internet at www.fao.org/agris/default32.htm; DA-DIS (Domestic Animal Diversity Information System) - communication, information and tools to improve use and sustainable conservation of animal genetic resources; available on Internet at www.fao.org/dad-is; EMPRES (Emergency Prevention System for Transboundary Animal and Plant Pests and Diseases) - global early warning system for combating pests and diseases that threaten livestock, crops and food security; available on Internet at www.fao.org/EMPRES/default.htm; FAO Documentation Catalogue - used to locate and access the entire text of important FAO documents and publications; available on Internet at www.fao.org/catweb; FAOSTAT - the most complete international statistical database on food and agriculture, providing access to more than 1 million time-series records; available on

Internet at apps.fao.org; FIVIMS (Food Insecurity and Vulnerability Information and Mapping Systems) - networks of systems that assemble, analyse and disseminate information about the problem of food insecurity and vulnerability; available on Internet at www.fivims.net; GIEWS (Global Information and Early Warning System on Food and Agriculture) - information on food crops and markets worldwide; available on internet at www.fao.org/WAICENT/faoinfo/economic/giews/english/giewse.htm; GPPIS (Global Plant and Pest Information System); available at pppis.fao.org/ResInit.htm on Internet; INPhO (Information Network on Post-harvest Operations) - information system to assist in preventing the loss of millions of tonnes of cereals, roots, tubers, fruits and vegetables in developing countries caused by inadequate handling and storage, pest damage, and transport and marketing problems; available on Internet at www.fao.org/inpho; WIEWS (World Information and Early Warning System on Plant Genetic Resources) - information system on national programmes on conservation and utilization of plant genetic resources for food and agriculture; available on Internet at apps2.fao.org/wiews **Service:** Internationally

1535   Rome, Italy
Fruit Tree Research Institute
Alberto Pirovano Library
Ciampino Aeroporto
00040 Rome

Location: Via Fioranello 52, 00134 Rome **Phone:** +39(6) 793-4811 **Fax:** +39(6) 7934-0158 **WWW:** www.inea.it/isf/index.html

Non-English Name: Istituto Sperimentale Frutticoltura, Biblioteca Alberto Pirovano **Founded:** 1927 **Type:** Government **Head:** Carlo Fideghelli *Phone:* +39(6) 600048 **Staff:** 1 Other **Holdings:** 8,000 books 70 journals **Subjects:** Horticulture **Loan:** Do not loan **Service:** Inhouse **Photocopy:** Yes

1536   Rome, Italy
International Fund for Agricultural Development
  (IFAD)
Documents Centre
107 Via del Serafico
00142 Rome

Phone: +39(6) 5459-2218 **Fax:** +39(6) 504-3463 **Email:** documents-centre@ifad.org **WWW:** www.ifad.org

Non-English Name: Fondo Internazional di Sviluppo Agricolo **Type:** International **Head:** Carla Secchi *Phone:* +39(6) 5459-2307 *Email:* c.secchi@ifad.org **Staff:** 1 Prof. 8 Other **Holdings:** 15,000 books 600 journals **Language of Collection/Services:** English **Subjects:** Agriculture (Tropics), Agricultural Development, Agricultural Economics, Animal Husbandry, Biotechnology, Crops, Education/Extension, Farming, Fisheries, Food Sciences, Forestry, Water Resources **Specializations:** Developing Countries, Development, Economics **Loan:** Inhouse and FAO/WFP **Service:** In country **Photocopy:** Yes

1537   Rome, Italy
International Plant Genetic Resources Institute
  (IPGRI)
HQ Library
Via delle Sette Chiese 142

00145 Rome
Phone: +39(6) 5189-2219 **Fax:** +39(6) 575-0309 **WWW:** www.cgiar.org/ipgri

Former Name: International Board for Plant Genetic Resources (IBPGR) **Founded:** 1990 **Type:** International **Head:** Elizabeth Goldberg *Email:* e.goldberg@cgiar.org *Phone:* +39(6) 5189-2237 **Staff:** 2 Prof. .5 Other **Holdings:** 5,000 books 40 journals **Language of Collection/Services:** English / English **Subjects:** Genetics, Plant Breeding **Specializations:** Plant Genetic Resources **Databases Developed:** IPGRI research and collecting mission reports **Databases Used:** Agricola; Agris; PlantGeneCD; TROPAG & RURAL **Loan:** Inhouse **Service:** Inhouse **Photocopy:** Yes

1538   Rome, Italy
Istituto per Studi, Recerche, e Informazioni sul
Mercato Agricolo (ISMEA)
Via Cornelio Celso 6
00187 Rome
Phone: +39(6) 8556-1280 **Fax:** +39(6) 4225-0613 **WWW:** www.ismea.it

Networks: AGRIS

1539   Rome, Italy
National Institute for Agricultural Economics
Library
Via Barberini 36
00187 Rome
Phone: +39(6) 4878561 **Fax:** +39(6) 4741984 **Email:** inea@inea.it **WWW:** www.inea.it

Non-English Name: Istituto Nazionale di Economia Agraria (INEA), Biblioteca **Founded:** 1928 **Type:** Government **Head:** Guido Bonati *Email:* bonati@inea.it *Phone:* +39(6) 47856520 **Staff:** 2 Prof. 1 Other **Holdings:** 26,000 books 300 journals **Language of Collection/Services:** Italian **Subjects:** Agribusiness, Agricultural Development, Agricultural Economics, Agricultural Policy, Statistics **Databases Developed:** RICA ITALIA - Italian farm accounting data network **Databases Used:** Agris; CABCD **Photocopy:** Yes **Loan:** Inhouse **Service:** Internationally

1540   Rovigo, Italy
Istituto Sperimentale per le Colture Industriali
(ISCI)
Bieticoltura-Rovigo
Via Amendola 82
45100 Rovigo
Fax: +39(425) 34681 **Email:** isciro@tecna.it **WWW:** www.inea.it/isci/ISCI_p1.htm

Former Name: Stazione Sperimentale di Bieticoltura **Type:** Government **Founded:** 1912 **Head:** E. Biancardi *Phone:* +39(425) 360113 *Email:* isciro@tecna.it **Staff:** 1 Prof. 1 Other **Holdings:** 20,000 books 54 journals **Language of Collection/Services:** Italian, English/Italian **Wubjects:** **Loan:** Do not loan **Photocopy:** Yes

1541   San Michele all'Adige, Italy
National Research Council, Wood Technology
Institute
Documentation Service - Library

Via Biasi, 75
38010 San Michele all'Adige (Trent)
Location: Via Biasi, 75 **Phone:** +39(461) 660222 **Fax:** +39(461) 650045 **Email:** biblio2@itl.tn.cnr.it **WWW:** www.itl.tn.cnr.it

Non-English Name: Consiglio Nazionale delle Ricerche, Instituto per la Tecnologia del Legno (CNR, ITL), Servizio Documentazione-Biblioteca **Founded:** 1981 **Type:** Government **Head:** Emanuela Rachello *Phone:* +39(461) 660222 *Email:* rachello@itl.tn.cnr.it **Staff:** 1 Prof. **Holdings:** 13,000 books 260 journals **Language of Collection/Services:** Italian, English, French, German **Subjects:** Forestry **Specializations:** Wood Technology **Databases Used:** Comprehensive **Loan:** Do not loan **Service:** Internationally **Photocopy:** Yes

1542   Sassari, Italy
University of Sassari, Agriculture Faculty
Main Library
Via E. De Nicola, 1
07100 Sassari
Phone: +39(79) 229205 **Fax:** +39(79) 229206 **WWW:** www.uniss.it

Non-English Name: Università degli Studi di Sassari, Facoltà di Agraria, Biblioteca Centrale **Founded:** 1979 **Type:** Academic **Head:** Prof. Sandro Dettori, Scientific Director; Dott. ssa Velia Pisanu, Co-ordinator *Phone:* +39(79) 218023 **Staff:** 1 Prof. 1 Other **Holdings:** 3,600 books 80 journals **Subjects:** Agricultural Economics, Agricultural Engineering, Agricultural Policy, Agronomy, Aquaculture, Animal Husbandry, Biotechnology, Climatology, Drainage, Ecology, Food Technology, Genetics, Horticulture, Irrigation, Machinery, Plants, Zoology **Loan:** Do not loan **Photocopy:** No

1543   Scafati, Italy
Istituto Sperimentale per il Tabacco (IST)
Biblioteca
Via Pasquale Vitiello, 66
84018 Scafati (Salerno)
Phone: +39(81) 856-86311 **Fax:** +39(81) 8580-6206 **Email:** istab@uniserv.uniplan.it **WWW:** www.inea.it/ist/home.htm

Founded: 1895 **Type:** Government **Staff:** 1 Other **Holdings:** 3,500 books **Subjects:** Crops, Genetics, Plant Pathology, Plant Breeding **Loan:** Do not loan **Photocopy:** No

1544   Torino, Italy
Experimental Institute for Plant Nutrition,
Operative Division of Turin
Library
Via Ormea 47
10125 Torino
Phone: +39(11) 6507026 **Fax:** +39(11) 6692995 **WWW:** www.isnp.it

Non-English Name: Istituto Sperimentale per la Nutrizione delle Piante, Sezione Operative Periferica di Torino (ISNP), Biblioteca **Founded:** 1875 **Type:** Government **Head:** Prof. Augusto Marchesini *Phone:* +39(11) 6504090 **Staff:** 1 Other **Holdings:** 20,000 books 20 journals **Subjects:** Agricultural Sciences, Biochemistry, Plant Nutrition, Plant Physiology

Specializations: Pharmacology (History - 1830-) **Loan:** Do not loan **Photocopy:** No

1545   Torino, Italy
University of Turin, Faculty of Agronomy and
    Forestry
Central Library
Via P. Giuria 15
10126 Torino

Phone: +39(11) 650-8789 **Fax:** +39(11) 670-8557 **WWW:** www.agraria.unito.it **OPAC:** hal9000.cisi.unito.it/wf/ BIBLIOTECH/Reti-di-OP/index.htm

Non-English Name: Università degli Studi di Torino, Facoltà di Scienze Agrarie, Biblioteca Centrale **Founded:** 1954 **Type:** Academic **Head:** Prof. Italo Currado *Phone:* +39(11) 670-8529 **Staff:** 1 Prof. **Holdings:** 3,000 books 190 journals **Loan:** Do not loan **Photocopy:** Yes

1546   Trieste, Italy
Municipal Museum of Natural History
Library
Piazza A. Hortis 4
34123 Trieste

Phone: +39(40) 301821 **Fax:** +39(40) 302563

Non-English Name: Museo Civico di Storia Naturale, Biblioteca **Founded:** 1848 **Type:** Government **Head:** Dr. Sergio Dolce *Phone:* +39(40) 301821 **Staff:** 1 Prof. 3 Other **Holdings:** 12,000 books 100 journals **Language of Collection/Services:** Italian/Italian **Subjects:** Comprehensive **Specializations:** Entomology **Loan:** Do not loan **Service:** Inhouse

1547   Valenzano, Italy
International Center for Advanced Mediterranean
    Agronomic Studies, Mediterranean
    Agronomic Institute of Bari
Centre for Documentation and Scientific
    Information
Via Ceglie 9
89919 Valenzano, Bari

Phone: +39(80) 4606-111 **Fax:** +39(80) 4606-206 **WWW:** www.iamb.it **OPAC:** netserver.iamb.it/library/search.asp

Non-English Name: Centre International de Hautes Etudes Agronomiques Méditerranéennes, Institut Agronomique Méditerranéen de Bari (CIHEAM, IAMB), Centre de Documentation et d'Information Scientifique **Founded:** 1964 **Type:** Research **Holdings:** 11,000 books 100 journals **Language of Collection/Services:** French, English, Italian/ French, English, Italian **Subjects:** Integrated Pest Management, Irrigated Farming, Land Resources, Organic Farming, Water Resources **Specializations:** Fruit Crops (Mediterranean Countries) **Databases Used:** SCI

1548   Vercelli, Italy
Experimental Institute of Cereal Crops
Experimental Section of Rice-Growing
Strada Starale per Torino km 2,5
13100 Vercelli

Fax: +39(161) 294206 **Email:** isc.rice@iol.it **WWW:** www.inea.it/isc/Vercelli1.htm

Non-English Name: Istituto Sperimentale per la Cerealicoltura (ISC), Sezione Specializzata per la Risicoltura **Founded:** 1908 **Type:** Government **Head:** Dr. Salvatore Russo *Phone:* +39(161) 391134, 391148 **Staff:** 1 Other **Holdings:** 5,000 books 17 journals **Subjects:** Agriculture (History), Biology, Chemistry, Hydrology **Specializations:** Rice **Loan:** Do not loan **Photocopy:** Yes

Jamaica

1549   Kingston, Jamaica
Coconut Industry Board (CIB)
Library
18 Waterloo Road
PB 204
Kingston 10

Phone: +1(876) 926-1770 **Fax:** +1(876) 906-1045 **Email:** cocomax@cwjamaica.com

Founded: 1960 **Holdings:** 134 books 52 journals **Subjects:** Agricultural Chemicals, Coconuts, Herbicides, Industry, Oil Plants, Plant Diseases, Plants, Soil Management

1550   Kingston, Jamaica
Coffee Industry Board (CIB)
Library
PO Box 508
Kingston

Location: Marcus Garvey Drive **Phone:** +1(876) 923-5850 /9 **Fax:** +1(876) 923-7587 **WWW:** www.jamaicancoffee. gov.jm **Email:** coffeeboard@jamaicancoffee.gov.jm

Founded: 1950 **Type:** Business **Language of Collection/ Services:** English **Subjects:** Agricultural Development, Extension, Crop Production, Marketing **Specializations:** Coffee **Photocopy:** Yes

1551   Kingston, Jamaica
Ministry of Agriculture and Mining
National Agricultural Information Centre
PO Box 480
K.6 Kingston

Location: 193 Old Hope Road **Phone:** +1(876) 927-1732, 927-1894 **Fax:** +1(876) 977-0580

Former Name: Ministry of Agriculture and Lands (MAL), Department of Public Gardens and Plantations, Department of Agriculture **Founded:** 1876 **Type:** Government **Head:** Trevor Wong *Phone:* +1(876) 977-0580 **Staff:** 3 Prof. 6 Other **Holdings:** 60,000 books 300 journals **Language of Collection/Services:** English / English **Subjects:** Agriculture (Tropics) **Networks:** AGRIS **Loan:** Internationally **Service:** Internationally **Photocopy:** Yes

♦**1552   Mandeville, Jamaica**
Sugar Industry Authority, Sugar Industry Research
    Institute (SIA, SIRI)
Library
Kendal Road
Mandeville

Phone: +1(876) 962-2241, 962-1287 **Fax:** +1(876) 962-1288

Founded: 1973 **Head:** D.W. Little *Phone:* +1(876) 962-2241, 962-1287 **Staff:** 1 Other **Holdings:** 527 books 120 journals **Language of Collection/Services:** English/English **Subjects:** Crop Production, Plant Protection, Sugarcane, Sugar Industry, Water Management **Loan:** Inhouse **Service:** Inhouse **Photocopy:** Yes

♦**1553   Port Antonio, Jamaica**
Ministry of Education, College of Agriculture
Library
PB 170
Passley Gardens
Port Antonio
Fax: +1(876) 993-2208

Founded: 1982 **Type:** Government **Head:** Mrs. Caseta Nelson *Phone:* +1(876) 993-2468 **Holdings:** 10,000 books 50 journals **Staff:** 1 Prof. 3 Other **Subjects:** Agricultural Engineering, Animal Production, Crop Production, Food Technology, Rural Sociology **Photocopy:** Yes

Japan

Aichi

1554   Nagakute, Aichi, Japan
Aichi Prefectural Agricultural Research Center
Library
1-1 Sagamine, Yazako
Nagakute, Aichi, Aichi 480-1193
Phone: +81(561) 62-0085 **Fax:** +81(561) 63-0815 **Email:** admin@agri-rc.pref.aichi.jp

Founded: 1967 **Type:** Government **Head:** Hidetoshi Goto *Phone:* +81(561) 62-0085 **Staff:** 1 Prof. **Holdings:** 10,700 books 136 journals **Language of Collection/Services:** Japanese / Japanese **Subjects:** Agricultural Economics, Agricultural Engineering, Crops, Horticulture, Plant Pathology, Soil **Networks:** NACSIS **Databases Used:** Agris; JASI **Loan:** Inhouse **Service:** Inhouse **Photocopy:** Yes

1555   Nagoya, Aichi, Japan
Meijo University (MU)
Library
1-501 Shiogamaguchi, Tempaku
Nagoya, Aichi 468-8502
Phone: +81(52) 832-1151 ext 6555 **Fax:** +81(52) 833-6046 **Email:** library@meijo-u.ac.jp **WWW:** www.meijo-u.ac.jp:10070/tosho/index.html

Former Name: Library of Faculty of Agriculture, Meijo University **Founded:** 1950 **Type:** Academic **Head:** Minoru Hashimoto *Email:* uldirect@meijo-u.ac.jp *Phone:* +81(52) 832-1151 ext 6500 **Staff:** 31 Prof. 21 Other **Holdings:** 761,673 books 7,484 journals **Language of Collection/Services:** Japanese / Japanese **Networks:** NACSIS **Subjects:** Comprehensive **Loan:** Internationally **Service:** Internationally **Photocopy:** Yes

1556   Nagoya, Aichi, Japan
Nagoya University, School of Agricultural
    Sciences
Library
Furo, Chikusa
Nagoya, Aichi 464-8601
Phone: +81(52) 789-4975 **Fax:** +81(52) 789-4012 **Email:** library@agr.nagoya-u.ac.jp **WWW:** www.agr.nagoya-u.ac.jp **OPAC:** www.nul.nagoya-u.ac.jp

Founded: 1952 **Type:** Academic **Staff:** 5 Prof. 2 Other **Holdings:** 118,990 books 694 journals **Language of Collection/Services:** Japanese/Japanese **Subjects:** Comprehensive **Networks:** NACSIS **Databases Used:** Comprehensive **Loan:** In country **Service:** In country **Photocopy:** Yes

Akita

1557   Akita, Akita, Japan
Akita Agricultural Experiment Station
Library and Information Section
111 Konakajima, Niida
Akita, Akita 010-1426
Phone: +81(188) 39-2121

Founded: 1891 **Type:** Government **Head:** Hiroshi Naganoma **Staff:** 1 Prof. **Holdings:** 11,500 books 25 journals **Language of Collection/Services:** Japanese / Japanese **Subjects:** Farm Management, Fertilizers, Horticulture, Insect Control, Plant Diseases, Rice, Soil Science **Loan:** Do not loan **Service:** Inhouse **Photocopy:** Yes

Aomori

1558   Hirosaki, Aomori, Japan
Hirosaki University (HU)
Library
3 Bunkyo
Hirosaki, Aomori 036
Phone: +81(172) 36-2111 ext 3187 **Fax:** +81(172) 34-7034 **WWW:** www.hirosaki-u.ac.jp

Founded: 1949 **Type:** Academic, Government **Head:** Professor Kunio Matsubara *Phone:* +81(172) 36-2111 **Staff:** 14 Prof. 8 Other **Holdings:** 589,917 books 4,203 journals **Language of Collection/Services:** Japanese/Japanese **Subjects:** Agribusiness, Agricultural Development, Agricultural Economics, Agricultural Engineering, Animal Husbandry, Biotechnology, Entomology, Horticulture, Plant Pathology, Crops, Plants, Soil Science **Loan:** In country **Service:** In country **Photocopy:** Yes

1559   Kuroishi, Aomori, Japan
Aomori Apple Experiment Station
Library
24 Fukutami
Kuroishi, Aomori 036-0332
Fax: +81(172) 52-5934

Founded: 1931 **Type:** Academic **Head:** Masateru Yamada *Phone:* +81(172) 52-2331 **Holdings:** 12,000 books 100 journals **Subjects:** Biotechnology, Entomology, Horticulture,

Plant Pathology, Soil Science **Loan:** Do not loan **Photocopy:** Yes

Chiba

1560   Chiba, Chiba, Japan
Chiba Prefectural Agricultural Experiment Station
Library
808 Daizenno, Midori
Chiba, Chiba 266-0006
Phone: +81(43) 291-0151 **Fax:** +81(43) 291-5319 **Email:** agrchiba@remus.dti.ne.jp

Founded: 1963 **Type:** Government **Head:** *Phone:* +81(43) 291-9985 **Staff:** 1 Prof. 2 Other **Holdings:** 60,000 books 70 journals **Language of Collection/Services:** Japanese / Japanese **Subjects:** Agricultural Research **Loan:** Do not loan **Photocopy:** Yes

1561   Matsudo, Chiba, Japan
Chiba University, Faculty of Horticulture
Library
648, Matsudo
Matsudo, Chiba 271
Phone: +81(473) 63-1490 **Fax:** +81(473) 66-2234 **WWW:** www.chiba-u.ac.jp

Founded: 1950 **Type:** Academic **Head:** Kazuya Hirano *Phone:* +81(473) 63-1221 **Staff:** 3 Prof. 1 Other **Holdings:** 77,630 books 1,289 journals **Language of Collection/Services:** Japanese / Japanese **Subjects:** Biology, Biochemistry, Economic Botany, Environmental Sciences, Landscape Architecture, Horticulture, Plant Biotechnology **Loan:** In country **Service:** In country **Photocopy:** Yes

Ehime

1562   Matsuyama, Ehime, Japan
Ehime University
Agricultural Library
3-5-7 Tarumi
Matsuyama, Ehime 790-8566
Phone: +81(89) 946-9914 **Fax:** +81(89) 947-2466 **Email:** agrlib@lib.ehime-u.ac.jp **WWW:** www.lib.ehime-u.ac.jp **OPAC:** opac.lib.ehime-u.ac.jp/ilis

Founded: 1954 **Type:** Academic **Head:** Teruo Henmi **Staff:** 2 Prof. 2 Other **Holdings:** 110,733 books 473 journals **Language of Collection/Services:** Japanese / Japanese **Subjects:** Comprehensive **Networks:** NACSIS **Databases Used:** Comprehensive **Loan:** In country **Service:** In country **Photocopy:** Yes

Fukuoka

1563   Fukuoka, Fukuoka, Japan
Kyushu University (KU)
Faculty of Agriculture
Library
6-10-1 Hakozaki
Higashi

Fukuoka, Fukuoka 812-8581
WWW: www.lib.kyushu-u.ac.jp/dep/agr/agrihp.html
OPAC: www.lib.kyushu-u.ac.jp/index-j.html

Former Name: Kyushu Imperial University **Founded:** 1921 **Type:** Academic **Head:** Professor Satoru Kuhara *Phone:* +81(92) 642-2817 *Email:* agri@lib.kyushu-u.ac.jp **Staff:** 5 Prof. 4 Other **Holdings:** 278,569 books 8,816 journals **Language of Collection/Services:** Japanese, English / Japanese **Subjects:** Agriculture (Tropics), Agricultural Chemistry, Agricultural Engineering, Agronomy, Animal Husbandry, Biological Control, Fisheries, Forestry, Forest Products, Food Sciences, Genetic Resources **Specializations:** Agricultural Economics, Entomology **Networks:** NACSIS **Databases Used:** Comprehensive **Loan:** In country **Service:** In country **Photocopy:** Yes

Fukushima

1564   Koriyama, Fukushima, Japan
Fukushima Prefecture Agricultural Experiment
Station (FAES)
Division of Research Planning and Information
(RPI)
20 Aza Wakamiyamae
Tomitamachi
Koriyama, Fukushima 963-8041
Phone: +81(249) 32-3020 **Fax:** +81(249) 31-3639

Founded: 1952 **Type:** Government **Head:** Mr. Kaoru Matsumoto *Phone:* +81(249) 32-3020 **Staff:** 2 Prof. 1 Other **Holdings:** 34,000 books 45 journals **Language of Collection/Services:** Japanese / Japanese **Loan:** Inhouse **Service:** Inhouse **Photocopy:** Yes

Gunma

1565   Azuma, Sawa, Gunma, Japan
Gunma Horticultural Experiment Station (GHES)
Library
Nishiobokata 493
Azuma, Sawa, Gunma 379-2224
Phone: +81(27) 62-1021 **Fax:** +81(27) 62-1021

Founded: 1970 **Type:** Government **Head:** Kinzoh Tsukui *Phone:* +81(370) 62-1021 **Staff:** 6 Other **Holdings:** 7,000 books 90 journals **Language of Collection/Services:** Japanese/Japanese **Subjects:** Horticulture **Loan:** Inhouse **Service:** Inhouse **Photocopy:** Yes

1566   Maebashi, Gunma, Japan
Gunma Agricultural Experiment Station
Library
1251 Egi
Maebashi, Gunma 371-0002
Phone: +81(27) 269-9121 **Fax:** +81(27) 269-9124

Former Name: Gunma Agricultural Research Center **Type:** Government **Founded:** 1983 **Head:** Ichio Senbongi *Phone:* +81(27) 269-9121 **Holdings:** 2,500 books 30 journals **Language of Collection/Services:** Japanese / Japanese **Loan:** In country **Photocopy:** Yes

Hiroshima

1567   Fukuyama, Hiroshima, Japan
Ministry of Agriculture, Forestry and Fisheries,
  Chugoku National Agricultural Experiment
  Station (MAFF)
Library and Documentation Section
6-12-1 Nishifukatu
Fukuyama, Hiroshima 721-8514
Phone: +81(849) 23-4100 **Fax:** +81(849) 24-7893 **WWW:**
iiss.cgk.affrc.go.jp

Founded: 1960 **Type:** Government **Head:** Nobumasa
Teraue *Email:* teraue1@cgk.affrc.go.jp *Phone:* +81(849)
23-4100 **Staff:** 1 Prof. 2 Other **Holdings:** 72,991 books
2,745 journals **Language of Collection/Services:** Japanese/
Japanese **Subjects:** Agricultural Economics, Animal Hus-
bandry, Entomology, Farming, Food Sciences, Meat and
Livestock Industry, Plant Pathology, Soil Science **Special-
izations:** Biotechnology **Networks:** NACSIS **Databases
Used:** Comprehensive **Loan:** Do not loan **Service:** Inhouse
Photocopy: Yes

1568   Higashi-Hiroshima, Hiroshima, Japan
Hiroshima University Library (HUL)
East Library (EL)
Kagamiyama 1-4-5
Higashi-Hiroshima, Hiroshima 732-8512
Phone: +81(824) 24-6226 **Fax:** +81(824) 24-6222 **Email:**
t-jservice-higashi@bur.hiroshima-u.ac.jp **WWW:** www.
lib.hiroshima-u.ac.jp **OPAC:** www.cat.op.nacsis.ac.jp

Founded: 1949 **Type:** Academic **Head:** Kunio Ito *Phone:*
+81(824) 24-6210 **Staff:** 2 Prof. 2 Other **Holdings:** 309,110
books 8,701 journals **Language of Collection/Services:**
Japanese, English / Japanese, English **Subjects:** Comprehensive **Networks:** NACSIS **Databases Used:** Comprehensive
Loan: In country **Service:** Internationally **Photocopy:** Yes

Hokkaido

1569   Abashiri, Hokkaido, Japan
Tokyo University of Agriculture, Faculty of
  Bioindustry
Library
196 Yasaka
Abashiri, Hokkaido 099-2493
Phone: +81(152) 48-3818 **Fax:** +81(152) 48-2263 **Email:**
k-yamamo@bioindustry.nodai.ac.jp

Founded: 1989 **Type:** Academic **Head:** Ren Kuwabara
Phone: +81(152) 48-3827 **Staff:** 2 Prof. 2 Other **Holdings:**
750,000 books 1,200 journals **Language of Collection/Ser-
vices:** Japanese / Japanese **Subjects:** Agricultural Economics, Animal Husbandry, Biotechnology, Crops, Farming,
Fisheries, Food Sciences, Forestry, Plant Pathology, Plants,
Soil, Veterinary Medicine **Networks:** NACSIS **Databases
Used:** Agricola **Loan:** In country **Service:** In country **Photocopy:** Yes

1570   Ebetsu, Hokkaido, Japan
Rakuno Gakuen University (RGU)

Library
582 Bunkyodai, Midorimachi
Ebetsu, Hokkaido 069-0851
Phone: +81(11) 386-1111 **Fax:** +81(11) 386-4038 **Email:**
rg-tosho@rakuno.ac.jp **WWW:** library.rakuno.ac.jp
OPAC: opac.rakuno.ac.jp

Former Name: College of Dairying **Founded:** 1950 **Type:**
Academic **Head:** Katsuhiro Yamamoto *Phone:* +81(11)
386-1111 *Email:* yamamoto@rakuno.ac.jp **Staff:** 10 Prof.
10 Other **Holdings:** 240,000 books 2,700 journals **Language of Collection/Services:** Japanese / Japanese **Subjects:** Agricultural Economics, Animal Husbandry, Dairy
Science, Veterinary Medicine **Networks:** NACSIS; OCLC
Databases Used: Comprehensive **Loan:** Among Hokkaido
universities **Service:** In country **Photocopy:** Yes

1571   Kunneppu, Toro, Hokkaido, Japan
Hokkaido Prefectural Kitami Agricultural
  Experiment Station
Library
52 Aza-Yayoi
Kunneppu, Toro, Hokkaido 099-14
Fax: +81(157) 47-2774

Founded: 1950 **Type:** Government **Head:** Dr. Takashi
Sanbuichi *Phone:* +81(157) 47-2146 **Staff:** 12 Other **Holdings:** 4,168 books 79 journals **Language of Collection/Ser-
vices:** Japanese / Japanese **Subjects:** Crops, Entomology,
Horticulture, Plant Breeding, Plant Nutrition, Plant Pathology, Soil Science **Loan:** Do not loan **Photocopy:** No

1572   Kushiro, Hokkaido, Japan
Ministry of Agriculture, Forestry and Fisheries,
  Hokkaido National Fisheries Research
  Institute (MAFF, HNFRI)
Research, Planning and Coordination Section
  Library
116, Katsurakoi
Kushiro, Hokkaido 085
Phone: +81(54) 91-9136 **Fax:** +81(54) 91-9355 **WWW:**
ss.hnf.affrc.go.jp

Former Name: Hokkaido Regional Fisheries Research Laboratory **Type:** Government **Head:** Yoshikazu Nakamura
Phone: +81(54) 91-9136 *Email:* yoshinak@hnf.affrc.go.jp
Staff: 2 Prof. 1 Other **Holdings:** 30,000 books 74 journals
Language of Collection/Services: Japanese / Japanese **Subjects:** Water Resources **Specializations:** Fisheries **Loan:** In
country **Service:** In country **Photocopy:** Yes

1573   Naganuma, Yuubari, Hokkaido, Japan
Hokkaido Central Agricultural Experiment Station
  (HAGRES)
Research Planning Coordination Office
Information Section
Naganuma, Yuubari, Hokkaido 069-1395

Founded: 1964 **Type:** Government **Head:** Hiroyuki Shiga
Email: shigahy@agri.pref.hokkaido.jp *Phone:* +81(1238) 9-
2001 **Staff:** 1 Prof. 3 Other **Holdings:** 25,000 books 1,200
journals **Language of Collection/Services:** Japanese / Japanese **Subjects:** Biotechnology, Crops, Entomology, Extension, Farm Machinery, Farm Management, Plant Pathology,

Soil **Databases Used:** CABCD **Loan:** Inhouse **Service:** Inhouse **Photocopy:** Yes

1574   Obihiro, Hokkaido, Japan
         Obihiro University of Agriculture and Veterinary
              Medicine
         University Library
         Inada
         Obihiro, Hokkaido 080-8555
Phone: +81(155) 49-5332 **Fax:** +81(155) 49-5349 **WWW:**
www.obihiro.ac.jp

Founded: 1949 **Type:** Academic **Head:** Takashi Kawabata
Staff: 7 Prof. 3 Other **Holdings:** 163,856 books 4,685 journals **Language of Collection/Services:** Japanese / Japanese
Subjects: Veterinary Science **Networks:** NACSIS **Databases Used:** Biosis; CABCD **Loan:** In country **Service:** In country **Photocopy:** Yes

1575   Sapporo, Hokkaido, Japan
         Hokkaido University, Faculty of Agriculture
         Library
         Nishi 9-chome, Kita 9-jo, Kita
         Sapporo, Hokkaido 060-8589
Phone: +81(11) 716-2111 **WWW:** www.lib.hokudai.ac.jp
OPAC: www.lib.hokudai.ac.jp/opac

Founded: 1957 **Type:** Academic **Staff:** 8 Prof. **Holdings:**
282,174 books 6,096 journals **Language of Collection/Services:** Japanese / Japanese **Subjects:** Comprehensive **Networks:** NACSIS **Databases Used:** Comprehensive **Loan:** In country **Service:** In country **Photocopy:** Yes

1576   Sapporo, Hokkaido, Japan
         Ministry of Agriculture, Forestry and Fisheries,
              Hokkaido National Agricultural Experiment
              Station (MAFF)
         Library and Information Section
         1 Hitsujigaoka, Toyohira
         Sapporo, Hokkaido 062-8555
Phone: +81(11) 857-9260 **Fax:** +81(11) 859-2178 **Email:**
rf@cryo.affrc.go.jp **WWW:** www.cryo.affrc.go.jp

Founded: 1929 **Type:** Government **Head:** Koichi Ohashi
Phone: +81(11) 857-9260 **Staff:** 4 Prof. 2 Other **Holdings:**
54,150 books 247 journals **Language of Collection/Services:** Japanese, English / Japanese **Subjects:** Agricultural Economics, Agricultural Engineering, Animal Husbandry, Biotechnology, Crops, Entomology, Fodder Crops, Grasslands, Horticulture, Plant Pathology, Soil Science **Networks:** NACSIS **Databases Used:** Agris; Biosis; CABCD
Loan: Inhouse **Service:** In country **Photocopy:** Yes

1577   Shintoku, Kamikawa, Hokkaido, Japan
         Hokkaido Prefectural Shintoku Animal Husbandry
              Experiment Station
         Library
         40 West 4 sen
         Shintoku, Kamikawa, Hokkaido 081-0038
Phone: +81(1566) 4-5321 **Fax:** +81(1566) 9-5118

Type: Government **Head:** Tatsushi Tsukamoto1 *Email:*
t.tsukamoto@agri.pref.hokkaido.jp *Phone:* +81(1566) 4532
Staff: 1.5 Prof. 10 Other **Holdings:** 101 journals **Language**

of Collection/Services: Japanese / Japanese **Subjects:** Animal Husbandry, Animal Wastes, Biotechnology, Grasses, Veterinary Medicine, Waste Utilization **Loan:** In country **Service:** In country **Photocopy:** Yes

1578   Takikawa, Hokkaido, Japan
         Hokkaido Plant Genetic Resource Center
              (HPGRC)
         Improvement and Utilization Section
         Minamani-Takinokawa 363-2
         Takikawa, Hokkaido 073-0013
WWW: www.agri.pref.hokkaido.jp

Founded: 1986 **Type:** Government **Head:** Hiroshi Sasaki
Phone: +81(125) 23-3195 **Staff:** .5 Other **Holdings:** 1,000 books 60 journals **Language of Collection/Services:** Japanese / Japanese **Subjects:** Crops **Specializations:** Plant Genetic Resources **Databases Developed:** Plant Genetic Resources database - available inhouse **Loan:** Inhouse **Service:** Inhouse **Photocopy:** Yes

1579   Takikawa, Hokkaido, Japan
         Takikawa Animal Experiment Station (TAESH)
         Library
         735 Higashitakikawa
         Takikawa, Hokkaido 073-0026
Phone: +81(125) 28-2211 **Fax:** +81(125) 28-2165

Founded: 1962 **Type:** Government **Head:** Keiichi Takaishi
Phone: +81(125) 28-2211 **Staff:** 1 Other **Holdings:** 5,000 books 230 journals **Language of Collection/Services:** Japanese / Japanese **Subjects:** Biotechnology, Plants, Veterinary Medicine **Specializations:** Animal Husbandry **Loan:** Inhouse **Service:** Inhouse **Photocopy:** No

Hyogo

1580   Kobe, Hyogo, Japan
         Kobe University
         Natural Sciences Library
         Rokkodai, Nada
         Kobe, Hyogo 657
Phone: +81(78) 881-7865 **WWW:** www.kobe-u.ac.jp

Founded: 1984 **Type:** Academic **Head:** Takayama Toshihiro *Phone:* +81(78) 881-1212 **Staff:** 14 Prof. 7 Other **Holdings:** 45,000 books 950 journals **Subjects:** Agricultural Chemistry, Agricultural Engineering, Horticulture, Plant Protection **Loan:** Do not loan **Photocopy:** Yes

1581   Kobe, Hyogo, Japan
         Konan University
         Biological Branch Library
         8-9-1 Okamoto, Higashinada
         Kobe, Hyogo
WWW: www.konan-u.ac.jp

Founded: 1918 **Head:** Isamu Kurosaki *Phone:* +81(78) 431-4341 **Staff:** 15 Prof. 13 Other **Subjects:** Biology, Genetics **Photocopy:** Yes

Ibaraki

1582   Ami, Inashiki, Ibaraki, Japan
Ibaraki University, Faculty of Agriculture
Library
3-21-1 Chuo
Ami, Inashiki, Ibaraki 300-0393
Phone: +81(298) 88-8531 **Fax:** +81(298) 88-8533 **Email:** ng01958@jim.ibaraki.ac.jp **WWW:** www.lib.ibaraki.ac.jp

Founded: 1952 **Type:** Academic **Head:** Prof. Masaki Takeharu **Staff:** 2 Prof. 1 Other **Holdings:** 77,763 books 1,641 journals **Language of Collection/Services:** Japanese, English/Japanese **Subjects:** Agricultural Development, Agricultural Economics, Agricultural Engineering, Biotechnology, Crops, Entomology, Food Sciences, Horticulture, Plant Pathology, Plants, Soil **Networks:** NACSIS **Databases Used:** Agricola; Agris **Loan:** In country **Service:** In country **Photocopy:** Yes

1583   Inashiki, Ibaraki, Japan
Ministry of Agriculture, Forestry and Fisheries, Forestry and Forest Products Research Institute (MAFF, FFPRI)
Library
PO Box 16, Tsukuba Norin Kenkyu Danchi-Nai
Inashiki, Ibaraki 305
Phone: +81(298) 73-3211 ext 237 **Fax:** +81(298) 74-8507 **Email:** ref@ffpri.affrc.go.jp **WWW:** ss.ffpri.affrc.go.jp

Founded: 1905 **Type:** Government **Head:** Koichi Natsui *Phone:* +81(298) 73-3211 ext 236 *Email:* ref@ffpri.affrc.go.jp **Staff:** 3 Prof. 4 Other **Holdings:** 202,000 books 1,600 journals **Subjects:** Forest Products, Forestry **Loan:** Do not loan **Service:** Internationally **Photocopy:** Yes

1584   Kashima, Ibaraki, Japan
Ministry of Agriculture, Forestry and Fisheries, Fisheries Agency of Japan, National Research Institute of Fisheries Engineering (MAFF, NRIFE)
Research Planning and Coordination Division
Ebidai, Hasaki
Kashima, Ibaraki 314-0421
Phone: +81(479) 44-5927 **Fax:** +81(479) 44-1875 **WWW:** www.nrife.affrc.go.jp

Founded: 1979 **Type:** Government **Head:** Kenichi Ishizima *Phone:* +81(479) 44-5927 *Email:* ishizima@nrife.affrc.go.jp **Staff:** 1 Prof. 1 Other **Holdings:** 90 journals **Language of Collection/Services:** Japanese/Japanese **Subjects:** Fisheries **Specializations:** Fishery Engineering **Networks:** NACSIS **Loan:** Inhouse **Service:** In country **Photocopy:** Yes

1585   Naka, Ibaraki, Japan
Ibaraki Prefectural Government Forestry Technology Center (IPGFTC)
Library
4692, To
Naka
Naka, Ibaraki 311-0122
Phone: +81(29) 298-0257 **Fax:** +81(29) 295-1325 **Email:** ibafor-c@net-ibaraki.ne.jp **WWW:** www.net-ibaraki.ne.jp

Former Name: Ibaraki Prefectural Forest Experiment Station (IFES) **Founded:** 1964 **Type:** Government **Head:** Sadao Ohtsu *Email:* ibafor-c@net-ibaraki.ne.jp *Phone:* +81(29) 298-0257 **Staff:** 25 Other **Holdings:** 45,000 books 25 journals **Language of Collection/Services:** Japanese / Japanese **Subjects:** Farming, Plants **Specializations:** Forestry **Loan:** Inhouse **Service:** Inhouse **Photocopy:** Yes

1586   Ohmiya, Naka, Ibaraki, Japan
Ministry of Agriculture, Forestry and Fisheries, National Institute of Agrobiological Resources, Institute of Radiation Breeding (MAFF, NIAR, IRB)
Library
PO Box 3
Ohmiya, Naka, Ibaraki 319-2293
Phone: +81(2955) 2-1138 ext 44 **Fax:** +81(2955) 3-1075 **Email:** www@irb.affrc.go.jp **WWW:** www.irb.affrc.go.jp

Founded: 1960 **Type:** Government **Staff:** 3 Other **Holdings:** 3,100 books 150 journals **Subjects:** Crops, Genetics, Mutations, Plant Breeding **Loan:** Do not loan **Photocopy:** Yes

1587   Tsukuba, Ibaraki, Japan
International Rice Research Institute (IRRI)
IRRI Japan Library Office
c/o Japan International Research Center for Agriculture, Forestry and Fisheries
1-2 Ohwashi
Tsukuba, Ibaraki 305-8686
Fax: +81(298) 38-6339 **Email:** k.morooka@jircas.affrc.go.jp **WWW:** www.cgiar.org/irri **OPAC:** ricelib.irri.cgiar.org

Founded: 1963 **Type:** International **Head:** Ms. Kazuko Morooka *Phone:* +81(298) 38-6637 *Email:* k.morooka@jircas.affrc.go.jp **Staff:** 2 Prof. 1 Other **Holdings:** 200 books 86 journals **Language of Collection/Services:** Japanese, English / Japanese, English **Subjects:** Rice **Databases Developed:** Japanese rice literature - about 18,000 references issued from 1990 to date **Databases Used:** Agris; Biosis; CABCD; JOIS **Networks:** NACSIS **Loan:** Do not loan **Service:** Internationally **Photocopy:** Yes

1588   Tsukuba, Ibaraki, Japan
Japan International Cooperation Agency, Tsukuba International Centre (JICA, TBIC)
Library
3-6 Koyadai
Tsukuba, Ibaraki 305-0074
Phone: +81(298) 38-1964 **Fax:** +81(298) 38-1776 **Email:** xt3n-ash@asahi-net.or.jp **WWW:** www.jica.go.jp

Former Name: Tsukuba International Agricultural Training Centre **Founded:** 1990 **Type:** Government **Head:** Masao Watanabe (temporary) **Staff:** 2 Prof. **Holdings:** 90 journals 17,000 books **Language of Collection/Services:** Japanese, English / Japanese, English **Subjects:** Crops, Agricultural Engineering, Horticulture **Specializations:** Farm Machinery, Irrigation, Rice, Vegetables **Networks:** NACSIS **Loan:** In country **Service:** In country **Photocopy:** No

1589 Tsukuba, Ibaraki, Japan
Ministry of Agriculture, Forestry and Fisheries,
Agriculture, Forestry and Fisheries Research
Council Secretariat, Tsukuba Office (MAFF)
Agriculture, Forestry and Fisheries Research
Information Center
2-1-2 Kannondai
Tsukuba, Ibaraki 305-8601
Phone: +81(298) 38-7284 **Fax:** +81(298) 38-7364 **Email:**
ric@affrc.go.jp **WWW:** ss.cc.affrc.go.jp/ric

Founded: 1978 **Type:** Government **Head:** Shizuyo Nanakida *Phone:* +81(298) 38-7315 **Staff:** 10 Prof. 2 Other **Holdings:** 39,608 books 1,712 journals **Networks:** AGRIS
Language of Collection/Services: Japanese/Japanese **Databases Used:** Agris **Loan:** In country **Photocopy:** Yes

1590 Tsukuba, Ibaraki, Japan
Ministry of Agriculture, Forestry and Fisheries,
Japan International Research Center for
Agricultural Sciences (MAFF, JIRCAS)
Library and Information Division
1-2 Ohwashi
Tsukuba, Ibaraki 305-8686
Phone: +81(298) 38-6341 **Fax:** +81(298) 38-6656 **Email:**
letter@jircas.affrc.go.jp **WWW:** ss.jircas.affrc.go.jp

Former Name: Tropical Agricultural Research Center
(TARC) **Founded:** 1970 **Type:** Government **Head:** Chuich
Sato *Phone:* +81(298) 38-6340 *Email:* kijimu@jircas.affrc.
go.jp **Staff:** 2 Prof. 4 Other **Holdings:** 45,000 books 300
journals **Language of Collection/Services:** English, Japa-
nese/English, Japanese **Subjects:** Entomology, Agricultural
Development, Horticulture Veterinary Medicine, Plant Pathology, **Specializations:** Agriculture (Tropics), Crops **Networks:** NACSIS **Databases Used:** Comprehensive **Service:**
Internationally **Loan:** In country **Photocopy:** Yes

1591 Tsukuba, Ibaraki, Japan
Ministry of Agriculture, Forestry and Fisheries,
National Agriculture Research Center
(MAFF, NARC)
Library and Information Division
3-1-1 Kannondai
Tsukuba, Ibaraki 305-8666
Phone: +81(298) 38-8849 **Fax:** +81(298) 38-8558 **WWW:**
www.nard.affrc.go.jp

Founded: 1981 **Type:** Government **Head:** Ms. Shizuyo
Nanakida *Phone:* +81(298) 38-8979 *Email:* nanakida@narc.
affrc.go.jp **Staff:** 4 Prof. 3 Other **Holdings:** 175,000 books
2,298 journals **Language of Collection/Services:** Japanese,
English/Japanese **Databases Used:** Comprehensive **Subjects:** Comprehensive **Loan:** Inhouse **Service:** Inhouse **Photocopy:** Yes

1592 Tsukuba, Ibaraki, Japan
Ministry of Agriculture, Forestry and Fisheries,
National Food Research Institute (MAFF,
NFRI)
Library
2-1-2 Kannondai
Tsukuba, Ibaraki 305

Phone: +81(298) 38-7993 **Fax:** +81(298) 38-7996 **WWW:**
ss.nfri.affrc.go.jp

Type: Government **Head:** Nobuo Ueno **Staff:** 2 Prof. 2
Other **Holdings:** 44,000 books 1,200 journals **Language of
Collection/Services:** Japanese / Japanese **Subjects:** Food
Sciences **Loan:** Inhouse **Service:** Inhouse **Photocopy:** Yes

1593 Tsukuba, Ibaraki, Japan
Ministry of Agriculture, Forestry and Fisheries,
National Institute of Agrobiological
Resources (MAFF, NIAR)
Documentation and Information Division
2-1-2 Kannondai
Tsukuba, Ibaraki 305-8602
Phone: +81(298) 38-7002 **Fax:** +81(298) 38-7044 **Email:**
niarl@abr.affrc.go.jp **WWW:** ss.abr.affrc.go.jp

Former Name: Institute for Plant Virus Research **Founded:**
1983 **Type:** Government **Head:** Shunsuke Fujimaki *Phone:*
+81(298) 38-7004 *Email:* fs1832@abr.affrc.go.jp **Staff:** 5
Prof. 3 Other **Holdings:** 8,612 books 123 journals **Language
of Collection/Services:** English, Japanese **Subjects:** Biochemistry, Biotechnology, Cytology, Genetics, Microbiology, Molecular Biology, Plant Pathology, Plant Physiology
Databases Used: Agris; Biosis; CABCD; CAS **Loan:** Inhouse **Photocopy:** No

1594 Tsukuba, Ibaraki, Japan
Ministry of Agriculture, Forestry and Fisheries,
National Institute of Agro-Environmental
Sciences (MAFF, NIAES)
Library and Information Division
Nogyo Kankyo Gijutsu Kenkyusho Toshokan
3-1-1 Kannondai
Tsukuba, Ibaraki 305-8604
Phone: +81(298) 38-8186 **Fax:** +81(298) 38-8186 **WWW:**
ss.niaes.affrc.go.jp

Founded: 1983 **Type:** Government **Head:** Eiichi Maeda
Phone: +81(298) 38-8185 **Staff:** 5 Prof. 3 Other **Holdings:**
74,519 books 1,539 journals **Subjects:** Agricultural Development, Environment **Databases Used:** Agris; Biosis;
CABCD **Networks:** NACSIS **Loan:** In country **Service:** In
country **Photocopy:** Yes

1595 Tsukuba, Ibaraki, Japan
Ministry of Agriculture, Forestry and Fisheries,
National Institute of Animal Health (MAFF,
NIAH)
Library
3-1-1 Kannondai
Tsukuba, Ibaraki 305-0856
Phone: +81(298) 38-7956 **Fax:** +81(298) 38-7907 **Email:**
ref@niah.affrc.go.jp **WWW:** ss.niah.affrc.go.jp

Founded: 1947 **Type:** Government **Staff:** 4 Prof. **Holdings:**
12,141 books 1,246 journals **Language of Collection/Ser-
vices:** Japanese / Japanese **Subjects:** Animal Husbandry, Biology **Specializations:** Veterinary Medicine **Networks:**
NACSIS **Databases Used:** Comprehensive **Photocopy:** Yes

1596 Tsukuba, Ibaraki, Japan
Ministry of Agriculture, Forestry and Fisheries,
National Institute of Animal Industry (MAFF,
NIAI)
Library and Information Section
Norin-kenkyu-danchi PO Box 5
Tsukuba, Ibaraki 305- 0901
Phone: +81(298) 38-8612 **Fax:** +81(298) 38-8628 **Email:**
endoh@niai.affrc.go.jp **WWW:** www.niai.affrc.go.jp
OPAC: www.niai.affrc.go.jp/jis/siryouka/journal.html

Founded: 1916 **Type:** Government **Head:** T. Miyanuma
Phone: +81(298) 38-8611 *Email:* miyanuma@niai.affrc.go.
jp **Staff:** 1 Prof. 2 Other **Holdings:** 51,264 books 1,194 journals **Language of Collection/Services:** Japanese, English/
Japanese, English **Subjects:** Animal Husbandry **Specializations:** Clones, Genomes, Methane Inhibitors, Milking Machines **Networks:** NACSIS **Databases Developed:** Animal
Genome Database in Japan - available via Internet at ws4.
niai.affrc.go.jp/jgbase.html **Databases Used:** Comprehensive **Loan:** In country **Service:** In country **Photocopy:** Yes

1597 Tsukuba, Ibaraki, Japan
Ministry of Agriculture, Forestry and Fisheries,
National Institute of Fruit Tree Science
(MAFF, NIFTS)
Library and Information Division
2-1 Fujimoto
Tsukuba, Ibaraki 305-8605
Phone: +81(298) 38-6454 **Fax:** +81(298) 38-6437 **WWW:**
ss.fruit.affrc.go.jp/new/index-e.html

Former Name: Fruit Tree Research Station (FTRS) **Type:**
Government **Head:** Masayoshi Wakou *Phone:* +81(298) 38-
6416 *Email:* wakou@fruit.affrc.go.jp **Staff:** 2 Prof. 2 Other
Holdings: 7,200 books 1,300 journals **Language of Collec-
tion/Services:** Japanese/Japanese **Subjects:** Horticulture
Specializations: Fruit Trees **Networks:** NACSIS **Databases Used:** Agris; Biosis; CABCD **Loan:** In country **Service:** In country **Photocopy:** Yes

1598 Tsukuba, Ibaraki, Japan
Ministry of Agriculture, Forestry and Fisheries,
National Institute of Sericultural and
Entomological Science (MAFF, NISES)
Library and Information Section
1-2 Ohwashi
Tsukuba, Ibaraki 305-8634
Phone: +81(298) 38-6013 **Fax:** +81(298) 38-6028 **WWW:**
www.nises.affrc.go.jp

Former Name: Sericultural Experiment Station **Type:** Government **Head:** Koichi Simokawa *Phone:* +81(298) 38-6011
Email: shi23@nises.affrc.go.jp **Staff:** 4 Prof. 2 Other **Holdings:** 25,778 books 2,027 journals **Language of Collection/
Services:** Japanese / Japanese **Subjects:** Entomology, Sericulture **Loan:** Inhouse **Service:** Inhouse **Photocopy:** Yes

1599 Tsukuba, Ibaraki, Japan
Ministry of Agriculture, Forestry and Fisheries,
National Research Institute of Agricultural
Engineering (MAFF, NRIAE)
Documentation and Information Section

2-1-2, Kannondai
Tsukuba, Ibaraki 305-8609
Fax: +81(298) 38-7609 **Email:** ref@nkk.affrc.go.jp
WWW: ss.nkk.affrc.go.jp

Founded: 1988 **Type:** Government **Head:** Nagaoka Shini-
chi *Phone:* +81(298) 38-7505 **Staff:** 2 Prof. **Holdings:** 1,415
journals 18,000 books **Language of Collection/Services:**
Japanese **Subjects:** Agricultural Engineering **Specializations:** Soil, Water Resources Engineering **Networks:**
NACSIS **Databases Used:** Agris **Loan:** In country **Service:**
In country **Photocopy:** Yes

1600 Tsukuba, Ibaraki, Japan
University of Tsukuba
Library
1-1-1 Tennodai
Tsukuba, Ibaraki 305
Phone: +81(298) 53-2784 **Fax:** +81(298) 53-6021 **WWW:**
www.tsukuba.ac.jp

Founded: 1973 **Type:** Government **Head:** Yasuo Kitahara
Phone: +81(298) 532340 **Staff:** 59 Prof. 23 Other **Holdings:**
1,780,000 books 1,100 journals **Language of Collection/
Services:** Japanese / Japanese **Subjects:** Agricultural Economics, Agriculture (History), Cultivation Methods, Forestry **Databases Used:** Biosis; Medline **Loan:**
Internationally **Service:** Internationally **Photocopy:** Yes

1601 Uchihara, Higashi-Ibaraki, Ibaraki, Japan
Association for Farmer's Education
Koibuchi College Library
5165 Koibuchi
Uchihara, Higashi-Ibaraki, Ibaraki 315-0323
Phone: +81(29) 259-2811 **Fax:** +81(29) 259-6965 **WWW:**
www.sphere.ad.jp/koibuchi

Founded: 1945 **Type:** Academic **Head:** Tsuneo Tsuchizaki
Staff: 1 Prof. 1 Other **Holdings:** 41,000 books 90 journals
Language of Collection/Services: Japanese / Japanese **Subjects:** Comprehensive **Loan:** Inhouse **Service:** Inhouse **Photocopy:** Yes

Ishikawa

1602 Nonoichi, Ishikawa, Japan
Ishikawa Agricultural College (IAC)
Library
1-308, Suematsu
Nonoichi, Ishikawa, Ishikawa 921-8836
Phone: +81(76) 248-3135 **Fax:** +81(76) 248-8402 **Email:**
kishimot@ishikawa-c.ac.jp **WWW:** www.ishikawa-c.ac.jp

Founded: 1971 **Type:** Academic **Head:** Tokukazu Izumi
Phone: +81(76) 248-3135 *Email:* kishimot@ishikawa-c.ac.
jp **Staff:** 2 Prof. 2 Other **Holdings:** 56,742 books 541 jour-
nals **Language of Collection/Services:** Japanese, English/
Japanese **Subjects:** Comprehensive **Networks:** NACSIS
Loan: In country **Service:** In country **Photocopy:** Yes

Iwate

1603   Morioka, Iwate, Japan
Iwate University
Library
3-18-8 Ueda
Morioka, Iwate 020-8550

Phone: +81(19) 621-6086 **Fax:** +81(19) 621-6088 **Email:** www-adm@news7l1.atm.iwate-u.ac.jp **WWW:** news7a1. atm.iwate-u.ac.jp/index-e.html or www.iwate-u.ac.jp

Founded: 1949 **Type:** Academic **Head:** Kubota Noriaki **Staff:** 10 Prof. 11 Other **Holdings:** 707,588 books 8,975 journals **Language of Collection/Services:** Japanese / Japanese **Subjects:** Comprehensive **Networks:** NACSIS **Loan:** In country **Service:** In country **Photocopy:** Yes

1604   Morioka, Iwate, Japan
Ministry of Agriculture, Forestry and Fisheries,
    Forestry and Forest Products Research
    Institute (MAFF, FFPRI)
Library
72 Nabeyashiki
Shimokuriyagawa
Morioka, Iwate 020-0123

Phone: +81(19) 648-3932 **Fax:** +81(19) 641-6747 **WWW:** www.ffpri.thk.affrc.go.jp

Founded: 1959 **Type:** Government **Head:** Teruhiko Kawahara **Staff:** 1 Prof. **Holdings:** 10,575 books 173 journals **Language of Collection/Services:** Japanese / Japanese **Subjects:** Forest Products, Forestry **Networks:** NACSIS **Loan:** Inhouse **Service:** Inhouse **Photocopy:** Yes

1605   Morioka, Iwate, Japan
Ministry of Agriculture, Forestry and Fisheries,
    Tohoku National Agricultural Experiment
    Station (MAFF, TNAES)
Documentation and Information Section
4 Akahira, Shimo-kuriyagawa
Morioka, Iwate 020-0123

Phone: +81(19) 643-3414 **Fax:** +81(19) 641-7794 **Email:** tnaeslib@tnaes.affrc.go.jp **WWW:** ss.tnaes.affrc.go.jp

Founded: 1957 **Type:** Government **Head:** Naoki Moriwaki *Phone:* +81(19) 643-3400 **Staff:** 5 Prof. 2 Other **Holdings:** 22,271 books 1,239 journals **Language of Collection/Services:** Japanese / Japanese **Subjects:** Agricultural Economics, Animal Husbandry, Edible Species **Loan:** In country **Service:** Internationally **Photocopy:** Yes

Kagawa

1606   Mikicho, Kida, Kagawa, Japan
Kagawa University, Faculty of Agriculture
Library
Ikedo
Mikicho, Kida, Kagawa 761-0795

Phone: +81(87) 891-3030 **Fax:** +81(87) 891-3035 **Email:** libbun@ao.kagawa-u.ac.jp **WWW:** www.kagawa-u.ac.jp /lib **OPAC:** telnet://opac.lib.kagawa-u.ac.jp

Founded: 1956 **Type:** Academic **Head:** Yukihiro Fujime *Phone:* +81(87) 891-3030 *Email:* libbun@ao.kagawa-u.ac. jp **Staff:** 2 Prof. 1 Other **Holdings:** 99,000 books 2,200 journals **Language of Collection/Services:** Japanese / Japanese **Subjects:** Agribusiness, Agricultural Engineering, Biotechnology **Loan:** In country **Photocopy:** Yes

1607   Takamatsu, Kagawa, Japan
Kagawa Prefecture Agricultural Experiment
    Station
Library and Database Management Section
220 Bushozan
Takamatsu, Kagawa 761-8078

Phone: +81(87) 889-1121 **Fax:** +81(87) 889-1125

Founded: 1963 **Type:** Government **Head:** Satoshi Onishi **Staff:** 1 Prof. 3 Other **Holdings:** 2,000 books 14 journals **Language of Collection/Services:** Japanese / Japanese **Subjects:** Agricultural Economics, Crops, Entomology, Horticulture, Plant Pathology, Soil **Loan:** In country **Service:** In country **Photocopy:** Yes

1608   Zentsuji, Kagawa, Japan
Ministry of Agriculture, Forestry and Fisheries,
    Shikoku National Agricultural Experiment
    Station (MAFF)
Library and Documentation Section
1-3-1 Senyu
Zentsuji, Kagawa 765

Fax: +81(877) 63-1683 **Email:** www@skk.affrc.go.jp **WWW:** ss.skk.affrc.go.jp

Founded: 1952 **Type:** Government **Head:** Kiyoshi Myogan *Phone:* +81(877) 62-0800 **Staff:** 2 Other **Holdings:** 17,923 books 1,257 journals **Language of Collection/Services:** Japanese, English / Japanese **Loan:** Inhouse **Service:** Inhouse **Photocopy:** No

Kagoshima

1609   Kagoshima, Kagoshima, Japan
Kagoshima University (KU)
Library
1-21-35 Korimoto
Kagoshima, Kagoshima 890-0065

Phone: +81(99) 285-7435 **Fax:** +81(99) 259-3442 **Email:** wwwadm@libws1.lib.kagoshima-u.ac.jp **WWW:** www.lib. kagoshima-u.ac.jp **OPAC:** websv.lib.kagoshima-u.ac.jp/ lib/search.html

Founded: 1949 **Type:** Academic **Head:** Satoshi Yamashita *Email:* yamashit@sci.kagoshima-u.ac.jp *Phone:* +81(99) 285-7400 **Staff:** 31 Prof. 1418 Other **Holdings:** 1,247,138 books 16,404 journals **Language of Collection/Services:** Japanese / Japanese **Subjects:** Comprehensive **Databases Used:** Comprehensive **Networks:** NACSIS **Loan:** In country **Service:** In country **Photocopy:** Yes

Kanagawa

1610   **Fujisawa, Kanagawa, Japan**
Nihon University, College of Bioresource
      Sciences (NUBS)
Library
1866 Kameino
Fujisawa, Kanagawa 252-3891
Phone: +81(466) 84-3851 **Fax:** +81(466) 84-3855 **WWW:** www.tosho.brs.nihon-u.ac.jp

Former Name: College of Agriculture and Veterinary Medicine **Founded:** 1943 **Type:** Academic **Head:** Professor Kiyoshi Imai *Phone:* +81(466) 84-3891 **Staff:** 15 Prof. 24 Other **Holdings:** 306,892 books 3,962 journals **Language of Collection/Services:** Japanese / Japanese **Subjects:** Agribusiness, Agricultural Development, Agricultural Economics, Agricultural Engineering, Agriculture (Tropics), Animal Husbandry, Biotechnology, Crops, Entomology, Farming, Fisheries, Food Sciences, Forestry, Horticulture, Plant Pathology, Plants, Soil, Veterinary Medicine, Water Resources **Networks:** NACSIS **Databases Used:** Comprehensive **Loan:** In country **Service:** In country **Photocopy:** Yes

1611   **Sagamihara, Kanagawa, Japan**
Azabu University (AU)
Library
1-17-71 Fuchinobe
Sagamihara, Kanagawa 229-8501
Fax: +81(427) 76-3059 **Email:** toshokan@azabu-u.ac.jp
OPAC: turf.azabu-u.ac.jp

Former Name: Azabu Veterinary College **Founded:** 1949 **Type:** Academic **Head:** Professor Hideo Fujitani *Phone:* +81(427) 69-1608 *Email:* toshokan@azabu-u.ac.jp **Staff:** 7 Prof. 5 Other **Holdings:** 134,337 books 2,355 journals **Language of Collection/Services:** Japanese/Japanese **Subjects:** Animal Husbandry, Food Sciences **Specializations:** Environment, Veterinary Medicine **Databases Used:** Medline **Loan:** In country **Service:** Internationally **Photocopy:** Yes

1612   **Yokohama, Kanagawa, Japan**
Ministry of Agriculture, Forestry and Fisheries,
      Yokohama Plant Protection Station (MAFF)
Research Division Library
1-16-10 Shinyamashita, Naka
Yokohama, Kanagawa 231-0801
Phone: +81(45) 622-8892 **Fax:** +81(45) 621-7560

Type: Government **Head:** Tetsuo Suetsuzu *Phone:* +81(45) 622-8892 **Holdings:** 50,000 books 50 journals **Language of Collection/Services:** Japanese/Japanese **Subjects:** Nematology, Food Sciences, **Specializations:** Entomology, Plant Pathology **Loan:** In country **Service:** Internationally **Photocopy:** Yes

Kochi

1613   **Nankoku, Kochi, Japan**
Kochi University, Faculty of Agriculture (KU)
Library
200 Otsu, Monobe
Nankoku, Kochi 783
Phone: +81(888) 64-5117 **Fax:** +81(888) 64-5202 **WWW:** www.koichi-u.ac.jp

Type: Academic **Staff:** 1 Prof. 2 Other **Holdings:** 31,109 books 3,568 journals **Language of Collection/Services:** Japanese, English/Japanese **Subjects:** Agriculture (Tropics), Agricultural Development, Agricultural Economics, Agricultural Engineering, Animal Husbandry, Biotechnology, Crops, Entomology, Farming, Fisheries, Food Sciences, Forestry, Horticulture, Plant Pathology, Plants, Soil Science, Water Resources **Loan:** In country **Service:** Internationally **Photocopy:** Yes

Kumamoto

1614   **Kumamoto, Kumamoto, Japan**
Shokei Women's Junior College
Library
2-6-78 Kuhonji
Kumamoto, Kumamoto 862-8678
Phone: +81(96) 362-2011 ext 356 **Fax:** +81(96) 363-6520

Type: Academic **Staff:** 4 Prof. 3 Other **Holdings:** 100,000 books 160 journals **Language of Collection/Services:** Japanese/Japanese **Subjects:** Food Sciences **Loan:** In country **Service:** In country **Photocopy:** Yes

1615   **Nishigoshi, Kikuchi, Kumamoto, Japan**
Ministry of Agriculture, Forestry and Fisheries,
      Kyushu National Agricultural Experiment
      Station (MAFF, KNAES)
Library
Suya 2421
Nishigoshi, Kikuchi, Kumamoto 861-1192
Phone: +81(96) 242-1150 **Fax:** +81(96) 249-1002 **WWW:** ss.knaes.affrc.go.jp

Founded: 1950 **Type:** Government **Head:** Professor Akihiro Yamashita *Phone:* +81(96) 242-1150 **Staff:** 3 Prof. 2 Other **Holdings:** 57,000 books 1,580 journals **Language of Collection/Services:** Japanese/Japanese **Subjects:** Crops, Biotechnology, Entomology, Food Sciences, Plant Pathology, Plants, Soil **Databases Used:** Comprehensive **Loan:** Inhouse **Service:** Inhouse **Photocopy:** Yes

Kyoto

1616   **Kyoto, Kyoto, Japan**
Kyoto Prefectural University (KPU)
Library
1-5 Shimogamohangi, Sakyo
Kyoto, Kyoto 606-8522
Phone: +81(75) 703-5130 **Fax:** +81(75) 703-5192 **WWW:** www.kpu.ac.jp

Founded: 1949 **Type:** Academic **Head:** Kazumi Saito *Phone:* +81(75) 703-5129 **Staff:** 4 Prof. 4 Other **Holdings:** 310,466 books 8,832 journals **Language of Collection/Services:** Japanese / Japanese **Subjects:** Comprehensive **Networks:** NACSIS **Loan:** In country **Service:** In country **Photocopy:** Yes

1617   Kyoto, Kyoto, Japan
Kyoto University, Faculty of Agriculture and
     Graduate School of Agriculture
Library
Kitashirakawa Oiwake, Sakyo
Kyoto, Kyoto 606-8502

Phone: +81(75) 753-6016 **Fax:** +81(75) 753-6025 **WWW:**
www.agril.kais.kyoto-u.ac.jp **OPAC:** kensaku.libnet.kulib.
kyoto-u.ac.jp/ibibser1.ja.html

Founded: 1923 **Type:** Academic **Head:** Shiro Inamoto
Phone: +81(75) 753-6293 **Staff:** 10 Prof. 3 Other **Holdings:**
300,000 books 3,400 journals **Language of Collection/Services:** Japanese / Japanese **Subjects:** Comprehensive **Networks:** NACSIS **Databases Used:** Comprehensive **Loan:** In
country **Service:** Inhouse **Photocopy:** Yes

Mie

1618   Anou, Age, Mie, Japan
Ministry of Agriculture, Forestry and Fisheries,
     National Research Institute of Vegetables,
     Ornamental Plants and Tea (MAFF, NIVOT)
Library and Information
360 Kusawa
Anou, Age, Mie 514-2392

Phone: +81(59) 268-1331 **Fax:** +81(592) 68-1339 **WWW:**
www.nivot.affrc.go.jp

Founded: 1986 **Type:** Government **Head:** Kiyoshi Myogan
Phone: +81(59) 268-1339 **Staff:** 1 Prof. 4 Other **Holdings:**
8,300 books 300 journals **Language of Collection/Services:**
Japanese, English/Japanese, English **Subjects:** Horticulture,
Biology, Plants **Networks:** NACSIS **Databases Used:**
Comprehensive **Loan:** Inhouse **Service:** Inhouse **Photocopy:** Yes

1619   Nansei, Watarai, Mie, Japan
Ministry of Agriculture, Forestry and Fisheries,
     National Research Institute of Aquaculture
     (MAFF, NRIA)
Research Planning and Coordination Division
Library
Nansei, Watarai, Mie 516-0193

Fax: +81(5996) 6-1962 **WWW:** www.nria.affrc.go.jp

Founded: 1979 **Type:** Government **Head:** Dr. Toshihiko
Matsusato *Email:* matsusato@nria.affrc.go.jp *Phone:* +81
(5996) 6-1830 ext 30 **Staff:** 2 Prof. 1 Other **Holdings:** 87
journals 43,771 books **Language of Collection/Services:**
Japanese/Japanese **Subjects:** Biotechnology, Farming, Fisheries, Food Sciences **Specializations:** Fish Culture **Databases Used:** ASFA; Biosis **Loan:** In country **Service:** In
country **Photocopy:** Yes

1620   Tsu, Mie, Japan
Mie University
Library
1515 Kamihariacho
Tsu, Mie 514-8507

Email: sanko@lib.mie-u.ac.jp **WWW:** www.lib.mie-u.ac.
jp **OPAC:** www.lib.mie-u.ac.jp/ilis/search/index.html

Founded: 1949 **Type:** Academic **Head:** Marami Shibata
Phone: +81(59) 232-4196 *Email:* director@lib.mie-u.ac.jp
Staff: 13 Prof. 16 Other **Holdings:** 850,000 books 14,000
journals **Language of Collection/Services:** Japanese / Japanese **Networks:** MILAI; NACSIS **Subjects:** Comprehensive **Databases Used:** Comprehensive **Loan:** Internationally
Service: Internationally **Photocopy:** Yes

Miyagi

1621   Sendai, Miyagi, Japan
Miyagi Agricultural College
Library
2-2-1 Hatatate, Taihaku
Sendai, Miyagi 982-0215

Phone: +81(22) 245-2211 **WWW:** ha6.seikyou.ne.jp/
home/miyano-tandai

Founded: 1952 **Type:** Academic **Head:** Michihisa Tomita
Staff: 1 Prof. 2 Other **Holdings:** 33,176 books 162 journals
Language of Collection/Services: Japanese / Japanese **Subjects:** Agricultural Economics, Agricultural Engineering,
Animal Husbandry, Horticulture **Networks:** NACSIS **Loan:**
Inhouse **Service:** Inhouse **Photocopy:** Yes

1622   Sendai, Miyagi, Japan
Tohoku University (TU)
Agricultural Library
1-1 Tsutsumidori Amamiyamachi
Aoba
Sendai, Miyagi 981-8555

Phone: +81(22) 717-8627 **Fax:** +81(22) 263-9296 **Email:**
alib@library.tohoku.ac.jp **WWW:** www.tohoku.ac.jp/
index-e.html **OPAC:** www.library.tohoku.ac.jp/library-e.
html

Founded: 1979 **Type:** Academic **Head:** Prof. Takayuki
Oritani *Email:* alib@library.tohoku.ac.jp *Phone:* +81(22)
717-8627 **Staff:** 4 Prof. 2 Other **Holdings:** 122,265 books
3,836 journals **Language of Collection/Services:** English/Japanese **Subjects:** Agricultural Economics, Food Sciences, Animal Husbandry, Biochemistry, Biotechnology,
Marine Sciences, Plants **Networks:** NACSIS **Databases
Used:** Comprehensive **Loan:** In country **Service:** In country
Photocopy: Yes

1623   Sendai, Miyagi, Japan
Tohoku University, Institute of Genetic Ecology
     (TU, IGE)
Library
2-1-1 Katahira, Aoga
Sendai, Miyagi 980-8577

Fax: +81(22) 263-9845 **WWW:** www.ige.tohoku.ac.jp

Former Name: Institute for Agricultural Research **Founded:** 1939 **Type:** Academic **Head:** Dr. Hironao Kataoka
Phone: +81(22) 217-5692 **Staff:** 1 Prof. **Holdings:** 30,000
books 611 journals **Language of Collection/Services:** Japanese, English **Subjects:** Biology, Plant Ecology, Plant Genetics **Loan:** Do not loan **Photocopy:** No

1624 Shiogama, Miyagi, Japan
Ministry of Agriculture, Forestry and Fisheries,
Fishery Agency, Tohoku National Fisheries
Research Institute (MAFF, TNFRI)
Library
3-27-5 Niihama
Shiogama, Miyagi 985-0001
Phone: +81(22) 365-7419 **Fax:** +81(22) 367-1250 **Email:**
tterui@myg.affrc.go.jp **WWW:** ss.myg.affrc.go.jp

Type: Government **Staff:** 1 Prof. **Holdings:** 19,000 books
40 journals **Language of Collection/Services:** Japanese,
English / Japanese, English **Subjects:** Fisheries **Service:** In
country **Loan:** In country **Photocopy:** Yes

Miyazaki

1625 Miyazaki, Miyazaki, Japan
Miyazaki University
Library
Gakuen-Kibanadai 1-1
Miyazaki, Miyazaki 889-2192
WWW: www.lib.miyazaki-u.ac.jp **OPAC:** www.lib.
miyazaki-u.ac.jp/ilis/search/Eindex.htm

Founded: 1949 **Type:** Academic **Head:** Yoshito Akashi
Staff: 10 Prof. 12 Other **Holdings:** 468,623 books 1,530
journals **Language of Collection/Services:** Japanese / Japanese **Subjects:** Comprehensive **Networks:** NACSIS **Databases Used:** JOIS **Loan:** In country **Service:** In country
Photocopy: Yes

1626 Takanabe, Koyu, Miyazaki, Japan
Minami Kyushu University (MKU)
Library
11609 Oaza Minami-Takanabe
Takanabe, Koyu, Miyazaki 884-0003
Phone: +81(983) 22-6812 **Fax:** +81(983) 22-0070 **Email:**
mint@nankyudai.ac.jp **WWW:** www.nankyudai.ac.jp

Type: Academic **Head:** Takao Shimizu *Phone:* +81(983)
23-0793 *Email:* takao-sz@nankyudai.ac.jp **Staff:** 3 Prof. 2
Other **Language of Collection/Services:** Japanese / Japanese **Subjects:** Comprehensive **Specializations:** Horticulture **Networks:** NACSIS **Loan:** In country **Service:** In
country **Photocopy:** Yes

Nagano

1627 Nagano, Nagano, Japan
Shinshu University, Faculty of Agriculture (SU,
FA)
Branch Library of Agriculture
8304 Minamiminowa
Nagano, Nagano 399-4598
Phone: +81(265) 72-1108 **Fax:** +81(265) 73-4901 **WWW:**
karamatsu.shinshu-u.ac.jp/nougakubu/library/index.html
OPAC: shinlis2.shinshu-u.ac.jp/opac

Founded: 1971 **Type:** Academic **Head:** Professor Katsuaki
Ota *Phone:* +81(265) 72-5255 **Staff:** 3 Prof. 2 Other **Hold-
ings:** 76,133 books 1,485 journals **Language of Collection/
Services:** Japanese, English/Japanese **Subjects:** Compre-

hensive **Specializations:** Agricultural Development, Agri-
cultural Economics, Agricultural Engineering, Agriculture
(Tropics), Animal Husbandry, Crops, Entomology, Farming,
Food Sciences, Forestry, Horticulture, Plant Pathology,
Plants, Soil, Veterinary Medicine **Databases Used:** Agris;
Biosis **Networks:** NACSIS **Loan:** In country **Service:** Inter-
nationally **Photocopy:** Yes

Niigata

1628 Joetsu, Niigata, Japan
Ministry of Agriculture, Forestry and Fisheries,
Hokuriku National Agricultural Experiment
Station (MAFF)
Library and Information Section
1-2-1 Inada
Joetsu, Niigata 943-0193
Phone: +81(255) 26-3215 **Fax:** +81(255) 24-8578 **WWW:**
www.inada.affrc.go.jp

Founded: 1944 **Type:** Government **Head:** Kyuzaburo
Takahashi *Phone:* +81(255) 23-4131 **Staff:** 3 Prof. **Holdings:** 60,000 books 1,560 journals **Language of Collection/
Services:** Japanese/Japanese **Subjects:** Agricultural Economics, Agricultural Engineering, Entomology, Horticulture, Plant Pathology, Plants, Soil Science **Databases Used:**
Agris; Biosis; CABCD **Loan:** Inhouse **Service:** Internationally **Photocopy:** Yes

1629 Maki, Nishikanbara, Niigata, Japan
Niigata Agricultural Junior College
School Library
12021 Maki-ko
Maki, Nishikanbara, Niigata 953-0041
Phone: +81(256) 72-3141 **Fax:** +81(256) 73-3001

Founded: 1963 **Head:** Toshio Saito *Phone:* +81(256) 72-
3141 **Type:** Academic **Staff:** 80 Other **Holdings:** 20 journals 4,500 books **Language of Collection/Services:** Japa-
nese/Japanese **Photocopy:** No

1630 Niigata, Niigata, Japan
Ministry of Agriculture, Forestry and Fisheries,
Japan Sea National Fisheries Research
Institute (MAFF, JSNFRI)
Library
1-5939-22 Suido
Niigata, Niigata 951-8121
Phone: +81(25) 228-0451 **Fax:** +81(25) 224-0950 **WWW:**
ss.jsnf.affrc.go.jp

Former Name: Japan Sea Regional Fisheries Research Laboratory **Type:** Government **Head:** Katsuhiko Ito *Phone:* +81
(25) 228-0451 **Staff:** 27 Prof. 37 Other **Holdings:** 50,000
books 600 journals **Language of Collection/Services:** Japa-
nese/Japanese **Subjects:** Fisheries **Loan:** Inhouse **Service:**
In country **Photocopy:** Yes

1631 Niigata, Niigata, Japan
Niigata University, Faculty of Agriculture
Branch Library
8050 Ikarashi 2-no-cho
Niigata, Niigata 950-2181

Phone: +81(25) 262-6607 **Email:** voice@lib.niigata-u.ac.jp **WWW:** www.niigata-u.ac.jp **OPAC:** www.lib.niigata-u.ac.jp

Founded: 1974 **Type:** Academic **Head:** Takashi Okuma *Phone:* +81(25) 262-6211 *Email:* okuma@eng.niigata-u.ac.jp **Staff:** 2 Other **Holdings:** 1,668 books 128 journals **Language of Collection/Services:** Japanese, English / Japanese **Loan:** Inhouse **Service:** Inhouse **Photocopy:** Yes

Okayama

1632   Kurashiki, Okayama, Japan
        Okayama University, Research Institute for
            Bioresources (RIB)
        Branch Library
        2-20-1 Chuo
        Kurashiki, Okayama 710-0046
Phone: +81(86) 434-1204 **Fax:** +81(86) 434-1249 **WWW:** www.okayama-u.ac.jp

Former Name: Institute for Agricultural and Biological Sciences **Founded:** 1914 **Type:** Government **Head:** Professor Hideaki Matsumoto *Phone:* +81(86) 434-1661 **Staff:** 4 Prof. **Holdings:** 153,870 books 223 journals **Language of Collection/Services:** Japanese/Japanese **Subjects:** Biotechnology, Entomology, Plant Pathology, Plants, Water Resources, Crops **Specializations:** Plant Physiology, Agriculture (History - China - Ancient), Agriculture (History - Japan - Edo Era), Agriculture (History - Japan - Meizi Era) **Databases Used:** Agris; Biosis **Loan:** In country **Service:** Internationally **Photocopy:** Yes

1633   Ushimado, Oku, Okayama, Japan
        Okayama Prefecture Fisheries Experiment Station
        Library
        35, Kashino
        Ushimado, Oku, Okayama 701-4303
Phone: +81(869) 34-3074 **Fax:** +81(869) 34-4733 **Email:** suishiken@pref.okayama.jp **WWW:** www.pref.okayama.jp/norin/suishiken/suishiken.htm

Founded: 1902 **Type:** Government **Head:** Shinsaku Matsumura *Email:* shinsaku_matsumura@pref.okayama.jp *Phone* +81(869) 34-3074 **Staff:** 1 Prof. **Holdings:** 70,000 books 200 journals **Language of Collection/Services:** Japanese/Japanese **Subjects:** Fisheries **Loan:** Internationally **Service:** Internationally **Photocopy:** Yes

Okinawa

1634   Nishihara, Nakagami, Okinawa, Japan
        University of the Ryukyus
        Library
        1 Senbaru
        Nishihara, Nakagami, Okinawa 903-0214
Phone: +81(98) 895-8166 **Fax:** +81(98) 895-8169 **WWW:** www.lib.u-ryukyu.ac.jp **OPAC:** www.lib.u-ryukyu.ac.jp

Founded: 1950 **Type:** Academic **Head:** Tommonori Ishikawa *Phone:* +81(98) 895-8150 **Staff:** 23 Prof. 3 Other **Holdings:** 750,053 books 5,848 journals **Language of Collection/Services:** Japanese, English / Japanese **Subjects:**

Comprehensive **Networks:** NACSIS **Photocopy:** yes **Databases Used:** Biosis **Loan:** In country **Service:** In country

Osaka

1635   Habikino, Osaka, Japan
        Osaka Agricultural and Forestry Research Center
        Library
        442 Shakudo
        Habikino, Osaka 583-0862
Phone: +81(729) 58-6551 **Fax:** +81(729) 56-9691

Former Name: Osaka Agricultural Research Center **Founded:** 1962 **Type:** Government **Head:** Yoshiji Okuda *Phone:* +81(729) 58-6551 **Staff:** 2 Other **Holdings:** 2,500 books 100 journals **Language of Collection/Services:** Japanese **Subjects:** Animal Husbandry, Crops, Forestry, Horticulture **Loan:** Inhouse **Service:** Inhouse **Photocopy:** No

1636   Sakai, Osaka, Japan
        Osaka Prefecture University (OPU)
        Library for the College of Agriculture (LCA)
        1-1 Gakuen
        Sakai, Osaka 599-8531
Phone: +81(722) 54-9403 **Fax:** +81(722) 54-9403 **WWW:** www.osakafu-u.ac.jp

Founded: 1949 **Type:** Academic **Head:** Professor Fumiaki Hata *Phone:* +81(722) 54-9403 **Holdings:** 103,106 books 2,164 journals **Language of Collection/Services:** Japanese/Japanese **Staff:** 4 Prof. **Subjects:** Entomology, Horticulture, Plants, Soil Science, Veterinary Medicine **Specializations:** Calcium, Metabolism **Databases Used:** CABCD; Medline **Networks:** NACSIS-CAT **Loan:** Inhouse **Service:** Inhouse **Photocopy:** Yes

Saga

1637   Saga, Saga, Japan
        Saga University, Faculty of Agriculture
        Library
        1 Honsho
        Saga, Saga 840
Phone: +81(952) 24-5191 ext 2719 **WWW:** www.cc.saga-u.ac.jp/agriculture

Founded: 1957 **Type:** Academic, Government **Staff:** 4 Prof. 1 Other **Holdings:** 16,654 books 37,600 journals **Loan:** Do not loan **Photocopy:** Yes

Saitama

1638   Omiya, Saitama, Japan
        Institute of Agricultural Machinery, Bio-oriented
            Technology Research Advancement
            Institution, Planning Department (IAM,
            BRAIN)
        Library / Planning Department
        1-40-2 Nisshin
        Omiya, Saitama 331-8537

Phone: +81(48) 654-7033 **Fax:** +81(48) 654-7130 **Email:** kyamamoto@iam.brain.go.jp **WWW:** www.iam.brain.go.jp

Founded: 1962 **Type:** Government **Head:** *Phone:* +81(48) 654-7030 *Email:* letters@iam.brain.go.jp **Holdings:** 24,500 books 167 journals **Language of Collection/Services:** Japanese, English/Japanese, English **Staff:** 2 Prof. **Subjects:** Agricultural Engineering, Farm Machinery **Specializations:** Farm Machinery Industry **Databases Used:** JOIS **Loan:** Inhouse **Service:** In country **Photocopy:** Yes

1639   Osato, Saitama, Japan
Saitama Prefectural Center of Animal Husbandry
Library and Information Section
784 Sugahiro
Konan
Osato, Saitama 360-0102
Phone: +81(485) 36-0311 **Fax:** +81(485) 36-0315

Founded: 1997 **Type:** Government **Head:** Ken Otaka *Phone:* +81(485) 36-0311 **Staff:** 1 Prof. **Holdings:** 39,426 books 44 journals **Language of Collection/Services:** Japanese / Japanese **Subjects:** Animal Husbandry **Loan:** Do not loan **Service:** Inhouse **Photocopy:** No

1640   Wako, Saitama, Japan
Institute of Physical and Chemical Research
     (RIKEN)
Library
2-1 Hirosawa
Wako, Saitama 351-0198
Phone: +81(48) 462-1111 ext 2396 **Fax:** +81(48) 462-4714 **Email:** library@postman.riken.go.jp **WWW:** www.riken.go.jp

Founded: 1917 **Type:** Academic **Head:** Hiroko Takada *Email:* takada@postman.riken.go.jp *Phone:* +81(48) 462-1111 ext 2621 **Staff:** 6 Prof. 2 Other **Holdings:** 100,000 books 320 journals **Language of Collection/Services:** English/Japanese **Subjects:** Biotechnology **Databases Used:** Biosis; CAS; Current Contents; Medline **Loan:** In country **Service:** Inhouse **Photocopy:** Yes

Shimane

1641   Matsue, Shimane, Japan
Shimane University (SU)
Library
1060 Nishikawatsu
Matsue, Shimane 690-8504
Fax: +81(852) 32-2781 **Email:** library@lib.shimane-u.ac.jp **WWW:** lisa.shimane-u.ac.jp

Founded: 1949 **Type:** Academic **Head:** Maretsugy Yamasaki *Email:* library@lib.shimane-u.ac.jp *Phone:* +81(852) 32-6080 **Staff:** 8 Prof. 15 Other **Holdings:** 663,000 books 10,000 journals **Language of Collection/Services:** Japanese /Japanese **Subjects:** Comprehensive **Networks:** NACSIS **Databases Used:** Comprehensive **Loan:** In country **Service:** In country **Photocopy:** Yes

Shizuoka

1642   Haibara, Shizuoka, Japan
Ministry of Agriculture, Forestry and Fisheries,
     National Research Institute of Vegetables,
     Ornamental Plants and Tea (MAFF, NIVOT)
Library and Information Section
2769 Kanaya, Kanaya
Haibara, Shizuoka 428-8401
Phone: +81(547) 45-4429 **Fax:** +81(547) 46-2169 **WWW:** www.nivot.affrc.go.jp

Former Name: National Research Institute of Tea, Documentation and Library **Founded:** 1972 **Type:** Government **Staff:** 1 Prof. 1 Other **Holdings:** 25,000 books 470 journals **Language of Collection/Services:** Japanese / Japanese **Subjects:** Tea, Tea Industry **Networks:** NACSIS **Databases Used:** Comprehensive **Loan:** Inhouse **Service:** Inhouse **Photocopy:** Yes

1643   Iwata, Shizuoka, Japan
Shizuoka Agricultural Experiment Station
Library
678-1 Tomigaoka, Toyoda
Iwata, Shizuoka 438-0803
Phone: +81(538) 35-7211 **Fax:** +81(538) 37-8466 **WWW:** www.u-shizuoka-ken.ac.jp/center/hougyou.html

Type: Government **Staff:** 1 Other **Holdings:** 34,000 books 65 journals **Language of Collection/Services:** Japanese/ Japanese **Subjects:** Agribusiness, Biotechnology, Crops, Entomology, Horticulture, Plant Pathology, Soil **Databases Used:** Comprehensive **Loan:** Inhouse **Service:** Inhouse **Photocopy:** Yes

1644   Iwata, Shizuoka, Japan
Shizuoka Prefectural Agriculture and Forestry
     College
Library
678-1 Tomioka
Toyoda
Iwata, Shizuoka 438-0803
OPAC: www6.shizuokanet.or.jp/usr/noudai/index.htm

Type: Academic **Head:** Akihiro Doi *Phone:* +81(538) 36-0211 **Staff:** 1 Other **Holdings:** 9,430 books 20 journals **Language of Collection/Services:** Japanese/Japanese **Subjects:** Animal Husbandry, Forestry, Fruit Trees, Horticulture, Tea **Loan:** Inhouse **Photocopy:** No

1645   Shimizu, Shizuoka, Japan
Ministry of Agriculture, Forestry and Fisheries,
     Fisheries Agency of Japan, National Research
     Institute of Far Seas Fisheries (MAFF,
     NRIFSF)
Library and Information Section
7-1 Orido 5-chome
Shimizu, Shizuoka 424-8633
Phone: +81(543) 36-6000 **Fax:** +81(543) 35-9642 **Email:** kiren@enyo.affrc.go.jp **WWW:** www.enyo.affrc.go.jp

Former Name: Far Seas Fisheries Research Laboratory **Founded:** 1967 **Type:** Government **Head:** Asuhiko Shimazu *Phone:* +81(543) 36-6000 **Holdings:** 31,919 books 200

journals **Language of Collection/Services:** Japanese, English/Japanese, English **Staff:** 1 Prof. 1 Other **Subjects:** Fisheries **Networks:** NACSIS **Databases Used:** ASFA **Loan:** In country **Service:** Internationally **Photocopy:** Yes

1646　Shimizu, Shizuoka, Japan
　　　　Tokai University, Faculty of Marine Science and
　　　　　　Technology
　　　　Library
　　　　3-20-1, Orido
　　　　Shimizu, Shizuoka 424-0902
Fax: +81(543) 34-0862 **WWW:** www.scc.u-tokai.ac.jp

Founded: 1962 **Type:** Academic **Head:** Masahisa Kubota *Phone:* +81(543) 34-0414 **Staff:** 6 Prof. 5 Other **Holdings:** 190,146 books 539 journals **Language of Collection/Services:** Japanese, English/Japanese **Subjects:** Biotechnology, Fisheries, Marine Engineering, Marine Resources, Marine Technology, Shipbuilding **Networks:** NACSIS **Loan:** In country **Service:** In country **Photocopy:** Yes

Tochigi

1647　Nishinasuno, Nasu, Tochigi, Japan
　　　　Ministry of Agriculture, Forestry and Fisheries,
　　　　　　National Grassland Research Institute
　　　　　　(MAFF, NGRI)
　　　　Library and Information Section
　　　　768 Senbonmatsu
　　　　Nishinasuno, Nasu, Tochigi 329-2793
Fax: +81(287) 36-6629 **WWW:** ss.ngri.affrc.go.jp

Founded: 1970 **Type:** Government **Head:** Miyoshi Nonoue *Phone:* +81(287) 36-0111 **Staff:** 2 Prof. 2 Other **Holdings:** 41,382 books 189 journals **Language of Collection/Services:** Japanese **Subjects:** Animal Husbandry, Grasslands **Loan:** Do not loan **Service:** Inhouse **Photocopy:** No

1648　Utsunomiya, Tochigi, Japan
　　　　Utsunomiya University
　　　　Library
　　　　350 Mine-machi
　　　　Utsunomiya, Tochigi 321-8505
Phone: +81(28) 649-5134 **WWW:** www.lib.utsunomiya-u.ac.jp

Founded: 1949 **Type:** Academic **Head:** Kazuhito Matsumura *Phone:* +81(28) 649-5128 **Staff:** 14 Prof. 9 Other **Holdings:** 512,000 books 5,600 journals **Language of Collection/Services:** Japanese, English/Japanese **Subjects:** Agribusiness, Agricultural Development, Crops, Agricultural Economics, Agricultural Engineering, Animal Husbandry, Biotechnology, Education/Extension, Entomology, Farming, Food Sciences, Forestry, Horticulture, Plant Pathology, Plants, Soil, Water Resources **Networks:** NACSIS **Loan:** In country **Service:** In country **Photocopy:** Yes

Tokyo

1649　Tokyo, Japan
　　　　Japan FAO Association
　　　　Library
　　　　Bajichikusan Kaikan
　　　　1-2 Kanda Surugadai, Chiyoda
　　　　Tokyo 101-0062
Phone: +81(3) 3294-2425 **Fax:** +81(3) 3294-2427 **Email:** mailbox@fao-kyokai.or.jp **WWW:** www.fao-kyokai.or.jp

Founded: 1952 **Type:** Association **Head:** Maiko Mori *Email:* jpnfao@infoweb.ne.jp **Staff:** 3 Prof. 7 Other **Holdings:** 20,000 books 7 journals **Language of Collection/Services:** English **Subjects:** Comprehensive **Specializations:** Fisheries, Forestry, Nutrition **Loan:** In country **Service:** Inhouse **Photocopy:** Yes

1650　Tokyo, Japan
　　　　Ministry of Agriculture, Forestry and Fisheries
　　　　　　(MAFF)
　　　　Library
　　　　1-2-1 Kasumigaseki, Chiyoda
　　　　Tokyo 100-8950
Phone: +81(3) 3502-8111 ext 3047

Founded: 1907 **Type:** Government **Head:** Yasuhiro Taga *Phone:* +81(3) 3502-8111 ext 3037 **Staff:** 21 Prof. **Holdings:** 280,000 books 1,100 journals **Language of Collection/Services:** Japanese/Japanese **Subjects:** Fisheries, Food Sciences, Forestry **Loan:** Do not loan **Photocopy:** Yes

1651　Tokyo, Japan
　　　　Ministry of Agriculture, Forestry and Fisheries,
　　　　　　National Research Institute of Agricultural
　　　　　　Economics (MAFF, NRIAE)
　　　　Library
　　　　2-2-1 Nishigahara, Kita
　　　　Tokyo 114-0024
Phone: +81(3) 3910-3946 **Fax:** +81(3) 3940-0232 **Email:** ref@nriae.affrc.go.jp **WWW:** ss.nriae.affrc.go.jp

Founded: 1946 **Type:** Government **Head:** Ikushiro Mineo *Phone:* +81(3) 3910-3962 **Staff:** 13 Prof. **Holdings:** 268,000 books 210 journals **Language of Collection/Services:** Japanese/Japanese **Specialization:** Agricultural Economics **Service:** Inhouse **Loan:** Inhouse **Photocopy:** No

1652　Tokyo, Japan
　　　　National Diet of Japan
　　　　National Diet Library (NDL)
　　　　1-10-1 Nagata, Chiyoda
　　　　Tokyo 100-8924
Phone: +81(3) 3581-2331 **Fax:** +81(3) 3597-9104 **WWW:** www.ndl.go.jp

Founded: 1948 **Type:** Government **Head:** Masao Tobari *Phone:* +81(3) 3581-2331 **Holdings:** 156,599 journals 6,766,250 books **Language of Collection/Services:** Japanese / Japanese, English **Staff:** 851 Prof. **Subjects:** Comprehensive **Databases Developed:** Fourteen systems including Debates Processing, Japanese Books and National Union Catalogue System for Braille and Recorded Books **Loan:** Internationally **Service:** Internationally **Photocopy:** Yes

1653　Tokyo, Japan
　　　　Rural Culture Association
　　　　Noubunkyou Library
　　　　14-34, Tatenochou, Nerima

Tokyo 177-0054

Phone: +81(3) 3928-7440 **Fax:** +81(3) 3928-7442 **WWW:** www.ruralnet.or.jp

Founded: 1981 **Type:** Association **Head:** Yasuo Kondo *Phone:* +81(3) 3928-7440 **Holdings:** 35,000 books 100 journals **Language of Collection/Services:** Japanese/Japanese **Staff:** 2 Prof. 2 Other **Subjects:** Agricultural Economics, Agricultural Development, Fisheries, Forestry **Specializations:** Environment, Food Sciences **Databases Developed:** Rural Electronic Library - full text database of articles and books for past 13 years; access with charges **Loan:** In country **Service:** In country **Photocopy:** Yes

1654   Tokyo, Japan

Tokyo University of Agriculture (TUA)
Library
1-1-1 Sakuragaoka, Setagaya
Tokyo 156-8502

Phone: +81(3) 5477-2528 **Fax:** +81(3) 5477-2639 **WWW:** www.nodai.ac.jp

Founded: 1891 **Type:** Academic **Head:** Tsuneo Maki *Phone:* +81(3) 5477-2525 **Holdings:** 400,000 books 3,000 journals **Language of Collection/Services:** Japanese/Japanese **Staff:** 15 Prof. 11 Other **Subjects:** Comprehensive **Networks:** NACSIS **Databases Used:** Comprehensive **Loan:** Inhouse **Service:** In country **Photocopy:** Yes

1655   Tokyo, Japan

Tokyo University of Fisheries (TUF)
Library
4-5-7 Konan, Minato
Tokyo 108-8477

Phone: +81(3) 5463-0444 **Fax:** +81(3) 5463-0445 **Email:** sabisu@tokyo-u-fish.ac.jp **WWW:** www.tokyo-u-fish.ac.jp/newwebpage/indel.html

Founded: 1949 **Type:** Academic **Head:** Ko Matuda **Staff:** 8 Prof. 3 Other **Holdings:** 263,180 books 2,794 journals **Language of Collection/Services:** Japanese/Japanese **Subjects:** Fisheries **Networks:** NACSIS **Loan:** Inhouse **Service:** Inhouse **Photocopy:** Yes

1656   Tokyo, Japan

University of Tokyo, Faculty of Agriculture
Library
1-1-1 Yayoi, Bunkyo
Tokyo 113-8657

Phone: +81(3) 3812-2111 ext 5427 **Fax:** +81(3) 3815-8392 **Email:** library@lib.a.u-tokyo.ac.jp **WWW:** www.lib.a.u-tokyo.ac.jp **OPAC:** opac.cc.u-tokyo.ac.jp

Founded: 1965 **Type:** Academic **Head:** Manabu Tanaka *Phone:* +81(3) 3812-2111 ext 5430 **Holdings:** 4,242 journals 335,620 books **Language of Collection/Services:** Japanese **Staff:** 16 Prof. 3 Other **Subjects:** Animal Husbandry, Agricultural Chemistry, Agricultural Economics, Agricultural Engineering, Biotechnology, Fisheries, Forestry, Forest Products, Veterinary Medicine, Water Resources **Networks:** NACSIS **Databases Used:** Comprehensive **Service:** Internationally **Loan:** Inhouse **Photocopy:** Yes

1657   Fuchu, Tokyo, Japan

Tokyo University of Agriculture and Technology (TUAT)
Library
3-5-8 Saiwai
Fuchu, Tokyo 183-8509

Phone: +81(42) 367-5577 **Fax:** +81(42) 367-5571 **Email:** library@cc.tuat.ac.jp **WWW:** www.tuat.ac.jp

Former Name: Branch Library of Agriculture **Founded:** 1949 **Type:** Academic **Head:** Prof. Atsushi Sawatari *Phone:* +81(42) 367-5568 *Email:* library@cc.tuat.ac.jp **Staff:** 7 Prof. 2 Other **Holdings:** 249,000 books 5,800 journals **Language of Collection/Services:** Japanese/Japanese **Subjects:** Agricultural Chemistry, Agricultural Engineering, Forestry, Plants, Veterinary Medicine **Loan:** Internationally **Service:** Internationally **Photocopy:** Yes

1658   Machida, Tokyo, Japan

Japan Agricultural Cooperatives (JA)
Library
4771 Aihara
Machida, Tokyo 194-0293

Phone: +81(42) 783-7032 **Fax:** +81(42) 783-7086 **WWW:** www.rim.or.jp/ci/ja

Founded: 1979 **Type:** Association **Head:** Kanji Fukuma **Staff:** 2 Prof. **Holdings:** 100,000 books 100 journals **Language of Collection/Services:** Japanese, English / Japanese **Subjects:** Agricultural Economics **Specializations:** Cooperatives **Loan:** Do not loan **Service:** Inhouse **Photocopy:** Yes

1659   Machida, Tokyo, Japan

Japan Agricultural Cooperatives, Central
     Cooperatives College (JAC)
Library
4771 Aihara
Machida, Tokyo 194-0293

Phone: +81(42) 783-7025 **Fax:** +81(42) 783-7086 **WWW:** www.rim.or.jp/ci/ja

Founded: 1970 **Type:** Academic **Head:** Kenryo Kaneda **Staff:** 2 Other **Holdings:** 72,000 books 100 journals **Language of Collection/Services:** Japanese/Japanese **Subjects:** Cooperatives **Loan:** Inhouse **Service:** In country **Photocopy:** Yes

1660   Mitaka, Tokyo, Japan

Kyorin University (KY)
Kyorin University Medical Library (KYMEL)
6-20-2 Shinkawa
Mitaka, Tokyo 181

Phone: +81(422) 47-5511 **Fax:** +81(422) 40-7281 **WWW:** www.kyorin-u.ac.jp

Type: Academic **Head:** Masamitsu Shimomura *Phone:* +81(422) 47-5511 **Staff:** 12 Prof. 1 Other **Holdings:** 2,000 journals 190,000 books **Language of Collection/Services:** English / Japanese **Subjects:** Biotechnology, Food Sciences, Veterinary Medicine **Databases Used:** Current Contents; Medline **Loan:** Internationally **Service:** Internationally **Photocopy:** Yes

1661 Musashino, Tokyo, Japan
Nippon Veterinary and Animal Science University
Library
1-7-1 Kyonan
Musashino, Tokyo 180-0023
Phone: +81(422) 31-4151 **Fax:** +81(422) 33-2035

Former Name: Nippon Veterinary and Zootechnical College (NVZC) **Founded:** 1949 **Type:** Academic **Head:** Professor Tomio Murata *Phone:* +81(422) 31-4151 **Staff:** 5 Prof. 2 Other **Holdings:** 92,897 books 398 journals **Language of Collection/Services:** Japanese, English / Japanese **Subjects:** Agriculture (Tropics), Agribusiness, Agricultural Development, Agricultural Economics, Agricultural Engineering, Animal Husbandry, Biotechnology, Education/Extension, Entomology, Farming, Fisheries, Food Sciences, Veterinary Medicine **Databases Used:** CABCD; FSTA; Biosis; Medline **Loan:** Inhouse **Service:** In country **Photocopy:** Yes

Toyama

1662 Kosugi, Imizu, Toyama, Japan
Toyama Prefectural University (TPU)
Library
Kosugi, Imizu, Toyama 939-0398
Phone: +81(766) 56-7500 **Fax:** +81(766) 56-8103

Founded: 1990 **Type:** Academic **Head:** Hiroshi Miyashiro *Phone:* +81(766) 56-7500 **Staff:** 4 Prof. **Holdings:** 134,000 books 2,055 journals **Language of Collection/Services:** Japanese **Subjects:** Agricultural Economics, Agricultural Engineering, Biotechnology, Crops, Water Resources **Networks:** NACSIS **Loan:** Inhouse **Service:** Inhouse **Photocopy:** Yes

Yamagata

1663 Tsuruoka, Yamagata, Japan
Yamagata University, Faculty of Agriculture (YU, FA)
Branch Library
1-23, Wakaba
Tsuruoka, Yamagata 997-8555
Phone: +81(235) 28-2810 **Fax:** +81(235) 28-2815 **WWW:** www.yamagata-u.ac.jp **OPAC:** klibs3.kj.yamagata-u.ac.jp/library

Founded: 1950 **Type:** Academic **Head:** Professor Tadaaki Fukushima *Phone:* +81(235) 28-2881 *Email:* fukushima@tdsl.tr.yamagata-u.ac.jp **Staff:** 2 Prof. 1 Other **Holdings:** 80,000 books 395 journals **Language of Collection/Services:** Japanese **Subjects:** Animal Husbandry, Agricultural Economics, Agricultural Engineering, Plants, Biotechnology, Crops, Entomology, Farming, Food Sciences, Forestry, Horticulture, Soil **Databases Used:** Current Contents **Networks:** NACSIS **Loan:** In country **Service:** In country **Photocopy:** Yes

Yamaguchi

1664 Yamaguchi, Yamaguchi, Japan
Yamaguchi Agricultural Experiment Station
Library
718 Ohuchi-Mihori
Yamaguchi, Yamaguchi 743-0214

Founded: 1910 **Type:** Government **Head:** Akinari Shigemune *Phone:* +81(839) 27-0211 **Staff:** 3 Other **Holdings:** 91,000 books 39 journals **Subjects:** Agricultural Economics, Crops, Horticulture, Soil Science **Loan:** In country

1665 Yamaguchi, Yamaguchi, Japan
Yamaguchi University (YU)
Library
Yoshida, 1677-1
Yamaguchi, Yamaguchi 753-8516
Phone: +81(839) 33-5183 **Fax:** +81(839) 33-5186 **Email:** toshokan@po.cc.yamaguchi-u.ac.jp **OPAC:** opac.lib-c.yamaguchi-u.ac.jp **WWW:** www.yamaguchi-u.ac.jp

Founded: 1949 **Type:** Academic **Head:** Masahiro Kawaguchi **Staff:** 15 Prof. 13 Other **Holdings:** 1,100,000 books 20,000 journals **Language of Collection/Services:** Japanese /Japanese **Subjects:** Comprehensive **Networks:** NACSIS **Databases Used:** Medline **Loan:** Internationally **Service:** Internationally **Photocopy:** Yes

Yamanashi

1666 Masuho, Minamikoma, Yamanashi, Japan
Yamanashi Forestry and Forest Products Institute
Library and Information Section
2290-1 Saishoji
Masuho, Minamikoma, Yamanashi 400-0502
Phone: +81(556) 22-8001 **Fax:** +81(556) 22-8002

Founded: 1935 **Type:** Government **Head:** Akio Yokoi *Email:* shin.souken@pref.yamanashi.jp *Phone:* +81(556) 22-8001 **Staff:** 2 Prof. 13 Other **Holdings:** 13,800 books 124 journals **Language of Collection/Services:** Japanese / Japanese **Subjects:** Forestry **Specializations:** Forest Products, Forest Resources, Protection of Forests **Loan:** Do not loan **Photocopy:** Yes

Jordan

1667 Amman, Jordan
Abdul Hameed Shoman Public Library (AHSF)
PO Box 940255
Amman 11194
Location: 11 August, Shmeissani **Phone:** +962(6) 567-9182 **Fax:** +962(6) 560-7368 **Email:** ahsf@shorman.org.jo

Founded: 1986 **Type:** Non-government **Head:** Ms. Yusra Abu Ajamieh *Phone:* +962(6) 560-7368 *Email:* ajamiehy@shoman.org.jo **Staff:** 7 Prof. 28 Other **Holdings:** 5,400 books 50 journals **Language of Collection/Services:** Arabic, English/Arabic, English **Subjects:** Crop Production, Animal Husbandry, Fertilizers, Horticulture, Soil Conservation **Networks:** Union Catalogue of Serials **Loan:** In country **Service:** Internationally **Photocopy:** Yes

1668 Amman, Jordan
University of Jordan
Library
Amman
Phone: +962(6) 843555 ext 3142 **WWW:** www.ju.edu.jo

Founded: 1962 **Type:** Academic **Staff:** 33 Prof. 75 Other **Holdings:** 30,000 books 187 journals **Subjects:** Agriculture (Tropics), Agribusiness, Agricultural Development, Crops, Agricultural Economics, Agricultural Engineering, Animal Husbandry, Biotechnology, Education/Extension, Entomology, Farming, Fisheries, Food Sciences, Forestry, Horticulture, Plant Pathology, Soil Science, Veterinary Medicine, Water Resources **Loan:** In country **Photocopy:** Yes

1669 Amman, Jordan
University of Jordan, Faculty of Agriculture
Library
Amman
Fax: +962(6) 535-5577 **Email:** dfoagr@ju.edu.jo **WWW:** www.ju.edu.jo

Founded: 1996 **Type:** Academic **Head:** Mr. Saleam Abo Zolof *Phone:* +962(6) 535-5000 ext 3017 *Email:* admin@ju.edu.jo **Staff:** 1 Prof. 1 Other **Holdings:** 1,000 books 10 journals **Language of Collection/Services:** English, Arabic/English, Arabic **Subjects:** Arid Lands, Animal Production, Farming, Food Processing, Horticulture, Nutrition, Soil, Water Resources **Loan:** Inhouse **Service:** Inhouse **Photocopy:** No

1670 Baqa'a, Jordan
Ministry of Agriculture, National Center for Agricultural Research and Technology Transfer (NCARTT)
Library
PO Box 639
Baqa'a 19381
Phone: +962(6) 725411/2 **Fax:** +962(6) 726099

Founded: 1958 **Type:** Government **Head:** Dr. Raid Jameel Yakub Sulieman *Phone:* +962(6) 725411/2 **Staff:** 2 Prof. 1 Other **Holdings:** 22,000 books 500 journals **Language of Collection/Services:** Arabic, English / Arabic, English **Subjects:** Agriculture (Tropics), Agribusiness, Agricultural Development, Agricultural Economics, Farming, Agricultural Engineering, Animal Husbandry, Biotechnology, Crops, Education/Extension, Entomology, Fisheries, Food Sciences, Forestry, Horticulture, Plant Pathology, Soil Science, Water Resources, Veterinary Medicine **Networks:** AGRIS **Databases Developed:** JORDOC–Jordan Agricultural Documentation Centre collection for AGRIS input **Databases Used:** Agricola; Agris; CABCD **Loan:** In country **Photocopy:** Yes

1671 Irbid, Jordan
Jordan University of Science and Technology
Library
PO Box 3030
Irbid
Fax: +962(2) 295123

Founded: 1986 **Type:** Academic **Head:** Dr. Farouq Mansour *Phone:* +962(2) 295111 ext 3737 **Holdings:** 55,000 books 450 journals **Language of Collection/Services:** English **Staff:** 3 Prof. 27 Other **Subjects:** Animal Husbandry, Animal Production, Crop Production, Crops, Nutrition **Databases Used:** Compendex; Medline **Loan:** Do not loan **Service:** In country **Photocopy:** Yes

Kazakhstan

1672 Akmola, Kazakhstan
S. Seifullin Akmola Agrarian University
Library
116 Pobeda Ave.
Akmola 473000

1673 Almaty, Kazakhstan
Academy of Sciences of the Republic of Kazakhstan
Kazak State Research Institute of Scientific and Technical Information (KSISTI)
Bogenbay Batry 221
480096 Almaty
Phone: +7(3272) 547172 **Fax:** +7(3272) 547059 **Email:** mgo@ksisti.kz

Networks: AGRIS

♦1674 Almaty, Kazakhstan
Kazak Scientific Research Institute of Agriculture
Documentation Centre
37, Erlepesov St., Almalybak
Kaskelen District
Almaty 483133

1675 Almaty, Kazakhstan
Kazakh Scientific Research Veterinary Institute (KazSRV)
Information Center (IC)
50th Year of October Av., 223
Almaty 480029
Phone: +7(3272) 329332 **Email:** kaznivi@itte.kz

Founded: 1926 **Type:** Government **Head:** Sultanov *Phone:* +7(3272) 321888 **Staff:** 2 Prof. 2 Other **Holdings:** 47,791 books 52,072 journals **Language of Collection/Services:** Russian / Russian **Subjects:** Veterinary Medicine **Databases Developed:** Database animal diseases (horses) for the years 1956-1995 in Kazakhstan - local commercial access **Loan:** In country **Service:** Internationally **Photocopy:** No

1676 Almaty, Kazakhstan
Kazakh State University of Agriculture
Library
8 Abai Ave.
Almaty 480100
Phone: +7(3272) 651948 **Fax:** +7(3272) 642409 **Email:** info@kgau.almaty.kz **WWW:** www.agriun.almaty.kz

Founded: 1930 **Type:** Academic **Holdings:** 68,800 books

1677   Almaty, Kazakhstan
National Academic Centre of Agrarian Research
  of the Republic of Kazakhstan (NACAR)
Republican Scientific Agricultural Library
  (RNSKHB)
Abylaikhan Avenue, 79
Almaty 480091
Phone: +7(2) 626943

Former Name: Kazakh Agricultural Academy, Kazakh Scientific Agricultural Library **Founded:** 1931 **Type:** Government **Head:** Koychumanova Trumtay Qmirserlkovna *Phone* +7(2) 621068 **Staff:** 20 Prof. 3 Other **Holdings:** 700,000 books 150,000 journals **Language of Collection/Services:** Russian / Kazakh, Russian **Subjects:** Agribusiness, Agricultural Development, Agricultural Engineering, Entomology, Education/Extension, Farming, Food Sciences, Forestry, Horticulture, Plant Pathology, Soil Science, Veterinary Medicine **Specializations:** Agricultural Economics, Biotechnology, Animal Husbandry, Crops **Service:** In country **Loan:** Internationally **Photocopy:** No

♦1678   Almaty District, Kazakhstan
Kazakh Scientific Research Institute of Plant
  Protection
Scientific Library
Rakhat Village
Kaskelen Region
Almaty District 483117

Founded: 1945 **Type:** Government **Staff:** 2 Prof. **Holdings:** 29,134 books 34 journals **Language of Collection/Services:** Russian, Kazakh / Russian, Kazakh **Subjects:** Biological Control, Biotechnology, Entomology, Pest Control, Plant Diseases **Specializations:** Plant Protection **Loan:** In country **Service:** In country **Photocopy:** No

1679   Chimkent District, Kazakhstan
Krasnovodopadskaya State Breeding Station
Library
Krasnovodopadskaya P/O
Sary-Agachskii Region
Chimkent District 4873200
Phone: +7() 22340

Founded: 1911 **Type:** Government **Holdings:** 6,100 books **Language of Collection/Services:** Russian / Russian **Subjects:** Agricultural Economics, Genetics, Plant Pathology, Biotechnology, Plants, Soil **Specializations:** Plant Breeding **Loan:** Inhouse **Service:** Inhouse **Photocopy:** No

♦1680   Dzhambul, Kazakhstan
Dzhambul Hydro Land Reclamation Building
  Institute (PGMSI)
Library
Satpaev str. 28
Dzhambul 484022
Phone: +7() 43651, 43652 **Fax:** +327() 24643

Founded: 1963 **Type:** Academic **Staff:** 20 Prof. 14 Other **Holdings:** 540,000 books 200 journals **Language of Collection/Services:** Kazakh, Russian / Kazakh, Russian **Subjects:** Agricultural Economics, Crops, Engineering, Fodder Crops,

Farming, Hydrology, Postharvest Storage, Reclamation, Soil Science **Loan:** In country **Service:** Inhouse **Photocopy:** Yes

1681   Uralsk, Kazakhstan
West Kazakhstan Agrarian University
Library
51 Volgogradskaya Str.
Uralsk 417025

Founded: 1963 **Type:** Academic **Holdings:** 46,000 books

Kenya

1682   Bukura, Kenya
Ministry of Agriculture, Livestock Development
  and Marketing, Bukura Agricultural College
  (MOAL&M, BAC)
Library
PO Box 23
Bukura via Kakamega
Location: S. Galagala - Butere Road **Phone:** +254(333) 20023, 20291

Former Name: Ministry of Agriculture, Bukura Institute of Agriculture **Founded:** 1974 **Type:** Academic **Head:** Jason Makanga *Phone:* +254(333) 20023, 20291 **Staff:** 1 Prof. 8 Other **Holdings:** 8,500 books 3,600 journals **Language of Collection/Services:** English **Subjects:** Agricultural Economics, Agricultural Engineering, Animal Husbandry, Farm Management, Crops, Education/Extension, Plant Pathology, Entomology, Home Economics, Horticulture **Loan:** In country **Photocopy:** Yes

♦1683   Eldoret, Kenya
Moi University
Library
PO Box 1125
Eldoret
Fax: +254(321) 43047

Founded: 1984 **Type:** Academic **Head:** Jafred S. Musisi *Phone:* +254(321) 63111/4 **Staff:** 4 Prof. 12 Other **Holdings:** 50 books **Language of Collection/Services:** English/ English **Subjects:** Agriculture (Tropics), Crops, Animal Husbandry, Education/Extension, Entomology, Food Sciences, Horticulture, Plant Pathology, Soil Science, Veterinary Medicine, Water Resources **Loan:** Internationally **Service:** Internationally **Photocopy:** Yes

1684   Embu, Kenya
Kenya Agricultural Research Institute, Regional
  Research Centre (KARI, RRC)
Library
PB 27
Embu PC 0161

Former Name: Embu Agricultural Research Station **Founded:** 1953 **Type:** Research **Head:** S.P. Gachanja *Phone:* +254(161) 20116, 20873 *Email:* icraf-embu@cgiar. org **Staff:** 1 Prof. 1 Other **Holdings:** 227 books 2 journals **Language of Collection/Services:** English / English **Subjects:** Animal Husbandry, Animal Production, Extension, Biotechnology, Crop Production, Entomology, Farming

Systems, Food Sciences, Horticulture, Plants, Plant Protection, Rural Sociology, Soil, Stored Products **Databases Used:** CABCD **Photocopy:** Yes

♦**1685 Kericho, Kenya**
Tea Research Foundation of Kenya (TRFK)
Library
PO Box 820
Kericho
Fax: +254(361) 20575

Former Name: Tea Research Institute of East Africa **Founded:** 1951 **Type:** Government **Head:** V. Sudoi *Phone:* +254(361) 20598/9 **Staff:** 1 Prof. 1 Other **Holdings:** 10,100 books 21 journals **Language of Collection/Services:** English/English **Subjects:** Tea **Loan:** Internationally **Service:** Internationally **Photocopy:** Yes

♦**1686 Kitale, Kenya**
Ministry of Agriculture, National Agricultural
    Research Centre - Kitale (MOA,
    NARC-Kitale)
Library
PO Box 450
Kitale, Rift Valley Province
Fax: +254(325) 20161

Founded: 1951 **Type:** Government **Head:** R.C. Butaki *Phone:* +254(325) 20107/9, 20160 **Staff:** 5 Other **Holdings:** 1,490 books 162 journals **Language of Collection/Services:** English **Subjects:** Agriculture (Tropics), Agricultural Development, Agricultural Economics, Biometry, Agricultural Engineering, Animal Husbandry, Biotechnology, Crops, Education/Extension, Entomology, Farming, Food Sciences, Horticulture, Plant Pathology, Statistics, Soil Science **Loan:** In country **Photocopy:** Yes

♦**1687 Londiani, Kenya**
Kenya Forestry College (KFC)
Library
PO Box 8
Londiani
Phone: +254(361) 64029

Former Name: Forest Training School **Founded:** 1960 **Type:** Academic **Head:** A.M. Njoroge *Phone:* +254(361) 64029 **Staff:** 1 Prof. 2 Other **Holdings:** 5,000 books 600 journals **Language of Collection/Services:** English / English **Subjects:** Crops, Extension, Engineering, Entomology, Farming, Forest Economics, Forest Management, Forestry, Plant Pathology, Plants, Soil Science, Surveying, Water Resources **Loan:** Inhouse **Service:** In country **Photocopy:** No

♦**1688 Mbita Point, Kenya**
International Centre of Insect Physiology and
    Ecology, Mbita Point Field Station
    (ICIPE-Mbita)
Library
PO Box 30
Mbita Point, South Nyanza

Founded: 1980 **Head:** Dorothy Achieng *Phone:* +254(35) 43281/2/6 **Type:** International **Staff:** 1 Prof. 1 Other **Holdings:** 1,500 books 30 journals **Language of Collection/Ser-**

vices: English **Subjects:** Agriculture (Tropics), Crops, Entomology **Specializations:** Pest Control, Pest Resistance **Databases Developed:** PMDISS - Pest Management Documentation and Information System and Service **Databases Used:** Agricola; Agris; CABCD **Loan:** In country **Photocopy:** Yes

♦**1689 Nairobi, Kenya**
Environment Liaison Centre International (ELCI)
Centre for Environment Development Information
    Exchange (CEDIE)
PO Box 72461
Nairobi
Location: Ndemi Road off Ngong Road **Phone:** +254(2) 562015/22 **Fax:** +254(2) 562175

Founded: 1975 **Head:** Dianah Macharia *Phone:* +254(2) 562015/22 **Type:** International **Staff:** 1 Prof. 1 Other **Holdings:** 3,500 books 500 journals **Language of Collection/Services:** English, French, Spanish **Subjects:** Agriculture (Tropics), Animal Husbandry, Biotechnology, Crops, Farming, Fisheries, Food Security, Food Supply, Forestry, Soil Science, Water Resources **Databases Developed:** NGO DATABANK - Profiles of 8,000 NGO contacts; available free to Southern NGO'S and for a charge to others **Loan:** Do not loan **Service:** Internationally **Photocopy:** Yes

1690   **Nairobi, Kenya**
International Centre for Research in Agroforestry
    (ICRAF)
Library
PO Box 30677
Nairobi
Location: ICRAF House, United Nations Avenue, Gigiri **Fax:** +254(2) 521001 **Email:** icraf@cgiar.org **WWW:** www.cgiar.org/icraf

Founded: 1978 **Type:** International **Head:** William Umbima *Phone:* +254(2) 521450 *Email:* wumbima@cgiar.org **Staff:** 5 Prof. 3 Other **Holdings:** 130 journals 40,000 books **Language of Collection/Services:** English / English **Subjects:** Agriculture (Tropics), Agricultural Development, Agricultural Economics, Agricultural Engineering, Animal Husbandry, Biotechnology, Crops, Education/Extension, Entomology, Farming, Forestry, Horticulture, Soil Science, Veterinary Medicine, Water Resources **Specializations:** Agroforestry, Arid Zones, Farming Systems, Land Use, Multipurpose Trees, Natural Resources Management, Semi-arid Zones, Soil Conservation **Databases Developed:** Multipurpose Trees Database; AFBIB - Agroforestry bibliography database **Databases Used:** Comprehensive **Loan:** Inhouse **Service:** Internationally **Photocopy:** Yes

1691   **Nairobi, Kenya**
International Centre of Insect Physiology and
    Ecology (ICIPE)
Information Resource Centre (IRC)
PO Box 30772
Nairobi
Location: Duduville, Kasarani, off Thika Road **Phone:** +254(2) 802501/3/9 **Fax:** +254(2) 803360 **Email:** icipe@cgiar.org **WWW:** www.icipe.org

Founded: 1973 **Type:** International **Head:** Dr. Annalee Mengech *Phone:* +254(2) 802501 ext 2125, 803753 *Email:* icipe@cgiar.org **Staff:** 3 Prof. 2 Other **Holdings:** 9,000 books 130 journals **Language of Collection/Services:** English / English **Subjects:** Entomology **Specializations:** Insect Pests, Integrated Control, Pest Control **Databases Developed:** PMDISS - Pest Management Documentation and Information Systems and Services **Databases Used:** Agris; CABCD; SCI **Loan:** In country **Service:** Internationally **Photocopy:** Yes

1692   Nairobi, Kenya
            International Livestock Research Institute (ILRI)
            Library
            PO Box 30709
            Nairobi
Location: Naivasha Road **Fax:** +254(2) 631499 **Email:** ilri-kenya@cgiar.org **WWW:** www.cgiar.org/ilri

Former Name: International Laboratory for Research on Animal Diseases (ILRAD) **Founded:** 1975 **Type:** International **Head:** Mr. Normand Demers *Phone:* +254(2) 632311 *Email:* n.demers@cgiar.org **Staff:** 2 Prof. 2 Other **Holdings:** 3,000 books 215 journals **Language of Collection/Services:** English / English **Subjects:** Agricultural Economics, Animal Husbandry, Entomology, Veterinary Medicine **Specializations:** Theileria, Trypanosomiasis **Databases Developed:** Database of tropical ruminant animal health and production literature; African Trypanosomiasis - not accessible internationally **Databases Used:** Agricola; Biosis; CABCD; Medline **Loan:** In country **Service:** Internationally **Photocopy:** Yes

♦**1693   Nairobi, Kenya**
            Kenya Agricultural Research Institute (KARI)
            Library and Scientific Literature Service
            PO Box 30148
            Nairobi
Location: Muguga

Former Name: East African Agriculture and Forestry Research Organization (EAAFRO) **Type:** Government **Founded:** 1929 **Head:** E.M. Kamumbu *Phone:* +254(2) 32880/6 ext 266 **Staff:** 3 Prof. 20 Other **Holdings:** 110,000 books 140 journals **Language of Collection/Services:** English **Subjects:** Agricultural Development, Agricultural Economics, Agriculture (Tropics), Agricultural Engineering, Biotechnology, Animal Husbandry, Crops, Entomology, Farming, Forestry, Horticulture, Plant Pathology, Soil Science, Veterinary Medicine, Water Resources **Loan:** Internationally **Photocopy:** Yes

♦**1694   Nairobi, Kenya**
            Kenya National Library Services (KNLS)
            PO Box 30573
            Nairobi
Location: Ngong Road **Phone:** +254(2) 718012 **Fax:** +254 (2) 721749

Founded: 1965 **Type:** Government **Head:** Mr. Stanley Ng'Ang'A *Phone:* +254(2) 718012 **Staff:** 31 Prof. 94 Other **Holdings:** 549,734 books 10 journals **Language of Collection/Services:** English / English **Subjects:** Agribusiness,

Agricultural Development, Agricultural Economics, Agricultural Engineering, Animal Husbandry, Crops, Farming, Biotechnology, Education/Extension, Entomology, Forestry **Specializations:** Africa **Loan:** Internationally **Service:** Internationally **Photocopy:** Yes

♦**1695   Nairobi, Kenya**
            Kenyatta University (KU)
            Moi Library
            PO Box 43844
            Nairobi
Phone: +254(2) 810900/19 ext 57043 **Fax:** +254(2) 810759

Former Name: Kenyatta University College **Founded:** 1972 **Type:** Academic **Head:** Mr. James M. Ngàngà *Phone:* +254(2) 810900/19 ext 57043 **Staff:** 19 Prof. 102 Other **Holdings:** 500 books 50 journals **Language of Collection/Services:** English **Subjects:** Agriculture (Tropics), Animal Husbandry, Biotechnology, Crops, Farming, Fisheries, Forestry, Horticulture, Soil Science **Loan:** In country **Service:** Inhouse **Photocopy:** Yes

1696   Nairobi, Kenya
            Ministry of Agriculture, Agricultural Information
                  Resource Centre (MOA)
            Kenya Agricultural Documentation Center
                  (KADOC)
            PO Box 14733
            Nairobi
Location: Cathedran Road **Phone:** +254(2) 446464 ext 105 **Fax:** +254(2) 446467

Former Name: Ministry of Agriculture and Livestock Development (MALD), Ministry of Agriculture, Livestock and Marketing Development (MALMD) **Founded:** 1979 **Type:** Government **Head:** Mrs. Nancy Kungu *Phone:* +254(2) 446464 ext 105 **Staff:** 1 Prof. 4 Other **Holdings:** 18,000 books 44 journals **Language of Collection/Services:** English / English **Subjects:** Comprehensive **Networks:** AGRIS **Databases Developed:** KADOC - database containing non-conventional technical and scientific material **Databases Used:** Comprehensive **Loan:** Internationally **Service:** Internationally **Photocopy:** Yes

1697   Nairobi, Kenya
            Ministry of Agriculture (MOA)
            Library Services
            PO Box 30028
            Nairobi
Location: Kilimo House, Cathedral Road **Phone:** +254(2) 718870 ext 48322

Former Name: Ministry of Agriculture, Livestock and Marketing Development (MALMD) **Type:** Government **Founded:** 1900 **Head:** Mr. D.P. Mathenge *Phone:* +254(2) 718870 ext 48364 **Staff:** 4 Prof. 5 Other **Holdings:** 60,000 books 33 journals **Language of Collection/Services:** English / English **Subjects:** Agricultural Economics, Animal Husbandry, Crops, Veterinary Medicine **Loan:** Inhouse **Service:** Internationally **Photocopy:** Yes

1698 Nairobi, Kenya
Ministry of Agriculture, Veterinary Research
Laboratory (MOA, Vet-Labs)
Vet-Labs Library
PO Kabete
Nairobi, Nairobi
Phone: +254(2) 631287, 631390 ext 46017 **Fax:** +54(2) 631273

Former Name: Ministry of Agriculture and Livestock Development (MALD), Ministry of Agriculture, Livestock and Marketing Development (MALMD) **Founded:** 1907 **Type:** Government **Head:** Fredrick N. Muthui *Phone:* +254(2) 631287, 631390 ext 46017 **Staff:** 1 Prof. 2 Other **Holdings:** 7,500 books 180 journals **Language of Collection/Services:** English / English **Subjects:** Animal Diseases, Animal Husbandry, Biotechnology, Veterinary Medicine **Loan:** Inhouse **Service:** Inhouse **Photocopy:** No

♦1699 Nairobi, Kenya
Ministry of Environment and Natural Resources, Forest Department
Library
PO Box 30513
Nairobi
Location: Karura Forest Station **Phone:** +254(2) 762195

Founded: 1902 **Type:** Government **Staff:** 1 Prof. 2 Other **Holdings:** 3,000 books 10 journals **Language of Collection/Services:** English / English **Subjects:** Extension, Farming, Forestry, Plant Pathology, Soil Science, Water Resources **Loan:** In country **Service:** Inhouse **Photocopy:** Yes

1700 Nairobi, Kenya
Ministry of Lands and Settlement, Survey of Kenya
Library
PO Box 30046
Nairobi, Nairobi

Founded: 1952 **Type:** Government **Head:** A.M. Masio *Phone:* +254(2) 802241/2 ext 241 **Staff:** 1 Prof. 1 Other **Subjects:** Mapping, Surveying **Loan:** Do not loan **Photocopy:** Yes

♦1701 Nairobi, Kenya
Ministry of Research, Technical Training and Technology, Kenya Industrial Research and Development Institute (KIRDI)
Library and Information Services
PO Box 30650
Nairobi
Location: Dunga, Lusaka Road **Phone:** +254(2) 557728, 557762 **Fax:** +254(2) 505546

Founded: 1942 **Type:** Research **Head:** Paul B. Imende *Phone:* +254(2) 557988, 557762 **Staff:** 5 Prof. 7 Other **Language of Collection/ Services:** English/English **Holdings:** 3,500 books 56 journals **Subjects:** Agricultural Engineering, Biotechnology, Fertilizers, Food Sciences, Machinery **Photocopy:** Yes **Loan:** In country

♦1702 Nairobi, Kenya
National Council for Science and Technology (NCST)
Kenya National Scientific Information, Documentation and Communication Center (KENSIDOC)
PO Box 30623
Nairobi
Location: 9th Floor, Utalii House, Uhuru Highway **Phone:** +254(2) 336173 **Fax:** +254(2) 330947

Founded: 1978 **Type:** Government **Head:** Mrs. E.K. Muthigani *Phone:* +254(2) 336173 **Staff:** 2 Prof. 2 Other **Holdings:** 1,000 books 4 journals **Language of Collection/ Services:** English / English **Loan:** Inhouse **Service:** Inhouse **Photocopy:** Yes

♦1703 Nairobi, Kenya
United Nations Environment Programme (UNEP)
Library and Documentation Centre
PO Box 30552
Nairobi
Location: United Nations Avenue, Gigiri **Phone:** +254(2) 622543 **Fax:** +254(2) 226890

Founded: 1973 **Type:** International **Head:** Mary Dwyer Rigby *Phone:* +254(2) 622541 **Staff:** 1 Prof. 6 Other **Holdings:** 50,000 books 280 journals **Language of Collection/ Services:** English / English **Subjects:** Biotechnology, Diversity, Pesticides, Range Management, Soil Science, Water Resources **Specializations:** Arid Zones, Dry Farming, Environment **Databases Developed:** EPDOC - Database provides bibliographic access to UNEP's documents; searches are free; presently must access inhouse **Loan:** Inhouse **Service:** Internationally **Photocopy:** Yes

♦1704 Nairobi, Kenya
United States Agency for International Development, Regional Economic Development Services Office for Eastern and Southern Africa (USAID, REDSO/ESA)
Library
PO Box 30261
Nairobi
Location: Union Towers, Moi Avenue **Phone:** +254(2) 331160 ext 2356

Type: Government **Head:** Patricia Wanzalla *Phone:* +254 (2) 331160 ext 2356 **Staff:** 1 Prof. **Holdings:** 10,000 books 100 journals **Language of Collection/Services:** English/ English **Subjects:** Agricultural Research, Food Aid, Forestry, Livestock, Natural Resources **Specializations:** Africa, East Africa, Southern Africa **Loan:** In country **Service:** In country **Photocopy:** Yes

1705 Naivasha, Kenya
Kenya Agricultural Research Institute, National Animal Husbandry Research Centre (KARI, NAHRC)
Library
PO Box 25
Naivasha

Phone: +254(311) 20165/6 ext 31 **Fax:** +254(311) 20102 **Email:** karinaiv@arcc.or.ke

Former Name: National Animal Husbandry Research Station (NAHRS) **Founded:** 1939 **Type:** Government **Head:** Francis Nyoike Kimani *Phone:* +254(311) 20165/6 *Email:* karinaiv@arcc.or.ke **Staff:** 1 Other **Holdings:** 300 books 20 journals **Language of Collection/Services:** English / English **Subjects:** Animal Husbandry **Loan:** Inhouse **Service:** Inhouse **Photocopy:** Yes

1706   Njoro, Kenya
         Egerton University
         Library
         PO Box 536
         Njoro
Phone: +254(37) 61620 **Fax:** +254(37) 61527 **Email:** egerton@users.africanonline.or.ke

Former Name: Egerton College **Founded:** 1939 **Type:** Academic **Head:** S.C. Otenya *Phone:* +254(37) 61620, 61282 **Staff:** 22 Prof. 92 Other **Holdings:** 150,000 books 30 journals **Language of Collection/Services:** English **Subjects:** Agricultural Economics, Agricultural Engineering, Animal Husbandry, Dairy Science, Education/Extension, Food Sciences **Databases Used:** Comprehensive **Loan:** In country **Service:** In country **Photocopy:** Yes

1707   Ruiru, Kenya
         Coffee Research Foundation, Coffee Research
            Station (CRF)
         Library
         PO Box 4
         Ruiru
Fax: +254(151) 55133

Type: Government **Head:** Mrs. L.W. Njeru *Phone:* +254 (151) 54631 ext 230 **Staff:** 1 Other **Holdings:** 1,552 books 24 journals **Language of Collection/Services:** English/ English **Subjects:** Agriculture (Tropics), Agribusiness, Agricultural Development, Agricultural Economics, Agricultural Engineering, Crops, Plant Pathology, Entomology, Education/Extension, Horticulture, Soil Science **Loan:** Inhouse **Service:** Inhouse **Photocopy:** Yes

Kiribati

1708   Tarawa, Kiribati
         Ministry of Natural Resources Development,
            Agriculture Division
         Library
         PO Box 267
         Bikenibeu
         Tarawa
Location: Agriculture Station, Tanaea, South Tarawa
Phone: +686 28108 **Fax:** +686 28121

Type: Government **Head:** Ms. Roota Collins

1709   Tarawa, Kiribati
         University of the South Pacific
         Kiribati Extension Centre
         PO Box 59

         Teaoraereke
         Tarawa
Phone: +686 21085 **WWW:** www.usp.ac.fj

Founded: 1973 **Type:** Government **Head:** R. Teiwaki **Staff:** 5 Other **Holdings:** 5,000 books **Subjects:** Extension

Korea, North

1710   Pyongyang, North Korea
         Academy of the Agricultural Sciences
         Institute for Science and Technology Information
            (ISTI)
         Chonggye-Dong
         Rongsong District
         Pyongyang
Fax: +850(2) 814660

Type: Government **Networks:** AGRIS

Korea, South

1711   Kwangju, South Korea
         Chonnam National University (CNU)
         Library
         318 Yang-Dong
         Kwangju
WWW: www.chonnam.ac.kr

Founded: 1952 **Type:** Academic **Holdings:** 158,000 books

1712   Seoul, South Korea
         Forestry Research Institute (FRI)
         Library
         207 Chongnyangni-dong
         Tongdaemun-gu
         Seoul 130-012
Phone: +82(2) 961-2715 **Fax:** +82(2) 967-5101 **Email:** friok@chollian.dacom.co.kr **WWW:** user.chollian.net/ ~frirok

Staff: 1 Prof. 1 Other **Holdings:** 18,311 books 102 journals **Subjects:** Forestry **Databases Used:** Current Contents

1713   Seoul, South Korea
         Kon-Kuk University
         Library
         93-1 Mojin-dong
         Seongdong-gu
         Seoul 133-701
Phone: +82(2) 450-3852/5 **Fax:** +82(2) 457-5411 **WWW:** www.konkuk.ac.kr

Founded: 1946 **Type:** Academic **Holdings:** 481,000 books 1,547 journals **Language of Collection/Services:** Korean, English / Korean, English **Subjects:** Agriculture (Tropics), Agricultural Development, Agricultural Economics, Agricultural Engineering, Animal Husbandry, Crops, Education/ Extension, Farming, Food Sciences, Forestry, Horticulture, Plant Pathology, Veterinary Medicine **Loan:** Inhouse **Service:** Inhouse **Photocopy:** Yes

1714   Seoul, South Korea
Korea University
Library
1, 5-ga, Anam-dong
Sungbuk-gu
Seoul
WWW: www.korea.ac.kr

Former Name: Posung College **Founded:** 1937 **Type:** Academic **Holdings:** 400,200 books

1715   Seoul, South Korea
Sung Kyun Kwan University
Library
53, 3-ga, Myungryun-dong
Chongno-gu
Seoul 110
WWW: www.akku.ac.kr/home/index_e.html

Founded: 1938 **Type:** Academic **Holdings:** 400,000 books

1716   Suwon, South Korea
Ministry of Agriculture and Forestry, Rural
    Development Administration
Agriculture Science Library
250 Seodun-Dong
Kwonsun-gu
Suwon, Kyonggi-do 441-707
Phone: +82(331) 299-2376 **Fax:** +82(331) 299-2384
Email: kslee@lib.rda.go.kr **WWW:** www.maf.go.kr,
lib.rda.go.kr

Founded: 1906 **Type:** Government **Holdings:** 35,800 books 980 journals **Subjects:** Rural Development

1717   Suwon, South Korea
Seoul National University, College of Agriculture
    and Life Sciences
Agricultural Library
#103 Seo Dum-Dong
Suwon 441-744
Fax: +82(331) 296-0130 **Email:** dglib@aginfo.snu.ac.kr
WWW: aglib.snu.ac.kr **OPAC:** aglib.snu.ac.kr

Founded: 1945 **Type:** Academic **Head:** Dr. Don Koo Lee
Phone: +82(331) 290-2327 *Email:* leedk@plaza.snu.ac.kr
Staff: 5 Prof. 7 Other **Holdings:** 1,130,000 books 4,500 journals **Subjects:** Comprehensive **Specializations:** Agricultural Engineering, Biotechnology, Food Engineering **Loan:** Internationally **Service:** Internationally **Photocopy:** No **Networks:** AGRIS

1718   Taegu, South Korea
Kyungpook National University (KNU)
Central Library
1370 Sanyuk-dong, Buk-gu
Taegu 635
WWW: www.kyungpook.ac.kr

Founded: 1946 **Type:** Academic

Kuwait

1719   Safat, Kuwait
Public Authority for Agriculture and Fishing
Library
PO Box 21422
Safat 13075

Type: Government **Networks:** AGRIS

Kyrgyzstan

1720   Bishkek, Kyrgyzstan
Bishkek Resource Center
National Library
ul. Sovetskaya 208, Rm 92
Bishkek 720000
Phone: +996(312) 223829 **Fax:** +996(312) 223829 **Email:** brcenter@adv.bishkek.su

Head: Ms. Janet Kilian, Adviser

1721   Bishkek, Kyrgyzstan
Kyrgyz Agrarian Academy
Academic Library
68, Mederova St.
Bishkek 720005
Fax: +996(312) 540545

Former Name: Kirghiz Agriculture Institute **Founded:** 1933 **Type:** Academic **Head:** Gulmira K. Tynalieva *Phone:* +996(312) 540538 **Holdings:** 626,140 books **Language of Collection/Services:** Kyrgyz, Russian / Kyrgyz, Russian **Loan:** Inhouse **Service:** Inhouse **Photocopy:** No

1722   Bishkek, Kyrgyzstan
Kyrgyz Agrarian Academy
Kirghiz Republik Scientific Agricultural Library
T. Frunze St., 91
Bishkek 720027
Phone: +996(331) 225-3185

Former Name: Kirghiz SSR Scientific Agricultural Library **Founded:** 1975 **Type:** Government **Head:** Olga Alekseevna Gerasko **Staff:** 25 Prof. 2 Other **Holdings:** 420,887 books 77 journals **Language of Collection/Services:** Kyrgyz, Russian / Kyrgyz, Russian **Subjects:** Agribusiness, Agricultural Development, Agricultural Economics, Crops, Agricultural Engineering, Animal Husbandry, Biotechnology, Education/Extension, Entomology, Farming, Fisheries, Food Sciences, Forestry, Horticulture, Plant Pathology, Poultry, Soil Science, Veterinary Medicine, Water Resources **Loan:** Inhouse **Photocopy:** No

1723   Jalal-Abad, Kyrgyzstan
Jalal-Abad State University
Library
57 Lenin Street
Jalal-Abad 715600
Phone: +996(3722) 32206 **Fax:** +996(3722) 33900

1724   Osh, Kyrgyzstan
Osh State University (OSU)
Library
331 Lenin Street
Osh 714000
Phone: +996(3222) 22273 **Fax:** +996(3222) 24605 **Email:** tvs@osupub.freenet.bishkek.su

Founded: 1992

Laos

1725   Vientiane, Laos
National Forestry Research Center
Information Services
PO Box 7174
Vientiane
Phone: +856(21) 215000 **Fax:** +856(21) 215004

Subjects: Forestry

Latvia

1726   Aizkraukles Region, Latvia
Latvian Scientific Research Institute of
        Agriculture (LVZZPI "Agra")
Scientific Library
Skriveri - 1
Aizkraukles Region LV-5126
Phone: +371(51) 97266

Former Name: Latvian Scientific Research Institute of Agriculture and Economics **Founded:** 1959 **Type:** Government **Head:** Gaida Grabe *Phone:* +371(51) 97522 **Staff:** .5 Prof. **Holdings:** 67,400 books 8 journals **Language of Collection/Services:** Russian / Latvian **Subjects:** Agricultural Economics, Crops, Horticulture, Plants, Soil Science **Specializations:** Crop Production, Plant Breeding **Loan:** In country **Service:** In country **Photocopy:** Yes

1727   Jelgava, Latvia
Latvian University of Agriculture
Fundamental Library
2 Liela Street
Jelgava LV-3001
Phone: +371(30) 05695 **Fax:** +371(30) 27238 **Email:** bibliogr@cs.llu.lv **Ariel IP:** 159.148.237.67 **WWW:** www.cs.llu.lv/Struktv/Fund_b/LLUFB.HTM

Non-English Name: Latvijas Lauksaimniecibas Universitate (LLU), Fundamentala Biblioteka (FB) **Former Name:** Latvian Academy of Agriculture **Founded:** 1939 **Type:** Academic **Head:** Mrs. Ilona Dobelniece *Phone:* +371(30) 25925 *Email:* ilona@cs.llu.lv **Staff:** 20 Prof. 23 Other **Holdings:** 107,785 books 230 journals **Language of Collection/Services:** Latvian, Russian / Latvian **Subjects:** Comprehensive **Networks:** AGRIS; Latvian national on-line union catalog **Databases Developed:** Bibliographic database of the publications of the teaching staff of the Latvian University of Agriculture - local access; Bibliographic database of articles published in Latvian periodicals - local access **Databases**

Used: Comprehensive **Loan:** Internationally **Service:** Internationally **Photocopy:** Yes

1728   Riga, Latvia
Latvian Academic Library
Rûobuecîbas str. 10
Riga LV-1235
Phone: +371 710-6206 **Fax:** +371 710-6202 **Email:** acadlib@lib.acad.ib.lv **WWW:** www.acadlib.lv/e **OPAC:** www.acadlib.lv/e/katalogs

Head: Venta Kocere *Email:* vkocere@lib.acadlib.lv *Phone:* +371 710-6217

1729   Riga, Latvia
Riga Technical University
Scientific Library
10 Kipsalas Street
Riga LV-1659
Phone: +371 708-9431 **Fax:** +371 708-9474 **Email:** rtusclib@acad.latnet.lv **WWW:** www.rtu.lv/www_zb/rtu_sl.htm

Head: Aija Janbicka *Phone:* +371 708-9443

1730   Salaspils, Latvia
Latvian Forestry Research Institute "Silava"
Library
111, Rigas Str.
Salaspils LV-2169
Phone: +371(2) 949771 **Fax:** +371(2) 901359 **Email:** lib@silava.lv **WWW:** www.silava.lv/main.html

Head: Ieva Svenne **Subjects:** Afforestation, Protection of Forests, Silviculture, Timbers, Tree Breeding

1731   Sigulda, Latvia
Latvian Scientific Research Institute of Breeding
        and Veterinary Science, Research Centre
        "Sigra"
Library
1 Instituta St.
Sigulda LV-2150
Phone: +371 790-1654 **Fax:** +371 790-1655 **Email:** sigra@lis.lv

Founded: 1946 **Type:** Government **Holdings:** 32,800 books **Subjects:** Animal Husbandry, Animal Nutrition, Biochemistry, Breeding, Veterinary Science

Lebanon

1732   Beirut, Lebanon
American University of Beirut
Science and Agriculture Library
PO Box 11-0236
Beirut
Phone: +961(1) 350000, 340460 **Fax:** +961(1) 351706 **Email:** ec00@aub.edu.lb **WWW:** www.aub.edu.lb

Founded: 1958 **Type:** Academic **Staff:** 3 Other **Holdings:** 25,000 books 400 journals **Subjects:** Agribusiness, Agricultural Economics, Animal Husbandry, Crops, Food Technology, Irrigation, Mechanization, Nutrition, Plant Protection, Soil Science **Loan:** In country **Photocopy:** Yes

1733   Beirut, Lebanon
National Council for Scientific Research (NCSR)
Documentation and Scientific Information Centre
PO Box 11-8281
Beirut
Location: Cité Sportive, Fakhry and Dagher Bldg. **Phone:** +961(1) 840260/4, 822665/75 **Fax:** +961(1) 822639 **Email:** docctr@cnrs.edu.lb **WWW:** www.cnrs.edu.lb

Non-English Name: Conseil National Recherche Scientifique (CNRS), Centre de Documentation et d'Information Scientifique (CEDIS) **Founded:** 1974 **Type:** Government **Head:** Ms. Amal Habib *Phone:* +961(1) 840260/4 *Email:* docctr@cnrs.edu.lb **Staff:** 2 Prof. 2 Other **Holdings:** 4,000 books **Language of Collection/Services:** English, French, Arabic / English, French, Arabic **Subjects:** Comprehensive **Specializations:** Nuclear Energy **Networks:** AGRIS **Databases Developed:** CARIN - research projects; LEBINIS - Energy; AGRIN - bibliography of agriculture **Databases Used:** Comprehensive **Loan:** Inhouse **Service:** Internationally **Photocopy:** Yes

Lesotho

1734   Maseru, Lesotho
Lesotho Agricultural College
Library
Private Bag A4
Maseru
Phone: +266 322484

Founded: 1978 **Type:** Academic **Head:** Joel T. Malelu *Phone:* +266 322484 **Staff:** 2 Prof. 3 Other **Holdings:** 10,000 books **Language of Collection/Services:** English **Subjects:** Agricultural Economics, Animal Husbandry, Forestry, Crops, Home Economics, Mechanization, Soil Science **Photocopy:** No

♦**1735   Maseru, Lesotho**
Lesotho Highlands Development Authority
(LHDA)
Library
PO Box 7332
Maseru 100
Location: Orpen Road, Sun Cabanas Office Complex **Phone:** +266 314324 **Fax:** +266 310050

Type: Government **Head:** Francinah M. Thabisi *Phone:* +266 314324 **Staff:** 1 Prof. 1 Other **Language of Collection/Services:** English / English **Subjects:** Dairying, Field Crops, Fisheries, Forestry, Fruit Growing, Gardens, Soil Conservation **Databases Developed:** Environmental Database **Loan:** Internationally **Service:** Internationally **Photocopy:** Yes

♦**1736   Maseru, Lesotho**
Ministry of Agriculture, Agricultural Research
Division
National Agricultural Library
PO Box 829

Maseru 100
Phone: +266 312395 **Fax:** +266 310362 **Email:** agrires@ lesoff.co.za

Former Name: Agricultural Research Library **Founded:** 1980 **Type:** Government **Staff:** 1 Prof. 2 Other **Holdings:** 16,500 books 430 journals **Language of Collection/Services:** English / English **Subjects:** Agricultural Economics, Animal Husbandry, Extension, Farm Management, Forestry, Grassland Management, Horticulture, Irrigation, Plant Protection, Rural Sociology, Soil Science **Specializations:** Botany, Economics, Nutrition, Sociology, Zoology **Databases Used:** Agris; CABCD **Loan:** In country **Service:** In country **Photocopy:** Yes

1737   Maseru, Lesotho
Ministry of Agriculture, Cooperatives and
Marketing and Youth Affairs, Agricultural
Research Division
Agricultural Information Library
PO Box 24
Maseru 100
Location: Main South 1, Cathedral Area **Phone:** +266 312330 **Fax:** +266 310362

Founded: 1980 **Type:** Government **Head:** Shoeshoe E. Kholopo *Phone:* +266 312330 **Staff:** 1 Prof. **Holdings:** 10 journals 4,000 books **Language of Collection/Services:** English / Sesotho **Subjects:** Agricultural Development, Botany, Education/Extension, Farm Management, Horticulture, Human Nutrition, Plants, Soil, Zoology **Specializations:** Animal Husbandry, Communication, Home Economics, Social Sciences **Networks:** AGRIS **Loan:** Inhouse **Service:** Inhouse **Photocopy:** Yes

♦**1738   Maseru, Lesotho**
Southern African Development Community,
Environment and Land Management Sector
Coordination Unit (SADC, ELMS)
Documentation Centre
PO Box 24
Maseru 100
Location: Thaba Bosiu Project Building, Industrial Area **Phone:** +266 312158 **Fax:** +266 310190

Former Name: Southern African Development Coordination Conference (SADCC), Soil and Water Conservation and Land Utilization (SWCLU) **Head:** Eduardo A. Coelho *Phone:* +266 312158 **Staff:** 1 Prof. **Type:** Inter-governmental **Holdings:** 2,000 books 15 journals **Language of Collection/Services:** English / English **Subjects:** Agricultural Development, Agricultural Economics, Agroforestry, Erosion, Cost Effectiveness Analysis, Desertification, Environment, Farming, Forestry, Hydrology, Water Resources, Soil Science, Watershed Management **Specializations:** Land Use, Environment, Land Management, Soil Conservation, Water Conservation **Loan:** In country **Photocopy:** Yes

1739   Roma, Lesotho
National University of Lesotho (NUL)
Thomas Mofolo Library
PO Roma 180
Roma

Phone: +266 340601, 340468 **Fax:** +266 340000 **WWW:** www.nul.ls **OPAC:** thaba.nul.ls/library

Former Name: Pius XII College **Type:** Academic **Head:** Mrs. 'Mampaila M. Lebotsa *Email:* mm.lebotsa@nul.ls **Staff:** 11 Prof. 17 Other **Holdings:** 170,000 books 500 journals **Databases Used:** Agricola; ERIC

1740   Roma, Lesotho
National University of Lesotho, Institute of
       Southern African Studies (NUL, ISAS)
Documentation Centre
PO Roma 180
Roma

Location: PO Box 1892, Maseru **Fax:** +266 340000, 340004 **Email:** m.mmoshoeshoe-chadzingwa@nul.ls **WWW:** www.nul.ls/isas/index.htm

Founded: 1981 **Type:** Academic **Head:** M.M. Moshoeshoe-Chadzingwa *Email:* m.mmoshoeshoe-chadzingwa@nul.ls *Phone:* +266 310601, 340247 **Staff:** 4 Prof. 2 Other **Holdings:** 10,000 books 530 journals **Language of Collection/Services:** English, Sesotho / English, Sesotho **Subjects:** Agricultural Economics, Animal Production, Development Policy, Households, Natural Resources, Rural Sociology, Water Management **Specializations:** Environment, Gender Issues, Human Rights, Land Use, Marketing, Occupational Disorders, SADCC Countries, Tenure Systems **Databases Developed:** Lesotho Index - over 3000 annotated entries of documents; Government Gazette; High Court Judgements; Lesotho Clippings **Loan:** Inhouse **Service:** Internationally **Photocopy:** Yes

Liberia

1741   Monrovia, Liberia
Cuttington University College (CUC)
William V.S. Tubman Library
c/o The Episcopal Chruch of Liberia
PO Box 10-0277
Monrovia

Location: Suacoco, Bong County **Phone:** +231 2227519 **Fax:** +231 2227519 **Email:** cuc@libnet.net **WWW:** www.cuttington.org

Former Name: Cuttington College and Divinity School **Founded:** 1948 **Type:** Academic **Head:** Mr. Emmanuel R.C. Nyamadi *Phone:* +231 224-243 **Staff:** 2 Prof. 8 Other **Holdings:** 390 books **Subjects:** Animal Husbandry, Crops, Fisheries, Forestry, Horticulture, Hunting **Loan:** In country **Photocopy:** Yes

1742   Monrovia, Liberia
Ministry of Agriculture
Information Division
PO Box 9010
Tubmand Blvd.
1000 Monrovia 10

Networks: AGRIS

♦1743   Monrovia, Liberia
Ministry of Agriculture, Central Agricultural
       Research Institute (CARI)
Library
Mailbag 3929
Monrovia, Suakoko Bong County

Founded: 1980 **Type:** Government **Head:** Miss Lucy J. Bondo *Phone:* +231 223443 **Staff:** 1 Prof. 2 Other **Holdings:** 7,800 books 40 journals **Subjects:** Agricultural Economics, Agricultural Engineering, Animal Husbandry, Crops, Plant Protection, Soil Science **Loan:** In country

Libya

1744   Tajura, Libya
Marine Biology Research Centre
Library
PO Box 30830
Tajura

Phone: +218(21) 369-0001, 369-0003 **Fax:** +218(21) 369-0002

Head: Mr. Mohamed N. Ben Musa

1745   Tripoli, Libya
Agricultural Research Centre
National AGRIS Centre
PO Box 2480
Tripoli

Type: Government **Networks:** AGRIS

Lithuania

1746   Babtai, Lithuania
Lithuanian Institute of Horticulture (LIH)
Library
Kauno g. 28
4335 Babtai, Kauno rajonas

Phone: +370(7) 555416 **Fax:** +370(7) 555176 **Email:** institutas@lsdi.lt **WWW:** www1.omnitel.net/zu/LIH.html

Non-English Name: Lietuvos sodininkystes ir darzininkystes institutas (LSDI), Biblioteka **Former Name:** Lithuanian Scientific Research Institute of Agriculture, Vitenskaya Fruit and Vegetable Experiment Station **Founded:** 1989 **Type:** Government **Head:** Mrs. Birute Olkstiniene *Phone:* +370(7) 555416 *Email:* institutas@lsdi.lt **Staff:** 1.5 Prof. **Holdings:** 30,000 books 50 journals **Language of Collection/Services:** Lithuanian, Russian, English / Lithuanian **Subjects:** Flowers, Gardening, Horticulture, Plant Protection **Databases Used:** Agricola; Agris; CARIS **Service:** In country **Loan:** In country **Photocopy:** Yes

1747   Baisogala, Lithuania
Lithuanian Institute of Animal Science (LIAS)
Library
R. Zebenkos g. 12
5125 Baisogala, Radviliskio rajonas

Phone: +370(92) 55837 **Fax:** +370(92) 55886 **Email:** lgi@saiuliai.omnitel.net **WWW:** www1.omnitel.net/zu/LIAS.html

Non-English Name: Lietuvos gyvulininkystes institutas **Former Name:** Lithuanian Scientific Research Institute of Stock Breeding **Founded:** 1956 **Type:** Government **Head:** Mrs. Regina Gedviliene *Phone:* +370(92) 55837 **Staff:** 1 Prof. **Holdings:** 73,700 books 17 journals **Language of Collection/Services:** Lithuanian, Russian, English / Lithuanian **Subjects:** Animal Feeding, Animal Husbandry, Veterinary Medicine **Specializations:** Cattle, Pigs **Databases Used:** Agricola; Agris; CARIS **Databases Developed:** Dissertations and scientific reports of research from institute **Loan:** In country **Service:** In country **Photocopy:** Yes

1748   Dotnuva, Lithuania
         Lithuanian Institute of Agriculture (LIA)
         Library
         Instituto aleja 1
         5051 Dotnuva, Kedainiu rajonas
Phone: +370(57) 37308 **Fax:** +370(57) 60996 **Email:** lzibibl@lzi.lt **WWW:** lzi-institutas.lzi.lt

Non-English Name: Lietuvos zemdirbystes institutas (LZI), Biblioteka **Founded:** 1956 **Type:** Government **Head:** Mrs. Birute Ruzgiene *Phone:* +370(57) 37287 *Email:* birute@lzi.lt **Staff:** 9 Prof. **Holdings:** 261,000 books 72 journals **Language of Collection/Services:** Lithuanian, Russian, English / Lithuanian, English, Russian **Subjects:** Agronomy, Biology, Plants **Specializations:** Beekeeping, Crops, Crop Production, Cropping Systems, Farming Systems, Fertilizers, Herbicides, Microbiology, Plant Anatomy, Plant Diseases, Plant Breeding, Plant Ecology, Plant Genetics, Plant Physiology, Soil **Databases Developed:** Historic Lituanian agricultural publications - bibliographic descriptions of 16,000 publications issued before 1941 **Databases Used:** Current Contents; VINITI Abstracts **Loan:** Internationally **Service:** Internationally **Photocopy:** Yes

1749   Girionys, Lithuania
         Lithuanian Institute of Forestry
         Library
         4312 Girionys, Kauno rajonas
Phone: +370(7) 547335 **Fax:** +370(7) 547446 **Email:** miskinst@mi.lt

Non-English Name: Lietuvos misku institutas (LMI), Biblioteka **Founded:** 1952 **Type:** Government **Head:** Mrs. Julija Saudiene *Phone:* +370(7) 547335 **Staff:** 1 Prof. **Holdings:** 58,400 books 18 journals **Language of Collection/Services:** Russian, Lithuanian, English / Lithuanian **Subjects:** Biology, Environment **Specializations:** Forestry **Networks:** CABCD **Databases Used:** Agricola; Agris; CARIS; TREECD **Loan:** In country **Service:** In country **Photocopy:** Yes

1750   Kaisiadorys, Lithuania
         Lithuanian Veterinary Institute
         Library
         Instituto g. 2
         4230 Kaisiadorys

Phone: +370(56) 51936 **Fax:** +370(56) 51440 **Email:** lvi@org.ktu.lt **WWW:** www1.omnitel.net/zu/LVI.html

Non-English Name: Lietuvos veterinarijos institutas (LVI), Biblioteka **Founded:** 1962 **Type:** Government **Head:** Mrs. Birute Salkauskiene *Phone:* +370(56) 51936 *Email:* lvi@org.ktu.lt **Staff:** 1 Prof. **Holdings:** 67,000 books 45 journals **Language of Collection/Services:** Lithuanian / Lithuanian **Subjects:** Biology, Medicine, Veterinary Science **Databases Used:** Agricola; Agris; CARIS **Loan:** In country **Service:** In country **Photocopy:** Yes

1751   Kaunas, Lithuania
         Lithuanian Food Institute
         Department of Information, Patents, Standards and
            Publication
         Taikos pr. 92
         3031 Kaunas
Phone: +370(7) 719758 **Fax:** +370(7) 719393 **Email:** maistas@lmai.lt **WWW:** www1.omnitel.net/zu/LMI.html

Non-English Name: Lietuvos maisto institutas (LMI), Informacijos, standartu, patentu, ir leidybos skyrius **Founded:** 1958 **Type:** Government **Head:** Mrs. Marija Paserpskiene *Phone:* +370(7) 719758 *Email:* maistas@lmai.lt **Staff:** 8 Prof. 2 Other **Holdings:** 67,000 books 18 journals **Language of Collection/Services:** Lithuanian, Russian, English / Lithuanian **Subjects:** Food Sciences **Specializations:** Milk Products **Databases Used:** Agris; CARIS; Food Safety Plus; FSTA **Loan:** In country **Service:** In country **Photocopy:** Yes

1752   Kaunas, Lithuania
         Lithuanian Veterinary Academy
         Library
         Tilzes g. 18
         3022 Kaunas
Phone: +370(7) 261145 **Fax:** +370(7) 261417 **Email:** biblioteka@mail.lva.lt **WWW:** www.lva.lt

Non-English Name: Lietuvos veterinarijos akademija (LVA), Biblioteka **Founded:** 1936 **Type:** Government **Head:** Mrs. Nijole Orzekauskiene *Phone:* +370(7) 261145 **Staff:** 9 Prof. **Holdings:** 244,400 books 59 journals **Language of Collection/Services:** Lithuanian, Russian, English / Lithuanian **Subjects:** Animal Husbandry, Medicine, Veterinary Science **Specializations:** Veterinary Medicine **Databases Used:** Agricola; Agris; CARIS; Medline **Loan:** Internationally **Service:** Internationally **Photocopy:** Yes

1753   Kaunas-Akademija, Lithuania
         Lithuanian University of Agriculture (LUA)
         Library
         4324 Kaunas-Akademija
Phone: +370(7) 397134 **Fax:** +370(7) 397531 **Email:** abon@nora.lzua.lt **WWW:** www.lzua.lt/bibl/bibl.html **OPAC:** www.lzua.lt/bibl/bibl.html

Non-English Name: Lietuvos zemès ukio universitetas (LZUU), Biblioteka **Former Name:** Academy of Agriculture **Founded:** 1924 **Type:** Academic **Head:** Mrs. Ausra Raguckaite *Phone:* +370(7) 296564 *Email:* ausra@nora.lzua.lt **Staff:** 31 Prof. **Holdings:** 551,000 books 200 journals **Language of Collection/Services:** Lithuanian, Russian, English

/Lithuanian **Subjects:** Agricultural Development, Agricultural Economics, Agricultural Engineering, Forestry, Home Economics, Water Resources **Databases Developed:** Publications of the university teaching staff and University in Print - local access **Databases Used:** Comprehensive **Loan:** Internationally **Service:** Internationally **Photocopy:** Yes

1754   Radviliskis, Lithuania
Lithuanian Institute of Agriculture, Radviliskskis
Experiment Station
Library
5120 Radviliskis

Type: Government **Holdings:** 2,200 books

1755   Raudondvaris, Lithuania
Lithuanian Institute of Agricultural Engineering
(LIAgEng)
Library
Instituto g. 20
4320 Raudondvaris, Kauno rajonas
Phone: +370(7) 549289 **Fax:** +370(7) 549366 **Email:** liageng@mei.lt **WWW:** dvaras.mei.lt

Non-English Name: Lietuvos zemes ukio inzinerijos institutas (LZUII), Biblioteka **Former Name:** Lithuanian Scientific Research Institute of Mechanization and Electrification of Agriculture **Founded:** 1956 **Type:** Government **Head:** Mrs. Kristina Povilaitiene *Phone:* +370(7) 549289 *Email:* liageng@mei.lt **Staff:** 1.5 Prof. **Holdings:** 20,300 books 32 journals **Language of Collection/Services:** Lithuanian, Russian, English / Lithuanian **Subjects:** Agricultural Development, Agricultural Engineering, Buildings, Crops, Soil Science, Education/Extension, Farming **Databases Used:** Agricola; Agris; CARIS **Databases Developed:** Dissertations and scientific reports of research from institute - local access **Loan:** In country **Service:** In country **Photocopy:** Yes

1756   Rumokai, Lithuania
Lithuanian Institute of Agriculture, Rumokai
Experiment Station
Library
4293 Rumokai, Vilkaviskio rajonas

Type: Government **Holdings:** 2,400 books

1757   Velzys, Lithuania
Baltic Zone Experiment Station of Poultry Raising
Library
Nevezio g. 54
5368 Velzys, Panevezio rajonas

Founded: 1963 **Type:** Government **Holdings:** 6,300 books **Subjects:** Poultry

1758   Vilainiai, Lithuania
Lithuanian Water Management Institute (LWMI)
Library
Parko g. 6
5048 Vilainiai, Kedainiu rajonas
Phone: +370(57) 68181 **Fax:** +370(57) 68105 **Email:** kutra@water.omnitel.net **WWW:** www1.omnitel.net/zu/LWMI.html

Non-English Name: Lietuvos vandens ukio institutas (LVUI), Biblioteka **Founded:** 1951 **Type:** Government **Head:** Mrs. Liuda Zarskyte *Phone:* +370(57) 68181 **Staff:** 1 Prof. **Holdings:** 22,100 books 32 journals **Language of Collection/Services:** Lithuanian, Russian, English / Lithuanian **Subjects:** Water Management, Water Pollution, Water Resources **Databases Developed:** Dissertations and scientific reports of institute's researchers - local access **Databases Used:** Agricola; Agris; CARIS **Loan:** In country **Service:** In country **Photocopy:** Yes

1759   Vilnius, Lithuania
Lithuanian Institute of Agrarian Economics
(LIAE)
Library
V. Kudirkos g. 18
2009 Vilnius
Phone: +370(2) 613539 **Fax:** +370(2) 614524 **Email:** bibliot@laei.lt **WWW:** www.laei.lt/indexe.html

Non-English Name: Lietuvos agrarines ekonomikos institutas (LAEI), Biblioteka **Former Name:** Lithuanian Scientific Research Institute of Agricultural Economics **Founded:** 1960 **Type:** Government **Head:** Mrs. Audrone Naraskeviciene *Phone:* +370(2) 613539 *Email:* bibliot@laei.lt **Staff:** 1 Prof. **Holdings:** 34,200 books 40 journals **Language of Collection/Services:** Lithuanian, English, Russian / Lithuanian **Subjects:** Agricultural Development, Agricultural Economics **Databases Used:** Agricola; Agris; CARIS; Unikat/Unimarc **Loan:** In country **Service:** In country **Photocopy:** Yes

1760   Vilnius, Lithuania
Lithuanian Ministry of Agriculture
Lithuanian Agricultural Library
Gedimino pr. 19
2025 Vilnius
Phone: +370(2) 391237 **Fax:** +370(2) 391236 **Email:** biblioteka@zum.lt **WWW:** www.zum.lt **OPAC:** www.libis.lt

Non-English Name: Lietuvos zemes ukio ministerija, Lietuvos zemes ukio biblioteka **Founded:** 1969 **Type:** Government **Head:** Mrs. Renata Niauriene *Phone:* +370(2) 391 236 *Email:* r.niauriene@zum.lt **Staff:** 3 Prof. **Holdings:** 154,000 books 60 journals **Language of Collection/Services:** Lithuanian, Russian, English / Lithuanian **Subjects:** Comprehensive **Specializations:** Animal Husbandry, Crops, Horticulture, Plants, Veterinary Medicine **Databases Developed:** Annual non-conventional scientific reports on agriculture in Lithuania **Databases Used:** Comprehensive **Networks:** AGRIS; LIBIS **Loan:** Internationally **Service:** In country **Photocopy:** Yes

Luxembourg

1761   Luxembourg
Administration des Services Techniques de
l'Agriculture (ASTA)
BP 1904
16 rte d'Esch

L-1019 Luxembourg
Fax: +352 457172341 **Email:** asta@asta.smtp.etat.lu

Type: Government **Networks:** AGRIS

1762　Luxembourg
Centre Universitaire de Luxembourg
Bibliothèque
162A, avenue de la Faïenceri
L-1511 Luxembourg
Phone: +352 466-6441 ext 520 **Fax:** +352 466-6441 ext
521 **WWW:** www.cu.lu/cu/generali/bib.htm

Head: Gilbert Graff *Phone:* +352 466-6441 ext 520

Macedonia, The Former Yugoslav Republic of

1763　Skopje, Macedonia
Ss. Cyril and Methodius University
National and University Library "St. Kliment
　　Ohridski"
bul. "Goce Delcev" 6
91000 Skopje
Phone: +389(91) 115 177, 133 418 **Fax:** +389(91) 226 846
Email: kliment@nubsk.edu.mk **WWW:** www.ukim.edu.
mk **OPAC:** nubsk.nubsk.edu.mk/cobiss

Non-English Name: Univerzitet Sv. Kiril i Metodij, Narod-
na i Univerzitetska Biblioteka Sv. Kliment Ohridski **Head:**
Mladen Srbinovski *Phone:* +389(91) 133 418 *Email:* mladen
@nubsk.edu.mk

Madagascar

1764　Antananarivo, Madagascar
Centre National de la Recherche Appliquée au
　　Développement Rural (CENRADERU)
Unité d'Information Scientifique et Technique
　　(UIST)
BP 1690
Antananarivo
Phone: +261(2) 40130, 40270 **Email:** fofifa@bow.dts.mg

Former Name: Centre de Documentation et d'Information
pour la Recherche Agricole **Founded:** 1976 **Type:** Research
Head: Raharimanana Minasoa *Email:* fofifa@bow.dts.mg
Phone: +261(2) 40130, 40270 **Staff:** 2 Prof. 4 Other **Holdings:** 10,000 books 10 journals **Subjects:** Agricultural Economics, Animal Husbandry, Crops, Farm Machinery, Fish
Culture, Farming, Fisheries, Forestry, Research, Rural Development, Soil, Veterinary Science, Zootechny **Photocopy:**
Yes

1765　Antananarivo, Madagascar
Chamber of Commerce, Industry and Agriculture
　　of Antananarivo (CCIA)
Library
20, Rue Paul Dussac, BP 166
Antananarivo 101

Phone: +261(2) 222-0211/2, 222-0281 **Fax:** +261(2) 222-
0213

Non-English Name: Chambre de Commerce, d'Industrie et
d'Agriculture d'Antananarivo (CCIA), Bibliothèque **Type:**
Public **Founded:** 1920 **Head:** Mr. Georges Rheal *Phone:*
+261(2) 222-0211/2, 222-0281 **Staff:** 1 Prof. **Holdings:** 100
books **Language of Collection/Services:** French **Subjects:**
Agriculture (Tropics), Agricultural Development, Agricultural Economics, Agribusiness, Animal Husbandry, Biotechnology, Crops, Plant Pathology, Veterinary Medicine
Photocopy: Yes

1766　Antananarivo, Madagascar
Ministère de l'Information, de la Culture et de la
　　Communication (MICC)
Bibliothèque Nationale (BN)
BP 257
Antananarivo 101
Location: Rue Me Stibbe, Anosy **Fax:** +261(2) 22448

Founded: 1961 **Type:** Government **Head:** Louis Ralaisaho-
limanana *Phone:* +261(2) 222-5872, 222-0511 **Staff:** 6 Prof.
23 Other **Holdings:** 230,000 books **Language of Collection/
Services:** Malagasy, French, English / Malagasy, French
Subjects: Agribusiness, Farming, Organic Farming, Subsistence Farming **Loan:** Internationally **Photocopy:** Yes

1767　Antananarivo, Madagascar
Ministry of Agriculture and Rural Development,
　　Department of Rural Infrastructure
Library
BP 1061
Antananarivo

Non-English Name: Ministère d'Etat à l'Agriculture et au
Développement Rural, Direction de l'Infrastructure Rurale
(MEADR, DIR), Bibliothèque **Former Name:** Ministère de
la Production Agricole et de la Réforme Agraire (MPARA)
Founded: 1983 **Type:** Government **Head:** Marcel Théo-
phile Raveloarijaona *Phone:* +261(2) 40180 **Staff:** 1 Prof.
Holdings: 1,000 books 6 journals **Subjects:** Agricultural
Engineering, Drainage, Water Resources

1768　Antananarivo, Madagascar
Ministry of Agriculture and Rural Development,
　　Department of Waters and Forests
Library
BP 243, Nanisana
Antananarivo 101
Location: Route de Nanisana **Fax:** +261(2) 40230

Non-English Name: Ministère d'Etat à l'Agriculture et au
Développement Rural, Direction des Eaux et Forêts
(MEADR, DEF), Bibliothèque **Former Name:** Ministère de
la Production Animale (Elevage et Pêche) et des Eaux et
Forêts (MPAEF) **Type:** Government **Head:** Mrs. Estelle
Raharinaivosoa *Phone:* +261(2) 40610 **Staff:** 1 Prof. 1 Other
Holdings: 15,000 books 50 journals **Language of Collec-
tion/Services:** French / French **Subjects:** Agroforestry, Bio-
technology, Ecology, Education/Extension, Entomology,
Environmental Protection, Horticulture, Natural Resources,
Plant Pathology, Water Resources **Specializations:** Envi-
ronment, Forestry, Soil Science, Water **Photocopy:** No

1769   Antananarivo, Madagascar
Ministry of Agriculture and Rural Development
Statistical Methodology and Processing Service
BP 7086
Antananarivo 101

Location: Anosy

Non-English Name: Ministère d'Etat à l'Agriculture et au Développement Rural (MEADR), Service de Méthodologie et du Traitement des Informations Statistiques (SMTIS) **Former Name:** Ministère de la Production Agricole et de la Réforme Agraire (MPARA) **Founded:** 1971 **Type:** Government **Head:** Guy Ranaivomanana *Phone:* +261(2) 24710 ext 4253 **Staff:** 3 Prof. 19 Other **Holdings:** 10,000 books 5 journals **Language of Collection/Services:** French / French **Subjects:** Agricultural Development **Specializations:** Statistics **Loan:** Inhouse **Service:** In country **Photocopy:** Yes

1770   Antananarivo, Madagascar
Ministry of Scientific Research
Scientific and Technical Information and
    Documentation Center
Rue Fernand Kasanga BP 6224
Andoharano Tsimbazaza
Antananarivo 101

Email: cidst@bow.dts.mg

Non-English Name: Ministère de la Recherche Scientifique (MRS), Centre d'Information et de Documentation Scientifique et Technique (CIDST) **Former Name:** Ministry of Higher Education and Scientific Research, International Information and Documentation Service **Founded:** 1987 **Type:** Government **Head:** Mrs. Juliette Ratsimandrava *Phone:* +261(2) 33288, 24919 **Holdings:** 9,808 books 60 **Staff:** 7 Prof. 65 Other journals **Language of Collection/Services:** French / French **Subjects:** Agriculture (Tropics), Agribusiness, Agricultural Development, Agricultural Economics, Agricultural Engineering, Animal Husbandry, Biotechnology, Cereals, Crops, Education/Extension, Fisheries, Entomology, Environment, Farming, Food Sciences, Forestry, Horticulture, Hydrology, Natural Resources, Plant Pathology, Plants, Rural Development, Soil Science, Veterinary Medicine, Water Resources **Networks:** AGRIS **Databases Used:** Agris **Loan:** In country **Service:** Internationally **Photocopy:** Yes

1771   Antananarivo, Madagascar
United Nations, Department of Information
United Nations Information Center
22 Rue Rainitovo
BP 1348, Antsahavola
Antananarivo 101

Fax: +261(2) 33315

Non-English Name: Nations Unies, Département de l'Information (DPI), Centre d'Information des Nations Unies (CINU) **Founded:** 1963 **Type:** International **Head:** René Rakotovoa *Phone:* +261(2) 24115 **Staff:** 1 Prof. **Holdings:** 50,000 books 20 journals

♦1772   Nosy-Bé, Madagascar
Ministry of Scientific and Technological Research
    for Development

Documentation Service
BP 68
Nosy-Bé 207

Non-English Name: Ministère de la Recherche Scientifique et Technologique pour le Développement (MRSTD), Service Documentation Générale (SDoc) **Former Name:** Ministère de l'Enseignement supérieur et de la Recherche Scientifique **Founded:** 1979 **Type:** Government **Head:** Mrs. Iarilalao Razafiarisoa *Phone:* +261 61373 **Holdings:** 15,000 books **Staff:** 3 Prof. **Subjects:** Fisheries **Loan:** In country **Photocopy:** Yes

1773   Nosy-Bé, Madagascar
National Oceanographic Research Center
Library
BP 68
Nosy-Bé 207

Non-English Name: Centre National de Recherches Océanographiques (CNRO), Bibliothèque **Former Name:** ORSTOM **Founded:** 1978 **Type:** Government **Head:** Ms. Rachel Raniriarison *Phone:* +261(20) 866-1373 **Staff:** 4 Prof. **Holdings:** 2,000 books 1,200 journals **Language of Collection/Services:** English / French **Subjects:** Farming, Fisheries, Marine Biology, Oceanography, Water Resources **Loan:** In country **Service:** In country **Photocopy:** Yes

Malawi

1774   Lilongwe, Malawi
Ministry of Agriculture, Department of
    Agricultural Research (MA, DAR)
Library System
PO Box 158
Lilongwe

Phone: +265 767252 **Fax:** +265 784184 **Email:** icrisat-malawi@cgiar.org

Former Name: Chitedze Agricultural Research Station Library **Founded:** 1967 **Type:** Government **Head:** *Phone:* +265 767222 **Staff:** 4 Prof. 8 Other **Holdings:** 20,000 books 270 journals **Language of Collection/Services:** English **Subjects:** Agriculture (Tropics), Agribusiness, Agricultural Development, Agricultural Economics, Crops, Agricultural Engineering, Animal Husbandry, Biotechnology, Education/Extension, Entomology, Farming, Fisheries, Food Sciences, Forestry, Horticulture, Plant Pathology, Soil Science, Veterinary Medicine, Water Resources **Specializations:** Malawi **Networks:** AGRIS **Databases Developed:** DAR Library System - online union catalog contains records of holdings of 8 DAR libraries **Databases Used:** Agricola **Loan:** In country **Service:** In country **Photocopy:** Yes

1775   Lilongwe, Malawi
Ministry of Agriculture, Natural Resources
    College (MA, NRC)
Library and Resources Centre
PO Box 143
Lilongwe

Phone: +265 722744

Former Name: Colby College of Agriculture, Likuni Farm Institute **Founded:** 1984 **Type:** Academic **Head:** C. Banda *Phone:* +265 722744 **Staff:** 1 Prof. 2 Other **Holdings:** 65 journals 25,000 books **Language of Collection/Services:** English **Subjects:** Agriculture (Tropics), Agricultural Development, Agricultural Economics, Farming, Agricultural Engineering, Animal Husbandry, Appropriate Technology, Education/Extension, Fisheries, Forestry, Food Sciences, Crops, Horticulture, Soil Science, Veterinary Medicine, Water Resources **Databases Used:** Agris **Loan:** In country **Service:** In country **Photocopy:** Yes

1776   Lilongwe, Malawi
Ministry of Agriculture and Irrigation (MAI)
Planning Division Library
PB 30134
Lilongwe 3
Email: moald@en.wn.apc.org

Former Name: Ministry of Agriculture and Livestock Development (MALD) **Type:** Government **Head:** S.W. Mtonga *Phone:* +265 784299 *Email:* moald@en.wn.apc.org **Staff:** 1 Other **Holdings:** 7,000 books 31 journals **Language of Collection/Services:** English **Subjects:** Agricultural Development, Agricultural Economics, Animal Production, Crop Production, Human Nutrition, Rural Sociology, Statistics **Databases Used:** Agricola; Agris; CABCD **Loan:** In country **Service:** In country **Photocopy:** No

1777   Lilongwe, Malawi
University of Malawi, Bunda College of
      Agriculture
Bunda College Library (BCL)
PO Box 219
Lilongwe
Phone: +265 277222 **Fax:** +265 277251 **Email:** bunda.library@unima.wn.apc.org, bundalibrary@malawi.net,

Founded: 1966 **Head:** Gray L. Nyali *Phone:* +265 277348 *Email:* bundalibrary@malawi.net **Type:** Academic **Staff:** 3 Prof. 10 Other **Holdings:** 38,000 books 104 journals **Language of Collection/Services:** English / English **Subjects:** Agricultural Economics, Nutrition, Rural Development **Specializations:** Women in Development, Maize, Malawi **Databases Developed:** Maize, Malawi Environment, and Women in Development bibliographic databases **Databases Used:** Comprehensive **Loan:** In country **Photocopy:** Yes

1778   Limbe, Malawi
Ministry of Agriculture, Bvumbwe Agricultural
      Research Station (BARS)
Library
PB 5748
Limbe
Phone: +265 606803 **Fax:** +265 662323

Founded: 1940 **Type:** Government **Head:** R.F.N. Sauti *Phone:* +265 606803 **Staff:** 2 Other **Holdings:** 3,400 books 120 journals **Language of Collection/Services:** English / English **Subjects:** Crops, Entomology, Horticulture, Plants, Root Crops, Seeds, Stored Products, Tubers **Specializations:** Malawi, Plant Diseases, Seed Testing, Vegetables **Loan:** In country **Service:** In country **Photocopy:** Yes

1779   Monkey Bay, Malawi
Fisheries Research Station (FRU)
Library
PO Box 27
Monkey Bay
Phone: +265 587371 **Fax:** +265 587249

Founded: 1962 **Type:** Government **Holdings:** 1,000 books 10 journals **Staff:** 1 Other **Language of Collection/Services:** English **Subjects:** Fisheries **Loan:** In country **Service:** Internationally **Photocopy:** No

♦1780   Mulanje, Malawi
Tea Research Foundation - Central Africa
      (TRFCA)
Library
PO Box 51
Mulanje
Fax: +265 462209

Founded: 1929 **Type:** Research **Head:** Dr. A.M. Whittle *Phone:* +265 462277 **Staff:** 1 Prof. **Holdings:** 12,000 books 23 journals **Language of Collection/Services:** English **Subjects:** Agricultural Development, Agricultural Engineering, Food Sciences, Horticulture, Plant Breeding, Plant Diseases, Plant Protection, Plants, Soil Science, Tea **Loan:** In country **Photocopy:** Yes

♦1781   Zomba, Malawi
Ministry of Forestry and Natural Resources,
      Forestry Research Institute of Malawi (FRIM)
Library
PO Box 270
Zomba
Location: Kufa Road **Phone:** +265 502866, 502548

Former Name: Silviculture Research Station, Malawi Forestry Research Institute **Founded:** 1957 **Type:** Government **Staff:** 1 Prof. 2 Other **Holdings:** 1,300 books 32 journals **Language of Collection/Services:** English **Subjects:** Entomology, Forestry, Plant Pathology, Soil Science **Loan:** In country **Service:** In country **Photocopy:** Yes

Malaysia

1782   Batu Maung, Malaysia
Fisheries Research Institute (FRI)
Library
11960 Batu Maung, Penang
Fax: +60(4) 6262210 **Email:** frilib1@po.jaring.my
WWW: www.spl.my/~fri

Non-English Name: Institut Penyelidikan Perikanan (IPP), Perpustakaan **Founded:** 1957 **Type:** Government **Head:** Nor Hadzirah Ramli *Phone:* +60(4) 6263925/26 *Email:* frilib1@po.jaring.my **Staff:** 1 Prof. 1 Other **Holdings:** 3,879 books 735 journals **Language of Collection/Services:** English / English, Bahasa Malaysia **Subjects:** Marine Biology, Aquaculture, Statistics **Specializations:** Fisheries, Oceanography, Pollution **Loan:** In country **Service:** In country **Photocopy:** Yes

1783   **Georgetown, Malaysia**
University of Science Malaysia (USM)
Library
Minden
11800 Georgetown, Penang
Phone: +60(4) 877888 ext 3720 or 3723, 870230 **Fax:** +60
(4) 871526 **Email:** chieflib@usm.my **WWW:** www.lib.
usm.my **OPAC:** telnet://lib.usm.my

Non-English Name: Universiti Sains Malaysia (USM),
Perpustakaan **Founded:** 1969 **Type:** Academic **Head:**
Rashidah Begum *Phone:* +60(4) 877888 ext 3700 *Email:*
rashidah@usm.my **Holdings:** 642,800 books 1,197 journals
Staff: 35 Prof. 148 Other **Language of Collection/Services:**
English, Bahasa Malaysia / English, Bahasa Malaysia **Sub-**
jects: Biotechnology, Ecology, Entomology, Fisheries, Food
Sciences, Mangrove Forests, Plant Pathology, Soil Science,
Water Resources **Databases Developed:** USM staff publi-
cations **Databases Used:** FSTA **Loan:** Internationally **Ser-**
vice: Internationally **Photocopy:** Yes

1784   **Ipoh, Malaysia**
Veterinary Research Institute (VRI)
VRI Library
59 Jalan Sultan Azlan Shah
PO Box 369
30740 Ipoh, Perak
Phone: +60(5) 545-7166 ext 122 **Fax:** +60(5) 546-3368

Non-English Name: Institut Penyelidikan Haiwan, Perpustakaan **Founded:** 1953 **Type:** Government **Head:** Mr. Abd.
Halim Idris *Phone:* +60(5) 5457166 ext 122 *Email:* halim@
jphvri.po.my **Staff:** 2 Other **Holdings:** 1,100 books 90 journals **Language of Collection/Services:** English / English
Subjects: Animal Husbandry, Veterinary Medicine **Special-**
izations: Veterinary Science **Loan:** In country **Service:** In
country **Photocopy:** Yes

1785   **Kelana Jaya, Malaysia**
Palm Oil Registration and Licensing Authority
(PORLA)
Library
PO Box 8073
46781 Kelana Jaya, Selangor
Location: Lot 6, SS 6, Jalan Perbandaran, 47301 Kelana
Jaya, Selangor **Phone:** +60(3) 703-5544 **Fax:** +60(3) 703-
3533 **WWW:** porla.gov.my

Non-English Name: Lembaga Pendaftaran dan Pelesenan
Minyak Kelapa Sawit, Perpustakaan PORLA **Type:** Govern-
ment **Head:** Syahrulhaida Yahya *Phone:* +60(3) 703-5544
ext 2883 *Email:* sya@porla.gov.my **Staff:** 1 Prof. 1 Other
Holdings: 6,000 books 60 journals **Language of Collection/**
Services: English / English **Subjects:** Cooking Oils, Fats,
Palm Oils, Plant Oils **Specializations:** Palm Oils (Malaysia -
Statistics) **Loan:** In country **Service:** Internationally **Photo-**
copy: Yes

1786   **Kota Kinabalu, Malaysia**
Ministry of of Agriculture and Fisheries, Sabah
Library
Menara Khidmat Building
88632 Kota Kinabalu, Sabah

Phone: +60(88) 55155 **WWW:** www.sabah.gov.my/maf

Founded: 1966 **Type:** Government **Staff:** 1 Other **Hold-**
ings: 200 books 30 journals **Subjects:** Agricultural Economics, Agricultural Engineering, Botany, Crops, Forestry, Plant
Protection, Soil Science **Loan:** Do not loan **Photocopy:** No

1787   **Kuala Lumpur, Malaysia**
ASEAN Institute of Forest Management (AIFM)
Library
Level 3, Block A, Forestry Department
Headquarters
Jalan Sultan Salahuddin
50660 Kuala Lumpur, Selangor
Phone: +60(3) 294-3477 **Fax:** +60(3) 294-3499 **Email:**
info@aifm.po.my **WWW:** www.jaring.my/aifm

Founded: 1986 **Head:** Harin Abu Hassan *Email:* fazali@
aifm.po.my **Holdings:** 5,000 books 79 journals **Subjects:**
Forest Management **Databases Used:** TREECD

1788   **Kuala Lumpur, Malaysia**
Fisheries Development Authority of Malaysia
(FDAM)
FDAM Library
PO Box 12630
50784 Kuala Lumpur
Location: 1st Floor, Wisma PKNS, Jalan Raja Laut **Fax:**
+60(3) 291-1931 **Phone:** +60(3) 294-9651, 291-8346
WWW: agrolink.moa.my/lkim

Non-English Name: Lembaga Kemajuan Ikan Malaysia
(LKIM, MAJUIKAN), Perpustakaan Majuikan **Type:** Government **Head:** *Phone:* +60(3) 292-4044 ext 820 **Staff:** 1
Other **Holdings:** 2,000 books 20 journals **Language of Col-**
lection/Services: English, Malay **Specializations:** Fisheries, Aquaculture **Loan:** Do not loan **Photocopy:** No

1789   **Kuala Lumpur, Malaysia**
Forest Research Institute Malaysia (FRIM)
Library
Karung Berkunci 201, Kepong
52109 Kuala Lumpur, Selangor
Phone: +60(3) 6342633 **Fax:** +60(3) 6367753 **WWW:**
frim.gov.my

Non-English Name: Institut Penyelidikan Perhutanan Malaysia, Perpustakaan **Former Name:** Forest Research Institute **Founded:** 1929 **Type:** Government **Head:** Mr. Moha-
mad Zaki *Email:* zaki@frim.gov.my *Phone:* +60(3) 630-
2222, 634-2628 **Staff:** 2 Prof. 6 Other **Holdings:** 140,000
books 319 journals **Language of Collection/Services:** English / English **Subjects:** Agriculture (Tropics), Agricultural
Economics, Crops, Education/Extension, Entomology, Horticulture, Plant Pathology, Soil Science, Water Resources
Specializations: Bamboos, Biomass, Botany, Forestry (Malaysia), Tropical Rain Forests, Biotechnology, Environment,
Extractives, Energy, Forest Management, Rattan, Wood
Residues **Databases Developed:** Index to Malaysian For-
ester, Commonwealth Forestry Review, Journal of Tropical
Forest Science, Journal of Tropical Forest Products, and Ma-
laysian Forestry Conference **Databases Used:** CABCD
Loan: Internationally **Service:** Internationally **Photocopy:**
Yes

1790 **Kuala Lumpur, Malaysia**
Malaysian Agricultural Research and
    Development Institute (MARDI)
Resource Centre/Management Information
    Systems
PO Box 12301
General Post Office
50774 Kuala Lumpur
Location: Serdang, Selangor **Phone:** +60(3) 943-7146
Fax: +60(3) 948-3664 **Email:** lib@mardi.my **WWW:**
www.mardi.my

Non-English Name: Institut Penyelidikan dan Kemajuan
Pertanian Malaysia, Unit Pemgangunan Sistem dan Pusat
Sumber **Former Name:** Systems Development and Re-
source Centre Unit **Founded:** 1971 **Type:** Research **Head:**
Mrs. Khadijah Ibrahim *Email:* khadijah@mardi.my *Phone:*
+60(3) 943-7149 **Staff:** 2 Prof. 9 Other **Holdings:** 35,000
books 300 journals **Language of Collection/Services:** Eng-
lish / Bahasa Malaysia **Subjects:** Agricultural Development,
Crops, Food Sciences, Plants **Specializations:** Biotechnol-
ogy, Horticulture, Livestock, Remote Sensing, Soil Science
Databases Developed: MAB - collection of abstracts on
MARDI publications **Databases Used:** Comprehensive
Loan: Internationally **Service:** In country **Photocopy:** Yes

1791 **Kuala Lumpur, Malaysia**
Malaysian Rubber Board (MRB)
Library
260 Jalan Ampang
PO Box 10150
50908 Kuala Lumpur
Phone: +60(3)4567033 ext 255 **WWW:** www.lgm.gov.my

Non-English Name: Lembaga Getah Malaysia (LGM) **For-
mer Name:** Rubber Research Institute of Malaysia (RRIM),
Malaysian Rubber Research and Development Board
(MRRDB), Malaysian Rubber Exchange and Licensing
Board **Founded:** 1925 **Type:** Government **Head:** Daw Hun
Woon *Phone:* +60(3) 4567033 **Staff:** 5 Prof. 11 Other **Hold-
ings:** 80,000 books 400 journals **Subjects:** Crops, Educa-
tion/Extension, Plant Protection, Rubber, Soil Science
Loan: In country **Service:** Internationally **Photocopy:** Yes

1792 **Kuala Lumpur, Malaysia**
Ministry of Agriculture
Library
1st Floor, Wisma Tani
Jalan Sultan Salahuddin
50624 Kuala Lumpur
Phone: +60(3) 2982011 ext 216, 217 **Fax:** +60(3) 2913758
WWW: agrolink.moa.my

Non-English Name: Kementerian Pertanian, Perpustakaan
Founded: 1906 **Type:** Government **Head:** Mrs. Norkhaton
Mohd. Yunus *Phone:* +60(3) 2982011 ext 215 **Staff:** 3 Prof.
8 Other **Holdings:** 90,000 books 240 journals **Language of
Collection/Services:** English **Subjects:** Agriculture (Trop-
ics), Agribusiness, Agricultural Development, Agricultural
Economics, Agricultural Engineering, Animal Husbandry,
Biotechnology, Crops, Education/Extension, Entomology,
Farming, Fisheries, Food Sciences, Forestry, Horticulture,
Plant Pathology, Soil Science **Loan:** Internationally **Ser-
vice:** Internationally **Photocopy:** Yes

1793 **Kuala Lumpur, Malaysia**
Palm Oil Research Institute of Malaysia (PORIM)
Palm Information Centre
P.P. Box 10620
50720 Kuala Lumpur
Location: No. 6 Persiaran Institusi, Bandar Baru Bangi,
43000 Kajang, Selangor Darul Ehsan **Phone:** +60(3) 825-
9155 ext 775 **Fax:** +60(3) 825-9446 **Email:** pms@porim.
gov.my **WWW:** porim.gov.my **OPAC:** netra.porim.gov.
my

Non-English Name: Institut Penyelidikan Minyak Kelapa
Sawit Malaysia, Pusat Maklumat Sawit **Founded:** 1979
Type: Government **Head:** Mardhiah Mohd Zin *Phone:*
+60(3) 825-9182 *Email:* mardhiah@porim.gov.my **Staff:** 3
Prof. 9 Other **Holdings:** 7,000 books 270 journals **Language
of Collection/Services:** English **Subjects:** Agricultural Economics, Agricultural Engineering, Biotechnology, Food Sciences, Education/Extension, Entomology, Plant Pathology,
Soil Science **Specializations:** Elaeis guineensis, Fats, Oil
Palms, Oils, Palm Oils **Databases Developed:** Palmoilis
(Palm Oil Information Online Servis) - information service
which includes a wide range of databases. Access via subscription over the Internet at netra.porim.gov.my. Databases
include:; PALMSEARCH - technical information with abstracts on oil palm/palm oil and other oils and fats; PALM-
CLIENT - directory-type data on business enterprises in the
industry; PALMCONSULT- directory-type information on
experts for consultation in the industry; Miscellaneous databases of palm oil-based recipes, palm oil/oil palm statistics,
PORIM approved palm-based products, etc. **Loan:** Inhouse
Service: In country (industry) **Photocopy:** Yes

1794 **Kuching, Malaysia**
Agriculture Institute, Sarawak
Library
Semonggok
93250 Kuching, Sarawak
Location: 12th mile, Kuching Serian Road **WWW:**
agrolink.moa.my/doa/english/latihan/ipsrwke.html

Founded: 1984 **Type:** Government **Staff:** 1 Prof. 1 Other
Subjects: Agricultural Economics, Animal Husbandry,
Crops, Plant Pathology, Veterinary Medicine **Loan:** Do not
loan **Photocopy:** No

1795 **Kuching, Malaysia**
Forest Department, Sarawak
Forest Research Library
Km. 10, Jalan Datuk Amar
Kalong Ningkan
Beg Berkunci 3126
93250 Kuching, Sarawak
Phone: +60(82) 442180 ext 405 **Fax:** +60(82) 617953

Non-English Name: Jabatan Perhutanan, Sarawak, Perpustakaan Penyelidikan Hutan **Founded:** 1978 **Type:** Government **Head:** Abang Haji Abdul Hamid Karim *Phone:* +60
(82) 442180 *Email:* jpsk@po.jaring.my **Staff:** 1 Other **Holdings:** 3,000 books 50 journals **Language of Collection/Ser-
vices:** English / English **Subjects:** Ecology, Entomology,
Botany, Forestry, Plant Pathology, Silviculture, Soil Science
Loan: Inhouse **Photocopy:** Yes

1796   Sandakan, Malaysia
Forest Department, Sabah
Library
Forest Research Center, PO Box 1407
90008 Sandakan, Sabah

Location: Sepilok, 23 km North Road **Phone:** +60(89) 531522 **Fax:** +60(89) 531068

Non-English Name: Jabatan Perhutanan, Sabah, Perpustakaan Penyelidikan **Former Name:** FRC Library **Founded:** 1965 **Type:** Government **Head:** Poon Ka Ling **Staff:** 3 Other **Holdings:** 2,000 books 72 journals **Subjects:** Chemistry, Entomology, Forestry, Plant Pathology, Plant Protection, Soil Science, Wildlife **Loan:** Do not loan **Service:** Inhouse **Photocopy:** Yes

1797   UPM Serdang, Malaysia
Universiti Putra Malaysia
Library
43400 UPM Serdang, Selangor Darul Ehsan

Phone: +60(3) 948-6101 **Fax:** +60(3) 948-3745 **Email:** lib@lib.upm.edu.my **WWW:** www.upm.edu.my **OPAC:** www.lib.upm.edu.my

Non-English Name: Universiti Putra Malaysia (UPM), Perpustakaan **Former Name:** Universiti Pertanian Malaysia, University of Agriculture Malyasia **Founded:** 1973 **Type:** Academic **Head:** Mrs. Kamariah Abdul Hamid *Phone:* +60(3)948-6688 *Email:* kah@lib.upm.edu.my **Holdings:** 450,000 books 2,133 journals **Staff:** 35 Prof. 93 Other **Language of Collection/Services:** English, Bahasa Malaysia / English, Bahasa Malaysia **Subjects:** Comprehensive **Specializations:** Animal Production, Engineering, Crops, Computer Science, Forestry, Information Technology, Horticulture, Management, Plant Pathology, Plant Protection, Veterinary Medicine **Networks:** AGRIS **Databases Developed:** Malaysian Agricultural Bibliography, Agricultural Waste Management **Databases Used:** Comprehensive **Loan:** In country **Service:** Internationally **Photocopy:** Yes

Mali

♦1798   Bamako, Mali
Canadian Embassy
Documentation Centre
BP 198
Bamako

Phone: +223(21) 213096 **Fax:** +223(21) 224362 **Email:** amb@scc.malinet.ml

Type: Government **Head:** Camara Oumou Kante **Staff:** 1 Prof. **Holdings:** 5,027 books 110 journals **Subjects:** Agricultural Economics, Agroforestry, Social Development, Statistics

♦1799   Bamako, Mali
Cellule de Planification Statistique (CPS)
Bibliothèque
BP 275
Bamako

Founded: 1980 **Head:** Boubacar Haidara *Phone:* +223 228240, 231939

♦1800   Bamako, Mali
Cellule Provisoire du Programme National de
        Lutte contre la Désertification (CPPNLCD)
Documentation
BP 275
Bamako

Type: Government **Head:** Djiré Ibrahima **Staff:** 2 Prof. **Holdings:** 2,482 books 6 journals **Language of Collection/Services:** French **Subjects:** Desertification, Environment, Forage, Natural Resources

♦1801   Bamako, Mali
Centre d'Etudes et de Recherche pour la
        Population et le Développement (CERPOD)
Centre de Documentation
BP 1530
Bamako

Fax: +223 228086

Founded: 1988 **Head:** Ouaidou G. Nassour *Phone:* +223 223043

♦1802   Bamako, Mali
Centre Djoliba, Recherche-Formation pour le
        Développement
Bibliothèque-Documentation
BP 298
Bamako

Location: Avenue du Fleuve

Founded: 1965 **Type:** Private **Head:** Francis Verstraete *Phone:* +223 228332 **Staff:** 4 Prof. 6 Other **Holdings:** 68 journals 22,000 books **Language of Collection/Services:** French **Subjects:** Cooperatives, Crop Production, Machinery, Crops, Plant Protection, Rural Development, Rural Economy **Loan:** Do not loan **Photocopy:** Yes

♦1803   Bamako, Mali
Centre National de Recherche Scientifique et
        Technologique (CNRST)
Centre de Documentation
BP 3052
Bamako

Head: Dontigui Samake *Phone:* +223 229085 **Founded:** 1986

1804   Bamako, Mali
Comité de Coordination des Actions des O.N.G.
        (CCA-ONG)
Documentation
BP E 3216
Bamako

Phone: +223 212112 **Fax:** +223 212359, 210414 **Email:** oca@malinet.ml

Founded: 1992 **Type:** Non-government **Head:** Mamadou Sékou Toure *Phone:* +223 212112, 218083 *Email:* oca@malinet.ml **Staff:** 2 Prof. 2 Other **Holdings:** 2,000 books 1 journals **Language of Collection/Services:** French / French **Subjects:** Economic Development, Social Development **Photocopy:** Yes **Loan:** Inhouse

♦1805 **Bamako, Mali**
Compagnie Malienne pour le Développement des
   Textiles (CMDT)
Documentation
BP 487
Bamako
Phone: +223 227919, 227280

Founded: 1981 **Head:** Diarisso Demba **Holdings:** 16 journals 3,436 books **Language of Collection/Services:** French
Staff: 3 Prof. **Type:** Business **Subjects:** Agribusiness, Ecology, Environment, Hydrology, Water Management

♦1806 **Bamako, Mali**
Direction National de l'Hydraulique et de
   l'Energie
Centre de Documentation
BP 66
Bamako

Founded: 1962 **Head:** Abdoulaye Djire *Phone:* +223 222-
588 **Subjects:** Energy, Hydrology **Subjects:** Machinery

♦1807 **Bamako, Mali**
Division du Machinisme Agricole
Bibliothèque
BP 155
Bamako

Founded: 1970 **Head:** Sidiki Lamine Kone

1808 **Bamako, Mali**
Institut d'Economie Rurale, Division de la
   Documentation de l'Information et de la
   Formation (IER)
Service Documentation Information Publication
   (SEDIP)
Avenue Mohamed V
BP 258
Bamako
Phone: +223 231905, 222606 **Fax:** +223 223775 **Email:**
ier.mali@cgiar.org

Former Name: Bureau Documentation Information Formation **Founded:** 1960 **Type:** Research **Head:** Cheik Dia
Phone: +223 222606 **Staff:** 5 Prof. 11 Other **Holdings:** 115
journals 6,000 books **Language of Collection/Services:**
French / French **Subjects:** Agricultural Development, Agricultural Economics, Crop Production, Rural Sociology **Networks:** AGRIS **Loan:** Inhouse **Service:** Internationally
Photocopy: Yes

♦1809 **Bamako, Mali**
Institut Polytechnique Rural (Annexe) (IPR)
Bibliothèque
BP 224
Bamako
Phone: +223 222655

Founded: 1972 **Type:** Government **Head:** Cheick Sidibe
Staff: 1 Prof. **Holdings:** 2,550 books **Language of Collec-
tion/Services:** French **Subjects:** Livestock Farming, Zootechny

♦1810 **Bamako, Mali**
Laboratoire Central Vétérinaire (LCV)
Bibliothèque
BP 2295
Bamako

Founded: 1979 **Head:** Rokoa Bodge *Phone:* +223 226653
Subjects: Veterinary Science

♦1811 **Bamako, Mali**
Ministère de l'Elevage et des Ressources Natur-
   elles, Direction Nationale de l'Elevage (DNE)
Bibliothèque
BP 265
Bamako
Location: Route de Roulouba

Founded: 1926 **Type:** Government **Head:** Mahaamadou
Touré *Phone:* +223 222022 **Staff:** 1 Prof. **Holdings:** 4,446
books 12 journals **Language of Collection/Services:** French
Subjects: Animal Health, Animal Production, Natural Resources, Pastoralism, Zootechny

♦1812 **Bamako, Mali**
Ministry of Agriculture, Rural Engineering
   Department
Library
BP 155
Bamako
Location: Avenue Mohamed V **Phone:** +223 222605 **Fax:**
+223 228549

Non-English Name: Ministère de l'Agriculture, Direction
Nationale du Génie Rural (DNGR), Bibliothèque **Founded:**
1960 **Type:** Government **Head:** Mamadou Bouba Camara
Phone: +223 222605 **Staff:** 2 Prof. 1 Other **Language of
Collection/Services:** French **Holdings:** 400 journals 5,600
books **Subjects:** Agricultural Engineering, Farm Machinery,
Rural Development, Water Management **Specializations:**
Irrigation **Photocopy:** Yes

♦1813 **Bamako, Mali**
Ministry of the Environment, National Direction
   of Forests and Water
Library and Documentation
BP 275
Bamako
Location: Rue Rochester

Non-English Name: Ministère de l'Environnement, Direc-
tion Nationale des Eaux et Forêts (DNEF), Bibliothèque et
Documentation **Founded:** 1940 **Type:** Government **Head:**
Drissa Kone *Phone:* +223 225973, 225850 **Staff:** 1 Prof. 1
Other **Holdings:** 2,398 books 18 journals **Language of Col-
lection/Services:** French **Subjects:** Aquaculture, Environment, Environmental Protection, Fisheries, Forestry, Natural
Resources, Water Resources **Specializations:** Agroforestry,
Aquaculture, Environmental Protection, Fauna, Forest Management, Pastoralism, Resource Development, Soil Conser-
vation **Photocopy:** yes

♦1814 **Bamako, Mali**
National Library
Research Studies Library

PO Box 159
Bamako

Location: Avenue Kassé keita **Phone:** +223 224963

Non-English Name: Bibliothèque Nationale, Bibliothèque d'Etudes et de Recherche **Founded:** 1960 **Type:** Government **Head:** Al Mady Keita *Phone:* +223 224963 **Language of Collection/Services:** French **Subjects:** Animal Production, Forage

1815 Bamako, Mali
Observatoire Economique et Statistique pour
l'Afrique Subsaharienne (AFRISTAT)
Centre de Documentation
PO Box E 1600
Bamako

Location: Niare'la Rue 499 Porte 23 **Phone:** +223 215580 **Fax:** +223 211140 **Email:** afristat@malinet.ml **WWW:** www.afristat.refer.ci

Founded: 1997 **Type:** International **Head:** Fatima Diallo *Phone:* +223 215500 **Staff:** 1 Prof. **Holdings:** 9,000 books 50 journals **Language of Collection/Services:** French **Subjects:** Agricultural Statistics **Specializations:** Economic Statistics, Social Development **Photocopy:** Yes **Databases Used:** FAOSTAT **Loan:** Internationally **Service:** Internationally

♦1816 Bamako, Mali
Office Malien du Bétail et de la Viande
(OMBEVI)
Centre d'Information et de Documentation
BP 1382
Bamako

Location: Route de Koulouba

Founded: 1978 **Type:** Government **Head:** Modibo Fofana *Phone:* +223 223858 **Staff:** 2 Prof. **Holdings:** 1,235 books 6 journals **Language of Collection/Services:** French **Subjects:** Animal Husbandry, Meat **Specializations:** Beef, Marketing, Goats, Sheep, Statistics

♦1817 Bamako, Mali
Opération Haute Vallée du Niger (OHVN)
Centre de Documentation
BP 178
Bamako

Founded: 1972 **Type:** Government **Head:** Alou Soumare *Phone:* +223 224064 **Staff:** 1 Prof. **Holdings:** 281 books 11 journals **Subjects:** Agricultural Economics, Rural Development, Rural Sociology

1818 Bamako, Mali
Research Institute for Development
Documentation and Scientific Exchange Center
BP 2528
Bamako

Location: Quartier du fleuve **Phone:** +223 225747 **Fax:** +223 227588

Non-English Name: Institut de Recherche pour le Développement (IRD), Atelier de Documentation et d'Echanges Scientifiques **Former Name:** Institut Français de Recherche Scientifique pour le Développement en Coopération (ORS-

TOM), French Scientific Research Institute for Development through Cooperation **Founded:** 1991 **Type:** Government **Head:** Diop Binta Diallo *Phone:* +223 225747 *Email:* diop @bamako.ird.ml **Holdings:** 3,740 books 30 journals **Language of Collection/Services:** French / French **Subjects:** Animal Husbandry, Forage, Hydrobiology

1819 Bamako, Mali
Sahel Institute
Sahelian Network for Documentation and
Scientific and Technical Information
BP 1530
Bamako

Phone: +223 222148, 235338 **Fax:** +223 230237 **Email:** insah@spider.toolnet.org

Non-English Name: Institut du Sahel (INSAH), Réseau Sahélien de Documentation et d'Information Scientifiques et Techniques (RESADOC) **Founded:** 1980 **Type:** Regional **Head:** A.A. Ly *Phone:* +223 235338 *Email:* insah@spider. toolnet.org **Staff:** 2 Prof. 4 Other **Holdings:** 20,000 books 35 journals **Language of Collection/Services:** French **Subjects:** Crop Production, Crops, Fertilization, Genetics, Marketing, Plant Pathology, Plant Protection, Soil Science, Storage **Loan:** Inhouse **Photocopy:** Yes

♦1820 Bamako, Mali
Station de Recherches Zootechniques (SRZ)
Bibliothèque
BP 262
Bamako

Phone: +223 222449

Former Name: Centre de Recherches Zootechniques **Type:** Government **Staff:** 1 Prof. **Holdings:** 1,000 books **Language of Collection/Services:** French **Subjects:** Animal Health, Animal Husbandry, Animal Production, Zootechny

♦1821 Bamako, Mali
United States Agency for International
Development (USAID)
Documentation Center
BP 34
Bamako

Location: Quartier du Fleuve **Phone:** +223 223602 **Fax:** +223 223933

Founded: 1975 **Type:** Government **Head:** Sékou Sidibe *Phone:* +223 223602 **Staff:** 1 Prof. **Holdings:** 5,404 books 30 journals **Language of Collection/Services:** English **Subjects:** Education, Health, Human Population, Women in Development **Loan:** Internationally

♦1822 Gao, Mali
Bibliothèque Lecture Publique (BLP)
Gao

Location: Près de la Mairie de Gao

Type: Public **Head:** Moussa A. Maiga **Holdings:** 2,085 books 10 journals **Staff:** 1 Prof. **Language of Collection/Services:** French **Subjects:** Animal Nutrition, Animal Production, Environment, Human Nutrition

♦**1823 Kayes, Mali**
Centre d'Apprentissage Agricole de Same
Centre de Documentation
BP 21
Kayes

Founded: 1983

♦**1824 Koulikoro, Mali**
Institut Polytechnique Rural de Katibougou
(IPR/Katibougou)
Bibliothèque
BP 6
Koulikoro

Founded: 1965 **Head:** Yacouba Doumbia *Phone:* +223 262012, 262015

1825 Koutiala, Mali
Institute of Rural Economy, Koutiala, Agronomy
Research Station of N'Tarla
Documentation
BP 28
Koutiala

Non-English Name: Institut d'Economie Rurale, Koutiala, Station de Recherche Agronomique de N'Tarla (IER, SRA N'Tarla), Documentation **Founded:** 1949 **Type:** Government **Head:** Dembélé Bakary **Staff:** 1 Prof. **Holdings:** 5,590 books **Language of Collection/Services:** French **Subjects:** Agronomy, Entomology, Plant Breeding, Plant Pathology, Soil Science **Databases Used:** Agris **Loan:** Inhouse **Service:** Internationally **Photocopy:** Yes

♦**1826 Mopti, Mali**
Bibliothèque Rizière Sevaré (BR - Sevaré)
BP 45
Mopti

Type: Government **Staff:** 1 Prof. **Head:** Jean de Dieu Dembélé **Holdings:** 3,532 books **Language of Collection/Services:** French

♦**1827 Mopti, Mali**
Centre Régional de Recherche Agronomique de
Mopti (CRRA/Mopti)
Centre de Documentation
BP 204
Mopti
Fax: +223 430197

Founded: 1996 **Head:** Lassina Toure *Phone:* +223 430357, 430260

♦**1828 Mopti, Mali**
ISSA BERR (BIB - Mopti)
Bibliothèque
BP 45
Mopti

Founded: 1973 **Head:** Sister Sopie Marie **Holdings:** 5,053 books 31 journals **Staff:** 1 Prof. **Language of Collection/Services:** French

♦**1829 Mopti, Mali**
Office Riz Mopti (ORM/Mopti)
Bibliothèque Centrale
BP 161
Mopti

Head: Oumar Baba Bouare *Phone:* +223 420187

♦**1830 Niono, Mali**
Centre Régional de Recherche Agronomique de
Niono (CRRA/Niono)
Centre de Documentation
BP 12
Niono

Founded: 1992 **Head:** Mohamed Diarra *Phone:* +223 355-055

♦**1831 Ségou, Mali**
Office du Niger (ON)
Centre de Documentation
BP 106
Ségou

Founded: 1932 **Head:** Samba Traore *Phone:* +223 320003

♦**1832 Ségou, Mali**
Operation Riz Segou
Bibliothèque
BP 94
Ségou

Founded: 1972 **Head:** Sadou Ongoiba *Phone:* +223 320326

♦**1833 Ségou, Mali**
Station de Recherche Agronomique de Cinzana
(SRA/Cinzana)
Bibliothèque
BP 214
Ségou

Founded: 1990 **Head:** Lasiné Sacko

1834 Sikasso, Mali
Centre Régional de Recherche Agronomique de
Sikasso (CRRA/Sikasso)
Centre de Documentation
BP 186
Sikasso
Phone: +223 620346 **Fax:** +223 620349 **Email:** bdiaw@sik-spgr.ier.ml

Founded: 1979 **Type:** Government **Head:** Boubacar Diaw *Phone:* +223 620028 *Email:* bdiaw@sik-spgr.ier.ml **Holdings:** 5,800 books 18 journals **Language of Collection/Services:** French **Subjects:** Agricultural Development, Animal Husbandry, Agricultural Economics, Agroforestry Rural Development **Specializations:** Cotton, Rice, Farming Systems, Forestry, Legumes **Databases Used:** Comprehensive **Loan:** Inhouse **Service:** Internationally **Photocopy:** Yes

1835 Sikasso, Mali
Compagnie Malienne pour le Développement des
Textiles (CMDT/Sikasso)
Bibliothèque

BP 27
Sikasso
Phone: +223 620224 **Fax:** +223 620458

Founded: 1995 **Type:** Government **Head:** Abou Traoré *Phone:* +223 620302, 620224 **Holdings:** 2,065 books 6 journals **Language of Collection/Services:** French/French **Subjects:** Cotton, Extension, Rural Development **Loan:** Inhouse **Photocopy:** Yes

1836   Sikasso, Mali
Direction Régionale de l'Aménagement et
Equipement Rural (DRAER)
Centre de Documentation
BP 38
Sikasso
Fax: +223 620265

Founded: 1982 **Head:** Adboulaye Coumare *Phone:* +223 620109 **Holdings:** 2,155 books 71 journals **Language of Collection/Services:** French / French **Subjects:** Agroforestry, Forestry, Traditional Medicines **Databases Developed:** REFOD - Documentation of Forestry Research

Malta

1837   Valletta, Malta
Department of Agriculture and Fisheries
Library
14 Mikiel Anton Vassalli Street
Valletta
Networks: AGRIS

1838   Msida, Malta
University of Malta
Library
Msida MAD 06
Phone: +356 3290-2050 **Fax:** +356 314306 **WWW:** www.lib.um.edu.mt **OPAC:** www.lib.um.edu.mt/opac.html

Head: Mr. Anthony Mangion *Phone:* +356 320-2317, 310-239 *Email:* dis@lib.um.edu.mt

Marshall Islands

1839   Majuro, Marshall Islands
College of the Marshall Islands, Land Grant
Program
Library
PO Box 1258
Majuro 96960
Phone: +692 625-3394, 625-3291, 615-3236 **Fax:** +692 625-2203

Type: Academic **Head:** Ms. Maxine Becker

1840   Majuro, Marshall Islands
Ministry of Resources and Development, Division
of Agriculture
Library
PO Box 1727

Majuro 96960
Phone: +692 625-3202, 625-3206, 625-3262 **Fax:** +692 625-3218

Type: Government

Mauritania

1841   Nouakchott, Mauritania
Centre National d'Elevage et de Recherche
Vétérinaire (CNERV)
Service de Documentation
BP 167
Nouakchott
Fax: +222(2) 52803 **Email:** cnrv10@calvapro.fr

Founded: 1984 **Type:** Research **Head:** Cheikh Diop *Phone:* +222(2) 52803, 52705 **Staff:** 2 Prof. 1 Other **Holdings:** 210 books 130 journals **Subjects:** Animal Breeding, Animal Production, Animal Feeding, Animal Husbandry, Biodiversity, Animal Health, Epidemiology, Veterinary Medicine **Databases Used:** RESADOC **Loan:** Do not loan **Photocopy:** No

♦1842   Nouakchott, Mauritania
Société Nationale pour le Développement Rural
(SONADER)
Service de Documentation et des Archives
BP 321
Nouakchott

Founded: 1969 **Staff:** 3 Other **Holdings:** 10 journals 2,351 books **Subjects:** Agricultural Development, Irrigated Farming, Agricultural Economics, Rural Sociology, Water Management, Water Resources

Mauritius

1843   Albion, Mauritius
Ministry of Fisheries and Cooperatives, Albion
Fisheries Research Centre (AFRC)
Fisheries Information and Documentation Centre
Albion, Petite Rivière
Phone: +230 238-4100 **Fax:** +230 238-4184 **Email:** fish@intnet.mu **WWW:** ncb.intnet.mu/fishco/index.htm

Former Name: Ministry of Fisheries and Marine Resources (Fisheries Division) **Founded:** 1982 **Type:** Government **Head:** Noel Wan Sai Cheong *Phone:* +230 238-4100 *Email:* fish@intnet.mu **Staff:** 2 Other **Holdings:** 10,000 books 100 journals **Language of Collection/Services:** English/English **Subjects:** Aquaculture, Fisheries, Marine Environment, Marine Sciences, Pollution **Databases Used:** Comprehensive **Loan:** Inhouse **Service:** Internationally **Photocopy:** No

1844   Port-Louis, Mauritius
Ministry of Environment, Human Resources
Development and Employment
Resource Centre
Ken Lee Tower, 4th Floor
Barracks Street
Port-Louis

Phone: +230 212-4385 **Fax:** +230 212-6671

Founded: 1992 **Language of Collection/Services:** English, French/English, French **Subjects:** Environment **Photocopy:** No

1845   Réduit, Mauritius
       Food and Agricultural Research Council (FARC)
       Documentation Centre
       Réduit

Phone: +230 465-1011 **Fax:** +230 465-3344 **Email:** farc@
intnet.mu **WWW:** ncb.intnet.mu/moa/farc.htm

Founded: 1985 **Type:** Parastatal **Head:** Naren Sakurdeep
Phone: +230 465-1011 *Email:* farc@intnet.mu **Staff:** 1 Prof.
Holdings: 3,000 books **Subjects:** Comprehensive **Databases Used:** Comprehensive **Loan:** Inhouse **Service:** Internationally **Photocopy:** Yes

1846   Réduit, Mauritius
       Mauritius Institute of Education
       Library
       Réduit
Fax: +230 465-7226

Founded: 1975 **Type:** Academic **Head:** B.R. Goordyal
Phone: +230 454-1031/32, 466-1940 **Staff:** 2 Prof. 6 Other
Holdings: 35,000 books 105 journals **Language of Collection/Services:** English **Subjects:** Agricultural Economics, Agriculture (Tropics), Animal Husbandry, Biotechnology, Crops, Farming, Food Sciences, Forestry, Plant Pathology, Plants, Soil Science **Specializations:** Education **Loan:** In country **Service:** In country **Photocopy:** Yes

1847   Réduit, Mauritius
       Mauritius Sugar Industry Research Institute
         (MSIRI)
       Library
       Réduit

Phone: +230 454-1061 **Fax:** +230 454-1971 **Email:** m.s.i.
r.i.@msiri.intnet.mu **WWW:** webmsiri.intnet.mu

Founded: 1953 **Type:** Research **Head:** Rosemay Ng Kee
Kwong *Phone:* +230 454-1061 *Email:* rng@msiri.intnet.mu
Staff: 3 Prof. 4 Other **Holdings:** 29,000 books 450 journals
Language of Collection/Services: English / English, French
Subjects: Agriculture (Tropics), Agricultural Economics,
Agricultural Engineering, Biotechnology, Crops, Education/
Extension, Entomology, Land Use, Plant Pathology, Plant
Protection, Plants, Soil Science, Water Resources **Specializations:** Intercropping, Sugarcane **Databases Used:** Agris;
Agricola; CABCD **Databases Developed:** MSIRI publications since 1953; Literature on potatoes since 1854 in Mauritius **Loan:** Inhouse **Service:** Internationally **Photocopy:** Yes

1848   Réduit, Mauritius
       Ministry of Agriculture, Food Technology and
         Natural Resources
       Library and Documentation Centre
       Agricultural Services
       Réduit
Phone: +230 466-2483 **Fax:** +230 464-8749 **WWW:** ncb.
intnet.mu/moa/index.htm

Former Name: Ministry of Agriculture, Fisheries and Co-operatives, Ministry of Agriculture and Natural Resources
Founded: 1985 **Type:** Government **Head:** Miss J. Hiu Sin
Nen *Phone:* +230 466-2483 **Staff:** 8 Other **Holdings:** 5,500
books 50 journals **Language of Collection/Services:** English, French / English **Subjects:** Agricultural Development, Agricultural Economics, Animal Production, Conservation, Crop Production, Forestry, Plant Protection **Specializations:** Mauritania **Databases Used:** TROPAG & RURAL **Loan:** Inhouse **Service:** Inhouse **Photocopy:** Yes

1849   Réduit, Mauritius
       University of Mauritius (UM)
       Library
       Royal Road
       Réduit

Phone: +230 454-1041 ext 1286 **Fax:** +230 454-0905
WWW: www.uom.ac.mu

Founded: 1965 **Head:** B.R. Goordyal *Phone:* +230 454-1041 ext 1229 *Email:* goordyal@uom.ac. mu **Staff:** 3 Prof.
20 Other **Holdings:** 95,000 books 350 journals **Language of Collection/Services:** English **Type:** Academic **Subjects:** Comprehensive **Specializations:** Agricultural Economics, Animal Breeding, Soil **Networks:** AGRIS **Loan:** Inhouse **Service:** Inhouse **Photocopy:** Yes

Mexico

1850   Celaya, México
       Secretary of Agriculture, Livestock and Rural
         Development
       Information and Documentation Center in
         Guanajuato State
       Avenida Irrigación s/n
       38030 Celaya, Guanajuato
Phone: +52(461) 21619 ext 362 **Email:**
gto_biblio@sagar.gob.mx

Non-English Name: Secretaría de Agricultura, Ganadería y
Desarrollo Rural (SAGAR), Centro de Información y Documentación en el Estado de Guanajuato (CID) **Former
Name:** Secretaría de Agricultura y Recursos Hidráulicos
(SARH) **Founded:** 1990 **Type:** Government **Head:** Lic.
Teresa Torres Solis **Staff:** 1 Prof. 2 Other **Holdings:** 5,000
books 45 journals **Language of Collection/Services:** Spanish / Spanish **Subjects:** Comprehensive **Specializations:** Official agricultural and livestock production statistics, both
national and state **Databases Used:** Agricola; Agris; Diario
Oficial de la Federación **Loan:** In country **Service:** In country **Photocopy:** Yes

1851   Celaya, México
       Secretary of Agriculture, Livestock and Rural
         Development, National Institute of Forestry
         and Agricultural Research
       National Agricultural Library
       Apdo. Postal No. 112
       38600 Celaya, Guanajuato
Location: Km 6.5 Carretara Celaya-San Miguel Allende
Phone: +52(461) 15323 ext 220 **Fax:** +52(461) 15431

Email: biblioa@cirpac.inifap.conacyt.mx **WWW:** www. inifap.conacyt.mx

Non-English Name: Secretaría de Agricultura, Ganadería y Desarrollo Rural, Instituto Nacional de Investigaciones Forestales, Agrícolas y Pecuarias (SAGAR, INIFAP), Biblioteca Agrícola Nacional **Former Name:** Secretaría de Agricultura y Recursos Hidráulicos (SARH), Instituto Nacional de Investigaciones Agrícolas (INIA), National Institute of Agricultural Research, Centro de Investigaciones Forestales y Agropecuarias del Estado de Guanajuato, Centro de Documentación Científica y Tecnológica **Founded:** 1949 **Type:** Government **Staff:** 3 Other **Holdings:** 954 journals 190,000 books **Language of Collection/Services:** English/Spanish **Subjects:** Agricultural Economics, Cereals, Entomology, Forage, Forestry, Fruit Trees, Genetics, Legumes, Livestock, Plant Pathology, Soil Science, Vegetables, Woodlands **Databases Used:** Comprehensive **Loan:** Internationally **Service:** Inhouse **Photocopy:** Yes

1852   Chapingo, México
         Autonomous University of Chapingo
         Marte R. Gomez Central Library
         56230 Chapingo, México
Phone: +52(595) 21500 ext 5741 **Fax:** +52(595) 50877

Non-English Name: Universidad Autónoma Chapingo (UACH), Biblioteca Central Marte R. Gómez **Former Name:** Escuela Nacional de Agricultura **Type:** Academic **Founded:** 1963 **Head:** Lic. Ramón Suárez Espinoza *Phone:* +52(595) 50877 *Email:* rsuarez@taurus1.chapingo.mx **Staff:** 10 Prof. 40 Other **Holdings:** 76,337 books 280 journals **Language of Collection/Services:** Spanish / Spanish **Subjects:** Comprehensive **Databases Used:** Agricola; Agris; CABCD **Loan:** In country **Service:** In country **Photocopy:** Yes

1853   Chapingo, México
         Post Graduate College
         Department of Documentation and Library
         Apdo 60
         56230 Chapingo, México
Location: Montecillos **Phone:** +52(595) 20200 ext 1102, 1128, 1129 **Fax:** +52(595) 20231 **Email:** bibliocp@colpos. colpos.mx **WWW:** www.colpos.mx

Non-English Name: Colegio de Posgraduados (CP), Departamento de Documentación y Biblioteca **Founded:** 1980 **Type:** Government **Head:** Lic. Raymundo M. Ruíz Melchor *Phone:* +52(595) 20231 **Staff:** 2 Prof. 14 Other **Holdings:** 60,000 books 1,200 journals **Subjects:** Agricultural Economics, Botany, Edaphic Factors, Plant Pathology, Cattle, Entomology, Genetics, Hydrology, Woodlands, Rural Development **Loan:** In country **Photocopy:** Yes

1854   Hermosillo, México
         University of Sonora, School of Agriculture and
               Livestock
         Library
         Carretera a Bahia Kino Km 25
         Hermosillo, Sonora
Phone: +52(62) 21046 **WWW:** www.uson.mx

Non-English Name: Universidad de Sonora, Escuela de Agricultura y Ganadería, Biblioteca **Founded:** 1946 **Type:** Academic **Staff:** 3 Prof. 1 Other **Holdings:** 2,500 books 2 journals **Subjects:** Farm Machinery, Fruits, Plants, Irrigation, Zootechny **Loan:** Inhouse **Photocopy:** Yes

1855   Jiutepec, México
         Institute of Water Technology
         National Center of Water Information
         Paseo Cuauhnahuac 8532
         62550 Jiutepec, Morelos
Phone: +52(9173) 19400 ext 140 **Fax:** +52(9173) 193881 **WWW:** www.imta.mx **OPAC:** cenca.imta.mx

Non-English Name: Instituto Mexicano de Tecnología del Agua (IMTA), Centro de Consulta del Agua (CENCA) **Language of Collection/Services:** English, Spanish / Spanish **Type:** Government **Holdings:** 23,725 books 300 journals **Subjects:** Agricultural Research, Aquatic Resources, Biotechnology, Biodeterioration, Microbiology, Safety, Natural Resources, Wastes, Water Resources **Photocopy:** Yes **Databases Developed:** IMTA books **Loan:** In country **Service:** In country

1856   Metepec, México
         Agriculture and Livestock Development
               Commission of the State of México
         Salvador Sanchez Colin Agriculture
               Documentation Center
         Apdo 34
         52140 Metepec, México
Location: Group SEDAGRO, RAnch San Lorenzo **Fax:** +52(72) 322657

Non-English Name: Comisión para el Desarrollo Agrícola y Ganadera del Estado de México (SEDAGRO), Centro de Documentación Agrícola "Ing. Salvador Sánchez Colín" **Founded:** 1980 **Type:** Government **Head:** Lic. David Reyes Marín *Phone:* +52(72) 322639 ext 587, 355 **Staff:** 1 Prof. 2 Other **Holdings:** 50,000 books 12 journals **Language of Collection/Services:** Spanish / Spanish **Subjects:** Comprehensive **Loan:** In country **Photocopy:** Yes

1857   México, México
         Autonomous Metropolitan University, Xochimilco
               Campus (AMU-X)
         Library
         Calzada del Hueso 1100
         Villa Quietud
         04960 México, Distrito Federal
Phone: +52(5) 724-5369 **Fax:** +52(5) 594-5346 **Email:** ojimenez@copitl.uam.mx **WWW:** cueyatl.uam.mx **OPAC:** telnet://148.206.107.3, longin: opac

Non-English Name: Universidad Autónoma Metropolitana, Unidad Xochimilco (UAM-X), Biblioteca **Founded:** 1975 **Type:** Academic **Head:** Lic. Rafael Pagaza García *Phone:* +52(5) 724-5361 *Email:* rpagaza@copitl.uam.mx **Staff:** 25 Prof. 79 Other **Holdings:** 170,000 books 400 journals **Language of Collection/Services:** Spanish, English / Spanish, English **Subjects:** Agronomy, Veterinary Medicine **Specializations:** Biology, Food Sciences **Databases Used:** ASFA;

CABCD; Life Science Collection; Medline **Loan:** Inhouse **Service:** Inhouse **Photocopy:** Yes

1858   México, México
International Maize and Wheat Improvement
        Center
Library
Lisboa 27, Apdo 6-641
06600 México, Distrito Federal
Location: Km. 45 Carretera México-Veracruz, 56130 El Batán, Texcoco **Phone:** +52(5) 5804-2004 ext 2021, +1 (650) 833-6655 ext 2021 (via USA) **Fax:** +52(5) 5804-7558/9, +1(650) 833-6656 (via USA) **WWW:** www. cimmyt.mx **Ariel IP:** 192.100.189.63

Non-English Name: Centro Internacional de Mejoramiento de Maíz y Trigo (CIMMYT), Biblioteca **Former Name:** Scientific Information Unit (SIU), Unidad de Información Científica **Founded:** 1984 **Type:** International **Head:** Mr. Efren Orozco (Acting Library Manager) *Phone:* +52(5) 5804-2004 ext 2022 *Email:* eorozco@cgiar.org **Staff:** 4 Prof. 7 Other **Holdings:** 30,000 books 225 journals **Language of Collection/Services:** English / English, Spanish **Subjects:** Agricultural Development, Agricultural Economics, Crops, Entomology, Food Sciences, Plant Pathology, Soil Science **Specializations:** Biotechnology, Maize, Natural Resources, Plant Breeding, Triticale, Wheat **Networks:** AGRIS; SERIUNAM **Databases Used:** Agris; CABCD; Current Contents **Loan:** In country and CIMMYT regional offices **Service:** Internationally **Photocopy:** Yes

1859   México, México
Mexican Institute of Renewable Natural
        Resources
Library
Av. Dr. Vertiz 724 Col. Narvarte
03020 México, Distrito Federal 12
Phone: +52(5) 519-1633 **Fax:** +52(5) 538-4520 **Email:** ebeltra1@mail.internet.com.mx **WWW:** www.teesa. imernar.com.mx

Non-English Name: Instituto Mexicano de Recursos Naturales Renovables, A.C. (IMERNAR), Biblioteca **Type:** Non-government **Founded:** 1952 **Head:** Lic. Francisco Acevedo R. *Phone:* +52(5) 519-4505 *Email:* ebeltra1@mail.internet. com.mx **Staff:** 2 Prof. **Holdings:** 3,700 books 50 journals **Language of Collection/Services:** Spanish / Spanish **Subjects:** Administration, Agricultural Development, Farming, Fruits, Horticulture **Specializations:** Forestry, Administration, Animal Husbandry **Loan:** In country **Service:** Inhouse **Photocopy:** Yes

1860   México, México
National Autonomous University of Mexico,
        Faculty of Veterinary Medicine
Library
Apdo. Postal 22-857
14000 México, Distrito Federal
Location: Circuito Exterior Ciudad Universitaria, Col. Coyoacan, 14510 México, D.F. **Phone:** +52(5) 622-5911, 622-5932 **Fax:** +52(5) 550-0057, 550-8697 **WWW:** www. veterin.unam.mx

Non-English Name: Universidad Nacional Autónoma de México (UNAM), Facultad de Medicina Veterinaria y Zootecnia, Biblioteca **Founded:** 1853 **Type:** Academic **Head:** Lic. María Ines Escalante Vargas *Phone:* +52(5) 622-5904 *Email:* miev@servidor.unam.mx **Staff:** 8 Prof. 32 Other **Holdings:** 49,000 books 500 journals **Language of Collection/Services:** Spanish, English / English, Spanish **Subjects:** Agriculture (Tropics), Agricultural Economics, Biotechnology, Education/Extension, Farming, Fisheries, Food Sciences, Veterinary Medicine **Specializations:** Bird Diseases, Anesthesia, Anatomy, Animal Behavior, Animal Production, Animal Husbandry, Anthelmintics, Antibiotics, Artificial Insemination, Aujeszky's Disease, Bovidae, Fractures, Cattle Diseases, Disease Prevention, Dog Diseases, Epidemiology, Equidae, Fishes, Hematology, Immunology, Laboratory Animals, Mastitis, Meat, Milk, Newcastle Disease, Nutrition, Physiology, Pigs, Poultry, Rabbits, Rabies, Radiography, Respiratory Diseases, Small Animal Practice, Surgery, Uterine Diseases, Veterinary Medicine, Zoonoses **Databases Used:** Agricola; CABCD **Loan:** Internationally **Service:** Internationally **Photocopy:** Yes

1861   México, México
Secretary of Agriculture, Livestock and Rural
        Development, National Institute of Forestry
        and Agricultural Research
Center for Scientific and Technological
        Documentation
Serapio Randón No. 83
Col. San Rafael
06470 México, Distrito Federal
Fax: +52(5) 592-5240 **Email:** zertur@inifap2.inifap. conacyt.mx **WWW:** www.inifap.conacyt.mx

Non-English Name: Secretaría de Agricultura, Ganadería y Desarrollo Rural, Instituto Nacional de Investigaciones Forestales, Agrícolas y Pecuarias (SAGAR, INIFAP), Centro de Documentación Científica y Tecnológica **Former Name:** Secretaría de Agricultura y Recursos Hidráulicos (SARH) **Founded:** 1958 **Type:** Government **Staff:** 2 Prof. 5 Other **Holdings:** 40,635 books 395 journals **Subjects:** Biology, Botany, Entomology, Genetic Improvement, Forestry, Forest Inventories, Forest Ecology, Forest Products **Networks:** AGRIS **Databases Used:** Agris **Loan:** In country **Photocopy:** Yes

1862   México, México
Secretary of Agriculture, Livestock and Rural
        Development, National Institute of Forestry
        and Agricultural Research
Department of Scientific and Technological
        Documentation
Apdo 41-652
11001 México, Distrito Federal
Location: Km 15.5 Carretera México-Toluca, México, DF 05110 **Fax:** +52(5) 570-0682 **WWW:** www.inifap.conacyt.mx

Non-English Name: Secretaría de Agricultura, Ganadería y Desarrollo Rural, Instituto Nacional de Investigaciones Forestales, Agrícolas y Pecuarias (SAGAR, INIFAP), Departamento de Documentación Científica y Tecnológica **Former Name:** Secretaría de Agricultura y Recursos Hidráulicos (SARH) **Founded:** 1970 **Type:** Government **Head:** Arturo García Fraustro *Phone:* +52(5) 570-3100 ext l32 **Staff:** 3 Prof. 3 Other **Holdings:** 10,000 books 175 journals **Language of Collection/Services:** English **Subjects:** Animal Husbandry, Fodder Crops, Veterinary Medicine **Databases Used:** Agris; CABCD; Medline **Loan:** In country **Photocopy:** Yes

1863   Morelia, México
Fund for the Development of Agricultural and
        Fishery Activities in Mexico (FDAF)
Library
Km. 8 Antigua Carretera Patzcuaro s/n
Ex-Hacienda La Huerta
58341 Morelia, Michoacan

Phone: +52(5243) 222348 **Fax:** +52(5243) 222338 **Email:** cie@correo.fira.gob.mx **WWW:** www.fira.gob.mx

Non-English Name: Fondo de Garantía y Fomento para la Agricultura, Ganadería y la Pesca (FIRA), Biblioteca **Type:** Government **Founded:** 1958 **Head:** Ing. Valentín Rebollo Gómez *Phone:* +52(5243) 222340 *Email:* vrebollo@correo. fira.gob.mx **Staff:** 5 Prof. 2 Other **Holdings:** 8,300 books 120 journals **Language of Collection/Services:** Spanish **Subjects:** Comprehensive **Specializations:** Agricultural Credit **Databases Developed:** Rentabilidad Agrícola - analysis of the profitability of the major agricultural crops; Indicadores Económicos - Updating for the main national economic indicators **Databases Used:** Comprehensive **Loan:** Internationally **Service:** In country **Photocopy:** Yes

1864   Querétaro, México
Monterrey Institute of Advanced Technological
        Studies, Queretaro Campus (Monterrey Tech)
Library
Apdo. Postal 37
76000 Querétaro, Querétaro
Location: Jesús Oviedo 10, Parques Industriales **Phone:** +52(42) 383196 **Fax:** +52(42) 173823 **Email:** biblioteca@ campus.qro.itesm.mx **WWW:** www.qro.itesm.mx **OPAC:** info04.rzc.ites.mx **Ariel IP:** ariel.qro.itesm.mx

Non-English Name: Instituto Tecnológico de Estudios Superiores de Monterrey, Campus Querétaro (ITESM), Biblioteca **Founded:** 1975 **Type:** Academic **Head:** Lic. Saúl H. Souto Fuentes *Email:* ssouto@ campus.qro.itesm.mx *Phone:* +52(42) 383170 **Staff:** 5 Prof. 16 Other **Holdings:** 60,000 books 450 journals **Language of Collection/Services:** Spanish/Spanish **Subjects:** Agribusiness, Biotechnology, Crops, Food Sciences, Horticulture, Plants, Soil Science **Loan:** Inhouse **Service:** Inhouse **Photocopy:** Yes

1865   Saltillo, México
Universidad Autónoma Agraria "Antonio Narro"
Biblioteca "Dr. Egidio G. Rebonato"
Apdo 342
Saltillo, Coahuila
Location: Buena Vista **Phone:** +52(84) 173022 ext 429 **Fax:** +52(84) 173003 **WWW:** www.uaaan.mx

Type: Academic **Head:** Ing. Arnoldo S. Rodriguez Villarreal *Phone:* +52(84) 173022 ext 429 **Staff:** 4 Prof. 35 Other **Holdings:** 20,719 books 136 journals **Language of Collec-**

tion/Services: Spanish, English / Spanish, English **Subjects:** Agricultural Statistics, Genetic Improvement, Horticulture, Irrigation, Zootechny **Databases Used:** Agricola **Loan:** In country **Photocopy:** Yes

1866   San Nicolás de los Garza, México
Universidad Autónoma de Nuevo León, Facultad
        de Agronomía (UANL, FA)
Biblioteca "Dr. Eduardo Aguirre Pequeño"
Apdo 358
66450 San Nicolás de los Garza, Nuevo León
Location: Carretera Zuazua-Marín Km 17, 66700 Marín
Fax: +52(824) 80022 **WWW:** www.dsi.uanl.mx

Founded: 1954 **Type:** Academic **Head:** Emma Melchor Rodriguez *Phone:* +52(824) 80099 **Staff:** 2 Prof. 16 Other **Holdings:** 33,990 books 157 journals **Language of Collection/Services:** Spanish **Subjects:** Agricultural Engineering, Food Industry, Parasitology, Plants, Rural Development, Zootechny **Databases Used:** CABCD **Loan:** Internationally **Photocopy:** Yes

Micronesia, Federated States of

1867   Chuuk, Micronesia
Chuuk Department of Resources and
        Development, Division of Agriculture
Library
PO Box 219
Weno
Chuuk 96942
Fax: +691 330-2233

Type: Government

1868   Kosrae, Micronesia
Kosrae Department of Agriculture and Land
Agriculture Resource Library
PO Box 82
Tofol
Kosrae 96944
Phone: +691 370-3017 **Fax:** +691 370-3952 **Email:** dalu @mail.fm

Former Name: Kosrae Department of Conservation and Development **Type:** Government

1869   Pohnpei, Micronesia
College of Micronesia
Library
PO Box 159
Kolonia
Pohnpei 96941
Type: Academic

1870   Pohnpei, Micronesia
Department of Resources and Development,
        Division of Agriculture
Library
PO Box PS-12
Palikir
Pohnpei 96941

Phone: +691 320-2646, 320-2697, 320-5133 **Fax:** +691 320-5854

Type: Government

1871   Pohnpei, Micronesia
Family Food Production and Nutrition Project
Library
PO Box 1028
Palikir
Pohnpei 96941
Location: Agriculture Station, Kolonia **Phone:** +691 320-2400 **Fax:** +691 320-5997

Type: Non-government

1872   Pohnpei, Micronesia
Micronesian Seminar
Library
PO Box 160
Kolonia
Pohnpei 96941
Phone: +691 320-4067 **Fax:** +691 320-6668 **WWW:** microstate.com/micsem/micsem.htm

Founded: 1972 **Type:** Academic **Head:** Rev. Francis X. Hezel, S. J. *Phone:* +691 320-4067 *Email:* fxhezel@mail.fm **Staff:** 1 Prof. **Holdings:** 12,500 books 30 journals **Language of Collection/Services:** English / English **Subjects:** Agriculture (Micronesia) **Specializations:** Traditional Society, Ethnography (Micronesia), **Loan:** Do not loan **Service:** Bibliographies and copies sent on request **Photocopy:** Yes

1873   Pohnpei, Micronesia
Nature Conservancy
Library
PO Box 216
Kolonia
Pohnpei 96941
Phone: +691 320-4267 **Fax:** +691 320-4267

Founded: 1992 **Type:** Non-government

1874   Pohnpei, Micronesia
Pohnpei Department of Conservation and Resources Surveillance, Division of Agriculture
Library
PO Box 1028
Palikir
Pohnpei 96941
Phone: +691 320-2400/2401 **Fax:** +691 320-5997

Type: Government

1875   Pohnpei, Micronesia
Ponape Agricultural Trade School (PATS)
Christopher Library
PO Box 39
Pohnpei 96941
Founded: 1965 **Type:** Academic **Head:** Bill Rolls **Staff:** 1 Other **Holdings:** 2,500 books 3 journals **Language of Collection/Services:** English / English **Subjects:** Horticulture (Tropics), Animal Husbandry **Photocopy:** No **Service:** Inhouse **Loan:** Inhouse

1876   Yap, Micronesia
Yap Department of Resources and Development
Library
PO Box 463
Colonia
Yap 96943
Type: Government

1877   Yap, Micronesia
Yap Institute of Natural Science
Library
PO Box 215
Colonia
Yap 96943
Phone: +691 841-3115 **Fax:** +691 841-4113
Type: Research

Moldova

1878   Anenii Noi, Moldova
Electromechanical College, Roscani
Library
Roscani
Anenii Noi 6530
Phone: +373(65) 98404

Head: Maria Bezerdîc

1879   Anenii Noi, Moldova
Scientific Research Institute of Zootechnics and Veterinary Science
Library
Maximovca
Anenii Noi 6525
Phone: +373(65) 237767 **Fax:** +373(65) 277600

Founded: 1957 **Type:** Government **Head:** Iraida Zeduic *Phone:* +373(65) 237767 **Language of Collection/Services:** Russian/Romanian **Holdings:** 18,800 books **Subjects:** Animal Breeding, Livestock, Veterinary Science **Loan:** Inhouse **Service:** Inhouse **Photocopy:** No

1880   Beltsy, Moldova
Scientific Research Institute of Field Crops
Library
Calea Iesilor str., 28
Beltsy 3100
Phone: +373(31) 34137 **Fax:** +373(31) 30221

Non-English Name: Institutul de cercetari pentry culturile de camp (ICCC), Bibliteca **Founded:** 1947 **Type:** Government **Head:** Svetlana Botezatu *Email:* selectia@beltsy.md **Holdings:** 63,000 books **Language of Collection/Services:** Romanian, English, French, Russian **Subjects:** Field Crops, Biochemistry, Biology, Farming, Genetics, Plant Breeding, Pedology **Networks:** AGRIS

1881   Cahul, Moldova
Agrarian Technical College, Cahul
Library
Dunarii str. 36

Cahul
Phone: +373(39) 23570
Head: Larisa Stavila

1882 Cahul, Moldova
Experiment Station of Aromatic Plants and
Essential Oils
Library
Sudica str. 17
Cahul 3900
Phone: +373(39) 21898

Subjects: Aromatic Plants, Essential Oils

1883 Chisinau, Moldova
Academy of Sciences of Moldova, Institute of
Biological Plant Protection (IBPP)
Library
Dacia Av., 58
Chisinau 2060
Phone: +373(2) 770466 **Fax:** +373(2) 779641 **Email:**
slipbp@cc.acad.md **WWW:** www.asm.md

Non-English Name: Academiei de Stiinte a Republicii Moldova, Institutul de Protectie Biologica a Plantelor (IPBP), Biblioteca **Former Name:** All-Union Scientific Research Institute of Biological Methods of Plant Protection **Founded:** 1946 **Type:** Government **Head:** Madame Tatiana Timacova *Phone:* +373(2) 770492 **Holdings:** 79,326 books 9 journals **Staff:** 153 Other 143 Prof. **Language of Collection/Services:** Russian, Moldavian, English, French / Moldavian, Russian **Subjects:** Biological Control, Entomology, Biotechnology, Plant Protection **Loan:** In country **Service:** In country **Photocopy:** Yes

1884 Chisinau, Moldova
National Agency of Geodesy and Cartography,
Project Institute of Territory Organization
Library
Ialoveni str. 100b
Chisinau 2070
Phone: +373(2) 723388

Type: Academic **Head:** Nina Roganov *Phone:* +373(2) 432-578 **Language of Collection/Services:** Moldavian, Russian **Staff:** 1 Prof. **Subjects:** Amelioration, Soil Science **Loan:** In country **Service:** In country **Photocopy:** No

1885 Chisinau, Moldova
National Institute of Wine and Viticulture
Library
Grenoble 128
Chisinau
Phone: +373(2) 721400

Founded: 1947 **Type:** Government **Head:** Sofia Ghertescu **Holdings:** 26,700 books **Subjects:** Vineyards, Viticulture, Winemaking

1886 Chisinau, Moldova
Research Station of Aromatic Plants and Essential
Oils
Library
Muncesti str. 426

Chisinau 2018
Head: Natalia Baranova *Phone:* +373(2) 532087 **Subjects:** Aromatic Plants, Essential Oils

1887 Chisinau, Moldova
Scientific Research Institute and Bureau of
Mechanization in Agricultural Complex
Library
M. Costin str. 7
Chisinau 2068
Phone: +373(2) 438856

Head: Nadejda Timoschin **Subjects:** Mechanization

1888 Chisinau, Moldova
Scientific Research Institute and Project Bureau of
Food Industry
Library
Cogalniceanu str. 63
Chisinau 2709
Fax: +373(2) 241688

Founded: 1957 **Type:** Government **Head:** Galina S. Kudryavtseva *Phone:* +373(2) 243592 **Holdings:** 46,108 books **Language of Collection/Services:** Russian **Subjects:** Food Sciences **Service:** Inhouse **Photocopy:** Yes

1889 Chisinau, Moldova
Scientific Research Institute of Fruit Growing
Library
Costiujeni 14
Chisinau 2019
Phone: +373(2) 787749

Founded: 1947 **Type:** Government **Head:** Antonina Ungureanov **Subjects:** Fruits

1890 Chisinau, Moldova
Scientific Research Institute of Soil Science and
Water Problems "N. Dimo"
Library
Ialoveni str. 100
Chisinau 2070
Phone: +373(2) 723844

Founded: 1965 **Type:** Government **Head:** Viorica Boraga **Holdings:** 39,900 books **Subjects:** Agricultural Chemistry, Soil Science

1891 Chisinau, Moldova
Scientific Research Institute of Tobacco and
Tobacco Industry, Gratiesti
Library
Gratiesti
Chisinau 2089
Phone: +373(48) 442104

Founded: 1968 **Type:** Government **Head:** Natalia Serdiuc **Holdings:** 3,500 books **Subjects:** Tobacco, Tobacco Industry

1892 Chisinau, Moldova
State Agrarian University of Moldova (SAUM)
Republican Agrarian Scientific Library (RASL)

Mircesti 42
Chisinau 2049
Phone: +373(2) 432592 **Fax:** +373(2) 246326 **Email:**
biblio@agro.net.md

Non-English Name: Universitatea Agrare de Stat din Moldova (UASM), Biblioteca Republicana Stiintifica Agrara (BRSA) **Former Name:** Institutul Agricol M.V. Frunze, Agrarian Scientific Library **Type:** Academic **Head:** Ludmila Costin *Email:* costin@agro.net.md *Phone:* +373(2) 432578 **Founded:** 1945 **Staff:** 5 Prof. 3 Other **Holdings:** 756,268 books 160 journals **Language of Collection/Services:** Romanian, Russian/Romanian, Russian **Subjects:** Agricultural Development, Agricultural Economics, Agricultural Engineering, Animal Husbandry, Biotechnology, Entomology, Fisheries, Forestry, Horticulture, Plant Pathology, Plants, Soil Science, Veterinary Medicine, Water Resources **Loan:** In country **Service:** Inhouse **Photocopy:** No

1893   Criuleni, Moldova
National College of Viticulture and Winemaking, Stauceni
Library
Gratiesti str. 1
Stauceni
Criuleni 4839
Phone: +373(48) 326366

Head: Ludmila Cires **Subjects:** Viticulture, Winemaking

1894   Criuleni, Moldova
Scientific Research Institute of Maize and Sorghum
Pascani
Criuleni 4834
Phone: +373(48) 222478 **Fax:** +373(48) 227302

Founded: 1975 **Type:** Government **Head:** Parascovia Ion Veresceac *Phone:* +373(48) 223284 **Staff:** 1 Prof. 3 Other **Holdings:** 18,922 books 11,723 journals **Language of Collection/Services:** Romanian, Russian / Romanian **Subjects:** Agribusiness, Agricultural Engineering, Crops, Farming, Biotechnology, Entomology, Plant Pathology **Specializations:** Maize, Seed Production, Sorghum **Loan:** In country **Service:** In country **Photocopy:** Yes

1895   Donduseni, Moldova
Agrarian College, Taul
Library
Taul
Donduseni 5141
Phone: +373(51) 61344

Head: Valentina Dadu

1896   Edinet, Moldova
College of Zootechnics, Bratuseni
Library
Bratuseni
Edinet 4600
Phone: +373(46) 231109

1897   Hâncesti, Moldova
Building College

Library
Mitropolitul Varlaam str. 51
Hâncesti 3401
Phone: +373(34) 23603

Head: Maria Urmanschi

1898   Ocnita, Moldova
Agrarian Industrial College, Grinauti
Library
Grinauti
Ocnita 7123
Phone: +373(72) 22513

Head: Valentina Kolibin

1899   Orhei, Moldova
Scientific Research Institute of Piglets Cultivation
Library
Nistreana str. 50
Orhei 3500
Phone: +373(35) 23196

Head: Iulia Pogonii **Subjects:** Piglets

1900   Rascani, Moldova
Agrarian Industrial College, Rascani
Library
Trandafirilor str. 30
Rascani 5601
Phone: +373(56) 28701

Head: Maria Ghilescu

1901   Soroca, Moldova
Agrarian Technical College, Soroca
Library
Calea Baltuni str. 28
Soroca 3001
Phone: +373(74) 32482

Head: Anastasia Drobusenco

1902   Taraclia, Moldova
Agrarian Technical College, Svetlâi
Library
Svetlâi
Taraclia 7400
Phone: +373(74) 32482

Head: Vera Lugovschi

Mongolia

1903   Ulan Bator, Mongolia
National Agricultural University
Library
Zaisan 53
Ulan Bator
Fax: +976(1) 341770

Networks: AGRIS

Morocco

1904   Casablanca, Morocco
Ministère de la Santé, Institut Pasteur du Maroc
Bibliothèque
1 Place Abou Kacem Ez-Zahraoui
Casablanca

Phone: +212(2) 269424, 275778, 275206 **Fax:** +212(2) 260957 **WWW:** www.maroc.net/ipm

Founded: 1929 **Type:** Government **Holdings:** 3,187 books **Subjects:** Animal Husbandry, Botany **Loan:** In country **Photocopy:** Yes

1905   Casablanca, Morocco
Université Hassan II, Faculté des Sciences II de
            Casablanca
Bibliothèque
Km 8 Route D'El Jadida
BP 5366 Mâarif
Casablanca

Phone: +212(2) 230680/84 **Fax:** +212(2) 230674 **WWW:** www.facsc-achok.ac.mas

Founded: 1984 **Type:** Government **Head:** Zakaria Rochd **Holdings:** 16,000 books **Subjects:** Plants, Zoology **Loan:** In country **Photocopy:** Yes

1906   Ifrane, Morocco
Al Akhawayn University in Ifrane
Library
PO Box 104
Hassan II Avenue
Ifrane 53000

Phone: +212(5) 862000 **Fax:** +212(5) 567150 **WWW:** www.alakhawayn.ma

Head: Wahiba Sebbane *Email:* w.sebbane@alakhawayn.ma *Phone:* +212(5) 862171

1907   Marrakech, Morocco
Ministère de l'Agriculture, du Développement
            Rural et des Pêches Maritimes, Office
            Régional de Mise en Valeur Agricole du
            Haouz (MADRP, ORMVAH)
Section Documentation
BP 22
Marrakech

Location: Avenue Hassan II **Phone:** +212(4) 21204 **Fax:** +212(4) 449793

Former Name: Ministère de l'Agriculture et de la Réforme Agraire (MARA) **Founded:** 1962 **Type:** Government **Head:** Chrouate Faiza *Phone:* +212(4) 449650, 449597 **Staff:** 1 Prof. 1 Other **Holdings:** 12,540 books 30 journals **Language of Collection/Services:** French, Arabic/French, Arabic **Subjects:** Agricultural Development, Agricultural Economics, Animal Husbandry, Entomology, Farming, Horticulture, Plant Pathology, Plants, Soil Science, Veterinary Medicine, Water Resources **Specializations:** Irrigation, Development Plans **Databases Used:** Agris **Loan:** Inhouse **Service:** Internationally **Photocopy:** Yes

1908   Meknès, Morocco
Ministry of Agriculture, Rural Development and
            Marine Fisheries, National School of
            Agriculture in Meknes
Documentation Center
BP S/40
Meknès

Phone: +212(5) 300239/41 **Fax:** +212(5) 300238 **Email:** ena@enameknes.ac.ma **WWW:** www.enameknes.ac.ma

Non-English Name: Ministère de l'Agriculture, du Développement Rural et des Pêches Maritimes, Ecole Nationale d'Agriculture de Meknès (MADRP, ENAM), Centre de Documentation-Information (CDI) **Former Name:** Ministère de l'Agriculture et de la Réforme Agraire **Founded:** 1948 **Type:** Government **Holdings:** 100 journals 16,000 books **Staff:** 1 Prof. 1 Other **Language of Collection/Services:** French, English / French **Subjects:** Botany, Agricultural Engineering, Animal Products, Animal Husbandry, Biology, Chemistry, Environmental Sciences, Physics, Extension, Entomology, Fisheries, Forestry, Geology, Machinery, Natural Resources, Pedology, Plant Pathology, Plants, Rural Economy, Zoology **Loan:** Internationally **Service:** In country **Photocopy:** Yes

1909   Mohammadia, Morocco
Université Hassan II - Mohammadia, Faculté des
            Sciences et Techniques - Mohammadia
            (FSTM)
Bibliothèque
BP 146
Route de Rabat
Mohammadia 20650

Phone: +212(3) 314705/8 **Fax:** +212(3) 315353 **WWW:** www.mp3m.gov.ma

1910   Oujda, Morocco
Université Mohammed Premier
Bibliothèque
Complexe Universitaire Hay El Qods
BP 524
Oujda 60000

Phone: +212(6) 500612, 500614 **Fax:** +212(6) 500609 **Email:** rogui@univ-oujda.ac.ma **WWW:** webserver1. univ-oujda.ac.ma

1911   Rabat, Morocco
Hassan II Institute of Agronomy and Veterinary
            Medicine
Agricultural Documentation Centre
BP 6214
Rabat-Instituts
Rabat

Phone: +212(7) 771758/9 **WWW:** www.iav.refer.org.ma/ accueil/iav.htm

Non-English Name: Institut Agronomique et Vétérinaire Hassan II (MADRP, IAVH II), Centre de Documentation Agricole (CDA) **Former Name:** Ministry of Agriculture and Agrarian Reform, Ministère de l'Agriculture et de la Réforme Agraire (MARA) **Founded:** 1968 **Type:** Government **Head:** Mohamed Lemallem *Email:* lemallem@iav.refer.org. ma *Phone:* +212(7) 771758/9 **Staff:** 4 Prof. 10 Other **Hold-**

ings: 39,000 books 120 journals **Language of Collection/Services:** English / French **Subjects:** Agriculture (Tropics), Agricultural Development, Agricultural Economics, Agricultural Engineering, Animal Husbandry, Biology, Biotechnology, Botany, Chemistry, Crops, Entomology, Farming, Fisheries, Food Sciences, Forestry, Plant Pathology, Soil Science, Horticulture, Water Resources, Veterinary Medicine **Specializations:** Agronomy, Veterinary Science **Databases Used:** Comprehensive **Service:** Internationally **Loan:** Inhouse **Photocopy:** Yes

1912   Rabat, Morocco
         House of Representatives
         Library
         Boulevard Mohamed V
         BP 431
         Rabat

Non-English Name: Chambre des Représentants, Bibliothèque **Founded:** 1971 **Type:** Government **Head:** Mohamed Loukili *Phone:* +212(7) 761101, 760960 **Staff:** 2 Prof. 2 Other **Holdings:** 9,642 books 136 journals **Language of Collection/Services:** Arabic, French / Arabic, French **Subjects:** Fisheries **Loan:** In country **Service:** In country **Photocopy:** Yes

1913   Rabat, Morocco
         Ministère de la Prévision Economique et du Plan,
              Direction de la Statistique (DS)
         Bibliothèque
         BP 178
         Rabat 10001
Location: Rue Mohamed Belhassan El Ouazzani, Haut-Agdal **Phone:** +212(7) 773606 **Fax:** +212(7) 773042 **Email:** asarti@statistic.gov.ma **WWW:** www.statistic.gov.ma

Founded: 1975 **Type:** Government **Head:** Berjali Karima *Phone:* +212(7) 773606 **Staff:** 7 Prof. 5 Other **Holdings:** 11,535 books 64 journals **Language of Collection/Services:** French, English/Arabic **Subjects:** Forestry **Specializations:** Demography, Economics, Social Sciences, Statistics **Loan:** Inhouse **Service:** Inhouse **Photocopy:** Yes

1914   Rabat, Morocco
         Ministère de la Prévision Economique et du Plan,
              Institut National des Statistiques et
              d'Economie Appliquée (INSEA)
         Bibliothèque
         BP 6217
         Madinat Al Irfane
         Rabat-Instituts
         Rabat
Phone: +212(7) 774859/60 **Fax:** +212(7) 779457 **WWW:** www.mpep.gov.ma

Founded: 1965 **Type:** Government **Holdings:** 28,700 books 207 journals **Loan:** In country **Photocopy:** Yes

1915   Rabat, Morocco
         Ministry of Agriculture, Rural Development and
              Marine Fisheries
         Documentation and Information Division

         Km 4, Route de Casablanca
         Rabat
Phone: +212(7) 690215/6 **Fax:** +212(7) 698401 **Email:** dpae@mtds.com

Non-English Name: Ministère de l'Agriculture, du Développement Rural et des Pêches Maritimes (MADRP), Division de Documentation et d'Information (DDI) **Staff:** 6 Prof. 20 Other **Type:** Government **Holdings:** 40,000 books 5 journals **Language of Collection/Services:** French / Arabic, French **Subjects:** Agricultural Development, Agricultural Economics, Agricultural Engineering, Animal Husbandry, Crops, Farming, Forestry, Horticulture **Networks:** AGRIS **Databases Used:** Agris **Loan:** Inhouse **Photocopy:** Yes

♦**1916   Rabat, Morocco**
         Ministry of Agriculture, Rural Development and
              Marine Fisheries, Guich Experiment Station
         Documentation Center
         Haut-Agdal
         Rabat

Non-English Name: Ministère de l'Agriculture, du Développement Rural et des Pêches Maritimes, Station Expérimentale du Guich, Bureau de Documentation **Founded:** 1938 **Type:** Government **Holdings:** 1,058 journals 11,087 books **Loan:** In country **Photocopy:** Yes

1917   Rabat, Morocco
         Ministry of Economic and Social Affairs
         National Documentation Centre
         Avenue Al Haj Ahmed Cherkaoui - Agdal
         BP 826-10004
         Rabat 10004
Phone: +212(7) 774944 **Fax:** +212(7) 773134 **Email:** khalloufi@cnd.mpep.gov.ma **WWW:** www.mpep.gov.ma

Non-English Name: Ministère de la Prévision Economique et du Plan, Centre National de Documentation (CND) **Former Name:** Ministère du Plan **Founded:** 1966 **Type:** Government **Staff:** 33 Prof. 76 Other **Holdings:** 8,000 books 55 journals **Language of Collection/Services:** French / French **Subjects:** Animal Husbandry, Beekeeping, Fisheries, Forestry **Databases Used:** Agris **Loan:** Internationally **Service:** Internationally **Photocopy:** Yes

♦**1918   Rabat, Morocco**
         National Institute of Agricultural Research
         Documentation Unit
         BP 6512 RI
         Rabat
Location: Haut Agdal **Phone:** +212(7) 775530 **Fax:** +212 (7) 774003 **WWW:** www.inra.org.ma

Non-English Name: Institut National de la Recherche Agronomique (INRA), Département de Documentation **Former Name:** Direction de la Recherche Agronomique, Bureau de Documentation **Founded:** 1924 **Type:** Government **Head:** Mr. Abderrahmane Lakrimi *Phone:* +212(7)774003, 775530 **Staff:** 5 Prof. 7 Other **Holdings:** 30,000 books 75 journals **Language of Collection/Services:** English, French /French **Subjects:** Agronomy, Crops, Entomology, Farming, Horticulture, Plant Pathology, Soil Science **Databases Used:**

Agricola; Agris **Loan:** Inhouse **Service:** In country **Photocopy:** Yes

1919   Settat, Morocco
National Institute of Agricultural Research,
Chaouia-Abda-Doukkala Regional Center
Library
PO Box 589, CRRA
Settat 26000
Location: Route tertiaire 1406 (vers Péitencier Ali Moumene) a 5 km de Settat **Phone:** +212(3) 403210/18 **Fax:** +212(3) 404087 **WWW:** www.inra.org.ma/settat.html

Non-English Name: Institut National de la Recherche Agronomique, Centre Régional de Chaouia-Abda-Doukkala (INRA), Bibliothèque

Mozambique

♦**1920   Maputo, Mozambique**
Eduardo Mondlane University, Agronomy Faculty
Library
CP 257
Maputo
Location: Av. Julius Nyerere **Phone:** +258(1) 490009 **Fax:** +258(1) 492176

Non-English Name: Universidade Eduardo Mondlane, Faculdade de Agronomia (UEM, FA), Biblioteca **Former Name:** Universidade de Lourenço Marques Cursos Superiores de Agronómica e Silvicultura **Founded:** 1956 **Type:** Academic **Head:** Miguel Salvador Muchanga *Phone:* +258 (1) 492142 ext 186 **Staff:** 2 Prof. 3 Other **Holdings:** 8,000 books 60 journals **Language of Collection/Services:** English / Portuguese **Subjects:** Agricultural Development, Agricultural Engineering, Forestry, Plant Protection, Plants, Soil Science **Databases Used:** Agricola; CABCD **Loan:** Inhouse **Service:** In country **Photocopy:** Yes

1921   Maputo, Mozambique
Eduardo Mondlane University, Centre of African Studies
Documentation and Information Center
CP 1993
Maputo
Location: Centro de Estudos Africanos, Campus Universitário **Phone:** +258(1) 490828 **Fax:** +258(1) 491896 **Email:** ceadid@zebra.uem.mz **WWW:** www.uem.mz

Non-English Name: Universidade Eduardo Mondlane, Centro de Estudos Africanos (UEM), Departamento de Documentação e Informação (DID) **Founded:** 1975 **Type:** Academic **Head:** Dr. Amélia Neves de Souto *Phone:* +258 (1) 490828 *Email:* ansouto@zebra.uem.mz **Staff:** 2 Prof. 2 Other **Holdings:** 5,000 books 100 journals **Language of Collection/Services:** English **Subjects:** Agricultural Development, Agricultural Economics, Land **Specializations:** Rural Development **Loan:** Inhouse **Photocopy:** Yes

1922   Maputo, Mozambique
Eduardo Mondlane University, Faculty of Veterinary Medicine (EMU, FVM)

Library
PO Box 257
Maputo
Location: Av. de Mocambique Km. 1.5 **Fax:** +258(1) 475360

Non-English Name: Universidade Eduardo Mondlane, Faculdade de Veterinária (UEM), Biblioteca **Founded:** 1964 **Type:** Academic **Head:** Dr. Paulo Bagassi *Phone:* +258(1) 475155, 475183 *Email:* pbg@impala.uem.mz **Staff:** 5 Other **Holdings:** 10,547 books 1,332 journals **Language of Collection/Services:** English / Portuguese **Subjects:** Animal Production, Veterinary Medicine **Specializations:** Animal Physiology, Wildlife **Photocopy:** Yes

1923   Maputo, Mozambique
Ministry of Agriculture and Fisheries
Centre for Agricultural Documentation and Information
PB 1406
Maputo
Location: Ministry of Agriculture and Fisheries, 3rd Floor, Praça dos Heroes Mocambicanos **Phone:** +258(1) 460137 **Fax:** +258(1) 460060 **Email:** cda@sdisa.vem.mz

Non-English Name: Ministério da Agricultura e Pescas, Centro de Documentação e Informação do Sector Agrário (CDA) **Founded:** 1988 **Type:** Government **Head:** Luis Majope **Staff:** 8 Prof. 6 Other **Holdings:** 40 journals 3,000 books **Language of Collection/Services:** Portuguese **Specializations:** Development Policy, National Technical Documents (Mozambique) **Networks:** AGRIS; VALMA - collective database for 8 libraries in SDISA Network; 20,000 records **Databases Used:** Agris **Photocopy:** Yes

♦**1924   Maputo, Mozambique**
National Institute of Agricultural Research
Documentation and Information Center (CDI)
CP 3658 Mavalane
Maputo 4
Location: Rua das Forças Populares, Mavalane

Non-English Name: Instituto Nacional de Investigação Agronómica (INIA), Centro de Documentação e Informação **Former Name:** Centro de Documentação de Agricultura, Silvicultura e Pesca (CEDASPE) **Founded:** 1978 **Type:** Government **Head:** Daniel de Sousa *Phone:* +258(1) 460100 460099 **Staff:** 4 Other **Holdings:** 11,176 books 4 journals **Language of Collection/Services:** Portuguese, English/ Portuguese **Loan:** In country **Service:** In country **Photocopy:** Yes

1925   Maputo, Mozambique
National Veterinary Research Institute
Library
PB 1922
Maputo
Location: Av. de Moçambique, Km. 1.5 **Phone:** +258(1) 475170/1 **Fax:** +258(1) 475172 **Email:** inive@tropical.co.mz

Non-English Name: Instituto Nacional de Investigação Veterinária (INIVE), Biblioteca **Founded:** 1908 **Type:** Government **Head:** Antonieta Nhamusso *Email:* inive@tropical.

co.mz *Phone:* +258(1) 475161, 475170/1 **Staff:** 1 Prof. 1 Other **Holdings:** 900 books 20 journals **Language of Collection/Services:** English / Portuguese **Subjects:** Animal Health, Animal Husbandry, Animal Production **Specializations:** Food Sciences, Parasitology, Pathology, Veterinary Microbiology **Loan:** Inhouse **Service:** Inhouse **Photocopy:** No

Namibia

1926   Windhoek, Namibia
      Ministry of Agriculture, Water and Development
         (MAWRD)
      Namibian Agriculture and Water Information
         Centre (NAWIC)
      Private Bag 13184
      Windhoek
Phone: +264(61) 208-7763 **Fax:** +264(61) 208-7068 **Email:** hoffmannm@mawrd.gov.na

Former Name: Department of Agriculture and Nature Conservation, National Agricultural Information Center (NAIC) **Founded:** 1974 **Type:** Government **Staff:** 1 Prof. 3 Other **Holdings:** 19,000 books 63 journals **Language of Collection/Services:** English / English **Subjects:** Comprehensive **Specializations:** Agriculture (Namibia) **Networks:** AGRIS; SABINET **Databases Used:** Agris; CABCD **Loan:** Inhouse **Service:** Internationally **Photocopy:** Yes

1927   Windhoek, Namibia
      Namibia Development Corporation (NDC)
      Information Centre
      Private Bag 13252
      Windhoek 9000
Phone: +264(61) 206-2232 **Fax:** +264(61) 247834 **Email:** ndc@iwwn.com.na **WWW:** www.ndc.org.na

Founded: 1993 **Type:** Parastatal **Head:** Linda Shaanika *Email:* linda.shaanika@ndc.org.na **Staff:** 3 Prof.

1928   Windhoek, Namibia
      University of Namibia (UNAM)
      Library
      Private Bag 13301
      Windhoek
Location: 340 Mandume Ndemufayo Avenue, Pioneers Park **Phone:** +264(61) 2063-8740 **Fax:** +264(61) 2063-8760 **Email:** library@unam.na **WWW:** www.unam.na

Type: Academic **Head:** Mr. Kwami E. Avafia *Phone:* +264 (61) 2063874 *Email:* kavafia@unam.na

Nepal

1929   Kathmandu, Nepal
      Forest Research and Survey Centre (FORESC)
      Central Forestry Library (FRIC)
      PO Box 3339
      Kathmandu
Location: Babar Mahal **Phone:** +977(1) 224943, 220479 **Fax:** +977(1) 220159 **Email:** foresc@wlink.com.np

Former Name: Forest Survey and Research Office (FSRO) **Founded:** 1965 **Type:** Government **Head:** Dasharath Thapa *Phone:* +977(1) 220671, 222601 *Email:* foresc@wlink.com. np **Staff:** 1 Prof. 3 Other **Holdings:** 8,500 books 16 journals **Language of Collection/Services:** English **Subjects:** Entomology, Forestry, Plant Pathology, Soil Science **Loan:** In country **Photocopy:** No

1930   Kathmandu, Nepal
      International Centre for Integrated Mountain
         Development (ICIMOD)
      Documentation, Information and Training Service
         (DITS)
      PO Box 3226
      Kathmandu
Location: 4/80 Jawalakhel, Lalitpur **Phone:** +977(1) 525 313 **Fax:** +977(1) 524509, 536747 **Email:** dits@icimod. org.np **WWW:** www.south-asia.com/icimod.html

Founded: 1984 **Type:** International **Head:** Shahid Akhtar *Phone:* +977(1) 521575 ext 461 *Email:* dits@icimod.org.np **Staff:** 1 Prof. 3 Other **Holdings:** 16,000 books 456 journals **Language of Collection/Services:** English **Subjects:** Agricultural Development, Agricultural Economics, Agricultural Engineering, Animal Husbandry, Biotechnology, Crops, Education/Extension, Food Sciences, Forestry, Horticulture, Rural Development, Soil Science, Water Resources, Women in Development **Specializations:** Ecology, Environment, Farming, Mountain Areas, Watershed Management **Loan:** Internationally **Service:** Internationally **Photocopy:** Yes

1931   Kathmandu, Nepal
      Nepal Agricultural Research Council (NARC)
      National Agricultural Documentation Centre,
         Central Agricultural Research Library
      PO Box 5459
      Kathmandu
Phone: +977 523041 **Fax:** +977(1) 521197 **Email:** narc@ ed.mos.com.np

Founded: 1977 **Type:** Government **Head:** Ms. Subarna K. Bajracharya *Phone:* +977 215971, 211741 **Staff:** 4 Prof. 8 Other **Holdings:** 20,000 books 60 journals **Subjects:** Agricultural Economics, Animal Husbandry, Crops, Horticulture, Soil Science **Networks:** AGRIS **Loan:** Internationally **Photocopy:** Yes

1932   Kirtipur, Nepal
      Tribhuvan University (TU)
      Central Library (TUCL)
      Kirtipur
Phone: +977 213277 ext 131, 132, 133 **Fax:** +977 226964

Founded: 1959 **Type:** Academic **Head:** Mr. K.M. Bhandary *Phone:* +977 212834 **Staff:** 5 Prof. 62 Other **Holdings:** 17,000 books 22 journals **Language of Collection/Services:** English, Nepali **Subjects:** Agriculture (Tropics), Agribusiness, Agricultural Development, Agricultural Economics, Agricultural Engineering, Animal Husbandry, Biotechnology, Crops, Education/Extension, Entomology, Fisheries, Food Sciences, Forestry, Horticulture, Plant Pathology, Soil Science, Veterinary Medicine, Water Resources **Loan:** In country **Service:** In country **Photocopy:** Yes

1933　Rampur, Nepal
　　　　Tribhuvan University, Institute of Agriculture and
　　　　　　Animal Science (TU, IAAS)
　　　　Central Library
　　　　PO Box 984
　　　　Rampur, Chitwan

Founded: 1974 **Type:** Academic **Head:** Bishnu Hari Devakota *Phone:* +977(56) 9302/3 **Holdings:** 27,000 books 60 journals **Staff:** 2 Prof. 10 Other **Language of Collection/ Services:** English **Subjects:** Agribusiness, Agricultural Development, Agricultural Economics, Agricultural Engineering, Agriculture (Tropics), Crops, Animal Husbandry, Biotechnology, Education/Extension, Entomology, Farming, Fisheries, Horticulture, Plant Pathology, Soil Science, Veterinary Medicine **Loan:** Do not loan **Service:** Inhouse **Photocopy:** Yes

Netherlands

1934　Aalsmeer, Netherlands
　　　　Research Institute for Floriculture and Glasshouse
　　　　　　Vegetables
　　　　Library
　　　　Linnaeuslaan 2a
　　　　1431 JV Aalsmeer

Phone: +31(297) 352214 **Fax:** +31(297) 352270 **Email:** pbg@pbg.agro.nl **WWW:** www.agro.nl/pbg/eindex.htm **OPAC:** www.agralin.nl/desktop

Non-English Name: Proefstation voor Bloemisterij en Glasgroente (PBGA), Bibliotheek **Type:** Government **Head:** M. van Oorde *Phone:* +31(297) 352214 **Staff:** 1 Prof. **Subjects:** Cut Flowers, Floriculture, Pot Plants **Loan:** In country **Photocopy:** Yes

1935　Amsterdam, Netherlands
　　　　Royal Tropical Institute
　　　　Information, Library and Documentation
　　　　PO Box 95001
　　　　1090 HA Amsterdam

Location: Mauritskade 63 **Phone:** +31(20) 568-8711, 568-8508, 568-8288 **Fax:** +31(20) 568-8444 **Email:** library@kit.nl **WWW:** www.kit.nl **OPAC:** www.kit.nl/ibd/html/catalogue_search.asp

Non-English Name: Koninklijk Instituut voor de Tropen (KIT) **Founded:** 1917 **Type:** Association **Head:** Drs. J. H. W. Van Hartevelt *Email:* library@kit.nl *Phone:* +31(20) 568-8290 **Staff:** 36 Prof. 11 Other **Holdings:** 200,000 books 5,000 journals **Language of Collection/Services:** English, French, Spanish, Portuguese, Dutch / English **Subjects:** Agricultural Development, Agriculture (Tropics), Education/ Extension, Rural Development **Databases Developed:** Tropag & Rural database of articles on tropical agriculture & rural development; available on CD-ROM **Databases Used:** TROPAG & RURAL **Loan:** In country **Photocopy:** Yes

1936　Amsterdam, Netherlands
　　　　University of Amsterdam
　　　　University Library
　　　　PO Box 19185

　　　　1000 GD Amsterdam
Location: Singel 425, 1012 WP Amsterdam **Phone:** +31 (20) 525-2266 **Fax:** +31(20) 525-2311 **WWW:** www.uva. nl **OPAC:** www.uba.uva.nl/en

Non-English Name: Universiteit van Amsterdam, Bibliotheek **Type:** Academic **Staff:** 1 Prof. **Holdings:** 220 journals 12,000 books **Loan:** Internationally **Photocopy:** Yes

1937　Arnhem, Netherlands
　　　　ARCADIS-Euroconsult BV
　　　　Information Center
　　　　PO Box 441
　　　　6800 AK Arnhem

Location: Beaulieustraat 22 **Phone:** +31(26) 357-7512 **Fax:** +31(26) 357-7577

Non-English Name: ARCADIS-Euroconsult BV, Informatie Centrum **Founded:** 1954 **Type:** Business **Head:** Mrs. M. van de Ven *Phone:* +31(26) 357-7512 **Staff:** 1 Prof. **Holdings:** 20,000 books 100 journals **Language of Collection/ Services:** English **Subjects:** Agricultural Economics, Agricultural Engineering, Aquaculture, Crops, Environmental Management, Groundwater, Hydrology, Institutional Development, Soil Science, Rural Development, Surface Water, Urban Development **Loan:** Do not loan **Service:** Inhouse **Photocopy:** No

1938　Delft, Netherlands
　　　　Delft University of Technology (DUT)
　　　　Library
　　　　PO Box 98
　　　　2600 MG Delft

Location: Prometheusplein 1 **Phone:** +31(15) 278-5678 **Fax:** +31(15) 257-2060 **Email:** info@library.tudelft.nl **WWW:** www.library.tudelft.nl **OPAC:** delfi.library. tudelft.nl:4505/ALEPH

Non-English Name: Technische Universiteit Delft (TU Delft), Bibliotheek **Founded:** 1842 **Type:** Academic **Head:** Dr. L.J.M. Waaijers *Phone:* +31(15) 278-5656 *Email:* info@ library.tudelft.nl **Holdings:** 861,000 books 10,500 journals **Staff:** 160 Prof. 40 Other **Language of Collection/Services:** English/Dutch **Subjects:** Agricultural Engineering, Biotechnology, Food Sciences, Water Resources **Specializations:** Environment **Databases Developed:** CTC - Central Technical Catalogue, i.e. the Dutch Catalogue of Technology **Databases Used:** Comprehensive **Loan:** Internationally **Service:** Internationally **Photocopy:** Yes

1939　Delft, Netherlands
　　　　WL/delft hydraulics
　　　　Document Information Department
　　　　PO Box 177
　　　　2600 MH Delft

Location: Rotterdamseweg 185 **Phone:** +31(15) 285-8585 **Fax:** +31(15) +31(15) 285-8582 **Email:** info@wldelft.nl **WWW:** www.wldelft.nl

Non-English Name: WL/delft hydraulics (WL), Sectie Documentaire Informatie **Former Name:** Waterloopkundig Laboratorium (WL), Delft Hydraulics Laboratory **Founded:** 1957 **Type:** Foundation **Staff:** 4 Prof. **Holdings:** 60,000 books 425 journals **Subjects:** Environmental Assessment,

Hydrology, Pollution, Water Resources **Loan:** In country **Service:** Inhouse **Photocopy:** No

1940   Deventer, Netherlands
International Agricultural College "Larenstein"
Library
PO Box 7
7400 AA Deventer

Location: Brinkgreverweg 69 **Phone:** +31(570) 684600 **Fax:** +31(570) 684608 **WWW:** www.larenstein.nl

Non-English Name: Internationale Agrarische School "Larenstein", Bibliotheek **Former Name:** International Agricultural College Deventer **Founded:** 1969 **Type:** Academic **Head:** L.H.C. Stokmans-Berteling *Phone:* +31(570) 684616 **Staff:** 2 Prof. **Holdings:** 10,000 books 125 journals **Language of Collection/Services:** English **Loan:** In country **Photocopy:** Yes

1941   Ede, Netherlands
NIZO Food Research
Library
PO Box 20
6710 BA Ede

Location: Kernhemseweg 2 **Phone:** +31(318) 659511 **Fax:** +31(318) 650400 **Email:** info@nizo.nl **WWW:** www.nizo.com

Non-English Name: NIZO Food Research (NIZO), Bibliotheek **Former Name:** Netherlands Institute for Dairy Research, Nederlands Instituut voor Zuivelonderzoek (NIZO) **Founded:** 1950 **Type:** Research **Head:** E. Otter *Phone:* +31 (318) 659511 *Email:* otter@nizo.nl **Staff:** 1.5 Prof. .5 Other **Holdings:** 6,000 books 255 journals **Language of Collection/Services:** English **Subjects:** Food Sciences **Specializations:** Dairy Science, Dairy Technology **Databases Used:** CABCD; FSTA **Networks:** AGRALIN **Loan:** In country **Service:** Inhouse **Photocopy:** Yes

1942   Groningen, Netherlands
University of Groningen
University Library
Postbus 559
9700 AN Groningen

Location: Broerstraat 4, 9712 CP Groningen **Phone:** +31 (50) 363-5017 **Fax:** +31(50) 363-4996 **WWW:** www.rug.nl **OPAC:** www.ub.rug.nl

Non-English Name: Rijksuniversiteit te Groningen (RuG), Universiteitsbibliotheek **Founded:** 1949 **Type:** Academic **Head:** Drs. Sybren Sybrandy *Email:* s.sybrandy@ub.rug.nl *Phone:* +31(50) 363-5025

1943   The Hague, Netherlands
Agricultural Economics Research Institute
Information Center
PO Box 29703
2502 LS The Hague

Location: Burgemeester Patynlaan 19, 2585 BE Den Haag **Phone:** +31(70) 330-8134 **Fax:** +31(70) 361-5624 **Email:** informatiecentrum@lei.dlo.nl **WWW:** www.lei.dlo.nl

Non-English Name: Landbouw-Econonisch Instituut (LEI), Informatiecentrum **Founded:** 1940 **Head:** S. Hogendorf

Email: s.j.hogendorf@lei.dlo.nl *Phone:* +31(70) 330-8176 **Type:** Government **Staff:** 3 Prof. **Holdings:** 17,000 books 480 journals **Language of Collection/Services:** Dutch, English/Dutch **Subjects:** Agricultural Economics **Databases Used:** Comprehensive **Loan:** In country **Service:** Inhouse **Photocopy:** Yes

1944   The Hague, Netherlands
International Service for National Agricultural
      Research (ISNAR)
Library and Documentation Centre
PO Box 93375
2509 AJ The Hague

Location: Laan van Niewe Oost Indie 133 **Fax:** +31(70) 381-9677 **Email:** isnar@cgiar.org **WWW:** www.cgiar.org/isnar

Founded: 1983 **Type:** International **Staff:** 1 Prof. 1 Other **Head:** Ms. Monica Allmand *Email:* m.allmand@cgiar.org *Phone:* +31(70) 349-6100 **Holdings:** 30,000 books 130 journals **Language of Collection/Services:** English, French, Spanish **Specializations:** Agricultural Research, Organizational Management, Research Institutes, Research Policy, Organization of Research **Databases Developed:** Agricultural research policy, organization and management **Databases Used:** Comprehensive **Loan:** Internationally **Service:** Internationally **Photocopy:** Yes

1945   Haren, Netherlands
University of Groningen, Department of
      Biological Sciences
Library
Postbus 14
9750 AA Haren

Location: Kerklaan 30, 9751 NN Haren **Phone:** +31(50) 363-2375 **Fax:** +31(50) 363-2412 **Email:** biolbibl@biol.rug.nl **WWW:** www.biol.rug.nl/bibliotheek **OPAC:** www.ub.rug.nl/bin/wwwlibmenu

Non-English Name: Rijksuniversiteit te Groningen, Afdeling Biologie (RuG), Bibliotheek **Founded:** 1972 **Type:** Academic **Head:** Mrs. T. Lemstra *Phone:* +31(50) 363-2377 **Staff:** 4 Prof. **Holdings:** 30,000 books 300 journals **Language of Collection/Services:** English **Subjects:** Animal Physiology, Biotechnology, Ecology, Education/Extension, Entomology, Fisheries, Genetics, Horticulture, Phylogeny, Marine Biology, Microbiology, Plant Pathology, Plant Physiology, Soil Science **Databases Used:** Biosis **Loan:** Internationally **Photocopy:** Yes

1946   Ijmuiden, Netherlands
Wageningen University and Research Centre,
      Netherlands Institute for Fisheries Research
      (Wageningen UR)
Library
PO Box 68
1970 AB Ijmuiden

Location: Haringkade 1, 1976 CP Ijmuiden **Phone:** +31 (255) 564646 **Fax:** +31(255) 564644 **Email:** postmaster@rivo.dlo.nl **WWW:** www.rivo.wageningen-ur.nl **OPAC:** www.agralin.nl/desktop/services

Non-English Name: Wageningen University and Research Centre, Rijksinstituut voor Visserijonderzoek (Wageningen UR, RIVO), Bibliotheek **Former Name:** Agricultural Research Department, Institute for Fishery Products, Dienst Landbouwkundig Onderzoek (DLO), Instituut voor Visserijprodukten **Head:** S.E. Koudenburg *Phone:* +31(255)564623 **Type:** Government **Holdings:** 200 journals **Language of Collection/Services:** Dutch, English **Subjects:** Fisheries **Loan:** In country **Service:** Inhouse **Photocopy:** Yes

1947   **Lelystad, Netherlands**
       Research Station for Arable Farming and Field
           Production of Vegetables
       Library
       PO Box 430
       8200 AK Lelystad

Location: Edelhertweg 1 **Fax:** +31(320) 230479 **WWW:** www.agro.nl/appliedresearch/pav

Non-English Name: Praktijkonderzoek voor de Akkerbouw en der Vollengrondsgroenteteelt (PAV), Bibliotheek **Founded:** 1974 **Type:** Government **Staff:** 1 Prof. **Head:** A. van der Kolk *Phone:* +31 (320) 291421 *Email:* j.van.der.kolk@pav.agro.nl **Holdings:** 4,000 books 300 journals **Subjects:** Agribusiness, Agricultural Development, Agricultural Economics, Agricultural Engineering, Farming, Horticulture, Plant Pathology, Soil Science **Loan:** In country **Photocopy:** Yes

1948   **Lelystad, Netherlands**
       Wageningen University and Research Centre,
           Institute for Animal Science and Health
           (Wageningen UR)
       Library
       PO Box 65
       8200 AB Lelystad

Location: Edelhertweg 15 **Fax:** +31(320) 238080 **Email:** s.j.langelaar@id.dlo.nl **WWW:** www.id.wageningen-ur.nl **OPAC:** www.agralin.nl/desktop/services

Non-English Name: Wageningen University and Research Centre, Instituut voor Dierhouderij en Diergezondheid (Wageningen UR, ID), Bibliotheek **Former Name:** Agricultural Research Department, Central Veterinary Institute, Dienst Landbouwkundig Onderzoek (DLO), Centraal Diergeneeskundig Instituut (CDI), Institute for Livestock Feeding and Nutrition Research, Stichting Instituut voor Veevoedingsonderzoek **Founded:** 1904 **Type:** Government **Head:** S.J. Langelaar *Email:* s.j.langelaar@id.dlo.nl *Phone:* +31(320) 238063, 238083 **Staff:** 2 Prof. **Holdings:** 20,000 books 350 journals **Language of Collection/Services:** English **Subjects:** Animal Husbandry, Biotechnology, Veterinary Medicine **Databases Used:** Comprehensive **Loan:** In country **Photocopy:** Yes

1949   **Leusden, Netherlands**
       Centre for Research and Information on Low
           External Input and Sustainable Agriculture
           (ILEIA)
       c/o ETC Foundation
       Kastanjelaan 5
       PO Box 64
       3830 AB Leusden

Phone: +31(33) 493086 **Fax:** +31(33) 940791 **Email:** ileia@ileia.nl **WWW:** www.oneworld.org/ileia **OPAC:** www.oneworld.org/ileia/catalog.htm

Former Name: Information Centre for Low External Input and Sustainable Agriculture **Founded:** 1990 **Type:** International **Head:** I. Huibers-Govaert *Email:* i.huibers@ileia.nl *Phone:* +31(33) 943086 **Staff:** 2 Prof. **Holdings:** 470 journals 8,500 books **Language of Collection/Services:** English /English **Subjects:** Low External Inputs, Sustainability **Networks:** AGRALIN **Loan:** Inhouse **Service:** Internationally **Photocopy:** Yes

1950   **Naaldwijk, Netherlands**
       Research Station for Floriculture and Glasshouse
           Vegetables
       Library
       PO Box 8
       2670 AA Naaldwijk

Location: Kruisbroekweg 5 **Phone:** +31(174) 636700 **Fax:** +31(174) 636835 **Email:** w.a.van.winden@pbgn.agro.nl **WWW:** www.agro.nl/appliedresearch/pbg

Non-English Name: Proefstation voor Bloemisterij en Glasgroente (PBG), Bibliotheek **Former Name:** Glasshouse Crops Research Station, Proefstation voor Tuinbouw onder Glas (PTG) **Founded:** 1900 **Type:** Government **Head:** Drs. W.A. van Winden *Phone:* +31(174) 636769 *Email:* w.a.van.winden@pbgn.agro.nl **Staff:** 2 Prof. 1 Other **Holdings:** 100 journals 2,500 books **Language of Collection/Services:** English / Dutch **Subjects:** Agricultural Economics, Agricultural Engineering, Crops, Entomology, Horticulture, Plant Pathology **Specializations:** Greenhouse Crops **Networks:** AGRALIN **Databases Developed:** WWE - Worldwide Encyclopedia for Floriculture and Glasshouse Vegetables in Dutch and English **Databases Used:** CABCD **Loan:** In country **Photocopy:** Yes

1951   **Utrecht, Netherlands**
       University of Utrecht
       Faculty of Veterinary Medicine Library
       PO Box 80159
       3508 TD Utrecht

Location: Yalelaan 1 **Phone:** +31(30) 253-4603 **Fax:** +31 (30) 253-1407 **Email:** uitleen.dgh@library.uu.nl **WWW:** www.library.vet.uu.nl/vetlib/en **OPAC:** www.library.uu.nl

Non-English Name: Universiteit Utrecht (UU), Bibliotheek Diergeneeskunde **Founded:** 1821 **Type:** Academic **Head:** Mrs. ir. G.B. de Jonge *Phone:* +31(30) 253-4638 *Email:* g.dejonge@library.uu.nl **Staff:** 9 Prof. **Holdings:** 75,000 books 1,200 journals **Subjects:** Animal Husbandry, Food Sciences, Veterinary Medicine **Specializations:** Infectious Diseases, Laboratory Animals **Databases Used:** Comprehensive **Loan:** Internationally **Service:** In country **Photocopy:** Yes

1952   **Wageningen, Netherlands**
       International Agricultural Centre (IAC)
       Library
       PO Box 88
       6700 AB Wageningen

Location: Lawickse Allee 11, 6701 AN Wageningen
Phone: +31(317) 490111 **Fax:** +31(317) 418552 **Email:** iac@iac.agro.nl **WWW:** www.iac-agro.nl **OPAC:** www.agralin.nl/desktop/services

Non-English Name: Internationaal Agrarisch Centrum (IAC), Bibliotheek **Founded:** 1951 **Head:** J.C.M. Mooij *Phone:* +31(317) 490267 *Email:* iac@iac.agro.nl **Staff:** 1 Prof. 1 Other **Holdings:** 7,500 books 300 journals **Type:** International **Language of Collection/Services:** English/Dutch, English **Subjects:** Agricultural Development, International Cooperation **Networks:** AGRALIN **Databases Developed:** GLOS - grey literature mainly publications on fisheries - available inhouse **Databases Used:** Comprehensive **Loan:** In country **Service:** In country **Photocopy:** Yes

1953   Wageningen, Netherlands
           International Institute for Land Reclamation and
                Improvement (ILRI)
           Drainage Information Network (DRAiNnet)
           PO Box 45
           6700 AA Wageningen

Location: Lawickse allee 11 **Phone:** +31(317) 490144 **Fax:** +31(317) 417187 **Email:** ilri@ilri.nl **WWW:** www.ilri.nl **OPAC:** www.ilri.nl/drainnet.html

Former Name: Staring Building Library **Founded:** 1967 **Type:** International **Language of Collection/Services:** English **Subjects:** Drainage, Hydrology, Irrigation, Water Resources **Databases Developed:** Network maintains several databases including: addresses of institutions, experts, manufacturers, and equipment suppliers; ongoing courses, training activities, and research projects; and 'grey literature' and computer models

1954   Wageningen, Netherlands
           International Soil Reference and Information
                Centre (ISRIC)
           PO Box 353
           6700 AJ Wageningen

Location: Duivendaal 9 **Phone:** +31(317) 471711 **Fax:** +31(317) 471700 **Email:** library@isric.nl **WWW:** www.isric.nl

Former Name: International Soil Museum **Founded:** 1966 **Type:** Academic **Head:** O.C. Spaargaren *Phone:* +31(317) 471704 *Email:* spaargaren@isric.nl **Staff:** 1 Prof. 3 Other **Holdings:** 17,000 books 100 journals **Language of Collection/Services:** English **Subjects:** Soil Science **Specializations:** Mapping, Soil Surveys **Databases Developed:** 6000 maps **Loan:** In country **Service:** Internationally **Photocopy:** Yes

1955   Wageningen, Netherlands
           Technical Centre for Agricultural and Rural
                Co-operation ACP-EU
           Documentation and Information Section
           PO Box 380
           6700 AJ Wageningen

Location: Agro Business Park 2 **Phone:** +31(317) 467138 **Fax:** +31(317) 460067 **Email:** cta@cta.nl **WWW:** www.cta.nl

Non-English Name: Centre Technique de Coopération Agricole et Rurale ACP-EU (CTA), Centre de Documentation et Information **Founded:** 1983 **Type:** International **Head:** Thiendou Niang *Email:* niang@cta.nl *Phone:* +31 (317) 467100 **Staff:** 38 Prof. **Holdings:** 4,000 books 350 journals **Language of Collection/Services:** French, English /French, English **Subjects:** Agroforestry, Agricultural Development, Agricultural Research, Animal Husbandry, Communication, Crops, Environment, Fisheries, Food Sciences, Documentation, Information Services, Farm Equipment, Mechanization, Organization of Research, Resource Management, Soil Management, Training, Water Resources **Specializations:** Crop Production, Extension, Project Management **Databases Developed:** Catalogs; Experts List; SPORE Mailing **Databases Used:** Agricola; Agris; Biosis; CABCD; Dissertation Abstracts; FSTA **Loan:** Do not loan **Service:** African, Caribbean and Pacific (ACP) States **Photocopy:** Yes

1956   Wageningen, Netherlands
           Wageningen Agricultural University (WAU)
           Centre for Agricultural Publishing and
                Documentation (PUDOC)
           PO Box 9100
           6700 HA Wageningen

Location: Gen. Foulkesweg 19 **Phone:** +31(317) 484440 **Fax:** +31(317) 484761 **Email:** de.helpdesk@pd.bib.wau.nl **WWW:** www.bib.wau.nl **OPAC:** www.bib.wau.nl

Non-English Name: Landbouwuniversiteit Wageningen **Type:** Academic **Staff:** 90 Prof. **Holdings:** 500,000 books 5,000 journals **Language of Collection/Services:** English, Dutch / English, Dutch **Subjects:** Comprehensive **Specializations:** Animal Husbandry, Forestry, Environmental Sciences **Networks:** AGRIS **Databases Developed:** Gender studies, home economics, land-soil-water **Databases Used:** Comprehensive **Loan:** Internationally **Photocopy:** Yes

1957   Wageningen, Netherlands
           Wageningen Agricultural University
           Library of Agronomy, Horticulture and Ecological
                Agriculture
           Postbus 341
           6700 AH Wageningen

Location: Haarweg 333, 6709 RZ Wageningen **Phone:** +31(317) 483051 **Email:** bluw.teelt@pd.bib.wau.nl **WWW:** www.wau.nl **OPAC:** www.agralin.nl/desktop

Non-English Name: Landbouwuniversiteit Wageningen, Bibliotheek TEELT **Former Name:** Department of Field Crops and Grassland Science, Department of Tropical Crop Science **Founded:** 1940 **Type:** Academic **Head:** A.S.A.A. Westermann-Welling *Email:* thuur.westermann@pd.bib.wau.nl *Phone:* +31(317) 482742 **Staff:** 1 Prof. **Holdings:** 13,500 books 1,200 journals **Subjects:** Crops, Ecology, Grasslands, Tropical Crops **Language of Collection/Services:** English **Loan:** In country **Photocopy:** Yes

1958   Wageningen, Netherlands
           Wageningen Agricultural University
           University Library
           PO Box 9100
           6700 HA Wageningen

Location: Jan-Kopshuis, Gen. Foulkesweg 19, 6703 BK Wageningen **Phone:** +31(317) 482250 **Fax:** +31(317) 484761 **Email:** bluw.ub@pd.bib.wau.nl **WWW:** www. wau.nl **OPAC:** www.agralin.nl/desktop **Ariel IP:** 137.224. 140.75

Non-English Name: Landbouwuniversiteit Wageningen, Universiteitsbibliotheek **Founded:** 1873 **Type:** Academic **Head:** M.C.A. van Boven *Phone:* +31(317) 482637 *Email:* marianne.vanboven@pd.bib.wau.nl **Staff:** 26 Prof. 76 Other **Holdings:** 400,000 books 18,000 journals **Language of Collection/Services:** English / English, Dutch **Subjects:** Comprehensive **Databases Developed:** IDRIS projects; FAO documentation **Databases Used:** Comprehensive **Loan:** In Western Europe **Service:** Internationally **Photocopy:** Yes

1959   Wageningen, Netherlands
         Wageningen Agricultural University, Laboratory
              for Spatial Analysis, Planning and Design
         De Hucht Library
         Gen. Foulkesweg 13
         6703 BJ Wageningen
Phone: +31(317) 483479 **Fax:** +31(317) 482166 **Email:** bluw.hucht@pd.bib.wau.nl **WWW:** www.wau.nl **OPAC:** www.bib.wau.nl

Non-English Name: Landbouwuniversiteit Wageningen, Labroatorium voor Ruimtelijke Planvorming, Bibliotheek De Hucht **Former Name:** Department of Physical Planning Library **Founded:** 1950 **Type:** Academic **Head:** A.S.A.A. Westermann-Welling *Email:* thuur.westermann@pd.bib. wau.nl *Phone:* +31(317) 482742 **Staff:** 2 Prof. **Holdings:** 20,000 books 110 journals **Language of Collection/Services:** Dutch, English, German / Dutch, English, German **Subjects:** Landscape Architecture, Leisure, Recreation, Regional Planning **Databases Used:** Comprehensive **Loan:** Internationally **Service:** Internationally **Photocopy:** Yes

1960   Wageningen, Netherlands
         Wageningen Agricultural University, Laboratory
              of Plant Breeding (WAU)
         Library
         PO Box 386
         6700 AJ Wageningen
Location: Lawickse Allee 166 **Phone:** +31(317) 482844 **Email:** bluw.player@pd.bib.wau.nl **WWW:** www.wau.nl **OPAC:** www.agralin.nl/desktop

Non-English Name: Landbouwuniversiteit Wageningen, Laboratorium voor Plantenveredeling (PLAVER), Bibliotheek **Founded:** 1924 **Type:** Academic **Head:** A.S.A.A. Westermann-Welling *Email:* thuur.westermann@pd.bib. wau.nl *Phone:* +31(317) 482742 **Staff:** 2 Prof. **Holdings:** 10,000 books 200 journals **Language of Collection/Services:** English **Subjects:** Crops, Plant Breeding, Plant Pathology, Horticulture **Service:** Internationally **Loan:** In country **Photocopy:** Yes

1961   Wageningen, Netherlands
         Wageningen Agricultural University, Plant
              Taxonomy Group (WAU, PLATAX)
         Library
         PO Box 8129

6700 EV Wageningen
Location: Gen. Foulkesweg 37 **Phone:** +31(317) 483181 **Fax:** +31(317) 484917 **WWW:** www.wau.nl **OPAC:** www.agralin.nl/desktop

Non-English Name: Landbouwuniversiteit Wageningen, Leerstoelgroep Plantentaxonomie **Founded:** 1918 **Type:** Government **Head:** G. Naber *Email:* ger.naber@pd.bib.wau. nl *Phone:* +31(317) 484106 **Staff:** 1 Prof. **Holdings:** 20,000 books 100 journals **Language of Collection/Services:** English **Subjects:** Taxonomy **Loan:** In country **Photocopy:** Yes

1962   Wageningen, Netherlands
         Wageningen University and Research Centre
              (Wageningen UR)
         Library
         PO Box 9100
         6700 AA Wageningen
Location: Jan-Kopshuis, Gen. Foulkesweg 19, 6703 BK Wageningen **Phone:** +31(317) 484440 **Fax:** +31(317) 484761 **Email:** de.helpdesk@pd.bib.wau.nl **WWW:** www. agralin.nl **OPAC:** www.agralin.nl/desktop **Ariel IP:** 137. 224.140.75

Type: Academic **Head:** M.C.A. van Boven *Phone:* +31 (317) 482637 *Email:* marianne.vanboven@pd.bib.wau.nl **Service:** Internationally

1963   Wageningen, Netherlands
         Wageningen University and Research Centre,
              Agrotechnological Research Institute
              (Wageningen UR)
         Library
         PO Box 17
         6700 AA Wageningen
Location: Bornsesteeg 56, 5708 PD Wageningen **Fax:** +31(317) 475347 **WWW:** www.ato.wageningen-ur.nl **OPAC:** www.agralin.nl/desktop/services

Non-English Name: Wageningen University and Research Centre, Instituut voor Agrotechnologisch Onderzoek (Wageningen UR, ATO), Bibliotheek **Former Name:** Agricultural Research Department, Institute for Research on Storage and Processing of Agricultural Produce, Dienst Landbouwkundig Onderzoek (DLO), Instituut voor Bewaring en Verwerking van Landbouwproducten (IBVL) **Type:** Government **Head:** Miss C.C. Snijder *Phone:* +31(317) 475134 *Email:* c.c.snijder@ato.dlo.nl **Staff:** 1 Prof. **Holdings:** 7,000 books 225 journals **Language of Collection/Services:** English / Dutch **Subjects:** Agricultural Engineering, Biochemistry, Biophysics, Biotechnology, Botany, Chemistry, Crops, Mathematics, Plants, Postharvest Systems **Specializations:** Food Sciences, Horticulture, Postharvest Technology **Loan:** In country **Photocopy:** Yes

1964   Wageningen, Netherlands
         Wageningen University and Research Centre,
              Institute of Agricultural and Environmental
              Engineering (Wageningen UR)
         Library Centre for Agricultural and Environmental
              Engineering
         PO Box 43
         6700 AA Wageningen

Location: Mansholtlaan 10-12 **Phone:** +31(317) 476426 **Fax:** +31(317) 425670 **Email:** bibcentec@imag.dlo.nl **WWW:** www.imag.wageningen-ur.nl **OPAC:** www. agralin.nl/desktop/services

Non-English Name: Wageningen University and Research Centre, Instituut voor Milieu- en Agritechniek (Wageningen UR, IMAG), Bibliotheek Centrum Techniek (CENTEC) **Former Name:** Agricultural Research Department, Institute of Agricultural Engineering, Dienst Landbouwkundig Onderzoek (DLO), Instituut voor Mechanisatie, Arbeid en Gebouwen (IMAG) **Founded:** 1974 **Type:** Research **Head:** H. Gunther *Phone:* +31(317) 476726 *Email:* louis.bouten@ pd.bib.wau.nl **Staff:** 6 Prof. **Holdings:** 12,000 books 300 journals **Language of Collection/Services:** English, German, Dutch **Subjects:** Agricultural Engineering, Environmental Engineering, Measurement **Specializations:** Farm Machinery **Networks:** AGRALIN **Databases Used:** Comprehensive **Loan:** In country **Service:** Internationally **Photocopy:** Yes

1965   Wageningen, Netherlands
           Wageningen University and Research Centre,
              Plant Research International (Wageningen
              UR)
           Library
           PO Box 16
           6700 ER Wageningen

Location: Droevendaalsesteeg 1 **Phone:** +31(317) 482264 **Fax:** +31(317) 484254 **Email:** bluw.fyto@pd.bib.wau.nl **WWW:** www.plant.wageningen-ur.nl **OPAC:** www. agralin.nl/desktop/services

Former Name: Research Institute for Plant Protection, Dienst Landbouwkundig Onderzoek (DLO), Instituut voor Planteziektenkundig Onderzoek (IPO), Centre for Agrobiological Research, Research Institute for Agrobiology and Soil Fertility, Centre for Plant Breeding and Reproduction Research (CPRO), Centrum voor Agrobiologisch Onderzoek (AB) **Type:** Academic **Head:** A.S.A.A. Westermann-Welling *Phone:* +31(317) 482742 *Email:* thuur.westermann @pd.bib.wau.nl **Language of Collection/Services:** English, Dutch **Subjects:** Beekeeping, Biotechnology, Crops, Entomology, Horticulture, Nematology, Plant Pathology, Plant Protection, Plant Physiology, Plants, Soil, Systems Analysis, Weeds **Networks:** AGRALIN **Loan:** Internationally **Service:** Internationally **Photocopy:** Yes

1966   Wageningen, Netherlands
           Wageningen University and Research Centre,
              State Institute for Quality Control of
              Agricultural Products (Wageningen UR)
           Library
           PO Box 230
           6700 AE Wageningen

Location: Bornsesteeg 45 **Phone:** +31(317) 475434 **Fax:** +31(317) 414717 **Email:** bibliotheek@rikilt.dlo.nl **WWW:** www.rikilt.dlo.nl

Non-English Name: Wageningen University and Research Centre, Rijkskwaliteitsinstituut voor Land- en Tuinbouwprodukten (Wageningen UR, RIKILT), Bibliotheek **Former Name:** Agricultural Research Department, Dienst Landbouwkundig Onderzoek (DLO) **Type:** Government **Head:**

Ir. G. Naber *Phone:* +31(317) 484106 **Holdings:** 120 journals **Language of Collection/Services:** Dutch, English **Subjects:** Agricultural Products, Quality Controls **Loan:** In country **Service:** Inhouse **Photocopy:** Yes

1967   Zeist, Netherlands
           TNO Division of Nutrition and Food Research
           Library
           PO Box 360
           3700 AY Zeist

Location: Utrechtseweg 48 **Phone:** +31(30) 695-2244 **Fax:** +31(30) 695-7224 **Email:** infofood@voeding.tno.nl **WWW:** www.voeding.tno.nl

Non-English Name: TNO Hoofdgroep Voeding en Voedingsmiddelen (TNO Voeding), Bibliotheek **Holdings:** 400 journals **Language of Collection/Services:** Dutch, English **Subjects:** Food Sciences **Loan:** Internationally **Service:** Inhouse **Photocopy:** Yes

New Caledonia

1968   Noumea, New Caledonia
           CIRAD-Forêt
           Bibliothèque
           BP 10001
           Montravel
           98805 Noumea Cédex

Phone: +687 274855 **Fax:** +687 284927 **WWW:** www. cirad.nc

Type: Government **Subjects:** forestry

1969   Noumea, New Caledonia
           Direction de l'Economie Rurale, Section de
              l'Agriculture et de la Forêt
           Bibliothèque
           BP 256
           98848 Noumea Cédex

Phone: +687 252434 **Fax:** +687 276394

Type: Government

1970   Noumea, New Caledonia
           Research Institute for Development
           Library
           BP A5
           98848 Noumea Cédex

Location: Promenade Roger Laroque, Anse Vata **Phone:** +687 261000 **Fax:** +687 264326 **Email:** bibliotheque@ noumea.ird.nc **WWW:** www.ird.nc

Non-English Name: Institut de Recherche pour le Développement (IRD), Bibliothèque **Former Name:** Institut Français de Recherche Scientifique pour le Développement en Cooperation (ORSTOM), French Scientific Research Institute for Development through Cooperation, ORSTOM Library **Founded:** 1946 **Type:** Government **Head:** Isabelle Gasser *Email:* gasser@noumea.ird.nc **Staff:** 2 Prof. **Holdings:** 12,500 books 150 journals **Language of Collection/Services:** French / French **Subjects:** Agronomy, Botany, Earth Sciences, Marine Biology, Remote Sensing **Special-**

izations: Oceanography **Service:** Internationally **Photocopy:** Yes

1971   **Noumea, New Caledonia**
Secretariat of the Pacific Community
Library
BP D5
98848 Noumea Cédex

Location: Anse Vata **Phone:** +687 262000 **Fax:** +687 263818 **WWW:** www.spc.org.nc

Former Name: South Pacific Commission **Founded:** 1949 **Type:** International **Head:** Mr. Mark Perkins *Phone:* +687 262000 *Email:* markp@spc.org.nc **Staff:** 2 Prof. 2 Other **Holdings:** 4,500 books 25 journals **Subjects:** Fisheries, Pacific Islands **Loan:** In country **Photocopy:** Yes

1972   **Païta, New Caledonia**
Centre for International Cooperation in
      Development-Oriented Agricultural Research
Library
BP 73
98890 Païta Cédex

Phone: +687 353684 **Fax:** +687 353223, 353255 **Email:** burzat@cirad.nc **WWW:** www.cirad.nc

Non-English Name: Centre de Coopération Internationale en Recherche Agronomique pour le Développement (CIRAD), Bibliothèque **Type:** Government **Head:** Mr. Daniel Burzat *Email:* burzat@cirad.nc

1973   **Pouembout, New Caledonia**
Pouembout Agricultural College
Information and Documentation Centre
BP 5
Pouembout Cédex

Phone: +687 355644 **Fax:** +687 355062

Non-English Name: Lycée Agricole de Pouembout, Centre de Documentation et d'Information **Type:** Academic

New Zealand

1974   **Auckland, New Zealand**
AgriQuality New Zealand
AgriQuality New Zealand Library Lynfield
PO Box 41
Auckland 1

Location: 131 Boundary Road, Blockhouse Bay **Fax:** +64 (9) 627-9750 **Email:** championn@agriquality.co.nz **WWW:** www.maf.govt.nz

Former Name: Department of Agriculture, Ministry of Agriculture and Fisheries (MAF), Lynfield Agricultural Centre, MAFQUAL Lynfield Library **Founded:** 1987 **Head:** Noeline Champion *Email:* championn@agriquality.co.nz *Phone:* +64 (9) 626-6026 ext 565, 627-2565 **Staff:** 1 Prof. **Holdings:** 26,000 books 150 journals **Language of Collection/Services:** English/English **Type:** Government **Subjects:** Plant Pathology, Botany, Entomology, Horticulture, Dairy Science, Nematology **Specializations:** Fish Diseases, Plant Diseases, Plant Pests, Veterinary Science **Networks:** NZBN **Databases Developed:** MAF Interloan Database **Databases**

Used: CABI; Pubmed **Loan:** Internationally **Service:** Internationally **Photocopy:** Yes

1975   **Auckland, New Zealand**
Horticulture and Food Research Institute of New
      Zealand, Mount Albert Research Centre
      (HortResearch, MARC)
Library
Private Bag 92169
Auckland

Location: 120 Mount Albert Road **Phone:** +64(9) 815-4200 **Fax:** +64(9) 815-4201 **Email:** alibrary@hort.cri.nz **WWW:** www.hort.cri.nz **OPAC:** library1.hort.cri.nz/libcat/newlib1.htm

Former Name: Department of Scientific and Industrial Research (DSIR) **Founded:** 1973 **Type:** Research **Head:** Ms. Michele Napier *Phone:* +64(9) 815-4200 ext 7038 *Email:* mnapier@hort.cri.nz **Staff:** 2.5 Prof. .5 Other **Holdings:** 120,000 books 1,800 journals **Language of Collection/Services:** English / English **Subjects:** Entomology, Food Technology, Fish Processing, Horticulture, Plant Breeding, Plant Pathology, Plant Pests **Specializations:** Fungi, Insects, Taxonomy, Kiwifruits **Databases Developed:** BUGS - Entomology in New Zealand; ACTINIDIA - Kiwifruit **Databases Used:** Agricola; CABCD; Current Contents; FSTA **Loan:** Internationally **Service:** Internationally **Photocopy:** Yes

1976   **Canterbury, New Zealand**
Lincoln University, College of Agriculture (LIU)
Library
PO Box 64
Canterbury 8150

Location: Cin Springs and Ellesmere Junction Roads **Phone:** +64(3) 325-2811 **Fax:** +64(3) 325-2944 **Email:** lib4@kea.lincoln.ac.nz **WWW:** www.lincoln.ac.nz **OPAC:** www.lincoln.ac.nz/libr/catalog.htm

Founded: 1960 **Head:** Isobel Mosley *Phone:* +64(3) 325-2811 ext 7833 **Type:** Academic **Staff:** 6 Prof. 7 Other **Holdings:** 76,000 books 2,600 journals **Language of Collection/Services:** English **Subjects:** Agriculture (Tropics), Agribusiness, Agricultural Development, Animal Husbandry, Agricultural Economics, Agricultural Engineering, Biotechnology, Crops, Education/Extension, Entomology, Farming, Food Sciences, Horticulture, Plant Pathology, Soil Science, Veterinary Medicine, Water Resources **Loan:** In country **Photocopy:** Yes

1977   **Christchurch, New Zealand**
University of Canterbury
Engineering Library
Private Bag 4800
Christchurch, Canterbury

Location: Creyke Road, Ilam **Phone:** +64(3) 364-2155, 366-7001 ext 6155 **Fax:** +64(3) 364-2755 **Email:** library-eng@libr.canterbury.ac.nz **OPAC:** library.canterbury.ac.nz **WWW:** www.canterbury.ac.nz

Founded: 1873 **Head:** Ms. Heather McCarrigan *Email:* h.mccarrigan@libr.canterbury.ac.nz *Phone:* +64(3) 366-7001 ext 7152 **Type:** Academic **Staff:** 3 Prof. 5 Other **Holdings:** 116,000 books 200 journals **Language of Collection/Ser-**

vices: English / English **Subjects:** Agricultural Engineering, Forestry **Networks:** Kinetica **Databases Used:** Compendex **Loan:** Internationally **Service:** Internationally **Photocopy:** Yes

1978   Hamilton, New Zealand
         AgResearch, Ruakura Agriculture Centre
         Library
         Private Bag 3123
         Hamilton
Phone: +64(7) 856-2836 **Fax:** +64(7) 838-5012 **Email:** ruaglib@agresearch.cri.nz **WWW:** www.agresearch.cri.nz

Head: Jackie Broughan *Email:* broughanj@agresearch.cri.nz

1979   Hamilton, New Zealand
         MIRINZ Food Technology and Research Limited
         MIRINZ Library
         PO Box 617
         Hamilton, Waikato
Location: East Street **Fax:** +64(7) 854-8560 **WWW:** www.mirinz.org.nz

Former Name: Meat Industry Research Institute of New Zealand, Inc. **Founded:** 1957 **Type:** Association **Head:** Val Hector *Phone:* +64(7) 854-8550 *Email:* v.hector@mirinz.org.nz **Staff:** 2 Prof. 1 Other **Holdings:** 20,000 books 280 journals **Language of Collection/Services:** English / English **Subjects:** Food Sciences, Meat, Microbiology **Networks:** NZBN **Databases Developed:** MICAS - current awareness service for staff, industrial members. Also available on subscription **Databases Used:** Comprehensive **Loan:** In country **Service:** Internationally **Photocopy:** Yes

1980   Lincoln, New Zealand
         Landcare Research New Zealand
         Library
         PO Box 69
         Lincoln, Canterbury
Location: Gerald Street **Phone:** +64(3) 325-6700 **Fax:** +64(3) 325-2418 **Email:** library@landcare.cri.nz **WWW:** www.landcare.cri.nz **OPAC:** www.library.landcare.cri.nz

Former Name: Lincoln Research Centre, Canterbury Agriculture and Science Centre, DSIR Division of Land and Soil Sciences Library, DSIR Lincoln Library, Forest Research Institute Library **Founded:** 1960 **Type:** Research **Head:** Margot Bowden *Phone:* +64(3) 325-6700 *Email:* bowdenm @landcare.cri.nz **Staff:** 5 Prof. 1 Other **Holdings:** 20,000 books 900 journals **Language of Collection/Services:** English / English **Subjects:** Algology, Botany, Crops, Cytology, Ecology, Entomology, Food Sciences, Genetics, Horticulture, Palynology, Pastures, Plant Breeding, Plant Morphology, Plant Pathology, Plant Physiology, Plants, Taxonomy, Soil Science **Specializations:** Flora, Herbaria **Networks:** NZBN **Databases Developed:** Publications database **Databases Used:** CABCD; Current Contents **Loan:** In country **Service:** Internationally **Photocopy:** Yes

1981   Mosgiel, New Zealand
         AgResearch, New Zealand Pastoral Agriculture
            Research Institute Ltd.

Invermay Library and Information Services
Invermay Agricultural Centre
Private Bag 50034
Mosgiel, Otago
Location: Puddle Alley **Phone:** +64(3) 489-3809 **Fax:** +64(3) 489-3739 **Email:** weddells@agresearch.cri.nz **WWW:** www.agresearch.cri.nz

Former Name: Ministry of Agriculture and Fisheries (MAF) **Founded:** 1961 **Type:** Research **Head:** Sue Weddell *Phone:* +64(3) 489-3809 *Email:* weddells@agresearch.cri.nz **Staff:** 1 Prof. 1 Other **Holdings:** 25,500 books 600 journals **Language of Collection/Services:** English / English **Subjects:** Animal Fibers, Animal Husbandry, Crops, Edible Fungi, Entomology, Plant Pathology, Soil Science, Zoology **Specializations:** Deer, Essential Oil Plants, Fungi, Medicinal Plants, Sheep, Wool, Soil Science, Veterinary Medicine **Networks:** NZBN **Databases Used:** Comprehensive **Loan:** Internationally **Service:** Internationally **Photocopy:** Yes

1982   Motueka, New Zealand
         Horticulture and Food Research Institute of New
            Zealand (HortResearch)
         Nelson Research Centre Library
         Old Mill Road, Brooklyn
         RD 3
         Motueka, Nelson
Phone: +64(3) 528-9106 **Fax:** +64(3) 528-7813

Former Name: Department of Scientific and Industrial Research (DSIR), DSIR Hop Research Station Library, DSIR Tobacco Research Station Library, Riwaka Research Station Library **Founded:** 1977 **Type:** Research **Head:** Mrs. Marilyn Green *Phone:* +64(3)528-9106 *Email:* mgreen@hort.cri.nz **Staff:** 1 Other **Holdings:** 1,700 books 84 journals **Language of Collection/Services:** English **Subjects:** Entomology, Food Sciences, Horticulture, Plant Pathology, Plant Protection, Crops, Soil Science **Specializations:** Humulus lupulus, Nicotiana tabacum **Loan:** In country **Photocopy:** Yes

1983   New Plymouth, New Zealand
         Dow AgroSciences (NZ) Ltd.
         Technical Library
         Private Bag 2017
         New Plymouth 4620
Location: 78 Parikiti Road **Phone:** +64(6) 751-2400 **Fax:** +64(6) 751-0442

Former Name: DowElanco (NZ) Ltd., Ivon Watkins-Dow Ltd. **Founded:** 1969 **Type:** Business **Head:** Elizabeth Isabel Fuller **Staff:** 1 Prof. **Holdings:** 2,000 books **Language of Collection/Services:** English / English **Subjects:** Agribusiness, Agricultural Development **Specializations:** Chemistry **Databases Developed:** DERBI - DowElanco Research and Business Index **Loan:** In country **Service:** Inhouse **Photocopy:** Yes

1984   Palmerston North, New Zealand
         Agriquality New Zealand (MAF)
         Library
         PO Box 536
         Palmerston North

Location: Tennent Drive **Phone:** +64(6) 351-7950 **Fax:** +64(6) 351-7910 **Email:** clarker@agriquality.co.nz **WWW:** www.agriquality.co.nz

Former Name: Ministry of Agriculture and Fisheries, Ministry of Agriculture and Forestry, Batchelar Information Centre **Founded:** 1977 **Type:** Government **Head:** Rosemary Clarke *Phone:* +64(6) 351-7950 *Email:* clarker@agriquality.co.nz **Staff:** 1 Prof. **Holdings:** 1,000 books 69 journals **Language of Collection/Services:** English / English **Subjects:** Animal Diseases, Crops, Food Industry, Horticulture, Meat and Livestock Industry, Seed Industry, Veterinary Medicine **Specializations:** Animal Health, Food Inspection, Seed Certification **Networks:** NZBN **Databases Developed:** LIMS (BRS-LOIS) - online catalogue for items held in the 4 MAF libraries in New Zealand, networked by PC by Telnet **Databases Used:** CABPESTCD; Pubmed; VETCD **Loan:** Internationally **Service:** Inhouse **Photocopy:** Yes

1985   Palmerston North, New Zealand
Crown Research Institutes (CRI)
Library
Private Bag 11060
Palmerston North

Location: Fitzherbert West **Phone:** +64(6) 356-8080 ext 7704 **WWW:** www.hort.cri.nz **OPAC:** library1.hort.cri.nz/libcat/newlib1.htm

Former Name: Department of Scientific and Industrial Research (DSIR) **Founded:** 1936 **Type:** Government **Head:** Steven A. Northover *Email:* snorthover@hort.cri.nz *Phone:* +64(6) 356-8080 ext 7704 **Staff:** 2 Prof. 1 Other **Holdings:** 35,000 books 400 journals **Language of Collection/Services:** English / English **Subjects:** Crops, Entomology, Food Sciences, Grasses, Horticulture, Soil Science, Weeds **Specializations:** Biotechnology, Grasslands, Plant Pathology, Plant Physiology **Databases Used:** Agricola; CABCD **Loan:** In country **Service:** In country **Photocopy:** Yes

1986   Palmerston North, New Zealand
Massey University
Library
Private Bag 11043
Palmerston North

Phone: +64(6) 356-9099 ext 7613 **Fax:** +64(6) 350-5601 **Email:** intloan@massey.ac.nz **WWW:** www.massey.ac.nz

Former Name: Massey Agricultural College **Founded:** 1927 **Type:** Academic **Head:** Helen Renwick *Phone:* +64(6) 356-9099 ext 7606 **Staff:** 29 Prof. 34 Other **Holdings:** 750,000 books 7,500 journals **Language of Collection/Services:** English/English **Subjects:** Agricultural Development, Agricultural Economics, Agricultural Engineering, Animal Husbandry, Agribusiness, Biotechnology, Crops, Entomology, Farming, Food Sciences, Horticulture, Plant Pathology, Plants, Soil Science **Specializations:** Agricultural Wastes, Animal Nutrition, Conservation Tillage, Fruiting, Environmental Control, Flowering, Immunology, Postharvest Treatment, Natural Resources, Renewable Resources, Ruminants, Veterinary Medicine **Databases Used:** CABCD **Loan:** Internationally **Service:** In country **Photocopy:** Yes

1987   Palmerston North, New Zealand
New Zealand Dairy Research Institute (NZDRI)
Information Services
Private Bag 11029
Palmerston North

Location: Dairy Farm Road, Fitzherbert West **Fax:** +64(6) 356-1476

Founded: 1927 **Type:** Association **Head:** Johnston Connelly *Phone:* +64(6) 350-4649 *Email:* j.connelly@nzdri.org.nz **Staff:** 4 Prof. 1 Other **Holdings:** 10,000 books 350 journals **Language of Collection/Services:** English / English **Subjects:** Dairy Science, Food Sciences **Databases Used:** Comprehensive **Loan:** In country **Service:** Inhouse **Photocopy:** Yes

1988   Palmerston North, New Zealand
New Zealand Institute for Crop and Food
    Research (C&FR)
Crop and Food Research Library
Private Bag 11600
Palmerston North 5301

Location: Batchelar Road, Fitzherbert Science Centre **Phone:** +64(6) 351-7066 ext 6177, 356-8300 ext 6177 **Fax:** +64(6) 351-7050 **WWW:** www.crop.cri.nz

Former Name: Levin Horticultural Research Centre **Type:** Government **Founded:** 1947 **Head:** Roberta Mayclair *Phone:* +64(6) 351-7066 *Email:* mayclairr@crop.cri.nz **Staff:** 2 Prof. **Holdings:** 5,000 books 120 journals **Language of Collection/Services:** English / English **Subjects:** Food Sciences, Horticulture **Databases Used:** Comprehensive **Loan:** In country **Photocopy:** Yes

1989   Palmerston North, New Zealand
New Zealand Leather and Shoe Research
    Association (LASRA)
Library
Private Bag 11-333
Palmerston North

Location: Fitzherbert Science Centre, Cnr Dairy Farm and Poultry Farm Roads **Fax:** +64(6) 354-1185 **Email:** lasra@xtra.co.nz

Type: Research **Head:** Mrs. Anne Odogwu *Phone:* +64(6) 355-9028 *Email:* lasra@xtra.co.nz **Staff:** 1 Prof. **Holdings:** 5,800 books 26 journals **Language of Collection/Services:** English/English **Subjects:** Hides and Skins, Leather, Skinning, Slaughter, Skin Diseases, Tanning, Tannery Sludge, Tannery Waste **Loan:** Within industry **Service:** Within industry **Photocopy:** Yes

1990   Rotorua, New Zealand
New Zealand Forest Research Institute Limited
National Forestry Library
Private Bag 3020
Rotorua

Location: Sala Street **Phone:** +64(7) 347-5847 **Fax:** +64(7) 347-9380 **Email:** library@fri.cri.nz **WWW:** www.forestresearch.cri.nz

Non-English Name: Forest Research **Former Name:** Ministry of Forestry, New Zealand Forest Service, Forest Research Institute **Founded:** 1947 **Type:** Government **Head:**

Beryl Anderson *Phone:* +64(7) 347-5849 *Email:* andersob@ fri.cri.nz **Staff:** 3 Prof. **Holdings:** 175,000 books 610 journals **Language of Collection/Services:** English / English **Subjects:** Agricultural Economics, Biotechnology, Entomology, Forest Products, Forestry, Plant Pathology, Pulp and Paper Industry, Soil Science **Networks:** NZBN **Databases Used:** Comprehensive **Loan:** Internationally **Service:** Internationally **Photocopy:** Yes

1991   Tokoroa, New Zealand
        Carter Holt Harvey Pulp and Paper
        Kinleith Technical Library
        Private Bag
        Tokoroa

Location: Kinleith Mill **Phone:** +64(7) 886-3815 **Fax:** +64 (7) 886-3614

Former Name: New Zealand Forest Products **Type:** Business **Head:** Maryanne Gilbert *Phone:* +64(7) 886-3815 **Staff:** 1 Prof. **Holdings:** 3,000 books 300 journals **Subjects:** Forestry **Loan:** Internationally **Photocopy:** Yes

1992   Upper Hutt, New Zealand
        Central Institute of Technology (CIT)
        Bateman Library
        PO Box 40 740
        Upper Hutt

Location: Somme Road, Heretaunga **Phone:** +64(4) 527-6398 ext 6726 **Fax:** +64(4) 527-6368

Founded: 1972 **Type:** Academic, Government **Head:** Sue Hirst *Phone:* +64(4) 527-7089 ext 8727 **Staff:** 7 Prof. 4 Other **Holdings:** 500 books 25 journals **Language of Collection/Services:** English / English **Subjects:** Botany, Farming, Forestry, Horticulture, Soil Science **Service:** In country **Loan:** Internationally **Photocopy:** Yes

1993   Upper Hutt, New Zealand
        New Zealand Pastoral Agriculture Research
            Institute (AgResearch)
        Wallaceville Animal Research Centre Library
        PO Box 40-771
        Upper Hutt

Location: 62 Ward Street **Phone:** +64(4) 528-6089 ext 878 **Fax:** +64(4) 528-6605

Former Name: Ministry of Agriculture and Fisheries (MAF), Agricultural Library and Information Centre (ALIC), MAF Central Library **Founded:** 1988 **Type:** Research **Head:** Carole Devine *Email:* devinec@agresearch. cri.nz *Phone:* +64(4) 528-6089 **Staff:** 4 Prof. 1 Other **Holdings:** 56,500 books 3,000 journals **Language of Collection/ Services:** English / English **Subjects:** Cellular Biology, Entomology, Microbiology, Molecular Biology, Parasitology **Databases Used:** Medline; Agris; CABCD **Loan:** In country **Service:** In country **Photocopy:** Yes

1994   Wellington, New Zealand
        Development Resource Centre (DRC)
        Information Service
        Box 11345
        Wellington

Location: 58-60 Victoria Street **Phone:** +64(4) 472-9549 **Fax:** +64(4) 472-3622 **Email:** drc@apc.org.nz

Former Name: New Zealand Coalition for Trade and Development, Centre for International Development Education and Action (IDEA) **Founded:** 1985 **Type:** Association **Head:** Phillip Hewitt *Phone:* +64(4) 472-9549 **Staff:** 2 Prof. **Holdings:** 6,000 books 250 journals **Language of Collection/Services:** English / English **Subjects:** Crops, Agribusiness, Biotechnology, Education/Extension, Fisheries, Food Sciences, Pesticides **Loan:** In country **Photocopy:** Yes

1995   Wellington, New Zealand
        Ministry of Agriculture and Forestry (MAF)
        MAF Information Bureau
        PO Box 2526
        Wellington

Location: ASB House, 101-103 The Terrace **Phone:** +64 (4) 474-4100 ext 8850 **Fax:** +64(4) 474-4111 **Email:** library@maf.govt.nz **WWW:** www.maf.govt.nz

Former Name: Ministry of Agriculture and Fisheries, Ministry of Forestry **Founded:** 1988 **Type:** Government **Head:** Mrs. Jackie Hill *Phone:* +64(4) 498-9850 *Email:* hillj@maf. govt.nz **Staff:** 4 Prof. 1 Other **Holdings:** 8,000 books 350 journals **Language of Collection/Services:** English/English **Subjects:** Agribusiness, Agricultural Economics, Agricultural Policy, Computer Science, Food Sciences, Forestry, Management, Marketing **Networks:** AGRIS; NZBN **Databases Used:** CABCD **Loan:** In country **Service:** In country **Photocopy:** Yes

1996   Wellington, New Zealand
        New Zealand Dairy Board (NZDB)
        Information Centre
        PO Box 417
        Wellington

Location: Pastoral House, 25 The Terrace **Phone:** +64(4) 471-8607 **Fax:** +64(4) 471-8555 **Email:** nzdblib@netlink. co.nz **WWW:** www.nzmilk.co.nz

Founded: 1968 **Type:** Business **Head:** Philippa Pointon *Phone:* +64(4) 471-8908 *Email:* ppoin@netlink.co.nz **Staff:** 3 Prof. 1 Other **Holdings:** 7,000 books 350 journals **Language of Collection/Services:** English / English **Subjects:** Dairy Technology, Food Industry, Food Sciences, Marketing **Specializations:** Marketing, Milk Products **Databases Used:** CABCD; FSTA **Loan:** In country **Service:** Internationally **Photocopy:** Yes

1997   Wellington, New Zealand
        New Zealand Horticulture Export Authority
            (HEA)
        Library
        PO Box 1417
        Wellington

Location: Huddart Parker Building, Post Office Square **Phone:** +64(4) 471-0451 ext 81 **Fax:** +64(4) 471-2474

Former Name: Horticultural Market Research Unit **Founded:** 1979 **Type:** Business, Government **Head:** Gerard Prendergast *Phone:* +64(4) 471-0451 *Email:* gerard@pims.co.nz **Staff:** 1 Prof. **Holdings:** 200 books 70 journals **Language of Collection/Services:** English **Subjects:** Horticulture **Spe-**

cialities: Exports, Horticultural Crops **Loan:** Inhouse **Service:** In country **Photocopy:** Yes

1998   Wellington, New Zealand
         New Zealand Seafood Industry Council
         Information Resource Centre
         Private Bag 24901
         Wellington
Location: Fishing Industry House, 74 Cambridge TCE
Phone: +64(4) 385-4005 **Fax:** +64(4) 385-2727 **Email:**
www.seafood.co.nz **WWW:** www.seafood.co.nz

Former Name: New Zealand Fishing Industry Board **Type:** Association **Founded:** 1963 **Head:** Lorraine Crozier *Phone:* +64(4) 385-4005 *Email:* lorraine@seafood.co.nz **Staff:** 2 Prof. 2 Other **Holdings:** 4,000 books 130 journals **Language of Collection/Services:** English/English **Subjects:** Fisheries, Food Sciences, Water Resources **Specializations:** Fish Industry, Aquaculture, Fish Processing, Fish Products, Fisheries (Statistics), Fishery Management, International Trade, Marketing **Databases Developed:** New Zealand Fishery Export Statistics **Loan:** In country **Service:** Internationally **Photocopy:** Yes

1999   Wellington, New Zealand
         New Zealand Wool Group
         Library
         PO Box 3225
         Wellington
Location: 10 Brandon Street **Phone:** +64(4) 472-6888 ext 8698 **Fax:** +64(4) 473-7872 **WWW:** www.sheepresearch. co.nz

Founded: 1980 **Type:** Government **Head:** Cathie Benson *Phone:* +64(4) 471-4698 *Email:* cathie.benson@woolgroup. co.nz **Staff:** 1 Prof. 2 Other **Holdings:** 3,500 books 385 journals **Language of Collection/Services:** English / English **Subjects:** Wool Industry, Wool Production **Specializations:** Wool **Databases Developed:** Wool and textile related materials **Loan:** Internationally **Service:** Internationally **Photocopy:** Yes

Nicaragua

2000   Managua, Nicaragua
         National Agricultural University
         National Center for Agricultural Information and
            Documentation
         Apdo l487
         Managua
Location: Km l2 Carretera Norte **Phone:** +505(2) 31473 ext l8 **Fax:** +505(2) 331871 **Email:** una@sdnnic.org.ni **WWW:** www.una.edu.ni

Non-English Name: Universidad Nacional Agraria, Centro Nacional de Información y Documentación Agropecuaria (CENIDA) **Former Name:** Escuela Nacional de Agricultura y Ganadería, National School of Agriculture and Livestock **Type:** Academic **Head:** Orlando Vargas-Soza *Phone:* +505 (2) 31473 **Staff:** 2 Prof. 19 Other **Holdings:** 18,000 books 30 journals **Subjects:** Animal Production, Disease Prevention,

Crop Production **Networks:** AGRIS **Loan:** In country **Photocopy:** Yes

Niger

2001   Kollo, Niger
         Institut Pratique de Développement Rural (IPDR)
         Centre de Documentation
         BP 76
         Kollo
Phone: +227 735157

Founded: 1979 **Type:** Government **Head:** Chaibou Abdou Dan Foussan, Director *Phone:* +227 735157 **Staff:** 2 Prof. 3 Other **Holdings:** 4,000 books 4 journals **Subjects:** Agricultural Engineering, Cooperatives, Forestry, Silviculture **Loan:** In country **Photocopy:** No

2002   Niamey, Niger
         Agrhymet-CILSS Regional Centre
         Documentation Centre
         BP 11011
         Niamey
Phone: +227 732181, 733116 **Fax:** +227 732436, 732237 **Email:** biblio@sahel.agrhymet.ne **WWW:** www.agrhymet. ne

Non-English Name: Centre Régional Agrhymet-CILSS, Centre de Documentation **Former Name:** Centre Régional de Formation et d'Application en Agrométéorologie et Hydrologie Opérationnelle, Centre Agrhymet **Founded:** 1976 **Type:** International **Head:** Tiemoko Issoufou *Phone:* +227 733116, 732436 *Email:* tiemoko@sahel.agrhymet.ne **Staff:** 2 Prof. 3 Other **Holdings:** 25,000 books 300 journals **Language of Collection/Services:** English, French **Subjects:** Atmospheric Sciences, Environmental Sciences, Farming, Hydrology, Water Resources **Specializations:** Agricultural Meteorology, Climatology, Desertification, Environment, Natural Resources, Plant Protection **Networks:** RESADOC **Databases Used:** CABCD; PolTox; TROPAG & RURAL **Loan:** Internationally **Service:** Internationally **Photocopy:** Yes

♦2003   Niamey, Niger
         Chambre de Commerce, d'Agriculture, d'Industrie
            et d'Artisanat du Niger (CCAIAN)
         Centre de Documentation
         BP 209
         Niamey
Fax: +227 734668

Founded: 1985

2004   Niamey, Niger
         International Crops Research Institute for the
            Semi-Arid Tropics (ICRISAT)
         Sahelian Center Library
         BP 12404
         Niamey
Phone: +227 722725 **Fax:** +227 734329 **Email:** icrisatsc@ cgiar.org **WWW:** www.icrisat.org

Non-English Name: Institut International de Recherche sur les Cultures des Zones Tropicales Semi-Arides, Bibliothèque du Centre Sahélien **Founded:** 1984 **Type:** International **Staff:** 2 Prof. 1 Other **Holdings:** 75 journals 3,800 books **Language of Collection/Services:** English, French **Subjects:** Agriculture (Tropics) **Loan:** Inhouse **Photocopy:** Yes

2005　Niamey, Niger
　　　　Ministère des Finances et du Plan
　　　　Centre d'Information et de Documentation
　　　　　　Economique et Sociale
　　　　BP 862
　　　　Niamey
Fax: +227 735983

Founded: 1985 **Type:** Government **Staff:** 2 Prof. 3 Other **Holdings:** 3,000 books 30 journals **Subjects:** Agricultural Development, Agricultural Economics, Economic Development, Investment, Rural Sociology

2006　Niamey, Niger
　　　　Ministère du Développement Rural, Institut
　　　　　　National de Recherche Agronomique du
　　　　　　Niger (INRAN)
　　　　Centre de Documentation
　　　　BP 429
　　　　Niamey
Fax: +227 934956

Founded: 1975 **Type:** Government **Staff:** 2 Prof. 3 Other **Holdings:** 5,000 books 46 journals **Language of Collection/Services:** French, English **Subjects:** Agricultural Research, Agronomy, Forestry, Horticulture, Plant Protection, Rural Economy, Soil Science, Veterinary Science **Photocopy:** Yes **Networks:** AGRIS **Loan:** In country **Service:** In country

2007　Niamey, Niger
　　　　Ministry of Agriculture and Livestock
　　　　Information and Documentation Center for Rural
　　　　　　Development
　　　　BP 12091
　　　　Niamey
Phone: +227 732058

Non-English Name: Ministère de l'Agriculture et de l'Elevage, Centre d'Information et de Documentation pour le Développement Rural (CIDR) **Founded:** 1981 **Type:** Government **Staff:** 3 Prof. 3 Other **Holdings:** 4,000 books 25 journals **Language of Collection/Services:** French **Subjects:** Agricultural Development, Agricultural Economics, Animal Production, Crop Production, Extension, Plant Protection, Rural Sociology **Networks:** AGRIS **Databases Used:** Agris **Photocopy:** Yes

2008　Niamey, Niger
　　　　Research Institute for Development
　　　　Documentation Center
　　　　BP 11416
　　　　Niamey
Fax: +227 772054 **WWW:** www.ird.ne

Non-English Name: Institut de Recherche pour le Développement (IRD), Centre de Documentation **Former Name:**

Institut Français de Recherche Scientifique pour le Développement en Coopération (ORSTOM), French Scientific Research Institute for Development through Cooperation **Founded:** 1991 **Head:** Mr. Amadou Tahirou *Phone:* +227 752804 *Email:* amadou@orstom.ne

2009　Niamey, Niger
　　　　Université Abdou Moumouni, Faculté
　　　　　　d'Agronomie
　　　　Bibliothèque
　　　　BP 10960
　　　　Niamey
Phone: +227 733238, 732713 **Fax:** +227 733238, 733862

Founded: 1982

2010　Niamey, Niger
　　　　Université de Niamey
　　　　Bibliothèque
　　　　BP 237
　　　　Niamey
Phone: +227 732713

Founded: 1982 **Type:** Academic **Staff:** 2 Other **Holdings:** 3,165 books 17 journals **Subjects:** Animal Husbandry, Soil Science, Plants

Nigeria

2011　Abeokuta, Nigeria
　　　　Federal University of Agriculture, Abeokuta
　　　　　　(UNAAB)
　　　　Library
　　　　PMB 2240
　　　　Abeokuta, Ogun State
Phone: +234(39) 240768, 244749, 23078 **Fax:** +234(39) 244299, 244054, 234650 **Email:** root@unaab.edu. ng

Head: Dr. Tunde Akinlade *Email:* akinlade@unaab.edu.ng **Type:** Academic

♦2012　Ado-Ekiti, Nigeria
　　　　Federal Polytechnic Ado-Ekiti
　　　　Polytechnic Library
　　　　Private Mail Bag 5351
　　　　Ado-Ekiti, Ondo State

Former Name: Federal Polytechnic, Akure **Founded:** 1978 **Type:** Academic **Staff:** 4 Prof. 16 Other **Holdings:** 10,000 books 300 journals **Language of Collection/Services:** English/English **Subjects:** Agriculture (Tropics), Animal Husbandry, Crops, Farming, Food Sciences, Horticulture, Soil Science, Water Resources **Specializations:** Agricultural Engineering **Loan:** Inhouse **Service:** Inhouse **Photocopy:** Yes

2013　Ado-Ekiti, Nigeria
　　　　Ondo State University
　　　　Library
　　　　PMB 5363
　　　　Ado-Ekiti, Ondo State
Phone: +234(30) 240370, 240711

Former Name: Obafemi Awolowo University **Founded:** 1983 **Type:** Academic **Head:** Mr. J.A. Arikenbi *Phone:* +234(30) 240662 **Staff:** 8 Prof. 27 Other **Holdings:** 2,325 books 29 journals **Language of Collection/Services:** English **Subjects:** Agricultural Economics, Crops, Agricultural Engineering, Biotechnology, Entomology, Education/Extension, Fisheries, Horticulture, Plant Pathology, Soil Science, Water Resources **Service:** Internationally **Photocopy:** Yes

2014　　Bauchi, Nigeria
　　　　Abubakar Tafawa Balewa University (ATBU)
　　　　Library
　　　　PMB 0248
　　　　Bauchi, Bauchi State
Phone: +234(77) 543500/1 ext 221, 222, 223 **Fax:** +234 (77) 542065

Former Name: Federal University of Technology, Bauchi **Founded:** 1981 **Type:** Academic **Head:** Mrs. Adebimpe O. Ike **Holdings:** 44,443 books 1,255 journals **Language of Collection/Services:** English/English **Subjects:** Agriculture (Tropics), Agricultural Economics, Agronomy, Animal Husbandry, Biotechnology, Crops **Loan:** Internationally **Service:** In country **Photocopy:** Yes

2015　　Benin City, Nigeria
　　　　Rubber Research Institute of Nigeria (RRIN)
　　　　Library
　　　　PMB 1049
　　　　Benin City, Edo State
Location: Iyanomo, km 19 Benin/Sapele Road **Phone:** +234(52) 41190 **Fax:** +234(52) 601885

Founded: 1961 **Type:** Government **Head:** Dr. Mustapha M. Nadoma **Staff:** 2 Prof. 3 Other **Holdings:** 724 books 76 journals **Language of Collection/Services:** English / English **Subjects:** Agriculture (Tropics), Agribusiness, Agricultural Development, Agricultural Economics, Agricultural Engineering, Crops, Entomology, Food Sciences, Forestry, Plant Pathology, Soil Science, Water Resources **Loan:** Internationally **Service:** Internationally **Photocopy:** Yes

2016　　Benin City, Nigeria
　　　　University of Benin
　　　　Library
　　　　PMB 1191
　　　　Benin City
Phone: +234(52) 200250

Founded: 1970 **Type:** Academic **Staff:** 25 Prof. 100 Other **Holdings:** 3,000 books 100 journals **Subjects:** Agriculture (Tropics), Agribusiness, Agricultural Engineering, Animal Husbandry, Crops, Entomology, Farming, Fisheries, Forestry, Horticulture, Plant Pathology, Soil Science **Loan:** In country **Photocopy:** Yes

2017　　Bida, Nigeria
　　　　National Cereals Research Institute (NCRI)
　　　　Library
　　　　Badeggi, Private Mail Bag 8
　　　　Bida, Niger State
Phone: +234(66) 461233 **Fax:** +234(66) 461234

Former Name: Federal Department of Agricultural Research (FDAR) **Founded:** 1954 **Type:** Government **Staff:** 1 Prof. 3 Other **Holdings:** 7,000 books 250 journals **Language of Collection/Services:** English **Subjects:** Agribusiness, Agriculture (Tropics), Agricultural Development, Crops, Agricultural Economics, Agricultural Engineering, Animal Husbandry, Biotechnology, Education/Extension, Entomology, Farming, Food Sciences, Plant Pathology, Soil Science **Specializations:** Cereals, Grain Legumes, Maize, Rice, Sugarcane **Loan:** In country **Service:** Internationally **Photocopy:** Yes

2018　　Garki-Abuja, Nigeria
　　　　Federal Ministry of Commerce and Tourism
　　　　　　(FMCT)
　　　　Technical Information Library (TIL)
　　　　Private Mail Bag 88
　　　　Garki-Abuja
Location: Block G, Room 322, Federal Secretariat, Area 1 **Phone:** +234(9) 234-1491 ext 130

Former Name: Federal Ministry of Trade **Founded:** 1951 **Type:** Government **Head:** Mr. A.U. Onyegbutulem *Phone:* +234(9) 234-1491 ext 130 **Staff:** 4 Prof. 4 Other **Holdings:** 20,000 books 50 journals **Language of Collection/Services:** English / English **Subjects:** Agricultural Development, Agricultural Economics, Animal Husbandry, Industry, Marketing, Rural Sociology **Loan:** Inhouse **Service:** Inhouse **Photocopy:** No

2019　　Ibadan, Nigeria
　　　　Cocoa Research Institute of Nigeria (CRIN)
　　　　Library, Information and Documentation Centre
　　　　　　(LIDC)
　　　　PMB 5244
　　　　Idi-Ayunre
　　　　Ibadan
Location: Idi-Ayunre, Oluyole Lga., via Ijebu-Ode, Oyo State **Phone:** +234(22) 410040 ext 110 **Fax:** +234(2) 241-3385 **Email:** sanyaolutogun@skannet.com.ng

Former Name: West African Cocoa Research Institute (WACRI) **Founded:** 1964 **Type:** Government **Head:** O.O. Fagbami *Email:* sanyaolutogun@skannet.com.ng *Phone:* +234(22) 410040 ext 158 **Staff:** 2 Prof. 2 Other **Holdings:** 25,375 books 45 journals **Language of Collection/Services:** English/English **Subjects:** Agricultural Chemistry, Agriculture (Tropics), Biochemistry, Biotechnology, Crops, Entomology, Farming Systems, Genetics, Plant Breeding, Plant Pathology, Soil Science, Tissue Culture **Specializations:** Anacardium Occidentale, Cocoa, Coffee, Cola, Soil Formation, Soil Injection, Tea **Databases Used:** Agris **Loan:** Internationally **Service:** Internationally **Photocopy:** Yes

2020　　Ibadan, Nigeria
　　　　Forestry Research Institute of Nigeria (FRIN)
　　　　Library and Documentation
　　　　PMB 5054
　　　　Jericho
　　　　Ibadan
Location: Jericho Hill **Phone:** +234(2) 241-1441, 241-4073, 241-3327 **Fax:** +234(2) 241-6036

Former Name: Federal Department of Forestry Research **Founded:** 1941 **Type:** Government **Staff:** 5 Prof. 12 Other **Holdings:** 12,000 books 121 journals **Language of Collection/Services:** English / English **Subjects:** Plant Pathology, Education/Extension, Entomology, Fisheries, Forestry, **Specializations:** Wood Technology **Loan:** In country **Service:** Internationally **Photocopy:** No

---

2021   Ibadan, Nigeria
      International Institute of Tropical Agriculture
        (IITA)
      Library and Documentation Centre
      PMB 5320
      Ibadan

Location: Oyo Road **Phone:** +234(2) 241-2626 ext 2582 **Fax:** +234(2) 241-2221 **Email:** y.adedigba@cgiar.org **WWW:** www.cgiar.org/iita

Founded: 1969 **Type:** International **Head:** Y.A. Adedigba *Email:* y.adedigba@cgiar.org *Phone:* +234(2) 241-2626 ext 236 **Staff:** 5 Prof. 10 Other **Holdings:** 41,352 books 200 journals **Language of Collection/Services:** English/English **Subjects:** Agriculture (Tropics), Agricultural Development, Agricultural Economics, Agricultural Engineering, Biotechnology, Crops, Education/Extension, Entomology, Farming, Food Sciences, Plant Pathology, Soil Science, Water Resources **Specializations:** Cassava, Cowpeas, Rice, Farming Systems, Maize **Databases Developed:** Integrated database with 114,000 records covering all books and pamphlets in stock or on order and selected journal articles in stock; database accessible on over 80 computer terminals in various locations in IITA **Databases Used:** Comprehensive **Loan:** In country **Service:** Internationally **Photocopy:** Yes

---

♦**2022   Ibadan, Nigeria**
      National Horticultural Research Institute
        (NIHORT)
      Library and Documentation Division
      Idi-Ishin
      Private Mail Bag 5432
      Ibadan, Oyo State

Founded: 1975 **Type:** Government **Staff:** 2 Prof. 4 Other **Holdings:** 5,000 books 20 journals **Language of Collection/Services:** English **Subjects:** Agriculture (Tropics), Agricultural Development, Agricultural Economics, Agricultural Engineering, Crops, Education/Extension, Food Sciences, Entomology, Plant Pathology, Soil Science **Specializations:** Horticulture **Loan:** In country **Photocopy:** Yes

---

2023   Ibadan, Nigeria
      Obafemi Awolowo University, Institute of
        Agricultural Research and Training (OAU,
        IAR&T)
      Library and Documentation Centre
      PMB 5029
      Ibadan, Oyo State

Location: Moor Plantation **WWW:** www.oauife.edu.ng

Former Name: University of Ife **Founded:** 1968 **Type:** Academic **Head:** Mrs. B.O. Ikhizama *Phone:* +234(22) 312 523, 312861 **Staff:** 2 Prof. 8 Other **Holdings:** 45,000 books 300 journals **Language of Collection/Services:** English

Subjects: Agriculture (Tropics), Agribusiness, Agricultural Development, Agricultural Economics, Agricultural Engineering, Animal Husbandry, Biotechnology, Entomology, Farming, Food Sciences, Horticulture, Plant Pathology, Veterinary Medicine, Water Resources **Specializations:** Crops, Education/Extension, Farming Systems, Soil Science **Loan:** In country **Photocopy:** Yes

---

2024   Ibadan, Nigeria
      University of Ibadan, Kenneth Dike Library (UI,
        KDI)
      Faculty of Agriculture, Forestry and Veterinary
        Medicine Library
      c/o Dean's Office
      Faculty of Agriculture and Forest Resources
        Management
      Ibadan, Oyo State

Phone: +234(2) 810-3118, 810-1100 **Fax:** +234(2) 810-3043 **Email:** library@kdl.ui.edu.ng **WWW:** www.ui.edu.ng

Former Name: College of Agriculture, Forestry and Veterinary Medicine Library **Type:** Academic **Head:** Mrs. O. Tamuno *Email:* tamuno@kdl.ui.edu.ng **Staff:** 2 Prof. 5 Other **Founded:** 1975 **Holdings:** 3,290 books 120 journals **Language of Collection/Services:** English / English **Subjects:** Agricultural Economics, Agronomy, Crops, Animal Husbandry, Extension, Fisheries, Forest Management, Veterinary Medicine **Specializations:** Plants, Soil Science **Photocopy:** Yes **Loan:** Inhouse

---

2025   Ile-Ife, Nigeria
      Obafemi Awolowo University (OAU)
      Hezekiah Oluwasanmi Library (HOL)
      Ile-Ife, Osun State

Fax: +234(36) 232401/232909 **Email:** +234(36) 23397, 232401

Former Name: University of Ife **Founded:** 1962 **Type:** Academic **Head:** Mr. M.A. Adelabu *Phone:* +234(36) 233974 **Staff:** 20 Prof. 175 Other **Holdings:** 1,545 books 275 journals **Language of Collection/Services:** English / English **Subjects:** Agricultural Economics, Animal Husbandry, Education/Extension, Plants, Rural Sociology, Soil Science **Photocopy:** Yes

---

2026   Ilorin, Nigeria
      Nigerian Stored Products Research Institute
        (NSPRI)
      Library
      PMB 1489
      Ilorin, Kwara State

Location: Km.3, Asa Dam Road **Phone:** +234(31) 222143 **Fax:** +234(31) 223912

Former Name: West African Stored Products Research Unit (WASPRU) **Founded:** 1970 **Type:** Research **Head:** Akande Femi **Staff:** 2 Prof. 5 Other **Holdings:** 3,110 books 15 journals **Language of Collection/Services:** English / English **Subjects:** Agribusiness, Agricultural Development, Agricultural Economics, Agricultural Engineering, Education/Extension, Entomology **Specializations:** Postharvest Systems, Stored Products **Databases Developed:** Database on

Nigerian abstracts of postharvest science **Loan:** Inhouse **Service:** Inhouse **Photocopy:** Yes

2027   Ilorin, Nigeria
University of Ilorin
Library
PMB 1515
Ilorin, Kwara State
Phone: +234(31) 221715 ext 512 **Fax:** +234(31) 222561

Founded: 1976 **Type:** Academic **Staff:** 16 Prof. 73 Other **Holdings:** 393 books **Subjects:** Agricultural Engineering, Agricultural Economics, Animal Husbandry, Crops, Farm Management, Soil **Loan:** In country **Photocopy:** Yes

2028   Lagos, Nigeria
Federal Ministry of Science and Technology
    (FMST)
Promotion Department
PMB 12793
Lagos
Location: 9 Kofo Abayomi Road

Type: Government **Networks:** AGRIS

2029   Lagos, Nigeria
Nigerian Institute for Oceanography and Marine
    Research (NIOMR)
Library
PMB 12729, Victoria Island
Lagos
Location: Wilmot Point Road, Bar Beach, Victoria Island
Phone: +234(1) 619530 **Fax:** +234(1) 616550 **Email:** niomr@linkserve.com.ng

Founded: 1975 **Type:** Government **Staff:** 4 Prof. 9 Other **Holdings:** 18,316 books 86 journals **Language of Collection/Services:** English **Subjects:** Fishery Management, Aquaculture **Specializations:** Fisheries **Loan:** Internationally **Service:** Internationally **Photocopy:** Yes

2030   Makurdi, Nigeria
University of Agriculture, Makurdi (UAM)
Library
PMB 2313
Makurdi, Benue State
Phone: +234(44) 33577, 33488, 33204/5

Former Name: University of Jos, Makurdi Campus **Founded:** 1981 **Type:** Academic **Head:** Mr. J.A. Achema *Phone:* +234(44) 31460 **Staff:** 6 Prof. 57 Other **Holdings:** 24,000 books 362 journals **Language of Collection/Services:** English / English **Subjects:** Agricultural Economics, Agricultural Engineering, Animal Husbandry, Crops, Education/ Extension, Entomology, Farming, Fisheries, Food Sciences, Forestry, Horticulture, Plant Pathology, Soil Science **Loan:** In country **Service:** Internationally **Photocopy:** Yes

2031   Nsukka, Nigeria
University of Nigeria
Library
Nsukka, Enugu State
Phone: +234(42) 771911 ext 59

Founded: 1960 **Type:** Academic **Head:** Dr. M.W. Anyakoha **Staff:** 1 Prof. 4 Other **Holdings:** 200 journals 6,000 books **Subjects:** Agricultural Economics, Crops, Fishery Management, Agricultural Engineering, Animal Husbandry, Extension, Soil Science, Veterinary Medicine **Loan:** Internationally **Photocopy:** Yes

♦2032   Nsukka, Nigeria
University of Nigeria, Nsukka (UNN)
Faculty of Agricultural Sciences Library
Nsukka, Enugu State

Founded: 1973 **Type:** Academic **Staff:** 1 Prof. 6 Other **Holdings:** 2,703 books 2,282 journals **Language of Collection/Services:** English / English **Subjects:** Agriculture (Tropics), Agribusiness, Agricultural Development, Agricultural Economics, Agricultural Engineering, Animal Husbandry, Biotechnology, Crops, Education/Extension, Entomology, Farming, Fisheries, Food Sciences, Forestry, Horticulture, Plant Pathology, Plants, Soil Science, Veterinary Medicine, Water Resources **Loan:** In country **Service:** Internationally **Photocopy:** No

2033   Owerri, Nigeria
Federal University of Technology, Owerri
    (FUTO)
Library
PMB 1526
Owerri, Imo State
Phone: +234(83) 232430, 2330564, 233456 **Fax:** +234(83) 233228 **Email:** root@futo.edu. ng

Founded: 1981 **Type:** Academic **Staff:** 9 Prof. 32 Other **Holdings:** 35,570 books 323 journals **Language of Collection/Services:** English **Subjects:** Agriculture (Tropics), Agricultural Economics, Agricultural Engineering, Animal Husbandry, Biology, Biotechnology, Crops, Education/Extension, Farming, Plants, Soil Science **Photocopy:** Yes

2034   Port Harcourt, Nigeria
University of Port Harcourt (Uniport)
Library
PMB 5323
Port Harcourt, Rivers State
Phone: +234(84) 334400

Founded: 1975 **Type:** Academic **Head:** Mr. George B. Affia **Staff:** 14 Prof. 100 Other **Holdings:** 64,416 books 2,036 journals **Language of Collection/Services:** English **Subjects:** Agricultural Development, Agricultural Research **Loan:** In country **Service:** Internationally **Photocopy:** Yes

2035   Sokoto, Nigeria
Usmanu Danfodiyo University
Library
PMB 2346
Sokoto
Phone: +234(60) 232058, 233221

Former Name: University of Sokoto **Founded:** 1977 **Type:** Academic **Head:** Mrs. S. S. Mukoshy, Acting University Librarian **Staff:** 18 Prof. 55 Other **Holdings:** 850 books 60 journals **Language of Collection/Services:** English **Subjects:** Agricultural Engineering, Crops, Soil Science, Veterinary Medicine **Loan:** In country **Service:** In country **Photocopy:** Yes

2036 Umuahia, Nigeria
Federal University of Agriculture, Umudike
(FUAU)
Library
PMB 7267
Umuahia, Abia State
Phone: +234(88) 220066 **Email:** root@fuau.edu. ng

♦**2037 Zaria, Nigeria**
Ahmadu Bello University (ABU)
Veterinary Medical Library
Zaria
Phone: +234(69) 51511

Type: Academic **Staff:** 3 Prof. 13 Other **Holdings:** 5,200 books 382 journals **Subjects:** Animal Health, Animal Husbandry

2038 Zaria, Nigeria
Ahmadu Bello University, Institute for
Agricultural Research
Agricultural Library
PMB 1044
Zaria
Location: Samaru **Phone:** +234(69) 50571/4 ext 4014
Fax: +234(69) 50022

Founded: 1922 **Type:** Research **Head:** Mr. T.M. Ndakotsu
Phone: +234(69) 50571/4 ext 4013 **Staff:** 4 Prof. 16 Other
Holdings: 29,249 books 768 journals **Subjects:** Agriculture
(Tropics), Agribusiness, Agricultural Development, Agricultural Economics, Agricultural Engineering, Education/
Extension, Crops, Entomology, Farming, Forestry, Food
Sciences, Horticulture, Plant Pathology, Soil Science, Water
Resources **Loan:** In country **Service:** Internationally **Photocopy:** Yes

2039 Zaria, Nigeria
Ahmadu Bello University, National Animal
Production Research Institute (ABU, NAPRI)
Library
PMB 1096
Zaria
Phone: +234(69) 50596 **Fax:** +234(69) 51272 **Email:**
lukman@abu.edu.ng

Former Name: Shika Research Station Library **Founded:**
1976 **Type:** Academic **Head:** Segun Adewole *Phone:* +234
(69) 50596 *Email:* olusegun@abu.edu.ng **Staff:** 3 Prof. 8
Other **Holdings:** 4,000 books 250 journals **Language of
Collection/Services:** English / English **Subjects:** Comprehensive **Specializations:** Animal Husbandry, Biotechnology, Veterinary Medicine **Databases Used:** CABCD **Loan:**
In country **Service:** Inhouse **Photocopy:** Yes

Niue

2040 Alofi, Niue
Department of Agriculture, Forestry and Fisheries

Library
PO Box 74
Alofi
Phone: +683 4032 **Fax:** +683 4079

Type: Government **Head:** Ms. Gaylene Mitikulena

Northern Mariana Islands

2041 Saipan, Northern Mariana Islands
Department of Natural Resources
Library
PO Box 1271
Saipan 96950
Fax: +670 322-5096

2042 Saipan, Northern Mariana Islands
Northern Marianas College
Library
PO Box 1250
Saipan 96950
Phone: +670 23334-9023/25 **Fax:** +670 235-7601

Type: Academic

Norway

2043 Ås, Norway
Agricultural University of Norway (AUN)
Library/Information Technology
PO Box 5012
N-1432 Ås
Location: Tårnbygningen **Phone:** +47(64) 947663 **Fax:**
+47(64) 947670 **Email:** biblutl@bibl.nlh.no **WWW:** www.
nlh.no/Biblioteket **OPAC:** www.nlh.no/Biblioteket/eng/
e_bibsys.htm

Non-English Name: Norges Landbrukshøgskole (NLH),
Bibliotek/IT-avd **Founded:** 1859 **Type:** Academic **Head:**
Paul Stray *Phone:* +47(64) 947667 *Email:* paul.stray@bibl.
nlh.no **Staff:** 9.5 Prof. 3 Other **Holdings:** 460,000 books
3,500 journals **Language of Collection/Services:** English/
Norwegian **Subjects:** Crops, Agriculture (Tropics), Agricultural Development, Agricultural Economics, Agricultural
Engineering, Animal Husbandry, Aquaculture, Biotechnology, Education/Extension, Entomology, Farming, Forestry,
Food Sciences, Horticulture, Landscape Architecture, Soil
Science, Planning, Plant Pathology, Plants, Surveying, Water Resources **Networks:** AGRIS **Loan:** Internationally **Service:** Internationally **Photocopy:** Yes

2044 Ås, Norway
Norwegian Food Research Institute
Library
Osloveien 1
N-1430 Ås
Phone: +47(64) 970100 **Fax:** +47(64) 970333 **WWW:**
www.matforsk.no

Non-English Name: Norsk Institutt for Nøringsmiddel
Forskning (MATFORSK), Biblioteket **Head:** Anne Arne-

berg *Email:* anne.rogstad@matforsk.no *Phone:* +47(64) 970 189 **Type:** Research **Holdings:** 13,000 books 350 journals **Language of Collection/Services:** English, Norwegian/ Norwegian **Subjects:** Biotechnology, Food Sciences **Databases Used:** FSTA; Medline **Service:** Inhouse **Photocopy:** Yes

2045   Ås, Norway
         Norwegian Forest Research Institute
         Library
         Høgskoleveien 12
         N-1432 Ås

Phone: +47 64 94 89 84 **Fax:** +47 64 94 29 80 **Email:** bibliotek@nisk.no **WWW:** www.nisk.no

Non-English Name: Norsk institutt for skogforskning (NISK), Biblioteket **Former Name:** Det norske Skogforsøksvesen **Founded:** 1917 **Type:** Government **Head:** Guri Rongen Woxholtt *Email:* guri.woxholtt@nisk.no *Phone:* +47 64 94 89 84 **Staff:** 1 Prof. 1 Other **Holdings:** 30,000 books 966 journals **Language of Collection/Services:** English / Norwegian **Subjects:** Environment, Forestry, Soil Science **Databases Used:** Comprehensive **Photocopy:** Yes **Loan:** Internationally **Service:** Internationally

2046   Oslo, Norway
         Norwegian College of Veterinary Medicine
         Library
         PO Box 8146 Dep
         N-0033 Oslo 1

Location: Ullevålsveien 72 **Phone:** +47 22 96 45 55 **Fax:** +47 22 96 45 31 **Email:** biblioteket@veths.no **WWW:** www.veths.no **OPAC:** wgate.bibsys.no/search/pub?lang=E

Non-English Name: Norges Veterinærhøgskole (NVH), Biblioteket **Founded:** 1891 **Type:** Academic **Head:** Anne Catherine Munthe *Phone:* +47 22 96 45 56 *Email:* anne.c.munthe@veths.no **Staff:** 3.5 Prof. 1 Other **Holdings:** 78,000 books 480 journals **Language of Collection/Services:** English / Norwegian **Subjects:** Animal Husbandry, Aquaculture, Food Sciences, Veterinary Medicine **Networks:** BIBSYS **Databases Developed:** BIBSYS - from 1990 - common catalogue for several Norwegian university and college libraries **Databases Used:** Comprehensive **Loan:** Internationally **Service:** In country **Photocopy:** Yes

2047   Oslo, Norway
         Norwegian Institute for Water Research
         Library
         PO Box 173 Kjelsås
         N-0411 Oslo

Location: Brekkevn. 19 **Phone:** +47(2) 2185100 **Fax:** +47 (2) 2185200 **WWW:** www.niva.no

Non-English Name: Norsk institutt for vannforskning, Biblioteket **Type:** Research **Staff:** 2 Prof. 1 Other **Holdings:** 35,000 books 380 journals **Language of Collection/Services:** Norwegian, English / Norwegian **Subjects:** Fisheries, Biotechnology, Water Resources **Specializations:** Water **Loan:** Internationally **Service:** Internationally **Photocopy:** Yes

2048   Oslo, Norway
         Norwegian Institute of Wood Technology
         Library
         PO Box 113 Blindern
         N-0314 Oslo

Location: Forskningsveien 3 B **Phone:** +47 22 96 56 12 **Fax:** +47 22 60 42 91 **Email:** firmapost@treteknisk.no **WWW:** www.treteknisk.no

Non-English Name: Norsk Treteknisk Institutt (NTI), Biblioteket **Founded:** 1949 **Head:** Liv Jakobsen Føyn *Email:* liv.foyn@treteknisk.no Holdings: 20,000 books 200 journals **Language of Collection/Services:** Norwegian, English, Swedish, German **Staff:** 1 Prof. **Type:** Academic **Subjects:** Forestry **Specializations:** Drying, Wood, Wood Anatomy, Wood Construction, Wood Preservation, Wood Technology **Databases Developed:** Rapportbase - all publications published by NTI, written by researchers in the employ of the Institute. It covers publications from 1949 up to 1988. **Databases Used:** CABCD **Loan:** Internationally **Service:** Internationally **Photocopy:** Yes

2049   Oslo, Norway
         Norwegian Nobel Institute (Nobel)
         Library
         Drammensveien 19
         N-0255 Oslo

Fax: +47 22 43 01 68 **Email:** ack@nobel.no **WWW:** www.nobel.no

Non-English Name: Det Norske Nobelinstitutt (Nobel), Biblioteket **Founded:** 1904 **Type:** Association **Head:** Anne C. Kjelling *Phone:* +47 22 44 20 63 *Email:* ack@nobel.no **Staff:** 3 Prof. **Holdings:** 180,000 books 220 journals **Language of Collection/Services:** English / Norwegian, English **Subjects:** Agricultural Development, Agricultural Economics, Fisheries, Food Sciences **Networks:** OCLC **Loan:** Internationally **Service:** Internationally **Photocopy:** Yes

2050   Ridabu, Norway
         Hedmark College, Agriculture and Natural
            Sciences
         Library
         N-2322 Ridabu

Location: Blæstad gård **Phone:** +47(62) 541630 **Fax:** +47 (62) 595942 **Email:** bibliotek.lnb@lnb.hihm.no **WWW:** www.hihm.no **OPAC:** wgate.bibsys.no/search/pub?lang=E

Non-English Name: Høgskolen i Hedmark, Avdeling for landbruks- og naturfag, Biblioteket **Former Name:** Statens Landbruksmaskinskole **Type:** Academic **Head:** Laila Bäckmark *Email:* laila.beckmark@lnb.hihm.no. **Holdings:** 4,200 books 110 journals **Language of Collection/Services:** Norwegian/Norwegian **Staff:** 2 Prof **Subjects:** Agricultural Engineering, Biotechnology, Crops, Environmental Factors, Farming, Food Sciences, Plants, Soil Science, Water Resources **Networks:** BIBSYS **Databases Used:** Agris **Loan:** Internationally **Service:** Internationally **Photocopy:** Yes

2051   Steinkjer, Norway
         North Trondelag College
         Library
         PO Box 145

N-7701 Steinkjer
Location: Kongens gt. 42, N-7700 Steinkjer **Phone:** +47 74 11 20 65 **Fax:** +47 74 11 20 03 **Email:** bibsteinkjer@ hint.no **WWW:** www.hint.no **OPAC:** wgate.bibsys.no/ search/pub?lang=E

Non-English Name: Høgskolen i Nord-Trøndelag (HiNT), Biblioteket **Former Name:** North Trondelag Regional College, Nord-Trøndelag distriktshøgskole (NTDH) **Founded:** 1980 **Type:** Academic **Head:** Geir Arne Rosvoll *Phone:* +47 74 11 20 61 *Email:* john.wold@hint.no **Staff:** 3 Prof. 1 Other **Holdings:** 25,000 books 350 journals **Language of Collection/Services:** Norwegian / Norwegian **Subjects:** Agricultural Economics, Animal Husbandry, Forestry, Natural Resources **Specializations:** Agricultural Economics (Norway), Agricultural Policy (Norway) **Networks:** BIBSYS; NOSP **Databases Used:** CABCD; CARL UnCover **Loan:** Internationally **Service:** Internationally **Photocopy:** Yes

Oman

♦2052   Muscat, Oman
  Ministry of Agriculture and Fisheries
  Main Library
  PO Box 467
  Muscat
Phone: +968 696265

2053   Muscat, Oman
  Ministry of Agriculture and Fisheries, Marine
    Science and Fisheries Centre
  Library
  PO Box 467
  Muscat
Phone: +968 740061 **Fax:** +968 740159

Type: Government **Subjects:** Fisheries

2054   Muscat, Oman
  Sultan Qaboos University (SQU)
  Main Library
  PO Box 37, Al-Khodh
  Muscat 123
Phone: +968 515521 **Fax:** +968 513413 **Email:** shoeb@ squ.edu.om **WWW:** www.squ.edu.om/main.html

Founded: 1986 **Type:** Academic **Head:** Muhammad H.N. Al-Amry *Phone:* +968 515502 *Email:* mhna@squ.edu.om **Staff:** 30 Prof. 23 Other **Holdings:** 1,400 journals 108,549 books **Language of Collection/Services:** English / Arabic **Subjects:** Comprehensive **Specializations:** Biotechnology, Crops, Fisheries, Plants, Soil, Water Resources **Databases Used:** Agricola; Biosis **Loan:** In country **Service:** In country **Photocopy:** Yes

2055   Seeb, Oman
  Ministry of Agriculture and Fisheries, Directorate
    General of Agricultural Research
  Documentation Centre
  Rumais, PO Box 50
  Seeb 121
Fax: +968 893097

Type: Government **Networks:** AGRIS

Pakistan

2056   Attock, Pakistan
  Barani Livestock Production Research Institute
  Library
  Kherimurat
  Attock
Phone: +92(57) 75890

Head: Mr. Dishad Hussain **Subjects:** Livestock

2057   Bahawalpur, Pakistan
  Regional Agricultural Research Institute,
    Bahawalpur (RARI, Bahawalpur)
  Library
  Post Box No. 18
  Tipu Shaheed Road, West End
  Model Town-A
  Bahawalpur, Punjab 63000
Location: Tipu Shaheed Road - Gulberg Road Intersection, Model Town-A **Phone:** +92(621) 6054, 876109

Former Name: Agricultural Research Station, Bahawalpur **Founded:** 1951 **Type:** Government **Head:** Dr. Sabir Zameer Siddiqi *Phone:* +92(621) 6054, 876109 **Holdings:** 1,800 books **Language of Collection/Services:** English, Urdu / English, Urdu **Subjects:** Agricultural Chemistry, Agricultural Economics, Agricultural Statistics, Agronomy, Botany, Crops, Genetics, Plant Breeding, Plant Pathology, Soil Science **Loan:** Inhouse **Service:** In country **Photocopy:** No

2058   Bhalwal, Pakistan
  Water and Power Development Authority, Mona
    Reclamation Experimental Project (WAPDA)
  Library
  WAPDA Mona Colony
  District Sargodha
  Bhalwal, Punjab
Phone: +92(455) 42756 **Fax:** +92(455) 42756

Founded: 1970 **Type:** Government **Staff:** 2 Other **Subjects:** Agricultural Economics, Agricultural Engineering, Crops, Soil Science **Loan:** Do not loan **Photocopy:** Yes

2059   Chakwal, Pakistan
  Barani Agricultural Research Institute (BARI)
  Library
  GPO Box 35
  Chakwal, Punjab 48800
Location: Talagang Road, Chakwal **Phone:** +92(573) 569367 **Fax:** +92(573) 569366

Founded: 1979 **Type:** Government **Head:** Mohammad Ijaz *Phone:* +92(573) 569367 **Staff:** 2 Other **Holdings:** 1,250 books 3 journals **Language of Collection/Services:** English /Urdu **Subjects:** Arid Lands **Service:** In country **Loan:** Inhouse **Photocopy:** Yes

2060   D.I. Khan, Pakistan
  Gomal University (GU)
  Faculty of Agriculture Library

D.I. Khan, North West Frontier Province

Phone: +92() 4395

Former Name: Government College of Science and Agriculture **Founded:** 1967 **Staff:** 1 Prof. **Holdings:** 12,000 books 57 journals **Type:** Academic **Language of Collection /Services:** English **Subjects:** Agricultural Chemistry, Agricultural Economics, Agricultural Engineering, Agronomy, Animal Husbandry, Botany, Entomology, Food Sciences, Horticulture, Plant Breeding, Plant Genetics, Plant Pathology, Soil Science, Statistics **Photocopy:** Yes

2061 Dokri, Pakistan
Rice Research Institute Dokri
Library
District Larkana
Dokri, Sind

Phone: +92() 60877 Larkana

Founded: 1974 **Type:** Government **Head:** *Phone:* +92() 07443 ext 328 **Staff:** 2 Prof. 3 Other **Holdings:** 3,450 books 15 journals **Subjects:** Agricultural Chemistry, Agricultural Engineering, Agricultural Meteorology, Crops, Grain Legumes, Plant Pathology, Plant Physiology, Rice, Soil Science, Statistics **Loan:** Do not loan **Photocopy:** No

2062 Faisalabad, Pakistan
Ayub Agricultural Research Institute (AARI)
Library
Faisalabad, Punjab 38950

Phone: +92(411) 624047

Former Name: Punjab Agricultural Research Institute (PARI) **Founded:** 1962 **Type:** Government **Head:** Amir Huhammad *Phone:* +92(411) 624359 **Staff:** 3 Prof. 10 Other **Holdings:** 32,000 books 150 journals **Language of Collection/Services:** English / English **Subjects:** Agriculture (Tropics), Biotechnology, Crops, Entomology, Food Sciences, Horticulture, Plant Pathology, Plants, Soil Science **Loan:** In country **Photocopy:** Yes **Databases Used:** Agricola; Agris

2063 Faisalabad, Pakistan
National Institute for Biotechnology and Genetic
     Engineering (NIBGE)
Library
PO Box 577, Jhang Road
Faisalabad

Phone: +92(41) 651475 **Fax:** +92(41) 651472 **Email:** root @nibgel.fsb.erum.com.pk

Head: Mr. M.D. Idrees **Subjects:** Biotechnology

2064 Faisalabad, Pakistan
Pakistan Atomic Energy Commission, Nuclear
     Institute for Agriculture and Biology (PAEC,
     NIAB)
Library
PO Box 128, Jhang Road
Faisalabad, Punjab

Fax: +92(411) 654213 **Email:** niab@paknet4.ptc.pk

Founded: 1972 **Type:** Government **Head:** Mr. Faqir Hussain *Phone:* +92(411) 654221/30 *Email:* niab@paknet4.ptc. pk **Staff:** 2 Prof. 2 Other **Holdings:** 6,664 books 36 journals **Language of Collection/Services:** English / English, Urdu

Subjects: Biochemistry, Biotechnology, Entomology, Food Sciences, Genetics, Mutations, Plant Breeding, Postharvest Systems, Plant Physiology, Soil Salinity, Soil Science **Databases Used:** Agricola; Agris **Loan:** In country **Photocopy:** Yes

2065 Faisalabad, Pakistan
University of Agriculture (AGRIVARSITY)
Library
Faisalabad

Phone: +92(41) 30281/9 **WWW:** www.members.tripod. com/~ahsanr/luaf

Former Name: Punjab Agricultural College, Lyallpur **Type:** Academic **Founded:** 1961 **Head:** Prof. Dr. Muhammad Ashfaq *Phone:* +92(41) 30281/9 ext 228, 328 *Email:* luaf@paknet4.ptc.pk **Staff:** 2 Prof. 32 Other **Holdings:** 180,800 books 237 journals **Language of Collection/Services:** English **Subjects:** Agriculture (Tropics), Agribusiness, Agricultural Development, Agricultural Economics, Biotechnology, Crops, Entomology, Farming, Fisheries, Forestry, Horticulture, Plant Pathology, Soil Science, Water Resources **Specializations:** Agricultural Engineering, Animal Husbandry, Education/Extension, Food Sciences, Veterinary Medicine **Databases Used:** Agricola; Agris; CABCD **Loan:** Do not loan **Service:** Inhouse **Photocopy:** Yes

2066 Hyderabad, Pakistan
Sindh Agriculture University
Central Library
Tandojam
Hyderabad, Sind

Phone: +92(2233) 5869 **Fax:** +92(2233) 5300

Founded: 1940 **Type:** Academic **Head:** Mr. Muhammad Idrees Khokhar *Phone:* +92(2233) 5869 **Staff:** 4 Prof. 14 Other **Holdings:** 100,000 books 78 journals **Subjects:** Agricultural Engineering, Animal Husbandry, Veterinary Medicine **Loan:** In country **Photocopy:** Yes

2067 Islamabad, Pakistan
Agricultural Development Bank of Pakistan
     (ADBP)
Research Library
PO Box 1400
Islamabad

Location: 1 Faisal Avenue

Founded: 1981 **Type:** Government **Head:** Mrs. Qamar Moin ul Islam *Phone:* +92(51) 820-6221 **Staff:** 1 Prof. 2 Other **Holdings:** 6,000 books 20 journals **Language of Collection/Services:** English **Subjects:** Agricultural Credit, Animal Husbandry, Crops, Dairy Industry, Fertilizers, Fisheries, Forestry, Horticulture, Poultry, Rural Development, Soil Science **Loan:** In country **Photocopy:** Yes

2068 Islamabad, Pakistan
Agricultural Prices Commission (APCom)
Library
Mandher Plaza, G-8 Markaz
PO Box 1739
Islamabad

Phone: +92(51) 926-1291 ext 241 **Fax:** +92(51) 926-1290

Founded: 1981 **Type:** Government **Head:** Sardar Arshad Hussain *Phone:* +92(51) 926-1291/7 **Staff:** 2 Prof. 2 Other **Holdings:** 1,000 books 80 journals **Subjects:** Agribusiness, Agricultural Development, Agricultural Economics, Agricultural Statistics, Censuses, Farm Management **Loan:** In country **Photocopy:** Yes

2069　Islamabad, Pakistan
　　　　Allama Iqbal Open University
　　　　Central Library
　　　　Sector H-8
　　　　Islamabad
Phone: +92(51) 435723 **Fax:** +92(51) 264319

Founded: 1974 **Type:** Academic **Head:** Mrs. Zamurat Mahmud *Phone:* +92(51) 264891/6 **Staff:** 9 Prof. 19 Other **Holdings:** 329 books 6 journals **Subjects:** Animal Husbandry, Farm Machinery, Forestry, Gardening, Soil Conservation, Vegetables **Loan:** In country **Photocopy:** Yes

2070　Islamabad, Pakistan
　　　　Federal Bureau of Statistics
　　　　Library
　　　　State Life Insurance Corporation Building
　　　　Plot No. 5, Blue Area, F-6/1
　　　　Islamabad
Phone: +92(51) 920-5627

Head: Mr. Shoukat Zaman

2071　Islamabad, Pakistan
　　　　Federal Seed Certification Department
　　　　Library
　　　　Mauve Road, G-9/4
　　　　Islamabad
Phone: +92(51) 853176

Head: Syed Irfan Ahmed *Phone:* +92(51) 853176 **Subjects:** Seed Certification

2072　Islamabad, Pakistan
　　　　National Center for Rural Development
　　　　Library
　　　　Park Road, Chackshahzad
　　　　Islamabad
Phone: +92(51) 240174, 140187 **Fax:** +92(51) 243140

Founded: 1983 **Type:** Government **Head:** Mr. Hamidullah Shah *Phone:* +92(51) 824721 **Staff:** 1 Prof. 2 Other **Holdings:** 500 books 6 journals **Subjects:** Agricultural Economics, Rural Development **Loan:** Internationally **Photocopy:** Yes

2073　Islamabad, Pakistan
　　　　National Centre for Rural Development (NCRD)
　　　　Library
　　　　Chak Shahzad
　　　　Islamabad
Founded: 1983 **Type:** Government **Head:** Hamid Ullah Khan **Staff:** 2 Prof. 3 Other **Holdings:** 20,000 books 5 journals **Language of Collection/Services:** English / English **Subjects:** Agricultural Development, Agricultural Economics **Specializations:** Local Government, Rural Development

2074　Islamabad, Pakistan
　　　　National Fertilizer Development Centre, Planning
　　　　　　and Development Division (NFDC)
　　　　Library
　　　　House No. 253, Street 52, F-10/4
　　　　Islamabad
Phone: +92(51) 449406 **Fax:** +92(51) 440042

Founded: 1979 **Type:** Government **Head:** Mr. Muhammad Saqiq *Email:* gcp075net@faopak.msm.cgiar.org *Phone:* +92 (51) 449407/11 **Staff:** 1 Prof. 1 Other **Holdings:** 600 books 50 journals **Subjects:** Agricultural Economics, Crops, Fertilizer Technology, Soil Fertility **Loan:** In country **Photocopy:** Yes

2075　Islamabad, Pakistan
　　　　National Library of Pakistan
　　　　Constitution Avenue
　　　　Islamabad 44000
Phone: +92(51) 920-6584 **Fax:** +92(51) 922-1375 **Email:** nlpiba@paknet2.ptc.pk

Founded: 1992 **Type:** Government **Head:** Mr. Abdul Hafeez Akhtar *Phone:* +92(51) 920-6584 *Email:* nlpiba@ paknet2.ptc.pk **Staff:** 18 Prof. 67 Other **Holdings:** 110,000 books **Language of Collection/Services:** Urdu, English/ Urdu, Punjabi, English **Specializations:** Pakistan **Loan:** Do not loan **Service:** In country **Photocopy:** Yes

2076　Islamabad, Pakistan
　　　　Pakistan Agricultural Research Council (PARC)
　　　　Headquarters Library
　　　　PO Box 1031
　　　　Shalimar G-5/1
　　　　Islamabad
Phone: +92(51) 920-3070/9 ext 2290 **Fax:** +92(51) 920-2968 **WWW:** www.parc.gov.pk

Founded: 1979 **Type:** Government **Head:** Syed Ghani Haider *Phone:* +92(51) 920-3070/9 *Email:* ch-parc@sdnpk. undp.org **Staff:** 1 Prof. 2 Other **Holdings:** 4,000 books 75 journals **Subjects:** Agricultural Development, Agricultural Planning **Loan:** In country **Photocopy:** Yes

2077　Islamabad, Pakistan
　　　　Pakistan Agricultural Research Council, National
　　　　　　Agricultural Research Centre (PARC, NARC)
　　　　Directorate of Scientific Information (DSI)
　　　　PO Box NARC, Park Road
　　　　Islamabad
Phone: +92(51) 242362, 241461 ext 3031, 3033 **Fax:** +92 (51) 240909 **Email:** siu%dsi-narc@sdnpk.undp.org, dsinarc@isb.comsats.net.pk **WWW:** www.parc.gov.pk

Former Name: Agricultural Research Centre (ARC), Scientific Information Unit **Founded:** 1973 **Type:** Research **Head:** Mr. Ashraf Tanvir *Phone:* +92(51) 240908, 241461 ext 3030 *Email:* siu%dsi-narc@sdnpk.undp.org **Staff:** 6 Prof. 9 Other **Holdings:** 30,000 books 36 journals **Language of Collection/Services:** English / English, Urdu **Subjects:** Comprehensive **Specializations:** Agricultural Development, Agricultural Economics, Agricultural Planning, Agricultural Research, Agronomy, Animal Diseases, Animal Husbandry, Beekeeping, Biotechnology, Dairy Science, Entomology,

Extension, Farm Machinery, Fisheries, Food Technology, Forestry, Horticulture, Plant Pathology, Poultry, Soil Science, Veterinary Science, Water Resources, Weed Control, Weeds **Networks:** AGRIS **Databases Developed:** Pakistan Agriculture Database — bibliographic database of more than 18,000 records containing references of publications (serial articles, monographs, theses, reports, etc.) published in Pakistan or elsewhere in the world about Pakistan's agriculture. From 1996 abstracts were also included; available at all major agricultural libraries in Pakistan; Union Database of Journals — database which includes data on about 3,000 journal titles along with their available volumes and issues in 29 libraries of Pakistan; available at all participating libraries **Databases Used:** Comprehensive **Loan:** Inhouse **Service:** Internationally **Photocopy:** Yes

2078   **Islamabad, Pakistan**
        Pakistan Council of Research in Water Resources
            (PCRWR)
        Library, Documentation and Informational Centre
        House No. 3&5, Street No. 17, F-6/2
        PO Box 1849
        Islamabad
Phone: +92(51) 921-8980/1 **Fax:** +92(51) 921-8939
Email: pcrwr@isb.comsats.net.pk

Former Name: Pakistan Council of Research in Irrigation, Drainage and Flood Control, National Documentation Centre, Library and Information Network (NADLIN) **Founded:** 1987 **Type:** Government **Head:** Mrs. Nuzhat Yasmin *Phone:* +92(51) 921-8982 *Email:* yasmin%nadlin@sdnpk. undp.org **Staff:** 3 Prof. 3 Other **Holdings:** 9,400 books 4 journals **Language of Collection/Services:** English / English, Urdu **Subjects:** Soil Science, Water Resources **Specializations:** Drainage, Hydrology, Irrigation, Water Resources Development **Databases Developed:** NIN - National database on water resources materials **Databases Used:** Agricola; Agris; Water Resources Abstracts; Waterlit **Loan:** In country **Service:** In country **Photocopy:** Yes

2079   **Islamabad, Pakistan**
        Pakistan Institute of Development Economics
            (PIDE)
        Library
        PO Box 1091, Quaid-e-Azam University Campus
        Islamabad
Phone: +92(51) 824070/80, 824087/89, 826911/14 **Fax:** +92(51) 210886

Head: Mr. Zafar Javed Naqvi *Email:* arshad%pide@sdnpk. undp.org

2080   **Islamabad, Pakistan**
        Pakistan Scientific and Technological Information
            Centre (PASTIC)
        PO Box 1217
        Quaid-e-Azam University Campus
        Islamabad
Phone: +92(51) 920-1340 **Fax:** +92(51) 920-1341 **Email:** pnc%pastic@sdnpk.undp.org

Former Name: PANSDOC **Type:** Government **Head:** Dr. Mohammad Afzal *Phone:* +92(51) 824161 **Staff:** 1 Prof. 2

Other **Holdings:** 5,000 books **Language of Collection/Services:** English **Subjects:** Agribusiness, Environment, Science, Technology **Databases Used:** Agricola; Agris **Loan:** Do not loan **Service:** Internationally **Photocopy:** Yes

2081   **Islamabad, Pakistan**
        Quaid-e-Azam University
        Library
        Islamabad
Phone: +92(51) 812563

Type: Academic **Head:** Sheikh Muhammad Hanif

2082   **Kala Shah Kaku, Pakistan**
        Punjab Department of Agriculture, Rice Research
            Institute (RRI)
        Library
        G.T. Road
        Kala Shah Kaku, Punjab 39030
Phone: +92(42) 290368

Founded: 1926 **Type:** Government **Staff:** 1 Prof. 1 Other **Holdings:** 1,000 books 10 journals **Language of Collection/Services:** English **Subjects:** Agriculture (Tropics), Agribusiness, Agricultural Development, Crops, Agricultural Economics, Agricultural Engineering, Cereals, Education/ Extension, Entomology, Farming, Food Sciences, Plant Pathology, Plant Breeding, Rice, Soil Science, Statistics, Water Resources **Loan:** In country **Photocopy:** Yes

2083   **Karachi, Pakistan**
        Department of Plant Protection
        Library
        Jinnah Avenue, Mlir Halt
        Karachi

Subjects: Plant Protection

2084   **Karachi, Pakistan**
        Marine Fisheries Department
        Library
        Fish Harbour, West Wharf
        Karachi, Sind
Fax: +92(21) 231-2923

Type: Government **Head:** Mr. Moazzam Khan *Phone:* +92 (21) 231-2923 **Staff:** 1 Prof. 3 Other **Holdings:** 2,000 books **Subjects:** Fisheries **Loan:** In country **Photocopy:** Yes

2085   **Karachi, Pakistan**
        Pakistan Central Cotton Committee
        Library
        Moulvi Tamizuddin Khan Road
        Karachi
Phone: +92(21) 568-4106, 568-4115, 568-4124 **Fax:** +92 (21) 568-5682

Subjects: Cotton

2086   **Karachi, Pakistan**
        Poultry Production and Research Institute
        Library
        PO Darul Uloom, Near Railway Station, Korangi
        Karachi, Sind 75180

Phone: +92(21) 311259

Founded: 1970 **Type:** Government **Staff:** 1 Prof. 1 Other **Holdings:** 1,200 books 10 journals **Subjects:** Animal Husbandry, Poultry **Loan:** In country **Photocopy:** Yes

2087   Karachi, Pakistan
Tropical Agricultural Research Institute
Library
PARC, Old Block 9-10
Karachi University Campus
Karachi
Phone: +92(21) 498-2509 **Fax:** +92(21) 498-8037

Head: Ms. Shahida Waheed

2088   Karachi, Pakistan
University of Karachi
Dr. Mahmud Husain Library
Karachi 32
Phone: +92(21) 479001/7 **Fax:** +92(21) 496-9277

Founded: 1952 **Type:** Government **Head:** Ms. Malahat Kaleem Sherwani *Phone:* +92(21) 479001/7 **Staff:** 22 Prof. 74 Other **Holdings:** 15,000 books 85 journals **Subjects:** Crops, Entomology, Horticulture, Plant Pathology, Plant Protection **Loan:** In country **Photocopy:** Yes

2089   Karachi, Pakistan
Zoological Survey Department
Library
Blok-61, Pak-Secretariat
Shahran-e-Iraq
Karachi

Head: Rubina Talat

2090   Lahore, Pakistan
Agricultural Census Organization (AgriCensus)
Library
Gulberg 3
Lahore
Phone: +92(42) 575-8030 **Fax:** +92(42) 575-2009

Founded: 1958 **Head:** Bashir Ali *Phone:* +92(42) 575-8030 **Type:** Government **Staff:** 2 Prof. 1 Other **Holdings:** 2,500 books 10 journals **Language of Collection/Services:** English / English **Subjects:** Agricultural Statistics **Service:** In country **Loan:** In country **Photocopy:** Yes

2091   Lahore, Pakistan
College of Veterinary Sciences
Library
Lahore
Phone: +92(42) 732-0248 **Email:** cvsl@brain.net.pk

Head: Mr. Muhammad Akram **Subjects:** Veterinary Science

2092   Lahore, Pakistan
Directorate of Fisheries
Library
2 Saandha Road
Lahore
Subjects: Fisheries

2093   Lahore, Pakistan
Directorate of Land Reclamation Punjab
Library
Canal Bank, Mughal Pura
Lahore
Phone: +92(42) 682-3025 **Fax:** +92(42) 482-3025 **Email:** dlr@paknet4.ptc.pk

Founded: 1945 **Type:** Government **Staff:** 1 Other **Language of Collection/Services:** English / English **Subjects:** Agricultural Development, Reclamation **Databases Used:** Comprehensive **Photocopy:** Yes

2094   Lahore, Pakistan
Fisheries Research and Training Institute
Library
G.T. Road, PO Box Batapur
Lahore
Subjects: Fisheries

2095   Lahore, Pakistan
International Water Management Institute (IWMI)
Library
IWMI - Pakistan
12 Km. Multan Road, Thokar Niaz Baig
Lahore 53700
Phone: +92(42) 541050 **Fax:** +92(42) 541054 **Email:** iimi-pak@cgiar.org **WWW:** www.cgiar.org/iwmi

Former Name: International Irrigation Management Institute (IIMI) **Founded:** 1995 **Head:** Samee Ullah *Email:* s.ullah@cgiar.org **Type:** International **Staff:** 1 Other **Holdings:** 2,754 books **Language of Collection/Services:** English **Subjects:** Agricultural Economics, Water Resources, Agricultural Engineering, Irrigation **Specializations:** Drainage, Soil Science **Service:** Inhouse **Photocopy:** Yes

2096   Lahore, Pakistan
International Waterlogging and Salinity Research
        Institute (IWASRI)
Library
13, West Wood Colony, Thokar Niaz Beg
Lahore, Punjab
Fax: +92(42) 522-1264, 522-1445

Founded: 1986 **Head:** Mr. Allah Bakhsh Sufi *Phone:* +92(42) 522-1061, 522-1063, 542-1446 *Email:* iwasri@brain.net.pk **Staff:** 1 Prof. 2 Other **Holdings:** 8,000 books 15 journals **Language of Collection/Services:** English / English **Subjects:** Community Involvement, Drainage, Environment, Irrigation, Salinity, Reclamation, Waterlogging **Loan:** Inhouse **Service:** Inhouse **Photocopy:** Yes

2097   Lahore, Pakistan
Irrigation and Power Department, Irrigation
        Research Institute Punjab
Library
Library Road
Lahore, Punjab
Phone: +92(42) 324477 **Fax:** +92(42) 312793

Founded: 1950 **Type:** Government **Staff:** 1 Prof. 3 Other **Holdings:** 5,441 books 60 journals **Language of Collection/Services:** English **Subjects:** Groundwater, Hydrology, Soil

Science **Loan:** In country **Service:** In country **Photocopy:** Yes

2098   Lahore, Pakistan
Pakistan Council of Scientific and Industrial
   Research Laboratories
Library
Complex
Lahore
Phone: +92(42) 575-7433 **Fax:** +92(42) 575-7429

2099   Lahore, Pakistan
Punjab Agriculture Department
Directorate of Agricultural Information Punjab
21 Sir Sultan Muhammad Shah Agha Khan III Rd.
Lahore
Phone: +92(42) 302941, 305914

Head: Muhammad Nawaz Bhatti

2100   Lahore, Pakistan
Punjab Forest Department
Punjab Forest Library
108-Ravi Road
Lahore, Punjab
Founded: 1930 **Type:** Government **Head:** Mr. Munawwar
Ali Khan *Phone:* +92(42) 772-3104 **Staff:** 2 Prof. 4 Other
Holdings: 35,000 books 5 journals **Language of Collection/
Services:** English **Subjects:** Biology, Forestry, Range Man-
agement, Sericulture, Silviculture, Soil Conservation, Wild-
life **Loan:** In country **Photocopy:** Yes

2101   Lahore, Pakistan
Soil Survey of Pakistan
Library
PO Box Shahnoor
Multan Road
Lahore

Subjects: Soil

2102   Lahore, Pakistan
University of Engineering and Technology, Centre
   of Excellence in Water Resources
   Engineering (UET, CEWRE)
Library
G.T. Road
Lahore, Punjab 54890
Phone: +92(42) 682-2558, 682-1100 **Fax:** +92(42) 682-
2024 **Email:** centre@cewre.edunet.sdnpk.undp.org

Founded: 1977 **Type:** Academic **Head:** Ms. Ruby Yamin
Email: librarian@cewre.edunet.sdnpk.undp.org *Phone:* +92
(42) 682-2024, 682-1100 **Staff:** 2 Prof. 1 Other **Holdings:**
6,000 books 18 journals **Language of Collection/Services:**
English / English, Urdu **Subjects:** Agricultural Engineering,
Soil, Water Resources **Specializations:** Civil Engineering,
Computers, Hydrology **Loan:** Inhouse **Service:** Internation-
ally **Photocopy:** Yes

2103   Lahore, Pakistan
University of the Punjab
Central Library

New Campus
Lahore, Punjab
Phone: +92(42) 586-8853 **Fax:** +92(42) 735-4428

Founded: 1882 **Type:** Academic **Head:** Mr. Jamil Ahmad
Shah **Staff:** 24 Prof. 67 Other **Holdings:** 2,000 books 6 journals **Subjects:** Agricultural Economics, Agricultural Engineering, Entomology, Fisheries, Plant Protection, Veterinary
Medicine **Loan:** In country **Photocopy:** Yes

2104   Lahore, Pakistan
Veterinary Research Institute
Library
Ghazi Road, Lahore Cantt.
Lahore, Punjab
Founded: 1962 **Type:** Government **Head:** Niaz Ali Shad
Phone: +92(42) 370006 ext 003 **Staff:** 1 Prof. 3 Other **Hold-
ings:** 10,000 books 18 journals **Subjects:** Veterinary Medi-
cine **Loan:** In country **Photocopy:** Yes

2105   Lahore, Pakistan
World Wildlife Fund for Nature Pakistan
   (WWF-Pakistan)
Library
Ferozepur Road
Lahore, Punjab 54600
Phone: +92(42) 586-9429 **Fax:** +92(42) 586-2358 **Email:**
qnaveed@wwfnet.org

Founded: 1992 **Type:** Non-government **Head:** Qammer
Naveed *Email:* qnaveed@wwfnet.org *Phone:* +92(42) 586-
9429, 586-2360 **Staff:** 1 Prof. 1 Other **Holdings:** 40 journals
3,000 books **Language of Collection/Services:** English
Subjects: Agricultural Development, Biotechnology, Crops,
Fisheries, Forestry, Horticulture, Plants, Water Resources
Specializations: Biodiversity, Environment **Databases Developed:** Union Database of Journals **Loan:** In country **Photocopy:** Yes

2106   Mardan, Pakistan
Pakistan Tobacco Board
Library
Tobacco Research Station
PO Box 36
Mardan
Phone: +92(521) 812435, 812491 **Fax:** +92(521) 810050

Subjects: Tobacco

2107   Mirpurkhas, Pakistan
Sindh Horticulture Research Institute
Library
Mirpurkhas, Sindh

Subjects: Horticulture

2108   Multan, Pakistan
Central Cotton Research Institute (CCRI)
Library
Old Shujabad Road
PO Box 572
Multan
Phone: +92(61) 545361, 545371 **Fax:** +92(61) 75153
Email: ccri@infolink.net.pk

Subjects: Cotton

2109   Nowshera, Pakistan
Cereal Crops Research Institute
Library
PO Box 43, Pirsabak
Nowshera, NWFP

Subjects: Cereals

2110   Okara, Pakistan
Livestock Production Research Institute
Library
Bahadurnagar
Okara

Phone: +92(442) 661181, 661093 **Fax:** +92(422) 661081

Head: Mr. Khadim Hussain **Subjects:** Livestock

2111   Peshawar, Pakistan
Agricultural Research Institute
Library
Tarnab
Peshawar, North West Frontier Province

Founded: 1962 **Type:** Government **Head:** Suttan Khan Jadoon *Phone:* +92(521) 64304 **Staff:** 1 Prof. 5 Other **Holdings:** 9,000 books 10 journals **Subjects:** Agricultural Development, Agricultural Economics, Biochemistry, Farming, Crops, Entomology, Food Sciences, Horticulture, Plant Pathology, Plant Physiology, Soil Science, Vegetables **Loan:** Do not loan **Photocopy:** Yes

2112   Peshawar, Pakistan
North West Frontier Province Agricultural
   University (NWFP-AU)
Library
Peshawar, North West Frontier Province 376
Phone: +92(521) 44490/99, 44590/99

Founded: 1962 **Type:** Academic **Head:** Attaullah **Staff:** 3 Prof. 5 Other **Holdings:** 50,000 books 120 journals **Language of Collection/Services:** English / English, Pushto, Urdu **Subjects:** Agriculture (Tropics), Agribusiness, Agricultural Development, Agricultural Economics, Agricultural Engineering, Animal Husbandry, Biotechnology, Crops, Education/Extension, Entomology, Farming, Fisheries, Food Sciences, Forestry, Horticulture, Plant Pathology, Soil Science, Water Resources **Databases Used:** Agricola; Agris; CABCD **Loan:** Inhouse **Service:** Inhouse **Photocopy:** Yes

2113   Peshawar, Pakistan
Nuclear Institute for Food and Agriculture (NIFA)
Library
PO Box 446
Peshawar
Location: G.T. Road, Tarnab **Phone:** +92(91) 296-4060/2 ext 44 **Fax:** +92(91) 296-4059 **Email:** nifa@packnet2.ptc.pk

Founded: 1982 **Type:** Government **Head:** Mr. Muhammad Asif *Email:* nifa@packnet2.ptc.pk *Phone:* +92(91) 296-4060/2 **Staff:** 2 Prof. 2 Other **Holdings:** 100 journals 3,500 books **Language of Collection/Services:** English/English **Subjects:** Entomology, Food Sciences, Plant Breeding, Soil

Science, Mutations **Loan:** In country **Service:** In country **Photocopy:** Yes

2114   Peshawar, Pakistan
Pakistan Academy for Rural Development
   (PARD)
Library
Academy Town
Peshawar
Phone: +92(521) 842639 ext 3010 **Email:** nipa@pknet1.ptc.pk

Head: Mr. Abul Ihsan **Subjects:** Rural Development

2115   Peshawar, Pakistan
Pakistan Forest Institute
Library
Peshawar
Phone: +92(521) 40580 **Fax:** +92(521) 844851 **Email:** kms.pfi@paknet.ptc.pk

Subjects: Forestry

2116   Peshawar, Pakistan
Veterinary Research Institute
Library
Charade Road
Peshawar

Subjects: Veterinary Science

2117   Peshawar-Cantt, Pakistan
Pakistan Tobacco Board
Library
PO Box 188
Peshawar-Cantt
Location: 46-B, Office Enclave-Phase V, Hyatabad Town, Peshawar **Phone:** +92(91) 812435 **Fax:** +92(91) 810050

Type: Research **Head:** Javed Iqbal *Phone:* +92(91) 812435 **Language of Collection/Services:** Urdu, English / Urdu, English **Subjects:** Agricultural Development **Specializations:** Tobacco **Service:** Inhouse **Photocopy:** Yes

2118   Quetta, Pakistan
Agricultural Research Institute
Library
Sariab
Quetta

Head: Mr. Abdul Qayum

2119   Quetta, Pakistan
Arid Zone Research Institute
Library
PO Box 363
Quetta, Baluchistan
Location: Brewery Road **Phone:** +92(81) 853620 **Fax:** +92(81) 853620

Head: Mr. Tariq Javed

2120   Rawalakot, Pakistan
University College of Agriculture
Library

Rawalakot, AJ & K

Phone: +92(576) 2688

Head: Mr. Muhammad Saleem Khan

2121   Rawalpindi, Pakistan
Agency for Barani Areas Development (ABAD)
Library
Murree Road
Rawalpindi, Punjab
Phone: +92(51) 840671 **Fax:** +92(51) 843696

Founded: 1978 **Type:** Government **Staff:** 2 Other **Holdings:** 1,000 books **Language of Collection/Services:** English, Urdu **Subjects:** Floriculture, Horticulture, Irrigation, Sericulture, Soil Conservation, Veterinary Science **Loan:** Inhouse **Service:** Inhouse **Photocopy:** Yes

2122   Rawalpindi, Pakistan
Directorate of Soil Conservation
Library
Murree Road
Rawalpindi

Subjects: Soil Conservation

2123   Rawalpindi, Pakistan
International Institute of Biological Control,
        Pakistan Agricultural Research Council
        (IIBC, PARC)
PARC-IIBC Station
PO Box 8
Rawalpindi, Punjab
Location: Data Gunj Baksh Road, Satellite Town **Fax:** +92 (51) 451147 **Email:** CABCDpak@isb.comsats.net.pk

Former Name: Commonwealth Institute of Biological Control **Founded:** 1957 **Type:** International **Head:** Farooq Nasir *Phone:* +92(51) 929-0332 **Staff:** 1 Other **Holdings:** 9,800 books 9 journals **Language of Collection/Services:** English **Subjects:** Biological Control, Ecology, Insect Pests, Pest Management, Weed Control **Specializations:** Entomology **Databases Used:** CABCD **Loan:** In country **Photocopy:** Yes

2124   Rawalpindi, Pakistan
Poultry Research Institute
Library
Shamsabad, Murree Road
Rawalpindi
Phone: +92(51) 450685 **Email:** dpr@paknet2.ptc.pk

Head: Mr. Muhammad Asif **Subjects:** Poultry

2125   Rawalpindi, Pakistan
University of Arid Agriculture
Library
Murree Road
Rawalpindi, Punjab
Phone: +92(51) 929-0151/2

Former Name: Barani Agricultural College **Founded:** 1979 **Type:** Academic **Head:** Muhammad Azam *Phone:* +92(51) 929-0151/2 **Staff:** 2 Prof. 6 Other **Holdings:** 10,000 books 20 journals **Subjects:** Crops, Food Technology, Genetics,

Horticulture, Plant Breeding, Plant Pathology, Soil Science
Loan: In country **Photocopy:** Yes

2126   Saidu-Sharif, Pakistan
Agricultural Research Station (North)
Library
PO Box 22
Saidu-Sharif, Swat
Fax: +92(936) 812625

Type: Research **Head:** Mujibur Rahman *Phone:* +92(936) 812611 **Staff:** 3 Prof. 4 Other **Holdings:** 6,000 books 20 journals **Language of Collection/Services:** English **Subjects:** Agricultural Development, Food Technology, Plant Breeding, Entomology **Specializations:** Agronomy, Horticulture, Biotechnology **Loan:** Internationally **Service:** In country **Photocopy:** Yes

2127   Swat, Pakistan
Project for Horticultural Promotion in NWFP
Library
PO Box 21, Saidu Sharif
Swat
Phone: +92(936) 812611, 813611 **Fax:** +92(936) 812625

Head: Mr. Abdul Rauf **Subjects:** Horticulture

2128   Tandojam, Pakistan
Agricultural Research Institute
Library
Tandojam

2129   Tandojam, Pakistan
Atomic Energy Agricultural Research Centre
Library
Tandojam 70060

2130   Tandojam, Pakistan
Pakistan Council of Research in Water Resources,
        Drainage Research Centre (DRC)
Library
Tando Qaiser Road
Tandojam, District Hyderabad 70060

Former Name: Drainage and Reclamation Institute of Pakistan **Founded:** 1975 **Type:** Government **Head:** Muhammed Ilyas Khan *Phone:* +92(2233) 5785 **Staff:** 3 Prof. 1 Other **Holdings:** 1,668 books 4 journals **Language of Collection/Services:** English **Subjects:** Drainage, Hydrology, Irrigation, Reclamation, Soil Science, Water Management **Loan:** Inhouse **Service:** Internationally **Photocopy:** Yes

2131   Yousafwala, Pakistan
Maize and Millets Research Institute
Library
Yousafwala, District Sahiwal
Fax: +92(441) 301028

Type: Government **Head:** Mr. Muhammad Hussain Ch. *Phone:* +92(441) 301141 **Holdings:** 700 books 15 journals **Language of Collection/Services:** English **Specializations:** Maize, Millets **Loan:** Do not loan **Service:** In country **Photocopy:** Yes

Palau

2132   **Koror, Palau**
Bureau of Resources and Development, Division
     of Agriculture
Library
PO Box 460
Koror PW 96940
Phone: +660 488-2504, 488-1517 **Fax:** +660 488-1725

Type: Government

2133   **Koror, Palau**
Palau Community Action Agency, Informal
     Employment and Sustainable Livlihoods
     Project (IESL)
Library
PO Box 3000
Koror PW 96940
Phone: +680 488-1170 **Fax:** +680 488-1169 **Email:**
iesl@palaunet.com

Former Name: Family Food Production and Nutrition Project **Founded:** 1987 **Type:** Non-government **Head:** Robert Bishop *Phone:* +680 448-4909 *Email:* iesl@palaunet.com **Language of Collection/Services:** English / English, Palauan **Holdings:** 300 books 7 journals **Subjects:** Agriculture (Tropics), Nutrition **Specializations:** Permaculture **Databases Developed:** Traditional agriculture; Traditional medicine **Loan:** In country **Service:** In country **Photocopy:** Yes

2134   **Koror, Palau**
Palau Community College (PCC)
Library
PO Box 9
Koror PW 96940
Phone: +860 448-2471 **Fax:** +680 448-3435, 488-2447

Former Name: Micronesian Occupational Center, Micronesian Occupational College **Founded:** 1969 **Type:** Academic **Head:** Ms. Jane Barnwell *Phone:* +680 488-2471 ext 261 *Email:* janeb@belau.org **Staff:** 1 Prof. 2 Other **Holdings:** 15,000 books 250 journals **Language of Collection/Services:** English / English, Palauan **Subjects:** Agriculture (Tropics) **Loan:** Internationally **Service:** Internationally **Photocopy:** Yes

Panama

2135   **Panamá, Panamá**
Instituto de Investigación Agropecuaria de
     Panamá (IDIAP)
Centro de Información Documental Agropecuaria
     (CIDAGRO)
Apartado 6-4391, El Dorado
Panamá 6A
Phone: +507 976-1279, 976-1168 **Fax:** +507 975-1587

Type: Government **Networks:** AGRIS

2136   **Panamá, Panamá**
Union of Banana Exporting Countries

Information and Documentation Center
Apdo 4273
Panamá 5
Location: Calle 50, Edificio Bancomer, 7° Piso **Phone:** +507 636266 **Fax:** +507 648355

Non-English Name: Unión de Países Exportadores de Banano (UPEB), Centro de Información y Documentación (CID) **Founded:** 1978 **Type:** International **Head:** Nitzia Barrantes *Phone:* +507 636310 **Staff:** 3 Prof. 3 Other **Holdings:** 15,000 books 90 journals **Language of Collection/Services:** Spanish, English, French, Portuguese **Subjects:** Agriculture (Tropics), Horticulture **Specializations:** Bananas **Loan:** Do not loan **Service:** Internationally **Photocopy:** Yes

Papua New Guinea

2137   **Bulolo, Papua New Guinea**
University of Technology, Bulolo University
     College (BUC)
Library (FORKOL)
PO Box 92
Bulolo, MP
Phone: +675 474-5226/5236 **Fax:** +675 474-5311

Former Name: PNG Forestry College **Type:** Academic **Founded:** 1964 **Head:** Ms. Kapi Lama *Phone:* +675 474-5226/5236 **Staff:** 1 Prof. 1 Other **Holdings:** 3,383 books **Language of Collection/Services:** English **Subjects:** Agriculture (Tropics), Forestry **Databases Used:** CABCD **Loan:** In country **Service:** In country **Photocopy:** Yes

2138   **Kainantu, Papua New Guinea**
Coffee Research Institute
Library
PO Box 105
Kainantu, EHP
Location: Aiyura, Eastern Highlands Province **Phone:** +675 737-3511, 737-3552, 737-3518 **Fax:** +675 373-3524

Type: Research **Head:** Mr. Jacob Taru **Subjects:** Coffee

2139   **Kerevat, Papua New Guinea**
National Agricultural Research Institute,
     Lowlands Agriculture Experiment Station
     (NARI, LAES)
Library
PO Box 204
Kokopo, ENBP
Location: Keravat **Phone:** +675 983-9145 **Fax:** +675 983-9129 **Email:** narilli@datec.com.pg

Former Name: Department of Agriculture and Livestock **Founded:** 1928 **Type:** Government **Head:** Ms. Medline Elisabeth Ling *Email:* narilli@datec.com.pg *Phone:* +675 983-9145 **Staff:** 1 Prof. **Holdings:** 2,034 books 83 journals **Language of Collection/Services:** English / English **Subjects:** Cocoa, Coconuts, Food Crops, Fruits, Pests, Plant Breeding, Plant Diseases, Tropical Crops **Databases Developed:** SCAINIP databases—developed by Pacific Islands collaborators **Databases Used:** CABCD; Current Contents **Loan:** In country **Service:** In country **Photocopy:** Yes

2140　Kerevat, Papua New Guinea
PNG Cocoa and Coconut Research Institute
Library
PO Box 1846
Rabaul, ENBP

Location: LAES, Kerevat **Phone:** +675 983-9131 **Fax:** +675 983-9115 **Email:** ccri@datec.com.pg

Type: Research **Head:** Mr. John Duigu

2141　Kerevat, Papua New Guinea
University of Vudal (UOV)
Library
Private Mail Bag
Rabaul, ENBP

Location: Kerevat **Phone:** +675 982-1444 **Fax:** +675 982-1119

Former Name: University of Technology, Vudal University College **Founded:** 1965 **Type:** Academic **Head:** Mr. Bruce Ningakun *Phone:* +675 982-1444 **Staff:** 5 Prof. **Holdings:** 14,000 books 130 journals **Language of Collection/Services:** English / English **Subjects:** Comprehensive **Specializations:** Agriculture (Tropics), Animal Husbandry, Crops **Loan:** Inhouse **Service:** Inhouse **Photocopy:** Yes

2142　Kimbe, Papua New Guinea
New Britain Palm Oil Development
Dami Oil Palm Research Station Library
PB 165
Kimbe, WNBP

Phone: +675 983-5203 **Fax:** +675 983-5476

Founded: 1968 **Type:** Business **Subjects:** Coconuts, Coffee, Crop Production, Oil Palms, Plant Protection, Plants

2143　Lae, Papua New Guinea
Appropriate Technology and Community
　　Development Institute, Lik Lik Buk
　　Information Centre
Library
Private Mail Bag, Unitech
Lae, MP

Location: University of Technology **Fax:** +675 473-4303 **Email:** jsabua@atdi.unitech.ac.pg

Founded: 1976 **Head:** Mrs. J. Sabua *Phone:* +675 473-4781 *Email:* jsabua@atdi.unitech.ac.pg **Type:** Academic **Staff:** 2 Other **Holdings:** 2,000 books **Language of Collection/Services:** Melanesian, Pidgin / English, Pidgin **Subjects:** Agribusiness, Animal Husbandry, Crops, Education/ Extension, Farming, Livestock, Plants, Processing **Loan:** Inhouse **Service:** Internationally **Photocopy:** Yes

2144　Lae, Papua New Guinea
Department of Agriculture and Livestock,
　　National Agricultural Research Institute,
　　Bubia Agricultural Research Centre (DAL,
　　NARI)
Library
PO Box 1639
Lae, MP

Location: Bubia, Morobe Province **Phone:** +675 475-1033 **Fax:** +675 475-1034

Type: Government **Head:** Ms. Clara Malangen Bandi

2145　Lae, Papua New Guinea
Department of Agriculture and Livestock,
　　National Agricultural Research Institute, Labu
　　Animal Husbandry Research Centre (DAL,
　　NARI)
Library
PO Box 1086
Lae, MP

Location: Wau Road, Bubia, Morobe Province **Phone:** +675 475-1066 **Fax:** +675 475-1185

Type: Government **Subjects:** Animal Husbandry

2146　Lae, Papua New Guinea
Forest Research Institute
Technical Support Services
PO Box 314
Lae, MP

Phone: +675 472-4188 **Fax:** +675 472-4357

Founded: 1989 **Type:** Research **Head:** Mr. Tinkepa Tumau **Subjects:** Forestry

2147　Lae, Papua New Guinea
Papua New Guinea University of Technology
　　(UNITECH)
Matheson Library
Private Mail Bag
Lae, MP

Phone: +675 473-4351 **Fax:** +675 475-7196 **WWW:** www.unitech.ac.pg

Founded: 1965 **Type:** Academic **Head:** Mr. Raphael Topagur *Email:* rtopagur@lib.unitech.ac.pg *Phone:* +675 473-4351 **Staff:** 7 Prof. 8 Other **Holdings:** 4,500 books 70 journals **Language of Collection/Services:** English **Subjects:** Agriculture (Tropics), Crop Production, Agricultural Engineering, Animal Production, Plant Protection, Soil Science, Tropical Crops **Databases Used:** Agricola; CABCD **Service:** Internationally **Loan:** Internationally **Photocopy:** Yes

2148　Lae, Papua New Guinea
Ramu Sugar Ltd.
Research Library
PO Box 2183
Lae, MP

Location: Gusap, Morobe Province **Phone:** +675 474-3299 **Fax:** +675 474-3295

Type: Business **Subjects:** Sugar

2149　Popondetta, Papua New Guinea
Department of Agriculture and Livestock,
　　Agricultural Education and Training Division,
　　Popondetta Agricultural College (DAL)
Library
PO Box 131
Popondetta, OP

Phone: +675 329-7139 **Fax:** +675 329-7674

Type: Academic **Head:** Mr. Topabi Upaiga

2150 **Port Moresby, Papua New Guinea**
Agricultural Bank of Papua New Guinea
Library
PO Box 6310
Somare Cr. Waigani
Boroko, NCD

2151 **Port Moresby, Papua New Guinea**
Department of Agriculture and Livestock,
    National Agricultural Research Institute, Land
    Use Section (DAL, NARI)
Library
PO Box 1860
Boroko, NCD
Location: Konedobu, National Capital District **Phone:**
+675 321-4673 **Fax:** +675 321-1755

Type: Government **Subjects:** Land Use

2152 **Port Moresby, Papua New Guinea**
Ministry of Agriculture, Department of
    Agriculture and Livestock (DAL)
Central Library
PO Box 417
Konedobu, NCD
Location: Konedobu, National Capital District **Phone:**
+675 321-4881 **Fax:** +675 321-4808

Former Name: Department of Primary Industry, Agricultural Education and Training Division **Type:** Government
Founded: 1960 **Head:** Mr. Nicks Maniha **Staff:** 4 Other
Holdings: 10,000 books 85 journals **Language of Collection/Services:** English **Subjects:** Agricultural Economics,
Crops, Entomology, Farming, Farming Systems, Livestock,
Plant Pathology, Vegetables, Veterinary Medicine **Networks:** AGRIS **Loan:** Internationally **Photocopy:** Yes

2153 **Port Moresby, Papua New Guinea**
National Agricultural Research Institute, Dry
    Lowlands Programme Laloki (NARI)
Library
PO Box 1828
Port Moresby, NCD
Location: Laloki, Central Province **Phone:** +675
328-1068, 328-1015 **Fax:** +675 328-1075

Type: Government

2154 **Port Moresby, Papua New Guinea**
University of Papua New Guinea
Michael Somare Library
Box 319
University Post Office, NCD
Location: Waigani, National Capital District **Fax:** +675
326-7187 **Email:** library@upng.ac.pg **WWW:** www.upng.
ac.pg

Head: Ms. Florence J. Griffin *Phone:* +675 326-7280 **Staff:**
15 Prof. 43 Other **Holdings:** 400,000 books 1,500 journals
Language of Collection/Services: English / English **Subjects:** Crop Production, Fisheries, Food Sciences, Plant Protection, Soil Science **Specializations:** Education/Extension
Databases Developed: South Pacific Legal Collection; Pa-

pua New Guinea Collection **Service:** Internationally **Loan:**
Inhouse **Photocopy:** Yes

2155 **Wau, Papua New Guinea**
Wau Ecology Institute
Library
PO Box 77
Wau, MP

Type: Non-government **Subjects:** Ecology

Paraguay

2156 **Asunción, Paraguay**
Ministerio de Agricultura y Ganadería
Biblioteca Nacional de Agricultura "Dr. Moisés S.
    Bertoni"
Presidente Franco 479
Casilla 825
Asunción
Phone: +595(21) 447250 **Fax:** +595(21) 441534 **Email:**
dgp_mag@infonet.com.py, dinamb@xoommail.com

Type: Government **Networks:** AGRIS

2157 **Asunción, Paraguay**
National University of Asuncion, Faculty of
    Veterinary Sciences
Library and Documentation Centre
Campus Universitario de San Lorenzo
Asunción
Phone: +595(21) 501516 **Fax:** +595(21) 585577 **Email:**
veterin@vet.una.py **WWW:** www.vet.una.py

Non-English Name: Universidad Nacional de Asunción,
Facultad de Ciencias Veterinarias, Biblioteca y Centro de
Documentación **Former Name:** Facultad de Agronomía y
Veterinaria **Founded:** 1958 **Type:** Academic **Holdings:**
8,000 books **Subjects:** Agricultural Economics, Agricultural
Production, Forestry, Soil Science **Loan:** In country **Photocopy:** Yes

Peru

2158 **Callao, Perú**
Instituto del Mar del Perú (IMARPE)
Biblioteca
Esq. Gamarra y Gral.Valle s/n Chucuito
Callao
Phone: +51(1) 429-7630 **Fax:** +51(1) 465-6023 **Email:**
imarpe-bib@imarpe.gob.pe **WWW:** www.imarpe.gob.pe

Former Name: Centro de Información y Documentación en
Ciencias Acuáticas y Pesqueras (CIDCAP) **Founded:** 1964
Type: Government **Holdings:** 4,000 books 21,000 journals
Subjects: Extraction, Fisheries, Limnology, Marine Areas,
Marine Sciences, Oceanography **Loan:** In country **Photocopy:** Yes

2159 **Cusco, Perú**
Centro Bartolomé de las Casas

Biblioteca
Pampa de la Alianza 465
Apartado 477
Cusco

Phone: +51(84) 222524 **Fax:** +51(84) 232544 **Email:** sid @apu.cbc.org.pe **WWW:** www.cbc.org.pe **OPAC:** www. cbc.org.pe/biblio

Former Name: Centro de Estudios Regionales Andinos "Bartolomé de Las Casas", Servicio de Biblioteca y Documentación (SERBIDOC) **Founded:** 1974 **Type:** Academic **Head:** Mr. Juan José Bellido *Phone:* +51(84) 236494 *Email:* juanjo@apu.cbc.org.pe **Staff:** 2 Prof. 2 Other **Holdings:** 30,000 books 70 journals **Language of Collection/Services:** Spanish / Spanish **Subjects:** Agrarian Reform, Agricultural Development, Agricultural Production, Agricultural Statistics, Commercial Farming, Education/Extension, Forestry, Water Resources **Specializations:** Andean Group (History), Anthropology (Andean Group), Farming (Andean Group), Rural Development **Databases Used:** Apice; Latin American Databases; Handbook of Latin American Studies; Hispanic American Books **Loan:** Do not loan **Photocopy:** Yes

2160   Huanuco, Perú
Hermilio Valdizan National University
Library
Dos de Mayo 680
Huanuco

Phone: +51(64) 512340/1 **Fax:** +51(64) 513360

Non-English Name: Universidad Nacional "Hermilio Valdizan", Biblioteca **Founded:** 1964 **Type:** Academic **Staff:** 2 Prof. 13 Other **Holdings:** 300 books **Subjects:** Botany, Cattle Husbandry, Herbs, Horticulture **Loan:** In country **Photocopy:** No

2161   Lima, Perú
Intermediate Technology Development Group
    (ITDG)
Documentation Center (CENDOC)
Apdo. Postal 18-0620
Lima 18

Location: Jorge Chávez 275, Miraflores, Lima **Fax:** +51 (1) 446-6621 **WWW:** www.itdg.org.pe **OPAC:** www.itdg. org.pe

Founded: 1986 **Type:** Non-government **Head:** Juan Fernando Bossio *Email:* juanf@itdg.org.pe *Phone:* +51(1) 444-7055, 447-5127 **Staff:** 1 Prof. **Holdings:** 5,500 books 70 journals **Language of Collection/Services:** Spanish, English / Spanish **Subjects:** Agribusiness, Agricultural Development, Agricultural Engineering, Animal Husbandry, Crops, Education/Extension, Farming, Food Sciences, Forestry, Horticulture, Irrigation, Soil, Veterinary Medicine, Water Resources **Specializations:** Appropriate Technology, Food Processing, Irrigation Management **Loan:** In country **Service:** Internationally **Photocopy:** Yes

2162   Lima, Perú
International Potato Center (CIP)
Library
Apartado 1558
Lima 12

Location: Av. La Universidad 795 **Fax:** +51(1) 349-5638 **Email:** cip-library@cgiar.org **WWW:** www.cipotato.org

Non-English Name: Centro Internacional de la Papa (CIP), Biblioteca **Former Name:** Information Unit **Founded:** 1973 **Type:** International **Head:** Cecilia Ferreyra *Phone:* +51(1) 349-6017, 349-5783 *Email:* c.ferreyra@cgiar.org **Staff:** 8 Prof. 2 Other **Holdings:** 13,000 books 100 journals **Language of Collection/Services:** English, Spanish, French / English, Spanish **Subjects:** Agriculture (Tropics), Agricultural Development, Agricultural Economics, Biotechnology, Crops, Education/Extension, Entomology, Farming, Food Sciences, Horticulture, Ipomoea, Plant Pathology, Soil Science, Solanum tuberosum **Specializations:** Potatoes, Sweet Potatoes, Root Crops (Andean Group), Tuberous Species (Andean Group) **Databases Used:** Agricola; Agris; CABCD **Loan:** In country **Service:** Internationally **Photocopy:** Yes

2163   Lima, Perú
National Agricultural University La Molina
Forestry Information Center
Apdo 456
Lima

Location: Av. La Molina **Email:** redinfor@lamolina.edu. pe **WWW:** www.lamolina.edu.pe **OPAC:** 196.40.0.244

Non-English Name: Universidad Nacional Agraria la Molina (UNALM), Centro de Información Forestal (CEDIF) **Founded:** 1984 **Type:** Academic **Staff:** 3 Prof. **Holdings:** 2,000 books 15 journals **Language of Collection/Services:** Spanish **Subjects:** Forestry **Loan:** Do not loan **Photocopy:** Yes

2164   Lima, Perú
National Agricultural University La Molina
National Agriculture Library
Apdo 14-0297
La Molina
Lima

Location: Av. la Universidad s/n, Lima 12 **Phone:** +51(14) 352035 ext 111 **Fax:** +51(14) 388012 **Email:** ban@ lamolina.edu.pe **WWW:** www.lamolina.edu.pe **OPAC:** 200.10.82.19/data/principal.htm

Non-English Name: Universidad Nacional Agraria La Molina (UNALM), Biblioteca Agrícola Nacional (BAN) **Founded:** 1962 **Type:** Government **Head:** William Hurtado de Mendoza Santander *Phone:* +51(14) 352035 ext 111, 342935 **Staff:** 9 Prof. 40 Other **Holdings:** 46,000 books 213 journals **Language of Collection/Services:** Spanish / Spanish **Subjects:** Agricultural Economics, Agricultural Engineering, Agricultural Planning, Fisheries, Food Industry, Forestry, Zootechny **Databases Developed:** SNIDA - Peruvian information from theses and journal articles **Databases Used:** Agricola; Agris; FSTA **Networks:** AGRIS **Loan:** In country **Service:** In country **Photocopy:** Yes

Philippines

2165   Banga, Philippines
Aklan State College of Agriculture (ASCA)
Library

Banga, Aklan 5601

Former Name: Banga Rural High School, Aklan Agricultural College **Type:** Government **Head:** Mrs. Patria Q. Aguilar **Staff:** 2 Prof. 6 Other

2166   Batac, Philippines
Cotton Development Administration (CODA)
Library
Batac, Ilocos Norte 2906
Phone: +63(77) 792-3137 **Fax:** +63(77) 792-3137 **Email:** coda@lc.amanet.net

Former Name: Cotton Research and Development Institute (CRDI) **Founded:** 1978 **Type:** Research **Head:** Myrna G. Acantilado *Email:* coda@lc.amanet.net *Phone:* +63(77) 793-2488 **Staff:** 1 Prof. **Holdings:** 10,000 books 27 journals **Language of Collection/Services:** English / English **Subjects:** Cotton **Specializations:** Gossypium **Photocopy:** No

2167   Batac, Philippines
Mariano Marcos State University
Library
Batac, Ilocos Norte 0305
Phone: +63(792) 3191

Founded: 1978 **Type:** Academic, Government **Head:** Professor Bucalen C. Saboy *Phone:* +63(792) 283 **Staff:** 10 Prof. 6 Other **Holdings:** 991 books 118 journals **Subjects:** Agribusiness, Agricultural Development, Agricultural Economics, Agricultural Engineering, Animal Husbandry, Education/Extension, Crops, Entomology, Fisheries, Forestry, Horticulture, Plant Pathology, Plant Protection, Range Management, Soil Science, Veterinary Medicine **Loan:** In country **Photocopy:** Yes

2168   Batac, Philippines
National Tobacco Administration (NTA)
Library
Batac, Ilocos Norte 2906
Phone: +63(792) 3076

Former Name: Philippine Tobacco Research and Training Center **Founded:** 1980 **Type:** Government **Head:** Evelyn E. Tacderan *Phone:* +63(792) 3076 **Staff:** 1 Prof. 1 Other **Holdings:** 2,500 books 26 journals **Language of Collection/Services:** English **Subjects:** Crops, Agribusiness, Agricultural Economics, Agricultural Engineering, Biotechnology, Education/Extension, Entomology, Farming, Horticulture, Plant Pathology, Soil Science, Water Resources **Specializations:** Agriculture (Tropics), Plants, Tobacco **Loan:** Do not loan **Service:** Inhouse **Photocopy:** Yes

2169   Baybay, Philippines
Visayas State College of Agriculture (VISCA)
Library
Baybay, Leyte 6521-A
Founded: 1924 **Type:** Academic **Head:** Linda K. Miranda *Phone:* +63(53) 335-2645 **Staff:** 7 Prof. 13 Other **Holdings:** 37,292 books 900 journals **Language of Collection/Services:** English **Subjects:** Agricultural Chemistry, Agricultural Engineering, Animal Husbandry, Botany, Education/Extension, Horticulture, Plant Breeding, Plant Protection **Specializations:** Cassava, Root Crops, Sweet Potatoes,

Gabi, Yams **Databases Developed:** RC - root crops; GABI - gabi; CAS - Cassava; YAM - Yams **Databases Used:** Agricola; TROPAG & RURAL **Loan:** In country **Photocopy:** Yes

2170   Borongan, Philippines
Eastern Samar State College (ESSC)
Library/Media Center
Borongan, Eastern Samar 6800
Phone: +63() 261-2731

Founded: 1960 **Type:** Academic **Head:** Florita C. Cabato *Phone:* +63() 261-2731 **Staff:** 4 Prof. 4 Other **Holdings:** 20,000 books 300 journals **Language of Collection/Services:** English / English **Subjects:** Agricultural Economics, Agriculture (Tropics), Animal Husbandry, Plants, Soil **Service:** Inhouse **Loan:** Inhouse **Photocopy:** Yes

2171   Bukidnon, Philippines
Central Mindanao University (CMU)
University Library
University Town, Musuan
Bukidnon 8710

Founded: 1952 **Type:** Academic **Head:** Mrs. Esther E. Dinampo **Staff:** 8 Prof. 10 Other **Holdings:** 17,536 books 180 journals **Language of Collection/Services:** English **Subjects:** Agribusiness, Agricultural Economics, Agricultural Engineering, Agronomy, Animal Husbandry, Crops, Biotechnology, Communication, Education/Extension, Entomology, Horticulture, Plant Pathology, Plant Protection **Specializations:** Biology, Chemistry, Engineering, Forestry, Soil, Veterinary Medicine **Photocopy:** Yes

2172   Cagayan de Oro City, Philippines
Department of Environment and Natural
        Resources (DENR)
Region X Library
Puntod
Cagayan de Oro City
Phone: +63(32366) 2020

Founded: 1978 **Type:** Government **Staff:** 1 Prof. **Subjects:** Environment, Natural Resources **Photocopy:** Yes

2173   Cagayan de Oro City, Philippines
Xavier University - Anteneo de Cagayan, College
        of Agriculture
Complex Library
Cagayan de Oro City, Misamis Oriental
WWW: www.cc.xu.edu.ph

Founded: 1953 **Type:** Academic **Head:** Ms. Annabelle P. Acedera *Phone:* +63(32366) 3133 **Staff:** 3 Prof. 6 Other **Holdings:** 6,000 books 50 journals **Subjects:** Agricultural Economics, Agricultural Engineering, Animal Husbandry, Crops, Soil Science **Loan:** Do not loan **Photocopy:** Yes

2174   Camiling, Philippines
Tarlac College of Agriculture (TCA)
Library
Camiling, Tarlac
Phone: +63(47) 216

Founded: 1952 **Type:** Academic **Head:** Mrs. Eledencia M. Rosete *Phone:* +63(47) 216 **Staff:** 1 Prof. 8 Other **Holdings:** 15,889 books **Language of Collection/Services:** English / Filipino, English **Subjects:** Agribusiness, Animal Husbandry, Fisheries, Horticulture, Veterinary Medicine, Soil Science **Loan:** In country

2175 Catarman, Philippines
University of Eastern Philippines
Library
University Town
Catarman, Northern Samar

Founded: 1964 **Type:** Government **Head:** Gloris T. Corocoto **Staff:** 3 Prof. 7 Other **Holdings:** 2,657 books 30 journals **Subjects:** Agricultural Economics, Animal Husbandry, Crops, Entomology, Fisheries, Forestry, Soil Science **Photocopy:** Yes

2176 College, Philippines
Ecosystems Research and Development Bureau
    (ERDB)
Library
College, Laguna 4031
Phone: +63(49) 536-2229 ext 204 **Fax:** +63(49) 536-2850 **Email:** ecosystems@gaia.psdn.iphil.net

Former Name: Forest Research Institute **Founded:** 1974 **Type:** Government **Head:** Praxedes L. Silvoza *Phone:* +63(49) 536-2229 ext 204 *Email:* ecosystems@gaia.psdn.iphil.net**Staff:** 2 Prof. 1 Other **Holdings:** 23,145 books 40 journals **Language of Collection/Services:** English / English **Subjects:** Agriculture (Tropics), Biotechnology, Crops, Farming, Entomology, Horticulture, Range Management, Plant Pathology, Soil Science, Water Resources, Wildlife Management **Specializations:** Ecosystems, Forestry, Natural Resources **Databases Used:** Fruit CD; TREECD **Service:** Inhouse **Loan:** Inhouse **Photocopy:** Yes

2177 College, Philippines
Forest Products Research and Development
    Institute, Department of Science and
    Technology (FPRDI, DOST)
Scientific Library and Documentation Service
    (SLDS)
Narra St.
College, Laguna 4031
Phone: +63(49) 536-2377 **Fax:** +63(49) 536-3630

Former Name: National Science Development Board (SDB) **Founded:** 1953 **Type:** Government **Head:** Olympia M. Molod *Phone:* +63(49) 536-2377 ext 111 **Staff:** 1 Prof. 4 Other **Holdings:** 6,604 books **Language of Collection/Services:** English **Subjects:** Forest Products, Forest Trees, Forestry, Furniture, Pulping, Veneering, Wood Chemistry, Wood Preservation, Wood Properties, Wood Technology, Wood Utilization, Wood Wool, Woodworking **Loan:** Inhouse **Service:** Inhouse **Photocopy:** Yes

2178 College, Philippines
National Institute of Molecular Biology and
    Biotechnology (BIOTECH)
BIOTECH Library

University of the Philippines at Los Baños
College, Laguna 4031
Fax: +63(49) 536-2721 **WWW:** www.laguna.net/~bioinfo

Former Name: National Institutes of Applied Microbiology and Biotechnology **Founded:** 1982 **Type:** Research **Head:** Ms. Concepcion dl. Saul *Phone:* +63(49) 536-2884 *Email:* cdls@biotech.uplb.edu.ph **Staff:** 1 Prof. 1 Other **Holdings:** 6,000 books **Language of Collection/Services:** English / English, Filipino **Subjects:** Biotechnology **Databases Developed:** BIOPUB - BIOTECH staff's technical publications; RESEARCH - completed biotechnology research in the Philippines **Loan:** Inhouse **Service:** Inhouse **Photocopy:** Yes

2179 College, Philippines
University of the Philippines Los Baños (UPLB)
University Library
College, Laguna 4031
Phone: +63(49) 536-2235, 536-3178 **Fax:** +63(49) 536-5081 **Email:** ill@library.uplb.edu.ph **WWW:** www.uplb.edu.ph/lib **OPAC:** 165.220.20.110 (Login twice: tinlib; then, opac)

Former Name: University of the Philippines College of Agriculture (UPCA) **Founded:** 1909 **Type:** Academic **Head:** Vilma Anday *Email:* vga@mudspring.uplb.edu.ph *Phone:* +63(49) 536-2326 **Staff:** 25 Prof. 30 Other **Holdings:** 285,464 books 2,749 journals **Language of Collection/Services:** English, Filipino / English, Filipino **Subjects:** Comprehensive **Networks:** DOST-ESEP **Databases Used:** Comprehensive **Loan:** In country **Service:** Internationally **Photocopy:** Yes

2180 College, Philippines
University of the Philippines Los Baños, College
    of Economics and Management, Research
    Management Center (UPLB, RMC)
Research Management Information Center
    (RM-IC)
College, Laguna 4030
Fax: +63(49) 536-3341 **Email:** rmc@laguna.net **WWW:** www.uplb.edu.ph

Founded: 1981 **Type:** Government **Head:** Lydia R. Lapastora *Phone:* +63(49) 536-3872 **Staff:** 1 Prof. 1 Other **Holdings:** 2,000 books 3 journals **Language of Collection/Services:** English / English **Subjects:** Management, Research Management **Photocopy:** Yes

2181 College, Philippines
University of the Philippines Los Baños, College
    of Forestry and Natural Resources (UPLB,
    CFNR)
Library
College, Laguna 4031
Phone: +63(49) 536-2266 **Fax:** +63(49) 536-3206 **Email:** feb@mudspring.uplb.edu.ph, florebel@laguna.net **WWW:** www.uplb.edu.ph/cfnr

Former Name: College of Forestry **Founded:** 1910 **Type:** Academic **Head:** Ms. Flor E. Belen *Phone:* +63(49) 536-2266 *Email:* feb@mudspring.uplb.edu.ph, florebel@laguna.net **Staff:** 3 Prof. 6 Other **Holdings:** 26,813 books 33 journals **Language of Collection/Services:** English/English **Subjects:** Forestry **Specializations:** Agroforestry, Forest Management, Forest Products, Forest Resources, Silviculture, Forest Soils, Social Forestry, Wood Technology **Databases Used:** Agris **Loan:** In country **Service:** In country **Photocopy:** Yes

2182 College, Philippines
University of the Philippines Los Baños, School of Environmental Science and Management (UPLB, SESAM)
Library
College, Laguna 4031

Phone: +63(49) 536-2251 **WWW:** www.uplb.edu.ph

Former Name: Institute of Environmental Science and Management **Founded:** 1984 **Type:** Academic **Head:** Ms. Evangeline L. Alcantara *Phone:* +63(49) 536-2251 **Staff:** 1 Prof. 1 Other **Holdings:** 3,500 books **Language of Collection/Services:** English **Subjects:** Sustainability **Specializations:** Environmental Management, Natural Resources Management, Policy **Loan:** Inhouse **Service:** Inhouse **Photocopy:** Yes

2183 Davao City, Philippines
Philippine Coconut Authority, Davao Research Center (PCA, DRC)
Library
PO Box 80437
Davao City 8000

Location: Bago Oshiro **Fax:** +63(82) 293-0118 **Email:** pca-drc@interasia.com.ph **WWW:** www.interasia.com.ph/clients/pca-drc

Former Name: PHILCORIN **Founded:** 1971 **Type:** Government **Head:** Ms. Esther Santos *Phone:* +63(82) 293-0119 *Email:* pca-drc@interasia.com.ph **Staff:** 1 Other **Holdings:** 629 books 15 journals **Language of Collection/Services:** English / English **Subjects:** Genetics, Plant Breeding, Plant Nutrition, Plant Protection **Specializations:** Coconuts **Databases Developed:** PROSEA - Plant Resources of South-East Asia **Loan:** Do not loan **Photocopy:** Yes

2184 Davao City, Philippines
Twin Rivers Plantation, Inc.
Research Center Library
PO Box 305
Davao City

Location: Madaum, Tagum **Phone:** +63(82) 850191, 855283

Founded: 1974 **Type:** Business **Head:** Mrs. Elenita G. Dablo **Staff:** 1 Prof. 1 Other **Holdings:** 50 books 6 journals **Subjects:** Fertilization, Horticulture, Irrigation, Pesticides, Plant Protection, Soil Science **Loan:** Do not loan **Photocopy:** Yes

2185 Dumaguete City, Philippines
Silliman University (SU)
College of Agriculture Library
Dumaguete City, Negros Oriental 6200

Phone: +63(35) 225-2516 **Fax:** +63(35) 225-2516 **Email:** sulib@su.edu.ph **WWW:** www.su.edu.ph

Founded: 1979 **Type:** Academic **Head:** Mrs. Violeta D. Rusiana **Staff:** 1 Prof. 4 Other **Holdings:** 5,000 books 12 journals **Language of Collection/Services:** English **Subjects:** Agribusiness, Animal Husbandry, Crops, Plant Pathology, Plant Protection **Loan:** Inhouse **Service:** Inhouse **Photocopy:** Yes

2186 Echague, Philippines
Isabela State University
Main Library
San Fabian
Echague, Isabela 3309

Former Name: Isabela State College of Agriculture (ISCA) **Founded:** 1954 **Type:** Academic **Head:** Dr. Oliva A. Karganilla *Phone:* +63(76) 22015 **Holdings:** 15,552 books 112 journals **Language of Collection/Services:** English, Filipino **Subjects:** Agribusiness, Crops, Agricultural Economics, Agricultural Engineering, Animal Husbandry, Farming, Education/Extension, Farm Management, Food Sciences, Horticulture, Plant Pathology, Plants, Soil Science, Veterinary Medicine **Loan:** Do not loan **Photocopy:** No

2187 Iloilo, Philippines
Central Philippine University (CPU)
University Library
Iloilo 5000

Location: Lopez Jaena Street, Jaro **Fax:** +63(33) 310-3582 **WWW:** users.iloilo.net/cpu/home.html

Founded: 1905 **Type:** Academic **Head:** Miss Victory D. Gabawa *Phone:* +63(33) 320-3582 *Email:* cpuhll@stealth.iloilo.net **Staff:** 11 Prof. 1 Other **Holdings:** 6,000 books 26 journals **Language of Collection/Services:** English **Subjects:** Agriculture (Tropics), Agricultural Development, Agricultural Engineering, Animal Husbandry, Crops, Farming **Loan:** In country **Service:** Internationally **Photocopy:** Yes

2188 Iloilo City, Philippines
Southeast Asian Fisheries Development Center, Aquaculture Department (SEAFDEC, AQD)
Library
PO Box 256
Iloilo City 5000

Location: Tigbauan, Iloilo 5021 **Phone:** +673(33) 335-1009, 336-2965, 336-2937 **Fax:** +63(33) 335-1008, 336-2891 **Email:** chief@i-iloilo.com.ph **WWW:** www.seafdec.org.ph, aqd.seafdec.org.ph

Founded: 1973 **Type:** Government **Head:** Ms. Amelia T. Arisola *Phone:* +63 (33) 335-1009, 336-2965, 336-2937 *Email:* library@aqd.seafdec.org.ph, aqdlib@i-iloilo.com.ph **Staff:** 3 Prof. 1 Other **Holdings:** 24,255 books 4,540 journals **Language of Collection/Services:** English **Subjects:** Fisheries **Specializations:** Aquaculture, Fish Culture, Fishery Management **Databases Developed:** BRAIS - bibliographic database on brackishwater aquaculture information; SEAFIS - bibliographic database on Philippines fisheries and aquatic sciences or written by a Filipino **Databases Used:** Comprehensive **Loan:** In country **Service:** Internationally **Photocopy:** Yes

2189   Indang, Philippines
Cavite State University
Library
Indang, Cavite 4122

Former Name: Don Severino Agricultural College (DSAC), Don Severino National Agricultural School, Indang Farm School, Indang Rural High School **Founded:** 1921 **Type:** Academic, Government **Head:** Mrs. Guillermina G. Astudillo **Staff:** 4 Prof. 1 Other **Holdings:** 4,809 books 100 journals **Language of Collection/Services:** English **Subjects:** Agriculture (Tropics), Agribusiness, Agricultural Development, Agricultural Economics, Agricultural Engineering, Biotechnology, Education/Extension, Plant Pathology, Entomology, Farming, Food Sciences, Forestry, Veterinary Medicine, Water Resources **Specializations:** Animal Husbandry, Crops, Horticulture, Plants, Soil Science **Loan:** In country **Photocopy:** Yes

2190   Isabela, Philippines
Isabela State University
Library
3328 Cabagan
Isabela, Northern Luzon 1303
Location: Garita Slopes

Founded: 1960 **Type:** Government **Head:** Ms. Corona Bagunu Zipagan **Staff:** 6 Prof. 2 Other **Holdings:** 10,108 books 100 journals **Subjects:** Agribusiness, Agricultural Research, Animal Husbandry, Communication, Crops, Education/Extension, Food Sciences, Forestry, Soil Science **Loan:** In country

2191   Kabacan, Philippines
University of Southern Mindanao, Agricultural
    Research Center (USM, ARC)
Library
Kabacan, Cotabato

Former Name: Mindanao Institute of Technology, Southern Mindanao Agricultural Research Center **Founded:** 1954 **Type:** Government **Head:** Mrs. Febe C. Braga **Staff:** 1 Prof. 13 Other **Holdings:** 30,000 books 3,824 journals **Language of Collection/Services:** English **Loan:** In country **Service:** In country **Photocopy:** Yes

2192   La Carlota City, Philippines
Department of Agriculture, Bureau of Plant
    Industry, La Granja National Crop Research
    and Development Center (DA, BPI,
    LGNCRDC)
Library
La Carlota City, Negros Occidental 6130

Former Name: La Granja Experiment Station **Founded:** 1950 **Type:** Government **Head:** Mrs. Nora T. Armones **Staff:** 1 Prof. 1 Other **Holdings:** 5,936 books 1,508 journals **Language of Collection/Services:** English / English **Subjects:** Agricultural Economics, Agricultural Engineering, Agronomy, Farming Systems, Horticulture, Plant Nutrition, Plant Protection, Soil **Loan:** In country **Service:** Inhouse **Photocopy:** No

2193   La Trinidad, Philippines
Benguet State University (BSU)
University Library Services (ULS)
La Trinidad, Benguet 2601
Phone: +63(74) 422-2402 **Fax:** +63(74) 422-2281 **Email:** bsu@burgos.slu.edu.ph **WWW:** www.slu.edu.ph/BSU

Former Name: Mountain State Agricultural College, Library Information Services (LIS) **Founded:** 1970 **Type:** Academic **Head:** Dr. Nora J. Claravall *Phone:* +63(74) 422-1121 *Email:* bsu@burgos.slu.edu.ph **Staff:** 3 Prof. 7 Other **Holdings:** 30,000 books 20 journals **Language of Collection/Services:** English / English **Subjects:** Agricultural Engineering, Agriculture (Tropics), Forestry, Social Sciences, Veterinary Medicine **Networks:** SLU-BSU Consortium **Databases Developed:** BSU theses collection **Loan:** In country **Photocopy:** Yes

2194   Lamut, Philippines
Ifugao State College of Agriculture and Forestry
    (ISCAF)
Main Library
Nayon
Lamut, Ifugao 3605

Founded: 1969 **Type:** Academic **Head:** Emily L. Sungduan **Staff:** 2 Prof. 3 Other **Holdings:** 5,222 books 3 journals **Subjects:** Comprehensive **Photocopy:** No

2195   Los Baños, Philippines
Philippine Council for Agriculture, Forestry and
    Natural Resources Research and
    Development (PCARRD)
Scientific Literature Services Program (SLS)
PO Box 425
Los Baños, Laguna 3732
Phone: +63(49) 536-0014/7 ext 276 **Fax:** +63(49) 536-0016, 536-0132 **Email:** pcarrd@ultra.pcarrd.ddost.gov.ph **WWW:** www.pcarrd.dost.gov.ph

Former Name: Philippine Council for Agriculture and Resources Research and Development **Founded:** 1973 **Type:** Government **Head:** Lilia G. Bayabos *Phone:* +63(49) 536-0014/7 **Staff:** 4 Prof. **Holdings:** 13,000 books 900 journals **Language of Collection/Services:** English **Subjects:** Animal Husbandry, Crops, Farming Systems, Forestry, Natural Resources **Databases Developed:** RETRES - Research Information Storage and Retrieval System, contains bibliographic information and abstracts of completed research generated in the national network **Databases Used:** CABCD **Loan:** In country **Photocopy:** Yes

2196   Los Baños, Philippines
Philippine Council for Aquatic and Marine
    Resources Development (PCAMRD)
Research Information Utilization Division (RIUD)
Alfonzo N. Eusebio Bldg., BPI
Economic Garden
Los Baños, Laguna
WWW: www.laguna.net/pcamrd

Head: Mrs. Zeny Pamulaklakin *Email:* zcp@sun1.dost.gov.ph

2197   Los Baños, Philippines
Southeast Asian Ministers of Education
        Organization, Regional Center for Graduate
        Study and Research in Agriculture
        (SEAMEO)
SEARCA Library
College
Los Baños, Laguna 4031
Phone: +63(49) 536-2317, 3459, 2554, 2576 **Fax:** +63(2)
817-0598, +53(49) 536-2914 **Email:** central@agri.searca.
org **WWW:** www.searca.org

Former Name: Southeast Asian Regional Center for Graduate Study and Research in Agriculture (SEARCA) **Founded:**
1990 **Type:** International **Head:** Ms. Alicia H. Rillo *Phone:*
+63(49) 536-2284 *Email:* ahr@agri.searca.org **Staff:** 2 Prof.
1 Other **Holdings:** 5,000 books **Language of Collection/**
Services: English / English **Subjects:** Agribusiness, Agricultural Development, Agricultural Economics, Agricultural
Engineering, Agriculture (Tropics), Animal Husbandry,
Biotechnology, Crops, Education/Extension, Entomology,
Farming, Fisheries, Food Sciences, Forestry, Horticulture,
Plant Pathology, Soil Science, Veterinary Medicine, Water
Resources **Specializations:** Agriculture (Southeast Asia)
Databases Developed: Agriasia - quarterly bibliography of
current agricultural literature.; Factual database on medicinal
and aromatic plants found in Asia and the Pacific. **Loan:** In-
house **Service:** Internationally **Photocopy:** Yes

2198   Magalang, Philippines
Pampanga Agricultural College (PAC)
Library
Magalang, Pampanga 2011
Phone: +63(12) 305-2618

Former Name: Pampanga National Agricultural School
Founded: 1954 **Type:** Government **Head:** Erlinda I. David
Staff: 2 Prof. 1 Other **Holdings:** 6,000 books 10 journals
Language of Collection/Services: English **Subjects:** Agri-
business, Agricultural Economics, Agricultural Engineering,
Animal Husbandry, Biotechnology, Crops, Education/Ex-
tension, Entomology, Food Sciences, Forestry, Horticulture,
Plant Pathology, Plants, Soil Science, Veterinary Medicine
Service: In country

2199   Makati City, Philippines
International Center for Living Aquatic Resources
        Management (ICLARM)
Ian R. Smith Memorial Library and
        Documentation Center (IRSMLDC)
MCPO Box 2631
Makati City 0718
Location: Ground Floor, Bloomingdale Building, 205
Salcedo Street, Legaspi Village **Phone:** +63(2) 818-0466,
818-9283, 817-5255 **Fax:** +63(2) 816-3183 **Email:** iclarm
@cgiar.org **WWW:** www.cgiar.org/iclarm

Founded: 1978 **Type:** International **Head:** Rosalinda M.
Temprosa *Phone:* +63(2) 812-8641 *Email:* l.temprosa@
cgiar.org **Staff:** 5 Prof. 1 Other **Holdings:** 21,834 books 90
journals **Language of Collection/Services:** English / English **Subjects:** Aquaculture, Coasts, Fisheries, Resource
Management **Specializations:** SFIS - Selective Fisheries Information Service **Databases Developed:** NAGA - 17,000+

bibliographic records on fisheries, aquaculture and coastal
resource management relevant to tropical and developing
countries; RED - bibliographic information on Indo-Pacific
Red Tides; CITEANAL - 17,000+ bibliographic records of
ICLARM publications or contributions series cited in articles from serials, mmonographs, proceedings and other materials to analyze the extent of usage and to determine the
bibliographic impact of the Center's publications **Databases**
Used: Comprehensive **Loan:** In country **Service:** Internationally **Photocopy:** Yes

2200   Mambusao, Philippines
Panay State Polytechnic College (PSPC)
Library Services
Mambusao, Capiz 5807

Former Name: Mambusao Agricultural and Technical Col-
lege (MATEC) **Founded:** 1963 **Type:** Government **Head:**
Mrs. Aurea G. Bernabe **Staff:** 3 Prof. 3 Other **Holdings:**
29,773 books 7,134 journals **Language of Collection/Ser-**
vices: English / English, Filipino **Subjects:** Agribusiness,
Agricultural Development, Agricultural Economics, Crops,
Agricultural Engineering, Animal Husbandry, Education/
Extension, Farming, Fisheries, Food Sciences, Forestry,
Horticulture, Plant Pathology, Soil Science, Veterinary Med-
icine **Loan:** In country **Service:** In country **Photocopy:** Yes

2201   Manila, Philippines
Department of Agriculture, Bureau of Fisheries
        and Aquatic Resources (BFAR)
Scientific Library and Documentation Service
        (SLDS)
PO Box 623
Manila 1103
Location: 860 Arcadia Building, Quezon Avenue, Quezon
City **Fax:** +63(2) 372-5009 **Email:** bfar@libv-link.net.ph

Founded: 1947 **Type:** Government **Head:** Philip E. Albano
Phone: +63(2) 965650 *Email:* bfar@libv-link.net.ph **Staff:** 1
Prof. 1 Other **Holdings:** 6,000 books 50 journals **Language**
of Collection/Services: English / English **Subjects:** Aquaculture, Fisheries **Loan:** In country **Photocopy:** Yes

2202   Manila, Philippines
Department of Environment and Natural
        Resources, National Mapping and Resource
        Information Authority (DENR, NAMRIA)
Library
National Cartography Authority Annex Building
1201 Fort Bonifacio, Makati
Manila
Phone: +63(2) 810-4831 ext 262 **WWW:** www.denr.gov.
ph

Former Name: Ministry of Natural Resources **Founded:**
1987 **Head:** Elizabeth P. De Leon *Phone:* +63(2) 810-4831
Type: Government **Staff:** 2 Prof. 4 Other **Holdings:** 650
books 4 journals **Language of Collection/Services:** English
Subjects: Fisheries, Forestry, Wildlife Conservation **Loan:**
In country **Photocopy:** Yes

2203   Manila, Philippines
Food and Agriculture Organization,
      ASEAN/UNDP/FAO Regional Small-Scale
      Coastal Fisheries Development Project (FAO)
Library
c/o FAO Representative's Office
PO Box 1864
Manila

Location: 860 Quezon Avenue, Arcadia Building, 3rd Floor, Quezon City

Founded: 1974 **Type:** International **Head:** Mrs. Paulina T. Zabala *Phone:* +63(2) 973617 **Holdings:** 12,000 books **Language of Collection/Services:** English **Staff:** 1 Prof. **Specializations:** Fisheries **Loan:** Do not loan **Service:** Inhouse **Photocopy:** Yes

2204   Manila, Philippines
International Rice Research Institute (IRRI)
Library and Documentation Service
PO Box 933
Manila 1099

Location: College, Los Baños, Laguna 4031 **Fax:** +63(2) 891-1292, 761-2404, 761-2406 **Email:** c.austria@cgiar.org **WWW:** www.cgiar.org/irri **OPAC:** ricelib.irri.cgiar.org **Ariel IP:** 198.93.230.21

Founded: 1960 **Type:** International **Head:** Ian M. Wallace *Phone:* +63(2) 845-0563 *Email:* i.wallace@cgiar.org **Staff:** 6.5 Prof. 9 Other **Holdings:** 110,000 books 2,250 journals **Language of Collection/Services:** English, Japanese, Chinese / English **Subjects:** Rice **Databases Developed:** Rice Bibliography - 170,000 references covering materials from 1970 to date; access via Internet or printed version, Rice Literature Update, published 3 times per year **Databases Used:** Comprehensive **Loan:** In country **Service:** Internationally **Photocopy:** Yes

2205   Munoz, Philippines
Central Luzon State University (CLSU)
Library
Munoz, Nueva Ecija 3120

Phone: +63(44) 4560-107 **Fax:** +63(44) 4560-107 **Email:** clsu@mozcom.com **WWW:** www2.mozcom.com/~clsu

Former Name: Central Luzon Agricultural School, Central Luzon Agricultural College **Type:** Academic, Government **Founded:** 1954 **Head:** Celia D. dela Cruz *Phone:* +63(44) 4560-107 **Staff:** 6 Prof. 9 Other **Holdings:** 45,000 books 150 journals **Language of Collection/Services:** English / Filipino **Subjects:** Agriculture (Tropics), Agribusiness, Agricultural Development, Agricultural Economics, Agricultural Engineering, Animal Husbandry, Biodiversity, Biotechnology, Crops, Education/Extension, Entomology, Farming, Fisheries, Food Sciences, Forestry, Horticulture, Plant Pathology, Soil Science, Water Resources, Veterinary Medicine **Loan:** Inhouse **Service:** Inhouse **Photocopy:** Yes

2206   Palawan, Philippines
State Polytechnic College of Palawan
Library
Aborlan
Palawan 5302

Former Name: Palawan National Agricultural College (PNAC) **Founded:** 1910 **Type:** Government **Head:** Efren Bautista **Staff:** 1 Prof. 3 Other **Holdings:** 25,000 books 59 journals **Language of Collection/Services:** English, Filipino **Subjects:** Agriculture (Tropics), Agribusiness, Crops, Agricultural Economics, Agricultural Engineering, Animal Husbandry, Education/Extension, Entomology, Farming, Fisheries, Food Sciences, Forestry, Horticulture, Plant Pathology, Plants, Statistics, Veterinary Medicine, Water Resources **Loan:** In country **Service:** Inhouse **Photocopy:** No

2207   Pasig City, Philippines
Agricultural Credit Policy Council (ACPC)
Library
3/F Agustin I Bldg., Emerald Avenue
Ortigas Center
Pasig City 1605

Phone: +63(2) 634-3319/21 **Fax:** +63(2) 633-4603 **Email:** acpc@manila-online.net

Former Name: Technical Board for Agricultural Credit **Founded:** 1989 **Type:** Government **Head:** Rowena C. Rueda *Email:* acpc@manila-online.net *Phone:* +63(2) 634-3320 ext 118 **Staff:** 1 Prof. 2 Other **Holdings:** 5,000 books 5 journals **Language of Collection/Services:** English / English, Filipino **Subjects:** Agricultural Credit, Rural Economy **Specializations:** Agribusiness, Economics, Land Reform, Public Finance, Sociology, Statistics **Loan:** Inhouse **Service:** In country **Photocopy:** Yes

2208   Pili, Philippines
Camarines Sur State Agricultural College
      (CSSAC)
Library
San Jose
Pili, Camarines Sur 4418

Phone: +63(5435) 756699, 777206 **Fax:** +63(5435) 773341

Founded: 1918 **Type:** Academic **Head:** Adoracion M. Villareal *Phone:* +63(5435) 756699 ext 205 **Staff:** 4 Prof. 16 Other **Holdings:** 15,000 books 4 journals **Language of Collection/Services:** English / English **Subjects:** Comprehensive **Photocopy:** Yes

2209   Quezon City, Philippines
Bureau of Animal Industry
Library
Visayas Avenue, Diliman
Quezon City

Phone: +63(2) 951844

Founded: 1932 **Type:** Government **Head:** Mrs. Bernandine M. Zamora *Phone:* +63(2) 952184 **Staff:** 3 Prof. 2 Other **Holdings:** 5,000 books 10 journals **Subjects:** Animal Husbandry, Veterinary Medicine **Loan:** Do not loan **Photocopy:** No

2210   Quezon City, Philippines
Department of Agriculture (DA)
Library
Elliptical Road, Diliman
Quezon City 1104

Phone: +63(2) 928-8741/65 ext 140

Former Name: Department of Agriculture and Natural Resources (DANR) **Founded:** 1953 **Type:** Government **Head:** Filipinas O. Bernal *Phone:* +63(2) 928-8741/65 ext 140 **Staff:** 2 Prof. 1 Other **Holdings:** 15,000 books 20 journals **Language of Collection/Services:** English / Filipino, English **Subjects:** Agribusiness, Agricultural Development, Agricultural Economics, Animal Husbandry, Fisheries, Plant Pathology, Horticulture, Plants, Soil Science **Specializations:** Crops, Farming **Loan:** In country **Service:** Internationally **Photocopy:** Yes

2211   Quezon City, Philippines
Department of Agriculture, Bureau of Agricultural
     Statistics (DA, BAS)
BAS Library
1184 Benlor Building
Quezon Avenue
Quezon City 1100
Phone: +63(2) 371-2075, 372-3801 ext 262 **Fax:** +63(2) 371-2086

Former Name: Bureau of Agricultural Economics **Founded:** 1968 **Type:** Government **Head:** Davina J. Salem / Renalyn Leal Peña *Phone:* +63(2) 371-2075, 372-3801 ext 262 **Staff:** 5 Prof. 1 Other **Holdings:** 250 books 60 journals **Language of Collection/Services:** English, Filipino **Subjects:** Agricultural Development, Agricultural Economics, Crops **Specializations:** Agricultural Statistics **Loan:** In country **Service:** In country **Photocopy:** Yes

2212   Quezon City, Philippines
Department of Agriculture, Fertilizer and Pesticide
     Authority (DA, FPA)
Planning and Information Division
PO Box 2582
Quezon City
Location: 4th Floor, Building B, NIA Complex, EDSA **Phone:** +63(2) 922-3364, 922-3362, 922-5877 **Fax:** +63(2) 922-3368 **Email:** pmdpfpa@skyinet.net **WWW:** www. fadinap.org/philippines **OPAC:** www.fadinap.org

Former Name: Fertilizer Industry Authority (FIA) **Founded:** 1994 **Type:** Government **Head:** *Phone:* +63(2) 922-3355 *Email:* pmdpfpa@skyinet.net **Staff:** 2 Prof. **Holdings:** 1,750 books 21 journals **Language of Collection/Services:** English / Filipino, English **Subjects:** Fertilizers, Pesticides **Databases Developed:** Fertilizer databases - includes licensed fertilizer handlers, fully registered fertilizer, licensed fertilizer and pesticide dealers, and fertilizer supply and demand; some available upon request and some via the Internet home page; Pesticide databases - includes licensed agricultural and household pesticide handlers, registered pesticide use patterns, licensed pest control operators and certified pesticide applicators, pesticide importation statistics, and list of accredited fertilizer/pesticide researchers; some available upon request and some via the Internet home page **Photocopy:** No

2213   Quezon City, Philippines
Department of Environment and Natural
     Resources (DENR)

Library
Visayas Avenue, Diliman
Quezon City 1100
Founded: 1974 **Type:** Government **Head:** Rosita O. De Guzman *Phone:* +63(2) 976626 ext 237 **Staff:** 5 Prof. 2 Other **Holdings:** 500 books 45 journals **Subjects:** Aquaculture, Forestry **Loan:** In country **Photocopy:** No

2214   Quezon City, Philippines
Department of Environment and Natural
     Resources, Bureau of Mines and
     Geo-Sciences (DENR)
Library
North Avenue
Diliman
Quezon City 1104
Fax: +63(2) 920-1635 **Email:** denr-mine@psdn.org.ph

Former Name: Department of Natural Resources **Founded:** 1950 **Type:** Government **Head:** Corazon M. Camat *Phone:* +63(2) 928-8344 *Email:* denr-mine@psdn.org.ph **Staff:** 2 Prof. 2 Other **Holdings:** 2,800 books 25 journals **Language of Collection/Services:** English **Subjects:** Agricultural Economics, Education/Extension, Forestry, Geology, Metallurgy, Mining, Soil Science, Water Resources **Loan:** In country **Service:** In country **Photocopy:** Yes

2215   Quezon City, Philippines
National Irrigation Administration (NIA)
Library
NIA Building, EDSA, Diliman
Quezon City 1100
Founded: 1976 **Type:** Government **Head:** Ambrosia A. Salcedo *Phone:* +63(2) 928-4287, 929-6071 ext 154 **Staff:** 1 Prof. **Holdings:** 2,800 books 6 journals **Specializations:** Irrigation **Loan:** In country **Photocopy:** Yes

2216   Quezon City, Philippines
Philippine Coconut Authority (PCA)
Library
Elliptical Road
Diliman
Quezon City 1100
Phone: +63(2) 928-4501/9 ext 212, 213 **Fax:** +63(2) 921-6173

Former Name: Philippine Coconut Administration (PHIL-COA) **Founded:** 1954 **Type:** Government **Head:** Harley Belarte Tuando *Phone:* +63(2) 928-4501/9 **Staff:** 1 Prof. 1 Other **Holdings:** 7,000 books 35 journals **Language of Collection/Services:** English / English, Filipino **Subjects:** Coconuts **Loan:** Internationally **Photocopy:** Yes

2217   Quezon City, Philippines
Sugar Regulatory Administration (SRA)
Library Division
PO Box 70, U.P., Diliman
Quezon City 1101
Location: North Avenue, Diliman **Phone:** +63(2) 990661 ext 214, 263

Former Name: Philippine Sugar Institute, Philippine Sugar Commission **Founded:** 1953 **Head:** Prescy S. David *Phone:*

+63(2) 990661/9 **Type:** Government **Staff:** 4 Prof. 2 Other **Holdings:** 9,020 books 70 journals **Language of Collection/Services:** English **Subjects:** Agriculture (Tropics), Agricultural Economics, Agricultural Engineering, Food Sciences, Plant Pathology, Soil Science **Specializations:** Sugar **Loan:** Inhouse **Service:** Inhouse **Photocopy:** Yes

2218   San Augustin, Pili, Philippines
Department of Agriculture
Region V Library
San Augustin, Pili, Camarines Sur

Type: Government **Head:** Ms. Emily B. Balilo *Phone:* +63 (54) 35254 **Staff:** 1 Prof. 2 Other **Holdings:** 800 books **Subjects:** Animal Husbandry, Crops, Fisheries, Plant Protection, Soil Science

2219   Tanay, Philippines
Rizal College of Agriculture and Technology
Library
Sampaloc
Tanay, Rizal 3138

Founded: 1959 **Type:** Academic **Staff:** 1 Prof. **Holdings:** 2,000+ books 11 journals **Subjects:** Agricultural Economics, Agricultural Engineering, Horticulture, Soil Science, Zoology **Loan:** Do not loan **Photocopy:** Yes

2220   Tuguegarao, Philippines
Department of Agriculture, Region Field Unit No. 2 (DA, RFU 2)
Agricultural Library
Nursery Compound
Tuguegarao, Cagayan 3500
Fax: +63(78) 844-1031

Founded: 1977 **Type:** Government **Head:** Ms. Gloria R. de Yro *Phone:* +63(78) 844-1324 ext 1312 **Staff:** 2 Prof. 6 Other **Holdings:** 3,453 books 1,152 journals **Language of Collection/Services:** English / English **Subjects:** Agricultural Engineering, Animal Husbandry, Environment, Extension, Fisheries, Forestry, Home Economics, Horticulture, Nutrition, Pest Management, Soil **Loan:** Do not loan **Photocopy:** Yes

2221   Victoria, Philippines
Mindoro State College of Agriculture and Technology (MinSCAT)
Library
Victoria, Oriental Mindoro 5205

Former Name: Mindoro College of Agriculture and Technology **Type:** Academic **Head:** Norma M. Caoli *Phone:* +63(912) 334-0292 **Staff:** 1 Prof. 1 Other **Language of Collection/Services:** English, Filipino / English, Filipino **Subjects:** Plants **Databases Developed:** Abstracts of research in agriculture and abstracts of theses **Loan:** Inhouse **Photocopy:** Yes

2222   Virac, Philippines
Catanduanes State College (CSC)
College Main Library (CML)
Virac, Catanduanes 4800

Founded: 1972 **Type:** Academic **Head:** Araceli T. Mendez *Phone:* +63(52) 811-1485 **Staff:** 3 Prof. 21 Other **Holdings:** 17,469 books **Language of Collection/Services:** English / English **Subjects:** Comprehensive **Loan:** Inhouse **Photocopy:** Yes

Poland

2223   Balice, Poland
National Research Institute of Animal Production
Main Library
32-083 Balice, k. Krakowa

Phone: +48(12) 285-6777 ext 447 **Fax:** +48(12) 285-6733 **Email:** izooinfo@izoo.krakow.pl **WWW:** www.izoo.krakow.pl

Non-English Name: Instytut Zootechniki (IZ), Biblioteka Główna **Former Name:** National Institute of Animal Production **Founded:** 1950 **Type:** Research **Head:** Mariola Kaczanowska **Staff:** 4 Prof. 3 Other **Holdings:** 13,045 books 103 journals **Language of Collection/Services:** Polish / Polish **Subjects:** Animal Husbandry **Specializations:** Animal Breeding, Animal Nutrition, Animal Physiology **Loan:** In country **Service:** In country **Photocopy:** Yes

2224   Bialowieza, Poland
Forestry Research Institute, Natural Forest Department
Library
6 Park Dyrekcyjny Str.
17-230 Bialowieza

Phone: +48(85) 681-2396 **Fax:** +48(85) 681-2203 **Email:** office@las.ibl.bialowieza.pl

Non-English Name: Instytut Badawczy Lesnictwa, Zaklad Lasów Naturalnych (IBL), Biblioteka **Founded:** 1937 **Type:** Government **Head:** Prof. Dr. A.W. Sokolowski **Staff:** 1 Prof. **Holdings:** 8,800 books 120 journals **Language of Collection/Services:** Polish / Polish **Subjects:** Entomology, Nature Conservation, Soil Science, Water Resources **Specializations:** Forestry **Loan:** In country **Service:** In country **Photocopy:** Yes

2225   Bialowieza, Poland
Polish Academy of Sciences, Mammal Research Institute
Library
17-230 Bialowieza

Phone: +48(85) 681-2287 **Fax:** +48(85) 681-2289 **Email:** library@bison.zbs.bialowieza.pl **WWW:** bison.zbs.bialowieza.pl

Non-English Name: Polska Akademia Nauk, Zaklad Badania Ssaków (PAN, ZBS), Biblioteka **Founded:** 1953 **Type:** Research **Head:** Malgorzata Rychlik **Staff:** 2 Prof. **Holdings:** 6,000 books 900 journals **Language of Collection/Services:** Polish, English **Subjects:** Ecology, Mammalogy, Zoology **Specializations:** European Bison and Hybrids **Loan:** Internationally **Service:** Internationally **Photocopy:** Yes

2226   Blonie, Poland
Plant Breeding and Acclimatization Institute
    Radzików
Scientific and Technical Information, Scientific
    Library
Radzików k. Warszawy
05-870 Blonie

Phone: +48(22) 725-3611 **Fax:** +48(22) 725-4714 **Email:**
postbox@ihar.edu.pl

Non-English Name: Instytut Hodowli i Aklimatyzacji
Roslin (IHAR), Dzial Informacji Naukowo-Technicznej,
Biblioteka Naukowa (B. Nauk.) **Founded:** 1951 **Type:** Government **Head:** Anna Iwona Sobczak *Email:* a.i.sobczak@
ihar.edu.pl **Staff:** 3 Prof. 1 Other **Holdings:** 10,000 books
120 journals **Language of Collection/Services:** Polish / Polish **Subjects:** Plant Genetics, Plant Breeding, Plant Pathology, Plant Physiology, Seed Production **Loan:** In country
Service: In country **Photocopy:** No

2227   Bonin, Poland
Plant Breeding and Acclimatization Institute -
    Branch Division Bonin
Science Information and Publication Division
76-009 Bonin, k. Koszalina

Phone: +48(94) 342-3031 **Fax:** +48(94) 342-7028 **Email:**
iziem@man.koszalin.pl **WWW:** www.ihar.edu.pl

Non-English Name: Instytut Hodowli i Aklimatyzacji Ros-
lin - Oddzial Bonin (IHAR-Bonin), Dzial Informacji Naukowej i Wydawnictw (DINiW) **Former Name:** Institute for
Potato Research, Zaklad Informacji Naukow-Technicznej i
Upowszechniania Postepu **Founded:** 1966 **Type:** Government **Head:** Mgr. Bogumila Wasilewska **Staff:** 2 Prof. 4
Other **Holdings:** 12,920 books 218 journals **Language of
Collection/Services:** Polish, English / Polish **Subjects:** Agricultural Economics, Biotechnology, Crops, Entomology,
Plant Pathology, Plants **Specializations:** Potatoes **Loan:** In
country **Service:** In country **Photocopy:** No

2228   Brwinów, Poland
National Advisory Centre for Agriculture and
    Rural Development (NACARD)
Library
ul. Pszczelinska 99
05-840 Brwinów

Phone: +48(22) 729-6634 ext 222 **Fax:** +48(22) 729-7251
Email: brwinow-biblioteka@cdr.gov.pl **WWW:** www.cdr.
gov.pl

Non-English Name: Krajowe Centrum Doradztwa Rozwoju
Rolnictwa i Obszarów Wiejskich (KCDRRiOW), Biblioteka
Former Name: Centralny Osrodek Oswiaty i Postepu w
Rolnictwie **Founded:** 1947 **Type:** Government **Head:** Mat-
gorzata Ustymowicz **Staff:** 2 Prof. **Holdings:** 20,000 books
45 journals **Language of Collection/Services:** Polish **Subjects:** Agribusiness, Agricultural Economics **Specializations:** Education/Extension **Loan:** In country **Service:** In
country **Photocopy:** Yes

2229   Bydgoszcz, Poland
Central Agricultural Library in Warsaw,
    Bydgoszcz Branch

PO Box 603
85-950 Bydgoszcz

Location: Pl. Weyssenhoffa 11, 85-072 Bydgoszcz **Fax:**
+48(52) 223909 **WWW:** www.cbr.edu.pl

Non-English Name: Centralna Biblioteka Rolnicza w War-
zawie, Oddziat w Bydgoszczy (CBR) **Founded:** 1955 **Type:**
Government **Head:** Anna Pilarska *Phone:* +48(52) 223909
Staff: 8 Prof. 1 Other **Holdings:** 36,110 books 200 journals
Language of Collection/Services: Polish / Polish **Subjects:**
Comprehensive **Loan:** In country **Service:** In country **Pho-
tocopy:** Yes

2230   Bydgoszcz, Poland
University of Technology and Agriculture (UTA)
Main Library
ul. prof. S. Kaliskiego 7
85-796 Bydgoszcz

Phone: +48(52) 440-8077 **Fax:** +48(52) 340-8063 **Email:**
bibinfo@atr.bydgszcz.pl **WWW:** www.bg.atr.bydgoszcz.
pl **OPAC:** telnet://bib.atr.bydgszcz.pl - login: tinlib;
password: tinlib

Non-English Name: Akademia Techniczno-Rolnicza
(ATR), Biblioteka Glówna **Founded:** 1969 **Type:** Academic
Head: Jan Kubinski *Email:* bibatr@atr.bydgoszcz.pl *Phone:*
+48(52) 340-8090 **Staff:** 40 Prof. 1 Other **Holdings:** 520
journals 145,000 books **Language of Collection/Services:**
Polish / Polish, English **Subjects:** Agricultural Economics,
Agricultural Engineering, Animal Husbandry, Crops, Ento-
mology, Horticulture, Plant Pathology, Plants, Soil Science,
Water Resources **Databases Used:** Agris **Loan:** In country
Service: In country **Photocopy:** Yes

2231   Jablonna, Poland
Polish Academy of Sciences, Jan Kielanowski
    Institute of Animal Physiology and Nutrition
Scientific Library
Instytucka 3
05-110 Jablonna, near Warsaw

Phone: +48(22) 782-4037, 782-4422 **Fax:** +48(22) 774-
2038 **Email:** infizyz@atos.warman.com.pl **WWW:** ciuw.
warman.net.pl/alf/infizyz/index_eng.html

Non-English Name: Polska Akademia Nauk, Instytut Fizjologii i Zywienia Zwierzat im. Jana Kielanowskiego Pan,
Biblioteka **Founded:** 1955 **Type:** Academic **Staff:** 1 Prof. 1
Other **Holdings:** 4,600 books 120 journals **Subjects:** Animal
Husbandry, Biotechnology, Veterinary Medicine **Specializations:** Animal Nutrition, Animal Physiology, Endocrinology, Microbiology, Reproduction, Rumen **Loan:** In country

2232   Katowice, Poland
Institute for Ecology of Industrial Areas
Library
6 Kossutha St.
40-832 Katowice

Phone: +48(32) 254-6251 **Fax:** +48(32) 254-1717 **Email:**
ietu@ietu.katowice.pl **WWW:** www.ietu.us.edu.pl

Non-English Name: Instytut Ekologii Terenów Uprzemy-
slowionych (IETU), Biblioteka **Former Name:** Institute of
Environmental Protection, Instytut Ochrony Srodowiska
Type: Government **Head:** Halina Griger *Email:* h.griger@

ietu.katowice.pl **Staff:** 2 Prof. **Holdings:** 690 books 20 journals **Language of Collection/Services:** Polish / Polish **Subjects:** Agriculture (Polluted Areas), Pollution **Loan:** In country **Service:** In country **Photocopy:** No

2233   Kórnik, Poland
Polish Academy of Sciences, Institute of
    Dendrology
Library
Ul. Parkowa 5
62-035 Kórnik
Phone: +48(61) 817-0033 **Fax:** +48(61) 817-0166 **Email:** idkornik@rose.man.poznan.pl

Non-English Name: Polska Akademia Nauk, Instytut Dendrologi (PAN, ID), Biblioteka **Founded:** 1933 **Type:** Government **Head:** Elzbieta Nowak **Staff:** 3 Prof. **Holdings:** 25,500 books 28 journals **Language of Collection/Services:** English / Polish **Subjects:** Forestry, Horticulture, Ornamental Woody Plants, Silvicultural Characters, Woody Plants **Specializations:** Silvicultural Characters **Databases Used:** TREECD **Loan:** In country **Service:** In country **Photocopy:** Yes

2234   Kraków, Poland
Central Laboratory of Tobacco Industry
Library
Al. Jana Pawla II 190
31-982 Kraków
Phone: +48(12) 644-3200 **Fax:** +48(12) 644-5970

Non-English Name: Centralne Laboratorium Przemyslu Tytoniowego (CLPT), Biblioteka **Founded:** 1962 **Type:** Government **Head:** Mgr. Lucyna Zamorska **Staff:** 1 Prof. **Holdings:** 4,942 books 30 journals **Language of Collection/Services:** Polish / Polish **Subjects:** Tobacco **Loan:** In country **Service:** Internationally **Photocopy:** Yes

2235   Kraków, Poland
H. Kollataj Agricultural University in Krakow
Main Library
Al. Mickiewicza 24/28
30-059 Kraków
Phone: +48(12) 633-3341 **Fax:** +48(12) 633-3341 **Email:** library@ar.krakow.pl **WWW:** www.ar.krakow.pl/bibl/biblfr.htm **OPAC:** telnet://victoria.uci.agh.edu.pl

Non-English Name: Akademia Rolnicza im. H. Kollataja w Krakowie (AR), Biblioteka Glówna **Founded:** 1954 **Type:** Academic **Head:** mgr. inz. Ewa Turczynska *Email:* eturczyn @ar.krakow.pl **Staff:** 27 Prof. 8 Other **Holdings:** 331,000 books 553 journals **Language of Collection/Services:** Polish, English / Polish **Subjects:** Comprehensive **Specializations:** Agriculture (History - Poland), Wildlife **Databases Developed:** Polish agricultural prints to 1900 **Databases Used:** Comprehensive **Loan:** Internationally **Service:** In country **Photocopy:** Yes

2236   Kraków, Poland
Polish Academy of Sciences, Botanical Institute,
    Jagiellonian University, Wladyslaw Szafer
    Institute of Botany
Library

ul. Lubicz 46
31-512 Kraków
Phone: +48(12) 421-5144 ext 246 **Fax:** +48(12) 421-9790 **Email:** mnowak@ib-pan.krakow.pl **WWW:** www.ib-pan.krakow.pl

Non-English Name: Polska Akademia Nauk (PAN), Universytet Jagiellonski, Instytut Botaniki im. Wladyslawa Szafera (IB), Biblioteka **Founded:** 1798 **Head:** dr. hab. Andrzej Jankun *Phone:* +48 (12) 421-5144 ext 218 *Email:* jankun@grodzki.phils.uj.edu.pl **Type:** Academic **Staff:** 6 Prof. 2 Other **Holdings:** 163,510 books 848 journals **Language of Collection/Services:** Polish, English/Polish **Subjects:** Biotechnology, Agriculture (Tropics), Forestry, Horticulture, Plant Pathology, Soil Science **Specializations:** Algology, Botany, Ecology, Mycology, Plant Protection, Palynology, Paleobotany, Physiology **Loan:** Internationally **Service:** Inhouse **Photocopy:** Yes

2237   Kraków, Poland
Polish Academy of Sciences, Franciszek Gorski
    Department of Plant Physiology
Library
Slawkowska 17
31-016 Kraków
Phone: +48(12) 227944 **Fax:** +48(12) 217901

Non-English Name: Polska Akademia Nauk, Zaklad Fizjologii Roslin im. Franciszka Górskiego, Biblioteka **Type:** Research **Staff:** 1 Prof. **Holdings:** 5,500 books 34 journals **Language of Collection/Services:** English/Polish **Subjects:** Crops, Photobiology, Plant Ecology, Plant Physiology **Loan:** Internationally **Service:** Internationally **Photocopy:** Yes

2238   Lublin, Poland
Polish Academy of Sciences, Institute of
    Agrophysics
Library
PO Box 201
20-290 Lublin 27
Location: Doswiadczalna 4 **Phone:** +48(81) 744-5061 **Fax:** +48(81) 744-5067 **Email:** agrof@demeter.ipan.lublin.pl **WWW:** www.ipan.lublin.pl

Non-English Name: Polska Akademia Nauk, Instytut Agrofizyki im. B. Dobrzanskiego (PAN, IA), Biblioteka **Type:** Research **Staff:** 1 Prof. **Holdings:** 2,500 books 40 journals **Language of Collection/Services:** English/Polish **Subjects:** Plants, Soil Biology, Soil Chemistry, Soil Mechanics, Soil Physics **Loan:** In country **Service:** In country **Photocopy:** Yes

2239   Lomianki, Poland
Polish Academy of Sciences, Institute of Ecology
Library
Dziekanów Lesny k/W-wy
05-092 Lomianki
Phone: +48(7) 513046 **Fax:** +48(7) 513046 **Email:** ekolog @warman.com.pl

Non-English Name: Polska Akademia Nauk, Instytut Ekologii (PAN, IE), Biblioteka **Founded:** 1953 **Type:** Research **Head:** Ewa Uchmanska *Email:* ekotom@polbox.com **Staff:**

3 Prof. 2 Other **Holdings:** 3,700 books 150 journals **Language of Collection/Services:** English / Polish **Subjects:** Ecology, Ecotoxicology, Environment, Hydrobiology, Soil, Plants, Pollution **Loan:** Internationally **Service:** Internationally **Photocopy:** Yes

2240   Kraków, Poland
            Polish Academy of Sciences, Institute of Nature
            Conservation
            Library
            Ul. Lubicz 46
            31-512 Kraków
Phone: +48(12) 215144 ext 275 **Fax:** +48(12) 210348
WWW: botan.ib-pan.krakow.pl/przyroda/incpas.htm

Non-English Name: Polska Akademia Nauk, Instytut Ochrony Przyrody, Biblioteka **Type:** Research **Staff:** 2 Prof. **Holdings:** 18,000 books 850 journals **Language of Collection/Services:** Polish / Polish **Subjects:** Acid Rain, Human Ecology, Air Pollution, Biological Control, Pollution, Protection of Forests, Soil Science **Specializations:** Botany, Ecology, Geography, Geology, National Parks, Nature Conservation, Reserved Areas, Water Resources, Zoology **Service:** In country **Loan:** In country **Photocopy:** No

2241   Kraków, Poland
            Polish Academy of Sciences, Institute of
            Systematics and Evolution of Animals
            ul. Slawkowska 17
            31-016 Kraków
Fax: +48(12) 422-4294 **Email:** office@isez.pan.krakow.pl

Non-English Name: Polska Akademia Nauk, Instytut Systematyki i Ewolucji Zwierzat **Former Name:** Institute of Systematic and Experimental Zoology **Founded:** 1870 **Type:** Government **Head:** Jolanta Palkowa *Phone:* +48(12) 422-7066 ext 219 *Email:* palka@isez.pan.krakow.pl **Staff:** 2 Prof. **Holdings:** 45,700 books 60 journals **Language of Collection/Services:** Polish, English / Polish **Subjects:** Biology, Entomology, Evolution, Paleontology, Taxonomy, Zoology **Loan:** In country **Service:** In country **Photocopy:** Yes

2242   Kraków, Poland
            Polish Academy of Sciences, K. Starmach
            Institute of Freshwater Biology
            Library
            Slawkowska 17
            31-016 Kraków
Phone: +48(12) 215082 **Fax:** +48(12) 222115

Non-English Name: Polska Akademia Nauk, Zaklad Biologii Wód im. K. Starmacha, Biblioteka **Former Name:** Institute of Freshwater Biology **Type:** Research **Staff:** 35 Prof. 15 Other **Holdings:** 29,000 books 50 journals **Language of Collection/Services:** Polish, English/Polish **Subjects:** Limnology, Hydrobiology, Algology, Ichthyology, Water, Microbiology **Photocopy:** Yes **Loan:** In country **Service:** In country

2243   Lublin, Poland
            University of Agriculture (UA)
            Main Library
            ul. 1, Radziszewskiego 11

            20-036 Lublin
Phone: +48(81) 445-6228 **Fax:** +48(81) 445 6229 **Email:** jalub@eos.umcs.lublin.pl **WWW:** priam.umcs.lublin.pl/ar/index.htm **OPAC:** telnet://priam.umcs.lublin.pl

Non-English Name: Akademia Rolnicza (AR), Biblioteka Glówna (BG) **Founded:** 1955 **Type:** Academic **Head:** Marta Kêsik *Email:* agrobibl@eos.umcs.lublin.pl **Staff:** 42 Prof. 1 Other **Holdings:** 220,000 books 1,500 journals **Language of Collection/Services:** Polish / Polish **Subjects:** Comprehensive **Specializations:** Biotechnology, Food Sciences, Horticulture, Soil Science, Veterinary Medicine **Databases Developed:** Bibliography of publications from Agricultural University - Lublin; available via Internet at prace.ar.lublin.pl/index.htm **Databases Used:** CABCD; Derwent Biotechnology Abstracts; FSTA; SIGZ **Loan:** Internationally **Service:** Internationally **Photocopy:** Yes

2244   Mroków, Poland
            Polish Academy of Sciences, Institute of Genetics
            and Animal Breeding
            Library
            Jastrzebiec
            05-551 Mroków
Phone: +48(22) 756-1711 **Fax:** +48(22) 756-1699 **Email:** panighz@atos.warman.com.pl **WWW:** ciuw.warman.net.pl/alf/igab

Non-English Name: Polska Akademia Nauk, Instytut Genetyki i Hodowli Zwierzat (PAN, IGiHZ), Biblioteka **Founded:** 1955 **Type:** Research **Head:** Maria Nowaczewska **Staff:** 1 Prof. **Holdings:** 6,470 books 131 journals **Language of Collection/Services:** Polish, English **Subjects:** Animal Husbandry, Biotechnology, Genetics, Veterinary Medicine **Databases Used:** Current Contents **Loan:** In country **Service:** Internationally **Photocopy:** Yes

2245   Olsztyn, Poland
            Warmia and Masuria University in Olsztyn
            Main Library
            ul. M. Oczapowskiego 4
            10-957 Olsztyn
Phone: +48(89) 523-3309 **Fax:** +48(89) 523-3882 **Email:** bib.post@art.olsztyn.pl**OPAC:** bart.uwm.edu.pl:4505/ALEPH/POL/ART/ART/ART/sysale **WWW:** www.art.olsztyn.pl

Non-English Name: Uniwersytet Warminsko-Mazurski w Olsztynie (UWM), Biblioteka Glówna **Former Name:** Olsztyn University of Agriculture and Technology, Akademia Rolniczo-Techniczna w Olsztynie (AR-T), Wyzsza Szkola Rolnicza **Founded:** 1951 **Type:** Academic **Head:** mgr. Irena Suchta *Email:* irenas@uwm.olsztyn.pl **Staff:** 34 Prof. 22 Other **Holdings:** 360,000 books 996 journals **Language of Collection/Services:** Polish/Polish, English **Subjects:** Agricultural Engineering, Animal Husbandry, Civil Engineering, Biology, Computer Science, Environmental Protection, Fisheries, Management, Marketing, Veterinary Medicine, Water Conservation **Specializations:** Agribusiness, Biotechnology, Ecology, Food Sciences, Property **Databases Developed:** Database of on-going and completed research; bibliography of publications of Olsztyn University researchers **Databases Used:** Comprehensive **Loan:** Internationally **Service:** In country **Photocopy:** Yes

2246   Olsztyn-Kortowo, Poland
Inland Fisheries Institute
Library and Scientific Information
ul. Michala Oczapowskiego 10
10-719 Olsztyn-Kortowo

Phone: +48(89) 527-3171 **Fax:** +48(89) 527-2505 **Email:** irs@art.olsztyn.pl

Non-English Name: Instytut Rybactwa Sródladowego (IRS), Biblioteka i Informacja Naukowa **Type:** Government **Founded:** 1951 **Head:** Jadinga Zdaksaska **Staff:** 3 Prof. **Holdings:** 19,900 books 151 journals **Language of Collection/Services:** English, Polish, German, French, Russian/ Polish, English, Russian **Subjects:** Fish Culture, Fishes, Hydrobiology, Water **Specializations:** Fisheries **Databases Developed:** SIGZ-IR - 10,000+ records on inland fisheries, biology of freshwater fish culture, hydrobiology and water ecology. **Databases Used:** Agris; ASFA **Loan:** In country **Service:** In country **Photocopy:** No

2247   Paledzie, Poland
National Research Institute of Animal Production, Poultry Research Branch at Zakrzewo near Poznan (NRIAP, PRB)
Library
Zakrzewo k/Poznania
ul. Poznanska 11
62-069 Paledzie

Phone: +48(61) 814-3011 **Fax:** +48(61) 814-3011 **Email:** cobrd@rose.man.poznan.pl **WWW:** www.izobd.poznan.pl

Non-English Name: Instytut Zootechniki, Oddzial Badawczy Drobiarstwa w Zakrzewie k. Poznania (IZ, OBD), Biblioteka **Former Name:** Poultry Research and Development Center, Branch Center for Scientific, Technical and Economical Information **Founded:** 1952 **Type:** Research **Head:** Krystyna Gawecka *Email:* center@izobd.poznan.pl **Staff:** 4 Prof. **Holdings:** 9,500 books 112 journals **Language of Collection/Services:** Polish / Polish **Subjects:** Animal Husbandry, Poultry **Specializations:** Animal Breeding, Animal Genetics, Egg Production, Egg Products, Poultry Industry, Poultry Products **Loan:** In country **Service:** In country **Photocopy:** Yes

2248   Poznan, Poland
Central Research Laboratory of Food Concentrates Industry "KONCLAB"
Center of Scientific, Technological and Economic Information
ul. Starolecka 40
61-361 Poznan

Phone: +48(61) 879-3241, 879-3472 **Fax:** +48(61) 879-3483 **Email:** remi@man.poznan.pl **WWW:** rose.man. poznan.pl/informator96

Non-English Name: Centralne Laboratorium Przemyslu Koncentratów Spozywczych "KONCLAB" (CLPKS KONCLAB), Branzowy Osrodek Informacji Naukowej, Technicznej i Ekonomicznej (BOINTE) **Founded:** 1962 **Type:** Research **Head:** Iwona Blasinska *Phone:* +48(61) 879-3241 ext 305 **Staff:** 2 Prof. 3 Other **Holdings:** 1,660 books 63 journals **Language of Collection/Services:** Polish, English/ Polish **Subjects:** Biotechnology, Food Additives, Food Sciences, Food Packaging, Food Technology **Specializations:**

Beverages, Cereals, Coffee, Convenience Foods, Desserts, Dietetic Foods, Extractives, Infant Foods **Databases Developed:** ITER - bibliographic database covering food science and technology for years 1980-1986; CL - bibliographic database covering food science and technology from 1992 to date; PROD - bibliographic database covering food industry producers from 1992 to date; MASZYN - database covering technical equipment for food industry from 1995 to date **Databases Used:** Agris; Food and Human Nutrition; FSTA **Loan:** In country **Service:** In country **Photocopy:** Yes

2249   Poznan, Poland
Industrial Institute of Agricultural Engineering Branch Center of Scientific, Technical and Economical Information
ul. Starolecka 31
60-963 Poznan

Fax: +48(61) 879 3262 **Email:** office@pimr.poznan.pl **WWW:** www.pimr.poznan.pl

Non-English Name: Przemyslowy Instytut Maszyn Rolniczych (PIMR), Branzowy Osrodek Informacji Naukowej, Technicznej i Ekonomicznej (BOINTE) **Former Name:** Institute of Agricultural Engineering, Instytut Maszyn Rolniczych **Founded:** 1954 **Type:** Government **Head:** Mr. Tadeusz Pawlicki *Email:* pawlicki@pimr.poznan.pl *Phone:* +48(61) 876 5517 **Staff:** 5 Prof. 1 Other **Holdings:** 130,000 books 310 journals **Language of Collection/Services:** Polish/Polish, English **Subjects:** Agricultural Engineering **Specializations:** Equipment, Tractors **Databases Developed:** Agrimach Multimedia - agricultural machinery database; available via internet at www.agrimach.com **Loan:** In country **Service:** Internationally **Photocopy:** Yes

2250   Poznan, Poland
Institute of Medicinal Plants
Scientific and Technical Information Section
ul. Libelta 27
61-707 Poznan

Phone: +48(61) 852-4003 **Fax:** +48(61) 852-7463 **Email:** jg-iripz@man.poznan.pl

Non-English Name: Instytut Roslin i Przetworów Zielarskich (IRiPZ), Branzowy Osrodek Informacji Naukowo-Technicznej (BOINT) **Founded:** 1948 **Type:** Government **Head:** Joanna Gilewicz **Staff:** 2 Prof. **Holdings:** 13,000 books 100 journals **Language of Collection/Services:** Polish **Subjects:** Medicinal Plants **Databases Developed:** HERBA - bibliographic database of medicinal plants **Loan:** Inhouse **Service:** In country **Photocopy:** No

2251   Poznan, Poland
Institute of Natural Fibres
Scientific Information Centre
ul. Wojska Polskiego 71 b
60-630 Poznan

Phone: +48(61) 822-4815 **Fax:** +48(61) 841-7830 **Email:** boint@iwn.inf.poznan.pl **WWW:** iwn.inf.poznan.pl

Non-English Name: Instytut Wlókien Naturalnych (IWN), Zaklad Informacji Naukowej i Technicznej **Former Name:** Instytut Krajowych Wlokien Naturalnych, Branzowy Osrodek Informacji Naukowej, Technicznej i Ekonomicznej

(BOINTE) **Founded:** 1945 **Type:** Research **Head:** Dobrostawa Gucia (Information Centre); Irena Wojciechowska (Library) *Email:* dgucia@iwn.inf.poznan.pl **Staff:** 6 Prof. **Holdings:** 20,196 books 7,406 journals **Language of Collection/Services:** Polish, English, German, Russian / Polish **Subjects:** Bast Fibers, Fibers, Fire Resistance, Flax, Hemp, Lignocellulose, Moisture Resistance, Natural Fibers, Silk, Toxic Substances, Waste Utilization, Wool **Databases Developed:** Unpublished scientific research of institute **Loan:** Internationally **Service:** Internationally **Photocopy:** Yes

2252 Poznan, Poland
Plant Protection Institute (PPI)
Library
ul. Miczurina 20
60-318 Poznan

Phone: +48(61) 864-9025 **Fax:** +48(61) 867-6301 **Email:** biblioteka@ior.poznan.pl **WWW:** www.ior.poznan.pl **OPAC:** www.ior.poznan.pl

Non-English Name: Instytut Ochrony Roslin (IOR), Biblioteka **Founded:** 1951 **Type:** Research **Head:** Olga Brzezinska-Gabler *Phone:* +48 (61) 864-9172 **Holdings:** 25,000 books 120 journals **Staff:** 5 Prof. **Language of Collection/Services:** Polish, English, Russian / Polish, English, Russian **Subjects:** Biochemistry, Ecology, Entomology, Environmental Protection, Plant Pathology, Plant Protection, Pollution **Databases Used:** Comprehensive **Loan:** Internationally **Service:** Internationally **Photocopy:** Yes

2253 Poznan, Poland
Polish Academy of Sciences, Institute of Plant
    Genetics
Library
ul. Strzeszynska 34
60-479 Poznan

Phone: +48(61) 823-3511 **Fax:** +48(61) 823-3671 **Email:** library@igr.poznan.pl **WWW:** www.igr.poznan.pl

Non-English Name: Polska Akademia Nauk, Instytut Genetyki Roslin (PAN, IGR), Biblioteka **Type:** Academic **Head:** Barbara Sadowska *Phone:* +48(61) 823-3511 ext 213 **Staff:** 2 Prof. **Holdings:** 35,000 books 140 journals **Language of Collection/Services:** Polish, English/Polish, English **Databases Used:** Current Contents; Life Science Collection **Subjects:** Biotechnology, Plant Genetics, Plant Pathology, Plants **Loan:** Internationally **Service:** Internationally **Photocopy:** Yes

2254 Poznan, Poland
Polish Academy of Sciences, Research Center for
    Agricultural and Forest Environment (PAS,
    RCAFE)
Library
Bukowska Street 19
60-809 Poznan

Phone: +48(61) 847-5601 **Fax:** +48(61) 847-3668 **Email:** zbsril@man.poznan.pl

Non-English Name: Polska Akademia Nauk, Zaklad Badan Srodowiska Rolniczego i Lesnego (PAN, ZBSRiL), Biblioteka **Former Name:** Department of Agrobiology and Forestry **Founded:** 1975 **Type:** Government **Head:** Prof. dr.

hab. Lech Ryszkowski *Email:* ryszagro@man.poznan.pl *Phone:* +48(61) 847-5603 **Staff:** 1 Prof. **Holdings:** 7,120 books **Language of Collection/Services:** English / Polish **Subjects:** Ecology, Forest Ecology **Specializations:** Environmental Protection, Soil Science, Water Resources **Loan:** In country **Service:** In country **Photocopy:** Yes

2255 Poznan, Poland
Starch and Potato Products Research Laboratory
Centre for Information and Documentation
ul. Zwierzyniecka 18
60-814 Poznan

Phone: +48(61) 866-8045 **Fax:** +48(61) 841-7610 **Email:** clpz@man.poznan.pl **WWW:** www.clpz.poznan.pl

Non-English Name: Centralne Laboratorium Przemyslu Ziemniaczanego (CLPZ), Branzowy Osrodek Informacji Naukowej, Technicznej i Ekonomicznej (BOINTE) **Founded:** 1962 **Type:** Research **Head:** Ms. Bogumila Ratajczak *Email:* rataj@man.poznan.pl **Staff:** 4 Prof. **Holdings:** 24 journals 19,060 books **Language of Collection/Services:** Polish / Polish **Subjects:** Food Sciences **Specializations:** Potatoes, Starch **Databases Developed:** InfoStarch - food technology, potato, starch information; local access; FIRMA - food products and machinery manufacturers in Poland; access via CD-ROM **Databases Used:** BAZVUP; FSTA **Service:** In country **Loan:** In country **Photocopy:** Yes

2256 Poznan, Poland
University of Agriculture in Poznan
Main Library and Center of Scientific Information
ul. Witosa 45
60-667 Poznan

Phone: +48(61) 848-7810 **Fax:** +48(61) 858-7802 **WWW:** swan.au.poznan.pl **OPAC:** 150.254.174.29/arka-cn.htm

Non-English Name: Akademia Rolnicza w Poznaniu (AR), Biblioteka Glówna i Centrum Informacji Naukowej **Former Name:** Wyzsza Szkola Rolnicza w Poznaniu **Founded:** 1952 **Type:** Academic **Head:** Wlodzimierz Golab *Phone:* +48(61) 848-7809 *Email:* wgolab@owl.au.poznan.pl **Staff:** 42 Prof. 4 Other **Holdings:** 648,000 books 1,000 journals **Language of Collection/Services:** Polish, English / Polish, English **Subjects:** Agriculture (Tropics), Agribusiness, Agricultural Development, Agricultural Economics, Agricultural Engineering, Animal Husbandry, Biotechnology, Crops, Education/Extension, Entomology, Farming, Fisheries, Food Sciences, Horticulture, Plant Pathology, Plants, Forestry, Soil Science, Veterinary Medicine, Water Resources, Wood Technology **Networks:** Horizon **Databases Developed:** Database of Polish periodical artical concerning nature and science **Databases Used:** Agris **Loan:** Internationally **Service:** Inhouse **Photocopy:** Yes

2257 Pulawy, Poland
Fertilizers Research Institute
Branch Center of Scientific and Technological
    Information
24-110 Pulawy

Location: al. 1000-lecia Panstwa Polskiego 13a **Phone:** +48(81) 887-6444 **Fax:** +48(81) 887-6566 **Email:** inte@atena.ins.pulawy.pl **WWW:** www.ins.pulawy.pl **OPAC:** 212.244.50.131/katalogi.htm

Non-English Name: Instytut Nawozow Sztucznych (INS), Branzowy Osrodek Informacji Naukowej, Technicznej i Ekonomicznej (BOINTE) **Founded:** 1958 **Type:** Government **Head:** Alicja Stolecka *Phone:* +48(831) 887-6609 **Staff:** 2 Prof. 1 Other **Holdings:** 1,500 books 20 journals **Language of Collection/Services:** Polish / Polish **Subjects:** Agricultural Development, Agricultural Engineering, Fertilizers **Loan:** In country **Service:** In country **Photocopy:** Yes

2258   Pulawy, Poland
Ministry of Agriculture and Rural Development, Central Agricultural Library
Pulawy Branch
ul. Czartoryskich 8
24-100 Pulawy
Phone: +48(81) 887-7290 **Fax:** +48(81) 887-7290 **WWW:** www.warman.com.pl/~cebibrol/index.html

Non-English Name: Ministerstwo Rolnictwa i Rozwoju Wsi, Centralna Biblioteka Rolnicza (CBR), Oddzial w Pulawach **Type:** Research **Head:** Zdzislaw Bort **Staff:** 13 Prof. **Holdings:** 99,000 books **Language of Collection/Services:** Polish / Polish, Russian, English **Service:** Internationally **Photocopy:** Yes

2259   Pulawy, Poland
National Veterinary Research Institute
Scientific Library
Partyzantów 57
24-100 Pulawy
Phone: +48(81) 886-3051 **Fax:** +48(81) 886-2595 **WWW:** www.piwet.pulawy.pl

Non-English Name: Panstwowy Instytut Weterynaryjny (PIWet), Biblioteka Naukowa **Former Name:** Instytut Weterynarii (IWet) **Founded:** 1945 **Type:** Research **Head:** Józefa Zelazna *Email:* zelazna@piwet.pulawy.pl **Staff:** 3 Prof. 1 Other **Holdings:** 18,500 books 185 journals **Language of Collection/Services:** Polish, English / Polish, English **Subjects:** Biotechnology, Veterinary Medicine, Food Sciences **Databases Used:** Current Contents **Loan:** In country **Service:** In country **Photocopy:** Yes

2260   Siedlce, Poland
University of Podlasie
Main Library
ul. Gen. Orlicz-Dreszera 19/21
08-110 Siedlce
Phone: +48(25) 643-1633 **Email:** infobib@ap.siedlce.pl **WWW:** www.wsrp.siedlce.pl

Non-English Name: Akademia Podlaska, Biblioteka Główna **Former Name:** Agricultural and Teachers University in Siedlce, Wyzsza Szkola Rolniczo-Pedagogiczna (WSRP) **Founded:** 1969 **Type:** Academic **Head:** Maria Nesiolowska *Phone:* +48 (25) 643-1623 *Email:* biblio@ap.siedlce.pl **Staff:** 29 Prof. **Holdings:** 300,000 books 445 journals **Language of Collection / Services:** Polish / Polish **Subjects:** Animal Husbandry, Crops, Environmental Protection **Photocopy:** Yes

2261   Skierniewice, Poland
Ministry of Agriculture and Rural Development, Research Institute of Vegetable Crops
Library
ul. Konstytucji 3 Maja 1/3
96-100 Skierniewice
Phone: +48(46) 833-2211 ext 285 **Fax:** +48(46) 833-3186 **Email:** bibliot@inwarz.skierniewice.pl **WWW:** www.inwarz.skierniewice.pl

Non-English Name: Ministerstwo Rolnictwa i Rozwoju Wsi, Instytut Warzywnictwa (MinRol, IWarz), Biblioteka **Former Name:** Ministerstwo Rolnictwa i Gospodarki Zywnosciowej, Ministry of Agriculture and Food Economy **Founded:** 1964 **Type:** Government **Head:** Maria Plucinska *Phone:* +48(46) 833-3434 **Staff:** 2 Prof. **Holdings:** 8,020 books 80 journals **Language of Collection/Services:** Polish /Polish **Subjects:** Horticulture, Vegetables **Databases Developed:** SIGZ (in cooperation with Central Library of Agriculture) - 7000 records on vegetables **Loan:** In country **Service:** In country **Photocopy:** Yes

2262   Skierniewice, Poland
Research Institute of Pomology and Floriculture
Library
18 Pomologiczna Street
96-100 Skierniewice
Fax: +48(46) 833-3238 **Email:** isad@insad.isk.skierniewice.pl **WWW:** www.isk.skierniewice.pl

Non-English Name: Instytut Sadownictwa i Kwiaciarstwa (ISK), Biblioteka **Founded:** 1951 **Type:** Government **Head:** Z. Rolewska*Phone:* +48(46) 833-2021 *Email:* zrolew@insad.isk.skierniewice.pl **Staff:** 4 Prof. 1 Other **Holdings:** 25,162 books 82 journals **Language of Collection/Services:** Polish/Polish **Subjects:** Horticulture **Specializations:** Nuts, Fruits, Ornamental Plants, Viticulture **Databases Used:** Current Contents; HORTCD **Loan:** In country **Service:** Internationally **Photocopy:** Yes

♦2263   Slupia Wielka, Poland
Research Centre for Cultivar Testing
Library
63-022 Slupia Wielka
Phone: +48(667) 52341 **Fax:** +48(667) 53558

Non-English Name: Centralny Osrodek Badania Odmian Roslin Uprawnych (COBORU), Biblioteka **Type:** Research **Staff:** 60 Prof. 60 Other **Holdings:** 6,100 books 1,200 journals **Language of Collection/Services:** Polish / Polish **Subjects:** Peanuts, Plant Breeding, Plants, Varieties **Loan:** In country **Service:** In country **Photocopy:** Yes

2264   Szczecin, Poland
University of Agriculture Szczecin
Main Library
ul. Janosika 8
71-424 Szczecin
Phone: +48(91) 220851 **Fax:** +48(91) 232417 **WWW:** www.libra.ar.szczecin.pl

Non-English Name: Akademia Rolnicza w Szczecinie, Biblioteka Główna **Type:** Research **Head:** Tadeusz Cieslak *Email:* cieslak@libsrv.libra.ar.szczecin.pl **Staff:** 7 Prof. 14

Other **Holdings:** 203,997 books 545 journals **Language of Collection/Services:** Polish / Polish **Subjects:** Agricultural Economics, Agricultural Engineering, Animal Husbandry, Biology, Biotechnology, Ecology, Food Sciences, Food Storage **Databases Used:** Comprehensive **Loan:** In country **Service:** In country **Photocopy:** No

2265   Warsaw, Poland
Central Laboratory for Grain Storage and
     Processing
Information Center for Grain and Milling Industry
ul. Rakowiecka 36
02-532 Warsaw
Phone: +48(22) 606-3868 **Fax:** +48(22) 849-0643 **Email:** cltpipz@polbox.com

Non-English Name: Centralne Laboratorium Technologii Przetwórstwa i Przechowalnictwa Zbóz (CLTPiPZ), Branzowy Osrodek Informacji Techniczno-Ekonomicznej (BOITE) **Founded:** 1956 **Type:** Research **Head:** Anna Gajewska **Staff:** 2 Prof. **Holdings:** 4,105 books 15 journals **Language of Collection/Services:** Polish / Polish **Subjects:** Cereals, Food Sciences **Specializations:** Food Technology, Grain, Grain Stores, Processing, Storage **Databases Developed:** SIGZ-91 - abstracts from Polish branch magazines; SIGZ-93 - abstracts from other than Polish languages branch magazines; SIBROL - papers of institute **Loan:** Internationally **Service:** Internationally **Photocopy:** Yes

2266   Warsaw, Poland
Forest Research Institute in Warsaw
Section of Scientific Information, Library
ul. Bitwy Warszawskiej 1920 r. Nr 3
00-973 Warsaw
Phone: +48(22) 822-3201 ext 142 **Fax:** +48(22) 822-4935 **Email:** biblioteka@ibles.waw.pl **WWW:** www.ibles.waw.pl/index_p.html

Non-English Name: Instytut Badawczy Lesnictwa (IBL), Zaklad Informacji Naukowej, Biblioteka (ZIN) **Former Name:** Instytut Badawczy Lasów Panstwowych, Zaklad Informacji Naukowej, Technicznej i Ekonomicznej Lesnictwa **Type:** Government **Head:** Elzbieta Surwara *Phone:* +48 (22) 822-3201 ext 350 **Staff:** 10 Prof. 1 Other **Holdings:** 324 journals 45,000 books **Language of Collection/Services:** Polish / Polish, English **Subjects:** Forestry **Specializations:** Biology, Environment, Forest Management, Forest Products, Forestry Engineering, Marketing, Mensuration, Occupational Hazards, Safety at Work, Silviculture, Wood **Loan:** In country **Photocopy:** Yes

2267   Warsaw, Poland
Horticulture Research and Development Centre
Library
ul. Grochowska 341
03-822 Warsaw
Phone: +48(22) 618-4154 **Fax:** +48(22) 618-3916

Non-English Name: Centralny Osrodek Badawezo-Roznojowy Ogrodnictwa (COBRO), Biblioteka **Type:** Research **Head:** Teresa Kruczak **Staff:** 1 Prof. **Holdings:** 1,175 books 14 journals **Language of Collection/ Services:** Polish / Polish **Subjects:** Agricultural Economics, Horticulture **Special-**

izations: Trade **Photocopy:** Yes **Loan:** Inhouse **Service:** Inhouse

2268   Warsaw, Poland
Institute for Building, Mechanization and
     Electrification of Agriculture
Department of Promotion of Agricultural Progress
Rakowiecka 32
02-532 Warsaw
Phone: +48(22) 849-3231 **Fax:** +48(22) 849-1737 **Email:** ibmer@ibmer.waw.pl **WWW:** www.ibmer.waw.pl

Non-English Name: Instytut Budownicta, Mechanizacji i Elektryfikacji Rolnictwa, Zaklad Upowszechniania Postepu Rolniczego (IBMER), Zaklad Promocji **Former Name:** Institute for Mechanization and Electrification of Agriculture **Founded:** 1950 **Type:** Research **Head:** Dr. Eng. Wieslaw Golka *Email:* selian@ibmer.waw.pl *Phone:* +48(22) 848-2539 **Staff:** 8 Prof. 3 Other **Holdings:** 33,500 books 110 journals **Language of Collection/Services:** Polish / Polish **Subjects:** Agricultural Engineering, Environmental Protection **Specializations:** Safety at Work **Databases Developed:** ITER - includes all subjects on the mechanization of technological processes in agriculture; MASZYNY ROLNICZE - includes all items concerning machines and equipment connected with plant and animal production offered by producers and distributors in Polish market **Loan:** In country **Service:** In country **Photocopy:** Yes

2269   Warsaw, Poland
Institute of Agricultural and Food Biotechnology
Department of Scientific and Technical
     Information
ul. Rakowiecka 36
02-532 Warsaw
Phone: +48(22) 606-3660 **Fax:** +48(22) 490426, 490428 **Email:** ibprs@ibprs.waw.pl

Non-English Name: Instytut Biotechnologii Przemyslu Rolno-Spozywczego (IBPRS), Zaklad Informacji Naukowo-Technicznej (ZINT) **Former Name:** Institute of Biotechnology of the Agricultural and Food Industry, Zaklad Organizacji Badan i Informacji Naukowo-Technicznej (ZOBINT) **Founded:** 1954 **Type:** Government **Head:** Wieslawa Ogórkiewicz **Staff:** 1 Prof. 2 Other **Holdings:** 23,000 books 110 journals **Language of Collection/Services:** Polish, English, German, Russian / Polish, English **Subjects:** Biotechnology, Food Sciences **Loan:** Internationally **Service:** In country **Photocopy:** Yes

♦2270   Warsaw, Poland
Institute of Agriculture and Food Economics
Information Center
20 Swietokrzyska Str.
00-002 Warsaw
Phone: +48(22) 265031 **Fax:** +48(22) 271960

Non-English Name: Instytut Ekonomiki Rolnictwa i Gospodarki Zywnosciowej (IERiGZ), Osrodek Informacji Naukowej (OIN) **Founded:** 1950 **Type:** Government **Staff:** 12 Prof. **Holdings:** 41,000 books **Language of Collection/ Services:** Polish, English / Polish **Subjects:** Agribusiness, Agricultural Development, Agricultural Economics, Farming **Databases Developed:** IE - Agricultural economics, food economics, agribusiness, farming, agricultural statistics, food policy; available inhouse **Loan:** In country **Service:** In country **Photocopy:** Yes

2271   Warsaw, Poland
Institute of Environmental Protection (IEP)
Library
ul. Krucza 5/11
00-548 Warsaw
Phone: +48(22) 628-1569 **Fax:** +48(22) 629-5263 **Email:** iosbibl@plearn.edu.pl **WWW:** ciuw.warman.net.pl/alf/ios **OPAC:** venus.cl.uw.edu.pl/book, ciuw.warman.net.pl/alf/biodiversit

Non-English Name: Instytut Ochrony Srodowiska (IOS), Biblioteka **Former Name:** Research Institute on Environmental Development **Founded:** 1986 **Head:** Anna Lukasik **Type:** Research **Staff:** 2 Prof. **Holdings:** 9,000 books 140 journals **Language of Collection/Services:** Polish, English / Polish, English **Subjects:** Air Pollution, Climatology, Environmental Management, Environmental Protection, Noise, Landscape, Plants, Soil Science, Waste Water, Wastes, Water Resources **Loan:** In country **Service:** Internationally **Photocopy:** Yes

2272   Warsaw, Poland
Institute of Food Processing Machinery
Information Center
ul. Otwocka 1 b
03-759 Warsaw
Phone: +48(22) 619-1261 **Fax:** +48(22) 619-8794

Non-English Name: Instytut Maszyn Spozywczych (IMS), Osrodek Informacji **Type:** Research **Head:** Zygmunt Malinowski **Staff:** 1 Prof. 1 Other **Holdings:** 11,500 books 15 journals **Language of Collection/Services:** Polish **Subjects:** Food Processing Equipment, Food Technology **Loan:** In country **Service:** In country **Photocopy:** Yes

2273   Warsaw, Poland
Institute of Meteorology and Water Management
(IMWM)
Specialized Centre of Scientific, Technical and
Economic Information
61 Podlesna St.
01-673 Warsaw
Fax: +48(22) 834-5466 **WWW:** www.imgw.pl/meteo/wstep.html

Non-English Name: Instytut Meteorologii i Gospodarki Wodnej (IMGW), Branzowy Osrodek Informacji Naukowej, Technicznej i Ekonomicznej (BOINTE) **Type:** Government **Founded:** 1919 **Head:** Barbara Sendrowicz, Krystyna Storozynska *Email:* bointe@imgw.pl *Phone:* +48(22) 834-2566 **Staff:** 5 Prof. 1 Other **Holdings:** 30,850 books 160 journals **Language of Collection/Services:** Polish / Polish **Subjects:** Water Resources **Specializations:** WMO Documents **Loan:** Internationally **Service:** Internationally **Photocopy:** Yes

♦**2274   Warsaw, Poland**
Institute of Sugar Industry

Center for Scientific, Technical and Economic
Information
ul. Rakowiecka 36
02-532 Warsaw
Phone: +48(22) 490093 ext 11 **Fax:** +48(22) 480901

Non-English Name: Instytut Przemyslu Cukrowniczego (IPC), Branzowy Osrodek Informacji Naukowej, Technicznej i Ekonomicznej (BOINTE) **Staff:** 2 Prof. **Type:** Research **Holdings:** 1,430 books 31 journals **Language of Collection/Services:** Polish/Polish **Subjects:** Food Sciences **Specializations:** Beets **Loan:** In country **Service:** In country **Photocopy:** Yes

2275   Warsaw, Poland
Meat and Fat Institute
Library
ul. Jubilerska 4
04-190 Warsaw
Phone: +48(22) 612-0452 **Fax:** +48(22) 610-2366 **Email:** ipmt@ipmt.waw.pl

Non-English Name: Instytut Przemyslu Miesnego i Tluszczowego (IPMiT), Biblioteka **Founded:** 1975 **Type:** Research **Head:** Ing. Barbara Pracz **Staff:** 1 Prof. 1 Other **Holdings:** 4,500 books 50 journals **Language of Collection/Services:** Polish / Polish **Subjects:** Agricultural Economics, Microbiology **Specializations:** Fats, Meat **Databases Used:** Agris; CELEX; Current Contents **Service:** Internationally **Photocopy:** Yes

2276   Warsaw, Poland
Ministry of Agriculture and Rural Development
Central Agricultural Library (CAL)
Krakowskie Przedmiescie 66
PO Box 360
00-950 Warsaw 40
Phone: +48(22) 826-6041 **Fax:** +48(22) 826-0157 **Email:** cebibrol@atos.warman.com.pl **WWW:** www.warman.com.pl/~cebibrol

Non-English Name: Ministerstwo Rolnictwa i Rozwoju Wsi, Centralna Biblioteka Rolnicza (CBR) **Former Name:** Ministry of Agriculture, Forestry and Food Economy, Ministerstwo Rolnictwa i Gospodarki Zywnosciowej (MRiGZ) **Founded:** 1955 **Type:** Government **Head:** dr. inz. Krystyna Kocznorowska *Phone:* +48(22) 826-9027 **Staff:** 47 Prof. 26 Other **Holdings:** 416,550 books 1,032 journals **Language of Collection/Services:** Polish/Polish, English **Subjects:** Comprehensive **Specializations:** Animal Husbandry, Crops, Soil Science, Plant Protection **Networks:** AGRIS **Databases Developed:** SIGZ - System Informacji o Gospodarce Zywnosciowej - database containing bibliographic indexing and abstracts issued in Poland from 1981 (in Polish); from 1993 onwards available on CD-ROM; PARC database (in Polish and English) - Polish Agricultural Research Completed covers the years from 1991-1995 and includes over 5,200 records; SIBROL database (in Polish and English) - Agricultural Research information System containing data about on-going and completed research from 1995 onwards, data on authors (experts), and data related to agricultural research centers in Poland **Databases Used:** Comprehensive **Loan:** Internationally **Service:** Internationally **Photocopy:** Yes

2277   Warsaw, Poland
Polish Academy of Sciences, Institute of
Biochemistry and Biophysics (PAS, IBB)
Library
ul. Pawinskiego 5A
02-106 Warsaw
Phone: +48(22) 658-2420 **Email:** bibl@ibbrain.ibb.waw.pl
WWW: www.ibb.waw.pl

Non-English Name: Polska Akademia Nauk, Instytut Biochemii i Biofizyki (PAN, IBB), Biblioteka **Founded:** 1962 **Type:** Academic **Head:** Ms. Teresa Zylka **Staff:** 2 Prof. 1 Other **Holdings:** 7,000 books 200 journals **Language of Collection/Services:** English/Polish **Subjects:** Biochemistry, Biotechnology, Microbiology, Plant Genetics, Plant Pathology, Plant Physiology, Plants, Virology **Databases Used:** Current Contents **Loan:** In country **Service:** In country **Photocopy:** Yes

2278   Warsaw, Poland
Polish Academy of Sciences, Institute of Rural
and Agricultural Development
Division for Documentation, Information
Handling and Popularization of Research
Findings
ul. Nowy Swiat 72
00-330 Warsaw
Location: Palac Staszica **Phone:** +48(22) 826-9436 **Fax:** +48(22) 826-6371 **Email:** irwir@irwirpan.waw.pl **WWW:** www.irwirpan.waw.pl/polski/glowna.htm

Non-English Name: Polska Akademia Nauk, Instytut Rozwoju Wsi i Rolnictwa (PAN, IRWiR), Pracownia Dokumentacji, Przetwarzania Informacji i Upowszechniania Wyników Badan **Type:** Research **Staff:** 25 Prof. 16 Other **Holdings:** 6,000 books 64 journals **Language of Collection/ Services:** Polish / Polish **Subjects:** Agricultural Development, Agricultural Economics, Agricultural Engineering, Education, Farming, Food Sciences, Rural Youth **Service:** In country **Photocopy:** No

2279   Warsaw, Poland
Polish Academy of Sciences, Nencki Institute of
Experimental Biology
Library
ul. Pasteura 3
02-093 Warsaw
Phone: +48(22) 659-8571 ext 218 **Fax:** +48(22) 822-5342 **Email:** bibl@nencki.gov.pl **WWW:** www.nencki.gov.pl **OPAC:** ciuw.warman.net.pl/webpac-1.2

Non-English Name: Polska Akademia Nauk, Instytut Biologii Doswiadczalnej im. M. Nenckiego (PAN, Nencki), Biblioteka **Type:** Research **Head:** Jan Bienias *Phone:* +48 (22) 659-3501 **Staff:** 3 Prof. **Holdings:** 66,000 books 240 journals **Language of Collection/Services:** Polish, English, French, German, Russian / Polish **Subjects:** Cellular Biology, Muscle Physiology **Databases Used:** Current Contents; Medline **Loan:** Internationally **Service:** Internationally **Photocopy:** Yes

2280   Warsaw, Poland
Polish Academy of Sciences, W. Stefanski
Institute of Parasitology
Library
Twarda St. 51/55
00-818 Warsaw
Phone: +48(22) 697-8888, 620-6226 **Fax:** +48(22) 620-6227 **Email:** libripar@twarda.pan.pl **WWW:** www.ipar.pan.pl

Non-English Name: Polska Akademia Nauk, Instytut Parazytologii im. Witolda Stefanskiego, Biblioteka **Former Name:** Research Centre of Parasitology **Founded:** 1952 **Type:** Academic **Head:** Malgorzata Woronowicz *Phone:* +48 (22) 697-8972 **Staff:** 3 Prof. **Holdings:** 12,000 books 144 journals **Language of Collection/Services:** English/ Polish, English **Subjects:** Veterinary Medicine **Loan:** Internationally **Photocopy:** No

2281   Warsaw, Poland
Warsaw Agricultural University (WAU)
Central Library
ul. Nowoursynowska 161
02-787 Warsaw
Phone: +48(22) 847-2671 **Fax:** +48(22) 847-2561 **Email:** bg-oin@alpha.sggw.waw.pl **WWW:** www.sggw.waw.pl **OPAC:** www.bg.sggw.waw.pl

Non-English Name: Szkola Glówna Gospodarstwa Wiejskiego (SGGW), Biblioteka Glówna (BG) **Founded:** 1911 **Type:** Academic **Head:** Mgr. Jerzy Lewandowski *Phone:* +48 (22) 847-2561 *Email:* lewandowskij@alpha.sggw.waw. pl **Staff:** 53 Prof. **Holdings:** 180,000 books 770 journals **Language of Collection/Services:** Polish / Polish **Subjects:** Comprehensive **Specializations:** Animal Husbandry, Food Sciences, Forestry, Horticulture, Human Nutrition, Land Improvement, Veterinary Medicine, Wood Technology **Databases Used:** Comprehensive **Loan:** Internationally **Service:** Internationally **Photocopy:** Yes

2282   Wroclaw, Poland
Agricultural Academy in Wroclaw
Main Library
ul. Norwida 29
50-375 Wroclaw
Phone: +48(71) 320-5156, 320-5443 **Fax:** +48(71) 320-5168 **Email:** sdi@bg.ar.wroc.pl **WWW:** www.bibl.ar.wroc.pl **OPAC:** www.bibl.ar.wroc.pl/kat/kat.htm

Non-English Name: Akademia Rolnicza we Wroclawiu (AR we Wroclawiu), Biblioteka Glówna **Former Name:** Wyzsza Szkola Rolnicza we Wroclawiu **Founded:** 1952 **Type:** Academic **Head:** Grazyna Talar *Phone:* +48(71) 320-5203, 320-5234 *Email:* talar@bg.ar.wroc.pl **Staff:** 31 Prof. 1 Other **Holdings:** 180,000 books 611 journals **Language of Collection/Services:** Polish, English/Polish **Subjects:** Comprehensive **Specializations:** Biotechnology, Ecology, Food Sciences, Veterinary Medicine **Databases Developed:** Agricultural University authors' bibliography **Databases Used:** Comprehensive **Loan:** Internationally **Service:** Internationally **Photocopy:** Yes

Portugal

2283   Coimbra, Portugal
Agriculture College of Coimbra (ACC)
Documentation and Information Centre
Bencanta
3040 Coimbra
Phone: +351(39) 444400 **Fax:** +351(39) 813612 **Email:** biblioteca@mail.esac.pt **WWW:** www.esac.pt

Non-English Name: Escola Superior Agrária de Coimbra (ESAC), Serviços de Documentação e Informação (SDI) **Former Name:** Escola de Regentes Agrícolas **Type:** Academic **Founded:** 1889 **Head:** Armando Augusto Alves Martinho *Phone:* +351(39) 444400 *Email:* martinho@mail.esac.pt **Staff:** 1 Prof. 3 Other **Holdings:** 19,000 books 60 journals **Language of Collection/Services:** Portuguese / Portuguese **Subjects:** Agribusiness, Agricultural Development, Agricultural Economics, Biotechnology, Entomology, Farming, Environment, Plant Pathology, Plants, Soil Science, Veterinary Medicine **Specializations:** Agricultural Engineering, Animal Husbandry, Crops, Food Sciences, Forestry, Horticulture **Databases Used:** Agricola; Agris; CABCD **Loan:** Internationally **Service:** Internationally **Photocopy:** Yes

2284   Coimbra, Portugal
University of Coimbra
Central Library
3049-447 Coimbra codex
Location: Largo da Porta Férrea **Phone:** +351(39) 859847 **Fax:** +351(39) 827135 **WWW:** www.uc.pt **OPAC:** scoweb.bg.uc.pt/cgi-bin/webopac/opac.pl

Non-English Name: Universidade de Coimbra (UC), Biblioteca Geral (BG) **Type:** Academic **Head:** Aníbal Pinto de Castro *Email:* acastro@scoweb.bg.uc.pt *Phone:* +351(39) 859848 **Staff:** 38 Prof. 40 Other **Holdings:** 1,000,000 books 315,000 journals **Language of Collection/Services:** Portuguese, French, English / Portuguese **Subjects:** Agricultural Development, Agricultural Statistics **Loan:** Internationally **Service:** Internationally **Photocopy:** Yes

2285   Elvas, Portugal
National Agrarian Research Institute, National
   Station for Plant Breeding
Information and Documentation Center
Apartado 6
7351 Elvas codex
Phone: +351(68) 622847, 622734 **Fax:** +351(68) 629295 **WWW:** www.inia.min-agricultura.pt/enmp.html **Email:** enmp@mail.telepac.pt

Non-English Name: Instituto Nacional de Investigação Agrária, Estação Nacional de Melhoramento de Plantas (INIA, ENMP), Centro de Documentação e Informação (CDI) **Former Name:** Estação de Melhoramento de Plantas **Founded:** 1942 **Type:** Government **Staff:** 2 Other **Holdings:** 15,000 books 200 journals **Subjects:** Biotechnology, Crops, Education, Plant Breeding, Plant Pathology **Loan:** In country **Photocopy:** Yes

2286   Faro, Portugal
University of Algarve
Library - Gambelas Campus
Campus de Gambelas
8000 Faro
Phone: +351(89) 800945 **Fax:** +351(89) 818803 **Email:** mvargues@ualg.pt **WWW:** www.ualg.pt

Non-English Name: Universidade do Algarve (UALG), Biblioteca - Câmpus de Gambelas (SDI) **Founded:** 1983 **Type:** Academic **Head:** Maria Margarida Vargues *Phone:* +351 (89) 800944 *Email:* mvargues@ualg.pt **Staff:** 3 Prof. **Holdings:** 22,000 books 20 journals **Language of Collection/Services:** Portuguese **Subjects:** Biotechnology, Soil Science, Aquaculture, Farming, Water Resources **Specializations:** Agricultural Engineering, Plant Pathology, Entomology, Horticulture, Fisheries, Plants **Databases Used:** HORTCD **Networks:** PORBASE **Loan:** Internationally **Photocopy:** Yes

2287   Lisbon, Portugal
Higher Institute of Agronomy
Library
Tapada da Ajuda
1300 Lisbon
Fax: +351(1) 3635031 **WWW:** www.isa.utl.pt

Non-English Name: Instituto Superior de Agronomia (ISA), Biblioteca **Former Name:** Instituto Agrícola de Lisboa **Founded:** 1853 **Type:** Academic **Head:** Luis de Gouveia Aveiro *Email:* laveiro@isa.utl.pt *Phone:* +351(1) 363-7824 ext 431 **Staff:** 7 Prof. 6 Other **Holdings:** 52,000 books 1,500 journals **Language of Collection/Services:** Portuguese/Portuguese **Subjects:** Agribusiness, Farming, Agricultural Development, Agricultural Economics, Agricultural Engineering, Animal Husbandry, Biotechnology, Crops, Education/ Extension, Entomology, Fisheries, Food Sciences, Forestry, Horticulture, Plant Pathology, Soil Science, Veterinary Medicine, Water Resources **Specializations:** Agriculture (Tropics) **Databases Used:** AGECON CD; CABCD **Loan:** In country **Photocopy:** Yes

2288   Lisbon, Portugal
Ministry of Agriculture, Rural Development and
   Fisheries, Secretary General (MARDF)
Division of Documentation and Information
Praca do Comércio
1149-010 Lisbon
Phone: +351(1) 346-3151 **Fax:** +351(1) 347-3798 **WWW:** www.min-agricultura.pt **OPAC:** www.min-agricultura.pt/menuframeset.asp?ID=2&Pos=1&Tipo=0

Non-English Name: Ministério da Agricultura, do Desenvolvimento Rural e das Pescas, Secretaria Geral (MADRP), Divisão de Documentação e Informação, Divisão de Documentação **Founded:** 1918 **Type:** Government **Head:** Ms. Manuela Pintão *Email:* mp@min-agricultura.pt *Phone:* +351 (1) 346-3151 **Staff:** 4 Prof. 3 Other **Holdings:** 40,000 books 2,000 journals **Language of Collection/ Services:** Portuguese **Subjects:** Comprehensive **Specializations:** Animal Husbandry, Food Technology, Forestry, Crops **Networks:** AGRIS **Databases Used:** Agris **Loan:** In country **Service:** Internationally **Photocopy:** Yes

2289　Lisbon, Portugal
National Agrarian Research Institute, National
　　Forestry Station
Central Library
Tapada das Necessidades
Buado Borja n° 2
1399-051 Lisbon
Phone: 213901661 **Fax:** +351(1) 213973163 **Email:**
rosefn@individual.eunet.pt **WWW:** www.ip.pt/efn

Non-English Name: Instituto Nacional de Investigação
Agrária, Estação Florestal Nacional (INIA, EFN), Biblioteca
Central (BC) **Type:** Academic **Staff:** 3 Prof. 1 Other **Holdings:** 23,100 books 3,900 journals **Language of Collection/
Services:** Portuguese / Portuguese **Subjects:** Forestry Engineering, Forestry Machinery **Loan:** In country **Service:** In
country **Photocopy:** Yes

2290　Lisbon, Portugal
Portuguese Marine Research Institute
Department of Scientific and Technical
　　Information and Documentation
Avenida de Brasília
1400 Lisbon
Phone: +351(1) 302-7000 **Fax:** +351(1) 301-5948 **Email:**
ipimar@ipimar.pt **WWW:** www.ipimar.pt

Non-English Name: Instituto Português de Investigação
Marítima (IPIMAR), Departamento de Informação e Documentação Cientifica e Técnica (DIDCT) **Former Name:**
Instituto Nacional de Investigação das Pescas (INIP) **Type:**
Research **Head:** Carmen Lima **Phone:** +351(1) 301-0814
Staff: 5 Prof. 4 Other **Holdings:** 10,000 books 62 journals
Language of Collection/Services: English/Portuguese **Subjects:** Fisheries, Food Sciences **Loan:** In country **Photocopy:** Yes

2291　Lisbon, Portugal
Technical University of Lisbon, Faculty of
　　Veterinary Medicine
Library
Rua Gomes Freire
1169-014 Lisbon codex
Phone: +351(1) 352-2591, 352-2596, 352-2589 **Fax:** +35
(1) 353-3088, 357-0334 **WWW:** www.utl.pt

Non-English Name: Universidade Tecnica de Lisboa,
Faculdade de Medicina Veterinária (UTL, FMV), Biblioteca
Founded: 1852 **Type:** Government **Head:** Dr. Leopoldo
Rocha **Email:** leorocha@fmv.utl.pt **Phone:** +351 (1) 356-
2596 **Staff:** 2 Prof. 2 Other **Holdings:** 213 journals 38,648
books **Language of Collection/Services:** Portuguese, English, French **Subjects:** Agricultural Economics, Animal Husbandry, Biotechnology, Entomology, Food Sciences, Water
Resources, Fisheries **Specializations:** Theses (Veterinary
Medicine), Veterinary Medicine, Veterinary Medicine (History - Portugal) **Loan:** In country **Service:** Internationally
Photocopy: Yes

2292　Lisbon, Portugal
Tropical Sciences Research Institute
Documentation and Information Center
Rua Jau, 47

1300 Lisbon
Phone: +351(1) 364-5031 **Fax:** +351(1) 363-1460 **Email:**
cdi@iict.pt **WWW:** www.iict.pt **OPAC:** www.iict.pt

Non-English Name: Instituto de Investigação Científica
Tropical (IICT), Centro de Documentação e Informação
(CDI) **Former Name:** Junta de Investigações Científicas do
Ultramar (JICU), Centro de Documentação Científica Ultramarina (CDCU) **Founded:** 1936 **Type:** Government **Head:**
Dr. Maria Virgínia Aires Magriço **Phone:** +351(1) 364-5326
Email: cdi@iict.pt **Staff:** 3 Prof. 4 Other **Holdings:** 36,500
books 110 journals **Language of Collection/Services:** Portuguese / Portuguese **Subjects:** Agricultural Sciences, Cattle, Entomology, Forestry, Horticulture, Plants, Veterinary
Science **Specializations:** Agriculture (Tropics), Soil **Loan:**
Do not loan **Photocopy:** Yes

2293　Oeiras, Portugal
Tropical Sciences Research Institute, Coffee Rusts
　　Research Center
Library
Quinta do Marquês
2780 Oeiras
Phone: +351(21) 442-3323 **Fax:** +351(21) 442-0867
WWW: www.iict.pt

Non-English Name: Instituto de Investigação Científica
Tropical, Centro de Investigação das Ferrugens do Cafeeiro
(CIFC), Biblioteca **Founded:** 1955 **Type:** Government
Head: Dr. Carlos José Rodrigues Jr. **Phone:** +351(21) 442-
3323 **Staff:** 1 Other **Holdings:** 5,712 books 20 journals **Language of Collection/Services:** English/Portuguese **Subjects:** Agriculture (Tropics), Agriculture (Subtropics),
Biotechnology, Plant Pathology, Subtropics **Specializations:** Coffee **Loan:** In country **Photocopy:** Yes

2294　Lisbon, Portugal
Tropical Sciences Research Institute, Garden
　　Museum of Tropical Agriculture
Library
Belém
1400-171 Lisbon
Location: Calçada do Galvão **Phone:** +351(1) 3637023
Fax: +351(1) 3631460 **WWW:** www.iict.pt

Non-English Name: Instituto de Investigação Científica
Tropical, Jardim-Museu Agrícola Tropical (IICT), Biblioteca **Founded:** 1914 **Staff:** 1 Prof. **Holdings:** 3,500 books
1,200 journals **Type:** Government **Language of Collection/
Services:** Portuguese, French, English, Spanish **Subjects:**
Agriculture (Tropics), Agribusiness, Agricultural Development, Agricultural Economics, Agricultural Engineering,
Crops, Entomology, Forestry, Horticulture, Soil Science
Loan: In country **Photocopy:** Yes

2295　Ponta Delgada, Portugal
University of the Azores
Documentation Services
Rua da Mãe de Deus
9502 Ponta Delgada codex, Azores
Phone: +351(296) 653245 **Fax:** +351(296) 653245 **Email:**
sdpd@notes.uac.pt **WWW:** www.uac.pt **OPAC:** www.uac.
pt/bbsoft2/bbhtm/pesqu02.htm

Non-English Name: Universidade dos Açores (UAC), Serviços de Documentação (SD) **Type:** Academic **Staff:** 16 Prof. 1 Other **Language of Collection/Services:** Portuguese **Holdings:** 69,466 books 122 journals **Subjects:** Agrarian Reform, Agricultural Economics, Agricultural Policy, Agronomy, Marketing, Property, Rural Development **Specializations:** Bovidae, Food Production, Food Industry, Forestry, Goats, Sheep **Photocopy:** Yes **Loan:** Internationally **Service:** Internationally

2296   Porto, Portugal
        Ministry of Agriculture, Rural Development and
            Fisheries, Port Wine Institute
        Library
        Rua de Ferreira Borges
        4050 Porto
Fax: +351(2) 208-0465 **Email:** ivp@mail.ivp.pt **WWW:** www.ivp.pt

Non-English Name: Ministério da Agricultura, do Desenvolvimento Rural e das Pescas, Instituto do Vinho do Porto, Biblioteca **Founded:** 1933 **Type:** Government **Head:** Deª Ana Brochado Coelho *Phone:* +351(2) 207-1600 ext 18 *Email:* abrochado@mail. ivp.pt **Staff:** 3 Other **Subjects:** Enology, Viticulture **Specializations:** Port Wine **Loan:** Do not loan **Photocopy:** Yes

2297   Santarèm, Portugal
        Instituto Nacional de Investigação Agrária,
            Estação Zootécnica Nacional (INIA, EZN)
        Centro de Documentação e Informação
        Fonte Boa
        2000 Santarèm
Phone: +351(43) 760202/5 **Fax:** +351(43) 760540 **WWW:** www.inia.min-agricultura.pt/ezn.html **Email:** ezn. inia@mail.telepac.pt

Founded: 1911 **Type:** Government **Staff:** 6 Prof. 4 Other **Holdings:** 5,000 books 57 journals **Subjects:** Animal Production **Loan:** Do not loan **Photocopy:** Yes

2298   Vila Real, Portugal
        Universidade de Trás-os-Montes e Alto Douro
            (UTAD)
        Biblioteca Central
        Apt. 206
        5001 Vila Real codex
Phone: +351(259) 352104/5 **Fax:** +351(259) 74480 **WWW:** www.utad.pt/utad.html **OPAC:** aquaeflaviae.utad. pt/sirius/sirius.exe

Founded: 1973 **Type:** Academic **Head:** Nuno Tavares Moreira *Email:* nmoreira@utad.pt **Staff:** 5 Prof. 5 Other **Holdings:** 40,000 books 42 journals **Subjects:** Agribusiness, Agriculture (Tropics), Agricultural Development, Agricultural Economics, Agricultural Engineering, Biotechnology, Animal Husbandry, Education/Extension, Entomology, Forestry, Crops, Farming, Fisheries, Food Sciences, Horticulture, Plant Pathology, Veterinary Medicine, Soil Science, Plants **Loan:** In country

Puerto Rico

2299   Mayagüez, Puerto Rico
        University of Puerto Rico, Mayaguez Campus
            (UPR)
        General Library
        PO Box 9022
        Mayagüez 00681-9022
Location: Post Street **Phone:** +1(787) 832-4040, 833-8600 **Fax:** +1(787) 834-3080 **WWW:** www.upr.clu.edu **OPAC:** www.upr.clu.edu/webpac

Non-English Name: Universidad de Puerto Rico, Universitario de Mayagüez (UPR, UM), Biblioteca General Recinto **Type:** Academic **Head:** Isabel M. Ruiz, Acting Director *Email:* isabel@rumlib.uprm.edu *Phone:* +1(787) 832-4040 ext 3568 **Staff:** 19 Prof. 65 Other **Holdings:** 224,000 books 2,248 journals **Language of Collection/Services:** English, Spanish / Spanish, English **Subjects:** Agriculture (Tropics), Agricultural Economics, Animal Husbandry, Agricultural Engineering, Biotechnology, Horticulture, Plant Pathology, Soil Science **Specializations:** Fisheries, Government Documents (USA), Water Resources **Databases Used:** Agricola **Networks:** OCLC **Loan:** Internationally **Service:** Internationally **Photocopy:** Yes

2300   Río Piedras, Puerto Rico
        United States Department of Agriculture, Forest
            Service, Southern Forest Experiment Station,
            International Institute of Tropical Forestry
            (IITF)
        Library
        Call Box 25000
        Río Piedras 00928-5000
Location: Agricultural Experiment Station Grounds, Guadalcanal St. **Phone:** +1(787) 766-5335 ext 208 **Fax:** +1 (787) 766-6302 **WWW:** www.fs.fed.us/global/iitf/library/ library.html

Non-English Name: Instituto Internacional de Dasonomía Tropical, Biblioteca **Former Name:** Institute of Tropical Forestry (ITF), Instituto de Dasonomía Tropical **Founded:** 1939 **Type:** Government **Head:** Gisel Reyes *Phone:* +1 (787) 766-5335 ext 350 *Email:* g-reyes@upr1.upr.clu.edu **Staff:** 2 Prof. 3 Other **Holdings:** 20,000 books 100 journals **Language of Collection/Services:** English / English, Spanish **Subjects:** Agroforestry **Specializations:** Tropical Forests **Loan:** Inhouse **Service:** Inhouse **Photocopy:** Yes

2301   Río Piedras, Puerto Rico
        University of Puerto Rico, Agricultural
            Experiment Station
        Library
        Box H
        Río Piedras 00928
Phone: +1(787) 767-9705 **Fax:** +1(787) 758-5158 **WWW:** www.upr.clu.edu

Non-English Name: Universidad de Puerto Rico, Estación Experimental Agrícola, Biblioteca **Founded:** 1915 **Type:** Academic **Head:** Joan P. Hayes *Phone:* +1(787) 767-9705 **Staff:** 1 Prof. 2 Other **Holdings:** 325,556 books 425 journals **Language of Collection/Services:** English / Spanish, English **Subjects:** Comprehensive **Specializations:** Agriculture (Tropics) **Databases Used:** Agricola; UPRENET; Current Contents **Loan:** Internationally **Photocopy:** Yes

2302 San Juan, Puerto Rico
University of Puerto Rico, Rio Piedras Campus
Jose Ma. Lazaro Library
PO Box 23302
San Juan 00931-3302
Location: Edif José M. Lázaro Biblioteca General, Tercer Piso, Recito de Piedras Negras **Phone:** +1(787) 764-0000 ext 3303, 3296, 3311 **Fax:** +1(787) 763-5685 **WWW:** www.upr.clu.edu **OPAC:** www.upr.clu.edu/webpac
Non-English Name: Universidad de Puerto Rico, Recinto de Río Piedras, Biblioteca José Ma. Lázaro **Founded:** 1969 **Type:** Academic **Staff:** 4 Prof. 9 Other **Loan:** Internationally

2303 San Juan, Puerto Rico
University of Puerto Rico, Rio Piedras Campus
Natural Sciences Library
Apartado 22446 Estación UPR
San Juan 00931-2446
Location: Edificio Nuevo Ciencias Naturales II **Phone:** +1 (787) 764-7307 **Fax:** +1(787) 764-2890 **WWW:** www. cnnet.clu.edu **OPAC:** www.upr.clu.edu/webpac
Non-English Name: Universidad de Puerto Rico, Recinto de Río Piedras, Biblioteca de Ciencias Naturales II **Founded:** 1954 **Type:** Academic **Head:** Evangelina Pérez *Phone:* +1(787) 764-0000 **Holdings:** 2,655,000 books 10,068 journals **Loan:** Internationally

Reunion

2304 Saint-Denis, Réunion
Université de la Réunion
Bibliothèque
Campus du Moufia
15, Avenue René Cassin
BP 7151
97 715 Saint-Denis messag cedex 9
Phone: +262 938332, 938377 **Fax:** +262 938333 **WWW:** www.univ-reunion.fr
Founded: 1966 **Type:** Academic **Head:** Anne-Marie Blanc *Phone:* +262 938361 **Staff:** 6 Prof. 9 Other **Holdings:** 2,000 books 20 journals **Subjects:** Agriculture (Tropics), Aquaculture, Biotechnology, Crops, Fisheries, Soil Science, Sugar, Zoology **Loan:** Internationally **Photocopy:** Yes

Romania

2305 Balotesti, Romania
Research and Production Institute for Bovine
Breeding
Library
Sect. Agricol Ilfov
8113 Balotesti
Phone: +40(179) 52028 **Fax:** +40(179) 51206

Non-English Name: Institutul de Cercetare si Productie pentru Cresteres Bovinelor (ICPCB), Biblioteca **Founded:** 1948 **Type:** Government **Head:** Lucia Cureu *Phone:* +40 (179) 51202 **Staff:** 1 Prof. **Holdings:** 1,500 books 30 journals **Language of Collection/Services:** English, French **Subjects:** Agricultural Engineering, Animal Husbandry, Biotechnology, Farming **Specializations:** Bovidae, Cattle, Artiodactyla, Mammals, Ruminants **Databases Used:** Agris **Loan:** In country **Photocopy:** Yes

2306 Braila, Romania
Central Research Station for the Improvement of
Salt-Affected Soils
Library
Soseaua Vizirului km. 9
6100 Braila
Fax: +40(39) 684744 **WWW:** www.icpa.ro/sccass
Non-English Name: Statiunea Centrala de Cercetari pentru Ameliorarea Solurilor Saraturate Braila (SCCASS Braila), Biblioteca **Head:** Nicolae Craciun *Phone:* +40(39) 684695 **Staff:** 1 Prof. **Holdings:** 1,300 books 19 journals **Subjects:** Soil Science **Specializations:** Soil Improvement, Soil Management **Photocopy:** Yes

2307 Brasov, Romania
Academy of Agricultural and Forestry Sciences
"Gheorghe Ionescu-Sisesti", Institute for
Potato Research and Production (AAFS)
Library
Str. Fundaturii 2
2200 Brasov
Phone: +40(68) 150095 **Fax:** +40(68) 151508 **Email:** icpc @potato.deltanet.ro **WWW:** www.potato.ro/indexr.htm
Non-English Name: Academia de Stiinte Agricole si Silvice "Gheorghe Ionescu Sisesti", Institutul de Cercetare si Productie a Cartofului (ASAS, ICPC), Biblioteca **Former Name:** Institutul de Ceretari pentru Cultura Cartofului si a Sfeclei de zahar **Founded:** 1967 **Type:** Government **Head:** Draica Domnica *Phone:* +40(68) 150095 ext 141 *Email:* icpc@potato.deltanet.ro **Staff:** 1 Prof. **Holdings:** 7,000 books 16 journals **Language of Collection/Services:** Romanian/Romanian, French, English **Subjects:** Agriculture (Tropics), Agricultural Development, Agricultural Economics, Agricultural Engineering, Animal Husbandry, Biotechnology, Crops, Education/Extension, Entomology, Farming, Food Sciences, Horticulture, Plant Pathology, Soil Science, Veterinary Medicine, Water Resources **Specializations:** Potatoes **Databases Used:** Agris **Loan:** Inhouse **Service:** In country **Photocopy:** Yes

2308 Brasov, Romania
Grassland Research Institute Brasov
Library
Cucului Str., nr. 5
2200 Brasov, Brasov
Phone: +40(68) 167055, 165379 **Fax:** +40(68) 150650
Non-English Name: Institutul de Cercetare si Productie pentry Cultura Pajistilor Brasov (ICPCP), Biblioteca **Holdings:** 968 books 1,151 journals **Subjects:** Agronomy, Bot-

any, Breeding, Pastures, Plant Nutrition, Soil Improvement **Photocopy:** Yes

2309   Brasov, Romania
Ministry of National Education, University "Transilvania" of Brasov
Central Library
B-dul Eroilor Nr. 9
2200 Brasov

Phone: +40(68) 150786 **Email:** libr@vega.unitbv.ro
WWW: www.unitbv.ro **OPAC:** www.unitbv.ro/biblio/bib_home.htm

Non-English Name: Ministerul Educatiei Nationale, Universitatea "Transilvania" din Brasov, Biblioteca Centrala **Founded:** 1948 **Type:** Government **Head:** Prof. dr. ing. Aurel Negrutiu *Phone:* +40(68) 150786 *Email:* negrutiu@ vega.unitbv.ro **Staff:** 1 Prof. 48 Other **Holdings:** 668,372 books 252 journals **Language of Collection/Services:** Romanian / Romanian **Subjects:** Agricultural Engineering **Specializations:** Silviculture **Loan:** Internationally **Service:** Internationally **Photocopy:** Yes

2310   Bucharest, Romania
Academy of Agricultural and Forestry Sciences "Gheorghe Ionescu-Sisesti", Department of Information, Documentation and Computing (AAFS)
Library
Bv. Marasti 61, sector 1
R-71331 Bucharest

Phone: +40(1) 222-9139 **Fax:** +40(1) 222-9139 **Email:** asas37@hotmail.com **WWW:** www.icpa.ro/asas/ASAS.htm

Non-English Name: Academia de Stiinte Agricole si Silvice "Gheorghe Ionescu Sisesti", Serviciul de Informare, Documentare si Informatizare (ASAS), Biblioteca **Founded:** 1928 **Type:** Academic **Head:** Cristian Kevorchian *Phone:* +40(1) 222- 7620 ext 224, 247 *Email:* c_kevorchian@ hotmail.com **Staff:** 5 Prof. 2 Other **Holdings:** 146,368 books 60 journals **Language of Collection/Services:** Romanian, French, English, Russian / Romanian **Subjects:** Comprehensive **Networks:** AGRIS **Databases Used:** Agris **Loan:** In country **Photocopy:** Yes

2311   Bucharest, Romania
Pasteur National Institute for Veterinary Medicine
Specialized Veterinary Library
Calea Giulesti 333, sector 6
77826 Bucharest

Phone: +40(1) 220-6920 ext 1238 **Fax:** +40(1) 220-6915

Non-English Name: Institutul National de Medicina Veterinara Pasteur (INMV Pasteur), Biblioteca de profil veterinar **Former Name:** Pasteur Institute for Veterinary Research and Biological Products, Institutul de Cercetari Veterinare si Biopreparate "Pasteur" **Founded:** 1909 **Type:** Government **Head:** Eva Codleanu *Phone:* +40 (1) 220-6920 ext 1238 **Staff:** 1 Prof. **Holdings:** 30,000 books 70 journals **Language of Collection/Services:** Romanian / Romanian, English **Subjects:** Animal Husbandry, Bacteriology, Fisheries, Biochemistry, Biotechnology, Chemistry, Entomology, Epi-

demiology, Genetics, Molecular Biology, Veterinary Medicine, Virology **Specializations:** 1250 translations of articles from periodicals, 650 doctoral theses **Loan:** Internationally **Photocopy:** Yes

2312   Bucharest, Romania
Research Institute for Soil Science and Agrochemistry
Library - National AGRIS Centre
Bd. Marasti, no. 61
71331 Bucharest sector 1

Phone: +40(1) 224-1790 **Fax:** +40(1) 222-5979 **Email:** icpa@icpa.ro **WWW:** www.icpa.ro

Non-English Name: Institutul de Cercetari pentru Pedologie si Agrochimie (ICPA), Biblioteca - Centrul National AGRIS **Founded:** 1969 **Type:** Government **Head:** Daniela Popa (Library); Virgil Vlad (National AGRIS Center) *Phone:* +40 (1) 224-1790 ext 264, 273 *Email:* dana@icpa.ro **Holdings:** 5,000 books 700 journals **Staff:** 1 Prof. **Subjects:** Environmental Protection, Fertilizers, Pollution, Soil **Networks:** AGRIS **Databases Used:** Comprehensive **Photocopy:** Yes

2313   Caracal, Romania
Agricultural Research Station Caracal
Library
V. Alecsandri str., nr. 106
0800 Caracal, Olt

Fax: +40(49) 410616 **Email:** sca_olt@romanati.ro

Non-English Name: Statiunea de Cercetari Agricole Caracal (SCA Caracal), Biblioteca **Head:** Ilie Ioana *Phone:* +40 (49) 511991 **Staff:** 1 Prof. **Holdings:** 4,300 books 9 journals **Subjects:** Agricultural Chemistry, Agroecology, Crops, Biotechnology, Environment, Genetics, Information Technology, Irrigation, Plant Breeding, Plant Protection **Photocopy:** Yes

2314   Comuna Baneasa, Romania
Research and Engineering Institute for Irrigation and Drainage
Library
8384 Comuna Baneasa, Giurgiu

Fax: +40(46) 285024

Non-English Name: Institutul de Cercetare si Inginerie Tehnologica pentru Irigatii si Drenaje (ICITID), Biblioteca **Founded:** 1948 **Type:** Government **Head:** Maria Nicolescu *Phone:* +40(46) 285023 **Staff:** 1 Prof. **Holdings:** 5,700 books 700 journals **Language of Collection/Services:** Romanian **Subjects:** Drainage, Environment, Groundwater, Irrigation, Hydrology **Loan:** Inhouse **Service:** Inhouse

2315   Comuna Dabuleni, Romania
Central Research Station for Agricultural Crops on Sands
Library
1185 Comuna Dabuleni, Dolj

Fax: +40(51) 270347

Non-English Name: Centrala de Cercetari pentru Cultura Plantelor pe Nisipuri Dabuleni (SCCCPN Dabuleni), Biblioteca **Head:** Ana Toma *Phone:* +40(51) 270347, 270402 ext 100 **Staff:** 1 Prof. **Holdings:** 4,981 books 1,436 journals

Subjects: Soil Science **Specializations:** Fruit Growing, Vegetable Growing, Vineyards **Photocopy:** Yes

2316   Galati, Romania
      Research and Design Center for Fish Culture,
         Fishing and Fish Processing, Galati
      Library
      Portului Str., nr. 2-4
      6200 Galati
Fax: +40(36) 414270

Non-English Name: Centrul de Cercetare Proiectare pentru Piscicultura, Pescuit si Industrializarea Pestelui Galati (CCPPPIP), Biblioteca **Head:** Catalina Patriciu, Despina Popescu *Phone:* +40(36) 416914 **Staff:** 2 Prof. **Holdings:** 11,705 books 8,121 journals **Subjects:** Fish Culture, Fishing **Photocopy:** Yes

2317   Iasi, Romania
      Viticulture Research Station - Jassy
      Library
      Str. Aleea M. Sadoveanu, nr. 48
      6600 Iasi
Fax: +40(32) 218774

Non-English Name: Statiunea de Cercetare Viti-Vinicola Iasi (SCVV Iasi), Biblioteca **Head:** Victoria Crisan *Phone:* +40(32) 219500 **Staff:** 1 Prof. **Holdings:** 10,707 books 4 journals **Subjects:** Enology, Viticulture **Photocopy:** Yes

2318   Livada, Romania
      Agricultural Research Station Livada
      Library
      Baia Mare str., nr. 7
      Livada, Satu Mare
Phone: +40(61) 734881 **Fax:** +40(61) 734881 **Email:** alivada@p5net.ro

Non-English Name: Statiunea de Cercetari Agricole Livada (SCA Livada), Biblioteca **Staff:** 1 Prof. **Holdings:** 7 journals 800 books **Subjects:** Crop Production, Plant Breeding, Plant Genetics, Plant Protection, Soil Science **Photocopy:** Yes

2319   Odobesti, Romania
      Viticulture and Oenology Research Station -
         Odobesti
      Library
      Str. Stefan cel Mare nr. 61
      5332 Odobesti, Vrancea
Fax: +40(37) 675474

Non-English Name: Statinnea de Cercetari Viti-Vinicole Odobesti (SCVV Odobesti), Biblioteca **Head:** Tica Costel *Phone:* +40(37) 675201 **Staff:** 1 Prof. **Holdings:** 700 journals 5,000 books **Subjects:** Enology, Viticulture

2320   Perisoru, Romania
      Marculeti Research Station for Irrigated Crops
      Library
      8577
      Perisoru, Calarasi
Fax: +40(42) 313915

Non-English Name: Statiunea de Cercetari pentru Culturi Irigate Marculesti - Calarasi (SCCI Marculesti), Biblioteca

Head: Vionea Leliana *Phone:* +40(42) 318293 **Staff:** 1 Prof. **Holdings:** 3,000 books 2 journals **Subjects:** Irrigated Farming, Mechanization, Plant Breeding, Plant Protection

2321   Pitesti-Maracineni, Romania
      Research Institute for Fruit Growing
      Library
      PO Box 73
      0312 Pitesti-Maracineni, Arges
Phone: +40(48) 634292, 632066 **Fax:** +40(48) 632492

Non-English Name: Institutul de Cercetari Pomicole, Biblioteca **Founded:** 1967 **Type:** Government **Head:** Maria Schwartz *Phone:* +40(48) 634292 **Staff:** 1 Prof. **Holdings:** 24,000 books 35 journals **Language of Collection/Services:** Romanian / Romanian, English **Subjects:** Agricultural Economics, Agricultural Engineering, Biochemistry, Biotechnology, Fruit Growing, Horticulture, Soil **Specializations:** Fruit Crops, Harvesting, Orchards, Plant Breeding, Plant Protection, Rootstocks **Photocopy:** No

2322   Podul Iloaiei, Romania
      Podul-Iloaiei Agricultural Research Station
      Library
      Soseaua Nationala de Sus, nr. 87
      6623 Podul Iloaiei, Iasi
Fax: +40(32) 740328

Non-English Name: Statiunea de Cercetari Agricole Podul Iloaiei, Biblioteca **Head:** Slonovschi Vintila *Phone:* +40(32) 740234 **Staff:** 2 Prof. **Holdings:** 6,000 books 9,500 journals **Subjects:** Crops, Erosion Control, Irrigation, Meadows, Mechanization, Pest Control, Plant Breeding, Plant Diseases, Plant Nutrition, Soil Fertility, Weed Control

2323   Tg. Bujor, Romania
      Viticulture and Enology Research Station - Tg.
         Bujor
      Library
      Str. G-ral Eremia Grigorescu, nr. 57
      Tg. Bujor, Galati
Fax: +40(36) 540642

Non-English Name: Statiunea de Cercetari Viti-Vinicole Tg. Bujor (SCVV Tg. Bujor), Biblioteca **Head:** Rodica Potarniche *Phone:* +40(36) 540640 **Staff:** 1 Prof. **Holdings:** 20 journals 2,500 books **Subjects:** Enology, Viticulture **Specializations:** Erosion, Fungicides, Growth Regulators, Herbicides, Insecticides, Irrigation, Plant Ecology, Plant Physiology, Plant Protection, Winemaking **Photocopy:** Yes

2324   Valea Calugareasca, Romania
      Research Institute for Viticulture and Enology
      Library
      Str. Valea Mantei, nr. 1
      2040 Valea Calugareasca, Prahova
Phone: +40(44) 236690 **Fax:** +40(44) 236389

Non-English Name: Institutului de Cercetari Pentru Viticultura si Vinificatie (ICVV Valea Calugareasca), Biblioteca **Founded:** 1967 **Head:** Maria Ivan *Phone:* +40(44) 236690 **Type:** Government **Staff:** 1 Prof. **Holdings:** 13,769 books 174 journals **Subjects:** Enology, Viticulture **Specializations:** Vineyards **Loan:** In country

Russia

2325   Adygeya Republic, Russia
Adygeisky Scientific Research Institute of
    Agriculture
Library
Lenin St., 48
PO Podgornoye
Maikop
Adygeya Republic 352764
Phone: +7() 22342

Founded: 1962 **Type:** Government **Holdings:** 7,400 books

2326   Adygeya Republic, Russia
Maikopskaya Experiment Station
Library
Shuntuk Settlement
Maikopsky District
Adygeya Republic 352772
Phone: +7() 56432

Type: Government **Holdings:** 21,200 books **Subjects:**
Plants

2327   Altay Area, Russia
Altay Scientific Research Veterinary Station
Library
Shevchenko St., 160
Barnaul 656031
Altay Area
Phone: +7(3852) 380935

Founded: 1938 **Type:** Government **Holdings:** 2,700 books
Subjects: Veterinary Science

2328   Altay Area, Russia
Altay State Agrarian University
Library
Krasnoarmeyskiy Av., 98
Barnaul 656099
Altay Area
Phone: +7(3852) 38-1228 **Fax:** +7(3852) 38-0600

Founded: 1942 **Type:** Academic **Holdings:** 98,200 books
Subjects: Agricultural Chemistry, Agricultural Economics,
Agronomy, Land Management, Mechanization, Reclamation, Soil Science, Veterinary Medicine, Water Management, Zootechny

2329   Altay Area, Russia
Gorno-Altay Research Institute of Agriculture
Library
Katunskaya St., 12
Maima 659701
Altay Area
Phone: +7() 22184

Type: Government **Holdings:** 7,400 books

2330   Altay Area, Russia
Russian Academy of Agricultural Sciences,
    Siberian Branch, Altay Research and

Technology Institute of Animal Husbandry
    (RAAS SB)
Library
Scientific Town
Barnaul 656910
Altay Area
Phone: +7(3852) 316806, 316803 **WWW:** www-sbras.ict.
nsk.su/eng/sbras/siberia/raas-sb.html

Type: Government **Holdings:** 10,400 books **Subjects:** Animal Breeding, Livestock

2331   Altay Area, Russia
Russian Academy of Agricultural Sciences,
    Siberian Branch, Altay Research Institute of
    Arable Farming and Selection (RAAS SB)
Library
Scientific Town, 32
Barnaul 656910
Altay Area
WWW: www-sbras.ict.nsk.su/eng/sbras/siberia/raas-sb.
html

Former Name: Altay Research Institute of Agriculture
Founded: 1975 **Type:** Government **Head:** Lidia I. Yego-
rova *Phone:* +7(3852) 316837 **Holdings:** 31,000 books **Subjects:** Breeding **Loan:** Inhouse **Photocopy:** Yes

2332   Altay Area, Russia
Russian Academy of Agricultural Sciences,
    Siberian Branch, Research Institute of
    Horticulture of Siberia (RAAS SB)
Library
Zmeiorsky Tract, 49
Barnaul 656045
Altay Area
Phone: +7(3852) 231986, 230690 **WWW:** www-sbras.ict.
nsk.su/eng/sbras/siberia/raas-sb.html

Founded: 1939 **Type:** Government **Holdings:** 12,600 books
Subjects: Horticulture

2333   Altay Area, Russia
West Siberian Vegetable Breeding Experiment
    Station
Library
Barnaul 656904
Altay Area
Phone: +7(3852) 26595

Type: Government **Holdings:** 5,500 books **Subjects:** Vegetables, Potatoes

2334   Amur Province, Russia
All-Russia Scientific Research Institute of
    Soybeans
Library
Ignatyevskoe Highway, 19
Blagoveshchensk
Amur Province 675027
Phone: +7(416-24) 52833

Founded: 1925 **Type:** Government **Holdings:** 11,100 books
Subjects: Soybeans

2335   Amur Province, Russia
Far East Scientific Research and Production
    Technology Institute of Mechanization and
    Electrification of Agriculture
Library
Vasilenko St., 5
Blagoveshchensk
Amur Province 675027
Phone: +7(4162) 41624, 54971

Subjects: Electrification, Mechanization

2336   Amur Province, Russia
Far East State Agrarian University
Library
Politekhnicheskaya St., 86
Blagoveshchensk
Amur Province 675005
Phone: +7(4162) 31-3211 **Fax:** +7(4162) 42-3179

Founded: 1950 **Type:** Academic **Holdings:** 53,900 books
Subjects: Agricultural Chemistry, Agricultural Economics,
Agricultural Engineering, Agricultural Technologies, Agro-
ecology, Biology, Electrification, Land Management, Nature
Conservation, Veterinary Medicine, Water Resources, Zoo-
techny

2337   Amur Province, Russia
Far Eastern Zone Scientific Research Veterinary
    Institute
Library
Northern, 112
Blagoveshchensk
Amur Province 675005
Phone: +7(4162) 22119

Founded: 1935 **Type:** Government **Holdings:** 9,600 books
Subjects: Veterinary Science

2338   Arkhangelsk, Russia
Arkhangelsk Scientific Research Institute of
    Agriculture
Library
Ilyich St., 43
Arkhangelsk 183054
Phone: +7(818-2) 245444, 245516

Founded: 1931 **Type:** Government **Holdings:** 4,200 books

2339   Astrakhan Province, Russia
All-Russia Scientific Research Institute of
    Irrigated Vegetable and Melon Growing
Library
Lyubich St., 16
Kamyzyak
Astrakhan Province 416306
Phone: +7(851-15) 28770

Founded: 1939 **Type:** Government **Holdings:** 12,300 books
Subjects: Irrigation, Melons, Vegetables

2340   Astrakhan Province, Russia
Prikaspiysky Scientific Research Institute of Arid
    Agriculture
Library

Solenoye Zaymishche Village
Chernoyarsk Region
Astrakhan Province 416231
Phone: +7(851-19) 22244

2341   Bashkortostan, Russia
Bashkir Scientific Research and Production
    Technology Institute of Animal Breeding and
    Forage Production
Library
Pushkin St., 86
Ufa 450025
Bashkortostan
Phone: +7(3472) 221723

Founded: 1984 **Type:** Government **Holdings:** 12,100 books
Subjects: Animal Breeding, Feeds, Livestock

2342   Bashkortostan, Russia
Bashkir Scientific Research Institute of
    Agriculture
Library
R. Zorge St., 19
Ufa 450059
Bashkortostan
Phone: +7(3472) 240708

Founded: 1956 **Type:** Government **Holdings:** 20,700 books
Subjects: Field Crops

2343   Bashkortostan, Russia
Bashkir State Agrarian University
Library
50 -letiya Oktyabrya St., 34
Ufa 450089
Bashkortostan
Phone: +7(3472) 28-0698 **Fax:** +7(3472) 28-9177 **Email:**
bgau@soros.bashedu.ru, bgau@poikc.bashnet.ru

Founded: 1930 **Type:** Academic **Holdings:** 100,900 books
Subjects: Agricultural Economics, Agronomy, Electrifica-
tion, Forestry, Mechanization, Veterinary Medicine,
Zootechny

2344   Belgorod Province, Russia
Alekseevka Experiment Station of Volatile Oils
Library
Alekseevka
Belgorod Province 309800
Phone: +7(7234) 30625

Type: Government **Subjects:** Oils

2345   Belgorod Province, Russia
Belgorod State Agricultural Academy
Library
Vavilov St., 24
Mayskiy Settlement
Belgorod Region
Belgorod Province 309103
Phone: +7(722) 39-2195 **Fax:** +7(722) 22-5129

Type: Academic **Holdings:** 10,200 books **Subjects:** Agricultural Engineering, Agronomy, Mechanization, Veterinary
Medicine, Zootechny

2346   Bryansk Province, Russia
All-Russia Scientific Research Institute of Lupin
Library
PO Michurinskoye
Bryansk Province 242024
Phone: +7(083-22) 911263 **Fax:** +7(083-22) 741447
Email: root@lupin.bitmcnit.bryansk.ru

Founded: 1958 **Type:** Government **Holdings:** 28,300 books

2347   Bryansk Province, Russia
Bryansk State Agricultural Academy
Library
Kokino Settlement
Vygonicheskiy Region
Bryansk Province 243365
Phone: +7(083) 41-24341

Founded: 1980 **Type:** Academic **Holdings:** 199,900 books
Subjects: Agricultural Economics, Agroecology, Agronomy, Equipment, Mechanization, Reclamation, Water Resources, Zootechny

2348   Bryansk Province, Russia
Pogarskaya Experiment Station
Library
Chaikino Settlement
Pogarsky Region
Bryansk Province 243566
Phone: +7(083-49) 91295

2349   Bryansk Province, Russia
Scientific Research Institute of Fertilizers and
      Agro-Soil Science, Novozybkovsky Branch
Library
PO Box 10
Novozybkov
Bryansk Province 243000
Phone: +7(083-43) 33225 **Fax:** +7(083-43) 33220

Subjects: Fertilizers, Soil Science

2350   Buryat Republic, Russia
Buryat Scientific Research Institute of Agriculture
Library
Kirov St., 35
Ulan-Ude 670000
Buryat Republic
Phone: +7(3012) 21608/9

Founded: 1932 **Type:** Academic **Holdings:** 130,600 books

2351   Buryat Republic, Russia
Buryat State Agricultural Academy
Library
Pushkin St., 8
Ulan-Ude 670020
Buryat Republic
Phone: +7(3012) 34-2341 **Fax:** +7(3012) 34-2254 **Email:**
bgha@eastsib.ru

Subjects: Agricultural Chemistry, Agricultural Economics,
Agronomy, Mechanization, Soil Science, Veterinary Medicine, Zootechny

2352   Buryat Republic, Russia
Eastern Siberian Scientific Industrial Centre for
      Fisheries
Library
Hahalov St., 4
Ulan-Ude 670034
Buryat Republic
Phone: +7(3012) 341931, 342533 **Fax:** +7(3012) 343116

Subjects: Fisheries

2353   Chechen Republic, Russia
All-Russia Scientific Research and Production
      Technology Institute of Lucerne and Rape
Library
Chikalo Settlement
Grozniy Region 366021
Chechen Republic
Phone: +7(712) 229038, 224481

Subjects: Lucerne, Rape

2354   Chechen Republic, Russia
Chechen Scientific Research Institute of
      Agriculture
Library
Lenin St., 1
Gikalo Settlement
Grozniy Region 366021
Chechen Republic

Founded: 1963 **Type:** Government **Holdings:** 11,800 books

2355   Chelyabinsk, Russia
Chelyabinsk State Agroengineering University
      (CSAU)
Library
Lenin Av., 75
Chelyabinsk 454080
Phone: +7(3512) 666557 **Fax:** +7(3512) 666512 **WWW:**
www.urc.ac.ru:8002/Universities/AGRO

Former Name: Ural Institute of Mechanization and Electrification of Agriculture **Founded:** 1930 **Type:** Academic
Head: Elena Lebedeva *Phone:* +7(3512) 666557 *Email:*
agroun@chel.surnet.ru **Staff:** 8 Prof. 21 Other **Holdings:**
407,975 books 200 journals **Language of Collection/Services:** Russian **Subjects:** Agribusiness, Agricultural Economics, Agricultural Engineering, Agronomy, Education,
Food Processing, Farming **Loan:** Inhouse **Service:** Inhouse
Photocopy: No

2356   Chelyabinsk, Russia
South Ural Scientific Research Institute of Fruit,
      Vegetable and Potato Breeding
Library
Gidrostroy St., 16
PO Shershny
Chelyabinsk 454902
Phone: +7(352-2) 606229

Type: Government **Holdings:** 3,700 books **Subjects:** Fruits,
Vegetables

2357   **Chelyabinsk Province, Russia**
Chelyabinsk Scientific Research Institute of
     Agriculture
Library
Timiryazevsky Settlement
Chebakul' Region
Chelyabinsk Province 456404
Phone: +7(351-2) 332316

Founded: 1936 **Type:** Government **Holdings:** 13,600 books

2358   **Chelyabinsk Province, Russia**
Institute of Agroecology
Library
Sovietskaya St., 8
Miasskoe Settlement
Krasnoarmeysk Region
Chelyabinsk Province 456660
Phone: +7(351-2) 22100

Subjects: Agroecology

2359   **Chelyabinsk Province, Russia**
Ural State Institute of Veterinary Medicine
Library
Gagarin St., 13
Troitsk
Chelyabinsk Province 457100
Phone: +7(351-63) 2-4418 **Fax:** +7(351-63) 2-0472

Founded: 1920 **Type:** Academic **Holdings:** 36,200 books
Subjects: Veterinary Science, Zootechny

2360   **Chita, Russia**
East Siberia Scientific Veterinary Research
     Institute
Library
Kirova St., 49
Chita 672039
Phone: +7(302-22) 96854

Subjects: Veterinary Science

2361   **Chita, Russia**
Irkutsk State Agricultural Academy, Chita Branch
Library
Yubileinaya St., 4
Vostochny Settlement
Chita 672023

Subjects: Agricultural Economics, Agronomy, Mechanization, Zootechny

2362   **Chita, Russia**
Zabaikalsky Scientific Research Institute of
     Agriculture
Library
Vostochny Settlement
Yubilleinaya St., 4
Chita 672023
Phone: +7(302-22) 42292, 40361

Founded: 1985 **Type:** Academic

2363   **Chuvash Republic, Russia**
Chuvash Scientific Research Institute of
     Agriculture
Library
Tsivilisk, PO Ivanovo
Opitniy Settlement
Tsivilsky Region 429911
Chuvash Republic
Phone: +7(835-45) 21626

Founded: 1971 **Type:** Government **Holdings:** 5,900 books

2364   **Chuvash Republic, Russia**
Chuvash State Agricultural Academy
Library
Karl Marx St., 29
Cheboksary 428000
Chuvash Republic
Phone: +7(8352) 62-2145

Founded: 1931 **Type:** Academic **Holdings:** 43,200 books
Subjects: Agricultural Economics, Agricultural Technologies, Agronomy, Mechanization, Zootechny

2365   **Chuvash Republic, Russia**
Scientific Research and Production Technology
     Institute of Hops
Library
Nikolayev St., 11
Tsivilsk 429900
Chuvash Republic
Phone: +7(813) 21844

Founded: 1971 **Type:** Government **Subjects:** Hops

2366   **Dagestan Republic, Russia**
Dagestan Production Technology Institute of
     Agriculture
Library
Akushinsky pr.
Nauchny Gorodok
Makhachkala 367014
Dagestan Republic
Phone: +7(872-00) 636660

Founded: 1956 **Type:** Government **Holdings:** 29,400 books

2367   **Dagestan Republic, Russia**
Dagestan State Agricultural Academy
Library
Gadzhiev St., 180
Makhachkala 367032
Dagestan Republic
Phone: +7(872-2) 682470, 682446

Founded: 1932 **Type:** Academic **Holdings:** 94,000 books
Subjects: Agricultural Economics, Agronomy, Crop Production, Fruits, Mechanization, Vegetables, Viticulture, Veterinary Medicine, Zootechny

2368   **Dagestan Republic, Russia**
Prikaspiysky Regional Scientific Veterinary
     Research Institute
Library
Dakhadayev St., 88

Makhachkala 367020
Dagestan Republic
Phone: +7(872-00) 679465 **Fax:** +7(872-00) 679465

Founded: 1968 **Type:** Government **Holdings:** 41,100 books
Subjects: Veterinary Science

2369 Ekaterinburg, Russia
Sverdlovsk Scientific Research Veterinary Station
Library
Belinsky St., 122a
Ekaterinburg 620142
Phone: +7(3432) 222044

Subjects: Veterinary Science

2370 Ekaterinburg, Russia
Ural Scientific Research Institute of Agriculture
Library
Glavnaya St., 21
Ekaterinburg 620061
Phone: +7(3432) 267170, 267461 **Fax:** +7(3432) 244906

Founded: 1956 **Type:** Government **Holdings:** 198,800 books

2371 Ekaterinburg, Russia
Ural State Agricultural Academy
Library
Karl Libknekht St., 42
Ekaterinburg 620219
Email: academy@usaca.ru

Founded: 1929 **Type:** Academic **Holdings:** 324,000 books
Subjects: Agricultural Economics, Agronomy, Mechanization, Veterinary Medicine, Vocational Training, Zootechny

2372 Irkutsk, Russia
Irkutsk Scientific Research Veterinary Station
Library
Botkin St., 4
Irkutsk 664005
Phone: +7(3952) 436613

Founded: 1957 **Type:** Government **Holdings:** 2,400 books
Subjects: Veterinary Science

2373 Irkutsk, Russia
Irkutsk State Agricultural Academy
Library
Molodezhny Settlement
Irkutsk 664038
Phone: +7(3952) 46-9488 **Fax:** +7(3952) 46-4645

Founded: 1934 **Type:** Academic **Holdings:** 96,200 books
Subjects: Agricultural Economics, Agronomy, Biology, Electrification, Mechanization, Zootechny

2374 Irkutsk, Russia
Russian Academy of Agricultural Sciences, Siberian Branch, Irkutsk Research Institute of Agriculture (RAAS SB)
Library
PO Pivovariha
Irkutsk 666011

Phone: +7(3952) 43-3410 **WWW:** www-sbras.ict.nsk.su/eng/sbras/siberia/raas-sb.html

Founded: 1957 **Type:** Government **Holdings:** 15,200 books

2375 Irkutsk, Russia
Russian Academy of Sciences, Siberian Branch, Siberian Institute of Plant Physiology and Biochemistry (SB RAS, SIPPB)
Library
PO Box 1243
Irkutsk 664033
Phone: +7(3952) 460721 **Fax:** +7(3952) 310754 **Email:** root@sifibr.irkutsk.su **WWW:** www.icc.ru/acad/sifibr/sifibr_e.htm

Type: Government **Subjects:** Biochemistry, Plant Physiology

2376 Irkutsk Province, Russia
Tulunskaya State Breeding Experiment Station
Library
Tula, 4
Tulunsky Region
Irkutsk Province 665210

2377 Ivanovo, Russia
Ivanovo Scientific Research Institute of Agriculture
Library
Central St., 2
Bogorodskoe Settlement
Ivanovo 155106
Phone: +7(932) 372185, 316396

Founded: 1935 **Type:** Government **Holdings:** 16,500 books

2378 Ivanovo, Russia
Ivanovo State Agricultural Academy
Library
Sovetskaya St., 45
Ivanovo 153467
Phone: +7(932) 32-8604

Founded: 1918 **Type:** Academic **Holdings:** 240,600 books
Subjects: Agricultural Economics, Agroecology, Agronomy, Land Management, Mechanization, Veterinary Medicine, Zootechny

2379 Kabardino-Balkarskaya Republic, Russia
Kabardino-Balkarian State Agricultural Academy
Library
Lev Tolstoy St., 185
Nalchik 360004
Kabardino-Balkarskaya Republic
Phone: +7(866-22) 9-4881 **Fax:** +7(866-22) 7-5692

Type: Academic **Holdings:** 17,500 books **Subjects:** Agricultural Economics, Agronomy, Fruits, Land Management, Reclamation, Vegetables, Veterinary Medicine, Viticulture, Zootechny

2380 Kabardino-Balkarskaya Republic, Russia
Kabardino-Balkarskiy Scientific Research Institute of Agriculture

Library
Mechnikov St., 130 A
Nalchik 360024
Kabardino-Balkarskaya Republic
Phone: +7(866-22) 52533, 50316 **Fax:** +7(866-22) 50886

2381   Kabardino-Balkarskaya Republic, Russia
North Caucasian Scientific Research Institute of
     Mountain and Foothill Horticulture
Library
PO Zatishye - 4
Nalchik 360000
Kabardino-Balkarskaya Republic
Phone: +7(866-22) 27590, 25294

Subjects: Horticulture

2382   Kaliningrad Province, Russia
Kaliningrad Scientific Research Institute of
     Agriculture
Library
Slavyanskoye Village
Polessky Region
Kaliningrad Province 238631
Phone: +7(011-58) 25447

Founded: 1950 **Type:** Government **Holdings:** 29,100 books

2383   Kaliningrad Province, Russia
Saint Petersburg State Agrarian University,
     Kaliningrad Branch of Correspondence
Library
Sovetskaya St., 12
Pollesk
Kaliningrad Province 238630

Type: Academic **Subjects:** Agricultural Economics, Agronomy, Mechanization, Zootechny

2384   Kalmik Republic, Russia
Kalmitsky Scientific Research Institute of
     Agriculture
Library
Gorodovikov pr., 5
Elista 358011
Kalmik Republic
Phone: +7(847-22) 20668 **Fax:** +7(847-22) 20673

Founded: 1967 **Type:** Government **Holdings:** 10,000 books
Subjects: Animal Breeding, Livestock

2385   Kaluga, Russia
Moscow Agricultural Academy, Kaluga Branch
Library
Vishnevskiy St., 27
Kaluga 248007

Founded: 1976 **Subjects:** Agricultural Economics, Agronomy, Zootechny

2386   Kaluga Province, Russia
All-Russia Scientific Research Institute of
     Agricultural Radiology and Agroecology
Library
Obninsk

Kaluga Province 249020
Phone: +7(084-39) 64802 **Fax:** +7(084-39) 48066 **Email:** riar@obninsk.org, acr@storm.iasnet.com **WWW:** www.obninsk.ru/science/nii_shr_en.html

Founded: 1971 **Subjects:** Agroecology

2387   Kaluga Province, Russia
All-Russia Scientific Research Institute of
     Physiology, Biochemistry and Feeding of
     Agricultural Animals
Library
Borovsk
Kaluga Province 249010
Phone: +7(095) 546-3415 **Fax:** +7(095) 546-3443 **Email:** bifip@kaluga.ru

Founded: 1961 **Type:** Government **Holdings:** 79,200 books
Subjects: Animal Husbandry, Animal Nutrition, Biochemistry, Feeds, Physiology

2388   Kaluga Province, Russia
Kaluga Scientific Research and Production
     Technology Institute of Agriculture
Library
Barrikad Str., 116
PO Experimental Agricultural Station
Peremishlbskiy Region
Kaluga Province 249202
Phone: +7() 96239, 96230

Founded: 1947 **Type:** Government **Holdings:** 13,200 books

2389   Kamchatka Province, Russia
Kamchatka Scientific Research Institute of
     Agriculture
Library
Sosnovka Village
Elizovsky Region
Kamchatka Province 684033
Phone: +7() 537544, 554320

Founded: 1962 **Type:** Government **Holdings:** 6,900 books

2390   Karachayevo-Cherkesskaya Republic, Russia
Karachayevo-Cherkessky Scientific Research
     Institute of Agriculture
Library
Lenin pr., 27
Kavkazsky Settlement
Prikubansk Region
Karachayevo-Cherkesskaya Republic 357111
Phone: +7(8-878-22) 32424

2391   Kemerovo, Russia
Novosibirsk State Agrarian University, Kemerovo
     Agricultural Institute
Library
Markovtsev St., 5
Kemerovo 650060
Phone: +7(3842) 51-4911 **Fax:** +7(3842) 51-3944

Type: Academic **Subjects:** Agricultural Economics, Agronomy, Mechanization, Natural Resources Management, Zootechny

2392   Kemerovo Province, Russia
Russian Academy of Agricultural Sciences,
   Siberian Branch, Kemerovo Research
   Institute of Agriculture (RAAS SB)
Library
PO Novostroika
Kemerovo Region
Kemerovo Province 652410
Phone: +7(3842) 537544, 554320 **WWW:** www-sbras.ict.
nsk.su/eng/sbras/siberia/raas-sb.html

Founded: 1945 **Type:** Government **Holdings:** 14,400 books

2393   Kemerovo Province, Russia
State Center of Agricultural Chemistry Service
   "Kemerovskiy"
Information Department
Central St., 15
P/O Novostroika, 10
Kemerovo Province 652410
Phone: +7(3842) 553781, 121248 **Fax:** +7(3842) 553781

Founded: 1964 **Type:** Government **Head:** Olga Prosiynni-
cova *Phone:* +7(3842) 553781, 121248 **Staff:** 70 Prof. 30
Other **Holdings:** 1,500 books **Language of Collection/Ser-
vices:** Russian / Russian **Subjects:** Agricultural Chemistry
Specializations: Soil Chemistry **Loan:** In country **Service:**
In country **Photocopy:** No

2394   Khabarovsk, Russia
Far Eastern Scientific Research Institute of
   Economy of Agro-industrial Complex
   Management
Library
K. Marx St., 107
Khabarovsk 680009
Phone: +7(4212) 371324

Subjects: Agricultural Economics

2395   Khabarovsky Area, Russia
Far Eastern Scientific Research Institute of
   Agriculture (FESRIA)
Library
Vostochny Settlement
Khabarovsky Area 682321
Phone: +7() 937666

Founded: 1939 **Type:** Government **Head:** Mrs. Donets
Tatyana **Staff:** 3 Prof. **Holdings:** 20,000 books 25 journals
Language of Collection/Services: Russian / Russian **Sub-
jects:** Comprehensive **Specializations:** Animal Husbandry,
Farming, Plants **Loan:** Internationally **Service:** Inhouse
Photocopy: Yes

2396   Kirov, Russia
All-Russia Scientific Research Institute of
   Hunting Economics and Fur Breeding
Library
PO Box 81
Engels St., 79
Kirov 610000
Phone: +7(833-2) 385594 **Fax:** +7(833-2) 381130

Subjects: Furbearing Animals, Hunting

2397   Kirov, Russia
North Eastern Scientific Methodology Centre
Library
Lenin St., 166 a
Kirov 610007
Phone: +7(833-2) 674334 **Fax:** +7(833-2) 674262

Founded: 1967 **Type:** Government **Holdings:** 32,500 books

2398   Kirov Province, Russia
Falenskaya Breeding Station
Library
Timirayzev St., 3
Falensky Region
Kirov Province 612500
Phone: +7(83-332) 12518 **Fax:** +7(83-332) 11185

Type: Government **Holdings:** 23,800 books

2399   Komi Republic, Russia
Ijmo-Pechera Scientific Research Veterinary
   Station
Library
Depovskaya St., 12
Pechera 169700
Komi Republic
Phone: +7(821-42) 24033

Type: Government **Subjects:** Veterinary Science

2400   Komi Republic, Russia
Scientific Research and Production Technology
   Institute of Agriculture
Library
Rucheynaya St., 27
Siktivkar 167003
Komi Republic
Phone: +7(821-22) 219069, 291520

2401   Kostroma, Russia
Kostroma State Agricultural Academy
Library
Karavayevo Settlement
Kostroma 157930
Phone: +7(094-2) 66-1236 **Fax:** +7(094-2) 54-3423
Email: biblio@staff.ksaa.edu.ru **WWW:** www.ksaa.edu.
ru:8101

Founded: 1949 **Type:** Academic **Head:** Natalia Egorova
Holdings: 500,000 books **Subjects:** Agricultural Econom-
ics, Agricultural Engineering, Agronomy, Electrification,
Mechanization, Veterinary Medicine, Zootechny

2402   Kostroma, Russia
Scientific Research Institute on Bast Fibre
   Processing
Library
Komsomolskaya St., 4
Kostroma 156000
Phone: +7(094-22) 72997

Subjects: Bast Fibers

2403   Kostroma Province, Russia
Kostroma Scientific Research Institute of
    Agriculture
Library
PO Minskoe Highway
Kostroma Region
Kostroma Province 157943
Phone: +7(094-2) 666251, 666261

Founded: 1963 **Type:** Government **Holdings:** 10,400 books

2404   Krasnodar, Russia
All-Russia Scientific Research Institute of
    Biological Plant Protection
Library
PO 39
Krasnodar 350039
Phone: +7(861-2) 508916

Subjects: Plant Protection

2405   Krasnodar, Russia
All-Russia Scientific Research Institute of
    Tobacco, Makhorka and Tobacco Products
Library
Moscovskaya St, 42
Krasnodar 350072
Phone: +7(862-2) 578882, 578579

Founded: 1913 **Type:** Government **Holdings:** 180,600
books **Subjects:** Tobacco

2406   Krasnodar, Russia
Krasnodar Scientific Research Institute of
    Agricultural Production Storage and
    Processing
Library
Topolinaya St., 2
Krasnodar 350072
Phone: +7(861-2) 579593 **Fax:** +7(861-2) 579844 **Email:**
kisp@kubannet.ru

2407   Krasnodar, Russia
Krasnodar Scientific Research Institute of Fishery
    Economy
Library
Gogol St., 46
Krasnodar 350000
Phone: +7(861-2) 573042 **Fax:** +7(861-2) 573003

Subjects: Fisheries

2408   Krasnodar, Russia
Krasnodar Scientific Research Veterinary Station
Library
Liniya St., 1
Krasnodar 350004
Phone: +7(861-2) 560978

Type: Government **Holdings:** 12,900 books **Subjects:** Veterinary Science

2409   Krasnodar, Russia
Kuban State Agrarian University
Library

Kalinin St., 13
Krasnodar 350044
Phone: +7(861-2) 502609 **Fax:** +7(861-2) 502935

Former Name: Kuban Agriculture Institute **Founded:** 1922
Type: Academic **Head:** Mrs. L. Butko **Staff:** 45 Prof. **Holdings:** 635,000 books 1,300 journals **Language of Collection
/Services:** Russian **Subjects:** Agricultural Economics, Agricultural Engineering, Animal Husbandry, Biotechnology,
Crops, Entomology, Farming, Horticulture, Plant Pathology,
Soil Science, Veterinary Medicine **Specializations:** Collection of old books and journals before 1917 **Loan:** In country
Service: Inhouse **Photocopy:** No

2410   Krasnodar, Russia
Lykyanenko Krasnodar Scientific Research
    Institute of Agriculture
Library
Krasnodar 350012
Phone: +7(861-2) 508104

Founded: 1956 **Type:** Government **Holdings:** 17,800 books

2411   Krasnodar, Russia
North Caucasian Scientific Research and Project
    Technological Institute of Agrochemistry and
    Soil Science
Library
Starokubanskaya St., 2
Krasnodar 350011
Phone: +7(861-2) 338249

Subjects: Agricultural Chemistry, Soil Science

2412   Krasnodar, Russia
North Caucasian Scientific Research Institute of
    Horticulture and Viticulture
Library
40 - letiya Pobedy St., 39
Krasnodar 350029
Phone: +7(861-2) 537074, 537286 **Fax:** +7(861-2) 535972

Founded: 1958 **Type:** Government **Holdings:** 24,300 books
Subjects: Horticulture, Vineyards, Viticulture

2413   Krasnodar, Russia
North Caucasian Scientific Research Institute of
    Sugar Beets and Sugar
Library
Krasnaya St., 113
Krasnodar 350680
Phone: +7(861-2) 554968

Subjects: Sugar, Sugarbeet

2414   Krasnodar, Russia
V.S. Pustovoyt All-Russia Scientific Research
    Institute of Oil-Producing Crops
Library
Filatov St., 17
Krasnodar 350038
Phone: +7(861-2) 555933/4

Founded: 1924 **Type:** Government **Holdings:** 67,200 books
Subjects: Oil Plants

2415   Krasnodar Area, Russia
All-Russia Scientific Research Institute of Rice
Library
Belozerny Settlement
Krasnodar Area 353204
Phone: +7(861-2) 500792 **Fax:** +7(861-2) 509423

Founded: 1967 **Type:** Government **Holdings:** 52,700 books
Subjects: Rice

2416   Krasnodar Area, Russia
All-Union Scientific Research Institute of
Floriculture and Subtropical Horticulture
Library
Fabritsius St., 2/28
Sochi
Krasnodar Area 354002
Phone: +7(862-2) 995221, 927361

Founded: 1894 **Type:** Government **Holdings:** 37,000 books
Subjects: Farming, Flowers, Horticulture, Mountain Areas

2417   Krasnodar Area, Russia
Krasnodar Scientific Research Institute of
Vegetables and Potato Economy
Library
PO Belozernoye
Krasnodar Area 350101
Phone: +7(861-2) 500490 **Fax:** +7(861-2) 509204

Subjects: Potatoes, Vegetables

2418   Krasnodar Area, Russia
North Caucasian Scientific Research Institute of
Animal Breeding
Library
Znamensky Settlement
Krasnodar Area 350055
Phone: +7(861-2) 371669, 376720 **Fax:** +7(861-2) 377503

Founded: 1965 **Type:** Government **Subjects:** Animal
Breeding, Livestock

2419   Krasnoyarsk, Russia
Krasnoyarsk State Agrarian University
Library
Mir Av., 88
Krasnoyarsk 660049
Phone: +7(3912) 45-0666, 27-2323 **Fax:** +7(3912) 27-
0386 **Email:** krasgay@public.krasnet.ru

Founded: 1953 **Subjects:** Agricultural Economics, Agricultural Engineering, Agronomy, Electrification, Food Technology, Food Processing Equipment, Land Management,
Mechanization, Management, Veterinary Medicine, Zootechny

2420   Krasnoyarsk, Russia
Russian Academy of Agricultural Sciences,
Siberian Branch, Krasnoyarsk Research
Institute of Agriculture (RAAS SB)
Library
Svobodny Pr., 66
Krasnoyarsk 660062

Phone: +7(3912) 49514, 449645 **WWW:** www-sbras.ict.
nsk.su/eng/sbras/siberia/raas-sb.html
Founded: 1956 **Type:** Government

2421   Krasnoyarsk, Russia
Russian Academy of Agricultural Sciences,
Siberian Branch, Technological Institute of
Animal Husbandry (RAAS SB)
Library
Svobodny pr., 66
Krasnoyarsk 660062
Phone: +7(3912) 449514, 449645 **WWW:** www-sbras.ict.
nsk.su/eng/sbras/siberia/raas-sb.html

Subjects: Animal Husbandry

2422   Krasnoyarsk, Russia
Russian Academy of Sciences, Siberian Branch,
V.N. Sukachev Institute of Forestry (SB RAS,
SIF)
Library
Krasnoyarsk 660036
Phone: +7(3912) 433686 **Fax:** +7(3912) 433686 **Email:**
ifor@krsk.infotel.ru **WWW:** www-sbras.nsc.ru/eng/sbras/
copan/ifor_main.html

Type: Government **Subjects:** Forestry

2423   Krasnoyarsk, Russia
Siberian Scientific Research Institute of Hydraulic
Engineering and Melioration
Library
Svobodny pr., 68
Krasnoyarsk 660062
Phone: +7(3912) 454448 **Fax:** +7(3912) 454371

Subjects: Hydraulic Engineering

2424   Krasnoyarsk Area, Russia
Russian Academy of Agricultural Sciences,
Siberian Branch, Far North Research Institute
of Agriculture (RAAS SB)
Scientific Library
Komsomolskaya St., 1
Norilsk
Krasnoyarsk Area 663302
Phone: +7(391-52) 463798 **WWW:** www-sbras.ict.nsk.su/
eng/sbras/siberia/raas-sb.html

Founded: 1937 **Type:** Academic **Head:** Olga G. Krylova
Phone: +7(391-52) 40148 **Staff:** 40 Prof. 46 Other **Hold-
ings:** 154 books **Subjects:** Biology, Deer, Deer Farming,
Fisheries, Forage, Grasses, Hunting, Livestock, Meadows,
Plant Pathology, Plant Pests, Plant Protection, Soil Science,
Technology, Vegetables, Veterinary Medicine **Loan:** In
country **Photocopy:** Yes

2425   Kurgan Province, Russia
Kurgan Scientific Research Institute of Grain
Farming
Library
Sadovoye Settlement
Ketovo Region
Kurgan Province 641325

Phone: +7(352-31) 22739 Fax: +7(352-31) 22656

Founded: 1962 Type: Government Holdings: 15,200 books
Subjects: Grain Crops

2426   Kurgan Province, Russia
Kurgan State Agricultural Academy
Library
Lesnikovo Settlement
Ketovo Region
Kurgan Province 641311
Phone: +7(352-31) 4-4264 Fax: +7(352-31) 4-4370

Subjects: Agricultural Economics, Agroecology, Agronomy, Mechanization, Zootechny

2427   Kurgan Province, Russia
Shadrinskaya Scientific Research Experiment
    Station
Library
Maltsevo Settlement
Shadrinsky Region
Kurgan Province 641854
Phone: +7(352-53) 478449

Founded: 1952 Type: Government Holdings: 9,200 books

2428   Kursk, Russia
All-Russia Scientific Research Institute of Land
    Use and Soil Protection
Library
K. Marx St., 70 B
Kursk 305021
Phone: +7(071-2) 334256

Founded: 1970 Type: Government Holdings: 10,000 books
Subjects: Erosion, Plant Protection

2429   Kursk, Russia
Kursk State Agricultural Academy
Library
Karl Marx St., 70
Kursk 305034
Phone: +7(071-2) 33-0954 Fax: +7(071-2) 33-8436

Founded: 1956 Subjects: Agricultural Economics, Agronomy, Agroecology, Mechanization, Plant Protection, Veterinary Medicine, Zootechny

2430   Kursk, Russia
Russian Scientific Research Institute of Sugar
    Industry
Library
Karl Marx St., 63
Kursk 305029
Phone: +7(071-2) 333186 Fax: +7(071-2) 332174

Subjects: Sugar Industry

2431   Kursk Province, Russia
Kursk Scientific Research Institute of Agricultural
    Manufacture
Library
PO Cheremushky
Kursk Region

Kursk Province 307026
Phone: +7(071-00) 63070, 331563

2432   Leningrad Province, Russia
Federal Selection - Genetics Center of Fishery
Library
Ropsha Settlement
Lomonosov Region
Leningrad Province 190000
Phone: +7(812) 767-2236, 767-2286

Type: Government Subjects: Fisheries

2433   Leningrad Province, Russia
Northwestern Scientific Research Institute of
    Agriculture
Library
Institutskaya St., 1
Belogorka Settlement
Gatchinsky Region
Leningrad Province 188231
Phone: +7(812) 51140

Founded: 1930 Type: Government Holdings: 39,700 books
Subjects: Plants

2434   Lipetsk, Russia
All-Russia Scientific Research and Production
    Technology Institute of Rape
Library
Boyevoy pr., 26
Lipetsk 398037
Phone: 7(074-2) 262361

Founded: 1956 Type: Government Holdings: 27,500 books
Subjects: Rape

2435   Magadan, Russia
Russian Academy of Agricultural Sciences,
    Siberian Branch, North-East Zonal
    Agricultural Institute (RAAS SB)
Library
Proletarskaya St., 17
Magadan 685000
Phone: +7(8413) 222-9105 Fax: +7(8413) 222-9881
WWW: www-sbras.ict.nsk.su/eng/sbras/siberia/raas-sb.
html

Founded: 1969 Type: Government Holdings: 9,500 books
Subjects: Agricultural Production, Animal Husbandry,
Livestock Specializations: Reindeer

2436   Mariy - El Republic, Russia
Mariyskiy Scientific Research Institute of
    Agriculture
Library
Ruem Settlement
Medvedevsky Region 425201
Mariy - El Republic
Phone: +7(836-2) 128010, 127928

2437 Moscow, Russia
A.N. Kostyakov All-Russia Scientific Research
Institute of Hydraulic Engineering and Land
Reclamation
Library
Bolshaya Academicheskaya, 44
Moscow 127550
Phone: +7(095) 153-9072

Subjects: Hydraulic Engineering, Reclamation

♦2438 Moscow, Russia
All-Russia Center for Translations of
Scientific-Technical Literature and
Documentation
Library
Krzhizhanovskogo St. 14, Bd. 1
Moscow 117218
Phone: +7(095) 221-1457

Former Name: Academy of Sciences of the USSR, All-Union Center for Translations of Scientific-Technical Literature and Documentation **Founded:** 1972 **Type:** Government **Holdings:** 350,000 books

2439 Moscow, Russia
All-Russia Institute of Construction Technology
and Management
Library
Leninsky pr., 156
Moscow 117471
Phone: +7(095) 438-4200

Former Name: All-Union Scientific Production Union of Rebuilding Mechanical Parts of Agricultural Machinery

♦2440 Moscow, Russia
All-Russia Institute of Instruments and
Technology of Measuring in Agriculture
Library
Skakovaya St., 36
Moscow 125040

Former Name: All-Union Institute of Instruments and Technology of Measuring in Agriculture **Founded:** 1958 **Type:** Government **Holdings:** 20,300 books **Subjects:** Measurement

2441 Moscow, Russia
All-Russia Research and Technological Institute
for Repair and Utilization of Tractors and
Farm Machinery
Library
1-st Institutskiy pr., 1
Moscow 109428
Phone: +7(095) 372-8639, 372-7461 **Fax:** +7(095) 170-4373, 371-0125

Former Name: State All-Union Scientific Research and Technology Institute of Machine Repair **Founded:** 1953 **Type:** Government **Holdings:** 280,200 books **Subjects:** Farm Machinery

2442 Moscow, Russia
All-Russia Research Institute for Nature
Protection
Library
Znamenskie Sadki
Moscow 113628
Phone: +7(095) 423-0322, 423-1955 **Fax:** +7(095) 423-2322

Former Name: All-Union Scientific Research Institute of Nature Protection and Preservation **Founded:** 1972 **Type:** Government **Holdings:** 28,000 books **Subjects:** Nature Conservation

♦2443 Moscow, Russia
All-Russia Scientific Research Institute
"Agrosystem"
Library
Yartsevskaya St., 30
Moscow 121552
Phone: +7(095) 149-5024

Founded: 1982 **Type:** Government **Holdings:** 9,600 books **Subjects:** Farm Machinery

♦2444 Moscow, Russia
All-Russia Scientific Research Institute of
Agricultural Biotechnology
Library
Pskovskaya St., 12/4
Moscow 125206

Former Name: All-Union Scientific Research Institute of Agricultural Biotechnology **Type:** Government **Holdings:** 1,000 books **Subjects:** Biotechnology

2445 Moscow, Russia
All-Russia Scientific Research Institute of
Agricultural Biotechnology
Library
Timeryazevskaya St., 42
Moscow 127266
Phone: +7(095) 229-2091, 276-6544, 977-0930 **Fax:** +7 (095) 977-0947

Subjects: Biotechnology

2446 Moscow, Russia
All-Russia Scientific Research Institute of
Agricultural Economics
Library
Khoroshevskoye Highway, 35
Moscow 123007
Phone: +7(095) 195-4221 **Fax:** +7(095) 195-6094

Former Name: All-Union Scientific Research Institute of Agricultural Economics **Founded:** 1955 **Type:** Government **Holdings:** 32,900 books **Subjects:** Agricultural Economics

2447 Moscow, Russia
All-Russia Scientific Research Institute of
Agricultural Electrification
Library
1st Veshnyakovski proezd, 2
Moscow 109456

Phone: +7(095) 174-8774 **Fax:** +7(095) 170-5101 **Email:** energy@viesh.su

Former Name: All-Union Scientific Research Institute of Agricultural Electrification **Founded:** 1961 **Type:** Government **Head:** Dr. N. Molosnov *Phone:* +7(095) 171-0274 **Staff:** 2 Prof. 2 Other **Holdings:** 134,000 books 420 journals **Language of Collection/Services:** Russian / Russian **Subjects:** Automation, Renewable Resources **Specializations:** Power Engineering **Loan:** In country **Service:** In country **Photocopy:** Yes

2448 Moscow, Russia
    All-Russia Scientific Research Institute of
        Agricultural Mechanization
    Library
    1-st Institutsky pr., 5
    Moscow 109428
Phone: +7(095) 171-1933, 174-8929, 170-4349 **Fax:** +7 (095) 170-8707

Former Name: All-Union Scientific Research Institute of Agricultural Mechanization **Founded:** 1930 **Type:** Government **Holdings:** 268,400 books **Subjects:** Mechanization

2449 Moscow, Russia
    All-Russia Scientific Research Institute of
        Brewing, Nonalcoholic and Winemaking
        Industry
    Library
    Rossolimo St., 7
    Moscow 119021
Phone: +7(095) 246-6769, 246-3307

Former Name: Scientific Industrial Union of Beverages and Mineral Waters **Founded:** 1947 **Type:** Government **Holdings:** 44,400 books **Subjects:** Beverages, Mineral Waters

2450 Moscow, Russia
    All-Russia Scientific Research Institute of
        Economics, Labor and Management in
        Agriculture
    Library
    Orenburgskaya St., 15
    Moscow 111621
Phone: +7(095) 700-1214 **Fax:** +7(095) 700-0671

Founded: 1965 **Type:** Government **Holdings:** 37,400 books **Subjects:** Agricultural Economics, Agricultural Manpower, Management

2451 Moscow, Russia
    All-Russia Scientific Research Institute of Food
        Biotechnology
    Library
    Samokatnaya Street, 4b
    Moscow 109033
Phone: +7(095) 362-4624 **Fax:** +7(095) 362-3700

Former Name: All-Union Scientific Research Institute of Food Biotechnology **Founded:** 1931 **Type:** Government **Holdings:** 38,300 books **Subjects:** Biotechnology, Food Sciences

2452 Moscow, Russia
    All-Russia Scientific Research Institute of Grain
        and Grain Processing
    Library
    Dmitrovskoe Highway, 11
    Moscow 127434
Phone: +7(095) 976-3349 **Fax:** +7(095) 976-1910

Subjects: Grain

2453 Moscow, Russia
    All-Russia Scientific Research Institute of
        Medicinal and Aromatic Plants
    Library
    Gagarin St., 7
    Moscow 113628
Phone: +7(095) 712-0909, 388-6309, 382-8318 **Fax:** +7 (095) 388-5509

Subjects: Aromatic Plants, Medicinal Plants

2454 Moscow, Russia
    All-Russia Scientific Research Institute of
        Veterinary Sanitation, Hygiene and Ecology
    Library
    Zvenigorodskoye Highway, 5
    Moscow 123022
Phone: +7(095) 256-0488, 256-4101 **Fax:** +7(095) 256-2020

Former Name: All-Union Scientific Regulatory Institute of Veterinary Procedures, All-Russia Scientific Research Institute of Veterinary Sanitation **Founded:** 1931 **Type:** Government **Holdings:** 14,000 books **Subjects:** Veterinary Science

2455 Moscow, Russia
    All-Russia Scientific Research Institute on Social
        and Personnel Problems of Agroindustrial
        Complex
    Library
    Sovkhoznaya St., 10
    Moscow 109382
Phone: +7(095) 359-0665

2456 Moscow, Russia
    All-Russia Selection and Technological Institute
        of Horticulture and Breeding
    Library
    Zagoje, 1
    Moscow 115598
Phone: +7(095) 329-5155

Founded: 1938 **Type:** Government **Holdings:** 14,900 books **Subjects:** Horticulture

♦**2457 Moscow, Russia**
    Central Institute of Agrochemical Services for
        Agriculture
    Library
    Pryanishnikova St. 2, Build 31
    Moscow 127550
Phone: +7(095) 976-0175 **Fax:** +7(095) 956-1626

Founded: 1970 **Type:** Government **Holdings:** 6,400 books **Subjects:** Agricultural Chemistry

2458　Moscow, Russia
Central Scientific Research Laboratory for
　　Hunting Husbandry and Reserves
Library
Losinoostrovskaya St.
Lesnaya Dacha, kv. 18
Moscow 129347
Phone: +7(095) 582-1308, 582-1844, 915-0886

Subjects: Hunting

♦2459　Moscow, Russia
Central Scientific Technical Library of the Food
　　Industry
Leningradskoe Highway, 8
Moscow 125875

Founded: 1918 **Type:** Government **Holdings:** 573,000
books **Subjects:** Food Sciences

2460　Moscow, Russia
D.N. Pryanishnikov All-Russia Scientific
　　Research Institute of Fertilizers and
　　Agricultural Soil Science
Library
Pryanishnikov Street, 31
Moscow 127550
Phone: +7(095) 976-4789, 976-0175 **Fax:** +7(095) 956-1626

Former Name: D.N. Pryanishnikov All-Union Scientific
Research Institute of Fertilizer and Agricultural Soil Science
Founded: 1931 **Type:** Government **Holdings:** 23,800 books
Subjects: Fertilizers, Soil Science

2461　Moscow, Russia
Engineering Scientific Production Centre on
　　Water Facilities, Reclamation and Ecology
Library
Baumanskaya St., 43/1
Moscow 107005
Phone: +7(095) 263-0920 **Fax:** +7(095) 263-0901

Subjects: Ecology, Reclamation, Water

♦2462　Moscow, Russia
Institute of Scientific and Technical Information
Library
Usievitcha St., 20a
Moscow 125219

Former Name: All-Union Institute of Scientific and Techni-
cal Information **Founded:** 1952 **Type:** Government **Head:**
A.I. Mikhailov *Phone:* +7(095) 155-4435 **Subjects:** Food
Production, Forestry **Holdings:** 1,000,000 books

♦2463　Moscow, Russia
International Centre for Scientific and Technical
　　Information
Kuusinena St., 21-b
Moscow 125252

2464　Moscow, Russia
K.I. Skryabin All-Russia Scientific Research
　　Institute of Helminthology

Library
Cheremushkinskaya St., 28
Moscow 117218
Phone: +7(095) 124-5811 **Fax:** +7(095) 124-5655

Former Name: K.I. Skryabin All-Union Scientific Research
Institute of Helminthology **Founded:** 1934 **Type:** Government **Holdings:** 77,000 books **Subjects:** Helminthology

2465　Moscow, Russia
Moscow Hydro Land Reclamation Institute
Library
Pryanihniskova St., 19
Moscow 127550
Phone: +7(095) 976-2348 **Fax:** +7(095) 154-3321

Non-English Name: Moskovskiji gidromeliorativnij institut
Founded: 1929 **Type:** Academic **Holdings:** 756,400 books
Subjects: Agricultural Engineering, Environmental Protec-
tion, Natural Resources Management, Nature Conservation,
Reclamation, Water Resources Engineering

2466　Moscow, Russia
Moscow State Agricultural Engineering
　　University
Library
Timirayazevskaya St., 58
Moscow 127550
Phone: +7(095) 976-2673 **Fax:** +7(095) 976-7874 **Email:**
mgau@mgau.msk.ru

Founded: 1930 **Type:** Academic **Holdings:** 82,000 books
Subjects: Agricultural Engineering, Electrification, Mechanization

2467　Moscow, Russia
Russian Academy of Agricultural Sciences
　　(RAAS)
Central Scientific Agricultural Library (CSAL)
B Orlikov pereulok, 3 Build. "B"
Moscow 107139
Phone: +7(095) 207-8500 **Fax:** +7(095) 207-8972 **Email:**
dir@cnshb.ru **WWW:** www.cnshb.ru

Former Name: All-Union Academy of Agricultural Sciences **Founded:** 1930 **Type:** Government **Head:** Vyatcheslav G. Pozdnyakov *Email:* pvg@cnshb.ru *Phone:* +7
(095) 207-8972 **Staff:** 237 Prof. 102 Other **Holdings:**
1,600,000 books 110,000 journals **Language of Collection/
Services:** Russian, English, French, German / Russian **Subjects:** Comprehensive **Specializations:** Agricultural Meteorology, Agricultural Research, Agricultural Statistics,
Biochemistry, Biology, Biophysics, Breeding, Dairy Science, Farm Machinery, Fertilizers, Irrigation, Mechanization, Plant Protection **Networks:** AGRIS **Databases Used:**
Agricola; Agris; CABCD; FSTA **Loan:** In country **Service:**
Internationally **Photocopy:** Yes

♦2468　Moscow, Russia
Russian Academy of Sciences, Zyzyn Main
　　Botanic Garden (RAS)
Library
Botanicheskaya St., 4
Moscow 127276

Former Name: Academy of Sciences of the USSR, Main Botanic Garden **Founded:** 1947 **Type:** Academic **Head:** O.Z. Fadeeva **Staff:** 8 Prof. 1 Other **Holdings:** 155,000 books 250 journals **Subjects:** Botany, Entomology, Floriculture, Horticulture, Plant Pathology **Loan:** Internationally **Photocopy:** No

2469   **Moscow, Russia**
        Russian Academy of Sciences (RAS)
        Library for Natural Sciences (LNS)
        Znamenka St., 11
        Moscow 119890

Fax: +7(095) 291-2289 **Email:** osiat@ben.irex.ru **WWW:** ben.irex.ru **OPAC:** 195.178.196.159/catalog/catalog_en.htm

Former Name: Academy of Sciences of the USSR **Founded:** 1973 **Type:** Academic **Head:** A.G. Zakharov *Phone:* +7(095) 291-2289 **Staff:** 30 Prof. 3 Other **Holdings:** 4,200 books **Language of Collection/Services:** Russian, English / Russian, English **Subjects:** Biotechnology, Entomology, Fisheries, Forestry, Plant Pathology, Plants, Range Management, Soil Science, Water Resources **Loan:** Internationally **Photocopy:** Yes

2470   **Moscow, Russia**
        Russian Scientific Research Institute of Dairy
            Industry
        Library
        Lyusinovskaya St., 35
        Moscow 113093

Phone: +7(095) 237-0383 **Fax:** +7(095) 236-3164

Former Name: All-Union Scientific Research Institute of Dairy Industry **Founded:** 1930 **Type:** Government **Holdings:** 21,000 books **Subjects:** Dairy Industry

♦2471   **Moscow, Russia**
        Russian Scientific Research Institute of
            Experimental Veterinary Science
        Library
        Kuzminky
        Moscow 109472

Former Name: All-Union Scientific Research Institute of Experimental Veterinary Science **Founded:** 1898 **Type:** Government **Holdings:** 128,900 books **Subjects:** Veterinary Science

2472   **Moscow, Russia**
        Russian Scientific Research Institute of Meat
            Industry
        Library
        Talalikhin St., 26
        Moscow 109316

Phone: +7(095) 276-6871, 276-9511 **Fax:** +7(095) 276-9551 **Email:** vniimp@glasnet.ru

Former Name: All-Union Scientific Research Institute of Meat Industry **Founded:** 1930 **Type:** Government **Holdings:** 33,200 books **Subjects:** Meat and Livestock Industry

♦2473   **Moscow, Russia**
        Scientific Production Center of Synthetic and
            Natural Aromatic Substances
        Library
        Profsoyuznaya St., 66
        Moscow 117939

Former Name: All-Union Scientific Research Institute of Synthetic and Natural Aromatic Substances **Founded:** 1946 **Type:** Government **Holdings:** 44,000 books **Subjects:** Fragrance, Perfumery

2474   **Moscow, Russia**
        Scientific Research Institute of Confectionery
            Industry
        Library
        Elektrozavodskaya St., 20
        Moscow 105023

Phone: +7(095) 962-1740, 963-6500 **Fax:** +7(095) 963-6535

Former Name: All-Union Scientific Research and Design Technology of Refrigeration Industry **Founded:** 1932 **Type:** Government **Holdings:** 65,100 books **Subjects:** Agricultural Engineering, Refrigeration

♦2475   **Moscow, Russia**
        Scientific Research Institute of Information and
            Technical-Economic Research on
            Agro-Industry
        Library
        Orlikov per., 3, corp. "A"
        Moscow 107139

Phone: +7(095) 204-4360 **Fax:** +7(095) 207-4839

Former Name: All-Union Scientific Research Institute of Information and Technical-Economic Research on Agriculture **Founded:** 1964 **Type:** Government **Head:** V.I. Nazarenko *Phone:* +7(095) 204-4360 **Staff:** 72 Prof. 40 Other **Holdings:** 642,200 books 34 journals **Language of Collection/Services:** Russian, English, German, French / Russian **Subjects:** Agribusiness, Agricultural Development, Crops, Agricultural Economics, Agricultural Engineering, Animal Husbandry, Biotechnology, Education/Extension, Entomology, Farming, Fisheries, Food Sciences, Forestry, Horticulture, Plant Pathology, Plants, Soil Science, Water Resources, Veterinary Medicine **Loan:** Internationally **Service:** Internationally **Photocopy:** Yes

2476   **Moscow, Russia**
        State Land Management University
        Library
        Kazakov St., 15
        Moscow 103063

Phone: +7(095) 261-9868 **Fax:** +7(095) 261-9545

Former Name: Moscow Land Tenure System Engineers Institute **Founded:** 1936 **Type:** Academic **Holdings:** 39,500 books **Subjects:** Land Management, Tenure Systems

2477   **Moscow, Russia**
        State Scientific Research Institute of Baking
            Industry
        Library

Cherkizovskaya St., 26 A
Moscow 107553
Phone: +7(095) 161-4144 **Fax:** +7(095) 161-4273/4

Subjects: Bakery Industry

2478   Moscow, Russia
Timiryazev Moscow Agricultural Academy
Library
Timiryazevskaya St., 49
Moscow 127550
Phone: +7(095) 976-1485 **Fax:** +7(095) 976-0428 **Email:**
timacad2@aha.ru **WWW:** www.timacad.ru

Founded: 1865 **Type:** Government **Holdings:** 176,800
books **Subjects:** Agricultural Chemistry, Agricultural Economics, Agroecology, Agronomy, Plant Genetics, Plant Protection, Soil Science, Zootechny

2479   Moscow, Russia
V.V. Dokuchayev Soil Science Research Institute
Library
Pyzhevsky pereulok, 7
Moscow 109017
Phone: +7(095) 951-5037, 230-8033 **Fax:** +7(095) 951-
5037

Founded: 1895 **Type:** Government **Holdings:** 141,200
books **Subjects:** Soil Science

2480   Moscow, Russia
Ya.R. Kovalenko All-Russia Scientific Research
        Institute of Experimental Veterinary Science
Library
Skryabin St., 23
Kuzminky
Moscow 109472
Phone: +7(095) 377-9432, 377-8492, 377-8320 **Fax:** +7
(095) 377-8084

Founded: 1948 **Subjects:** Biochemistry, Biophysics, Veterinary Science, Zootechny

2481   Moscow Province, Russia
A.G. Lorkh All-Russia Scientific Research
        Institute of Potato Production
Library
PO Korenevo
Lyuberetsky Region
Moscow Province 140052
Phone: +7(095) 557-5001

Founded: 1930 **Type:** Government **Holdings:** 77,400 books
Subjects: Potatoes

2482   Moscow Province, Russia
All-Russia Research Institute of Poultry
        Processing Industry (RRIPPI)
Library
PO Rzhavki
Solnechnogorsk Region
Moscow Province 141552
Phone: +7(095) 535-1538 **Fax:** +7(095) 534-4712 **Email:**
vniipp@orc.ru

Non-English Name: Vserossiysky Nauchno-Issledovatelsky Institut Ptitsepererabativayushchey Promyshlennosty
(VNIIPP), Biblioteka **Former Name:** Scientific Research
Institute of Poultry Processing and the Gelatin Industry, Scientific and Technical Library **Founded:** 1928 **Type:** Academic **Head:** Natalia Sazonova *Phone:* +7(095) 535-9444
Holdings: 40,500 books 52 journals **Language of Collec-
tion/Services:** Russian / Russian **Subjects:** Poultry **Databases Developed:** Journal on agriculture and poultry - access
inhouse **Loan:** Inhouse **Service:** Inhouse **Photocopy:** Yes

2483   Moscow Province, Russia
All-Russia Research Institute of Swine Breeding
Library
Bikovo Settlement
Podolsk Region
Moscow Province 142023
Phone: +7(095) 546-7047/8

Former Name: All-Union Breeding-Genetic Center **Founded:** 1929 **Type:** Government **Holdings:** 3,000 books **Subjects:** Animal Breeding, Genetics, Livestock

2484   Moscow Province, Russia
All-Russia Scientific Production Institute of Waste
        Water Use
Library
Sovetskaya St., 1a
Staraya Kupavna Settlement
Noginsk Region
Moscow Province 142450
Phone: +7(095) 524-0976

Subjects: Waste Water

♦**2485   Moscow Province, Russia**
All-Russia Scientific Research and Design and
        Technological Institute of Agricultural
        Chemistry
Library
Nemchinovka P/O
Agrohimikov St., 6
Odintsovo Region
Moscow Province 143013

Former Name: All-Russian Scientific Research and Technology Institute of Agricultural Chemistry **Type:** Government **Holdings:** 5,900 books **Subjects:** Agricultural
Chemistry

2486   Moscow Province, Russia
All-Russia Scientific Research and Production
        Technology Institute of Animal Breeding
        Mechanization
Library
PO Znamya Oktyabrya, 31
Podolsk Region
Moscow Province 142004
Phone: +7(095) 119-7604 **Fax:** +7(095) 119-7517

Founded: 1964 **Type:** Government **Holdings:** 21,300 books
Subjects: Animal Breeding, Livestock

2487   Moscow Province, Russia
All-Russia Scientific Research and Project
Technological Institute of Agricultural
Chemicals
Library
Agrokhimiki St., 6
Nemchinovka Settlement
Odintsovo Region
Moscow Province 143013
Phone: +7(095) 591-9159, 591-8430, 591-8409 **Fax:** +7
(095) 991-9173

Type: Government **Holdings:** 5,900 books **Subjects:** Agricultural Chemicals

2488   Moscow Province, Russia
All-Russia Scientific Research and Technological
Institute of Biological Industry
Library
PO Kashintsevo
Shchelkovo Region
Moscow Province 141142
Phone: +7(096-56) 32885 **Fax:** +7(096-56) 32419 **Email:**
chiefmen@mtu-net.ru

Former Name: All-Union Scientific Research Institute of
Biology Industry **Founded:** 1971 **Type:** Government **Holdings:** 84,700 books **Subjects:** Biology

2489   Moscow Province, Russia
All-Russia Scientific Research and Technology
Institute of Poultry Breeding
Library
Ptitsegradskaya St., 10
Sergiev Posad - 11
Moscow Province 141300
Phone: +7(096-54) 7770 **Fax:** +7(096-54) 61138

Former Name: All-Union Scientific Research and Technology Institute of Poultry Raising **Founded:** 1930 **Type:** Government **Holdings:** 21,900 books **Subjects:** Poultry

2490   Moscow Province, Russia
All-Russia Scientific Research Institute of Animal
Breeding
Library
Dubrovitsy Settlement
Podolsk Region
Moscow Province 142012
Phone: +7(096-7) 651242 **Fax:** +7(096-7) 651424

Former Name: All-Union Scientific Research Institute of
Stock Breeding **Founded:** 1929 **Type:** Government **Holdings:** 165,300 books **Subjects:** Animal Breeding, Livestock

2491   Moscow Province, Russia
All-Russia Scientific Research Institute of
Canning and Vegetable Drying Industries
Library
Shkolnaya St., 78
Vidnoye
Moscow Province 142703
Phone: +7(095) 541-0892 **Fax:** +7(095) 541-0892

Former Name: All-Union Scientific Research Institute of
Canning and Vegetable Drying Industry **Founded:** 1930
Type: Government **Holdings:** 36,100 books **Subjects:** Canning, Vegetables

♦**2492   Moscow Province, Russia**
All-Russia Scientific Research Institute of
Feedstuffs, Dedinovskaya Experiment Station
of Flood Land Meadow Cultivation
Library
Krasnaya Poima P/O
Lukhovitskii Region
Moscow Province 140514
Phone: +7(096-63) 12323

Former Name: All-Union Scientific Research Institute of
Feedstuffs **Founded:** 1956 **Type:** Government **Holdings:**
300 books **Subjects:** Flooded Land

♦**2493   Moscow Province, Russia**
All-Russia Scientific Research Institute of
Fertilizer and Agricultural Soil Science,
Central Experiment Station
Library
Domodedovo Region
Moscow Province 140062

Former Name: All-Union Scientific Research Institute of
Fertilizer and Agricultural Soil Science **Type:** Government
Holdings: 20,600 books **Subjects:** Fertilizers, Soil Science

2494   Moscow Province, Russia
All-Russia Scientific Research Institute of
Irrigated Fish Farming
Library
Vorovskoy Settlement
Noginsk Region
Moscow Province 142460

Former Name: All-Union Scientific Research Institute of
Irrigated Fish Farming **Founded:** 1980 **Type:** Government
Holdings: 1,200 books **Subjects:** Fish Farming

2495   Moscow Province, Russia
All-Russia Scientific Research Institute of
Irrigation Systems and Agricultural Water
Supply "Raduga"
Library
Paduzhny Settlement, 38
Kolomna Region
Moscow Province 140400
Phone: +7(096-6) 156479 **Fax:** +7(096-6) 156029

Subjects: Irrigation, Water Supply

2496   Moscow Province, Russia
All-Russia Scientific Research Institute of
Phytopathology
Library
PO Vayzemy
Odintsovo Region
Moscow Province 143050
Phone: +7(095) 592-9287 **Fax:** +7(095) 40902

Subjects: Plant Pathology

2497   Moscow Province, Russia
All-Russia Scientific Research Institute of Plant
    Growing, Moscow Branch
Library
PO Mikhnevo
Stupino Region
Moscow Province 142840
Phone: +7(096-64) 3540

Subjects: Plants

2498   Moscow Province, Russia
All-Russia Scientific Research Institute of Plant
    Quarantine
Library
Pogranichnaya St., 32
Bykovo Settlement
Ramensky Region
Moscow Province 140150
Phone: +7(095) 558-4453

Former Name: All-Union Scientific Research Institute of
Quarantine and Plant Protection **Founded:** 1934 **Type:** Government **Holdings:** 28,000 books **Subjects:** Plant Protection,
Quarantine

2499   Moscow Province, Russia
All-Russia Scientific Research Institute of Starch
    Products
Library
Nekrasov St., 11
Korenevo Settlement
Lyubertsi Region
Moscow Province 140052
Phone: +7(095) 557-1509, 557-2385 **Fax:** +7(095) 557-0544

Founded: 1933 **Type:** Government **Holdings:** 19,900 books
Subjects: Starch

2500   Moscow Province, Russia
All-Russia Scientific Research Institute of Stock
    Breeding
Library
PO Lesniye Polyany
Pushkin Region
Moscow Province 141212
Phone: +7(095) 515-9543, 515-9557

Founded: 1977 **Type:** Government **Holdings:** 17,600 books
Subjects: Breeding

2501   Moscow Province, Russia
All-Russia Scientific Research Institute of
    Vegetable Crop Breeding and Seed
    Production
Library
P/O Lesnoy Gorodok
Odintsovo Region
Moscow Province 143080
Phone: +7(095) 599-2442 **Fax:** +7(095) 599-2277 **Email:**
vniissok@cea.ru

Former Name: All-Union Scientific Research Institute of
Vegetable Crop Breeding and Seed Production **Founded:**

1925 **Type:** Academic **Head:** *Email:* vniissok@cea.ru
Holdings: 24,500 books **Language of Collection/Services:**
Russian / Russian **Subjects:** Biotechnology, Farming, Plant
Breeding, Plant Pathology, Seed Production, Vegetables
Photocopy: Yes

2502   Moscow Province, Russia
All-Russia Scientific Research Institute of
    Vegetable Growing
Library
PO Vereya, str. 500
Ramenskoye Region
Moscow Province 114153
Phone: +7(095) 558-4537, 246-243-04 **Fax:** +7(095) 246-243-64

Subjects: Vegetable Growing

♦**2503   Moscow Province, Russia**
All-Russia Scientific Research Station of Meat
    and Poultry Raising
Library
50-letiya Komsomola St., 34
Pushkino
Moscow Province 141280

Type: Government **Subjects:** Poultry, Meat

2504   Moscow Province, Russia
Central Machine Testing Station
Library
Central St., 1
Solnechnogorsk
Moscow Province 141500
Phone: +7(095) 539-7458 **Fax:** +7(095) 539-3616

2505   Moscow Province, Russia
Centre of Scientific Research, Moscow Scientific
    Research and Project Technological Institute
    of Land Use
Library
Novaya St., 3
Mytishchy
Moscow Province 141017
Phone: +7(095) 583-6448

Founded: 1968 **Type:** Government **Holdings:** 32,900 books
Subjects: Land Resources

2506   Moscow Province, Russia
Institute of Soil Sciences and Photosynthesis
Library
Pushchino
Moscow Province 142292
Phone: +7(095) 923-3558 **Email:** sokolov@issp.
serpukhov.su **WWW:** www.grid.unep.org/arci0090.htm

Subjects: Photosynthesis, Soil Science

2507   Moscow Province, Russia
Moscow Breeding Experiment Station
Library
Uzunovo Settlement
Serebryano-Prudsky Region

Moscow Province 142960
Phone: +7(096-67) 23867

Former Name: All-Union Scientific Research Institute of Feedstuffs **Founded:** 1939 **Type:** Government **Holdings:** 10,800 books **Subjects:** Feeds, Fodder

2508   Moscow Province, Russia
Russian State Agrarian Correspondence
    University
Library
U. Fuchik St., 8
Balashikha - 8
Moscow Province 143900
Phone: +7(095) 521-4921 **Fax:** +7(095) 521-2456

Former Name: All-Union Agriculture Institute of Extramural Education **Founded:** 1945 **Type:** Academic **Holdings:** 108,300 books **Subjects:** Agricultural Economics, Agronomy, Electrification, Fruits, Information Systems, Mechanization, Plant Protection, Vegetables, Viticulture, Water Management

2509   Moscow Province, Russia
Scientific Industrial Biotechnological Centre on
    Animal Industries
Library
PO Gorki Leninskiye
Leninsky Region
Moscow Province 142712
Phone: +7(095) 548-9045 **Fax:** +7(095) 548-9232

Subjects: Animal Biotechnology, Animal Husbandry

2510   Moscow Province, Russia
Scientific Research Design and Project
    Technological Institute of Liquid Fertilizers
Library
Maydanovo Settlement
Klin
Moscow Province 141600
Phone: +7(096-24) 398316

Subjects: Fertilizers

2511   Moscow Province, Russia
Scientific Research Institute of Agriculture of the
    Central Regions of the Non-Chernozem Zone
Library
Agrokhimiki St., 6
Nemchinovka Settlement
Odintsovo Region
Moscow Province 143013
Phone: +7(095) 591-8391, 591-8661 **Fax:** +7(095) 591-9287

Founded: 1935 **Type:** Government **Holdings:** 88,600 books

2512   Moscow Province, Russia
V.A. Afanasyev Scientific Research Institute of
    Fur Farming and Rabbit Breeding
Library
Trudovaya St., 2
Udelnaya Settlement
Ramensk Region

Moscow Province 140143
Phone: +7(095) 558-5936, 558-7283

Founded: 1932 **Type:** Government **Holdings:** 28,200 books **Subjects:** Furbearing Animals, Furs, Pelts, Rabbits

2513   Moscow Province, Russia
V.R. Vilayms All-Russia Feed Research Institute
Scientific Library
Lugovaya St.
Mitishchi Region
Moscow Province 141740
Phone: +7(095) 577-7337 **Fax:** +7(095) 577-0107 **Email:** korma@com2com.ru

Former Name: All-Union Scientific Research Institute of Feedstuffs **Founded:** 1922 **Type:** Government **Head:** Ms. Georgiadi *Phone:* +7(095) 577-7337 **Staff:** 2 Prof. **Holdings:** 200,000 books 10 journals **Language of Collection/Services:** Russian / Russian **Subjects:** Animal Production, Feeds, Fodder **Loan:** In country **Service:** In country **Photocopy:** No

2514   Murmansk Province, Russia
Murmansk State Reindeer Breeding Experiment
    Station
Library
Sovkhoznaya St., 1
Molochny Settlement
Kolsky Region
Murmansk Province 184365
Phone: +7(81553) 91324

Type: Government **Holdings:** 22,100 books **Subjects:** Deer Farming

2515   Murmansk Province, Russia
Polar Experiment Station
Library
Kozlov St., 2
Apatity
Murmansk Province 184200
Phone: +7(815-55) 40842

Type: Government **Holdings:** 16,100 books **Subjects:** Plants

2516   Nizhniy Novgorod, Russia
Nizhniy Novgorod State Agricultural Academy
Library
Gagarin Av., 97
Nizhniy Novgorod 603078
Phone: +7(8312) 66-0773 **Fax:** +7(8312) 66-0684 **Email:** root@dagri.sci.nnov.ru

Founded: 1927 **Type:** Academic **Holdings:** 97,700 books **Subjects:** Agricultural Chemistry, Agricultural Economics, Agroecology, Forest Management, Mechanization, Soil Science, Veterinary Medicine, Zootechny

2517   Nizhniy Novgorod, Russia
Scientific Research Veterinary Institute of
    Non-Black Soil Zone of Russian Federation
Library
Veterinary St., 3

GSP 847
Nizhniy Novgorod 603600
Phone: +7(831-2) 339588 **Fax:** +7(831-2) 334107

Founded: 1925 **Type:** Government **Holdings:** 31,200 books
Subjects: Veterinary Science

2518   Nizhniy Novgorod Province, Russia
Gorkov State Regional Agriculture Experiment
      Station
Library
P/O Roika
Selektsionniy Village
Ketovsky Region
Nizhniy Novgorod Province 606216
Phone: +7() 694377, 665434

Founded: 1950 **Type:** Government **Holdings:** 8,700 books

2519   North Osetiya-Alanya Republic, Russia
Gorsky State Agrarian University
Library
Kirova St., 37
Vladikavkaz 362000
North Osetiya-Alanya Republic
Phone: +7(867-22) 339039 **Fax:** +7(867-22) 539004

Former Name: Gorskii Agriculture Institute **Founded:**
1918 **Type:** Academic **Holdings:** 510,000 books **Subjects:**
Agricultural Economics, Agricultural Engineering, Agronomy, Crop Production, Electrification, Forest Economics,
Fruits, Mechanization, Vegetables, Veterinary Medicine, Viticulture, Zootechny

2520   North Osetiya-Alanya Republic, Russia
North Caucasian Scientific Research Institute of
      Mountain and Foothill Village Horticulture
Library
Vilyams St., 1
Mikhailovskoe Settlement 363110
North Osetiya-Alanya Republic
Phone: +7(864-22) 730420, 730105

Founded: 1932 **Type:** Government **Holdings:** 21,800 books
Subjects: Farming, Mountain Areas

2521   Novgorod Province, Russia
Novgorod Scientific Research and Production
      Technology Institute of Agriculture
Library
PO Borki
Novgorod Region
Novgorod Province 174116
Phone: +7(816-00) 72439 **Fax:** +7(816-00) 72439

Founded: 1954 **Type:** Government **Holdings:** 19,600 books

2522   Novosibirsk, Russia
Novosibirsk State Agrarian University
Library
Dobrolubov St., 160
Novosibirsk 630039
Phone: +7(3832) 67-0910 **Fax:** +7(3832) 67-3922 **Email:**
public@nsau.edu.ru **WWW:** www.nsau.edu.ru

Founded: 1936 **Type:** Academic **Holdings:** 88,300 books
Subjects: Agricultural Economics, Agronomy, Agricultural
Technologies, Equipment, Land Improvement, Mechaniza-
tion, Plant Genetics, Plant Protection, Veterinary Medicine,
Zootechny

2523   Novosibirsk, Russia
West Siberian Territorial Scientific Research and
      Production Technology Institute of
      Agro-industrial Complex
Library
Nemirovich - Danchenko St., 165
Novosibirsk 630087

2524   Novosibirsk Province, Russia
Centre of Information Provision - Computing
      Maintenance
Library
Krasnoobsk
Novosibirsk Province 633128
Phone: +7(3832) 483460

2525   Novosibirsk Province, Russia
North Kulunda Experiment Station
Library
Kuibyshev St., 31
Bagan Settlement
Novosibirsk Province 632770
Phone: +7(38353) 91384

Founded: 1962 **Type:** Government **Holdings:** 6,100 books
Subjects: Reclamation, Salt

2526   Novosibirsk Province, Russia
Novosibirsk Centre "Agroprogress"
Library
Krasnoobsk
Novosibirsk Province 633128
Phone: +7(3832) 481927

2527   Novosibirsk Province, Russia
Russian Academy of Agricultural Sciences,
      Siberian Research Institute of Fodder Crops
      (RAAS)
Library
Krasnoobsk
Novosibirsk Province 633128
Phone: +7(3832) 483409 **Subjects:** Fodder Crops

2528   Novosibirsk Province, Russia
Russian Academy of Agricultural Sciences,
      Siberian Research Institute of Physical and
      Technical Problems (RAAS)
Library
Krasnoobsk
Novosibirsk Province 633128
Phone: +7(3832) 383552

2529   Novosibirsk Province, Russia
Russian Academy of Agricultural Sciences,
      Siberian Branch, Siberian Research Institute

of Experimental Veterinary Science of Siberia
and the Far East (RAAS SB)
Library
Krasnoobsk
Novosibirsk Province 633128
Phone: +7(3832) 484462 **WWW:** www-sbras.ict.nsk.su/
eng/sbras/siberia/raas-sb.html

Founded: 1940 **Type:** Government **Holdings:** 17,000 books
Subjects: Veterinary Science

2530   Novosibirsk Province, Russia
Russian Academy of Agricultural Sciences,
Siberian Branch, Siberian Research, Design
and Technological Institute of Animal
Husbandry (RAAS SB)
Library
Krasnoobsk
Novosibirsk Province 633128
Phone: +7(3832) 484709 **WWW:** www-sbras.ict.nsk.su/
eng/sbras/siberia/raas-sb.html

Founded: 1931 **Type:** Government **Holdings:** 15,000 books
Subjects: Animal Breeding, Livestock

2531   Novosibirsk Province, Russia
Russian Academy of Agricultural Sciences,
Siberian Branch, Siberian Research Institute
of Arable Farming and Use of Agrochemicals
(RAAS SB)
Library
Krasnoobsk
Novosibirsk Province 633128
Phone: +7(3832) 480744, 481262 **WWW:** www-sbras.ict.
nsk.su/eng/sbras/siberia/raas-sb.html

Founded: 1971 **Type:** Government **Holdings:** 15,000 books
Subjects: Agricultural Chemicals

2532   Novosibirsk Province, Russia
Russian Academy of Agricultural Sciences,
Siberian Branch, Siberian Research Institute
of Economics of Agriculture (RAAS SB)
Library
Krasnoobsk
Novosibirsk Province 633128
Phone: +7(3832) 484693 **WWW:** www-sbras.ict.nsk.su/
eng/sbras/siberia/raas-sb.html

Founded: 1956 **Type:** Government **Holdings:** 10,100 books
Subjects: Agricultural Economics

2533   Novosibirsk Province, Russia
Russian Academy of Agricultural Sciences,
Siberian Branch, Siberian Research Institute
of Mechanization and Electrification of
Agriculture (RAAS SB)
Library
Krasnoobsk
Novosibirsk Province 633128
Phone: +7(3832) 481963 **WWW:** www-sbras.ict.nsk.su/
eng/sbras/siberia/raas-sb.html

Founded: 1960 **Type:** Government **Holdings:** 44,600 books
Subjects: Electrification, Mechanization

2534   Novosibirsk Province, Russia
Russian Academy of Agricultural Sciences,
Siberian Branch, Siberian Research Institute
of Plant Breeding and Selection (RAAS SB)
Library
Krasnoobsk
Novosibirsk Province 633126
Phone: +7(3832) 480883 **WWW:** www-sbras.ict.nsk.su/
eng/sbras/siberia/raas-sb.html

Founded: 1937 **Type:** Government **Holdings:** 21,900 books
Subjects: Plant Breeding

2535   Novosibirsk Province, Russia
Russian Academy of Agricultural Sciences,
Siberian Branch, Siberian Research
Technological Design Institute of Processing
of Agricultural Products (RAAS SB)
Library
Krasnoobsk
Novosibirsk Province 633128
Phone: +7(3832) 480409 **WWW:** www-sbras.ict.nsk.su/
eng/sbras/siberia/raas-sb.html

Subjects: Agricultural Products

2536   Novosibirsk Province, Russia
Siberian Experiment Station
Library
Lekarstvennoe Settlement
Toguchinsky Region
Novosibirsk Province 633430
Phone: +7(3832) 26423

2537   Omsk, Russia
Omsk State Agrarian University
Library
Institutskaya Av., 2
Omsk 644008
Phone: +7(3812) 65-4656 **Fax:** +7(3812) 55-1072 **Email:**
adm@omgau.omsk.su

Founded: 1918 **Type:** Academic **Holdings:** 273,500 books
Subjects: Agricultural Chemistry, Agricultural Economics,
Fruits, Geodesy, Land Management, Mechanization, Milk
Production, Plant Genetics, Vegetables, Veterinary Medi-
cine, Water Resources Engineering, Zootechny

2538   Omsk, Russia
Omsk State Veterinary Institute
Library
Octyabrskaya St., 92
Omsk 644007
Phone: +7(3812) 23-7762

Founded: 1918 **Type:** Academic **Holdings:** 54,500 books
Subjects: Veterinary Science

2539   Omsk, Russia
Russian Academy of Agricultural Sciences,
    Siberian Branch, Siberian Research Institute
    of Agriculture (RAAS SB)
Library
Korolyov St., 2
Omsk 644012

Phone: +7(3812) 241787 **WWW:** www-sbras.ict.nsk.su/
eng/sbras/siberia/raas-sb.html

Founded: 1926 **Type:** Government **Holdings:** 44,600 books

2540   Omsk, Russia
Russian Academy of Agricultural Sciences,
    Siberian Branch, Research Institute of
    Brucellosis and Tuberculosis of Agricultural
    Animals (RAAS SB)
Scientific Library
Lermontov St., 93
Omsk 644001

Phone: +7(3812) 563260 **Fax:** +7(3812) 563260 **WWW:**
www-sbras.ict.nsk.su/eng/sbras/siberia/raas-sb.html

Founded: 1921 **Type:** Government **Head:** Nina I. Kjuba-
kowa **Staff:** 3 Prof. 1 Other **Holdings:** 42,894 books 17,285
journals **Subjects:** Animal Diseases, Brucellosis, Tuberculo-
sis **Loan:** In country **Photocopy:** No

2541   Omsk Province, Russia
Siberian Experiment Station
Library
Stroitely St., 2
Isilkul
Omsk Province 646000

Phone: +7() 21413

Type: Government **Holdings:** 3,200 books **Subjects:** Oil
Plants

2542   Orel, Russia
All-Russia Scientific Research Institute of Grain
    Legumes and Cereal Crops
Library
PO Streletskoe
Orel 303112

Phone: +7(086-00) 403330, 99300 **Fax:** +7(086-00)
403130, 99481 **Email:** zbk@valley.ru **WWW:** www.
valley.ru

Founded: 1962 **Subjects:** Cereals, Grain Crops, Legumes

2543   Orel, Russia
All-Russia Scientific Research Institute of
    Horticultural Breeding
Scientific Library
PO Zilina
Orel 303130

Phone: +7(086-2) 414479, 90022

Former Name: Orlov Fruit-Berry Experiment Station
Founded: 1935 **Type:** Government **Head:** Olga V. Novikova *Phone:* +7(086-2) 414479 **Staff:** 2 Prof. **Holdings:**
71,850 books 143 journals **Language of Collection/Ser-
vices:** Russian **Subjects:** Agricultural Development, Agricultural Economics, Biotechnology, Crops, Entomology,

Fruits, Heavy Metals, Plant Pathology, Soil **Specializations:**
Horticulture **Photocopy:** Yes

2544   Orel, Russia
Department of Agriculture and Food, All-Russia
    Scientific Research Institute of Labor
    Protection (ARSRILP)
Library
Komsomolskaya St., 127
Orel 302016

Phone: +7(086) 222-4672, 222-4789 **Fax:** +7(086) 222-
4798

Former Name: All-Union Scientific Research Institute of
Work Protection in Agriculture **Founded:** 1973 **Type:** Government **Head:** Elena Korotkaja **Holdings:** 79,000 books 15
journals **Language of Collection/Services:** Russian / Russian **Subjects:** Agricultural Manpower **Loan:** Do not loan
Photocopy: Yes

2545   Orel, Russia
Orel State Agricultural Academy
Library
General Rodin St., 69
Orel 302019

Phone: +7(086-22) 9-6899 **Fax:** +7(086-22) 9-4064

Founded: 1975 **Type:** Academic **Holdings:** 30,300 books
Subjects: Agricultural Economics, Agronomy, Equipment,
Mechanization, Veterinary Medicine, Zootechny

2546   Orel, Russia
State Scientific Research and Project
    Technological Institute on Creation of Fruit
    and Vegetable Production Storage and
    Processing Structures and Nurseries
Library
Komsomolskaya St., 66
Orel 302026

Phone: +7(086) 694192 **Fax:** +7(086) 73263

Subjects: Nurseries, Postharvest Storage

2547   Orel Province, Russia
Orel Scientific Research Institute of Agriculture
Library
Znamenka Settlement
Orel Province 303112

Phone: +7(086-00) 17890, 12094

Founded: 1962 **Type:** Government **Holdings:** 47,400 books
Subjects: Grain Crops, Legumes

2548   Orenburg, Russia
All-Russia Scientific Research Institute of Meat
    Cattle Breeding
Library
9 Janvuarya St., 29
Orenburg 460000

Phone: +7(353-2) 474641

Founded: 1931 **Type:** Government **Holdings:** 60,900 books
Subjects: Animal Breeding, Cattle

2549   Orenburg, Russia
Orenburg Scientific Research Institute of
     Agriculture
Library
Gagarin pr., 27/1
Orenburg 460051
Phone: +7(353-2) 770550 **Fax:** +7(353-2) 710200

Founded: 1948 **Type:** Government **Holdings:** 20,100 books

2550   Orenburg, Russia
Orenburg State Agrarian University
Library
Cheluskintsev St., 18
Orenburg 460795
Phone: +7(353-2) 77-2744 **Email:** kotov@esso.ru

Founded: 1930 **Type:** Academic **Holdings:** 525,700 books
Subjects: Agricultural Economics, Agronomy, Forest Management, Mechanization, Veterinary Medicine, Zootechny

2551   Penza, Russia
Penza State Agricultural Academy
Library
Botanicheskaya St., 30
Penza 440014
Phone: +7(8412) 59-6360 **Fax:** +7(8412) 59-6354 **Email:**
psaca@sura.com.ru

Founded: 1951 **Type:** Academic **Holdings:** 68,000 books
Subjects: Agricultural Economics, Agricultural Technologies, Agroecology, Agronomy, Mechanization, Zootechny

2552   Penza Province, Russia
Penza Scientific Research Institute of Agriculture
Library
Michurin St.
PO Lunino
Penza Province 442730
Phone: +7(841-61) 22425

Founded: 1935 **Type:** Government **Holdings:** 19,000 books

2553   Penza Province, Russia
Petrovskaya Breeding Experiment Station
Library
Vekhovo Settlement
Danilovka
Lopatinsky Region
Penza Province 442564
Phone: +7(84148) 22290

Type: Government **Holdings:** 17,100 books

2554   Perm, Russia
Perm State Agricultural Academy
Library
Communisticheskaya St., 23
Perm 614000
Phone: +7(3422) 12-8334 **Fax:** +7(3422) 12-4779 **Email:**
psaa@pstu.ac.ru

Founded: 1931 **Type:** Academic **Holdings:** 173,500 books
Subjects: Agricultural Chemistry, Agricultural Economics,

Agronomy, Fruits, Land Management, Mechanization, Vegetables, Veterinary Science, Viticulture

2555   Perm Province, Russia
Perm Scientific Research Institute of Agriculture
Library
Kultury St., 12
Lobanovo Settlement
Perm Region
Perm Province 618032
Phone: +7(3422) 963464, 975230 **Fax:** +7(3422) 975136

Founded: 1945 **Type:** Government **Holdings:** 20,500 books

2556   Primorskiy Area, Russia
Far Eastern Scientific Research Institute of Plant
     Protection
Library
Mir St., 42 A
Hankansky Region
Kamen-Ryibolov 692280
Primorskiy Area
Phone: +7(213) 91160

Type: Government **Holdings:** 2,400 books **Subjects:** Plant
Protection

2557   Primorskiy Area, Russia
Seaside Scientific Research Institute of
     Agriculture
Library
Volozgenin St., 30
Timiryazevsky Settlement
Ussuriyskiy Region 692539
Primorskiy Area
Phone: +7(423-41) 92710 **Fax:** +7(423-41) 24378 **Email:**
fe.smcnf@ml.ussuriisk.ru

Founded: 1912 **Type:** Government **Holdings:** 19,800 books

2558   Primorskiy Area, Russia
Seaside State Agricultural Academy
Library
Blukher Av., 44
Ussuriysk 692510
Primorskiy Area
Phone: +7(423-41) 29854 **Email:** bitmaster@pgsa.
usuriisk.ru

Founded: 1957 **Type:** Academic **Holdings:** 59,300 books
Subjects: Agricultural Economics, Agroecology, Agronomy, Forest Management, Land Management, Mechanization, Water Resources Engineering, Veterinary Medicine, Zootechny

2559   Pskov, Russia
Velikie Luky State Agricultural Academy
Library
Lenin Square, 1
Velikie Luky
Pskov 182100
Phone: +7(81153) 36565 **Fax:** +7(81153) 32673 **Email:**
vgsha@mart.ru

Founded: 1958 **Type:** Academic **Head:** V.A. Kozlova **Staff:** 17 Prof. 12 Other **Holdings:** 253,251 books 168 journals **Language of Collection/Services:** Russian / Russian **Subjects:** Comprehensive **Loan:** Inhouse **Service:** Inhouse **Photocopy:** Yes

2560   Pskov Province, Russia
Pskov Scientific Research Institute of Agriculture
Library
PO Rodina
Mir St., 1
Pskov Region
Pskov Province 181201
Phone: +7(8112) 467251, 173110

Founded: 1950 **Type:** Government **Holdings:** 7,100 books

2561   Rostov Province, Russia
All-Russia Scientific Research and Production
    Technology Institute of Agricultural
    Mechanization and Electrification
Library
Lenin St., 14
Zernograd
Rostov Province 347720
Phone: +7(863-59) 32285, 32404

Founded: 1930 **Type:** Government **Holdings:** 50,300 books **Subjects:** Electrification, Mechanization

2562   Rostov Province, Russia
All-Russia Scientific Research Institute of
    Sorghum Breeding and Seed Production
Library
Lenin St., 19
Zernograd
Rostov Province 347720
Phone: +7(863-59) 31758

Type: Government **Holdings:** 3,300 books **Subjects:** Sorghum

2563   Rostov Province, Russia
Azov-Black Sea State Agroengineering Academy
Library
Lenin St., 21
Zernograd
Rostov Province 347720
Phone: +7(863-59) 33254 **Fax:** +7(863-59) 33-380 **Email:** nauch@ACHGAA.zern.donpac.ru

Founded: 1930 **Type:** Government **Holdings:** 93,000 books **Subjects:** Agricultural Economics, Electrification, Equipment, Mechanization

2564   Rostov Province, Russia
Donskoy Regional Scientific Research Institute of
    Agriculture
Library
Rassvet Settlement
Aksay Region
Rostov Province 346714
Phone: +7(863-50) 37019 **Fax:** +7(863-50) 37175

Founded: 1956 **Type:** Government **Holdings:** 89,100 books

2565   Rostov Province, Russia
Donskoy State Agrarian University
Library
Persiyanovka
Oktyabrskaya Region
Rostov Province 346493
Phone: +7(863-52) 9-3579 **Fax:** +7(863-52) 9-4350

Founded: 1962 **Type:** Academic **Holdings:** 70,500 books **Subjects:** Agricultural Economics, Agricultural Technologies, Agronomy, Fruits, Meat Technology, Vegetables, Veterinary Medicine, Viticulture, Zootechny

2566   Rostov Province, Russia
North Caucasian Regional Scientific Veterinary
    Research Institute
Library
Rostov Highway. 26
Novocherkassk
Rostov Province 346421
Phone: +7(863-52) 22070, 45170

Founded: 1929 **Type:** Government **Holdings:** 14,500 books **Subjects:** Veterinary Science

2567   Rostov Province, Russia
Southern Scientific Research Institute of
    Hydraulic Engineering and Land Reclamation
Library
Rostovskoe Highway, 21
Novocherkassk
Rostov Province 346421
Phone: +7(863-52) 22070, 45170

Founded: 1930 **Type:** Academic **Holdings:** 74,200 books **Subjects:** Reclamation

2568   Rostov Province, Russia
Ya.N. Potapenko All-Russia Scientific Research
    Institute of Viticulture and Winemaking
Library
Baklanovsky pr., 166
Novocherkassk
Rostov Province 346421
Phone: +7(863-52) 22088 **Fax:** +7(863-52) 24459

Founded: 1936 **Type:** Government **Holdings:** 38,500 books **Subjects:** Vineyards, Viticulture, Winemaking

2569   Ryazan, Russia
All-Russia Scientific Research and Project
    Institute on Mineral Fertilizers Storage
    Economy, Transportation and Use
    Mechanization
Library
Nakhimov St., 13
Ryazan 390025
Phone: +7(091-2) 724631 **Fax:** +7(091-2) 724631

Founded: 1965 **Type:** Government **Holdings:** 12,400 books **Subjects:** Fertilizers, Soil Science

2570   Ryazan, Russia
All-Russia Scientific Research Institute on
    Organization, Economy and Material and

Technical Supply Technology of
Agroindustrial Complex
Library
Shchors St., 38/11
Ryazan 390025
Phone: +7(091-2) 285607 **Fax:** +7(091-2) 285704 **Email:**
vniims@mis.ryasan.ru **Founded:** 1965

2571   Ryazan, Russia
Central Experimental Design Technological
Bureau, All-Russia Scientific Research
Institute of Machine Tractor Parts Repair and
Operation
Library
Polevaya St., 1
Ryazan 391110
Phone: +7(091-2) 446964

Type: Government **Subjects:** Machinery, Tractors

2572   Ryazan, Russia
Ryazan State Agricultural Academy
Library
Kostichev St., 1
Ryazan 390044
Phone: +7(091-2) 7-5790 **Fax:** +7(091-2) 55-3501 **Email:**
library@aal.ryazan.su

Founded: 1949 **Type:** Academic **Holdings:** 56,500 books
Subjects: Agricultural Economics, Agricultural Technologies, Agronomy, Mechanization, Zootechny

2573   Ryazan Province, Russia
All-Russia Scientific Research Institute of Horse
Breeding
Library
PO Institut Konevodstva
Rybnoye Region
Ryazan Province 391128
Phone: +7(13) 32211 **Fax:** +7(096) 904-7788

Founded: 1928 **Type:** Government **Holdings:** 37,000 books
Subjects: Horse Breeding

2574   Ryazan Province, Russia
Ryazan Scientific Research and Production
Technology Institute of Agriculture
Library
PO Podvyazie
Ryazan Region
Ryazan Province 391002
Phone: +7(091-2) 266133, 946133, 946231

Founded: 1962 **Type:** Government **Holdings:** 14,100 books

2575   Ryazan Province, Russia
Scientific Research Institute of Beekeeping
Library
Pochtovaya St., 22
Rybnoe
Ryazan Province 391110
Phone: +7(091-37) 51547

Founded: 1930 **Type:** Academic **Head:** Mrs. A.I. Lazarewa
Staff: 1 Prof. **Holdings:** 60,000 books 9,000 journals **Lan-**

guage of Collection/Services: Russian **Subjects:** Beekeeping **Databases Developed:** Manual database on beekeeping
Loan: In country **Service:** Internationally **Photocopy:** No

2576   Saha Republic, Russia
Russian Academy of Agricultural Sciences,
Siberian Branch, Yakutsk Research Institute
of Agriculture (RAAS SB)
Library
Kalandarashvili St., 5
Yakutsk 677891
Saha Republic
Phone: +7(4112) 61308 **WWW:** www-sbras.ict.nsk.su/
eng/sbras/siberia/raas-sb.html

Type: Academic

2577   Saha Republic, Russia
Yakutsk Scientific Research Institute of
Agriculture (YSRIA)
Library
Bestuzheva-Marlinskogo, 23/1
Yakutsk 677001
Saha Republic
Phone: +7(4112) 464574 **Fax:** +7(4112) 464572 **Email:**
nord@sakha.ru

Founded: 1956 **Type:** Government **Head:** Sergey P.
Ammosov *Phone:* +7(4112) 464577 *Email:* nord@sakha.ru
Staff: 1 Prof. 1 Other **Holdings:** 43,000 books 5,000 journals
Language of Collection/Services: Yakut, Russian, English /
Yakut, Russian **Subjects:** Comprehensive **Specializations:**
Animal Breeding, Horse Breeding, Veterinary Medicine,
Plants **Databases Developed:** 59 patents and authorized cer-
tificates for 16 plant varieties **Databases Used:** Comprehen-
sive **Loan:** In country **Service:** In country **Photocopy:** No

2578   Saha Republic, Russia
Yakutskaya State Agricultural Academy
Library
Krasilnikov St., 15
Yakutsk 677013
Saha Republic
Phone: +7(4112) 26-4719 **Fax:** +7(4112) 26-4949

Subjects: Agricultural Economics, Agronomy, Crop Production, Equipment, Veterinary Medicine, Zootechny

2579   Saint Petersburg, Russia
Agrophysics Scientific Research Institute
Library
Gusarskih St., 9
Pushkin
Saint Petersburg 189620
Phone: +7(812) 465-5875

2580   Saint Petersburg, Russia
Agrophysics Scientific Research Institute
Scientific and Technical Library (STL)
Grazhdanskiy Av., 14
Saint Petersburg 195220
Phone: +7(812) 534-1841 **Fax:** +7(812) 535-5220

Founded: 1947 **Type:** Government **Head:** I.B. Uskov *Phone:* +7(812) 534-4630 **Staff:** 194 Prof. 69 Other **Holdings:** 62,100 books 48 journals **Language of Collection/Services:** Russian **Subjects:** Agricultural Engineering, Agricultural Meteorology, Farming, Physics, Plants, Soil Science, Water Resources **Service:** In country **Photocopy:** Yes

2581   Saint Petersburg, Russia
All-Russia Scientific Research Institute of
    Agricultural Microbiology
Library
Podbelsky Highway, 3
Pushkin
Saint Petersburg 189620
Phone: +7(812) 470-5100 **Fax:** +7(812) 470-4362

Founded: 1930 **Type:** Government **Subjects:** Microbiology

2582   Saint Petersburg, Russia
All-Russia Scientific Research Institute of Fats
Library
Chernaykhovsky St., 10
Saint Petersburg 191119
Phone: +7(812) 164-1524 **Fax:** +7(812) 112-0113

Founded: 1932 **Type:** Government **Holdings:** 40,800 books **Subjects:** Butter, Milk Fat

2583   Saint Petersburg, Russia
All-Russia Scientific Research Institute of Food
    Aromatizers, Acids and Dyes
Library
Liteyni pr., 55
Saint Petersburg 191104
Phone: +7(812) 273-7524 **Fax:** +7(812) 273-7524

Founded: 1961 **Type:** Government **Holdings:** 13,100 books **Subjects:** Food Sciences

2584   Saint Petersburg, Russia
All-Russia Scientific Research Institute of Genet-
    ics and Breeding of Agricultural Animals
Library
Moscowskoie Highway, 55-a
Pushkin
Saint Petersburg 189620
Phone: +7(812) 470-7663 **Fax:** +7(812) 465-9969

Former Name: All-Union Scientific Research Institute of Breeding and Genetics of Agricultural Animals **Founded:** 1963 **Type:** Government **Holdings:** 36,200 books **Subjects:** Animal Breeding, Genetics

2585   Saint Petersburg, Russia
All-Russia Veterinary Institute of Poultry
    Breeding
Library
Chernikov St., 3
Lomonosov
Saint Petersburg 189510
Phone: +7(812) 422-0669 **Fax:** +7(812) 422-7677

Founded: 1918 **Type:** Government **Holdings:** 40,900 books **Subjects:** Poultry

2586   Saint Petersburg, Russia
Leningrad Fruit and Vegetable Experiment Station
Library
Krasnaya Slavaynka Settlement
Pavlovsk
Saint Petersburg 189623
Phone: +7(812) 466-7053 **Fax:** +7(812) 466-7093

Subjects: Fruits, Vegetables

2587   Saint Petersburg, Russia
N.I. Vavilov All-Russia Scientific Research
    Institute of Plant Growing
Library
Bolshaya Morskaya St., 44
Saint Petersburg 190000
Phone: +7(812) 312-7548 **Fax:** +7(812) 311-8728

Founded: 1895 **Type:** Government **Holdings:** 362,300 books **Subjects:** Plants

2588   Saint Petersburg, Russia
North-West Research Institute of Agricultural
    Engineering and Electrification
Library/Information Center
Filtrovskoe Highway, 3
PO Tiarlevo
Pavlovsk
Saint Petersburg 189625
Phone: +7(812) 466-6244 **Fax:** +7(812) 466-5666 **Email:** nii@nevsky.net

Non-English Name: Severo-Zapadny Nauchno-Issledovatelskij Institut Mekhanizatsii i Elektrifikatsii Selskogo Khoziajstva (SZNIIMESK), Nauchno-tekhnicheskaja Biblioteka /Informatsionny Tsentr (NTB/ITs) **Founded:** 1962 **Type:** Government **Head:** Guenrikh V. Agapov *Phone:* +7(812) 466-7804 *Email:* nii@nevsky.net **Staff:** 3 Prof. 2 Other **Holdings:** 24,000 books 21,000 journals **Language of Collection/Services:** Russian/Russian, English **Subjects:** Comprehensive **Specializations:** Equipment, Farm Buildings, Farm Machinery **Databases Developed:** Research reports of the institute **Loan:** In country **Service:** In country **Photocopy:** Yes

2589   Saint Petersburg, Russia
Northern Scientific Research Institute of
    Hydraulic Engineering and Land Reclamation
Library
PO Novoselye
Saint Petersburg 188323
Phone: +7(812) 138-9836

Subjects: Hydraulic Engineering, Reclamation

2590   Saint Petersburg, Russia
Northwestern Scientific Research Institute of
    Economy and Agricultural Production
    Management
Library
Podbelsky St., 7
Pushkin
Saint Petersburg 189620
Phone: +7(812) 470-4374 **Fax:** +7(812) 466-6644

Subjects: Agricultural Production

2591   Saint Petersburg, Russia
Russian Academy of Agricultural Sciences, North-Western Research Center (RAAS, NWRC)
Saint Petersburg Central Scientific Agricultural Library (St.-Pet. Sci. Agr. Lib.)
Bolshaya Morskaya St., 42
Saint Petersburg 190000

Phone: +7(812) 314-4914 **Fax:** +7(812) 466-6476

Non-English Name: Rossyiskoi Akademii selskokhoziast-vennykh nauk, Severo-Zapadny Nauchny Zentr (RASKHN, SZNZ), Sankt-Peterburgskaya Zentralnaya nauchnaya selskokhozaistvennaya biblioteka (SPB ZNSKHB) **Former Name:** All-Union Academy of Agricultural Sciences, Central Scientific Agricultural Library, Leningrad Branch **Founded:** 1838 **Type:** Government **Head:** Liudmila Dobranskaya *Phone:* +7(812) 314-4914 **Staff:** 24 Prof. 11 Other **Holdings:** 455,087 books 4,580 journals **Language of Collection/Services:** Russian / Russian **Subjects:** Comprehensive **Databases Developed:** Agriculture of pre-revolutionary Russia (18th-20th centuries); Catalogue of the Library of the Scientific Committee (1758-1917); Documents on St. Petersburg and Petrograd provinces and Leningrad region (1779-1997); Rural associations (1850-1917); Spinning crops (1786-1926); Horticulture and fruit crops (1779-1917); Apiculture (18th century-1996); Horse breeding and horse husbandry (1778-1917); Veterinary medicine (18th century-1917); N.I. Vavilov bibliography (1910-1998) **Loan:** Inhouse **Service:** Inhouse **Photocopy:** Yes

2592   Saint Petersburg, Russia
Russian Scientific Research Institute of Plant Protection
Library
Podbelsky Highway, 3
Pushkin - 8
Saint Petersburg 189620

Phone: +7(812) 470-5110 **Fax:** +7(812) 470-4384 **Email:** vizrspb@spb.cityline.ru

Subjects: Plant Protection

2593   Saint Petersburg, Russia
Saint Petersburg State Academy of Veterinary Medicine
Library
Chernigovskaya St., 5
Saint Petersburg 196084

Phone: +7(812) 298-2513, 298-3631 **Fax:** +7(812) 294-1176 **Email:** vetacademy@crosswinds.net **WWW:** www.crosswinds.net/~vetacademy, vetacademy.home.dhs.org

Founded: 1922 **Type:** Academic **Holdings:** 245,000 books
Subjects: Veterinary Medicine

2594   Saint Petersburg, Russia
Saint Petersburg State Agrarian University
Library
Saint Petersburg Highway, 2
Pushkin

Saint Petersburg 189620

Phone: +7(812) 476-2877 **Fax:** +7(812) 465-0505 **Email:** shkrabak@glusnet.ru

Founded: 1905 **Type:** Academic **Holdings:** 200,700 books
Subjects: Agricultural Chemistry, Agricultural Economics, Agronomy, Electrification, Fruits, Mechanization, Plant Protection, Land Management, Vegetables, Viticulture, Zootechny

2595   Saint Petersburg, Russia
State Scientific Research Institute of Lake and River Fisheries
Library
Naberezhnaya Makarova, 26
Saint Petersburg 199053

Phone: +7(812) 328-0762 **Fax:** +7(812) 328-0742 **Email:** nirkh@mail.dux.ru

Subjects: Fisheries

2596   Samara Province, Russia
All-Russia Scientific Research and Production Technology Institute of Swine Breeding
Library
Povolzhskoye Association
Tolyatti
Samara Province 445680

Phone: +7(846-2) 371715

Subjects: Pigs

2597   Samara Province, Russia
Povolzhkaya Agroforestry Experiment Station
Library
PO Berezki Settlement
Volzhsky Region
Samara Province 443099

Phone: +7(37) 52410

Subjects: Agroforestry

2598   Samara Province, Russia
Povolzhsky Scientific Research Institute of Selection and Seed Production "Konstantinov"
Library
Shosseynaya St., 76
Ust-Kinelsky Settlement
Kinel - 4
Samara Province 446409

Phone: +7(846-63) 281383 **Fax:** +7(846-63) 46248

Subjects: Seed Production, Seeds

2599   Samara Province, Russia
Samara Scientific Research Institute of Agriculture
Library
K. Marx St., 41
Bezenchyk Settlement
Samara Province 446080

Phone: +7(846-76) 21140 **Fax:** +7(846-76) 22633

Founded: 1903 **Type:** Government **Holdings:** 42,700 books

2600 Samara Province, Russia
Samara State Agricultural Academy
Library
Ust-Kinel' Settlement
Kinel' Region
Samara Province 446409
Phone: +7(846-63) 46-134

Founded: 1920 **Type:** Academic **Holdings:** 94,200 books
Subjects: Agricultural Economics, Agricultural Technologies, Agronomy, Mechanization, Storage, Zootechny

2601 Samara Province, Russia
Sredne-Volzhskaya Experiment Station
Library
Polevaya St., 19
Antonovka Settlement
Sergievsky Region
Samara Province 446554
Phone: +7(846-5) 23306

2602 Saratov, Russia
Povolzhsky Scientific Research and Production
    Technology Institute of Sorghum and Corn
Library
Zonalny Settlement
Saratov 410050
Phone: +7(845-2) 281383

Subjects: Maize, Sorghum

2603 Saratov, Russia
Povolzhsky Scientific Research Institute of
    Agroindustrial Complex Economy and
    Organization
Library
Shekhurdin St., 12
Saratov 410020
Phone: +7(845-2) 640647

2604 Saratov, Russia
Povolzhsky Scientific Research Institute of
    Animal Breeding and Biotechnology
Library
Selektsionny pr., 5
Saratov 410020
Phone: +7(845-2) 640431

Subjects: Animal Biotechnology, Animal Breeding

2605 Saratov, Russia
Saratov Scientific Research Veterinary Station
Library
Str 53 Rifle Divisions, 6
Saratov 410028
Phone: +7(845-2) 250866

Type: Government **Subjects:** Veterinary Science

2606 Saratov, Russia
Saratov State Agrarian University
Library
Teatralnaya Av., 1
Saratov 410600

Phone: +7(845-2) 241228, 260490 **Fax:** +7(845-2) 267488
Email: agm@ssau.saratov.su **WWW:** www.ic.sgu.ru/
library

Founded: 1913 **Type:** Academic **Holdings:** 137,300 books
Subjects: Comprehensive

2607 Saratov, Russia
Scientific Research Institute of South-East
    Agriculture
Library
Tulaykov St., 7
Saratov 410020
Phone: +7(845-2) 647739 **Fax:** +7(845-2) 647688

Founded: 1923 **Type:** Government **Holdings:** 30,200 books

2608 Saratov Province, Russia
Arkadakskaya Agriculture Experiment Station
Library
Rostoshi Settlement
Arkadaksky Region
Saratov Province 412214
Phone: +7(84542) 23625

Type: Government **Holdings:** 20,100 books

2609 Saratov Province, Russia
Ershov Experiment Station
Library
Tulyikovo Settlement
Ershov
Saratov Province 413500
Phone: +7(84564) 21800

Holdings: 7,200 books **Subjects:** Irrigation

2610 Saratov Province, Russia
Krasnoutskaya Breeding Experiment Station
Library
Semennoy Settlement
Krasnoutskaya Region
Saratov Province 413241
Phone: +7(84560) 36333

Type: Government **Holdings:** 11,600 books

2611 Saratov Province, Russia
Volzhsky Scientific Research Institute of
    Agriculture of Hydraulic Engineering
Library
Engels
Saratov Province 413123
Phone: +7(745) 14420 **Fax:** +7(745) 14420

Subjects: Hydraulic Engineering

2612 Smolensk, Russia
Smolensk Agricultural Institute
Library
Bolshaya Sovietskaya St., 27/20
Smolensk 214000
Phone: +7(8200) 3-4557

Type: Academic **Holdings:** 25,000 books **Subjects:** Agricultural Economics, Agricultural Technologies, Agronomy, Zootechny

2613   Smolensk, Russia
Smolensk Scientific Research Institute of
     Agricultural Economics
Library
Nakhimov St., 21
Smolensk 214025
Phone: +7(081-00) 68902

Subjects: Agricultural Economics

2614   Smolensk Province, Russia
Smolensk State Experiment Station
Library
Sovetskaya St., 117
Stodolishche
Pochinkovsky Region
Smolensk Province 216470
Phone: +7(8149) 47172 **Fax:** +7(8149) 47134

Founded: 1945 **Type:** Government **Holdings:** 20,900 books

2615   Stavropol, Russia
All-Russia Scientific Research Institute of Sheep
     and Goat Breeding
Library
Zootehnicheskiy per., 15
Stavropol 355017
Phone: +7(865-22) 347688 **Fax:** +7(865-22) 347688
Email: vniiok@minas.rosmail.com

Founded: 1932 **Type:** Government **Holdings:** 52,000 books
Subjects: Animal Breeding, Goats, Sheep

2616   Stavropol, Russia
Stavropol Scientific Research Institute of Animal
     Breeding and Forage Production
Library
Abramov St., 2
Stavropol 355005
Phone: +7(865-22) 324001 **Fax:** +7(865-22) 324001

Subjects: Animal Breeding, Forage

2617   Stavropol, Russia
Stavropol Scientific Research Institute of
     Hydraulic Engineering and Land Reclamation
Library
Lenin St., 480
Stavropol 355027

Subjects: Hydraulic Engineering, Reclamation

2618   Stavropol, Russia
Stavropol State Agricultural Academy
Library
Zootechnicheskaya Pereulok, 10
Stavropol 355017
Phone: +7(865-22) 34-5935 **Fax:** +7(865-22) 35-2286
Email: sgsa@minas.rosmail.com

Founded: 1932 **Type:** Academic **Holdings:** 78,600 books
Subjects: Agricultural Economics, Agronomy, Electrification, Mechanization, Zootechny

2619   Stavropol Area, Russia
All-Russia Scientific Research Institute of Corn
Library
Yermolav St., 14
Pyatigorsk
Stavropol Area 357528
Phone: +7(865-33) 78584

Type: Government **Holdings:** 26,600 books **Subjects:** Maize

2620   Stavropol Area, Russia
Scientific Research Institute of Preparation and
     Primary Processing of Wool
Library
Mayakovsky St., 20
Nevinnomyssk
Stavropol Area 357030
Phone: +7(865-54) 27630

Subjects: Wool

2621   Stavropol Area, Russia
Stavropol Scientific Research Institute of
     Agriculture
Library
PO Shpakovskoe
Stavropol Region
Stavropol Area 356200
Phone: +7(865-53) 32297, 365019 **Fax:** +7(865-53)
363312

Founded: 1962 **Type:** Government **Holdings:** 16,000 books

2622   Stavropol Area, Russia
Stavropol Scientific Research Institute of
     Agriculture, Prikumsky Branch
Library
Budyennovsk
Stavropol Area 357920
Location: Village POSS (PBES), Vavilov Street 4 **Phone:**
+7(86559) 42858

Former Name: Prikumskaya Breeding Experiment Station
Type: Government **Head:** Zoya I. Dubinina *Phone:* +7
(86559) 42944 **Staff:** 60 Prof. 140 Other **Holdings:** 5,000
books 4,000 journals **Language of Collection/Services:**
Russian / Russian **Subjects:** Agricultural Development, Biotechnology, Education/Extension, Farming, Food Sciences,
Plant Pathology, Plant Protection, Plants, Soil Conservation,
Soil Science **Specializations:** Breeding, Crops, Fertilizers
Loan: In country **Service:** In country **Photocopy:** No

2623   Sverdlovsk Province, Russia
Krasnoufimskaya Breeding Station
Library
Seleksionnaya St., 8
Krasnoufimsk
Sverdlovsk Province 623300
Type: Government **Holdings:** 22,900 books

2624   Tambov, Russia
        All-Russia Scientific Research and Production
            Technology Institute on Machine Use and Oil
            Products Use in Agriculture
        Library
        Gagarin St., 1A
        Tambov 392022
Phone: +7(0752) 240248 **Fax:** +7(0752) 246203

Founded: 1980 **Type:** Government **Holdings:** 41,300 books
Subjects: Oils

2625   Tambov Province, Russia
        Ekaterininskaya Experiment Station
        Library
        Ekaterinino Settlement
        Nikiforovsky Region
        Tambov Province 393023
Phone: +7(0752) 34223

2626   Tambov Province, Russia
        I.V. Michurin All-Russia Scientific Research
            Institute of Horticulture
        Library
        Michurin St., 30
        Michuninsk
        Tambov Province 393740
Phone: +7(075-45) 20761 **Fax:** +7(075-45) 52635

Founded: 1931 **Type:** Government **Holdings:** 52,100 books
Subjects: Horticulture

2627   Tambov Province, Russia
        Michurinskaya State Agricultural Academy
        Library
        Internatsionalnaya St., 101
        Michurinsk
        Tambov Province 393740
Phone: +7(075-45) 53137 **Fax:** +7(075-45) 52635

Type: Academic **Subjects:** Agricultural Economics,
Agroecology, Agronomy, Fruits, Mechanization, Plant Genetics, Vegetables, Zootechny

2628   Tambov Province, Russia
        Tambov State Regional Agriculture Experiment
            Institute
        Library
        PO Chakino
        Rzhaksa Region
        Tambov Province 393510
Phone: +7() 61130

Former Name: Russian Academy of Agricultural Sciences
Founded: 1913 **Type:** Academic **Staff:** 2 Prof. 1 Other
Holdings: 57,900 books 7,000 journals **Language of Col-
lection/Services:** Russian / Russian **Subjects:** Agricultural
Development, Cropping Systems, Fertilizers, Plants, Rota-
tions, Selection **Loan:** In country **Photocopy:** Yes

2629   Tatarstan Republic, Russia
        All-Russia Scientific Research Veterinary Institute
        Library
        Nauchniy gorodok - 2

Kazan 420075
Tatarstan Republic
Phone: +7(8432) 792632, 792521 **Fax:** +7(8432) 792571

Founded: 1874 **Type:** Academic **Holdings:** 411,100 books
Subjects: Veterinary Science

2630   Tatarstan Republic, Russia
        Kazan State Academy of Veterinary Medicine
        Library
        Sibirskiy St., 35
        Kazan 420075
        Tatarstan Republic
Phone: +7(8432) 761633 **Fax:** +7(8432) 761693 **Email:**
kgavm@kgavm.kcn.ru

Type: Academic **Subjects:** Veterinary Science, Zootechny

2631   Tatarstan Republic, Russia
        Kazan State Agricultural Academy
        Library
        Karl Marx St., 65
        Kazan 420015
        Tatarstan Republic
Phone: +7(8432) 34-1670 **Fax:** +7(8432) 36-6651

Founded: 1919 **Type:** Academic **Holdings:** 421,500 books
Subjects: Agricultural Economics, Agronomy, Mechanization

2632   Tatarstan Republic, Russia
        Tatar Scientific Research Institute of Agriculture
        Library
        NPO "Niva Tatarstan"
        Kazan 420048
        Tatarstan Republic
Phone: +7(843-2) 373244 **Fax:** +7(843-2) 373216

Founded: 1925 **Type:** Government **Holdings:** 17,400 books

2633   Tomsk, Russia
        Novosibirsk State Agrarian University, Tomsk
            Branch
        Library
        Solenaya Area, 11
        Tomsk 634008

Subjects: Agricultural Economics, Agronomy, Mechanization, Zootechny

2634   Tomsk, Russia
        Siberian Scientific Research Institute of Peat
        Library
        Gagarin St., 3
        Tomsk 634050
Phone: +7() 233390

Subjects: Peat

2635   Tomsk Province, Russia
        Narymskaya State Breeding Station
        Library
        Nauka St., 20
        PO Kolpashevo
        Tomsk Province 634420

Phone: +7(38254) 53109

Founded: 1946 **Type:** Government **Holdings:** 15,300 books

2636 Tula Province, Russia
Tula Scientific Research Institute of Agriculture
Library
PO Molochniye dvory
Plavsk Region
Tula Province 301053
Phone: +7(087-52) 52322

Founded: 1956 **Type:** Government **Holdings:** 10,000 books

2637 Tver, Russia
All-Russia Scientific Research Institute of
    Agricultural Utilization of Reclaimed Land
Library
PO Emmaus
Tver 171330
Phone: +7(082-22) 371544 **Fax:** +7(082-22) 360763

Type: Government **Holdings:** 10,200 books **Subjects:** Land Use, Reclamation

2638 Tver, Russia
Central Scientific Research and Project
    Technological Institute of Flax Cultivation
    Mechanization (NPO
    "Nechernozemagropromlen")
Library
Komsomolsky pr., 17/56
Tver 170041
Phone: +7(082-22) 14396, 11546

Type: Government **Subjects:** Flax

2639 Tver, Russia
Tver Agricultural Academy
Library
Saharovo Settlement
Tver 171314
Phone: +7(082-22) 9-1320 **Fax:** +7(082-22) 9-1236
Email: taa@tversu.ac.ru **WWW:** www.tversu.ac.ru/
Education/TAA/Overview.html

Founded: 1972 **Type:** Academic **Holdings:** 37,500 books
Subjects: Agricultural Economics, Agronomy, Mechanization, Zootechny

2640 Tver Province, Russia
All-Russia Scientific Research Institute of Flax
Library
Lunacharsky St., 35
Torzhok
Tver Province 172060
Phone: +7(082-51) 51844 **Fax:** +7(082-51) 44458

Founded: 1930 **Type:** Government **Staff:** 2 Prof. **Holdings:** 43,000 books 2,750 journals **Subjects:** Flax

2641 Tyumen, Russia
All-Russia Scientific Research Institute of
    Veterinary Entomology and Arachnology
Library

Institutskaya St., 2
Tyumen 625041
Phone: +7(3452) 430529, 230738, 230529

Founded: 1968 **Type:** Government **Subjects:** Entomology, Veterinary Science

2642 Tyumen, Russia
Russian Academy of Agricultural Sciences,
    Siberian Branch, Research Institute of Land
    Improvement and Rational Use of Nature
    (RAAS SB)
Library
Institutskaya St., 4
Tyumen 625057
Phone: +7(3452) 232821 **WWW:** www-sbras.ict.nsk.su/
eng/sbras/siberia/raas-sb.html

Subjects: Land Improvement

2643 Tyumen, Russia
Siberian Scientific Research and Project Design
    Institute of Fisheries
Library
Odesskaya St., 33
Tyumen 625023
Phone: +7(345-2) 224116, 225443 **Fax:** +7(345-2) 226196
Subjects: Fisheries

2644 Tyumen, Russia
Tyumen State Agricultural Academy
Library
Respublica St., 7
Tyumen 625007
Phone: +7(3452) 46-1650

Founded: 1959 **Type:** Academic **Holdings:** 36,800 books
Subjects: Agricultural Economics, Agroecology, Agronomy, Aquaculture, Land Management, Mechanization, Veterinary Medicine, Water Resources, Zootechny

2645 Tyumen Province, Russia
Russian Academy of Agricultural Sciences,
    Siberian Branch, Research Institute of
    Agriculture of North Urals (RAAS SB)
Library
Burlaki St., 2
Moscovsky Settlement
Tyumen Province 625001
Phone: +7(423-41) 764054 **Fax:** +7(423-41) 76454
WWW: www-sbras.ict.nsk.su/eng/sbras/siberia/raas-sb.
html

Founded: 1952 **Type:** Government **Holdings:** 18,200 books

2646 Udmurtiya Republic, Russia
Izhevsk State Agricultural Academy
Library
Studencheskaya St., 11
Izhevsk 426069
Udmurtiya Republic
Phone: +7(3412) 43-0077 **Fax:** +7(3412) 58-9947 **Email:**
root@izhsa.udm.ru

Subjects: Agricultural Economics, Agronomy, Electrification, Forest Economics, Mechanization, Veterinary Medicine, Zootechny

2647   Udmurtiya Republic, Russia
Udmurt State Scientific Research Institute of
   Agriculture
Library
Lenin St., 1
Pervomayskiy Settlement
Zavyalovsky Region 427007
Udmurtiya Republic
Phone: +7(3412) 318132 **Fax:** +7(3412) 318417 **Email:**
ugniish@udmnet.ru

Founded: 1961 **Type:** Government **Holdings:** 20,300 books

2648   Ulyanovsk, Russia
Ulyanovsk State Agricultural Academy
Library
Noviy Venets Settlement, 1
Ulyanovsk 432063
Phone: +7(842-2) 31-3012 **Email:** academy@rnv.ru

Founded: 1944 **Type:** Academic **Holdings:** 74,100 books
Subjects: Agricultural Economics, Agronomy, Equipment,
Mechanization, Zootechny

2649   Ulyanovsk Province, Russia
Ulyanovsk Scientific Research Institute of
   Agriculture
Library
Timiryazevsky Village
Ulyanovsk Region
Ulyanovsk Province 433315
Phone: +7(842-2) 34116 **Fax:** +7(842-2) 317858

2650   Viatka, Russia
Viatka State Agriculture Academy
Library
October Av., 133
Viatka 610017
Phone: +7(8332) 694986 **Fax:** +7(8332) 622317

Former Name: Kirov Agriculture Institute **Founded:** 1901
Type: Academic **Head:** Z.N. Borozdina **Staff:** 31 Prof.
Holdings: 344,840 books 59,783 journals **Language of Collection/Services:** Russian / Russian **Subjects:** Comprehensive **Loan:** Inhouse **Photocopy:** No

2651   Vladimir, Russia
All-Russia Scientific Research Institute of Animal
   Protection
Library
PO Yurjevets
Vladimir 600900
Phone: +7(092-2) 260753 **Fax:** +7(092-2) 243675 **Email:**
sinko@arriah.elcom.ru

2652   Vladimir Province, Russia
All-Russia Scientific Research and Production
   Technology Institute of Organic Fertilizers
   and Peat

Library
Vyatkino Settlement
Sudogda Region
Vladimir Province 601242
Phone: +7(092-22) 296010

Type: Government **Holdings:** 4,700 books **Subjects:** Fertilizers, Peat

2653   Vladimir Province, Russia
All-Russia Scientific Research Institute of
   Veterinary Virology and Microbiology
Library
Pokrov
Vladimir Province 601120
Phone: +7(092-43) 967-9755 **Fax:** +7(092-43) 967-9755

Subjects: Microbiology, Veterinary Science, Virology

2654   Vladimir Province, Russia
Vladimir Scientific Research Institute of
   Agriculture
Library
Noviy Settlement
PO Seltso
Suzdal Region
Vladimir Province 601261
Phone: +7(092-31) 21915 **Fax:** +7(092-31) 21825 **Email:**
mazirov@vnisx.vladimir.ru

Founded: 1939 **Type:** Government **Holdings:** 29,900 books

2655   Vladivostok, Russia
Far East Scientific Research Institute of Hydraulic
   Engineering and Melioration
Library
Krasnoe Znamya prospect, 66
Vladivostok 690014
Phone: +7(42322) 251441 **Fax:** +7(42322) 251441

Subjects: Hydraulic Engineering

2656   Vladivostok, Russia
Far Eastern Experiment Station
Library
Vavilov St., 9
Vladivostok 690040

Type: Government **Holdings:** 4,500 books

2657   Vladivostok, Russia
Seaside Scientific Research Veterinary Station
Library
PO 206
Uborevich St., 36
Vladivostok 690106
Phone: +7(42322) 68465

Type: Government **Subjects:** Veterinary Science

2658   Volgograd, Russia
All-Russia Scientific Research Institute of
   Agroforest Land Reclamation
Library
Krasnopresnenskaya St., 39

Volgograd 400062
Phone: +7(844-2) 434002 **Fax:** +7(844-2) 433472 **Email:**
vnialmi@advent.avtlg.ru

Former Name: All-Union Scientific Research Institute of
Agroforest Land Reclamation **Founded:** 1931 **Type:** Government **Head:** Marina Pleskatchova *Phone:* +7(8442)
434002 **Staff:** 2 Prof. **Holdings:** 62,000 books 300 journals
Language of Collection/Services: Russian **Subjects:** Agroforestry, Crops, Desertification, Erosion Control, Forestry,
Pastures, Reclamation, Remote Sensing, Woody Plants
Loan: In country **Service:** In country **Photocopy:** Yes

2659   Volgograd, Russia
All-Russia Scientific Research Institute of
Irrigated Agriculture
Library
Timiryazev St., 9
Volgograd 400002
Phone: +7(844-2) 436120 **Fax:** +7(844-2) 433475

Founded: 1968 **Type:** Government **Holdings:** 33,100 books
Subjects: Irrigation

2660   Volgograd, Russia
Volgograd Scientific Research and Technological
Institute of Meat - Dairy Cattle Breeding and
Animal Industries Production Processing
Library
Rokossovsky St., 6
Volgograd 400086
Phone: +7(844-2) 321324 **Fax:** +7(844-2) 321142

Subjects: Animal Breeding, Dairy Cattle, Meat and Livestock Industry

2661   Volgograd, Russia
Volgograd State Agricultural Academy
Library
Institutskaya St., 8
Volgograd 400041
Phone: +7(844-2) 433006 **Fax:** +7(844-2) 430851

Founded: 1944 **Type:** Government **Head:** Nina M.
Zhmurina **Staff:** 15 Prof. 20 Other **Holdings:** 542,599 books
72,108 journals **Subjects:** Agricultural Economics, Agricultural Engineering, Agronomy, Electrification, Fruits, Mechanization, Natural Resources Management, Reclamation,
Technology, Vegetables, Viticulture, Zootechny, Water Resources **Loan:** In country **Photocopy:** No

2662   Volgograd Province, Russia
Bykovo Melon Breeding Experiment Station
Library
Zeleny Settlement
Bykovsky Region
Volgograd Province 404067
Phone: +7(844-2) 31644

Type: Government **Holdings:** 9,500 books **Subjects:** Vegetables

2663   Volgograd Province, Russia
Nizhne-Volzhsky Scientific Research Institute of
Agriculture

Library
Opitnaya Stantsiya Settlement
Gorodishe Region
Volgograd Province 404013
Phone: +7(844-2) 336156

Type: Government **Holdings:** 31,000 books

2664   Volgograd Province, Russia
Volgogradskaya Experiment Station
Library
Sverdlov St., 51
Krasnoslobodsk
Volgograd Province 404153
Phone: +7(884-79) 77338, 77638

Type: Government **Holdings:** 25,500 books **Subjects:**
Plants

2665   Vologda, Russia
Northwestern Scientific Research Institute of
Dairy Farming and Cultivation of Meadows
Facilities
Library
Levin St., 14
Molochnoye Settlement
Vologda 160091
Phone: +7(8172) 761007

Founded: 1948 **Type:** Government **Subjects:** Dairy Farming, Pastures

2666   Vologda, Russia
Vologda Scientific Research Veterinary Station
Library
Chekhov St., 10
Vologda 160009
Phone: +7(8172) 720432

Type: Government **Subjects:** Veterinary Science

2667   Vologda Province, Russia
Vologda State Dairy Academy
Library
Shmidt St., 2
Molochnoe Settlement
Vologda Province 160901
Phone: +7(81727) 61237 **Fax:** +7(81727) 61069

Founded: 1912 **Type:** Academic **Holdings:** 375,600 books
Subjects: Agronomy, Dairy Science, Marketing, Mechanization, Milk Production, Veterinary Medicine, Zootechny

2668   Voronezh, Russia
All-Russia Scientific Research Institute of
Pathology, Pharmacology and Therapy
Library
Lomonosov St., 114 B
Voronezh 394043
Phone: +7(073-2) 539316 **Fax:** +7(073-2) 539306

Subjects: Pathology, Pharmacology

2669   Voronezh, Russia
Scientific Research Institute of Central Black-Soil
Zone Agroindustrial Complex Organization
and Economy
Library
Serafimovich St., 26 A
Voronezh 394028
Phone: +7(073-2) 231031

2670   Voronezh, Russia
Voronezh State Agricultural University (VSAU)
Library
Michurin St., 1
Voronezh 394612
Phone: +7(073-2) 538779 **Fax:** +7(073-2) 538139 **WWW:**
www.vsau.ru

Founded: 1913 **Type:** Academic **Holdings:** 163,600 books
Subjects: Agricultural Economics, Agricultural Engineering, Agronomy, Land Management, Veterinary Medicine, Zootechny

2671   Voronezh Province, Russia
A.L. Mazlunov All-Russia Scientific Research
Institute of Sugarbeets and Sugar
Library
PO Ramon
Ramon Region
Voronezh Province 396030
Phone: +7(073-40) 21993 **Fax:** +7(073-40) 21993 **Email:**
vniiss@vrn.ru

Founded: 1923 **Type:** Government **Holdings:** 19,600 books
Subjects: Sugar, Sugarbeet

2672   Voronezh Province, Russia
All-Russia Scientific Research Institute of Plant
Protection
Library
Ramon
Voronezh Province 396030
Phone: +7(073) 21147 **Fax:** +7(073) 27596

Type: Government **Holdings:** 7,600 books **Subjects:** Plant
Protection

2673   Voronezh Province, Russia
Rossoshanskaya Experiment Station of Gardening
Library
Rossosh
Voronezh Province 396600
Phone: +7(073-96) 24666 **Fax:** +7(073-96) 24666

Type: Government **Holdings:** 5,200 books **Subjects:** Fruits

2674   Voronezh Province, Russia
V.V. Dokuchayev Scientific Research Institute of
Black-Soil Zone Agriculture
Library
Dokuchayev Institute Settlement
Talovsky Region
Voronezh Province 397463
Phone: +7(073-52) 45535

Founded: 1936 **Type:** Government **Holdings:** 70,100 books

2675   Voronezh Province, Russia
Voronezh Scientific Research Experiment Station
Library
Opytnoe Settlement
Horholsky Region
Voronezh Province 396835
Phone: +7(217) 90251

2676   Voronezh Province, Russia
Voronezh Vegetable Experiment Station
Library
Spasskoe Settlement
Verkhnehavsky Region
Voronezh Province 396116
Phone: +7(80743) 22443 **Fax:** +7(80743) 22443

Type: Government **Holdings:** 4,600 books **Subjects:** Vegetables

2677   Yaroslavl', Russia
Yaroslavl Scientific Research Institute of
Agricultural Perspective Technologies
Automation
Library
Flotskaya St., 3a
Yaroslavl' 150028
Phone: +7(085-2) 256824, 257434 **Fax:** +7(085-2) 256815

Subjects: Automation

2678   Yaroslavl', Russia
Yaroslavl Scientific Research Institute of Animal
Industries and Feedstuffs Breeding
Library
PO Mikhaylovskoe
Yaroslavl' 152217
Phone: +7(085-2) 662567

Founded: 1953 **Type:** Government **Holdings:** 26,800 books
Subjects: Animal Breeding, Feeds, Fodder, Livestock

2679   Yaroslavl', Russia
Yaroslavl State Agricultural Academy
Library
Tutayevskoe Road, 58
Yaroslavl' 150017
Phone: +7(085-2) 30-1874

Type: Academic **Holdings:** 29,700 books **Subjects:** Agricultural Economics, Agronomy, Mechanization, Zootechny

2680   Yaroslavl' Province, Russia
All-Russia Research Institute for Butter and
Cheesemaking
Library
Krasnoarmeiskiy Boulevard, 19
Uglich
Yaroslavl' Province 152620
Phone: +7(085-32) 50435 **Fax:** +7(085-32) 50439

Non-English Name: Vserossiiskii Nauchno-Issledovatel-
skii Institut Maslodeliya Syrodeliya (VNIIMS) **Former
Name:** All-Union Research Institute of the Dairy and
Cheesemaking Industry **Founded:** 1944 **Type:** Government
Head: N.V. Grigorova *Phone:* +7(085-32) 38375 **Staff:** 1

Prof. **Holdings:** 59,000 books **Language of Collection/Services:** Russian / Russian **Subjects:** Butter, Cheesemaking, Dairy Industry, Whey **Loan:** Inhouse **Service:** Inhouse **Photocopy:** Yes

2681   Yzhno-Sahalinsk, Russia
Sakhalin Scientific Research Institute of
    Agriculture
Library
Novoaleksandrovsk, 22
Yzhno-Sahalinsk 693022
Phone: +7(424-00) 796383

Rwanda

2682   Butare, Rwanda
Ecole Agricole et Vétérinaire de Kabutaré
    (EAVK)
Bibliothèque
BP 119
Butare

Founded: 1937 **Type:** Government **Staff:** 1 Other **Holdings:** 5,000 books 13 journals **Subjects:** Animal Husbandry, Animal Health, Animal Production, Crop Production, Plants

2683   Butare, Rwanda
National University of Rwanda
Main Library
BP 117
Butare
Phone: +250 32160 ext 1050 **Fax:** +250 30870 **Email:** biblio@nur.ac.rw **WWW:** www.nur.ac.rw/index.html
Non-English Name: Université Nationale de Rwanda, Bibliothèque **Founded:** 1964 **Type:** Academic **Head:** Mr. Emmanuel Serugendo **Staff:** 2 Prof. 33 Other **Holdings:** 5,158 books 29 journals **Language of Collection/Services:** French / French **Subjects:** Agricultural Engineering, Animal Biotechnology, Fish Culture, Plant Biotechnology, Plants, Soil Science, Zootechny **Loan:** In country **Photocopy:** Yes

♦**2684   Butare, Rwanda**
Rwanda Agricultural Sciences Institute,
    Department of Forestry
Forestry and Agroforestry Research Library
BP 617
Butare
Phone: +250 30642 **Fax:** +250 30643, 30391
Non-English Name: Institut des Sciences Agronomiques du Rwanda, Department de Foresterie (ISAR), Bibliothèque de la Recherche Forestière et Agroforestière **Founded:** 1980 **Type:** Research **Staff:** 1 Prof. 1 Other **Holdings:** 4,427 books 40 journals **Language of Collection/Services:** English, French / French **Subjects:** Agricultural Development, Agroforestry, Forestry **Loan:** Inhouse **Service:** Inhouse **Photocopy:** Yes

2685   Butare, Rwanda
Rwanda Agricultural Sciences Institute, Rubona
    Station

Library
BP 138
Butare
Non-English Name: Institut des Sciences Agronomiques du Rwanda, Station de Rubona (ISAR), Bibliothèque **Founded:** 1932 **Type:** Government **Head:** Mathias Sibomana **Staff:** 2 Prof. 1 Other **Holdings:** 2,000 books 75 journals **Language of Collection/Services:** French, English / French, English **Subjects:** Agricultural Research, Horticulture, Soil Science **Databases Used:** Agris; Biosis; CABCD **Loan:** In country **Service:** Inhouse **Photocopy:** Yes

2686   Kigali, Rwanda
Ministère de l'Agriculture, de l'Elevage et des
    Forêts (MINAGRI)
Centre National de Documentation Agricole
    (CNDA)
Rue de la Nyabugogo
BP 621
Kigali
Phone: +250 85008 **Fax:** +250 85057

Founded: 1982 **Type:** Government **Staff:** 5 Other **Holdings:** 3,600 books 10 journals **Subjects:** Agricultural Development, Agricultural Economics, Animal Production, Crop Production, Fisheries, Forestry **Networks:** AGRIS

Saint Lucia

2687   Castries, Saint Lucia
Windward Islands Banana Development and
    Exporting Co. Ltd (WIBDECO)
Library
PB 115
Castries
Location: Roseau **Phone:** +1(809) 451-4255 **Fax:** +1(809) 451-4601 **Email:** wibdecord@wibdeco.com

Former Name: Windward Islands Banana Growers Association (WINBAN) **Founded:** 1978 **Type:** Association **Head:** Mrs. Ianthe Mondesir *Phone:* +1(809) 451-4255 **Staff:** 1 Prof. 1 Other **Holdings:** 5,000 books 25 journals **Language of Collection/Services:** English / English **Subjects:** Crop Production, Fruit Crops, Marketing, Plant Pathology, Plant Protection, Quality, Stored Products **Specializations:** Bananas **Databases Developed:** Special collection of 1300 items on bananas **Loan:** Inhouse **Service:** In country **Photocopy:** Yes

Saint Vincent and the Grenadines

2688   Kingstown, Saint Vincent and the Grenadines
Ministry of Finance
National Documentation Centre
Administrative Centre
Kingstown
Phone: +1(809) 456-1689 **Fax:** +1(809) 457-2943 **Email:** document@caribsurf.com

Founded: 1981 **Type:** Government **Head:** Gail B. Nurse *Phone:* +1(809) 456-1689 *Email:* document@caribsurf.com **Staff:** 1 Prof. 2 Other **Holdings:** 5,610 books 70 journals **Language of Collection/Services:** English / English **Subjects:** Agricultural Development, Agricultural Economics, Animal Production, Crop Production **Specializations:** Agribusiness, Agricultural Policy, Extension, Markets **Loan:** Inhouse **Service:** In country **Photocopy:** Yes

Samoa

2689   Apia, Samoa
         Ministry of Agriculture, Forests and Fisheries,
             Forestry Division (MAFF)
         Library
         PO Box 1874
         Apia
Phone: +685 22561 **Fax:** +685 22565

Former Name: Ministry of Agriculture, Forests, Fisheries and Meteorology (MAFFM) **Type:** Government **Staff:** 1 Prof. **Subjects:** Agricultural Development, Agricultural Economics, Agriculture (Tropics), Fisheries, Food Sciences, Horticulture

2690   Apia, Samoa
         Ministry of Agriculture, Forests and Fisheries,
             Information and Communications Section
             (MAFF)
         Headquarters Library
         PO Box 206
         Apia
Phone: +685 22561 **Fax:** +685 25268 **Email:** infowesam @pactok.peg.apc.org

Type: Government **Head:** Ms. Sii Laufiso

2691   Apia, Samoa
         Ministry of Agriculture, Forests and Fisheries,
             Livestock Division (MAFF)
         Library
         PO Box 1874
         Apia
Location: Avele, Upolu **Phone:** +685 21052 **Fax:** +685 26532

Former Name: Ministry of Agriculture, Forests, Fisheries and Meteorology (MAFFM) **Type:** Government **Staff:** 1 Prof. **Holdings:** 100 books 200 journals **Language of Collection/Services:** English / English, Samoan **Subjects:** Agriculture (Tropics), Animal Husbandry, Education/Extension, Farming, Veterinary Medicine **Photocopy:** Yes

2692   Apia, Samoa
         Ministry of Agriculture, Forests and Fisheries,
             Nu'u Crop Development Centre (MAFF)
         Library
         PO Box 1587
         Apia
Location: Nu'u, Upolu **Phone:** +685 20605 **Fax:** +685 20607

Type: Government **Head:** Ms. Susana Tekori **Networks:** AGRIS

2693   Apia, Samoa
         South Pacific Regional Environment Programme
             (SPREP)
         Library
         PO Box 240
         Apia
Phone: +685 21929 **Fax:** +685 20231 **Email:** sprep@ samoa.net

Founded: 1994 **Type:** Regional **Head:** Ms. Satui Bentin **Staff:** 2 Prof.

2694   Apia, Samoa
         University of the South Pacific, School of
             Agriculture (USP, SOA)
         Alafua Library
         Private Bag
         Apia
Location: Alafua, Upolu **Phone:** +685 21671, 26697 **Fax:** +685 22933 **Email:** valasi_m@samoa.net

Former Name: South Pacific Regional College of Tropical Agriculture (SPRCTA), Alafua Library **Founded:** 1978 **Type:** Academic **Head:** Mr. Suaesi (Mikki) Valasi *Phone:* +685 21671 *Email:* valasi_m@samoa.net **Staff:** 1 Prof. 4 Other **Holdings:** 13,000 books 100 journals **Language of Collection/Services:** English / English **Subjects:** Agricultural Economics, Agricultural Engineering, Crops, Animal Husbandry, Crop Production, Education/Extension, Entomology, Horticulture, Plant Pathology, Plant Protection, Plants, Soil Science, Tissue Culture **Databases Developed:** RFF (Regional Resource File) - Database of locally produced materials both published and unpublished papers **Databases Used:** Agricola; Agris; CABCD; TROPAG & RURAL **Loan:** In country **Service:** Inhouse **Photocopy:** Yes

Senegal

2695   Bambey, Sénégal
         Senegal Institute of Agricultural Research,
             National Center for Agronomy Research
         Documentation and Information Service (DIS)
         BP 53
         Bambey
Fax: +221 973-6052

Non-English Name: Institut Sénégalais de Recherches Agricoles, Centre National de Recherches Agronomiques (ISRA, CNRA), Service de Documentation et d'Information (SDI) **Founded:** 1964 **Type:** Government **Head:** Rosalie Diouf *Email:* isracnra@telecomplus.sn *Phone:* +221 973-6050/1 **Staff:** 1 Other **Holdings:** 16,000 books 50 journals **Language of Collection/Services:** French, English / French **Subjects:** Agricultural Economics, Crop Production, Agricultural Engineering, Natural Resources, Plant Diseases, Plant Protection, Plants, Soil Science **Specializations:** Agronomy, Cereals, Entomology, Legumes, Plant Breeding,

Plant Pathology, Plant Physiology, Storage **Loan:** Inhouse **Photocopy:** Yes

2696　Dahra-Djoloff, Sénégal
　　　Institut Sénégalais de Recherches Agricoles,
　　　　　Centre de Recherches Zootechniques de
　　　　　Dahra (ISRA, CRZ)
　　　Cellule de Documentation
　　　BP 2057
　　　Dahra-Djoloff
Phone: +221 686111 **Fax:** +221 686111

Head: Dr. Racine Samba Sow **Holdings:** 2,000 books 30 journals **Subjects:** Animal Husbandry

2697　Dakar, Sénégal
　　　African Regional Center of Technology (ARCT)
　　　Information Service (IS)
　　　BP 2435
　　　Dakar
Location: Immeuble Fahd Ben ABdel Aziz, Avenue Djily Mbaye **Phone:** +221 823-7712 **Fax:** +221 823-7713 **Email:** arct@sonatel.senet.net

Non-English Name: Centre Régional Africain de Technologie (CRAT), Division Information et Documentation **Founded:** 1980 **Type:** International **Staff:** 3 Prof. 1 Other **Holdings:** 5,000 books **Language of Collection/Services:** English, French **Subjects:** Biomass, Harvesting **Loan:** Do not loan **Photocopy:** Yes

2698　Dakar, Sénégal
　　　Council for the Development of Social Science
　　　　　Research in Africa (CODESRIA)
　　　CODESRIA Documentation and Information
　　　　　Center (CODICE)
　　　BP 3304
　　　Dakar
Location: Avenue Chekh Anta Diop angle Canal 4 **Phone:** +221 825-9822/23 **Fax:** +221 824-1289 **Email:** codesria@telecomplus.sn **WWW:** www.sas.upenn.edu/African_studies/codesria/codes_Menu.html

Founded: 1983 **Type:** Research **Head:** Abou Moussa Ndongo *Phone:* +221 825-9822/23 *Email:* abou.ndongo@codesria.sn **Staff:** 3 Prof. 1 Other **Holdings:** 21,000 books 120 journals **Language of Collection/Services:** English, French / English, French **Subjects:** Agricultural Development, Agricultural Economics, Forestry, Land Reform, Water Resources **Specializations:** Environment **Databases Developed:** Database of African social science researchers; Database of research and training institutes in Africa; Database of research projects in Africa **Loan:** Inhouse **Photocopy:** Yes

2699　Dakar, Sénégal
　　　Ecole Inter-Etats des Sciences et Médecine
　　　　　Vétérinaires (EISMV)
　　　Bibliothèque
　　　BP 5077
　　　Dakar
Phone: +221 824-9545, 825-6692 **Fax:** +221 825-4283 **WWW:** www.refer.org/sngal_ct/edu/eismv/eismv.htm

Founded: 1968 **Type:** Academic **Head:** Mme Mariam Diouf *Email:* mariamd@eismv.refer.sn **Staff:** 1 Prof. 1 Other **Holdings:** 7,508 books 57 journals **Subjects:** Feeding, Food Technology, Parasitology, Veterinary Medicine, Veterinary Science, Zoology, Zootechny **Loan:** Internationally **Photocopy:** No

2700　Dakar, Sénégal
　　　Environment and Development in the Third World
　　　　　(ENDA TM)
　　　Documentation Center
　　　BP 3370
　　　Dakar
Location: 54, Rue Carnot **Phone:** +221 823-6391 **Fax:** +221 822-2695 **Email:** docs@enda.sn **WWW:** www.enda.sn

Founded: 1983 **Type:** Private **Head:** Mamane Boukari *Phone:* +221 823-6391 *Email:* docs@enda.sn **Staff:** 2 Prof. 2 Other **Holdings:** 30,000 books 60 journals **Language of Collection/Services:** French **Subjects:** Agriculture (Tropics), Agricultural Economics, Forestry, Horticulture, Natural Resources **Networks:** IBISCUS **Photocopy:** Yes

2701　Dakar, Sénégal
　　　Institut Sénégalais de Recherches Agricoles,
　　　　　Laboratoire National de l'Elevage et de
　　　　　Recherches Vétérinaires (ISRA, LNERV)
　　　Service de Documentation
　　　BP 2057
　　　Dakar
Location: Route du Front de Terre **Phone:** +221 320524, 325146 **Fax:** +221 320524

Founded: 1953 **Type:** Government **Staff:** 1 Prof. 4 Other **Holdings:** 83 journals **Language of Collection/Services:** French **Subjects:** Animal Husbandry, Biotechnology, Entomology, Veterinary Medicine **Loan:** In country **Photocopy:** Yes

2702　Dakar, Sénégal
　　　International Development Research Centre, West
　　　　　and Central Africa Regional Office (IDRC,
　　　　　WCARO)
　　　Library
　　　BP 11007 CD Annexe
　　　Dakar
Location: Avenue Cheikh Anta Diop, Angle Boulevard de l'Est **Phone:** +221 864-0000 **Fax:** +221 825-3255 **WWW:** www.idrc.ca/index_e.html

Non-English Name: Centre de Recherche pour le Développement International, Bureau Régional pour l'Afrique Centrale et Occidentale (CRDI, BRACO), Bibliothèque **Type:** International **Head:** Mr. Moussa Dramé *Phone:* +221 864-2241 *Email:* mdrame@idrc.org.sn **Staff:** 1 Prof. **Holdings:** 4,000 books 200 journals **Language of Collection/Services:** English / French **Subjects:** Agriculture (Tropics), Agricultural Development, Crops, Entomology, Environment, Forestry, Plant Pathology, Soil Science, Water Resources **Specializations:** Agricultural Economics, Farmer Participation, Rural Development **Databases Developed:** IDRIS - projects database; BRAIN - institute and regional

database **Loan:** In country **Service:** In country **Photocopy:**
Yes

♦**2703   Dakar, Sénégal**
Ministère de l'Education Nationale, Ecole
Nationale d'Economie Appliquée (MEN)
Bibliothèque
Rue C.A. Diop
BP 5084
Dakar

Founded: 1964**Staff:** 1 Other **Type:** Government **Holdings:**
2,500 books 10 journals **Subjects:** Communication, Agricultural Development, Agricultural Economics, Demography, Economic Developmen, Land Use Planningt, Statistics
Photocopy: Yes

2704   Dakar, Sénégal
Ministère de l'Environnement et de la Protection
de la Nature, Direction des Eaux, Forêts,
Chasses et de la Conservation des Sols
(MEPN, DEFC)
Bibliothèque
Route des Pères Maristes
BP 1834
Dakar

Location: Parc Forestier de Hann **WWW:** www.refer.org/
sngal_ct/cop/mepn

Founded: 1982 **Type:** Government **Staff:** 1 Prof. **Holdings:**
1,352 books 20 journals **Subjects:** Afforestation, Aquaculture, Desertification, Fisheries, Forestry, Hunting

2705   Dakar, Sénégal
Ministry of Agriculture, Agricultural Policy Unit
(MA, APU)
Documentation and Communication Centre
BP 4005
Dakar

Location: Adm. Building, 3rd Floor, Roume Street **Phone:**
+221 823-4216 **Fax:** +221 823-7596 **Email:**
upadeux@pop.telecomplus.sn

Non-English Name: Ministère de l'Agriculture, Unité de
Politique Agricole (MA, UPA), Centre de Documentation et
de Communication (CDOC) **Founded:** 1981 **Type:** Govern-
ment **Head:** Mr. Raymond Salla Dione *Phone:* +221 630-
0804, 823-4216 *Email:* rsdione@hotmail.com **Staff:** 2 Other
Holdings: 11,000 books 69 journals **Language of Collec-
tion/Services:** French / French **Subjects:** Agricultural Fi-
nancial Policy, Agricultural Production, Breeding, Ecology,
Environment, Extension, Forestry, Hydrology, International
Cooperation, Livestock, Marketing, Plant Protection, Rural
Sociology, Women **Specializations:** Agricultural Policy,
Agroforestry, Crop Production, Crops, Environment, Fish-
eries **Networks:** AGRIS **Databases Developed:** AGRIN-
MA - database on information on agriculture **Databases
Used:** Agris **Loan:** Inhouse **Service:** Internationally **Photo-
copy:** Yes

2706   Dakar, Sénégal
National Archives Directorate of Senegal
Information Center of National Archives

Avenue L.S. Senghon
Dakar

Non-English Name: Direction des Archives du Sénégal
(DAS), Centre de Documentation des Archives du Sénégal
(CDAS) **Founded:** 1962 **Type:** Public **Head:** Waly Ndiaye
Phone: +221 821-5072 **Staff:** 4 Prof. **Holdings:** 24,400
books 1,302 journals **Language of Collection/Services:**
French / French **Subjects:** Administration, Agricultural De-
velopment, Biology, Ecology, Economic Development **Pho-
tocopy:** Yes

♦**2707   Dakar, Sénégal**
Office de Recherches sur l'Alimentation et la
Nutrition Africaines (ORANA)
Bibliothèque
39 Avenue Pasteur
PB 2089
Dakar

Phone: +221 225892

Founded: 1956 **Staff:** 1 Prof. 1 Other **Holdings:** 123 jour-
nals 2,400 books **Language of Collection/Services:** French
/French **Subjects:** Human Nutrition, Public Health **Loan:**
Inhouse **Service:** Internationally **Photocopy:** Yes

2708   Dakar, Sénégal
Senegal Institute of Agricultural Research
Documentation Service
BP 3120
Dakar

Location: Dakar, Bel Air **Phone:** +221 332431 **Fax:** +221
322427

Non-English Name: Institut Sénégalais de Recherches
Agricoles (ISRA), Service de Documentation (SD) **Founded:** 1978 **Type:** Research **Staff:** 1 Prof. 13 Other **Holdings:**
5,000 books 230 journals **Language of Collection/Services:**
French / French **Subjects:** Agricultural Economics, Animal
Husbandry, Forestry, Plants, Rural Sociology **Loan:** Internationally **Service:** Internationally **Photocopy:** Yes

2709   Dakar, Sénégal
United States Agency for International
Development (USAID)
Mission Documentation Center
c/o American Embassy
BP 49
Dakar

Location: Department of State, Avenue Jean XXIII and
Rue Kleber **Phone:** +221 823-5880 **Fax:** +221 823-2965
WWW: www.info.usaid.gov/regions/afr

Founded: 1980 **Type:** Government **Staff:** 2 Prof. **Holdings:**
10,000 books **Language of Collection/Services:** English
Subjects: Agricultural Economics, Agricultural Production
Loan: Inhouse **Photocopy:** Yes

2710   Dakar, Sénégal
Université Cheikh Anta Diop
Bibliothèque Universitaire, Section Sciences
(BUCAD)
BP 2006
Dakar

Phone: +221 824-6981 **Fax:** +221 824-2379 **Email:** biblicad@ucad.sn **WWW:** www.ucad.sn

Former Name: Université de Dakar **Founded:** 1967 **Type:** Academic **Head:** M. Louis Edouard Dniaye *Phone:* +221 824-6981 ext 34 *Email:* biblicad@ucad.sn **Staff:** 5 Prof. 4 Other **Holdings:** 37,000 books 106 journals **Language of Collection/Services:** French, English/French **Subjects:** Entomology, Fisheries, Plants, Soil Science, Veterinary Medicine, Zoology, Zootechny **Loan:** Internationally **Photocopy:** Yes

2711 Dakar-Hann, Sénégal
Food Technology Institute
Information Department
Route des Pères Maristes
BP 2765
Dakar-Hann
Phone: +221 832-0070

Non-English Name: Institut de Technologie Alimentaire (ITA), Département Information et Vulgarisation **Founded:** 1963 **Staff:** 5 Other **Holdings:** 5,000 books 50 journals **Subjects:** Agricultural Economics, Food Technology, Human Nutrition

2712 Dakar-Hann, Sénégal
Research Institute for Development
Documentation Centre
Route des Pères Maristes
BP 1386
Dakar-Hann
Phone: +221 832-5864 **Fax:** +221 832-4307 **Email:** crdo@orstom.sn **WWW:** www.ird.sn

Non-English Name: Institut de Recherche pour le Développement (IRD), Centre de Documentation (CRDO) **Former Name:** Office de la Recherche Scientifique et Technique d'Outre-Mer (ORSTOM), Institut Français de Recherche Scientifique pour le Développement en Coopération (ORSTOM), French Scientific Research Institute for Development through Cooperation **Founded:** 1944 **Staff:** 1 Prof. 2 Other **Holdings:** 5,661 books **Subjects:** Biology, Oceanography, Social Sciences, Soil Science

2713 Dakar-Hann, Sénégal
Senegal Institute of Agricultural Research,
   Research Department for Forest Production
Documentation and Information Service
BP 2312
Dakar-Hann
Location: Route des Pères Maristes **Phone:** +221 323219 ext 346 **Fax:** +221 329617

Non-English Name: Institut Sénégalais de Recherches Agricoles, Centre National de Recherches Forestières (ISRA), Service de Documentation et d'Information (SDI) **Former Name:** Département des Recherches sur les Productions Forestières e l'Hydrobiologie (DRPF), Bibliothèque **Founded:** 1975 **Type:** Government **Staff:** 1 Prof. **Holdings:** 1,000 books 10 journals **Language of Collection/Services:** French **Subjects:** Forestry **Loan:** In country **Service:** In country **Photocopy:** Yes

2714 Dakar-Thiaroye, Sénégal
Dakar-Thiaroye Oceanographic Research Center
Documentation Center
BP 2241
Dakar-Thiaroye
Phone: +221 834-3383 **Fax:** +221 834-2792

Non-English Name: Centre de Recherches Océanographiques de Dakar-Thiaroye (CRODT), Centre de Documentation **Founded:** 1973 **Type:** Government **Staff:** 1 Prof. **Holdings:** 12,000 books 66 journals **Language of Collection/Services:** English/French **Subjects:** Aquaculture, Fisheries, Fishery Management, Water Resources, Oceanography **Loan:** Internationally **Service:** Internationally **Photocopy:** Yes

2715 Thiès, Sénégal
Ministry of National Education, National School
   of Agriculture
Library
BP 296-A
Thiès
Location: Km 7 route de Khombole **Fax:** +221 511551
WWW: www.refer.org/sngal_ct/edu/ensa/accueil.htm

Non-English Name: Ministère de l'Education Nationale, Ecole Nationale Supérieure d'Agriculture (ENSA), Bibliothèque **Former Name:** Institut National de Développement Rural (INDR), National Institute for Rural Development **Founded:** 1983 **Type:** Government **Head:** Abdoul Aziz Hanne *Phone:* +221 511257 *Email:* ensath@telecomplus.sn **Staff:** 1 Prof. 2 Other **Holdings:** 6,000 books 50 journals **Language of Collection/Services:** French, English / French **Subjects:** Agricultural Economics, Animal Husbandry, Agricultural Engineering, Crops, Entomology, Forestry, Horticulture, Plants, Soil Science **Databases Developed:** MEMO - database on students' work after their studies **Loan:** In country **Service:** Internationally **Photocopy:** No

Serbia and Montenegro

2716 Belgrade, Serbia and Montenegro
Institute for Plant Protection and Environment
Library
Teodora Drajzera 9
PO Box 33-79
11040 Belgrade
Phone: +381(11) 660049, 660079 **Fax:** +381(11) 669860
Email: info@izbizs.co.yu **WWW:**
www.izbizs.co.yu/first.html

Non-English Name: Institut za Zastitu Bilja i Zivotnu, Biblioteka **Former Name:** Institute for Plant Protection, Institut za Zastitu Bilja **Founded:** 1945 **Type:** Academic **Staff:** 2 Prof. 1 Other **Holdings:** 20,000 books 3,000 journals **Subjects:** Environment, Plant Protection **Loan:** Internationally **Photocopy:** Yes

2717 Belgrade, Serbia and Montenegro
Institute of Forestry
Library
Kneza Viseslave 3

11030 Belgrade
Phone: +381(11) 553355 **Fax:** +381(11) 545969 **Email:** inszasum@eunet.yu

Non-English Name: Institut za Sumarstvo i Drvnu Industriju, Biblioteka **Founded:** 1946 **Type:** Government **Staff:** 1 Prof. **Holdings:** 15,770 books 120 journals **Subjects:** Entomology, Horticulture, Plant Pathology, Soil Science **Specializations:** Forestry **Loan:** Inhouse **Photocopy:** Yes

2718 Belgrade, Serbia and Montenegro
University of Belgrade, Faculty of Agriculture
Central Library
Nemanjina 6
PO Box 127
11080 Belgrade, Zemun
Phone: +381(11) 615363 **Fax:** +381(11) 193659 **WWW:** www.bg.ac.yu

Non-English Name: Beogradski Universitet, Poljoprivredni Fakultet, Centralna Biblioteka **Founded:** 1945 **Type:** Academic **Staff:** 2 Prof. 2 Other **Holdings:** 50,000 books 350 journals **Language of Collection/Services:** Serbian / Serbian, English, Russian **Subjects:** Agricultural Economics, Animal Husbandry, Arable Farming, Food Technology, Fruits, Plant Protection, Soil Management, Tobacco Industry **Loan:** Internationally **Photocopy:** Yes

2719 Beli Potok Belgrade, Serbia and Montenegro
"Jaroslav Cerni" Institute for the Development of
    Water Resources
YUWAT
PO Box 33-54
11223 Beli Potok Belgrade
Phone: +381(11) 649265 **Email:** jcerni@bglink.com

Founded: 1947 **Type:** Association **Staff:** 2 Prof. 1 Other **Holdings:** 500 books 20 journals **Subjects:** Drainage, Hydrology, Irrigation, Soil Physics, Water Management, Water Resources **Loan:** In country **Photocopy:** Yes

2720 Cacak, Serbia and Montenegro
Fruit and Grape Research Institute
Library
Kralja Petra I/9
32000 Cacak
Phone: +381(32) 21375, 21413 **Fax:** +381(32) 29391
Email: vocinsca@emi.yu

Non-English Name: Institut za Vocarstvo i Vinogradarstvo, Biblioteka **Former Name:** Fruit and Viticulture Research Institute **Founded:** 1949 **Type:** Government **Head:** Mirjana Radovanovic *Phone:* +381(32) 21375 *Email:* vocinsca@emi.yu **Staff:** 1 Prof. 1 Other **Holdings:** 2,260 books 20 journals **Language of Collection/Services:** Serbian / Serbian **Subjects:** Plant Breeding, Plant Protection **Specializations:** Fruit Growing **Loan:** Do not loan **Service:** Inhouse **Photocopy:** Yes

2721 Novi Sad, Serbia and Montenegro
Institute of Field and Vegetable Crops, Novi Sad
    (IFVC)
Library
Maksima Gorkog 30

21000 Novi Sad
Phone: +381(21) 421717 **Fax:** +381(21) 621212 **Email:** institut@ifvcns.ns.ac.yu

Non-English Name: Institut za Ratarstvo i Povrtarstvo, Novi Sad, Biblioteka **Founded:** 1938 **Type:** Government **Head:** Mrs. Zora Dzilitov *Phone:* +381(21) 421717 *Email:* institut@ifvcns.ns.ac.yu **Staff:** 1 Prof. **Holdings:** 8,000 books 21 journals **Language of Collection/Services:** English, Serbian/Serbian, English **Subjects:** Plant Breeding, Crops **Specializations:** Field Crops, Vegetables **Loan:** Inhouse **Service:** Internationally **Photocopy:** Yes

2722 Novi Sad, Serbia and Montenegro
University at Novi Sad, Faculty of Agriculture
Central Library
Trg Dositeja Obradovica
21000 Novi Sad
Phone: +381(21) 450-355, 450-366 **Fax:** +381(21) 59761
WWW: www.ns.ac.yu, polj.ns.ac.yu

Non-English Name: Univerzitet u Novom Sadu, Poljoprivredni Fakultet, Centralnu Biblioteku **Networks:** AGRIS

2723 Novi Sad, Serbia and Montenegro
Yugoslav National Library
Matice Srpske, br. 1
21000 Novi Sad
Phone: +381(21) 615599 **Fax:** +381(21) 28574

Non-English Name: Biblioteka Matice Srpske (BMS) **Founded:** 1826 **Type:** Government **Staff:** 100 Prof. 50 Other **Language of Collection/Services:** Serbian / Serbian **Subjects:** Agribusiness, Biotechnology, Fisheries, Horticulture **Specializations:** Agricultural Development, Agricultural Economics, Agricultural Engineering, Food Sciences, Animal Husbandry, Crops, Entomology, Farming, Forestry, Plant Pathology, Soil Science, Veterinary Medicine **Databases Used:** Agris **Loan:** Inhouse **Service:** Inhouse **Photocopy:** Yes

Seychelles

2724 Mahe, Seychelles
Ministry of Agriculture and Marine Resources
    (MAMR)
Agricultural Documentation Centre (AGRIDOC)
PO Box 166
Mahe
Location: Union Vale **Phone:** +248 322411/2 **Fax:** +248 324030 **Email:** statmamr@sey.net

Non-English Name: Ministere l'Agrikiltir ek Resours Maren (MARM), Sant Dokimantasyon **Founded:** 1991 **Type:** Government **Head:** Ms. M. Arissol *Phone:* +248 322411/2 *Email:* statmamr@sey.net **Staff:** 2 Other **Holdings:** 5,000 books 25 journals **Language of Collection/Services:** English / Creole **Subjects:** Agricultural Development, Agricultural Economics, Animal Production, Aquaculture, Crop Production, Extension, Fisheries, Forestry, Natural Resources, Plant Protection, Plants, Veterinary Science **Networks:** AGRIS **Databases Developed:** AGRIN database; SECAT database - all journals in AGRIDOC; SOURCE database - directory of other documentation centers **Databases Used:** Agris **Loan:** In country **Service:** In country **Photocopy:** Yes

◆**2725 Mont Fleuri, Seychelles**
Botanical Gardens, Environment Division
Environment Documentation Centre
PO Box 445
Mont Fleuri

Fax: +248 224500

Type: Government

2726 Victoria, Seychelles
Ministry of Industry, Seychelles Bureau of
Standards (SBS)
Centre for Industrial, Scientific and Technological
Information and Documentation (CISTID)
PO Box 953
Victoria

Location: Pointe Larue, Mahé **Fax:** +248 375151 **Email:** sbsorg@seychelles.net

Founded: 1990 **Type:** Government **Head:** Mrs. Amy Quatre *Phone:* +248 375333 *Email:* sbsorg@seychelles.net **Staff:** 3 Prof. 4 Other **Holdings:** 3,548 books 27 journals **Language of Collection/Services:** English / English **Subjects:** Science, Technology **Loan:** In country **Service:** In country **Photocopy:** Yes

2727 Victoria, Seychelles
Seychelles Fishing Authority (SFA)
SFA Documentation Centre
PO Box 449
Fishing Port
Victoria

Phone: +248 224597 **Fax:** +248 224508 **Email:** sfasez@seychelles.net

Founded: 1989 **Type:** Government **Head:** Mrs. Josette Confait *Phone:* +248 224597 *Email:* jconfait@hotmail.com **Holdings:** 1,000 books 40 journals **Language of Collection/Services:** English / English **Subjects:** Fisheries, Marine Resources **Specializations:** Aquaculture, Fishery Management, Oceanography **Photocopy:** Yes **Loan:** In country **Service:** Internationally

Sierra Leone

◆**2728 Bo, Sierra Leone**
Ministry of Agriculture, Forestry and Marine
Resources
Regional Agricultural Documentation Centre
PO Box 29
Bo

Founded: 1986 **Type:** Government **Staff:** 1 Prof. 6 Other **Holdings:** 100 books 10 journals **Subjects:** Agricultural Research, Agricultural Economics, Education/Extension **Loan:** Do not loan **Photocopy:** No

2729 Freetown, Sierra Leone
Department of Agriculture and Forestry (DAF)

National Agricultural Documentation Centre
(NADOC)
Rooms M209/M211, 2nd Floor
Youyi Building, Brookfields
Freetown

Phone: +232(22) 241612, 242141 **Fax:** +232(22) 241613

Former Name: Ministry of Agriculture, Natural Resources and Forestry **Founded:** 1986 **Type:** Government **Staff:** 1 Prof. 5 Other **Language of Collection/Services:** English/ English **Subjects:** Agricultural Engineering, Animal Husbandry, Crops, Drainage, Fisheries, Forestry, Irrigation, Health Hazards, Nutrition, Plant Protection, Soil Science, Veterinary Medicine **Specializations:** Appropriate Technology, Mangrove Swamps, Subsistence Farming, Swamps (Sierra Leone), Tenure Systems, Women in Agriculture **Networks:** AGRIS **Databases Developed:** Developing national agricultural database **Databases Used:** Agris; CABCD; Dissertation Abstracts **Loan:** Do not loan **Service:** Internationally **Photocopy:** Yes

◆**2730 Freetown, Sierra Leone**
Rice Research Station, Rokupr (RRS)
Library
PMB 736
Freetown

Location: Station, Rokupr

Former Name: West African Rice Research Station, Rokupr, Njala University College, Rice Research Station, Rokupr **Founded:** 1934 **Type:** Government **Staff:** 1 Prof. 2 Other **Holdings:** 2,000 books 125 journals **Language of Collection/Services:** English, French, German, Italian, Chinese, Spanish, Portuguese / English, French **Subjects:** Agriculture (Tropics), Agricultural Development, Agricultural Economics, Agricultural Engineering, Crops, Education/Extension, Entomology, Farming, Farming Systems Research, Forestry, Plant Pathology, Plant Protection, Postharvest Technology, Rice, Soil Science **Loan:** In country **Photocopy:** Yes

◆**2731 Freetown, Sierra Leone**
University of Sierra Leone, Fourah Bay College
(USL, FBC)
Library
PO Box 87
Freetown

Location: Mount Aureol

Founded: 1827 **Type:** Academic **Staff:** 5 Prof. 15 Other **Holdings:** 1,108 books 4 journals **Language of Collection/Services:** English **Subjects:** Animal Husbandry, Biotechnology, Crop Production, Crops, Dairying, Farming, Fisheries, Forestry, Fruit Growing, Horticulture, Plant Pathology, Poultry, Soil Conservation, Soil Science, Veterinary Medicine **Loan:** In country **Service:** Internationally **Photocopy:** Yes

Singapore

2732 Singapore, Singapore
National University of Singapore

Science Library
12 Kent Ridge Crescent
Singapore 119275

Phone: +65 874-2454 **Fax:** +65 777-3571 **Email:** slbfrm01
@nus.edu.sg **WWW:** www.lib.nus.edu.sg **OPAC:** linc.nus.
edu.sg

Founded: 1986 **Type:** Academic **Head:** Mrs. Loy Shiow
Yong **Holdings:** 202,000 books 2,106 journals **Networks:**
AGRIS

Slovakia

2733 **Banská Bystrica, Slovakia**
Grassland and Mountain Agriculture Research
Institute (GMARI)
Library
Mládeznícka 36
974 21 Banská Bystrica

Phone: +421(88) 413-2541 **Fax:** +421(88) 413-2544
Email: kniznica@nmost.vutphp.sk **WWW:** www.vutphp.
sk/english/indexe.html

Non-English Name: Výskumný ústav travnych porastov a
horskeho polnohospodarstva (VÚTPHP), Kniznica **Former
Name:** Grassland Research Institute, Výskumný ústav lúk a
pasienkov (VÚLP) **Founded:** 1962 **Type:** Research **Head:**
Daniela Feriencíková *Phone:* +421(88) 413-2541 *Email:*
kniznica@nmost.vutphp.sk **Staff:** 2 Prof. **Holdings:** 9,000
books 35 journals **Language of Collection/Services:** Slovak, Czech, English, German, Russian/ Slovak, English **Subjects:** Agricultural Development, Crops, Animal Husbandry,
Biotechnology, Farming Systems, Plant Physiology, Soil Biology, Soil Science, Veterinary Medicine **Specializations:**
Grasses, Grassland Management, Grassland Improvement,
Grasslands **Loan:** Inhouse **Photocopy:** Yes **Service:** Inhouse

2734 **Bratislava, Slovakia**
Central Institute for Control and Testing in
Agriculture
Scientific Information Centre
Matúskova 21
833 16 Bratislava

Phone: +421(7) 5477-5485 **Fax:** +421(7) 5477-7436
Email: uksup@internet.sk

Non-English Name: Ústredny kontrolny a skusobny ústav
polnohospodársky (ÚKSUP), Stredisko vedeckych informácií **Former Name:** Státní vyzkumné ústavy zemedelské,
Státne vyskumné ústavu polnohhospodárske, Ústredny kontrolny ústav polnohospodársky **Founded:** 1951 (library);
1975 (information center) **Type:** Government **Staff:** 2 Prof.
1 Other **Holdings:** 14,429 books 200 journals **Language of
Collection/Services:** Czech, Slovak **Subjects:** Agricultural
Development, Agricultural Economics, Animal Husbandry,
Biotechnology, Crops, Entomology, Farming, Horticulture,
Plant Pathology, Soil Science **Specializations:** Forecasting,
Monitoring, Testing **Databases Used:** Agricola; Agris; Biosis; CABCD; CAS; FSTA **Loan:** Internationally **Service:** In
country **Photocopy:** Yes

2735 **Bratislava, Slovakia**
Research Institute of Agriculture and Food
Economics (RIAFE)
Information Centre
Trencianska 55
824 80 Bratislava

Phone: +421(7) 524-3208 **Fax:** +421(7) 521-6408 **Email:**
subinova@vuepp.sk **WWW:** www.vuepp.sk **OPAC:**
infoware.uvtip.sk

Non-English Name: Výskumný ústav ekonomiky polno-
hospodárstva a potravinárstva (VÚEPP), Útvar VTEI **Type:**
Government **Founded:** 1919 **Head:** Mgr. Anna Zemanová
Phone: +421(7) 524-3237 *Email:* zemanova@vuepp.sk
Staff: 3 Prof. **Holdings:** 16,500 books 100 journals **Lan-
guage of Collection/Services:** Slovak / Slovak **Subjects:**
Agribusiness, Agricultural Development, Agricultural Eco-
nomics, Agricultural Engineering, Biotechnology, Educa-
tion/Extension, Farming, Food Sciences **Networks:**
Agrokatalog **Databases Used:** Agris; CELEX; FAOSTAT
Loan: In country **Service:** In country **Photocopy:** Yes

♦2736 **Bratislava, Slovakia**
Research Institute of Viticulture and Enology
Information Center for Viticulture and Enology
Matúskova 25
833 11 Bratislava

Phone: +421(7) 375292, 375866, 375982 **Fax:** +421(7)
375436

Non-English Name: Výskumný ústav vinohradnícky a
vinársky (VÚVV), Oborové informacné stredisko pre vinohradníctvo a vinárstvo (OBIS VTEI) **Founded:** 1924 **Type:**
Business **Staff:** 5 Prof. **Holdings:** 17,000 books 59 journals
Language of Collection/Services: Slovak / Slovak, French,
German, English, Spanish, Czech, Russian **Subjects:** Biotechnology, Breeding, Enology, Microbiology, Nutrition,
Plant Pathology, Soil Science, Viticulture **Databases Developed:** Annotations from foreign journals accessible by
computer **Loan:** In country **Service:** In country **Photocopy:**
Yes

2737 **Bratislava, Slovakia**
Slovak Academy of Sciences, Institute of Zoology
Library
Dubravska cesta 9
84 206 Bratislava

Phone: +421(7) 5478-9756 **Fax:** +421(7) 5478-9757
Email: uzaelabu@savba.sk

Subjects: Zoology

2738 **Bratislava, Slovakia**
Slovak Land Fund
Information Center
Búdkova 36
817 15 Bratislava

Phone: +421(7) 371302, 371320

Non-English Name: Slovensky pozemkovy fond, Informacné stredisko **Staff:** 1 Prof. **Holdings:** 5,000 books **Language of Collection/Services:** Slovak **Subjects:** Drainage,
Irrigation, Soil Management, Soil Science, Water Resources
Photocopy: Yes

2739 Bratislava, Slovakia
Soil Science and Conservation Research Institute
Department of Scientific, Economic and Technical
    Information - Library
Gagarinova 10
827 13 Bratislava
Phone: +421(7) 434 20 866 **Fax:** +421(7) 432 95 487
Email: sci@vupu.sk **WWW:** www.uvtip.sk/english/rezort/
vupu/index.html

Non-English Name: Výskumný ústav pôdoznalectva a
ochrany pôdy, Oddelenie vedecko-technických informácií -
kniznica **Former Name:** Soil Fertility Research Center,
Výskumný centrum podnej urodnosti, Soil Science and Plant
Nutrition Research Institute, Irrigation Management Research Institute, Grassland Management Research Institute
Founded: 1959 **Type:** Government **Staff:** 17 Prof. **Holdings:** 70,000 books 400 journals **Subjects:** Grasslands, Irrigation, Soil Science **Loan:** In country **Photocopy:** Yes

♦2740 Bratislava, Slovakia
State Forest Products Research Institute
Library
Lamacska 1
833 30 Bratislava
Phone: +42(7) 3706363 **Fax:** +42(7) 3706363

Non-English Name: Statny drevarsky výzkumný ústav
(SDVÚ), Kniznica **Founded:** 1947 **Type:** Government
Staff: 1 Prof. 3 Other **Holdings:** 16,000 books 325 journals
Language of Collection/Services: Slovak **Subjects:** Bio-
technology, Wood Chemistry **Specializations:** Forest Prod-
ucts **Loan:** In country **Photocopy:** Yes

2741 Bratislava, Slovakia
Water Research Institute (WRI)
Information Center
Nábr. arm. gen. L. Svobodu 5
812 49 Bratislava
Fax: +421(7) 544-15743 **Email:** veda@vuvh.sk

Non-English Name: Výskumný ústav vodného hospodárstva (VÚVH), Vedecko-technické Informácie (VTI)
Type: Research **Founded:** 1952 **Head:** PhDr. E. Kovaci-
ková **Phone:** +421(7) 534-3340 **Email:** veda@vuvh.sk
Staff: 4 Prof. 2 Other **Holdings:** 27,000 books 79 journals
Language of Collection/Services: Slovak **Subjects:** Biotechnology, Water Resources **Databases Developed:** Various databases of water parameters **Databases Used:** Agris
Loan: In country **Service:** In country **Photocopy:** Yes

♦2742 Ivanka pri Dunaji, Slovakia
Feedstuffs Research Institute
Information Center
Nádrazná 36
900 28 Ivanka pri Dunaji
Fax: +421(7) 943128

Non-English Name: Výskumný ústav krmivársky (VÚK),
Stredisko vedeckych, technickhych a ekonomickych informácií (VTEI) **Former Name:** Výskumný ústav Krmivárs-
keho priemyslu a s luzieb, Oborové informacné stredisko
(OBIS) **Founded:** 1976 **Type:** Research **Staff:** 6 Prof. **Holdings:** 4,650 books 130 journals **Subjects:** Biotechnology,

Cereals, Feed Industry, Feeds, Feed Mixing, Postharvest
Technology **Loan:** Internationally **Photocopy:** Yes

2743 Ivanka pri Dunaji, Slovakia
Poultry Research Institute
Library
900 28 Ivanka pri Dunaji
Fax: +421(7) 4594-3131

Non-English Name: Výskumný ústav hydinárstva, Oborové
informacní stredisko (OBIS) **Founded:** 1951 **Type:** Government **Head:** Viera Lukácová **Phone:** +421(7) 4594-3121 ext
20 **Email:** baumgart@ivanka.vuzv.sk **Staff:** 1 Other **Holdings:** 12,000 books 87 journals **Language of Collection/
Services:** Slovak, Czech, English, German, Russian / Slovak
Subjects: Animal Husbandry, Environment, Poultry, Veterinary Medicine **Loan:** In country **Photocopy:** Yes

2744 Košice, Slovakia
Research Institute of Veterinary Medicine (RIVM)
Basic Information Center
Hlinkova 1/A
040 01 Košice
Phone: +421(95) 633-2011 **Fax:** +421(95) 633-1853
Email: vuvm@vuvm.sk **WWW:** www.vuvm.sk

Non-English Name: Výskumný ústav veterinárnej medicí-
ny (VÚVM), Základné informacné stredisko (ZIS) **Former
Name:** Ústav experimentálnej veterinárnej medicíny
(ÚEVM), Research Institute of Experimental Veterinary
Medicine **Founded:** 1970 **Type:** Government **Head:** Dr.
Amália Ruzíková **Phone:** +421(95) 633-2011 **Email:** vuvm
@vuvm.sk **Staff:** 2 Prof. **Holdings:** 3,500 books 56 journals
Language of Collection/Services: Slovak / Slovak **Sub-
jects:** Agricultural Economics, Biotechnology, Food Sci-
ences, Gastroenteritis, Genetics, Immunology, Nutrition,
Microbiology, Plants, Reproduction **Specializations:** Veter-
inary Medicine **Databases Used:** Current Contents **Loan:**
Internationally **Service:** In country **Photocopy:** Yes

2745 Košice, Slovakia
Slovak Academy of Sciences, Parasitological
    Institute
Library
Hlinkova 3
040 01 Košice
Phone: +421(95) 63 344 55 **Fax:** +421(95) 63 314 14
Email: pausav@saske.sk **WWW:** www.saske.sk/
~pauwww/pau.html

Non-English Name: Slovenská akadémia vied, Parazitologicky ústav (SAV, PaÚ), Kniznica **Former Name:** Hel-
minthological Institute, Helmintologický ústavne (HELÚ)
Founded: 1953 **Type:** Academic **Head:** Bozena Mráziková
Phone: +42(95) 63 314 11 **Staff:** 1 Prof. **Holdings:** 16,800
books 20 journals **Language of Collection/Services:** English **Subjects:** Nematoda, Plant Pathology, Veterinary Medicine **Specializations:** Helminths, Plant Parasitic Nematodes
Loan: In country **Service:** In country **Photocopy:** Yes

2746 Košice, Slovakia
University of Veterinary Medicine (UVM)

Library and Institute of Scientific Information
(LISI)
Komenského 73
041 81 Košice
Phone: +421(95) 633-9689 **Fax:** +421(95) 633-9689
WWW: www.uvm.sk

Non-English Name: Univerzita veterinárskeho lekárstva
(UVL), Ústav vedeckých informácií a kniznica (ÚVIK)
Founded: 1949 **Type:** Academic **Head:** MVD Sona Lemá-
ková *Phone:* +421(95) 633-9689 *Email:* lemakova@uvik.
uvm.sk **Staff:** 11 Prof. 1 Other **Holdings:** 99,604 books 241
journals **Language of Collection/Services:** Slovak, Czech,
German, English, French / Slovak, English **Subjects:** Animal Husbandry, Education/Extension, Farming, Fisheries,
Food Sciences, Plant Pathology **Specializations:** Veterinary
Medicine **Databases Developed:** List of publication activity
of UVM **Databases Used:** CABCD; Medline **Loan:** Internationally **Service:** In country **Photocopy:** Yes

2747   Liptovský Hrádok, Slovakia
Research Institute of Animal Production, Institute
of Apiculture (RIAP, IofAp)
Information Center of Beekeeping - Library
Gasperíkova 599
033 80 Liptovský Hrádok
Phone: +421(844) 221141 **Fax:** +421(844) 222120
WWW: www.uvtip.sk/slovak/rezort/vuzv/index.html

Non-English Name: Výskumný ústav zivocísnej výroby,
Ústav vcelárstva (VÚZV, ÚVc), Vcelárske informacné stredisko - kniznica (VIS-K) **Former Name:** Výskumný ústav
vcelársky v Liptovskom Hrádku, Zakladne informacné stredisko (ZIS) **Founded:** 1934 **Type:** Government **Head:** Dr.
Ivan Popovic *Email:* popovic@vcelari.vuzv.sk *Phone:*
+421(844) 221141 **Staff:** 1 Prof. **Holdings:** 2,600 books 26
journals **Language of Collection/Services:** Slovak / Slovak,
English **Subjects:** Beekeeping **Loan:** Internationally **Service:** Internationally **Photocopy:** Yes

2748   Nitra, Slovakia
Institute of Scientific and Technical Information
for Agriculture (ISTIA)
Department of Scientific and Technical
Information
Samova 9
950 10 Nitra
Phone: +421(87) 772-1805 **Fax:** +421(87) 772-1742
Email: uvtip@uvtip.sk **WWW:** www.uvtip.sk **OPAC:**
infoware.uvtip.sk:8888/WWWisis/iis.htm

Non-English Name: Ústav vedecko-technických informácií
pre pôdohospodárstvo (ÚVTIP) **Founded:** 1952 **Type:** Government **Head:** Ing. Eva Vokurková *Phone:* +421(87) 772-
1752 *Email:* skfaolib@uvtip.sk, vokurkova@uvtip.sk **Staff:**
17 Prof. 24 Other **Holdings:** 4,600 books 61 journals **Language of Collection/Services:** Slovak, Czech, German,
English, Hungarian **Subjects:** Agribusiness, Agricultural
Development, Agricultural Economics, Crops, Horticulture,
Soil Science, Veterinary Medicine **Networks:** AGRIS **Databases Developed:** AGROINDEX - National Agricultural
Database **Databases Used:** Agricola; Agris; Agrisearch
Loan: Internationally **Service:** Internationally **Photocopy:**
Yes

2749   Nitra, Slovakia
Ministry of Agriculture
Library of Agroinstitute
Akademická c. 4
949 01 Nitra
Phone: +421(87) 534 851/4 **Fax:** +421(87) 36742 **Email:**
public@agroinst.sk **WWW:** www.agroinst.sk

Non-English Name: Ministerstvo podohospodárstva SR,
Kniznica agroinstitútu **Former Name:** Oborové informacné
stredisko vedeckotechnichych a ekonomickych informácií
(OBIS-VTEI) **Founded:** 1979 **Type:** Government **Head:**
Ildikó Pongóová *Phone:* +421(87) 534 851 ext 227 *Email:*
pongoova@agroinst.sk **Staff:** 2 Prof. 1 Other **Holdings:**
3,800 books 98 journals **Language of Collection/Services:**
Slovak / Slovak **Subjects:** Agribusiness, Agricultural Development, Agricultural Economics, Education **Loan:** In country **Service:** In country **Photocopy:** Yes

2750   Nitra, Slovakia
Research Institute of Animal Production (RIAP)
Department of Scientific-Technical Information
(DSTI)
Hlohovská 2
949 92 Nitra
Phone: +421(87) 515240, 515246 **Fax:** +421(87) 519032
WWW: www.uvtip.sk/slovak/rezort/vuzv/index.html

Non-English Name: Výskumný ústav zivocísnej výroby
(VÚZV), Oddelenie vedecko-technických informácií (OV-
TEI) **Former Name:** Centre of Scientific-Technical Information, Oborové informacné stredisko (OBIS) **Founded:**
1947 **Type:** Government **Staff:** 5 Prof. 1 Other **Holdings:**
28,000 books 130 journals **Language of Collection/Ser-
vices:** English, German, Slovak / Slovak **Subjects:** Animal
Breeding, Animal Husbandry, Biotechnology, Genetic Engineering, Reproduction **Specializations:** Agricultural Economics, Ecology, Farming, Veterinary Medicine **Databases
Developed:** Bibliography of publications of scientists of
RIAP, Nitra **Databases Used:** Agris; CABCD **Loan:** Internationally **Service:** Internationally **Photocopy:** Yes

2751   Nitra, Slovakia
Slovak Agricultural University
Slovak Agricultural Library
PO Box 20 B
949 59 Nitra
Location: Stúrova 51 **Phone:** +421(87) 523337, 26732
Fax: +421(87) 517743, 528539 **Email:** slpk@uniag.sk
WWW: www.uniag.sk/~slpk **OPAC:** sun.uniag.sk/
en-katalog/start.htm

Non-English Name: Slovenská pol'nohospodárska univer-
zita (SPU), Slovenská pol'nohospodárska kniznica (SlPK)
Former Name: Vysoká skola pol'nohospodárska (VSP),
Ústredná pôdohospodárska kniznica SR, Central Agricul-
tural Library of SR **Founded:** 1946 **Type:** Academic **Head:**
Ing. Dana Petrásová *Email:* dpetraso@uniag.sk *Phone:* +421
(87) 517743 **Staff:** 45 Prof. **Holdings:** 517,000 books 700
journals **Language of Collection/Services:** Slovak / Slovak
Subjects: Agribusiness, Agricultural Development, Crops,
Agricultural Economics, Agricultural Engineering, Animal
Husbandry, Biotechnology, Education/Extension, Entomol-
ogy, Farming, Horticulture, Plant Pathology, Plants, Soil

Science, Water Resources **Specializations:** Fisheries, Food Sciences, Forestry, Veterinary Medicine **Databases Developed:** Agrobibliografia - database of the Slovak Agricultural Bibliography and database of the Slovak Agricultural Citation Index **Databases Used:** Agricola; CABCD **Loan:** Internationally **Service:** Internationally **Photocopy:** Yes

2752   Nové Zámky, Slovakia
         Research Institute of Vegetables (RIV)
         Institute Library
         Andovská 6
         940 01 Nové Zámky

Location: Murgašova 102 **Phone:** +421(817) 420352 **Fax:** +421(817) 401892

Non-English Name: Výskumný ústav zeleninársky (VÚZ), Kniznica ústavu (KÚ) **Former Name:** Research Institute of Vegetables and Special Plants **Founded:** 1952 **Type:** Nongovernment **Head:** Ladislav Kelemen *Phone:* +421(817) 426248 ext 37 **Staff:** 1 Prof. **Holdings:** 4,500 books 69 journals **Language of Collection/Services:** Czech, Slovak, Hungarian / Slovak **Subjects:** Horticulture, Medicinal Plants, Vegetables **Specializations:** Important vegetables in Middle Europe **Databases Used:** Agricola **Loan:** In country **Service:** In country **Photocopy:** Yes

2753   Piestany, Slovakia
         Research Institute of Plant Production (RIPP)
         Scientific Information Unit (SIU)
         Bratislavská 122
         921 68 Piestany

Fax: +421(838) 772-2311 **Email:** vti@vurv.sk **WWW:** www.mpsr.sk

Non-English Name: Výskumný ústav rastlinnej výroby (VÚRV), Oddelenie vedecko-technických informácií (VTI) **Founded:** 1951 **Type:** Research **Head:** Mária Amberská *Phone:* +421(838) 722531 *Email:* vti@vurv.sk **Staff:** 3 Prof. **Holdings:** 25,000 books 62 journals **Language of Collection/Services:** Slovak, English **Subjects:** Agricultural Engineering, Agronomy, Biochemistry, Biotechnology, Cereals, Alternative Farming, Cultivation, Cytology, Fodder Crops, Gene Banks, Grasses, Legumes, Oil Plants, Plant Breeding, Plant Genetics, Plant Nutrition, Plant Pathology, Plant Physiology, Plant Protection **Databases Used:** Agricola **Loan:** In country **Service:** In country **Photocopy:** Yes

♦**2754   Trencín, Slovakia**
         Research Institute for Sheep Husbandry
         Library
         Opatovska 53
         911 43 Trencín

Fax: +421(831) 32842

Non-English Name: Výskumný ústav ovciarsky (VÚO Trencín), Oborové informacní stredisko, Kniznica (OBIS) **Founded:** 1935 **Type:** Research **Staff:** 1 Prof. **Holdings:** 10,000 books 50 journals **Language of Collection/Services:** Slovak **Subjects:** Agricultural Economics, Agricultural Engineering, Biotechnology, Farming, Veterinary Medicine **Specializations:** Animal Husbandry, Goats, Sheep **Databases Developed:** Sheep and goat farming - books, journals, proceedings, statistics, etc. mainly from Slovak and Czech

Republics **Loan:** Internationally **Service:** Internationally **Photocopy:** Yes

2755   Zvolen, Slovakia
         Forest Research Institute (FRI)
         Department of Scientific and Technical
             Information
         Masaryk Street No. 22
         960 62 Zvolen

Phone: +421(855) 531-4117 **Fax:** +421(855) 532-1883 **Email:** katarina.sladekova@fris.sk **WWW:** www.fris.sk

Non-English Name: Lesnícky výskumný ústav (LVÚ), Oddelenie vedecko-technických informácií - kniznica **Former Name:** Výskumný ústav lesného hospodárstva (VÚLH) **Founded:** 1924 **Type:** Research **Head:** Ing. Katarína Sládeková *Email:* katarina.sladekova@fris.sk *Phone:* +421(855) 532-0316/8, 531-4190 **Staff:** 52 Prof. 1 Other **Holdings:** 86 journals 70,000 books **Language of Collection/Services:** Slovak, Czech **Subjects:** Horticulture, Plants, Plant Pathology, Soil, Veterinary Medicine, Water Resources **Specializations:** Environment, Forest Products, Forestry, Wildlife Management **Databases Developed:** Bibliography of published works of staff for 100 years **Databases Used:** Agris **Loan:** Internationally **Service:** In country **Photocopy:** Yes

2756   Zvolen, Slovakia
         Technical University
         Slovak Library of Forestry and Wood Science
         T.C. Masaryka 20
         961 02 Zvolen

Phone: +421(855) 5206 641 **Fax:** +421(855) 5479 942 **WWW:** sldk.tuzvo.sk **OPAC:** sldk.tuzvo.sk/e/index2.html

Non-English Name: Technická univerzita (TU), Slovenská lesnícka a drevárska kniznica (SLDK) **Former Name:** University College of Forestry and Wood Technology, Vysoká skola lesnícka a drevárska (VSLD) **Founded:** 1952 **Type:** Academic **Head:** Ing. Elena Ihlavniková *Phone:* +421(855) 5206 641 *Email:* ezihlav@vsld.tuzvo.sk **Staff:** 36 Prof. 15 Other **Holdings:** 350,000 books **Language of Collection/Services:** Czech, Slovak **Subjects:** Agriculture (Tropics), Ecology, Education/Extension, Entomology, Forestry, Plant Pathology, Soil Science, Water Resources **Loan:** In country **Service:** In country **Photocopy:** Yes

Slovenia

2757   Ljubljana, Slovenia
         Agricultural Institute of Slovenia
         Library and INDOC
         PO Box 2553
         SI 1001 Ljubljana

Location: Hacquetova ul. 17 **Fax:** +386(61) 137-5413 **Email:** lili.marincek@kis-h2.si **WWW:** www.kis-h2.si **OPAC:** izumw.izum.si/scripts/cobiss?ukaz=NEWS&id=12 [English], izumw.izum.si/scripts/cobiss?ukaz=NEWS&id= 3 [Slovenian]

Non-English Name: Kmetijski institut Slovenije, Knjiznica in INDOK **Founded:** 1964 **Type:** Research **Head:** Lili Marincek *Phone:* +386(61) 137-5435 *Email:* lili.marincek@

kis-h2.si **Staff:** 2 Prof. **Holdings:** 21,000 books 135 journals **Language of Collection/Services:** Slovenian, English / Slovenian, English, German **Subjects:** Agribusiness, Farming, Agricultural Development, Agricultural Economics, Agricultural Engineering, Animal Husbandry, Crops, Horticulture, Plant Pathology, Plants **Networks:** COBISS; OCLC **Databases Developed:** Electronic bibliography of institute researchers; access via OPAC **Loan:** Internationally **Service:** Internationally **Photocopy:** Yes

2758   Ljubljana, Slovenia
           National Institute of Biology, University of
              Ljubljana, Biotechnical Faculty, Biology
              Department
           Biology Library
           PO Box 141
           SI-1001 Ljubljana
Location: Vecna pot 111, SI 1000 Ljubljana **Fax:** +386 (61) 123-5038 **WWW:** www.uni-lj.si **OPAC:** izumw.izum. si/scripts/cobiss?ukaz=NEWS&id=12 [English], izumw. izum.si/scripts/cobiss?ukaz=NEWS&id=3 [Slovenian]

Non-English Name: Nacionalni institut za biologijo, Univerza v Ljubljani, Biotehniska fakulteta, Oddelek za biologijo (NIB), Bioloska knjiznica **Type:** Academic **Founded:** 1961 **Head:** Barbara Cernac *Phone:* +386(61) 123- 3388 *Email:* barbara.cernac@uni-lj.si **Staff:** 2 Prof. **Holdings:** 39,000 books 413 journals **Language of Collection/Services:** Slovenian, English / Slovenian, English **Subjects:** Biology, Biotechnology, Ecology, Marine Environment, Wildlife **Databases Developed:** Electronic bibliography of researchers and professors - access via OPAC **Databases Used:** Comprehensive **Networks:** COBISS; OCLC **Loan:** Internationally **Service:** Internationally **Photocopy:** Yes

2759   Ljubljana, Slovenia
           Slovenian Forestry Institute, University of
              Ljubljana, Biotechnical Faculty, Department
              of Forestry and Renewable Forest Resources
           Forestry Library and INDOC Service
           PO Box 2985
           SI-1001 Ljubljana
Location: Vecna pot 2, SI 1000 Ljubljana **Phone:** +386 (61) 123-1161, 123-1343 **Fax:** +386(61) 273-589 **Email:** gisinfo@gozdis.si **WWW:** www.uni-lj.si **OPAC:** izumw. izum.si/scripts/cobiss?ukaz=NEWS&id=12 [English], izumw.izum.si/scripts/cobiss?ukaz=NEWS&id=3 [Slovenian]

Non-English Name: Gozdarski inštitut Slovenije, Univerza v Ljubljani, Biotehniska fakulteta, Oddelek za gozdarstvo in obnovijive gozdne vire (GIS), Gozdarska Knjiznica in INDOK dejavnost **Founded:** 1949 **Type:** Academic **Head:** Teja Koler-Povh *Email:* teja.koler@gozdis.si *Phone:* +386 (61) 123-1161, 123-1343 **Staff:** 2 Prof. **Holdings:** 35,300 books 308 journals **Language of Collection/Services:** Slovenian, English, German / Slovenian, English, German **Subjects:** Ecology, Forestry, Wildlife **Networks:** COBISS; OCLC **Databases Developed:** Electronic bibliogriphy of Institute and Department researchers and professors; access via OPAC address **Databases Used:** Comprehensive **Loan:** Internationally **Service:** Internationally **Photocopy:** Yes

2760   Ljubljana, Slovenia
           University of Ljubljana, Biotechnical Faculty
           Central Biotechnical Library, Slovenian National
              AGRIS Center (CBL)
           PO Box 2995
           SI-1001 Ljubljana
Location: Jamnikarjeva 101, SI 1000 Ljubljana **Phone:** +386(61) 123-1161 **Fax:** +386(61) 265-782 **WWW:** www .bf.uni-lj.si **OPAC:** izumw.izum.si/scripts/cobiss?ukaz= NEWS&id=12 [English], izumw.izum.si/scripts/cobiss? ukaz=NEWS&id=3 [Slovenian]

Non-English Name: Univerza v Ljubljani, Biotehniska fakulteta, Centralna biotehniska knjiznica, Slovenski nacionalni AGRIS center (CBK) **Former Name:** Univerza Edvarda Kardelja v Ljubljani, University Edvarda Kardelja of Ljubljana, Central Library and INDOC Service, Centralna Knjiznica and INDOK Center **Founded:** 1947 **Type:** Academic **Head:** Jana Bradac (Library), Tomaz Bartol (AGRIS Center) *Phone:* +386(61) 123-1161 *Email:* jana.bradac@bf. uni-lj.si, tomaz.bartol@bf.uni-lj.si **Staff:** 2 Prof. **Holdings:** 12,000 books 125 journals **Language of Collection/Services:** Slovenian, English/Slovenian, English, German, Italian, French, Spanish **Subjects:** Comprehensive **Specializations:** Theses, Documentation, Information Science, Legislation, Standards, Thesauri **Networks:** AGRIS; COBISS; OCLC **Databases Developed:** Electronic bibliography of researchers and professors; access via OPAC **Databases Used:** Comprehensive **Loan:** Internationally **Service:** Internationally **Photocopy:** Yes

2761   Ljubljana, Slovenia
           University of Ljubljana, Biotechnical Faculty,
              Agronomy Department
           Library
           PO Box 2995
           SI-1001 Ljubljana
Location: Jamnikarjeva 101, SI 1000 Ljubljana **Phone:** +386(61) 123-1161 **Fax:** +386(61) 123-1088 **Email:** btflj. cobissbfagr@cobiss.izum.si **WWW:** www.bf.uni-lj.si/ cgi-bin/slo/ag.htm **OPAC:** izumw.izum.si/scripts/cobiss? ukaz=NEWS&id=12 [English], izumw.izum.si/scripts/ cobiss?ukaz=NEWS&id=3 [Slovenian]

Non-English Name: Univerza v Ljubljani, Biotehniska fakulteta, Oddelek za agronomijo, Knjiznica **Former Name:** Univerza Edvarda Kardelja, University Edvarda Kardelja **Founded:** 1979 **Type:** Academic **Head:** prof. dr. Franc Bati[1]; Karmen Stopar (INDOC); Tatjana Ge[1] (Library) *Email:* karmen.stopar@bf.uni-lj.sv *Phone:* +386(61) 123- 1161 **Staff:** 3 Prof. **Holdings:** 58,000 books 270 journals **Language of Collection/Services:** Slovenian, English/Slovenian, English **Subjects:** Agribusiness, Agricultural Development, Agricultural Economics, Agricultural Engineering, Biotechnology, Crops, Ecology, Education/Extension, Entomology, Farming, Horticulture, Meteorology, Plant Pathology, Plants, Rural Sociology, Soil Science, Water Resources **Networks:** COBISS; OCLC **Databases Developed:** Electronic bibliography of researchers and professors - access via OPAC; Slovenian information system for plant protection - access via Internet at www.bf.uni-lj.si/ag/fito; Soil maps of Slovenia - access via Internet at www.bf.uni-lj.si/cgi-bin/slo/ ag/cpvo/xahxcpvo.htm **Databases Used:** Comprehensive

Loan: Internationally **Service:** Internationally **Photocopy:** Yes

2762 Ljubljana, Slovenia
University of Ljubljana, Biotechnical Faculty,
    Department of Food Science and Technology
Library and INDOC
PO Box 2995
SI-1001 Ljubljana
Location: Jamnikarjeva 101, SI 1000 Ljubljana **Phone:** +386(61) 123-1161 **Fax:** +386(61) 266-296 **Email:** ivica. hocevar@bf.uni-lj.sv **WWW:** www.bf.uni-lj.si/cgi-bin/ slo/zi.htm **OPAC:** izumw.izum.si/scripts/cobiss?ukaz= NEWS&id=12 [English], izumw.izum.si/scripts/cobiss? ukaz=NEWS&id=3 [Slovenian]

Non-English Name: Univerza v Ljubljani, Biotehniska fakulteta, Oddelek za zivilstvo, Knjiznica in INDOK **Former Name:** Univerza Edvarda Kardelja v Ljubljani, University Edvarda Kardelja of Ljubljana **Founded:** 1979 **Type:** Academic **Head:** Ivica Hocevar *Phone:* +386(61) 123-1161 *Email:* ivica.hocevar@bf.uni-lj.sv **Staff:** 2 Prof. **Holdings:** 32,000 books 220 journals **Language of Collection/Services:** Slovenian, English / Slovenian, English, French **Subjects:** Biotechnology, Food Sciences **Networks:** COBISS; OCLC **Databases Developed:** Electronic bibliography of researchers and professors; access via OPAC **Databases Used:** Comprehensive **Loan:** Internationally **Service:** Internationally **Photocopy:** Yes

2763 Ljubljana, Slovenia
University of Ljubljana, Biotechnical Faculty,
    Department of Wood Science and Technology
INDOC Service and Library
PO Box 2995
SI-1001 Ljubljana
Location: Rozna dolina, C. VIII/34, SI 1000 Ljubljana **Phone:** +386(61) 123-1161 **Fax:** +386(61) 272-297 **WWW:** www.bf.uni-lj.si/cgi-bin/slo/les/bf_new.htm? language-winee **OPAC:** izumw.izum.si/scripts/cobiss? ukaz=NEWS&id=12 [English], izumw.izum.si/scripts/ cobiss?ukaz=NEWS&id=3 [Slovenian]

Non-English Name: Univerza v Ljubljani, Biotehniska fakulteta, Oddelek za lesarstvo, INDOK sluzba in knjiznica **Former Name:** Univerza Edvarda Kardelja, University Edvarda Kardelja **Founded:** 1978 **Type:** Academic **Head:** Zoran Trošt (Director); Maja Cimerman (INDOC); Darja Vranjek (Library) *Phone:* +386(61) 123-1161 *Email:* maja. cimerman@uni-lj.sv, darja.vranjek@uni-lj.si **Staff:** 2 Prof. **Holdings:** 15,500 books 91 journals **Language of Collection/Services:** Slovenian, English, German/Slovenian, English, German **Subjects:** Wood Technology **Networks:** COBISS; OCLC **Databases Developed:** Electronic bibliography of researchers and professors - access via OPAC **Databases Used:** Comprehensive **Loan:** Internationally **Service:** Internationally **Photocopy:** Yes

2764 Ljubljana, Slovenia
University of Ljubljana, Biotechnical Faculty,
    Zootechnical Department
INDOC Service and Library
PO Box 2995

SI-1001 Ljubljana
Location: Groblje 3, SI 1230 Domzale **Phone:** +386(61) 717-875 **Fax:** +386(61) 721-005 **Email:** bfzolib@uni-lj.si, karmela.malinger@bfro.uni-lj.si **WWW:** www.bfro.uni-lj. si, zlomek.bfro.uni-lj.si/zoo/indok **OPAC:** izumw.izum.si/ scripts/cobiss?ukaz=NEWS&id=12 [English], izumw.izum. si/scripts/cobiss?ukaz=NEWS&id=3 [Slovenian]

Non-English Name: Univerza v Ljubljani, Biotehniska fakulteta, Oddelek za zootehniko, INDOK in knjiznica za zivinorejo **Former Name:** Univerza Edvarda Kardelja, University Edvarda Kardelja **Founded:** 1974 **Type:** Academic **Head:** Natasa Siard *Phone:* +386 (61) 717-873 *Email:* natasa.siard@bfro.uni-lj.si **Staff:** 4 Prof. **Holdings:** 38,000 books 312 journals **Language of Collection/Services:** Slovenian, English, German **Subjects:** Education/Extension, Animal Husbandry, Biotechnology, Farming, Fisheries **Networks:** COBISS; OCLC **Databases Developed:** Electronic bibliography of researchers and professors; access via OPAC **Databases Used:** Comprehensive **Loan:** Internationally **Service:** Internationally **Photocopy:** Yes

2765 Ljubljana, Slovenia
University of Ljubljana, Faculty of Veterinary
    Medicine
Library and INDOC Service
PO Box 3425
SI 1001 Ljubljana
Location: Gerbiceva 60, SI 1000 Ljubljana **Phone:** +386 (61) 177-9254 **Fax:** +386(61) 177-9255, 332-243 **WWW:** www.vf.uni-lj.si/veterina/index.htm **OPAC:** izumw.izum. si/scripts/cobiss?ukaz=NEWS&id=12 [English], izumw. izum.si/scripts/cobiss?ukaz=NEWS&id=3 [Slovenian]

Non-English Name: Univerza v Ljubljani, Veterinarska fakulteta, Knjiznica in INDOK **Former Name:** University Edvarda Kardelja, Biotechnical Faculty, Veterinary Department **Founded:** 1947 **Type:** Academic **Head:** Gita Grecs-Smole *Email:* smolegi@vf.uni-lj.si *Phone:* +386 (61) 177-9336 **Staff:** 3 Prof. **Holdings:** 49,000 books 163 journals **Language of Collection/Services:** Slovenian, English/Slovenian, English, French **Subjects:** Veterinary Medicine **Networks:** COBISS; OCLC **Databases Developed:** Electronic bibliography of Department researchers and professors; access via OPAC **Databases Used:** Comprehensive **Loan:** Internationally **Service:** Internationally **Photocopy:** Yes

2766 Ljubljana, Slovenia
University of Maribor, Faculty of Agriculture
Library
PO Box 222
SI-1001 Ljubljana
Location: Vrbanska 30, SI 2000 Maribor **Phone:** +386(62) 229-60-30-43 **Fax:** +386(62) 229-60-71 **Email:** umbl. cobissfkmb@mb.si, fk@uni-mb.si **WWW:** www.uni-mb/si **OPAC:** www.ukm.uni-mb.si/katalogi.html

Non-English Name: Univerza v Maribor, Fakulteta za kmetijstvo (FK), Knjiznica **Former Name:** Univerza Edvarda Kardelja v Ljubljani, University Edvarda Kardelja of Ljubljana **Founded:** 1960 **Type:** Academic **Head:** Ksenija Savinc *Email:* ksenija.savinc@uni-mb.sv *Phone:* +386(62) 229-60-30-51 **Staff:** 2 Prof. **Holdings:** 19,900 books 135 journals **Language of Collection/Services:** Slovenian, English / Slovenian, English, French, German, Italian, Spanish **Subjects:** Agribusiness, Agricultural Development, Agricultural Economics, Agricultural Engineering, Animal Husbandry, Crops, Farming, Food Sciences, Horticulture, Plant Pathology, Plants **Networks:** COBISS; OCLC **Databases Developed:** Electronic bibliography of researchers and professors; access via OPAC **Databases Used:** Comprehensive **Loan:** Internationally **Service:** Internationally **Photocopy:** Yes

2767 Zalec, Slovenia
         Institute of Hop Research and Brewing, Zalec
         Library
         PO Box 51
         SI 3310 Zalec

Location: Cesta Zalskega tabora 2 **Phone:** +386(63) 715-214 **Fax:** +386(63) 712-163 **Email:** iztok.kosir@guest.arnes.si **WWW:** www.hmelj-giz.si **OPAC:** izumw.izum.si/scripts/cobiss?ukaz=NEWS&id=12 [English], izumw.izum.si/scripts/cobiss?ukaz=NEWS&id=3 [Slovenian]

Non-English Name: Institut za hmeljarstvo in pivovarstvo Zalec (IHP Zalec), Knjiznica **Founded:** 1958 **Type:** Research **Holdings:** 5,000 books 54 journals **Language of Collection/Services:** Slovenian, English / Slovenian, English, German **Subjects:** Beers, Beverages, Brewing Industry, Humulus lupulus, Hops **Networks:** COBISS; OCLC **Databases Developed:** Electronic bibliography of institute researchers; access via OPAC **Loan:** Internationally **Service:** Internationally **Photocopy:** Yes

Solomon Islands

2768 Auki, Solomon Islands
         Solomon Islands College of Higher Education,
             School of Natural Resources, National
             Agricultural Training Institute
         Library
         PO Box 18
         Auki, Malaita Province
Location: Fote, North Malaita

Type: Academic

2769 Gizo, Solomon Islands
         Solomon Islands College of Higher Education,
             School of Natural Resources, National
             Forestry Training Institute
         Library
         PO Box 73
         Gizo, Western Province
Location: Poitete, Kolombangara Island **Phone:** +677 39152 (SICHE Honiara)

Founded: 1987 **Type:** Academic **Subjects:** Forestry

2770 Honiara, Solomon Islands
         Ministry of Agriculture and Fisheries, Dodo Creek
             Research Station (MAF, DCRS)
         Library
         PO Box G13
         Honiara

Location: Tenaru, Guadalcana, 121 kms east of Honiara **Phone:** +677 31037, 31111 **Fax:** +677 31037

Founded: 1973 **Type:** Government **Head:** Mr. Francis Kolopala *Phone:* +677 31111 **Staff:** 1 Prof. **Holdings:** 4,200 books 220 journals **Language of Collection/Services:** English / English, Pidgin English **Subjects:** Animal Husbandry, Agricultural Economics, Agricultural Research, Entomology, Farming Systems, Plant Pathology, Soil Science **Networks:** AGRIS **Databases Used:** PAIS **Loan:** Do not loan **Photocopy:** Yes

2771 Honiara, Solomon Islands
         Ministry of Natural Resources, Forestry Division
         Library
         PO Box G24
         Honiara

Type: Government **Subjects:** Forestry

2772 Honiara, Solomon Islands
         Solomon Islands College of Higher Education,
             School of Natural Resources (SICHE, SNR)
         Library Service
         PO Box G23
         Honiara

Location: Ranadi, Guadalcanal **Phone:** +677 30111 **Fax:** +677 30502, 30390, 30037 **Email:** siche_snr@pactok.peg.apc.org

Founded: 1984 **Type:** Academic **Head:** Hudson G. Dwalea *Phone:* +677 30111 *Email:* siche@welkam.solomon.com.sb **Staff:** 9 Prof. 15 Other **Language of Collection/Services:** English **Subjects:** Comprehensive **Service:** Inhouse **Photocopy:** Yes

2773 Munda, Solomon Islands
         Ministry of Natural Resources, Forestry Division
         Munda Forest Research Library
         PO Box 79
         Munda, Western Province

Founded: 1968 **Type:** Government **Staff:** 1 Prof. 1 Other **Holdings:** 3,000 books 15 journals **Subjects:** Forestry, Silviculture **Loan:** In country **Photocopy:** Yes

Somalia

2774 Afgoi, Somalia
         Agricultural Research Institute
         Library
         Afgoi

Type: Government **Networks:** AGRIS

♦2775 Mogadishu, Somalia
         Somalia National University, Faculty of
             Agriculture
         Library
         PB 801 MOG
         Mogadishu

Founded: 1972 **Type:** Academic **Head:** Mohamed Ali Abdi **Staff:** 1 Prof. **Holdings:** 5,000 books 500 journals **Subjects:**

Animal Production, Crop Production, Natural Resources, Pastures

South Africa

2776   **Bethlehem, South Africa**
            Agricultural Research Council, Small Grain
                  Institute (ARC)
            Library
            Private Bag X 29
            Bethlehem 9700
Phone: +27(58) 307-3400 **Fax:** +27(58) 303-3952 **Email:** juliette@kgs1.agric.za **WWW:** www.arc.agric.za

Non-English Name: Landbounavorsingsraad, Kleingraan-instituut, Biblioteek **Former Name:** Grain Crops Research Institute, Small Grain Centre Library **Founded:** 1952 **Type:** Parastatal **Head:** Mrs. Juliette Kilian *Phone:* +27(58) 307-3400 *Email:* juliette@kgs1.agric.za **Staff:** 1 Prof. **Holdings:** 1,500 books 60 journals **Language of Collection/Services:** English/English **Subjects:** Agricultural Development, Entomology, Crops, Food Sciences, Plant Pathology, Soil Science **Loan:** In country **Service:** In country **Photocopy:** Yes

2777   **Bloemfontein, South Africa**
            University of the Orange Free State
            Rabie Saunders Library
            PO Box 339
            Bloemfontein 9300
Location: University of the Orange Free State, Faculty of Agriculture **Phone:** +27(51) 401-2533 **Fax:** +27(51) 480692 **Email:** land@hbib.uovs.ac.za **WWW:** www.uovs. ac.za

Non-English Name: Universiteit van die Oranje Vrystaat (UOVS), Rabie Saunders-biblioteek **Founded:** 1958 **Type:** Academic **Head:** Ms. Radilene le Grange *Phone:* +27(51) 401-2533 *Email:* radilene@hbib.uovs.ac.za **Staff:** 2 Prof. 1.5 Other **Holdings:** 15,000 books 418 journals **Language of Collection/Services:** English / English, Afrikaans **Subjects:** Agribusiness, Agricultural Development, Farming, Agricultural Economics, Agricultural Engineering, Biotechnology, Entomology, Crops, Horticulture, Irrigation, Plant Breeding, Veterinary Medicine, Plant Pathology **Specializations:** Animal Husbandry, Agronomy, Farm Management, Food Sciences, Soil Science, Sustainability **Networks:** SABINET **Databases Developed:** Kovsidex - bibliographic information retrieval database of South African publications and other information available in the library **Databases Used:** Agricola; Biosis; CABCD; Medline **Loan:** Internationally **Service:** In country **Photocopy:** Yes

2778   **Cape Town, South Africa**
            National Botanical Institute
            Harry Molteno Library
            Kirstenbosch
            Private Bag X7, Claremont
            Cape Town 7735
Fax: +27(21) 762-3229, 762-0646 **Email:** library@nbict. nbi.ac.za **WWW:** www.nbi.ac.za

Founded: 1913 **Type:** Parastatal **Head:** Yvonne Reynolds *Phone:* +27(21) 762-1166 *Email:* library@nbict.nbi.ac.za **Staff:** 1 Prof. **Holdings:** 16,000 books 400 journals **Language of Collection/Services:** English **Subjects:** Botany, Environmental Education, Conservation, Ecology, Horticulture **Networks:** SABINET **Databases Used:** Current Contents **Loan:** In country **Service:** Inhouse **Photocopy:** Yes

2779   **Cascades, South Africa**
            Department of Agriculture, Directorate of Animal
                  Health
            Allerton Provincial Veterinary Library (Allerton
                  PVL)
            Private Bag X2
            Cascades 3202
Location: 458 Townbush Road, Pietermaritzburg 3201 **Phone:** +27(331) 471931 **Fax:** +27(331) 471633 **Email:** jbridgla@vetnl.agric.za **WWW:** www.agric.za

Former Name: Allerton Regional Veterinary Library **Type:** Government **Head:** Mrs. J. Bridgall *Email:* jbridgla@vetnl. agric.za *Phone:* +27(331) 471931 **Staff:** 1 Other **Holdings:** 497 books 12 journals **Language of Collection/Services:** English / English **Subjects:** Veterinary Medicine **Databases Developed:** Reference database of articles of interest **Loan:** In country **Service:** In country **Photocopy:** Yes

2780   **Durban, South Africa**
            Sugar Milling Research Institute (SMRI)
            Library
            University of Natal
            King George V Avenue
            Durban 4041
Phone: +27(31) 261-6882 **Fax:** +27(31) 261-6886 **WWW:** www.smri.org/home.asp

Founded: 1949 **Type:** Research **Head:** M.J. Kort *Phone:* +27(31) 261-6882 ext 301 *Email:* mjkort@smri.org **Staff:** 1 Prof. **Holdings:** 35 journals **Language of Collection/Services:** English **Subjects:** Sugar **Loan:** In country **Service:** In country **Photocopy:** Yes

2781   **Irene, South Africa**
            Agricultural Research Council, Animal Nutrition
                  and Animal Products Institute (ARC)
            Library
            Private Bag X2
            Irene 1675
Phone: +27(12) 672-9241 **Fax:** +27(12) 665-1563 **WWW:** www.arc.agric.za

Former Name: Animal and Dairy Science Research Institute, Irene Animal Production Institute **Founded:** 1962 **Type:** Parastatal **Head:** Mr. Andries Labuschagne *Phone:* +27(12) 672-9241 *Email:* alabusch@idpi1.agric.za **Staff:** 1 Prof. 2 Other **Holdings:** 8,459 books 223 journals **Subjects:** Animal Breeding, Animal Nutrition, Dairy Science, Genetics, Meat, Reproduction **Loan:** In country **Photocopy:** Yes

2782   **Middelburg, South Africa**
            Grootfontein Agricultural Development Institute
            Library
            Private Bag X529

Middelburg 5900

Phone: +27(4924) 21113 **Fax:** +27(4924) 24352 **Email:** bib1@karoo3.agric.za

Non-English Name: Grootfontein Landbou-ontwikkelings-instituut, Biblioteek **Former Name:** Departement van Landbou, Biblioteek Karoostreek **Type:** Government **Head:** Ms. Elsa Badenhorst *Phone:* +27(4924) 21113 **Staff:** 1 Prof. **Language of Collection/Services:** English / English **Subjects:** Agricultural Development, Agricultural Engineering, Animal Husbandry, Crops **Specializations:** Arid Lands **Networks:** SABINET **Databases Developed:** Agricultural literature in the Karoo Region **Loan:** Internationally **Service:** Internationally **Photocopy:** Yes

♦**2783　Mmabatho, South Africa**
　　　Department of Agriculture, Northwest Province
　　　Central Information Centre
　　　Private Bag X 2039
　　　Mmabatho 8681

Location: Agricentre **Phone:** +27(140) 895022 **Fax:** +27 (140) 21732

Former Name: Department of Agriculture and Natural Resources, Department of Agriculture, Lands and Rural Development **Founded:** 1985 **Type:** Government **Staff:** 2 Prof. 2 Other **Holdings:** 3,500 books 1,250 journals **Language of Collection/Services:** English / English **Subjects:** Agricultural Development, Agricultural Economics, Animal Husbandry, Agricultural Engineering, Farming, Entomology, Education/Extension, Crops, Food Sciences, Forestry, Horticulture, Natural Resources, Plant Pathology, Soil Science, Resource Conservation, Veterinary Medicine, Water Resources, Wildlife Conservation **Networks:** SABINET **Service:** Inhouse **Loan:** In country **Photocopy:** Yes

2784　Mount Edgecombe, South Africa
　　　South African Sugar Association, Experiment
　　　　　Station (SASA)
　　　H.H. Dodds Library
　　　Private Bag X02
　　　Mount Edgecombe, KwaZulu-Natal 4300

Phone: +27(31) 593205 **Fax:** +27(31) 595406 **Email:** library@sugar.org.za **WWW:** www.sugar.org.za

Founded: 1925 **Type:** Research **Head:** Poovie Govender *Phone:* +27(31) 593205 *Email:* sasex@sugar.org.za **Staff:** 1 Prof. 1 Other **Holdings:** 4,500 books 110 journals **Language of Collection/Services:** English **Subjects:** Agricultural Engineering, Biotechnology, Education/Extension, Entomology, Farming, Irrigation, Plant Breeding, Plant Pathology, Plants, Soil Science, Water Resources **Specializations:** Sugar Industry, Sugarcane **Databases Used:** Current Contents **Loan:** In country **Service:** Inhouse **Photocopy:** Yes

2785　Nelspruit, South Africa
　　　Agricultural Research Council, Institute for
　　　　Tropical and Subtropical Crops (ARC, ITSC)
　　　Library
　　　Private Bag X11208
　　　Nelspruit 1200

Location: Rivier Street **Phone:** +27(13) 753-2071 **Fax:** +27(13) 752-3854 **WWW:** www.arc.agric.za

Non-English Name: Landbounavorsingsraad, Instituut vir Tropiese en Subtropiese Gewasse (LNR, ITSG), Biblioteek **Former Name:** Department of Agriculture and Water Supply, Citrus and Subtropical Fruit Research Institute **Type:** Parastatal **Head:** Mrs. Lucinda Rabie *Phone:* +27(13) 753-2071 *Email:* lucinda@itsg1.agric.za **Staff:** 1 Prof. **Holdings:** 5,332 books 74 journals **Language of Collection/Services:** Afrikaans / Afrikaans **Subjects:** Avocados, Citrus Fruits, Coconuts, Coffee, Entomology, Ginger, Litchi, Macadamia, Mangoes, Pawpaws, Peanuts, Pineapples, Plant Pathology, Soil Science, Tea, Turmeric **Networks:** SABINET **Loan:** Internationally **Service:** In country **Photocopy:** Yes

2786　Nelspruit, South Africa
　　　Department of Agriculture, Lowveld College of
　　　　Agriculture
　　　Library
　　　Private Bag X 11283
　　　Nelspruit 1200

Location: Friendenheim **Fax:** +27(13) 755-1110

Non-English Name: Departement van Landbou, Landbou-kollege Laeveld, Biblioteek **Founded:** 1991 **Type:** Academic **Head:** Miss Z. de Beer *Phone:* +27(13) 753-3064 *Email:* zelda@laeveld1.agric.za **Staff:** 1 Prof. 1 Other **Holdings:** 2,400 books 174 journals **Language of Collection/Services:** English / Afrikaans, English **Subjects:** Agricultural Engineering, Farm Management, Horticulture, Irrigation, Soil Science **Loan:** In country **Service:** In country **Photocopy:** Yes

2787　Onderstepoort, South Africa
　　　Agricultural Research Council, Onderstepoort
　　　　Veterinary Institute (ARC, OVI)
　　　Library
　　　Private Bag X 05
　　　Onderstepoort 0110

Location: Arnold Theiler Avenue, Onderstepoort, North of Pretoria, Transvaal **Phone:** +27(12) 529-9282 **Fax:** +27 (12) 565-6573 **Email:** library@moon.ovi.ac.za **WWW:** www.arc.agric.za

Non-English Name: Landbounavorsingsraad, Onderstepoort Veeartsenykunde-instituut (LNR, OVI), Biblioteek **Founded:** 1908 **Type:** Parastatal **Head:** David A. Swanepoel *Phone:* +27(12) 529-9279 *Email:* david@moon.ovi.ac.za **Staff:** 2 Prof. 5 Other **Holdings:** 97,500 books 282 journals **Language of Collection/Services:** English / Afrikaans, English **Subjects:** Bacteriology, Protozoology, Toxicology, Virology **Specializations:** Veterinary Medicine **Networks:** SABINET **Databases Used:** Medline **Loan:** Internationally **Service:** Internationally **Photocopy:** Yes

2788　Onderstepoort, South Africa
　　　University of Pretoria
　　　Faculty of Veterinary Science Library
　　　Private Bag X04
　　　Onderstepoort 0110

Phone: +27(12) 529-8009 **Fax:** +27(12) 323-8243, 529-8302 **Email:** vetbib@op1.up.ac.za **WWW:** www.up.ac.za **OPAC:** explore.up.ac.za

Head: Erica van der Westhuizen *Phone:* +27(12) 529-8007 *Email:* bib1@op1.up.ac.za **Subjects:** Veterinary Science

2789 Pietermaritzburg, South Africa
Department of Agriculture
Cedara Library
Private Bag X9059
Pietermaritzburg 3200

Location: Cedara College of Agriculture **Phone:** +27(331) 33371 ext 112 **Fax:** +27(331) 431253

Former Name: Department of Agriculture and Water Supply **Founded:** 1906 **Type:** Government **Head:** Patricia L. Weston *Email:* pweston@cedaral.agric.za *Phone:* +27(331) 33371 **Staff:** 2 Prof. 2 Other **Holdings:** 26,064 books 340 journals **Language of Collection/Services:** English **Subjects:** Agricultural Economics, Agricultural Engineering, Agricultural Meteorology, Cattle, Education/Extension, Entomology, Horticulture, Irrigation, Pastures, Plant Pathology, Rural Development, Sheep, Small Farms, Soil Science, Weeds **Networks:** SABINET **Databases Used:** CABCD **Loan:** In country **Service:** Inhouse **Photocopy:** Yes

2790 Pietermaritzburg, South Africa
Natal Town and Regional Planning Commission (TRPC)
Library
Private Bag X9038
Pietermaritzburg, KwaZulu-Natal 3200

Location: Floor 12, North Tower, Natalia Building, c/o Longmarket and Boshoff Streets **Phone:** +27(33) 395-2666 **Fax:** +27(33) 342-8825 **WWW:** www.kznplanning.co.za

Founded: 1975 **Type:** Government **Head:** Carol Ferguson *Phone:* +27(33) 395-2664 *Email:* fergusoc@natalia.kzntl.gov.za **Staff:** 1 Prof. **Holdings:** 2,000 books 65 journals **Language of Collection/Services:** English / English **Subjects:** Education/Extension, Farming, Forestry, Planning, Soil Science, Urbanization, Water Resources **Networks:** SABINET **Loan:** Internationally **Service:** In country **Photocopy:** Yes

2791 Port Elizabeth, South Africa
Council for Scientific and Industrial Research, Textile Technology (CSIR, TEXTEK)
Library
PO Box 1124
Port Elizabeth 6000

Location: Gomery Avenue, Summerstrand **Phone:** +27 (41) 583-2131 **Fax:** +27(41) 583-2325 **WWW:** www.csir.co.za

Former Name: Division of Processing and Chemical Manufacturing Technology, South African Wool and Textile Research Institute **Founded:** 1952 **Type:** Parastatal **Head:** Jenny Wooldridge *Email:* jwoold@csir.co.za *Phone:* +27 (41) 583-2131 ext 2240 **Staff:** 1 Prof. 2 Other **Holdings:** 70 journals 1,000 books **Language of Collection/Services:** English **Subjects:** Cotton, Textiles, Wool **Loan:** Internationally **Photocopy:** Yes

2792 Potchefstroom, South Africa
Department of Agriculture and Environmental Affairs, North West Agricultural Development Institute (NWADI)
Library
Private Bag X804
Potchefstroom 2520

Location: Botha Street **Phone:** +27(18) 299-6695 **Fax:** +27(18) 299-7135 **Email:** biblb@potch1.agric.za

Non-English Name: Departement van Landbou & Omgewingsake, Noord-Wes Landbou-Ontwikkelingsinstituut, Biblioteek, Hoëveldstreek-biblioteek **Head:** Mrs. Lucia M. Botha *Phone:* +27(18) 299-6695 **Type:** Research **Staff:** 2 Prof. 1 Other **Holdings:** 7,000 books 105 journals **Language of Collection/Services:** English / English **Subjects:** Cattle, Extension, Grain, Oilseeds, Pastures, Training, Veld **Networks:** SABINET **Loan:** Internationally **Service:** Internationally **Photocopy:** Yes

2793 Pretoria, South Africa
Agricultural Research Council, Institute for Agricultural Engineering (ARC)
Library and Information Service
Private Bag X 519, Silverton
Pretoria 0127

Location: Cresswell Road 141, Weavind Park **Phone:** +27 (12) 842-4023 **Fax:** +27(12) 842-4216 **Email:** bib2@ing1.agric.za **WWW:** www.arc.agric.za

Non-English Name: Landbounavorsingsraad, Instituut vir Lanbou-ingenieurswese (LNR), Biblioteek en Ingligtingsdiens **Former Name:** Department of Agricultural Technical Services, Department of Agriculture, Division of Agricultural Mechanization and Engineering, Division of Agricultural Engineering **Founded:** 1964 **Type:** Semi-government **Head:** Mrs. Erika van Heerden *Phone:* 842-4000 *Email:* bib2@ing1.agric.za **Staff:** 1 Prof. 1 Other **Holdings:** 4,600 books 200 journals **Language of Collection/Services:** English / English, Afrikaans **Subjects:** Agricultural Economics, Aquaculture, Engineering, Extension, Energy, Greenhouses, Instrumentation, Irrigation, Mechanization, Soil Conservation, Water Conservation **Specializations:** Agricultural Engineering **Networks:** SABINET **Service:** Internationally **Loan:** Internationally **Photocopy:** Yes

2794 Pretoria, South Africa
Agricultural Research Council, Plant Protection Research Institute (ARC, PPRI)
Library
Private Bag X134
Pretoria 0001

Location: Roodeplaat **Phone:** +27(12) 808-0952 **Fax:** +27 (12) 808-1489 **Email:** nipbkg@plant1.agric.za **WWW:** www.arc.agric.za

Non-English Name: Landbounavorsingsraad, Navorsingsinstituut vir Plantbeskerming (LNR, NIPB), Bibliotheek **Former Name:** Department of Agriculture and Water Supply, Entomology Library **Founded:** 1910 **Type:** Parastatal **Head:** Mrs. J.H. Combrink *Phone:* +27(12) 808-1685 **Staff:** 1 Prof. 1 Other **Holdings:** 10,000 books 143 journals **Language of Collection/Services:** English / English, Afrikaans **Subjects:** Herbicides, Microbiology, Pesticides, Plant Pathology, Weeds **Specializations:** Entomology, Mycology **Networks:** SABINET **Loan:** Internationally **Service:** Internationally **Photocopy:** Yes

2795　Pretoria, South Africa
　　　Agricultural Research Council, Roodeplaat
　　　　　Vegetable and Ornamental Plant Institute
　　　　　(ARC, VOPI)
　　　Library
　　　Private Bag X293
　　　Pretoria 0001

Location: Roodeplaat **Phone:** +27(12) 841-9611 **Fax:** +27 (12) 808-0844 **Email:** estia@vopi.agric.za **WWW:** www. arc.agric.za

Non-English Name: Landbouavorsingsraad, Instituut vir Groente en Sierplante (LNR, IGS), Bibliotheek **Former Name:** Horticultural Research Institute **Founded:** 1962 **Type:** Parastatal **Staff:** 1 Prof. **Holdings:** 3,140 books 70 journals **Language of Collection/Services:** English **Subjects:** Biotechnology, Entomology, Plant Pathology **Specializations:** Horticulture **Networks:** SABINET **Loan:** In country **Service:** Internationally **Photocopy:** Yes

2796　Pretoria, South Africa
　　　Department of Water Affairs and Forestry
　　　Library
　　　Private Bag X313
　　　Pretoria

Location: Residensie Building, Room 75, Schoeman Street **Phone:** +27(12) 336-7500 **Fax:** +27(12) 328-4254 **WWW:** www-dwaf.pwv.gov.za/idwaf

Former Name: Department of Water Affairs **Founded:** 1950 **Type:** Government **Staff:** 1 Prof. 2 Other **Holdings:** 14,700 books 200 journals **Subjects:** Irrigation **Specializations:** Water Resources **Networks:** SABINET **Loan:** In country **Photocopy:** Yes

2797　Pretoria, South Africa
　　　Die Suid-Afrikaanse Akademie Vir Wetenskap en
　　　　　Kuns
　　　Library
　　　PO Box 538
　　　Pretoria 0001

Location: Ziervogelstreet, Arcadia **Phone:** +27(12) 28-5082 **Fax:** +27(12) 28-5091 **Email:** akademie@mweb.co. za **WWW:** www.akademie.co.za

Former Name: S.A. Akademie Vir Wetenskap en Kuns **Founded:** 1972 **Type:** Academic **Staff:** 1 Prof. **Subjects:** Crops, Soil Science, Zoology **Loan:** Do not loan **Photocopy:** Yes

2798　Pretoria, South Africa
　　　National Botanical Institute
　　　Mary Gunn Library
　　　Private Bag X101
　　　Pretoria 0001

Location: 2 Cussonia Avenue, Brummeria, Pretoria 0002 **Fax:** +27(12) 804-3211 **WWW:** www.kirstenbosch.com/ index.html

Former Name: Botanical Research Institute **Founded:** 1916 **Type:** Parastatal **Head:** Mrs. E. Potgieter *Phone:* +27 (12) 804-3200 *Email:* ep@nbi.pre.ac.za **Staff:** 2 Prof. **Holdings:** 29,239 books 101 journals **Language of Collection/ Services:** English **Subjects:** Anatomy, Botany, Conservation, Cytology, Ecology, Morphology, Paleobotany, Taxonomy **Networks:** SABINET **Loan:** In country **Service:** In country **Photocopy:** Yes

2799　Pretoria, South Africa
　　　National Department of Agriculture
　　　Information Services Division
　　　Private Bag X388
　　　Pretoria 0001

Location: Agricultural Buildings, Beatrix Street **Phone:** +27(12) 319-7060 **Fax:** +27(12) 323-2516 **Email:** gerda@ hoof2.agric.za **WWW:** www.nda.agric.za

Non-English Name: Nasionale Departement van Landbou, Afdeling Inligtingsdienste **Former Name:** Department of Agricultural Technical Services, Department of Agriculture and Fisheries, Department of Agriculture and Water Supply, Department of Agricultural Development, Department of Agriculture, Central Agricultural Library, Sentrale Landbou-biblioteek **Founded:** 1910 **Type:** Government **Head:** Miss M.M. Koen *Phone:* +27(12) 319-6886 *Email:* daleen@ hoof2.agric.za **Staff:** 8 Prof. 10 Other **Holdings:** 48,000 books 200 journals **Language of Collection/Services:** English / English, Afrikaans **Subjects:** Comprehensive **Specializations:** Government Documents (South Africa), Theses (South Africa) **Networks:** AGRIS; SABINET **Databases Used:** Agris; CABCD; CARIS **Loan:** Internationally **Service:** Inhouse **Photocopy:** Yes

2800　Pretoria, South Africa
　　　Technikon Pretoria
　　　Gold Fields Technobib
　　　Private Bag X680
　　　Pretoria 0001

Location: State Artillery Road, Pretoria-West **Phone:** +27 (12) 318-5240 **Fax:** +27(12) 318-5285 **WWW:** local. techpta.ac.za

Former Name: Tegniese Kollege vir Gevorderde, Tegniese Onderwys **Type:** Educational **Head:** Mr. M. Swanepoel *Phone:* +27(12) 318-5240 **Staff:** 16 Prof. **Holdings:** 35,000 books 12,000 journals **Language of Collection/Services:** English / English **Subjects:** Agricultural Engineering, Animal Husbandry, Crops, Horticulture **Databases Used:** FSTA **Loan:** Internationally **Service:** Internationally **Photocopy:** Yes

2801　Pretoria, South Africa
　　　University of Pretoria (PU)
　　　Agricultural Library
　　　Agricultural Sciences Building Annexe, East
　　　　　Campus
　　　Pretoria 0002

Phone: +27(12) 420-3293 **Fax:** +27(12) 362-5161 **Email:** lanpos@acinfo.up.ac.za **WWW:** www.up.ac.za **OPAC:** explore.up.ac.za

Non-English Name: Universiteit van Pretoria, Landbou Biblioteek **Type:** Academic **Head:** Mrs. A. Viljoen, Agricultural Specialist *Email:* alviljoe@ais.up.ac.za *Phone:* +27 (12) 420-3614 **Staff:** 3 Prof. 3 Other **Holdings:** 19,200 books 312 journals **Language of Collection/Services:** English / Afrikaans **Subjects:** Agricultural Development, Agricultural Economics, Animal Husbandry, Biotechnology, Agribusiness, Crops, Entomology, Farming, Fisheries, Food Sciences, Genetics, Horticulture, Microbiology, Plant Pathology, Plant Breeding, Soil Science **Databases Used:** Agricola **Loan:** Internationally **Service:** Internationally **Photocopy:** Yes

2802   Residensie, South Africa
          Department of Water Affairs and Forestry,
             Forestry Branch
          Library
          185 Schoeman Street
          Residensie 1065

Phone: +27(12) 336-8752 **Fax:** +27(12) 336-8942 **Email:** xfb@dwaf.pwv.gov.za **WWW:** www-dwaf.pwv.gov.za/idwaf

Former Name: Department of Environment Affairs **Type:** Government **Staff:** 1 Prof. 2 Other **Holdings:** 50,000 books 160 journals **Subjects:** Environmental Policy, Forestry **Loan:** In country **Photocopy:** Yes

2803   Rogge Bay, South Africa
          Department of Environmental Affairs and
             Tourism, Marine and Coastal Management
             (MCM)
          Gilchrist Library
          Private Bag X2
          Rogge Bay 8012

Location: 414 Foretrust House, Martin Hammerschlag Road, Cape Town **Phone:** +27(21) 402-3249 **Fax:** +27(21) 217406 **Email:** library@sfri.wcape.gov.za **WWW:** www.environment.gov.za/mcm/index.html

Former Name: Department of Agriculture and Fisheries, Sea Fisheries Research Institute (SFRI), Division of Sea Fisheries, Sea Fisheries Institute **Founded:** 1920 **Type:** Government **Head:** B. Wessels *Phone:* +27(21) 402-3250 **Staff:** 2 Prof. 1 Other **Holdings:** 5,000 books 750 journals **Language of Collection/Services:** English / English **Subjects:** Aquaculture, Fisheries **Specializations:** Marine Biology, Marine Pollution, Oceanography **Networks:** SABINET **Loan:** In country **Service:** Inhouse **Photocopy:** Yes

2804   Rustenburg, South Africa
          Agricultural Research Council, Tobacco and
             Cotton Research Institute (ARC, TCRI)
          Library
          Private Bag X82075
          Rustenburg 0300

Location: Farm 10 km outside Rustenburg **Phone:** +27 (142) 993150 **Fax:** +27(142) 993113 **Email:** petrie@nitk.agric.za **WWW:** www.arc.agric.za

Non-English Name: Landbounavorsingsraad, Navorsingsinstituut vir Tabak en Katoen (LNR, NITK), Biblioteek **Type:** Research **Head:** Mrs. Ansie Ellis *Phone:* +27(142)

993150 *Email:* ansie@nitk1.agric.za **Staff:** 1 Prof. 1 Other **Holdings:** 3,000 books 140 journals **Language of Collection/Services:** English / Afrikaans **Subjects:** Agricultural Development, Agronomy, Biotechnology, Entomology, Nematology, Plant Breeding, Plant Protection, Soil Science, Water **Specializations:** Cotton, Tobacco **Photocopy:** Yes

2805   Scottsville, South Africa
          Institute for Commercial Forestry Research
             (ICFR)
          Library
          PO Box 100281
          Scottsville 3209

Location: University of Natal, Agric Avenue, off Epworth Road **Phone:** +27(33) 386-2314 **Fax:** +27(33) 386-8905 **Email:** desiree@icfr.unp.ac.za **WWW:** www.icfrnet.unp.ac.za

Former Name: Wattle Research Institute (WRI) **Founded:** 1948 **Type:** Academic **Head:** Ms. Desirée Lamoral *Phone:* +27(33) 386-2314 *Email:* desiree@icfr.unp.ac.za **Staff:** 1 Prof. 1 Other **Holdings:** 3,000 books 65 journals **Language of Collection/Services:** English / English **Subjects:** Forestry **Specializations:** Genetics, Mensuration, Silviculture, Forestry (South Africa) **Networks:** SABINET **Databases Used:** Comprehensive **Loan:** In country **Service:** Inhouse **Photocopy:** Yes

2806   Scottsville, South Africa
          University of Natal, Pietermaritzburg (UNP)
          Life Sciences Library
          Private Bag X014
          Scottsville 3209

Location: 3rd Floor, John Bews Building, Carbis Road **Phone:** +27(33) 260-5163 **Fax:** +27(33) 260-5161 **WWW:** www.unp.ac.za **OPAC:** www.unp.ac.za/UNPDepartments/Library/lib_base03.htm

Former Name: Agriculture Faculty Library **Founded:** 1947 **Type:** Academic **Head:** Mr. C.E. Merrett *Phone:* +27(33) 260-5264 *Email:* merrett@library.unp.ac.za **Staff:** 3 Prof. 4 Other **Holdings:** 60,000 books 500 journals **Language of Collection/Services:** English **Subjects:** Agriculture (Tropics), Agribusiness, Agricultural Development, Agricultural Economics, Agricultural Engineering, Animal Husbandry, Biotechnology, Crops, Entomology, Farming, Food Sciences, Horticulture, Plant Pathology, Soil Science, Water Resources **Specializations:** Natural History (Southern Africa) **Networks:** CATNIP; SABINET **Databases Used:** CABCD; Life Science Collection **Loan:** In country **Service:** Inhouse **Photocopy:** Yes

2807   Springs, South Africa
          SAPPI Ltd.
          Research and Development Technical Library
          PO Box 3252
          Springs 1560

Location: East Geduld Road **Phone:** +27(11) 360-0279 **Fax:** +27(11) 816-2604 **WWW:** www.sappi.com

Type: Business **Head:** Mrs. H. Humphries *Phone:* +27(11) 816-2100 **Staff:** 1 Prof. **Holdings:** 2,000 books 50 journals **Language of Collection/Services:** English **Subjects:** Forestry, Water Resources **Specializations:** Paper, Pulp and Paper Industry **Databases Developed:** SAPLIND - paper-making, forestry, chemical engineering, etc. - articles, conference papers, patents, reports. Access via library and head office. **Loan:** In country **Service:** Internationally **Photocopy:** Yes

2808   Stellenbosch, South Africa
         Agricultural Research Council, Fruit, Vine and
              Wine Research Institute (ARC,
              Infruitec/Nietvoorbij)
         Library
         Private Bag X 5026
         Stellenbosch 7599
Location: Adam Tas Road (R44) and Helshoogte Road **Phone:** +27(21) 809-3311 **Fax:** +27(21) 809-3400 **Email:** karlien@infruit.agric.za **WWW:** www.agric.za

Non-English Name: Landbounavorsingsraad, Instituut vir Vrigte, Wingerd en Wyn (LNR), Biblioteek **Former Name:** Department of Agriculture and Water Supply, Viticultural and Oenological Research Institute, Nietvoorbij Institute for Oenology and Viticulture **Founded:** 1960 **Type:** Research **Head:** Karlien Coertzen *Phone:* +27(21) 809-3311 *Email:* karlien@infruit.agric.za **Staff:** 1 Prof. 2 Other **Holdings:** 8,000 books 150 journals **Language of Collection/Services:** English / Afrikaans, English **Subjects:** Biotechnology, Microbiology, Plant Diseases, Plant Physiology, Soil Science **Specializations:** Deciduous Tree Fruits, Enology, Olives, Viticulture **Networks:** SABINET **Loan:** In country **Service:** Internationally **Photocopy:** Yes

2809   Stellenbosch, South Africa
         Department of Agriculture, Winter Rainfall
              Region
         Library
         Private Bag, Elsenburg
         Stellenbosch 7607
Fax: +27(2231) 94226 **WWW:** www.wcape.agric.za

Former Name: Department of Agriculture and Water Supply **Founded:** 1974 **Type:** Government **Staff:** 1 Prof. 1 Other **Holdings:** 5,000 books 400 journals **Language of Collection/Services:** English, Afrikaans **Subjects:** Agricultural Development, Animal Husbandry, Crops, Education/Extension, Entomology, Soil Science **Networks:** SABINET **Loan:** In country **Service:** In country **Photocopy:** Yes

2810   Stellenbosch, South Africa
         Stellenbosch Farmers Winery (SFW)
         Library
         PO Box 46
         Stellenbosch 7599
Location: Oude Libertas, Adam Tas Road **Phone:** +27(21) 808-7911 **Fax:** +27(21) 228-7318 **Email:** jastarke@sfw.co.za **WWW:** www.sfw.co.za

Type: Association **Head:** Christine Dippenaar *Phone:* +27(21) 808-7409 **Staff:** 1 Prof. **Holdings:** 200 journals 2,500 books **Language of Collection/Services:** English / English **Subjects:** Chemistry, Enology, Microbiology, Viticulture **Loan:** Inhouse **Service:** Inhouse **Photocopy:** Yes

2811   Stellenbosch, South Africa
         University of Stellenbosch (US)
         J S Gericke Library
         Private Bag 5036
         Stellenbosch 7600
Location: Victoria Street **Phone:** +27(21) 808-4345 **Fax:** +27(21) 808-4336 **Email:** mt@bib.sun.ac.za **WWW:** www.sun.ac.za **OPAC:** www.sun.ac.za/local/library **Ariel IP:** 146.232.73.148

Non-English Name: Universiteit van Stellenbosch (US), J S Gericke Biblioteek **Former Name:** Victoria College, Carnegie Library **Founded:** 1876 **Type:** Academic **Head:** Professor J.H. Viljoen *Phone:* +27(21) 808-4880 *Email:* jhv@bib.sun.ac.za **Staff:** 2 Prof. **Holdings:** 28,000 books 300 journals **Language of Collection/Services:** English / Afrikaans **Subjects:** Agricultural Economics, Animal Husbandry, Crops, Entomology, Food Sciences, Forestry, Genetics, Horticulture, Plant Pathology, Plants, Soil Science, Winemaking **Networks:** SABINET **Databases Used:** Comprehensive **Loan:** In country **Service:** Inhouse **Photocopy:** Yes

2812   Stutterheim, South Africa
         Department of Agriculture, Dohne Agricultural
              Development Institute
         Library
         Private Bag X15
         Stutterheim 4930
Location: Agricultural Research Institute **Phone:** +27(43) 683-1240 **Fax:** +27(43) 683-2890

Founded: 1961 **Type:** Government **Head:** Mrs. Dorothy A. Kingman *Phone:* +27(43) 683-1240 *Email:* dorothy@dohne.agric.za **Staff:** 1 Prof. 1 Other **Holdings:** 3,000 books 142 journals **Language of Collection/Services:** English / English, Afrikaans **Subjects:** Animal Husbandry, Extension, Crop Production, Pastures, Resource Development **Networks:** SABINET **Databases Developed:** Bibliography of agricultural literature of Eastern Cape, 1935 to date **Loan:** In country **Service:** Inhouse **Photocopy:** Yes

♦2813   Taung, South Africa
         University of the Northwest, Faculty of
              Agriculture
         Resource Center
         Private Bag X532
         Taung 8584
Former Name: University of Bophuthatswana **Founded:** 1981 **Type:** Academic **Staff:** 2 Prof. 4 Other **Subjects:** Agricultural Economics, Animal Health, Animal Production, Education/Extension, Management, Plants **Loan:** In country **Photocopy:** Yes

2814   Umtata, South Africa
         University of Transkei (UNITRA)
         Library
         Private Bag X1, Unitra
         Umtata 5100
Location: East London Road **Phone:** +27(471) 302-2733 **Fax:** +27(471) 25747 **WWW:** www.utr.ac.za

Founded: 1976 **Type:** Academic **Language of Collection/Services:** English / English **Subjects:** Biochemistry, Biology, Botany, Chemistry, Entomology, Zoology **Networks:** SABINET **Loan:** Internationally **Service:** Internationally **Photocopy:** Yes

Spain

2815   Almeria, Spain
Higher Council for Scientific Research, Arid
        Zones Experiment Station
Library
General Segura, 1
04001 Almeria
Phone: +34(950) 276400, 281045 **Fax:** +34(950) 277100
WWW: www.eeza.csic.es **OPAC:** www.eeza.csic.es/eeza/
Biblioteca.htm

Non-English Name: Consejo Superior de Investigaciones
Científicas, Estación Experimental de Zonas Aridas (CSIC,
EEZA), Biblioteca **Founded:** 1958 **Type:** Government
Head: Isabel Jiménez Borrajo *Email:* isabel@eeza.csic.es
Staff: 1 Prof. 2 Other **Holdings:** 1,500 books 54 journals
Subjects: Animal Husbandry, Entomology, Forestry, Soil
Science, Water Resources **Specializations:** Botany **Loan:**
Inhouse

♦**2816   Barcelona, Spain**
Catalan Agricultural Institute of St. Isidre
Library
Plaza Sant Josep Oriol, 4
08002 Barcelona
Fax: +34(4) 319-3005

Non-English Name: Instituto Agricola Catalan de Sant
Isidre, Biblioteca **Founded:** 1851 **Type:** Academic **Staff:** 1
Prof. 1 Other **Holdings:** 15,500 books 200 journals **Subjects:** Agricultural Economics, Forestry, Livestock **Loan:** In
country **Photocopy:** Yes

2817   Barcelona, Spain
Escola Superior d'Agricultura de Barcelona
        (ESAB)
Biblioteca
c/ Urgell, 187
08036 Barcelona
Phone: +34(3) 430-4207 **Fax:** +34(3) 419-2601 **Email:**
biblioteca@esab.upc.es **WWW:** www.esab.upc.es

Founded: 1912 **Type:** Academic **Head:** Assumpció Juan
Phone: +34(3) 430-4207 **Staff:** 3 Prof. 1 Other **Holdings:**
37,000 books 250 journals **Language of Collection/Ser-
vices:** Spanish **Subjects:** Comprehensive **Databases Used:**
CABCD; FSTA **Loan:** In country **Photocopy:** Yes

2818   Barcelona, Spain
Higher Council for Scientific Research, Institute
        of Marine Sciences
Library
Passeig Joan de Borbo, s/n
08039 Barcelona
Fax: +34(3) 221-7340 **Email:** bib@icm.csic.es **WWW:**
www.icm.csic.es **OPAC:** olivo.csic.es:4500/ALEPH,
telnet://olivo.csic.es

Non-English Name: Consejo Superior de Investigaciones
Científicas, Instituto de Ciencias del Mar (CSIC, ICM),
Biblioteca **Former Name:** Instituto de Investigaciones Pes-
queras **Founded:** 1949 **Type:** Government **Head:** Marta
Ezpeleta *Phone:* +34(3) 221-6416 ext 277 *Email:* ezpeleta@
icm.csic.es **Staff:** 2 Other **Holdings:** 5,600 books 108 jour-
nals **Language of Collection/Services:** English **Subjects:**
Fisheries, Marine Sciences **Databases Used:** ASFA; Current
Contents; Marine Literature Review **Photocopy:** Yes

2819   Barcelona, Spain
Municipal Museum of Natural Sciences, Botanical
        Institute of Barcelona
Library
Avda. dels Muntanyans, s/n
08038 Barcelona
Location: Parque de Montjuic **Fax:** +34(3) 426-9321
Email: jarbot@ija.csic.es

Non-English Name: Museo Municipal de Ciencias Naturales, Instituto Botanico de Barcelona, Biblioteca **Founded:**
1934 **Type:** Government **Head:** Teresa Formenti Pedrerol
Phone: +34(3) 325-8050, 325-8104 *Email:* jarbot@ija.csic.
es **Staff:** 1 Prof. **Holdings:** 30,000 books 60 journals **Subjects:** Botany **Loan:** Do not loan **Photocopy:** Yes

2820   Barcelona, Spain
University of Barcelona
Library
Edifici Biblioteca
Baldiri Reixac, 2
08028 Barcelona
Phone: +34(3) 402-1566, 403-5715, 402-1568, 403-4592
Fax: +34(3) 490-8274 **Email:** infobio@d3.bib.ub.ex
WWW: www.bib.ub/es/bub/bub/htm **OPAC:** www.bib.ub.
es/bub/abub4.htm

Non-English Name: Universitat de Barcelona (UB), Biblio-
teca **Former Name:** Instituto de Edafologia y Fisiologia
Founded: 1958 **Type:** Academic **Head:** Dolors Lamarca
Phone: +34(3) 403-5716 *Email:* dolors@bib.ub.es **Staff:** 10
Prof. 2 Other **Holdings:** 1,000 books 10 journals **Language
of Collection/Services:** English/Spanish, Catalan **Subjects:**
Plant Physiology **Loan:** Inhouse **Service:** Inhouse **Photo-
copy:** Yes

2821   Bellaterra, Spain
Autonomous University of Barcelona
Veterinary Library
Campus Universitari
Edifici V
08193 Bellaterra, Barcelona
Fax: +34(3) 581-2006 **Email:** iybv1@cc.uab.es **WWW:**
www.bib.uab.es/veter/veter.htm **OPAC:** www.bib.uab.es/
opac.htm

Non-English Name: Universitat Autonoma de Barcelona
(UAB), Biblioteca de Veterinaria **Founded:** 1985 **Type:**
Government **Head:** Vicenç Allue i Blanch *Phone:* +34(3)
581-2545 *Email:* vicenc.allue@uab.es **Staff:** 2 Prof. 4 Other
Holdings: 13,000 books 450 journals **Language of Collec-
tion/Services:** Spanish / Spanish, Catalan **Subjects:** Animal
Husbandry, Food Sciences, Veterinary Medicine **Specializa-**

tions: Mycology **Networks:** CCUC - available on Internet at www.cbuc.es/virtua/english **Databases Used:** Comprehensive **Loan:** Internationally **Service:** Inhouse **Photocopy:** Yes

2822　Burjassot, Spain
　　　　Higher Council for Scientific Research, Institute
　　　　　　for Agrochemistry and Food Technology
　　　　Library and Scientific Documentation
　　　　Apartado de Correos 73
　　　　46100 Burjassot (Valencia)
Location: Polígono de "La Coma", s/n., 46980 Paterna (detrás de la Televisión Valenciana) **Phone:** +34(6) 390-0022 **Fax:** +34(6) 363-6301 **WWW:** www.iata.csic.es **OPAC:** www.csic.es/cbic/cbic.htm

Non-English Name: Consejo Superior de Investigaciones Científicas, Instituto Agroquímica Tecnología Alimentos (CSIC, IATA), Biblioteca y Documentación **Founded:** 1952 **Type:** Government **Head:** Rafael Gavara **Email:** rgavara@iata.csic.es **Staff:** 3 Prof. 1 Other **Holdings:** 2,200 books 69 journals **Language of Collection/Services:** English **Subjects:** Agricultural Economics, Agricultural Engineering, Biotechnology, Crop Production, Food Sciences, Plant Pathology, Plant Protection, Soil Science **Specializations:** Canning, Cereals, Meat, Molecular Biology, Plants, Postharvest Physiology **Loan:** Do not loan **Service:** Inhouse **Photocopy:** No

2823　Cabrils, Spain
　　　　Institute for Food and Agricultural Research and
　　　　　　Technology
　　　　Documentation Service
　　　　Ctra. de Cabrils, s/n
　　　　08348 Cabrils, Barcelona
Phone: +34(3) 750-7511 **Fax:** +34(3) 753-3954 **Email:** xantal@cabrils.irta.es **WWW:** www.irta.es

Non-English Name: Institut de Recerca i Tecnologia Agroalimentàries (IRTA), Servei de Documentació **Founded:** 1985 **Type:** Government **Head:** Xantal Romaguera **Phone:** +34(3) 750-7511 **Email:** xantal@cabrils.irta.es **Staff:** 1 Prof. **Holdings:** 10,000 books 202 journals **Language of Collection/Services:** English / Catalan, Spanish, French, English **Subjects:** Animal Biotechnology, Animal Nutrition, Animal Production, Cereals, Ecology, Food Sciences, Forestry, Fruit Crops (Mediterranean Countries), Meat, Nut Crops (Mediterranean Countries), Plant Biotechnology, Plant Genetics, Plant Pathology, Plant Protection **Specializations:** Horticulture, Integrated Pest Management, Ornamental Plants, Plant Breeding, Temperate Fruits **Databases Used:** Comprehensive **Loan:** Do not loan **Service:** Internationally **Photocopy:** Yes

2824　Cordova, Spain
　　　　University of Cordova
　　　　University Library
　　　　Campus Rabanales
　　　　Ctra. Madrid-Cadiz km 396-A
　　　　14071 Cordova
Phone: +34(57) 218135 **Fax:** +34(57) 218136 **Email:** biblioteca@uco.es **WWW:** www.uco.es **OPAC:** www.uco.eswebuco/buc/catalogos/index.htm

Non-English Name: Universidad de Córdoba, Biblioteca Universitaria **Head:** Daniel Rodriguez **Phone:** +34(57) 218135 **Email:** bg1rocid@uco.es

2825　Cordova, Spain
　　　　University of Cordova, Department of Agronomy
　　　　Library
　　　　Apartado 3048
　　　　14080 Cordova
Location: Alameda del Obispo s/n **Phone:** +34(57) 218438 **Fax:** +34(57) 218563 **WWW:** www.uco.es

Non-English Name: Universidad de Córdoba, Escuela Técnica Superior de Ingenieros Agrónomos y Montes (ETSIAM), Biblioteca **Founded:** 1970 **Type:** Academic **Head:** Juan Alfredo Guzmán Garcìa **Phone:** +34(57) 218438 **Email:** am3gugaj@uco.es **Staff:** 2 Prof. 3 Other **Holdings:** 36,556 books 346 journals **Language of Collection/Services:** Spanish **Subjects:** Agricultural Economics, Crops, Agricultural Engineering, Entomology, Forestry, Horticulture, Plant Pathology **Loan:** In country **Photocopy:** Yes

2826　El Ejido, Spain
　　　　Horticultural Research and Development Center
　　　　Library - Information Center
　　　　Apdo. Correos 91
　　　　04700 El Ejido, Almeria
Location: Autovía Mediterráneo, Salida 420 La Mojonera, Almería **Phone:** +34(3950) 558014 **Fax:** +34(3950) 558055 **Email:** formagro@arrakis.es

Non-English Name: Centro de Investigación y Formación Hortícola (CIFH), Biblioteca - Centro de Documentación **Former Name:** Estación de Investigación sobre Cultivos Hortícolas Intensivos, Centro de Investigación y Desarrollo Hortícola (CIDH) **Founded:** 1980 **Type:** Research **Staff:** 1 Prof. 1 Other **Holdings:** 5,000 books 32 journals **Language of Collection/Services:** Spanish / Spanish **Subjects:** Agricultural Economics, Entomology, Horticulture, Integrated Pest Management, Plant Pathology, Soil Science, Water Resources **Databases Developed:** 25,000 specialized items in ornamental horticulture; 3,000 slides of different items **Loan:** Inhouse **Service:** Internationally **Photocopy:** Yes

2827　Granada, Spain
　　　　Higher Council for Scientific Research, Zaidin
　　　　　　Experiment Station
　　　　Library
　　　　c/o Professor Albareda, no. 1
　　　　18008 Granada
Phone: +34(958) 121011 **Fax:** +34(958) 129600 **Email:** bibzaidin@eez.csic.es **WWW:** www.eez.csic.es **OPAC:** www.eez.csic.es/~biblio

Non-English Name: Consejo Superior de Investigaciones Científicas, Estación Experimental del Zaidín (CSIC, EEZ), Biblioteca **Founded:** 1955 **Type:** Government **Head:** Ana Mª. de la Fuente Navarro **Phone:** +34(958) 121011 ext 239 **Email:** ana@eez.csic.es **Staff:** 3 Prof. **Holdings:** 75 journals 5,150 books **Subjects:** Biology **Loan:** Do not loan **Photocopy:** Yes

♦**2828 Jerez de la Frontera, Spain**
Experiment Station Ranch of Merced
Library
Apto de Correos 589
11480 Jerez de la Frontera, Cadiz
Location: Carretera de Trebujena km. 3.200 **Phone:** +34 (56) 310000, 310236 **Fax:** +34(56) 182352

Non-English Name: Estación Experimental Rancho de la Merced, Biblioteca **Founded:** 1890 **Type:** Government **Staff:** 1 Other **Holdings:** 1,981 books 38 journals **Language of Collection/Services:** Castellano **Subjects:** Enology, Viticulture **Databases Developed:** Collective catalog of periodical publications **Loan:** Do not loan **Photocopy:** Yes

2829 La Alberca, Spain
Institute for Agricultural and Agrofood Industry
Research and Development
Library
Apartado Oficial
30150 La Alberca, Murcia
Location: Estación Sericicola **Phone:** +34(68) 840250 ext 127 **Fax:** +34(68) 844802 **Email:** enavarro@forodigital.ex **WWW:** burete.forodigital.es/cida/cida/cida.htm

Non-English Name: Centro de Investigación y Desarrollo Agroalimentario (CIDA), Biblioteca **Former Name:** Centro Regional de Investigación y Desarrollo Agrario (CRIDA), Centro Regional de Investigaciones Agrarias (CRIA), Regional Agricultural Research Center **Founded:** 1975 **Type:** Government **Head:** Fuensanta Gonzalez Gómez **Phone:** +34(68) 840150, 840250 **Staff:** 2 Other **Holdings:** 4,500 books 379 journals **Language of Collection/Services:** Spanish / Spanish **Subjects:** Agricultural Development, Animal Husbandry, Biotechnology, Crops, Horticulture, Soil Science, Plant Pathology, Water Resources **Specializations:** Citrus Fruits, Fruit Growing, Vegetable Growing **Databases Used:** Agris; CABI **Loan:** Inhouse **Service:** In country **Photocopy:** Yes

2830 La Coruña, Spain
Agricultural Research Center
Library
Apdo 10
15080 La Coruña
Location: Carr. Betanzos - Santiago, Mabegondo **Phone:** +34(81) 673000 **Fax:** +34(81) 673656 **Email:** biblioteca_ciam@igatel.igape.es

Non-English Name: Centro de Investigaciones Agrarias de Mabegondo (CIAM), Biblioteca **Type:** Government **Holdings:** 8,000 books 652 journals **Language of Collection/Services:** Spanish / Spanish **Subjects:** Agricultural Economics, Animal Husbandry, Crops, Farming, Pastures, Plant Pathology **Databases Used:** Agris; CABCD **Loan:** In country **Service:** Inhouse **Photocopy:** Yes

2831 Léon, Spain
University of Léon, Advanced Technical School
of Agricultural Engineering
Library
Corretera Circonvaldción s/n
24071 Léon

Phone: +34(87) 291808, 291690 **Fax:** +34(87) 210126 **Email:** bueia@unileon.es **WWW:** www.unileon.es **OPAC:** www.unileon.es/servicios/indice.html

Non-English Name: Universidad de Léon, Escuela Superior y Técnica de Ingeniería Agraria (UNLE), Biblioteca **Type:** Academic **Head:** D. Santiago Asenjo Rodríguez **Phone:** +34 (87) 291133 **Email:** bu@unileon.es **Holdings:** 6,300 books 100 journals **Language of Collection/Services:** Spanish **Subjects:** Agribusiness, Agricultural Engineering, Animal Husbandry, Crops, Entomology, Farming, Food Sciences, Horticulture, Plant Pathology, Plants, Soil Science

2832 Lleida, Spain
University of Lleida, Lleida Advanced School of
Agricultural Engineering
Library
Av. Rovira Roure, 177
25198 Lleida
Location: Escuela Técnica Superior de Ingenieros Agrónomos **Phone:** +34(73) 702516 **Fax:** +34(73) 238264 **Email:** etsea@sbd.udl.es **WWW:** www.udl.es **OPAC:** www.bib.udl.es/cataleg/catalan

Non-English Name: Universitat de Lleida, Escola Tècnica Superior d'Enginyeria Agrària de Lleida (UdL, ETSEA), Biblioteca **Former Name:** Universidad Politécnica de Cataluña, Escuela Superior de Agricultura **Founded:** 1975 **Type:** Government **Head:** Loli Manciñeiras **Phone:** +34(73) 702178 **Email:** loli@sbd.udl.es **Staff:** 1 Prof. 2 Other **Holdings:** 16,000 books 283 journals **Language of Collection/Services:** Spanish, English / Catalan **Subjects:** Agricultural Development, Agricultural Economics, Agricultural Engineering, Animal Husbandry, Biotechnology, Crops, Entomology, Farming, Food Sciences, Food Technology, Forest Products Industries, Forestry, Forests, Horticulture, Plant Pathology, Soil Science, Water Resources **Databases Developed:** Agricultura; Ramaderia; Alimentació **Loan:** Inhouse **Photocopy:** Yes

2833 Lugo, Spain
University of Santiago de Compostela,
Polytechnic School
Library
Avda de Madrid, 81
27002 Lugo
Phone: +34(82) 563100 ext 23503 **Fax:** +34(82) 241835 **Email:** intprest@sialpha1.usc.es **WWW:** www.usc.es **OPAC:** busc.usc.es/busc/catalogo.htm

Non-English Name: Universidad de Santiago de Compostela, Escuela Politécnica Superior, Biblioteca **Former Name:** Escuela Universitaria de Ingeniería Técnica Agrícola, Escuela Técnica Superior de Ingenieros Agrónomos **Type:** Academic **Staff:** 2 Prof. 2 Other **Holdings:** 9,000 books 120 journals **Language of Collection/Services:** Spanish, French, English / Spanish **Subjects:** Agricultural Development, Agricultural Economics, Agricultural Engineering, Crops, Farming, Fisheries, Food Sciences, Forestry, Horticulture, Plant Pathology, Plants, Soil Science, Water Resources **Loan:** Internationally **Photocopy:** Yes

2834   Lugo, Spain
University of Santiago de Compostela, Veterinary
   Faculty
Library
Campus Universitario s/n
27002 Lugo
Phone: +34(82) 252303 ext 22005 **Fax:** +34(82) 252195
WWW: www.usc.es **OPAC:** busc.usc.es/busc/catalogo.
htm

Non-English Name: Universidad de Santiago de Compostela, Facultad de Veterinaria, Biblioteca **Type:** Academic
Head: Julia Cantalapiedra Alvarez *Phone:* +34(82) 252303
ext 22202 **Staff:** 2 Prof. 2 Other **Holdings:** 6,000 books 117
journals **Language of Collection/Services:** Spanish, English, French/Spanish **Subject:** Animal Husbandry, Farming,
Fisheries **Specializations:** Veterinary Medicine **Databases
Used:** Agris **Loan:** Internationally **Photocopy:** Yes

2835   Madrid, Spain
Complutense University of Madrid, Faculty of
   Veterinary Medicine
Library
Ciudad Universitaria, s/n
28040 Madrid
Phone: +34(1) 394-3875 **Fax:** +34(1) 394-3828 **Email:**
buc_vet@buc.ucm.es **WWW:** www.ucm.es **OPAC:** www.
ucm.es/BUCM/frames03.htm

Non-English Name: Universidad Complutense de Madrid,
Facultad de Veterinaria, Biblioteca **Founded:** 1944 **Type:**
Academic **Head:** Raquel Benito Alonso *Phone:* +34(1) 394-
3877 *Email:* rbenito@buc.ucm.es **Staff:** 6 Prof. 6 Other
Holdings: 35,395 books 248 journals **Language of Collec-
tion/Services:** Spanish, English **Subjects:** Food Sciences,
Animal Husbandry, Farming, Fisheries, Veterinary Medi-
cine **Databases Used:** BEASTCD; Current Contents; FSTA;
Medline; VETCD **Loan:** Internationally **Service:** Interna-
tionally **Photocopy:** Yes

2836   Madrid, Spain
Complutense University of Madrid, Faculty of
   Biology and Geology, Royal Society of
   Natural History
Library
Cuidad Universitaria
28040 Madrid
Phone: +34(1) 394-4900 **Fax:** +34(1) 543-9162 **Email:**
rsehno@eucmax.sim.ucm.es **WWW:** www.ucm.es/info/
rsehn/index.htm

Non-English Name: Universidad Complutense de Madrid,
Facultad de Biología y Geología, Real Sociedad Española de
Historia Natural (RSEHN), Biblioteca **Former Name:**
Sociedad Española de Historia Natural **Type:** Association
Head: Margarita Costa Tenorio **Staff:** 4 Prof. 7 Other **Hold-
ings:** 685 journals **Language of Collection/Services:** Span-
ish, French / Spanish, French **Subjects:** Biotechnology,
Crops, Entomology, Fisheries, Food Sciences, Forestry,
Plants, Soil Science, Water Resources **Specializations:** Biol-
ogy, Geology, Natural History **Photocopy:** Yes

2837   Madrid, Spain
Higher Council for Scientific Research, Centre for
   Environmental Sciences
Documentation and Library Service
Serrano 115 bis
28006 Madrid
Phone: +34(1) 562-5020 **Fax:** +34(1) 564-0800 **WWW:**
www.ccma.csic.es **OPAC:** www.csic.es/cbic/areas.htm

Non-English Name: Consejo Superior de Investigaciones
Científicas, Centro de Ciencias Medioambientales (CSIC,
CCMA), Servicio de Documentación y Biblioteca **Former
Name:** Instituto de Edafología y Biología Vegetal **Founded:**
1942 **Type:** Association **Staff:** 3 Prof. **Holdings:** 200,000
books 1,400 journals **Subjects:** Biology, Ecology, Plant
Breeding, Soil Science **Photocopy:** Yes

2838   Madrid, Spain
Higher Council for Scientific Research
Centre for Scientific Information and
   Documentation
C/ Pinar, 25, 3 Planta
28006 Madrid
Phone: +34(1) 411-2220 **Fax:** +34(1) 562-5567 **WWW:**
www.cindoc.csic.es **OPAC:** www.cindoc.csic.es/prod/
dbsconx.html

Non-English Name: Consejo Superior de Investigaciones
Científicas (CSIC), Centro de Información y Documentación
Científica (CINDOC) **Former Name:** Centro Nacional de
Información y Documentación Científica (CENIDOC),
Instituto de Información y Documentación en Ciencia y
Tecnología (ICYT), Instituto de Información y Documenta-
ción en Ciencias Sociales y Humanidades (ISOC) **Founded:**
1953 **Type:** Government **Head:** Carmen Vidal Perucho, Di-
rector; Elena Primo Peña, Library Director *Email:* direc-
tor.cindoc@csic.es; eprimo@cindoc.csic.es

2839   Madrid, Spain
Higher Council for Scientific Research, Institute
   of Economics and Geography
Library
Pinar 25
28006 Madrid
Phone: +34(1) 411-2220 **Fax:** +34(1) 562-5567 **WWW:**
www.ieg.csic.es **OPAC:** www.csic.es/cbic/acceso.htm

Non-English Name: Consejo Superior de Investigaciones
Científicas, Instituto de Economía y Geografía (CSIC, IEG),
Biblioteca **Former Name:** Instituto de Economía y Geo-
grafía Aplicadas (IEGA), Institute of Economics and Ap-
plied Geography, Centro de Investigaciones sobre la
Economía, la Sociedad y el Medio (CIESM) **Founded:** 1987
Type: Government **Head:** Matilde Vilarroig Aroca *Phone:*
+34(1) 411-1098 ext 206 *Email:* mvilarroig@bib.csic.es
Staff: 9 Prof. 4 Other **Holdings:** 4,000 books 70 journals
Subjects: Agricultural Economics, Farming **Loan:** Inhouse
Photocopy: Yes

2840   Madrid, Spain
Higher Council for Scientific Research, Royal
   Botanic Garden
Archives Library Unit

Plaza de Murillo, 2
28014 Madrid

Phone: +34(1) 420-3017 **Fax:** +34(1) 420-0157 **Email:** bib_jardin@bib.csic.es **WWW:** www.rjb.csic.es **OPAC:** www.rjb.csic.es/Biblioteca/catalogos.htm

Non-English Name: Consejo Superior de Investigaciones Científicas, Real Jardín Botánico (CSIC, RJB), Unidad Archivo-Biblioteca **Founded:** 1781 **Type:** Government **Head:** Mª Pilar de San Pío Aladrén *Phone:* +34(1) 4203017 ext 229 *Email:* san_pio@ma-rjb.csic.es **Staff:** 1 Prof. 4 Other **Holdings:** 19,239 books 1,600 journals **Language of Collection/Services:** Spanish, English **Subjects:** Forestry, Horticulture, Plant Pathology, Soil Science **Specializations:** Botany **Loan:** In country **Service:** Internationally **Photocopy:** Yes

2841   **Madrid, Spain**
Ministry of Agriculture, Fisheries and Nutrition, National Institute of Agricultural and Nutrition Research
Documentation Service and Library
Carretera de La Coruña, Km. 7,5
28040 Madrid

Phone: +34(1) 347-1496 **Fax:** +34(1) 357-2293 **Email:** biblinia@inia.es **WWW:** www.inia.es **Ariel IP:** ariel@inia.es

Non-English Name: Ministerio de Agricultura, Pesca y Alimentación, Instituto Nacional de Investigación y Tecnología Agraria y Alimentaria (MAPyA, INIA), Servicio de Documentación y Biblioteca **Former Name:** National Institute of Agricultural Research, Instituto Nacional de Investigaciones Agrarias (INIA) **Founded:** 1925 **Type:** Government **Head:** Carmen Perez Muñoz *Phone:* +34(1) 347-3907 *Email:* perezm@inia.es **Staff:** 6 Prof. 6 Other **Holdings:** 30,000 books 4,400 journals **Subjects:** Agriculture (Tropics), Agribusiness, Agricultural Development, Agricultural Economics, Agricultural Engineering, Animal Husbandry, Crops, Biotechnology, Education/Extension, Entomology, Farming, Food Sciences, Horticulture, Plant Pathology, Soil Science, Veterinary Medicine, Water Resources **Networks:** AGRIS **Databases Used:** Agris **Loan:** Internationally **Service:** Internationally **Photocopy:** Yes

2842   **Madrid, Spain**
Polytechnic University of Madrid, Agricultural Engineering High School
Library
Cuidad Universitaria
28040 Madrid

Phone: +34(1) 336-5610, 336-5611 **Fax:** +34(1) 543-4879 **Email:** maria@bib.etsia.upm.es **WWW:** www.etsia.upm.es **OPAC:** www.upm.es/servicios

Non-English Name: Universidad Politécnica de Madrid, Escuela Técnica Superior de Ingenieros Agrónomos (UPM, ETSIA), Biblioteca **Type:** Government **Head:** Mª Carmen Martínez Utesa *Phone:* +34(1) 336-5609 *Email:* mutesa@bib.etsia.upm.es **Staff:** 9 Prof. **Holdings:** 32,050 books 180 journals **Language of Collection/Services:** Spanish / Spanish **Subjects:** Agribusiness, Agricultural Development, Agricultural Economics, Biotechnology, Crops, Entomology, Food Sciences, Water Resources **Specializations:** Agricul-

tural Engineering **Networks:** DOBIS-LIBIS **Databases Used:** Agris **Loan:** Internationally **Service:** Internationally **Photocopy:** Yes

2843   **Madrid, Spain**
Polytechnic University of Madrid, Technical High School of Forestry
Library and Documentation Center
Ramiro de Maeztu, s/n
Ciudad Universitaria
28040 Madrid

Phone: +34(1) 336-7085 **Fax:** +34(1) 544-6025 **WWW:** www.upm.es **OPAC:** www.upm.es/servicios/biblioteca.html

Non-English Name: Universidad Politécnica de Madrid, Escuela Técnica Superior de Ingenieros de Montes (ETSIM), Biblioteca y Centro de Documentación **Former Name:** Escuela Especial Ingenieros de Montes **Founded:** 1846 **Type:** Academic **Head:** Dña. Mª Dolores Guío Moreno *Phone:* +34(1) 336-7540 *Email:* dguio@forestales.upm.es **Staff:** 3 Prof. 2 Other **Holdings:** 40,000 books 308 journals **Language of Collection/Services:** Spanish **Subjects:** Ecology, Farming, Fisheries, Grasslands, Plant Pathology, Soil Science, Water Resources, Wood Technology **Specializations:** Botany, Entomology, Forestry **Databases Developed:** Bibliografia Forestal Español - 35,000 analytical references of 70 forest reviews, 1965 - date **Loan:** Internationally **Photocopy:** Yes

2844   **Mérida, Spain**
Government of Extremadura, Ministry of Agriculture and Environment
Library
Avenida de Portugal, s/n
06800 Mérida (Badajoz)

Phone: +34(924) 382562, 382564 **Fax:** +34(924) 382800 **WWW:** www.juntaex.es/consejerias/aym/home.htm

Non-English Name: Junta de Extremadura, Consejería de Agricultura y Medio Ambiente, Biblioteca **Head:** Sara Espina Hidalgo *Phone:* +34(924) 382589 *Email:* sespina@bme.es **Language of Collection/Services:** Spanish, English /Spanish **Subjects:** Agricultural Development, Animal Husbandry, Biotechnology, Food Sciences, Horticulture, Soil Science, Veterinary Medicine

2845   **Pamplona, Spain**
Navarra Public University
University Library
Campus de Arrosadía, s.m.
31006 Pamplona, Navarra

Phone: +34(48) 169626 **Fax:** +34(48) 169069 **Email:** bupna@unavarra.es **WWW:** www.unavarra.es **OPAC:** brocar.unavarra.es/biblio5.htm

Non-English Name: Universidad Pública de Navarra, Nafarroako Unibertsitate Publikoa (UPNa), Biblioteca Universitaria, Unibertsitateko Liburutegia **Type:** Government **Head:** Guillermo Sánchez-Martínez *Phone:* +34(48) 169060 **Staff:** 24 Prof. 18 Other **Holdings:** 128,000 books 1,850 journals **Language of Collection/Services:** Spanish, English / Spanish, Basque **Subjects:** Agricultural Economics,

Agricultural Engineering, Animal Husbandry, Enology, Crops, Food Sciences, Forestry, Plant Physiology, Plants, Soil Science, Water Resources **Databases Used:** Agricola; Agris; CABCD; Compendex; FSTA **Loan:** Internationally **Photocopy:** Yes

2846　Pontevedra, Spain
　　　Higher Council for Scientific Research, Biological
　　　　　Mission of Galicia
　　　Library
　　　Apartado de Correos, 28
　　　36080 Pontevedra
Location: c/Carballeira 8, Palacio Salcedo, 36143 Ponte-
vedra **Phone:** +34(86) 854800 **Fax:** +34(86) 841362
Email: bib_mision@bib.csic.es **WWW:** www.mbg.csic.es
OPAC: www.csic.es/cbic/areas.htm

Non-English Name: Consejo Superior de Investigaciones Científicas, Misión Biológica de Galicia (CSIC, MBG), Biblioteca **Founded:** 1927 **Type:** Government **Head:** Julia Fuentes González **Staff:** 1 Prof. **Holdings:** 2,925 books 60 journals **Language of Collection/Services:** English, Spanish, French, German **Subjects:** Biotechnology, Genetics, Crops, Horticulture, Plant Physiology, Soil Science, Viticulture **Loan:** In country **Photocopy:** Yes

2847　Salamanca, Spain
　　　Higher Council for Scientific Research, Institute
　　　　　of Natural Resources and Agriculture of
　　　　　Salamanca
　　　Documentation and Library
　　　Cordel de Merinas, 40
　　　37008 Salamanca
Phone: +34(23) 219606 **Fax:** +34(23) 219609 **Email:**
inarb15@gugu.usal.es **WWW:** www.irnasa.csic.es

Non-English Name: Consejo Superior de Investigaciones Científicas, Instituto de Recursos Naturales y Agrobiología de Salamanca (CSIC, IRNASA), Documentación y Biblioteca **Founded:** 1954 **Type:** Government **Head:** Mª Teresa Bárez Hernandez *Phone:* +34(23) 219606 ext 225 **Holdings:** 2,500 books 100 journals **Subjects:** Biology, Natural Resources **Loan:** Inhouse

2848　San Pedro del Pinatar, Spain
　　　Ministry of Agriculture, Fisheries and Nutrition,
　　　　　Spanish Institute of Oceanography,
　　　　　Oceanographic Center of Murcia
　　　Library
　　　PO Box 22
　　　30740 San Pedro del Pinatar, Murcia
Location: c/ Magallanes, 2 **Phone:** +34(968) 180500 **Fax:**
+34(968) 184441 **Email:** comu.ieo.sp@mx2.redestb.es
WWW: www.ieo.es

Non-English Name: Ministerio de Agricultura, Pesca y Alimentación, Instituto Español de Oceanografía, Centro Oceanográfico de Murcia (MAPA, IEO), Biblioteca **Type:** Government **Staff:** 1 Prof. **Holdings:** 900 books 13 journals **Language of Collection/Services:** Spanish / Spanish **Subjects:** Aquaculture, Fisheries

2849　Santiago de Compostela, Spain
　　　Government of Galicia, Ministry of Agriculture,
　　　　　Cattle Breeding and Land and Food Policy
　　　Department of Studies and Publications
　　　San Lázaro, s/n
　　　Santiago de Compostela
Phone: +34(81) 546692 **Fax:** +34(81) 546699 **Email:**
publications.agri@xunta.es **WWW:** www.xunta.es/
conselle/ag/index.htm

Non-English Name: Xunta de Galicia, Consellería de Agricultura, Ganadería e Política Agroalimentaria, Servicio de Estudios e Publicacións **Type:** Government **Head:** Elvira Fernández Díaz *Phone:* +34(81) 546692 **Staff:** 10 Prof. **Holdings:** 5,000 books 100 journals **Language of Collection/Services:** Galician / Galician **Subjects:** Cattle, Animal Breeding **Loan:** Do not loan **Photocopy:** Yes

2850　Santiago de Compostela, Spain
　　　Higher Council for Scientific Research, Institute
　　　　　of Agrobiological Research of Galicia
　　　Library
　　　Apartado de Correos, 122
　　　15780 Santiago de Compostela
Location: Avda de Vigo s/n, Campus Universitario Sur
Phone: +34(81) 590958 **Fax:** +34(81) 592504 **Email:**
bib_iiag@cesga.es **WWW:** www.iiag.csic.es **OPAC:**
www.csic.es/cbic/areas.htm

Non-English Name: Consejo Superior de Investigaciones Científicas, Instituto de Investigaciones Agrobiológicas de Galicia (CSIC, IIAG), Biblioteca **Founded:** 1959 **Type:** Government **Head:** Maria Teresa Porto Torres *Phone:* +34(81) 590958 ext 26 **Staff:** 1 Prof. **Holdings:** 9,214 books 122 journals **Subjects:** Agricultural Development, Biotechnology, Crops, Forestry, Soil Science **Loan:** Inhouse **Service:** Inhouse **Photocopy:** Yes

2851　Santiago de Compostela, Spain
　　　University of Santiago de Compostela, Faculty of
　　　　　Biology
　　　Library
　　　Campus Universitario Sur
　　　15706 Santiago de Compostela
Phone: +34(81) 563100 ext 13246 **Fax:** +34(81) 547063
Email: bubio@usc.es, bioprest@sialpha1.usc.es **WWW:**
www.usc.es **OPAC:** busc.usc.es/busc/catalogo.htm

Non-English Name: Universidade de Santiago de Compostela, Facultade de Bioloxía, Biblioteca **Founded:** 1983 **Type:** Academic **Head:** Carmen Bermejo Díaz de Rábago *Phone:* +34(81) 563100 ext 2597 *Email:* cbermejo@usc.es **Staff:** 2 Prof. 3 Other **Holdings:** 2,000 books 50 journals **Language of Collection/Services:** English / Spanish **Subjects:** Biotechnology, Entomology, Fisheries, Food Sciences, Horticulture, Plant Pathology, Plants, Soil Science **Databases Used:** Biosis; Current Contents **Loan:** Inhouse **Service:** Internationally **Photocopy:** Yes

2852　Seville, Spain
　　　Higher Council for Scientific Research, Institute
　　　　　of Natural Resources and Agriculture of
　　　　　Seville

Library
Apartado 1052
41080 Seville

Location: Avenida de Reina Mercedes, 10 **Phone:** +34(54) 624711 **Fax:** +34(54) 624002 **Email:** bibirna@cica.es **WWW:** www.irnase.csic.es **OPAC:** www.csic.es/cbic/acceso.htm

Non-English Name: Consejo Superior de Investigaciones Científicas, Instituto de Recursos Naturales y Agrobiología de Sevilla (CSIC, IRNAS), Biblioteca **Founded:** 1953 **Type:** Government **Head:** Adela Sabido Corro **Staff:** 1 Other **Holdings:** 3,500 books 42 journals **Subjects:** Plant Physiology, Soil Science **Loan:** Inhouse **Photocopy:** Yes

2853   Seville, Spain
Technical Library of Agriculture
Juan Ramón Jimenez No. 11
41011 Seville

Phone: +34(5) 427-9570 **Fax:** +34(5) 427-1510 **Ariel IP:** agrotec@zoom.es

Non-English Name: Librería Técnica Agrícola **Founded:** 1983 **Type:** Business **Head:** Teresa Maza Burgos *Phone:* +34(5) 427-1510, 427-9570 **Staff:** 2 Prof. **Holdings:** 4,000 books 30 journals **Subjects:** Agribusiness, Agricultural Development, Agricultural Economics, Animal Husbandry, Agricultural Engineering, Crops, Forestry, Plant Pathology, Soil Science **Loan:** Do not loan **Photocopy:** No

2854   Seville, Spain
University of Seville, School of Agricultural Engineering
Library
Ctra. Utrera, Km. 1 (ant. Univ. Laboral)
41013 Seville

Phone: +34(54) 233669, 237587 **Fax:** +34(54) 232644 **WWW:** www.us.es **OPAC:** www.bib.us.es

Non-English Name: Universidad de Sevilla, Escuela Universitaria de Ingeniería Agrícola, Biblioteca **Former Name:** Escuela Universitaria de Ingeniería Técnica Agrícola (EUITA) **Founded:** 1968 **Type:** Government **Head:** Manuel Bravo Borrego *Phone:* +34(54) 233669 ext 19, 237640 *Email:* mbravo@cica.es **Staff:** 1 Prof. 1 Other **Holdings:** 10,000 books 150 journals **Language of Collection/Services:** Spanish / Spanish, English **Subjects:** Agricultural Engineering, Animal Husbandry, Entomology, Horticulture, Plant Pathology **Loan:** Inhouse **Service:** Inhouse **Photocopy:** No

2855   Tarragona, Spain
University Rovira and Virgili, Faculty of Enology
Library
Ramón y Cajal, 70
43005 Tarragona

Phone: +34(977) 250352 **Fax:** +34(977) 250347, 250353 **Email:** bibeno@bib.urv.es **WWW:** www.urv.es **OPAC:** www.urv.es/sgenerals/biblioteca/Bib_Enologia/index.html

Non-English Name: Universitat Rovira i Virgili, Facultat d'Enologia, Biblioteca **Founded:** 1988 **Type:** Academic **Head:** Josefa Rius Masip *Phone:* +34(977) 250352 **Staff:** 1 Prof. 1 Other **Holdings:** 3,500 books 175 journals **Language**

of Collection/Services: English, French, Spanish / Catalan, Spanish, English, French **Subjects:** Food Sciences **Specializations:** Enology, Viticulture **Networks:** CCUC **Databases Used:** Current Contents; FSTA **Loan:** Internationally **Service:** Internationally **Photocopy:** Yes

2856   Valencia, Spain
Polytechnic University of Valencia
Library
Camí de Vera s/n
46022 Valencia

Phone: +34(6) 387-7080 **Fax:** +34(6) 387-7089 **Email:** biblio@bib.upv.es **OPAC:** biblioteca.upv.es/bib/bib_menu /v **WWW:** www.upv.es

Non-English Name: Universitat Politècnica València, Universidad Politécnica de Valencia (UPV), Biblioteca **Type:** Government **Head:** Prof. José Llorens *Phone:* +34(6) 387-7081 *Email:* jllorens@dsic.upv.es **Staff:** 9 Prof. 35 Other **Holdings:** 150,000 books 950 journals **Language of Collection/Services:** English / Spanish **Subjects:** Agricultural Economics, Agricultural Engineering, Animal Husbandry, Biotechnology, Crops, Food Sciences, Horticulture, Plant Pathology, Soil Science **Databases Used:** Agricola; FSTA **Loan:** Internationally **Service:** In country **Photocopy:** Yes

2857   Vigo, Spain
Higher Council for Scientific Research, Institute of Marine Research
Library
Eduardo Cabello, 6
36208 Vigo

Fax: +34(86) 292762 **Email:** bib_iim@iim.csic.es **WWW:** www.iim.csic.es **OPAC:** www.csic.es/cbic/areas.htm **Ariel IP:** 193.144.47.48

Non-English Name: Consejo Superior de Investigaciones Científicas, Instituto de Investigaciones Marinas (CSIC, IIM), Biblioteca **Former Name:** Instituto Investigaciones Pesqueras **Founded:** 1951 **Type:** Government **Head:** Mª Angeles García Calvo *Phone:* +34(86) 292758 ext 228 **Staff:** 2 Other **Holdings:** 3,200 books 172 journals **Language of Collection/Services:** English **Subjects:** Aquaculture, Biotechnology, Fisheries, Food Sciences **Databases Used:** ASFA; CAS; Current Contents **Loan:** In country **Photocopy:** Yes

2858   Vitoria, Spain
Basque Government, Department of Agriculture and Fisheries
Library - Agriculture
Duque de Wellington, 2
01010 Vitoria

Phone: +34(45) 189686 **Fax:** +34(45) 188252 **Email:** e-bacaicoa@ej-gv.es **WWW:** www.euskadi.net

Non-English Name: Gobierno Vasco, Departamento de Agricultura y Pesca, Biblioteca-Agricultura **Founded:** 1985 **Type:** Government **Head:** Esther Bacaicoa *Phone:* +34(45) 189686 *Email:* e-bacaicoa@ej-gv.es **Staff:** 2 Prof. **Holdings:** 4,000 books 100 journals **Language of Collection/Services:** Spanish/Spanish **Subjects:** Agricultural Development, Agricultural Economics, Agricultural Engineering,

Fisheries **Databases Used:** Agris; CABCD **Loan:** Internationally **Service:** Internationally **Photocopy:** Yes

2859 Zaragoza, Spain
Higher Council for Scientific Research, Aula Dei
Experiment Station
Library and Documentation Support Unit
Apartado 202
50080 Zaragoza

Location: Avda. de Montañana, 177 **Fax:** +34(76) 575620 **Email:** bib_aula@eead.csic.es **WWW:** www.eead.csic.es **OPAC:** olivo.csic.es (user name ALEPH)

Non-English Name: Consejo Superior de Investigaciones Científicas, Estación Experimental de Aula Dei (CSIC, EEAD), Unidad de Apoyo de Biblioteca y Documentación **Founded:** 1948 **Type:** Government **Head:** José Carlos Martínez Giménez *Phone:* +34(76) 576511 *Email:* martinez@eead.csic.es **Staff:** 4 Prof. 2 Other **Holdings:** 6,000 books 308 journals **Language of Collection/Services:** English, Spanish **Subjects:** Biotechnology, Crops, Horticulture, Plant Nutrition, Soil Science, Water Resources **Databases Used:** Comprehensive **Networks:** CIRBIC **Loan:** In country **Service:** Inhouse **Photocopy:** Yes

2860 Zaragoza, Spain
Mediterranean Agronomic Institute of Zaragoza
Library
Apartado 202
50080 Zaragoza

Location: Situated on the Aula Dei Campus **Phone:** +34 (76) 576013 **Fax:** +34(76) 576377 **Email:** iamz@iamz.ciheam.org **WWW:** iamz.ciheam.org

Non-English Name: Instituto Agronómico Mediterráneo de Zaragoza (IAMZ), Biblioteca **Type:** International **Staff:** 2 Prof. **Holdings:** 8,000 books 100 journals **Language of Collection/Services:** English, French, Spanish / Spanish **Subjects:** Agribusiness, Agricultural Development, Animal Husbandry, Crops, Fisheries, Natural Resources **Specializations:** Animal Production, Marketing, Plant Breeding, Rural Planning **Databases Used:** Agris; CABCD **Loan:** Inhouse **Service:** Internationally **Photocopy:** Yes

2861 Zaragoza, Spain
University of Zaragoza, Faculty of Veterinary
Medicine
Library
Miguel Servet, 177
50013 Zaragoza

Phone: +34(76) 761606 **Fax:** +34(76) 761612 **Email:** bibvetez@posta.unizar.es **WWW:** www.unizar.es **OPAC:** aneto.unizar.es

Non-English Name: Universidad de Zaragoza, Facultad de Veterinaria, Biblioteca **Founded:** 1861 **Type:** Academic **Head:** Mª Josefa Yusta Bonilla *Phone:* +34(76) 761606 *Email:* mjyusta@posta.unizar.es **Staff:** 2 Prof. 5 Other **Holdings:** 18,000 books 466 journals **Language of Collection/Services:** Spanish **Subjects:** Agricultural Economics, Biotechnology, Food Sciences, Veterinary Medicine **Databases Used:** Biosis; CABCD; Current Contents **Loan:** Internationally **Service:** In country **Photocopy:** Yes

Sri Lanka

2862 Agalawatta, Sri Lanka
Rubber Research Institute of Sri Lanka (RRISL)
Library
Dartonfield
Agalawatta

Phone: +94(34) 47426, 47383 **Fax:** +94(34) 47427 **Email:** director@rri.ac.lk

Founded: 1936 **Type:** Government **Staff:** 2 Prof. 4 Other **Holdings:** 8,567 books 76 journals **Language of Collection/Services:** English / Sinhala, English **Subjects:** Agriculture (Tropics), Agricultural Development, Agricultural Economics, Biotechnology, Crops, Entomology, Horticulture, Plant Pathology, Rubber, Soil Science **Databases Developed:** BIN - RRISL Bulletin Index **Loan:** In country **Photocopy:** Yes

2863 Aturugiriya, Sri Lanka
National Institute of Plantation Management
(NIPM)
Library
PO Box 1
M.D.H. Jayawardena Mawatha
Aturugiriya

Phone: +94(1) 438009 **Fax:** +94(1) 074-403429 **Email:** nipm@srilanka.net

Type: Training **Head:** Ms. Chandani Ranaweera **Staff:** 1 Prof. **Holdings:** 1,800 books 12 journals **Language of Collection/Services:** English / English **Subjects:** Plantation Management **Specializations:** Computers **Loan:** Inhouse **Service:** Inhouse **Photocopy:** No

♦2864 Battaramulla, Sri Lanka
Forest Department
Library
Rajamalwatte Road
Battaramulla

Fax: +94(1) 566633

Type: Government **Head:** Ms. S. Geekiyanage *Phone:* +94 (1) 566632, 566628 **Staff:** 1 Prof. **Holdings:** 8,700 books 80 journals **Language of Collection/Services:** English / English **Subjects:** Crops, Environment, Forestry **Loan:** In country **Service:** In country

2865 Colombo, Sri Lanka
Central Environmental Authority (CEA)
National Environmental Information Center
(NEIC)
Parisara Mawatha
Maligawatte
Colombo 10

Type: Government **Head:** Mrs. A.C.P. Dabare *Phone:* +94 (1) 449455/6 *Email:* cen_aut@sll.lk **Staff:** 3 Prof. 2 Other **Holdings:** 6,150 books 100 journals **Language of Collection/Services:** English / English **Subjects:** Conservation, Forestry, Irrigation, Pollution, Waste Disposal **Databases Developed:** UNICEB - Union Catalogue of Environmental Books; UNILEP - Union List of Environmental Periodicals;

IND-Environmental Index; EXPT-Directory of Environmental Experts in Sri Lanka **Loan:** In country **Service:** Internationally **Photocopy:** Yes

2866   Colombo, Sri Lanka
         Hector Kobbekaduwa Agrarian Research and
             Training Institute (HARTI)
         National Centre for Information on Agrarian
             Development (NACIAD)
         114, Wijerama Mawatha
         Colombo 7
Phone: +94(1) 698539/41, 696437, 696981, 698565 **Fax:** +94(1) 692423

Former Name: Agrarian Research and Training Institute (ARTI) **Founded:** 1972 **Type:** Government **Head:** Gamini H. Karunaratne *Phone:* +94(1) 698539 **Staff:** 5 Prof. 2 Other **Holdings:** 16,000 books 64 journals **Language of Collection/Services:** English **Subjects:** Agricultural Development, Agricultural Economics, Crops, Education/ Extension, Farm Management, Farming, Fisheries, Food Research, Nutrition, Forestry, Irrigation, Rural Development, Rural Sociology, Water Management, Water Resources, Women **Loan:** In country **Service:** In country **Photocopy:** Yes

2867   Colombo, Sri Lanka
         International Water Management Institute (IWMI)
         Library and Documentation Service
         PO Box 2075
         Colombo
Location: 127, Sunil Mawatha, Pelawatte via Colombo
Phone: +94(1) 867404 **Fax:** +94(1) 866854 **Email:** iwmi@ cgiar.org **WWW:** www.cgiar.org/iwmi **OPAC:** www. cgiar.org/iwmi/libcat.htm

Former Name: International Irrigation Management Institute (IIMI) **Founded:** 1986 **Type:** International **Head:** Ms. Ramya de Silva *Phone:* +94(1) 867404 *Email:* r.desilva@ cgiar.org **Staff:** 4 Prof. 1 Other **Holdings:** 9,034 books 80 journals **Language of Collection/Services:** English / English **Subjects:** Agricultural Development, Farming, Irrigation, Rural Development, Rural Sociology, Soil Science, Water Resources **Specializations:** Irrigation Management, Water Management **Databases Developed:** IMIN - Cooperative database comprising collections at IWMI Headquarters in Sri Lanka, IWMI Pakistan, IWMI Nigeria, the Overseas Development Institute (ODI) Library in London, and the ICID Central Office in New Delhi **Databases Used:** Comprehensive **Loan:** Internationally **Service:** Internationally **Photocopy:** Yes

2868   Colombo, Sri Lanka
         Irrigation Department (ID)
         Library
         PO Box 1138
         Bauddhaloka Mawatha
         Colombo 7
Fax: +94(1) 584984

Founded: 1948 **Type:** Government **Head:** Ms. Gamanayake *Phone:* +94(1) 5883301/4 **Staff:** 1 Prof. 3 Other **Holdings:** 6,150 books 7 journals **Language of Collection/Services:** English / English **Subjects:** Drainage, Irrigation,

Water Management **Loan:** In country **Service:** In country **Photocopy:** Yes

2869   Colombo, Sri Lanka
         National Aquatic Resources Research and
             Development Agency (NARA)
         Library
         Crow Island
         Colombo 15
Phone: +94(1) 522000/6 **Fax:** +94(1) 552932 **WWW:** www.naresa.ac.lk/nara/profile.htm

Founded: 1981 **Type:** Semi-Government **Head:** Mr. H. Tilakabandu *Email:* tbandu@nara.ac.lk **Holdings:** 7,000 books 463 journals **Language of Collection/Services:** English / English **Subjects:** Aquatic Resources, Fisheries **Loan:** In country **Service:** In country **Photocopy:** Yes

2870   Kamburupitiya, Sri Lanka
         University of Ruhuna, Faculty of Agriculture
             (UR)
         Library
         Mapalana
         Kamburupitiya
Phone: +94(41) 92381 **Fax:** +94(41) 92384 **Email:** sandya @aglib.ruh.ac.lk

Founded: 1980 **Type:** Academic **Head:** G. de Silva *Phone:* +94(41) 27028 *Email:* mainlib@libruh.ac.lk **Staff:** 1 Prof. 8 Other **Holdings:** 10,825 books 67 journals **Language of Collection/Services:** English / English **Subjects:** Agricultural Economics, Agricultural Engineering, Animal Husbandry, Crops, Entomology, Fisheries, Horticulture, Plant Pathology, Plant Protection, Soil Science **Loan:** In country **Photocopy:** No

2871   Lunuwila, Sri Lanka
         Coconut Research Institute (CRI)
         Library
         Lunuwila
Fax: +94(31) 57391 **Email:** libcri@sri.lanka.net **WWW:** www.naresa.ac.lk/cri/profile.htm

Former Name: Coconut Information Centre (CIC) **Founded:** 1929 **Type:** Government **Head:** Mrs. Sunethra Perera *Phone:* +94(1) 253795 *Email:* libcri@sri.lanka.net **Staff:** 4 Prof. 3 Other **Holdings:** 5,160 books 67 journals **Language of Collection/Services:** English / English **Subjects:** Agriculture (Tropics), Crops, Entomology, Horticulture, Plant Pathology, Soil Science **Specializations:** Coconut Products, Coconuts **Databases Developed:** Database of coconut research workers and research projects; Bibliographic database on coconuts **Databases Used:** Agricola **Loan:** In country **Service:** Internationally **Photocopy:** Yes

2872   Peradeniya, Sri Lanka
         Department of Agriculture
         Central Library
         PO Box 47, Gannoruwa
         Peradeniya
Location: Central Agricultural Research Institute, Gannoruwa

Founded: 1810 **Type:** Government **Head:** Mrs. Srimathie Gunasekera *Phone:* +94(8) 88011 ext 20 **Staff:** 4 Prof. 5 Other **Holdings:** 16,000 books 75 journals **Language of Collection/Services:** English / English **Subjects:** Comprehensive **Specializations:** Food and Agriculture Organization Documents, International Crops Research Institute for the Semi-Arid Tropics Documents **Networks:** AGRIS **Databases Used:** Agris **Loan:** Internationally through National AGRIS Centers **Photocopy:** Yes

2873   Peradeniya, Sri Lanka
          Department of Animal Production and Health,
              Veterinary Research Institute (VRI)
          Library
          PO Box 28
          Gannoruwa
          Peradeniya
Phone: +94(8) 88311, 88037 **Fax:** +94(8) 88125

Founded: 1978 **Type:** Government **Head:** Ms. V.S. Wijesekera *Phone:* +94(8) 88125 **Staff:** 1 Prof. 1 Other **Holdings:** 10,000 books 13 journals **Language of Collection/Services:** English / English **Subjects:** Animal Diseases, Animal Husbandry, Bacteriology, Buffaloes, Cattle, Extension, Parasitology, Poultry, Veterinary Medicine **Loan:** In country **Service:** In country **Photocopy:** Yes

2874   Peradeniya, Sri Lanka
          University of Peradeniya
          Agriculture Library
          Old Galaha Road
          Peradeniya
Fax: +94(8) 388318 **Email:** congress@pgia.pdn.ac.lk
WWW: www.pdn.ac.lk

Former Name: University of Ceylon, University of Sri Lanka **Founded:** 1947 **Type:** Academic **Head:** Ms. I. Mudannayake *Phone:* +94(8) 388956 **Staff:** 3 Prof. 10 Other **Holdings:** 33,463 books 150 journals **Language of Collection/Services:** English **Subjects:** Agricultural Economics, Agricultural Engineering, Animal Husbandry, Biometry, Biotechnology, Crops, Entomology, Environment, Extension, Farming Systems, Forestry, Horticulture, Management, Plant Pathology, Rural Sociology, Soil Science, Statistics **Specializations:** Agriculture (Sri Lanka) **Databases Used:** CABCD **Loan:** In country **Photocopy:** Yes

2875   Peradeniya, Sri Lanka
          University of Peradeniya, Faculty of Veterinary
              Medicine
          Library
          Old Galaha Road
          Peradeniya
Phone: +94(8) 88685 **Fax:** +94(8) 88789 **WWW:**
www.pdn.ac.lk

Founded: 1956 **Type:** Government **Staff:** 2 Other **Holdings:** 30,000 books **Language of Collection/Services:** English **Subjects:** Animal Husbandry, Microbiology, Veterinary Medicine, Public Health **Loan:** Do not loan **Photocopy:** No

2876   Talawakelle, Sri Lanka
          Tea Research Institute (TRI)
          Library
          Talawakelle
Phone: +94(51) 2601 **Email:** postmaster@tri.ac.lk

Former Name: Tea Research Institute of Ceylon **Founded:** 1925 **Type:** Government **Head:** Mrs. W. Illangantileke *Phone:* +94(52) 58385, 58386 *Email:* wasantha@tri.ac.lk **Staff:** 2 Prof. 2 Other **Holdings:** 3,913 books 60 journals **Language of Collection/Services:** English **Subjects:** Agriculture (Tropics), Agricultural Development, Agricultural Economics, Agricultural Engineering, Crops, Biotechnology, Extension, Entomology, Food Sciences, Plant Pathology, Plants, Processing, Soil Science, Water Resources **Specializations:** Tea **Loan:** In country **Service:** In country **Photocopy:** Yes

2877   Uda Walawe, Sri Lanka
          Sugarcane Research Institute (SRI)
          Library
          Uda Walawe
Phone: +94(47) 33233 **Fax:** +94(47) 33233

Founded: 1984 **Type:** Research **Head:** A.P. Keerthipala *Phone:* +94(47) 33233 *Email:* keerthi@sugar.ac.lk **Staff:** 1 Prof. **Holdings:** 10,000 books 14 journals **Language of Collection/Services:** English / English **Subjects:** Agricultural Economics, Agricultural Engineering, Biometry, Biotechnology, Crops, Education/Extension, Entomology, Fermentation, Pest Management, Plant Breeding, Plant Pathology, Plants, Soil Science **Specializations:** Sugarcane **Databases Used:** HORTCD **Loan:** In country **Service:** In country **Photocopy:** Yes

2878   Welisera, Sri Lanka
          Department of Animal Production and Health, Sri
              Lanka School of Animal Husbandry
          Library
          Welisera, Ragama
Phone: +94(1) 958340 **Fax:** +94(1) 958340

Founded: 1980 **Type:** Government **Staff:** 2 Other **Holdings:** 5,000 books **Language of Collection/Services:** English **Subjects:** Animal Husbandry, Crops, Extension **Loan:** In country **Photocopy:** Yes

Sudan

2879   Juba, Sudan
          University of Juba
          Library
          PO Box 82
          Juba, Equatoria
Phone: +249(11) 451351 ext 2113 **Fax:** +249(11) 451351

Founded: 1977 **Type:** Academic **Head:** Alfred D. Lado **Staff:** 7 Prof. 25 Other **Holdings:** 20,000 books 500 journals **Subjects:** Agricultural Economics, Animal Husbandry, Crops, Entomology, Fisheries, Plant Pathology, Plant Protection, Soil Science, Wildlife **Loan:** In country **Photocopy:** Yes

2880   **Khartoum, Sudan**
Arab Organization for Agricultural Development
    (AOAD)
Arab Center for Agricultural Documentation and
    Information (ACADI)
PO Box 474
Khartoum 11111
Location: St. No. 7 - Al-Amarat **Phone:** +249(11) 452177
Fax: +249(11) 451402 **Email:** aoad@sudanet.net

Founded: 1980 **Type:** Government **Head:** Dr. Monir A.
El-Agezi *Phone:* +249(11) 452176 *Email:* aoad@sudanet.
net **Staff:** 6 Prof. 5 Other **Holdings:** 42,900 books 854 jour-
nals **Language of Collection/Services:** Arabic, English,
French / Arabic, English **Subjects:** Agriculture (Tropics),
Agribusiness, Agricultural Engineering, Biotechnology,
Crops, Education/Extension, Entomology, Farming, Fish-
eries, Food Sciences, Forestry, Horticulture, Plant Pathol-
ogy, Soil Science, Veterinary Medicine, Water Resources
Specializations: Agricultural Development, Agricultural
Economics, Animal Husbandry, Rural Development **Data-
bases Developed:** Arab Agricultural Experts; Arab Agricul-
tural Dictionary; Arab Agricultural Extension **Databases
Used:** Agris; Singer; World Development Resources **Loan:**
In country **Service:** Arab countries **Photocopy:** Yes

♦**2881**   **Khartoum, Sudan**
National Centre for Research
Documentation and Information Centre
PO Box 2404
Khartoum
Location: Near Council of Ministers **Phone:** +249 70701

Former Name: National Council for Research, National
Documentation Centre **Founded:** 1974 **Type:** Government
Staff: 15 Prof. 7 Other **Holdings:** 24,000 books 65 journals
Language of Collection/Services: English / English **Databases Developed:** Sudan Science Abstracts; National Register of Current Research; National bibliographic database
relating to Sudan including dissertations, conference papers,
journal article. **Databases Used:** Agricola; Agris; CABCD;
Medline **Loan:** Inhouse **Service:** In country **Photocopy:** No

2882   **Shambat, Sudan**
University of Khartoum, Agricultural Studies
    Campus (U of K)
Shambat Library
PO Box 32
Shambat
Phone: +249 310101 (Faculty of Agriculture) **Email:** info
@uofk.edu **WWW:** www.uofk.edu/uofk.htm

Founded: 1938 **Type:** Academic **Staff:** 2 Prof. 14 Other
Holdings: 10,664 books 12,000 journals **Language of Col-
lection/Services:** English / English **Subjects:** Animal Husbandry, Forestry, Veterinary Medicine **Loan:** Internationally
Service: In country

2883   **Wad Medani, Sudan**
Agricultural Research Corporation (ARC)
Central Library
PO Box 126
Wad Medani

Phone: +249(51) 42226 **Fax:** +249(51) 43213 **Email:**
arcsudan@sudanet.net
Founded: 1930 **Type:** Government **Head:** Ahlam Ismail
Musa *Phone:* +249(51) 42226 *Email:* arcsudan@sudanet.net
Staff: 1 Prof. 4 Other **Holdings:** 12,000 books 75 journals
Language of Collection/Services: English, Arabic / Eng-
lish, Arabic **Subjects:** Comprehensive **Specializations:** Ag-
ricultural Research, Crop Production, Crops, Forestry,
Horticulture, Plant Protection, Soil, Water **Networks:**
AGRIS **Databases Used:** Agris **Loan:** Inhouse **Service:** In-
house **Photocopy:** Yes

2884   **Wad Medani, Sudan**
University of Gezira (UG)
Library
PO Box 20
Wad Medani
Phone: +249(51) 43174 **Fax:** +249(51) 43862 **Email:**
lib@ugezira.gn.apc.org

Founded: 1975 **Type:** Academic **Head:** Mr. A.M. Hamouda
Email: lib@ugezira.gn.apc.org **Staff:** 5 Prof. 56 Other **Hold-
ings:** 50,000 books 5 journals **Language of Collection/Ser-
vices:** English, Arabic **Subjects:** Agricultural Economics,
Animal Production, Crop Production, Plant Breeding, Plant
Physiology **Specializations:** Plant Protection, Rural Devel-
opment, Sudan, Tropics **Loan:** Inhouse **Service:** In country
Photocopy: Yes

Suriname

2885   **Nieuw Nickerie, Suriname**
Foundation for Rice Research in Suriname
Anne van Dijk Rice Research Centre Nickerie
PO Box 6093
Nieuw Nickerie
Location: Europolder-noord, serie 1 no 31, Nickerie
Phone: +597 804535 **Fax:** +597 804575 **Email:** adron@sr.
net **WWW:** www.cgiar.org/isnar/hosted/adron/adron.htm

Non-English Name: Stichting Nationaal Rijstonderzoeks
Instituut (SNRI), Anne van Dijk Rijstonderzoekscentrum
Nickerie (ADRON) **Former Name:** Foundation for the
Development of Agricultural Mechanics in Suriname, Rice
Research and Breeding Station **Founded:** 1994 **Type:** Gov-
ernment **Head:** Jerry Tjoe-Awie *Phone:* +597 804535
Email: adron@sr.net **Staff:** 2 Other **Holdings:** 600 books 2
journals **Language of Collection/Services:** English / Dutch
Subjects: Agriculture (Tropics), Rice **Loan:** Inhouse **Ser-
vice:** In country **Photocopy:** Yes

2886   **Paramaribo, Suriname**
Anton de Kom University of Suriname
Library
PO Box 9212
Paramaribo
Location: Leysweg 26 **Phone:** +597 464547 **Fax:** +597
434211 **WWW:** www.sr.net/adekbib

Founded: 1968 **Type:** Academic **Head:** Ms. Ine I.S. Tsai-
Meu-Chong *Phone:* +597 464547 *Email:* adekbib@sr.net
Staff: 8 Prof. 7 Other **Holdings:** 83,000 books **Language of**

Collection/Services: English / Dutch **Subjects:** Comprehensive **Specializations:** Economics, Sociology **Networks:** AGRIS; BIREME; SIAMAZ **Databases Used:** Agris; CABCD **Photocopy:** Yes

2887 Paramaribo, Suriname
Ministry of Agriculture, Animal Husbandry and Fisheries
Central Library
PO Box 160
Paramaribo

Location: Cultuurtuinlaan 8 **Phone:** +597 74177

Founded: 1903 **Type:** Government **Staff:** 1 Prof. 3 Other **Holdings:** 14,936 books 289 journals **Subjects:** Animal Husbandry, Fisheries, Forestry, Pests, Plant Diseases **Loan:** In country **Photocopy:** Yes

Swaziland

2888 Luyengo, Swaziland
University of Swaziland, Faculty of Agriculture (UNISWA)
Agriculture Library
Luyengo

Phone: +268 528-3021/3 **Fax:** +268 628-5276 **Email:** uniswapgs@uniswa.sz **WWW:** www.uniswa.sz **OPAC:** library.uniswa.sz/cgi-bin/urica1?V7OPACMENU

Founded: 1971 **Type:** Academic **Head:** M.R. Mavuso, University Librarian; J.J. Massawe, Head Agriculture *Phone:* +268 528-3021 **Staff:** 4 Other **Holdings:** 27,000 books 100 journals **Language of Collection/Services:** English / English **Subjects:** Agricultural Economics, Animal Husbandry, Crops, Education/Extension, Home Economics, Land Use, Mechanization **Databases Developed:** Thesis/Dissertation List compiled in Procite **Databases Used:** Agris; CABCD **Loan:** Internationally **Photocopy:** Yes

2889 Malkerns, Swaziland
Ministry of Agriculture, Malkerns Research Station
Library
PO Box 4
Malkerns

Phone: +268 83017 **Fax:** +268 83360 **Email:** malkernsresearch@iafrica.sz

Former Name: Ministry of Agriculture and Cooperatives (MOAC) **Founded:** 1959 **Type:** Government, Research **Staff:** 1 Other **Holdings:** 7,000 books 10 journals **Language of Collection/Services:** English / English **Subjects:** Extension, Food Sciences, Fodder Crops, Plant Pathology **Specializations:** Crops, Entomology, Horticulture **Loan:** In country **Service:** Inhouse **Photocopy:** No

2890 Mananga, Swaziland
Managa Centre for Regional Integration and Management Development
Youdale Library
PO Box 20
Mhlume

Mananga

Phone: +268 313-1011, 313-1133/4, 313-1491 **Fax:** +268 313-1335

Former Name: Managa Agricultural Management Centre **Founded:** 1972 **Type:** Academic **Staff:** 2 Prof. 1 Other **Holdings:** 5,000 books 30 journals **Subjects:** Accounting, Agricultural Economics, Farm Management, Rural Development

2891 Matata, Swaziland
Ministry of Agriculture, Lowveld Experiment Station (LES)
Library
PB 11
Matata

Location: Loop Road to Matata Store **Phone:** +268 36311 **Fax:** +268 36450 **Email:** les@iafrica.za

Former Name: Ministry of Agriculture and Cooperatives (MOAC) **Founded:** 1964 **Type:** Government **Head:** Benedict M. Bhembe *Phone:* +268 36311 *Email:* les@iafrica.za **Staff:** 4 Prof. 20 Other **Holdings:** 400 books 7 journals **Language of Collection/Services:** English **Subjects:** Africa, Cotton, Crop Production, Dry Farming, Irrigation, Pest Control, Plant Breeding, Plant Protection **Databases Used:** CABCD **Loan:** Inhouse **Photocopy:** Yes

2892 Mbabane, Swaziland
Ministry of Education
Swaziland National Library Service (SNLS)
PO Box 1461
Mbabane

Location: Warner Street **Phone:** +268 404-2633 **Fax:** +268 43863 **Email:** snissz@realnet.co.sz

Founded: 1970 **Type:** Government **Head:** Mrs. D. Kunene *Email:* dijkunene@realent.co.sz **Staff:** 5 Prof. 65 Other **Holdings:** 500,000 books 300 journals **Subjects:** Agriculture (Swaziland) **Databases Developed:** DEVSZ - Development Swaziland **Photocopy:** Yes **Loan:** Internationally **Service:** Internationally

Sweden

2893 Alnarp, Sweden
Swedish University of Agricultural Sciences
Alnarp Library
PO Box 51
SE 230 53 Alnarp

Location: Sundsvägen 6 **Phone:** +46(40) 415050 **Fax:** +46 (40) 465058 **Email:** alnarpsbiblioteket@bibal.slu.se **WWW:** www.bib.slu.se/index.html?alnarp/alnbibl **OPAC:** lukas.slu.se:1600/ALEPH

Non-English Name: Sveriges Lantbruksuniversitet (SLU), Alnarpsbiblioteket **Former Name:** Lantbrukshögskolan, Jordbrukets högskolor **Founded:** 1936 **Type:** Academic **Head:** Lennart Hultin *Phone:* +46(40) 415047 *Email:* lennart.hultin@bibal.slu.se **Staff:** 7 Prof. 3 Other **Holdings:** 114,000 books 467 journals **Language of Collection/Services:** English / Swedish, English **Subjects:** Comprehensive **Specializations:** Horticulture, Landscaping **Networks:**

LIBRIS **Databases Used:** Comprehensive **Loan:** Internationally **Service:** Internationally **Photocopy:** Yes

2894 Alnarp, Sweden
Swedish University of Agricultural Sciences,
Department of Agricultural Biosystems and
Technology
Library
PO Box 43
SE 230 53 Alnarp
Phone: +46 40 41 50 00 **Fax:** +46 40 46 04 21 **Email:**
mailbox @jbt.slu.se

Non-English Name: Sveriges Lantbruksuniversitet, Institutionen för Jordbrukets Biosystem och Teknologi (JBT), Biblioteket **Former Name:** Department of Farm Buildings, Institutionen för Lantbrukets Byggnadsteknik (LBT), Division of Education in Agricultural and Rural Management, Southern Animal Experimental District, Agricultural Experimental District of Southern Sweden **Founded:** 1960 **Type:** Academic **Staff:** 1 Prof. 1 Other **Holdings:** 25 journals **Language of Collection/Services:** Swedish / English **Subjects:** Agricultural Engineering, Animal Husbandry, Fisheries, Horticulture **Loan:** In country **Service:** In country **Photocopy:** Yes

2895 Garpenberg, Sweden
Dalarna University
Garpenberg Library
SE 776 98 Garpenberg
Location: Herrgårdsuägen 122 **Fax:** +46(225) 26100
Email: bka@du.se **WWW:** www.garpenbergs-utv.se
OPAC: www.libris.kb.se/home.html

Non-English Name: Högskolan Dalarna, Garpenbergsbiblioteket **Former Name:** Swedish University of Agricultural Sciences, Sveriges Lantbruksuniversitet (SLU) **Type:** Academic **Head:** Bodil Karlström **Email:** bka@du.se **Phone:** +46(225) 26030 **Staff:** 1 Prof. **Holdings:** 12,200 books 500 journals **Language of Collection/Services:** Swedish, English **Subjects:** Forestry **Databases Used:** TREECD **Loan:** Internationally **Service:** Internationally **Photocopy:** Yes

2896 Göteborg, Sweden
Gothenburg University Library
Botanical Library
Box 461
SE 405 30 Göteborg
Location: Carl Skottsbergs gata 22B **Phone:** +46(31)
733-2541 **Fax:** +46(31) 733-2544 **Email:** botanical.
library@ub.gu.se, gb.best@ub.gu.se **WWW:** www.ub.gu.
se/Gb

Non-English Name: Göteborgs Universitetsbibliotek (Gb), Botaniska Biblioteketet **Founded:** 1969 **Type:** Academic **Head:** Monika Ivarsson Almgren **Phone:** +46(31) 733-2542 **Email:** monika.ivarsson.almgren@ub.gu.se **Staff:** 4 Prof. **Holdings:** 50,000 books 300 journals **Language of Collection/Services:** English / Swedish **Subjects:** Chemical Ecology, Horticulture, Marine Biology, Microbiology, Plant Ecology, Plant Physiology, Taxonomy **Databases Used:** Biosis; Current Contents; Medline **Loan:** Internationally **Service:** Internationally **Photocopy:** Yes

2897 Jönköping, Sweden
Swedish Board of Agriculture
Forestry and Agriculture Library
Vallgatan 8
SE 551 82 Jönköping
Phone: +46(36) 155171 **Fax:** +46(36) 150082 **WWW:**
www.sjv.se

Non-English Name: Statens jordbruksvsrk (SJV), Skogs- och jordbruksbiblioteket **Founded:** 1975 **Type:** Government **Head:** Inga Hedström **Phone:** +46(36) 155171 **Email:** inga.hedstrom@sjv.se **Staff:** 1 Prof. 1 Other **Holdings:** 400 journals 25,000 books **Language of Collection/Services:** Swedish / Swedish **Subjects:** Comprehensive **Loan:** Internationally **Service:** Internationally **Photocopy:** Yes

2898 Malmö, Sweden
Danisco Sugar AB
Biblioteket
SE 205 04 Malmö
Location: Sockerbruksgatan, Arlov **Fax:** +46(40) 436717
Email: sven.eric.zethson@danisco.com **WWW:** www.
danisco.sugar.se

Former Name: Sockerbolaget AB **Founded:** 1933 **Type:** Business **Head:** Sven Eric Zethson **Phone:** +46(40) 537000 **Email:** sven.eric.zethson@danisco.com **Staff:** 1 Prof. **Holdings:** 5,000 books 400 journals **Language of Collection/Services:** Swedish, English / Swedish **Subjects:** Food Sciences **Databases Developed:** STID - references, including abstracts, to articles about sweetners **Databases Used:** Comprehensive **Loan:** Internationally **Photocopy:** Yes

2899 Skara, Sweden
Swedish University of Agricultural Sciences
Skara Veterinary Library
PO Box 234
SE 532 23 Skara
Location: The Veterinary Institution **Phone:** +46(511)
67240 **Fax:** +46(511) 67243 **Email:** veterinarbiblioteket@
bibsk.slu.se **WWW:** www.bib.slu.se **OPAC:** lukas.slu.se:
1600/ALEPH

Non-English Name: Sveriges Lantbruksuniversitet (SLU), Skara Veterinärbibliotek **Type:** Academic **Head:** Beata Akersten **Phone:** +46(511) 67240 **Email:** beata.akersten@ bibsk.slu.se **Staff:** 1 Prof. 1 Other **Holdings:** 8,300 books 200 journals **Language of Collection/Services:** English, Swedish **Subjects:** Animal Husbandry, Veterinary Medicine **Specializations:** Veterinary Medicine (History) **Loan:** Internationally **Service:** Internationally **Photocopy:** Yes

2900 Stockholm, Sweden
Ministry of Agriculture
Library
SE 103 33 Stockholm
Location: Drottninggatan 21 **Phone:** +46(8) 763-1115
Fax: +46(8) 206496 **WWW:** jordbruk.regeringen.se

Non-English Name: Jordbruksdepartementet, Biblioteket **Founded:** 1970 **Type:** Government **Head:** Christina Hedman **Phone:** +46(8) 763-1115 **Staff:** 2 Prof. **Holdings:** 6,000 books 325 journals **Language of Collection/Services:** Swedish **Subjects:** Agribusiness, Agricultural Development, Agricultural Economics, Agricultural Engineering, Animal Husbandry, Biotechnology, Crops, Education/Extension, Farming, Fisheries, Food Sciences, Forestry, Horticulture, Reindeer, Soil Science, Veterinary Medicine, Water Resources **Specializations:** European Communities Directory **Databases Developed:** RKBIBL - database between the Ministries libraries **Loan:** Inhouse **Photocopy:** Yes

2901   Stockholm, Sweden
Royal Swedish Academy of Agriculture and
      Forestry
Library
Box 6806
SE 113 86 Stockholm

Location: Drottninggatan 95 B **Phone:** +46(8) 300708 **Fax:** +46(8) 335377 **Email:** kslab@ksla.se **WWW:** www.kslab.ksla.se

Non-English Name: Kungl. Skogs- och Lantbruksakademien (KSLA), Biblioteket **Former Name:** Royal Swedish Academy of Agriculture, Kungl. Lantbruksakademien **Founded:** 1813 **Type:** Research **Head:** Lars Ljunggren *Phone:* +46(8) 300708 *Email:* lars.ljunggren@ksla.se **Staff:** 3 Prof. **Holdings:** 90,000 books 400 journals **Language of Collection/Services:** Swedish, English, German, French / Swedish, English **Subjects:** Agriculture (History), Agriculture (Sweden), Forestry (History) **Specializations:** Runs the Academy's historical archive and publishes the index to books in the history of agriculture and forestry **Networks:** LIBRIS **Databases Used:** LIBRIS **Loan:** Internationally **Service:** Internationally **Photocopy:** Yes

2902   Stockholm, Sweden
Swedish Institute for Wood Technology Research
Library
P.O. Box 5609
SE 114 86 Stockholm

Fax: +46(8) 762-1801 **Email:** laila.gunnare@tratek.se **WWW:** www.tratek.se

Non-English Name: Institutet för Träteknisk Forskning (Trätek), Biblioteket **Type:** Association **Head:** Mrs. Laila Gunnare *Phone:* +46(8) 762-1800 *Email:* laila.gunnare@tratek.se **Staff:** 1 Prof. **Holdings:** 6,000 books 150 journals **Language of Collection/Services:** English **Subjects:** Forest Products, Forestry, Structural Engineering **Databases Developed:** TRADOK - Books, research reports, and conference papers in the libraries collection for reference searching on a personal computer **Databases Used:** Comprehensive **Loan:** In country **Service:** In country **Photocopy:** Yes

2903   Svalöv, Sweden
Svalöf Weibull AB (SWAB)
Library
SE 268 81 Svalöv

Phone: +46(418) 667000 **Fax:** +46(418) 667100 **Email:** svalofweibull@swseed.se **WWW:** www.swseed.se

Former Name: Svalöf AB, W Weibull AB **Founded:** 1904 **Type:** Business **Staff:** 1 Prof. 1 Other **Holdings:** 2,800 books 400 journals **Language of Collection/Services:** English/Swedish **Subjects:** Crops **Specializations:** Plant Breeding **Loan:** Do not loan **Service:** Inhouse **Photocopy:** Yes

2904   Umeå, Sweden
Swedish University of Agricultural Sciences
      (SUAS)
Forestry Library
SE 901 83 Umeå

Location: Faculty of Forestry **Phone:** +46(90) 786-5802 **Fax:** +46(90) 786-5925 **Email:** skogsbiblioteket@bibum.slu.se **WWW:** www.bib.slu.se **OPAC:** lukas.slu.se:1600/ALEPH

Non-English Name: Sveriges Lantbruksuniversitet (SLU), Skogsbiblioteket **Former Name:** Skogshögskolan **Founded:** 1918 **Type:** Academic **Head:** Monica Danielsson *Email:* monica.danielsson@bibum.slu.se *Phone:* +46(90) 786-5803 **Staff:** 5 Prof. 2 Other **Holdings:** 110,000 books 1,800 journals **Language of Collection/Services:** Swedish, English / Swedish **Subjects:** Forestry **Loan:** Internationally **Service:** Internationally **Photocopy:** Yes

2905   Uppsala, Sweden
Forestry Research Institute of Sweden
Library
4 Science Park
SE 751 83 Uppsala

Location: Dag Hammarskjölds Väg 36A **Phone:** +46(18) 188500 **Fax:** +46(18) 188600 **Email:** skogforsk@skogforsk.se **WWW:** www.skogforsk.se

Non-English Name: Stiftelsen Skogsbrukets Forskningsinstitut (SkogForsk), Biblioteket **Former Name:** Forest Operations Institute, Forskningsstiftelsen Skogsarbeten **Type:** Association **Founded:** 1964 **Head:** Ingemar Nordansjö *Email:* ingemar.nordansjo@skogforsk.se *Phone:* +46 (18) 188530 **Staff:** 1 Other **Holdings:** 1,200 books 50 journals **Language of Collection/Services:** Swedish / Swedish **Subjects:** Forestry **Specializations:** Forest Management, Forestry Practices, Forest Products Industries, Tree Breeding **Loan:** Inhouse **Service:** Internationally **Photocopy:** Yes

2906   Uppsala, Sweden
Swedish University of Agricultural Sciences
      (SUAS)
Ultuna Library
PO Box 7071
SE 750 07 Uppsala

Location: Undervisningsplan 10 **Phone:** +46(18) 671090 **Fax:** +46(18) 672853 **Email:** infosok@bibul.slu.se **WWW:** www.bib.slu.se **OPAC:** lukas.slu.se:1600/ALEPH

Non-English Name: Sveriges Lantbruksuniversitet (SLU), Ultunabiblioteket **Type:** Academic **Head:** Jan Hagerlid *Phone:* +46(18) 671000 *Email:* jan.hagerlid@bibul.slu.se **Staff:** 31 Prof. 11 Other **Holdings:** 342,400 books 2,200 journals **Language of Collection/Services:** Swedish, English **Subjects:** Comprehensive **Networks:** LIBRIS **Databases Used:** Comprehensive **Loan:** Internationally **Service:** Internationally **Photocopy:** Yes

2907   Uppsala, Sweden
Swedish University of Agricultural Sciences,
      National Veterinary Institute (SUAS)
Veterinary Medical Library
PO Box 7073

S-750 07 Uppsala
Location: Ulls Väg 2 **Phone:** +46(18) 674112 **Fax:** +46
(18) 303239 **Email:** sva-biblioteket@bibul.slu.se **WWW:**
www.sva.se **OPAC:** lukas.slu.se:1600/ALEPH

Non-English Name: Sveriges Lantbruksuniversitet, Statens
Veterinärmedicinska Anstalt (SLU, SVA), Veterinärmedicinska Biblioteket **Founded:** 1911 **Type:** Academic **Head:**
Gunnel Erne *Phone:* +46(18) 674111 *Email:* gunnel.erne@
bibul.slu.se, gunnel.erne@sva.se **Staff:** 2 Prof. 1 Other
Holdings: 27,000 books 540 journals **Language of Collec-
tion/Services:** English, Swedish **Subjects:** Epidemiology,
Food Sciences, Medicine, Microbiology, Pathology, Veterinary Medicine **Databases Used:** Comprehensive **Networks:**
LIBRIS **Loan:** Internationally **Service:** Internationally **Photocopy:** Yes

Switzerland

2908   Bern, Switzerland
Federal Department for Environment, Transport,
Energy and Communication, Federal Office
for the Environment, Forests and Landscape
Library
CH-3003 Bern

Location: Papiermühlestrasse 172, 3063 Ittigen **Phone:**
+41(31) 322 93 15 **Fax:** +41(31) 323 03 46 **Email:** ueli.
tschannen@buwal.admin.ch **WWW:** www.buwal.admin.ch

Non-English Name: Eidgenössisches Departement für Umwelt, Verkehr, Energie und Kommunikation, Bundesamt für
Umwelt, Wald und Landschaft, Département fédéral de
l'Environnement, des Transports, de l'Energie et de la Communication, Office fédéral de l'Environnement, des Forêts et
du Paysage, Dipartimento federale dell'Ambiente, dei Trasporti, dell'Energia e delle Comunicazioni, Ufficio federale
dell'Ambiente, delle Foreste e del Paesaggio (UVEK,
BUWAL, DETEC, OFEFP, DATEC, UFAFP), Bibliothek
Former Name: Bundesamt für Forstwesen und Landschaftsschutz (BFL), Bundesamt für Umweltschutz **Type:**
Government **Head:** Ueli Tschannen *Phone:* +41(31) 322 93
15 *Email:* ueli.tschannen@buwal.admin.ch **Staff:** 1 Prof. 2
Other **Holdings:** 10,000 books 200 journals **Language of
Collection/Services:** German / German **Subjects:** Environ-
mental Protection, Forestry, Nature Conservation **Loan:**
Internationally **Service:** Internationally **Photocopy:** Yes

2909   Bern, Switzerland
Federal Department for Environment, Transport,
Energy and Communication, Federal Office
for the Environment, Forests and Landscape,
Federal Dairy Research Station
Library
Liebefeld
CH-3003 Bern

Location: Schwarzenburgstrasse 161 **Phone:** +41(31) 323-
8162 **Fax:** +41(31) 323-8227 **Email:** info@fam.admin.ch
WWW: www.admin.ch/sar/fam

Non-English Name: Eidgenössisches Departement für Umwelt, Verkehr, Energie und Kommunikation, Bundesamt für
Umwelt, Wald und Landschaft, Eidgenössische Forschungs-

anstalt für Milchwirtschaft, Département fédéral de l'Environnement, des Transports, de l'Energie et de la Communication, Office fédéral de l'Environnement, des Forêts et du
Paysage, Station fédérale de Recherches Laitières, Dipartimento federale dell'Ambiente, dei Trasporti, dell'Energia e
delle Comunicazioni, Dipartimento federale dell'Ambiente,
dei Trasporti, dell'Energia e delle Comunicazioni, Ufficio
federale dell'Ambiente, delle Foreste e del Paesaggio, Stazione di Ricerche Lattiere (UVEK, BUWAL, FAM, DETEC,
OFEFP, DATEC, UFAFP), Bibliothek, Bibliothèque **Type:**
Government **Founded:** 1901 **Head:** Dr. Pierre Lavanchy
Email: pierre.lavanchy@fam.admin.ch Phone: +41(31) 323-
8162 **Holdings:** 6,000 books 170 journals **Language of Col-
lection/Services:** German, English, French / German **Subjects:** Animal Husbandry, Biotechnology, Dairy Industry,
Entomology, Farming, Food Sciences, Veterinary Medicine
Specializations: Dairy Science **Databases Used:** Compre-
hensive **Photocopy:** Yes

2910   Bern, Switzerland
Federal Department of Economics, Federal Office
for Agriculture
Library
Mattenhofstrasse 5
CH-3003 Bern

Phone: +41(31) 322 25 30 **Fax:** +41(31) 322 26 34
WWW: www.blw.admin.ch

Non-English Name: Eidgenössisches Volkswirtschaftsde-
partement, Bundesamt für Landwirtschaft, Departement
fédéral de l'Economique, Office fédéral de l'Agriculture,
Dipartimento federale dell'Economia, Ufficio federale dell'
Agricoltura (EVD, DFE), Bibliothek und Dokumentation
Type: Government **Head:** Andre Megert *Phone:* +41(31)
322 25 30 *Email:* andre.megert@blw.admin.ch **Staff:** 1 Prof.
Holdings: 6,000 books 300 journals **Language of Collec-
tion/Services:** German / German **Subjects:** Agricultural
Economics, Agricultural Engineering, Farming, Law, Politics, Soil Science **Loan:** Inhouse **Service:** Inhouse **Photo-
copy:** No

2911   Bern, Switzerland
Federal Department of Economics, Federal Office
for Agriculture, Federal Research Station for
Agroecology and Agriculture, Institute of
Environmental Protection and Agriculture
Library
Liebefeld
Schwarzenburgstrasse 161
CH-3003 Bern

Phone: +41(31) 323 84 23 **Fax:** +41(31) 323 84 15 **Email:**
judith.kaufmann@iul.admin.ch **WWW:**
www.admin.ch/sar/fal

Non-English Name: Eidgenössisches Volkswirtschaftsdepartement, Bundesamt für Landwirtschaft, Eidgenössische
Forschungsanstalt für Agrarökologie und Landbau, Institut
für Umweltschutz und Landwirtschaft, Departement fédéral
de l'Economique, Office fédéral de l'Agriculture, Station
fédérale de Recherches en Agroécologie et Agriculture,
Institut de Recherches en Protection de l'Environnement et
en Agriculture, Dipartimento federale dell'Economia, Ufficio federale dell'Agricoltura, Stazione federale di Ricerche

in Agroecologia e Agricoltura, Instituto per la Protezione dell'Ambiente e per l'Agricultura (EVD, BLW, FAL, IUL, DFE), Bibliothek, Bibliothèque **Former Name:** Swiss Federal Research Station for Agricultural Chemistry and Hygiene of Environment, Eidgenössische Forschungsanstalt für Agrikulturchemie und Umwelthygiene (FAC), Station fédérale de Recherches en Chimie Agricole et sur l'Hygiène de l'Environnement **Founded:** 1897 **Type:** Government **Head:** Mrs. Judith Kaufmann Chassot *Phone:* +41(31) 323 84 23 *Email:* judith.kaufmann@iul.admin.ch **Staff:** 1 Prof. **Holdings:** 5,000 books 60 journals **Language of Collection/Services:** German / German **Subjects:** Agricultural Chemistry, Air Pollution, Environment, Soil Science, Water **Loan:** Internationally **Photocopy:** Yes

2912   Birmensdorf, Switzerland
         Federal Department of the Interior, Group for
            Science and Research, Federal Institute for
            Forest, Snow and Landscape Research
         Library
         CH-8903 Birmensdorf
Location: Zürcherstrasse 111 **Phone:** +41(1) 739-2380 **Fax:** +41(1) 739-2215 **Email:** bibliothek@wsl.ch **WWW:** www.nebis.ch **OPAC:** ethio3270.eth2.ch/cgi/HEstartN?

Non-English Name: Eidgenössisches Departement des Inneren, Gruppe für Wissenschaft und Forschung, Eidgenössische Forschungsanstalt für Wald, Schnee und Landschaft, Département fédéral de l'Interieur, Groupement de la Science et de la Recherche, Institut fédéral de Recherches sur la Forêt, la Niege et le Paysage, Dipartimento federale dell' Interno, Gruppo della Scienza e dell Ricerca, Instituto federale di Ricerca per la Foresta, la Neve e il Paesaggio (EDI, GWF, WSL, DFI, GSR, FNP), Bibliothek **Former Name:** Swiss Federal Institute of Forestry Research, Eidgenössische Anstalt für das forstliche Versuchswesen (EAFV), Schweizerische (Centraal-) Anstalt für das forstliche Versuchsween **Founded:** 1908 **Type:** Academic **Head:** *Phone:* +41(1) 739-2207, 739-2111 **Staff:** 3 Prof. 1 Other **Holdings:** 8,500 books 739 journals **Language of Collection/Services:** German/German **Subjects:** Entomology, Forestry, Plant Pathology, Plant Protection, Soil Science, Water Resources **Specializations:** Environment, Landscaping **Databases Developed:** "Landscape-related database" and "National forest inventory" **Loan:** Internationally **Service:** Internationally **Photocopy:** Yes

2913   Brugg, Switzerland
         Swiss Farmers' Union
         Library and Documentation Service
         Laurstrasse 10
         CH-5200 Brugg
Fax: +41(56) 441 53 48 **Email:** gakuba@agri.ch, mayr@agri.ch **WWW:** www.bauernverband.ch

Non-English Name: Schweizerischer Bauernverband (SBV), Bibliothek und Dokumentation **Founded:** 1897 **Type:** Association **Head:** Dr. Michel Gakuba / Rosmarie Mayr *Phone:* +41(56) 462 51 11 *Email:* gakuba@agri.ch, mayr@agri.ch **Staff:** 2 Prof. **Holdings:** 70,000 books 500 journals **Language of Collection/Services:** German, English, French, Italian **Subjects:** Agricultural Law, Agricultural Economics, Alternative Farming, Ecology, Politics,

Environment, Politics, Rural Law, Rural Planning, Rural Sociology **Loan:** Internationally **Service:** Internationally **Photocopy:** Yes

2914   Frick, Switzerland
         Research Institute of Organic Agriculture
         Library
         CH-5070 Frick
Phone: +41(62) 865 72 72 **Fax:** +41(62) 865 72 73 **Email:** admin@fibl.ch **WWW:** www.fibl.ch

Non-English Name: Forschungsinstitut für Biologischen Landbau (FiBL), Bibliothek **Founded:** 1974 **Type:** Non-government **Head:** Anne Merz *Phone:* +41(62) 865 72 72 *Email:* admin@fibl.ch **Staff:** 1 Prof. **Holdings:** 3,000 books 175 journals **Language of Collection/Services:** German / German, English, French **Subjects:** Agricultural Development, Agricultural Economics, Biological Control, Crop Production, Education/Extension, Ecology, Horticulture, Landscape, Plant Pathology, Soil Science, Veterinary Medicine **Specializations:** Organic Farming **Databases Used:** Agris; Biosis; CABCD **Photocopy:** Yes

2915   Nyon, Switzerland
         Federal Department of Economics, Federal Office
            for Agriculture, Federal Research Station for
            Plant Production
         Bibliothèque
         Route de Duillier
         PO Box 254
         CH-1260 Nyon 1
Phone: +41(22) 363-4444 **Fax:** +41(22) 362-1325 **Email:** rac@rac.admin.ch **WWW:** www.admin.ch/sar/rac

Non-English Name: Eidgenössisches Volkswirtschaftsdepartement, Bundesamt für Landwirtschaft, Eidgenössische Forschungsanstalt für Pflanzenbau, Departement fédéral de l'Economique, Office fédéral de l'Agriculture, Station fédérale de Recherches en Production Végétale, Dipartimento federale dell'Economia, Ufficio federale dell' Agricultura, Stazione federale di Ricerche per la Produzione Vegetale (EVD, BLW, DFE) **Former Name:** Station fédérale de Recherches Agronomiques de Changins (RAC) **Type:** Government **Head:** A. Maillard *Phone:* +41(22) 363-4153 *Email:* andre.maillard@rac.admin.ch **Staff:** 1 Prof. 2 Other **Holdings:** 20,000 books **Subjects:** Arboriculture, Biology, Entomology, Horticulture, Viticulture **Loan:** In country **Photocopy:** Yes

2916   Posieux, Switzerland
         Federal Department of Economics, Federal Office
            for Agriculture, Federal Research Station for
            Animal Production (RAP)
         Library and Documentation
         CH-1725 Posieux
Fax: +41(26) 407 73 00 **Email:** gerhard.mangold@rap.admin.ch **WWW:** www.admin.ch/sar/rap

Non-English Name: Eidgenössisches Volkswirtschaftsdepartement, Bundesamt für Landwirtschaft, Eidgenössische Forschungsanstalt für Nutztiere, Departement fédéral de l'Economique, Office fédéral de l'Agriculture, Station fédérale de Recherches en Production Animale, Dipartimento federale dell'Economia, Ufficio federale dell'Agricoltura, Stazione federale di Ricerche per la Produzione Animale (EVD, BLW, DFE), Bibliothek und Dokumentation **Founded:** 1974 **Type:** Government **Head:** Gerhard Mangold *Phone:* +41(26) 407 71 11 *Email:* gerhard. mangold@rap. admin.ch **Staff:** 2 Prof. **Holdings:** 10,000 books 250 journals **Language of Collection/Services:** German / German, English, French **Subjects:** Animal Feeding, Animal Husbandry, Animal Nutrition, Crops, Veterinary Medicine **Loan:** In country **Service:** In country **Photocopy:** Yes

2917 Tänikon, Switzerland

Federal Department of Economics, Federal Office for Agriculture, Federal Research Station for Agricultural Economics and Engineering
Library and Documentation
CH-8356 Tänikon

Phone: +41(52) 368 31 31 **Fax:** +41(52) 365 11 90 **Email:** info@fat.admin.ch **WWW:** www.admin.ch/sar/fat

Non-English Name: Eidgenössisches Volkswirtschaftsdepartement, Bundesamt für Landwirtschaft, Eidgenössische Forschungsanstalt für Agrarwirtschaft und Landtechnik, Departement fédéral de l'Economique, Office fédéral de l'Agriculture, Station fédérale de Recherches en Economie et Technologie Agricoles, Dipartimento federale dell' Economia, Ufficio federale dell'Agricoltura, Stazione federale di Ricerche in Economia e Tecnologia Agricole (EVD, BLW, DFE, FAT), Bibliothek und Dokumentation **Former Name:** Swiss Federal Station for Farm Management and Agricultural Engineering, Eidgenössische Forschungsanstalt für Betriebswirtschaft und Landtechnik **Founded:** 1969 **Type:** Government **Head:** Dr. Louis Hürlimann *Phone:* +41(52) 368 31 31 *Email:* louis.huerlimann@fat.admin.ch **Staff:** 1 Prof. 1 Other **Holdings:** 4,000 books 150 journals **Language of Collection/Services:** German **Subjects:** Agricultural Economics, Agricultural Engineering, Animal Husbandry **Networks:** AGRIS **Databases Used:** Agricola; Agris; CABCD **Loan:** Inhouse **Service:** Inhouse **Photocopy:** Yes

2918 Wädenswil, Switzerland

Federal Department of Economics, Federal Office for Agriculture, Federal Research Station for Fruit-Growing, Viticulture and Horticulture
Library
Schloss
CH-8820 Wädenswil

Phone: +41(1) 783-6219 **Fax:** +41(1) 780-6341 **WWW:** www.admin.ch/sar/faw

Non-English Name: Eidgenössisches Volkswirtschaftsdepartement, Bundesamt für Landwirtschaft, Eidgenössische Forschungsanstalt für Obst-, Wein- und Gartenbau, Departement fédéral de l'Economique, Office fédéral de l'Agriculture, Station fédérale de Recherches en Arboriculture, Viticulture et Horticulture, Dipartimento federale dell' Economia, Ufficio federale dell'Agricoltura, Stazione federale di Ricerche in Frutticoltura, Viticoltura e Orticoltura (EVD, BLW, DFE, FAW), Bibliothek **Former Name:** Eidgenössische Veruchsanstalt für Obst-, Wein- und Gartenbau **Founded:** 1890 **Type:** Government **Staff:** 1 Prof. **Hold-**

ings: 11,050 books 550 journals **Language of Collection/Services:** German, English / German, English, French, Italian **Subjects:** Agricultural Economics, Crops, Food Sciences, Plants, Soil Science **Specializations:** Entomology, Fruit Growing, Horticulture, Plant Pathology **Loan:** Internationally **Service:** In country **Photocopy:** Yes

2919 Wädenswil, Switzerland

University of Applied Sciences
Library
Gruental
PO Box 335
CH-8820 Wädenswil

Phone: +41(1) 789 99 00 **Fax:** +41(1) 789 99 50 **Email:** bibliothek@hswzfh.ch **WWW:** www.hswzfh.ch

Non-English Name: Hochschule Wädenswil (HSW), Bibliothek **Former Name:** Ingenieurschule Wädenswil (ISW) **Type:** Academic **Head:** Rosmarie Schwager *Phone:* +41(1) 789 99 99 *Email:* r.schwager@hswzfh.ch **Staff:** 2 Prof. **Holdings:** 8,000 books 200 journals **Language of Collection/Services:** German / German **Subjects:** Arboriculture, Biotechnology, Ecology, Enology, Food Sciences, Horticulture, Viticulture **Networks:** ETHICSplus **Loan:** Inhouse **Service:** Inhouse **Photocopy:** Yes

2920 Zollikofen, Switzerland

Swiss College of Agriculture (SCA)
Library
Länggasse 85
CH-3052 Zollikofen

Phone: +41(31) 910-2111 **Fax:** +41(31) 910-2299 **WWW:** www.shl.bfh.ch/homefranz.htm

Non-English Name: Schweizerische Hochschule für Landwirtschaft, Haute école suisse d'agronomie (SHL, HESA), Bibliothek **Type:** Academic **Staff:** 20 Prof. 30 Other **Holdings:** 13,000 books 90 journals **Language of Collection/Services:** German / German **Subjects:** Agriculture (Tropics), Agribusiness, Agricultural Development, Agricultural Economics, Agricultural Engineering, Animal Husbandry, Crops, Entomology, Plant Pathology, Plants, Soil Science **Databases Used:** Agris **Loan:** Inhouse **Service:** Inhouse **Photocopy:** Yes

2921 Zürich, Switzerland

Federal Department for Environment, Transport, Energy and Communication, Federal Office for the Environment, Forests and Landscape, Swiss Agency for the Environment, Forests and Landscape
Swiss Wildlife Information Service (SWIS)
Strickhofstrasse 39
CH-8057 Zürich

Fax: +41(1) 635 68 19 **Email:** wild@wild.unizh.ch **WWW:** www.wild.unizh.ch

Non-English Name: Eidgenössisches Departement für Umwelt, Verkehr, Energie und Kommunikation, Bundesamt für Umwelt, Wald und Landschaft, Département fédéral de l'Environnement, des Transports, de l'Energie et de la Communication, Office fédéral de l'Environnement, des Forêts et du Paysage, Dipartimento federale dell'Ambiente, dei Tras-

dell'Ambiente, delle Foreste e del Paesaggio (UVEK, BU-WAL, DETEC, OFEFP, DATEC, UFAFP), Schweizerische Dokumentationsstelle für Wildforschung **Founded:** 1971 **Type:** Academic **Head:** Christa Mosler *Phone:* +41(1) 635 61 31 *Email:* wild@wild.unizh.ch **Staff:** 3 Prof. 2 Other **Holdings:** 85,000 books 500 journals **Language of Collection/Services:** English / English, German **Subjects:** Forestry **Specializations:** Wildlife **Networks:** NISC Wildlife Worldwide **Databases Used:** Wildlife Worldwide **Loan:** In country **Service:** Internationally **Photocopy:** Yes

2922 Zürich, Switzerland
Federal Department of Economics, Federal Office for Agriculture, Federal Research Station for Agroecology and Agriculture
Library
Reckenholzstrasse 191
CH-8046 Zürich
Fax: +41(1) 377 72 01 **WWW:** www.admin.ch/sar/fal

Non-English Name: Eidgenössisches Volkswirtschaftsdepartement, Bundesamt für Landwirtschaft, Eidgenössische Forschungsanstalt für Agrarökologie und Landbau, Departement fédéral de l'Economique, Office fédéral de l'Agriculture, Station Fédérale de Recherches en Agroécologie et Agriculture, Dipartimento federale dell'Economia, Ufficio federale dell'Agricoltura, Stazione Federale di Ricerche in Agroecologia e Agricoltura (EVD, BLW, FAL, DFE), Bibliothek **Former Name:** Swiss Federal Research Station for Agronomy, Eidgenössische Forschungsanstalt für Landw. Pflanzenbau **Founded:** 1878 **Type:** Government **Head:** Mrs. Dr. Regina Schallberger *Email:* regina.schallberger@fal.admin.ch *Phone:* +41(1) 377-7111 **Staff:** 1.5 Prof. **Holdings:** 6,000 books 280 journals **Language of Collection/Services:** German / German **Subjects:** Comprehensive **Specializations:** Air Pollution, Climatology, Farming Systems, Ecotoxicology, Field Crops, Grasslands, Landscape Ecology, Plant Breeding, Soil Conservation, Water Conservation **Databases Developed:** Slide collection of 2000 slides; accessible inhouse **Databases Used:** Comprehensive **Loan:** Internationally **Service:** Internationally **Photocopy:** Yes

2923 Zürich, Switzerland
Swiss Federal Institute of Technology Zurich
Library
Rämistrasse 101
CH-8092 Zürich
Phone: +41(1) 632-2135 **Fax:** +41(1) 632-1357 **Email:** info@library.ethz.ch **WWW:** www.ethz.ch **OPAC:** www.nebis.ch/WebOPAC.html

Non-English Name: Eidgenössische Technische Hochschule Zürich (ETH), Bibliothek **Founded:** 1855 **Type:** Academic **Head:** Dr. Wolfram Neubauer *Phone:* +41(1) 632-2549 *Email:* neubauer@library.ethz.ch **Holdings:** 100,000 books 4,000 journals **Staff:** 160 Prof. **Subjects:** Agriculture (Tropics), Agribusiness, Agricultural Development, Agricultural Economics, Agricultural Engineering, Animal Husbandry, Biotechnology, Education/Extension, Entomology, Crops, Farming, Fisheries, Food Sciences, Forestry, Horticulture, Plant Pathology, Soil Science, Veterinary Medicine, Water Resources **Loan:** Internationally **Photocopy:** Yes

2924 Zürich, Switzerland
Swiss Federal Institute of Technology Zurich, Department of Forest and Wood Sciences
Forestry Library
ETH-Zentrum
CH-8092 Zürich
Location: Rämistrasse 101 **Fax:** +41(1) 632 11 27 **WWW:** www.ethz.ch **OPAC:** www.nebis.ch/WebOPAC.html

Non-English Name: Eidgenössische Technische Hochschule Zürich, Departement Wald- und Holzforschung (ETH), Forstbibliothek **Former Name:** Abteilung für Forstwirtschaft, Handbibliothek der Abteilung für Forstwirtschaft **Founded:** 1855 **Type:** Academic **Head:** Mrs. Rosmarie Louis *Phone:* +41(1) 632 32 09 *Email:* louis@waho.ethz.ch **Staff:** 1 Prof. 1 Other **Holdings:** 14,000 books 550 journals **Language of Collection/Services:** German, English, French /German, English, French **Subjects:** Forestry **Specializations:** Deer, Forest Ecology, Silviculture **Loan:** In country **Networks:** ETHICS **Photocopy:** Yes

2925 Zürich, Switzerland
University of Zürich, Faculty of Veterinary Medicine
Library
Winterthurerstr. 260
CH-8057 Zürich
Phone: +41(1) 356-1321 **Fax:** +41(1) 356-1323 **WWW:** www.unizh.ch

Non-English Name: Universität Zürich, Veterinär-medizinische Fakultät, Bibliothek **Type:** Academic **Staff:** 1 Prof. **Holdings:** 180 journals **Subjects:** Veterinary Medicine **Photocopy:** Yes **Loan:** In country

Syria

2926 Aleppo, Syria
International Center for Agricultural Research in the Dry Areas (ICARDA)
Library and Information Services (LIS)
PO Box 5466
Aleppo
Phone: +963(21) 235221, 213433 **Fax:** +963(21) 425105 **Email:** icarda@cgiar.org **WWW:** www.icarda.org

Founded: 1977 **Type:** International **Head:** Mr. Nick Maliha *Phone:* +963(21) 213433 ext 375 *Email:* n.maliha@cgiar.org **Staff:** 1 Prof. 6 Other **Holdings:** 14,000 books 160 journals **Language of Collection/Services:** English / English, Arabic **Subjects:** Agricultural Development, Agricultural Economics, Agricultural Engineering, Animal Husbandry, Biotechnology, Crops, Education/Extension, Entomology, Farming, Plant Pathology, Soil Science, Water Resources **Specializations:** Barley, Faba Beans, Fodder Crops, Lentils, Wheat **Databases Used:** Comprehensive **Loan:** In country **Service:** Internationally **Photocopy:** Yes

2927 Damascus, Syria
Arab Center for the Studies of Arid Zones and Dry Lands (ACSAD)

Library
PO Box 2440
Damascus

Phone: +963(11) 755-713/4 **Fax:** +963(11) 755-712

Founded: 1971 **Subjects:** Arid Zones, Deserts, Dry Lands

2928   Damascus, Syria
Damascus University
Central Library
Damascus

WWW: www.nyu.edu/rectors/damas.html

Type: Academic **Staff:** 5 Prof. 20 Other **Holdings:** 4,000 books **Subjects:** Animal Husbandry, Dairy Industry, Farm Machinery, Farming, Field Crops, Forestry, Horticulture, Plant Disorders, Poultry, Veterinary Medicine **Loan:** Do not loan

2929   Damascus, Syria
Ministry of Agriculture and Agrarian Reform
    (MAAR)
National Center for Agricultural Information and
    Documentation (NCAID)
PO Box 31570
Al Abed Street - Saba Bahrat
Damascus

Phone: +963(11) 224-4729 ext 267 **Fax:** +963(11) 224-7542

Founded: 1988 **Type:** Government **Head:** Dr. Nahi Al Sheibani *Phone:* +963(11) 224-4729 ext 260 **Staff:** 8 Prof. 4 Other **Language of Collection/Services:** Arabic / Arabic **Networks:** AGRIS **Databases Used:** Agricola; Agris **Loan:** Inhouse **Service:** Internationally **Photocopy:** Yes

Taiwan

2930   Chia-yi, Taiwan
National Chia-yi Institute of Technology (NCIT)
Library
300 University Road
Chia-yi 600

Phone: +886(5) 276-6141 ext 225 **Fax:** +886(5) 277-9106
Email: hsust@rice.cit.edu.tw **WWW:** www.cit.edu.tw

Former Name: National Chia-yi Institute of Technology **Founded:** 1921 **Type:** Academic **Head:** Tsai-mu Shen *Phone:* +886(5) 276-6141 ext 225 *Email:* tmshen@rice.cit.edu.tw **Staff:** 7 Prof. 6 Other **Holdings:** 10,000 books 290 journals **Language of Collection/Services:** Chinese, English, Japanese / Chinese, English, Japanese **Subjects:** Comprehensive **Databases Used:** Agricola; Agris **Loan:** In country **Service:** Inhouse **Photocopy:** Yes

2931   Chia-yi, Taiwan
Taiwan Agricultural Research Institute, Chia-yi
    Agricultural Experiment Station (TARI,
    CAES)
2 Min-Cheng Road
Chia-yi 600

Phone: +886(5) 277-1341 ext 127 **Fax:** +886(5) 277-3630
Email: caes76@mail.ttn.com.tw **WWW:** www.tari.gov.tw
OPAC: www.tari.gov.tw

Founded: 1984 **Type:** Government **Head:** Yung-Hsiung Cheng *Phone:* +886(5) 277-1341 *Email:* caes76@mail.ttn.com.tw **Staff:** 1 Other **Holdings:** 7,500 books 60 journals **Language of Collection/Services:** Chinese, English, Japanese/Chinese, English, Japanese **Subjects:** Agriculture (Tropics), Agricultural Development, Entomology, Horticulture, Crops, Plant Pathology **Specializations:** Agronomy, Diseases, Functional Disorders, Growth, Pests, Nitrogen Fixation, Varietal Resistance, Varieties **Loan:** Inhouse **Service:** In country **Photocopy:** Yes

2932   Chiuju, Taiwan
Taiwan Banana Research Institute (TBRI)
Library
PO Box 18
Chiuju, Pingtung 904

Phone: +886(8) 739-2111/3 **Fax:** +886(8) 739-0595
Email: tbri@ksts.seed.net.tw

Founded: 1976 **Type:** Research **Head:** Shih Mei-Hsiu *Phone:* +886 (8) 739-2111 *Email:* tbri@ksts.seed.net.tw **Staff:** 1 Prof. 1 Other **Holdings:** 2,580 books 40 journals **Language of Collection/Services:** Chinese / Chinese **Subjects:** Agriculture (Tropics), Entomology, Farming, Horticulture, Plant Breeding, Plant Pathology **Photocopy:** Yes

2933   Chunan, Taiwan
Pig Research Institute Taiwan (PRIT)
Library
PO Box 23
Chunan, Miaoli 35099

Phone: +886(5) 767-2352 ext 260 **Fax:** +886(5) 766-0104
Email: library@mail.prit.org.tw **WWW:** www.prit.org.tw
OPAC: telnet://202.39.232.1

Founded: 1970 **Type:** Research **Head:** En-Chung Lin *Phone:* +886(3) 767-2352 ext 265, 260 *Email:* clin@mail.prit.org.tw **Staff:** 1 Prof. **Holdings:** 4,000 books 90 journals **Language of Collection/Services:** English / Chinese, English **Subjects:** Animal Husbandry, Veterinary Medicine **Databases Used:** Agricola; Medline **Loan:** In country **Service:** In country **Photocopy:** Yes

2934   Chungli, Taiwan
Agricultural Engineering Research Center
    (AERC)
Agricultural Engineering Technical Information
    Center (AETIC)
196-1, Chun-Yuan Rd.
Chungli 320

Phone: +886(3) 452-1314 **Fax:** +886(3) 452-6583 **Email:** aerccom@ms8.hinet.net **WWW:** www.aerc.org.tw

Founded: 1971 **Type:** Academic **Head:** Lan-Hsiang Chen *Phone:* +886(3) 452-1314 ext 222 *Email:* chenlany@aerc.org.tw **Staff:** 1 Prof. **Holdings:** 5,500 books 61 journals **Language of Collection/Services:** Chinese / Chinese **Subjects:** Agricultural Development, Soil Science, Education/Extension, Farming, Fisheries, Water Resources **Specializa-**

tions: Agricultural Engineering **Loan:** Inhouse **Service:** Inhouse **Photocopy:** No

2935   Hsinhua, Taiwan
Taiwan Livestock Research Institute (TLRI)
Library
112 Muchang
Hsinhua, Tainan 712
Phone: +886(6) 591-1211 ext 258 **Fax:** +886(6) 591-2452
Email: pdaf0302@mail.tpg.gov.tw **WWW:**
www.tpg.gov.tw/tlri/tlri.htm

Founded: 1958 **Type:** Government **Head:** C.C. Cheng
Phone: +886(6) 591-1211 ext 255 *Email:* pdaf0302@mail.
tpg.gov.tw **Staff:** 1 Prof. 3 Other **Holdings:** 2,650 books 200
journals **Language of Collection/Services:** English, Chinese, Japanese / Chinese **Subjects:** Biotechnology, Animal
Husbandry, Fodder Crops, Extension **Specializations:** Animal Production **Loan:** Inhouse **Service:** In country **Photocopy:** Yes

2936   I-Lan, Taiwan
National I-Lan Institute of Technology (NIIT)
Library
1, Shen-Lung Road
I-Lan 26015
Phone: +886(3) 935-7400 **Fax:** +886(3) 935-2419 **Email:**
kshuang@mail.ilantech.edu.tw **WWW:** www.ilantech.edu.
tw **OPAC:** libnt.ilantech.edu.tw/lib/index.html

Former Name: National I-Lan Institute of Agriculture and
Technology **Founded:** 1988 **Type:** Academic **Head:** K.S.
Huang *Phone:* +886(3) 935-7400 ext 310 *Email:* kshuang@
mail.ilantech.edu.tw **Staff:** 4 Prof. 3 Other **Holdings:** 88,000
books 839 journals **Language of Collection/Services:** Chinese, English, Japanese / Chinese **Subjects:** Agricultural
Economics, Agricultural Engineering, Animal Husbandry,
Food Sciences, Forestry, Horticulture **Networks:** STICNET
Databases Used: Agricola; Biosis; FSTA **Loan:** In country
Service: In country **Photocopy:** Yes

2937   Kaohsiung, Taiwan
Taiwan Agricultural Research Institute (TARI)
Fengshan Tropical Horticultural Experiment
    Station
Fengshan
Kaohsiung 83017
Phone: +886(7) 731-0191 **Fax:** +886(7) 731-5590 **Email:**
fth111@ms4.hinet.net **WWW:** www.tari.gov.tw

Founded: 1940 **Type:** Government **Head:** Liou Tsung Dao
Phone: +886(7) 731-0191 *Email:* fth111@ms4.hinet.net
Staff: 30 Prof. 7 Other **Holdings:** 3,200 books 20 journals
Language of Collection/Services: Chinese / Chinese, English **Subjects:** Agriculture (Tropics), Biotechnology, Crops,
Education/Extension, Entomology, Food Sciences, Plant Pathology, Soil Science, Water Resources **Specializations:**
Horticulture **Loan:** Inhouse **Service:** Internationally **Photocopy:** Yes

2938   Keelung, Taiwan
National Taiwan Ocean University (NTOU)
Library

2 Pei Ning Road
Keelung 202
Phone: +886(2) 2462-2192 ext 1189 **Fax:** +886(2) 2462-
4651 **Email:** jenny@www.lib.ntou.edu.tw **WWW:** www.
lib.ntou.edu.tw **OPAC:** 140.121.140.5

Former Name: National Taiwan College of Marine Science
and Technology (NTCMST) **Founded:** 1964 **Type:** Academic **Head:** Yang Wen-Bin *Phone:* +886(2) 2462-2192 ext
1180 *Email:* yang@ntoubb.ntou.edu.tw **Holdings:** 195,804
books 1,815 journals **Staff:** 6 Prof. 6 Other **Language of
Collection/Services:** English, Chinese, Japanese, German /
Chinese, English **Subjects:** Aquaculture, Fisheries, Food
Sciences **Specializations:** Marine Engineering, Marine
Technology **Networks:** IDS; OCLC; STICNET **Databases
Used:** Comprehensive **Loan:** Internationally **Service:** Internationally **Photocopy:** Yes

2939   Keelung, Taiwan
Taiwan Fisheries Research Institute (TFRI)
Library
199 Hou-Ih Road
Keelung 202
Phone: +886(2) 2462-2101 ext 2513 **Fax:** +886(2) 2462-
9388 **Email:** tfrilib@mail.tfrin.gov.tw **WWW:** www.tfrin.
gov.tw

Founded: 1952 **Type:** Academic **Head:** Dr. I-Chiu Liao
Phone: +886(2) 2462-2101 *Email:* icliao@mail.tfrin.gov.tw
Staff: 1 Prof. 1 Other **Holdings:** 20,000 books 120 journals
Language of Collection/Services: Chinese, Japanese, English / Chinese **Subjects:** Aquaculture, Marine Technology,
Fisheries, Food Sciences **Networks:** IDS; STICNET **Databases Used:** Comprehensive **Loan:** Internationally **Service:**
Internationally **Photocopy:** Yes

2940   Kung-Kuan, Taiwan
Taiwan Miaoli District Agricultural Improvement
    Station (TMDAIS)
Library
261 Kuan-nan
Kung-Kuan, Miaoli 307
Phone: +886(37) 222111 **Fax:** +886(37) 221277 **Email:**
mldais04@mail.tpg.gov.tw

Former Name: Taiwan Agricultural and Sericultural Experiment Station (TASES) **Founded:** 1984 **Type:** Government
Head: Liou Shin-Miau *Phone:* +886(37) 222111 *Email:*
mldais08@mail.tpg.gov.tw **Staff:** 1 Prof. 1 Other **Holdings:**
5,000 books 60 journals **Language of Collection/Services:**
Chinese, English, Japanese / Chinese, English **Subjects:** Entomology **Specializations:** Beekeeping, Sericulture **Loan:**
In country **Service:** In country **Photocopy:** Yes

2941   Pingtung, Taiwan
National Pingtung University of Science and
    Technology (NPUST)
Yuh-Gang Memento Library
1, Hsueh Fu Road
Nei-pu Hsiang Pingtung
Pingtung, Shiann 91207
Phone: +886(8) 770-3202 ext 7213 **Fax:** +886(8) 774-
0149 **WWW:** www.nppi.edu.tw **OPAC:** 140.127.23.2

Former Name: National Pingtung Institute of Agriculture, National Pingtung Polytechnic Institute (NPPI) **Founded:** 1954 **Type:** Academic **Head:** Liou Rong Jye *Phone:* +886(8) 770-3202 ext 7260 *Email:* ldhwang@mail.npust. edu.tw **Staff:** 5 Prof. 5 Other **Holdings:** 169,370 books 720 journals **Language of Collection/Services:** Chinese / Chinese **Subjects:** Agriculture (Tropics), Agribusiness, Agricultural Development, Agricultural Economics, Agricultural Engineering, Animal Husbandry, Biotechnology, Crops, Education/Extension, Entomology, Farming, Fisheries, Food Sciences, Forestry, Horticulture, Plant Pathology, Soil Science, Veterinary Medicine, Water Resources **Databases Used:** Agricola **Loan:** In country **Service:** In country **Photocopy:** Yes

2942 Pingtung, Taiwan
Taiwan Fisheries Research Institute, Tungkang
Marine Laboratory
Library
Tungkang
Pingtung 928
Phone: +886(8) 832-4121 **Fax:** +886(8) 832-0234 **WWW:** www.tfrin.gov.tw

Type: Government **Head:** Mao-Sen Su *Phone:* +886(8) 832-4121 ext 211 **Staff:** 1 Prof. 2 Other **Holdings:** 1,460 books 200 journals **Language of Collection/Services:** Chinese, English / Chinese, English **Subjects:** Aquaculture **Loan:** In country **Service:** In country **Photocopy:** Yes

2943 Shanhua, Taiwan
Asian Vegetable Research and Development
Center (AVRDC)
Information and Documentation
PO Box 42
Shanhua, Tainan 741
Location: 60 I-Men-Liao **Phone:** +886(6) 583-7801/9 ext 531-533 **Fax:** 8866(6) 583-0009, 585-0060 **Email:** avrdcbox@netra.avrdc.org.tw **WWW:** www.avrdc.org.tw **Ariel IP:** 203.64.245.140

Former Name: Library and Documentation Services **Type:** International **Founded:** 1972 **Head:** Teng-Hui Hwang *Phone:* +886(6) 583-7801/9 ext 530 *Email:* thhwang@netra. avrdc.org.tw **Staff:** 5 Prof. **Holdings:** 50,000 books 100 journals **Language of Collection/Services:** English, Chinese, Japanese / English **Subjects:** Agriculture (Tropics), Agricultural Economics, Biotechnology, Crops, Entomology, Food Sciences, Horticulture, Plant Pathology, Soil Science **Specializations:** Cabbages, Capsicum, Mung Beans, Chinese Cabbages, Eggplants, Garlic, Onions, Shallots, Soybeans, Tomatoes, Vegetables (Tropics) **Databases Used:** Agricola; Agris; CABCD **Databases Developed:** Bibliographic, thesaurus, institution, and serials holdings **Loan:** In country **Service:** Internationally **Photocopy:** Yes

2944 Shin-Shieh, Taiwan
Taiwan Seed Improvement and Propagation
Station (TSIPS)
Library
46 Hsing Chung Street
Ta-Nan
Shin-Shieh, Taichung 42603

Fax: +886(4) 581-1577 **WWW:** www.tsips.tpg.gov.tw

Former Name: Taiwan Seed Service (TSS) **Founded:** 1913 **Type:** Government **Head:** Chang Yih-horng *Phone:* +886 (4) 581-1311 **Staff:** 3 Prof. **Holdings:** 6,000 books 120 journals **Language of Collection/Services:** Chinese, English / Chinese, English **Subjects:** Biotechnology, Crops, Horticulture, Plant Pathology, Seeds **Databases Developed:** Seed and seedling production **Loan:** Inhouse **Service:** In country **Photocopy:** Yes

2945 Taichung, Taiwan
National Chung Hsing University (NCHU)
Library
250 Kuo Kuang Road
Taichung 402
Phone: +886(4) 287-3181 ext 293 **Fax:** +886(4) 287-3454 **WWW:** www.lib.nchu.edu.tw **OPAC:** 140.120.80.4

Founded: 1961 **Type:** Academic **Head:** Lin Woei *Phone:* +886(4) 287-3454 **Staff:** 12 Prof. 14 Other **Holdings:** 230,000 books 611 journals **Language of Collection/Services:** Chinese / Chinese **Subjects:** Agricultural Economics, Agricultural Engineering, Animal Husbandry, Biotechnology, Crops, Entomology, Education/Extension, Food Sciences, Forestry, Horticulture, Marketing, Plant Pathology, Soil Conservation, Soil Science, Veterinary Medicine, Water Conservation **Databases Used:** Comprehensive **Loan:** In country **Service:** In country **Photocopy:** Yes

2946 Tainan, Taiwan
Tainan District Agricultural Improvement Station
(Tainan DAIS)
Library
350, Linsen Road, Sect. 1
Tainan 701
Phone: +886(6) 267-9526 ext 207 **Fax:** +886(6) 269-6523 **Email:** tndais@mail.tndais.gov.tw **WWW:** www.tndais. gov.tw

Former Name: Tainan County Agricultural Experiment Station **Founded:** 1945 **Type:** Government **Head:** C.C. Yeh *Phone:* +886(6) 269-6520 *Email:* ccyeh@mail.tndais.gov. tw **Staff:** 1 Prof. **Holdings:** 3,000 books 50 journals **Language of Collection/Services:** Chinese, English / Chinese, English **Subjects:** Agronomy, Biotechnology, Extension, Farm Machinery, Farming, Horticulture, Plant Pathology, Statistics **Service:** In country **Photocopy:** Yes

2947 Taipei, Taiwan
Academia Sinica
Life Science Library
Nankang
Taipei 11529
Phone: +886(2) 2789-9829 **Fax:** +886(2) 2653-5662 **Email:** lsl@gate.sinica.edu.tw **WWW:** www.sinica.edu.tw **OPAC:** las.sinica.edu.tw (140.109.4.14) **Ariel IP:** 140.109. 195.15

Founded: 1996 **Type:** Academic **Head:** Lee Te-Chang *Phone:* +886(2) 2789-9843 *Email:* mbtok@ibms.sinica.edu. tw **Staff:** 8 Prof. 2 Other **Holdings:** 25,000 books 820 journals **Language of Collection/Services:** Chinese, English **Subjects:** Comprehensive **Databases Used:** Comprehensive

Loan: Internationally **Service:** Internationally **Photocopy:** Yes

2948   Taipei, Taiwan
Agricultural Science Information Center (ASIC)
14, 3rd Floor Wen-Chou Street
Taipei 10616

Phone: +886(2) 2362-6222 **Fax:** +886(2) 2363-2459
WWW: www.asic.gov.tw

Founded: 1976 **Type:** Association **Head:** Wan-Jiun Wu *Phone:* +886(2) 2362-6226 **Staff:** 18 Prof. 13 Other **Holdings:** 11,046 books 847 journals **Language of Collection/Services:** Chinese/Chinese **Subjects:** Agriculture (Tropics), Agribusiness, Agricultural Development, Agricultural Economics, Agricultural Engineering, Animal Husbandry, Ecology, Crops, Entomology, Farming, Fisheries, Food Sciences, Forestry, Horticulture, Plant Pathology, Soil Science, Veterinary Medicine, Water Resources **Databases Developed:** FASTEP - Files on Agricultural Science and Technology Personnel; FASTEJ - Files on Agricultural Science and Technology Research Projects; FASTEL - Files on Agricultural Science and Technology Literature (1962-1997); FASTET - Files on Agricultural Science and Technology Thesaurus; FASTRR - Files on Agricultural Science and Technology Research Reports; FAAPP - Files on the Automation of Agricultural Production Personnel; FAAPL - Files on Automation of Agricultural Production Literature **Databases Used:** Comprehensive **Loan:** Do not loan **Service:** In country **Photocopy:** Yes

2949   Taipei, Taiwan
China Grain Products Research and Development
    Institute (CGPRDI)
Walter L. Frey Memorial Library
12-6 Hsia Ku Tze, Pali Hsiang
Taipei 249

Phone: +886(2) 2610-1010 **Fax:** +886(2) 2610-3351
Email: cgprdi01@ms13.hinet.net **WWW:** www.cgprdi.org.tw

Former Name: China Wheat Products Research and Development Institute **Founded:** 1984 **Type:** Academic **Head:** Paul H.C. Hsu *Phone:* +886(2) 2610-1010 *Email:* cgprdi01 @ms13.hinet.net **Staff:** 1 Prof. 1 Other **Holdings:** 250 books 12 journals **Language of Collection/Services:** Chinese, English, Japanese / Chinese **Subjects:** Education/Extension, Food Sciences **Specializations:** Baking, Cereals **Loan:** Inhouse **Service:** Inhouse **Photocopy:** No

2950   Taipei, Taiwan
Development Center for Biotechnology (DCB)
Library
81 Chang Hsing Street
Taipei 106

Phone: +886(2) 2732-5123 **Fax:** +886(2) 2732-5181
WWW: www.dcb.org.tw

Founded: 1987 **Type:** Association **Head:** Nancy Kuo *Phone:* +886(2) 2732-5123 *Email:* nancykuo@mail.dcb.org. tw **Staff:** 2 Prof. 2 Other **Holdings:** 6,500 books 300 journals **Language of Collection/Services:** English / Chinese **Subjects:** Comprehensive **Specializations:** Drugs, Biotechnology, Medicine, Pharmaceutical Industry **Networks:** CSA; IAC; ISICCC; STN **Databases Developed:** Taiwan Biotech Business News; Taiwan Biotechnology Company Directory; Biotechnology Literature Collection **Databases Used:** Comprehensive **Loan:** In country **Service:** In country **Photocopy:** Yes

2951   Taipei, Taiwan
National Taiwan University (NTU)
Library
1, Section 4, Roosevelt Road
Taipei 106

Phone: +886(2) 2362-7383 **Fax:** +886(2) 2362-4344
Email: tul@ccms.ntu.edu.tw **WWW:** www.lib.ntu.edu.tw
OPAC: tulips.ntu.edu.edu.tw

Former Name: Taipei Imperial University **Founded:** 1928 **Type:** Academic **Head:** Ming-der Wu *Phone:* +886(2) 2363-6810 *Email:* mdwu@ccms.ntu.edu.tw **Staff:** 122 Prof. **Holdings:** 2,333,969 books 10,728 journals **Language of Collection/Services:** Chinese, English / Chinese **Subjects:** Comprehensive **Networks:** NBINET; OCLC **Databases Developed:** List of publications of the faculty and staff members of the National Taiwan University; available via Library's web site **Databases Used:** Comprehensive **Loan:** Internationally **Service:** Internationally **Photocopy:** Yes

2952   Taipei, Taiwan
Taipei Zoo
Library
30, Hsin-Kuang Road Sec. 2
Taipei 11628

Phone: +886(2) 2938-2300 ext 393 **Fax:** +886(2) 2938-2316 **Email:** lib@mail.zoo.gov.tw **WWW:** www.zoo.gov.tw

Founded: 1988 **Type:** Government **Head:** *Phone:* +886(2) 2938-2300 ext 301 *Email:* lib@mail.zoo.gov.tw **Staff:** 1 Prof. 2 Other **Holdings:** 12,000 books 200 journals **Language of Collection/Services:** English, Chinese, Japanese **Subjects:** Animal Husbandry, Biodiversity, Ecology, Education/Extension, Horticulture, Plants, Veterinary Medicine **Photocopy:** Yes

2953   Taipei, Taiwan
Taiwan Floriculture Development Association
    (TFDA)
Library
18F-1 No. 102 Sung Lung Road
Taipei 110

Phone: +886(2) 2762-1755 **Fax:** +886(2) 2748-6690
Email: tfda@ms14.hinet.net **WWW:** www.tfda.org.tw
OPAC: www.tfda.org.tw

Type: Association **Head:** Chih-Hui Liu *Phone:* +886(2) 2762-1755 *Email:* tfda@ms14.hinet.net **Staff:** 3 Prof. 2 Other **Holdings:** 1,000 books 50 journals **Language of Collection/Services:** Chinese, English / Chinese, English **Subjects:** Agribusiness, Agricultural Development, Agricultural Economics, Biotechnology, Farming, Horticulture, Landscaping, Plant Pathology, Plants, Soil, Trees **Specializations:** Floriculture, Flower Industry **Databases Developed:**

Taiwan flower industry information, grower name list, trader list **Loan:** Inhouse **Service:** Internationally **Photocopy:** No

2954 Taipei, Taiwan
Taiwan Forestry Research Institute (TFRI)
Library
53 Nan-hai Road
Taipei 100
Phone: +886(2) 2381-7107 ext 892 **Fax:** +886(2) 2305-2027 **Email:** library@serv.tfri.gov.tw **WWW:** www.tfri.gov.tw/index-e.html

Founded: 1927 **Type:** Government **Head:** Hui-Yung Chang *Phone:* +886(2) 2381-7107 ext 887 *Email:* library@serv.tfri.gov.tw **Staff:** 2 Prof. 2 Other **Holdings:** 31,000 books 90 journals **Language of Collection/Services:** Chinese, English, Japanese / Chinese, English **Subjects:** Forestry **Specializations:** Forest Utilization, Forest Management, Forest Cellulose, Forest Biology, Forest Chemistry, Forest Economics, Forest Extension, Protection of Forests **Loan:** Inhouse **Service:** Internationally **Photocopy:** Yes

2955 Wufeng, Taiwan
Taiwan Agricultural Chemicals and Toxic
    Substances Research Institute (TACTRI)
Office of Technical Service (OTS)
11, Kuang Ming Road
Wufeng, Taichung 431
Fax: +886(4) 330-6542 **WWW:** www.tactri.gov.tw

Type: Government **Head:** Wen-Chi Fei *Phone:* +886(4) 330-2101 **Staff:** 4 Prof. 12 Other **Holdings:** 6,500 books 300 journals **Language of Collection/Services:** English / Chinese **Subjects:** Pesticides, Plant Protection, Toxicology **Databases Developed:** ALIS - integrated library processing and information provision system offering on-line query; LSINFO - pesticide registered information in Taiwan. **Databases Used:** Comprehensive **Loan:** In country **Service:** In country **Photocopy:** Yes

2956 Wufeng, Taiwan
Taiwan Agricultural Research Institute (TARI)
Library
189 Chung-Cheng Road
Wufeng, Taichung 41301
Fax: +886(4) 333-8162 **Email:** lcc@wufeng.tari.gov.tw **WWW:** www.tari.gov.tw

Former Name: Government Agricultural Research Institute Taiwan Nippon **Founded:** 1895 **Type:** Academic **Head:** Ching-Liang Liaw *Phone:* +886(4) 330-2301 ext 218 *Email:* lcc@wufeng.tari.gov.tw **Staff:** 1 Prof. 1 Other **Holdings:** 30,000 books 300 journals **Language of Collection/Services:** English/Chinese **Subjects:** Agriculture (Tropics), Agricultural Economics, Agricultural Engineering, Agronomy, Biotechnology, Entomology, Germplasm, Plants, Horticulture, Plant Pathology, Soil Science **Databases Developed:** Special collection of the reports of the Department of Agriculture, Government Research Institute, Formosa, Japan **Databases Used:** Agricola **Loan:** In country **Service:** In country **Photocopy:** Yes

2957 Yangmei, Taiwan
Taiwan Tea Experiment Station (TTES)
Library
324, Chung Hsin Road
Pushin
Yangmei, Taoyuan 326
Phone: +886(3) 482-2059 ext 228 **Fax:** +886(3) 482-4716 **WWW:** www.tpg.gov.tw/tea

Founded: 1968 **Type:** Government **Head:** Mai-Chin Tsai *Phone:* +886(3) 482-2059 ext 228 **Staff:** 1 Prof. **Holdings:** 5,500 books 40 journals **Language of Collection/Services:** Chinese / Chinese **Subjects:** Crops, Food Sciences **Specializations:** Tea **Loan:** In country **Service:** In country **Photocopy:** Yes

Tajikistan

♦2958 Dushanbe, Tajikistan
Tajik Agricultural University (TAU)
Library
PO Box 464
Rudaki Av., 146
Dushanbe 734017
Phone: +992(372) 243771, 246249

Former Name: Tadzhik Agriculture Institute **Founded:** 1931 **Type:** Academic **Staff:** 48 Prof. **Holdings:** 380,000 books 410 journals **Language of Collection/Services:** Russian / Tajik, Russian **Subjects:** Agribusiness, Agricultural Development, Agricultural Economics, Crops, Agricultural Engineering, Animal Husbandry, Biotechnology, Farming, Plants, Soil Science, Veterinary Medicine, Water Resources **Loan:** In country **Service:** In country **Photocopy:** Yes

2959 Dushanbe, Tajikistan
Tajik Scientific Research Institute of Agriculture
Library
Gissarski Region
Dushanbe 735022

Founded: 1957 **Type:** Government **Holdings:** 10,400 books

2960 Dushanbe, Tajikistan
Tajik Scientific Research Veterinary Institute
Library
40 Years of Tadzhik St.
Dushanbe 734005

Founded: 1956 **Type:** Government **Holdings:** 9,100 books **Subjects:** Veterinary Science

♦2961 Khodzhent, Tajikistan
Tajik Scientific Research Institute of Agriculture,
    Leninabad Experiment Station of Cotton
    Growing
Library
Leninabad District
Khodzhent 735700

Type: Government **Holdings:** 4,200 books **Subjects:** Cotton

Tanzania

2962   Arusha, Tanzania
Forestry Training Institute, Olmotonyi (FTI)
Library
PB 943
Arusha

Location: Olmotonyi, Arusha

Founded: 1950 **Type:** Government **Head:** Dr. Ismail K. Aloo *Phone:* +255() 3441 **Staff:** 4 Other **Holdings:** 10,000 books 4 journals **Language of Collection/Services:** English **Subjects:** Forestry, Rural Sociology **Loan:** Inhouse **Service:** Inhouse **Photocopy:** Yes

2963   Arusha, Tanzania
Ministry of Agriculture and Cooperatives,
    Ministry of Agriculture Training Institute,
    Tengeru (MAC, MATI Tengeru)
Library
PB 3101
Arusha

Location: Tengeru Area **Phone:** +255() 34 Duluti ext 41

Former Name: Ministry of Agriculture and Livestock Development (MALD), Livestock Training Institute Tengeru (LTIT) **Founded:** 1942 **Type:** Government **Head:** Mr. Matua E. Mhina *Email:* gilbertmaeda@haberi.co.tz (Attn: MATI Tengeru Arusha) *Phone:* +255() 34 Duluti **Staff:** 2 Prof. **Holdings:** 4,500 books 2,000 journals **Language of Collection/Services:** English / English, Swahili **Subjects:** Afforestation, Animal Breeding, Ecology, Land Use, Livestock, Pastures, Soil Conservation, Training **Specializations:** Animal Production, Animal Health, Farm Machinery, Irrigation **Loan:** Inhouse **Service:** Inhouse **Photocopy:** No

♦2964   Arusha, Tanzania
Ministry of Agriculture and Cooperatives,
    Tengeru Horticultural Research and Training
    Institute (HORTI)
Library
PO Box 1253
Arusha

Former Name: Ministry of Agriculture and Livestock Development (MALD) **Founded:** 1980 **Type:** Academic **Staff:** 2 Prof. 1 Other **Holdings:** 1,500 books 15 journals **Language of Collection/Services:** English, Swahili **Subjects:** Agricultural Economics, Food Sciences, Fruit Growing, Horticulture, Land Use, Mechanization, Ornamental Plants, Plant Protection, Propagation, Vegetables **Loan:** In country **Photocopy:** Yes

2965   Arusha, Tanzania
Tropical Pesticides Research Institute (TPRI)
Library and Documentation Center
PO Box 3024
Arusha

Phone: +255(57) 3557/8 ext 132, 133, 8813/5 **Fax:** +255 (57) 8217

Founded: 1945 **Type:** Government **Staff:** 3 Prof. 5 Other **Holdings:** 20,000 books 30 journals **Subjects:** Biology, Agricultural Chemistry, Pesticides, Pests, Physics **Loan:** In country **Photocopy:** Yes

2966   Dar-Es-Salaam, Tanzania
Ministry of Agriculture and Cooperatives
Agricultural Library
PO Box 2066
Dar-Es-Salaam

Location: Pamba House Road **Phone:** +255(51) 865323 **Fax:** +255(51) 864976 **Email:** drt@costech.gn.apc.org

Former Name: Ministry of Agriculture and Livestock Development (MALD) **Founded:** 1930 **Type:** Government **Staff:** 1 Prof. 4 Other **Holdings:** 8,000 books 25 journals **Language of Collection/Services:** English **Subjects:** Comprehensive **Networks:** AGRIS **Loan:** In country **Service:** Internationally **Photocopy:** No

♦2967   Dar-Es-Salaam, Tanzania
Ministry of Tourism, Natural Resources and
    Environment, Forestry and Beekeeping
    Division
Library
PB 426
Dar-Es-Salaam

Type: Government **Holdings:** 2,500 books **Language of Collection/Services:** English / English **Subjects:** Agricultural Development, Agricultural Economics, Beekeeping, Animal Production, Extension, Forestry, Natural Resources **Loan:** In country **Service:** In country **Photocopy:** Yes

♦2968   Dar-Es-Salaam, Tanzania
Tanzania Library Service (TLS)
Tanzania National Documentation Centre
    (TANDOC)
PO Box 9283
Dar-Es-Salaam

Location: National Central Library, Uwt Street **Phone:** +255(51) 26121/2

Founded: 1975 **Type:** Government **Staff:** 6 Prof. 7 Other **Holdings:** 100,000 books 200 journals **Language of Collection/Services:** English **Subjects:** Administration, Agricultural Engineering, Animal Husbandry, Mechanization, Plant Breeding, Plant Protection, Soil Science **Loan:** Internationally **Service:** Internationally **Photocopy:** No

♦2969   Dar-Es-Salaam, Tanzania
Tanzania Livestock Research Organization,
    Animal Diseases Research Institute
    (TALIRO, ADRI)
Library
PO Box 9254
Dar-Es-Salaam

Location: Opposite RTD Alumium Africa Limited, along the Port Access Road

Former Name: Central Veterinary Laboratory (CVL) **Type:** Government **Founded:** 1962 **Staff:** 1 Prof. 1 Other **Holdings:** 2,600 books 40 journals **Language of Collection/Services:** English **Subjects:** Animal Feeding, Animal Health, Animal Husbandry, Immunology, Parasitology, Toxicology **Specializations:** Veterinary Medicine **Loan:** Inhouse

2970   Kilosa, Tanzania
Ministry of Agriculture and Cooperatives,
    Ministry of Agriculture Training Institutes
    (MAC, MATI)
Library
MATI - Ilonga
Private Bag, Kilosa
Kilosa
Phone: +255() 64 Kilosa

Former Name: Ministry of Agriculture and Livestock Development (MALD) **Founded:** 1972 **Type:** Academic **Head:** Pamba House **Staff:** 1 Prof. 1 Other **Holdings:** 5,639 books 125 journals **Language of Collection/Services:** English/ English, Swahili **Subjects:** Agricultural Economics, Agricultural Engineering, Animal Husbandry, Biochemistry, Chemistry, Crops, Horticulture, Extension, Farm Management, Food Sciences, Nutrition, Soil Science **Loan:** In country **Service:** In country **Photocopy:** No

◆**2971   Mbeya, Tanzania**
Ministry of Agriculture and Cooperatives, Uyole
    Agricultural Centre (UAC)
Library
Mbeya Iringa Road
PB 400
Mbeya
Phone: +255() 3087

Former Name: Ministry of Agriculture and Livestock Development (MALD) **Founded:** 1970 **Staff:** 1 Prof. 2 Other **Type:** Government **Holdings:** 9,934 books 33 journals **Subjects:** Agricultural Development, Agricultural Economics, Agricultural Policy, Animal Production, Cereals, Crop Production, Farming Systems, Legumes, Livestock, Pesticides

◆**2972   Morogoro, Tanzania**
Ministry of Agriculture and Cooperatives
Library
PO Box 603
Morogoro
Phone: +255(56) 4367

Former Name: Ministry of Agriculture and Livestock Development (MALD) **Founded:** 1968 **Type:** Academic, Government **Staff:** 30 Prof. 2 Other **Holdings:** 5,100 books 10 journals **Language of Collection/Services:** English / Swahili **Subjects:** Entomology, Veterinary Medicine **Specializations:** Animal Husbandry, Education/Extension, Range Management **Loan:** In country **Photocopy:** Yes

◆**2973   Morogoro, Tanzania**
Sokoine University of Agriculture
Library
PO Box 3022
Morogoro
Phone: +255(56) 4639, 3511/4

Founded: 1965 **Type:** Academic **Staff:** 6 Prof. 24 Other **Holdings:** 50,000 books 600 journals **Subjects:** Forestry, Veterinary Medicine **Loan:** Do not loan **Photocopy:** Yes

2974   Morogoro, Tanzania
Tanzania Forestry Research Institute (TAFORI)

Library
PB 1854
Morogoro

Founded: 1983 **Type:** Research **Head:** F.H. Mgumia *Phone* +255(56) 3122 *Email:* tafori@turiga.com **Staff:** 1 Prof. 2 Other **Holdings:** 500 books 15 journals **Language of Collection/Services:** English / English, Swahili **Subjects:** Forestry, Wood **Databases Used:** CABCD **Photocopy:** Yes **Loan:** Inhouse **Service:** Inhouse

2975   Moshi, Tanzania
College of African Wildlife Management, Mweka
    (CAWM Mweka)
Library
PO Box 3031
Moshi
Fax: +255(55) 5113

Founded: 1965 **Type:** Academic **Head:** Mrs. Nellie J. Mwandoloma *Phone:* +255() 18, 24 Kibosho **Staff:** 3 Other **Holdings:** 12,000 books 15 journals **Language of Collection/Services:** English / English **Subjects:** Range Management, Soil Science, Veterinary Medicine **Specializations:** Agribusiness, Wildlife, Zoology **Networks:** EPIO **Loan:** Inhouse **Photocopy:** Yes

2976   Moshi, Tanzania
Ministry of Agriculture and Cooperatives,
    Lyamungu Agricultural Research and
    Training Institute (MOC, LARTI)
Lyamungu Library
PO Box 3004
Moshi
Phone: +255(55) 53444 **Fax:** +255(55) 53033

Founded: 1945 **Type:** Academic **Head:** Amelda Kimaro *Phone:* +255(55) 53444 **Staff:** 1 Prof. 1 Other **Holdings:** 1,773 books 24 journals **Language of Collection/Services:** English / English **Subjects:** Agronomy, Entomology, Plant Breeding, Plant Pathology, Soil Science **Loan:** Inhouse **Service:** Inhouse **Photocopy:** No

◆**2977   Mpwapwa, Tanzania**
Tanzania Livestock Research Organization,
    Livestock Training Institute (TALIRO, LITI)
Library
Private Mail Bag
Mpwapwa

Founded: 1930 **Type:** Academic **Staff:** 2 Prof. 5 Other **Holdings:** 2,500 books 100 journals **Subjects:** Animal Husbandry, Livestock **Loan:** In country **Photocopy:** No

◆**2978   Mpwapwa, Tanzania**
Zonal Research and Training Centre (ZRTC)
LPRI/LTI Joint Library
PO Box 202
Mpwapwa
Phone: +255() 21

Former Name: Tanzania Livestock Research Organization (TALIRO), Livestock Production Research Institute (LPRI) **Type:** Research **Staff:** 20 Prof. 152 Other **Holdings:** 5,000 books 50 journals **Language of Collection/Services:** English **Subjects:** Farming Systems Research **Loan:** In country **Service:** In country **Photocopy:** Yes

♦2979　Mwanza, Tanzania
　　　Agriculture Research Institute Ukiriguru,
　　　　　Research and Training Division (ARIU)
　　　Ukiriguru Research Library (URL)
　　　PO Box 1433
　　　Mwanza
Location: Ukiriguru - 17 miles south of Mwanza along Shinyanga Road **Phone:** +255(68) 40596/7

Former Name: Tanzania Agriculture Research Organization (TARO), Agricultural Research and Training Division, Western Research Center Library **Founded:** 1961 **Type:** Government **Staff:** 1 Other **Holdings:** 2,200 books 57 journals **Language of Collection/Services:** English **Subjects:** Agriculture (Tropics), Agricultural Economics, Animal Husbandry, Extension, Entomology, Farming, Horticulture, Soil Science, Plant Pathology, **Loan:** In country **Photocopy:** No

2980　Tanga, Tanzania
　　　Ministry of Agriculture and Cooperatives, Tsetse
　　　　　and Trypanosomiasis Research Institute
　　　　　(MAC, TTRI)
　　　TTRI Library
　　　Korogwe Road
　　　PB 1026
　　　Tanga
Phone: +255(53) 44572/3 **Fax:** +255(53) 42577 **Email:** tsetse@costech.gn.apc.org

Former Name: Tanzania Livestock Research Organization (TALIRO) **Founded:** 1981 **Type:** Government **Head:** Dr. Atway Msangi *Email:* amasangi@costech.gn.apc.org *Phone* +255 (53) 44572/3 **Staff:** 1 Prof. **Holdings:** 384 books 63 journals **Language of Collection/Services:** English / English **Subjects:** Entomology, Extension, Glossina, Pest Control, Trypanosomiasis **Service:** In country **Photocopy:** Yes

Thailand

2981　Bangkok, Thailand
　　　Bank for Agriculture and Agricultural
　　　　　Cooperatives (BAAC)
　　　Agriculture and Agricultural Cooperatives Library
　　　469 Nakorn Sawan Road
　　　Dusit
　　　Bangkok 10300
Phone: +66(2) 280-0180 ext 2810-12 **Fax:** +66(2) 280-0442, 280-5320 **WWW:** www.baac.mof.go.th

Founded: 1983 **Type:** Government **Head:** Miss Worawan Kumyaem *Phone:* +66(2) 280-0180 ext 2813 **Staff:** 2 Prof. 5 Other **Holdings:** 24,050 books 119 journals **Language of Collection/Services:** English, Thai / Thai **Subjects:** Agricultural Credit, Finance, Rural Economy **Loan:** In country **Service:** In country **Photocopy:** No

2982　Bangkok, Thailand
　　　Chulalongkorn University (CU)
　　　Center of Academic Resources (CAR)

Phayathai Road
Bangkok 10330
Phone: +66(2) 218-2929 **Fax:** +66(2) 215-3617 **Email:** webmaster@car.chula.ac.th **WWW:** www.car.chula.ac.th **OPAC:** library.car.chula.ac.th

Former Name: Academic Resource Center **Founded:** 1916 **Type:** Academic **Head:** Dr. Kamales Santivejkul *Phone:* +66(2) 218-2905 *Email:* kamales@mail.car.chula.ac.th **Staff:** 36 Prof. 103 Other **Holdings:** 773,716 books 423 journals **Language of Collection/Services:** Thai, English / Thai, English **Subjects:** Agricultural Development, Agricultural Economics, Animal Husbandry, Crops, Fisheries, Forestry, Plant Pathology, Soil Science, Veterinary Medicine, Water Resources **Databases Developed:** Thesis and Periodical indexes database **Databases Used:** Comprehensive **Loan:** In country **Service:** Internationally **Photocopy:** Yes

2983　Bangkok, Thailand
　　　Chulalongkorn University, Center of Academic
　　　　　Resources (CU, CAR)
　　　Thailand Information Center (TIC)
　　　Phayathai Road
　　　Bangkok 10330
Phone: +66(2) 218-2959 **Fax:** +66(2) 215-3617 **Email:** kultida@mail.car.chula.ac.th **WWW:** www.car.chula.ac.th

Former Name: Academic Resource Center **Founded:** 1968 **Type:** Government **Head:** Kultida Boon-Itt *Phone:* +66(2) 2182956 *Email:* kultida@mail.car.chula.ac.th **Staff:** 9 Prof. 4 Other **Holdings:** 70,000 books **Language of Collection/Services:** English, Thai / Thai, English **Subjects:** Agribusiness, Agricultural Development, Agricultural Economics, Farming, Fisheries, Forestry, Water Resources **Specializations:** Politics **Databases Developed:** TIC Database - provides information social sciences and behavioral sciences relating to Thailand. **Databases Used:** CABCD **Loan:** In country **Service:** Internationally **Photocopy:** Yes

2984　Bangkok, Thailand
　　　Chulalongkorn University, Faculty of Veterinary
　　　　　Sciences
　　　Veterinary Library and Information Center
　　　Henri Dunant Road
　　　Bangkok 10330
Phone: +66(2) 252-0980, 218-9556 **Fax:** +66(2) 252-8853, 218-9557 **Email:** pkourwan@netserve.ac.th **WWW:** www. vet.chula.ac.th **OPAC:** 161.200.145.1

Founded: 1935 **Type:** Academic **Head:** Miss Pringsri Ingkaninun *Email:* ipringsr@pioneer.netserv.ac.th *Phone:* +66 (2) 252-0980, 218-9554 **Staff:** 4 Prof. 4 Other **Holdings:** 18,721 books 768 journals **Language of Collection/Services:** English, Thai **Subjects:** Animal Husbandry, Food Sciences, Veterinary Medicine **Databases Developed:** Veterinary Research Database **Databases Used:** Agricola; Agris; CABCD **Loan:** In country **Photocopy:** Yes

2985　Bangkok, Thailand
　　　Department of Agriculture (DOA)
　　　Technical Information Center (TIC)
　　　Paholyothin Road, Chatuchak
　　　Bangkok 10900

Phone: +66(2) 579-8539 **Fax:** +66(2) 561-4624 **Email:** doa-info@mozart.inet.co.th **WWW:** www.disc.doa.go.th

Founded: 1987 **Type:** Government **Head:** Mrs. Saowalak Arunsri *Phone:* +66 (2) 579-8539 **Staff:** 2 Prof. 2 Other **Holdings:** 12,230 books 13 journals **Language of Collection/Services:** Thai, English / Thai **Subjects:** Agriculture (Tropics), Agricultural Development, Agricultural Economics, Agricultural Engineering, Biotechnology, Crops, Entomology, Farming, Horticulture, Plant Pathology, Plants, Soil Science **Databases Developed:** Research database - contains the results of research work done by DOA **Databases Used:** Agris; CABCD **Loan:** Inhouse **Service:** Internationally **Photocopy:** Yes

2986   Bangkok, Thailand
          Department of Agriculture Extension
          Library
          Phaholyothin Road
          Chatuchak
          Bangkok 10900
Phone: +66(2) 579-2594 **WWW:** www.doae.go.th

Type: Government **Head:** Mrs. Siritorn Thamluxme *Phone:* +66(2) 579-2594 **Staff:** 1 Prof. 1 Other **Holdings:** 20,000 books 80 journals **Language of Collection/Services:** English, Thai/English, Thai **Subjects:** Extension **Loan:** In country **Service:** In country **Photocopy:** Yes

2987   Bangkok, Thailand
          Department of Fisheries
          W.E. Johnson Library
          Paholyothin Road
          Chatuchak
          Bangkok 10900
Phone: +66(2) 579-2151 ext 5121 **Fax:** +66(2) 579-6439 **WWW:** www.fisheries.go.th

Former Name: Marine Fisheries Division, National Inland Fisheries Institute **Founded:** 1901 **Type:** Government **Head:** Mr. Satitpong Boonmeesuwan *Phone:* +66(2) 579-8211 *Email:* satitpob@fisheries.go.th **Staff:** 1 Prof. 1 Other **Holdings:** 7,100 books 98 journals **Language of Collection/Services:** English, Thai **Subjects:** Aquaculture, Fisheries **Loan:** Inhouse **Service:** Inhouse **Photocopy:** Yes

2988   Bangkok, Thailand
          Department of Fisheries, Marine Fisheries
               Division
          Library
          89/1 Soi Sapan Pla, Yannawa
          Bangkok 10120
Phone: +66(2) 2114981/2

Founded: 1965 **Type:** Government **Holdings:** 900 books 45 journals **Subjects:** Fisheries **Loan:** In country **Photocopy:** No

2989   Bangkok, Thailand
          Department of Livestock Development (DLD)
          Library
          Phayathai Road
          Rat Thewi
          Bangkok 10400

Phone: +66(2) 254-2664 **Fax:** +66(2) 254-2664

Founded: 1957 **Type:** Government **Head:** Mrs. Prapushsorn Timtong *Phone:* +66(2) 254-2664, 251-5136/8 ext 110 **Staff:** 1 Prof. 2 Other **Holdings:** 6,000 books 10 journals **Language of Collection/Services:** English, Thai / Thai **Subjects:** Livestock **Specializations:** Veterinary Science **Loan:** In country **Service:** In country **Photocopy:** Yes

2990   Bangkok, Thailand
          Food and Agriculture Organization, Regional
               Office for Asia and the Pacific (FAO)
          Library
          Maliwan Mansion
          Phra Atit Road
          Bangkok 10200
Phone: +66(2) 281-7844 ext 190 **Fax:** +66(2) 280-0455 **Email:** fao-rap@field.fao.org **WWW:** www.fao.org

Type: International **Head:** Ms. Praneet Gunatilaka *Phone:* +66(2) 281-7844 ext 222 *Email:* praneet.gunatiloke@fao.org **Staff:** 1 Prof. 2 Other **Holdings:** 50,000 books 20 journals **Language of Collection/Services:** English / English, Thai **Subjects:** Agricultural Development, Agricultural Economics, Agricultural Engineering, Economic Development, Rural Sociology, Water Resources **Databases Used:** Agricola; Agris; VLibrary **Photocopy:** Yes

2991   Bangkok, Thailand
          Horticultural Research Institute
          Library
          Paholyothin Road
          Chatuchak
          Bangkok 10900
Phone: +66(2) 579-8553 ext 129 **Fax:** +66(2) 561-4667 **Email:** hortdoa@mozart.inet.co.th **WWW:** www.doa.go.th

Founded: 1985 **Type:** Government **Head:** Mrs. Kanokrat Sittipoch *Phone:* +66(2) 579-7531 **Staff:** 2 Other **Holdings:** 1,200 books 30 journals **Language of Collection/Services:** English, Thai / English, Thai **Subjects:** Horticulture **Loan:** In country **Service:** In country **Photocopy:** Yes

2992   Bangkok, Thailand
          International Board for Soil Research and
               Management (IBSRAM)
          Information Center
          PO Box 9-109
          Paholyothin Road
          Bangkok 10900
Phone: +66(3) 941-2500 **Fax:** +66(2) 561-1230 **Email:** info@ibsram.org **WWW:** www.ibsram.org

Type: International **Head:** Kanchana Laparat *Phone:* +66(2) 941-2500 *Email:* kanchana@ibsram.org **Staff:** 1 Prof. 2.5 Other **Holdings:** 3,500 books 200 journals **Language of Collection/Services:** English / English, Thai **Subjects:** Soil Science **Specializations:** Land Management, Sustainability **Databases Developed:** SALAD - Soil and Land Database; available via Internet only **Loan:** Internationally **Service:** Internationally **Photocopy:** Yes

2993   Bangkok, Thailand
          Kasetsart University (KU)

Kasetsart Main Library
PO Box 1084 Kasetsart
Bangkok 10903

Location: Paholyothin Road **Phone:** +66(2) 942-8614 **Fax:** +66(2) 561-1369 **Email:** libnt@ku.ac.th **WWW:** www.lib.ku.ac.th **OPAC:** intanin.lib.ku.ac.th

Founded: 1943 **Type:** Academic **Head:** Mrs. Piboonsin Watanapongse *Email:* upvp@nontri.ku.ac.th *Phone:* +66(2) 942-8615 **Staff:** 33 Prof. 85 Other **Holdings:** 250,648 books 2,025 journals **Language of Collection/Services:** English, Thai / Thai, English **Subjects:** Comprehensive **Specializations:** Buffaloes **Networks:** AGRIS **Databases Developed:** IBIC - International Buffalo Information Center **Databases Used:** Agris; DAO; FSTA **Loan:** Internationally **Service:** Internationally **Photocopy:** Yes

2994   Bangkok, Thailand
King Mongkut's Institute of Technology, Faculty of Agricultural Technology (KMITL)
Library and Information Center
Ladkrabang
Bangkok 10520

Phone: +66(2) 326-7341 **Fax:** +66(2) 326-7341 **Email:** kcjirapo@kmitl.ac.th **WWW:** www.kmitl.ac.th **OPAC:** 161.246.37.11

Founded: 1978 **Type:** Academic **Head:** Mrs. Jiraporn Chuenpreechar *Phone:* +66(2) 326-7341 *Email:* kcjirapo@chaokhun.kmitl.ac.th **Staff:** 2 Prof. 6 Other **Holdings:** 418 journals 24,491 books **Language of Collection/Services:** Thai, English **Subjects:** Agribusiness, Animal Husbandry, Biotechnology, Crops, Entomology, Food Sciences, Horticulture, Plant Pathology, Soil Science **Loan:** In country **Service:** Inhouse **Photocopy:** Yes

2995   Bangkok, Thailand
Land Development Department
Library
Phaholyothin Road
Chatuchak
Bangkok 10900

Phone: +66(2) 579-0111 ext 1274 **Fax:** +66(2) 941-2139

Founded: 1963 **Type:** Government **Head:** Mrs. Kesorn Suansri *Phone:* +66(2) 579-0111 ext 1274 **Staff:** 1 Prof. 4 Other **Holdings:** 25,000 books 30 journals **Language of Collection/Services:** English, Thai/Thai **Subjects:** Geology **Specializations:** Soil Science **Loan:** In country **Service:** In country **Photocopy:** No

2996   Bangkok, Thailand
Ministry of Agriculture and Cooperatives (MOAC)
Library
3 Ban Phan Thom, Ratchadamnoen Nok
Phra Nakhon
Bangkok 10200

Phone: +66(2) 629-9040 **Fax:** +66(2) 282-8827 **WWW:** www.moac.go.th

Type: Government **Head:** Mrs. Panita Liangpandh *Phone:* +66(2) 629-9040 **Staff:** 1 Prof. 2 Other **Holdings:** 10,000 books 40 journals **Language of Collection/Services:** English, Thai/Thai **Loan:** Inhouse **Service:** Inhouse **Photocopy:** No

2997   Bangkok, Thailand
Ministry of Agriculture and Cooperatives, Office of Agricultural Economics
Library
Paholyothin Road
Chatuchak
Bangkok 10900

Phone: +66(2) 940-6919, 940-7242 **Fax:** +66(2) 940-7241 **WWW:** www.oae.go.th

Founded: 1979 **Type:** Government **Head:** Mr. Thawat Thongmak *Phone:* +66(2) 940-7239 **Staff:** 1 Prof. **Holdings:** 9,000 books 12 journals **Language of Collection/Services:** English, Thai / English, Thai **Subjects:** Agricultural Development, Agricultural Economics, Agricultural Statistics **Loan:** Inhouse **Service:** Inhouse **Photocopy:** No

2998   Bangkok, Thailand
National Institute of Animal Health (NIAH)
Library
Kaset Klang
Chatuchak
Bangkok 10900

Phone: +66(2) 579-8908/14 **Fax:** +66(2) 579-8919

Former Name: National Animal Health and Production Institute **Founded:** 1986 **Type:** Government **Head:** Mr. Patiporn Thapanagulsak *Phone:* +66 (2) 579-8908/14 ext 201 *Email:* pornpana@mozart.inet.co.th **Language of Collection/Services:** Thai, English **Subjects:** Animal Diseases, Animal Production, Marketing

2999   Bangkok, Thailand
Rice Research Institute (RRI)
Library
Paholyothin Road
Chatuchak
Bangkok 10900

Phone: +66(2) 579-7593 **Fax:** +66(2) 561-1732 **WWW:** www.doa.go.th

Founded: 1984 **Type:** Government **Head:** Mr. Wiset Chanyanuwat *Phone:* +66(2) 579-7593 *Email:* rrida@kkk.a-net.net.th **Staff:** 1 Other **Holdings:** 1,000 books 15 journals **Language of Collection/Services:** English, Thai / English, Thai **Subjects:** Rice **Loan:** In country **Service:** In country **Photocopy:** Yes

3000   Bangkok, Thailand
Royal Forest Department (RFD)
Library
Phaholyothin Road
Chatuchak
Bangkok 10900

Phone: +66(2) 579-4301 **Fax:** +66(2) 579-4301 **WWW:** www.forest.go.th

Founded: 1896 **Type:** Government **Head:** Mrs. Sermsagul Boonthaveekun *Phone:* +66(2) 579-4301 **Staff:** 2 Prof. 6 Other **Holdings:** 10,000 books 120 journals **Language of**

Collection/Services: English, Thai/Thai **Subjects:** Forestry **Loan:** Inhouse **Service:** Inhouse **Photocopy:** Yes

---

3001   Bangkok, Thailand
Rubber Research Institute (RRI)
Library
Phaholyothin Road
Chatuchak
Bangkok 10900
Phone: +66(2) 579-7557 **Fax:** +66(2) 561-4744 **WWW:** www.doa.go.th

Type: Government **Head:** Mr. Bodee Napawongs Na Ayutthaya *Phone:* +66(2) 579-7557 **Staff:** 2 Prof. 18 Other **Holdings:** 1,000 books **Language of Collection/Services:** English, Thai / Thai, English **Subjects:** Rubber **Loan:** Inhouse **Service:** Inhouse **Photocopy:** Yes

---

3002   Bangkok, Thailand
Sericultural Research Institute
Library
Paholyothin Road
Chatuchak
Bangkok 10900
Phone: +66(2) 940-6655 **Fax:** +66(2) 579-5595

Type: Government **Head:** Mrs. Pojana Werasopon *Phone:* +66(2) 940-6655 **Staff:** 1 Prof. **Holdings:** 1,000 books 20 journals **Language of Collection/Services:** English, Thai / Thai **Subjects:** Sericulture **Loan:** In country **Service:** In country **Photocopy:** Yes

---

3003   Bangkok, Thailand
Thailand Institute of Scientific and Technological
        Research (TISTR)
Thai National Documentation Center (TNDC)
196 Phaholyothin Road
Chatuchak
Bangkok 10900
Phone: +66(2) 579-5515, 579-1121 ext 1231 **Fax:** +66(2) 679-8594 **Email:** tistr@mozart.inet.co.th **WWW:** www. tistr.or.th

Former Name: Applied Scientific Research Corporation of Thailand (ASRCT) **Founded:** 1963 **Type:** Government **Head:** Mrs. Bang-on Theimsiri *Phone:* +66(2) 579-1121, 579-5515 ext 1231 *Email:* tistr@mozart.inet.co.th **Staff:** 8 Prof. 10 Other **Holdings:** 110,830 books 332 journals **Language of Collection/Services:** Thai, English / Thai **Subjects:** Agriculture (Tropics), Agribusiness, Agricultural Economics, Agricultural Engineering, Animal Husbandry, Crops, Entomology, Education/Extension, Farming, Fisheries, Forestry, Horticulture, Plants, Soil Science, Water Resources **Specializations:** Agricultural Development, Aromatic Plants, Biotechnology, Food Sciences, Medicinal Plants, Rubber **Databases Developed:** LIST - List of scientific and technical literature relating to Thailand; GAZETTE - Index of Thail Official Gazette; DIRECT - directory of scientific and technical libraries in Thailand; APM - bibliographies on medicinal and aromatic plants in Asian and Pacific retion; TECH - abstracts of TISTR reports; SERIALS - union list of scientific serials in Thai libraries **Databases Used:**

Comprehensive **Loan:** Internationally **Service:** Internationally **Photocopy:** Yes

---

3004   Bangkok, Thailand
United Nations Economic and Social Commission
        for Asia and the Pacific (ESCAP)
United Nations ESCAP Library
United Nations Building
Rajadamnern Nok Avenue
Bangkok 10200
Phone: +66(2) 288-1360 **Fax:** +66(2) 288-3036 **Email:** library-escap@un.org **WWW:** www.unescap.org

Former Name: United Nations Economic Commission for Asia and the Far East (ECAFE) **Founded:** 1949 **Type:** International **Head:** Ms. Evelyn Domingo-Barker *Phone:* +66(2) 288-1799 *Email:* domingo-barker.unescap@un.org **Staff:** 2 Prof. 11 Other **Holdings:** 255,000 books 400 journals **Language of Collection/Services:** English / English **Subjects:** Agricultural Development, Agricultural Economics, Fertilizers, Irrigation, Water Resources **Loan:** In country **Service:** UN staff, ESCAP member countries, researchers **Photocopy:** Yes

---

3005   Bangkok, Thailand
United Nations Economic and Social Commission
        for Asia and the Pacific, Fertilizer Advisory,
        Development and Information Network for
        Asia and the Pacific (ESCAP, FADINAP)
FADINAP/ARSAP Documentation Unit
United Nations Building
Rajadamnern Nok Avenue
Bangkok 10200
Phone: +66(2) 282-9161 ext 1343 **Fax:** +66(2) 281-2403 **WWW:** www.fadinap.org **OPAC:** www.fadinap.org/ onlinedbases.htm

Founded: 1978 **Type:** International **Head:** Ms. Ivy Rodricks *Phone:* +66(2) 282-9161 ext 1348 **Staff:** 2 Prof. 2 Other **Holdings:** 5,000 books 150 journals **Language of Collection/Services:** English / English **Subjects:** Fertilizers, Pesticides **Databases Developed:** Agro-pesticides - Active ingredients, trade names, importing or formulating companies, use, toxicity and antidotes, residue limits; available in nine Asian countries: China, Malaysia, Pakistan, Philippines, Republic of Korea, Singapore, Sri Lanka, and Thailand; Fertilizer Prices and Trade - Asia and the Pacific; 1985 to date; includes information on origin or loading port, destination, price/ton, quantity purchased, date and supplier; Nutrient and Product Database - Asia; 1970 to date; includes data on production, consumption/off-take, import and export, by nutrient, by product and by country **Loan:** In country **Service:** Internationally **Photocopy:** Yes

---

3006   Buriram, Thailand
Buriram College of Agriculture and Technology
Library
Amphur Muang
Buriram 31000
Phone: +66(2) 611159

Former Name: Buriram Agricultural College **Type:** Academic, Government **Staff:** 1 Prof. 2 Other **Holdings:** 8,012

books 35 journals **Subjects:** Agribusiness, Animal Husbandry, Crops, Education/Extension, Farm Machinery **Photocopy:** No **Loan:** In country

3007　Chaiyaphum, Thailand
　　　　Chaiyaphum College of Agriculture and
　　　　　　Technology
　　　　Chaiyaphum Agricultural Information Center
　　　　115 Niwaterat Road
　　　　Amphur Muang
　　　　Chaiyaphum

Former Name: Chaiyaphum Agricultural College **Founded:** 1977 **Type:** Government **Staff:** 1 Prof. **Holdings:** 54 journals 15,740 books **Subjects:** Crops, Animal Husbandry **Loan:** In country **Photocopy:** Yes

3008　Chanthaburi, Thailand
　　　　Chanthaburi Horticultural Research Center
　　　　　　(CHRC)
　　　　Library
　　　　Chanthaburi 22190
Phone: +66(39) 397030, 397146 **Fax:** +66(39) 397236
Email: chrc@ksc.th.com

Founded: 1986 **Type:** Government **Head:** Cholathee Numnhoo *Phone:* +66 (39) 397030 **Staff:** 2 Other **Holdings:** 6 books 8 journals **Language of Collection/Services:** Thai / Thai **Subjects:** Crops, Entomology, Soil Science, Water Resources **Specializations:** Horticulture **Loan:** Inhouse **Service:** In country **Photocopy:** Yes

3009　Chanthaburi, Thailand
　　　　Rajamangala Institute of Technology, Chanthaburi
　　　　　　Camput (RIT)
　　　　Library
　　　　Bamrat Naradun Road
　　　　Chanthaburi 22210
WWW: www.rit.ac.th

Founded: 1964 **Type:** Academic **Head:** Mr. Weerasak Nonmuang *Phone:* +66(39) 452387/8 ext 126 **Staff:** 1 Prof. 3 Other **Holdings:** 13,000 books 85 journals **Language of Collection/Services:** English, Thai / Thai **Subjects:** Animal Husbandry, Fisheries, Food Sciences, Landscaping, Plants **Loan:** In country **Service:** In country **Photocopy:** Yes

3010　Chiang Mai, Thailand
　　　　Chiang Mai University (CMU)
　　　　Main Library
　　　　239 Huaykaew Road
　　　　Muang District
　　　　Chiang Mai 50200
Phone: +66(53) 944501 **Fax:** +66(53) 222766 **WWW:** www.cmu.ac.th **OPAC:** www.lib.cmu.ac.th

Founded: 1964 **Type:** Academic **Head:** Asst. Prof. Prasit Malumpong *Email:* prasit@lib.cmu.ac.th **Staff:** 41 Prof. 64 Other **Holdings:** 651,608 books 2,359 journals **Language of Collection/Services:** Thai, English / Thai, English **Subjects:** Agricultural Economics, Animal Husbandry, Crops, Education/Extension, Entomology, Food Sciences, Horticulture, Plant Pathology, Soil Science **Databases Developed:** Union List of Serials in PULINET Libraries; Thai Encyclopedia In-

dex; Thai Periodical Index of CMUL **Databases Used:** Comprehensive **Loan:** Internationally **Service:** Internationally **Photocopy:** Yes

3011　Chiang Mai, Thailand
　　　　Chiang Mai University, Faculty of Agriculture
　　　　　　(CMU)
　　　　Library
　　　　Suthep Road
　　　　Chiang Mai 50200
Phone: +66(53) 944075, 944096 **Fax:** +66(53) 944078
WWW: www.cmu.ac.th **OPAC:** isisweb.lib.cmu.ac.th

Founded: 1971 **Type:** Academic **Head:** Mrs. Prapapun Plaichan *Email:* prapapun@lib.cmunet.edu *Phone:* +66(53) 944075, 944096 **Staff:** 2 Prof. 3 Other **Holdings:** 30,000 books 44 journals **Language of Collection/Services:** English, Thai / Thai **Subjects:** Agriculture (Tropics), Farming, Agricultural Economics, Animal Husbandry, Crops, Education/Extension, Entomology, Food Sciences, Horticulture, Plant Pathology, Soil Science, Water Resources **Loan:** In country **Service:** In country **Photocopy:** Yes

3012　Chiang Mai, Thailand
　　　　Maejo University
　　　　Central Library (CELIB)
　　　　Chiang Mai 50290
Location: 63 Maejo, Tambon Nong Harn, Amphoe Sansai
Phone: +66(53) 498755 **Fax:** +66(53) 498147 **WWW:** www.mju.ac.th

Former Name: Maejo Institute of Agricultural Technology (MIAT) **Founded:** 1978 **Type:** Academic **Head:** Dr. Boonrawd Supa-Udomlerk *Email:* penapa@maejo.mju.ac.th *Phone:* +66(53) 498147 **Staff:** 8 Prof. 25 Other **Holdings:** 70,000 books 800 journals **Language of Collection/Services:** Thai, English / Thai, English **Subjects:** Agribusiness, Agriculture (Tropics), Agricultural Development, Agricultural Economics, Agricultural Engineering, Biotechnology, Animal Husbandry, Crops, Education/Extension, Farming, Entomology, Fisheries, Food Sciences, Forestry, Horticulture, Plant Pathology, Plants, Soil Science, Veterinary Medicine, Water Resources **Databases Developed:** Thai Journal Index **Databases Used:** Agris **Loan:** Internationally **Service:** Internationally **Photocopy:** Yes

3013　Chiang Mai, Thailand
　　　　Rajamangala Institute of Technology, Northern
　　　　　　Campus (RIT)
　　　　Library
　　　　Huai-kaeo Road
　　　　Muang
　　　　Chiang Mai 50300
Phone: +66(53) 221576, 213112, 213134, 892780 ext 1330
Fax: +66(53) 213183 **WWW:** www.rit.ac.th

Founded: 1957 **Type:** Academic **Head:** Mrs. Wipawan Paladkhun *Phone:* +66(53) 221576, 213112, 213134, 892 780 ext 1330 **Staff:** 2 Prof. 7 Other **Holdings:** 34,000 books 70 journals **Language of Collection/Services:** English, Thai /Thai **Subjects:** Agricultural Engineering **Loan:** Inhouse **Service:** Inhouse **Photocopy:** Yes

3014 **Chiangrai, Thailand**
Chiangrai Horticulture Research Centre (CHRC)
Library
PO Box 39
Muang
Chiangrai 57000
Phone: +66(53) 715200 **Fax:** +66(53) 714024 **Email:**
crhort@ksc.th.com

Founded: 1982 **Type:** Government **Head:** Nattarat Suppa-
kumnerd *Phone:* +66(53) 715200 *Email:* crhort@ksc.th.com
Staff: 1 Prof. **Holdings:** 1,000 books **Language of Collec-
tion/Services:** English, Thai / Thai **Subjects:** Horticulture
Loan: In country **Service:** In country **Photocopy:** Yes

3015 **Chonburi, Thailand**
Burapha University (BUU)
Library
PO Box 8 Burapha University
Muang
Chonburi 20131
Phone: +66(38) 390060, 391163, 391560, 391352 **Fax:**
+66(38) 390049 **Email:** library@bucc.buu.ac.th **WWW:**
www.buu.ac.th/~library

Former Name: Srinakarinwirot University, Bangsaen Campus **Founded:** 1955 **Type:** Academic **Head:** Mrs. Sriwan
Meekhun *Phone:* +66(38) 390049, 745796 *Email:* library@
bucc4.buu.ac.th **Staff:** 8 Prof. 46 Other **Holdings:** 177,824
books 1,467 journals **Language of Collection/Services:**
Chinese, English, Japanese, Thai / Thai **Subjects:** Comprehensive **Loan:** Inhouse **Service:** Inhouse **Photocopy:** Yes

3016 **Chonburi, Thailand**
Rajamangala Institute of Technology (RIT)
Library
Amphur Sri Racha
Chonburi 20210
Phone: +66(38) 311808 **WWW:** www.rit.ac.th

Former Name: Institute of Technology and Vocational Education **Type:** Academic **Staff:** 2 Prof. 4 Other **Holdings:**
8,644 books 94 journals **Subjects:** Animal Husbandry, Edu-
cation/Extension, Crops, Fisheries, Horticulture, Soil Science **Loan:** In country **Photocopy:** No

3017 **Kalasin, Thailand**
Rajamangala Institute of Technology (RIT)
Library
Nua
Muang
Kalasin 46000
Phone: +66(43) 811128 **Fax:** +66(43) 812972 **WWW:**
www.rit.ac.th

3018 **Kamphaengphet, Thailand**
Kamphaengphet College of Agriculture and
Technology (KCAT)
Library
Muang
Kamphaengphet 62000
Phone: +66(56) 712264

Former Name: Kamphaengphet Agricultural College
(KAC) **Founded:** 1977 **Type:** Academic **Head:** Ms. Sree-
phan Tonkao *Phone:* +66(56) 712264 **Staff:** 1 Prof. 1 Other
Holdings: 6,800 books 12 journals **Language of Collection/
Services:** English, Thai / Thai **Subjects:** Agribusiness, Agri-
cultural Economics, Agricultural Engineering, Animal Hus-
bandry, Computer Science, Food Sciences, Plants **Loan:**
Inhouse **Service:** Inhouse **Photocopy:** Yes

3019 **Khon Kaen, Thailand**
Khon Kaen University (KKU)
Instructional Resources Center (IRC)
Mittraphap Road
Khon Kaen 40002
Phone: +66(43) 237302 **Fax:** +66(43) 237302 **WWW:**
library.kku.ac.th **OPAC:** kkulib.kku.ac.th

Founded: 1964 **Type:** Academic **Head:** Mr. Aphai Prakob-
pol *Phone:* +66(43) 237302 *Email:* aphpra@kku1.kku.ac.th
Staff: 45 Prof. 92 Other **Holdings:** 200,000 books 1,016
journals **Language of Collection/Services:** Thai, English /
Thai **Subjects:** Comprehensive **Databases Used:** Comprehensive **Loan:** In country **Service:** In country **Photocopy:**
Yes

3020 **Khon Kaen, Thailand**
Khonkaen College of Agriculture and Technology
(KCAT)
Academic Resource Center
Pancha Kiri
Khon Kaen 40160
Phone: +66(43) 289193 **Fax:** +66(43) 289194

Former Name: Khon Kaen Agriculture College (KKAC)
Founded: 1977 **Type:** Academic **Head:** Mr. Manop Silla-
patiwat *Phone:* +66(43) 289193 **Holdings:** 26,000 books
140 journals **Staff:** 1 Prof. 2 Other **Language of Collection/
Services:** English, Thai / Thai **Subjects:** Agribusiness, Ani-
mal Husbandry, Crops, Dairy Cattle, Education/Extension,
Fisheries, Horticulture, Orchards, Sericulture, Soil Science,
Vegetables, Veterinary Medicine **Loan:** Inhouse **Service:**
Inhouse **Photocopy:** Yes

3021 **Khon Kaen, Thailand**
Rajamangala Institute of Technology (RIT)
Library
Nai-Muang
Muang
Khon Kaen 40000
Phone: +66(43) 237483, 237492, 236451 **Fax:** +66(43)
237483 **WWW:** www.kkc.rit.ac.th

3022 **Klong Luang, Thailand**
Asian Institute of Technology (AIT)
Center for Library and Information Resources
(CLAIR)
PO Box 4
Klong Luang, Pathumthani 12120
Location: 42 km Paholyothin Highway, Klong Luang,
Patumthani 12120 **Phone:** +66(2) 524-5878 **Fax:** +66(2)
524-5870 **Email:** ref@ait.ac.th **WWW:** www.ait.ac.th/clair
OPAC: telnet://clair.ait.ac.th

Former Name: SEATO Graduate School of Engineering, Library and Information Center, Library and Regional Documentation Center (LRDC) **Founded:** 1959 **Type:** Academic **Head:** F.J. Devadason *Email:* devdsn@ait.ac.th *Phone:* +66 (2) 524-5853 **Staff:** 20 Prof. 33 Other **Holdings:** 22,000 books 650 journals **Language of Collection/Services:** English / English **Subjects:** Aquaculture, Farming, Postharvest Technology **Specializations:** Agricultural Engineering, Biotechnology, Environmental Sciences, Food Technology, Water Resources **Databases Developed:** BOOKCAT - technical books and documents on civil engineering; ENSC - water supply and environmental sanitation documents; RERI - renewable energy resources documents; AGE - geotechnical engineering documents; INFC - ferrocement publications **Databases Used:** ABI/Inform; Compendex **Loan:** Internationally **Service:** Internationally **Photocopy:** Yes

3023   Lampang, Thailand
          Rajamangala Institute of Technology, Lampang
              Agricultural Research and Training Center
              (RIT, LARTC)
          Library
          PO Box 89
          Amphur Muang
          Lampang 52000

Location: Phaholyothin Road **Phone:** +66(54) 218570 **Fax:** +66(54) 218570 **WWW:** www.rit.ac.th

Founded: 1982 **Type:** Government **Head:** Mrs. Srismorn Chooduang *Phone:* +66(54) 218570 **Staff:** 1 Prof. 1 Other **Holdings:** 7,000 books 85 journals **Language of Collection/ Services:** Thai, English / Thai **Subjects:** Agricultural Development, Agricultural Economics, Agricultural Engineering, Crops, Food Sciences, Pomology, Sericulture, Vegetables **Loan:** Inhouse **Service:** In country **Photocopy:** Yes

3024   Lamphun, Thailand
          Lamphun College of Agriculture and Technology
          Library
          Amphur Maetha
          Lamphun 51140

Former Name: Lamphun Agricultural College **Founded:** 1980 **Type:** Academic **Staff:** 1 Prof. 4 Other **Holdings:** 9,000 books 40 journals **Subjects:** Agribusiness, Crops, Animal Husbandry, Irrigation **Loan:** Inhouse **Photocopy:** Yes

3025   Nakhon Pathom, Thailand
          Kasetsart University (KU)
          Kamphaeng Saen Campus Library
          Nakhon Pathom 73140

Phone: +66(34) 351401 **Fax:** +66(34) 351401 **Email:** libctp@nontri.ku.ac.th **WWW:** www.ku.ac.th

Founded: 1979 **Type:** Academic **Head:** Miss Chantipa Pumechantra *Phone:* +66(34) 351884 *Email:* libctp@nontri. ku.ac.th **Staff:** 6 Prof. 17 Other **Holdings:** 1,100 journals 90,000 books **Language of Collection/Services:** Thai, English **Subjects:** Agriculture (Tropics), Agricultural Development, Agricultural Engineering, Animal Husbandry, Crops, Biotechnology, Education/Extension, Entomology, Farming, Food Technology, Horticulture, Irrigation, Plant Pathology, Plants, Soil Science, Veterinary Medicine, Water

Resources **Specializations:** Agriculture (Thailand) **Databases Used:** Agricola; Agris; CABCD **Loan:** In country **Service:** In country **Photocopy:** Yes

3026   Nakhon Pathom, Thailand
          Kasetsart University, Kamphaeng Saen Campus,
              National Agricultural Machinery Center
          Library
          Nakhon Pathom 73140

Phone: +66(34) 351397 **Fax:** +66(34) 351946 **Email:** rdispn@nontri.ku.ac.th **WWW:** www.ku.ac.th **Ariel IP:** 158.108.201.9

Founded: 1985 **Type:** Academic **Head:** Mr. Suttiporn Niamhom *Phone:* +66(34) 351397 *Email:* rdispn@nontri. ku.ac.th **Staff:** 1 Other **Holdings:** 1,000 books 3 journals **Language of Collection/Services:** English, Thai/Thai **Subjects:** Agricultural Engineering, Farm Machinery **Loan:** In country **Service:** In country **Photocopy:** Yes

3027   Nakhon Phanom, Thailand
          Nakhonphanom College of Agriculture and
              Technology
          Information Center
          Tambon Khamthao
          Muang
          Nakhon Phanom 48000

Phone: +66(42) 513258 **Fax:** +66(42) 513258

Former Name: Nakhonphanom Agricultural College **Founded:** 1974 **Type:** Academic **Head:** Mrs. Thasamalee Buntoa *Phone:* +66(42) 513258 **Staff:** 1 Prof. 1 Other **Holdings:** 12,000 books 23 journals **Language of Collection/ Services:** English, Thai / Thai **Subjects:** Agribusiness, Animal Husbandry, Crops, Education/Extension, Entomology, Fisheries, Horticulture **Loan:** Inhouse **Service:** Inhouse **Photocopy:** No

3028   Nakhon Ratchasima, Thailand
          Nakhonrajsrima College of Agriculture and
              Technology (NCT)
          Library
          Lat Bua Luang, Sikiu
          Nakhon Ratchasima 30340

Phone: +66(44) 325495/6 **Fax:** +66(44) 325497

Former Name: Nakhonrajsrima Agricultural College **Founded:** 1929 **Type:** Academic **Head:** Mr. Artit Sudachan *Phone:* +66(44) 325495/6 **Staff:** 1 Prof. 2 Other **Holdings:** 13,500 books 12 journals **Language of Collection/Services:** English, Thai / Thai **Subjects:** Agriculture (Tropics), Agribusiness, Agricultural Economics, Animal Husbandry, Entomology, Crops, Farming, Fisheries, Food Sciences, Forestry, Horticulture, Plant Pathology, Soil Science, Veterinary Medicine **Loan:** Inhouse **Service:** Inhouse **Photocopy:** No

3029   Nakhon Ratchasima, Thailand
          Nakornratchasima Sericultural Research Center
              (Korat Seri. Res. Cen.)
          Library
          1887 Mittraphap Road
          Muang
          Nakhon Ratchasima 30000

Phone: +66(44) 2141023 **Fax:** +66(44) 214100

Former Name: Nakornratchasima Experiment Station **Founded:** 1982 **Type:** Government **Head:** Mrs. Thong-kum Pholpanit *Phone:* +66(44) 299527, 336145 **Staff:** 1 Prof. **Holdings:** 1,880 books 100 journals **Language of Collection/Services:** English, Japanese, Thai / Thai **Subjects:** Sericulture **Loan:** In country **Service:** In country **Photocopy:** Yes

3030   Nakhon Ratchasima, Thailand
         Rajamangala Institute of Technology,
              Northeastern Campus, Nakhon Ratchasima
              (RIT)
         Library
         Muang
         Nakhon Ratchasima 30000
Phone: +66(44) 242978/9 ext 2230, 2232/4 **Email:** korat@nec.rit.ac.th **WWW:** www.rit.ac.th

Founded: 1957 **Type:** Academic **Head:** Mrs. Ratanakorn Yimpraserd *Phone:* +66(44) 242978/9 ext 2230, 2232/4 *Email:* ratakorn@nec.rit.ac.th **Staff:** 3 Prof. 8 Other **Holdings:** 68,000 books 48 journals **Language of Collection/Services:** English, Thai / Thai **Subjects:** Agricultural Engineering, Agricultural Technologies **Loan:** In country **Service:** In country **Photocopy:** No

3031   Nakhon Ratchasima, Thailand
         Suranaree University of Technology (SUT)
         Center for Library Resources and Educational
              Media
         Mahawitthayalai Road
         Nakhon Ratchasima 30000
Phone: +66(44) 223061 **Fax:** +66(44) 223060 **WWW:** sutlib1.sut.ac.th **OPAC:** telnet://203.158.6.33 login library

Founded: 1993 **Type:** Academic **Head:** Dr. Prapavadee Suebsonthi *Phone:* +66(44) 223062 *Email:* prapava@ccs.sut.ac.th **Staff:** 10 Prof. 15 Other **Holdings:** 50,000 books 330 journals **Language of Collection/Services:** English, German, Thai / English, Thai **Subjects:** Agricultural Technologies **Specializations:** Animal Husbandry, Biotechnology, Crop Production, Food Technology **Databases Used:** Comprehensive **Loan:** Internationally **Service:** Internationally **Photocopy:** Yes

3032   Nakorn Si Thammarat, Thailand
         Rajamangala Institute of Technology, Nakhon
              Sithammarat Campus (RIT)
         Library
         Thung Song
         Nakhon Si Thammarat 80110
Phone: +66(75) 329597 **Fax:** +66(75) 411745 **WWW:** www.rit.ac.th

Non-English Name: Nakhon Sithammarat Saiyai **Former Name:** Institute of Technology and Vocational Education **Founded:** 1961 **Type:** Academic **Head:** Ms. Suvannee Koungthoung *Phone:* +66(75) 411144, 329597 **Staff:** 2 Prof. 2 Other **Holdings:** 23,955 books 251 journals **Language of Collection/Services:** English, Thai / Thai **Subjects:** Animal Husbandry, Crops, Fisheries, Plants **Loan:** In country **Service:** In country **Photocopy:** Yes

3033   Nakorn Si Thammarat, Thailand
         Southern Veterinary Research and Diagnostic
              Center (SVRDC)
         Library
         Tung Song Huai-Yot Road
         Nakhon Si Thammarat 80110
Phone: +66(75) 363423/4, 538035/6 **Fax:** +66(75) 353486

Founded: 1979 **Type:** Government **Head:** Miss Umai Bilamoad *Phone:* +66(75) 363423/4, 538035/6 **Staff:** 1 Other **Holdings:** 1,800 books 5 journals **Language of Collection/Services:** English, Thai / Thai **Subjects:** Animal Husbandry, Veterinary Medicine **Specializations:** Animal Diseases **Loan:** In country **Service:** In country **Photocopy:** Yes

3034   Nan, Thailand
         Rajamangala Institute of Technology (RIT)
         Library
         Fai-Kaeo
         Muang
         Nan 55000
Phone: +66(54) 710259 **Fax:** +66(54) 771398 **WWW:** www.rit.ac.th

3035   Narathiwat, Thailand
         Narathiwat College of Agriculture and
              Technology
         Library
         Amphur Rangae
         Narathiwat 96130
Phone: +66(73) 671165 **Fax:** +66(73) 671165

Former Name: Narathiwat Agricultural College **Founded:** 1976 **Type:** Academic **Head:** Mrs. Thitsanita Bangwichit *Phone:* +66(73) 671165 **Holdings:** 9,157 books 70 journals **Language of Collection/Services:** Thai / Thai **Subjects:** Animal Husbandry, Crops, Farming, Fisheries, Plants **Loan:** In country **Photocopy:** No

3036   Pathum Thani, Thailand
         Pathum Thani Rice Research Center (PTT RRC)
         Library
         Thanya Buri
         Pathum Thani 12110
Phone: +66(2) 577-1688/9 **Fax:** +66(2) 577-1300

Former Name: Rangsit Rice Experiment Station **Founded:** 1985 **Type:** Government **Head:** Mr. Sarayouth Phumiphon *Phone:* +66(2) 577-1688/9 **Staff:** 1 Prof. **Holdings:** 2,000 books 50 journals **Language of Collection/Services:** Thai, English / Thai, English **Subjects:** Agriculture (Tropics), Agricultural Development, Biotechnology, Crops, Entomology, Farming, Plant Pathology, Plants, Soil Science **Specializations:** Rice, Seed Production **Loan:** Internationally **Service:** Internationally **Photocopy:** Yes

3037   Pathum Thani, Thailand
         Rajamangala Institute of Technology (RIT)
         Library
         Prachathipat, Thanya Buri
         Pathum Thani 12130
Phone: +66(2) 531-2988 **Fax:** +66(2) 531-2989 **WWW:** www.rit.ac.th

3038   Phangnga, Thailand
Phangnga College of Agriculture and Technology
Library
Amphur Takua Tung
Phangnga 82130
Phone: +66(76) 591151 **Fax:** +66(76) 591239

Former Name: Phangnga Agricultural College **Founded:**
1977 **Type:** Academic **Head:** Miss Sutham Boonhok *Phone:*
+66(76) 591151 **Staff:** 1 Prof. 2 Other **Holdings:** 12,000
books 50 journals **Language of Collection/Services:** Thai /
Thai **Subjects:** Animal Husbandry, Fisheries, Plants **Loan:**
Inhouse **Service:** Inhouse **Photocopy:** Yes

3039   Phatthalung, Thailand
Phatthalung College of Agriculture and
    Technology
Library
Muang
Phatthalung 93000
Phone: +66(74) 612348

Former Name: Phatthalung Agricultural College **Founded:**
1973 **Type:** Academic **Head:** Mrs. Chiraporn Sangnak
Staff: 1 Prof. 3 Other **Holdings:** 12,090 books 21 journals
Language of Collection/Services: Thai / Thai **Subjects:**
Animal Husbandry, Crops, Farming, Fisheries, Horticulture
Loan: Inhouse **Service:** Inhouse **Photocopy:** No

3040   Phatthalung, Thailand
Rice Research Institute, Phatthalung Rice
    Research Center
Library
Amphur Muang
Phatthalung 93000
Fax: +66(74) 622795

Founded: 1987 **Type:** Government **Head:** Mr. Manoon
Anekachai *Phone:* +66 (74) 622795/6 **Staff:** 25 Prof. 20
Other **Subjects:** Agriculture (Tropics), Agribusiness, Agri-
cultural Development, Biotechnology, Crops, Entomology,
Plant Pathology, Plants, Rice, Soil Science **Loan:** Do not
loan **Photocopy:** No

3041   Phitsanulok, Thailand
Naresuan University (NU)
Library
Phitsanulok-Nakhon Sawan Road
Phitsanulok 65000
Phone: +66(55) 261055 **Fax:** +66(55) 261049 **Email:**
khwantrakulk@nu.ac.th **WWW:** www.lib.nu.ac.th **OPAC:**
telnet://203.149.14.227 login: library

Former Name: Srinakarinwirot University, Phitsanulok
Campus **Founded:** 1968 **Type:** Academic **Head:** Mr.
Nikom Thatree *Phone:* +66(55) 261048 *Email:* nikomt@nu.
ac.th **Staff:** 8 Prof. 33 Other **Holdings:** 200,000 books 380
journals **Language of Collection/Services:** Chinese, English, French, Thai / Thai **Subjects:** Comprehensive **Databases Used:** Comprehensive **Loan:** In country **Service:** In
country **Photocopy:** Yes

3042   Phitsanulok, Thailand
    Phitsanulok Rice Research Center (PSL RRC)

Library and Information Service (LIS)
Wang Thong
Phitsanulok 65130
Phone: +66(55) 311184 **Fax:** +66(55) 311185

Former Name: Phitsanuloke Rice Experiment Station
Founded: 1987 **Type:** Government **Head:** Mrs. Porntip
Nualsiri *Phone:* +66(55) 311184 **Staff:** 1 Prof. 1 Other **Hold-
ings:** 2,900 books 20 journals **Language of Collection/Ser-
vices:** English, Thai / Thai **Specializations:** Rice **Subjects:**
Farming **Loan:** Inhouse **Service:** Inhouse **Photocopy:** No

3043   Phitsanulok, Thailand
Rajamangala Institute of Technology, Phitsanulok
    Campus (RIT Phitsanulok)
Library
Muang
Phitsanulok 65000
Phone: +66(55) 298438 **Fax:** +66(55) 298439 **WWW:**
www.rit.ac.th

Type: Academic **Head:** Warangkana Gruyrungroj *Phone:*
+66(76) 244446 **Staff:** 1 Prof. 4 Other **Holdings:** 15,000
books 66 journals **Language of Collection/Services:** Thai /
Thai **Subjects:** Animal Husbandry, Fisheries, Plants **Loan:**
Inhouse **Service:** Inhouse **Photocopy:** Yes

3044   Phrae, Thailand
Phrae Rice Research Center (PRRC)
Library
PO Box 54
Phrae 54000
Location: Yantarakitkosol Road, Muang District **Phone:**
+66(54) 646033/36 **Fax:** +66(54) 646033 **Email:** rrcpre@
phrae.ksc.co.th

Founded: 1983 **Type:** Government **Head:** Mr. Jitakorn
Nuankaew *Phone:* +66(54) 646033/36 **Staff:** 1 Other **Holdings:** 5,374 books 94 journals **Language of Collection/Ser-
vices:** Thai, English / Thai **Subjects:** Agriculture (Tropics),
Agricultural Development, Biotechnology, Crops, Entomology, Farming, Food Sciences, Plant Pathology, Soil Science
Specializations: Seed Industry, Seeds, Postharvest Technology, Rice **Loan:** Inhouse **Service:** Inhouse **Photocopy:** Yes

3045   Phranakorn Si Ayutthaya, Thailand
Rajamangala Institute of Technology (RIT)
Library
60 Mu 3, Hantra
Phranakorn Si Ayutthaya 13000
Phone: +66(35) 242554 **Fax:** +66(35) 242654 **WWW:**
www.rit.ac.th

Former Name: Institute of Technology and Vocational Education **Founded:** 1933 **Type:** Academic **Holdings:** 24,000
books 72 journals **Language of Collection/Services:** Thai,
English

3046   Phuket, Thailand
Phuket Marine Biological Center (PMBC)
Library
PO Box 60
Phuket 83000

Location: 51 Sakdej, Tambon Vichit, Muang District
Phone: +66(76) 391128 **Fax:** +66(76) 391127 **Email:** pmbcnet@sun.phuket.ksc.co.th

Founded: !971 **Type:** Government **Head:** Miss Pin Tong-ratana *Email:* pmbcnet@sun.phuket.ksc.co.th *Phone:* +66 (76) 391128 **Staff:** 1 Prof. 1 Other **Holdings:** 2,500 books 180 journals **Language of Collection/Services:** English / Thai, English **Subjects:** Fisheries, Marine Biology, Marine Ecology, Pollution **Loan:** In country **Service:** Internationally **Photocopy:** Yes

3047   Prachin Buri, Thailand
          Rice Research Institute, Prachin Buri Rice
              Research Center (PCRC)
          Prachin Buri Deepwater Rice Library
          Bangsang
          Prachin Buri 25150
Phone: +66(37) 271231 **Fax:** +66(37) 271385

Founded: 1982 **Type:** Government **Head:** Mr. Prayote Chareondham *Phone:* +66(37) 271232 *Email:* prayote@mozart.inet.co.th **Staff:** 1 Prof. 1 Other **Holdings:** 1,500 books 10 journals **Language of Collection/Services:** Thai / Thai, English **Subjects:** Rice **Loan:** Inhouse **Service:** In country **Photocopy:** Yes

3048   Roi-Et, Thailand
          Roi-Et College of Agriculture and Technology
              (RCAT)
          Library
          Chaeng Sanit Road
          Thawatchaburi
          Roi-Et 45170
Phone: +66(43) 569117 **Fax:** +66(43) 569118 **Email:** agrroiet@msu.ac.th

Former Name: Roi-Et Agricultural College **Founded:** 1979 **Type:** Academic **Head:** Miss Wipaporn Sungkhayanon **Staff:** 1 Prof. 2 Other **Holdings:** 14,000 books 20 journals **Language of Collection/Services:** English, Thai / Thai **Subjects:** Agribusiness, Animal Husbandry, Crops, Fisheries, Horticulture, Landscape **Loan:** Inhouse **Service:** Inhouse **Photocopy:** Yes

3049   Sakon Nakhon, Thailand
          Sakon Nakorn Agricultural Research and Training
              Center (SARTC)
          Information Center
          PO Box 3
          Phang Khon
          Sakon Nakhon 47160
Phone: +66(42) 771450 **Fax:** +66(42) 771460 **Email:** dm516@shane.net, kva@health2.moph.co.th

Founded: 1995 **Type:** Government **Head:** Mr. Pramote Laolapha *Phone:* +66(42) 771450 ext 114 **Staff:** 1 Prof. 1 Other **Holdings:** 1,800 books 25 journals **Language of Collection/Services:** Thai / Thai **Subjects:** Animal Husbandry, Fisheries, Plants **Loan:** Inhouse **Service:** Inhouse **Photocopy:** Yes

3050   Samutprakan, Thailand
          Southeast Asian Fisheries Development Center,
              Training Department (SEAFDEC)
          Southeast Asian Fisheries Information System
              (SEAFIS)
          PO Box 97
          Phrasmutchedi
          Samutprakan 10290
Location: Suksawasdi Road, Pom Phrachullachomlkao, Phrapradaeng, Samut Prakan **Phone:** +66(2) 425-8040/5 **Fax:** +66(2) 425-9919, 425-8561 **Email:** td@seafdec.org **WWW:** www.seafdec.org

Founded: 1984 **Type:** International **Head:** Ms. Rungtiwa Saranyapipat *Email:* rungtiwa@seafdec.org *Phone:* +66(2) 425-4040/5 ext 423 **Staff:** 2 Prof. 2 Other **Holdings:** 7,000 books 200 journals **Language of Collection/Services:** Thai, English / English, Thai **Subjects:** Fisheries **Specializations:** Fishing Methods, Marine Engineering, Marine Fisheries Extension **Networks:** Union Catalog of Fisheries Serial Holdings in Asia (ICLARM) **Databases Developed:** Marine Fisheries Abstracts Database **Databases Used:** Agris **Loan:** In country **Service:** Internationally **Photocopy:** Yes

3051   Saraburi, Thailand
          ASEAN Forest Tree Seed Centre (AFTSC)
          Library
          Muak-Lek
          Saraburi 18180
Phone: +66(36) 341305 **Fax:** +66(36) 341859 **WWW:** www.asean.or.id

Former Name: ASEAN - Canada Forest Tree Seed Centre (ACFTSC) **Founded:** 1983 **Type:** Government **Head:** Ms. Nopharat Inthongchai *Phone:* +66(36) 341305 **Staff:** 1 Prof. **Holdings:** 3,000 books 106 journals **Language of Collection/Services:** English / English, Thai **Subjects:** Forestry **Specializations:** Diversity, Forest Management, Genetics, Pollination, Seeds, Tropical Forests **Databases Used:** Agris; CABCD; Current Contents **Loan:** Do not loan **Service:** Internationally **Photocopy:** Yes

3052   Songkhla, Thailand
          National Institute of Coastal Aquaculture (NICA)
          Library
          Kao Saen Soi 1, Muang District
          Songkhla 90000
Phone: +66(74) 312036, 322895, 312091 **Fax:** +66(74) 442054 **Email:** nicas@t-rex.hatyai.inct.co.th

Former Name: Songkhla Fisheries Station **Founded:** 1981 **Type:** Government **Head:** Mrs. Chulaporn Ratanachai *Phone:* +66(74) 311895, 312032 **Staff:** 1 Prof. **Holdings:** 5,000 books 35 journals **Language of Collection/Services:** Thai / Thai **Subjects:** Aquaculture, Fisheries **Specializations:** Coastal Areas, Groupers, Plankton Cultures, Sea Bass **Loan:** Inhouse **Service:** Inhouse **Photocopy:** No

3053   Songkhla, Thailand
          Prince of Songkla University (PSU)
          Lady Atthakraweesuntorn Library
          Hat-yai Campus
          PO Box 13 Tambon Kho Hong

Songkhla 90110
Phone: +66(74) 211030 ext 2920, 2924, 2925 **Fax:** +66 (74) 211805, 446694 **Email:** library.ref@ratree.psu.ac.th **WWW:** www.psu.ac.th **OPAC:** telnet://203.154.134.2 login: pub

Type: Academic **Head:** Mr. Sittichai Lumtansub *Phone:* +66(74) 211030 ext 2921 *Email:* lsittich@ratree.psu.ac.th **Staff:** 18 Prof. 44 Other **Holdings:** 623 journals 148,789 books **Language of Collection/Services:** English, Thai / English, Thai **Subjects:** Comprehensive **Specializations:** Natural Resources **Databases Used:** Comprehensive **Loan:** Internationally **Service:** Internationally **Photocopy:** Yes

3054   Songkhla, Thailand
Rajamangala Institute of Technology (RIT)
Library
Ratchadammoen-nok, Boyang
Muang
Songkhla 90000
Fax: +66(74) 324245 **WWW:** www.rit.ac.th

3055   Songkhla, Thailand
Tinnssulanonda Fishery College
Library
Tambon Pa-wong
Amphur Muang
Songkhla 90100
Phone: +66(74) 333642, 333800 **Fax:** +66(74) 333525

Founded: 1986 **Type:** Government **Head:** Mrs. Kanjana Suthi *Phone:* +66(74) 447884 **Staff:** 2 Other **Holdings:** 800 books 50 journals **Language of Collection/Services:** Thai / Thai **Subjects:** Agricultural Development, Biotechnology, Fisheries **Loan:** Internationally **Service:** In country **Photocopy:** No

3056   Suphan Buri, Thailand
Department of Agriculture, Suphan Buri Field
        Crops Research Centre
Library
Amphur U-Thong
Suphan Buri 72160
Phone: +66(35) 551433 **Fax:** +66(35) 551543 **Email:** onipon@nontri.ku.ac.th **WWW:** www.geocities.com/ researchtriangle/lab/2419

Founded: 1965 **Type:** Government **Head:** Charlermpol Lairungreong *Email:* onipon@nontri.ku.ac.th *Phone:* +66 (35) 551543 **Staff:** 1 Prof. 3 Other **Holdings:** 10,000 books 10 journals **Language of Collection/Services:** Thai, English /Thai, English **Subjects:** Biotechnology, Field Crops, Sorghum, Sugarcane, Tobacco **Loan:** In country **Service:** In country **Photocopy:** Yes

3057   Surat Thani, Thailand
Surat Thani Horticulture Research Center
Library
PO Box 53
Surat Thani 84000
Phone: +66(77) 286933 **Fax:** +66(77) 286933

Founded: 1987 **Type:** Government **Staff:** 1 Prof. **Holdings:** 2,000 books 3 journals **Language of Collection/Services:**

English, Thai/Thai **Subjects:** Fruits, Horticulture, Oil Palms **Loan:** In country **Service:** In country **Photocopy:** Yes

3058   Surin, Thailand
Rajamangala Institute of Technology, Surin
        Campus (RIT Surin)
Library
Surin-Prasat Road
Muang
Surin 32000
WWW: www.rit.ac.th

Former Name: Institute of Technology and Vocational Education, Surin Campus **Type:** Academic **Head:** Thongchai Phabu *Phone:* +66(44) 511022 ext 109 **Staff:** 3 Prof. 3 Other **Holdings:** 30,000 books 200 journals **Language of Collection/Services:** Thai, English / Thai **Subjects:** Agribusiness, Agricultural Economics, Agricultural Engineering, Animal Husbandry, Computer Science, Fisheries, Food Sciences, Landscape Architecture, Plants **Loan:** Internationally **Service:** Internationally **Photocopy:** Yes

3059   Tak, Thailand
Rajamangala Institute of Technology (RIT)
Library
41 Mu 7, Phaholyothin Road
Mai-ngam, Muang
Tak 63000
Phone: +66(55) 511862, 511832 **Fax:** +66(55) 511833 **WWW:** www.rit.ac.th

3060   Trang, Thailand
Rajamangala Institute of Technology (RIT)
Library
179 Mu 3, Mai-fat
Sikao
Trang 92150
Phone: +66(75) 212510 **WWW:** www.rit.ac.th

3061   Ubonratchathani, Thailand
Ubonratchathani Field Crops Research Center
        (UBFCRC)
Library
PO Box 69
Ubonratchathani 34000
Location: Satitnimankan Street, Tambon Tachang, Amphur Varinchamrap **Phone:** +66(45) 202187/9 **Fax:** +66 (45) 202187 **Email:** ubfcrc@ubon.a-net.net.th, ubfcre@ thaimail.com **WWW:** www.geocities.com/capecanaveral/ lab/3911

Founded: 1975 **Type:** Government **Head:** Boonguar Poosri *Phone:* +66(45) 202187 *Email:* ubfcrc@yahoo.com **Staff:** 2 Prof. 3 Other **Holdings:** 2,900 books 40 journals **Language of Collection/Services:** Thai / Thai **Subjects:** Agricultural Development, Agricultural Economics, Agricultural Engineering, Agriculture (Tropics), Biotechnology, Crops, Plant Pathology, Plants, Soil Science **Loan:** In country **Service:** In country **Photocopy:** Yes

3062   Ubonratchathani, Thailand
Ubonratchathani University (UBU)
Instructional Resources Centre

Sathonman Road
Ubonratchathani 34190
Phone: +66(45) 288397 **Fax:** +66(45) 288397 **Email:** maliwan@Li1.ubu.ac.th **WWW:** www.lib.ubu.ac.th **Ariel IP:** 203.148.223.6

Founded: 1990 **Type:** Academic **Head:** Mr. Supachai Hatongkum *Phone:* +66(45) 288397 *Email:* supah@li1.ubu.ac.th **Staff:** 7 Prof. 12 Other **Language of Collection/Services:** English, Thai/Thai **Databases Used:** Comprehensive **Loan:** Internationally **Service:** Internationally **Photocopy:** Yes

Togo

3063   **Agou, Togo**
        Institut National Zootechnique et Vétérinaire
            (INZV)
        Cellule de Documentation
        BP 27
        Agou
Location: site Aventonou **Phone:** +228 215287

Subjects: Veterinary Science

3064   **Anié-Mono, Togo**
        Institut Togolais de Recherche Agronomique,
            Centre de Recherche Agronomique des
            Savanes Humides (ITRA, CRA-SH)
        Bibliothèque
        BP 01 et 02
        Anié-Mono
Fax: +228 269405

Former Name: Direction Nationale de la Recherche Agronomique (DNRA), Institut de Recherches du Coton et des Textiles Exotiques (IRCT) **Founded:** 1948 **Head:** Pamazi K. Laodjassondo *Phone:* +228 269405 **Staff:** 1 Prof. 1 Other **Holdings:** 500 books **Language of Collection/Services:** French, English **Subjects:** Agricultural Economics, Agricultural Statistics, Agriculture (Tropics), Fertilization, Genetics, Plant Protection, Tropical Crops **Specializations:** Animal Breeding, Cotton, Grain Legumes, Sheep **Loan:** Do not loan **Photocopy:** No

♦**3065**   **Atakpame, Togo**
        Société Togolaise du Coton (SOTOCO)
        Bibliothèque
        BP 219
        Atakpame
Phone: +228 400153

Subjects: Cotton

3066   **Kpalimé, Togo**
        Ministère du Développement Rural, Institut
            Togolais de Recherche Agricole, Institut de
            Recherche Café-Cacao (MDR, ITRA, IRCC)
        Bibliothèque
        BP 90
        Kpalimé
 Phone: +228 410034 **Fax:** +228 410060

Founded: 1967 **Type:** Government **Staff:** 1 Other **Holdings:** 204 books 8 journals **Subjects:** Cocoa, Coffee, Tea

3067   **Kpalimé, Togo**
        Structure Nationale d'Appui à la Filière
            Café-Cacao (SAFICC)
        Service de Documentation
        BP 86
        Kpalimé
Phone: +228 410037

Subjects: Cocoa, Coffee

3068   **Lomé, Togo**
        Chambre de Commerce d'Agriculture et
            d'Industrie du Togo (CCAIT)
        Service d'Information et de Documentation
        BP 360
        Lomé
Location: Avenue de la Présidence 360 **Phone:** +228 212065, 217065 **Fax:** +228 214730

Founded: 1921 **Type:** Association **Head:** Tata Boukary *Phone:* +228 212065 **Staff:** 1 Prof. 1 Other **Holdings:** 100 books 25 journals **Subjects:** Agriculture (Tropics), Agricultural Statistics, Plant Protection, Tropical Crops **Loan:** Do not loan **Photocopy:** No

♦**3069**   **Lomé, Togo**
        Direction de la Production Forestière (DPF)
        Service de Documentation
        BP 393
        Lomé
Phone: +228 223924

Subjects: Forestry

3070   **Lomé, Togo**
        Direction de la Protection des Végétaux
        Bibliothèque
        BP 1263
        Lomé
Phone: +228 253773

Subjects: Plant Protection

♦**3071**   **Lomé, Togo**
        Direction Générale du Plan et du Développement
            (DGPD)
        Centre de Documentation Technique (CDT)
        BP 2818
        Lomé
Location: Immeuble CASEF, Avenue du 24 Janvier **Fax:** +228 213751

Former Name: Service de Documentation Technique **Type:** Government **Founded:** 1972 **Head:** Yawo Assigbley *Phone:* +228 215595 **Staff:** 4 Prof. 11 Other **Holdings:** 2,500 books 40 journals **Language of Collection/Services:** French, English **Subjects:** Agriculture (Tropics), Agribusiness, Agricultural Development, Agricultural Economics, Animal Husbandry, Education/Extension, Farming, Fisheries, Food Sciences, Forestry, Plant Pathology, Water Resources **Databases Developed:** CDT - Compilation de la Documentation TG; DOSET - Documentation Scientifique et Technologique; CAPET - Catalogue des Articles du Périodiques Techniques **Loan:** Internationally **Photocopy:** Yes

♦**3072   Lomé, Togo**
Direction Régionale du Développement Rural -
Région Maritime
Unité de Documentation
BP 446
Lomé
Phone: +228 213467

3073   Lomé, Togo
Institut de Nutrition et de Technologie Alimentaire
(INTA)
Unité de Documentation
BP 1242
Lomé
Phone: +228 254118 **Fax:** +228 218792

Subjects: Food Technology, Nutrition

3074   Lomé, Togo
Institut National des Cultures Vivrières (INCV)
Unité de Documentation
BP 2318
Lomé
Phone: +228 250043 **Fax:** +228 218792

3075   Lomé, Togo
Institut National des Sols (INS)
Centre de Documentation
BP 1026
Lomé
Phone: +228 253096 **Fax:** +228 251559

Subjects: Soil

3076   Lomé, Togo
Institut Togolais de Recherche Agricole (ITRA)
Division de la Documentation et Information
Scientifique et Technique (DIST)
BP 1163
Lomé
Phone: +228 252148 **Fax:** +228 251559 **Email:** itra@
cafe.tg

Former Name: Direction Nationale de la Recherche Agronomique (DNRA)

3077   Lomé, Togo
International Fertilizer Development Center for
Africa (IFDC-A)
Library
BP 4483
Lomé
Location: 86, Boulevard du Mono **Phone:** +228 217971
Fax: +228 217817 **Email:** ifdctogo@cafe.tg

Non-English Name: Centre International pour la Gestion de
la Fertilité des Sols en Afrique, Bibliothèque **Founded:** 1987
Type: International **Head:** Mme Cunégonde Kayi Koulekey
Phone: +228 217971 *Email:* ifdctogo@cafe.tg **Staff:** 1 Prof.
1 Other **Holdings:** 3,500 books 55 journals **Language of
Collection/Services:** English / English, French **Subjects:**

Farm Inputs, Fertilizers, Input Output Analysis, Soil
Analysis, Soil Fertility, Soil Science **Loan:** Internationally
Service: Internationally **Photocopy:** Yes

3078   Lomé, Togo
Ministère du Développement Rural et de
l'Hydraulique Villageoise
Centre de Documentation et d'Information
Agricoles (CDIA)
BP 341
Lomé
Phone: +228 215286 **Fax:** +228 211062

Type: Government **Networks:** AGRIS

♦**3079   Lomé, Togo**
Research Institute for Development
Documentation Center
BP 375
Lomé
Location: Avenue du Général de Gaulle **Phone:** +228
212344, 212346 **Fax:** +228 210343

Non-English Name: Institut de Recherche pour le Développement (IRD), Centre de Documentation **Former Name:**
Institut Français de Recherche Scientifique pour le Développement en Coopération (ORSTOM), French Scientific
Research Institute for Development through Cooperation
Founded: 1950 **Type:** Association **Head:** Mr Kokou M.
Devatchagni *Phone:* +228 212344 **Staff:** 2 Prof. **Holdings:**
5,000 books 45 journals **Language of Collection/Services:**
French / French **Subjects:** Agriculture (Tropics), Agribusiness, Agricultural Development, Agricultural Economics,
Animal Husbandry, Biotechnology, Crops, Education/Extension, Entomology, Fisheries, Food Sciences, Horticulture, Plant Pathology, Soil Science, Water Resources **Loan:**
Do not loan **Photocopy:** Yes

3080   Lomé, Togo
Université du Bénin, Ecole Supérieure
d'Agronomie
Bibliothèque
BP 1515
Lomé
Phone: +228 254843, 254197 **Fax:** +228 250183, 250072
Email: biblio-ub@syfed.tg.refer.org

♦**3081   Sokode, Togo**
Direction Regionale du Développement Rural -
Région Centrale (DRDR/RC)
Centre de Documentation
BP 86
Sokode
Phone: +228 500023

Tonga

3082   Nuku'alofa, Tonga
Ministry of Agriculture, Vaini Research Station
Library
PO Box 14

Nuku'alofa
Location: Vaini, Tongatapu **Phone:** +676 32125, 32153
Fax: +676 32132, 24271

Founded: 1982 **Type:** Government **Head:** Ms. Meleane
Vea

3083   Nuku'alofa, Tonga
University of the South Pacific, Tonga Centre
(USP Centre Tonga)
USP Centre Tonga Library
PO Box 278
Nuku'alofa
Location: 'Atele, Nuku'alofa, Tongatapu **Phone:** +676
29055, 29240 **Fax:** +676 29249 **Email:** postmaster@
tonga.usp.ac.fj

Founded: 1971 **Type:** Academic **Head:** Ms. Judy Ma'ilei
Phone: +676 29240 ext 17 *Email:* judy@tonga.usp.ac.fj
Staff: 2 Other **Holdings:** 10,000 books 30 journals **Language of Collection/Services:** English / Tongan, English
Subjects: Comprehensive **Specializations:** Tongan and Pacific Collection **Loan:** Inhouse **Service:** Inhouse **Photocopy:** Yes

3084   'Onohua, Tonga
Hango Agricultural College
Library
PO Box 16
'Onohua, 'Eua
Phone: +676 50050

Type: Academic **Head:** Mr. Ken J. Blackman

Trinidad and Tobago

3085   Trinidad and Tobago
CAB International (CABI)
Library
Gordon Street
Curepe
Phone: +1(868) 662-4173 **Fax:** +1(868) 663-2859 **Email:**
cabi-bio@carib-link.net **WWW:** www.cabi.org

Former Name: CAB Institute of Biological Control (CIBC)
Founded: 1949 **Type:** International **Head:** Anne DeGazon
Phone: +1(868) 662-4173 *Email:* cabi-bio@carib-link.net
Holdings: 600 books 30 journals **Language of Collection/
Services:** English / English **Subjects:** Aquaculture, Entomology, Pest Control, Plant Protection, Plants, Weeds **Databases Developed:** Caribbean Plant Protection Commission
Database - describes agricultural pests and diseases of the region as well as possible control measures **Databases Used:**
CABCD **Loan:** In country **Service:** Internationally **Photocopy:** Yes

3086   Trinidad and Tobago
Caribbean Agricultural Research and
Development Institute (CARDI)
Information Centre (CIC)
University Campus
St. Augustine
Fax: +1(868) 645-1208 **Email:** infocentre@cardi.org

Former Name: Regional Research Centre (RRC), Information and Documentation Centre **Founded:** 1975 **Type:** Research **Head:** Mrs. M. Gosine-Boodoo *Phone:* +1(868) 645-1205/7 *Email:* infocentre@cardi.org **Staff:** 1 Prof. 2 Other
Holdings: 10,000 books 300 journals **Language of Collection/Services:** English / English **Subjects:** Agriculture
(Tropics), Agricultural Development, Agricultural Economics, Animal Husbandry, Biotechnology, Crops, Education/Extension, Entomology, Farming, Horticulture, Plant
Pathology, Plants **Specializations:** Agriculture (Caribbean),
Fruit Crops, Root Crops, Ruminants, Technology Transfer,
Tree Fruits **Databases Developed:** Non-conventional literature and information generated and documented by CARDI
Databases Used: Agricola; Agris; CABCD **Loan:** Regionally **Service:** Regionally **Photocopy:** Yes

3087   Trinidad and Tobago
Ministry of Agriculture, Land and Marine
Resources, Agricultural Planning Division
(MAL&MR, APD)
Library
St. Clair Circle
St. Clair
Phone: +1(868) 622-1221/5 **Fax:** +1(868) 622-8762

Former Name: Ministry of Food Production, Marine Exploitation, Forestry and the Environment (MFPMEFE)
Type: Government **Head:** Sarah Maharaj *Phone:* +1(868)
622-1221, 622-5481 **Staff:** 1 Prof. **Holdings:** 800 books 15
journals **Language of Collection/Services:** English/English
Subjects: Agricultural Development, Agricultural Economics, Finance, Marketing, Statistics **Specializations:** Agriculture (Trinidad and Tobago) **Service:** Internationally **Loan:**
Inhouse **Photocopy:** Yes **Databases Used:** Comprehensive

3088   Trinidad and Tobago
Ministry of Agriculture, Land and Marine
Resources (MAL&MR)
Central Experiment Station Library (CES Library)
Caroni North Bank Road
via Arima PO
Centeno
Phone: +1(868) 646-4334/5, 646-7656 **Fax:** +1(868) 646-1646

Former Name: Ministry of Food Production, Marine Exploitation, Forestry and the Environment (MFPMEFE)
Founded: 1945 **Type:** Government **Head:** Ms. Claudette
Barrington *Phone:* +1(868) 646-1643 **Staff:** 2 Prof. 5 Other
Holdings: 50,286 books 20 journals **Language of Collection/Services:** English / English **Subjects:** Agriculture (Tropics), Agricultural Engineering, Entomology, Extension,
Crops, Horticulture, Plant Pathology, Plant Protection, Soil
Science **Specializations:** Agriculture (Caribbean), Agriculture (Trinidad and Tobago) **Networks:** AGRIS **Databases
Developed:** FARM - Local non-conventential literature; Serials
Database - holdings of Ministry libraries **Databases Used:**
Agricola; Agris **Loan:** In country **Service:** In country **Photocopy:** Yes

3089   Trinidad and Tobago
Ministry of Agriculture, Land and Marine
Resources, East Caribbean Institute of

Agriculture and Forestry (MAL&MR, ECIAF)
Library
Centeno
Via Arima PO

Location: Coroni North Bank Road **Phone:** +1(868) 646-2650 **Fax:** +1(868) 646-3964

Former Name: Ministry of Food Production, Marine Exploitation, Forestry and the Environment (MFPMEFE) **Head:** Mrs. Angela Titus *Phone:* +1(868) 646-2650 **Staff:** 1 Prof. 2 Other **Holdings:** 5,418 books 364 journals **Language of Collection/Services:** English / English **Subjects:** Crops, Agriculture (Tropics), Animal Husbandry, Education/Extension, Farming, Forestry **Databases Used:** Agricola; Agris; CABCD **Loan:** In country **Service:** In country **Photocopy:** Yes

3090   Trinidad and Tobago
Ministry of Agriculture, Land and Marine
Resources, Fisheries Division (MAL&MR)
Library
West Main Road
Chaguaramas

Phone: +1(868) 634-4505 **Fax:** +1(868) 634-4488 **Email:** msau2sd@tstt.net.tt **WWW:** www.cep.unep.org/fisheries/trini-tbgo/index.htm

Former Name: Ministry of Food Production, Marine Exploitation, Forestry and the Environment (MFPMEFE) **Head:** Wendy McIntyre *Phone:* +1(868) 634-4505 **Staff:** 1 Prof. **Holdings:** 2,500 books 20 journals **Subjects:** Agricultural Development, Agricultural Economics, Fisheries

3091   Trinidad and Tobago
Ministry of Agriculture, Land and Marine
Resources (MAL&MR)
Forestry Library
Long Circular Rd.
St. James

Phone: +1(868) 622-7476, 622-4521 **Fax:** +1(868) 628-5503 **Email:** forestry@tstt.net.tt

Former Name: Ministry of Food Production, Marine Exploitation, Forestry and the Environment (MFPMEFE) **Head:** Ms. Margaret Griffith **Staff:** 1 Prof. **Holdings:** 6,000 books 30 journals **Subjects:** Agricultural Development, Agricultural Economics, Forestry, Water Resources

3092   Trinidad and Tobago
Ministry of Agriculture, Land and Marine
Resources, Veterinary Diagnostic Laboratory
(MAL&MR)
Library
Eric Williams Medical Sciences Complex
School of Veterinary Medicine, Building 47-50
Mt. Hope

Phone: +1(868) 662-5678 **Fax:** +1(868) 645-4593

Former Name: Ministry of Food Production, Marine Exploitation, Forestry and the Environment (MFPMEFE) **Head:** Ms. Deidre Hewitt-Williams *Phone:* +1(868) 662-5678 **Staff:** 1 Other **Holdings:** 857 books 181 journals **Subjects:** Animal Health, Animal Husbandry, Livestock, Microbiology

3093   Trinidad and Tobago
University of the West Indies (UWI)
Main Library, Agriculture Division
St. Augustine

Phone: +1(868) 663-1439 ext 2132 **Fax:** +1(868) 662-9238 **Email:** mainlib@library.uwi.tt **WWW:** www.uwi.tt

Founded: 1960 **Type:** Academic **Head:** Dr. M. Rouse-Jones *Email:* mainlib@library.uwi.tt *Phone:* +1 (868) 662-2020 ext 2009 **Staff:** 2 Prof. 5 Other **Holdings:** 17,000 books 2,500 journals **Language of Collection/Services:** English **Subjects:** Comprehensive **Specializations:** Crops, Animal Husbandry, Agriculture (Tropics), Horticulture **Networks:** OCLC **Databases Developed:** Caribbean Information System for the Agricultural Sciences; CARINDEX - Science and Technology **Databases Used:** Comprehensive **Loan:** Internationally **Service:** Internationally **Photocopy:** Yes

Tunisia

3094   Ariana, Tunisia
Agency for Agricultural Training, National
Institute of Research in Agriculture, Water
and Forests
Library
BP 10
2080 Ariana

Location: Avenue de l'Indépendance **Phone:** +216(1) 230039 **Fax:** +216(1) 717951

Non-English Name: Agence de Vulgarisation et de Formation Agricoles, Institut National de Recherches en Génie Rural, Eaux et Forêts, Bibliothèque **Former Name:** Centre de Recherche du Génie Rural **Founded:** 1963 **Type:** Government **Staff:** 1 Prof. 1 Other **Holdings:** 1,200 books 43 journals **Subjects:** Energy Conservation, Irrigation Water, Waste Water, Water Conservation, Water Resources **Loan:** Do not loan **Photocopy:** No

3095   Ariana, Tunisia
National Agricultural Research Institute of Tunisia
Library
Rue Hédi Karray
2049 Ariana

Fax: +216(1) 231686

Non-English Name: Institut National de la Recherche Agronomique de Tunisie (INRAT), Bibliothèque **Former Name:** Service Botanique et Agronomique de Tunisie (SBAT) **Founded:** 1914 **Type:** Government **Head:** Mrs. Aïda Kaabia *Phone:* +216(1) 230024 **Staff:** 1 Prof. 6 Other **Holdings:** 6,750 books 100 journals **Language of Collection/Services:** French, English **Subjects:** Agricultural Economics, Animal Husbandry, Crops, Entomology, Farming, Horticulture, Plant Pathology, Soil Science **Loan:** Do not loan **Service:** Internationally **Photocopy:** Yes

3096 **Médenine, Tunisia**
Agency for Agricultural Training, Arid Regions
Institute
Arid Regions Information and Documentation
Centre
km 22, route de Jorf-el Fje
4110 Médenine
Phone: +216(5) 640664, 640687 **Fax:** +216(5) 640435

Non-English Name: Agence de Vulgarisation et de Forma-
tion Agricoles, Institut des Régions Arides (IRA), Centre de
l'Information et de la Documentation des Régions Arides
(CIDRA) **Founded:** 1976 **Type:** Government **Staff:** 80 Prof.
120 Other **Holdings:** 7,000 books 50 journals **Language of
Collection/Services:** French / French **Subjects:** Agricultural
Development, Agricultural Economics, Animal Husbandry,
Plants, Soil Science, Water Resources **Specializations:** Ani-
mal Production, Crop Production, Desertification, Ecology,
Environment, Forestry, Rural Development, Social Sciences
Photocopy: Yes

♦**3097** **Sidi Thabet, Tunisia**
National School of Veterinary Medicine
Library
Sidi Thabet 2020
Phone: +216() 552460 **Fax:** +216() 552441

Non-English Name: Ecole Nationale de Médecine Vétérinaire, Bibliothèque **Founded:** 1975 **Type:** Academic **Staff:**
1 Prof. 2 Other **Holdings:** 300 books 60 journals **Language
of Collection/Services:** French, English / French **Subjects:**
Botany, Plants, Veterinary Medicine **Loan:** Internationally
Photocopy: Yes

3098 **Tunis, Tunisia**
Ministry of Agriculture
National Agricultural Documentation Centre
30 Rue Alain Savary
1002 Tunis
Phone: +216(1) 680559 **Fax:** +216(1) 785127

Non-English Name: Ministère de l'Agriculture, Centre National de Documentation Agricole (CNDA) **Founded:** 1975
Type: Government **Staff:** 8 Prof. 17 Other **Holdings:** 50,000
books **Language of Collection/Services:** French **Subjects:**
Comprehensive **Networks:** AGRIS **Databases Developed:**
CARIST - Tunisian agricultural research; CNDABIB - Bibliographical reference database; JORTAGRI - Agricultural
law database **Loan:** Do not loan **Service:** Inhouse **Photocopy:** Yes

3099 **Tunis, Tunisia**
National Agricultural Institute of Tunisia
Central Library
43 Avenue Charles Nicolle
1082 Cité Mahrajène
Tunis
Phone: +216(1) 280950 **Fax:** +216(1) 289166

Non-English Name: Institut National Agronomique de
Tunisie (INAT), Bibliothèque Centrale **Founded:** 1898
Type: Academic **Head:** Mme Labiadh Essia **Staff:** 1 Prof. 3
Other **Holdings:** 7,000 books 90 journals **Language of Col-
lection/Services:** French **Subjects:** Agricultural Economics,

Agricultural Engineering, Animal Husbandry, Crops,
Entomology, Farming, Food Sciences, Horticulture, Plant
Pathology, Soil Science **Loan:** Internationally **Photocopy:**
Yes

Turkey

3100 **Adana, Turkey**
Çukurova Tarimsal Arastirma Enstitüsü
Kütüphanesi
Adana
Phone: +90(322) 334-0055 **Fax:** +90(322) 334-0057

Founded: 1980 **Type:** Government **Staff:** 1 Prof. **Holdings:**
750 books 3 journals **Language of Collection/Services:**
English / Turkish **Subjects:** Crops, Plant Pathology, Plant
Protection **Specializations:** Agronomy, Animal Husbandry,
Plant Breeding **Loan:** In country **Service:** In country **Photo-
copy:** Yes

3101 **Ankara, Turkey**
Forest Research Institute
Library Directorate
PO Box 24, Bahçelievler
06501 Ankara
Fax: +90(312) 212-2944

Non-English Name: Ormancilik Arastirma Enstitüsü
(OAE), Kütüphane Müdürlügü (Küt. Müd.) **Founded:** 1955
Type: Government **Head:** Nihat Yilmaz *Phone:* +90(312)
212-6300 ext 2024 **Staff:** 2 Prof. 1 Other **Holdings:** 6,500
books 140 journals **Language of Collection/Services:** English, German, Turkish, French / Turkish **Subjects:** Entomology, Forest Fires, Forest Management, Forest Products,
Forestry Practices, Forestry, Logging, Protection of Forests,
Soil Science, Watershed Management **Loan:** Inhouse **Service:** In country **Photocopy:** Yes

3102 **Ankara, Turkey**
Ministry of Agriculture and Rural Affairs
Agricultural Documentation and Information
Centre
Ivedik cad. Bankacilar sok. No. 10 P.K. 124
Yenimahalle
06170 Ankara
Phone: +90(312) 344-7359 **Fax:** +90(312) 344-8140
Email: hkucukcakar@tb-yayin.gov.tr

Non-English Name: Tarim ve Köyisleri Bakanligi **Former
Name:** Ministry of Food, Agriculture and Animal Hus-
bandry, Ministry of Agriculture and Forestry, Agricultural
Library and Documentation Center, Uluslararasi Tarimsal
Dokümantasyon ve Enformasyon Merkezi **Founded:** 1985
Type: Government **Head:** Mustafa Pamuk *Phone:* +90(4)
1183259, 1170207 **Staff:** 1 Prof. 10 Other **Holdings:** 12,000
books 300 journals **Language of Collection/Services:** Turk-
ish, English **Subjects:** Comprehensive **Networks:** AGRIS
Loan: In country **Service:** Internationally **Photocopy:** Yes

3103 **Ankara, Turkey**
Plant Protection Research Institute
Library

Yenimahalle
Ankara

Phone: +90(312) 344-7430\ **Fax:** +90(312) 315-1513

Non-English Name: Diyarbakir Zirai Mücadele Arastirma Enstitüsü Müdürlügü **Founded:** 1956 **Type:** Government **Holdings:** 704 books **Subjects:** Entomology, Plant Pathology, Plant Protection **Loan:** Do not loan **Photocopy:** No

♦**3104   Antalya, Turkey**
Citrus Research Institute
Plant Protection Division Library
PO Box 35
07100 Antalya

Location: Calli Mevkii **Phone:** +90(242) 345-2884 **Fax:** +90(242) 321-1512

Non-English Name: Narenciye Arastirma Enstitüsü (NAE), Bitki Koruma Subesi Kitapligi **Former Name:** Biyolojik Mücadele Arastirma Enstitüsü, Biological Control Research Institute **Founded:** 1968 **Type:** Government **Head:** Gülen Günal *Phone:* +90(242) 334-1861 **Staff:** 16 Prof. 1 Other **Holdings:** 119 books 10 journals **Language of Collection/Services:** Turkish, English / Turkish **Subjects:** Biological Control, Entomology, Horticulture, Plant Pathology **Loan:** Inhouse **Service:** Internationally **Photocopy:** Yes

3105   **Balcalý, Turkey**
Cukurova University
Library and Documentation Center
01330 Balcalý, Adana

Phone: +90(322) 338-6651 **Fax:** +90(322) 338-6945
WWW: www.cu.edu.tr

Non-English Name: Çukurova Üniversitesi, Kütüphane ve Dokümantasyon Dairesi **Founded:** 1979 **Type:** Academic **Head:** Mr. Turhan Yýlmaz *Email:* tyilmaz@pamuk.cu.edu.tr **Staff:** 6 Prof. 12 Other **Holdings:** 6,000 books 148 journals **Subjects:** Agricultural Economics, Agricultural Engineering, Animal Husbandry, Crops, Education/Extension, Entomology, Farming, Food Sciences, Horticulture, Plant Pathology, Plant Protection, Plants, Soil Science **Databases Used:** Agricola; Agris **Loan:** In country **Photocopy:** Yes

3106   **Bornova, Turkey**
Olive Research Institute
Library
Universite Cad. No. 43
35100 Bornova, Izmir

Phone: +90(51) 161035

Non-English Name: Zeytincilik Arastirma Enstitüsü, Kütüphanesi **Founded:** 1937 **Type:** Government **Staff:** 1 Other **Holdings:** 1,749 books 8 journals **Language of Collection/Services:** Turkish **Subjects:** Olives **Loan:** In country **Service:** Internationally **Photocopy:** Yes

3107   **Bursa, Turkey**
Sericulture Research Institute
Library
PO Box I
16371 Bursa

Location: Hürriyet **Phone:** +90(224) 246-4802 **Fax:** +90 (224) 246-4803

Non-English Name: Ipekböcekçiligi Arastirma Enstitüsü, Kütüphane **Founded:** 1888 **Type:** Government **Staff:** 1 Other **Holdings:** 2,424 books **Head:** Mumin Kara *Phone:* +90(224) 246-4802 **Language of Collection/Services:** English **Subjects:** Sericulture **Loan:** In country **Service:** In country **Photocopy:** Yes

♦**3108   Erzurum, Turkey**
Ataturk University, College of Agriculture
Library
Erzurum

Phone: +90(11) 13423 **Fax:** +90(11) 83647

Non-English Name: Atatürk Üniversitesi, Ziraat Fakültesi (AÜ, ZF), Kütüphane **Founded:** 1960 **Type:** Academic **Head:** Dr. Ziya Yurttas *Phone:* +90(11) 13423 **Staff:** 3 Prof. 3 Other **Holdings:** 5,000 books 150 journals **Language of Collection/Services:** English **Subjects:** Field Crops, Horticulture, Plant Protection, Soil Science **Loan:** In country **Photocopy:** No

3109   **Eskisehir, Turkey**
Anadolu Agricultural Research Institute (AARI)
Library
P.K. 17
26001 Eskisehir

Fax: +90(222) 324-0301

Non-English Name: Anadolu Tarimsal Arastirma Enstitüsü (ATAE), Kütüphane **Founded:** 1925 **Type:** Government **Head:** Sermin Dönmez *Phone:* +90(222) 324-0300 **Staff:** 2 Other **Holdings:** 3,000 books 22 journals **Language of Collection/Services:** English / English, Turkish **Subjects:** Barley, Agronomy, Cereals, Chickpeas, Dry Beans, Industrial Crops, Legumes, Lentils, Opium, Plant Breeding, Plant Pathology, Safflower, Sunflowers, Wheat **Loan:** Do not loan **Service:** Inhouse **Photocopy:** Yes

♦**3110   Istanbul, Turkey**
Animal Diseases Central Research Institute
Library
Pendik
Istanbul

Phone: +90(1) 390-1280 **Fax:** +90(1) 354-7692

Non-English Name: Hayvan Hastaliklari Merkez Arastirma Enstitüsü, Kütüphane **Founded:** 1914 **Type:** Government **Staff:** 1 Prof. **Holdings:** 4,965 books 32 journals **Language of Collection/Services:** English, Turkish **Subjects:** Animal Diseases **Loan:** In country **Photocopy:** Yes

♦**3111   Izmir, Turkey**
Aegean Agricultural Research Institute (AARI)
Library
PO Box 9
Menemen
35661 Izmir

Non-English Name: Ege Tarimsal Arastirma Enstitüsü, Kütüphane **Former Name:** Aegean Regional Agricultural Research Institute (ARARI) **Founded:** 1963 **Type:** Government **Head:** Dr. A. Semsettin Tan *Phone:* +90(51) 849131, 22790 **Staff:** 1 Prof. **Holdings:** 5,000 books 600 journals **Subjects:** Animal Husbandry, Beekeeping, Field Crops,

Gene Banks, Horticulture, Ornamental Plants, Plants **Loan:** Internationally **Photocopy:** Yes

3112   Izmir, Turkey
           Ege University, Agricultural Research and
              Extension Center (AREC)
           Documentation Unit
           Ziraat Fakültesi, C Blok, 3. Kat
           Bornova
           35100 Izmir
Phone: +90(232) 342-5713 **Fax:** +90(232) 339-0600
Email: tuam@ziraat.ege.edu.tr **WWW:** www.agr.ege.
edu.tr/~tuam

Non-English Name: Ege Universitesi, Tarimsal Uygulama ve Araflorintirma Merkezi (TUAM), Dökümantasyon Birimi **Former Name:** Agricultural Extension and Communication Documentation Unit **Founded:** 1980 **Type:** Academic, Government **Head:** Dr. Tayfun Özkaya *Phone:* +90 (232) 342-5713 *Email:* ozkaya@ziraat.ege.edu.tr **Staff:** 1 Prof. 1 Other **Holdings:** 8,000 books 70 journals **Language of Collection/Services:** Turkish **Subjects:** Agricultural Development, Agricultural Economics, Education/Extension **Loan:** In country **Service:** In country **Photocopy:** Yes

3113   Izmit, Turkey
           Poplar and Fast Growing Exotic Forest Trees
              Research Institute
           Library
           P.K. 93
           Kocaeli
           41001 Izmit
Phone: +90(262) 335-0885 **Fax:** +90(262) 335-0885
Email: kavak@turnet.net.tr

Non-English Name: Kavak Ve Hizli Gelisen Orman Agaçlari Arastirma Enstitüsü, Kütüphane **Founded:** 1966 **Type:** Government **Head:** Doc. Dr. A. Sencer Birler *Phone:* +90(262) 335-0885 *Email:* kavak@turnet.net.tr **Staff:** 1 Prof. 3 Other **Holdings:** 3,000 books 200 journals **Subjects:** Economics, Entomology, Forestry, Genetics, Plant Pathology, Plant Protection, Soil Science **Loan:** In country **Photocopy:** Yes

♦**3114   Rize, Turkey**
           Ministry of Finance and Customs, General
              Directorate of Tea Organization
           Tea Institute Library
           PO Box 23
           53100 Rize
Location: Zihniderin Caddesi

Non-English Name: Maliye ve Gümrük Bakanligi, Çay Isletmeleri Genel Müdürlügü, Çay Enstitüsü Kütüphane **Former Name:** Arastirma Enstitüsü Baskanligi **Founded:** 1958 **Type:** Government **Head:** Hayri Pirimoglu *Phone:* +90(54) 30284, 30286 **Holdings:** 1,500 books **Language of Collection/Services:** Turkish **Subjects:** Biotechnology, Entomology, Plant Pathology, Soil Science, Tea **Loan:** Do not loan **Photocopy:** Yes

♦**3115   Samsun, Turkey**
           Black Sea Agricultural Research Institute

           Library
           PO Box 39
           Gelemen
           Samsun
Location: Gelemen/SAMSUN **Fax:** +90(36) 360516

Non-English Name: Karadeniz Tarimsal Arastirma Enstitüsü, Kütüphane **Former Name:** Tohum Islah Istasyonu-Karadeniz Bölge Zirai Arastirma Esntitüsü **Founded:** 1944 **Type:** Government **Head:** Yüksel Bas *Phone:* +90(36) 360514/5 **Staff:** 1 Other **Holdings:** 3,700 books 11 journals **Language of Collection/Services:** English / Turkish **Subjects:** Agricultural Economics, Horticulture, Agricultural Engineering, Crops, Entomology, Farming, Plant Pathology, Soil Science **Loan:** Do not loan **Service:** Inhouse **Photocopy:** No

Turkmenistan

♦**3116   Ashgabat, Turkmenistan**
           Turkmen Agriculture Institute
           Library
           I May St., 62
           Ashgabat 744012
Founded: 1930 **Type:** Government **Holdings:** 63,300 books

♦**3117   Ashgabat, Turkmenistan**
           Turkmen Scientific Research Institute of Stock
              Breeding and Veterinary Science
           Library
           Pervomaiskaya St., 70
           Ashgabat 744608
Founded: 1966 **Type:** Government **Holdings:** 16,100 books **Subjects:** Animal Breeding, Livestock, Veterinary Science

♦**3118   Bairam-Ali, Turkmenistan**
           Turkmen Scientific Research Institute of
              Agriculture, Maryiskaya Agriculture
              Experiment Station
           Library
           I May P/O
           Bairam-Ali 746006
Type: Government **Holdings:** 3,000 books

♦**3119   Chardzhev District, Turkmenistan**
           Turkmen Scientific Research Institute of
              Agriculture, Chardzhev Experiment Station
           Library
           Sakar P/O
           Chardzhev District 746122
Type: Government **Holdings:** 9,100 books

♦**3120   Dashkhovuz, Turkmenistan**
           Turkmen Scientific Research Institute of
              Agriculture, Dashkhovuz Agriculture
              Experiment Station
           Library
           P/O 3
           Tashauz District

Dashkhovuz 746300

Type: Government **Holdings:** 8,100 books

♦**3121   Gyaursk Region, Turkmenistan**
Turkmen Scientific Research Institute of
    Agriculture
Library
Sovkhoz of "9 Ashkhabad Commissar"
Gyaursk Region 745205

Founded: 1957 **Type:** Government **Holdings:** 29,100 books

♦**3122   Kara-Kala, Turkmenistan**
N.I. Vavilov All-Union Scientific Research
    Institute of Plant Growing, Turkmen
    Experiment Station
Library
Druzhby Narodov St., 47
Kara-Kala 745160

Type: Government **Holdings:** 8,400 books **Subjects:** Plants

Tuvalu

3123   Funafuti, Tuvalu
Ministry of Natural Resources, Department of
    Agriculture
Library
Private Mail Bag
Funafuti, Vaitupu

Location: Vaitupu Atoll **Phone:** +688 20186, 20825 **Fax:**
+688 20826

Type: Government **Head:** Mr. Uatea Vave

Uganda

3124   Kampala, Uganda
Makerere University
University Library Service
PO Box 7062
Kampala

Phone: +256(41) 532752 **Fax:** +256(41) 533640 **Email:**
mmlib@starcom.co.ug **WWW:** www.muk.ac.ug

Head: Mr. James Mutazindwa

♦**3125   Kampala, Uganda**
Ministry of Agriculture, Animal Industry and
    Fisheries, Namulonge Research Station
Library
PO Box 7084
Kampala

Former Name: Ministry of Agriculture and Forestry
Founded: 1950 **Type:** Government **Staff:** 1 Prof. 1 Other
Holdings: 4,000 books **Subjects:** Agriculture (Tropics), An-
imal Husbandry, Cotton, Entomology, Plant Pathology,
Plant Physiology **Loan:** In country **Photocopy:** Yes

3126   Kampala, Uganda
National Agricultural Research Organization,
    Kawanda Agricultural Research Station
National Agricultural Documentation and
    Information Centre (NADIC)
PO Box 11098
Kampala

Phone: +256(41) 567622 **Fax:** +256(41) 566049 **Email:**
nadic@imul.com

Type: Government **Networks:** AGRIS

3127   Kampala, Uganda
Uganda Martyrs University
Library
PO Box 5498
Kampala

Phone: +256(481) 21894/5 **Fax:** +256(481) 21898 **Email:**
umu@imul.com **WWW:** www.muk.ac.ug

Ukraine

3128   Cherkassk District, Ukraine
Instiue of Sugar Beets, Central Breeding-Genetics
    Experiment Station
Research Library
Internatsionalnaya St., 4
P/O Sophievka Uman
Cherkassk District 258900

Former Name: Central Breeding-Genetics Experiment Station **Type:** Research **Head:** Tetyana V. Demiedyuk *Phone:*
+380() 54598 **Staff:** 1 Prof. **Holdings:** 11,495 books 8,328
journals **Language of Collection/Services:** Ukrainian, Russian / Russian, Ukrainian **Subjects:** Ecology, Genetics, Selection, Seeds, Sugarbeet **Loan:** In country **Service:** In
country **Photocopy:** No

♦**3129   Chernigov, Ukraine**
Ukrainian Academy of Agricultural Sciences,
    Agricultural Microbiology Institute (UAAS)
Sciences Library
Shevchenko St., 97
Chernigov 250027
Phone: +380(4622) 31749

Former Name: Ukrainian Scientific Research Institute of
Agricultural Microbiology **Founded:** 1962 **Type:** Government **Head:** N.P. Bogdan *Phone:* +380(4622) 31749 **Holdings:** 15,900 books 2,800 journals **Language of Collection/
Services:** Russian, Ukrainian **Subjects:** Biotechnology, Entomology, Microbiology, Soil Science, Veterinary Medicine,
Plants

3130   Chernigov District, Ukraine
Institute of Potato Chernigov Experimental Station
Research Library
Sednev Village
Lenin St., 13
Chernigov Region
Chernigov District 251922
Phone: +380(4622) 74974

Non-English Name: Chernigivska Doslidna stantsiya, Naukova biblioteka **Former Name:** Ukrainian Scientific Research Institute of Potato Economics, Chernigov Experiment Station of Potato **Type:** Research **Head:** Grigory H. Klimenyuk *Phone:* +380(4622) 62795 **Staff:** 1 Prof. **Holdings:** 94,990 books 6,613 journals **Language of Collection/Services:** Russian, Ukrainian / Russian, Ukrainian **Subjects:** Agricultural Chemistry, Biochemistry, Biology, Plant Protection, Potatoes **Loan:** In country **Service:** In country

3131　Chernovtsy District, Ukraine
　　　　Institute of Plant Protection, Ukrainian
　　　　　　Experiment Station of Plant Quarantine
　　　　　　(UESPQ)
　　　　Research Library
　　　　Boyany Village
　　　　Novoselitskii Region
　　　　Chernovtsy District 275224
Phone: +380(3733) 21034

Non-English Name: Ukraiinska Doslidna Stantsia karantynu roslin (UDSKR), Naukova biblioteka **Former Name:** All-Union Institute of Plant Protection, All-Union Scientific Research Station of Cancer of Potatoes and the Colorado Beetle **Type:** Government **Head:** Galina Z. Pinzaru *Phone:* +380(3733) 25224 **Staff:** 1 Prof. **Holdings:** 5,494 books 8,227 journals **Language of Collection/Services:** Russian, Ukrainian/Russian, Ukrainian **Subjects:** Biochemistry, Biophysics, Biotechnology, Cancer, Coleoptera, Entomology, Plant Pathology, Plant Physiology, Plant Protection, Potatoes **Loan:** In country **Photocopy:** No

3132　Crimea Republic, Ukraine
　　　　Crimea State Agriculture Experiment Station
　　　　Research Library
　　　　Klepinino P/O
　　　　Krasnogvardeysky District
　　　　Crimea Republic 334061
Phone: +380(6556) 76228

Non-English Name: Krymska Derzhavna Sieskogospodarska Stantsiya, Naukova biblioteka **Former Name:** Crimea State Regional Agriculture Experiment Station **Founded:** 1924 **Type:** Research **Head:** Lubov T. Tumarova *Phone:* +380(6556) 97915 **Staff:** 1 Prof. **Holdings:** 29,441 books 35,658 journals **Language of Collection/Services:** Russian, Ukrainian / Russian, Ukrainian **Subjects:** Agricultural Economics, Agronomy, Forage, Oils, Plant Breeding, Plant Protection **Loan:** In country **Service:** In country **Photocopy:** No

3133　Crimea Republic, Ukraine
　　　　Institute of Essential Oil and Medicinal Plants
　　　　Scientific Library
　　　　Kievskaya Str., 150
　　　　Simferopol
　　　　Crimea Republic 333620
Phone: +380(652) 269146

Non-English Name: Institut efiromaslichnykh i lekarstvennykh rastenij (IELR), Naukova Biblioteka **Former Name:** All-Union Research Institute of Essential Oil Plants, Department of Scientific-Technical Information **Founded:** 1965 **Type:** Research **Head:** Irina Georgievna Skachkova *Phone:*

+380(652) 269178 **Staff:** 3 Prof. **Holdings:** 123,920 books 66 journals **Language of Collection/Services:** Russian, Ukrainian/Russian, Ukrainian **Subjects:** Agribusiness, Agricultural Development, Agricultural Economics, Agricultural Engineering, Biotechnology, Crops, Entomology, Plants, Plant Pathology, Plant Physiology, Plant Breeding, Plant Genetics **Specializations:** Essential Oil Plants, Medicinal Plants **Databases Developed:** Foreign Firms database **Service:** Internationally **Photocopy:** Yes

3134　Crimea Republic, Ukraine
　　　　Institute of Grape Vine and Wine "Magarach"
　　　　Scientific Library
　　　　Kirov Str., 31
　　　　Yalta
　　　　Crimea Republic 334200
Phone: +380(654) 326120 **Fax:** +380(654) 327054

Former Name: All-Union Research Institute of Vine and Products of Its Processing "Magarach" **Type:** Research **Head:** Larisa Petrovna Klimova-Donchuk *Phone:* +380 (654) 327083 **Staff:** 3 Prof. 1 Other **Holdings:** 41,070 books 84,302 journals **Language of Collection/Services:** Russian/ Russian **Subjects:** Economics, Vineyards, Winemaking **Databases Developed:** Grape Vine

3135　Crimea Republic, Ukraine
　　　　M.I. Kalinin Crimean Agriculture Institute
　　　　Research Library
　　　　Michurina St.
　　　　Agrarnoe P/O
　　　　Simferopol
　　　　Crimea Republic 333030
Phone: +380(652) 227267, 263356 **Fax:** +380(652) 223966 **Email:** csau@pop.cris.net

Former Name: Crimea Agriculture Institute **Founded:** 1931 **Type:** Academic **Head:** Anna P. Sumenko *Phone:* +380(652) 63324 **Staff:** 42 Other **Holdings:** 359,196 books 131,915 journals **Language of Collection/Services:** Russian, Ukrainian / Russian, Ukrainian **Subjects:** Accounting, Agricultural Economics, Amelioration, Horticulture, Plant Protection, Seed Production, Selection, Soil, Viticulture **Service:** In country **Loan:** In country **Photocopy:** No

♦**3136　Crimea Republic, Ukraine**
　　　　Nikita State Botanical Gardens
　　　　Scientific Library
　　　　Botanichne
　　　　Yalta
　　　　Crimea Republic 334267
Phone: +380(654) 335518 **Fax:** +380(654) 335386

Founded: 1812 **Type:** Research **Head:** Natalie Georgievna Lobova *Phone:* +380(654) 335535 **Staff:** 4 Prof. 2 Other **Holdings:** 210,000 books 2,540 journals **Language of Collection/Services:** Russian/Russian **Subjects:** Biochemistry, Cytology, Flowers, Fruit Growing, Horticulture, Ornamental Plants, Plant Breeding, Plant Genetics, Plant Pathology, Plant Protection, Silvicultural Characters, Soil Science **Service:** In country **Loan:** In country **Photocopy:** No

3137   Crimea Republic, Ukraine
        Nikitskii State Botanical Garden, Crimea
            Pomology Station
        Research Library
        Vavilov Settlement, 1
        Sevastopol
        Crimea Republic 335049
Phone: +380(692) 722128

Former Name: All-Union Institute of Peanuts **Type:** Research **Head:** Nina V. Reznichenko *Phone:* +380(692) 722883, 722316 **Staff:** 1 Prof. **Holdings:** 10,515 journals 6,886 books **Language of Collection/Services:** Russian, Ukrainian / Russian, Ukrainian **Subjects:** Agroclimatology, Fruit Growing, Horticulture, Plant Protection **Loan:** In country **Service:** In country **Photocopy:** No

3138   Crimea Republic, Ukraine
        Scientific Industrial Union "Tobacco", Crimea
            Experiment Station
        Library
        Tabachnoe Village
        Bakhchisarai Region
        Crimea Republic 334423
Location: Sovetskaya St., 3 **Phone:** +380(6554) 98366

Type: Government **Head:** Mihailov Anatoliy Petrovich *Phone:* +380(6554) 43730 **Staff:** 7 Prof. 10 Other **Holdings:** 4,300 books 1,500 journals **Language of Collection/Services:** Russian / Russian **Subjects:** Farming, Plants **Specializations:** Seeds, Tobacco **Databases Developed:** Collection of the Crimea Americans and Crimea Dubecs cross breeds **Loan:** Internationally **Service:** Internationally **Photocopy:** Yes

3139   Dnepropetrovsk, Ukraine
        Dnepropetrovsk State Agricultural University
        Research Library
        Voroshilov St., 25
        Dnepropetrovsk 49027
Phone: +380(562) 44-8132 **Fax:** +380(562) 45-5357
Email: dm@dsau.dp.ua

Non-English Name: Dnepropetrovsk Derzhavny agrarny universytet, Naukova biblioteka **Former Name:** Dnepropetrovsk Agriculture Institute **Founded:** 1922 **Type:** Academic **Head:** Zinaida E. Dudchenko *Phone:* +380(562) 463122 **Staff:** 42 Prof. **Holdings:** 264,605 books 55,271 journals **Language of Collection/Services:** Ukrainian, Russian / Russian, Ukrainian **Subjects:** Agricultural Chemistry, Agricultural Economics, Animal Husbandry, Crops, Farming, Mechanization, Soil Science, Veterinary Medicine **Loan:** In country **Service:** In country **Photocopy:** Yes

3140   Dnepropetrovsk, Ukraine
        Institute of Maize
        Scientific Library
        Dzerzhinsky Str., 14
        Dnepropetrovsk 320600
Phone: +380(562) 450236

Former Name: All-Union Institute of Maize **Founded:** 1930 **Type:** Government **Head:** Antonina Lobanova *Phone:* +380(562) 459189 **Staff:** 1 Prof. 1 Other **Holdings:** 55,941

books 33,514 journals **Language of Collection/Services:** Russian, Ukrainian/Russian, Ukrainian **Subjects:** Biochemistry, Botany, Crop Production, Maize, Plant Breeding, Plant Physiology

3141   Dnepropetrovsk District, Ukraine
        Institute of Corn, Erastovskaya Experiment
            Station
        Research Library
        Vishnevo P/O
        Pyatinatka Region
        Dnepropetrovsk District 322515
Phone: +380(565) 102790

Former Name: All-Union Scientific Research Institute of Corn **Type:** Government **Head:** Valentina M. Malovetska *Phone:* +380(565) 94151 **Staff:** 1 Prof. **Holdings:** 17,300 books **Language of Collection/Services:** Russian, Ukrainian / Russian, Ukrainian **Subjects:** Agricultural Chemistry, Agricultural Production, Maize, Plant Protection **Loan:** In country

3142   Dnepropetrovsk District, Ukraine
        Sinelnikovskaya Maize Breeding Experiment
            Station
        Research Library
        Synelinykove P/O
        Dnepropetrovsk Region
        Dnepropetrovsk District 323118
Phone: +380(5615) 22031

Non-English Name: Synelinykivska Doslidna stantsiya, Naukova biblioteka **Former Name:** All-Union Scientific Research Institute of Corn, Sinelnikovskaya Breeding Experiment Station **Type:** Research **Head:** Ludmila S. Tikhtina *Phone:* +380(5615) 3122 **Staff:** 1 Prof. **Holdings:** 10,902 books 10,773 journals **Language of Collection/Services:** Russian, Ukrainian / Russian, Ukrainian **Subjects:** Cereals, Crop Production, Fodder Crops, Maize, Plant Protection **Loan:** In country

3143   Ivano-Frankivsk District, Ukraine
        Ivano-Frankovsk State Agricultural Experiment
            Station
        Research Library
        V. Pyadyki
        Kolomyivskij Region
        Ivano-Frankivsk District 285240
Phone: +380(3422) 23804

Non-English Name: Ivano-Frankivska derzhavna sieskogospodarska doslidna stantsiya, Naukova biblioteka **Former Name:** Ivano-Frankovsk State Regional Agricultural Experiment Station **Founded:** 1956 **Type:** Research **Head:** Svetlana A. Yatsyk *Phone:* +380(3422) 20390 **Staff:** 1 Prof. **Holdings:** 19,421 books 14,632 journals **Language of Collection/Services:** Russian, Ukrainian / Russian, Ukrainian **Subjects:** Agricultural Economics, Crop Production, Forage, Mechanization, Plant Breeding **Loan:** In country **Service:** In country **Photocopy:** No

3144   Kharkov, Ukraine
        Kharkiv State Technical University of Agriculture

Research Library
45, Moskovskij Pr.
Kharkov 61050

Phone: +380(572) 219963 **Email:** romanov@khstua.
kharkov.ua

Founded: 1930 **Type:** Academic **Head:** Tatiyana V.
Novikova **Staff:** 37 Prof. **Holdings:** 330,000 books 6,779
journals **Language of Collection/Services:** Ukrainian, Russian **Subjects:** Electrification, Machinery, Maintenance,
Management, Marketing, Mechanization, Storage **Loan:** In
country **Service:** Internationally

3145   Kharkov, Ukraine
Kharkov State University
Central Scientific Library
pl. Svobody 4
Kharkov 61077

Phone: +380(572) 457420 **Fax:** +380(572) 471272
WWW: www.univer.kharkov.ua/main/library

Former Name: Kharkov Agriculture Institute **Founded:**
1816 **Type:** Academic **Head:** Elvira V. Bella **Staff:** 46 Prof.
Holdings: 608,725 books 137,102 journals **Language of
Collection/Services:** Russian, Ukrainian **Subjects:** Agricultural Chemistry, Agricultural Economics, Seed Production,
Soil Science, Crop Production, Farming **Loan:** In country
Service: In country

3146   Kharkov, Ukraine
Ukrainian Academy of Agricultural Sciences,
    Institute of Experimental and Clinical
    Veterinary Medicine (UAAS, IECVM)
Scientific Library
Pushkinskaya Str., 83
Kharkov 310023

Phone: +380(572) 403249 **WWW:** iekvm.kharkov.ua

Former Name: Ukrainian Research Institute of Experimental Veterinary Medicine **Founded:** 1923 **Type:** Research
Head: Galina Vasilievna Shamayeva *Phone:* +380(572)
403241 **Staff:** 2 Prof. **Holdings:** 38,755 books **Language of
Collection/Services:** Russian, Ukrainian / Russian, Ukrainian **Subjects:** Biochemistry, Microbiology, Parasitology,
Veterinary Medicine **Loan:** Inhouse

3147   Kharkov, Ukraine
Ukrainian Institut for Soil Science and
    Agrochemistry Research "A.N. Sokolovsky"
    (UkrISSAR)
Scientific Library (SL)
Chaikovsky Str., 4
Kharkov 310024

Phone: +380(572) 433392 **Fax:** +380(572) 478563 **Email:**
itl93@online.kharkov.ua

Former Name: A.N. Sokolovsky Institute of Soil Science
and Agrochemistry **Founded:** 1956 **Type:** Research **Head:**
Tamara Ivanovna Kisel *Phone:* +380(572) 470531 *Email:*
itl93@online.kharkov.ua **Staff:** 2 Prof. **Holdings:** 38,000
books 19,000 journals **Language of Collection/Services:**
Russian, Ukrainian / Russian, Ukrainian **Subjects:** Ecology,
Geography, Geology **Specializations:** Agricultural Chemistry, Soil Science **Photocopy:** Yes

3148   Kharkov, Ukraine
V.Ya. Yuryev Institute of Plant Science (YUPSI)
Scientific Library
Moskovshk pr. 142
Kharkov 310044

Phone: +380(572) 900220

Former Name: V.Ya. Yuryev Ukrainian Research Institute
of Plant Science, Breeding and Genetics **Founded:** 1910
Type: Research **Head:** Valentina Nikolaevna Ozherelieva
Phone: +380(572) 900272 **Staff:** 1 Prof. 1 Other **Holdings:**
51,528 books 3,091 journals **Language of Collection/Services:** Russian, Ukrainian / Russian, Ukrainian **Subjects:**
Plant Breeding, Plant Physiology, Plant Protection **Databases Developed:** Gene Fund **Loan:** In country **Service:** In
country **Photocopy:** Yes

3149   Kharkov District, Ukraine
Institute of Poultry Raising
Scientific Technical Library
Smilvsky Region
Borki S/O
Kharkov District 313410

Phone: +380(5747) 24439 **Fax:** +380(5747) 34958

Former Name: Ukrainian Scientific Research Institute of
Poultry Raising **Founded:** 1959 **Type:** Research **Head:** Alla
P. Ponomorova *Phone:* +380(5747) 22365 **Staff:** 1 Other
Holdings: 21,455 books 28,462 journals **Language of Collection/Services:** Russian, Ukrainian / Russian, Ukrainian
Subjects: Animal Breeding, Animal Husbandry, Biochemistry, Biology, Biotechnology, Poultry **Loan:** In country **Service:** Internationally **Photocopy:** Yes

3150   Kharkov District, Ukraine
Institute of Sericulture
Research Technical Library
c. Merepha
Kharkov District 312060

Phone: +380(572) 243570

Former Name: Ukrainian Scientific Research Institute of
Sericulture **Type:** Research **Head:** Lidia S. Birca *Phone:*
+380(572) 243238 **Staff:** 1 Other **Holdings:** 12,638 books
4,252 journals **Language of Collection/Services:** Russian,
Ukrainian / Russian, Ukrainian **Subjects:** Mechanization,
Plant Breeding, Plant Genetics, Sericulture, Silkworms
Loan: In country **Service:** In country **Photocopy:** No

3151   Kharkov District, Ukraine
Kharkiv Zooveterinary Institute
Library
Malaya Danilovka P/O
Dergachev Region
Kharkov District 312050

Phone: +380(263) 57537

Former Name: Kharkov Zoo-Veterinary Institute **Founded:** 1920 **Type:** Academic **Head:** Galina V. Sviridenko
Staff: 35 Prof. **Holdings:** 356,908 books 44,140 journals
Language of Collection/Services: Russian, Ukrainian /
Russian, Ukrainian **Subjects:** Animal Breeding, Veterinary
Science, Zootechny **Loan:** In country **Service:** In country
Photocopy: No

3152   Kharkov Region, Ukraine
Institute of Vegetable and Melon Growing (IVM)
Scientific Technical Library (STL)
P/O Selectsionniy
Kharkov Region 312155
Phone: +380(572) 489891 **Fax:** +380(572) 493740

Non-English Name: Institut Ovochivnitstva e Bashtannictva (IOB), Naukovo-Technitchna Biblioteka (NTB) **Former Name:** Ukrainian Scientific Research Institute of Vegetable and Melon Growing **Founded:** 1947 **Type:** Government **Head:** Lidia I. Romanenko *Phone:* +380(572) 489858 **Staff:** 2 Prof. 1 Other **Holdings:** 40,548 books 48,902 journals **Language of Collection/Services:** Russian, Ukrainian/Russian, Ukrainian **Subjects:** Agricultural Economics, Horticulture, Melons, Plant Physiology, Plant Protection, Potatoes, Vegetables **Loan:** In country **Service:** In country **Photocopy:** No

3153   Kharkov Region, Ukraine
Kharkov State Agrarian University "V.V.
    Dokuchajev"
Fundamental Library
Komunist-1
Kharkov Region 62482
Phone: +380(572) 997123 **Fax:** +380(572) 936067 **Email:** cau@kharkov.com

Former Name: Kharkov Agricultural Institute "V.V. Dokuchajev" **Founded:** 1816 **Type:** Academic **Head:** Olga Grigorievna Ivancha *Phone:* +380(572) 997123 *Email:* cau@kharkov.com **Staff:** 11 Prof. 27 Other **Holdings:** 474,070 books 107,546 journals **Language of Collection/Services:** Ukrainian, Russian / Ukrainian, Russian **Subjects:** Comprehensive **Specializations:** Forestry **Databases Developed:** University proceedings database **Service:** Internationally **Photocopy:** Yes

3154   Kharkov Region, Ukraine
Ukrainian Academy of Agricultural Sciences,
    Institue of Animal Science (UAAS)
Scientific Library
PO Kulynychi
Kharkov District
Kharkov Region 312120
Phone: +380(572) 953401, 953181 **Fax:** +380(572) 627094, 953066 **WWW:** www.awu.kiev.ua/ias.htm

Former Name: Ukrainian Research Institute of Animal Science **Founded:** 1929 **Type:** Research **Head:** Lidiya Nikolaevna Tatyanchenko *Phone:* +380(572) 959951 **Staff:** 2 Prof. **Holdings:** 108,603 books 45,430 journals **Language of Collection/Services:** Russian, Ukrainian **Subjects:** Animal Breeding, Animal Physiology, Economics, Genetics, Livestock, Veterinary Medicine, Zootechny

3155   Khenitskii District, Ukraine
Kamenets-Podilskii Agriculture Institute
Research Library
Shevchenko St., 13
Kamenets-Podilskii
Khenitskii District 281900
Phone: +380(3849) 25218 **Fax:** +380(3849) 25218

Type: Academic **Head:** Lidiya I. Malina *Phone:* +380 (3849) 68392, 68343 **Staff:** 33 Other **Holdings:** 457,926 books 6,052 journals **Language of Collection/Services:** Russian, Ukrainian **Subjects:** Agronomy, Animal Breeding, Animal Feeding, Electrification, Farming, Mechanization, Seed Production, Selection, Veterinary Medicine **Loan:** In country **Service:** In country **Photocopy:** No

3156   Kherson, Ukraine
Institute of Irrigated Agriculture
Research Technical Library
Naddnipryansky Settlement
Kherson 325908
Phone: +380(552) 553045

Former Name: Ukrainian Scientific Research Institute of Irrigated Agriculture **Founded:** 1879 **Type:** Research **Head:** Natalia P. Matsko *Phone:* +380(552) 554113 **Staff:** 4 Other **Holdings:** 81,173 books 2,885 journals **Language of Collection/Services:** Russian, Ukrainian / Russian, Ukrainian **Subjects:** Agricultural Chemistry, Botany, Irrigation, Plant Physiology, Plant Protection, Vegetable Growing **Loan:** In country **Service:** In country

3157   Kherson, Ukraine
Kherson Agricultural Institute
Research Library
Rosy Lyuksemburg St., 23
Kherson 73006
Phone: +380(552) 226471 **Fax:** +380(552) 263289 **Email:** hgau@selena.kherson.ua

Former Name: G. Tsyuryupa Kherson Agricultural Institute **Founded:** 1924 **Type:** Academic **Head:** Natallia Ya. Barsukova *Phone:* +380(552) 225504 **Staff:** 42 Other **Holdings:** 291,858 books 59,921 journals **Language of Collection/Services:** Russian, Ukrainian / Russian, Ukrainian **Subjects:** Agricultural Chemistry, Agronomy, Animal Breeding, Crop Production, Farming, Seed Production, Selection, Soil Science **Loan:** In country **Service:** In country **Photocopy:** No

3158   Kherson District, Ukraine
Institute of Vegetable and Melon Growing,
    Kherson Watermelon Growing Experiment
    Station
Research Library
Krasnoarmeiskaya St., 71
Gola Pristan
Kherson District 326240
Phone: +380(5539) 26222

Former Name: All-Union Scientific Research Institute of Vegetable Crop Breeding and Seed Production, Kherson Melon Breeding and Growing Experiment Station **Type:** Research **Head:** Nina A. Bobrova *Phone:* +380(5539) 26312 **Staff:** 1 Prof. **Holdings:** 2,891 books 1,062 journals **Language of Collection/Services:** Russian, Ukrainian / Russian, Ukrainian **Subjects:** Melons, Seeds, Selection, Vegetables **Loan:** In country **Photocopy:** No

3159   Kherson District, Ukraine
M.F. Ivanov Institute of Animal Breeding in
    Steppe Regions "Ascania Nova"

Scientific Library
Ascania-Nova P/O
Chaplynka Region
Kherson District 326332
Phone: +380(5538) 61144 **Fax:** +380(5538) 22675 **Email:** asknov@public.kherson.ua

Former Name: M.F. Ivanov Ukrainian Scientific Research Institute of Animal Breeding in Steppe Regions "Ascania Nova" **Founded:** 1921 **Type:** Research **Head:** Olena Kovalyk *Email:* asknov@public.kherson.ua *Phone:* +380(5538) 61294 **Staff:** 4 Prof. **Holdings:** 47,337 books 71,948 journals **Language of Collection/Services:** Russian, Ukrainian **Subjects:** Anatomy, Animal Breeding, Animal Husbandry, Livestock, Morphology, Veterinary Medicine **Service:** In country **Loan:** In country **Photocopy:** No

3160 Kherson District, Ukraine
Rice Experiment Station
Scientific Library
Antonivka
Skadovsk Region
Kherson District 326401

Former Name: Ukrainian Scientific Research Station of Rice **Founded:** 1935 **Type:** Research **Head:** Ludmila L. Zyryanova *Phone:* +380(5532) 95348 **Staff:** 1 Prof. **Holdings:** 7,900 books 4,100 journals **Language of Collection/Services:** Russian, Ukrainian, English **Subjects:** Comprehensive **Specializations:** Rice **Loan:** In country **Photocopy:** No

3161 Kiev, Ukraine
Institute of Agroecology and Biotechnology
Scientific Library
Metrologichna Str., 12
Kiev 252143
Phone: +380(44) 266-0287 **Fax:** +380(44) 266-2338

Type: Research **Head:** Alexandra Vasilyevna Zarytska *Phone:* +380(44) 266-1192 **Staff:** 2 Prof. **Holdings:** 3,150 books 2,730 journals **Language of Collection/Services:** Russian, Ukrainian / Russian, Ukrainian **Subjects:** Biotechnology, Cytology, Ecology, Fertilizers, Plant Genetics

3162 Kiev, Ukraine
Institute of Hydraulic Engineering and
    Reclamation
Scientific Library
Vasylkivska Str., 37
Kiev 252022
Phone: +380(44) 263-8733

Former Name: Ukrainian Research Institute of Hydraulic Engineering and Reclamation **Type:** Research **Head:** Lyudmila Grigorievna Zaika *Phone:* +380(44) 263-8733 **Staff:** 2 Prof. **Holdings:** 33,215 books 32,702 journals **Language of Collection/Services:** Russian, Ukrainian **Subjects:** Ecology, Hydraulic Engineering, Hydrology, Reclamation, Water Resources

3163 Kiev, Ukraine
Institute of Plant Protection
Scientific Library

Vasylkivska St., 33
Kiev 252022
Phone: +380(44) 263-1370, 263-1124 **Fax:** +380(44) 263-2185

Former Name: Ukrainian Research Institute of Plant Protection **Founded:** 1946 **Type:** Government **Head:** Lyudmila Petrovna Shelihova *Phone:* +380(44) 263-1370 **Staff:** 1 Prof. **Holdings:** 39,732 books 40,766 journals **Language of Collection/Services:** Russian, Ukrainian / Ukrainian, Russian **Subjects:** Biology, Chemistry, Entomology, Plant Genetics, Plant Pathology, Plant Physiology, Plant Protection **Loan:** Inhouse **Service:** Inhouse **Photocopy:** No

3164 Kiev, Ukraine
Institute of Sugar Beet (ISB)
Scientific Library
Klinichna Str., 25
Kiev 252000
Phone: +380(44) 277-5388

Former Name: All-Union Research Institute of Sugar Beet **Founded:** 1922 **Type:** Research **Head:** Alexandra Yurievna Minert *Phone:* +380(44) 277-5355 **Staff:** 1 Prof. **Holdings:** 80,161 books 30,411 journals **Language of Collection/Services:** Russian, Ukrainian / Russian, Ukrainian **Subjects:** Crop Production, Plant Breeding, Plant Genetics, Plant Protection, Seed Production, Sugarbeet **Loan:** In country **Service:** In country **Photocopy:** No

3165 Kiev, Ukraine
National Agricultural University
Scientific Research Library
Geroev Oboroni St., 13
Kiev 02241
Phone: +380(44) 263-5175, 267-8242 **Fax:** +380(44) 263-7155 **Email:** rector@nauu.kiev.ua **WWW:** www.nauu.kiev.ua

Former Name: Ukrainian Agriculture Academy **Type:** Academic **Head:** Victor V. Dovgopol *Phone:* +380(44) 263-5175 **Staff:** 38 Prof. **Holdings:** 856,453 books 111,986 journals **Language of Collection/Services:** Russian, Ukrainian / Russian, Ukrainian **Subjects:** Agricultural Chemistry, Agricultural Economics, Electrification, Mechanization, Plant Protection, Seed Production, Selection, Soil Science **Loan:** In country **Service:** In country **Photocopy:** Yes

3166 Kiev, Ukraine
Ukrainian Academy of Agricultural Sciences
    (UAAS)
Central Scientific Agricultural Library (CSAL)
Geroiv Oborony Str., 10
Kiev 127 2522650
Phone: +380(44) 267-8082 **Fax:** +380(44) 226-3284 **Email:** ucsal@nauu.kiev.ua

Non-English Name: Ukraiin'ska Akademia Agrarnykh Nauk (UAAN), Tsentral'na Naukova Sil'skohospodars'ka Biblioteka (TsNSHB) **Former Name:** V.I. Lenin All-Union Academy of Agricultural Sciences, Republican Scientific Agricultural Library **Founded:** 1921 **Type:** Research **Head:** Mykhaylo Semenovych Slobodianyk *Phone:* +380(44) 266-0509 *Email:* slobod@csl.freenet.kiev.ua **Staff:** 22 Other 72

Prof. **Holdings:** 541,042 books 4,412,057 journals **Language of Collection/Services:** Russian, Ukrainian, English/Ukrainian **Subjects:** Comprehensive **Databases Developed:** Agroindustrial complex of new Ukrainian agricultural books **Loan:** Internationally **Service:** Internationally **Photocopy:** Yes

3167　Kiev, Ukraine
　　　　Ukrainian Academy of Agricultural Sciences,
　　　　　　Dairy and Meat Technological Institute
　　　　　　(UAAS)
　　　　Library
　　　　Mariny Raskovoi St., 4a
　　　　Kiev 253002
Phone: +380(44) 517-1737 **Fax:** +380(44) 517-0228
Email: timm@public.ua.net

Former Name: Ukrainian Scientific Research Institute of Meat and Dairy Industry **Founded:** 1960 **Type:** Academic **Head:** Elena Frantsevna Bosko **Staff:** 1 Prof. **Holdings:** 25,000 books 5 journals **Language of Collection/Services:** Russian, Ukrainian / Russian, Ukrainian **Subjects:** Animal Husbandry, Biotechnology, Food Sciences **Specializations:** Dairy Technology, Food Processing, Meat Technology, Starters **Loan:** In country **Service:** Inhouse **Photocopy:** No

3168　Kiev, Ukraine
　　　　Ukrainian Academy of Agricultural Sciences,
　　　　　　Institute of Agricultural Economics (UAAS)
　　　　Scientific Library
　　　　Geroiv Oborony Str., 10
　　　　Kiev 252127
Phone: +380(44) 266-0519, 261-4821, 261-3202 **Fax:** +380(44) 266-0528, 265-0565, 267-8446 **Email:** agroecon@ukrpack.net

Former Name: Ukrainian Research Institute of Agrobusiness Industry **Founded:** 1956 **Type:** Research **Head:** Lyudmila Alexandrovna Stepanenko *Phone:* +380(44) 266-0538 **Staff:** 2 Prof. 5 Other **Holdings:** 38,850 books 23,482 journals **Language of Collection/Services:** Russian, Ukrainian/Russian, Ukrainian **Subjects:** Agricultural Economics, Agricultural Statistics, Computer Techniques, Management, Mathematics **Databases Developed:** Economy of Agricultural Enterprises **Loan:** In country

3169　Kiev, Ukraine
　　　　Ukrainian Academy of Agricultural Sciences,
　　　　　　Institute of Horticulture (UAAS)
　　　　Scientific Library
　　　　Settl. Novosyolky
　　　　Kiev 252027
Phone: +380(44) 266-3692 **Fax:** +380(44) 266-6549
Email: ih@uaas.rel.com

Former Name: Ukrainian Research Institute of Horticulture **Type:** Research **Head:** Vera Ivanovna Prudka *Phone:* +380 (44) 266-2308 *Email:* ih@uaas.rel.com **Staff:** 1 Other 1 Prof. **Holdings:** 15,291 books 13,326 journals **Language of Collection/Services:** Russian, Ukrainian **Subjects:** Berries, Fruit Crops, Horticulture, Plant Protection, Plant Breeding, Plant Genetics **Databases Used:** Agris **Loan:** Inhouse **Photocopy:** No

3170　Kiev, Ukraine
　　　　Ukrainian Academy of Agricultural Sciences,
　　　　　　Land Use Institute (UAAS)
　　　　Scientific and Technical Information Department
　　　　Narodnogo Opolchevya, 3
　　　　Kiev 252151
Phone: +380(44) 277-7344 **Fax:** +380(44) 277-7333
Email: kyiv@zempro.relc.com

Former Name: Ukrainian Land Project Institute **Type:** Research **Head:** Sergei P. Pogurelsky *Phone:* +380(44) 277-7566 *Email:* kyiv@zempro.relc.com **Staff:** 1 Prof. 5 Other **Holdings:** 21,649 books 2,400 journals **Language of Collection/Services:** Russian, Ukrainian, English, German/Russian, Ukrainian **Subjects:** Agricultural Development, Agricultural Economics, Geography, Geology, Land Use, Soil Science **Loan:** In country **Service:** In country **Photocopy:** Yes

3171　Kiev, Ukraine
　　　　Ukrainian Institute of Scientific, Technical and
　　　　　　Economic Information
　　　　Centre for Information Resources
　　　　180 Antonovych Str.
　　　　Kiev 252150
Phone: +380(44) 261-0930, 268-2153 **Fax:** +380(44) 258-2541 **Email:** agro@icr.ukrpack.net

Networks: AGRIS

3172　Kiev, Ukraine
　　　　Veterinary Medicine Institute (VMI)
　　　　Research Library
　　　　Donetsk St., 30
　　　　Kiev 252070
Phone: +380(44) 277-1588

Former Name: Ukrainian Scientific Research Veterinary Institute **Type:** Research **Head:** Irina V. Krysuk *Phone:* +380(44) 272-3563 **Staff:** 1 Other **Holdings:** 5,336 books 11,341 journals **Language of Collection/Services:** Russian, Ukrainian **Subjects:** Biology, Microbiology, Veterinary Medicine **Loan:** In country **Service:** In country

3173　Kiev District, Ukraine
　　　　Bila Tserkva State Agricultural University
　　　　Research Library
　　　　Svobody Square 8/1
　　　　c. Bila Tserkva
　　　　Kiev District 09100
Phone: +380(263) 52587, 55957 **Email:** rector@btsau.kiev.ua **WWW:** www.btsau.kiev.ua

Type: Academic **Head:** Zoya N. Denisenko *Phone:* +380 (263) 32368 **Staff:** 36 Other **Holdings:** 42,053 books 84,509 journals **Language of Collection/Services:** Ukrainian, Russian / Russian, Ukrainian **Subjects:** Agricultural Chemistry, Animal Feeding, Animal Husbandry, Electrification, Farming, Mechanization, Plant Protection, Selection, Seed Production, Soil Science, Veterinary Science **Loan:** In country **Service:** In country **Photocopy:** No

3174　Kiev District, Ukraine
　　　　Institute of Potato Growing

Research Technical Library
Nemeshaevo P/O
Borodyanskii Region
Kiev District 255740
Location: Chkalova St., 22 **Phone:** +380(277) 41569

Former Name: Ukrainian Scientific Research Institute of Potato Economy **Founded:** 1968 **Type:** Research **Head:** Olga M. Opanasenko *Phone:* +380(277) 41464 **Staff:** 1 Other **Holdings:** 19,364 books 20,664 journals **Language of Collection/Services:** Russian, Ukrainian **Subjects:** Biology, Biochemistry, Plant Physiology, Vegetable Growing, Potatoes **Loan:** In country **Service:** In country **Photocopy:** No

3175   Kiev District, Ukraine
Institute of Vegetable and Melon Growing, Skvira
    Experiment Station
Research Library
Selectionnaya Str. 1, 1
Skvira
Kiev District 256450
Phone: +380(268) 51333

Former Name: Ukrainian Scientific Research Institute of Vegetable and Melon Growing, Skvira Vegetable Breeding and Growing Experiment Station **Type:** Research **Head:** Nina B. Gandzha *Phone:* +380(268) 51333 **Staff:** 8 Prof. **Holdings:** 28,986 books 7,262 journals **Language of Collection/Services:** Russian, Ukrainian / Russian, Ukrainian **Subjects:** Crop Production, Melons, Plant Protection, Vegetables **Loan:** In country

3176   Kiev Region, Ukraine
Institute for Mechanization and Electrification of
    Agriculture
Scientific Library
Glevaha-1, Vasilkovsky District
Kiev Region 255133
Phone: +380(271) 36330

Former Name: Ukrainian Research Institute for Mechanization and Electrification of Agriculture **Founded:** 1944 **Type:** Government **Head:** Valentina Sergeyevna Dubovik *Phone:* +380(271) 36273 **Holdings:** 55,229 books 45,398 journals **Language of Collection/Services:** Ukrainian, Russian **Subjects:** Electrification, Electrical Engineering, Mechanization

3177   Kiev Region, Ukraine
Institute of Agriculture
Scientific Library
Settl. Chabany
Kiev-Svyatoshin District
Kiev Region 255205
Phone: +380(44) 266-1107, 266-2277 **Fax:** +380(44) 263-2185, 266-2025

Former Name: Ukrainian Research Institute of Agriculture **Founded:** 1934 **Type:** Government **Head:** Salina Stepanovna Sokorenko *Phone:* +380(44) 263-2185 **Staff:** 3 Prof. **Holdings:** 39,373 books 38,681 journals **Language of Collection/Services:** Russian, Ukrainian / Russian, Ukrainian **Subjects:** Agricultural Economics, Agronomy, Plant Genetics, Plant Breeding, Plant Physiology

3178   Kiev Region, Ukraine
Institute of Animal Rearing and Genetics
Scientific Library
Settl. Chubynskye
Boryspil District
Kiev Region 256319
Phone: +380(4495) 290-2242 **Fax:** +380(4495) 290-4255

Former Name: Ukrainian Research Institute of Animal Rearing and Artificial Insemination **Type:** Research **Head:** Nataliya Vladimirovna Zaitseva **Staff:** 2 Prof. **Holdings:** 41,332 books 31,043 journals **Language of Collection/Services:** Russian, Ukrainian **Subjects:** Animal Husbandry, Biology, Genetics, Veterinary Medicine, Zootechny

3179   Kiev Region, Ukraine
Mironovskiy Institute of Wheat
Scientific Library
Mironovka
Mironovsky District
Kiev Region 256816
Phone: +380(44) 220-9402

Former Name: Mironovskiy Research Institute of Wheat Breeding and Seed Production **Founded:** 1912 **Type:** Research **Head:** Lyudmila Pavlovna Maktulova **Staff:** 1 Prof. **Holdings:** 25,195 books 23,204 journals **Language of Collection/Services:** Russian, Ukrainian **Subjects:** Mechanization, Plant Breeding, Plant Genetics, Wheat

3180   Kiev Region, Ukraine
Ukrainian State Center for Testing and Prognosis
    of Equipment and Technologies for
    Agricultural Production
Library
Doslidnitske Settlement
Vasilkolsky District
Kiev Region 255171
Phone: +380(4471) 60840 **Fax:** +380(44) 295-7133, +380(4471) 60840

Founded: 1976 **Type:** Government **Holdings:** 28,000 books **Subjects:** Animal Breeding, Farm Machinery, Feeds, Livestock

3181   Kirovograd District, Ukraine
Kirovograd State Agricultural Experiment Station
Research Library
Sazonivka P/O
Kirovograd Region
Kirovograd District 317125
Phone: +380(522) 227782

Non-English Name: Kirovogradska Derzhavna Silskogospodazskz Dislidna Stantsia, Naukova biblioteka **Former Name:** Kirovograd State Regional Agriculture Experiment Station **Founded:** 1947 **Type:** Research **Head:** Ludmila N. Pernak *Phone:* +380(522) 227782 **Staff:** 1 Prof. **Holdings:** 19,470 books 24 journals **Language of Collection/Services:** Russian, Ukrainian **Subjects:** Agricultural Development, Agricultural Economics, Animal Husbandry, Crops, Mechanization, Plant Pathology, Plants, Soil Science **Loan:** In country **Service:** In country **Photocopy:** No

3182 Lugansk, Ukraine
Lugansk Agriculture Institute
Research Library
P/O CXU
Lugansk 348008
Phone: +380(642) 952040 **Email:** lshi@cci.lg.ua

Former Name: Voroshilovgrad Agriculture Institute **Type:** Academic **Head:** Valentina M. Fesechko *Phone:* +380(642) 952151 **Staff:** 30 Other **Holdings:** 269,954 books 43,722 journals **Language of Collection/Services:** Ukrainian, Russian, Ukrainian / Russian, Ukrainian **Subjects:** Agricultural Chemistry, Agricultural Economics, Animal Feeding, Animal Husbandry, Electrification, Mechanization, Plant Protection, Seed Production, Selection **Service:** In country **Loan:** In country **Photocopy:** No

3183 Lugansk, Ukraine
Soil Protection Institute
Research Library
Pushkina St., 8
Lugansk 348008
Phone: +380(642) 953356

Former Name: Ukrainian Scientific Research Institute of the Erosion Protection of Soils **Type:** Research **Head:** Zinaida S. Kuzmenko *Phone:* +380(642) 954013 **Staff:** 1 Other **Holdings:** 15,124 books 15,140 journals **Language of Collection/Services:** Russian, Ukrainian **Subjects:** Agronomy, Erosion, Erosion Control, Soil Conservation, Soil Science **Loan:** In country **Photocopy:** No

3184 Lugansky District, Ukraine
Lugansky State Agriculture Experiment Station
Research Library
Metalist P/O
Slavyanoserbsky Region
Lugansky District 349020
Phone: +380(6425) 526078

Non-English Name: Luganska Derzhavna Seiskogospodarska Doslidna Stantsia, Naukova Biblioteka **Type:** Research **Head:** Tatyana V. Polphorova *Phone:* +380(6425) 517119 **Staff:** 1 Prof. **Holdings:** 1,096 books 4,990 journals **Language of Collection/Services:** Russian, Ukrainian / Russian, Ukrainian **Subjects:** Agricultural Chemistry, Fruit Growing, Mechanization, Plant Protection, Soil Science **Loan:** In country **Service:** In country **Photocopy:** No

3185 Lviv, Ukraine
Institute of Physiology and Biochemistry of Farm
Animals
Research Technical Library
St. Stusa 38
Lviv 290034
Phone: +380(322) 798235

Former Name: Ukrainian Scientific Research Institute of Physiology and Biochemistry of Farm Animals **Founded:** 1960 **Type:** Research **Head:** Maria V. Oliynik *Phone:* +380 (322) 425192 **Staff:** 2 Other **Holdings:** 27,277 books 32,057 journals **Language of Collection/Services:** Ukrainian, Russian / Russian, Ukrainian **Subjects:** Animal Breeding, Animal Physiology, Biochemistry, Veterinary Medicine **Loan:** Internationally **Photocopy:** No

3186 Lviv, Ukraine
Lviv Academy of Veterinary Medicine (LAVM)
Scientific Research Library
Pekarskaya St., 50
Lviv 290601
Phone: +380(322) 756735

Former Name: Lviv Zoo-Veterinary Institute **Founded:** 1881 **Type:** Academic **Head:** Vasyl I. Zorenko *Phone:* +380(322) 793539 **Staff:** 1 Prof. **Holdings:** 244,564 books 70 journals **Language of Collection/Services:** Russian, Ukrainian **Subjects:** Animal Husbandry, Artificial Insemination, Biochemistry, Veterinary Medicine, Zoology **Loan:** In country **Service:** In country **Photocopy:** No

3187 Lviv, Ukraine
Ukrainian Academy of Agricultural Sciences,
    State Scientific-Research Control Institute of
    Veterinary Preparations and Fodder Additives
Library
Donetska Str., 11
Lviv 290019
Phone: +380(322) 590994 **Fax:** +380(322) 592-92 **Email:** mail@scivp.lviv.ua **WWW:** www.icmp.lviv.ua/scivp

Type: Research **Subjects:** Animal Breeding, Animal Physiology, Biochemistry, Veterinary Medicine **Loan:** Internationally **Photocopy:** No

3188 Lviv District, Ukraine
Institute of Agriculture and Stock Breeding of
    West Regions
Research Library
Ubroshino
Pustomyty Region
Lviv District 292084
Phone: +380(322) 396221, 396265, 798297

Former Name: Scientific Research Institute of Agriculture and Stock Breeding of West Regions **Founded:** 1956 **Type:** Research **Head:** Olga Vasilivna Panctushina *Phone:* +380 (322) 396207 **Staff:** 4 Other **Holdings:** 46,858 books 70,976 journals **Language of Collection/Services:** Ukrainian, Russian/ Russian, Ukrainian **Subjects:** Animal Breeding, Genetics, Livestock, Seeds **Photocopy:** No **Loan:** Internationally **Service:** Internationally

3189 Lviv District, Ukraine
Lviv Agriculture Institute
Scientific Research Library
Dublyany
Zhovtkivskii Region
Lviv District 292040
Phone: +380(322) 793345, 793160 **Fax:** +380(322) 793231 **Email:** lday@icmp.lviv.ua **WWW:** www.lviv.uar. net/~lday

Founded: 1947 **Type:** Academic **Head:** Pynda Lubov A. *Phone:* +380(322) 793539 **Staff:** 42 Other **Language of Collection/Services:** Russian, Ukrainian **Holdings:** 465,868 books 27,057 journals **Subjects:** Agricultural Economics,

Agronomy, Mechanization **Loan:** In country **Service:** In country **Photocopy:** No

3190   Melitopol, Ukraine
Institute of Irrigated Fruit Growing (IIFG)
Research Library (RL)
99 Vakulenchuk St.
Melitopol, Zaporizhzhya Region 332311
Phone: +380(6142) 31378

Non-English Name: Instytut Zroshuvanoho Sadivnytstva (IZS), Naukova Bibliteka (NB) **Former Name:** Ukrainian Scientific Research Institute of Irrigated Horticulture **Type:** Research **Founded:** 1932 **Head:** Lydia A. Zahurska *Phone:* +380(6142) 35067 **Staff:** 1 Prof. **Holdings:** 24,541 books 27,300 journals **Language of Collection/Services:** Russian, Ukrainian **Subjects:** Comprehensive **Specializations:** Horticulture **Loan:** Inhouse **Service:** Inhouse **Photocopy:** No

3191   Melitopol, Ukraine
Melitopol Institute of Agricultural Mechanization
Research Library
B. Khmelnitskogo Av., 18
Melitopol, Zaporozhe Region 332339
Phone: +380(6142) 22411

Founded: 1934 **Type:** Academic **Head:** Ludmila A. Petrova *Phone:* +380(6142) 21345 **Staff:** 37 Other **Holdings:** 22,689 journals 256,108 books **Language of Collection/ Services:** Russian, Ukrainian **Subjects:** Electrification, Machinery, Maintenance, Mechanization **Loan:** In country **Service:** In country **Photocopy:** No

3192   Melitopol, Ukraine
Takvriya State Agrotechnical Academy
Library
18, Khmelnytsky Ave.
Melitopol, Zaporozhe Region 72312
Phone: +380(6142) 22411 **Fax:** +380(6142) 21311 **Email:** tsaa@melitopol.net, tgatashm@mediana.net.us **WWW:** www.users.melitopol.net/~tsaa

Type: Academic

3193   Mycolav District, Ukraine
Institute of Feeds, Mycolaiv Experiment Station of Feedstuff Production
Research Library
v. Yastrebinove Voznesensky Retion
Mycolav District 329620
Phone: +380(5134) 91332

Non-English Name: Mykolaivska Doslidna Stantsia Kormovyrobnytstva, Naukova Biblioteka **Former Name:** Rovenskaya State Regional Agricultural Experiment Station **Type:** Research **Head:** Valentina D. Gruschenko *Phone:* +380(5134) 91566 **Staff:** 1 Prof. **Holdings:** 3,874 books 1,166 journals **Language of Collection/Services:** Russian, Ukrainian / Russian, Ukrainian **Subjects:** Agricultural Economics, Amelioration, Soil Science **Loan:** In country **Service:** In country **Photocopy:** No

3194   Nikolaev, Ukraine
Mykolaiiv State Agricultural Institute

Research Library
Karpenko St., 73
Nikolaev 327021
Phone: +380(512) 343146, 341082 **Fax:** +380(512) 343146 **Email:** rector@mdaa.mk.ua, admin@mdaa.mk.ua **WWW:** www.mdaa.mk.ua

Non-English Name: Mykolaiivski Silskogospodarskii Instytut, Naukova Biblioteka **Former Name:** Odessa Agriculture Institute, Nikolaev Branch **Type:** Academic **Head:** *Phone:* +380(512) 341140 **Staff:** 23 Other **Holdings:** 140,322 books 22,942 journals **Language of Collection/ Services:** Russian, Ukrainian /Russian, Ukrainian **Subjects:** Agricultural Economics, Agronomy, Mechanization, Veterinary Science, Zootechny **Loan:** In country **Service:** In country **Photocopy:** No

3195   Odessa, Ukraine
Institute of Animal Clinical Biochemistry and Sanitation
Research Library
Svobody Av., 2
Odessa 270037
Phone: +380(482) 446052

Former Name: Ukrainian Scientific Research Institute of Experimental Veterinary Science, Odessa Scientific Research Veterinary Station **Type:** Research **Head:** Natallya Boyko *Phone:* +380(482) 446052 **Staff:** 1 Other **Holdings:** 6,474 books 41 journals **Language of Collection/Services:** Russian, Ukrainian **Subjects:** Biochemistry, Biology, Poultry, Sanitation, Veterinary Science **Loan:** In country **Service:** In country **Photocopy:** No

3196   Odessa, Ukraine
Institute of Plant Breeding and Genetics
Scientific Library
Ovidiopolska Doroga, 3
Odessa 270036
Phone: +380(482) 656187 **Fax:** +380(482) 657084

Former Name: All-Union Breeding and Genetic Institute **Founded:** 1932 **Type:** Research **Head:** Elena Fedorovna Svirska *Phone:* +380(482) 694424 **Staff:** 2 Prof. **Holdings:** 81,009 books 25,381 journals **Language of Collection/Services:** Russian, Ukrainian / Russian, Ukrainian **Subjects:** Biochemistry, Cereals, Entomology, Fodder Crops, Genetics, Plant Pathology

3197   Odessa, Ukraine
Institute of Plant Protection, Experiment Station of Grapes and Breeits Quarantine
Research Library
Perekopskoi Divizii St., 49
Odessa 270049
Phone: +380(48) 631704

Non-English Name: Doslidna Stantsiya po Karantyny Vynograda i Plodovych Kultur, Naukova Biblioteka **Former Name:** All-Union Scientific Research Station of Anti-Phylloxera **Type:** Research **Head:** Valentina D. Gruschenko *Phone:* +380(48) 631704 **Staff:** 1 Prof. **Holdings:** 6,426 books 7,264 journals **Language of Collection/Services:** Russian, Ukrainian **Subjects:** Fruit Growing, Plant Protection, Viticulture **Loan:** In country **Service:** In country **Photocopy:** No

3198 Odessa, Ukraine
Odessa Agriculture Institute
Scientific Research Library
Sverdlova St., 99
Odessa 270039

Phone: +380(482) 223723 **Fax:** +380(482) 224802

Founded: 1921 **Type:** Academic **Head:** Svetlana S. Dzhuganova *Phone:* +380(482) 296503 **Holdings:** 561,325 books 161,343 journals **Staff:** 31 Other **Language of Collection/Services:** Russian, Ukrainian **Subjects:** Agricultural Chemistry, Agricultural Economics, Crop Production, Farming, Fruit Growing, Horticulture, Plant Protection, Seed Production, Selection, Veterinary Medicine, Viticulture **Loan:** In country **Service:** In country **Photocopy:** No

3199 Odessa, Ukraine
Odessa State Academy of Food Technology
(OSAFT)
Library
Kanatnaya St. 112
Odessa

Phone: +380(482) 291088 **Fax:** +380(482) 253284
WWW: www/osaft.odessa.ua

3200 Odessa, Ukraine
V.E. Tairov Institute of Vineyards and
Winemaking
Research Technical Library
Tairov S/O
St. 40-richy Peremogy, 27
Odessa 270103

Phone: +380(482) 662267

Former Name: V.E. Tairov Ukrainian Scientific Research Institute of Viticulture and Winemaking **Founded:** 1905 **Type:** Research **Staff:** 3 Other **Holdings:** 48,888 books 45,704 journals **Language of Collection/Services:** Russian, Ukrainian **Subjects:** Agricultural Chemistry, Horticulture, Plant Protection, Selection, Vineyards, Winemaking, Viticulture **Loan:** In country **Service:** In country **Photocopy:** No

3201 Poltava, Ukraine
Institute of Pig Science
Scientific Library
Shvedska Mogila, 25
Poltava 314006

Phone: +380(5322) 21439

Former Name: Poltava Research Institute of Pig Science **Founded:** 1930 **Type:** Research **Head:** Lyudmila Nikolayevna Cherednyk *Phone:* +380(5322) 21523 **Staff:** 2 Prof. **Holdings:** 18,327 books 90 journals **Language of Collection/Services:** Russian, Ukrainian / Russian, Ukrainian **Subjects:** Cattle, Mechanization, Pigs, Veterinary Medicine **Specializations:** Animal Breeding, Genetics, Nutrition, Selection **Loan:** In country **Service:** In country

3202 Poltava, Ukraine
Poltava State Agricultural Experiment Station
Research Library
Shvedskaya St., 86
Poltava 314601

Phone: +380(5322) 26891

Non-English Name: Poltavska Derzhavna Sieskogospodarska Doslidna Stantsia, Naukova Biblioteka **Former Name:** Poltava State Regional Agricultural Experiment Station **Founded:** 1884 **Type:** Research **Head:** Svetlana K. Isaeva *Phone:* +380(5322) 26891 **Staff:** 1 Prof. **Holdings:** 40,354 books 26,595 journals **Language of Collection/Services:** Russian, Ukrainian **Subjects:** Agricultural Chemistry, Horticulture, Plant Breeding, Plant Protection, Soil **Loan:** In country **Service:** In country **Photocopy:** No

3203 Poltava, Ukraine
Poltava State Agricultural Institute
Research Library
Skovorody St., 1/3
Poltava 36003

Phone: +380(5322) 73146, 22994 **Fax:** +380(5322) 22957
Email: psai@atv.net.ua

Founded: 1920 **Type:** Academic **Head:** Sereda Galina K. *Phone:* +380(5322) 22991 **Staff:** 1 Prof. **Holdings:** 291,623 books 35,292 journals **Language of Collection/Services:** Russian, Ukrainian / Russian, Ukrainian **Subjects:** Agricultural Chemistry, Agronomy, Farming, Mechanization, Plant Protection, Seed Production, Selection, Soil **Loan:** In country **Service:** In country **Photocopy:** No

3204 Rivne District, Ukraine
Rivenska State Agricultural Experiment Station
Research Library
Shubkov P/O
Rovensky Region
Rivne District 265226

Phone: +380(3622) 26085

Non-English Name: Rivenska Derzhavna Sieskogospodarska Doslidna Stantsia, Naukova Biblioteka **Former Name:** Rovenskaya State Regional Agriculture Experiment Station **Type:** Research **Head:** Zoya V. Pavluk *Phone:* +380(3622) 26085 **Staff:** 1 Prof. **Holdings:** 15,171 books 15,766 journals **Language of Collection/Services:** Russian, Ukrainian/ Russian, Ukrainian **Subjects:** Agricultural Economics, Crop Husbandry, Electrification, Forage, Meadows, Mechanization, Plant Protection, Seed Production, Soil **Loan:** In country **Service:** In country **Photocopy:** No

3205 Rovno, Ukraine
Ukrainian Academy of Agricultural Sciences,
Institute of Epizootology (UAAS, IE)
Library
Knyazya Volodimira St., 16/18
Rovno 266028

Phone: +380(362) 223134 **Fax:** +380(362) 266564

Former Name: Ukrainian Scientific Research Institute of Experimental Veterinary Science, West Branch **Founded:** 1959 **Type:** Government **Head:** Ludmilla Litwinowich *Phone:* +380(362) 266568 **Holdings:** 24,775 books 6 journals **Language of Collection/Services:** Russian, Ukrainian / Ukrainian **Subjects:** Veterinary Science **Loan:** Inhouse **Service:** Inhouse **Photocopy:** Yes

3206 Sumy, Ukraine
Sumy Agriculture Institute
Scientific Research Library
Petropavlivska Str., 57
Sumy 40030
Phone: +380(542) 221707, 223530, 226319, 225537
Email: admin@sau.sumy.ua **WWW:** www.sau.sumy.ua

Former Name: Kharkov Agriculture Institute, V.V. Dokuchaev Sumy Branch **Type:** Academic **Head:** Lubov G. Suitchenko *Phone:* +380(542) 296238 **Staff:** 28 Prof. **Holdings:** 140,000 books 29,866 journals **Language of Collection/Services:** Russian, Ukrainian **Subjects:** Agricultural Chemistry, Agricultural Economics, Electrification, Farming, Mechanization, Plant Protection, Seed Production, Selection, Soil Science **Loan:** In country **Service:** In country **Photocopy:** No

♦3207 Sumy District, Ukraine
All-Union Scientific Research Institute of Sugar
     Beets, Ivanovo Breeding Experiment Station
Library
Solnechnoe P/O
Akhtyzskii Region
Sumy District 245524
Phone: +380(54) 462-3288 **Fax:** +380(54) 462-3394

Type: Government **Head:** Vladimir F. Panchenko *Phone:* +380(54) 462-3394 **Holdings:** 15,800 books 45 journals **Language of Collection/Services:** Ukrainian / Ukrainian **Subjects:** Sugarbeet **Photocopy:** No

3208 Sumy District, Ukraine
Institute of Bast Crops
Library
Lenin St., 45
Glukhov
Sumy District 245130
Fax: +380(5444) 22643

Former Name: All-Union Scientific Research Institute of Fiber Crops **Founded:** 1931 **Type:** Research **Head:** Nina Nikolayevna Basanets *Phone:* +380(5444) 22135 **Staff:** 1 Prof. **Holdings:** 35,000 books 18,000 journals **Language of Collection/Services:** Russian, Ukrainian **Subjects:** Biotechnology, Farming, Fiber Plants **Loan:** In country **Photocopy:** Yes

3209 Sumy District, Ukraine
Institute of Fiber Crops
Scientific Library
Lenin Str., 45
Gluchov
Sumy District 245130
Phone: +380(5444) 22135

Former Name: All-Union Research Institute of Fiber Crops **Type:** Research **Head:** Nina Nikolayevna Basanets *Phone:* +380(5444) 22135 **Staff:** 2 Prof. **Holdings:** 34,459 books 28,200 journals **Language of Collection/Services:** Russian,

Ukrainian/Russian, Ukrainian **Subjects:** Agricultural Chemistry, Biochemistry, Cropping Systems, Fiber Plants, Plant Breeding, Plant Genetics

♦3210 Ternopol District, Ukraine
Ukrainian Experiment Station of Tobacco
Library
Melnitsa-Podolskaya
Ternopol District 283670
Phone: +380(3541) 41362, 41151

Non-English Name: Ukrainska Doslidna **Former Name:** Stancia Tutunnictva **Type:** Academic **Staff:** 28 Prof. 60 Other **Holdings:** 5,500 books 2,000 journals **Language of Collection/Services:** Ukrainian, Russian / Ukrainian **Subjects:** Agricultural Development, Agricultural Economics, Agricultural Engineering, Entomology, Plant Pathology **Specializations:** Tobacco **Loan:** Internationally

3211 Uman, Ukraine
Uman Agriculture Institute
Scientific Research Library
Sophievka P/O, 5
Cherkassk District
Uman 20300
Phone: +380(4744) 54281, 52202 **Fax:** +380(4744) 53170, 54367 **Email:** adm@usga.ip2.kiev.ua

Founded: 1859 **Type:** Academic **Head:** Anna P. Stolyarenko *Phone:* +380(4744) 53328 **Staff:** 27 Other **Holdings:** 189,665 books 8,738 journals **Language of Collection/Services:** Russian, Ukrainian **Subjects:** Agricultural Chemistry, Agricultural Economics, Farming, Crop Production, Plant Breeding, Seed Production, Selection, Soil Science **Loan:** In country **Service:** In country **Photocopy:** No

3212 Vinnitsa, Ukraine
Vinnitsa Agriculture Institute
Research Library
Sonyachna 3
Vinnitsa 286008
Phone: +380(432) 460003, 464782 **Fax:** +380(432) 464782, 438025 **Email:** office@vsau.org, olbi@vinnitsa.sovat.com **WWW:** www.vsau.org

Non-English Name: Vinnytssky Silskogospodarsky Instytyt, Naukova Biblioteka **Former Name:** Ukrainian Agriculture Academy, Vinnitsa Branch **Type:** Academic **Head:** Nadezhda P. Kotsyubinska *Phone:* +380(432) 465103 **Staff:** 22 Other **Language of Collection/Services:** Russian, Ukrainian / Russian, Ukrainian **Subjects:** Agricultural Economics, Agronomy, Mechanization, Veterinary Science **Loan:** In country **Service:** In country **Photocopy:** No

3213 Vinnitsa District, Ukraine
Institute of Sugar Beets, Uladovo-Lylinetska
     Breeding Experiment Station (ULBES)
Research Library
Uladovske P/O
Kalinivskii Region
Vinnitsa District 287080
Phone: +380(4333) 22868

Non-English Name: Uladovo-Lylinetska Doslidno Select-siyna Station (ULDSS), Naukova Biblioteka **Former Name:** All-Union Scientific Research Institute of Sugar Beets **Founded:** 1946 **Type:** Research **Head:** Maria I. Bondarchuk *Phone:* +380(4333) 27598 **Staff:** 1 Prof. **Holdings:** 11,541 books 3,634 journals **Language of Collection/Services:** Russian, Ukrainian/Ukrainian **Subjects:** Selection, Sugarbeet **Specializations:** Agricultural Development **Loan:** In country **Service:** In country **Photocopy:** Yes

3214　Vinnitsa District, Ukraine
Institute of Sugar Beets, Yaltushkiv Breeding Experiment Station
Research Library
Yaltusihkiv P/O
Barsky Region
Vinnitsa District 288613
Phone: +380(434) 103039

Non-English Name: Yaltushkivska Doslidno-selektsiyna Stantsia, Naukova Biblioteka **Former Name:** All-Union Scientific Research Institute of Sugar Beets **Type:** Research **Head:** Nadiya P. Goncharuk *Phone:* +380(434) 92399 **Staff:** 1 Prof. **Holdings:** 1,304 books 746 journals **Language of Collection/Services:** Russian, Ukrainian **Subjects:** Farming, Sugarbeet **Loan:** In country

3215　Vinnitsa District, Ukraine
Vinnitsa State Agriculture Experiment Station
Research Library
Agronomicheskoe Village
Vinnitsky Region
Vinnitsa District 287119
Phone: +380(1322) 26924

Non-English Name: Vinnytska Dertzhavna Sieialskogospodarska Doslidna Stantsia, Naukova Biblioteka **Type:** Research **Head:** Zoya P. Pavlovich *Phone:* +380(1322) 944283 **Staff:** 1 Prof. **Holdings:** 11,017 books 1,200 journals **Language of Collection/Services:** Russian, Ukrainian / Russian, Ukrainian **Subjects:** Agricultural Chemistry, Agricultural Economics, Animal Feeding, Animal Husbandry, Plant Protection, Seed Production, Selection, Soil Science **Loan:** In country **Service:** In country **Photocopy:** No

3216　Volynsk Region, Ukraine
Volynska State Agriculture Experiment Station
Research Technical Library
Rokyny Village
Lutsky District
Volynsk Region 264208
Phone: +380(3322) 99316

Founded: 1956 **Type:** Research **Head:** Galina M. Jaremiy *Phone:* +380(3322) 99324 **Staff:** 1 Prof. **Holdings:** 17,484 books 6,161 journals **Language of Collection/Services:** Russian, Ukrainian / Russian **Subjects:** Agricultural Chemistry, Fruit Growing, Mechanization, Pig Farming, Plant Protection, Seeds, Selection, Soil Science, Tillage **Service:** In country

3217　Zaporozhe, Ukraine
Institute of Stock Breeding Mechanization
Research Technical Library
Khortitsa
Zaporozhe 330017
Phone: +380(612) 605324

Former Name: Central Scientific Research Project Technology Institute of Mechanization and Electrification of Stock Breeding **Type:** Research **Head:** Ludmila Oleksandrivna Anokhina *Phone:* +380(612) 605344 **Staff:** 3 Prof. **Holdings:** 42,688 books 33,213 journals **Language of Collection/Services:** Russian, Ukrainian / Russian, Ukrainian **Subjects:** Electrification, Farm Buildings, Farm Equipment, Mechanization **Loan:** In country **Photocopy:** Yes

3218　Zaporozhe, Ukraine
Zaporozhe State Agriculture Experiment Station
Research
Library Zaporozhe 330031
Phone: +380(612) 961946

Non-English Name: Zaporozska Derzhavna Silskogospodarska Doslidna Stansia, Naukova Biblioteka **Former Name:** Zaporozhe State Regional Agriculture Experiment Station **Founded:** 1958 **Type:** Research **Head:** Natalia I. Dmytrenko *Phone:* +380(612) 953361 **Staff:** 1 Prof. **Holdings:** 29,100 books 12,214 journals **Language of Collection/Services:** Russian, Ukrainian **Subjects:** Agricultural Chemistry, Animal Feeding, Fruit Growing, Irrigated Farming, Pig Farming, Soil Science, Vegetable Growing, Viticulture **Loan:** In country **Service:** In country **Photocopy:** No

3219　Zaporozhe District, Ukraine
Institute of Corn, Rozovka Experiment Station
Scientific Library
Rozovka P/O
Rozovsky Region
Zaporozhe District 332930
Phone: +380(6162) 97168

Former Name: All-Union Scientific Research Institute of Corn **Type:** Research **Head:** Olena V. Mihlyaeva *Phone:* +380(6162) 97722 **Staff:** 1 Prof. **Holdings:** 6,516 books 1,495 journals **Language of Collection/Services:** Russian, Ukrainian **Subjects:** Agricultural Chemistry, Maize, Plant Protection, Soil Science **Loan:** In country

3220　Zhitomir, Ukraine
Institute of Hop Growing
Research Technical Library
Lenina Str., 289
Zhitomir 262007
Phone: +380(412) 366231

Former Name: Scientific Research and Technology Institute of Hop Growing **Founded:** 1927 **Type:** Research **Head:** Tetyana Ivanovna Shevchuk *Phone:* +380(412) 959951 **Staff:** 3 Prof. **Holdings:** 18,228 books 5,919 journals **Language of Collection/Services:** Russian, Ukrainian **Subjects:** Biochemistry, Biology, Hops, Plant Physiology **Loan:** In country **Service:** In country **Photocopy:** No

3221　Zhitomir, Ukraine
State Academy of Agriculture and Ecology of Ukraine

Library
Stary Bulvar St.
Zhitomir 10001
Phone: +380(412) 374931, 220457 **Fax:** +380(412)
221402, 220417 **Email:** ecos@ecos.zhitomir.ua

Type: Academic **Subjects:** Ecology

3222   **Zhitomir, Ukraine**
Zhitomir Agriculture Institute
Research Library
50 Years of October St., 9
Zhitomir 262001

Founded: 1922 **Type:** Academic **Head:** Eugeniya I. Konarska *Phone:* +380(412) 21651 **Staff:** 29 Other **Holdings:** 203,275 books 27,855 journals **Language of Collection/Services:** Russian, Ukrainian / Russian, Ukrainian **Subjects:** Agricultural Chemistry, Agricultural Economics, Farming, Animal Husbandry, Crop Production, Seed Production, Selection, Soil Science **Loan:** In country **Service:** In country

3223   **Zhitomir District, Ukraine**
Institute of Agriculture of the Polisya
Research Library
Grozino P/O
Korostenski Region
Zhitomir District 260103
Phone: +380(4142) 43017

Former Name: Scientific Research Institute of Agriculture of the Non-Chernozem Zone **Type:** Research **Head:** Svetlana N. Shevchuk *Phone:* +380(4142) 61322 **Staff:** 2 Prof. **Holdings:** 24,237 books 40,897 journals **Language of Collection/Services:** Russian, Ukrainia / Russian, Ukrainiann **Subjects:** Agricultural Economics, Agronomy, Marketing, Mechanization, Plants, Soil Science **Loan:** In country **Service:** In country **Photocopy:** No

United Kingdom

3224   **Aberdeen, UK**
Macaulay Land Use Research Institute (MLURI)
Library
Craigiebuckler
Aberdeen, Scotland AB15 8QH
Fax: +44(1224) 311556 **WWW:** www.mluri.sari.ac.uk

Former Name: Macaulay Institute for Soil Research **Type:** Government, Research **Founded:** 1930 **Head:** Mrs. Lorraine Robertson *Email:* l.robertson@mluri.sari.ac.uk *Phone:* +44 (1224) 318611 ext 2202 **Staff:** 2 Prof. **Holdings:** 10,000 books 200 journals **Language of Collection/Services:** English **Subjects:** Agricultural Economics, Crops, Farming, Forestry, Plant Pathology, Soil Science **Databases Used:** Biosis; Current Contents **Loan:** Internationally **Photocopy:** Yes

3225   **Aberdeen, UK**
Scottish Agricultural College, Campus - Aberdeen
(SAC)
Library
Craibstone, Bucksburn

Aberdeen, Scotland AB21 9YA
Phone: +44(1224) 711039 **Fax:** +44(1224) 711291 **Email:** library@ab.sac.ac.uk **WWW:** www.sac.ac.uk **OPAC:** actalis.ab.sac.ac.uk:8001

Former Name: Scottish Farm Buildings Investigation Unit **Founded:** 1972 **Type:** Academic **Head:** Elizabeth Buchan *Email:* e.buchan@ab.sac.ac.uk **Staff:** 1 Prof. **Holdings:** 89 journals 14,200 books **Language of Collection/Services:** English **Subjects:** Agricultural Engineering, Animal Husbandry **Specializations:** Animal Welfare, Building Construction, Farm Buildings **Loan:** In country **Photocopy:** Yes

3226   **Aberdeen, UK**
Scottish Office Agriculture, Environment and
Fisheries Department (SOAEFD)
Marine Laboratory Library
PO Box 101
Victoria Road
Torry
Aberdeen, Scotland AB9 9DB
Phone: +44(1224) 295391 **Fax:** +44(1224) 295511
WWW: www.marlab.ac.uk

Former Name: Department of Agriculture and Fisheries for Scotland (DAFS) **Founded:** 1886 **Type:** Government **Head:** Ms. Sarah P. Heath *Email:* heaths@marlab.ac.uk **Staff:** 2 Prof. 2 Other **Holdings:** 40,000 books 45 journals **Language of Collection/Services:** English / English **Subjects:** Fish Diseases, Fisheries, Fishing Gear, Fishing Methods, Marine Biology, Oceanography **Databases Developed:** Ogilvie collection on diatomaceae, 90 books, 130 pamphlets **Loan:** Inhouse **Service:** Inhouse **Photocopy:** Yes

3227   **Aberdeen, UK**
University of Aberdeen
MacRobert Library
581 King Street
Aberdeen, Scotland AB24 5UA
Phone: +44(1224) 272600 **Fax:** +44(1224) 273282 **Email:** library@abdn.ac.uk **WWW:** www.abdn.ac.uk **OPAC:** www.abdn.ac.uk/diss/infoserv/eres/webpac

Type: Academic **Head:** Graham Pryor *Phone:* +44(1224) 273384 *Email:* g.pryor@abdn.ac.uk **Staff:** 1 Prof. 4 Other **Holdings:** 14,570 books 423 journals **Language of Collection/Services:** English **Subjects:** Agribusiness, Agricultural Development, Agronomy, Aquaculture, Conservation, Biotechnology, Farming, Plant Breeding, Plant Pathology, Veterinary Medicine **Specializations:** Agricultural Economics, Animal Husbandry, Crops **Databases Used:** Agricola; CABCD **Loan:** Internationally **Service:** Internationally **Photocopy:** Yes

3228   **Aberystwyth, UK**
Institute of Grassland and Environmental
Research (IGER)
Stapledon Library and Information Service
Plas Gogerddan
Aberystwyth, Dyfed, Wales SY23 3EB
Phone: +44(1970) 823000 **Fax:** +44(1970) 828357
WWW: www.iger.bbsrc.ac.uk

Former Name: Institute of Grassland and Animal Products (IGAP), Grassland Research Institute (GRI), Welsh Plant Breeding Station (WPBS) **Type:** Research **Head:** Caroline Moss-Gibbons *Phone:* +44(1970) 823051 **Staff:** 2 Prof. 4 Other **Holdings:** 114,000 books 2,000 journals **Language of Collection/Services:** English **Subjects:** Agriculture (Tropics), Agricultural Development, Animal Husbandry, Crops, Entomology, Forestry **Specializations:** Biotechnology, Flora, Genetics, Grasslands, Herbaria, Plants, Plant Pathology, Soil Science **Databases Developed:** PUBS - Staff publications; FLOR - county and country flora, mainly antiquarian **Databases Used:** Agricola; Agris; CABCD **Loan:** Internationally **Service:** Internationally **Photocopy:** Yes

3229 Aberystwyth, UK
         The National Library of Wales
         Library
         Penglais
         Aberystwyth, Ceredigion, Wales SY23 3BU
Phone: +44(1970) 632800 **Fax:** +44(1970) 615709 **Email:** ymh.pb@llgc.org.uk **WWW:** www.llgc.org.uk **OPAC:** geacweb.llgc.org.uk:8000

Founded: 1907 **Type:** Academic **Head:** Mr. Andrew M.W. Green *Phone:* +44(1970) 623816 **Staff:** 80 Prof. 130 Other **Language of Collection/Services:** English / English, Welsh **Subjects:** Comprehensive **Specializations:** Law (UK) **Databases Developed:** URICA - printed materials; CAIRS - non-print materials **Loan:** Do not loan **Photocopy:** Yes

3230 Aberystwyth, UK
         University of Wales Aberystwyth, Welsh Institute
              of Rural Studies (WIRS)
         Thomas Parry Library
         Llanbadarn Fawr
         Aberystwyth, Ceredigion, Wales SY23 3AS
Phone: +44(1970) 622412 **Fax:** +44(1970) 622190 **Email:** tplib@aber.ac.uk **WWW:** www.wirs.aber.ac.uk **OPAC:** www.aber.ac.uk/!tplwww

Former Name: University College of Wales, Welsh Agricultural College, Joint Library **Founded:** 1971 **Type:** Academic **Head:** Alan Clark *Phone:* +44(1970) 622417 *Email:* alan.clark@aber.ac.uk **Staff:** 3 Prof. 2.5 Other **Holdings:** 46,793 books 566 journals **Language of Collection/Services:** English / English **Subjects:** Agricultural Engineering, Animal Husbandry, Biotechnology, Education/Extension, Crops, Equidae, Forestry **Specializations:** Farming, Horses, Rural Communities, Rural Planning, Wildlife Conservation **Databases Developed:** UPDATE - farming and countryside index: database on practical, technical and managerial press of land based industries; topics include agriculture, conservation, estate and countryside management, and organic husbandry **Loan:** Internationally **Photocopy:** Yes

3231 Addlestone, UK
         Veterinary Laboratories Agency (VLA)
         Library
         New Haw
         Addlestone, Surrey KT15 3NB
Phone: +44(1932) 341111 ext 2505 **Fax:** +44(1932) 347046 **WWW:** www.maff.gov.uk/aboutmaf/agency/vla

Former Name: Ministry of Agriculture, Fisheries and Food (MAFF), Central Veterinary Laboratory **Founded:** 1955 **Type:** Government **Head:** Mrs. H.J. Hulse *Phone:* +44 (1932) 341111 ext 2313 **Staff:** 4 Prof. 5 Other **Holdings:** 90,000 books 350 journals **Language of Collection/Services:** English **Subjects:** Animal Husbandry, Veterinary Medicine **Databases Developed:** VETIND - inhouse database on veterinary literature; includes journal articles and books from 1984 **Databases Used:** CABCD; Medline **Loan:** In country **Photocopy:** Yes

3232 Antrim, UK
         Department of Agriculture and Rural
              Development, Greenmount Agricultural and
              Horticultural College (DARD)
         Library
         22 Greenmount Road
         Antrim, Northern Ireland BT41 4PU
Phone: +44(28) 9442 6700 **WWW:** www.greenmount.ac.uk

Former Name: Ministry of Agriculture, Department of Agriculture for Northern Ireland (DANI) **Type:** Government **Staff:** 1 Prof. 1 Other **Holdings:** 6,000 books 70 journals **Language of Collection/Services:** English **Subjects:** Animal Husbandry, Crops, Horticulture **Databases Used:** CABCD **Loan:** Inhouse **Service:** Inhouse **Photocopy:** Yes

3233 Ascot, UK
         CAB International, Imperial College (CABI, IC)
         Michael Way Library
         Silwood Park, Buckhurst Road
         Ascot, Berkshire SL5 7TA
Location: Approximately 25 miles west of London **Phone:** +44(1491) 829112 ext 51 208 **Fax:** +44(1491) 829123 **Email:** library@cabi.org **WWW:** www.lib.ic.ac.uk/depts/siindex.htm

Former Name: International Institute of Entomology **Founded:** 1988 **Type:** Non-profit **Head:** Elizabeth Wheater *Email:* e.wheater@CABCD.org **Staff:** 3 Prof. 4 Other **Holdings:** 150,000 books 1,020 journals **Language of Collection/Services:** English / English **Subjects:** Agriculture (Tropics), Plant Pathology, Veterinary Medicine **Specializations:** Biological Control, Entomology, Integrated Control, Plant Protection **Databases Used:** CABCD **Loan:** In country **Service:** Internationally **Photocopy:** Yes

3234 Ashford, UK
         University of London, Wye College
         Library
         Wye
         Ashford, Kent TN25 5AH
Phone: +44(1233) 813555 ext 515 **Fax:** +44(1233) 813074 **Email:** w.sage@wye.ac.uk **WWW:** www.wye.ac.uk **OPAC:** www.wye.ac.uk/Library/wye.1.html

Founded: 1900 **Type:** Academic **Head:** Mrs. E.M. Lucas *Phone:* +44(1233) 812401 *Email:* m.lucas@wye.ac.uk **Language of Collection/Services:** English **Staff:** 3 Prof. 2.5 Other **Holdings:** 35,000 books 600 journals **Subjects:** Agriculture (Tropics), Agribusiness, Agricultural Development, Agricultural Economics, Animal Husbandry, Crops, Farming, Horticulture, Soil Science **Databases Used:** Agricola; CABCD **Loan:** In country **Service:** Inhouse **Photocopy:** Yes

3235   Ayr, UK
            Hannah Research Institute (HRI)
            Library
            Hannah Research Park
            Mauchline Road
            Kirkhill, St. Quivox
            Ayr, Scotland KA6 5HL
Phone: +44(1292) 674000 **Fax:** +44(1292) 674004
WWW: www.hri.sari.ac.uk/hri.htm

Founded: 1928 **Type:** Government **Head:** Mrs. E. Barbour *Email:* barboure@hri.sari.ac.uk **Staff:** 1 Prof. **Holdings:** 20,000 books 100 journals **Language of Collection/Services:** English **Subjects:** Animal Husbandry, Biotechnology, Farming, Food Sciences **Loan:** In country **Photocopy:** Yes

3236   Ayr, UK
            Scottish Agricultural College, Camput -
                Auchincruive (SAC)
            Library
            Donald Hendrie Building
            Auchincruive
            Ayr, Scotland KA6 5HW
Phone: +44(1292) 525209 **Fax:** +44(1292) 525211 **Email:** library@au.sac.ac.uk **WWW:** www.sac.ac.uk **OPAC:** actalis.ab.sac.ac.uk:8001

Former Name: West of Scotland Agricultural College **Founded:** 1899 **Type:** Academic, Government **Head:** Miss Elaine P. Muir *Phone:* +44(1292) 525208 *Email:* e.muir@au.sac.ac.uk **Staff:** 1 Prof. 4 Other **Holdings:** 18,000 books 350 journals **Language of Collection/Services:** English **Subjects:** Agribusiness, Agricultural Development, Agricultural Economics, Agricultural Engineering, Animal Husbandry, Biotechnology, Education/Extension, Environment, Crops, Farming, Fisheries, Forestry, Leisure, Plant Pathology, Recreation, Soil Science, Tourism **Specializations:** Food Sciences, Horticulture **Databases Used:** CABCD **Loan:** In country **Service:** Inhouse **Photocopy:** Yes

3237   Bangor, UK
            University of Wales Bangor (UWB)
            Deiniol Road Library
            Deiniol Road
            Bangor, Gwynedd LL57 2UW
Phone: +44(1248) 351151 ext 2984 **Fax:** +44(1248) 383826 **Email:** enquiries@bangor.ac.uk **WWW:** www.bangor.ac.uk **OPAC:** library.bangor.ac.uk

Former Name: University College of North Wales **Type:** Academic **Head:** P. Brady *Phone:* +44(1248) 351151 *Email:* p.r.brady@bangor.ac.uk **Staff:** 2 Prof. 4 Other **Holdings:** 656 journals **Language of Collection/Services:** English **Subjects:** Agricultural Economics, Agroforestry, Animal Husbandry, Entomology, Farming, Fisheries, Forestry, Plant Pathology, Plants, Soil Science, Wood **Databases Used:** ASFA; Biosis; CABCD **Loan:** Inhouse **Service:** Inhouse **Photocopy:** Yes

3238   Bedford, UK
            Cranfield University of Technology, Silsoe
                College
            Library
            Silsoe
            Bedford MK45 4DT
Phone: +44(1525) 863022 **Fax:** +44(1525) 863001
WWW: www.silsoe.cranfield.ac.uk **OPAC:** www.silsoe.cranfield.ac.uk/courses/academic/library.htm

Former Name: Cranfield Institute of Technology **Founded:** 1963 **Type:** Academic **Head:** Christopher Napper *Phone:* +44(1525) 863000 ext 3606 *Email:* c.napper@cranfield.ac.uk **Staff:** 2 Prof. 4 Other **Holdings:** 70,000 books 425 journals **Language of Collection/Services:** English / English **Subjects:** Comprehensive **Specializations:** Agricultural Engineering, Drainage, Erosion, Farm Machinery, Irrigation, Mechanization, Soil Conservation **Databases Used:** CABCD **Loan:** In country **Photocopy:** Yes

3239   Belfast, UK
            Department of Agriculture and Rural
                Development (DARD)
            Library
            Room 615 Dundonald House
            Upper Newtownards Road
            Belfast, Northern Ireland BT4 3SB
Phone: +44(1232) 524401 **Fax:** +44(1232) 525546 **Email:** library@dardni.gov.uk **WWW:** www.nics.gov.uk/dani

Former Name: Department of Agriculture for Northern Ireland (DANI) **Founded:** 1921 **Type:** Government **Head:** Mr. Noel Menary *Phone:* +44(1232) 524402 **Staff:** 3 Prof. 5 Other **Holdings:** 50,000 books 600 journals **Language of Collection / Services:** English **Subjects:** Comprehensive **Service:** Inhouse **Loan:** Internationally **Photocopy:** Yes

3240   Belfast, UK
            Queen's University of Belfast (QUB)
            Agriculture and Food Science Library
            Newforge Lane
            Belfast, Northern Ireland BT9 5PX
Phone: +44(1232) 255227 **Fax:** +44(1232) 255400
WWW: www.qub.ac.uk/lib **OPAC:** library.qub.ac.uk/qu_www-bin/www_talis32

Founded: 1850 **Type:** Academic **Head:** Elizabeth Traynor *Phone:* +44 (1232) 255226 *Email:* e.traynor@qub.ac.uk **Staff:** 3 Prof. 4 Other **Holdings:** 20,000 books 750 journals **Language of Collection/Services:** English **Subjects:** Agriculture (Tropics), Agribusiness, Agricultural Development, Agricultural Economics, Agricultural Engineering, Animal Husbandry, Aquaculture, Biotechnology, Crops, Entomology, Farming, Fisheries, Food Sciences, Forestry, Horticulture, Plant Pathology, Soil Science, Veterinary Medicine, Water Resources **Networks:** BLCMP **Databases Used:** Agricola; Biosis; CABCD; CAS; FSTA **Loan:** Internationally **Service:** Internationally **Photocopy:** Yes

3241   Bradford, UK
            University of Bradford, Development and Project
                Planning Centre (DPPC)
            J B Priestley Library, DPPC Collection

Bradford, West Yorkshire BD7 1DP
Phone: +44(1274) 233984 **Fax:** +44(1274) 235280 **Email:**
dppc-library@bradford.ac.uk **WWW:** www.brad.ac.uk/
acad/dppc/homepage.html **OPAC:** www.brad.ac.uk/library/
news/catalogue.htm

Former Name: Project Planning Centre for Developing
Countries **Founded:** 1971 **Type:** Academic **Head:** Mrs. N.
Matthews *Email:* n.matthews@bradford.ac.uk **Staff:** 2 Prof.
1 Other **Holdings:** 17,000 books 200 journals **Language of
Collection/Services:** English **Subjects:** Agriculture (Trop-
ics), Agribusiness, Agricultural Development, Agricultural
Economics, Water Resources **Loan:** Inhouse **Service:** Inter-
nationally **Photocopy:** Yes

3242   Brighton, UK
University of Sussex, Institute of Development
Studies (IDS)
British Library for Development Studies (BLDS)
Andrew Cohen Building
Falmer
Brighton, Sussex BN1 9RE
Phone: +44(1273) 678263 **Fax:** +44(1273) 621202 **Email:**
blds@ids.ac.uk **WWW:** www.ids.ac.uk **OPAC:** nt1.ids.ac.
uk/dbases/bldsdb0.htm

Former Name: Documentation and Library Centre, IDS Li-
brary **Founded:** 1966 **Type:** Academic **Head:** Ms. Maureen
Mahoney *Phone:* +44(1273) 678665 *Email:* m.mahoney@
ids.ac.uk **Staff:** 2 Prof. 8 Other **Holdings:** 250,000 books
12,000 journals **Language of Collection/Services:** English /
English **Subjects:** Agribusiness, Agricultural Development,
Agricultural Economics, Education/Extension **Databases
Developed:** DEVBASE - bibliographic database on devel-
opment related to third world. Available on-site and via
Internet at www.ids.ac.uk/blds/blds.html **Databases Used:**
Comprehensive **Loan:** Internationally **Service:** Internation-
ally **Photocopy:** Yes

3243   Bristol, UK
University of Bristol, Department of Agricultural
Sciences, Institute of Arable Crops Research,
Long Ashton Research Station (IACR,
LARS)
Treharne Library
Wildcountry Lane, Long Ashton
Bristol BS41 9AF
Phone: +44(1275) 392181 **Fax:** +44(1275) 394007 **Email:**
library.larslib@bbsrc.ac.uk **WWW:** www.iacr.bbsrc.ac.uk/
lars/tlarshome.html **OPAC:** saffron.res.bbsrc.ac.uk/brs/
search.htm

Founded: 1903 **Type:** Academic **Head:** Mr. S.P. Smith
Staff: 1 Prof. 3 Other **Holdings:** 20,000 books 220 journals
Language of Collection/Services: English / English **Sub-
jects:** Agriculture (Tropics), Agricultural Development,
Biochemistry, Biotechnology, Crops, Ecology, Entomology,
Farming, Forestry, Horticulture, Plant Protection, Plants
Specializations: Pesticides, Plant Pathology, Plant Physiol-
ogy, Weeds **Databases Used:** Comprehensive **Loan:** In
country **Service:** Inhouse **Photocopy:** Yes

3244   Cambridge, UK
Ministry of Agriculture, Fisheries and Food,
National Institute of Agricultural Botany
(MAFF, NIAB)
Library
Huntingdon Road
Cambridge CB3 0LE
Phone: +44(1223) 276381 **Fax:** +44(1223) 277602 **Email:**
n.niablibrary@pvs.maff.gov.uk

Founded: 1921 **Type:** Association **Head:** E.J. Murfitt **Staff:**
1 Prof. 1 Other **Language of Collection/Services:** English/
English **Subjects:** Botany, Crops, Horticulture, Plant Pathology, Seed Certification, Seed Testing, Variety Trials **Loan:**
Internationally **Service:** Internationally **Photocopy:** Yes

3245   Cambridge, UK
University of Cambridge
Cambridge University Library, Scientific
Periodicals Library, Buttress Collection of
Applied Biology
Benet Street
Cambridge CB2 3PY
Phone: +44(1223) 334742 **Fax:** +44(1223) 344748 **Email:**
library@ula.cam.ac.uk **WWW:** www.lib.cam.ac.uk

Former Name: Department of Applied Biology Library
Type: Academic **Head:** Mr. M.L. Wilson *Phone:* +44(1223)
334744 *Email:* mlw1003@cus.cam.ac.uk **Staff:** 2 Prof. 12
Other **Holdings:** 40,000 books 500 journals **Language of
Collection/Services:** English **Subjects:** Crops, Horticulture,
Plant Pathology **Specializations:** Plant Breeding **Loan:** In-
house **Service:** Inhouse **Photocopy:** Yes

3246   Cambridge, UK
University of Cambridge, Department of Land
Economy
Land Economy Library
19 Silver Street
Cambridge CB2 1SD
Location: Laundress Lane **Phone:** +44(1223) 337110 **Fax:**
+44(1223) 337130 **Email:** lan1@ula.cam.ac.uk **WWW:**
www.landecon.cam.ac.uk

Founded: 1965 **Type:** Academic **Head:** Wendy Thurley
Email: wt10000@cus.cam.ac.uk **Staff:** 1 Prof. **Language of
Collection/Services:** English **Holdings:** 20,000 books 100
journals **Subjects:** Agricultural Development, Agricultural
Economics, Forestry **Specializations:** Environmental Legis-
lation, Environmental Policy **Loan:** In country **Photocopy:**
Yes

3247   Cambridge, UK
W.S. Atkins Agriculture
Library
Wellbrook Court
Girton Road
Cambridge CB3 0NA

Former Name: Atkins Land and Water Management **Type:**
Business **Founded:** 1982 **Head:** Mrs. A.L. Sawalhi *Phone:*
+44(1223) 276002 ext 40 **Staff:** 1 Prof. **Holdings:** 6,000
books 30 journals **Language of Collection/Services:** English **Subjects:** Agriculture (Tropics), Animal Husbandry,

Agricultural Development, Agricultural Economics, Agricultural Engineering, Education/Extension, Fisheries, Crops, Forestry, Horticulture, Soil Science, Water Resources **Loan:** Do not loan **Photocopy:** Yes

3248   Cardiff, UK
International Bee Research Association (IBRA)
Eva Crane IBRA Library
18 North Road
Cardiff, Wales CF1 3DY
Fax: +44(29) 2066 5522 **Email:** ibra@cardiff.ac.uk
WWW: www.cf.ac.uk/ibra

Founded: 1949 **Type:** Association **Head:** Ms. Salma Zabaneh *Phone:* +44(29) 2037 2409 *Email:* ibra@cardiff.ac.uk **Staff:** 1 Prof. 1 Other **Holdings:** 35,000 books 5,000 journals **Language of Collection/Services:** English **Subjects:** Beekeeping **Databases Developed:** APICABS (1973-date) - apicultural abstracts reviewing the world's literature on bees, beekeeping and related subjects; access is chargeable. **Loan:** Internationally **Photocopy:** Yes

3249   Chelmsford, UK
Writtle Agricultural College
Learning Information Services
Lordship Lane
Writtle
Chelmsford, Essex CM1 3RR
Phone: +44(1245) 424200 **Fax:** +44(1245) 420456
WWW: www.writtle.ac.uk **OPAC:** www.writtle.ac.uk/learningresources/Libar.htm

Founded: 1945 **Type:** Academic **Head:** Rachel Hewings *Phone:* +44(1245) 424200 ext 26009 **Staff:** 2 Prof. 3 Other **Holdings:** 35,000 books 300 journals **Subjects:** Agricultural Engineering, Horticulture **Loan:** In country **Photocopy:** Yes

3250   Chippenham, UK
Lackham College
Library
Lacock
Chippenham, Wiltshire SN15 2NY
Phone: +44(1249) 650812 **Fax:** +44(1249) 444474

Founded: 1948 **Type:** Academic **Head:** Stella M. Vain *Phone:* +44(1249) 443111 **Staff:** 1 Prof. 3 Other **Holdings:** 19,500 books 240 journals **Language of Collection/Services:** English / English **Subjects:** Agricultural Economics, Agricultural Engineering, Animal Husbandry, Conservation, Crop Husbandry, Forestry, Horticulture **Loan:** Internationally **Photocopy:** Yes

3251   Chipping Campden, UK
Campden and Chorleywood Food Research
      Association (CCFRA)
Information and Legislation Department
Chipping Campden, Gloucestershire GL55 6LD
Fax: +44(1386) 842100 **Email:** information@campden.co.uk **WWW:** www.campden.co.uk

Former Name: Campden Food Preservation Research Association, Campden Food and Drink Research Association (CFDRA) **Founded:** 1952 **Type:** Research **Head:** Miss C.J. Willcox *Phone:* +44(1386) 842000 *Email:* information@

campden.co.uk **Staff:** 1 Prof. 5 Other **Holdings:** 10,000 books 300 journals **Language of Collection/Services:** English **Subjects:** Food Sciences, Food Technology **Databases Developed:** Flour Milling and Baking Abstracts - available on subscription **Databases Used:** Comprehensive **Loan:** Members only **Service:** Members only **Photocopy:** Yes

3252   Compton, UK
Biotechnology and Biological Sciences Research
      Council, Institute for Animal Health (BBSRC,
      IAH)
Library
Compton Laboratory
Compton, Near Newbury, Berkshire RG20 7NN
Phone: +44(1635) 578411 **Fax:** +44(1635) 577304, 577237 **Email:** compton.library@bbsrc.ac.uk **WWW:** www.iah.bbsrc.ac.uk

Former Name: Agricultural and Food Research Council (AFRC) **Type:** Research **Head:** Diane Collins **Staff:** 1 Prof. 1.5 Other **Holdings:** 1,000 books 140 journals **Language of Collection/Services:** English **Subjects:** Animal Pathology, Immunology, Infectious Diseases, Livestock, Microbiology, Molecular Biology, Virology **Photocopy:** Yes

3253   Cookstown, UK
Loughry College - The Food Centre
Library
Cookstown, Co. Tyrone, Northern Ireland BT80
      9AA
Phone: +44(28) 8676 2491 ext 222 **Fax:** +44(28) 8676 1043 **WWW:** www.loughrycollege.ac.uk/core/loughry.htm

Former Name: Loughry College of Agriculture and Food Technology **Type:** Academic **Staff:** 1 Prof. .5 Other **Holdings:** 10,000 books 100 journals **Language of Collection/Services:** English / English **Subjects:** Communication, Food Technology **Loan:** In country **Photocopy:** Yes

3254   Coventry, UK
Royal Agricultural Society of England (RASE)
Library
Stoneleigh Park
Coventry, Warwickshire CV8 2LZ
Phone: +44(24) 7685 8262, 7669 6969 ext 262 **Fax:** +44(24) 7669 6900 **WWW:** www.rase.org.uk

Founded: 1838 **Type:** Association, Private **Head:** Phillip Sheppy *Email:* phillips@rase.org.uk **Staff:** 1 Prof. **Holdings:** 10,000 books **Language of Collection/Services:** English / English **Subjects:** Agriculture (Tropics), Agribusiness, Agricultural Development, Agricultural Economics, Agricultural Engineering, Animal Husbandry, Biotechnology, Crops, Education/Extension, Entomology, Farming, Fisheries, Food Sciences, Forestry, Horticulture, Plant Pathology, Soil Science, Veterinary Medicine, Water Resources **Databases Developed:** Gilbey Pamphlets - 150 bound volumes from 1750-1840 on a variety of agricultural, rural, and related topics; will eventually be available on microfiche. **Loan:** Do not loan **Service:** Inhouse **Photocopy:** Yes

3255   Cupar, UK
Elmwood College

Library
Carslogie Road
Cupar, Scotland KY15 4JB

Phone: +44(1334) 658810 **Fax:** +44(1334) 658888 **Email:** library@elmwood.ac.uk **WWW:** www.elmwood.ac.uk

Former Name: Fife Regional Council, Elmwood Agricultural and Technical College **Founded:** 1971 **Type:** Academic **Head:** Mrs. Christine A. Barclay **Staff:** 1 Prof. 1 Other **Holdings:** 11,200 books 95 journals **Language of Collection/Services:** English **Subjects:** Amenity Planting, Conservation, Engineering, Food Research, Leisure **Databases Developed:** SAMI modular guidance system **Loan:** In country **Photocopy:** Yes

3256   Dorchester, UK
Dorset Natural History and Archaeological
    Society
Dorset County Museum
High West Street
Dorchester DT1 1XA

Fax: +44(1305) 257180 **Email:** dorsetcountymuseum@ dor-mus.demon.co.uk **WWW:** home.clara.net/dorset. museum

Founded: 1846 **Type:** Academic **Head:** R. de Peyer *Phone:* +44(1305) 262735 **Holdings:** 150 books **Language of Collection/Services:** English **Specializations:** Agriculture (UK - Dorset County) **Loan:** Do not loan **Photocopy:** Yes

3257   Dundee, UK
Scottish Executive Rural Affairs Department,
    Scottish Crop Research Institute (SERAD,
    SCRI)
Library
Invergowrie
Dundee, Scotland DD2 5DA

Phone: +44(1382) 562731 ext 2013 **Fax:** +44(1382) 562426 **Email:** s.stephens@scri.sari.ac.uk **WWW:** www. scri.sari.ac.uk

Former Name: Scottish Horticultural Research Institute, Scottish Plant Breeding Station **Founded:** 1981 **Type:** Government **Head:** Ms. S.E. Stephens *Email:* s.stephens@scri. sari.ac.uk *Phone:* +44(1382) 562731 ext 2013 **Staff:** 2 Prof. **Holdings:** 7,500 books 200 journals **Language of Collection/Services:** English / English **Subjects:** Biotechnology, Entomology, Crops, Plant Pathology, Soil **Databases Used:** Comprehensive **Loan:** In country **Service:** Inhouse **Photocopy:** Yes

3258   Durham, UK
Durham College of Agriculture and Horticulture
    (DCAH)
Library
Houghall
Durham DH1 3SG

Founded: 1938 **Type:** Academic **Staff:** 2 Other **Holdings:** 6,000 books 156 journals **Language of Collection/Services:** English **Subjects:** Arboriculture, Floriculture, Environmental Management, Horse Riding, Horticulture, Land Use, Recreation **Loan:** Internationally **Photocopy:** Yes

3259   Easter Bush, UK
University of Edinburgh, Centre for Tropical
    Veterinary Medicine (CTVM)
Library
Easter Bush, Scotland EH25 9RG

Location: Between Roslin and the Pentland Hills, 11 km south of Edinburgh **Phone:** +44(131) 650-6410 **WWW:** www.ed.ac.uk **OPAC:** www.lib.ed.ac.uk/lib/resources/ catalogues/index.shtml

Founded: 1970 **Type:** Academic **Head:** Fiona Brown *Phone:* +44(131) 650-6410 **Staff:** 1 Prof. **Holdings:** 4,500 books 69 journals **Language of Collection/Services:** English **Subjects:** Agriculture (Tropics), Agricultural Development, Agricultural Economics, Agricultural Engineering, Animal Husbandry, Biotechnology, Education/Extension, Entomology, Farming, Fisheries **Specializations:** Animal Production, Veterinary Medicine (Tropics), Tropics **Databases Used:** CABCD **Loan:** In country **Photocopy:** Yes

3260   Edinburgh, UK
Biotechnology and Biological Sciences Research
    Council, Institute for Animal Health,
    Neuropathogenesis Unit (BBSRC, IAH)
Library
Ogston Building
West Mains Road
Edinburgh, Scotland EH9 3JF

Phone: +44(131) 667-5204 **Fax:** +44(131) 668-3871 **WWW:** www.iah.bbsrc.ac.uk

Type: Government **Subjects:** Molecular Biology, Pathology

3261   Edinburgh, UK
National Library of Scotland (NLS)
Scottish Science Library (SSL)
33 Salisbury Place
Edinburgh, Scotland EH9 1SL

Location: Causewayside Building **Phone:** +44(131) 226-4531 **Fax:** +44(131) 622-0644 **Email:** enquiries@nls.uk **WWW:** www.nls.ac.uk **OPAC:** www.nls.ac.uk

Type: Government **Head:** John Coll *Phone:* +44(131) 226-4531 ext 3512 *Email:* j.coll@nls.uk **Staff:** 8 Prof. 5 Other **Language of Collection/Services:** English / English **Specializations:** Environmental Management, Environmental Protection, Pollution **Databases Used:** Biosis **Loan:** Do not loan **Service:** Internationally **Photocopy:** Yes

3262   Edinburgh, UK
Natural Environment Research Council, Centre for
    Ecology and Hydrology, Institute of
    Terrestrial Ecology, Edinburgh Research
    Station (NERC, CEH, ITE)
Library
Bush Estate, Penicuik
Edinburgh, Midlothian, Scotland EH26 0QB

Fax: +44(131) 445-3943 **WWW:** mwnta.nmw.ac.uk **OPAC:** www.nmw.ac.uk/ITE/library/html/unicorn.htm

Founded: 1973 **Type:** Government **Head:** S. Scobie *Phone:* +44(131) 445-4343 ext 210 *Email:* ssco@ceh.ac.uk **Staff:** 1 Prof. 1 Other **Holdings:** 2,350 books 300 journals **Language of Collection/Services:** English / English **Subjects:** Fisheries, Forestry **Specializations:** Ecology, Environment **Databases Developed:** TFSDIS - record of all ITE staff publications, contract reports and project information; in-house access only. **Databases Used:** Comprehensive **Loan:** Inhouse **Photocopy:** Yes

3263   Edinburgh, UK
Royal Botanic Garden, Edinburgh (RBGE)
Library
Inverleith Row
Edinburgh, Scotland EH3 5LR
Fax: +44(131) 248-2901 **Email:** library@rbge.org.uk
WWW: www.rbge.org.uk

Founded: 1670 **Type:** Government **Head:** Dr. C.D. Will
Phone: +44 (131) 248-2850 *Email:* library@rbge.org.uk
Staff: 3 Prof. 3 Other **Holdings:** 200,000 books 1,700 journals **Language of Collection/Services:** English **Subjects:** Botany, Horticulture **Loan:** In country **Photocopy:** Yes

3264   Edinburgh, UK
Royal Highland and Agricultural Society of
Scotland
Library
Royal Highland Centre, Ingliston
Edinburgh, Scotland EH28 8NF
Phone: +44(131) 333-2444 ext 237 **Fax:** +44(131) 333-5236 **Email:** info@rhass.org.uk **WWW:** www.rhass.org.uk/Site/MainFrame.cfm

Founded: 1784 **Type:** Academic **Staff:** 1 Other **Holdings:** 10,000 books 50 journals **Language of Collection/Services:** English **Subjects:** Agricultural Education, Agriculture (History) **Loan:** Do not loan **Service:** Inhouse **Photocopy:** Yes

3265   Edinburgh, UK
Scottish Agricultural College (SAC)
Edinburgh School of Agriculture Library and
Information Centre
West Mains Road
Edinburgh, Scotland EH9 3JG
Phone: +44(131) 535-4117 **Fax:** +44(131) 535-4246
WWW: www.sac.ac.uk **OPAC:** actalis.ab.sac.ac.uk:8001

Founded: 1790 **Type:** Academic, Government **Head:** Marilyn Mullay *Phone:* +44(131) 535-4116 *Email:* m.mullay@ed.sac.ac.uk **Staff:** 3 Prof. 1.5 Other **Holdings:** 35,000 books 310 journals **Language of Collection/Services:** English **Subjects:** Agriculture (Tropics), Agribusiness, Agricultural Economics, Agricultural Engineering, Animal Husbandry, Crops, Education/Extension, Entomology, Environmental Sciences, Farming, Food Sciences, Horticulture, Plant Pathology, Soil Science **Databases Developed:** AGDEX - an information service for the applied agriculturalist; covers agricultural trade and business literature, popular farming press; inquire for access **Databases Used:** Comprehensive **Loan:** In country **Photocopy:** Yes

3266   Edinburgh, UK
Scottish Agricultural Science Agency (SASA)
Library
82 Craigs Road
Edinburgh, Scotland EH12 8NJ

Fax: +44(131) 244-8940 **Email:** library@sasa.gov.uk

Former Name: Department of Agriculture and Fisheries for Scotland (DAFS), Agricultural Scientific Services, East Craigs **Type:** Government **Head:** Mrs. Lynda Clark *Phone:* +44(131) 244-8826 *Email:* clark@sasa.gov.uk **Staff:** 1 Prof. 1 Other **Holdings:** 5,000 books 150 journals **Language of Collection/Services:** English **Subjects:** Biotechnology, Entomology, Herbicides, Microbiology, Nematology, Pest Control, Pesticides, Plant Pathology, Plant Protection **Specializations:** Potatoes, Seed Testing **Databases Used:** Comprehensive **Loan:** In country **Photocopy:** Yes

3267   Edinburgh, UK
Scottish Beekeepers Association (SBA)
Moir Library
Fountainbridge Library
Dundee Street
Edinburgh, Scotland EH11 1BG
Phone: +44(131) 529-5616 **WWW:** www.users.zetnet.co.uk/scottish-beekeepers

Founded: 1916 **Type:** Association **Staff:** 1 Other **Holdings:** 6,700 books 3 journals **Subjects:** Entomology **Specializations:** Apidae, Husbandry, Hymenoptera, Insects **Loan:** Inhouse **Service:** In country **Photocopy:** Yes

3268   Edinburgh, UK
University of Edinburgh
Edinburgh University Library, Darwin Library
King's Buildings
Mayfield Road
Edinburgh, Scotland EH9 3JU
Phone: +44(131) 667-1081 ext 2716 **Fax:** +44(131) 650-6702 **WWW:** www.ed.ac.uk **OPAC:** www.lib.ed.ac.uk/lib/resources/catalogues/index.shtml

Type: Academic **Head:** Dr. D.M. Carroll *Phone:* +44(131) 650-5785 *Email:* d.carroll@ed.ac.uk **Staff:** 1 Prof. 3 Other **Language of Collection/Services:** English **Subjects:** Agriculture (Tropics), Agroforestry, Biotechnology, Botany, Ecology, Fisheries, Forestry, Molecular Biology, Plant Pathology, Soil Science, Water Resources, Wildlife Management **Loan:** In country **Service:** Inhouse **Photocopy:** No

3269   Edinburgh, UK
University of Edinburgh
Edinburgh University Library, Royal (Dick)
School of Veterinary Studies Library (EUL)
Summerhall
Edinburgh, Scotland EH9 1QH
Phone: +44(131) 650-6175 **Fax:** +44(131) 650-6593
Email: vet.summerhall.library@ed.ac.uk **WWW:** www.lib.ed.ac.uk **OPAC:** www.lib.ed.ac.uk/lib/resources/catalogues/index.shtml

Founded: 1823 **Type:** Academic **Head:** Mrs. M.A. Kennett *Phone:* +44 (131) 650-6176 *Email:* a.kennett@ed.ac.uk **Staff:** 1 Prof. 4 Other **Holdings:** 27,000 books 109 journals **Language of Collection/Services:** English/English **Subjects:** Animal Health, Animal Husbandry, Animal Production **Databases Used:** CABCD; Medline **Loan:** Internationally **Photocopy:** Yes

3270   Glasgow, UK
Department for International Development (DFID)
Library
Room AH 219, Abercrombie House
Eaglesham Road, East Kilbride
Glasgow G75 8EA

Phone: +44(1355) 843132 **Fax:** +44(1355) 843632 **Email:** enquiry@dfid.gtnet.gov.uk **WWW:** www.dfid.gov.uk

Former Name: Overseas Development Administration (ODA) **Type:** Government **Head:** Mrs. Anne Fraser *Phone:* +44(1355) 843167 **Staff:** 7 Prof. 5 Other **Holdings:** 50,000 books 850 journals **Language of Collection/Services:** English/English **Subjects:** Developing Countries **Databases Developed:** Shared catalogue with Foreign and Commonwealth Office Library - available in-house only **Loan:** In country **Service:** Inhouse **Photocopy:** Yes

3271   Glasgow, UK
Glasgow University
Library
Hillhead Street
Glasgow, Scotland G12 8QE

Phone: +44(141) 330-6704 **Fax:** +44(141) 330-4952 **Email:** library@lib.gla.ac.uk **WWW:** www.gla.ac.uk **OPAC:** eleanor.lib.gla.ac.uk/search

Founded: 1451 **Type:** Academic **Head:** Andrew Wale *Phone:* +44(141) 330-5635 *Email:* a.wale@lib.gla.ac.uk **Staff:** 3 Prof. 5.5 Other **Holdings:** 3,500 books 80 journals **Subjects:** Agricultural Chemistry, Agricultural Economics, Animal Husbandry, Soil Science **Loan:** Internationally **Photocopy:** Yes

3272   Glastonbury, UK
Somerset County Museums Service Library
Somerset Rural Life Museum
Abbey Farm
Chilkwell Street
Glastonbury, Somerset BA6 8DB

Phone: +44(1458) 831197 **Fax:** +44(1458) 834684 **Email:** county-museums@somerset.gov.uk

Founded: 1976 **Type:** Government **Staff:** 1 Other **Holdings:** 150 books 4 journals **Specializations:** Agriculture (History - UK - 19th Century), Agriculture (History - UK - 20th Century) **Loan:** Do not loan **Photocopy:** Yes

3273   Harpenden, UK
Biotechnology and Biological Sciences Research
    Council, Institute of Arable Crops Research
    (BBSRC, IACR)
Rothamsted Library
Harpenden, Hertfordshire AL5 2JQ

Phone: +44(1582) 763133 ext 2659 **Fax:** +44(1582) 760981 **WWW:** www.res.bbsrc.ac.uk

Former Name: Agricultural and Food Research Council (AFRC) **Founded:** 1911 **Type:** Government **Head:** Mrs. S. E. Allsopp *Email:* liz.allsopp@bbsrc.ac.uk *Phone:* +44 (1582) 763133 ext 2657 **Staff:** 3 Prof. 5 Other **Holdings:** 100,000 books 1,700 journals **Subjects:** Crops, Entomology, Plant Pathology **Specializations:** Arable Farming, Biotechnology, Plant Nutrition, Plant Protection, Soil Science **Data-**

bases Developed: IACR Book Catalogue, Rothamsted Staff Publications **Databases Used:** Comprehensive **Loan:** In country **Photocopy:** Yes

3274   Hatfield, UK
Royal Veterinary College (RVC)
Library
Hawkshead Campus, Hawkshead House
Hawkshead Lane, North Mymms
Hatfield, Herts AL9 7TA

Phone: +44(1707) 666214 **Fax:** +44(1707) 652090 Attn: Library **WWW:** www.rvc.ac.uk **OPAC:** www.rvc.ac.uk/general/library/libfront.htm

Type: Academic **Head:** Mr. Simon Jackson *Phone:* +44 (1707) 666214 *Email:* sjackson@rvc.ac.uk **Staff:** 8 Prof. 4 Other **Holdings:** 40,000 books 200 journals **Language of Collection/Services:** English/English **Subjects:** Veterinary Medicine **Databases Developed:** LIBERTAS - member of University of London Libertas Consortium; accessible via JANET network **Databases Used:** Comprehensive **Loan:** Inhouse **Service:** Inhouse **Photocopy:** Yes

3275   Hertford, UK
Tun Abdul Razak Research Centre (TARRC)
Library
Brickendonbury
Hertford, Herts SG13 8NL

Fax: +44(1992) 554837 **Email:** general@tarrc.tcom.co.uk **WWW:** www.tcom.co.uk/tarrc

Former Name: Malaysian Rubber Research and Development Board (MRRDB), Malaysian Rubber Producers' Research Association (MRPRA) **Founded:** 1938 **Type:** Association **Head:** Ms. Kristina Lawson *Phone:* +44(1992) 584966 *Email:* lawson@tarrc.tcom.co.uk **Staff:** 2 Prof. 2 Other **Holdings:** 300 books 2 journals **Language of Collection/Services:** English **Specializations:** Rubber **Databases Used:** Comprehensive **Loan:** In country **Service:** Internationally **Photocopy:** Yes

3276   Hungerford, UK
Holt Studios International Ltd.
Photographic Library
The Courtyard, 24 High Street
Hungerford, Berkshire RG17 0NF

Phone: +44(1488) 683523 **Fax:** +44(1488) 683511 **Email:** library@holt-studios.co.uk **WWW:** www.holt-studios.co.uk/library

Type: Business **Head:** Mr. Nigel Cattlin **Staff:** 3 Prof. 3 Other **Holdings:** 80,000 transparencies books **Language of Collection/Services:** English / English **Subjects:** Agriculture (Tropics), Agribusiness, Agricultural Development, Agricultural Engineering, Animal Husbandry, Biotechnology, Crops, Entomology, Farming, Forestry, Horticulture, Plant Pathology, Plants **Databases Developed:** All pictures catalogued on PC database; no public access; searches by request only **Loan:** Internationally **Service:** Internationally **Photocopy:** Yes

3277 Langford, UK
University of Bristol, School of Veterinary
　　Science
Veterinary Science Library
Churchill Building
Langford BS40 5DU
Phone: +44(117) 928-9205 **Fax:** +44(117) 928-9505
Email: lib-vet@bris.ac.uk **WWW:** www.bris.ac.uk
OPAC: www.bris.ac.uk/Depts/Library/catalogue/linkcat.
htm

Founded: 1950 **Type:** Academic **Head:** Sue Barefoot
Phone: +44(117) 928-7945 *Email:* s.j.barefoot@bris.ac.uk
Staff: 3 Other **Holdings:** 10,000 books 120 journals **Language of Collection/Services:** English **Subjects:** Animal
Husbandry, Meat, Pathology, Veterinary Science **Databases
Used:** Medline **Loan:** In country **Service:** Inhouse **Photocopy:** Yes

3278 Leeds, UK
University of Leeds
Edward Boyle Library
Leeds, Yorkshire LS2 9JT
Location: Woodhouse Lane **Phone:** +44(113) 233-5533
Fax: +44(113) 233-5539 **Email:** beesciences@library.
leeds.ac.uk **WWW:** www.leeds.ac.uk **OPAC:** lib.leeds.
ac.uk

Former Name: South Library **Type:** Academic **Head:** Mr.
Adrian Smith *Phone:* +44(113) 233-5531 *Email:* a.smith@
leeds.ac.uk **Holdings:** 2,000,000 books 2,500 journals **Language of Collection/Services:** English / English **Subjects:**
Animal Husbandry, Biotechnology, Food Sciences, Soil Science, Water Resources **Specializations:** Cookery, Biochemistry, Flora, Molecular Biology **Databases Developed:**
Oncology - LMI; Education - BEI **Databases Used:** Biosis;
CABCD; Medline **Loan:** Internationally **Service:** Inhouse
Photocopy: Yes

3279 Liverpool, UK
Liverpool John Moores University
Avril Robarts Learning Resource Centre
Tithebarn Street
Liverpool L2 2ER
Phone: +44(151) 231-4022 **Fax:** +44(151) 231-4479
WWW: www.livjm.ac.uk **OPAC:** www.livjm.ac.uk/lea/
lionpage.htm

Former Name: Liverpool Polytechnic, Byrom Street
Learning Resource Centre **Founded:** 1964 **Type:** Academic
Head: Jim Ainsworth *Phone:* +44(151) 231-4020 *Email:*
j.w.ainsworth@livjm.ac.uk **Staff:** 5 Prof. 9.5 Other **Holdings:** 1,000 books 20 journals **Language of Collection/Services:** English **Subjects:** Animal Husbandry, Entomology,
Biotechnology, Crops, Plant Pathology, Soil Science **Databases Used:** Agricola; Biosis; CABCD **Loan:** Do not loan
Photocopy: Yes

3280 London, UK
British Library (BL)
Science Technology and Business (STB)
The British Library at St. Pancras
96 Euston Road

London NW1 2DB
Phone: +44(20) 7412 7288 (Life Sciences); 7412 7494
(Physical Sciences and Engineering); 7412 7454 (British
Library-Lloyds/TSB Business Line); 7412 7536 (Social
Policy Information Service); 7412 7919 (Patents) **Fax:**
+44(20) 7412 7217 (Life Sciences); 7412 7495 (Physical
Sciences and Engineering) **Email:** STB-Marketing@bl.uk
WWW: www.bl.uk **OPAC:** opac97.bl.uk

Former Name: Patent Office Library **Founded:** 1973 **Type:**
Government **Head:** Alan Gomersall **Staff:** 60 Prof. 225
Other **Holdings:** 251,000 books 67,000 journals **Subjects:**
Agriculture (Tropics), Agribusiness, Agricultural Development, Agricultural Engineering, Animal Husbandry, Biotechnology, Education/Extension, Entomology, Farming,
Crops, Fisheries, Food Sciences, Forestry, Horticulture,
Plant Pathology, Soil Science, Veterinary Medicine, Water
Resources **Databases Developed:** IRS - Dialtech, UK national centre for the European Space Agency **Databases
Used:** Biosis; CABCD **Loan:** Do not loan **Photocopy:** Yes

3281 London, UK
Department for International Development (DFID)
Library
Room V221
94, Victoria Street
London SW1E 5JL
Phone: +44(20) 7917 0005 **Fax:** +44(20) 7917 0639
Email: library@dfid.gtnet.gov.uk **WWW:** www.dfid.gov.
uk

Former Name: Overseas Development Administration
(ODA) **Founded:** 1962 **Type:** Government **Head:** Mr. John
Lehane **Holdings:** 50,000 books 850 journals **Language of
Collection/Services:** English **Subjects:** Developing Countries **Databases Developed:** Shared catalogue with Foreign
and Commonwealth Office Library; available in-house only.
Loan: In country **Service:** Inhouse **Photocopy:** Yes

3282 London, UK
Imperial College of Science, Technology and
　　Medicine
Central Library, Life Sciences and Medicine
　　Collection
Prince Consort Road
London SW7 2AZ
Phone: +44(20) 7594 8842 **Fax:** +44(20) 7584 3763
WWW: www.ic.ac.uk **OPAC:** www.lib.ic.ac.uk/catalogue/
cataccess.htm

Type: Academic **Head:** Magda Czigany *Email:* m.czigany
@ic.ac.uk **Subjects:** Biochemistry, Biology, Botany, Cellular Biology, Environmental Sciences, Genetics, Immunology, Microbiology, Molecular Biology, Parasitology, Plant
Pathology, Zoology

3283 London, UK
International Coffee Organization (ICO)
Library
22 Berners Street
London W1P 4DD
Phone: +44(20) 7580 8591 **Fax:** +44(20) 7580 6129
Email: info@ico.org **WWW:** www.ico.org

Founded: 1963 **Type:** International **Staff:** 3 Prof. 2 Other **Holdings:** 12,000 books 200 journals **Subjects:** Coffee **Databases Developed:** Coffeeline - online bibliographical database, file 164 on DIALOG **Loan:** Do not loan **Photocopy:** Yes

3284   London, UK
    Linnean Society of London
    Library
    Burlington House
    Piccadilly
    London W1V 0LQ
Phone: +44(20) 7434 4479 **Fax:** +44(20) 7287 9364
WWW: www.linnean.org.uk

Founded: 1788 **Type:** Association **Head:** Gina Douglas *Email:* gina@linnean.demon.co.uk **Staff:** 1.5 Other **Holdings:** 90,000 books 100 journals **Language of Collection/Services:** English / English **Subjects:** Biology, Botany, Natural History, Taxonomy, Zoology **Specializations:** Biology (History - pre-1750) **Loan:** Fellows only **Service:** Internationally **Photocopy:** Yes

3285   London, UK
    Ministry of Agriculture, Fisheries and Food
        (MAFF)
    Economics Library
    3 Whitehall Place
    London SW1A 2HH
Fax: +44(20) 7270 8558 **WWW:** www.maff.gov.uk

Type: Government **Head:** Evan Bull *Phone:* +44(20) 7270 8634 **Staff:** 1 Prof. 1 Other **Holdings:** 24,000 books 300 journals **Language of Collection/Services:** English / English **Subjects:** Agricultural Economics, Agricultural Statistics **Databases Used:** Comprehensive **Loan:** Inhouse **Service:** Inhouse **Photocopy:** Yes

3286   London, UK
    Ministry of Agriculture, Fisheries and Food
        (MAFF)
    Nobel House Library
    Nobel House
    17 Smith Square
    London SW1P 3JR
Phone: +44(20) 7270 8961 **Fax:** +44(20) 7270 8419
Email: helpline@inf.maff.gov.uk **WWW:** www.maff.gov.uk

Type: Government **Holdings:** 30,000 books 620 journals **Subjects:** Food Sciences, Nutrition **Loan:** Inhouse **Photocopy:** Yes

3287   London, UK
    Ministry of Agriculture, Fisheries and Food
        (MAFF)
    Whitehall Place Library
    3-8 Whitehall Place (West Block)
    London SW1A 2HH
Phone: +44(20) 7270 8000 **Fax:** +44(20) 7270 8419
Email: helpline@inf.maff.gov.uk **WWW:** www.maff.gov.uk

Type: Government **Staff:** 9 Prof. 15 Other **Holdings:** 200,000 books 2,000 journals **Language of Collection/Services:** English / English **Subjects:** Agribusiness, Animal Husbandry, Crops, Farming, Fisheries, Food Sciences, Horticulture, Nutrition, Soil Science **Networks:** AGRIS **Loan:** In country **Service:** In country **Photocopy:** Yes

3288   London, UK
    Natural History Museum (NHM)
    Department of Library and Information Services
        (DLIS)
    Cromwell Road
    London SW7 5BD
Phone: +44(20) 7942 5207 (General and Zoology Libraries); 7942 5220 (Botany Library); 7942 5241 (Entomology Library; 7942 5269 (Earth Sciences Library) **Fax:** +44(20) 7942 5559 **Email:** library@nhm.ac.uk **WWW:** www.nhm.ac.uk **OPAC:** library.nhm.ac.uk **Ariel IP:** 157.140.9.57

Former Name: British Museum (Natural History) (BMNH) **Founded:** 1881 **Type:** Government **Head:** Dr. Ray Lester *Phone:* +44(20) 7942 5261 *Email:* rayl@nhm.ac.uk **Staff:** 27 Prof. 19 Other **Holdings:** 1,000,000 books 10,000 journals **Language of Collection/Services:** English / English **Subjects:** Agriculture (Tropics), Entomology, Fisheries, Forestry, Plant Pathology, Plants, Soil **Specializations:** Entomology, Medical Entomology, Taxonomy **Databases Used:** Biosis; CABCD **Loan:** Do not Loan **Photocopy:** Yes

3289   London, UK
    Overseas Development Institute (ODI)
    Library
    Portland House, Stag Place
    London SW1E 5DP
Phone: +44(20) 7393 1643 **Fax:** +44(20) 7393 1699
Email: library@odi.org.uk **WWW:** www.oneworld.org/odi **OPAC:** nt1.ids.ac.uk/eldis/odi/index.htm

Type: Research **Staff:** 2 Prof. 1 Other **Holdings:** 35,500 books 450 journals **Language of Collection/Services:** English **Subjects:** Agricultural Research, Conflict, Extension, Forestry, Livestock, Natural Disasters, Water Management **Specializations:** Agroforestry, Developing Countries, Non-governmental Organizations, Natural Resources, Pastoralism, Water Management **Loan:** Inhouse **Service:** Internationally **Photocopy:** Yes

3290   London, UK
    Royal College of Veterinary Surgeons (RCVS)
    Wellcome Library
    Belgravia House
    62-64 Horseferry Road
    London SW1P 2AF
Phone: +44(20) 7222 2021 **Fax:** +44(20) 7222 2004
Email: library@rcvs.org.uk **WWW:** www.rcvs.org.uk/rcvs **OPAC:** 212.212.145.2

Founded: 1844 **Type:** Association **Head:** Tom Roper *Phone:* +44(20) 7222-2021 *Email:* tom@rcvs.org.uk **Staff:** 3 Prof. 2 Other **Holdings:** 25,000 books 250 journals **Language of Collection/Services:** English / English **Subjects:** Animal Husbandry, Veterinary Science **Databases Used:**

Comprehensive **Loan:** In country **Service:** Internationally **Photocopy:** Yes

3291   London, UK
Royal Horticultural Society (RHS)
Lindley Library
80 Vincent Square
London SW1P 2PE

Phone: +44(20) 7821 3050 **Fax:** +44(20) 7828 3022
Email: library_enquiries@rhs.org.uk **WWW:** www.rhs.org.uk

Former Name: Horticultural Society of London **Founded:** 1868 **Type:** Association **Head:** Dr. Brent Elliott *Phone:* +44 (20) 7821 3050 *Email:* library-enquiries@rhs.org.uk **Staff:** 4 Prof. 2 Other **Holdings:** 51,000 books 350 journals **Language of Collection/Services:** English **Subjects:** Horticulture **Loan:** Inhouse **Photocopy:** Yes

3292   London, UK
Royal Society of Chemistry (RSC)
Library and Information Centre (LIC)
Burlington House
Piccadilly
London W1V 0BN

Phone: +44(20) 7437 8656 **Fax:** +44(20) 7287 9798
Email: library@rsc.org **WWW:** www.rsc.org/library
OPAC: www.rsc.org/lic/collections.htm

Former Name: Chemical Society **Founded:** 1841 **Type:** Academic **Head:** Mr. P.O'N. Hoey **Staff:** 3 Prof. 4 Other **Holdings:** 20,000 books 750 journals **Language of Collection/Services:** English/English **Subjects:** Agribusiness, Animal Pathology, Biotechnology, Chemistry, Food Sciences, Plant Pathology, Plant Protection, Water **Databases Used:** Comprehensive **Loan:** Members only **Service:** Internationally **Photocopy:** Yes

3293   London, UK
Royal Veterinary College (RVC)
Library
Camden Campus
Royal College Street
London NW1 0TU

Phone: +44(20) 7468 5161 **Fax:** +44(20) 7388 2342
WWW: www.rvc.ac.uk **OPAC:** www.rvc.ac.uk/general/library/libfront.htm

Founded: 1791 **Type:** Academic **Head:** Mr. Simon Jackson *Email:* sjackson@rvc.ac.uk **Staff:** 6 Prof. 6 Other **Holdings:** 40,000 books 200 journals **Language of Collection/Services:** English / English **Subjects:** Veterinary Medicine **Networks:** LIBERTAS **Databases Used:** CABCD; Medline **Loan:** Inhouse **Service:** Inhouse **Photocopy:** Yes

3294   London, UK
Science Museum
Library
Imperial College Road
South Kensington
London SW7 5NH

Phone: +44(20) 7942 4242 **Fax:** +44(20) 7942 4243
Email: smlinfo@nmsi.ac.uk **WWW:** www.nmsi.ac.uk/library **OPAC:** www.nmsi.ac.uk/library/smlcats.html

Founded: 1883 **Type:** Government **Staff:** 13 Prof. 35 Other **Holdings:** 2,250 books 25 journals **Language of Collection/Services:** English **Subjects:** Agricultural Engineering, Agriculture (History) **Loan:** Inhouse **Service:** Internationally **Photocopy:** Yes

3295   London, UK
Transport and General Workers Union (TGWU)
Rural Agricultural and Allied Workers Trade
    Group (RAAW)
Transport House, Palace Street
Victoria
London SWIE 5JD

Fax: +44(20) 7630 5861 **WWW:** www.tgwu.org.uk

Type: Business **Head:** E. Durkin *Phone:* +44(20) 7828 7788 *Email:* edurkin@tgwu.org.uk **Holdings:** 500 books 20 journals **Subjects:** Agricultural Trade Unions, Health Protection, Safety **Specializations:** Agricultural Trade Unions (History - UK) **Loan:** Do not loan **Photocopy:** Yes

3296   London, UK
Zoological Society of London
Library
Regents Park
London NW1 4RY

Phone: +44(20) 7449 6293 **Fax:** +44(20) 7586 5743
WWW: www.zsl.org

Founded: 1826 **Type:** Academic **Head:** Ann Sylph *Phone:* +44(20) 7449 6293 *Email:* a.sylph@ucl.ac.uk **Staff:** 3 Prof. **Holdings:** 200,000 books 1,500 journals **Language of Collection/Services:** English **Subjects:** Animal Husbandry, Conservation, Ecology, Extension, Fisheries, Veterinary Medicine, Zoology **Specializations:** Primates, Zoology (History - 19th Century) **Loan:** In country **Photocopy:** Yes

3297   Loughborough, UK
University of Nottingham
James Cameron-Gifford Library of Agricultural
    and Food Sciences
Sutton Bonington Campus
Loughborough, Leicestershire LE12 5RD

Phone: +44(115) 951-6392 **Fax:** +44(115) 951-6389
WWW: www.nottingham.ac.uk

Founded: 1948 **Type:** Academic **Head:** Mrs. E.A. Dodds *Email:* elizabeth.dodds@nottingham.ac.uk *Phone:* +44(115) 951-6388 **Staff:** 2 Prof. 7 Other **Holdings:** 75,000 books 500 journals **Language of Collection/Services:** English **Subjects:** Agriculture (Tropics), Agribusiness, Agricultural Development, Agricultural Economics, Agricultural Engineering, Animal Husbandry, Biotechnology, Education/Extension, Crops, Entomology, Environmental Sciences, Farming, Fisheries, Food Sciences, Forestry, Horticulture, Plant Pathology, Soil Science, Veterinary Medicine, Water Resources **Databases Used:** Comprehensive **Loan:** In country **Photocopy:** Yes

3298　Lowestoft, UK
Ministry of Agriculture, Fisheries and Food,
　Centre for Environment, Fisheries and
　Aquaculture Sciences, Lowestoft Laboratory
　(MAFF, CEFAS)
Information Unit
Pakefield Road
Lowestoft, Suffolk NR33 0HT
Phone: +44(1502) 562244 **Fax:** +44(1502) 513865
WWW: www.cefas.co.uk

Founded: 1921 **Type:** Government **Staff:** 2 Prof. 3 Other
Holdings: 1,000 journals **Subjects:** Fisheries, Water Pollution **Databases Developed:** FISHLAB - database covering fisheries and allied topics **Loan:** In country **Photocopy:** Yes

3299　Midlothian, UK
Moredun Research Institute (MRI)
Library
Pentlands Science Park
Bush Loan
Midlothian, Scotland EH26 0PZ
Phone: +44(131) 445 5111 **Fax:** +44(131) 445 6111
Email: library@mri.sari.ac.uk **WWW:** www.mri.sari.ac.uk

Founded: 1922 **Type:** Government **Head:** Diane Donaldson *Phone:* +44(131) 665 6157 *Email:* library@mri.sari.ac.uk **Staff:** 1 Prof. 1 Other **Holdings:** 7,000 books 150 journals **Language of Collection/Services:** English / English **Subjects:** Animal Husbandry, Microbiology, Immunology, Molecular Biology, Parasitology, Ruminants, Sheep, Veterinary Medicine, Virology **Databases Developed:** Staff publications database **Databases Used:** Comprehensive **Loan:** In country **Photocopy:** Yes

3300　Millport, UK
University of London/Glasgow University,
　University Marine Biological Station
Library
Millport, Isle of Cumbrae, Scotland KA28 0EG
Fax: +44(1475) 530601 **WWW:** www.gla.ac.uk/Acad/Marine

Former Name: Scottish Marine Biological Association **Founded:** 1970 **Type:** Academic **Head:** Ms. Kathryn Stevenson *Phone:* +44(1475) 530581/2 *Email:* kstevens@udcf.gla.ac.uk **Staff:** 1 Prof. **Holdings:** 3,000 books 40 journals **Language of Collection/Services:** English / English **Subjects:** Aquaculture, Water Resources **Specializations:** Fisheries, Marine Ecology **Loan:** Do not loan **Service:** Inhouse **Photocopy:** Yes

3301　Newmarket, UK
Animal Health Trust (AHT)
Library
Lanwades Park, Kentford
Newmarket, Suffolk CB8 7UU
Fax: +44(1638) 750410 **WWW:** www.aht.org.uk

Former Name: Equine Research Station **Type:** Non-profit **Head:** Sandra Tatum *Phone:* +44(1638) 751000 *Email:* sandra.tatum@aht.org.uk **Staff:** 1 Prof. **Holdings:** 3,000 books 40 journals **Language of Collection/Services:** English **Subjects:** Veterinary Medicine **Specializations:** Equidae **Data-**

bases Used: Medline; VETCD **Loan:** Inhouse **Photocopy:** Yes

3302　Newport, UK
Harper Adams Agricultural College
Library
Newport, Shropshire TF10 8NB
Phone: +44(1952) 815933 **Fax:** +44(1952) 814783 **Email:** libhelp@harper-adams.ac.uk **WWW:** www.haac.ac.uk

Founded: 1901 **Type:** Academic **Head:** Kathryn Greaves *Email:* kgreaves@harper-adams.ac.uk **Staff:** 3.5 Prof. 3.5 Other **Holdings:** 24,000 books 586 journals **Language of Collection/Services:** English **Subjects:** Agriculture (Tropics), Agribusiness, Agricultural Development, Agricultural Economics, Agricultural Engineering, Animal Husbandry, Biotechnology, Crops, Education/Extension, Entomology, Estates, Farming, Fisheries, Food Sciences, Forestry, Horticulture, Land Management, Plant Pathology, Soil Science, Veterinary Medicine, Water Resources **Specializations:** Poultry (History) **Databases Used:** Agricola; CABCD **Loan:** In country **Photocopy:** Yes

3303　Newton Abbot, UK
University of Plymouth
Seale-Hayne Library
Devon
Newton Abbot, Devon TQ12 6NQ
Phone: +44(1626) 325828 **Fax:** +44(1626) 325836
WWW: www.plym.ac.uk **OPAC:** telnet://lib.plym.ac.uk

Former Name: Seale-Hayne College **Founded:** 1920 **Type:** Academic **Head:** A.J. Blackman *Phone:* +44(1626) 325825 *Email:* ablackman@plymouth.ac.uk **Staff:** 3 Prof. 6 Other **Holdings:** 55,000 books 400 journals **Language of Collection/Services:** English **Subjects:** Estates, Food Technology, Hospitality Industry, Land Use, Tourism **Databases Used:** CABCD; ECODISC; FSTA; WHATT **Loan:** Inhouse **Photocopy:** Yes

3304　Norwich, UK
Biotechnology and Biological Sciences Research
　Council, John Innes Centre (BBSRC, JIC)
Library
Norwich Research Park
Colney
Norwich NR4 7UH
Phone: +44(1603) 452571 ext 2673 **Fax:** +44(1603) 456844 **WWW:** www.jic.bbsrc.ac.uk

Former Name: John Innes Institute **Type:** Research **Head:** Mrs. I.C. Walton *Email:* ingrid.walton@bbsrc.ac.uk **Staff:** 3 Prof. 3 Other **Holdings:** 60,000 books 700 journals **Language of Collection/Services:** English / English **Subjects:** Biotechnology, Crops, Entomology, Plants, Virology **Specializations:** Agricultural Chemistry, Cellular Biology, Genome Analysis, Molecular Genetics, Plant Pathology, Plant Protection **Databases Used:** Agricola; Medline **Loan:** Inhouse **Service:** In country **Photocopy:** Yes

3305　Oxford, UK
British Potato Council
Library

4300 Nash Court
John Smith Drive
Oxford Business Park
Oxford, Oxfordshire OX4 2RT
Phone: +44(1865) 714455 **Fax:** +44(1865) 782283
WWW: www.potato.org.uk

Former Name: Potato Marketing Board (PMB) **Founded:**
1961 **Type:** Association **Head:** S.H. Gerrish *Email:* sgerrish
@potato.org.uk **Staff:** 1 Prof. 1 Other **Holdings:** 40 journals
4,000 books **Subjects:** Potatoes **Specializations:** Potato
Products, Potato Stores **Loan:** Do not loan **Service:** Inhouse
Photocopy: Yes

3306 Oxford, UK
University of Oxford, Department of Plant
Sciences and Oxford Forestry Institute (OFI)
Plant Sciences Library
South Parks Road
Oxford, Oxfordshire OX1 3RB
Phone: +44(1865) 275082 **Fax:** +44(1865) 275074 **Email:**
library@plants.ox.ac.uk **WWW:** www.ox.ac.uk **OPAC:**
www.lib.ox.ac.uk/olis

Former Name: Commonwealth Forestry Institute, Botany
School, Department of Agricultural Science **Founded:** 1621
Type: Academic **Head:** Roger A. Mills *Phone:* +44(1865)
275080 *Email:* roger.mills@plants.ox.ac.uk **Staff:** 3 Prof. 7
Other **Holdings:** 200,000 books 2,000 journals **Language of
Collection/Services:** English **Subjects:** Agricultural Devel-
opment, Animal Husbandry, Biotechnology, Entomology,
Crops, Farming, Plant Pathology, Soil Science **Specializa-
tions:** Forest Products, Forestry **Databases Used:** Agricola;
Biosis; CABCD; CAS **Loan:** Inhouse **Service:** Internation-
ally **Photocopy:** Yes

3307 Oxford, UK
University of Oxford, Queen Elizabeth House,
International Development Centre (QEH,
IDC)
Library
21 St. Giles
Oxford, Oxfordshire OX1 3LA
Phone: +44(1865) 273590 **Fax:** +44(1865) 273607 **Email:**
library@qeh.ox.ac.uk **WWW:** www.qeh.ox.ac.uk/library
OPAC: www.lib.ox.ac.uk/olis

Former Name: Institute of Agricultural Economics Library
Founded: 1989 **Type:** Academic **Head:** Mrs. Sheila All-
cock *Phone:* +44(1865) 273629 *Email:* sheila.allcock@qeh.
ox.ac.uk **Staff:** 1 Prof. 3 Other **Holdings:** 60,000 books 600
journals **Language of Collection/Services:** English **Subjects:** Agriculture (Tropics), Agricultural Development, Agricultural Economics, Crops, Education/Extension, Farming
Networks: OCLC **Databases Used:** Comprehensive **Loan:**
In country **Service:** Internationally **Photocopy:** Yes

3308 Peterborough, UK
English Nature
Information and Library Services
Northminster House
Peterborough PE1 1UA

Phone: +44(1733) 455000 **Fax:** +44(1733) 568834
WWW: www.english-nature.org.uk **Email:** enquiries@
english-nature.org.uk

Former Name: Nature Conservancy Council (NCC) **Type:**
Government **Founded:** 1973 **Head:** Mr. J. Creedy *Phone:*
+44(1733) 455098 **Staff:** 5 Prof. 4 Other **Language of Col-
lection/Services:** English **Subjects:** Nature Conservation
Loan: Inhouse **Photocopy:** Yes

3309 Pitlochry, UK
Scottish Executive Rural Affairs Department,
Fisheries Research Services, Freshwater
Fisheries Laboratory (SERAD, FRS, FFL)
Library
Faskally
Pitlochry, Perthshire PH16 5LB
Phone: +44(1796) 472060 **Fax:** +44(1796) 473523
WWW: www.marlab.ac.uk/Freshwater/FFL.html

Former Name: Department of Agriculture and Fisheries for
Scotland (DAFS), Scottish Office Agriculture and Fisheries
Department **Founded:** 1948 **Type:** Government **Staff:** 1
Prof. 1 Other **Holdings:** 8,000 books 160 journals **Language
of Collection/Services:** English / English **Subjects:** Environment, Fishes, Fisheries **Loan:** In country **Service:** Internationally **Photocopy:** Yes

3310 Plymouth, UK
Centre for Coastal and Marine Studies, Plymouth
Marine Laboratory, Marine Biological
Association (PML, MBA, CCMS)
National Marine Biological Library (NMBL)
Citadel Hill
Plymouth, Devon PL1 2PB
Fax: +44(1752) 633102 **Email:** nmbl@pml.ac.uk **WWW:**
www.pml.ac.uk/pml

Former Name: Marine Biological Association of the United
Kingdom, Institute for Marine Environmental Research, Marine Biological Association Library **Founded:** 1888 **Type:**
Academic, Government **Head:** Linda Noble *Phone:* +44
(1752) 633266 *Email:* lno@wpo.nerc.ac.uk **Staff:** 4 Prof. 3
Other **Holdings:** 16,000 books 1,150 journals **Language of
Collection/Services:** English **Subjects:** Fisheries, Water
Resources **Specializations:** Marine Sciences, Water Pollution **Databases Developed:** British Waters Marine Pollution
on MOFR CD-ROM **Databases Used:** Comprehensive **Service:** Internationally **Loan:** In country **Photocopy:** Yes

3311 Preston, UK
Myerscough College
Library
Myerscough Hall
Bilsborrow
Preston, Lancashire PR3 0RY
Phone: +44(1995) 642222 **Fax:** +44(1995) 642333
WWW: www.myerscough.ac.uk/default.htm

Former Name: Lancashire College of Agriculture and Horticulture **Founded:** 1894 **Type:** Academic **Staff:** 1 Prof. 5
Other **Holdings:** 25,000 books 150 journals **Language of
Collection/Services:** English / English **Subjects:** Agribusiness, Agricultural Development, Agricultural Economics,

Animal Husbandry, Crops, Farming, Forestry, Land Use, Mechanization, Plant Pathology, Small Animal Rearing, Soil Science **Specializations:** Arboriculture, Horses, Horticulture, Leisure, Tourism **Databases Used:** CABCD **Loan:** Inhouse **Service:** Inhouse **Photocopy:** Yes

3312 Reading, UK
University of Reading
Library
Whiteknights
PO Box 223
Reading, Berkshire RG6 2AE
Phone: +44(118) 931-8779 **Fax:** +44(118) 931-6636
Email: library@reading.ac.uk **WWW:** www.rdg.ac.uk
OPAC: www.unicorn.rdg.ac.uk

Founded: 1926 **Type:** Academic **Head:** Ms. Sheila Corrall *Phone:* +44(118) 931-8772 *Email:* s.m.corrall@reading.ac.uk **Staff:** 20 Prof. 62 Other **Language of Collection/Services:** English **Subjects:** Agriculture (Tropics), Agricultural Development, Agribusiness, Agricultural Economics, Agricultural Engineering, Animal Husbandry, Biotechnology, Crops, Education/Extension, Entomology, Farming, Fisheries, Food Sciences, Forestry, Horticulture, Plant Pathology, Soil Science, Veterinary Medicine, Water Resources **Loan:** Inhouse **Photocopy:** Yes

3313 Reading, UK
University of Reading, Rural History Centre
Library
Whiteknights
PO Box 229
Reading RG6 6AG
Phone: +44(118) 931-8664 **Fax:** +44(118) 975-1264
Email: rhc@reading.ac.uk **WWW:** www.rdg.ac.uk/Instits/im/ **OPAC:** www.rdg.ac.uk/Instits/im/ruhist/cat.htm

Former Name: Institute of Agricultural History and Museum of English Rural Life **Founded:** 1966 **Type:** Academic **Head:** John S. Creasey *Phone:* +44(118) 931-8664 *Email:* j.s.creasey@reading.ac.uk **Staff:** 2 Prof. 1 Other **Holdings:** 50,000 books 70 journals **Language of Collection/Services:** English/English **Subjects:** Comprehensive **Specializations:** Agriculture (History - UK - 1750-) **Loan:** Inhouse **Service:** Internationally **Photocopy:** Yes

3314 Richmond, UK
Royal Botanic Gardens, Kew (RBG Kew)
Library and Archives
Richmond, Surrey TW9 3AE
Phone: +44(20) 8332 5414 **Fax:** +44(20) 8332 5278
Email: library@rbgkew.org.uk **WWW:** www.rbgkew.org.uk

Founded: 1852 **Type:** Government **Head:** Miss S.M.D. FitzGerald *Phone:* +44(20) 8332 5411 *Email:* s.fitzgerald@rbgkew.org.uk **Holdings:** 130,000 books 1,600 journals **Staff:** 8 Prof. 8 Other **Language of Collection/Services:** English, Latin, German, Spanish, French, Arabic, Hebrew, Chinese, Japanese, Russian / English **Subjects:** Agriculture (Tropics), Biotechnology, Conservation, Economic Botany, Forestry, Horticulture, Plants, Taxonomy **Specializations:** Botany, Endangered Species, Flora, Forest Products, Gene

Banks, Genetics, Mycology, Plant Anatomy, Plants (Tropics), Propagation, Seed Germination, Systematic Botany **Databases Developed:** Index Kewensis - names of seed-bearing plants, ferns and fern allies; printed and CD-ROM versions available; Kew Record of Taxonomic Literature - printed and CD-ROM versions available; SEPASAL (Survey of Economic Plants for Arid and Semi-Arid Lands) - database from Kew's Centre for economic Botany (CEB) which focuses on "wild" and semi-domesticated useful plants of tropical and subtropical drylands; available via the internet at www.rbgkew.org.uk/ceb/sepasal **Loan:** Do not loan **Service:** Internationally **Photocopy:** Yes

3315 Roslin, UK
Biotechnology and Biological Sciences Research
   Council, Roslin Institute (BBSRC, RI)
Library and Information Service
Roslin, Midlothian, Scotland EH25 9PS
Phone: +44(131) 527-4424 **Fax:** +44(131) 440-0434
Email: roslin.library@bbsrc.ac.uk **WWW:** www.ri.bbsrc.ac.uk

Former Name: Agricultural and Food Research Council (AFRC), Institute of Animal Physiology and Genetics Research (IAPGR), Edinburgh Research Station **Founded:** 1948 **Type:** Government **Head:** Mr. M. McKeen *Email:* mike.mckeen@bbsrc.ac.uk **Staff:** 1 Prof. 2 Other **Holdings:** 8,000 books 225 journals **Language of Collection/Services:** English **Subjects:** Animal Behavior, Animal Breeding, Animal Nutrition, Animal Physiology, Animal Welfare, Genetic Markers, Genetics, Growth, Molecular Biology, Poultry, Reproduction **Databases Used:** Medline **Loan:** Internationally **Service:** Inhouse **Photocopy:** Yes

3316 Silsoe, UK
Biotechnology and Biological Sciences Research
   Council, Silsoe Research Institute (BSSRC,
   SRI)
Library and Information Service
Wrest Park
Silsoe, Bedford MK45 4HS
Phone: +44(1525) 860000 **Fax:** +44(1525) 860156 **Email:** sri.pr@bbsrc.ac.uk **WWW:** www.sri.bbsrc.ac.uk **Ariel IP:** 149.155.182

Former Name: Agricultural and Food Research Council (AFRC), Institute of Engineering Research **Founded:** 1924 **Type:** Government **Head:** Anne Jarvis *Phone:* +44(1525) 860000 ext 2212 *Email:* anne.jarvis@bbsrc.ac.uk **Staff:** 2 Prof. 2 Other **Holdings:** 40,000 books 300 journals **Language of Collection/Services:** English / English **Subjects:** Agricultural Engineering **Databases Developed:** Library catalogue of 21,000 records available on network within BSSRC only. **Databases Used:** Comprehensive **Loan:** In country **Service:** Internationally **Photocopy:** Yes

3317 Somerset, UK
Royal Bath and West of England Society
Library
Showground, Shepton Mallet
Somerset BA4 6QN
Location: Bath University, Claverton Down **Phone:** +44 (1749) 822200 **Fax:** +44(1749) 823169 **Email:** general.

office@bathandwest.co.uk **WWW:** www.bathandwest.co.
uk/index.htm

Former Name: Royal Bath and West and Southern Counties
Society **Founded:** 1777 **Type:** Association **Head:** Tony
Holbrook *Phone:* +44(1749) 826826 **Staff:** 1 Prof. **Hold-
ings:** 1,000 books **Subjects:** Agricultural Economics, Soil
Science, Agricultural Engineering, Crops, Horticulture, Vet-
erinary Medicine, Zoology **Loan:** In country **Photocopy:**
Yes

3318   Southampton, UK
         University of Southampton
         Perkins Agricultural Library
         Hartley Library
         Highfield
         Southampton SO17 1BJ

Fax: +44(23) 8059 3007 **WWW:** www.soton.ac.uk **Email:**
library@uk.ac.southhampton **OPAC:** www.soton.ac.uk/
~library/index.shtml

Founded: 1935 **Type:** Academic **Head:** B. Naylor *Phone:*
+44(23) 8059 3335 *Email:* b.naylor@soton.ac.uk **Staff:** 1
Prof. **Holdings:** 2,000 books **Language of Collection/Ser-
vices:** English/English **Subjects:** Agricultural Development
(History - pre-1900), Agricultural Economics (History -
pre-1900), Agricultural Engineering (History - pre-1900),
Animal Husbandry (History - pre-1900), Biotechnology
(History - pre-1900), Crops (History - pre-1900), Educa-
tion/Extension (History - pre-1900), Farming (History -
pre-1900), Soil Science (History - pre-1900), Veterinary
Medicine (History - pre-1900) **Specializations:** Agriculture
(History - pre-1900) **Loan:** Do not loan **Photocopy:** Yes

3319   Surrey, UK
         Biotechnology and Biological Sciences Research
             Council, Institute for Animal Health (BBSRC,
             IAH)
         Pirbright Laboratory Library
         Ash Road, Pirbright
         Woking
         Surrey GV24 0NF
Phone: +44(1483) 232441 **Fax:** +44(1483) 232448
WWW: www.iah.bbsrc.ac.uk

Former Name: Agricultural and Food Research Council
(AFRC), Institute for Animal Disease Research, Animal Virus Research Institute (AVRI) **Founded:** 1950 **Type:** Government **Staff:** 1 Prof. 1 Other **Holdings:** 2,000 books 100
journals **Language of Collection/Services:** English **Subjects:** Biotechnology, Veterinary Medicine **Specializations:**
Virology **Databases Developed:** Virology Databases - over
70,000 references on mostly exotic virus diseases; inquire for
access **Loan:** Internationally **Service:** Inhouse **Photocopy:**
Yes

3320   Wallingford, UK
         CAB International (CABI)
         Information Services
         PO Box 100
         Wallingford, Oxon OX10 8DE
Phone: +44(1491) 832111 **Fax:** +44(1491) 833508 **Email:**
cabi@cabiorg **WWW:** www.cabi.org/infolib/infolib.htm

Founded: 1929 **Type:** International **Head:** Dr. Colin P.
Ogbourne **Language of Collection/Services:** English **Sub-
jects:** Agriculture (Tropics), Agribusiness, Crops, Agricul-
tural Development, Agricultural Economics, Agricultural
Engineering, Animal Husbandry, Biotechnology, Education/
Extension, Entomology, Farming, Fisheries, Food Sciences,
Forestry, Horticulture, Plant Pathology, Soil Science, Veteri-
nary Medicine, Water Resources **Databases Used:** CABCD
Service: Internationally **Photocopy:** Yes

3321   Wellesbourne, UK
         Horticulture Research International (HRI)
         Wellesbourne Library
         Wellesbourne, Warwick CV35 9EF
Phone: +44(1789) 470382 **Fax:** +44(1789) 470552 **Email:**
wellesbourne.library@hri.ac.uk **WWW:** www.hri.ac.uk

Former Name: National Vegetable Research Station, Institute of Horticultural Research (IHR) **Founded:** 1952 **Type:**
Government **Head:** Rhona Floate *Phone:* +44(1789) 472006
Email: rhona.floate@hri.ac.uk **Staff:** 2 Prof. 2 Other **Holdings:** 40,000 books 600 journals **Language of Collection/
Services:** English **Subjects:** Biotechnology, Crops, Entomology, Horticulture, Plant Pathology, Soil Science **Databases Developed:** Staff Publications - papers published by
staff **Databases Used:** Agricola; Biosis; CABCD **Loan:** In
country **Photocopy:** Yes

3322   West Malling, UK
         Horticulture Research International East Malling
             (HRI)
         Library
         East Malling
         West Malling, Kent ME19 6BJ
Phone: +44(1732) 843833 **Fax:** +44(1732) 849067
WWW: www.hri.ac.uk

Former Name: East Malling Research Station, Agricultural
and Food Research Council (AFRC), Institute of Horticultural Research (IHR) **Founded:** 1920 **Type:** Government
Staff: 1 Prof. 1 Other **Holdings:** 40,000 books 300 journals
Language of Collection/Services: English **Subjects:** Entomology, Horticulture, Plant Pathology **Specializations:**
Temperate Fruits **Loan:** In country **Photocopy:** Yes

3323   Wetherby, UK
         British Library (BL)
         Document Supply Centre (BLDSC)
         Boston Spa
         Wetherby, West Yorkshire LS23 7BQ
Phone: +44(1937) 546060 **Fax:** +44(1937) 546333 **Email:**
dsc-customer-services@bl.uk **WWW:** www.bl.uk **OPAC:**
opac97.bl.uk

Former Name: National Lending Library of Science and
Technology **Founded:** 1961 **Type:** Government **Head:** Mr.
Malcolm Smith **Staff:** 110 Prof. 538 Other **Holdings:**
6,000,000 books 49,000 journals **Language of Collection/
Services:** English **Subjects:** Comprehensive **Networks:**
OCLC **Databases Developed:** British Reports, Translations
and Theses; Translations Index - contains records of serial
articles and books translated from all languages into English,
especially Russian and Japanese; Monograph Acquisitions

and Record System (MARS) - books published from 1980 onwards, some Official Publications and the Centre's collection of conference proceedings are all recorded; Serials File - includes entries from the rest of the British Library, Cambridge University and the Science Museum Library as well as DSC stock. **Loan:** Registered customers only **Service:** Internationally **Photocopy:** Yes

3324   York, UK
Askham Bryan College
Learning Resource Centre
Askham Bryan
York, North Yorkshire YO23 3FR
Phone: +44(1904) 772234 **Fax:** +44(1904) 772287
WWW: www.askham-bryan.ac.uk

Founded: 1960 **Type:** Academic **Head:** Ms. Julie Amery *Phone:* +44(1904) 772277 **Staff:** 2 Prof. 4 Other **Holdings:** 27,000 books 200 journals **Language of Collection/Services:** English **Subjects:** Agriculture (Tropics), Agribusiness, Agricultural Development, Agricultural Engineering, Animal Husbandry, Biotechnology, Crops, Education/Extension, Entomology, Farming, Fisheries, Forestry, Food Sciences, Horticulture, Lawns and Turf, Management, Plant Pathology, Soil Science, Veterinary Medicine, Water Resources **Loan:** Inhouse **Service:** In country **Photocopy:** Yes

3325   York, UK
University of York
J.B. Morrell Library
Heslington
York, North Yorkshire YO10 5DD
Phone: +44(1904) 433865 **Fax:** +44(1904) 433866
WWW: www.york.ac.uk **OPAC:** www.york.ac.uk/
services/library

Founded: 1962 **Type:** Academic **Head:** Elizabeth Heaps *Phone:* +44(1904) 433863 *Email:* aemh1@york.ac.uk **Staff:** 13 Prof. 30 Other **Holdings:** 3,500 books 12 journals **Language of Collection/Services:** English / English **Subjects:** Entomology, Environmental Management, Food Sciences, Plants, Water Resources **Databases Used:** Biosis; CAS **Loan:** Internationally **Photocopy:** Yes

United States

Alabama

3326   Auburn, Alabama, US
Auburn University
Charles Allen Cary Veterinary Medical Library
101 Greene Hall
Auburn, Alabama 36849-5606
Phone: +1(334) 844-1749 **Fax:** +1(334) 844-1758 **Email:** vetlib@vetmed.auburn.edu **WWW:** www.auburn.edu
OPAC: aubiecat.auburn.edu

Type: Academic **Head:** Yvonne Kozlowski *Phone:* +1(334) 844-1750ykozlow@lib.auburn.edu **Staff:** 1 Prof. 3 Other **Holdings:** 30,000 books 500 journals **Language of Collection/Services:** English / English **Subjects:** Acupuncture, Biochemistry, Infectious Diseases, Neoplasms, Parasitoses,

Pathology, Veterinary Medicine **Networks:** OCLC **Databases Developed:** Database of non-classified documents related to biological detection - access through Auburn University Institute for Biological Detection Systems **Databases Used:** CABCD; Medline **Loan:** In country **Service:** Internationally **Photocopy:** Yes

3327   Auburn, Alabama, US
Auburn University
Ralph Brown Draughon Library (RBD Library)
231 Mell Street
Auburn, Alabama 36849
Phone: +1(334) 844-1747 **Fax:** +1(334) 844-4424 **WWW:** www.lib.auburn.edu **OPAC:** aubiecat.auburn.edu

Type: Academic **Head:** Dr. Stella Bentley *Phone:* +1(334) 844-4500 *Email:* bentley@lib.auburn.edu **Staff:** 37 Prof. 84 Other **Holdings:** 2,504,000 books 18,739 journals **Language of Collection/Services:** English **Subjects:** Agribusiness, Agriculture (Tropics), Agricultural Development, Agricultural Economics, Agricultural Engineering, Animal Husbandry, Biotechnology, Crops, Education/Extension, Entomology, Environmental Sciences, Food Sciences, Forestry, Horticulture, Plant Pathology, Soil Science, Veterinary Medicine, Water Resources **Specializations:** Fisheries **Networks:** OCLC **Databases Used:** Comprehensive **Loan:** Internationally **Service:** Internationally **Photocopy:** Yes

3328   Auburn, Alabama, US
Auburn University, Water Resources Research
         Institute
Information Center
101 Comer Hall
Auburn, Alabama 36849
Phone: +1(334) 844-5075 **Fax:** +1(334) 844-4462 **WWW:** www.auburn.edu

Head: Howard A. Clonts *Phone:* +1(334) 844-5611 *Email:* hclonts@acesag.auburn.edu **Subjects:** Water Resources

3329   Birmingham, Alabama, US
Birmingham Botanical Gardens
Horace Hammond Historical Library
2612 Lane Park Road
Birmingham, Alabama 35223
Phone: +1(205) 414-3920 **Fax:** +1(205) 879-3751 **Email:** bbsed@aol.com **WWW:** www.bbgardens.org **OPAC:** www.jclc.org

Founded: 1971 **Type:** Government **Holdings:** 3,150 books **Subjects:** Forestry, Horticulture **Databases Developed:** BG-BASE **Photocopy:** Yes

3330   Muscle Shoals, Alabama, US
International Fertilizer Development Center
         (IFDC)
Travis P. Hignett Memorial Library
PO Box 2040
Muscle Shoals, Alabama 35662
Location: TVA Reservation **Fax:** +1(256) 381-7408 **Email:** general@ifdc.org **WWW:** www.ifdc.org

Founded: 1976 **Type:** Association **Head:** Jean S. Riley *Phone:* +1(256) 381-6600 ext 263 *Email:* jriley@ifdc.org

Staff: 1 Prof. 1 Other **Holdings:** 14,000 books 286 journals **Language of Collection/Services:** English / English **Subjects:** Agriculture (Tropics), Agribusiness, Agricultural Economics, Crops, Education/Extension, Farming, Plants, Soil Science **Specializations:** Fertilizers, Agricultural Development **Networks:** OCLC **Databases Developed:** IFDC Current Awareness - current journal articles; IFDC Doc File - country, organization, and audio-visual material; IFDC Patent Database - 900 U.S. and foreign patents; TVA publications and document file. **Databases Used:** Agricola; Agris; CABCD; Medline **Loan:** In country **Service:** Internationally **Photocopy:** Yes

3331   Normal, Alabama, US
Alabama A&M University (AAMU)
Joseph F. Drake Memorial Learning Resources
    Center (LRC)
PO Box 489
Normal, Alabama 35762
Location: 4900 Meridian Street, Huntsville **Phone:** +1 (205) 851-5760 **Fax:** +1(205) 851-5768 **WWW:** www. aamu.edu

Former Name: Joseph F. Drake Memorial Library **Type:** Academic **Head:** Ms. Patgricia D. Ford, Interim Director *Phone:* +1(205) 851-5764 *Email:* pford@aamu.edu **Staff:** 10 Prof. 14 Other **Holdings:** 362,000 books 1,664 journals **Language of Collection/Services:** English / English **Subjects:** Agricultural Development, Agricultural Economics, Agriculture (Tropics), Crops, Entomology, Forestry, Horticulture, Plant Pathology, Water Resources **Specializations:** Agribusiness, Animal Husbandry, Food Sciences, Home Economics, Plants, Soil Science **Databases Used:** ABI/Inform; Agricola; Dissertation Abstracts **Loan:** Inhouse **Service:** Inhouse **Photocopy:** Yes

3332   Tuskegee, Alabama, US
Tuskegee University (TU)
Hollis Burke Frissell Library
Tuskegee, Alabama 36088
Phone: +1(334) 727-8896 **Fax:** +1(334) 727-9282 **WWW:** www.tusk.edu **OPAC:** svmc107.tusk.edu/library/ TuskUnivlib.html

Former Name: Tuskegee Institute **Type:** Academic **Head:** Ms. Juanita Roberts *Phone:* +1(334) 727-8892 **Staff:** 11 Prof. 13 Other **Holdings:** 346,154 books 1,193 journals **Language of Collection/Services:** English / English **Subjects:** Animal Husbandry, Biotechnology, Education/Extension, Crops, Food Sciences, Poultry, Veterinary Medicine **Databases Used:** Agricola; Biosis; CABCD; FSTA **Loan:** Internationally **Service:** Internationally **Photocopy:** Yes

3333   Tuskegee, Alabama, US
Tuskegee University (TU)
National Sweetpotato Information Center (NSPIC)
104 Campbell Hall
Tuskegee, Alabama 36088
Fax: +1(334) 727-4452 **Email:** nspic@acd.tusk.edu
WWW: agriculture.tusk.edu/NSPIC/NSPIC.html

Former Name: Tuskegee Institute **Founded:** 1991 **Type:** Academic **Head:** Sibyl J. Caldwell *Phone:* +1(334) 727-

8445 Staff: 2 Prof. 2 Other **Holdings:** 2,000 books **Language of Collection/Services:** English **Subjects:** Sweet Potatoes **Specializations:** Cultivars, Plant Diseases, Root Crops **Service:** Internationally **Photocopy:** Yes

3334   Tuskegee, Alabama, US
Tuskegee University (TU)
T.S. Williams Veterinary Medical Library
Patterson Hall
Tuskegee, Alabama 36088
Phone: +1(334) 727-8780 **Fax:** +1(334) 727-8442 **WWW:** www.tusk.edu **OPAC:** svmc107.tusk.edu/library/ TuskUnivlib.html

Former Name: Tuskegee Institute **Type:** Academic **Head:** Margaret K. Alexander *Phone:* +1(334) 727-8780 *Email:* dealex@acd.tusk.edu **Staff:** 1 Prof. 6 Other **Holdings:** 16,100 books 335 journals **Language of Collection/Services:** English / English **Subjects:** Veterinary Medicine **Specializations:** Large Animal Practice, Small Animal Practice, Surgery **Databases Developed:** Biomedical Information Management System **Photocopy:** Yes

Alaska

3335   Anchorage, Alaska, US
Alaska Resources Library and Information
    Services (ARLIS)
3150 C Street, Suite 100
Anchorage, Alaska 99503
Phone: +1(907) 272-7547 **Fax:** +1(907) 271-4742 **Email:** reference@arlis.org **WWW:** www.arlis.org **OPAC:** www.arlis.org

Former Name: United States Fish and Wildlife Service Library, Alaska Department of Fish and Game Habitat Library, United States Bureau of Land Management Alaska Resources Library, United States Minerals Management Service Library, United States National Park Service Library, United States Geological Survey Library, Arctic Environmental Information and Data Center Library, Oil Spill Public Information Center **Founded:** 1997 **Type:** Government **Staff:** 8 Prof. 7 Other **Holdings:** 150,000 books 300 journals **Language of Collection/Services:** English **Subjects:** Fisheries, Forestry, Plants, Soil, Water Resources **Specializations:** Fisheries (Alaska) **Networks:** OCLC **Databases Used:** Comprehensive **Loan:** Internationally **Service:** Internationally **Photocopy:** Yes

3336   Douglas, Alaska, US
Alaska Department of Fish and Game
Library
Box 240020
Douglas, Alaska 99824-0020
Location: 904 Third Street **Phone:** +1(907) 465-4119 **Fax:** +1(907) 586-9522 **WWW:** www.state.ak.us/local/akpages/ FISH.GAME/adfghome.html

Founded: 1954 **Type:** Government **Head:** Paul DeSloover *Email:* paul_desloover@fishgame.state.ak.us *Phone:* +1 (907) 465-4119 **Staff:** 1 Prof. 1 Other **Holdings:** 16,000 books 40 journals **Language of Collection/Services:** English / English **Subjects:** Aquaculture, Fisheries, Fishery Management **Loan:** Internationally **Service:** Inhouse

3337   Fairbanks, Alaska, US
University of Alaska, Fairbanks (UAF)
BioSciences Library
PO Box 757060
Fairbanks, Alaska 99775

Location: Arctic Health Research Building, South Koyukuk Drive **Phone:** +1(907) 474-7442 **Fax:** +1(907) 474-7820 **Email:** fybmlib@uaf.edu **WWW:** www.uaf.edu **OPAC:** www.uaf.edu/library/ril/catalogs/index.html

Former Name: Alaska Agricultural College and School of Mines, Bio-Medical Library, Arctic Health Research Center Library **Founded:** 1949 **Type:** Academic **Head:** James H. Anderson *Phone:* +1(907) 474-7442 *Email:* ffjha@uaf.edu **Staff:** 2 Prof. 4 Other **Holdings:** 50,000 books 511 journals **Language of Collection/Services:** English / English **Subjects:** Animal Husbandry, Crops, Entomology, Food Sciences, Forestry, Horticulture, Plant Pathology, Soil Science, Veterinary Medicine **Specializations:** Ecology, Fisheries, Marine Fishes, Plant Physiology, Plants, Wildlife, Wildlife Management **Networks:** OCLC **Databases Used:** Comprehensive **Loan:** Internationally **Service:** Internationally **Photocopy:** Yes

3338   Juneau, Alaska, US
United States Department of Agriculture, Forest
    Service, Forestry Sciences Laboratory
    (USDA, FS)
FS-INFO Alaska
2770 Sherwood Lane, Suite 2A
Juneau, Alaska 99801-8545

Phone: +1(907) 586-8545 **Fax:** +1(907) 586-7848 **WWW:** www.urova.fi/home/arktinen/polarweb/polar/lbusfsia.htm

Former Name: Pacific Northwest Research Station **Founded:** 1948 **Type:** Government **Head:** Lillian V. Petershoare *Phone:* +1(907) 586-8811 ext 265 *Email:* lpetershoare/r10@fs.fed.us **Staff:** 1 Prof. 1 Other **Holdings:** 35,000 books 200 journals **Language of Collection/Services:** English **Subjects:** Alaska (History), Cultural Heritage, Entomology, Fisheries, Forestry, Plant Pathology, Wildlife **Databases Developed:** Sitka Spruce; vertical files on papyrus; FS-INFO database - bibliographic memory of the Forest Service **Loan:** Internationally **Photocopy:** Yes

3339   Kodiak, Alaska, US
National Marine Fisheries Service (NMFS)
W.F. Thompson Memorial Library
301 Research Court
Kodiak, Alaska 99615-1638

Phone: +1(907) 481-1712 **Fax:** +1(907) 481-1702 **WWW:** www.afsc.noaa.gov/kodiak/library/libraryhomepage.htm

Founded: 1971 **Type:** Government **Head:** Beverly A. Burns *Email:* beverly.a.burns@noaa.gov **Staff:** 1 Prof. **Holdings:** 5,800 books 90 journals **Language of Collection/Services:** English / English **Subjects:** Fisheries **Loan:** Inhouse **Service:** Inhouse **Photocopy:** Yes

Arizona

3340   Flagstaff, Arizona, US
Northern Arizona University (NAU)
Cline Library
Box 6022
Flagstaff, Arizona 86011-6022

Phone: +1(520) 523-6805 **Email:** ann.eagan@nau.edu **WWW:** www.nau.edu/library **OPAC:** vista.nau.edu

Type: Academic **Head:** Jean D. Collins *Phone:* +1(520) 523-6802 *Email:* jean.collins@nau.edu **Subjects:** Forestry **Databases Used:** TREECD

3341   Phoenix, Arizona, US
Desert Botanical Garden (DES)
Richter Library
1201 North Galvin Parkway
Phoenix, Arizona 85008

Phone: +1(602) 941-1225 **Fax:** +1(602) 754-8124 **WWW:** www.dbg.org

Former Name: Desert Botanical Garden of Arizona, Desert Botanical Garden Library **Founded:** 1937 **Type:** Association **Head:** Dianne Bean *Phone:* +1(602) 754-8133 *Email:* beandp@primenet.com **Staff:** 1 Prof. **Holdings:** 50 journals 6,000 books **Language of Collection/Services:** English / English **Subjects:** Deserts, Dry Farming, Ethnobotany **Specializations:** Deserts, Farming (Sonoran Desert), Natural History, Plants (Sonoran Desert) **Networks:** OCLC **Loan:** Do not loan **Service:** Internationally **Photocopy:** Yes

3342   Phoenix, Arizona, US
United States Department of Agriculture,
    Agricultural Research Service, United States
    Water Conservation Laboratory (USDA,
    ARS)
Library
4331 East Broadway Road
Phoenix, Arizona 85040

Phone: +1(602) 379-4356 **Fax:** +1(602) 379-4355 **WWW:** www.uswcl.ars.ag.gov

Founded: 1961 **Type:** Government **Head:** Shirley Rish *Email:* srish@uswcl.ars.ag.gov **Holdings:** 2,100 books 75 journals **Subjects:** Climatic Change, New Crops, Remote Sensing, Water Conservation

3343   Tempe, Arizona, US
Arizona State University (ASU)
Daniel E. Noble Science and Engineering Library
Box 171006
Tempe, Arizona 85287-1006

Phone: +1(480) 965-7607 **Fax:** +1(480) 965-0883 **Email:** sciinfo@asu.edu **WWW:** www.asu.edu/lib/noble **OPAC:** catalog.lib.asu.edu

Founded: 1983 **Type:** Academic **Head:** Sherrie Schmidt *Phone:* +1(480) 965-3956 *Email:* sherrie.schmidt@asu.edu **Holdings:** 400,000 books 2,600 journals **Language of Collection/Services:** English / English **Subjects:** Agribusiness, Agricultural Economics, Fisheries, Horticulture, Plants, Soil Science **Databases Developed:** Map Index and Solar Energy

Index - access through ASU online catalog **Databases Used:** Agricola; Biosis **Photocopy:** Yes

3344   Tucson, Arizona, US
           Arabian Horse Owners Foundation (AHOF)
           W.R. Brown Memorial Library
           PO Box 31391
           Tucson, Arizona 85751
Location: 4101 North Bear Canyon Road **Phone:** +1(520) 760-0682, +1(800) 892-0682 **Email:** ahof001@aol.com **WWW:** www.ahof.org

Founded: 1957 **Type:** Business **Head:** Howard F. Shenk *Phone:* +1(520) 760-0682 **Staff:** 1 Other **Holdings:** 1,500 books **Subjects:** Horses **Loan:** Do not loan **Service:** Inhouse **Photocopy:** Yes

3345   Tucson, Arizona, US
           Native Seeds/SEARCH (NS/S)
           Library
           526 N. 4th Avenue
           Tucson, Arizona 85705
Phone: +1(520) 622-5561 **Fax:** +1(520) 622-5591 **Email:** nss@azstarnet.com **WWW:** desert.net/seeds/home.htm

Founded: 1986 **Type:** Association **Head:** Kevin Gaither-Banchoff *Phone:* +1(520) 622-5561 *Email:* nss@azstarnet.com **Staff:** 1 Other **Holdings:** 500 books 4 journals **Language of Collection/Services:** English / English **Subjects:** Crops, Farming **Specializations:** Agriculture (History - Native Americans), Agriculture (Native Americans) **Databases Developed:** Seed catalog of native American crops **Loan:** Do not loan **Service:** Internationally **Photocopy:** Yes

3346   Tucson, Arizona, US
           United States Department of Agriculture,
              Agricultural Research Service, Carl Hayden
              Bee Research Center (USDA, ARS)
           Library
           2000 East Allen Road
           Tucson, Arizona 85719
Phone: +1(520) 670-6481 **Fax:** +1(520) 670-6493 **WWW:** 198.22.133.109

Founded: 1966 **Type:** Government **Head:** Deborah Schulte *Phone:* +1(520) 629-6380 ext 125 **Staff:** 1 Other **Holdings:** 1,000 books 25 journals **Subjects:** Beekeeping, Pollination **Loan:** Do not loan **Photocopy:** No

3347   Tucson, Arizona, US
           University of Arizona (UA)
           Science-Engineering Library (SEL)
           1510 E University
           Tucson, Arizona 85720-0055
Phone: +1(520) 621-6384 **Fax:** +1(520) 621-3655 **Email:** askref@bird.library.arizona.edu **WWW:** www.arizona.edu **OPAC:** www.library.arizona.edu

Founded: 1963 **Type:** Academic **Head:** Karen Holloway *Phone:* +1(520) 621-6394 **Staff:** 15 Prof. 2 Other **Holdings:** 1,000,000 books 7,000 journals **Language of Collection/Services:** English / English **Subjects:** Agriculture (Tropics), Agribusiness, Agricultural Development, Agricultural Economics, Agricultural Engineering, Animal Husbandry, Bio-

technology, Education/Extension, Entomology, Farming, Crops, Fisheries, Food Sciences, Forestry, Horticulture, Plant Pathology, Soil Science, Veterinary Medicine **Specializations:** Arid Lands, Water Resources **Networks:** OCLC **Databases Used:** Comprehensive **Loan:** Internationally **Service:** Internationally **Photocopy:** Yes

3348   Tucson, Arizona, US
           University of Arizona, Environmental Research
              Laboratory (UA, ERL)
           Library
           2601 East Airport Drive
           Tucson, Arizona 85706
Fax: +1(520) 573-0852 **WWW:** ag.arizona.edu/azaqua/erlhome.html, architecture.arizona.edu/planning/project/d+d_planning **OPAC:** www.library.arizona.edu

Type: Academic **Head:** Sandra E. Menke *Phone:* +1(520) 626-2656 *Email:* smenk@ag.arizona.edu **Staff:** 1 Prof. **Holdings:** 1,800 books 75 journals **Language of Collection/Services:** English / English **Subjects:** Fisheries, Horticulture **Specializations:** Aquaculture, Halophytes **Loan:** Inhouse **Service:** Internationally **Photocopy:** Yes

3349   Tucson, Arizona, US
           University of Arizona, Office of Arid Lands
              Studies (UA, OALS)
           Arid Lands Information Center (ALIC)
           1955 East Sixth Street
           Tucson, Arizona 85719
Phone: +1(520) 621-7897 **Fax:** +1(520) 621-3816 **WWW:** ag.arizona.edu/OALS/oals/alic/alic.html

Founded: 1968 **Type:** Academic **Head:** Barbara Hutchinson *Phone:* +1(520) 621-8578 *Email:* barbarah@ag.arizona.edu **Staff:** 4 Prof. 2 Other **Holdings:** 30,000 books 20 journals **Language of Collection/Services:** English **Subjects:** Agricultural Development, Agricultural Economics, Agricultural Engineering, Soil Science, Water Resources **Specializations:** Desertification, Dry Farming, Forestry, Jojoba, Parthenium argentatum, Water Harvesting **Databases Used:** CABCD **Service:** Internationally **Photocopy:** Yes

Arkansas

3350   Arkadelphia, Arkansas, US
           Ouachita Baptist University (OBU)
           Riley-Hickingbotham Library
           410 Ouachita Street
           Arkadelphia, Arkansas 71998-0001
Phone: +1(870) 245-5119 **Fax:** +1(870) 245-5500 **WWW:** www.obu.edu **OPAC:** www.obu.edu/library/usersguidetoalis.htm

Former Name: Ouachita Baptist College **Type:** Academic **Head:** Ray Granade *Email:* granade@alpha.obu.edu *Phone:* +1(870) 245-5121 **Staff:** 7 Prof. 2 Other **Holdings:** 1,100 journals **Language of Collection/Services:** English / English **Subjects:** Government Documents (USA) **Loan:** Internationally **Service:** Inhouse **Photocopy:** Yes

3351   Conway, Arkansas, US
           University of Central Arkansas (UCA)

Torreyson Library
201 Donaghey Ave.
Conway, Arkansas 72035
Phone: +1(501) 450-5224, 450-3129 **Fax:** +1(501) 450-5208 **WWW:** www.uca.edu **OPAC:** ucark.uca.edu

Former Name: State College of Arkansas, Arkansas State Teachers College **Type:** Academic **Head:** Dr. Willie Hardin *Phone:* +1(501) 450-5202 *Email:* willieh@mail.uca.edu **Staff:** 13 Prof. 22 Other **Holdings:** 405,000 books 2,700 journals **Language of Collection/Services:** English / English **Subjects:** Agricultural Research, Food Supply, Plant Physiology, Soil Conservation **Databases Used:** Agricola; Dissertation Abstracts; Medline **Loan:** Internationally **Service:** Internationally **Photocopy:** Yes

3352   Fayetteville, Arkansas, US
National Center for Appropriate Technology
    (NCAT)
Appropriate Technology Transfer for Rural Areas
    Resource Center (ATTRA Resource Center)
PO Box 3657
Fayetteville, Arkansas 72703
Location: 1175 W. Cleaveland, University of Arkansas, 4th Floor Hatz, Fayetteville 72701 **Phone:** +1(501) 442-9824 **Fax:** +1(501) 442-9842 **WWW:** www.attra.org

Type: Research **Head:** Rose Sullivan *Phone:* +1(501) 442-9824 **Staff:** 1 Prof. 1 Other **Holdings:** 3,000 books 475 journals **Language of Collection/Services:** English / English **Subjects:** Sustainability **Loan:** In country **Service:** In country **Photocopy:** Yes

3353   Fayetteville, Arkansas, US
University of Arkansas, Fayetteville
University Libraries
Fayetteville, Arkansas 72701-1201
Phone: +1(501) 575-6645, 575-3177 **Fax:** +1(501) 575-6656 **Email:** ref@saturn.uark.edu **WWW:** www.uark.edu **OPAC:** library.uark.edu

Former Name: Mullins Library **Founded:** 1872 **Type:** Academic **Head:** Juana Young, Interim Director *Phone:* +1(501) 575-3079 *Email:* jyoung@comp.uark.edu **Staff:** 27 Prof. **Holdings:** 1,392,403 books 16,540 journals **Language of Collection/Services:** English / English **Subjects:** Agricultural Development, Agricultural Economics, Agricultural Engineering, Animal Husbandry, Biochemistry, Education/Extension, Biotechnology, Entomology, Biology, Cellular Biology, Crops, Farming, Fisheries, Food Sciences, Forestry, Horticulture, Plant Pathology, Plants, Soil Science, Veterinary Medicine, Water Resources **Specializations:** Apples, Biological Control, Cattle, Grapes, Poultry, Rice, Seeds, Soybeans **Networks:** OCLC; RLIN **Databases Developed:** Arkansas Periodicals Index **Databases Used:** Agricola; Agris; Biosis; CABCD; Medline **Loan:** In country and Canada **Service:** Internationally **Photocopy:** Yes

3354   Little Rock, Arkansas, US
Heifer Project International (HPI)
Library
PO Box 808
Little Rock, Arkansas 72203

Location: 1015 South Louisiana **Phone:** +1(501) 376-6836 **Email:** info@heifer.org **WWW:** www.heifer.org

Type: Association **Head:** Amy Davenport *Phone:* +1(501) 376-6836 *Email:* amyd@heifer.org **Staff:** 1 Prof. **Holdings:** 1,000 books 55 journals **Language of Collection/Services:** English / English **Subjects:** Agricultural Development, Farming, Fisheries, Veterinary Medicine **Specializations:** Animal Husbandry, Management **Loan:** Do not loan **Service:** Internationally **Photocopy:** Yes

3355   Magnolia, Arkansas, US
Southern Arkansas University
Magale Library
SAU Box 1401
Magnolia, Arkansas 71753-5000
Location: 100 East University **Phone:** +1(870) 235-5083 **Fax:** +1(870) 235-5018 **WWW:** www.saumag.edu **OPAC:** www.saumag.edu/library/default.htm

Type: Academic **Head:** Peggy Walters *Email:* ppwalters@saumag.edu **Staff:** 5 Prof. 5 Other **Holdings:** 435,000 books 850 journals **Language of Collection/Services:** English/English **Subjects:** Agricultural Economics, Agricultural Engineering, Animal Husbandry, Crops, Horticulture **Networks:** OCLC **Photocopy:** Yes

3356   Morrilton, Arkansas, US
Winrock International Institute for Agricultural
    Development
Library
38 Winrock Drive
Morrilton, Arkansas 72110
Phone: +1(501) 727-5435 **Fax:** +1(501) 727-5242 **Email:** information@winrock.org **WWW:** www.winrock.org

Former Name: Agricultural Development Council, International Agricultural Development Service, Winrock International Livestock Research and Training Center **Founded:** 1975 **Type:** Non-profit **Head:** Melinda Pennington *Phone:* +1(501) 727-5435 ext 303 *Email:* mpennington@winrock.org **Staff:** 1 Prof. 1 Other **Holdings:** 40,000 books 350 journals **Language of Collection/Services:** English / English **Subjects:** Agriculture (Tropics), Agribusiness, Agricultural Development, Agricultural Economics, Agricultural Policy, Animal Husbandry, Crops, Farming, Farming Systems, Forestry, Plants, Water Resources **Networks:** OCLC **Loan:** Internationally **Service:** Internationally **Photocopy:** Yes

3357   Pine Bluff, Arkansas, US
University of Arkansas, Pine Bluff (UAPB)
John Brown Watson Memorial Library
1200 N. University Blvd.
US Highway 79
Pine Bluff, Arkansas 71601-2703
Phone: +1(870) 543-8896 **WWW:** www.uapb.edu **OPAC:** www.uapb.edu/lib/index.html

Type: Academic **Head:** E.J. Fontenette *Phone:* +1(870) 543-8411 *Email:* fontenette_e@vx4500.uapb.edu

3358   Russellville, Arkansas, US
Arkansas Tech University (ATU)
Pendergraft Library and Technology Center

Russellville, Arkansas 72801-2222
Phone: +1(501) 968-0289 **Fax:** +1(501) 968-2185 **Email:**
libp@atuvm.atu.edu **WWW:** www.atu.edu **OPAC:**
webvoyage.atu.edu

Founded: 1909 **Type:** Academic **Head:** Bill Parton *Phone:*
+1(501) 968-0417 *Email:* bill.parton@mail.atu.edu **Staff:** 5
Prof. 6 Other **Holdings:** 10,500 books 35 journals **Language
of Collection/Services:** English **Networks:** OCLC **Loan:** In
country **Photocopy:** Yes

California

3359   Albany, California, US
         United States Department of Agriculture, Agri-
            cultural Research Service, Western Regional
            Research Center (USDA, ARS, WRRC)
         Library
         800 Buchanan Street
         Albany, California 94710
Phone: +1(510) 559-5600 **Fax:** +1(510) 559-5766 **WWW:**
www.pw.usda.gov

Founded: 1940 **Type:** Government **Head:** Rena Schonbrun
Phone: +1(510) 559-5603 *Email:* rschonbrun@pw.usda.gov
Staff: 1 Prof. 2 Other **Language of Collection/Services:**
English **Subjects:** Biotechnology, Food Sciences, Plant Pa-
thology, Plants **Networks:** OCLC **Databases Used:** Agri-
cola; Current Contents; FSTA **Photocopy:** Yes

3360   Arcata, California, US
         Humboldt State University (HSU)
         Library
         Arcata, California 95521
Phone: +1(707) 826-3418 **Fax:** +1(707) 826-3440 **Email:**
askus@library.humboldt.edu **OPAC:** library.humboldt.edu/
library_catalogs.html

Founded: 1913 **Type:** Academic **Head:** Sharon Kenyon
Phone: +1(707) 826-3441 *Email:* shk1@axe.humboldt.edu
Staff: 10 Prof. 20 Other **Holdings:** 750,000 books 2,000
journals **Language of Collection/Services:** English **Sub-
jects:** Aquaculture, Fisheries, Forestry, Range Management,
Rural Development, Soil Science, Water Resources, Wild-
life **Specializations:** Salmon Culture, Sequoia sempervirens,
Shellfish Culture **Networks:** OCLC **Databases Used:**
LEXIS-NEXIS; Agricola **Loan:** Internationally **Service:**
Internationally **Photocopy:** Yes

3361   Berkeley, California, US
         Bio-Integral Resource Center (BIRC)
         Library of Least-Toxic Pest Management
            Resources
         PO Box 7414
         Berkeley, California 94707
Location: 1307 Acton Street **Phone:** +1(510) 524-2567
Fax: +1(510) 524-1758 **WWW:** www.birc.org

Founded: 1978 **Type:** Association **Staff:** 5 Prof. 3 Other
Holdings: 5,000 books 200 journals **Language of Collec-
tion/Services:** English, Chinese/English, Chinese **Subjects:**
Pest Management **Specializations:** Biological Control, Integrated Pest Management **Databases Developed:** Integrated

Pest Management - products, options, services, analysis, and
recommendations **Loan:** Do not loan **Service:** Members
only **Photocopy:** Yes

3362   Berkeley, California, US
         University of California, Berkeley
         Marian Koshland Bioscience and Natural
            Resources Library
         2101 VLSB #6500
         Berkeley, California 94720
Phone: +1(510) 642-0456 **Fax:** +1(510) 642-8217 **Email:**
bios@library.berkeley.edu **WWW:** www.lib.berkeley.edu/
bios **OPAC:** gladis.berkeley.edu

Former Name: BioSciences Library, Forestry Library, En-
tomology Library **Founded:** 1995 **Type:** Academic **Head:**
Beth Weil *Phone:* +1(510) 642-9706 *Email:* bweil@library.
berkeley.edu **Staff:** 3 Prof. 14 Other **Holdings:** 450,000
books 7,000 journals **Language of Collection/Services:**
English / English **Subjects:** Agricultural Economics, Cellular Biology, Ecology, Environment, Forestry, Microbiology,
Molecular Biology, Natural Resources, Nutrition, Plants
Networks: OCLC; RLIN **Databases Developed:** Rudy
Grah Agroforestry Database **Databases Used:** Comprehen-
sive **Loan:** Internationally **Photocopy:** Yes

3363   Berkeley, California, US
         University of California, Berkeley, Botanical
            Garden
         Library
         200 Centennial Drive #5045
         Berkeley, California 94720-5045
Phone: +1(510) 643-2755 **Fax:** +1(510) 642-5045 **Email:**
garden@uclink4.berkeley.edu **WWW:** www.mip.berkeley.
edu/garden

Founded: 1890 **Type:** Academic **Head:** Ms. Holly Forbes
Email: hforbes@uclink4.berkeley.edu *Phone:* +1(510) 643-
8040 **Holdings:** 1,000 books 12 journals **Language of Col-
lection/Services:** English / English **Subjects:** Horticulture,
Taxonomy **Loan:** Inhouse **Service:** Reference use only **Photocopy:** No

3364   Berkeley, California, US
         University of California, Berkeley, Giannini
            Foundation of Agricultural Economics
         Library
         248 Giannini Hall #3310
         Berkeley, California 94720-3310
Phone: +1(510) 642-7121 **Fax:** +1(510) 643-8911 **Email:**
dote@are.berkeley.edu **WWW:** are.berkeley.edu/library

Founded: 1930 **Type:** Academic **Head:** Grace Dote *Phone:*
+1(510) 642-7121 *Email:* dote@are.berkeley.edu **Staff:** 1
Prof. 2 Other **Holdings:** 19,500 books 1,500 journals **Language of Collection/Services:** English / English **Subjects:**
Agribusiness, Agricultural Development, Agricultural Economics, Biotechnology, Commodities Marketing, Crops,
Development Economics, Education/Extension, Fisheries,
Natural Resources, Water Resources **Loan:** Do not loan **Service:** Internationally **Photocopy:** Yes

3365   Chico, California, US
California State University, Chico (CSUC)
Meriam Library
Chico, California 95929
Phone: +1(916) 895-5834 **Fax:** +1(916) 898-4443 **WWW:**
www.csuchico.edu **OPAC:** www.csuchico.edu/library

Founded: 1887 **Type:** Academic **Head:** Carolyn Dusenbury
Phone: +1(916) 898-6487 *Email:* cdusenbury@csuchico.
edu **Staff:** 15 Prof. 38 Other **Holdings:** 22,000 books 180
journals **Language of Collection/Services:** English **Subjects:** Agricultural Economics, Almonds, Citrus, Rice **Networks:** OCLC **Databases Used:** Agricola **Photocopy:** Yes
Loan: Internationally

3366   Claremont, California, US
Rancho Santa Ana Botanic Garden
Library
1500 North College Avenue
Claremont, California 91711-3157
Phone: +1(909) 625-8767 **Fax:** +1(909) 626-7670 **WWW:**
www.rsabg.org

Founded: 1927 **Type:** Academic **Head:** Mrs. Beatrice M.
Beck *Email:* bea.beck@cgu.edu *Phone:* +1(909) 625-8767
ext 2361 **Staff:** 1 Prof. 1 Other **Holdings:** 40,000 books 500
journals **Language of Collection/Services:** English **Subjects:** Botany, Drought Resistance, Ethnobotany (Native
Americans), Horticulture, Landscaping, Water Resources
Networks: BLAIS; OCLC **Databases Used:** Agricola
Loan: Do not loan **Photocopy:** Yes

3367   Davis, California, US
Monsanto
Monsanto Information Resources and Services -
       Davis (MIRS-Davis)
Monsanto - Calgene Campus
1920 Fifth Street
Davis, California 95616
Phone: +1(530) 792-2207 **Fax:** +1(530) 792-2453 **WWW:**
www.monsanto.com

Former Name: Calgene Inc. **Founded:** 1983 **Type:** Business **Head:** Deanna Johnson *Phone:* +1(530) 792-2206
Email: deanna.johnson@monsanto.com **Staff:** 1 Prof. 1
Other **Holdings:** 2,000 books 100 journals **Language of
Collection/Services:** English / English **Subjects:** Biotechnology, Plant Oils, Plant Physiology, Plants **Databases
Used:** Comprehensive **Loan:** Inhouse **Photocopy:** Yes

3368   Davis, California, US
University of California, Davis (UCD)
Agricultural and Resource Economics Library
One Shields Avenue
Davis, California 95616-8512
Email: arel@primal.ucdavis.edu **WWW:** www.lib.
ucdavis.edu **OPAC:** www.agecon.ucdavis.edu/Library/
Catalogs.htm

Founded: 1951 **Type:** Academic **Head:** Susan Casement
Phone: +1(530) 752-1540 *Email:* sdcasement@ucdavis.edu
Staff: 1 Prof. 2 Other **Holdings:** 7,847 books 205 journals
Language of Collection/Services: English **Subjects:** Agricultural Economics **Loan:** Do not loan **Photocopy:** Yes

3369   Davis, California, US
University of California, Davis (UCD)
General Library
Davis, California 95616
Phone: +1(530) 752-6196 **Fax:** +1(530) 752-5251 **Email:**
bioag@ucdavis.edu **WWW:** www.lib.ucdabis.edu **OPAC:**
www.lib.ucdavis.edu/catalogs.html **Ariel IP:** Shields
Library - slariel.ucdavis.edu; Physical Sciences Library -
pslariel.ucdavis.edu; Health Sciences Library -
hslariel.ucdavis.edu

Founded: 1908 **Type:** Academic **Head:** Marilyn J. Sharrow, Ted S. Sibia, Head, Biological and Agricultural Sciences Department; Axel Borg, Wine Bibliographer *Email:*
tssibia@ucdavis.edu, aeborg@ucdavis.edu *Phone:* +1(530)
752-2110 **Staff:** 40 Prof. 150 Other **Holdings:** 2,399,415
books 44,672 journals **Language of Collection/Services:**
English / English **Subjects:** Agriculture (Tropics), Agribusiness, Agricultural Development, Agricultural Economics,
Agricultural Engineering, Animal Husbandry, Biotechnology, Crops, Education/Extension, Entomology, Farming,
Fisheries, Food Sciences, Forestry, Horticulture, Plant Pathology, Soil Science, Water Resources, Veterinary Medicine **Specializations:** Apis, Enology, Nematoda, Vitis,
Winemaking **Networks:** OCLC **Databases Used:** Comprehensive **Loan:** Internationally **Service:** Internationally **Photocopy:** Yes

3370   Davis, California, US
University of California, Davis (UCD)
Loren D. Carlson Health Sciences Library
One Shields Avenue
Davis, California 95616-5291
Phone: +1(530) 752-1162 **Fax:** +1(530) 752-4718 **Email:**
hslref@ucdavis.edu **WWW:**
www.lib.ucdavis.edu/hsl/hshome.html **OPAC:**
www.melvyl.ucop.edu

Founded: 1956 **Type:** Academic **Head:** Jo Anne Boorkman
Phone: +1(530) 752-6383 *Email:* jaboorkman@ucdavis.edu
Staff: 6.5 Prof. 16.5 Other **Holdings:** 280,319 books 2,369
journals **Language of Collection/Services:** English / English **Subjects:** Veterinary Medicine **Networks:** DOCLINE;
OCLC **Databases Used:** Comprehensive **Loan:** Internationally **Service:** Internationally **Photocopy:** Yes

3371   Fresno, California, US
United States Department of Agriculture,
       Agricultural Research Service, Horticultural
       Crops Research Laboratory (USDA, ARS,
       HCRL)
Library
2021 South Peach Avenue
Fresno, California 93727-5999
Phone: +(559) 453-3000 **Fax:** +1(559) 453-3088 **WWW:**
pwa.ars.usda.gov/fresno/index.html

Type: Government **Holdings:** 10,000 books 25 journals
Language of Collection/Services: English **Subjects:** Entomology, Plant Pathology, Plant Physiology **Specializations:**
Postharvest Technology **Databases Used:** Agricola **Loan:**
Inhouse **Service:** Inhouse **Photocopy:** Yes

3372 Healdsburg, California, US
Sonoma County Library
Sonoma County Wine Library
Piper and Center Streets
Healdsburg, California 95448
Phone: +1(707) 433-3772 **Fax:** +1(707) 433-7946 **WWW:**
www.sonoma.lib.ca.us/wine.html **OPAC:** telnet://sonoma.
lib.ca.us

Founded: 1988 **Type:** Business **Head:** Bo Simons *Phone:*
+1(707) 433-3772 *Email:* bo@sonoma.lib.ca.us **Staff:** 1
Prof. 3 Other **Holdings:** 4,000 books 80 journals **Language
of Collection/Services:** English **Subjects:** Agricultural Economics, Enology, Viticulture, Wine Industry, Winemaking,
Wines **Networks:** OCLC **Databases Developed:** Wine Information Files **Databases Used:** Agricola; FSTA **Loan:**
Internationally **Service:** Internationally **Photocopy:** Yes

3373 La Jolla, California, US
National Oceanic and Atmospheric Administration, National Marine Fisheries Service,
Southwest Fisheries Science Center (NOAA,
NMFS, SWFSC)
Library
PO Box 271
La Jolla, California 92038-0271
Location: 8604 LaJolla Shores Drive **Phone:** +1(858) 546-
7038, 546-7000 **Fax:** +1(858) 546-7003 **Email:** debra.
losey@noaa.gov **WWW:** swfsc.ucsd.edu

Former Name: Fishery-Oceanography Center, United
States Department of the Interior, Bureau of Commercial
Fisheries, Southwest Fisheries Center (SWFC) **Founded:**
1965 **Type:** Government **Head:** Debra A. Losey *Phone:*
+1(858) 546-7196 *Email:* debra.losey@noaa.gov **Staff:** 1
Prof. **Holdings:** 15,000 books 180 journals **Language of
Collection/Services:** English / English **Subjects:** Fisheries,
Marine Biology, Marine Mammals **Specializations:** Anchovies, Dolphins, Fisheries, Sardines, Tuna **Networks:**
FEDLINK; OCLC **Databases Developed:** SWFSC and
SWFC Administrative report and technical memorandum reports databases **Databases Used:** Comprehensive **Loan:**
Internationally **Service:** Internationally **Photocopy:** Yes

3374 Lafayette, California, US
Soyfoods Center
Library and Archives
PO Box 234
Lafayette, California 94549
Location: 1021 Dolores Drive **Fax:** +1(925) 283-9091

Founded: 1976 **Type:** Business **Head:** William Shurtleff
Phone: +1(925) 283-2991 **Staff:** 3 Prof. **Holdings:** 40,000
books 24 journals **Language of Collection/Services:** English, Japanese / English **Subjects:** Food Sciences **Specializations:** Soybean Products, Soybeans **Databases Developed:**
SoyaScan - search for a fee - inquire; SoyaScan Publications
- bibliographic database listing more than 56,300 publications on soyfoods and soybeans from 1100 B.C. to the present; SoyaScan Products - details on more than 12,200
commercial soyfoods from 1546 A.D. to the present;
SoyaScan Directory and Mailing List - contains over 16,700
names and addresses **Loan:** Do not loan **Photocopy:** Yes

3375 Los Angeles, California, US
Educational Communications, Inc.
Environmental Resource Library
PO Box 351419
Los Angeles, California 90035-9119
Phone: +1(310) 559-9160 **Fax:** +1(310) 559-9160 **Email:**
ecnp@aol.com **WWW:** home.earthlink.net/~dragonflight/
ecoprojects.htm

Founded: 1959 **Type:** Non-profit **Head:** Nancy Pearlman
Phone: +1(310) 559-9160 *Email:* ecnp@aol.com **Holdings:**
900 books **Language of Collection/Services:** English **Subjects:** Environmental Impact, Organic Farming, Organic
Gardening, Regeneration

3376 Los Angeles, California, US
Los Angeles Public Library, Science, Technology,
and Patents Department (LAPL)
630 West Fifth Street
Los Angeles, California 90071
Phone: +1(213) 228-7200 **Fax:** +1(213) 228-7209 **Email:**
science@lapl.org **WWW:** www.lapl.org **OPAC:** www.
lapl.org

Founded: 1872 **Type:** Government **Head:** Billie M. Connor
Phone: +1(213) 228-7201 *Email:* bconnor@lapl.org **Staff:** 7
Prof. **Holdings:** 325,000 books 1,200 journals **Language of
Collection/Services:** English / English **Subjects:** Comprehensive **Specializations:** Food Sciences, Patents **Networks:**
OCLC **Databases Used:** Biological and Agricultural Abstracts **Loan:** Internationally **Service:** Internationally **Photocopy:** Yes

3377 Modesto, California, US
E. & J. Gallo Winery
Library
Box 1130
Modesto, California 95353
WWW: www.Gallo.Com/USA

Founded: 1969 **Type:** Business **Head:** Susan Van Till
Phone: +1(209) 341-3266 **Staff:** 2 Prof. **Holdings:** 13,950
books **Subjects:** Agriculture (Tropics), Agribusiness, Agricultural Development, Agricultural Economics, Agricultural
Engineering, Animal Husbandry, Biotechnology, Crops, Education/Extension, Enology, Entomology, Farming, Food
Sciences, Forestry, Horticulture, Plant Pathology, Soil Science, Viticulture, Water Resources **Loan:** Inhouse **Service:**
In country **Photocopy:** Yes

3378 Napa, California, US
Napa Valley Grape Growers Association
(NVGGA)
Library
811 Jefferson St.
Napa, California 94559
Phone: +1(707) 944-8311 **Fax:** +1(707) 224-7836 **Email:**
claudia@i-cafe.net **WWW:** www.napagrowers.org

Founded: 1975 **Type:** Association **Subjects:** Viticulture
Loan: Do not loan **Service:** Inhouse to members only **Photocopy:** Yes

3379   National City, California, US
Pacific Southwest Biological Services, Inc.
    (PSBS)
Beauchamp Botanical Library
PO Box 985
National City, California 91951-0985
Location: 1434 East 24th Street **Fax:** +1(935) 477-5380
Email: bio@psbs.com **WWW:** www.psbs.com

Founded: 1933 **Type:** Private **Head:** Mr. R. Mitchel Beauchamp *Phone:* +1(935) 477-0295, 477-5333 *Email:* mitch@psbs.com **Staff:** 1 Other **Holdings:** 8,000 books 15 journals **Language of Collection/Services:** English **Subjects:** Horticulture **Loan:** Do not loan **Photocopy:** No

3380   Palo Alto, California, US
Peninsula Conservation Center Foundation
    (PCCF)
Environmental Library
3921 East Bayshore
Palo Alto, California 94303
Phone: +1(650) 962-9876 **Fax:** +1(650) 962-8234 **Email:** library@pccf.org **WWW:** www.pccf.org

Founded: 1971 **Type:** Association **Head:** Rosemary Jorde *Phone:* +1(650) 962-9876 *Email:* library@pccf.org **Staff:** .5 Prof. **Holdings:** 5,136 books 30 journals **Language of Collection/Services:** English / English **Subjects:** Agriculture (Tropics), Biotechnology, Environment, Fisheries, Forestry, Water Resources **Specializations:** Endangered Species, Environmental Education, Trails, Wildlife **Loan:** In country **Service:** In country **Photocopy:** Yes

3381   Parlier, California, US
University of California
Kearney Agricultural Center (KAC)
9240 South Riverbend Avenue
Parlier, California 93648
Fax: +1(209) 646-6513 **WWW:** www.uckac.edu/danrcvr

Type: Academic **Head:** A. Charles Crabb *Phone:* +1(209) 646-6543 *Email:* ccrabb@uckac.edu **Staff:** 27 Prof. 40 Other **Holdings:** 12,000 books **Language of Collection/Services:** English / English **Subjects:** Entomology, Horticulture, Plant Pathology, Water Resources **Loan:** Inhouse **Photocopy:** Yes

3382   Pomona, California, US
California Polytechnic State University (Cal Poly
    Pomona)
University Library
3801 W. Temple Avenue
Pomona, California 91768
Phone: +1(909) 869-3074 **Fax:** +1(909) 869-6922 **Email:** libref@csupomona.edu **WWW:** www.csupomona.edu/~library **OPAC:** opac.lib.csupomona.edu

Founded: 1938 **Type:** Academic **Head:** Harold B. Schleifer *Phone:* +1(909) 869-3088 *Email:* hbschleifer@csupomona.edu **Databases Developed:** Wine and Wine Industry Collection - documents and the Southern California wine industry

3383   Richmond, California, US
University of California, Berkeley (UCB)

Forest Products Library
1301 South 46th Street
Richmond, California 94804-4698
Phone: +1(510) 215-4255 **Fax:** +1(510) 215-4299 **Email:** fpro@library.berkeley.edu **WWW:** www.ucfpl.ucop.edu

Founded: 1963 **Type:** Academic **Head:** Miriam Aroner *Phone:* +1(510) 643-6475 *Email:* miriam.aroner@ucop.edu **Staff:** 1 Prof. **Holdings:** 8,000 books 120 journals **Language of Collection/Services:** English / English **Subjects:** Forest Products, Pulps, Wood Preservation, Wood Properties **Databases Used:** TREECD **Loan:** UC only **Service:** Internationally **Photocopy:** Yes

3384   Richmond, California, US
ZENECA Ag Products, Western Research Center
Information Services
1200 South 47th Street
Richmond, California 94804
Fax: +1(105)231-1332 **WWW:** www.zeneca.com/page.asp

Former Name: ICI Americas Inc. **Type:** Research **Head:** Judy Secor *Phone:* +1(105) 231-1301 *Email:* judy.secor@agna.zeneca.com **Staff:** 1 Prof. 2.5 Other **Holdings:** 15,000 books 319 journals **Language of Collection/Services:** English **Subjects:** Agribusiness, Biotechnology, Crops, Food Sciences, Entomology, Horticulture, Plant Pathology **Networks:** OCLC **Loan:** Inhouse **Service:** Inhouse **Photocopy:** Yes

3385   Riverside, California, US
University of California, Riverside
Science Library
PO Box 5900
Riverside, California 92517-5900
Phone: +1(909) 787-3316 **Fax:** +1(909) 787-6378 **Email:** sciref@ucr.edu **WWW:** library.ucr.edu **OPAC:** library.ucr.edu

Former Name: Bio-Agricultural Library **Founded:** 1907 **Type:** Academic **Head:** Charlene M. Baldwin *Phone:* +1(909) 787-3238 *Email:* charlene.baldwin@ucr.edu **Staff:** 8 Prof. 25 Other **Holdings:** 450,000 books 3,500 journals **Language of Collection/Services:** English **Subjects:** Comprehensive **Specializations:** Agricultural Development, Arid Lands, Biotechnology, Citrus, Crops, Entomology, Environmental Sciences, Horticulture (Semi-Tropics), Horticulture (Sub-Tropics), Plant Pathology, Soil Science, Water Resources **Networks:** California Digital Library; OCLC **Databases Used:** Comprehensive **Loan:** Internationally **Service:** Internationally **Photocopy:** Yes

3386   Sacramento, California, US
California Kiwifruit Commission
Kiwifruit Reference File
9845 Horn Road, Suite #160
Sacramento, California 95758
Phone: +1(916) 362-7490 **Fax:** +1(916) 362-7993 **Email:** info@kiwifruit.org **WWW:** www.kiwifruit.org

Founded: 1980 **Type:** Association **Staff:** 1 Prof. **Holdings:** 250 books **Subjects:** Agricultural Development, Crops, Education/Extension, Entomology, Farming, Horticulture, Food

Sciences, Plant Pathology, Soil Science **Loan:** In country
Photocopy: Yes

3387 Sacramento, California, US
California State University, Sacramento (CSUS)
Reference Department
2000 Jed Smith Drive
Sacramento, California 95819-6309
Phone: +1(916) 278-5673 **Fax:** +1(916) 278-7089 **Email:**
budgewd@csus.edu **WWW:** www.csus.edu/csuslibr
OPAC: eureka.lib.csus.edu

Former Name: Sacramento State University **Founded:**
1927 **Type:** Academic **Staff:** 4 Prof. 2 Other **Holdings:**
306,652 books **Language of Collection/Services:** English/
English **Subjects:** Agricultural Economics, Biotechnology,
Fisheries, Food Sciences, Forestry, Plant Pathology, Plants,
Water Resources **Databases Used:** ABI/Inform; Medline;
LEXIS-NEXIS **Loan:** In country **Service:** In country **Photo-copy:** Yes

3388 Sacramento, California, US
United States Department of the Interior, Bureau
of Reclamation
Library
2800 Cottage Way, W-1522
Sacramento, California 95825
Phone: +1(916) 978-5593 **Fax:** +1(916) 978-5599 **Email:**
sjones@mp.usbr.gov **WWW:** www.mp.usbr.gov

Founded: 1946 **Type:** Government **Head:** Stephen E. Jones
Phone: +1(916) 978-5593 *Email:* sjones@mp.usbr.gov
Staff: 1 Prof. **Holdings:** 18,000 books 2,000 journals **Lan-guage of Collection/Services:** English / English **Loan:** In
country **Service:** In country **Photocopy:** Yes

3389 San Diego, California, US
Kelco Biopolymers
Information and Technical Services
8355 Aero Drive
San Diego, California 92123
Fax: +1(619) 467-6570 **WWW:** www.kelco.com

Type: Business **Head:** Susan J. Shepherd *Phone:* +1(619)
467-6470 **Staff:** 2 Prof. 3 Other **Holdings:** 4,000 books 400
journals **Language of Collection/Services:** English / Eng-lish **Subjects:** Biotechnology, Food Technology, Pesticides
Loan: Inhouse **Service:** Open to public by appointment only
Photocopy: Yes

3390 San Diego, California, US
San Diego State University (SDSU)
Malcolm A. Love Library, Science Division
5500 Campanile Drive
San Diego, California 92182-8050
Phone: +1(619) 594-6715 **Fax:** +1(619) 594-0719 **WWW:**
libweb.sdsu.edu **OPAC:** libpac2.sdsu.edu

Former Name: San Diego State College (SDSC), Teachers
College, San Diego, California State University, San Diego
Founded: 1897 **Type:** Academic **Head:** Karen Kinney;
Jerry Palsson, Division Head *Phone:* +1(619) 594-6014;
594-2535 *Email:* gpalsson@mail.sdsu.edu **Staff:** 20 Prof. 75
Other **Holdings:** 714,898 books 4,800 journals **Language of**

Collection/Services: English / English **Subjects:** Fisheries,
Food Sciences, Plants, Water Resources **Networks:** OCLC
Databases Used: Comprehensive **Loan:** Internationally
Service: Inhouse **Photocopy:** Yes

3391 San Francisco, California, US
Bio-dynamic Farming and Gardening Association,
Inc.
Library
PO Box 29135
San Francisco, California 94129-0135
Location: Building 1002B, Thoreau Center, The Presidio
Phone: +1(888) 516-7797 **Fax:** +1(888) 561-7796 **Email:**
biodynamic@aol.com **WWW:** www.biodynamics.com

Founded: 1941 **Type:** Association **Head:** Charles Beedy
Staff: 1 Prof. **Holdings:** 250 books 12 journals **Language of
Collection/Services:** English **Subjects:** Horticulture **Spe-cializations:** Diversity **Loan:** Do not loan **Photocopy:** Yes

3392 San Francisco, California, US
California Academy of Sciences (CAS)
J.W. Mailliard, Jr. Library and Biodiversity
Resource Center
Golden Gate Park
San Francisco, California 94118
Phone: +1(415) 750-7102 (Library); 750-7361
(Biodiversity) **Fax:** +1(415) 750-7106 **Email:** library@
calacademy.org, biodiversity@calacademy.org **WWW:**
www.calacademy.org **OPAC:** www.calacademy.org/
research/library/service.htm

Founded: 1853 (Library); 1991 (Biodiversity Resource
Center) **Type:** Research **Head:** Anne Marie Malley *Phone:*
+1(415) 750-7101 *Email:* amalley@calacademy.org **Staff:** 7
Prof. 4.8 Other **Holdings:** 185,000 books 2,700 journals
Language of Collection/Services: English **Subjects:** Ani-mal Husbandry, Education, Entomology, Plants, Taxonomy
Networks: OCLC **Databases Developed:** Catalog of Fishes
- access via Internet at www.calacademy.org/research/ich-thyology/catalog; Neuropterida Species in California Collec-tions, Bibliography of Sphecidae, World Checklist of Extant
Mecoptera Species, Catalog of Neuropteroid Genera of the
World, World Neuropteroid Bibliography, World Dryopoid
Bibliography - access via Internet at www.calacademy.org/
research/entomology; Diatom Database - access via Internet
at www.calacademy.org/research/diatoms **Databases Used:**
Fish and Fisheries Worldwide; Wildlife Worldwide; Zoolog-ical Record **Loan:** Internationally **Service:** Internationally
Photocopy: Yes

3393 San Francisco, California, US
Strybing Arboretum Society
Helen Crocker Russell Library
Golden Gate Park
9th Avenue & Lincoln Way
San Francisco, California 94122
Phone: +1(415) 661-1316 ext 303 **Fax:** +1(415) 661-3539
Email: bphcrl@ix.netcom.com **WWW:** www.strybing.org

Founded: 1972 **Type:** Association **Head:** Barbara M.
Pitschel *Phone:* +1(415) 661-1316 ext 303 *Email:* bpitschel
@strybing.org **Staff:** 1.8 Prof. **Holdings:** 18,000 books 450

journals **Language of Collection/Services:** English / English **Subjects:** Horticulture, Plants **Networks:** OCLC **Loan:** Do not loan **Service:** Internationally **Photocopy:** Yes

3394   San Luis Obispo, California, US
California Polytechnic State University (Cal Poly)
Robert E. Kennedy Library
San Luis Obispo, California 93407
Phone: +1(805) 756-2649 **Fax:** +1(805) 756-1415 **WWW:** www.calpoly.edu **OPAC:** www.lib.calpoly.edu

Founded: 1903 **Type:** Academic **Head:** Hiram Davis *Phone:* +1(805) 546-2649 *Email:* hldavis@library.calpoly.edu **Staff:** 16 Prof. 46 Other **Holdings:** 618,000 books 2,200 journals **Language of Collection/Services:** English / English **Subjects:** Agribusiness, Agricultural Education, Animal Husbandry, Crops, Dairies, Food Sciences, Nutrition, Natural Resources, Ornamental Plants, Soil Science **Databases Used:** LEXIS-NEXIS **Loan:** Inhouse **Photocopy:** Yes

3395   San Marino, California, US
Huntington Library, Art Collections, Botanical
    Gardens
Library
1151 Oxford Road
San Marino, California 91108
Phone: +1(626) 405-2191 **Fax:** +1(626) 405-5720 **WWW:** www.huntington.org

Founded: 1919 **Type:** Association **Head:** David S. Zeidberg *Phone:* +1(626) 405-2176 **Staff:** 21.4 Prof. 23.7 Other **Holdings:** 9,000 books 180 journals **Language of Collection/Services:** English / English **Subjects:** Botany, Horticulture **Specializations:** Nursery Catalogs **Networks:** RLIN **Loan:** Do not loan **Photocopy:** Yes

3396   Santa Barbara, California, US
Santa Barbara Botanic Garden
Library
1212 Mission Canyon Road
Santa Barbara, California 93105
Phone: +1(805) 682-4726 ext 107 **Fax:** +1(805) 563-0352 **WWW:** www.sbbg.org

Founded: 1942 **Type:** Non-profit **Head:** Laurie Hannah *Phone:* +1(805) 682-4726 **Staff:** 1 Prof. **Holdings:** 9,000 books 120 journals **Language of Collection/Services:** English / English **Subjects:** Botany, Flora (California), Horticulture **Networks:** OCLC **Loan:** Do not loan **Photocopy:** Yes

3397   Santa Barbara, California, US
University of California, Santa Barbara (UCSB)
Sciences-Engineering Library
Santa Barbara, California 93106
Phone: +1(805) 893-2762 **Fax:** +1(805) 893-8620 **Email:** sel@library.ucsb.edu **WWW:** www.library.ucsb.edu **OPAC:** www.library.ucsb.edu **Ariel IP:** 128.111.96.85

Founded: 1966 **Type:** Academic **Head:** Andrea Duda *Phone:* +1(805) 893-2762 *Email:* duda@library.ucsb.edu **Staff:** 4 Prof. 3 Other **Holdings:** 978,500 books **Language of Collection/Services:** English / English **Subjects:** Soil Science, Water Resources **Networks:** OCLC **Databases**

Used: Comprehensive **Loan:** Internationally **Service:** Inhouse **Photocopy:** Yes

3398   Santa Cruz, California, US
University of California, Santa Cruz (UCSC)
Science Library
Santa Cruz, California 95064
Phone: +1(831) 429-2886 **Fax:** +1(831) 429-3354 **WWW:** www.ucsc.edu **OPAC:** library.ucsc.edu

Founded: 1969 **Type:** Academic **Head:** Catherine Soehner *Phone:* +1(831) 459-2554 *Email:* soehner@cats.ucsc.edu **Staff:** 5 Prof. 4 Other **Holdings:** 8,000 books 200 journals **Language of Collection/Services:** English **Loan:** Internationally **Photocopy:** Yes

3399   St. Helena, California, US
Saint Helena Public Library
Napa Valley Wine Library
1492 Library Lane
St. Helena, California 94574
Phone: +1(707) 963-5244 **Fax:** +1(707) 963-5264 **Email:** ref@shpl.org, questions about the collection: napawine@fcs.net **WWW:** www.shpl.org **OPAC:** www.shpl.org/winlib.htm

Founded: 1963 **Type:** Association **Head:** Mrs. Clayla Davis *Phone:* +1(707) 963-5244 *Email:* clayla@shpl.org **Staff:** 5 Prof. 11 Other **Holdings:** 4,000 books 50 journals **Language of Collection/Services:** English / English **Subjects:** Viticulture, Wines, Winemaking **Networks:** OCLC; SNAP **Loan:** In country **Service:** Within California **Photocopy:** Yes

3400   Tiburon, California, US
United States National Marine Fisheries Service
Tiburon Laboratory Library
3150 Paradise Drive
Tiburon, California 94920
Phone: +1(415) 435-3149 ext 220 **Fax:** +1(415) 435-3675 **WWW:** swfsc.ucsd.edu

Founded: 1962 **Type:** Government **Staff:** 1 Prof. **Holdings:** 25,000 books 50 journals **Language of Collection/Services:** English / English **Subjects:** Water Resources **Specializations:** Fisheries, Marine Biology, Pollution **Networks:** OCLC **Databases Developed:** Sebastes Bibliography; Sablefish Bibliography **Loan:** In country **Service:** Internationally **Photocopy:** Yes

Colorado

3401   Akron, Colorado, US
United States Department of Agriculture,
    Agricultural Research Service, Central Great
    Plains Research Station (USDA, ARS)
Research Station Library
Box 400
Akron, Colorado 80720-0400
Location: 40335 County Road GG **Phone:** +1(970) 345-2259 **Fax:** +1(970) 345-2088 **Email:** mharms@lamar.colostate.edu **WWW:** www.akron.ars.usda.gov

Founded: 1907 **Type:** Government **Head:** R.L. Anderson *Phone:* +1(970) 345-2259 **Staff:** 6 Prof. 17 Other **Holdings:** 250 books **Language of Collection/Services:** English / English **Subjects:** Crops, Soil Science, Water **Specializations:** Weather Data **Loan:** Inhouse **Service:** Inhouse **Photocopy:** No

3402   Denver, Colorado, US
Denver Botanic Gardens
Helen K. Fowler Library
909 York Street
Denver, Colorado 80206

Location: 1005 York Street **Phone:** +1(303) 370-8014 **Fax:** +1(303) 370-8196 **WWW:** www.botanicgardens.org **Email:** library@denverbotanicgardens.org

Founded: 1945 **Type:** Non-profit **Head:** Susan C. Eubank *Email:* eubanks@denverbotanicgardens.org **Staff:** 2 Prof. **Holdings:** 27,000 books 500 journals **Language of Collection/Services:** English / English **Subjects:** Entomology, Agriculture (Tropics), Forestry, Plant Pathology, Soil Science **Specializations:** Botany, Flora (Colorado), Horticulture **Networks:** OCLC **Databases Used:** Agricola **Loan:** Internationally **Service:** Internationally **Photocopy:** Yes

3403   Denver, Colorado, US
Environmental Protection Agency, National
    Enforcement Investigations Center (EPA,
    NEIC)
Library
Denver Federal Center, Building 53
Box 25227
Denver, Colorado 80225

Phone: +1(303) 236-6136 **Fax:** +1(303) 236-3218 **WWW:** www.epa.gov/oeca/oceft/neic **OPAC:** www.epa.gov/natlibra/ols.htm

Founded: 1972 **Type:** Government **Head:** Kimberly O'Neill *Email:* oneill.kim@epa.gov **Staff:** 1 Prof. 2 Other **Holdings:** 5,000 books 135 journals **Language of Collection/Services:** English / English **Subjects:** Biotechnology, Pesticides **Networks:** EPA Library Network; OCLC **Databases Used:** Comprehensive **Loan:** Via ILL **Service:** Inhouse **Photocopy:** Yes

3404   Denver, Colorado, US
National Bison Association
Library
4701 Marion St., Suite 100
Denver, Colorado 80216

Phone: +1(303) 292-2833 **Fax:** +1(303) 292-2564 **Email:** info@nbabison.org **WWW:** www.nbabison.org

Former Name: American Bison Association, National Buffalo Association **Founded:** 1995 **Type:** Association **Staff:** 1 Prof. **Holdings:** 2,000 books 20 journals **Subjects:** Bison **Loan:** Do not loan **Photocopy:** Yes

3405   Englewood, Colorado, US
American Sheep Industry Association (ASIA)
Library
6911 South Yosemite, Suite 200
Englewood, Colorado 80112-1414

Fax: +1(303) 771-8200 **Email:** info@sheepusa.org **WWW:** www.sheepusa.org

Former Name: American Sheep Producers Council (ASPC) **Founded:** 1955 **Type:** Association **Head:** Mary Jensen *Phone:* +1(303) 771-3500 *Email:* mjensen@sheepusa.org **Staff:** 8 Prof. **Holdings:** 1 journals **Subjects:** Animal Husbandry, Food Sciences **Photocopy:** Yes

3406   Fort Collins, Colorado, US
Colorado State University (CSU)
Morgan Library
Fort Collins, Colorado 80523-1019

Phone: +1(970) 491-1841 **Fax:** +1(970) 491-1195 **WWW:** manta.library.colostate.edu **OPAC:** manta.library.colostate.edu/sage **Ariel IP:** 129.82.242.120

Former Name: Colorado Agricultural College, Colorado A & M **Founded:** 1870 **Type:** Academic **Head:** Camila Alire *Phone:* +1(970) 491-1833 *Email:* calire@manta.colostate.edu **Staff:** 37 Prof. 82 Other **Holdings:** 1,708,109 books 21,455 journals **Language of Collection/Services:** English **Subjects:** Environment, Fisheries, Forestry, Wildlife **Specializations:** Irrigation, Soil Science, Veterinary Medicine **Networks:** OCLC **Databases Used:** Comprehensive **Loan:** Internationally **Service:** Inhouse **Photocopy:** Yes

3407   Fort Collins, Colorado, US
Colorado State University (CSU)
Veterinary Teaching Hospital Branch Library
    (VTHBL)
300 West Drake Road
Fort Collins, Colorado 80523

Phone: +1(970) 491-1213 **Fax:** +1(970) 491-4141 **WWW:** manta.library.colostate.edu **OPAC:** manta.library.colostate.edu/sage

Former Name: Colorado Agricultural College, Colorado A & M **Type:** Academic **Head:** Tom Moothart *Phone:* +1(970) 491-1877 *Email:* tmoothart@manta.colostate.edu **Staff:** 1 Prof. 4 Other **Holdings:** 5,889 books 156 journals **Language of Collection/Services:** English / English **Subjects:** Veterinary Medicine **Specializations:** Veterinary Science **Networks:** OCLC **Databases Used:** CABCD; Medline **Loan:** Inhouse **Service:** Inhouse **Photocopy:** Yes

3408   Fort Collins, Colorado, US
United States Department of Agriculture, Forest
    Service, Rocky Mountain Forest and Range
    Experiment Station (USDA, FS)
Library
240 West Prospect Street
Fort Collins, Colorado 80526

Phone: +1(970) 498-1205 **Fax:** +1(970) 498-1010 **WWW:** www.fs.fed.us/rm

Founded: 1966 **Type:** Government **Head:** Carin Batt *Phone:* +1(970) 498-1205 *Email:* cbatt/rmrs@fs.fed.us **Holdings:** 36,050 books **Subjects:** Forestry

3409   Longmont, Colorado, US
Novartis Seeds, Inc., Longmont Plant
Research Library
11939 Sugarmill Road

Longmont, Colorado 80501
Phone: +1(303) 776-1802 **Fax:** +1(303) 776-0392 **WWW:** www.seeds.novartis.com

Former Name: Mono-Hy Sugar Beet Seed Inc., Great Western Sugar Co., Hilleshog Mono-Hy Inc. (HiMH) **Founded:** 1910 **Type:** Business **Holdings:** 6,850 books 10 journals **Language of Collection/Services:** English **Subjects:** Agricultural Economics, Crops, Entomology, Farming, Horticulture, Plant Pathology **Specializations:** Plant Breeding, Sugarbeet **Loan:** Internationally **Photocopy:** Yes

3410   Westminster, Colorado, US
Arabian Horse Trust
Library and Special Collections
12000 Zuni Street
Westminster, Colorado 80234-2300
Phone: +1(303) 450-4710 **Fax:** +1(303) 450-4707 **Email:** information@arabianhorsetrust.com **WWW:** www.arabianhorsetrust.com

Founded: 1975 **Type:** Association **Staff:** 1 Prof. 1 Other **Holdings:** 1,500 books 36 journals **Language of Collection/Services:** English **Subjects:** Horses **Specializations:** Arab Horse (History) **Databases Developed:** Index to Arabian Horse Photographs in Trust Collection - Indexed by name and registration number.; Library runs photograph reprint program, book restoration program, and pioneer scrapbook/keepsake programs. Write to Trust for information. **Loan:** Do not loan **Service:** In country **Photocopy:** Yes

Connecticut

3411   Groton, Connecticut, US
Pfizer Inc., Central Research
Information Resources
Eastern Point Road
Groton, Connecticut 06340
Fax: +1(203) 441-5729 **WWW:** www.pfizer.com

Founded: 1960 **Type:** Business **Head:** Dr. Roger P. Nelson *Phone:* +1(203) 441-8096 **Staff:** 17 Prof. 5 Other **Holdings:** 39,500 books 2,100 journals **Language of Collection/Services:** English / English **Subjects:** Animal Health, Drug Research, Vaccines **Specializations:** Pharmaceutical research for human and animal health **Databases Used:** Comprehensive **Loan:** Inhouse **Photocopy:** Yes

3412   Middlebury, Connecticut, US
Uniroyal Chemical Company Inc.
Management and Technical Information Services / Library (IS/L)
World Headquarters
Middlebury, Connecticut 06749
Fax: +1(203) 573-2890 **WWW:** www.uniroyalchemical.com

Former Name: Uniroyal Inc. **Type:** Business **Head:** Patricia Ann Harmon *Email:* ann_harmon@uniroyalchemical.com *Phone:* +1(203) 573-4508 **Staff:** 1 Prof. 1.5 Other **Holdings:** 14,200 books 200 journals **Language of Collection/Services:** English / English **Subjects:** Agribusiness, Agricultural Chemicals, Biotechnology, Crops, Entomol-

ogy, Horticulture, Plant Pathology, Soil Science **Loan:** In country **Service:** Inhouse **Photocopy:** Yes

3413   New Haven, Connecticut, US
Connecticut Agricultural Experiment Station
Thomas B. Osborne Library
PO Box 1106
New Haven, Connecticut 06504
Location: 123 Huntington Street **Phone:** +1(203) 974-8447 **Fax:** +1(203) 974-8504 **WWW:** www.state.ct.us/caes

Founded: 1910 **Head:** Ms. Vickie M. Bomba-Lewandoski *Email:* vickie.bomba@po.state.ct.us **Type:** Government **Staff:** 1 Prof. 1 Other **Holdings:** 23,000 books 800 journals **Language of Collection/Services:** English **Subjects:** Entomology, Crops, Farming, Food Sciences, Horticulture, Plant Pathology, Forestry, Soil Science, Water Resources **Databases Used:** Agricola **Loan:** In country **Photocopy:** Yes

3414   New Haven, Connecticut, US
Yale School of Forestry and Environmental Studies
Henry S. Graves Memorial Library
205 Prospect Street
New Haven, Connecticut 06511
Phone: +1(203) 432-5130 **Fax:** +1(203) 432-5942 **WWW:** www.yale.edu **OPAC:** webpac.library.yale.edu/webpac/orbis.htm

Founded: 1919 **Type:** Academic **Head:** Rochelle Smith *Phone:* +1(203) 432-5132 *Email:* rochelle.smith@yale.edu **Holdings:** 135,000 books 650 journals **Subjects:** Environment, Forestry

3415   Stamford, Connecticut, US
University of Connecticut, Bartlett Arboretum
Library
151 Brookdale Road
Stamford, Connecticut 06903
WWW: bartlett.arboretum.uconn.edu

Founded: 1965 **Type:** Academic **Head:** Joseph A. Castronuovo *Phone:* +1(203) 322-6971 *Email:* baradm01@uconnvm.uconn.edu **Staff:** 1 Other **Holdings:** 2,000 books 30 journals **Language of Collection/Services:** English **Subjects:** Horticulture **Specializations:** Conifers, Dwarf Cultivars, Rhododendron **Loan:** Do not loan **Photocopy:** No

3416   Storrs, Connecticut, US
University of Connecticut
Homer Babbidge Library
Storrs, Connecticut 06269-1005
Location: Fairfield Road, Box 5RI **Phone:** +1(860) 486-2513 **Fax:** +1(860) 486-3593 **WWW:** www.uconn.edu **OPAC:** homerweb.lib.uconn.edu

Type: Academic **Head:** Paul Kobulnicky *Phone:* +1(860) 486-5099 *Email:* paul.kobulnicky@uconn.edu **Staff:** 36 Prof. 60 Other **Holdings:** 4,100,000 books 9,000 journals **Language of Collection/Services:** English / English **Subjects:** Agricultural Economics, Agricultural Engineering, Entomology, Food Sciences, Horticulture, Plants, Soil Science, Water Resources **Specializations:** Biotechnology,

Forestry **Databases Used:** Agricola **Loan:** Internationally **Service:** Internationally **Photocopy:** Yes

Delaware

3417 **Dover, Delaware, US**
Delaware Agricultural Museum and Village
(DAMV)
Library
866 North DuPont Highway
Dover, Delaware 19901
Phone: +1(302) 734-1618 **Fax:** +1(302) 734-0457 **Email:** damv@dol.net **WWW:** www.agriculturalmuseum.org

Founded: 1974 **Type:** Non-profit, Private **Head:** Jennifer C. Griffin *Phone:* +1(302) 734-1618 *Email:* damv@dol.net **Staff:** 1 Prof. .5 Other **Holdings:** 4,100 books 35 journals **Language of Collection/Services:** English **Subjects:** Agricultural Technologies, Agriculture (History) **Specializations:** Agriculture (Delaware - 19th Century), Agriculture (Delaware - 20th Century), Poultry (History - 19th Century), Poultry (History - 20th Century), Rural Society **Loan:** Educational institutions **Photocopy:** Yes

3418 **Dover, Delaware, US**
Delaware State University (DSU)
William C. Jason Library - Learning Center
1200 N. Dupont Highway
Dover, Delaware 19901-2277
Phone: +1(302) 739-3571 **Fax:** +1(302) 739-3533 **WWW:** www.dsc.edu **OPAC:** www.dsc.edu/library/dsccat.html

Former Name: Delaware State College **Type:** Academic **Head:** Gertrude Winston Jackson *Phone:* +1(302) 739-6175 *Email:* gjackson@dsc.edu **Staff:** 11 Prof. 14 Other **Holdings:** 180,000 books 1,269 journals **Language of Collection /Services:** English **Networks:** OCLC **Photocopy:** Yes

3419 **Newark, Delaware, US**
E.I. du Pont de Nemours & Company, Inc.,
Agricultural Products Department,
Stine-Haskell Research Center
Stine 135 Library
PO Box 30
Newark, Delaware 19714-0030
Location: Elkton Road **Phone:** +1(302) 366-5353 **Fax:** +1 (302) 366-5739

Founded: 1947 **Type:** Business **Head:** Debbie Carman *Phone:* +1(302) 366-5229 **Staff:** 1 Prof. 1 Other **Holdings:** 2,200 books 250 journals **Language of Collection/Services:** English **Subjects:** Crops, Entomology, Farming, Horticulture, Plant Pathology, Soil Science **Loan:** In country **Service:** Inhouse **Photocopy:** Yes

3420 **Newark, Delaware, US**
University of Delaware
Agriculture Library
Hugh M. Morris Library
Newark, Delaware 19717-5267
Location: 002 Townsend Hall **Phone:** +1(302) 831-2530 **Fax:** +1(302) 831-6322 **WWW:** www.lib.udel.edu **OPAC:** www.lib.udel.edu/databases/delcat.html

Founded: 1888 **Type:** Academic **Head:** Frederick B. Getze *Phone:* +1(302) 831-2530 *Email:* fritzg@udel.edu **Staff:** 1 Prof. 1 Other **Holdings:** 25,000 books 325 journals **Language of Collection/Services:** English **Subjects:** Agribusiness, Agricultural Economics, Agricultural Engineering, Animal Husbandry, Biotechnology, Crops, Entomology, Farming, Horticulture, Plant Pathology, Plants, Veterinary Medicine, Water Resources **Specializations:** Agricultural Entomology, Genetic Engineering, Insects, Ornamental Plants, Plant Diseases, Plant Physiology, Poultry Diseases, Soil Science **Networks:** OCLC **Databases Used:** Comprehensive **Loan:** Internationally **Service:** Inhouse **Photocopy:** Yes

3421 **Wilmington, Delaware, US**
E.I. du Pont de Nemours & Company, Inc.
(DUPONT)
Lavoisier Library
PO Box 80301
Wilmington, Delaware 19880-0301
Location: Route 141, Henry Clay **Phone:** +1(302) 695-3391 **Fax:** +1(302) 695-1350

Founded: 1973 **Type:** Research **Staff:** 10 Prof. 14 Other **Holdings:** 30,000 books 800 journals **Language of Collection/Services:** English / English **Subjects:** Agribusiness, Biotechnology, Plant Pathology **Databases Developed:** Proprietary database of company reports. Restricted access even within company. **Loan:** Inhouse **Service:** Inhouse **Photocopy:** Yes

District of Columbia

3422 **Washington, District of Columbia, US**
American Forests
Richard E. McArdle Memorial Library and
Forestry Information Center
PO Box 2000
Washington, District of Columbia 20013
Location: 910 17th Street, NW #600 **Phone:** +1(202) 955-4500 **Fax:** +1(202) 955-4588 **Email:** info@amfor.org **WWW:** www.americanforests.org

Former Name: American Forestry Association **Founded:** 1985 **Type:** Association **Head:** Deborah Gangloff *Email:* gangloff@amfor.org **Staff:** 1 Prof. **Holdings:** 6,000 books **Subjects:** Agricultural Development, Entomology, Fisheries, Forestry, Horticulture, Plant Pathology, Soil Science, Water Resources **Loan:** Do not loan **Photocopy:** Yes

3423 **Washington, District of Columbia, US**
American Seed Trade Association (ASTA)
Reference Collection and Conference Proceeding
Collection
601 13th Street, NW, Suite 570 South
Washington, District of Columbia 20005-3807
Phone: +1(202) 638-3128 **Fax:** +1(202) 638-3171 **WWW:** www.amseed.com

Founded: 1883 **Type:** Association **Head:** Bona Park *Email:* bpark@ix.netcom.com **Staff:** 5 Prof. 5 Other **Holdings:** 100 books 6 journals **Language of Collection/Services:** English **Subjects:** Seeds **Loan:** Do not loan **Photocopy:** Yes

3424　Washington, District of Columbia, US
District of Columbia Public Library
Martin Luther King Memorial Library,
　　Technology and Science Division
901 G Street NW
Washington, District of Columbia 20001-4599
Phone: +1(202) 727-1175 **Fax:** +1(202) 727-1129 **WWW:**
www.dclibrary.org **OPAC:** citycat.dclibrary.org/uhtbin/
cgisirsi/vcNEyd7ynh/1766005/60/69

Founded: 1907 **Type:** Government **Holdings:** 62,127 books
225 journals **Photocopy:** Yes

3425　Washington, District of Columbia, US
Environmental Protection Agency
Headquarters Information Resource Center
401 M Street SW (3404)
Room 2904
Washington, District of Columbia 20460
Phone: +1(202) 260-5922 **Fax:** +1(202) 260-5153 **Email:**
library-hq@epamail.epa.gov **WWW:** www.epa.gov/
natlibra/hqirc **OPAC:** www.epa.gov/natlibra/ols.htm

Founded: 1971 **Type:** Government **Head:** Ted Sherman
Phone: +1(202) 260-6947 *Email:* sherman.ted@epa.gov
Staff: 15 Prof. 4 Other **Holdings:** 400,000 books 200 jour-
nals **Language of Collection/Services:** English **Subjects:**
Environment **Networks:** OCLC **Databases Used:** Agricola
Loan: Inhouse **Service:** Internationally **Photocopy:** Yes

3426　Washington, District of Columbia, US
International Food Policy Research Institute
　　(IFPRI)
Library
2033 K Street NW
Washington, District of Columbia 20006
Phone: +1(202) 862-5614 **Fax:** +1(202) 467-4439 **Email:**
t.klosky@cgiar.org **WWW:** www.ifpri.org

Founded: 1977 **Type:** International **Head:** Patricia Klosky
Phone: +1(202) 862-5614 *Email:* t.klosky@cgiar.org **Staff:**
2 Prof. .5 Other **Holdings:** 7,500 books 160 journals **Lan-
guage of Collection/Services:** English / English **Subjects:**
Agricultural Development, Agricultural Economics, Water
Resources **Specializations:** Environment, Food Policy, Mar-
kets, International Trade **Networks:** OCLC **Databases
Used:** AGECON CD; Agricola; Econlit **Loan:** In country
Service: Internationally **Photocopy:** Yes

3427　Washington, District of Columbia, US
National Grange
Library
1616 H Street NW
Washington, District of Columbia 20006-4999
Phone: +1(888) 447-2643 **Fax:** +1(202) 347-1091 **WWW:**
www.nationalgrange.org

Type: Non-profit **Head:** Barbara Jones *Phone:* +1(202)
628-3507 **Language of Collection/Services:** English **Subjects:** The Grange (Organization), Horticulture **Specializations:** Old horticulture reference books of first national
master **Loan:** Inhouse **Service:** Inhouse **Photocopy:** No

3428　Washington, District of Columbia, US
Public Lands Council (PLC)
Library
1301 Pennsylvania Avenue NW, Suite 300
Washington, District of Columbia 20004
Fax: +1(202) 638-0607 **WWW:** www.beef.org

Founded: 1968 **Type:** Non-profit **Head:** Lance Kotschwar
Phone: +1(202) 347-5355 *Email:* lkotschwar@beef.org
Staff: 3 Prof. **Holdings:** 300 books 20 journals **Language of
Collection/Services:** English / English **Subjects:** Animal
Husbandry, Livestock Farming **Specializations:** Public Do-
main **Loan:** Inhouse **Photocopy:** Yes

3429　Washington, District of Columbia, US
Smithsonian Institution Libraries (SIL)
National Museum of Natural History Branch
10th & Constitution Avenue, Room 51
Washington, District of Columbia 20560-0154
Phone: +1(202) 357-1496 **Fax:** +1(202) 357-1896 **Email:**
libmail@sil.si.edu **WWW:** www.sil.si.edu **OPAC:** www.
siris.si.edu **Ariel IP:** 160.111.88.63

Founded: 1968 **Type:** Government **Head:** Ann Juneau
Phone: +1(202) 357-1496 **Staff:** 5 Prof. 4 Other **Holdings:**
220,000 books 1,000 journals **Language of Collection/Ser-
vices:** English **Subjects:** Entomology **Specializations:**
Anatomy, Ecology, Evolution, Invertebrates, Taxonomy,
Vertebrates **Networks:** OCLC **Databases Used:** Agricola;
Biosis; Dissertation Abstracts **Loan:** Internationally **Ser-
vice:** Internationally **Photocopy:** Yes

3430　Washington, District of Columbia, US
Sugar Association Inc.
Library
1101 15th Street NW
Suite 600
Washington, District of Columbia 20005
Phone: +1(202) 785-1122 **Fax:** +1(202) 785-5019 **WWW:**
www.sugar.org

Founded: 1943 **Type:** Business **Holdings:** 2,500 books
Subjects: Sugar

3431　Washington, District of Columbia, US
United States Agency for International
　　Development (USAID)
Information Center
Ronald Reagan Building
Washington, District of Columbia 20523-0016
Phone: +1(202) 712-4810 **Fax:** +1(202) 216-3524 **Email:**
pinquiries@usaid.gov **WWW:** www.info.usaid.gov

Former Name: A.I.D. Library, Development Information
Center **Founded:** 1967 **Type:** Government **Staff:** 4 Prof. 8
Other **Holdings:** 9,000 books 425 journals **Language of
Collection/Services:** English **Subjects:** Agricultural Development **Networks:** OCLC **Databases Developed:** DIS - Development Information System - AID project descriptions
and bibliographic citations to AID-generated or AID-funded
publications **Databases Used:** LEXIS-NEXIS; Agricola
Loan: In country **Service:** Internationally **Photocopy:** Yes

3432 Washington, District of Columbia, US
United States Department of Agriculture,
    Agricultural Research Service, National
    Agricultural Library (USDA, ARS, NAL)
District of Columbia Reference Center (DCRC)
Room 1052 South
14th and Independence Avenue SW
Washington, District of Columbia 20250-7201
Location: South Agriculture Building **Phone:** +1(202)
720-3200 **Fax:** +1(202) 720-0342 **Email:** dcrc@nal.usda.
gov **WWW:** www.nal.usda.gov

Type: Government **Staff:** 4 Prof. 1 Other **Holdings:** 10,000
books 200 journals **Language of Collection/Services:** English/English **Databases Used:** ABI/Inform; Agricola; Agris;
FSTA; Medline **Loan:** Do not loan **Service:** Internationally
Photocopy: Yes

3433 Washington, District of Columbia, US
United States Department of the Interior
Library
MS 1151
1849 C Street, NW
Washington, District of Columbia 20240
Phone: +1(202) 208-5815 **Fax:** +1(202) 208-6773 **Email:**
library@nbc.gov **WWW:** www.doi.gov/indexj.html
OPAC: library.doi.gov/catalog.html

Founded: 1949 **Type:** Government **Holdings:** 1,058,000
books

3434 Washington, District of Columbia, US
United States Food and Drug Administration,
    Center for Food Safety and Applied Nutrition
    (US FDA, CFSAN)
Library
200 C Street SW
Room 3321 hff-37
Washington, District of Columbia 20204
WWW: vm.cfsan.fda.gov/list.html

Type: Government **Head:** Michele L. Chatfield *Phone:*
+1(202) 205-4349 *Email:* mrc@cfsan.fda.gov **Staff:** 5 Prof.
3 Other **Holdings:** 31,500 books **Subjects:** Biotechnology,
Food Sciences

3435 Washington, District of Columbia, US
United States National Arboretum
National Arboretum Library
3501 New York Avenue NE
Washington, District of Columbia 20002
Phone: +1(202) 245-4534 **Fax:** +1(202) 245-4579 **WWW:**
www.ars-grin.gov/na/index.html

Type: Government **Staff:** 2 Prof. **Holdings:** 7,500 books
200 journals **Language of Collection/Services:** English /
English **Subjects:** Botany, Cytogenetics, Horticulture, Plant
Breeding, Plant Pathology, Taxonomy **Specializations:** Ikebana Rare Book Collection **Databases Used:** Agricola **Service:** Open to public by appointment **Photocopy:** Yes

3436 Washington, District of Columbia, US
World Bank, International Bank for
    Reconstruction and Development (IBRD)

Sectoral Library
1818 H Street NW
MC-C3-220
Washington, District of Columbia 20433
Location: 801 19th Street NW, Room N-145 **Phone:** +1
(202) 473-8670 **Fax:** +1(202) 522-1160 **WWW:** www.
worldbank.org **OPAC:** jolis.worldbankimflib.org

Founded: 1984 **Type:** International **Head:** Pamela Tripp-Melby *Phone:* +1(202) 473-6646 **Staff:** 9 Prof. 5 Other
Holdings: 58,000 books 650 journals **Language of Collection/Services:** English/English **Subjects:** Agribusiness, Agriculture (Tropics), Agricultural Development, Agricultural
Economics, Agricultural Engineering, Animal Husbandry,
Biotechnology, Education/Extension, Entomology, Crops,
Farming, Fisheries, Food Sciences, Forestry, Horticulture,
Plant Pathology, Soil Science, Veterinary Medicine, Water
Resources **Networks:** OCLC **Databases Developed:** JOLIS
- catalog of the Joint Bank-Fund Library Network **Databases
Used:** Comprehensive **Loan:** In country **Service:** Inhouse
Photocopy: Yes

3437 Washington, District of Columbia, US
World Resources Institute (WRI)
Library/Information Center
10 G Street, NE, Suite 800
Washington, District of Columbia 20002
Phone: +1(202) 729-7600 **Fax:** +1(202) 729-7610 **Email:**
front@wri.org **WWW:** www.wri.org

Founded: 1982 **Type:** Research **Head:** *Phone:* +1(202)
729-7601 *Email:* beckym@wri.org **Staff:** 1 Prof. 1.3 Other
Holdings: 10,000 books 450 journals **Language of Collection/Services:** English **Subjects:** Agriculture (Tropics),
Agricultural Development, Agricultural Economics, Biotechnology, Climate, Environment, Fisheries, Forestry, Soil
Science, Water Resources **Specializations:** Environment
(Gray Literature), Natural Resources (Gray Literature)
Loan: In country **Service:** Internationally **Photocopy:** Yes

3438 Washington, District of Columbia, US
World Wildlife Fund–United States (WWF)
Library
1250 24th Street NW
Washington, District of Columbia 20037
Fax: +1(202) 293-9211 **WWW:** www.wwf.org

Founded: 1949 **Type:** Private **Staff:** 2 Prof. 1 Other **Holdings:** 10,000 books 300 journals **Language of Collection/
Services:** English, Spanish **Subjects:** Agricultural Development, Soil Science, Water Resources **Specializations:** Agricultural Policy, Conservation **Networks:** OCLC **Loan:** In
country **Service:** In country **Photocopy:** Yes

Florida

3439 Belle Glade, Florida, US
University of Florida, Institute of Food and
    Agricultural Sciences (UF, IFAS)
Everglades Research and Education Center, Belle
    Glade (EREC/BG)
PO Box 8003
Belle Glade, Florida 33430

Location: 3200 E. Palm Beach Road **Fax:** +1(561) 996-0339 **WWW:** EREC.ifas.ufl.edu

Former Name: Agricultural Research and Education Center (AREC) **Type:** Academic **Head:** Mrs. Kathleen Krawchuk *Phone:* +1(561) 996-3062 est 159 *Email:* klkr@gnv.ifas.ufl.edu **Staff:** 1 Prof. **Holdings:** 8,000 books 100 journals **Language of Collection/Services:** English / English **Subjects:** Entomology, Horticulture, Water Resources, Plant Pathology **Specializations:** Rice, Sugarcane **Networks:** LUIS **Databases Used:** Comprehensive **Loan:** Inhouse **Service:** Inhouse **Photocopy:** Yes

3440　Bradenton, Florida, US
　　　University of Florida, Institute of Food and
　　　　　Agricultural Sciences (UF, IFAS)
　　　Gulf Coast Research and Education Center
　　　　　(GCREC)
　　　5007 60th Street East
　　　Bradenton, Florida 34203
Fax: +1(941) 751-6739 **WWW:** gcrec.ifas.ufl.edu

Founded: 1965 **Type:** Academic **Head:** Tracey Revels *Phone:* +1(941) 751-7636 **Staff:** 2 Other **Holdings:** 13 journals **Language of Collection/Services:** English **Subjects:** Agricultural Economics, Agricultural Engineering, Crops, Entomology, Horticulture, Plant Pathology, Soil Science, Water Resources **Loan:** Do not loan **Service:** Inhouse **Photocopy:** No

3441　Brooksville, Florida, US
　　　Southwest Florida Water Management District
　　　Library
　　　2379 Broad Street
　　　Brooksville, Florida 34609-6899
Phone: +1(352) 756-7211 ext 4051 **Fax:** +1(352) 754-6884 **Email:** rick.mccleery@swfwmd.state.fl.us **WWW:** www.swfwmd.state.fl.us

Type: Government **Staff:** 1 Prof. 1 Other **Holdings:** 5,000 books 100 journals **Subjects:** Fisheries, Irrigation, Water Resources **Loan:** Inhouse **Service:** Open to public **Photocopy:** Yes

3442　Dania Beach, Florida, US
　　　International Game Fish Association (IGFA)
　　　International Library of Fishes (ILF)
　　　300 Gulf Stream Way
　　　Dania Beach, Florida 33004
Phone: +1(954) 927-2628 **Fax:** +1(954) 924-4299 **WWW:** www.igfa.org

Founded: 1939 **Type:** Association **Staff:** 2 Prof. **Holdings:** 9,000 books 1,000 journals **Language of Collection/Services:** English **Subjects:** Fisheries **Specializations:** Angling (Recreational Fishing), Fishing **Loan:** Inhouse **Photocopy:** Yes

3443　Fort Lauderdale, Florida, US
　　　University of Florida, Institute of Food and
　　　　　Agricultural Sciences, Agricultural Research
　　　　　and Education Center, Fort Lauderdale (UF,
　　　　　IFAS, AREC)
　　　Library

　　　3205 College Avenue
　　　Fort Lauderdale, Florida 33314
Phone: +1(954) 475-8990 **Fax:** +1(954) 475-4125 **Email:** jslane@ufl.edu **WWW:** www.ftld.ufl.edu

Type: Academic **Staff:** 1 Other **Holdings:** 1,560 books **Language of Collection/Services:** English **Loan:** Inhouse **Photocopy:** No

3444　Fort Pierce, Florida, US
　　　United States Department of Agriculture,
　　　　　Agricultural Research Service, Horticultural
　　　　　Research Laboratory (USDA, ARS)
　　　Library
　　　2001 South Rock Road
　　　Fort Pierce, Florida 34945
Phone: +1(561) 462-5800 **WWW:** www.ars-grin.gov/ars/SoAtlantic/fp

Founded: 1970 **Type:** Government **Staff:** 1 Prof. **Holdings:** 2,500 books **Language of Collection/Services:** English/English **Subjects:** Entomology, Horticulture, Plant Pathology **Loan:** Inhouse **Service:** Inhouse **Photocopy:** No

3445　Gainesville, Florida, US
　　　Florida Department of Agriculture and Consumer
　　　　　Services, Division of Plant Industry (FDACS,
　　　　　DPI)
　　　Library
　　　PO Box 147000
　　　Gainesville, Florida 32608-1268
Location: 1911 SW 34th Street **Phone:** +1(352) 372-3505 **Fax:** +1(352) 955-2301 **Email:** dpilib@doacs.state.fl.us **WWW:** doacs.state.fl.us

Former Name: State Plant Board of Florida **Founded:** 1936 **Type:** Government **Head:** Beverly Pope *Phone:* +1(352) 372-3505 *Email:* popeb@doacs.state.fl.us **Staff:** 1 Prof. 1 Other **Holdings:** 14,500 books 350 journals **Language of Collection/Services:** English **Subjects:** Plant Pathology, Entomology, Nematology **Specializations:** Classification, Identification, Plant Protection, Taxonomy **Databases Used:** Agricola **Loan:** Internationally **Service:** Internationally **Photocopy:** Yes

3446　Gainesville, Florida, US
　　　University of Florida (UF)
　　　Marston Science Library (MSL)
　　　PO Box 117011
　　　Gainesville, Florida 32611-2020
Location: Newell Drive **Phone:** +1(352) 392-2836 **Fax:** +1(352) 392-4787 **Email:** battiste@mail.uflib.ufl.edu **WWW:** www.ufl.edu **OPAC:** www.uflib.ufl.edu **Ariel IP:** 128.227.238.20

Former Name: Central Science Library (CSL) **Founded:** 1987 **Type:** Academic **Head:** Carol Drum *Phone:* +1(352) 335-8501 *Email:* cdrum@mail.uflib.ufl.edu **Staff:** 10 Prof. 15 Other **Holdings:** 700,000 books 5,000 journals **Language of Collection/Services:** English / English **Subjects:** Comprehensive **Specializations:** Entomology **Networks:** OCLC; RLIN **Databases Used:** Comprehensive **Loan:** Internationally **Service:** Internationally **Photocopy:** Yes

3447   Gainesville, Florida, US
University of Florida, Center for Aquatic and
    Invasive Plants
Aquatic Plant Information Retrieval System
    (APIRS)
7922 NW 71st Street
Gainesville, Florida 32653-3071
Fax: +1(352) 392-3462 **WWW:** aquat1.ifas.ufl.edu
OPAC: aquat1.ifas.ufl.edu/database.html

Former Name: Aquatic Weed Program **Founded:** 1979
Type: Academic **Head:** Karen Brown *Phone:* +1(352) 392-
1799 *Email:* kpb@gnv.ifas.ufl.edu **Staff:** 3 Prof. 2 Other
Holdings: 50,000 books **Language of Collection/Services:**
English/English **Subjects:** Aquatic Plants, Water Resources,
Wetlands **Specializations:** Aquatic Weeds, Weed Control
Databases Developed: APIRS - Largest computerized bib-
liographic database devoted to aquatic plants in the world;
available via Internet at aquat1.ifas.ufl.edu **Databases Used:**
APIRS **Loan:** Inhouse **Service:** Internationally **Photocopy:**
Yes

3448   Gulf Breeze, Florida, US
Environmental Protection Agency, Gulf Ecology
    Division (EPA, GED)
Library
1 Sabine Island Drive
Gulf Breeze, Florida 32561-5299
Phone: +1(850) 934-9218 **Fax:** +1(850) 934-9201 **Email:**
pinnell.liz@epamail.epa.gov **WWW:** www.epa.gov/ged,
www.epa.gov/ged/bld42.htm **OPAC:** www.epa.gov/
natlibra/ols.htm

Founded: 1967 **Type:** Government **Head:** Elizabeth Pinnell
Phone: +1(850) 934-9218 *Email:* pinnell.liz@epamail.epa.
gov **Staff:** 1 Prof. 2 Other **Holdings:** 7,000 books 200 jour-
nals **Language of Collection/Services:** English / English
Subjects: Fisheries, Water Resources **Networks:** EPA OLS;
OCLC **Databases Developed:** GED Contributions Database
- citations and abstracts of laboratory research publications
Databases Used: Comprehensive **Loan:** Internationally
Service: Internationally **Photocopy:** Yes

3449   Homestead, Florida, US
University of Florida, Institute of Food and
    Agricultural Sciences, Tropical Research and
    Education Center, Homestead (IFAS, TREC)
Library
18905 Southwest 280th Street
Homestead, Florida 33031
Phone: +1(305) 246-6340 **Fax:** +1(305) 246-7003 **WWW:**
www.ifas.ufl.edu/~trecweb

Type: Academic **Holdings:** 3,950 books

3450   Lake Alfred, Florida, US
University of Florida, Institute of Food and
    Agricultural Sciences, Citrus Research and
    Education Center (UF, IFAS, CREC)
Library
700 Experiment Station Road
Lake Alfred, Florida 33850

Phone: +1(863) 956-1151 **Fax:** +1(863) 956-4631 **WWW:**
tangelo.lal.ufl.edu **OPAC:** tangelo.lal.ufl.edu/library/
library.htm

Former Name: Agricultural Research and Education Center
Founded: 1947 **Type:** Academic **Head:** Pamela K. Russ
Phone: +1(863) 956-4311 wait for a dial tone and enter the
extension number 226 *Email:* pkr@icon.lal.ufl.edu **Staff:** 1
Prof. **Holdings:** 13,500 books 80 journals **Language of Col-
lection/Services:** English **Subjects:** Agriculture (Tropics),
Agribusiness, Agricultural Economics, Agricultural Engi-
neering, Biotechnology, Entomology, Food Sciences, Horti-
culture, Plant Pathology, Soil Science **Specializations:**
Citrus **Databases Used:** Agricola; CABCD **Loan:** Inhouse
Photocopy: Yes

3451   Lake Placid, Florida, US
Archbold Biological Station (ABS)
Library
Box 2057
Lake Placid, Florida 33862
Location: 123 Main Drive, Venus, FL 33960 **Phone:** +1
(863) 465-2571 **Fax:** +1(863) 699-1927 **WWW:** www.
archbold-station.org

Founded: 1941 **Type:** Research **Head:** Fred E. Lohrer
Email: flohrer@archbold-station.org **Staff:** 1 Prof. **Holdings:** 7,000 books 250 journals **Language of Collection/
Services:** English / English **Subjects:** Agroecology, Fisheries, Forestry **Specializations:** Conservation Biology, Ecology, Entomology, Herpetology, Ichthyology, Mammalogy,
Ornithology, Plant Ecology **Databases Developed:** Bibliography of the Archbold Biological Station - 1100 items online
Databases Used: Current Contents **Loan:** In country **Service:** Inhouse **Photocopy:** Yes

3452   Miami, Florida, US
Fairchild Tropical Garden (FTG)
Montgomery Library
11935 Old Cutler Road
Miami, Florida 33156-4299
Phone: +1(305) 667-1651 **Fax:** +1(305) 661-8953 **WWW:**
www.ftg.org

Founded: 1940 **Type:** Private **Head:** Dr. Scott Zona *Phone:*
+1(305) 665-2844 *Email:* zonas@fiu.edu **Holdings:** 8,000
books 100 journals **Language of Collection/Services:** English / English **Subjects:** Botany, Horticulture, Plants (Tropics) **Loan:** Inhouse **Service:** Inhouse **Photocopy:** No

3453   Miami, Florida, US
United States National Marine Fisheries Service,
    Southeast Fisheries Center, Miami Laboratory
Library
75 Virginia Beach Drive
Miami, Florida 33149
Phone: +1(305) 361-5761 **WWW:** www.sefsc.noaa.gov
OPAC: www.aoml.noaa.gov/general/lib/sefcw.html **Ariel
IP:** 199.242.233.33

Founded: 1965 **Type:** Government **Head:** Harriet Corvino,
Library Technician *Email:* harriet.crvino@noaa.gov *Phone:*
+1(305) 361-4229 **Holdings:** 3,200 books 300 journals **Subjects:** Fisheries

3454   Miami, Florida, US
University of Miami, Dorothy and Lewis
        Rosenstiel School of Marine and Atmospheric
        Sciences (RSMAS)
Library
4600 Rickenbacker Causeway
Miami, Florida 33149-1098
Phone: +1(305) 361-4021 **Fax:** +1(305) 361-9306 **WWW:**
www.rsmas.miami.edu **OPAC:** ibisweb.miami.edu **Ariel
IP:** 129.171.101.139

Founded: 1941 **Type:** Academic **Head:** Kay K. Hale
Phone: +1(305) 361-4021 *Email:* khale@rsmas.miami.edu
Staff: 2 Prof. 3 Other **Holdings:** 68,000 books 600 journals
Language of Collection/Services: English / English **Sub-
jects:** Aquaculture, Atmospheric Sciences, Fisheries, Ma-
rine Sciences **Specializations:** Oceanography **Networks:**
OCLC **Databases Developed:** Biscayne Bay Bibliography -
WWW access forthcoming **Databases Used:** Comprehen-
sive **Loan:** Internationally **Service:** Inhouse **Photocopy:**
Yes

3455   Panama City, Florida, US
United States National Marine Fisheries Service,
        Southeast Fisheries Center, Panama City
        Laboratory
Library
3500 Delwood Beach Road
Panama City, Florida 32408
Fax: +1(850) 235-3559 **WWW:** www.sefsc.noaa.gov
OPAC: www.aoml.noaa.gov/general/lib/sefcw.html

Founded: 1972 **Type:** Government **Head:** Rosalie Shaffer
Phone: +1(850) 234-6541 ext 227 *Email:* rosalie.shaffer@
noaa.gov **Staff:** 1 Prof. **Holdings:** 29,085 books 400 journals
Language of Collection/Services: English / English **Subjects:** Fisheries **Networks:** OCLC **Loan:** In country **Service:** Internationally **Photocopy:** Yes

3456   St. Petersburg, Florida, US
Florida Fish and Wildlife Conservation
        Commission, Florida Marine Research
        Institute (FMRI)
Library
100 Eighth Avenue SE
St. Petersburg, Florida 33701-5095
Phone: +1(727) 896-8626 **Fax:** +1(727) 823-0166 **Email:**
info@fmri.usf.edu **WWW:** www.fmri.usf.edu

Founded: 1955 **Type:** Government **Staff:** 1 Prof. 4 Other
Holdings: 48,000 books 150 journals **Language of Collec-
tion/Services:** English / English **Subjects:** Aquaculture,
Fisheries **Loan:** Marine related libraries **Service:** Inhouse
Photocopy: Yes

3457   Tallahassee, Florida, US
Florida A&M University
        Samuel H. Coleman Memorial Library
        Tallahassee, Florida 32307-4700
Fax: +1(850) 561-2293 **WWW:** www.famu.edu **OPAC:**
www.famu2.famu.edu/acad/coleman/index.html

Type: Academic **Head:** Dr. Lauren Sapp *Phone:* +1(850)
599-3370 *Email:* lsapp@famu.edu

3458   Tallahassee, Florida, US
Florida Geological Survey
Research Library
903 West Tennessee Street
Tallahassee, Florida 32304-7700
Fax: +1(850) 488-8086 **WWW:** www.dep.state.fl.us/geo

Former Name: Florida Bureau of Geology **Type:** Government **Head:** Deborah Mekeel *Email:* mekeel_d@dep.state.
fl.us *Phone:* +1(850) 488-9380 **Staff:** 1 Prof. .5 Other **Holdings:** 40,000 books 50 journals **Language of Collection/
Services:** English / English **Subjects:** Geology, Geology
(Florida), Water Resources **Loan:** Inhouse **Photocopy:** Yes

3459   Tallahassee, Florida, US
Florida State University
Paul A.M. Dirac Science Library
Tallahassee, Florida 32306-4140
Phone: +1(850) 644-5334 **Fax:** +1(850) 644-0025 **WWW:**
www.fsu.edu **OPAC:** www.fcla.edu

Founded: 1988 **Type:** Academic **Head:** Sharon W.
Schwerzel *Phone:* +1(850) 644-5334 *Email:* sschwerz@
mailer.fsu.edu **Staff:** 3 Prof. 14 Other **Holdings:** 550,000
books 3,200 journals **Language of Collection/Services:**
English **Subjects:** Biology, Computer Science, Environmental Sciences, Food Sciences, Geology, Mathematics, Meteorology, Nursing, Nutrition, Oceanography **Specializations:**
Physical Sciences **Networks:** OCLC; RLG **Databases
Used:** Comprehensive **Loan:** Inhouse **Service:** FSU affili-
ates, local community **Photocopy:** Yes

3460   Vero Beach, Florida, US
University of Florida, Institute of Food and
        Agricultural Sciences, Florida Medical
        Entomology Laboratory (UF, IFAS, FMEL)
Library
200 9th Street SE
Vero Beach, Florida 32960
WWW: www.ifas.ufl.edu/~VEROWEB

Type: Research **Head:** Lena C. Zimmerman *Phone:* +1(561)
778-7200 *Email:* caz@icon.vero.ufl.edu **Staff:** 1 Other
Holdings: 5,000 books 130 journals **Language of Collec-
tion/Services:** English / English **Subjects:** Education/Exten-
sion **Specializations:** Culicidae, Entomology, Psychodidae
Loan: Do not loan **Service:** Inhouse **Photocopy:** No

3461   West Palm Beach, Florida, US
American Orchid Society
Library
6000 South Olive Avenue
West Palm Beach, Florida 33405
Fax: +1(407) 585-0654 **WWW:** orchidweb.org/mainpage.
html

Founded: 1921 **Type:** Association **Head:** Ned Nash *Phone:*
+1(407) 585-8666 *Email:* theaos.compuserve.com **Staff:** 1
Prof. 19 Other **Holdings:** 900 books 20 journals **Language
of Collection/Services:** English / English **Subjects:** Horticulture, Orchidaceae, Ornamental Orchids **Databases Developed:** Inventory Database - Accessible by title, author,
several subjects **Loan:** Do not loan **Service:** Inhouse/mem-
bership **Photocopy:** Yes

Georgia

3462 Athens, Georgia, US
University of Georgia (UGA)
Science Library
Graduate Studies Building
Athens, Georgia 30602-7412

Phone: +1(706) 542-0698 **Fax:** +1(706) 542-6523, 542-7907 **Email:** sciref@arches.uga.edu **WWW:** www.uga.edu **OPAC:** www.libs.uga.edu

Founded: 1967 **Type:** Academic **Head:** Lucy M. Rowland *Phone:* +1(706) 542-6643 *Email:* lrowland@uga.arches.edu **Staff:** 7 Prof. 20 Other **Holdings:** 750,000 books 4,200 journals **Language of Collection/Services:** English / English **Subjects:** Agriculture (Tropics), Agribusiness, Agricultural Development, Agricultural Economics, Agricultural Engineering, Animal Husbandry, Biotechnology, Entomology, Crops, Education/Extension, Farming, Fisheries, Food Sciences, Forestry, Horticulture, Plant Pathology, Soil Science, Veterinary Medicine, Water Resources **Networks:** OCLC **Databases Used:** Comprehensive **Loan:** Internationally **Photocopy:** Yes

3463 Atlanta, Georgia, US
Coca-Cola Company
Technical Information Services (TIS)
PO Drawer 1734
Atlanta, Georgia 30301

Location: One Coca-Cola Plaza **Phone:** +1(404) 676-2008 **Fax:** +1(404) 515-2572 **WWW:** www.coke.com/alternate.html

Founded: 1967 **Type:** Business **Head:** Kenneth Koubek *Phone:* +1(404) 676-2183 *Email:* kkoubek@na.ko.com **Staff:** 2 Prof. 1 Other **Holdings:** 33,700 books 350 journals **Language of Collection/Services:** English / English **Subjects:** Food Sciences **Specializations:** Beverages, Chemistry, Fruit Juices, Nutrition, Soft Drinks **Networks:** OCLC **Databases Used:** Comprehensive **Loan:** Inhouse **Service:** Within company internationally **Photocopy:** Yes

3464 Atlanta, Georgia, US
Environmental Protection Agency (EPA)
Region IV Library
Sam Nunn Atlanta Federal Center Tower - 9th floor
61 Forsyth Street, SW
Atlanta, Georgia 30303-8909

Phone: +1(404) 562-8190 **Fax:** +1(404) 562-8114 **Email:** library-reg4@epa.gov **WWW:** www.epa.gov **OPAC:** www.epa.gov/natlibra/ols.htm

Founded: 1973 **Type:** Government **Staff:** 3 Prof. 3 Other **Holdings:** 200,000 books 60 journals **Language of Collection/Services:** English / English **Subjects:** Pesticides **Specializations:** Hazardous Wastes, Maps, Pollution Control, Solid Wastes, Environmental Protection Agency (USA) Documents, Geological Survey (USA) Documents, Soil Surveys (USA) **Loan:** Internationally **Service:** Inhouse **Photocopy:** Yes

3465 Atlanta, Georgia, US
Technical Association of the Pulp and Paper Industry (TAPPI)
James d'A. Clark Library
PO Box 105113
Atlanta, Georgia 30348-5113

Phone: +1(800) 332-8686 **WWW:** www.tappi.org

Type: Association **Staff:** 2 Prof. .5 Other **Holdings:** 4,500 books 180 journals **Language of Collection/Services:** English / English **Subjects:** Forestry **Specializations:** Pulp and Paper Industry **Databases Developed:** Pulp and Paper Research **Loan:** Members only **Service:** Internationally **Photocopy:** Yes

3466 Fort Valley, Georgia, US
American Camellia Society
Library
100 Massee Lane
Fort Valley, Georgia 31030

Phone: +1(912) 967-2722 **Fax:** +1(912) 967-2083 **Email:** acs@alltel.net, acs@mail.peach.public.lib.ga.us **WWW:** camellias-acs.com

Type: Association **Head:** Ann Blair Brown *Phone:* +1(912) 967-2358 **Staff:** 2 Prof. 4 Other **Holdings:** 3,000 books 10 journals **Language of Collection/Services:** English / English **Subjects:** Horticulture **Specializations:** Camellia **Loan:** Inhouse **Service:** Inhouse **Photocopy:** Yes

3467 Fort Valley, Georgia, US
Fort Valley State University (FVSU)
Hunt Memorial Learning Resources Center
1005 State University Drive
Fort Valley, Georgia 31030

Phone: +1(912) 825-6761 **Fax:** +1(912) 825-6916 **WWW:** www.fvsu.edu

Former Name: State Teachers and Agriculture College, Fort Valley High and Industrial School **Founded:** 1895 **Type:** Academic **Head:** Carole R. Taylor *Phone:* +1(912) 825-6342/3 *Email:* taylorc@mail.fvsu.edu **Staff:** 5 Prof. 9 Other **Holdings:** 191,806 books 805 journals **Language of Collection/Services:** English / English **Subjects:** Agribusiness, Agricultural Economics, Agricultural Engineering, Animal Husbandry, Horticulture, Plants, Soil Science, Veterinary Science **Networks:** GALILEO; OCLC **Loan:** In country **Service:** Inhouse **Photocopy:** Yes

3468 Griffin, Georgia, US
University of Georgia, Georgia Experiment Station
Library
Griffin, Georgia 30228-1797

Phone: +1(770) 228-7238 **Fax:** +1(770) 229-3213 **Email:** librgrf@gaes.griffin.peachnet.edu **WWW:** www.griffin.peachnet.edu/homepage.html **OPAC:** www.libs.uga.edu

Founded: 1889 **Type:** Academic **Staff:** 1 Prof. 1 Other **Holdings:** 40,000 books 250 journals **Subjects:** Agricultural Economics, Agricultural Engineering, Crops, Entomology, Horticulture, Plant Pathology, Soil Science **Loan:** In country **Photocopy:** Yes

3469   Savannah, Georgia, US
Skidaway Institute of Oceanography
Library
10 Ocean Science Circle
Savannah, Georgia 31411
Phone: +1(912) 598-2453 **Fax:** +1(912) 598-2310 **Email:** library@skio.peachnet.edu **WWW:** www.galileo.peachnet. edu **OPAC:** www.skio.peachnet.edu/index.html

Founded: 1970 **Type:** Academic **Head:** Elizabeth B. Cooksey *Phone:* +1(912) 598-2474 **Staff:** 1 Prof. **Holdings:** 4,000 books 110 journals **Language of Collection/Services:** English **Subjects:** Fisheries, Water Resources **Loan:** In country and Canada **Service:** In country and Canada **Photocopy:** Yes

3470   Tifton, Georgia, US
Abraham Baldwin Agricultural College (ABAC)
Baldwin Library
ABAC Station
Tifton, Georgia 31793-4401
Location: Moore Highway **Fax:** +1(912) 386-7471
WWW: stallion.abac.peachnet.edu **OPAC:** stallion.abac. peachnet.edu/library/database.htm

Founded: 1933 **Type:** Academic **Head:** Brenda J. Sellers *Phone:* +1(912) 386-3934 *Email:* bsellers@c.abac.peachnet. edu **Staff:** 3 Prof. 7 Other **Holdings:** 2,500 books 69 journals **Subjects:** Forestry, Horticulture, Veterinary Science, Wildlife Management **Loan:** In country **Photocopy:** Yes

3471   Tifton, Georgia, US
University of Georgia, College of Agricultural and
        Environmental Sciences Tifton Campus,
        Coastal Plain Experiment Station
Library
PO Box 748
Tifton, Georgia 31793
Location: Moore Highway **Phone:** +1(912) 386-3447 **Fax:** +1(912) 386-7005 **Email:** librtif@tifton.cpes.peachnet.edu **WWW:** sacs.cpes.peachnet.edu

Founded: 1924 **Type:** Academic **Head:** Duncan McClusky *Email:* mcclusky@tifton.cpes.peachnet.edu *Phone:* +1(912) 386-3833 **Staff:** 1 Prof. 1 Other **Holdings:** 16,800 books 200 journals **Language of Collection/Services:** English/English **Subjects:** Agriculture (Tropics), Agricultural Engineering, Animal Husbandry, Biotechnology, Crops, Entomology, Farming, Fisheries, Horticulture, Plant Pathology, Soil Science, Water Resources **Databases Developed:** Peanut Library Database - 30,000+ records dealing with all aspects of peanuts, e.g., production, processing, marketing. **Databases Used:** Agricola; CABCD **Loan:** Inhouse **Service:** Inhouse **Photocopy:** Yes

Hawaii

3472   Aiea, Hawaii, US
Hawaii Agriculture Research Center (HARC)
Library
99-193 Aiea Heights Drive #300
Aiea, Hawaii 96701-3911

Phone: +1(808) 486-5370 **Fax:** +1(808) 486-5020 **Email:** amarsteller@harc-hspa.com **WWW:** www.hawaiiag.org/ harc

Former Name: Hawaiian Sugar Planters' Association (HSPA) **Founded:** 1907 **Type:** Association **Head:** Ann L. Marsteller *Phone:* +1(808) 486-5370 *Email:* amarsteller@ harc-hspa.com **Staff:** 1 Prof. **Holdings:** 80,000 books 400 journals **Language of Collection/Services:** English/English **Subjects:** Agriculture (Tropics), Plant Pathology, Plant Physiology, Sugarcane **Databases Used:** Comprehensive **Loan:** Do not loan **Service:** Inhouse **Photocopy:** Yes

3473   Honolulu, Hawaii, US
Bernice P. Bishop Museum (BPBM)
Library
1525 Bernice Street
Honolulu, Hawaii 96817-2704
Phone: +1(808) 848-4148 **Fax:** +1(808) 847-8241 **Email:** library@bishop.bishop.hawaii.org **WWW:** www.bishop. hawaii.org **OPAC:** telnet://uhcarl.lib.hawaii.edu

Founded: 1889 **Type:** Non-profit **Head:** Mr. Duane Wenzel *Phone:* +1(808) 848-4152 *Email:* dwenzel@bishop.bishop. hawaii.org **Staff:** 5 Prof. 5 Other **Holdings:** 110,000 books 1,100 journals **Language of Collection/Services:** English / English **Subjects:** Agriculture (Tropics), Entomology, Forestry, Horticulture **Specializations:** Insects, Plants, Taxonomy **Networks:** OCLC **Loan:** Inhouse **Photocopy:** Yes

3474   Honolulu, Hawaii, US
Hawaii Department of Land and Natural Re-
        sources, Anuenue Fisheries Research Center
Library
1039 Sand Island Parkway
Honolulu, Hawaii 96819
Fax: +1(808) 845-4334 **WWW:** www.hawaii.gov/dlnr/ Welcome.html

Type: Government **Head:** Janet Yasumatsu *Phone:* +1(808) 845-9561 **Staff:** 1 Prof. **Holdings:** 2,450 books 17 journals **Language of Collection/Services:** English **Subjects:** Aquaculture, Fisheries, Livestock Enhancement **Loan:** Inhouse **Service:** Internationally **Photocopy:** Yes

3475   Honolulu, Hawaii, US
National Marine Fisheries Service, Southwest
        Fisheries Science Center (NMFS, SWFSC)
Honolulu Laboratory
2570 Dole Street
Honolulu, Hawaii 98622-2396
Phone: +1(808) 983-5307 **Fax:** +1(808) 982-2902 **WWW:** swfsc.ucsd.edu

Founded: 1950 **Type:** Government **Head:** Sandra L. Abbott-Stout *Phone:* +1(808) 983-5307 *Email:* sstout@ honlab.nmfs.hawaii.edu **Staff:** 1 Prof. **Holdings:** 3,800 books 70 journals **Language of Collection/Services:** English / English **Subjects:** Fisheries **Networks:** OCLC **Databases Used:** Agricola; ASFA **Loan:** Inhouse **Service:** Internationally **Photocopy:** Yes

3476   Honolulu, Hawaii, US
University of Hawaii at Manoa

Library, Science and Technology Reference Department
2550 The Mall
Honolulu, Hawaii 96822

Phone: +1(808) 956-8263 **Fax:** +1(808) 956-2547 **Email:** sciref@hawaii.edu **WWW:** www.hawaii.edu/lib **OPAC:** www.hawaii.edu/uhlib2/external/resources_catalogs.html **Ariel IP:** 128.171.56.140

Founded: 1908 **Type:** Academic **Head:** John Haak *Phone:* +1(808) 956-7205 *Email:* haak@hawaii.edu **Staff:** 4 Prof. 1 Other **Holdings:** 365,000 books 2,400 journals **Language of Collection/Services:** English / English **Subjects:** Agribusiness, Agricultural Economics, Agricultural Development, Agricultural Engineering, Animal Husbandry, Biotechnology, Crops, Entomology, Fisheries, Food Sciences, Horticulture, Nutrition, Plants, Water Resources **Specializations:** Agriculture (Asia), Agriculture (Latin America), Agriculture (Pacific Rim), Agriculture (Tropics), Aquaculture **Databases Developed:** PRAISE - Gray literature project; access via internet at larna.kcc.hawaii.edu/ praise/grayweb2.html **Databases Used:** Comprehensive **Networks:** OCLC **Service:** Inhouse **Loan:** In country **Photocopy:** Yes

3477 Lawai, Hawaii, US
National Tropical Botanical Garden (NTBG)
Library
PO Box 340
Lawai, Hawaii 96765

Location: Papalina Road, Kalaheo, Kauai **Phone:** +1(808) 332-7324 ext 118 **Fax:** +1(808) 332-9765 **WWW:** www.ntbg.org

Former Name: Pacific Tropical Botanical Garden (PTBG) **Founded:** 1971 **Type:** Association **Head:** Richard E. Hanna *Phone:* +1(808) 332-7324 ext 118 *Email:* rhanna@aloha.net **Staff:** 1 Prof. 2 Other **Holdings:** 10,000 books 500 journals **Language of Collection/Services:** English **Subjects:** Agriculture (Tropics), Botany, Horticulture, Plants (Tropics), Taxonomy **Loan:** Do not loan **Service:** Internationally **Photocopy:** Yes

Idaho

3478 Kimberly, Idaho, US
United States Department of Agriculture, Agricultural Research Service, Northwest Irrigation and Soils Laboratory (USDA, ARS)
Library
3793 North 3600 East
Kimberly, Idaho 83341

Phone: +1(208) 423-5582 **Fax:** +1(208) 423-6555 **Email:** kimberly@kimberly.ars.pn.usbr.gov **WWW:** kimberly.ars.usda.gov

Former Name: Snake River Conservation Research Center **Type:** Government **Head:** Kara VanderLinden *Phone:* +1(208) 423-5582 **Staff:** 12 Prof. 30 Other **Holdings:** 2,800 books 35 journals **Language of Collection/Services:** English / English **Subjects:** Agribusiness, Agricultural Engineering, Crops, Farming, Food Sciences, Horticulture, Plant Pathology, Soil Science, Water Resources **Loan:** Inhouse **Service:** Internationally **Photocopy:** No

3479 Moscow, Idaho, US
University of Idaho (UI)
Library
Moscow, Idaho 83844-2350

Phone: +1(208) 885-6235 **Fax:** +1(208) 885-6817 **Email:** libref@uidaho.edu **WWW:** www.lib.uidaho.edu **OPAC:** www.lib.uidaho.edu/booksarticles.htm **Ariel IP:** 129.101.79.150

Former Name: Library - Science and Technology **Founded:** 1892 **Type:** Academic **Head:** Ronald W. Force *Phone:* +1(208) 885-6534 *Email:* rforce@uidaho.edu **Staff:** 19 Prof. 34 Other **Holdings:** 110,000 books 4,310 journals **Language of Collection/Services:** English / English **Subjects:** Agriculture (Tropics), Agribusiness, Agricultural Development, Agricultural Economics, Agricultural Engineering, Animal Husbandry, Biotechnology, Crops, Education/Extension, Entomology, Farming, Fisheries, Food Sciences, Forestry, Horticulture, Plant Pathology, Soil Science, Veterinary Medicine, Water Resources **Networks:** OCLC **Databases Developed:** Salmonid aquaculture - access via internet at db.lib.uidaho.edu **Databases Used:** Comprehensive **Loan:** Internationally **Photocopy:** Yes

Illinois

3480 Bloomington, Illinois, US
Illinois Farm Bureau (IFB)
Information Research Center (IRC)
PO Box 2901
Bloomington, Illinois 61702-2901

Location: 1701 Towanda Avenue **Phone:** +1(309) 557-2552 **Fax:** +1(309) 557-3185 **WWW:** www.fb.com/ilfb

Former Name: Affiliated Companies Library **Founded:** 1958 **Type:** Business **Head:** Vince L. Sampson *Phone:* +1(309) 557-2551 *Email:* vsampson@davesworld.net **Staff:** 1 Prof. 4 Other **Holdings:** 12,000 books 450 journals **Language of Collection/Services:** English **Subjects:** Biotechnology, Crops **Specializations:** Agribusiness, Agricultural Economics, Environment **Networks:** OCLC **Databases Developed:** Political Information Network - demographic data by political boundaries **Databases Used:** Comprehensive **Loan:** Internationally **Service:** Inhouse **Photocopy:** Yes

3481 Carbondale, Illinois, US
Southern Illinois University at Carbondale
Morris Library, Science Division
Carbondale, Illinois 62901-6632

Phone: +1(618) 453-2700 **Fax:** +1(618) 453-2704 **Email:** sciref@lib.siu.edu **WWW:** www.lib.siu.edu **OPAC:** www.lib.siu.edu/hpage/Morris.Library.Catalog.html **Ariel IP:** 131.230.72.3

Founded: 1954 **Type:** Academic **Head:** Kathleen Fahey *Phone:* +1(618) 453-2706 *Email:* kfahey@lib.siu.edu **Staff:** 4 Prof. 2.5 Other **Holdings:** 32,700 books 530 journals **Language of Collection/Services:** English / English **Subjects:** Agribusiness, Agricultural Development, Agricultural Economics, Animal Husbandry, Crops, Education/Extension, Entomology, Farming, Fisheries, Food Sciences, Forestry, Horticulture, Plant Pathology, Soil Science **Networks:**

OCLC **Databases Used:** Comprehensive **Loan:** Internationally **Service:** Internationally **Photocopy:** Yes

3482   Champaign, Illinois, US
University of Illinois at Urbana-Champaign,
    Illinois State Natural History Survey (UIUC)
Library
196 Natural Resources Building
607 East Peabody
Champaign, Illinois 61820
Phone: +1(217) 333-5856 **Fax:** +1(217) 333-4949 **WWW:** www.inhs.uiuc.edu **OPAC:** www.library.uiuc.edu/nhx/default.asp

Founded: 1858 **Type:** Academic **Head:** Beth Wohlgemuth *Phone:* +1(217) 333-6892, 334-4907 *Email:* wohlgemu@mail.inhs.uiuc.edu **Staff:** 1 Prof. 1 Other **Holdings:** 39,000 books 180 journals **Language of Collection/Services:** English / English **Subjects:** Forestry, Plant Pathology, Soil, Water Resources **Specializations:** Aquaculture, Entomology, Environment, Fisheries **Networks:** DRA net; OCLC **Databases Used:** Comprehensive **Loan:** In country **Service:** Internationally **Photocopy:** Yes

3483   Chicago, Illinois, US
Chicago Mercantile Exchange (CME)
Library/Resource Center (L/RC)
30 South Wacker Drive
Chicago, Illinois 60606
Phone: +1(312) 930-8239 **Fax:** +1(312) 466-7436 **Email:** dfri@cme.com **WWW:** www.cme.com

Founded: 1977 **Type:** Association **Head:** Bruce Q. Frost *Phone:* +1(312) 930-3441 *Email:* bfrost@cme.com **Staff:** 4 Prof. 3 Other **Holdings:** 3,500 books 700 journals **Language of Collection/Services:** English **Subjects:** Agricultural Economics **Specializations:** Futures Trading, Options Trading **Networks:** OCLC **Databases Used:** LEXIS-NEXIS **Loan:** In country **Photocopy:** Yes

3484   Chicago, Illinois, US
Environmental Protection Agency (EPA)
Region V Library
77 West Jackson Blvd, 12th Floor
Chicago, Illinois 60604-3590
Phone: +1(312) 353-2023 **Fax:** +1(312) 353-2001 **Email:** library.reg5@epa.gov **WWW:** www.epa.gov **OPAC:** www.epa.gov/natlibra/ols.htm

Founded: 1972 **Type:** Government **Head:** Penny Boyle *Phone:* +1(312) 353-2022 *Email:* boyle.penny@epa.gov **Staff:** 2 Prof. 3 Other **Holdings:** 27,976 books 250 journals **Language of Collection/Services:** English / English **Subjects:** Air Pollution, Drinking Water, Hazardous Wastes, Solid Wastes, Tanks, Toxic Substances, Waste Disposal, Water Resources **Networks:** OCLC **Databases Developed:** OLS - Online Library System - all EPA libraries holdings **Loan:** Internationally **Service:** Inhouse **Photocopy:** Yes

3485   Chicago, Illinois, US
Metropolitan Water Reclamation District of
    Greater Chicago
Technical Library

100 East Erie Street
Chicago, Illinois 60611
Phone: +1(312) 751-6659 **Fax:** +1(312) 751-6635 **WWW:** www.mwrdgc.dst.il.us

Founded: 1966 **Type:** Government **Head:** Gerald Austiff *Phone:* +1(312) 751-6658 *Email:* gaustiff@mwrdgc.dst.il.us **Staff:** 1 Prof. 1 Other **Holdings:** 6,550 books 235 journals **Language of Collection/Services:** English / English **Subjects:** Soil Mechanics, Water Resources **Loan:** In country **Photocopy:** Yes

3486   Chicago, Illinois, US
National Cattlemen's Beef Association (NCPA)
Beef Industry Information Center
444 North Michigan Avenue
Chicago, Illinois 60611
Phone: +1(312) 670-9273 **Fax:** +1(312) 670-9729 **WWW:** www.beef.org

Former Name: National Livestock and Meat Board (NLSMB), National Cattlemen's Association, Meat Industry Information Center **Founded:** 1976 **Type:** Association **Head:** William D. Siarny, Jr. *Phone:* +1(312) 670-9272 *Email:* wsiarny@beef.org **Staff:** 2 Prof. 2 Other **Holdings:** 15,000 books 450 journals **Language of Collection/Services:** English / English **Subjects:** Agribusiness, Animal Husbandry, Food Sciences **Specializations:** Beef, Meat, Nutrition **Databases Developed:** Beef Industry Information System **Databases Used:** Agricola; Dow Jones; Medline **Loan:** Do not loan **Service:** Internationally by appointment **Photocopy:** Yes

3487   Chicago, Illinois, US
Quaker Oats Company, Marketing Information
    Department (MID)
Library
321 N Clark St. 15-8
Chicago, Illinois 60604-9001
Location: 321 North Clark

Type: Business **Head:** Duncan J. McKenzie *Phone:* +1(312) 222-7029

3488   Chicago, Illinois, US
University of Chicago (UC)
John Crerar Library (JCL)
5730 South Ellis Avenue
Chicago, Illinois 60637
Phone: +1(773) 702-7715 **Fax:** +1(773) 702-3317 **Email:** crerar-reference@lib.uchicago.edu **WWW:** www.lib.uchicago.edu/e/crerar/home.html **OPAC:** www.lib.uchicago.edu/e **Ariel IP:** 128.135.96.233

Founded: 1889 **Type:** Academic **Head:** Kathleen A. Zar *Phone:* +1(773) 702-7469 *Email:* kzar@midway.uchicago.edu **Staff:** 7 Prof. 30 Other **Holdings:** 1,800,000 books 5,000 journals **Language of Collection/Services:** English / English **Subjects:** Plants, Veterinary Science **Specializations:** Agricultural Economics, Strong historical collection for monographs and serials from 1850 to present **Networks:** OCLC; RLIN **Databases Used:** Comprehensive **Service:** Internationally **Photocopy:** Yes

3489   Chicago, Illinois, US
Wm. Wrigley Jr. Company
Corporate Library
410 North Michigan Avenue
Chicago, Illinois 60611
Phone: +1(312) 644-2121 **Fax:** +1(212) 644-0081 **WWW:**
www.wrigley.com

Founded: 1978 **Type:** Business **Head:** Linda G. Hanrath
Phone: +1(312) 645-3921 *Email:* lhanrath@wrigley.com
Staff: 1 Prof. 1 Other **Holdings:** 2,500 books 100 journals
Language of Collection/Services: English **Subjects:** Confectionery Industry **Loan:** Inhouse **Photocopy:** Yes

3490   Decatur, Illinois, US
A.E. Staley Manufacturing Company (AES)
Technical Information Center
2200 East Eldorado Street
Decatur, Illinois 62525-1801
Phone: +1(217) 421-2543 **Fax:** +1(217) 421-2519 **Email:**
rewallace@aestaley.com **WWW:** www.aestaley.com

Founded: 1953 **Type:** Business **Head:** Richard E. Wallace
Phone: +1(217) 421-3283 *Email:* rewallace@aestaley.com
Staff: 1 Prof. **Holdings:** 12,000 books 50 journals **Language of Collection/Services:** English / English **Subjects:**
Food Sciences **Specializations:** Analytical Chemistry, Food
Grains, Food Technology, Oilseeds, Organic Chemistry,
Starch **Databases Developed:** FAMULUS - Index to internal documents - inhouse use only **Databases Used:** Comprehensive **Networks:** OCLC **Service:** Internationally **Loan:** In
country **Photocopy:** Yes

3491   Downers Grove, Illinois, US
Armour Swift-Eckrich, Product Development Lab
PDL Research Library
3131 Woodcreek Drive
Downers Grove, Illinois 60515
Phone: +1(630) 512-1084 **Fax:** +1(630) 512-1125 **Email:**
ebreen@crfc.com

Former Name: Swift-Eckrich Incorporated **Type:** Business
Head: Eileen MM. Breen *Phone:* +1(630) 512-1084 *Email:*
ebreen@crfc.com **Staff:** 1 Prof. **Holdings:** 3,000 books 66
journals **Language of Collection/Services:** English / English **Subjects:** Food Sciences **Specializations:** Microbiology
Networks: OCLC **Databases Used:** Comprehensive **Loan:**
In country **Service:** In country **Photocopy:** Yes

3492   Glencoe, Illinois, US
Chicago Horticultural Society
Chicago Botanic Garden Library
1000 Lake Cook Road
Glencoe, Illinois 60022
Phone: +1(847) 835-8200 **Fax:** +1(847) 835-6885 **WWW:**
www.chicago-botanic.org

Type: Non-profit **Head:** Edward J. Valauskas *Phone:* +1
(847) 835-8202 *Email:* evalausk@chicagobotanic.org **Staff:**
2.5 Prof. 1 Other **Holdings:** 15,000 books 200 journals **Language of Collection/Services:** English / English **Subjects:**
Gardening, Horticulture **Networks:** OCLC **Loan:** In country
Service: Internationally **Photocopy:** Yes

3493   Hamilton, Illinois, US
Dadant & Sons, Inc.
Apicultural Library
51 South Second Street
Hamilton, Illinois 62341
Phone: +1(217) 847-3324 **Fax:** +1(217) 847-3660 **WWW:**
www.dadant.com

Founded: 1900 **Type:** Business **Head:** Tim Dadant *Phone:*
+1(217) 847-3324 *Email:* dadant@dadant.com **Staff:** 2
Other **Holdings:** 1,500 books 20 journals **Language of Collection/Services:** English **Subjects:** Beekeeping **Loan:** Do
not loan **Photocopy:** No

3494   Lisle, Illinois, US
Morton Arboretum
Sterling Morton Library
3100 Illinois Route 53
Lisle, Illinois 60532-1923
Phone: +1(630) 719-2427 **Fax:** +1(630) 719-7950 **WWW:**
www.mortonarb.org

Founded: 1963 **Type:** Non-profit **Head:** Michael Stieber
Phone: +1(630) 719-2427 *Email:* mstieber@mortonarb.org
Staff: 3 Prof. **Holdings:** 31,800 books 287 journals **Language of Collection/Services:** English / English **Subjects:**
Botany, Horticulture, Plant Pathology, Soil Science **Specializations:** Arboriculture **Networks:** OCLC **Databases Used:**
Comprehensive **Loan:** In country **Photocopy:** Yes

3495   Macomb, Illinois, US
Western Illinois University
Library
Western Avenue
Macomb, Illinois 61455
Phone: +1(309) 298-2700 **Fax:** +1(309) 298-2791 **WWW:**
www.wiu.edu **OPAC:** www.wiu.edu/library/catalogs

Founded: 1899 **Type:** Academic **Staff:** 18 Prof. 39 Other
Holdings: 9,000 books 96 journals **Language of Collection/
Services:** English **Subjects:** Agricultural Economics, Rural
Sociology **Networks:** OCLC **Databases Used:** Agricola
Loan: Internationally **Photocopy:** Yes

3496   Moline, Illinois, US
Deere & Company
Library
One John Deere Place
Moline, Illinois 61265
Phone: +1(309) 765-4733 **Fax:** +1(309) 765-4088 **WWW:**
www.deere.com

Founded: 1958 **Type:** Business **Head:** Betty S. Hagberg
Email: hagbergbettys@jdcorp.deere.com *Phone:* +1(309)
765-4881 **Staff:** 5 Prof. 6 Other **Holdings:** 20,000 books 800
journals **Language of Collection/Services:** English / English **Subjects:** Agricultural Economics, Agricultural Engineering **Networks:** OCLC **Databases Developed:** John
Deere Archives **Databases Used:** Comprehensive **Loan:** In
country **Service:** In country **Photocopy:** Yes

3497   Morton, Illinois, US
American Shetland Pony Club - American
       Miniature Horse Registry (ASPC)

Library
81 B Queenwood Road
Morton, Illinois 61550

Phone: +1(309) 263-4044 **Fax:** +1(309) 263-5113 **Email:** aspcamhr@dpc.net **WWW:** www.shetlandminiature.com

Founded: 1888 **Type:** Association **Staff:** 2 Prof. 2 Other **Holdings:** 1,400 journals **Specializations:** Horses, Shetland Pony **Loan:** Do not loan

3498 **Mossville, Illinois, US**
Caterpillar Inc.
Technical Information Center
Technical Center TC-K
14009 Old Galena Road
Mossville, Illinois 61552

WWW: www.cat.com

Type: Business **Head:** Shirley Streib *Phone:* +1(309) 578-6118 *Email:* streib_shirley_l@cat.com

3499 **Normal, Illinois, US**
Illinois State University
Milner Library
Campus Box 8900
Normal, Illinois 61790-8900

Phone: +1(309) 438-2869 **Fax:** +1(309) 438-3676 **Email:** mlberef@exchange1.mlb.ilstu.edu **WWW:** www.ilstu.edu **OPAC:** www.mlb.ilstu.edu/online/home.htm

Type: Academic **Head:** Cheryl Elzy *Phone:* +1(309) 438-3481 *Email:* caelzy@ilstu.edu **Holdings: Databases Used:** Agricola; Biological and Agricultural Abstracts **Loan:** In country **Service:** Inhouse **Photocopy:** Yes

3500 **Park Ridge, Illinois, US**
American Farm Bureau Federation (AFBF)
Library
Public Policy Division
225 Touhy Avenue
Park Ridge, Illinois 60068

Phone: +1(847) 685-8700 **Fax:** +1(847) 485-8969 **Email:** sue@fb.com **WWW:** www.fb.com

Founded: 1981 **Type:** Association **Head:** Susan Schultz *Phone:* +1(847) 685-8781 *Email:* sue@fb.com **Staff:** 1 Prof. 1 Other **Holdings:** 6,500 books 150 journals **Language of Collection/Services:** English / English **Subjects:** Agricultural Economics, Farming **Databases Used:** Comprehensive **Loan:** Do not loan **Photocopy:** Yes

3501 **Peoria, Illinois, US**
United States Department of Agriculture,
Agricultural Research Service, National
Center for Agricultural Utilization Research
(USDA, ARS, NCAUR)
Library
1815 North University Street
Peoria, Illinois 61604

Phone: +1(309) 681-6526 **Fax:** +1(309) 681-6881 **WWW:** www.ncaur.usda.gov

Former Name: Northern Regional Research Laboratory **Founded:** 1940 **Type:** Government **Head:** Joyce Blumenshine *Email:* blumenj@mail.ncaur.usda.gov *Phone:* +1(309)

681-6526 **Staff:** 1 Prof. 1 Other **Holdings:** 26,000 books 188 journals **Language of Collection/Services:** English **Subjects:** Biotechnology, Entomology, Food Sciences, Plant Pathology **Specializations:** Organic Chemistry, Plant Physiology **Networks:** OCLC **Databases Used:** Agricola; CAS; Current Contents **Loan:** Internationally **Service:** Internationally **Photocopy:** Yes

3502 **Schaumburg, Illinois, US**
American Veterinary Medical Association
(AVMA)
Library
1931 North Meacham Road, Suite 100
Schaumburg, Illinois 60173-4360

Fax: +1(847) 925-9329 **WWW:** www.avma.org

Type: Association **Head:** Diane A. Fagen *Phone:* +1(847) 925-8070 ext 245 *Email:* dfagen@avma.org **Staff:** 1 Prof. **Holdings:** 5,000 books 400 journals **Language of Collection/Services:** English **Subjects:** Animal Husbandry, Food Sciences, Veterinary Medicine **Databases Developed:** Complete issues of the Journal of the AVMA from 1855 to present **Databases Used:** Comprehensive **Loan:** Do not loan **Photocopy:** Yes

3503 **Urbana, Illinois, US**
University of Illinois at Urbana-Champaign
(UIUC)
Agricultural, Consumer and Environmental
Sciences Library (ACES Library)
226 Mumford
1301 West Gregory Drive
Urbana, Illinois 61801

Phone: +1(217) 244-2249 **Fax:** +1(217) 333-0588 **Email:** aceslib@aces.uiuc.edu **WWW:** www.library.uiuc.edu/agx **OPAC:** gateway.library.uiuc.edu

Founded: 1912 **Type:** Academic **Head:** Robert S. Allen *Phone:* +1(217) 333-2416 *Email:* allen2@uiuc.edu **Staff:** 2 Prof. 4.5 Other **Holdings:** 200,000 books 3,000 journals **Language of Collection/Services:** English / English **Subjects:** Comprehensive **Networks:** OCLC **Databases Used:** Comprehensive **Loan:** Internationally **Service:** Internationally **Photocopy:** Yes

3504 **Urbana, Illinois, US**
University of Illinois at Urbana-Champaign
(UIUC)
Biology Library
101 Burrill Hall
407 South Goodwin
Urbana, Illinois 61801

Phone: +1(217) 244-3591 **Fax:** +1(217) 333.3662 **Email:** biolib@uiuc.edu **WWW:** www.library.uiuc.edu/bix **OPAC:** gateway.library.uiuc.edu **Ariel IP:** 130.126.33.21

Founded: 1884 **Type:** Academic **Head:** Diane C. Schmidt *Phone:* +1(217) 333-3654 *Email:* dcschmid@uiuc.edu **Staff:** 2 Prof. 4 Other **Holdings:** 125,000 books 6,000 journals **Language of Collection/Services:** English / English **Subjects:** Animal Husbandry, Biology, Biotechnology, Plant Pathology, Plants **Specializations:** Birds, Botany, Entomology, Zoology **Networks:** OCLC **Databases Used:**

Comprehensive **Loan:** Internationally **Service:** Internationally **Photocopy:** Yes

3505   Urbana, Illinois, US
University of Illinois at Urbana-Champaign
(UIUC)
Veterinary Medicine Library
2001 South Lincoln Avenue
Urbana, Illinois 61802
Phone: +1(217) 333-2598 **Fax:** +1(217) 333-2286 **WWW:** www.library.uiuc.edu/vex **OPAC:** pac.library.uiuc.edu

Founded: 1952 **Type:** Academic **Head:** Mitsuko Williams *Phone:* +1(217) 333-2193 *Email:* mwillms1@uiuc.edu **Staff:** 1.5 Prof. 2.5 Other **Holdings:** 46,000 books 400 journals **Language of Collection/Services:** English **Subjects:** Animal Husbandry, Toxicology, Veterinary Medicine **Networks:** DOCLINE; OCLC **Databases Developed:** Plants toxic to animals - access via Internet at www.library.uiuc.edu/vex/vetdocs/toxic.htm; Veterinary abbreviations and acronyms - access via Internet at www.library.uiuc.edu/vex/vetdocs/abbs.htm **Databases Used:** Comprehensive **Loan:** Internationally **Service:** Internationally **Photocopy:** Yes

Indiana

3506   Fort Wayne, Indiana, US
Central Soya Company, Inc.
Research and Development Library
PO Box 1400
Fort Wayne, Indiana 46801-1400
Location: 1946 West Cook Road **Phone:** +1(219) 425-5346 **Fax:** +1(219) 425-5301 **WWW:** www.centralsoya.com

Founded: 1940 **Type:** Business **Staff:** 1 Prof. **Holdings:** 8,816 books 75 journals **Language of Collection/Services:** English **Subjects:** Agribusiness, Agricultural Development, Biotechnology, Food Sciences **Photocopy:** Yes

3507   Greenfield, Indiana, US
Eli Lilly and Company
Greenfield Intelligence Center
Greenfield Laboratories
Box 708
Greenfield, Indiana 46140
Location: 2001 W. Main **Phone:** +1(317) 277-4215 **Fax:** +1(317) 277-5137 **Email:** wss@lilly.com **WWW:** www.lilly.com

Founded: 1957 **Type:** Business **Head:** Wanda Sullivan *Phone:* +1(317) 277-4215 *Email:* wss@lilly.com **Staff:** 1 Prof. 2 Other **Holdings:** 6,000 books 400 journals **Language of Collection/Services:** English **Subjects:** Animal Health, Biotechnology, Chemistry, Plant Pathology, Toxicology **Networks:** OCLC **Databases Developed:** Company Agricultural Products **Databases Used:** Agricola; Biosis; CAB-CD; CAS **Loan:** Inhouse **Photocopy:** Yes

3508   Indianapolis, Indiana, US
Dow Agrosciences (DAS)
Information Management Center (IMC)
9330 Zionsville
Indianapolis, Indiana 46268-1054

Phone: +1(317) 337-3691 **Fax:** +1(317) 337-3245 **WWW:** www.dowagro.com

Former Name: DowElanco, Dow Chemical Company, Eli Lilly and Company, Technical Information Services **Founded:** 1920 **Type:** Business **Head:** Margaret Hentz *Phone:* +1(317) 337-3517 *Email:* mhentz@dowagro.com **Staff:** 4 Prof. 1 Other **Holdings:** 3,800 books 200 journals **Language of Collection/Services:** English / English **Subjects:** Agricultural Chemicals **Specializations:** Chemistry **Networks:** OCLC **Databases Used:** Comprehensive **Loan:** Internationally **Service:** Inhouse **Photocopy:** Yes

3509   Indianapolis, Indiana, US
Indianapolis-Marion County Public Library
Business, Science and Technology Service Section
PO Box 211
Indianapolis, Indiana 46206-0211
Location: 40 East St. Clair Street **Phone:** +1(317) 269-1741 **Fax:** +1(317) 269-1768 **Email:** webmaster@imcpl.lib.in.us **WWW:** www.imcpl.lib.in.us **OPAC:** www.imcpl.lib.in.us/catalog.htm

Founded: 1921 **Type:** Government **Head:** Mark Leggett *Phone:* +1(317) 269-1706 *Email:* mleggett@imcpl.lib.in.us **Staff:** 10 Prof. **Holdings:** 60,000 books 50 journals **Language of Collection/Services:** English / English **Subjects:** Agribusiness, Animal Husbandry, Crops, Farming, Forestry, Horticulture, Soil Science **Networks:** OCLC **Databases Used:** Comprehensive **Loan:** Internationally **Service:** Internationally **Photocopy:** Yes

3510   Reelsville, Indiana, US
American North Country Cheviot Sheep
Association, Inc.
Library
8708 S. Co. Rd. 500W
Reelsville, Indiana 46171
Phone: +1(765) 672-8205 **Email:** yuccafl@ccrtc.com

Founded: 1962 **Type:** Association **Staff:** 1 Other **Holdings:** 2 books **Specializations:** Cheviot Sheep **Photocopy:** Yes

3511   West Lafayette, Indiana, US
J.C. Allen & Son, Inc.
Rural Life Photo Service
PO Box 2061
West Lafayette, Indiana 47906
Location: 4750 Jackson Hiway

Founded: 1912 **Type:** Business **Head:** John Allen *Phone:* +1(765) 463-9614, 583-2316 **Staff:** 2 Prof. 1 Other **Language of Collection/Services:** English **Subjects:** Agribusiness, Agricultural Development, Agricultural Economics, Agricultural Engineering, Animal Husbandry, Biotechnology, Buildings, Crops, Education/Extension, Entomology, Farming, Fisheries, Food Sciences, Forestry, Horticulture, Farm Machinery, Insects, Plant Pathology, Rural Life Photography, Soil Science, Veterinary Medicine, Water Resources **Specializations:** Historic agricultural photographs **Databases Developed:** 1,000,000 photos under 77,000 subject topics **Loan:** Rent **Photocopy:** Yes

3512   West Lafayette, Indiana, US
Purdue University
Life Sciences Library
1323 Lilly Hall
West Lafayette, Indiana 47907-1323
Phone: +1(765) 494-2910 **Fax:** +1(765) 494-9007 **Email:**
liblife@omni.cc.purdue.edu **WWW:** www.purdue.edu
OPAC: www1.lib.purdue.edu

Founded: 1959 **Type:** Academic **Head:** Sarah A. Kelly
Phone: +1(765) 494-2912 *Email:* sakelly@purdue.edu
Staff: 3 Prof. 6 Other **Holdings:** 72,000 books 1,200 journals
Language of Collection/Services: English **Subjects:** Agri-
cultural Development, Animal Husbandry, Biotechnology,
Crops, Education/Extension, Farming, Fisheries, Plant Pa-
thology, Soil Science, Water Resources **Specializations:**
Agricultural Engineering, Biochemistry, Biology, Botany,
Entomology, Food Sciences, Forestry, Horticulture, Natural
Resources, Zoology **Networks:** OCLC **Databases Used:**
Comprehensive **Loan:** In country **Service:** Internationally
Photocopy: Yes

3513   West Lafayette, Indiana, US
Purdue University
Management and Economics Library
1340 Krannert Building
West Lafayette, Indiana 47907-1340
Phone: +1(765) 494-2920 **Fax:** +1(765) 494-9058 **WWW:**
www.lib.purdue.edu **OPAC:** www.lib.purdue.edu **Ariel
IP:** 128.210.63.101

Founded: 1959 **Type:** Academic **Head:** Judith M. Nixon
Phone: +1(765) 494-2922 *Email:* jnixon@purdue.edu **Staff:**
3 Prof. 6 Other **Holdings:** 103,646 books 802 journals **Language of Collection/Services:** English / English **Subjects:**
Agribusiness, Agricultural Development, Agricultural Economics **Networks:** OCLC **Databases Developed:** Working
papers received at library and annual reports to shareholders
received at library - available on library's web page at www.
lib.purdue.edu **Databases Used:** Comprehensive **Loan:** In
country **Service:** Inhouse **Photocopy:** Yes

3514   West Lafayette, Indiana, US
Purdue University
Veterinary Medical Library
1537 Lynn Hall, Room 1133
West Lafayette, Indiana 47907-1537
Phone: +1(765) 494-2853 **Fax:** +1(765) 494-0781 attn: G.
Stephens **WWW:** www.lib.purdue.edu **OPAC:** www.lib.
purdue.edu

Type: Academic **Head:** Gretchen Stephens *Phone:* +1(765)
494-2852 *Email:* gms@purdue.edu **Staff:** 2 Prof. 2 Other
Holdings: 31,679 books 564 journals **Language of Collec-
tion/Services:** English / English **Subjects:** Veterinary Medicine **Specializations:** Anatomy, Immunology, Animal
Welfare, Physiology, Laboratory Animals, Pathology, Virology **Networks:** OCLC **Databases Used:** Medline **Loan:**
Internationally **Service:** Internationally **Photocopy:** Yes

Iowa

3515   Ames, Iowa, US
Iowa State University (ISU)
Parks Library
Ames, Iowa 50011-2140
Phone: +1(515) 294-3642 **Fax:** +1(515) 294-5525 **WWW:**
www.iastate.edu **OPAC:** www.lib.iastate.edu **Ariel IP:**
129.186.11.39

Founded: 1870 **Type:** Academic **Head:** Olivia M.A. Madison *Phone:* +1(515) 294-1442 *Email:* omadison@iastate.edu
Staff: 43.5 Prof. 164 Other **Holdings:** 2,125,000 books
21,975 journals **Language of Collection/Services:** English /
English **Subjects:** Agriculture (Tropics), Agribusiness, Ag-
ricultural Development, Agricultural Economics, Agricul-
tural Engineering, Animal Husbandry, Biotechnology,
Crops, Education/Extension, Entomology, Farming, Fish-
eries, Food Sciences, Forestry, Horticulture, Plant Pathol-
ogy, Plants, Soil Science, Veterinary Medicine, Water
Resources **Networks:** OCLC **Databases Developed:** AAFF
- American Archives of the Factural Film **Databases Used:**
Agricola; Agris; CABCD **Loan:** Internationally **Service:**
Internationally **Photocopy:** Yes

3516   Ames, Iowa, US
Iowa State University (ISU)
Veterinary Medical Library
2280 College of Veterinary Medicine
Ames, Iowa 50011-2150
Phone: +1(515) 294-2225 **WWW:** www.iastate.edu
OPAC: www.lib.iastate.edu

Type: Academic **Head:** William Wiese *Phone:* +1(515)
294-2233 *Email:* wwiese@iastate.edu **Holdings:** 34,000
books 900 journals **Subjects:** Veterinary Medicine

3517   Ames, Iowa, US
United States Department of Agriculture, Agricul-
      tural Research Service, National Animal
      Disease Center (USDA, ARS, NADC)
Library
PO Box 70
Ames, Iowa 50010
Location: 2300 Dayton Ave. **Phone:** +1(515) 663-7200
WWW: www.nadc.ars.usda.gov

Founded: 1961 **Type:** Government **Head:** Janice K. Eifling
Phone: +1(515) 663-7744/7271 **Staff:** 1 Prof. 1.5 Other
Holdings: 5,000 books 200 journals **Language of Collec-
tion/Services:** English / English **Subjects:** Veterinary Medi-
cine **Databases Used:** Agricola; Medline **Loan:** In country
Service: Internationally **Photocopy:** Yes

3518   Ankeny, Iowa, US
Soil and Water Conservation Society
H. Wayne Pritchard Library
7515 NE Ankeny Road
Ankeny, Iowa 50021
Phone: +1(515) 289-2331 **Fax:** +1(515) 289-1227 **Email:**
swcs@swcs.org **WWW:** www.swcs.org

Former Name: Soil Conservation Society of America
Founded: 1961 **Type:** Association **Holdings:** 1,750 books

20 journals **Subjects:** Land Management, Water Management **Loan:** Do not loan **Photocopy:** No

3519   Clinton, Iowa, US
Bickelhaupt Arboretum
Free Lending Library
340 South 14th Street
Clinton, Iowa 52732

Founded: 1970 **Type:** Association **Head:** Peter J. van der Linden *Email:* bickelarb@clinton.net *Phone:* +1(319) 242-4771 **Staff:** 1 Prof. **Holdings:** 800 books 10 journals **Language of Collection/Services:** English / English **Subjects:** Entomology, Horticulture, Plant Pathology **Loan:** Internationally **Photocopy:** Yes

3520   Des Moines, Iowa, US
Kemin Industries, Inc.
Scientific Information Group (SIG)
2100 Maury Street
Box 70
Des Moines, Iowa 50301

Phone: +1(515) 266-2111 **Fax:** +1(515) 266-8354 **Email:** info@kemin.com **WWW:** www.keminfoods.com/food/index.htm

Type: Business **Staff:** 3 Prof. **Holdings:** 500 books 40 journals **Language of Collection/Services:** English / English **Subjects:** Agribusiness, Animal Husbandry, Biotechnology, Chemistry, Crops, Farming, Fisheries, Food Sciences, Microbiology **Databases Used:** Agricola; Biosis; CABCD; CAS **Loan:** Inhouse **Service:** Inhouse

3521   Iowa City, Iowa, US
University of Iowa
Biological Sciences Library
100 Biological Sciences Library
Iowa City, Iowa 52242-1324

Phone: +1(319) 335-3083 **Fax:** +1(319) 335-5900 **Email:** lib-biology@uiowa.edu **WWW:** www.uiowa.edu **OPAC:** www.lib.uiowa.edu/biology

Type: Academic **Head:** Jeff Dodd *Email:* john-dodd@uiowa.edu

3522   Johnston, Iowa, US
Pioneer Hi-Bred International, Inc.
Research Library
7300 North West 62nd Avenue
Box 1004
Johnston, Iowa 50131

Fax: +1(515) 253-2184 **WWW:** www.pioneer.com/index_ns.htm

Founded: 1981 **Type:** Business **Head:** Dana Smith *Phone:* +1(515) 270-4199 *Email:* smithde@phibred.com **Staff:** 3 Prof. 2 Other **Holdings:** 6,000 books 500 journals **Language of Collection/Services:** English **Subjects:** Biotechnology, Crops, Entomology, Plant Pathology **Networks:** OCLC **Loan:** Internationally **Photocopy:** Yes

3523   Milo, Iowa, US
American Hampshire Sheep Association
Library

1557 173rd Ave.
Milo, Iowa 50166
Phone: +1(515) 942-6402 **Fax:** +1(515) 942-5402

Founded: 1889 **Type:** Association **Head:** Karey Claghorn, Executive Secretary **Subjects:** American Hampshire Sheep, Sheep **Loan:** Do not loan **Photocopy:** No

3524   Muscatine, Iowa, US
Grain Processing Corporation
Technical Information Center
1600 Oregon Street
Muscatine, Iowa 52761-1494

Phone: +1(319) 264-4265 **Fax:** +1(319) 264-4130 **WWW:** www.grainprocessing.com

Type: Business **Head:** Rosemary A. Hollatz *Phone:* +1(319) 264-4389 *Email:* gpcrnd@muscanet.com **Holdings:** 6,000 books 250 journals **Language of Collection/Services:** English **Staff:** 1 Prof. **Subjects:** Alcohols, Food Grains, Foods, Starch **Specializations:** Agribusiness, Biotechnology, Food Sciences **Loan:** Inhouse **Service:** Inhouse **Photocopy:** Yes

Kansas

3525   Kansas City, Kansas, US
Environmental Protection Agency
Region VII Information Resources Center
901 North 5th Street
Kansas City, Kansas 66101-2798

Phone: +1(913) 551-7241 **Fax:** +1(913) 551-7215, 551-9241 **Email:** r7-library@epa.gov **WWW:** www.epa.gov **OPAC:** www.epa.gov/region07/newsinfo/irc/index.htm

Founded: 1970 **Type:** Government **Head:** Sharyl McMillian-Nelson *Email* mcmillian-nelson.sharyl@epa.gov *Phone* +1(913) 551-7358 **Staff:** 3 Prof. 3 Other **Holdings:** 150,000 books 125 journals **Language of Collection/Services:** English **Subjects:** Pesticides, Wetlands **Networks:** OCLC **Loan:** Via ILL **Service:** Internationally **Photocopy:** Yes

3526   Lawrence, Kansas, US
University of Kansas
Government Documents and Maps Library
6001 Malott Hall
Lawrence, Kansas 66045

Phone: +1(785) 864-4660 **Fax:** +1(785) 864-5380, 864-5154 **Email:** govdocs-ref@mail.lib.ukans.edu **WWW:** www.ukans.edu/cwis/units/kulib/docs/govdocs.html **OPAC:** www.lib.ukans.edu/ocatconn.html

Founded: 1869 **Type:** Academic **Head:** Ms. Donna Koepp *Phone:* +1(785) 864-4660 *Email:* dkoepp@ukans.edu **Staff:** 3 Prof. 5 Other **Holdings:** 2,200,000 books **Language of Collection/Services:** English **Subjects:** European Communities Documents, Food and Agriculture Organization Documents, Government Documents (USA), International Organizations' Documents, OECD Documents, UN Documents **Specializations:** Geographic Information Systems, Mapping, Maps **Networks:** OCLC **Loan:** Internationally **Photocopy:** Yes

3527   Manhattan, Kansas, US
American Institute of Baking (AIB)
Ruth Emerson Library
PO Box 3999
Manhattan, Kansas 66505-3999
Location: 1213 Bakers Way **Phone:** +1(785) 537-4750 ext
126 **Fax:** +1(785) 537-1493 **WWW:** www.aibonline.org

Former Name: Louis Livingston Library **Founded:** 1919
Type: Non-profit **Head:** Julie Goings *Phone:* +1(785) 537-
4750 ext 126 *Email:* jgoings@aibonline.org **Staff:** 2 Prof. 1
Other **Holdings:** 4,800 books 250 journals **Language of
Collection/Services:** English, German, French **Subjects:**
Baking, Food Sciences **Databases Developed:** Baking and
Food Science Database - includes some abstracts, 1960 to
date **Databases Used:** FSTA **Loan:** Inhouse **Service:** Open
to public, serve internationally **Photocopy:** Yes

3528   Manhattan, Kansas, US
Kansas State University (KSU)
Hale Library
Manhattan, Kansas 66506
Phone: +1(785) 532-7422, 532-0548 (Science reference)
Fax: +1(785) 532-6144 **Email:** jeneenw@lib.ksu.edu
WWW: www.lib.ksu.edu **OPAC:** www.lib.ksu.edu/
catalog

Former Name: Farrell Library **Founded:** 1863 **Type:** Aca-
demic **Head:** Dr. Brice Hobrock *Phone:* +1(785) 532-7400
Email: hobrock@ksu.edu **Staff:** 41 Prof. 58 Other **Hold-
ings:** 100,000 books 500 journals **Language of Collection/
Services:** English **Subjects:** Agricultural Economics, Crops,
Agricultural Engineering, Animal Husbandry, Entomology,
Horticulture, Plant Pathology, Soil Science **Specializations:**
Grain Crops, Food Sciences, Veterinary Medicine **Net-
works:** OCLC **Databases Developed:** Farming Systems;
Post Harvest Documentation; **Databases Used:** Compre-
hensive **Loan:** In country and Canada **Photocopy:** Yes

3529   Manhattan, Kansas, US
Kansas State University (KSU)
Information Support Services for Agriculture
        (ISSA)
118 Hale Library
Manhattan, Kansas 66506-1200
Phone: +1(785) 532-7452 **Fax:** +1(785) 532-6144 **Email:**
issa@ksu.edu **WWW:** www.lib.ksu.edu/depts/issa

Former Name: Post-Harvest Documentation Service
(PHDS), Farrell Library Resources for Developing Countries **Founded:** 1994 **Type:** Academic **Head:** Donna
Schenck-Hamlin *Phone:* +1(785) 532-7452 *Email:* issa@
ksu.edu **Staff:** 2 Prof. **Holdings:** 33,000 books **Language of
Collection/Services:** English / English **Subjects:** Agricultural Engineering, Agriculture (Tropics), Agricultural Economics, Entomology, Food Sciences, Plant Pathology
Databases Developed: PHDS Database - Contains bibliographic citations and abstracts or content notes to all documents in the collection; access via the Internet **Databases
Used:** Comprehensive **Loan:** Do not loan **Service:** Internationally **Photocopy:** Yes

3530   Manhattan, Kansas, US
Kansas State University, College of Veterinary
        Medicine (KSU)
Veterinary Medical Library
408 Trotter Hall
1700 Denison Ave.
Manhattan, Kansas 66506-5614
Phone: +1(785) 532-6006 **Fax:** +1(785) 532-2838 **Email:**
vetlib@vet.ksu.edu **WWW:** www.vet.ksu.edu/depts/library
OPAC: www.lib.ksu.edu/catalog

Founded: 1936 **Type:** Academic **Head:** Gayle K. Willard
Phone: +1(785) 532-6006 **Staff:** 1 Prof. 2.5 Other **Holdings:**
40,000 books 725 journals **Language of Collection/Ser-
vices:** English **Subjects:** Veterinary Medicine **Specializations:** Animal Nutrition, Animal Welfare, Cattle Diseases,
Management **Networks:** OCLC **Databases Used:** Comprehensive **Loan:** In country and Canada **Photocopy:** Yes

3531   Manhattan, Kansas, US
Kansas State University, Department of
        Agricultural Economics and Economics
        (KSU)
Agricultural Economics and Economics Reference
        Room
337 Waters Hall
Manhattan, Kansas 66506-4011
Fax: +1(785) 532-6925 **WWW:** www.agecon.ksu.edu/
default.htm

Former Name: Kansas State Agricultural College, Grimes
Reading Room **Founded:** 1970 **Type:** Academic **Head:**
Deana Foster *Phone:* +1(785) 532-6702 *Email:* dfoster@
agecon.ksu.edu **Staff:** 1.5 Other **Holdings:** 5,000 books 40
journals **Language of Collection/Services:** English **Sub-
jects:** Agribusiness, Agricultural Development, Farming,
Water Resources **Specializations:** Agricultural Economics,
Economics **Loan:** Inhouse **Service:** Inhouse **Photocopy:** No

3532   Manhattan, Kansas, US
Kansas State University, Department of Grain
        Science and Industry (KSU)
Swanson Resource Room
303 Shellenberger Hall
Manhattan, Kansas 66506-2201
Fax: +1(785) 532-7010 **WWW:** www.oznet.ksu.edu/
dp_grsi

Former Name: Swanson Reading Room **Founded:** 1950
Type: Academic **Head:** Kay Taylor *Phone:* +1(785) 532-
4068 *Email:* kkt@wheat.ksu.edu **Staff:** 1 Prof. 1 Other
Holdings: 8,100 books 75 journals **Language of Collection/
Services:** English **Subjects:** Bakery Industry, Baking, Ex-
trusion, Feeds, Food Sciences, Milling, Value Added **Loan:**
Inhouse **Service:** Inhouse **Photocopy:** Yes

Kentucky

3533   Frankfort, Kentucky, US
Kentucky State University
Paul G. Blazer Library
400 East Main Street
Frankfort, Kentucky 40601

Phone: +1(502) 227-6857 **Fax:** +1(502) 564-5068 **WWW:** www.kysu.edu **OPAC:** kysu.kcvl.org **Ariel IP:** 198.83.26. 229

Type: Academic **Head:** Mrs. Karen McDaniel *Phone:* +1(502) 227-6857 *Email:* kmcdaniel@gwmail.kysu.edu **Staff:** 12 Prof. 8 Other **Holdings:** 600,000 books 1,105 journals **Language of Collection/Services:** English / English **Subjects:** Comprehensive **Networks:** OCLC **Databases Used:** Comprehensive **Service:** In country **Photocopy:** Yes

3534   Lexington, Kentucky, US
American Saddle Horse Museum (ASHM)
American Saddlebred Library
4093 Iron Works Parkway
Lexington, Kentucky 40511
WWW: www.american-saddlebred.com

Founded: 1985 **Type:** Association **Head:** Tolley Graves *Phone:* +1(606) 259-2746 *Email:* ashm@mis.net **Staff:** .2 Other **Holdings:** 1,000 books 10 journals **Language of Collection/Services:** English / English **Subjects:** Animal Husbandry **Specializations:** American Saddlebred Horses, Horses **Loan:** Inhouse **Photocopy:** Yes

3535   Lexington, Kentucky, US
Keeneland Association Inc.
Keeneland Association Library
Box 1690 Versailles Road
Lexington, Kentucky 40588-1690
Location: 4201 Versailles Road **Phone:** +1(606) 288-4223 **Fax:** +1(606) 288-4348 **WWW:** www.keenland.com/ framehome.html

Founded: 1939 **Type:** Special **Head:** Ms. Cathy Schenck *Phone:* +1(606) 254-3412 **Staff:** 1 Prof. 1 Other **Holdings:** 6,000 books 20 journals **Language of Collection/Services:** English **Subjects:** Horse Racing, Horses, Thoroughbred **Loan:** Do not loan **Photocopy:** Yes

3536   Lexington, Kentucky, US
Kentucky Horse Park (KHP)
International Museum of the Horse (IMH)
4089 Iron Works Pike
Lexington, Kentucky 40511
WWW: www.imh.org

Founded: 1978 **Head:** Jenifer Raisor *Phone:* +1(606) 259-4247 *Email:* khp6@mis.net **Staff:** 1 Prof. 3 museum staff Other **Holdings:** 1,400 books 35 journals **Language of Collection/Services:** English / English **Subjects:** Animal Husbandry **Specializations:** Horses, Veterinary Medicine **Loan:** Inhouse **Service:** Inhouse **Photocopy:** Yes

3537   Lexington, Kentucky, US
University of Kentucky (UK)
Agriculture Information Center (AIC)
N-24 Agricultural Science Center North
Lexington, Kentucky 40546-0091
Phone: +1(606) 257-2758 **Fax:** +1(606) 323-4719 **WWW:** www.ca.uky.edu/AIC, www.uky.edu **OPAC:** commonweb. uky.edu:8000 **Ariel IP:** 128.163.192.115

Former Name: Agriculture Library **Founded:** 1905 **Type:** Academic **Head:** Antoinette Paris Powell *Phone:* +1(606)

257-2758 *Email:* apowell@ca.uky.edu **Staff:** 3 Prof. 4 Other **Holdings:** 108,000 books 2,000 journals **Language of Collection/Services:** English / English **Subjects:** Agriculture (Tropics), Agribusiness, Agricultural Development, Agricultural Economics, Agricultural Engineering, Animal Husbandry, Biotechnology, Education/Extension, Entomology, Crops, Farming, Fisheries, Food Sciences, Forestry, Horticulture, Plant Pathology, Soil Science, Veterinary Medicine, Water Resources **Networks:** OCLC **Databases Developed:** Kentucky Agricultural Research (1900's) **Databases Used:** Agricola; Agris; Biosis; CABCD **Loan:** Internationally **Service:** Internationally **Photocopy:** Yes

3538   Lexington, Kentucky, US
University of Kentucky (UK)
John A. Morris Memorial Library
200 Gluck Equine Research Center
Lexington, Kentucky 40546-0099
Phone: +1(606) 257-1192 **Fax:** +1(606) 257-8542 **WWW:** www.uky.edu/agriculture/vetscience/morris.htm

Founded: 1989 **Type:** Academic **Head:** Gracie Hale *Phone:* +1(606) 257-1192 *Email:* ghale@ca.uky.edu **Staff:** 1 Prof. 1 Other **Holdings:** 300 books 50 journals **Language of Collection/Services:** English / English **Subjects:** Veterinary Medicine **Specializations:** Horses **Networks:** OCLC **Databases Used:** Comprehensive **Loan:** Do not loan **Service:** Internationally **Photocopy:** No

3539   Lexington, Kentucky, US
University of Kentucky (UK)
Shaver Engineering Library
355 Anderson Hall
Lexington, Kentucky 40506-0046
Phone: +1(606) 257-2965 **Fax:** +1(606) 323-1911 **Email:** pwilson@pop.uky.edu **WWW:** www.uky.edu/Libraries **OPAC:** commonweb.uky.edu:8000

Type: Academic **Head:** James Manasco *Phone:* +1(606) 257-8358 *Email:* manasco@pop.uky.edu **Staff:** 2 Prof. 1.4 Other **Language of Collection/Services:** English / English **Subjects:** Engineering **Networks:** OCLC **Databases Used:** Comprehensive **Loan:** Internationally **Service:** Internationally **Photocopy:** Yes

3540   Morehead, Kentucky, US
Morehead State University (MSU)
Camden-Carroll Library (CCL)
Morehead, Kentucky 40351
Phone: +1(606) 783-5491 **Fax:** +1(606) 783-2799 **Email:** library@morehead-st.edu **WWW:** www.morehead-st.edu **OPAC:** www.morehead-st.edu/units/library **Ariel IP:** 147. 133.37.106

Former Name: Johnson Camden Library **Founded:** 1931 **Type:** Academic **Head:** Larry X. Besant *Phone:* +1(606) 783-5100 *Email:* l.besant@morehead-st.edu **Staff:** 14 Prof. 26 Other **Holdings:** 431,803 books 2,523 journals **Language of Collection/Services:** English / English **Subjects:** Animal Husbandry, Horticulture, Veterinary Science, Zoology **Networks:** OCLC **Databases Used:** Comprehensive **Loan:** In country **Photocopy:** Yes

3541   Murray, Kentucky, US
Murray State University
Waterfield Library
PO Box 9
Murray, Kentucky 42071-0009
Location: North 14th Street **Phone:** +1(502) 762-2053
Fax: +1(502) 762-3736 **Email:** jeff.cottingham@
murraystate.edu **WWW:** www.murraystate.edu **OPAC:**
www.murraystate.edu/msml/msml.htm **Ariel IP:** 204.148.
124.124

Founded: 1931 **Type:** Academic **Head:** Dr. Coy Harmon
Email: coy.harmon@murraystate.edu *Phone:* +1(502) 762-
2291 **Staff:** 12 Prof. 28 Other **Holdings:** 592,000 books
2,400 journals **Language of Collection/Services:** English
Subjects: Crops, Farming, Fisheries, Horticulture, Soil Science, Veterinary Medicine **Networks:** OCLC **Databases
Used:** Comprehensive **Loan:** In country **Photocopy:** Yes

Louisiana

3542   Baton Rouge, Louisiana, US
Louisiana State University (LSU)
Libraries
Baton Rouge, Louisiana 70803
Phone: +1(225) 388-8875 **Fax:** +1(225) 334-3598 **WWW:**
www.lsu.edu **OPAC:** www.lib.lsu.edu

Founded: 1860 **Type:** Academic **Head:** Jennifer Cargill
Phone: +1(225) 388-2217 *Email:* cargill@lsu.edu **Staff:** 48
Prof. 88 Other **Holdings:** 35,000 books **Language of Col-
lection/Services:** English / English **Subjects:** Agriculture
(Tropics), Agribusiness, Agricultural Development, Agri-
cultural Economics, Agricultural Engineering, Animal Hus-
bandry, Biotechnology, Education/Extension, Entomology,
Crops, Farming, Food Sciences, Forestry, Horticulture, Plant
Pathology, Soil Science, Veterinary Medicine, Water Re-
sources **Specializations:** Aquaculture, Fisheries, Wetlands,
Rice, Sugar **Networks:** OCLC **Databases Used:** Agricola;
ABI/Inform; Medline; CARL UnCover **Loan:** Internation-
ally **Service:** Inhouse **Photocopy:** Yes

3543   Baton Rouge, Louisiana, US
Louisiana State University (LSU)
School of Veterinary Medicine Library
South Stadium Drive at River Road
Baton Rouge, Louisiana 70803-8414
Phone: +1(225) 346-3173 **Fax:** +1(225) 346-3295 **WWW:**
www.lsu.edu **OPAC:** www.lib.lsu.edu

Type: Academic **Head:** Sue Loubiere *Phone:* +1(225)
346-3172 *Email:* vtllou@lsu.edu **Staff:** 1 Prof. 6.25 Other
Holdings: 38,000 books 600 journals **Language of Collec-
tion/Services:** English / English **Subjects:** Veterinary Medicine **Networks:** OCLC **Databases Used:** CABCD; Medline
Loan: Internationally **Service:** Internationally **Photocopy:**
Yes

3544   Baton Rouge, Louisiana, US
Southern University and A & M College
John B. Cade Library
167 Roosevelt Steptoe Avenue
Baton Rouge, Louisiana 70813

Phone: +1(225) 771-4875 **Fax:** +1(225) 771-4113 **Email:**
ref@subr.cmq.com **WWW:** www.subr.edu **OPAC:** www.
subr.cmq.com/data/eleclib.htm

Type: Academic **Head:** Emma Bradford Perry *Phone:*
+1(225) 771-4990 *Email:* eperry@subr.cmq.com

3545   Monroe, Louisiana, US
University of Louisiana at Monroe (ULM)
Sandel Library
4100 Northeast Drive
Monroe, Louisiana 71209-0720
Phone: +1(318) 342-1069 **Fax:** +1(318) 342-1075 **WWW:**
www.ulm.edu **OPAC:** www.ulm.edu/~dosmith/
SANDELIN.HTM

Former Name: Northeast Louisiana University **Founded:**
1931 **Type:** Academic **Head:** Donald R. Smith *Phone:* +1
(318) 342-1050 *Email:* libdsmith@ulm.edu **Staff:** 12 Prof.
16 Other **Holdings:** 900,000 books 2,900 journals **Language of Collection/Services:** English **Networks:** OCLC
Loan: Internationally **Photocopy:** Yes

3546   Natchitoches, Louisiana, US
Northwestern State University of Louisiana (NSU)
Eugene P. Watson Memorial Library
College Avenue
Natchitoches, Louisiana 71497
Phone: +1(318) 357-4574 **Fax:** +1(318) 357-4470 **WWW:**
www.nsula.edu/departments/watson_library/index.html
OPAC: www.lsu.edu/web-opac

Former Name: Louisiana State Normal School, Louisiana
State Normal College, Northwestern State College of Louisi-
ana **Founded:** 1885 **Type:** Academic **Head:** Ada D. Jarred
Phone: +1(318) 357-4403 *Email:* jarred@alpha.nsula.edu
Staff: 11 Prof. 7 Other **Holdings:** 4,200 books 50 journals
Language of Collection/Services: English **Subjects:** Agri-
culture (Tropics), Agribusiness, Agricultural Development,
Agricultural Economics, Agricultural Engineering, Animal
Husbandry, Biotechnology, Crops, Education/Extension,
Entomology, Farming, Fisheries, Food Sciences, Forestry,
Horticulture, Plant Pathology, Soil Science, Veterinary Med-
icine, Water Resources **Networks:** OCLC **Loan:** In country
Service: In country **Photocopy:** Yes

3547   New Orleans, Louisiana, US
United States Department of Agriculture,
      Agricultural Research Service, Southern
      Regional Research Center (USDA, ARS,
      SRRC)
Library
PO Box 19687
New Orleans, Louisiana 70179
Location: 1100 Robert E. Lee Boulevard **Phone:** +1(504)
286-4287 **Fax:** +1(504) 286-4396 **WWW:** msa.ars.usda.
gov/la/srrc/index.htm **Ariel IP:** 199.78.118.231

Founded: 1941 **Type:** Government **Head:** Suhad Wojkow-
ski *Phone:* +1(504) 286-4288 *Email:* suhad@nola.srrc.usda.
gov **Staff:** 1 Prof. 2 Other **Holdings:** 35,000 books 500 journals **Language of Collection/Services:** English **Subjects:**
Biochemistry, Chemistry, Crops (USA - South), Isoptera,
Physics, Plant Physiology, Textiles **Networks:** OCLC **Data-**

bases Developed: Reprint database - access to publications authored by Center staff **Databases Used:** Comprehensive **Loan:** Internationally **Photocopy:** Yes

3548   Ruston, Louisiana, US
Louisiana Tech University
Prescott Memorial Library
PO Box 10408
Ruston, Louisiana 71272
Phone: +1(318) 257-3555 **Fax:** +1(318) 257-2579 **WWW:** www.latech.edu **OPAC:** www.latech.edu/tech/library/catalog.htm

Founded: 1895 **Type:** Academic **Head:** Rebecca L. Stenzel *Phone:* +1(318) 257-2577 *Email:* stenzel@latech.edu **Staff:** 15 Prof. 16 Other **Holdings:** 10,000 books **Subjects:** Agribusiness, Animal Husbandry, Forestry, Horticulture **Loan:** In country **Photocopy:** Yes

Maine

3549   Orono, Maine, US
University of Maine
Raymond H. Fogler Library, Science and
     Engineering Center
5929 Fogler Library
Orono, Maine 04469-5729
Phone: +1(207) 581-1673 **Fax:** +1(207) 581-1653 **Email:** ref.questions@umit.maine.edu **WWW:** www.umaine.edu **OPAC:** libraries.maine.edu/umaine

Founded: 1865 **Type:** Academic **Head:** Elaine Albright *Email:* elaine.albright@umit.maine.edu *Phone:* +1(207) 581-1660 **Staff:** 21 Prof. 45 Other **Holdings:** 25,000 books 500 journals **Language of Collection/Services:** English / English **Subjects:** Agribusiness, Agricultural Economics, Agricultural Engineering, Animal Husbandry, Aquaculture, Biotechnology, Crops, Entomology, Environmental Sciences, Farming, Forestry, Plant Pathology, Soil Science, Water Resources **Specializations:** Spruce Budworm **Networks:** OCLC **Databases Developed:** Bibliography of materials on the Spruce Budworm **Databases Used:** Agricola **Loan:** Internationally **Service:** Internationally **Photocopy:** Yes

3550   West Boothbay Harbor, Maine, US
Maine State Department of Marine Resources
Library
McKown Point
West Boothbay Harbor, Maine 04575
Phone: +1(207) 633-9551 **Fax:** +1(207) 633-7109 **WWW:** janus.state.me.us/dmr

Type: Government **Staff:** 1 Prof. 1 Other **Holdings:** 10,000 books 255 journals **Language of Collection/Services:** English **Subjects:** Food Sciences, Water Resources **Specializations:** Fisheries **Loan:** In country **Service:** Internationally **Photocopy:** Yes

Maryland

3551   Beltsville, Maryland, US
Agricultural Network Information Center,
     Secretariat (AgNIC)
10301 Baltimore Ave.
Beltsville, Maryland 20705
Email: agnic@agnic.org **WWW:** www.agnic.org

Founded: 1995 **Type:** Association **Head:** Melanie Gardner, Coordinator *Phone:* +1(305) 504-6813 *Email:* mgardner@nal.usda.gov **Language of Collection/Services:** English / English **Subjects:** Comprehensive **Specializations:** Animal Husbandry, Economic Development, Entomology, Food Sciences, Forestry, Nutrition, Plants, Statistics, Water Quality **Databases Developed:** AgNIC — this discipline specific virtual information center provides Internet access to important sources regardless of their physical location. Sites selected for participation in AgNIC are reviewed and evaluated for reliability, quality, and timeliness.

3552   Beltsville, Maryland, US
United States Department of Agriculture,
     Agricultural Research Service (USDA, ARS)
Biological Control Documentation Center
     (BCDC)
National Agricultural Library, 4th Floor
10301 Baltimore Ave.
Beltsville, Maryland 20705
Fax: +1(301) 504-6355 **Email:** jcoulson@nal.usda.gov **WWW:** www.ars-grin.gov/nigrp/bcdc.html

Founded: 1982 **Type:** Government **Head:** Jack R. Coulson *Phone:* +1(301) 504-6350 *Email:* jcoulson@nal.usda.gov **Holdings:** 1,000 books 6 journals **Language of Collection/Services:** English **Subjects:** Biological Control, Entomology, Pests, Weed Control **Databases Developed:** ROBO - Releases of Beneficial Organisms; NAIAD - North American Immigrant Arthropod Database **Photocopy:** Yes

3553   Beltsville, Maryland, US
United States Department of Agriculture,
     Agricultural Research Service (USDA, ARS)
National Agricultural Library (NAL)
10301 Baltimore Avenue
Beltsville, Maryland 20705-2351
Phone: +1(301) 504-5479 **Fax:** +1(301) 504-6927 **Email:** info@nal.usda.gov **WWW:** www.nal.usda.gov **OPAC:** www.nal.usda.gov/isis, telnet://opac.nal.usda.gov

Former Name: USDA Library **Founded:** 1862 **Type:** Government **Head:** Pamela André *Phone:* +1(301) 504-5248 *Email:* pandre@nal.usda.gov **Staff:** 110 Prof. 80 Other **Holdings:** 2,000,000 books 22,000 journals **Subjects:** Comprehensive **Specializations:** National Agricultural Text Digitizing Program, Specialized Information Centers **Databases Developed:** AGRICOLA - 3,000,000 records indexing agricultural literature; accessed through DIALOG; available on CD-ROM from Silver Platter Information, Inc.; Plant Genome Databases **Databases Used:** Comprehensive **Networks:** AGRIS; OCLC **Loan:** Internationally **Service:** Internationally **Photocopy:** Yes

3553a   Beltsville, Maryland, US
United States Department of Agriculture,
Agricultural Research Service, National
Agricultural Library (USDA, ARS, NAL)
Alternative Farming Systems Information Center
(AFSIC)
10301 Baltimore Boulevard, Room 304
Beltsville, Maryland 20705-2351
Phone: +1(301) 504-6559 **Fax:** +1(301) 504-6409 **Email:**
afsic@nal.usda.gov **WWW:** www.nal.usda.gov

Founded: 1986 **Type:** Government **Head:** Jane Potter Gates
Phone: +1(301) 504-5724 *Email:* jgates@nal.usda.gov
Staff: 2 Prof. 1 Other **Language of Collection/Services:**
English / English **Subjects:** Alternative Crops, Alternative
Farming, Aquaculture, Farming Systems, Sustainability
Specializations: Videocassettes of Sustainable Agriculture
pioneers (interviews) **Networks:** OCLC **Databases Developed:** AGRICOLA - comprehensive catalog of agricultural documents; access on-line or via CD-ROM **Databases
Used:** Agricola **Loan:** In country **Service:** Internationally
Photocopy: Yes

3553b   Beltsville, Maryland, US
United States Department of Agriculture,
Agricultural Research Service, National
Agricultural Library (USDA, ARS, NAL)
Animal Welfare Information Center (AWIC)
10301 Baltimore Boulevard, 5th Floor
Beltsville, Maryland 20705-2351
Phone: +1(301) 504-6212 **Fax:** +1(301) 504-7125 **Email:**
awic@nal.usda.gov **WWW:** www.nal.usda.gov/awic

Founded: 1986 **Type:** Government **Head:** Jean Larson
Phone: +1(301) 504-5215 *Email:* jlarson@nal.usda.gov
Staff: 5 Prof. 1 Other **Language of Collection/Services:**
English **Subjects:** Animal Husbandry, Animal Experiments,
Ethics of Animal Use, Veterinary Medicine **Specializations:**
Animal Testing Alternatives, Animal Welfare, Bioethics,
Laboratory Animals **Databases Used:** Comprehensive
Loan: In country **Service:** In country **Photocopy:** Yes

3553c   Beltsville, Maryland, US
United States Department of Agriculture,
Agricultural Research Service, National
Agricultural Library (USDA, ARS, NAL)
Food and Nutrition Information Center (FNIC)
10301 Baltimore Boulevard, Room 304
Beltsville, Maryland 20705-2351
Phone: +1(301) 504-5719 **Fax:** +1(301) 504-6409 **Email:**
fnic@nal.usda.gov **WWW:** www.nal.usda.gov/fnic

Founded: 1971 **Type:** Government **Head:** Shirley K. Evans, Acting *Phone:* +1(301) 504-6369 **Staff:** 12 Prof. **Language of Collection/Services:** English / English **Subjects:**
Food Sciences, Human Nutrition **Specializations:** Food
Safety, Food Service, Nutrition Education **Databases Developed:** Foodborne Illness Education; WIC **Databases
Used:** Comprehensive **Loan:** In country and Canada **Service:** Internationally **Photocopy:** Yes

3553d   Beltsville, Maryland, US
United States Department of Agriculture,
Agricultural Research Service, National
Agricultural Library (USDA, ARS, NAL)
Plant Genome Data and Information Center
(PGDIC)
10301 Baltimore Avenue, 4th Floor
Beltsville, Maryland 20705-2351
Phone: +1(301) 504-6613 **Fax:** +1(301) 504-5022 **Email:**
pgenome@nal.usda.gov **WWW:** www.nal.usda.gov
OPAC: www.nal.usda.gov/ag98

Founded: 1990 **Type:** Government **Head:** Dr. Susan McCarthy *Phone:* +1(301) 504-6613 *Email:* smccarth@nal.
usda.gov **Staff:** 3 Prof. **Language of Collection/Services:**
English / English **Subjects:** Biochemistry, Genetics, Plants
Specializations: Genetic Mapping, Nucleotide Sequences
Databases Developed: Plant Genome Databases, Agricultural Genome Information Server **Databases Used:** Comprehensive **Service:** Limited free searching, extensive fee-for-service **Photocopy:** Yes

3553e   Beltsville, Maryland, US
United States Department of Agriculture,
Agricultural Research Service, National
Agricultural Library (USDA, ARS, NAL)
Rural Information Center (RIC)
10301 Baltimore Boulevard, Room 304
Beltsville, Maryland 20705-2351
Phone: +1(301) 633-7701 **Fax:** +1(301) 504-5181 **Email:**
ric.@nal.usda.gov **WWW:** www.nal.usda.gov/ric

Founded: 1987 **Type:** Government **Head:** Patricia LaCaille
John *Phone:* +1(301) 504-5372 *Email:* pjohn@nal.usda.gov
Staff: 9 Prof. 3 Other **Language of Collection/Services:**
English / English **Subjects:** Agribusiness, Community Development, Diversification, Economic Development, Education/Extension, Health Services, Local Government, Rural
Development, Rural Sociology, Water Issues **Loan:** Internationally **Service:** Internationally **Photocopy:** Yes

3553f   Beltsville, Maryland, US
United States Department of Agriculture,
Agricultural Research Service, National
Agricultural Library (USDA, ARS, NAL)
Special Collections
10301 Baltimore Boulevard
Beltsville, Maryland 20705-2351
Phone: +1(301) 504-5876 **Fax:** +1(301) 504-7593 **Email:**
speccoll@nal.usda.gov **WWW:** www.nal.usda.gov

Former Name: Rare Book Section, Rare Book Section
Type: Government **Head:** Susan H. Fugate *Phone:* +1(301)
504-5876 *Email:* sfugate@nal.usda.gov **Staff:** 4 Prof. 3
Other **Holdings:** 60,000 books **Language of Collection/
Services:** English / English **Networks:** OCLC **Databases
Used:** Agricola **Loan:** Do not loan **Service:** Internationally
Photocopy: Yes

3553g   Beltsville, Maryland, US
United States Department of Agriculture,
Agricultural Research Service, National
Agricultural Library (USDA, ARS, NAL)

Technology Transfer Information Center (TTIC)
10301 Baltimore Boulevard, 4th Floor
Beltsville, Maryland 20705-2351
Phone: +1(301) 504-6875 **Fax:** +1(301) 504-7098 **Email:** ttic@nal.usda.gov **WWW:** www.nal.usda.gov/ttic

Founded: 1989 **Type:** Government **Head:** Kathleen Hayes *Phone:* +1(301) 504-6875 *Email:* khayes@nal.usda.gov **Staff:** 2 Prof. 1 Other **Language of Collection/Services:** English **Subjects:** Agricultural Technologies, Entrepreneurship, Intellectual Property, Science and Technology Policy, Venture Capital **Specializations:** Business Management, Government Research, Innovation, Laboratories, New Products, Patents, Research Policy, Technology Diffusion of Research, Technology Transfer **Networks:** OCLC **Databases Developed:** Automated Patent System - the patent database produced by the PS Patent and Trademark Office; TEK-TRAN - Technology Transfer Automated Retrieval System - available via Internet at www.nal.usda.gov/ttic/tektran/tektran.html **Databases Used:** Comprehensive **Loan:** Internationally **Service:** Internationally **Photocopy:** Yes

3553h   Beltsville, Maryland, US
United States Department of Agriculture,
    Agricultural Research Service, National
    Agricultural Library (USDA, ARS, NAL)
Water Quality Information Center (WQIC)
10301 Baltimore Boulevard, 4th Floor
Beltsville, Maryland 20705-2351
Phone: +1(301) 504-6077 **Fax:** +1(301) 504-7098 **Email:** wqic@nal.usda.gov **WWW:** www.nal.usda.gov/wqic

Founded: 1990 **Type:** Government **Head:** Joe Makuch *Phone:* +1(301) 504-6077 *Email:* jakuch@nal.usda.gov **Staff:** 2 Prof. **Language of Collection/Services:** English **Subjects:** Nonpoint Source Pollution, Water Resources **Specializations:** Agricultural Wastes, Water Erosion, Water Policy, Water Pollution, Water Quality **Databases Used:** Agricola; Water Resources Abstracts **Loan:** Internationally **Service:** Internationally **Photocopy:** Yes

3554   Bethesda, Maryland, US
Society of American Foresters (SAF)
Library
5400 Grosvenor Lane
Bethesda, Maryland 20814
Fax: +1(301) 897-3690 **WWW:** www.safnet.org

Type: Association **Head:** Dr. Jennifer L. Plyler *Phone:* +1 (301) 897-8720 ext 117 *Email:* plylerj@safnet.org **Holdings:** 6 journals **Language of Collection/Services:** English/English **Subjects:** Forestry **Photocopy:** Yes

3555   Cambridge, Maryland, US
University of Maryland, Horn Point
    Environmental Laboratory
Horn Point Library
PO Box 775
Cambridge, Maryland 21613
Phone: +1(410) 221-8450 **Fax:** +1(410) 221-8490 **Email:** windsor@hpl.umces.edu **WWW:** www.hpl.umces.edu

Former Name: Center for Environmental and Estuarine Studies **Founded:** 1973 **Type:** Academic **Head:** Darlene

Windsor *Phone:* +1(410) 221-8450 *Email:* windsor@hpl.umces.edu **Staff:** 1 Prof. **Holdings:** 31,697 books 72 journals **Language of Collection/Services:** English / English **Subjects:** Aquaculture, Botany, Estuaries, Fisheries, Marine Sciences, Oceanography, Seafoods **Databases Used:** Comprehensive **Loan:** Inhouse **Service:** Inhouse **Photocopy:** Yes

3556   Chevy Chase, Maryland, US
Rachel Carson Council Inc.
Library
8940 Jones Mill Road
Chevy Chase, Maryland 20815
WWW: members.aol.com/rccouncil/ourpage/rcc_page.htm

Former Name: Rachel Carson Trust for the Living Environment **Founded:** 1965 **Type:** Non-profit **Head:** Dr. Diana Post *Phone:* +1(301) 652-1877 *Email:* rccouncil@aol.com **Holdings:** 3,500 books **Language of Collection/Services:** English / English **Subjects:** Pesticides **Loan:** Inhouse **Service:** Internationally **Photocopy:** Yes

3557   College Park, Maryland, US
University of Maryland
McKeldin Library
College Park, Maryland 20742
Phone: +1(301) 405-9075 **Fax:** +1(301) 314-7111 **Email:** www.lib.umd.edu/UMCP/PUBSERV/eref.html **WWW:** www.lib.umd.edu/UMCP **OPAC:** victorweb.lib.umd.edu:9000

Founded: 1856 **Type:** Academic **Head:** Dr. Charles Lowry *Phone:* +1(301) 405-9128 *Email:* clowry@deans.umd.edu **Staff:** 90 Prof. 148 Other **Holdings:** 13,000 books 400 journals **Language of Collection/Services:** English / English **Subjects:** Comprehensive **Databases Used:** Comprehensive **Loan:** Internationally **Photocopy:** Yes

3558   Princess Anne, Maryland, US
University of Maryland, Eastern Shore (UMES)
Frederick Douglass Library (FDL)
Princess Anne, Maryland 21853-1299
Location: Backbone Road **Phone:** +1(410) 651-6607, 651-7937 **Fax:** +1(410) 651-6269 **Email:** rpolk@fdl.umes.umd.edu **WWW:** www.fdl.umes.umd.edu **OPAC:** www.fdl.umes.umd.edu

Former Name: Maryland State College (MSC) **Founded:** 1968 **Type:** Academic **Head:** Theodosia T. Shields *Phone:* +1(410) 651-6622 *Email:* ttshields@mail.umes.edu **Staff:** 12 Prof. 23 Other **Language of Collection/Services:** English / English **Subjects:** Agriculture (Tropics), Agricultural Economics, Agricultural Engineering, Animal Husbandry, Entomology, Farming, Fisheries, Food Sciences, Horticulture, Plant Pathology, Soil Science **Specializations:** Agribusiness, Agricultural Development, Biotechnology, Crops, Education/Extension, Plants **Networks:** OCLC **Databases Used:** Comprehensive **Loan:** Internationally **Service:** Internationally **Photocopy:** Yes

3559 Solomons, Maryland, US
University of Maryland, Center for Environmental
Science, Chesapeake Biological Laboratory
(UM, CES, CBL)
Library
Box 38
Solomons, Maryland 20688-0038
Location: 1 Williams Street **Phone:** +1(410) 326-7287
Fax: +1(410) 326-7302 **WWW:** www.co.cees.edu

Former Name: Natural Resources Institute, Center for Environmental and Estuarine Studies (CEES) **Founded:** 1925
Type: Academic **Head:** Kathleen Heil *Phone:* +1(401)
326-7287 *Email:* heil@cbl.cees.edu **Staff:** 1 Prof. **Holdings:**
50,000 books 420 journals **Language of Collection/Services:** English **Subjects:** Cost Effectiveness Analysis, Ecology, Ecosystems, Fisheries, Immunology, Toxicology
Specializations: Aquatic Invertebrates, Fresh Water, Shellfish, Sponges **Loan:** Inhouse **Photocopy:** Yes

3560 Westminster, Maryland, US
Carroll County Farm Museum
Burns Research Library
500 South Center Street
Westminster, Maryland 21157
Phone: +1(410) 876-2667 **Fax:** +1(410) 848-7775

Founded: 1986 **Type:** Government **Subjects:** Farm Machinery (History - 19th Century), Farm Machinery (History - 20th Century), Farming, Rural Society (History - 19th Century), Rural Society (History - 20th Century) **Loan:** Do not loan **Service:** Inhouse **Photocopy:** Yes

Massachusetts

3561 Amherst, Massachusetts, US
University of Massachusetts
Biological Sciences Library
214 Morrill Science Center
Amherst, Massachusetts 01003
Phone: +1(413) 545-2674 **Fax:** +1(413) 549-7126 **WWW:**
www.umass.edu **OPAC:** umlibr.library.umass.edu

Type: Academic **Head:** Laurence Feldman *Phone:* +1(413)
545-0284 *Email:* larry.feldman@library.umass.edu

3562 Boston, Massachusetts, US
Environmental Protection Agency (EPA)
Region I Library
1. Congress St., Suite 1100
Boston, Massachusetts 02114-2023
Phone: +1(617) 918-1990 **Fax:** +1(617) 918-1992 **Email:**
library-reg1@epamail.epa.gov **WWW:** www.epa.gov
OPAC: www.epa.gov/region01/oarm/rlinks.html

Founded: 1970 **Type:** Government **Staff:** 2 Prof. 2 Other
Holdings: 20,000 books 100 journals **Language of Collection/Services:** English / English **Subjects:** Air Pollution, Air Quality, Environment, Fisheries, Hazardous Wastes, Solid Wastes, Water Pollution, Water Quality, Water Resources
Specializations: Wetlands **Networks:** OCLC **Databases Developed:** Wetlands database and collection; Test Methods

- EPA analytical procedures; inhouse access only **Loan:**
Internationally **Service:** Inhouse **Photocopy:** Yes

3563 Boston, Massachusetts, US
Massachusetts Horticulture Society
Library
Horticultural Hall
300 Massachusetts Avenue
Boston, Massachusetts 02115
Phone: +1(617) 536-9280 ext 225 **Fax:** +1(617) 262-8780
Email: library@masshort.org **WWW:** www.masshort.org

Founded: 1829 **Type:** Association **Staff:** 1 Prof. 1 Other
Holdings: 39,000 books **Language of Collection/Services:**
English / English **Subjects:** Gardening, Horticulture, Landscape Architecture **Networks:** OCLC **Loan:** Internationally
Service: Inhouse **Photocopy:** Yes

3564 Boston, Massachusetts, US
Tufts University
Health Sciences Library
Arthur M. Sackler Center for Health
Communications
145 Harrison Avenue
Boston, Massachusetts 02111
Phone: +1(617) 636-6705 **Fax:** +1(617) 636-4039 **WWW:**
www.library.tufts.edu **OPAC:** www.library.tufts.edu/hsl/
hsl.html

Type: Academic **Head:** Elizabeth K. Eaton *Phone:* +1(617)
636-2481 *Email:* eeaton@opal.tufts.edu **Staff:** 11.2 Prof. 18
Other **Holdings:** 120,500 books 1,468 journals **Language of Collection/Services:** English / English **Subjects:** Veterinary Medicine **Specializations:** Biology, Dentistry, Medicine, Nutrition **Networks:** OCLC **Databases Developed:** OVID MEDLINE **Databases Used:** Comprehensive **Loan:** Internationally **Service:** In country **Photocopy:** Yes

3565 Boylston, Massachusetts, US
Worcester County Horticultural Society
Library
Tower Hill Botanic Garden
PO Box 598
Boylston, Massachusetts 01505-0598
Location: 11 French Drive **Phone:** +1(508) 869-6111 **Fax:**
+1(508) 869-0314 **WWW:** www.towerhillbg.org

Founded: 1842 **Type:** Association **Head:** Jane Milligan
Phone: +1(508) 869-6111 **Staff:** 1 Prof. **Holdings:** 7,700
books 45 journals **Language of Collection/Services:** English / English **Subjects:** Horticulture **Networks:** OCLC
Loan: Members only **Service:** Inhouse **Photocopy:** Yes

3566 Cambridge, Massachusetts, US
Arthur D. Little Inc.
Life Sciences Library
Acorn Park
Cambridge, Massachusetts 02140
Fax: +1(617) 498-7241 **WWW:**
www.arthurdlittle.com/default.htm

Founded: 1954 **Type:** Business **Head:** Jenny T. Baker
Phone: +1(617) 498-6006 *Email:* jenny@adlittle.com **Staff:**
2 Prof. 1 Other **Holdings:** 2,935 books 250 journals **Lan-**

guage of Collection/Services: English **Subjects:** Animal Husbandry, Biotechnology, Entomology, Fisheries, Plant Pathology, Soil Science, Veterinary Medicine **Loan:** In country **Service:** Inhouse **Photocopy:** Yes

3567   Cambridge, Massachusetts, US
Harvard University, Arnold Arboretum, Farlow Herbarium, Gray Herbarium, Botanical Museum
Botany Libraries
22 Divinity Avenue
Cambridge, Massachusetts 02138
Phone: +1(617) 495-2366 **Fax:** +1(617) 495-8654 **Email:** botref@oeb.harvard.edu **WWW:** www.herbaria.harvard. edu/Libraries/libraries.html **OPAC:** www-hcl.harvard.edu/ catalogs.html

Founded: 1890 **Type:** Academic **Head:** Judith A. Warnement *Email:* warnemen@oeb.harvard.edu *Phone:* +1(617) 495-2640 **Staff:** 4 Prof. 3 Other **Holdings:** 250,000 books 1,200 journals **Language of Collection/Services:** English / English **Subjects:** Agriculture (Tropics), Botany, Crops, Horticulture, Plant Pathology, Plants, Taxonomy **Networks:** OCLC **Databases Developed:** Gray Herbarium Index - Taxonomic names of American plants (formerly "Gray Card Index") available via Internet. **Loan:** Do not loan **Photocopy:** Yes

3568   Cambridge, Massachusetts, US
Harvard University, Harvard College Libraries
    (HCL)
Cabot Science Library
1 Oxford St.
Cambridge, Massachusetts 02138
Phone: +1(617) 495-5353 **Fax:** +1(617) 495-5324 **WWW:** www-hcl.harvard.edu **OPAC:** www-hcl.harvard.edu/ catalogs.html

Type: Academic **Head:** Lynne M. Schmelz, Librarian for the Sciences, Acting Head *Phone:* +1(617) 495-5324 *Email:* schmelz@fas.harvard.edu **Networks:** OCLC

3569   Cambridge, Massachusetts, US
Harvard University
Oakes Ames Orchid Library
University Herbarium
Cambridge, Massachusetts 02138
Phone: +1(617) 495-2366 **Fax:** +1(617) 495-8654 **Email:** botref@oeb.harvard.edu **WWW:** www.herbaria.harvard. edu/Libraries/oakes_ames.html **OPAC:** www-hcl.harvard. edu/catalogs.html

Type: Academic **Holdings:** 4,891 books

3570   Cambridge, Massachusetts, US
Massachusetts Institute of Technology
Science Library
Room 14S-134
77 Massachusetts Ave.
Cambridge, Massachusetts 02139-4307
Phone: +1(617) 253-5685 **Fax:** +1(617) 251-1657 **WWW:** www.mit.edu **OPAC:** libraries.mit.edu/services/barton. html

Type: Academic **Head:** E. Louisa Worthington *Phone:* +1(617) 253-6575, 253-9795 *Email:* elworthi@mit.edu **Holdings:** 871,380 books

3571   Framingham, Massachusetts, US
New England Wild Flower Society Inc. (NEWFS)
Lawrence Newcomb Library
Garden in the Woods
180 Hemenway Road
Framingham, Massachusetts 01701-2699
WWW: www.newfs.org

Type: Non-profit **Head:** Mary M. Walker and John I. Benson *Phone:* +1(508) 877-7630 *Email:* newfs@newfs.org **Staff:** 2 Prof. 4 Other **Holdings:** 4,000 books 30 journals **Language of Collection/Services:** English / English **Subjects:** Gardening, Horticulture, Native Plants Conservation, Native Plants (Canada), Native Plants (USA), Plants **Specializations:** Comprehensive flora of U.S. regions and states, Extensive collection of gardening with native plants, Unique collection of the periodical publications of some 90 botanical clubs and native plant societies in the US and Canada **Databases Developed:** Database of botanical collection; Database of rare and endangered plants and their conservation **Loan:** Inhouse **Service:** Members only **Photocopy:** No

3572   Lincoln, Massachusetts, US
Massachusetts Audubon Society
Hatheway Environmental Resource Library
208 South Great Road
Lincoln, Massachusetts 01773
Phone: +1(800) 283-8266, +1(617) 259-9500 ext 7253 **Fax:** +1(617) 259-8899 **WWW:** www.massaudubon.org

Founded: 1967 **Type:** Association **Head:** Martha J. Cohen *Phone:* +1(617) 259-9500 **Staff:** 1 Prof. .5 Other **Holdings:** 11,000 books **Language of Collection/Services:** English **Subjects:** Agriculture (Tropics), Agricultural Economics, Education/Extension, Farming, Fisheries, Forestry, Soil Science, Water Resources **Loan:** Internationally **Service:** Internationally **Photocopy:** Yes

3573   North Grafton, Massachusetts, US
Tufts University School of Veterinary Medicine
    (TUSVM)
Webster Veterinary Medical Library
200 Westboro Road
North Grafton, Massachusetts 01536
Phone: +1(508) 839-7957 **Fax:** +1(508) 839-7987 **Email:** soelschl@opal.tufts.edu **WWW:** www.tufts.edu/vet **OPAC:** www.library.tufts.edu/vet

Founded: 1982 **Type:** Academic **Head:** Melinda Saffer Marchand *Phone:* +1(508) 839-7988 *Email:* msaffer@opal. tufts.edu **Staff:** 2 Prof. 2.5 Other **Holdings:** 6,000 books 437 journals **Language of Collection/Services:** English / English **Subjects:** Biotechnology, Veterinary Medicine **Networks:** OCLC **Databases Used:** Comprehensive **Loan:** Internationally **Service:** Internationally **Photocopy:** Yes

3574   Petersham, Massachusetts, US
Harvard University
Harvard Forest Library

PO Box 68
Petersham, Massachusetts 01366-0068
Location: 324 North Main Street **Phone:** +1(978) 724-3302 **Fax:** +1(978) 724-3595 **WWW:** LTERnet.edu/hfr

Founded: 1908 **Type:** Academic **Head:** Barbara Flye *Phone:* +1(978) 724-3302 **Staff:** 1 Other **Holdings:** 28,000 books 150 journals **Language of Collection/Services:** English **Subjects:** Forestry **Loan:** Inhouse **Photocopy:** Yes

3575   Woods Hole, Massachusetts, US
Marine Biological Laboratory, Woods Hole
        Oceanographic Institution (MBL, WHOI)
Library
Woods Hole, Massachusetts 02543
Location: 7 MBL Street **Phone:** +1(508) 289-7435 **Fax:** +1(508) 540-6902 **Email:** library@mbl.edu **WWW:** www.mbl.edu/vhosts/LIBRARY/index2.shtml **OPAC:** www.mbl.edu/vhosts/LIBRARY/LibraryURLS.html **Ariel IP:** 128.128.172.33 (MBL), 128.128.16.165 (WHOI)

Founded: 1859 **Type:** Research **Head:** Catherine Norton *Phone:* +1(508) 548-3705, 289-7341 *Email:* cnorton@mbl.edu **Staff:** 10 Prof. 16 Other **Holdings:** 50,000 books 2,000 journals **Subjects:** Biology, Chemistry, Oceanography, Fish Farming, Geology, Physiology, Water Resources **Networks:** BLC; OCLC; Uncover **Databases Used:** Comprehensive **Loan:** In country **Service:** Internationally **Photocopy:** Yes

3576   Worcester, Massachusetts, US
Worcester Polytechnic Institute (WPI)
George C. Gordon Library
100 Institute
Worcester, Massachusetts 01609
Phone: +1(508) 831-6700 **WWW:** www.wpi.edu **OPAC:** www.WPI.EDU/Academics/Library

Founded: 1865 **Type:** Academic **Head:** Helen M. Shuster *Phone:* +1(508) 831-5058 *Email:* hshuster@wpi.edu **Staff:** 9 Prof. 15 Other **Language of Collection/Services:** English **Subjects:** Biotechnology, Water Resources **Networks:** OCLC **Loan:** Internationally **Photocopy:** Yes

Michigan

3577   Ann Arbor, Michigan, US
Michigan State Department of Natural Resources,
        Institute for Fisheries Research (IFR)
Library
212 Museums Annex
1109 North University
Ann Arbor, Michigan 48109-1084
Fax: +1(734) 663-9399 **WWW:** www.dnr.state.mi.us/www/ifr/ifrlibra/ifrlibra.htm

Type: Government **Head:** Tina M. Tincher *Phone:* +1(734) 663-3554 *Email:* tinchert@state.mi.us **Staff:** 1 Prof. **Holdings:** 120,000 books 28 journals **Language of Collection/Services:** English / English **Subjects:** Fisheries, Water Resources **Specializations:** Fisheries (Great Lakes) **Databases Developed:** Bibliographic database with over 30,000 entries for fisheries and related citations using Papyrus software **Loan:** Inhouse **Service:** Inhouse **Photocopy:** Yes

3578   Ann Arbor, Michigan, US
United States Geological Survey, Great Lakes
        Science Center (USGS, GLSC)
John Van Oosten Library
1451 Green Road
Ann Arbor, Michigan 48105
Phone: +1(734) 994-3331 ext 210 **Fax:** +1(734) 994-8780 **WWW:** www.glsc.usgs.gov

Former Name: United States Fish and Wildlife Service (FWS), National Fisheries Research Center - Great Lakes, National Biological Service **Founded:** 1965 **Type:** Government **Head:** Ann Zimmerman *Phone:* +1(734) 994-3331 ext 210 *Email:* ann_zimmerman@usgs.gov **Staff:** 1 Prof. **Holdings:** 45,100 books 100 journals **Language of Collection/Services:** English **Subjects:** Fisheries, Water Resources **Networks:** OCLC **Databases Developed:** 23,000 reprint collection on fish **Databases Used:** Comprehensive **Loan:** Internationally **Service:** Internationally **Photocopy:** Yes

3579   Ann Arbor, Michigan, US
University of Michigan
Shapiro Science Library
3175 Shapiro Bldg.
919 South University Avenue
Ann Arbor, Michigan 48109-1185
Phone: +1(734) 936-2327 **Fax:** +1(734) 763-9813 **Email:** science.library@umich.edu **WWW:** www.umich.edu/~scilib **OPAC:** www.lib.umich.edu/libhome/mirlyn/mirlynpage.html

Founded: 1917 **Type:** Academic **Head:** Kitty Bridges *Phone:* +1(734) 763-6054 *Email:* bridges@umich.edu **Staff:** 3 Prof. 7 Other **Language of Collection/Services:** English **Subjects:** Fisheries, Forestry, Plant Pathology, Soil Science, Water Resources **Networks:** RLIN **Databases Used:** Agricola; Biosis **Service:** Inhouse **Photocopy:** Yes

3580   Detroit, Michigan, US
Detroit Garden Center
Library
Moross House
1460 East Jefferson Avenue
Detroit, Michigan 48207
Phone: +1(313) 259-6363 **Fax:** +1(313) 259-0107

Founded: 1932 **Type:** Association **Head:** Beverly Donaldson *Phone:* +1(313) 259-6363 **Staff:** 1 Prof. **Language of Collection/Services:** English / English **Holdings:** 5 journals 5,000 books **Subjects:** Horticulture **Specializations:** Bonsai, Cut Flowers, Gardening, Home Gardens **Loan:** Inhouse **Photocopy:** Yes

3581   East Lansing, Michigan, US
Michigan State University (MSU)
Agricultural Economics Reference Room
Department of Agricultural Economics
219 Agriculture Hall
East Lansing, Michigan 48824-1039
Phone: +1(517) 355-6650 **Fax:** +1(517) 336-1800 **Email:** agecon@mainlib3.lib.msu.edu **WWW:** www.lib.msu.edu/coll/branches/agecon **OPAC:** magic.lib.msu.edu

Founded: 1958 **Type:** Academic **Head:** Judith Dow *Phone:* +1(517) 355-6650 *Email:* dowj@pilot.msu.edu **Staff:** .5 Prof. .5 Other **Holdings:** 2,500 books 100 journals **Language of Collection/Services:** English **Subjects:** Agribusiness, Agricultural Development, Agricultural Economics **Networks:** OCLC **Databases Used:** Comprehensive **Loan:** Internationally **Service:** Internationally **Photocopy:** Yes

3582   East Lansing, Michigan, US
      Michigan State University (MSU)
      Animal Industries Reference Room
      3285 Anthony Hall
      East Lansing, Michigan 48824
Phone: +1(517) 355-8483 **Fax:** +1(517) 353-1699, 432-7587 **Email:** animalind@mail.lib.msu.edu **WWW:** www.lib.msu.edu **OPAC:** magic.lib.msu.edu

Founded: 1956 **Type:** Academic **Head:** Jane Meyer *Phone:* +1(517) 355-8483 *Email:* meyerl@pilot.msu.edu **Staff:** 1 Other **Holdings:** 10,000 books 250 journals **Language of Collection/Services:** English **Subjects:** Animal Husbandry, Beef, Dairy Farming, Food Sciences, Horses, Nutrition, Poultry, Pigs **Specializations:** Electronic databases and journals **Networks:** Magic; OCLC **Databases Used:** Agricola **Loan:** Do not loan **Service:** Inhouse **Photocopy:** Yes

3583   East Lansing, Michigan, US
      Michigan State University (MSU)
      Chemistry Library
      426 Chemistry Building
      East Lansing, Michigan 48824
Phone: +1(517) 355-9715 ext 363 **Fax:** +1(517) 432-0439 **WWW:** www.lib.msu.edu **OPAC:** magic.lib.msu.edu

Type: Academic **Head:** James W. Oliver *Phone:* +1(517) 355-9715 ext 364 *Email:* oliver@pilot.msu.edu **Staff:** 1 Prof. 14 Other **Holdings:** 58,000 books 120 journals **Language of Collection/Services:** English / English **Subjects:** Chemistry **Specializations:** Organic Chemistry **Loan:** Internationally **Service:** Internationally **Photocopy:** Yes

3584   East Lansing, Michigan, US
      Michigan State University (MSU)
      Main Library
      100 Library
      East Lansing, Michigan 48824-1048
Phone: +1(517) 355-2347, 353-8818, 355-2345 (outreach) **Fax:** +1(517) 432-3693 **WWW:** www.lib.msu.edu **OPAC:** magic.lib.msu.edu

Former Name: Michigan State College **Founded:** 1965 **Type:** Academic **Head:** Clifford H. Haka, Director; Amy Blair, Agriculture Bibliographer *Phone:* +1(517) 355-2344 (Haka); 432-1644 (Blair) *Email:* hakac@pilot.msu.edu, blaira@pilot.msu.edu **Staff:** 54 Prof. 78 Other **Holdings:** 4,000,000 books 28,000 journals **Language of Collection/Services:** English **Subjects:** Comprehensive **Specializations:** Lawns and Turf, Veterinary Medicine (History) **Networks:** OCLC **Databases Developed:** TGIF - Turfgrass Information File, access to over 59,000 bibliographic records on turfgrass; document delivery from the MSU collection to subscribers; available via the Internet at www.lib.msu.edu/

tgif **Databases Used:** Comprehensive **Loan:** Internationally **Service:** Internationally **Photocopy:** Yes

3585   East Lansing, Michigan, US
      Michigan State University (MSU)
      Veterinary Medical Center Library
      G201 Veterinary Medical Center
      East Lansing, Michigan 48824-1314
Phone: +1(517) 353-5099 **Fax:** +1(517) 432-3797 **WWW:** www.lib.msu.edu/coll/branches/vetmed **OPAC:** magic.lib.msu.edu

Founded: 1978 **Type:** Academic **Head:** Leslie M. Behm *Phone:* +1(517) 353-5099 *Email:* behm@pilot.msu.edu **Staff:** .5 Prof. 1 Other **Holdings:** 2,600 books 70 journals **Language of Collection/Services:** English **Subjects:** Veterinary Medicine **Networks:** OCLC **Databases Used:** Comprehensive **Loan:** Internationally **Service:** Internationally **Photocopy:** Yes

3586   Fremont, Michigan, US
      Gerber Products Company
      Resource Center
      445 State Street
      Fremont, Michigan 49413
Phone: +1(231) 928-2631 **Fax:** +1(231) 928-2964 **WWW:** www.gerber.com

Founded: 1946 **Type:** Business **Head:** Sherrie Harris *Phone:* +1(231) 928-2000 *Email:* sherrie.harris@gerber.novartis.com **Staff:** 1 Prof. 1 Other **Holdings:** 10,000 books 750 journals **Language of Collection/Services:** English / English **Databases Used:** Agricola; LEXIS-NEXIS; Medline **Loan:** Internationally **Service:** Inhouse **Photocopy:** Yes

3587   Hickory Corners, Michigan, US
      Michigan State University, W.K. Kellogg
        Biological Station (MSU, KBS)
      Walter F. Morofsky Memorial Library
      3700 East Gull Lake Drive
      Hickory Corners, Michigan 49060
Phone: +1(616) 671-2310 **Fax:** +1(616) 671-2309 **Email:** webermel@pilot.msu.edu **WWW:** kbs.msu.edu **OPAC:** magic.lib.msu.edu

Founded: 1966 **Type:** Academic **Head:** Diane Donham *Phone:* +1(517) 432-0808 *Email:* ddonham@kbs.msu.edu **Staff:** 1 Prof. **Holdings:** 11,117 books 150 journals **Subjects:** Crops, Entomology, Plants, Soil Science, Water Resources **Loan:** Inhouse **Service:** Inhouse **Photocopy:** Yes

3588   Houghton, Michigan, US
      Michigan Technological University (MTU)
      J. Robert Van Pelt Library
      Houghton, Michigan 49931
Phone: +1(906) 487-2507 **Fax:** +1(906) 487-2357 **Email:** reflib@mtu.edu **WWW:** www.mtu.edu **OPAC:** www.lib.mtu.edu/jrvp/aboutjrvp/libguide.htm

Former Name: Michigan School of Mines, Michigan College of Mining and Technology **Founded:** 1885 **Type:** Academic **Head:** Phyllis Johnson *Phone:* +1(906) 487-2500 **Staff:** 11 Prof. 21 Other **Holdings:** 6,000 books 3,000 journals **Language of Collection/Services:** English **Subjects:**

Conservation, Forestry, Logging, Soil Science, Wildlife **Specializations:** Biotechnology, Entomology, Plants, Plant Pathology, Soil, Water Resources **Networks:** OCLC **Databases Used:** Comprehensive **Loan:** Internationally **Photocopy:** Yes

3589   Midland, Michigan, US
Chippewa Nature Center
Library
400 South Badour Road
Midland, Michigan 48640
Phone: +1(517) 631-0830 **Fax:** +1(517) 631-7070 **WWW:** www.chippewanaturecenter.com

Founded: 1977 **Type:** Association **Head:** Dennis Pilaske *Email:* dpilaske@chippewanaturecenter.com *Phone:* +1(517) 631-0830 **Staff:** 3 Prof. 3 Other **Holdings:** 1,750 books 25 journals **Language of Collection/Services:** English / English **Subjects:** Entomology, Forestry, Horticulture, Organic Gardening, Plant Pathology, Water Resources **Loan:** Do not loan **Service:** Inhouse **Photocopy:** Yes

Minnesota

3590   Bemidji, Minnesota, US
Bemidji State University
A.C. Clark Library
Bemidji, Minnesota 56601
Phone: +1(218) 755-3342 **Fax:** +1(218) 755-2051 **WWW:** cswww.bemidji.msus.edu/~library **OPAC:** cswww. bemidji.msus.edu/~library/pals/catalogs.html

Type: Academic **Head:** Dr. Jon Quistgaard *Phone:* +1(218) 755-2955 *Email:* jonq@vax1.bemidji.msus.edu **Staff:** 12 Prof. **Holdings:** **Loan:** Internationally **Photocopy:** Yes

3591   Chanhassen, Minnesota, US
University of Minnesota Libraries
Andersen Horticultural Library
Minnesota Landscape Arboretum
3675 Arboretum Drive, Box 39
Chanhassen, Minnesota 55317
Phone: +1(952) 443-2440 **Fax:** +1(952) 443-2521 **WWW:** www.lib.umn.edu **OPAC:** mncat.lib.umn.edu

Founded: 1971 **Type:** Academic **Head:** Richard T. Isaacson *Phone:* +1(952) 443-2440 *Email:* r-isaa@tc.umn.edu **Staff:** 1 Prof. 5 Other **Holdings:** 10,500 books 525 journals **Language of Collection/Services:** English / English **Subjects:** Horticulture **Databases Developed:** Plant Information Online — includes sources in North American nurseries for over 60,000 plants, over 150,000 citations to current plant science literature, and listings for more than 1000 North American seed and nursery firms; available by subscription via the Internet at http://plantinfo.umn.edu **Loan:** Do not loan **Service:** Internationally **Photocopy:** Yes

3592   Falcon Heights, Minnesota, US
Minnesota State Horticultural Society
Library
1755 Prior Avenue North
Falcon Heights, Minnesota 55113-5549

Location: St. Paul Campus, University of Minnesota **Fax:** +1(651) 643-3538 **Phone:** +1(800) 676-6747 **Email:** info @northerngardener.org **WWW:** www.northerngardener. org

Founded: 1977 **Type:** Association **Head:** Terri Goodfellow-Heyer *Phone:* +1(800) 676-6747 **Subjects:** Horticulture **Holdings:** 2,000 books **Loan:** In country **Photocopy:** Yes

3593   Fergus Falls, Minnesota, US
Communicating for Agriculture
Information and Resource Center
PO Box 677
Fergus Falls, Minnesota 56537
Location: 112 East Lincoln **Fax:** +1(218) 739-3832 **WWW:** www.cainc.org

Founded: 1977 **Type:** Association **Head:** Coleen Speer *Phone:* +1(218) 739-3241 *Email:* babbe@unique/software. com **Staff:** 1 Prof. 1 Other **Language of Collection/Services:** English **Subjects:** Agricultural Crises, Agricultural Development, Agricultural Financial Policy, Agricultural Land, Farming, Ranching **Loan:** Internationally **Photocopy:** Yes

3594   Minneapolis, Minnesota, US
Cargill, Inc.
Cargill Information Center (CIC)
PO Box 5670
Minneapolis, Minnesota 55440
Location: 15407 McGinty Road West, Wayzata, Minnesota 55391-2399 **Phone:** +1(612) 742-6498 **Fax:** +1(612) 742-6062 **WWW:** www.cargill.com

Former Name: Research Library **Founded:** 1956 **Type:** Business **Head:** Peter Sidney *Phone:* +1(612) 742-5224 *Email:* peter_sidney@cargill.com **Staff:** 10 Prof. 3 Other **Holdings:** 25,000 books 1,000 journals **Language of Collection/Services:** English **Subjects:** Agribusiness, Agricultural Economics, Animal Husbandry, Biotechnology, Finance, Food Sciences, Marketing, Meat **Specializations:** Commodities, Dusts, Explosions, Feed Grains, Food Grains, Grain Stores, Oilseeds **Databases Developed:** Cargill Internal Report Database - Internal research, not available to non-company users; Cargill Technical Network - 400+ scientists and engineers in the company and their areas of expertise, not available to non-company users. **Databases Used:** Comprehensive **Loan:** Internationally **Service:** Inhouse **Photocopy:** Yes

3595   Minneapolis, Minnesota, US
General Mills Inc. (GMI)
Business Information Center (BIC)
Box 1113
Minneapolis, Minnesota 55440-1113
Location: #1 General Mills Boulevard **Fax:** +1(612) 764-5742 **WWW:** www.genmills.com

Type: Business **Head:** Colin McQuillan *Phone:* +1(612) 764-3536 *Email:* mcqui000@mail.genmills.com **Staff:** 5 Prof. 1 Other **Holdings:** 1,500 books 150 journals **Language of Collection/Services:** English / English **Subjects:** Advertising, Business, Government Documents (USA), Marketing

Networks: OCLC **Databases Used:** LEXIS-NEXIS **Loan:** Inhouse **Service:** Inhouse **Photocopy:** Yes

3596   Minneapolis, Minnesota, US
General Mills Inc., James Ford Bell Technical
    Center (GMI)
Technical Information Services (JFB Library)
9000 Plymouth Avenue North
Minneapolis, Minnesota 55427
Phone: +1(612) 540-2938 **Fax:** +1(612) 540-3166 **WWW:** www.genmills.com

Founded: 1961 **Type:** Business **Head:** Laura Baird *Phone:* +1(612) 540-2938 *Email:* baird000@mail.genmills.com **Staff:** 6 Prof. 4 Other **Holdings:** 12,000 books 900 journals **Language of Collection/Services:** English / English **Subjects:** Cereal Products, Food Sciences, Food Technology **Networks:** GMI; OCLC **Databases Used:** Comprehensive **Loan:** In country **Service:** Inhouse **Photocopy:** No

3597   Minneapolis, Minnesota, US
International Alliance for Sustainable Agriculture
    (IASA)
Resource Information Center
Newman Center, Room 202
1701 University Avenue SE
Minneapolis, Minnesota 55414
Phone: +1(612) 331-1099 **Fax:** +1(612) 379-1527 **Email:** iasa@mtn.org **WWW:** www.mtn.org/iasa

Founded: 1983 **Type:** Association **Head:** Terry Gips *Phone:* +1(612) 331-1099 **Staff:** 3 Other **Holdings:** 6,000 books 200 journals **Language of Collection/Services:** English / English **Subjects:** Agriculture (Tropics), Agribusiness, Agricultural Chemicals, Agricultural Development, Agricultural Economics, Animal Husbandry, Biotechnology, Entomology, Farming, Plants, Soil Science, Water Resources **Specializations:** Alternative Farming, Fertilizers, Organizations, Pest Management, Pesticides, Sustainability **Networks:** OCLC **Databases Developed:** Planting the Future - resource guide to sustainable agriculture in the Third World and natural step sustainability network **Databases Used:** Comprehensive **Loan:** Inhouse **Service:** Internationally **Photocopy:** Yes

3598   Minneapolis, Minnesota, US
Minneapolis Grain Exchange (MGE)
Library
400 South Fourth Street, Suite 130
Minneapolis, Minnesota 55415-1413
Phone: +1(612) 321-7101 **Fax:** +1(612) 339-1155 **Email:** mgex@ix.netcom.com **WWW:** www.mgex.com

Founded: 1986 **Type:** Association **Head:** Joe O'Neill *Phone:* +1(612) 321-7101 **Staff:** 5 Prof. **Holdings:** 750 books 15 journals **Language of Collection/Services:** English / English **Subjects:** Agribusiness, Agricultural Economics **Specializations:** Commodities, Futures Trading **Loan:** Inhouse **Service:** Inhouse **Photocopy:** No

3599   Minneapolis, Minnesota, US
Pillsbury Company
Technology Knowledge Center

330 University Avenue SE
Minneapolis, Minnesota 55414
Fax: +1(612) 330-8245 **WWW:** www.pillsbury.com

Former Name: Technical Information Center **Founded:** 1941 **Type:** Business **Head:** James B. Tchobanoff *Phone:* +1(612) 330-8081 *Email:* jtchobanoff@pillsbury.com **Staff:** 2 Prof. 3 Other **Holdings:** 96,800 books 325 journals **Language of Collection/Services:** English / English **Subjects:** Food Sciences **Specializations:** Analytical Chemistry, Food Chemistry, Food Engineering, Food Microbiology **Databases Developed:** Pillsbury technical reports and research documents - inhouse access only **Databases Used:** FSTA **Loan:** Inhouse **Service:** Inhouse **Photocopy:** No

3600   St. Paul, Minnesota, US
Land O' Lakes Inc.
Corporate Library
PO Box 64101
St. Paul, Minnesota 56164-0101
Location: 4001 Lexington Avenue North, Arden Hills, Minnesota 55126 **Phone:** +1(651) 481-2691 **Fax:** +1(651) 766-1346 **WWW:** www.landolakes.com

Type: Business **Head:** Donna Koenig *Phone:* +1(651) 481-2691 *Email:* dkoen@landolakes.com **Staff:** 1 Prof. 2 Other **Holdings:** 2,500 books 300 journals **Subjects:** Agribusiness, Biotechnology, Food Sciences **Specializations:** Dairies **Databases Used:** Medline **Loan:** Inhouse **Service:** Inhouse **Photocopy:** Yes

3601   St. Paul, Minnesota, US
Minnesota Canola Council
Library
1306 W. Co. Rd. F
St. Paul, Minnesota 55112
Phone: +1(651) 638-9883

Founded: 1997 **Type:** Association **Head:** Beth Nelson, President *Phone:* +1(651) 638-9883 **Staff:** 4 Other **Language of Collection/Services:** English **Subjects:** Rape **Loan:** In country **Photocopy:** Yes

3602   St. Paul, Minnesota, US
Minnesota Cultivated Wild Rice Council
Library
1306 W. Co. Rd. F
St. Paul, Minnesota 55112
Phone: +1(651) 638-1955 **Fax:** +1(651) 638-1955

Former Name: Minnesota Paddy Wild Rice Council **Founded:** 1974 **Type:** Association **Head:** Beth Nelson, President *Phone:* +1(651) 638-1955 **Staff:** 4 Other **Language of Collection/Services:** English **Subjects:** Wild Rice **Loan:** In country **Photocopy:** Yes

3603   St. Paul, Minnesota, US
Minnesota Department of Trade and Economic
    Development
Library
500 Metro Square Building
121 7th Place East
St. Paul, Minnesota 55101

Fax: +1(651) 296-7952 **WWW:** www.dted.state.mn.us
OPAC: www.pals.msus.edu

Former Name: Minnesota Department of Energy and Economic Development **Founded:** 1976 **Type:** Government **Head:** Pat Fenton *Phone:* +1(651) 296-8902 *Email:* pat.fenton@state.mn.us **Staff:** 2 Prof. **Holdings:** 10,000 books 250 journals **Language of Collection/Services:** English **Subjects:** Economic Development, Energy, Public Utilities **Networks:** OCLC **Databases Used:** Comprehensive **Loan:** Internationally **Photocopy:** Yes

3604   St. Paul, Minnesota, US
Minnesota State Department of Natural Resources
  (DNR)
Library
500 Lafayette Road
St. Paul, Minnesota 55155-4021

Phone: +1(651) 297-4929 **Fax:** +1(651) 297-4946 **Email:** char.feist@dnr.state.mn.us **WWW:** www.dnr.state.mn.us
OPAC: www.pals.msus.edu

Former Name: Minnesota State Department of Conservation (1931-1972) **Founded:** 1985 **Type:** Government **Head:** Char Feist *Phone:* +1(651) 297-4929 **Staff:** 1 Prof. 1 Other **Language of Collection/Services:** English **Holdings:** 15,000 books 350 journals **Subjects:** Fisheries, Forestry, Geology, Water Resources **Specializations:** Fishery Management, Wildlife Management **Networks:** OCLC **Databases Used:** Comprehensive **Loan:** Internationally **Service:** In-house **Photocopy:** Yes

3605   St. Paul, Minnesota, US
University of Minnesota
Entomology, Fisheries and Wildlife Library (EFW
  Library)
1980 Folwell Avenue
375 Hodson Hall
St. Paul, Minnesota 55108

Phone: +1(612) 624-9288 **WWW:** www.lib.umn.edu
OPAC: www.lib.umn.edu

Founded: 1905 **Type:** Academic **Head:** Loralee Kerr *Phone:* +1(612) 624-5376 *Email:* l-kerr@tc.umn.edu **Staff:** 1 Prof. 1.5 Other **Holdings:** 70,456 books 900 journals **Language of Collection/Services:** English **Specializations:** Biological Conservation, Endangered Species, Entomology, Fisheries, Wildlife **Networks:** OCLC; RLIN **Databases Used:** Comprehensive **Loan:** Internationally **Service:** Internationally **Photocopy:** Yes

3606   St. Paul, Minnesota, US
University of Minnesota
Forestry Library
B-50 NRAB
2003 Upper Buford Circle
St. Paul, Minnesota 55108

Phone: +1(612) 624-3222 **WWW:** www.umn.edu **OPAC:** www.lib.umn.edu

Founded: 1899 **Type:** Academic **Head:** Jean Albrecht *Phone:* +1(612) 624-2779 *Email:* j-albr@tc.umn.edu **Staff:** 1 Prof. 1 Other **Holdings:** 109,000 books 1,114 journals **Language of Collection/Services:** English **Subjects:** For-

estry, Outdoor Recreation, Pulp and Paper Industry, Range Management, Remote Sensing, Wood Chemistry, Woody Plants **Networks:** OCLC **Databases Developed:** Social Sciences in Forestry (SSiF) - bibliographic database of over 50,000 references from 1985 to date; accessible electronically over the world-wide Internet. Other bibliographies available via Internet include Trail Planning, Construction and Maintenance (1992-date), Tropical Forest Conservation and Development (1984-date), and Urban Forestry (1982-date). **Databases Used:** Comprehensive **Photocopy:** Yes

3607   St. Paul, Minnesota, US
University of Minnesota
Magrath Library
1984 Buford Avenue
St. Paul, Minnesota 55108

Phone: +1(612) 624-1212 **Fax:** +1(612) 624-9245, 625-3134 **Email:** stpref@zazu.lib.umn.edu **WWW:** www.umn.edu **OPAC:** www.lib.umn.edu **Ariel IP:** 134.84.136.50

Founded: 1890 **Type:** Academic **Head:** Jo Ann DeVries *Phone:* +1(612) 624-7446 *Email:* j-devr@tc.umn.edu **Staff:** 9 Prof. 19 Other **Holdings:** 656,861 books 6,213 journals **Language of Collection/Services:** English **Subjects:** Agriculture (Tropics), Agribusiness, Agricultural Development, Agricultural Engineering, Animal Husbandry, Biotechnology, Crops, Education/Extension, Entomology, Farming, Fisheries, Food Sciences, Horticulture, Soil Science, Water Resources **Specializations:** Agricultural Economics, Botany, Forestry, Plant Pathology, Veterinary Medicine **Networks:** OCLC; RLIN **Databases Developed:** Social Sciences in Forestry; Urban Forestry; Tropical Forestry, Conservation and Development; Trail Planning, Construction and Maintenance; AgEcon Search **Databases Used:** Comprehensive **Loan:** Internationally **Service:** Internationally **Photocopy:** Yes

3608   St. Paul, Minnesota, US
University of Minnesota
Plant Pathology Library
Borlaug Hall
1991 Upper Buford Circle
St. Paul, Minnesota 55108

Phone: +1(612) 625-9777 **Email:** pplibrar@puccini.crl.umn.edu **WWW:** www.umn.edu
OPAC: www.lib.umn.edu

Type: Academic **Head:** Melissa Pauna *Phone:* +1(612) 625-9777 *Email:* pauna001@tc.umn.edu **Staff:** 1 Prof. **Holdings:** 10,000 books 100 journals **Language of Collection/Services:** English / English **Subjects:** Mycology, Plant Pathology **Networks:** OCLC **Databases Used:** Comprehensive **Photocopy:** Yes

3609   St. Paul, Minnesota, US
University of Minnesota
Veterinary Medical Library
1971 Commonwealth Avenue
450 Veterinary Science Bldg.
St. Paul, Minnesota 55108

Phone: +1(612) 624-4281 **Fax:** +1(612) 625-5203, 624-9782 **Email:** vetlib@tc.umn.edu **WWW:** www-stp.lib. umn.edu/vetmed **OPAC:** mncat.lib.umn.edu

Type: Academic **Head:** Livija Carlson *Phone:* +1(612) 624-3078 *Email:* l-carl@tc.umn.edu **Staff:** 1 Prof. 2 Other **Holdings:** 80,000 books 1,258 journals **Language of Collection/Services:** English / English **Subjects:** Veterinary Medicine **Specializations:** Animal Welfare, Animal Behavior, Human-Animal Bond, Reproduction **Databases Used:** Comprehensive **Photocopy:** Yes

3610   St. Paul, Minnesota, US
University of Minnesota
Waite Library
Department of Applied Economics
232 Classroom Office Building
1994 Buford Avenue
St. Paul, Minnesota 55108
Phone: +1(612) 625-1705 **Fax:** +1(612) 625-6245 **WWW:** www.umn.edu

Founded: 1950 **Type:** Academic **Head:** Louise Letnes *Phone:* +1(612) 625-1705 *Email:* lletnes@dept.agecon.umn.edu **Staff:** 2 Prof. .5 Other **Holdings:** 20,000 books 40 journals **Language of Collection/Services:** English / English **Subjects:** Agribusiness, Agricultural Development, Agricultural Economics, Retail Food Industry, International Trade **Loan:** Inhouse **Service:** Inhouse **Photocopy:** Yes

3611   St. Paul, Minnesota, US
University of Minnesota, Minnesota Extension
    Service
Yard and Garden Line
240 Coffey Hall
1420 Eckles Avenue
St. Paul, Minnesota 55108-6070
Phone: +1(612) 624-4771 **Fax:** +1(612) 625-5299 **WWW:** www.extension.umn.edu/yardandgarden

Former Name: Dial U Insect and Plant Information **Founded:** 1983 **Type:** Academic **Head:** Dr. Mark E. Ascerno *Phone:* +1(612) 624-3278 **Staff:** 4 Prof. 10 Other **Holdings:** 200 books 15 journals **Language of Collection/Services:** English / English **Subjects:** Entomology, Horticulture, Plant Pathology, Urban Areas **Databases Developed:** Dial U is a telephone diagnostic clinic for urban insect and plant questions from the general public in Minnesota; US$2.99 service fee for each inquiry. **Loan:** Do not loan **Service:** In state **Photocopy:** No

Mississippi

3612   Alcorn State, Mississippi, US
Alcorn State University (ASU)
John Dewey Boyd Library
1000 ASU Drive #539
Alcorn State, Mississippi 39096-7500
Phone: +1(601) 877-6357 **Fax:** +1(601) 877-3885 **Email:** mharris@lorman.alcorn.edu **WWW:** www.alcorn.edu

Former Name: Alcorn A & M College **Founded:** 1970 **Type:** Academic **Head:** Mrs. Jessie Burks Arnold *Phone:* +1(601) 877-6350 *Email:* jarnold@lorman.alcorn.edu **Staff:** 6 Prof. 11 Other **Holdings:** 234,000 books 1,000 journals **Language of Collection/Services:** English **Subjects:** Agribusiness, Animal Husbandry, Food Sciences, Forestry, Hor-

ticulture, Plant Pathology, Soil Science **Specializations:** Agricultural Economics, Crops, Education/Extension, Farming **Networks:** OCLC **Databases Used:** Agricola; CABCD; Current Contents **Loan:** In country **Service:** In country **Photocopy:** Yes

3613   Mississippi State, Mississippi, US
Mississippi State University
College of Veterinary Medicine Library
PO Box 9825
Mississippi State, Mississippi 39762
Phone: +1(662) 325-1256 **Fax:** +1(662) 325-1141 **Email:** library@cvm.msstate.edu **WWW:** www.msstate.edu **OPAC:** nt.library.msstate.edu/galaxy.htm

Type: Academic **Head:** John Cruickshank, Acting Head *Email:* cruickshank@cvm.msstate.edu *Phone:* +1(662) 325-1240 **Subjects:** Veterinary Medicine

3614   Mississippi State, Mississippi, US
Mississippi State University
Mitchell Memorial Library
PO Box 5408
Hardy Road
Mississippi State, Mississippi 39762
Phone: +1(662) 325-7667 **Email:** reference@library.msstate.edu, ag-ref@nt.library.msstate.edu **WWW:** www.msstate.edu **OPAC:** nt.library.msstate.edu/galaxy.htm

Type: Academic **Head:** Frances Coleman *Phone:* +1(662) 325-7661 *Email:* fcoleman@library.msstate.edu

3615   Ocean Springs, Mississippi, US
University of Southern Mississippi, Institute of
    Marine Sciences, Gulf Coast Research
    Laboratory (USM, IMS, GCRL)
Gordon Gunter Library
PO Box 7000
Ocean Springs, Mississippi 39566-7000
Location: 703 Fast Beach Blvd. **Fax:** +1(228) 872-4264 **WWW:** www.ims.usm.edu

Founded: 1955 **Type:** Academic **Head:** Joyce M. Shaw *Phone:* +1(228) 872-4213 *Email:* joyce.shaw@usm.edu **Staff:** 1 Prof. 2 Other **Holdings:** 24,000 books 166 journals **Language of Collection/Services:** English **Subjects:** Fisheries, Food Sciences, Marine Biology, Plant Pathology, Water Resources **Databases Used:** Comprehensive **Loan:** Internationally **Service:** Internationally **Photocopy:** Yes

3616   Oxford, Mississippi, US
United States Department of Agriculture,
    Agricultural Research Service, National
    Sedimentation Laboratory (USDA, ARS,
    NSL)
Library
PO Box 1157
Oxford, Mississippi 38655-1157
Location: 598 McElroy Drive **Phone:** +1(662) 232-2920 **Fax:** +1(662) 232-2915 **Email:** teague@sedlab.olemiss.edu **WWW:** www.sedlab.olemiss.edu **Ariel IP:** 130.74.184.96

Founded: 1963 **Type:** Government **Head:** Dr. Mathias Römkens, Laboratory Director *Phone:* +1(662) 232-2901

Email: romkens@sedlab.olemiss.edu **Staff:** 1 Prof. **Holdings:** 20,000 books 92 journals **Language of Collection/Services:** English **Subjects:** Agricultural Engineering, Biotechnology, Crops, Farming, Fisheries, Soil Science, Water Resources **Loan:** In country **Service:** Inhouse **Photocopy:** Yes

3617   Stoneville, Mississippi, US
Mississippi State University, Agricultural and
    Forestry Experiment Station, Delta Research
    and Extension Center (DREC)
Library
PO Box 197
Stoneville, Mississippi 38776
Location: 384 Stoneville Road **Phone:** +1(662) 686-9311
Fax: +1(662) 686-7336 **Email:** ecook@drec.msstate.edu
WWW: www.msstate.edu/dept/drec

Former Name: Delta Branch Experiment Station **Founded:** 1966 **Type:** Academic **Head:** Rhonda H. Watson *Phone:* +1(662) 686-3260/1 *Email:* rhwatson@drec.msstate.edu **Staff:** 1 Prof. 1 Other **Holdings:** 22,000 books 250 journals **Language of Collection/Services:** English / English **Subjects:** Agricultural Economics, Agricultural Engineering, Crops, Education/Extension, Entomology, Farming, Fisheries, Forestry, Horticulture, Plant Pathology, Soil Science **Specializations:** Weeds **Databases Used:** Agricola **Loan:** In country **Service:** Inhouse **Photocopy:** Yes

Missouri

3618   Columbia, Missouri, US
University of Missouri, Columbia (UMC)
Elmer Ellis Library, Science Library, Agriculture
    Collection
Columbia, Missouri 65201-5149
Phone: +1(573) 882-4581 **Fax:** +1(573) 882-6034 **Email:** ellisref@showme.missouri.edu **WWW:** www.missouri.edu/~elliswww **OPAC:** merlin.missouri.edu

Founded: 1849 **Type:** Academic **Head:** Martha Alexander *Phone:* +1(573) 882-4701 *Email:* alexanderms@missouri.edu **Staff:** 33 Prof. 91 Other **Holdings:** 100,000 books 500 journals **Language of Collection/Services:** English / English **Subjects:** Comprehensive **Specializations:** Agricultural Economics, Animal Physiology, Crops, Entomology, Food Sciences, Forestry, Horticulture, Molecular Genetics, Plant Pathology, Plant Physiology, Soil Science, Wildlife **Networks:** OCLC **Databases Used:** Agricola; Biosis; CABCD **Loan:** Internationally **Photocopy:** Yes

3619   Columbia, Missouri, US
University of Missouri, Columbia (UMC)
Veterinary Medical Library
W218 Veterinary Medicine
Columbia, Missouri 65211
Fax: +1(573) 881-2950 **Email:** vetlib@showme.missouri.edu **WWW:** www.missouri.edu/~elliswww **OPAC:** merlin.missouri.edu

Type: Academic **Head:** C. Trenton Boyd *Phone:* +1(573) 882-2461 **Staff:** 1 Prof. 2 Other **Holdings:** 45,500 books 312 journals **Language of Collection/Services:** English / English **Subjects:** Veterinary Medicine **Loan:** Internationally **Service:** Internationally **Photocopy:** Yes

3620   Jefferson City, Missouri, US
Lincoln University
Inman E. Page Library
PO Box 29
820 Chestnut
Jefferson City, Missouri 65102-0029
Phone: +1(573) 681-5512 **Fax:** +1(573) 681-5511 **WWW:** www.lincolnu.edu **OPAC:** arthur.missouri.edu **Ariel IP:** 150.167.21.2

Type: Academic **Head:** Mrs. Elizabeth B. Wilson *Phone:* +1(573) 681-5502 *Email:* wilsone@lincolnu.edu **Staff:** 10 Prof. 7 Other **Holdings:** 164,782 books 640 journals **Language of Collection/Services:** English / English **Subjects:** Comprehensive **Networks:** OCLC **Databases Used:** Agricola **Loan:** In country **Service:** In country **Photocopy:** Yes

3621   Kansas City, Missouri, US
Linda Hall Library (LHL)
5109 Cherry Street
Kansas City, Missouri 64110-2498
Phone: +1(816) 363-4600, 926-8764 **Fax:** +1(816) 926-8785, 926-8790 **Email:** reference@lindahall.org, reference@lhl.lib.mo.us **WWW:** www.lhl.lib.mo.us **OPAC:** www.lhl.lib.mo.us

Founded: 1946 **Type:** Private **Head:** C. Lee Jones *Email:* leejones@lbl.lib.mo.us, leejones@lindahall.org *Phone:* +1(816) 926-8742 **Staff:** 19 Prof. 42 Other **Holdings:** 1,376,000 books 16,000 journals **Language of Collection/Services:** English / English **Subjects:** Agricultural Engineering, Biotechnology, Crops, Fisheries, Food Sciences, Horticulture, Plant Pathology, Plants **Specializations:** Chemistry, Entomology, Forestry, Mechanics, Soil Science, Water Resources **Networks:** OCLC; RLIN; WLN **Databases Used:** Compendex **Loan:** Internationally **Service:** Internationally **Photocopy:** Yes

3622   Maryville, Missouri, US
Northwest Missouri State University
B.D. Owens Library
Maryville, Missouri 64468
Phone: +1(816) 562-1591 **Fax:** +1(816) 562-2153 **WWW:** www.nwmissouri.edu **OPAC:** www.nwmissouri.edu/library/catalog/owens.htm

Founded: 1906 **Type:** Academic **Head:** Dr. Patt VanDyke *Email:* vandyke@mail.nwmissouri.edu, vandyke@acad.nwmissouri.edu *Phone:* +1(816) 562-1590 **Staff:** 10 Prof. 13 Other **Holdings:** 2,500 books 70 journals **Subjects:** Agribusiness, Agricultural Economics, Agricultural Engineering, Animal Husbandry, Crops, Farming, Food Sciences, Horticulture, Plant Pathology, Soil Science **Networks:** OCLC **Loan:** In country **Photocopy:** Yes

3623   Saint Joseph, Missouri, US
Boehringer Ingelheim Animal Health Inc.
    (BIAHI)
Library
2621 North Belt Highway

Saint Joseph, Missouri 64506
Phone: +1(816) 233-2571 ext 572 **Fax:** +1(816) 233-4767
WWW: www.boehringer-ingelheim.com/corporate/home/
home.asp

Type: Business **Staff:** 1 Prof. 1 Other **Holdings:** 65,750
books 150 journals **Language of Collection/Services:** English **Subjects:** Veterinary Medicine **Loan:** Inhouse **Service:**
Internationally **Photocopy:** Yes

3624   Springfield, Missouri, US
Southwest Missouri State University (SMSU)
Duane G. Meyer Library
Box 175
901 S. National Ave.
Springfield, Missouri 65804-0095
Phone: +1(417) 836-4535 **WWW:** www.smsu.edu **OPAC:**
library.smsu.edu

Founded: 1905 **Type:** Academic **Head:** Karen Horny
Phone: +1(417) 836-4525 *Email:* karenhorny@mail.smsu.
edu, klh533f@mail.smsu.edu **Staff:** 20 Prof. 24 Other **Subjects:** Agricultural Economics, Animal Husbandry **Networks:** OCLC **Loan:** Internationally **Photocopy:** Yes

3625   St. Louis, Missouri, US
Missouri Botanical Garden
Library
PO Box 299
St. Louis, Missouri 63166
Location: 4500 Shaw Boulevard **Phone:** +1(314) 577-
5155 **Fax:** +1(314) 577-0840 **Email:** molibref@mobot.org,
stiffler@mbot.org **WWW:** www.mobot.org **OPAC:** www.
mobot.org/mobot/molib/catalog.html

Founded: 1859 **Type:** Academic **Head:** Constance P. Wolf
Phone: +1(314) 577-5156 *Email:* wolf@mobot.org **Staff:** 5
Prof. 4 Other **Holdings:** 123,000 books 1,800 journals **Language of Collection/Services:** English / English **Subjects:**
Botany, Floriculture, Taxonomy **Specializations:** Herbs
(History - pre-1753) **Networks:** OCLC **Databases Developed:** TROPICOS - database of taxonomic information;
Internet access: mobot.mobot.org/pick/search/pick.html
Databases Used: Comprehensive **Loan:** Internationally
Service: Internationally **Photocopy:** Yes

3626   St. Louis, Missouri, US
Monsanto Company
Monsanto Information Organization (MIO)
Box 7090
St. Louis, Missouri 63177
Location: 800 North Lindbergh Boulevard **Phone:** +1
(314) 694-4747 **Fax:** +1(314) 694-8748 **Email:** c.c.library
@monsanto.com **WWW:** www.monsanto.com

Former Name: Monsanto Information Center **Founded:**
1961 **Type:** Business **Head:** Mark H. Williams *Phone:* +1
(314) 694-5704 *Email:* mark.h.williams@monsanto.com
Staff: 16 Prof. 6 Other **Holdings:** 45,000 books 800 journals
Language of Collection/Services: English / English **Subjects:** Agribusiness, Crops, Plant Pathology **Specializations:** Biotechnology **Networks:** OCLC **Databases Used:**
Biosis; Medline **Loan:** In country **Service:** Inhouse **Photocopy:** Yes

3627   St. Louis, Missouri, US
National Corn Growers Association (NCGA)
Library
1000 Executive Parkway, Suite 105
St. Louis, Missouri 63141
Phone: +1(314) 275-9915 **Fax:** +1(314) 275-7061 **Email:**
corninfo@ncga.com **WWW:** www.ncga.com

Founded: 1984 **Type:** Association **Staff:** .33 Prof. .33 Other
Holdings: 100 books 50 journals **Subjects:** Maize **Loan:** Do
not loan **Photocopy:** Yes

3628   St. Louis, Missouri, US
Ralston Purina Company
Library and Information Services
Checkerboard Square
St. Louis, Missouri 63164
Phone: +1(314) 982-2150 **Fax:** +1(314) 982-3259 **WWW:**
www.ralston.com

Founded: 1929 **Type:** Business **Staff:** 2.6 Prof. 2 Other
Holdings: 5,000 books 75 journals **Subjects:** Animal Nutrition, Food Sciences, Human Nutrition **Loan:** Internationally
Photocopy: Yes

3629   Warrensburg, Missouri, US
Central Missouri State University (CMSU)
James C. Kirkpatrick Library
Warrensburg, Missouri 64093
Phone: +1(660) 543-4154 **Fax:** +1(660) 543-8001 **Email:**
reference@libserv.cmsu.edu **WWW:** www.cmsu.edu

Founded: 1871 **Type:** Academic **Head:** Dr. Pal Rao *Phone:*
+1(660) 543-4140 *Email:* pal@libserv.cmsu.edu **Staff:** 17
Prof. 25 Other **Holdings:** 2,800 books 67 journals **Language
of Collection/Services:** English / English **Subjects:** Crops,
Agribusiness, Agricultural Development, Agricultural Economics, Animal Breeding, Animal Husbandry, Entomology,
Horticulture, Soil Science, Technology, Veterinary Medicine, Vocational Training, Water Management **Loan:** In
country **Service:** In region **Photocopy:** Yes

3630   Willow Springs, US
Scottish Blackface Sheep Breeders' Association
Library
1699 HH Highway
Willow Springs, Missouri 65793
Founded: 1982 **Type:** Association **Head:** R. J. Horwards,
Secretary *Phone:* +1(417) 962-5466 **Subjects:** Scottish
Blackface Sheep, Sheep

Montana

3631   Bozeman, Montana, US
Montana State University
Library
Bozeman, Montana 59717-0022
Phone: +1(406) 994-3171 **Fax:** +1(406) 994-2851 **WWW:**
www.montana.edu **OPAC:** www.lib.montana.edu

Former Name: Montana State College **Type:** Academic
Head: Bruce Morton *Email:* bmorton@montana.edu *Phone:*
+1(406) 994-3110 **Staff:** 21 Prof. 40 Other **Holdings:**

500,000 books 4,000 journals **Language of Collection/Services:** English / English **Subjects:** Agribusiness, Agricultural Development, Agricultural Economics, Agricultural Engineering, Animal Husbandry, Biotechnology, Crops, Education/Extension, Entomology, Farming, Food Sciences, Horticulture, Plant Pathology, Soil Science, Veterinary Medicine, Water Resources **Databases Developed:** MSU Agriculture Extension database - Montguides **Databases Used:** Agricola; Biosis; CAS; Medline **Service:** Internationally **Photocopy:** Yes

3632   Hamilton, Montana, US
National Institutes of Health, National Institute of Allergy and Infectious Diseases (NIH, NIAID)
Rocky Mountain Laboratories Library (RML Library)
903 South Fourth Street
Hamilton, Montana 59840
Phone: +1(406) 363-9211 **Fax:** +1(406) 363-9336 **WWW:** www.niaid.nih.gov

Type: Government **Staff:** 1 Prof. 1 Other **Holdings:** 5,000 books 287 journals **Language of Collection/Services:** English **Subjects:** Allergies, Bacteriology, Genetics, Immunology, Medical Entomology, Microbiology, Parasitology, Venereal Diseases, Veterinary Science, Virology **Specializations:** Biotechnology, Entomology, Veterinary Medicine **Databases Used:** Medline; Current Contents **Loan:** Internationally **Service:** Internationally **Photocopy:** Yes

3633   Helena, Montana, US
Montana State Library (MSL)
Natural Resource Information System (NRIS)
1515 East Sixth Avenue
Helena, Montana 59620-1800
Phone: +1(406) 444-5354 **Fax:** +1(406) 444-0581 **WWW:** nris.state.mt.us

Founded: 1985 **Type:** Government **Head:** Jim Stimson *Phone:* +1(406) 444-5355 *Email:* jstimson@state.mt.us **Staff:** 15 Prof. 3 Other **Language of Collection/Services:** English **Subjects:** Agricultural Economics, Animal Husbandry, Climate, Crops, Fisheries, Forestry, Grazing, Livestock, Pesticides, Plant Pathology, Plants, Soil Science, Water Resources, Weeds **Databases Developed:** Natural Heritage - flora and fauna **Loan:** Upon request **Service:** Open to public **Photocopy:** Yes

3634   Missoula, Montana, US
University of Montana
Maureen and Mike Mansfield Library
32 Campus Drive #9936
Missoula, Montana 59812-9936
Phone: +1(406) 243-6866 **Fax:** +1(406) 243-2060 **WWW:** www.umt.edu **OPAC:** www.lib.umt.edu/catalog1.htm

Founded: 1892 **Type:** Academic **Head:** Frank D'Andraia *Phone:* +1(406) 243-6800 *Email:* dandraia@selway.umt. edu **Staff:** 14 Prof. 40 Other **Holdings:** 1,500,000 books 4,500 journals **Language of Collection/Services:** English / English **Subjects:** Fisheries, Forestry, Soil Science **Speciali-**

zations: Montana (History), Government Documents (USA) **Loan:** Internationally **Service:** Inhouse **Photocopy:** Yes

3635   Sidney, Montana, US
American Polypay Sheep Association
609 South Central Avenue
Suite 9
Sidney, Montana 59270
Phone: +1(406) 482-7768 **Fax:** +1(406) 482-7768

Type: Association **Head:** Marty Dunn *Phone:* +1(406) 482-7768 **Staff:** 1 Prof. **Language of Collection/Services:** English **Subjects:** American Polypay Sheep, Sheep

Nebraska

3636   Anselmo, Nebraska, US
Hungarian Horse Association of America, Inc.
Registration Office - Business Office
HC 71 Box 108
Anselmo, Nebraska 68813
Phone: +1(308) 749-2411

Founded: 1957 **Type:** Association **Head:** Wanda Cooksley, Registrar *Phone:* +1(308) 749-2411 **Staff:** 1 Other **Language of Collection/Services:** English **Subjects:** Hungarian Horses **Loan:** Do not loan **Photocopy:** Yes

3637   Clay Center, Nebraska, US
United States Department of Agriculture, Agricultural Research Service, Meat Animal Research Center (USDA, ARS, MARC)
Library
Box 166
Clay Center, Nebraska 68933
Phone: +1(402) 762-4106 **Fax:** +1(402) 762-4148 **Email:** library@email.marc.usda.goc **WWW:** www.ars.usda.gov

Type: Government **Staff:** 2 Other **Holdings:** 4,050 books 150 journals **Language of Collection/Services:** English **Subjects:** Meat Production **Photocopy:** Yes

3638   Lincoln, Nebraska, US
Nebraska Library Commission (NLC)
The Atrium, 1200 N Street, Suite 120
Lincoln, Nebraska 68508-2023
Phone: +1(402) 471-4016, 471-6244 **Fax:** +1(402) 471-2083 **WWW:** www.nlc.state.ne.us

Type: Government **Head:** Rod Wagner *Phone:* +1(402) 471-4001 *Email:* rwagner@neon.nlc.state.ne.us **Staff:** 15 Prof. 34 Other **Holdings:** 375,000 books 180 journals **Language of Collection/Services:** English **Subjects:** Agricultural Censuses **Specializations:** Government Documents (Nebraska), USDA Documents **Databases Developed:** Nebraska Online - calendar of events, job listings, census and legislative databases, the NLC catalog, development services directory, files for downloading; Telnet: neon.nlc.state.ne.us - dial +1(402) 471-4020 **Loan:** In country **Service:** In country **Photocopy:** Yes

3639   Lincoln, Nebraska, US
Nebraska State Game and Parks Commission

Library
2200 North 33rd Street
Lincoln, Nebraska 68503
Phone: +1(402) 471-5587 **Fax:** +1(402) 471-5528 **WWW:** www.ngpc.state.ne.us

Founded: 1970 **Type:** Government **Head:** Barbara Voeltz *Phone:* +1(402) 471-5587 *Email:* bvoeltz@ngpsun.ngpc.state.ne.us **Staff:** 1 Prof. .5 Other **Holdings:** 17,000 books 50 journals **Language of Collection/Services:** English **Subjects:** Fisheries, Horticulture, Natural Resources, Wetlands, Soil Science, Wildlife **Databases Developed:** Bibliography of Nebraska Fishery publications and reports (1930- 1990) **Loan:** In state **Photocopy:** Yes

3640   Lincoln, Nebraska, US
Nebraska State Historical Society
Library/Archives
PO Box 82554
Lincoln, Nebraska 68501
Location: 1500 'R' Street **Phone:** +1(402) 471-4771 **Fax:** +1(402) 471-3100 **Email:** lanshs@nebraskahistory.org **WWW:** www.nebraskahistory.org

Founded: 1878 **Type:** Government **Head:** Andrea Faling *Phone:* +1(402) 471-4785 *Email:* lanshs@nebraskahistory.org **Staff:** 6 Prof. 13 Other **Holdings:** 117,000 books 125 journals **Language of Collection/Services:** English **Subjects:** Agribusiness, Agricultural Development, Agricultural Economics, Agricultural Manpower, Agricultural Research, Experimental Stations, Machinery **Databases Developed:** Nebraska Newspapers including those with agricultural emphasis such as "The Nebraska Farmer"; Government agency records especially Department of Agriculture, Board of Agriculture, State Horticultural Society, Poultry Association, Department of Water Resources **Loan:** Microfilmed materials only **Service:** Internationally **Photocopy:** Yes

3641   Lincoln, Nebraska, US
University of Nebraska - Lincoln (UNL)
Biological Sciences Library
402 Manter Hall
Lincoln, Nebraska 68588-0119
Phone: +1(402) 472-2756 **Fax:** +1(402) 472-0225 **Email:** biolmail@unllib.unl.edu **WWW:** www.unl.edu **OPAC:** iris.unl.edu

Founded: 1890 **Type:** Academic **Head:** Richard E. Voeltz *Phone:* +1(402) 472-2739 *Email:* dickv@unllib.unl.edu **Staff:** 1 Prof. 3 Other **Holdings:** 76,000 books 750 journals **Language of Collection/Services:** English **Subjects:** Biotechnology, Plants **Loan:** Internationally **Photocopy:** Yes

3642   Lincoln, Nebraska, US
University of Nebraska - Lincoln (UNL)
C.Y. Thompson Library (CYT)
38th & Holdrege Streets
East Campus
Lincoln, Nebraska 68583-0717
Phone: +1(402) 472-4407 **Fax:** +1(402) 472-7005 **Email:** cytref@unllib.unl.edu **WWW:** www.unl.edu **OPAC:** iris.unl.edu **Ariel IP:** 129.43.16.90

Founded: 1872 **Type:** Academic **Head:** Rebecca A. Bernthal *Phone:* +1(402) 472-4404 *Email:* rebecca@unllib.unl.edu **Staff:** 5 Prof. 5 Other **Holdings:** 3,451,000 books 4,020 journals **Language of Collection/Services:** English / English **Subjects:** Agribusiness, Agricultural Development, Agricultural Economics, Agricultural Engineering, Agriculture (Tropics), Animal Husbandry, Biotechnology, Crops, Education/Extension, Entomology, Farming, Fisheries, Food Sciences, Forestry, Horticulture, Plant Pathology, Plants, Soil Science, Veterinary Medicine, Water Resources **Networks:** OCLC **Databases Used:** Comprehensive **Loan:** Internationally **Service:** Internationally **Photocopy:** Yes

3643   Lincoln, Nebraska, US
University of Nebraska - Lincoln (UNL)
Engineering Library
204 West Nebraska Hall
Lincoln, Nebraska 68588-0410
Location: City Campus 0516 (On 16th Street between Vine and Y Streets) **Phone:** +1(402) 472-3411 **Fax:** +1 (402) 472-0663 **Email:** englibm@unllib.unl.edu **WWW:** www.unl.edu **OPAC:** iris.unl.edu

Type: Academic **Staff:** 2 Prof. 3 Other **Holdings:** 311,000 books 1,000 journals **Language of Collection/Services:** English / English **Subjects:** Agricultural Engineering, Water Resources **Specializations:** Patents **Databases Used:** Compendex **Loan:** Internationally **Service:** Internationally **Photocopy:** Yes

3644   Lincoln, Nebraska, US
University of Nebraska - Lincoln (UNL)
Love Library
Lincoln, Nebraska 68588-0496
Phone: +1(402) 472-2848 **Fax:** +1(402) 472-5131 **WWW:** www.unl.edu **OPAC:** iris.unl.edu

Type: Academic **Head:** Kent Hendrickson *Phone:* +1(402) 472-2526 *Email:* khendrickson1@unl.edu, khendric@unlnotes.unl.edu, **Staff:** 35 Prof. 90 Other **Holdings:** 21,000 journals 2,000,000 books **Language of Collection/Services:** English **Subjects:** Agribusiness, Agricultural Development, Agricultural Economics **Networks:** OCLC **Databases Used:** Agricola; Biosis; Medline **Loan:** Internationally **Service:** Internationally **Photocopy:** Yes

3645   Omaha, Nebraska, US
Omaha Public Library (OPL)
Business, Science and Technology Department (BST)
215 South 15th Street
Omaha, Nebraska 68102-1601
Phone: +1(402) 444-4817 **Fax:** +1(402) 444-4504 **Email:** bst@omaha.lib.ne.us **WWW:** www.omaha.lib.ne.us

Founded: 1952 **Type:** Public **Head:** Lowell Greunke *Phone:* +1(402) 444-4815 **Staff:** 5 Prof. 5 Other **Holdings:** 337,249 books 300 journals **Language of Collection/Services:** English **Subjects:** Soil Surveys, Water Resources **Loan:** Inhouse **Service:** Inhouse **Photocopy:** Yes

3646   Scottsbluff, Nebraska, US
University of Nebraska, Panhandle Research and
      Extension Center (PHREC)
D.A. Murphy Library
4502 Avenue I
Scottsbluff, Nebraska 69361

Fax: +1(308) 632-1315 **WWW:** www.ianr.unl.edu/ianr/
phrec

Type: Government **Head:** Cheryl Burkhart-Kriesel *Phone:*
+1(308) 632-1319 *Email:* phrc004@unlvm.unl.edu **Staff:** 1
Other **Language of Collection/Services:** English / English
Subjects: Dry Beans, Dry Farming Crops, Potatoes, Sugarbeet, Wheat **Loan:** Inhouse **Photocopy:** Yes

Nevada

3647   Carson City, Nevada, US
Nevada State Library and Archives (NSLA)
Library
Capitol Complex
100 North Stewart Street
Carson City, Nevada 89701-4285

Phone: +1(775) 684-33k60 **Fax:** +1(775) 684-3330, 684-
3311 **WWW:** dmla.clan.lib.nv.us **OPAC:** dmla.clan.lib.nv.
us/docs/nsla/catalogs.htm

Founded: 1865 **Type:** Government **Head:** Monteria High-
tower *Phone:* +1(775) 684-3315 *Email:* mhightow@clan.
sslib.nv.us **Staff:** 4 Prof. 1 Other **Holdings:** 490,000 books
484 journals **Language of Collection/Services:** English
Subjects: Government Documents (Nevada) **Loan:** Internationally **Service:** Internationally **Photocopy:** Yes

3648   Ely, Nevada, US
American Bashkir Curly Registry
Library
Box 246
Ely, Nevada 89301

Location: 371 Clark Street **Phone:** +1(775) 289-4999 **Fax:**
+1(775) 289-8579 **Email:** secretary@abcregistry.org
WWW: www.abcregistry.org/default.htm

Founded: 1971 **Type:** Association **Head:** Deborah Mitchell
Staff: 1 Prof. 2 Other **Holdings:** 25 books **Subjects:** Animal
Husbandry **Specializations:** Bashkir Horse, Horses **Data-
bases Developed:** Curly or American Abshkir Horses **Loan:**
In country **Photocopy:** Yes

3649   Reno, Nevada, US
University of Nevada Reno (UNR)
Life and Health Sciences Library (LHSL)
301 Fleischmann Agriculture Building
Reno, Nevada 89557

Phone: +1(775) 784-6616 **Fax:** +1(775) 784-1046 **WWW:**
www.unr.edu **OPAC:** catalog.library.unr.edu

Founded: 1961 **Type:** Academic **Head:** Amy W. Shannon
Phone: +1(775) 784-6616 *Email:* ashannon@unr.edu **Staff:**
1 Prof. 2 Other **Holdings:** 108,000 books 625 journals **Language of Collection/Services:** English / English **Subjects:**
Agricultural Economics, Animal Husbandry, Biotechnology, Crops, Education/Extension, Entomology, Farming,

Food Sciences, Forestry, Horticulture, Plant Pathology, Soil
Science, Veterinary Medicine **Networks:** OCLC **Databases
Developed:** Nevada State Documents including all state ag-
ricultural documents **Databases Used:** Agricola; Biosis
Loan: Internationally **Service:** In state **Photocopy:** Yes

New Hampshire

3650   Durham, New Hampshire, US
University of New Hampshire (UNH)
Grinnel Library, Biological Sciences Branch
      Library
Kendall Hall
129 Main St.
Durham, New Hampshire 03824

Phone: +1(603) 862-1018 **Fax:** +1(603) 862-2789 **Email:**
dml2@cisunix.unh.edu **WWW:** unhinfo.unh.edu **OPAC:**
library.unh.edu

Type: Academic **Head:** David Lane *Phone:* +1(603) 862-
3718 *Email:* david.lane@unh.edu **Language of Collection/
Services:** English **Staff:** 1 Prof. 2 Other **Holdings:** 70,000
books 800 journals **Subjects:** Animal Husbandry, Biotech-
nology, Crops, Entomology, Fisheries, Forestry, Genetics,
Horticulture, Microbiology, Nutrition, Plant Pathology,
Plants, Soil Science, Veterinary Medicine, Water Resources,
Wildlife Management **Networks:** OCLC **Databases Used:**
Agricola; Biosis; Medline **Loan:** In country **Photocopy:** Yes

3651   Durham, New Hampshire, US
University of New Hampshire (UNH)
Water Resource Research Center (WRRC)
311 Thompson Hall
Durham, New Hampshire 03824-3525

Phone: +1(603) 862-2144 **WWW:** www.unh.edu/wrrc/
index.html

Founded: 1964 **Type:** Academic **Staff:** 1 Other **Holdings:**
12,000 books 3 journals **Language of Collection/Services:**
English **Subjects:** Water Resources **Loan:** Inhouse **Photocopy:** Yes

3652   Hillsboro, New Hampshire, US
New Hampshire Department of Resources and
      Economic Development, Division of Forests
      and Lands
Fox Forest Library
Fox State Forest
Hillsboro, New Hampshire 03244

WWW: dred.state.nh.us

Founded: 1933 **Type:** Government **Head:** J.B. Cullen
Phone: +1(603) 271-3457 **Subjects:** Forestry

New Jersey

3653   East Hanover, New Jersey, US
R.J. Reynolds RJR Foods Inc., Nabisco Brands
      Inc.
Information Resource Center (IRC)
Box 1944
200 DeForest Avenue

East Hanover, New Jersey 07936
Phone: +1(201) 503-3070, 503-3539 **Fax:** +1(201) 428-8950 **Email:** silvan@nabisco.com

Former Name: Technology Center Library **Founded:** 1922 **Type:** Business **Staff:** 2 Prof. 2 Other **Holdings:** 15,000 books 300 journals **Language of Collection/Services:** English **Subjects:** Food Sciences **Databases Used:** Medline; LEXIS-NEXIS **Loan:** In country **Service:** Internationally **Photocopy:** Yes

3654   Highlands, New Jersey, US
United States National Marine Fisheries Service, Northeast Fisheries Science Center, James J. Howard Marine Sciences Laboratory at Sandy Hook
Lionel A. Walford Library
74 Magruder Road, Sandy Hook
Highlands, New Jersey 07732
Phone: +1(732) 872-3000 **WWW:** www.nmfs.gov

Founded: 1961 **Type:** Government **Holdings:** 24,500 books **Subjects:** Fisheries

3655   New Brunswick, New Jersey, US
Rutgers, The State University of New Jersey
Stephen and Lucy Chang Science Library
59 Dudley Road
New Brunswick, New Jersey 08901-8520
Location: Walter E. Foran Hall, Cook Campus **Phone:** +1(732) 932-0305 **Fax:** +1(732) 932-0311 **Email:** rgardner@rci.rutgers.edu **WWW:** www.libraries.rutgers.edu **OPAC:** www.iris.rutgers.edu/iris.html

Founded: 1995 **Type:** Academic **Staff:** 2 Prof. 2 Other **Holdings:** 280 journals **Language of Collection/Services:** English / English **Subjects:** Comprehensive **Networks:** RLIN **Databases Used:** Comprehensive **Loan:** In country **Service:** Internationally **Photocopy:** Yes

3656   Piscataway, New Jersey, US
Rutgers, The State University of New Jersey
Library of Science and Medicine
165 Bevier Road
Piscataway, New Jersey 08854-8009
Location: Bevier Road, Busch Campus **Phone:** +1(732) 445-3854 **Fax:** +1(732) 445-5703 **WWW:** www.libraries.rutgers.edu **OPAC:** www.iris.rutgers.edu/iris.html

Founded: 1970 **Type:** Academic **Head:** Mary Page *Phone:* +1(732) 445-3856 *Email:* mspage@rutgers.edu **Staff:** 13 Prof. 22 Other **Holdings:** 677,500 books 4,106 journals **Language of Collection/Services:** English **Subjects:** Agricultural Engineering, Agricultural Production, Aquaculture, Animal Husbandry, Biotechnology, Horticulture, Marine Sciences, Soil Science **Specializations:** Environmental Protection, Food Sciences, Forestry, Marine Environment, Nutrition, Sustainability **Networks:** OCLC; RLIN **Databases Developed:** PenPages - Rutgers Cooperative Extension Bulletin Board **Databases Used:** Compendex; Medline **Loan:** Internationally **Service:** Internationally **Photocopy:** Yes

3657   Princeton, New Jersey, US
FMC Corporation, Chemical Research and Development Center
Technical Information Services
Box 8
Princeton, New Jersey 08543
Location: US Route 1 at Plainsboro Road **Phone:** +1(609) 951-3236 **Fax:** +1(609) 951-3003 **WWW:** www.fmc.com

Founded: 1956 **Type:** Business **Head:** Coleen J. Dazé *Phone:* +1(609) 951-3238 **Staff:** 4 Prof. 2 Other **Holdings:** 30,000 books 200 journals **Language of Collection/Services:** English

3658   Somerset, New Jersey, US
CPC International, Best Foods Technical Center
Information Center
150 Pierce St.
Call Box 6710
Somerset, New Jersey 08873-6710
Fax: +1(908) 627-8506 **WWW:** www.bestfoods.com

Founded: 1970 **Type:** Business **Head:** Anne Troop *Phone:* +1(908) 627-8604 **Staff:** 5 Prof. 1 Other **Holdings:** 6,000 books 350 journals **Language of Collection/Services:** English **Subjects:** Food Sciences **Databases Developed:** Project documentation (proprietary) **Loan:** Inhouse **Service:** Inhouse **Photocopy:** Yes

3659   Trenton, New Jersey, US
Delaware River Basin Commission
Technical Library
25 State Police Drive
Box 7360
Trenton, New Jersey 08628
Phone: +1(609) 883-9500 ext 263 **Fax:** +1(609) 883-9522 **Email:** drbc@drbc.state.nj.us **WWW:** www.state.nj.us/drbc

Founded: 1962 **Type:** Government **Head:** Judith Strong *Phone:* +1(609) 883-9500 *Email:* jstrong@drbc.state.nj.us **Staff:** 1 Prof. **Holdings:** 12,000 books 70 journals **Language of Collection/Services:** English **Subjects:** Water Resources **Specializations:** Delaware River Basin **Loan:** Via ILL **Service:** Internationally **Photocopy:** Yes

New Mexico

3660   Albuquerque, New Mexico, US
University of New Mexico (UNM)
Centennial Science and Engineering Library (CSEL)
Albuquerque, New Mexico 87131-1466
Phone: +1(505) 277-4412 **Fax:** +1(505) 277-0702 **Email:** cselref@mail.unm.edu **WWW:** www.unm.edu **OPAC:** eLibrary.unm.edu/libinfo/Libraries/catalogs.html

Founded: 1963 **Type:** Academic **Head:** Johann van Reenen *Phone:* +1(505) 277-8310 *Email:* jreenen@unm.edu

3661   Las Cruces, New Mexico, US
New Mexico State University (NMSU)
University Library

Box 30006 - Department 3475
Las Cruces, New Mexico 88003-0006
Location: 15 Frenger Street **Phone:** +1(505) 646-5791
Fax: +1(505) 646-7477 **Email:** answers@lib.nmsu.edu
WWW: lib.nmsu.edu

Founded: 1888 **Type:** Academic **Head:** Tim McKimmie, Agriculture Librarian *Phone:* +1(505) 646-7483 *Email:* tmckimmi@lib.nmsu.edu **Staff:** 25 Prof. 74 Other **Holdings:** 1,200,000 books 6,000 journals **Language of Collection/Services:** English / English **Subjects:** Agricultural Economics, Agronomy, Animal Husbandry, Entomology, Fisheries, Home Economics, Horticulture, Plant Pathology, Rangelands, Weeds, Wildlife **Specializations:** Chillies, Cotton, Onions, Pecans, Rangelands **Networks:** OCLC **Databases Developed:** Aggie - extension documents; available via Internet at lib.nmsu.edu **Databases Used:** Agricola **Loan:** Internationally **Photocopy:** Yes

3662   Las Cruces, New Mexico, US
New Mexico Water Resources Research Institute
(WRRI)
Reference Room
Box 30001, Department 3167
Las Cruces, New Mexico 88003
Location: Stuckey Hall, New Mexico State University, Espina St. **Phone:** +1(505) 646-4334 **Fax:** +1(505) 646-6418 **WWW:** wrri.nmsu.edu **OPAC:** wrri.nmsu.edu/wrdis/wrdis.html

Founded: 1963 **Type:** Academic **Head:** Michelle Ford-Del Rio *Phone:* +1(505) 646-1813 *Email:* mfdelrio@wrri.nmsu.edu **Staff:** 1 Prof. **Holdings:** 9,000 books **Language of Collection/Services:** English **Subjects:** Fisheries, Irrigation, Soil Science, Water Resources **Loan:** Inhouse **Photocopy:** Yes

3663   Portales, New Mexico, US
Eastern New Mexico University (ENMU)
Golden Library
Station 32
Portales, New Mexico 88130
Phone: +1(505) 562-2638 **Fax:** +1(505) 562-2647 **WWW:** www.enmu.edu **OPAC:** goldenweb.enmu.edu

Founded: 1934 **Type:** Academic **Head:** Malveta Walker, Interim Director *Email:* melveta.walker@enmu.edu *Phone:* +1(505) 562-2624 **Staff:** 8 Prof. 13 Other **Holdings:** 750,000 books 3,685 journals **Language of Collection/Services:** English / English **Networks:** OCLC **Loan:** In country **Service:** In country **Photocopy:** Yes

New York

3664   Albany, New York, US
New York State Education Department (NY SED)
New York State Library (NYSL)
Cultural Education Center
Empire State Plaza
Albany, New York 12230
Phone: +1(518) 474-5355 **Fax:** +1(518) 474-5786 **WWW:** www.nysl.nysed.gov **OPAC:** www.nysl.nysed.gov **Ariel IP:** 149.10.146.151

Founded: 1818 **Type:** Government **Head:** Liz Lane *Phone:* +1(518) 473-1189 **Staff:** 67 Prof. 106 Other **Holdings:** 7,000,000 books 14,379 journals **Language of Collection/Services:** English / English **Specializations:** Biotechnology, Crops, Entomology, Farming, Fisheries, Forestry, Plants, Soil Science, Water Resources **Networks:** OCLC; RLIN **Databases Used:** ABI/Inform; LEXIS-NEXIS; Biosis; Medline **Loan:** In country **Service:** In country **Photocopy:** Yes

3665   Alfred, New York, US
State University of New York, College of
Technology at Alfred (SUNY)
Walter C. Hinkle Memorial Library
Alfred, New York 14802-1193
Phone: +1(607) 587-4313 **Fax:** +1(607) 587-4351 **Email:** library@alfredtech.edu **WWW:** www.alfredtech.edu

Founded: 1911 **Type:** Academic **Head:** David Haggstrom *Phone:* +1(607) 587-4313 *Email:* haggstdg@alfredtech.edu **Staff:** 7 Prof. 7 Other **Holdings:** 3,125 books 135 journals **Subjects:** Agriculture (Tropics), Agribusiness, Agricultural Development, Agricultural Economics, Agricultural Engineering, Animal Husbandry, Biotechnology, Crops, Entomology, Education/Extension, Farming, Food Sciences, Horticulture, Plant Pathology, Water Resources, Soil Science **Networks:** OCLC **Loan:** Internationally **Photocopy:** Yes

3666   Bronx, New York, US
New York Botanical Garden (NYBG)
LuEsther T. Mertz Library
Bronx, New York 10458-5126
Location: 200th Street & Southern Boulevard **Phone:** +1(718) 817-8753 **Fax:** +1(718) 817-8956 **Email:** libref@nybg.org **WWW:** www.nybg.org **OPAC:** librisc.nybg.org

Founded: 1900 **Type:** Association **Head:** John F. Reed *Phone:* +1(718) 817-8729 *Email:* jfreed@nybg.org **Staff:** 10 Prof. 10 Other **Holdings:** 261,000 books 2,000 journals **Language of Collection/Services:** English / English **Subjects:** Botany, Forestry, Gardening, Horticulture, Plant Pathology, Plants, Soil Science **Specializations:** Flora, Plant Taxonomy **Networks:** OCLC **Databases Developed:** Lord & Burnham architectural drawings of glass houses; index available locally **Databases Used:** Agricola; Biosis **Loan:** Internationally **Photocopy:** Yes

3667   Brooklyn, New York, US
Brooklyn Botanic Garden
Science Library
Science Center at 109 Montgomery Street
Brooklyn, New York 11225
Phone: +1(718) 623-7302 **Fax:** +1(718) 622-7839 **Email:** library@bbg.org **WWW:** www.bbg.org **OPAC:** www.bbg.org/library

Founded: 1911 **Type:** Private **Head:** Brenda Oakley *Email:* brendaoakley@bbg.org **Staff:** 3 Prof. **Holdings:** 150 journals 30,000 books **Language of Collection/Services:** English **Subjects:** Botany, Horticulture **Photocopy:** Yes **Loan:** Inhouse

3668 **Brooklyn, New York, US**
Domino Sugar
Research Library
266 Kent Avenue
Brooklyn, New York 11211-4131
Phone: +1(718) 486-4492 **WWW:** www.dominosugar.
com/dhtml/index.html

Founded: 1948 **Type:** Business **Holdings:** 2,260 books 250
journals **Language of Collection/Services:** English **Subjects:** Agribusiness, Biotechnology, Crops, Food Sciences
Databases Developed: Research Report Database - inhouse
Loan: Inhouse **Service:** In country **Photocopy:** No

3669 **Buffalo, New York, US**
Buffalo Museum of Science
Research Library
1020 Humboldt Parkway
Buffalo, New York 14211-1293
Phone: +1(716) 896-5200 ext 280 **Fax:** +1(716) 897-6723
Email: reslib@buffnet.net **WWW:** www.sciencebuff.org
OPAC: lepac1.brodart.com/search/yr

Founded: 1861 **Type:** Association **Head:** Lisa A. Seivert
Phone: +1(716) 896-5200 *Email:* seivert@sciencebuff.org
Staff: 1 Prof. 1 Other **Holdings:** 2,100 books 25 journals
Subjects: Botany, Entomology, Fisheries, Forestry, Horticulture, Plant Pathology, Soil Science **Databases Developed:** TAXACOM - Free online service for systematic
botany and phytogeography; available 24 hours daily, 7 days
a week; included are searchable herbarium databases, bibliographies, full-text articles from FLORA ONLINE (botanical journal), electronic mail, conferences and symposia, etc.
Loan: Internationally **Photocopy:** Yes

3670 **Chazy, New York, US**
Wm. H. Miner Agricultural Research Institute
FitzPatrick Library
1034 Route 191
PO Box 100
Chazy, New York 12921-0100
Fax: +1(518) 846-7774 **WWW:** www.whminer.com

Founded: 1972 **Type:** Academic **Head:** Linda J. Masters
Phone: +1(518) 846-7144 *Email:* mastersl@westelcom.com
Staff: 1 Prof. 4 Other **Holdings:** 5,400 books 82 journals
Language of Collection/Services: English / English **Subjects:** Agribusiness, Agricultural Development, Animal
Husbandry, Animal Nutrition, Crops, Ecology, Education/
Extension, Equidae, Farming, Forestry, Plant Pathology,
Soil Science, Water Resources **Specializations:** Dairy Cattle
Databases Developed: Farm Report Database - accesses
parent institution's monthly newsletter via title and subject
Databases Used: Current Contents **Loan:** Inhouse **Service:**
Inhouse **Photocopy:** Yes

3671 **Cobleskill, New York, US**
State University of New York, College of
Agriculture and Technology at Cobleskill
(SUNY Cobleskill)
Jared van Wagenen Jr. Hall Learning Resource
Center (LRC)
Cobleskill, New York 12043

Phone: +1(518) 255-5841 **Fax:** +1(518) 255-5843 **WWW:**
www.cobleskill.edu/lrc **OPAC:** albweb2.sunyconnect.
suny.edu/coble

Founded: 1912 **Type:** Academic **Head:** Nancy VanDeusen,
Acting *Email:* vandeun@cobleskill.edu *Phone:* +1(518)
255-5841 **Staff:** 4 Prof. 4 Other **Holdings:** 90,000 books 500
journals **Language of Collection/Services:** English **Subjects:** Animal Husbandry, Farming, Fisheries, Horticulture,
Plants **Networks:** OCLC **Databases Used:** Agricola; Biological and Agricultural Abstracts; Biosis **Loan:** Internationally **Service:** Internationally **Photocopy:** Yes

3672 **Cold Spring Harbor, New York, US**
Cold Spring Harbor Laboratory (CSHL)
Library
1 Bungtown Road
Cold Spring Harbor, New York 11724-2203
Phone: +1(516) 367-8352 **Fax:** +1(516) 367-6843 **Email:**
pollock@cshl.org **WWW:** www.cshl.org **OPAC:** nucleus.
cshl.org/worldpac/eng/wphome.htm

Founded: 1890 **Type:** Research **Head:** Ludmila Pollock
Phone: +1(516) 367-8493 *Email:* pollock@cshl.org **Staff:** 2
Prof. 5 Other **Holdings:** 9,500 books 275 journals **Language
of Collection/Services:** English/English **Subjects:** Biotechnology, Genetics **Databases Used:** Biosis; GeoRef; SCI;
Medline **Loan:** Internationally **Service:** Internationally **Photocopy:** Yes

3673 **Cooperstown, New York, US**
New York Center for Agricultural Medicine and
Health (NYCAMH)
Library and Information Center
One Atwell Road
Cooperstown, New York 13326
Phone: +1(607) 547-6023, +1(800) 353-7527 **Fax:** +1
(607) 547-6087 **Email:** nycamh@lakenet.org **WWW:**
www.nycamh.com

Founded: 1988 **Type:** Research **Head:** Bernadette Hodge
Phone: +1(800) 353-7527 *Email:* bhodge@lakenet.org
Staff: 1 Prof. **Holdings:** 600 books 42 journals **Language of
Collection/Services:** English/English **Subjects:** Health Protection, Occupational Hazards, Safety at Work **Specializations:** Respiratory Diseases, Safety Education **Networks:**
Docline; OCLC **Databases Developed:** Scientific and popular articles on topics from Allergy to Zoonosis **Databases
Used:** Agricola; HIOSH; Medline; OSHA **Loan:** Inhouse
Service: In country **Photocopy:** Yes

3674 **Cooperstown, New York, US**
New York State Historical Association (NYSHA)
Library
Lake Road
PO Box 800
Cooperstown, New York 13326
Phone: +1(607) 547-1470 **Fax:** +1(607) 547-1405 **WWW:**
www.nysha.org

Type: Association **Head:** Wayne Wright *Phone:* +1(607)
547-1470 **Staff:** 3 Prof. 3 Other **Holdings:** 5,000 books **Language of Collection/Services:** English **Subjects:** Agricul-

ture (History - New York - 19th Century) **Loan:** Inhouse **Service:** Inhouse **Photocopy:** Yes

3675   Delhi, New York, US
State University of New York, College of
     Technology at Delhi (SUNY)
Resnick Library
Bush Hall
Delhi, New York 13753-1190
Phone: +1(607) 746-4644 **Fax:** +1(607) 746-4327 **Email:** library@delhi.edu **WWW:** www.delhi.edu **OPAC:** www. delhi.edu/page/lib/catalog.htm

Founded: 1913 **Type:** Academic **Head:** Pamela J. Peters *Phone:* +1(607) 746-4643 *Email:* peterspj@delhi.edu **Staff:** 4 Prof. 4 Other **Holdings:** 57,788 books 600 journals **Language of Collection/Services:** English **Subjects:** Biotechnology, Food Sciences, Horticulture, Veterinary Medicine **Networks:** OCLC **Loan:** In country **Service:** Internationally **Photocopy:** Yes

3676   DeRuyter, New York, US
American Finnsheep Breeders Association
Library
HC 65 Box 495
DeRuyter, New York 13052
Phone: +1(315) 852-3344 **Email:** stillmeadowfinns@ hotmail.com **WWW:** www.finnsheep.org

Founded: 1971 **Type:** Association **Head:** Elizabeth Luke **Subjects:** Finnish Landrace Sheep, Sheep **Photocopy:** Yes

3677   Farmingdale, New York, US
State University of New York at Farmingdale
     (SUNY)
Thomas D. Greenley Library
Melville Road
Farmingdale, New York 11735
Phone: +1(516) 420-2184 **Fax:** +1(516) 420-2473 **Email:** reference@farmingdale.edu **WWW:** www.farmingdale.edu **OPAC:** albweb2.sunyconnect.suny.edu/farmi

Founded: 1910 **Type:** Academic **Head:** Michael G. Knauth *Phone:* +1(516) 420-2040 *Email:* knauthmg@farmingdale. edu **Holdings:** 298,000 books

3678   Flushing, New York, US
City University of New York, Queens College
     (CUNY, QC)
Benjamin S. Rosenthal Library
65-30 Kissena Boulevard
Flushing, New York 11367-0904
Phone: +1(718) 997-3799 **Fax:** +1(718) 997-3753 **Email:** library@qc.edu, libqc@cunyvm.cuny.edu **WWW:** www. qc.edu **OPAC:** libraries.cuny.edu/lib-cpl.htm

Type: Academic **Head:** Sharon Bonk *Phone:* +1(718) 997-3760 *Email:* sharon_bonk@qc.edu **Subjects:** Food Sciences, Home Economics

3679   Geneva, New York, US
Cornell University, New York State Agriculture
     Experiment Station
Library

West North Street
Geneva, New York 14456-0462
Phone: +1(315) 787-2214 **Fax:** +1(315) 787-2276 **Email:** lib@nysaes.cornell.edu **WWW:** www.nysaes.cornell.edu/ library

Founded: 1882 **Type:** Government **Head:** Mary Schlabach *Email:* mls5@cornell.edu **Staff:** 2 Prof. 2 Other **Holdings:** 55,000 books 900 journals **Language of Collection/Services:** English / English **Subjects:** Biotechnology, Crops, Entomology, Food Sciences, Horticulture, Pomology, Viticulture **Networks:** RLIN **Databases Used:** Comprehensive **Loan:** In country **Service:** In state **Photocopy:** Yes

3680   Greenport, New York, US
United States Department of Agriculture,
     Agricultural Research Service, North Atlantic
     Area, Plum Island Animal Disease Center
     (USDA, ARS, NAA, PIADC)
Research Library
PO Box 848
Greenport, New York 11944-0848
Phone: +1(631) 323-2500 ext 475 **Fax:** +1(631) 323-9790 **WWW:** www.ars.usda.gov

Founded: 1953 **Type:** Government **Head:** Honoré McILvain *Email:* hmcilvain@piadc.ars.usda.gov *Phone:* +1 (631) 323-2500 ext 475 **Staff:** 1 Prof. **Holdings:** 20,000 books 125 journals **Language of Collection/Services:** English **Subjects:** African Horse Sickness, African Swine Fever, Foot and Mouth Disease, Virology **Networks:** OCLC **Databases Used:** Agricola; Current Contents; Current Protocols; Medline **Loan:** Internationally **Service:** Inhouse **Photocopy:** Yes

3681   Ithaca, New York, US
Cornell University
Albert R. Mann Library
Ithaca, New York 14853-4301
Phone: +1(607) 255-5406 **Fax:** +1(607) 255-0318, Attention Reference **Email:** mann_ref@cornell.edu **WWW:** www.mannlib.cornell.edu **OPAC:** campusgw. library.cornell.edu **Ariel IP:** 128.253.78.105 (ILL lending); 128.243.78.106 (ILL borrowing)

Founded: 1952 **Type:** Academic **Head:** Janet A. McCue *Phone:* +1(607) 255-2285 *Email:* jam7@cornell.edu **Staff:** 32 Prof. 33 Other **Holdings:** 645,358 books 9,168 journals **Language of Collection/Services:** English **Subjects:** Agriculture (Tropics), Agribusiness, Agricultural Economics, Agricultural Engineering, Animal Husbandry, Biotechnology, Crops, Education/Extension, Entomology, Farming, Fisheries, Food Sciences, Forestry, Horticulture, Nutrition, Plant Pathology, Soil Science, Water Resources **Specializations:** Agricultural Development, Beekeeping, Biology, Poultry **Networks:** RLIN **Databases Developed:** Mann Library Gateway - computer system that provides easy access to over 200 databases **Databases Used:** Comprehensive **Loan:** In country **Service:** Internationally **Photocopy:** Yes

3682   Ithaca, New York, US
Cornell University
Comstock Memorial Library of Entomology

Comstock Hall
Ithaca, New York 14853-2601
Phone: +1(607) 255-3265 **Fax:** +1(607) 255-0850 **Email:** entomologylib@cornell.edu **WWW:** entomology.library.cornell.edu **OPAC:** campusgw.library.cornell.edu

Founded: 1914 **Type:** Academic **Head:** Marty Schlabach *Phone:* +1(607) 255-7959 *Email:* mls5@cornell.edu **Staff:** 1 Prof. 5 Other **Holdings:** 35,000 books 600 journals **Language of Collection/Services:** English / English **Subjects:** Entomology **Specializations:** Ecology, Medical Entomology, Nomenclature, Parasitology, Toxicology **Networks:** RLIN **Databases Used:** Agricola; Biosis; CABCD **Loan:** In country **Service:** Internationally **Photocopy:** Yes

3683 Ithaca, New York, US
Cornell University
Flower-Sprecher Library
College of Veterinary Medicine
Ithaca, New York 14853-6401
Phone: +1(607) 253-3510 **Fax:** +1(607) 253-3080 **Email:** veterinary-library@cornell.edu **WWW:** www.library.cornell.edu **OPAC:** campusgw.library.cornell.edu **Ariel IP:** 128.253.14.18

Former Name: Flower Veterinary Library **Founded:** 1897 **Type:** Academic **Head:** Erla P. Heynes *Phone:* +1(607) 253-3515 *Email:* eph8@cornell.edu **Staff:** 2 Prof. 4 Other **Holdings:** 90,000 books 1,000 journals **Language of Collection/Services:** English / English **Subjects:** Veterinary Medicine **Networks:** OCLC; RLIN **Databases Developed:** Consultant - Veterinary Diagnostic Databases **Databases Used:** Comprehensive **Loan:** In country **Service:** Internationally **Photocopy:** Yes

3684 Ithaca, New York, US
Cornell University
L.H. Bailey Hortorium Library
Room 467 Mann Library
Ithaca, New York 14853
Phone: +1(607) 255-7781 **Fax:** +1(607) 255-7979 **Email:** pf13@cornell.edu **WWW:** www.bio.cornell.edu/hortorium/hortlibe.html **OPAC:** campusgw.library.cornell.edu

Founded: 1935 **Type:** Academic **Head:** Jerrold I. Davis *Phone:* +1(607) 255-7988 *Email:* jid1@cornell.edu **Staff:** 1 Prof. 1 Other **Holdings:** 40,000 books 90 journals **Language of Collection/Services:** English / English **Subjects:** Botany, Horticulture, Paleobotany **Specializations:** Flora, Palmae, Plants **Networks:** OCLC; RLIN **Databases Used:** Comprehensive **Loan:** Inhouse **Service:** Inhouse **Photocopy:** Yes

3685 Ithaca, New York, US
Cornell University, Boyce Thompson Institute for Plant Research (BTI)
Library
Tower Road
Ithaca, New York 14853
Phone: +1(607) 254-1250 **Fax:** +1(607) 254-1242 **Email:** kpk3@cornell.edu **WWW:** bti.cornell.edu

Type: Academic **Head:** Kathleen Kramer *Phone:* +1(607) 254-1250 *Email:* kpk3@cornell.edu **Staff:** 1 Prof. 1 Other **Holdings:** 5,000 books 250 journals **Language of Collec-**

tion/Services: English / English **Subjects:** Biochemistry, Biotechnology, Entomology, Microbiology, Molecular Biology, Plant Pathology, Plant Physiology, Plants **Databases Used:** Biosis; Agricola; Current Contents **Loan:** Inhouse **Service:** Internationally **Photocopy:** Yes

3686 Millbrook, New York, US
Institute of Ecosystem Studies
Library
PO Box AB
Millbrook, New York 12545-0129
Fax: +1(914) 677-5976 **WWW:** www.ecostudies.org/index.html

Founded: 1976 **Type:** Research **Head:** Annette R. Frank *Phone:* +1(914) 677-5343 **Staff:** 1 Prof. 2 Other **Holdings:** 12,000 books 240 journals **Subjects:** Fisheries, Forestry, Plant Pathology, Plant Protection, Soil Science **Loan:** In country **Photocopy:** Yes

3687 Morrisville, New York, US
State University College of Agriculture and Technology, Morrisville
Donald G. Butcher Library
PO Box 902
Morrisville, New York 13408-0902
Phone: +1(315) 684-6055, 684-6060 **Fax:** +1(315) 684-6115 **WWW:** www.morrisville.edu **OPAC:** laip.hscsyr.edu

Former Name: State University of New York (SUNY), Agriculture and Technical College at Morrisville **Founded:** 1948 **Type:** Academic **Head:** Marion Hildebrand *Phone:* +1(315) 684-6055 *Email:* hildebme@morrisville.edu **Staff:** 5 Prof. 3 Other **Holdings:** 4,000 books 100 journals **Language of Collection/Services:** English **Subjects:** Agribusiness, Animal Husbandry, Farming, Fisheries, Food Sciences, Horticulture **Specializations:** Aquaculture, Forestry **Networks:** OCLC **Databases Used:** Agricola **Loan:** Internationally **Service:** Internationally **Photocopy:** Yes

3688 New York, New York, US
American Museum of Natural History (AMNH)
Department of Library Services
Central Park West at 79th Street
New York, New York 10024-5192
Phone: +1(212) 769-5400 **Fax:** +1(212) 769-5009 **Email:** libref@amnh.org **WWW:** www.amnh.org **OPAC:** nimidi.amnh.org/webvoy.htm

Founded: 1869 **Type:** Museum **Head:** Roscoe Thompson **Staff:** 10 Prof. 18 Other **Holdings:** 500,000 books 4,000 journals **Language of Collection/Services:** English **Networks:** OCLC **Loan:** Inhouse **Photocopy:** Yes

3689 New York, New York, US
Columbia University
Biological Sciences Library
601 Fairchild Building
New York, New York 10027
Phone: +1(212) 854-4812 **Email:** biology@libraries.cul.columbia.edu **WWW:** www.columbia.edu **OPAC:** www.columbia.edu/cu/libraries/indexes/clio.html

Founded: 1912 **Type:** Academic **Head:** Kathleen Kehoe *Phone:* +1(212) 854-4182 *Email:* kehoe@columbia.edu **Holdings:** 52,000 books 335 journals **Subjects:** Biochemistry, Cellular Biology, Molecular Biology, Microbiology, Neurobiology, Population and Evolutionary Biology, Plant Physiology

3690   New York, New York, US
Horticultural Society of New York (HSNY)
Public Reference Library
128 West 58th Street
New York, New York 10019
Fax: +1(212) 246-1207 **Email:** hsny@hsny.org **WWW:** newyork.citysearch.com/E/V/NYCNY/0006/01/15/1.html

Founded: 1922 **Type:** Association **Head:** Katherine Powis *Phone:* +1(212) 757-0915 **Staff:** 1 Prof. .5 Other **Holdings:** 15,000 books 90 journals **Language of Collection/Services:** English **Subjects:** Horticulture **Databases Used:** Agricola **Loan:** Inhouse **Service:** In country **Photocopy:** Yes

3691   New York, New York, US
New York Public Library
Science, Industry and Business Library (SIBL)
188 Madison Avenue
New York, New York 10016
Phone: +1(212) 592-7000 **WWW:** www.nypl.org **OPAC:** www.nypl.org/catalogs/catalogs.html

Type: Public **Databases Used:** FSTA; Water Resources Abstracts

3692   Paul Smiths, New York, US
Paul Smith's College
Frank L. Cubley Library
Box 257
Paul Smiths, New York 12970
Fax: +1(518) 327-6350 **Email:** conleys@paulsmiths.edu **WWW:** www.paulsmiths.edu **OPAC:** www.paulsmiths.edu/uhtbin/webcat

Founded: 1946 **Type:** Academic **Head:** Theodore D. Mack *Phone:* +1(518) 327-6313 *Email:* mackt@paulsmiths.edu **Staff:** 2 Prof. 4 Other **Holdings:** 3,000 books 100 journals **Language of Collection/Services:** English **Subjects:** Forestry **Specializations:** Logging **Networks:** OCLC **Databases Developed:** 19,000 pamphlets on forestry **Loan:** Internationally **Service:** Internationally **Photocopy:** Yes

3693   Riverhead, New York, US
Cornell University, Long Island Horticultural
    Research Laboratory (LIHRL)
Library
3059 Sound Avenue
Riverhead, New York 11901-1115
Phone: +1(516) 727-3595 **Fax:** +1(516) 727-3611 **WWW:** www.osp.cornell.edu/VPR/CenterDir/CenterDir.html

Type: Government **Head:** Joseph Sieczka *Phone:* +1(516) 727-3595 *Email:* jbs5@cornell.edu **Holdings:** 200 books 12 journals **Language of Collection/Services:** English **Subjects:** Crops, Entomology, Farming, Horticulture, Plant Pathology, Plants **Loan:** Inhouse **Photocopy:** Yes

3694   Rochester, New York, US
Garden Center of Rochester, Inc.
Library
5 Castle Park
Rochester, New York 14620

Founded: 1945 **Type:** Association **Head:** Regina Campbell *Phone:* +1(716) 473-5130 **Staff:** 1 Prof. 6 Other **Holdings:** 3,000 books 11 journals **Subjects:** Gardens, Horticulture, Landscaping **Loan:** Do not loan **Photocopy:** Yes

3695   Syracuse, New York, US
Borden Inc.
Corporate Science and Technology Research
    Center Library
1 Gail Borden Drive
Syracuse, New York 13204
Phone: +1(315) 477-0218

Founded: 1958 **Type:** Business **Staff:** 2 Prof. 2 Other **Holdings:** 2,000 books 75 journals **Language of Collection/Services:** English **Subjects:** Food Sciences **Specializations:** Analytical Chemistry, Dairy Science, Food Engineering, Food Microbiology, Pasta **Loan:** Inhouse **Photocopy:** Yes

3696   Syracuse, New York, US
State University of New York, College of
    Environmental Science and Forestry (SUNY,
    ESF)
F. Franklin Moon Library
1 Forestry Drive
Syracuse, New York 13210
Phone: +1(315) 470-6712 **Fax:** +1(315) 470-6512 **Email:** moon@esf.edu **WWW:** www.esf.edu **OPAC:** libwww.syr.edu/summit.htm

Founded: 1911 **Type:** Academic **Head:** Elizabeth A. Elkins *Phone:* +1(315) 470-6715 *Email:* eaelkins@esf.edu **Staff:** 6 Prof. 5 Other **Holdings:** 120,000 books 900 journals **Language of Collection/Services:** English **Subjects:** Agriculture (Tropics), Biotechnology, Entomology, Fisheries, Forestry, Plant Pathology, Soil Science, Water Resources **Networks:** OCLC **Databases Used:** Comprehensive **Loan:** Internationally **Service:** In country **Photocopy:** Yes

North Carolina

3697   Chapel Hill, North Carolina, US
University of North Carolina
John N. Couch Biology Library
CB#3280 Coker Hall
Chapel Hill, North Carolina 27599-3280
Location: Coker Hall (Botany Section), 213 Wilson Hall (Zoology Section) **Phone:** +1(919) 962-3783 (Botany); 962-2264 (Zoology) **Fax:** +1(919) 962-1625 **Email:** bioref@listserv.unc.edu **WWW:** www.unc.edu **OPAC:** library.unc.edu

Founded: 1902 **Type:** Academic **Head:** William R. Burk, Botany Librarian; David Romito, Zoology Librarian *Email:* billburk@email.unc.edu; dromito@email.unc.edu **Staff:** 1 Prof. 1 Other **Holdings:** 800 books 30 journals **Language of Collection/Services:** English **Subjects:** Biotechnology,

Horticulture, Plant Pathology, Soil Science **Networks:** OCLC **Databases Used:** Agricola; Biosis **Loan:** Internationally **Photocopy:** Yes

3698   **Durham, North Carolina, US**
Duke University
Biological and Environmental Sciences Library
   (BES)
Box 90336
Durham, North Carolina 27708-0336
Location: 101 Biological Sciences Bldg., Science Drive
Phone: +1(919) 660-5970 **Fax:** +1(919) 681-7606 **Email:** biofor@acpub.duke.edu **WWW:** www.lib.duke.edu/bes
OPAC: www.lib.duke.edu/online_catalog.html

Former Name: Biology-Forestry Library **Founded:** 1938 **Type:** Academic **Head:** Carol Fineman, Interim Librarian *Phone:* +1(919) 660-5971 *Email:* carolf@mc.duke.edu **Staff:** 1 Prof. 2 Other **Holdings:** 190,000 books 750 journals **Language of Collection/Services:** English / English **Subjects:** Biology, Botany, Environmental Sciences, Forestry, Plant Pathology, Soil Science, Water Resources, Zoology **Networks:** OCLC **Databases Used:** Comprehensive **Loan:** Internationally **Service:** Internationally **Photocopy:** Yes

3699   **Durham, North Carolina, US**
Forest History Society
Library
701 Vickers Avenue
Durham, North Carolina 27701-3162
Phone: +1(919) 682-9319 **Fax:** +1(919) 682-2349 **WWW:** www.lib.duke.edu/forest

Former Name: Forest Products History Foundation (1952), American Forest History Foundation (1954), Forest History Foundation (1955) **Founded:** 1946 **Type:** Educational **Head:** Cheryl Oakes *Email:* coakes@acpub.duke.edu *Phone* +1(919) 682-9319 **Staff:** 2 Prof. 1 Other **Holdings:** 507,000 books 125 journals **Language of Collection/Services:** English / English **Subjects:** Forestry **Specializations:** Conservation (History), Forestry (History) **Databases Developed:** Bibliography of North American Forest and Conservation History; A guide to Archives and Manuscripts in the US and Canada relating to Forest and Conservation History **Databases Used:** Agricola **Loan:** Inhouse **Service:** Internationally **Photocopy:** Yes

3700   **Greensboro, North Carolina, US**
North Carolina Agricultural & Technical State
   University (NC A&T)
F.D. Bluford Library
1601 E. Market Street
Greensboro, North Carolina 27411
Phone: +1(336) 334-7159 **Fax:** +1(336) 334-7783 **Email:** ref@luford.library.ncat.edu, refemail@ncat.edu **WWW:** www.ncat.edu **OPAC:** www.library.ncat.edu

Type: Academic **Head:** Waltrene Canada *Phone:* +1(336) 334-7782 *Email:* canadaw@ncat.edu **Holdings:** 529,084 books

3701   **Pittsboro, North Carolina, US**
American Livestock Breeds Conservancy (ALBC)

Resource Center
PO Box 477
Pittsboro, North Carolina 27312
Location: 15 Hillsboro Street **Phone:** +1(919) 542-5704 **Fax:** +1(919) 542-0022 **Email:** albc@albc-usa.org **WWW:** albc-usa.org

Former Name: American Minor Breeds Conservancy (AMBC) **Founded:** 1977 **Type:** Non-profit **Head:** Donald E. Bixby *Phone:* +1(919) 542-5704 *Email:* albc@albc-usa.org **Staff:** 5 Prof. 1 Other **Holdings:** 300 books 50 journals **Language of Collection/Services:** English / English **Subjects:** Animal Husbandry, Farming **Specializations:** Genetics, Livestock, Rare Breeds, Sustainability **Loan:** Do not loan **Service:** Internationally **Photocopy:** Yes

3702   **Raleigh, North Carolina, US**
North Carolina State University (NCSU)
Natural Resources Library (NRL)
Box 7114
Raleigh, North Carolina 27695-7114
Location: 1102 Jordan Hall, Faucette & Morrill Drives
Phone: +1(919) 515-2306 **Fax:** +1(919) 515-7802 **Email:** kneer@unity.ncsu.edu **WWW:** www.lib.ncsu.edu/natural
OPAC: www.lib.ncsu.edu

Former Name: Forest Resources Library **Founded:** 1971 **Type:** Academic **Head:** Katherine Fordham Neer, Interim Head *Phone:* +1(919) 515-2306 *Email:* katherine_neer@ncsu.edu **Staff:** 1 Prof. 2 Other **Holdings:** 29,000 books 300 journals **Language of Collection/Services:** English / English **Subjects:** Forestry, Geographic Information Systems, Geology, Marine Sciences, Meteorology, Recreation, Water Resources **Networks:** OCLC **Databases Used:** Comprehensive **Loan:** Internationally **Service:** Internationally **Photocopy:** Yes

3703   **Raleigh, North Carolina, US**
North Carolina State University (NCSU)
North Carolina State University Libraries
NCSU Box 7111
Raleigh, North Carolina 27695-7111
Location: 2205 Hillsborough Street **Phone:** +1(919) 515-2935 **Fax:** +1(919) 515-3628 **Email:** libref@ncsu.edu **WWW:** www.ncsu.edu **OPAC:** www.lib.ncsu.edu

Former Name: D.H. Hill Library **Founded:** 1889 **Type:** Academic **Head:** Susan K. Nutter *Phone:* +1(919) 515-2843 *Email:* susan_nutter@ncsu.edu **Staff:** 51 Prof. 175 Other **Holdings:** 2,228,195 books 17,442 journals **Language of Collection/Services:** English / English **Subjects:** Agriculture (Tropics), Agribusiness, Agricultural Development, Agricultural Economics, Agricultural Engineering, Animal Husbandry, Biotechnology, Crops, Education/Extension, Entomology, Farming, Fisheries, Food Sciences, Forestry, Horticulture, Plant Pathology, Soil Science, Veterinary Medicine, Water Resources **Networks:** OCLC **Databases Developed:** BIS Online Catalog (Database of North Carolina State University, Duke University, and University of North Carolina) **Loan:** Inhouse or interlibrary loan **Service:** Internationally **Photocopy:** Yes

3704　Raleigh, North Carolina, US
North Carolina State University (NCSU)
Veterinary Medical Library
College of Veterinary Medicine
Box 8401
4700 Hillsborough St.
Raleigh, North Carolina 27606
Phone: +1(919) 513-6218 **Fax:** +1(919) 513-6400 **WWW:** www.lib.ncsu.edu **OPAC:** www.lib.ncsu.edu

Type: Academic **Head:** Laura M. Osegueda *Phone:* +1(919) 513-6219 *Email:* laura_osegueda@ncsu.edu **Subjects:** Veterinary Medicine **Networks:** OCLC

3705　Research Triangle Park, North Carolina, US
Aventis CropScience
Library and Information Services (LIS)
Box 12014
Research Triangle Park, North Carolina
　　　27709-2014
Location: 2 Alexander Drive **Phone:** +1(919) 549-2648 **Fax:** +1(919) 549-4168 **WWW:** www2.aventis.com/cropsc/cro_main.htm

Former Name: Union Carbide Agricultural Products Company Inc., Rhone-Poulenc Ag Company (RPAC), AgrEvo **Founded:** 1981 **Type:** Business **Head:** Valerie Eslyn Wolford *Email:* vwolford@rp-agro.com **Staff:** 1 Prof. 4 Other **Holdings:** 17,000 books 300 journals **Language of Collection/Services:** English **Subjects:** Agricultural Chemicals, Biochemistry, Biotechnology, Entomology, Plant Pathology **Specializations:** Agricultural Chemicals **Loan:** In country **Service:** Inhouse **Photocopy:** Yes

3706　Research Triangle Park, North Carolina, US
Research Triangle Institute
Technical Library
Box 12194
Research Triangle Park, North Carolina
　　　27709-2194
Phone: +1(919) 485-2666 **WWW:** www.rti.org

Founded: 1960 **Type:** Business **Holdings:** 40,000 books 1,200 journals

North Dakota

3707　Bismarck, North Dakota, US
North Dakota State Library
Library Memorial Building
604 East Boulevard - Dept. 250
Bismarck, North Dakota 58505-0800
Phone: +1(701) 328-4622 **Fax:** +1(701) 328-2040 **Email:** ndsladmn@state.nd.us **WWW:** ndsl.lib.state.nd.us **OPAC:** ndsl.lib.state.nd.us

Founded: 1907 **Type:** Government **Head:** Mike Jaugstetter *Phone:* +1(701) 224-2492 *Email:* mjaugste@state.nd.us **Staff:** 10 Prof. 14.5 Other **Holdings:** 635 books 5 journals **Language of Collection/Services:** English **Loan:** Internationally **Service:** Internationally **Photocopy:** Yes

3708　Bottineau, North Dakota, US
Minot State University, Bottineau Branch (MSU - Bottineau)
Fossum Foundation Library
105 Simrall Boulevard
Bottineau, North Dakota 58318-1198
Fax: +1(701) 228-5438 **WWW:** www.misu-b.nodak.edu **OPAC:** www.odin.nodak.edu

Former Name: North Dakota State University (NDSU), Bottineau Branch **Type:** Academic **Head:** Jan Wysocki *Phone:* +1(701) 228-5454 *Email:* wysocki@misu.nodak.edu **Staff:** 1 Prof. .5 Other **Holdings:** 25,000 books 25 journals **Language of Collection/Services:** English **Subjects:** Forestry, Horticulture **Networks:** OCLC **Loan:** In country **Service:** In country **Photocopy:** Yes

3709　Fargo, North Dakota, US
North Dakota State University (NDSU)
Libraries
PO Box 5599
Fargo, North Dakota 58105
Phone: +1(701) 231-8886 **Fax:** +1(701) 231-7138 **WWW:** www.lib.ndsu.nodak.edu/index.nojs.shtml **OPAC:** www.lib.ndsu.nodak.edu **Ariel IP:** 134.129.115.34

Former Name: North Dakota Agriculture College **Founded:** 1889 **Type:** Academic **Head:** Kathie Richardson, Agricultural Sciences Librarian *Phone:* +1(701) 231-8879 *Email:* krichard@plains.nodak.edu **Staff:** 14 Prof. 26 Other **Holdings:** 300,000 books 2,400 journals **Language of Collection/Services:** English **Subjects:** Agribusiness, Agricultural Development, Agricultural Economics, Agricultural Engineering, Animal Husbandry, Biotechnology, Crops, Education/Extension, Entomology, Farming, Fisheries, Food Sciences, Forestry, Horticulture, Plant Pathology, Soil Science, Veterinary Medicine, Water Resources **Networks:** OCLC **Databases Developed:** Germans from Russia; North Dakota Institute for Regional Studies **Databases Used:** Comprehensive **Loan:** Internationally **Service:** Internationally **Photocopy:** Yes

Ohio

3710　Cincinnati, Ohio, US
Environmental Protection Agency, Andrew W.
　　　Breidenbach Environmental Research Center
　　　Cincinnati
Technical Library
26 West Martin Luther King Dr.
Cincinnati, Ohio 45268

Founded: 1971 **Type:** Government **Head:** Stephena Harmony *Phone:* +1(513) 569-7705 **Holdings:** 125,000 books 635 journals **Photocopy:** Yes

3711　Cincinnati, Ohio, US
Lloyd Library and Museum
917 Plum Street
Cincinnati, Ohio 45202
Phone: +1(513) 721-3707 **Fax:** +1(513) 721-6575 **Email:** michael.flannery@uc.edu **WWW:** www.libraries.uc.edu/lloyd

Founded: 1864 **Type:** Non-profit, Private **Head:** Michael A. Flannery *Email:* michael.flannery@uc.edu **Staff:** 2 Prof. 4 Other **Holdings:** 200,000 books **Language of Collection/Services:** English **Subjects:** Agriculture (Tropics), Economic Botany, Entomology, Forestry, Horticulture, Plant Pathology, Soil Science **Specializations:** Ethnobotany, Medicinal Plants, Pharmacognosy **Networks:** OCLC **Loan:** Do not loan **Photocopy:** Yes

3712   Cleveland, Ohio, US
         Cleveland Botanical Garden
         Eleanor Squire Library
         11030 East Boulevard
         Cleveland, Ohio 44106
Fax: +1(216) 721-2056 **WWW:** www.cbgarden.org

Former Name: Garden Center of Greater Cleveland **Founded:** 1930 **Type:** Non-profit **Head:** Mary Ellen Armentrout *Phone:* +1(216) 721-1600 **Staff:** 1 Prof. 2 Other **Holdings:** 16,000 books 200 journals **Language of Collection/Services:** English **Subjects:** Gardening, Horticulture **Loan:** Inhouse **Service:** In country **Networks:** OCLC

3713   Cleveland, Ohio, US
         Cleveland Public Library
         Science and Technology Department
         325 Superior Avenue
         Cleveland, Ohio 44114-1271
Fax: +1(216) 623-7029 **Email:** sci2@library.cpl.org **WWW:** www.cpl.org **OPAC:** www.cpl.org

Founded: 1912 **Type:** Government **Head:** Jean Z. Piety *Phone:* +1(216) 623-2932 *Email:* jean.piety@cpl.org **Staff:** 5 Prof. 9 Other **Holdings:** 289,142 books 1,353 journals **Language of Collection/Services:** English **Subjects:** Agriculture (Tropics), Agribusiness, Agricultural Development, Agricultural Economics, Agricultural Engineering, Animal Husbandry, Biotechnology, Crops, Education/Extension, Entomology, Farming, Fisheries, Food Sciences, Forestry, Horticulture, Plant Pathology, Soil Science, Veterinary Medicine, Water Resources **Networks:** OCLC **Databases Used:** Comprehensive **Loan:** Internationally **Photocopy:** Yes

3714   Columbus, Ohio, US
         Ohio State University
         Agriculture Library
         2120 Fyffe Road
         Columbus, Ohio 43210-1066
Location: 45 Agricultural Administration Building **Fax:** +1(614) 292-0590 **Email:** logan.2@osu.edu **WWW:** www.osu.edu **OPAC:** www.lib.ohio-state.edu

Founded: 1956 **Type:** Academic **Head:** Susan Logan *Phone:* +1(614) 292-3955 *Email:* logan.2@osu.edu **Staff:** 1 Prof. 2 Other **Holdings:** 83,419 books 1,192 journals **Language of Collection/Services:** English **Subjects:** Agribusiness, Agricultural Development, Agricultural Engineering, Agriculture (Tropics), Animal Husbandry, Crops, Biotechnology, Education/Extension, Farming, Fisheries, Food Sciences, Forestry, Horticulture, Plant Pathology, Soil Science, Veterinary Medicine, Water Resources **Specializations:** Agricultural Economics **Networks:** OCLC **Databases Developed:** ACTS - Agricultural Capital and Technology

Studies is a unique collection of reprint articles, papers, and pamphlets dealing with agricultural capital, technological change, savings, credit, and policy worldwide with a concentration on developing countries. The file is maintained by the Department of Agricultural Economics and Rural Sociology. **Databases Used:** Comprehensive **Loan:** Internationally **Photocopy:** Yes

3715   Columbus, Ohio, US
         Ohio State University (OSU)
         Biological Sciences/Pharmacy Library
         102 Riffe Building
         496 W. 12th Avenue
         Columbus, Ohio 432101214
Phone: +1(614) 292-1744 **Fax:** +1(614) 688-3123 **WWW:** www.osu.edu **OPAC:** www.lib.ohio-state.edu

Founded: 1994 **Type:** Academic **Head:** Bruce Leach *Email:* baleach@pop.service.ohio-state.edu, leach.5@osu.edu *Phone:* +1(614) 292-1744 **Staff:** 2 Prof. 4 Other **Holdings:** 116,000 books 1,300 journals **Language of Collection/Services:** English **Subjects:** Biochemistry, Botany, Biotechnology, Entomology, Microbiology, Molecular Genetics, Pharmacy, Zoology **Networks:** OhioLINK **Databases Used:** Comprehensive **Loan:** In country **Photocopy:** Yes

3716   Columbus, Ohio, US
         Ohio State University (OSU)
         Veterinary Medicine Library
         229 Sisson Hall
         1900 Coffey Road
         Columbus, Ohio 43210-1092
Phone: +1(614) 292-6107 **Fax:** +1(614) 292-7476 **WWW:** www.osu.edu **OPAC:** www.lib.ohio-state.edu

Founded: 1929 **Type:** Academic **Head:** Norma J. Bruce *Phone:* +1(614) 292-6107 *Email:* bruce.6@osu.edu **Staff:** 1 Prof. 1.5 Other **Holdings:** 42,000 books 630 journals **Language of Collection/Services:** English / English **Subjects:** Agricultural Production, Animal Welfare, Biology, Management, Veterinary Medicine **Specializations:** Animal Health **Networks:** OhioLink; OSCAR **Databases Used:** Comprehensive **Loan:** Internationally **Service:** Inhouse **Photocopy:** Yes

3717   Delaware, Ohio, US
         United States Department of Agriculture, Forest Service, Northeastern Research Station, Forestry Sciences Laboratory
         Library
         359 Main Road
         Delaware, Ohio 43015
Phone: +1(740) 368-0140 **Fax:** +1(740) 368-0152 **WWW:** www.fs.fed.us/ne

Founded: 1961 **Type:** Government **Head:** Sheryl A. Dew *Phone:* +1(740) 368-0124 *Email:* sdew/ne_de@fs.fed.us **Staff:** 1 Prof. 1 Other **Holdings:** 170 journals **Language of Collection/Services:** English **Subjects:** Agribusiness, Agricultural Development, Agricultural Economics, Agricultural Engineering, Biotechnology, Entomology, Forestry **Net-**

works: OCLC **Databases Used:** Agricola; TREECD **Loan:** Inhouse **Service:** Internationally **Photocopy:** Yes

3718 Kirtland, Ohio, US
The Herb Society of America, Inc.
Library
9019 Kirtland Chardon Road
Kirtland, Ohio 44094
Phone: +1(440) 256-0514 **Fax:** +1(440) 256-0541 **Email:** library@herbsociety.org **WWW:** www.herbsociety.org

Founded: 1933 **Type:** Association **Head:** Michele M. Meyers *Phone:* +1(440) 256-0514 **Staff:** 1 Prof. **Holdings:** 2,000 books 40 journals **Language of Collection/Services:** English **Subjects:** Botany, Herbs, Horticulture, Medicinal Plants **Specializations:** Rare book collection of herbals **Loan:** Members **Service:** Internationally **Photocopy:** Yes

3719 Kirtland, Ohio, US
The Holden Arboretum
Warren H. Corning Library
9500 Sperry Road
Kirtland, Ohio 44094-5172
Phone: +1(440) 256-1110 ext 225 **Fax:** +1(440) 256-5836 **Email:** holdlib@holdenarb.org **WWW:** www.holdenarb.org

Type: Association **Head:** Nadia Aufderheide *Phone:* +1 (440) 256-1110 ext 225 *Email:* holdlib@holdenarb.org **Staff:** 1.5 Prof. **Holdings:** 8,500 books 65 journals **Language of Collection/Services:** English **Subjects:** Horticulture **Loan:** Inhouse **Service:** Inhouse **Photocopy:** Yes

3720 Lucas, Ohio, US
Ohio State University, Ohio Department of
    Natural Resources (OSU, ODNR)
The Louis Bromfield Sustainable Agriculture
    Library
4050 Bromfield Road
Lucas, Ohio 44843
Phone: +1(419) 892-2784 **Fax:** +1(419) 892-3988 **Email:** malabar@richnet.net **WWW:** www.malabarfarm.org

Founded: 1991 **Type:** Academic **Staff:** 1 Prof. **Holdings:** 1,600 books 20 journals **Language of Collection/Services:** English / English **Subjects:** Crops, Soil Science **Specializations:** Education, Farming, Grazing Intensity **Loan:** Do not loan **Service:** Inhouse **Photocopy:** Yes

3721 Mansfield, Ohio, US
Kingwood Center
Library
900 Park Avenue West
Mansfield, Ohio 44906
Fax: +1(419) 522-0211

Founded: 1953 **Type:** Association **Head:** William W. Collins *Phone:* +1(419) 522-0211 **Staff:** 2 Prof. **Holdings:** 8,500 books 125 journals **Subjects:** Environment, Horticulture, Gardening, Nature **Loan:** In country **Photocopy:** Yes

3722 Marysville, Ohio, US
The Scotts Company
Information Services
14111 Scottslawn Road
Marysville, Ohio 43041
Phone: +1(937) 644-7506 **Fax:** +1(937) 644-7075 **WWW:** www.scottscompany.com/scottshome.htm

Type: Business **Staff:** 1 Prof. **Holdings:** 3,000 books 100 journals **Language of Collection/Services:** English / English **Subjects:** Horticulture **Specializations:** Lawns and Turf **Networks:** OCLC **Loan:** Internationally **Service:** Internationally **Photocopy:** No

3723 Painesville, Ohio, US
Ricerca, Inc.
Information Services
7528 Auburn Road
Box 1000
Painesville, Ohio 44077
Phone: +1(440) 357-3475 **Fax:** +1(440) 354-4415 **Email:** infoserv@ricerca.com **WWW:** www.ricerca.com

Founded: 1980 **Type:** Business **Head:** Susan Branchick *Phone:* +1(440) 357-3462 *Email:* branchick_s@ricerca.com **Staff:** 1 Prof. 1 Other **Holdings:** 10,000 books 50 journals **Language of Collection/Services:** English **Subjects:** Agribusiness, Agricultural Development, Biotechnology **Specializations:** Pesticides **Databases Used:** Comprehensive **Loan:** Inhouse **Service:** Internationally **Photocopy:** Yes

3724 Put-In-Bay, Ohio, US
Ohio State University
Franz Theodore Stone Laboratory Library
Box 119
Put-In-Bay, Ohio 43456
Phone: +1(419) 285-2341 **Fax:** +1(419) 292-1744 **WWW:** www.sg.ohio-state.edu

Founded: 1896 **Type:** Academic **Head:** Bruce Leach *Phone:* +1(419) 292-1744 **Staff:** 1 Prof. **Holdings:** 4,200 books 50 journals **Language of Collection/Services:** English / English **Subjects:** Biology, Botany, Entomology, Great Lakes, Ichthyology, Lake Erie, Limnology, Ohio, Zoology **Loan:** Inhouse **Photocopy:** No

3725 Toledo, Ohio, US
Toledo Zoological Society
Library and Archives
PO Box 4010
Toledo, Ohio 43609
Location: 2700 Broadway **Phone:** +1(419) 385-5721 ext 2043 **Fax:** +1(419) 389-8670 **WWW:** www.toledozoo.org

Founded: 1981 **Type:** Non-profit **Head:** Lynda Trabbic *Phone:* +1(419) 385-5721 ext 2043 **Staff:** 1 Prof. **Holdings:** 3,800 books 40 journals **Language of Collection/Services:** English **Subjects:** Animal Husbandry, Horticulture, Zoological Gardens **Specializations:** Ecology, Habitats, Natural History, Wildlife **Loan:** Inhouse **Service:** Inhouse **Photocopy:** Yes

3726 Westerville, Ohio, US
National Ground Water Association
National Ground Water Information Center
    (NGWIC)
601 Dempsey Road

Westerville, Ohio 43081
Phone: +1(614i) 898-7791, +1(800) 551-7379 (toll free)
Fax: +1(614) 898-7786 **Email:** ngwa@ngwa.org **WWW:**
www.h2o-ngwa.org

Founded: 1979 **Type:** Association **Staff:** 3 Prof. 5 Other
Holdings: 40,000 books 350 journals **Language of Collection/Services:** English **Subjects:** Soil Science, Water Resources **Specializations:** Groundwater **Networks:** OCLC
Databases Developed: Ground Water Online - Over 70,000
citations on ground water and water well technology;
searches available for fee on request or by dialup; subscriptions available. **Loan:** Internationally **Photocopy:** Yes

3727   Wooster, Ohio, US
Ohio State University, Agricultural Technical
Institute (OSU, ATI)
Library
1328 Dover Road
Wooster, Ohio 44691-2000
Phone: +1(330) 264-3911 ext 291 **Fax:** +1(330) 262-0859
WWW: ati.ag.ohio-state.edu **OPAC:** www.lib.ohio-state.
edu

Founded: 1972 **Type:** Academic **Head:** Mrs. Ella Copeland
Phone: +1(330) 264-3911 ext 224 *Email:* copeland.6@osu.
edu **Staff:** 1 Prof. 4 Other **Holdings:** 19,000 books 520 journals **Language of Collection/Services:** English **Subjects:**
Agribusiness, Agricultural Engineering, Animal Husbandry,
Construction, Crops, Entomology, Farming, Horticulture,
Soil Science **Specializations:** Cut Flowers, Golf Courses,
Landscaping, Lawns and Turf **Networks:** OhioLink **Databases Used:** Comprehensive **Loan:** In country **Service:**
Internationally **Photocopy:** Yes

3728   Wooster, Ohio, US
Ohio State University, Ohio Agricultural Research
and Development Center (OSU, OARDC)
Library
1680 Madison Avenue
Wooster, Ohio 44691-4096
Fax: +1(330) 263-3689 **WWW:** www.oardc.ohio-state.edu
OPAC: library.ohio-state.edu

Former Name: Ohio Agricultural Experiment Station
Founded: 1892 **Type:** Academic **Head:** Constance J. Britton *Phone:* +1(330) 263-3773 *Email:* britton.4@osu.edu
Staff: 1 Prof. 2 Other **Holdings:** 70,000 books 300 journals
Language of Collection/Services: English / English **Subjects:** Agricultural Engineering, Animal Husbandry, Biotechnology, Crops, Entomology, Forestry, Horticulture,
Plant Pathology, Soil Science, Veterinary Medicine **Networks:** OCLC **Databases Developed:** Agricultural Documents - Primarily U.S. and state agriculture publications;
inhouse only **Databases Used:** Comprehensive **Loan:** Internationally **Service:** Internationally **Photocopy:** Yes

Oklahoma

3729   Ada, Oklahoma, US
Environmental Protection Agency, Subsurface
Protection and Remediation Division
Library

Box 1198
Ada, Oklahoma 74820
Location: 919 Kerr Research Drive **Phone:** +1(580) 436-8505 **Fax:** +1(580) 436-8529

Former Name: Robert S. Kerr Environmental Research
Center **Founded:** 1966 **Type:** Government **Staff:** 1 Prof. 3
Other **Holdings:** 90,000 books 155 journals **Language of
Collection/Services:** English / English **Subjects:** Aquifers,
Chemistry, Biology, Groundwater, Simulation Models **Specializations:** Environmental Protection Agency (USA) Documents **Networks:** OCLC **Databases Developed:** EPA/
NOAA CD-ROM from Bibliofile; EPA Online Library System; EPA/DOC CD-ROM; Exposure Models CD-ROM;
Risk Assessment; EPA Toxic Release Inventory - CD-ROM
Databases Used: Compendex **Loan:** Internationally **Service:** Inhouse **Photocopy:** Yes

3730   Alva, Oklahoma, US
Northwestern Oklahoma State University
J.W. Martin Library
709 Oklahoma Boulevard
Alva, Oklahoma 73717
Phone: +1(580) 327-8573 **Fax:** +1(580) 327-8501 **Email:**
clgottsch@nwosu.edu **WWW:** www.nwalva.edu **OPAC:**
www.auto-graphics.com/cgipac/mmx/yzus

Founded: 1897 **Type:** Academic **Head:** Ray D. Lau *Phone:*
+1(580) 327-8570 *Email:* rdlau@ranger2.nwalva.edu **Staff:**
5 Prof. 2 Other **Holdings:** 2,000 books 40 journals **Subjects:**
Animal Husbandry **Loan:** In country **Photocopy:** Yes

3731   Ardmore, Oklahoma, US
Samuel Roberts Noble Foundation (NF)
Library
2510 Sam Noble Parkway
Ardmore, Oklahoma 73401
Location: 919 Kerr Research Drive **Phone:** +1(580) 221-7334 **Fax:** +1(580) 221-7483 **Email:** nksprehe@noble.org
WWW: www.noble.org **OPAC:** www.noble.org

Founded: 1945 **Type:** Private **Head:** Patrick W. Brennen
Phone: +1(580) 221-7333 *Email:* pbrennen@noble.org
Staff: 2 Prof. 2.5 Other **Holdings:** 26,100 books 501 journals
Language of Collection/Services: English / English **Subjects:** Animal Husbandry, Fisheries, Forage, Horticulture,
Livestock, Soil Science, Wildlife **Specializations:** Molecular Biology **Networks:** OCLC; OKNET **Databases Developed:** Specimen identity collection for flora and fauna
Databases Used: Comprehensive **Loan:** Internationally
Service: Internationally **Photocopy:** Yes

3732   Finley, Oklahoma, US
Southwest Spanish Mustang Association
Gilbert H. Jones Library
PO Box 148
Finley, Oklahoma 74543-0148

Founded: 1930 **Type:** Association **Holdings:** 600 books 10
journals **Subjects:** Cattle Farming (History - USA), Horse
Breeds (History), Horses, Mustang Horse, Native Americans, Saddles, USA (History - West) **Loan:** Inhouse **Photocopy:** Yes

3733 Langston, Oklahoma, US
Langston University (LU)
General Lamar Harrison Library
PO Box 1600
Langston, Oklahoma 73050
Phone: +1(405) 466-3292 **Email:** library@lunet.edu
WWW: www.lunet.edu **OPAC:** www.auto-graphics.com/
cgipac/mmx/odol

Founded: 1947 **Type:** Academic **Head:** Njambi Kamoche
Phone: +1(405) 466-3294 *Email:* nckamoche@lunet.edu
Staff: 1 Prof. 7 Other **Holdings:** 5,000 books 1,205 journals
Language of Collection/Services: English **Subjects:** Agribusiness, Agricultural Development, Agricultural Economics, Animal Husbandry, Crops, Food Sciences, Education/Extension, Farming, Fisheries, Horticulture, Plant Pathology, Soil Science, Water Resources **Loan:** In country **Service:** In country **Photocopy:** Yes

3734 Stillwater, Oklahoma, US
Oklahoma State University (OSU)
Edmon Low Library, Science and Engineering
Division
Stillwater, Oklahoma 74078-1071
Phone: +1(405) 744-6309 **Fax:** +1(405) 744-5183 **WWW:**
pio.okstate.edu **OPAC:**
www.library.okstate.edu/info/pete.htm

Founded: 1891 **Type:** Academic **Head:** Vicki W. Phillips
Phone: +1(405) 744-6309 *Email:* vicki@okway.okstate.edu
Staff: 9 Prof. 4 Other **Holdings:** 160,303 books 540 journals
Language of Collection/Services: English **Subjects:** Agriculture (Tropics), Agribusiness, Agricultural Development, Agricultural Economics, Agricultural Engineering, Animal Husbandry, Biotechnology, Crops, Education/Extension, Entomology, Farming, Fisheries, Food Sciences, Forestry, Horticulture, Plant Pathology, Soil Science, Veterinary Medicine, Water Resources **Databases Used:** Agricola **Loan:** In country **Service:** In country **Photocopy:** Yes

3735 Stillwater, Oklahoma, US
Oklahoma State University (OSU)
Veterinary Medicine Library
102 Veterinary Medicine Building
Stillwater, Oklahoma 74078-2013
Phone: +1(405) 744-6655 **Fax:** +1(405) 744-5609 **WWW:**
pio.okstate.edu **OPAC:** www.library.okstate.edu/info/pete.
htm

Type: Academic **Head:** Pat Mullen *Email:* pmullen@
okstate.edu **Subjects:** Veterinary Medicine

3736 Tulsa, Oklahoma, US
Palomino Horse Breeders of America, Inc.
(PHBA)
Library
15253 East Skelly Drive
Tulsa, Oklahoma 74116-2620
Phone: +1(918) 438-1234 **Fax:** +1(918) 438-1232 **Email:**
yellahrses@aol.com **WWW:** www.palominohba.com

Founded: 1941 **Type:** Association **Staff:** 5 Prof. **Holdings:**
250 books **Specializations:** Horses, Palomino Horse **Loan:**
Do not loan **Photocopy:** No

Oregon

3737 Beaverton, Oregon, US
Oregon Graduate Institute of Science and
Technology (OGI)
Samuel L. Diack Library
20000 NW Walker Road
Beaverton, Oregon 97006-8921
Phone: +1(503) 748-1383 **Fax:** +1(503) 748-1029 **Email:**
library@admin.ogi.edu **WWW:** www.ogi.edu **OPAC:**
www.ogi.edu/library **Ariel IP:** 129.95.65.27

Former Name: Oregon Graduate Center **Founded:** 1968
Type: Academic **Head:** Carol S. Resco *Phone:* +1(503)
448-1060 *Email:* resco@admin.ogi.edu **Staff:** 2 Prof. 4
Other **Holdings:** 30,000 books 400 journals **Language of
Collection/Services:** English **Subjects:** Soil Science, Water
Resources **Networks:** OCLC **Databases Used:** Agricola;
Biosis **Loan:** Inhouse **Service:** Inhouse **Photocopy:** Yes

3738 Corvallis, Oregon, US
Oregon State University
The Valley Library
Corvallis, Oregon 97331-4501
Phone: +1(541) 737-7293 **Fax:** +1(541) 737-7300 **WWW:**
www.orst.edu **OPAC:** oasis.orst.edu

Former Name: Kerr Library **Founded:** 1868 **Type:** Academic **Head:** Karyle Butcher *Phone:* +1(541) 737-7300
Email: karyle.butcher.orst.edu **Staff:** 35 Prof. 56 Other
Holdings: 1,200,000 books 12,000 journals **Language of
Collection/Services:** English / English **Subjects:** Agriculture (Tropics), Agribusiness, Agricultural Development, Agricultural Economics, Agricultural Engineering, Animal
Husbandry, Biotechnology, Crops, Education/Extension,
Entomology, Farming, Fisheries, Food Sciences, Forestry,
Horticulture, Natural Resources, Pests, Plant Pathology,
Range Management, Resource Management, Soil Science,
Veterinary Medicine, Water Resources, Weeds, Wildlife
Networks: OCLC **Databases Used:** Agricola; Biosis;
CABCD; Medline **Loan:** In country **Service:** Internationally
Photocopy: Yes

3739 Corvallis, Oregon, US
Oregon State University, Integrated Plant
Protection Center (OSU, IPPC)
IPM Information Research Unit
Cordley 2040
Corvallis, Oregon 97331-2915
Phone: +1(541) 737-3541 **Fax:** +1(541) 737-3080 **Email:**
ippc@bcc.orst.edu **WWW:** www.ippc.orst.edu

Former Name: Oregon Agricultural College, International
Plant Protection Center **Founded:** 1969 **Type:** Academic
Head: Marcos Kogan *Phone:* +1(541) 737-6271 *Email:*
koganm@bcc.orst.edu **Staff:** 1 Prof. 1 Other **Holdings:**
9,000 books 5 journals **Language of Collection/Services:**
English / English **Subjects:** Agricultural Development, Agricultural Economics, Crops, Integrated Pest Management,
Mulching, Sustainability **Specializations:** Ecology, Insects,
Pest Management, Pesticides, Plant Pathogens, Weeds, Plant
Protection **Databases Developed:** Extoxnet - Toxicological
information on pesticides; SELECTV - Pesticide selectivity

to natural enemies **Loan:** In country **Service:** Inhouse **Photocopy:** Yes

3740   Corvallis, Oregon, US
United States Department of Agriculture,
    Agricultural Research Service (USDA, ARS)
Hop Genetic Research Project
Oregon State University
Department of Crop and Soil Science
Corvallis, Oregon 97331-3002
Phone: +1(541) 737-5841 **Fax:** +1(541) 737-1334 **WWW:** hops.css.orst.edu

Founded: 1930 **Type:** Academic **Head:** Dr. John A. Henning *Phone:* +1(541) 750-8726 *Email:* john.henning@orst.edu **Staff:** 2 Prof. 3 Other **Holdings:** 2,300 books 5 journals **Language of Collection/Services:** English / English **Subjects:** Chemistry, Crops, Genetics, Plant Breeding, Plant Pathology **Specializations:** Hops **Databases Developed:** Hop chemistry and genetics database **Loan:** Do not loan **Service:** Inhouse

3741   Cottage Grove, Oregon, US
Aprovecho Research Center
Library
80574 Hazelton Road
Cottage Grove, Oregon 97424
Phone: +1(541) 942-81998 **Fax:** +1(541) 942-0302 **Email:** apro@efn.org **WWW:** www.efn.org/~apro/index.html

Founded: 1978 **Staff:** 2-3 Prof. **Holdings:** 500 books 38 journals **Type:** Educational **Language of Collection/Services:** English **Subjects:** Appropriate Technology, Bamboos, Fuelwood, Stoves **Service:** Internationally **Loan:** Inhouse **Photocopy:** Yes

3742   Eugene, Oregon, US
University of Oregon
John E. Jaqua Law Library, Ocean and Coastal
    Law Center Collection
1221 University of Oregon
Eugene, Oregon 97403-1221
Location: 1515 Agate Street **Phone:** +1(541) 346-1567 **Fax:** +1(541) 346-1564 **Email:** acoffman@law.uoregon.edu **WWW:** oceanlaw.uoregon.edu **OPAC:** janus.uoregon.edu/search

Former Name: Ocean Resources Law Program **Founded:** 1968 **Type:** Academic **Head:** Andrea G. Coffman *Phone:* +1(541) 346-1567 *Email:* acoffman@law.uoregon.edu **Staff:** 1 Prof. 1 Other **Holdings:** 6,000 books 168 journals **Language of Collection/Services:** English / English **Subjects:** Aquaculture, Fisheries **Networks:** OCLC **Loan:** Internationally **Service:** Internationally **Photocopy:** Yes

3743   Newport, Oregon, US
Oregon State University, Hatfield Marine Science
    Center (OSU, HMSC)
Marilyn Potts Guin Library
2030 South Marine Science Drive
Newport, Oregon 97365

Phone: +1(541) 867-0249 **Fax:** +1(541) 867-0105 **Email:** hmsc.library@orst.edu **WWW:** www.hmsc.orst.edu **OPAC:** oasis.orst.edu **Ariel IP:** 128.193.170.35

Founded: 1966 **Type:** Academic **Head:** Janet Webster *Phone:* +1(541) 867-0108 *Email:* janet.webster@orst.edu **Staff:** 1 Prof. 1 Other **Holdings:** 30,000 books 310 journals **Language of Collection/Services:** English / English **Subjects:** Aquaculture, Fisheries **Networks:** OCLC **Databases Developed:** Yaguina Bay Bibliography **Databases Used:** Comprehensive **Loan:** Internationally **Service:** Inhouse **Photocopy:** Yes

3744   Salem, Oregon, US
Oregon State Library
State Library Building
250 Winter St. NE
Salem, Oregon 97310-0640
Phone: +1(503) 378-4277 **Fax:** +1(503) 585-8059 **WWW:** www.osl.state.or.us/oslhome.html **OPAC:** webpac.osl.state.or.us

Founded: 1848 **Type:** Government **Head:** James Scheppke *Phone:* +1(503) 378-4243 *Email:* jim.b.scheppke@state.or.us **Staff:** 15 Prof. 30 Other **Holdings:** 65,000 books 80 journals **Language of Collection/Services:** English **Specializations:** Government Documents (Oregon), Government Documents (USA) **Networks:** OCLC **Databases Developed:** Oregon Index - index to Oregon publications covering articles relating to Oregon; access via OPAC in Oregon only **Loan:** Internationally **Service:** In state **Photocopy:** Yes

3745   Tigard, Oregon, US
Home Orchard Society (HOS)
Library
PO Box 230192
Tigard, Oregon 97281-0192
Location: 15305 NE Springbrook Road, Newberg, Oregon 97132 **Phone:** +1(503) 639-6250 **WWW:** www.wvi.com/~dough/HOS/HOS1.html

Founded: 1975 **Type:** Association **Head:** Loren Mills *Phone:* +1(503) 630-3392 *Email:* lmills@europa.com **Language of Collection/Services:** English **Subjects:** Education/Extension, Horticulture **Specializations:** Orchards **Databases Developed:** Database of Cultivars - in cooperation with the National Council Germplasm Repository **Loan:** Do not loan **Photocopy:** No

Pennsylvania

3746   Avondale, Pennsylvania, US
American Mushroom Institute (AMI)
Pamphlet Collection
1284 Gap Newport Pike, Suite 2
Avondale, Pennsylvania 19311
Phone: +1(610 268-7483 **Email:** mushroomnews@kennett.net **WWW:** www.americanmushroominst.org

Founded: 1955 **Type:** Association **Holdings:** 100 books 3 journals **Subjects:** Education/Extension **Specializations:** Mushrooms **Loan:** Do not loan **Service:** Inhouse **Photocopy:** Yes

3747   Doylestown, Pennsylvania, US
Delaware Valley College
Joseph Krauskopf Memorial Library
Doylestown, Pennsylvania 18901
Phone: +1(215) 489-2994 **WWW:** www.devalcol.edu/
index.htm **OPAC:** krauscat.devalcol.edu

Founded: 1896 **Type:** Academic **Head:** Peter Kupersmith
Phone: +1(215) 489-2254 **Holdings:** 50,000 books 400 journals **Subjects:** Agribusiness, Animal Husbandry, Biology, Chemistry, Crops, Horticulture, Plant Pathology, Soil Science **Networks:** OCLC **Loan:** In country **Photocopy:** Yes

3748   Harrisburg, Pennsylvania, US
State Library of Pennsylvania
Library
PO Box 1601
Harrisburg, Pennsylvania 17105
Location: Forum Building, Commonwealth & Walnut
Phone: +1(717) 783-5950 **Fax:** +1(717) 783-2070 **Email:** ra-reference@state.pa.us **WWW:** www.statelibrary.state.pa.us **OPAC:** accesspa.brodart.com **Ariel IP:** 164.156.106.88

Founded: 1745 **Type:** Government **Head:** Alice L. Lubrecht *Phone:* +1(717) 783-5968 *Email:* alubrecht@state.pa.us **Staff:** 19 Prof. 70 Other **Holdings:** 48,000 books 70 journals **Language of Collection/Services:** English **Subjects:** Agricultural Development, Agricultural Engineering, Biotechnology, Crops, Education/Extension, Entomology, Farming, Fisheries, Forestry, Horticulture, Soil Science, Veterinary Medicine, Water Resources **Networks:** OCLC **Databases Used:** Comprehensive **Loan:** In state or via ILL **Service:** Inhouse **Photocopy:** Yes

3749   Kennett Square, Pennsylvania, US
Longwood Gardens
Library
Route 1, PO Box 501
Kennett Square, Pennsylvania 19348-0501
Phone: +1(610) 388-1000 **WWW:** www.longwoodgardens.org

Founded: 1961 **Type:** Association **Staff:** 1 Prof. 2 Other **Holdings:** 18,000 books 277 journals **Subjects:** Horticulture **Loan:** In country **Photocopy:** Yes

3750   Philadelphia, Pennsylvania, US
Academy of Natural Sciences
Ewell Sale Stewart Library
1900 Benjamin Franklin Parkway
Philadelphia, Pennsylvania 19103
Phone: +1(215) 299-1040 **Fax:** +1(215) 299-1144 **Email:** library@acnatsci.org **WWW:** www.acnatsci.org **OPAC:** www.auto-graphics.com/cgipac/mmx/ans

Founded: 1812 **Type:** Association **Head:** Carol M. Spawn *Phone:* +1(215) 299-1041 **Staff:** 3 Prof. 5 Other **Holdings:** 6,280 books 460 journals **Language of Collection/Services:** English **Subjects:** Entomology, Water Resources **Specializations:** Environmental Sciences, Paleontology, Taxonomy **Networks:** OCLC **Databases Used:** Biosis **Loan:** In country with restrictions **Photocopy:** Yes

3751   Philadelphia, Pennsylvania, US
Drexel University
W.W. Hagerty Library
33rd and Market Streets
Philadelphia, Pennsylvania 19104
Phone: +1(215) 895-2755 **Fax:** +1(215) 895-2070 **WWW:** www.drexel.edu **OPAC:** dulib.library.drexel.edu:8080/marion.html

Founded: 1966 **Head:** Carol Montgomery *Phone:* +1(215) 895-2750 *Email:* montgoch@drexel.edu **Staff:** 2 Prof. 3 Other **Holdings:** 110,000 books 2,400 journals **Subjects:** Biology, Biotechnology, Chemistry, Environment, Nutrition **Networks:** OCLC **Loan:** In country **Service:** Inhouse **Photocopy:** Yes

3752   Philadelphia, Pennsylvania, US
Environmental Protection Agency, Region 3
Regional Center for Environmental Information
1650 Arch Street (3PM52)
Philadelphia, Pennsylvania 19103-2029
Location: southeast corner of 17th and Arch Streets
Phone: +1(215) 814-5254 **Fax:** +1(215) 814-5253 **Email:** library-reg3@epa.gov **WWW:** www.epa.gov/region3 **OPAC:** www.epa.gov/region3/r3lib/genlib/catalog.htm

Founded: 1972 **Type:** Government **Head:** Diane M. McCreary *Email:* mccreary.diane@epa.gov *Phone:* +1(215) 814-5519 **Staff:** 1 Prof. 2 Other **Holdings:** 25,000 books 300 journals **Subjects:** Environment, Toxicology, Wetlands **Databases Used:** Medline **Loan:** In country **Service:** Inhouse **Photocopy:** Yes

3753   Philadelphia, Pennsylvania, US
Library Company of Philadelphia
1314 Locust Street
Philadelphia, Pennsylvania 19107
Phone: +1(215) 546-2456 **Fax:** +1(215) 546-5167 **Email:** refdept@librarycompany.org **WWW:** www.librarycompany.org **OPAC:** www.librarycompany.org/catalogFrameset.htm

Founded: 1731 **Type:** Private **Head:** Dr. Cathy D. Matson *Email:* cmatson@librarycompany.org *Phone:* +1(215) 546-3181 **Staff:** 8 Prof. 5 Other **Holdings:** 1,500 books **Language of Collection/Services:** English **Subjects:** Crops (History - pre-1860), Agriculture (History - pre-1860), Animal Husbandry (History - pre-1860), Farming (History - pre-1860), Fisheries (History - pre-1860), Food Sciences (History - pre-1860), Forestry (History - pre-1860), Horticulture (History - pre-1860) **Networks:** RLIN **Loan:** Do not loan **Service:** Open to public **Photocopy:** Yes

3754   Philadelphia, Pennsylvania, US
Pennsylvania Horticultural Society (PHS)
McLean Library
100 N 20th Street - 5th Floor
Philadelphia, Pennsylvania 19103-1495
Location: 325 Walnut Street (between 3rd and 4th **Phone:** +1(215) 988-8772, 988-8779 **Fax:** +1(215) 988-8783 **WWW:** www.libertynet.org/phs **OPAC:** atlas.hslc.org/phrfil

Founded: 1827 **Type:** Non-profit, Private **Head:** Janet Evans *Email:* janeteva@libertynet.org **Staff:** 2 Prof. 3 Other **Holdings:** 14,000 books 200 journals **Subjects:** Horticulture **Specializations:** Horticulture (History - Pennsylvania), Nursery Catalogs (pre-1950), Seed Catalogs (pre-1950) **Loan:** In country **Service:** Internationally **Photocopy:** Yes

3755 Philadelphia, Pennsylvania, US
University of Pennsylvania, Morris Arboretum
Library
9414 Meadowbrook Avenue
Philadelphia, Pennsylvania 19118
Fax: +1(215) 248-4439 **WWW:** www.upenn.edu/morris

Founded: 1933 **Type:** Academic **Head:** Ann F. Rhoads *Phone:* +1(215) 247-5777 ext 134 *Email:* rhoadaf@pobox.upenn.edu **Staff:** 1 Prof. 2 Other **Holdings:** 6,000 books 50 journals **Language of Collection/Services:** English **Subjects:** Horticulture, Landscape Architecture, Plant Pathology **Databases Developed:** Flora of Pennsylvania - Database on the native and naturalized plants of the state **Loan:** Do not loan **Service:** Inhouse **Photocopy:** Yes

3756 Philadelphia, Pennsylvania, US
University of Pennsylvania, School of Veterinary
     Medicine
C.J. Marshall Memorial Library, Jean Austin
     DuPont Library
3800 Spruce Street
Philadelphia, Pennsylvania 19104-6008
Phone: +1(215) 898-8895 **Fax:** +1(215) 573-2007 **Email:** vetlib@pobox.upenn.edu **WWW:** www.library.upenn.edu **OPAC:** www.franklin.library.upenn.edu

Founded: 1908 and 1963 **Type:** Academic **Head:** Lillian D. Bryant *Email:* bryant@pobox.upenn.edu *Phone:* +1(215) 898-8874 **Staff:** 1 Prof. 3 Other **Holdings:** 32,000 books 365 journals **Language of Collection/Services:** English **Subjects:** Veterinary Medicine **Databases Used:** Agricola; Biosis; CABCD; Medline **Loan:** In country **Service:** In country **Photocopy:** Yes

3757 Pittsburgh, Pennsylvania, US
Carnegie-Mellon University
Hunt Institute for Botanical Documentation, Hunt
     Botanical Library
5000 Forbes Ave.
Pittsburgh, Pennsylvania 15213-3890
Phone: +1(412) 268-2436 **Fax:** +1(412) 268-5677 **WWW:** huntbot.andrew.cmu.edu **OPAC:** webcat.library.cmu.edu

Founded: 1961 **Type:** Academic **Head:** Charlotte A. Tancin *Phone:* +1(412) 268-7301 *Email:* ct0u@andrew.cmu.edu **Staff:** 7 Prof. 6 Other **Holdings:** 22,000 books 650 journals **Language of Collection/Services:** English / English **Specializations:** Agriculture (History), Botany (History), Horticulture (History) **Networks:** OCLC **Loan:** Internationally **Photocopy:** Yes

3758 Pittsburgh, Pennsylvania, US
Carnegie Museum of Natural History
Library
4400 Forbes Avenue
Pittsburgh, Pennsylvania 15213-4080
Phone: +1(412) 622-3284 **Fax:** +1(412) 622-8837 **Email:** cmnhlib@clpgh.org, cmnhlib@carnegiemuseums.org **WWW:** www.clpgh.org/cmnh **OPAC:** www.clpgh.org

Founded: 1898 **Type:** Non-profit, Research **Head:** Bernadette G. Callery *Phone:* +1(412) 622-8870 *Email:* calleryb@clpgh.org, calleryb@carnegiemuseums.org **Staff:** 1.3 Prof. 1.8 Other **Holdings:** 23,000 books 1,500 journals **Language of Collection/Services:** English **Subjects:** Forestry, Plants **Specializations:** Entomology **Networks:** OCLC **Databases Used:** Comprehensive **Loan:** Internationally **Service:** Internationally **Photocopy:** Yes

3759 Pittsburgh, Pennsylvania, US
H.J. Heinz Company
Technical Information Center
1062 Progress Street
Box 57
Pittsburgh, Pennsylvania 15230-0057
Phone: +1(412) 287-5725 **WWW:** www.heinz.com

Founded: 1903 **Type:** Business **Head:** Nancy Winstanley *Email:* 102167.1336@compuserve.com *Phone:* +1(412) 237-5757 **Holdings:** 27,700 books

3760 Pittsburgh, Pennsylvania, US
Pittsburgh Garden Place
Library
1059 Shady Avenue
Pittsburgh, Pennsylvania 15232
Phone: +1(412) 441-4442 **Fax:** +1(412) 665-2368 **Email:** garden@trfn.clpgh.org **WWW:** trfn.clpgh.org/garden

Former Name: Pittsburgh Civic Garden Center **Founded:** 1935 **Type:** Association **Head:** Jean Aiken *Phone:* +1(412) 441-4442 *Email:* garden@trfn.clpgh.org **Staff:** 1 Prof. **Holdings:** 3,000 books 20 journals **Language of Collection/Services:** English **Subjects:** Gardening, Horticulture **Loan:** Members only **Photocopy:** Yes

3761 University Park, Pennsylvania, US
Pennsylvania State University (PSU)
Life Sciences Library
401 Paterno Library
University Park, Pennsylvania 16802-1801
Phone: +1(814) 865-7056 **Fax:** +1(814) 863-9684 **WWW:** www.psu.edu **OPAC:** www.lias.psu.edu

Former Name: Pennsylvania State College, Agricultural Library, Agricultural and Biological Sciences Library **Founded:** 1888 **Type:** Academic **Head:** Amy L. Paster *Phone:* +1 (814) 865-3708 *Email:* alp@psulias.psu.edu **Staff:** 5 Prof. 3 Other **Holdings:** 280,000 books 2,500 journals **Language of Collection/Services:** English **Subjects:** Agriculture (Tropics), Agribusiness, Agricultural Development, Agricultural Economics, Agricultural Engineering, Animal Husbandry, Biotechnology, Crops, Education/Extension, Entomology, Farming, Fisheries, Food Sciences, Forestry, Horticulture, Plant Pathology, Soil Science, Veterinary Medicine, Water Resources **Specializations:** Mushrooms, Mycology **Networks:** OCLC **Databases Used:** Comprehensive **Loan:** In country **Service:** Inhouse **Photocopy:** Yes

3762   University Park, Pennsylvania, US
Pennsylvania State University, Department of
     Entomology, Frost Entomological Museum
Taxonomic Research Library
501 Ag Sciences and Industries Building
University Park, Pennsylvania 16802-3508
Phone: +1(814) 863-2863 **Fax:** +1(814) 865-3048 **WWW:**
www.cas.psu.edu

Founded: 1972 **Type:** Academic **Head:** Ke Chung Kim
Phone: +1(814) 865-1895 *Email:* kck@psu.edu **Staff:** 4
Prof. **Holdings:** 1,000 books **Subjects:** Entomology, Taxonomy **Photocopy:** Yes

3763   Wyndmoor, Pennsylvania, US
United States Department of Agriculture,
     Agricultural Research Service, Eastern
     Regional Research Center (USDA, ARS)
Library
600 East Mermaid Lane
Wyndmoor, Pennsylvania 19038-8598
Phone: +1(215) 233-6602/4 ext 60, 233-6400 **Fax:**
+1(215) 233-6606, 233-6777 **WWW:** www.ars.usda.gov

Founded: 1940 **Type:** Government **Head:** Wendy H.
Kramer *Email:* wkramer@arsercc.gov *Phone:* +1(215) 233-
6602 **Staff:** 1 Prof. 2 Other **Holdings:** 30,000 books 250
journals **Subjects:** Biochemistry, Biotechnology, Botany,
Chemical Engineering, Chemistry, Dairy Science, Food
Safety, Food Sciences, Hides and Skins, Leather, Microbiology, Fisheries, Wool **Networks:** OCLC **Databases Used:**
Agricola **Loan:** Internationally **Photocopy:** Yes

Rhode Island

3764   Kingston, Rhode Island, US
University of Rhode Island
Library
15 Lippitt Road
Kingston, Rhode Island 02881-0803
Phone: +1(401) 874-2653 **Fax:** +1(401) 874-4608 **WWW:**
www.uri.edu **OPAC:** library.uri.edu

Founded: 1892 **Type:** Academic **Head:** Paul Gandel
Phone: +1(401) 874-2666 *Email:* gandel@uri.edu **Staff:** 19
Prof. 55 Other **Holdings:** 8,000 books 450 journals **Language of Collection/Services:** English / English **Subjects:**
Aquaculture, Fisheries, Food Sciences, Horticulture, Plant
Pathology, Veterinary Science **Specializations:** Fisheries,
Water Resources **Networks:** HELIN; OCLC **Databases
Used:** Comprehensive **Loan:** Internationally **Service:** In
state **Photocopy:** Yes

3765   Providence, Rhode Island, US
Brown University
Sciences Library
Box I
Providence, Rhode Island 02912-9109
Location: 201 Thayer Street (corner of Waterman and
Thayer) **Phone:** +1(401) 863-3333 **Fax:** +1(401) 863-2753
Email: sciences@brown.edu **WWW:** www.brown.edu/
Facilities/University_Library **OPAC:** library.brown.edu
Ariel IP: 128.148.41.3

Founded: 1971 **Type:** Academic **Head:** Florence Kell
Doksansky *Email:* florence_doksansky@brown.edu *Phone:*
+1(401) 863-2405 **Staff:** 8 Prof. 20 Other **Holdings:**
612,927 books 4,012 journals **Language of Collection/Services:** English **Subjects:** Biology, Engineering, Physical
Sciences **Specializations:** Food Supply, Hunger **Networks:**
OCLC **Databases Used:** Agricola; Biosis **Loan:** Internationally **Service:** Internationally **Photocopy:** Yes

South Carolina

3766   Clemson, South Carolina, US
Clemson University
University Libraries
Clemson, South Carolina 29634-3001
Phone: +1(864) 656-3024 **Fax:** +1(864) 656-7608 **WWW:**
www.lib.clemson.edu **OPAC:** www.lib.clemson.edu/
oncat.htm

Founded: 1983 **Type:** Academic **Head:** Joseph F. Boykin,
Jr. *Phone:* +1(864) 656-3026 *Email:* jboykin@clemson.edu
Staff: 32 Prof. 70 Other **Holdings:** 1,700,000 books 6,600
journals **Language of Collection/Services:** English **Subjects:** Agricultural Economics, Agricultural Engineering,
Animal Husbandry, Aquaculture, Fisheries, Horticulture,
Plant Pathology **Networks:** OCLC **Databases Used:** Comprehensive **Loan:** Internationally **Service:** Inhouse **Photocopy:** Yes

3767   Orangeburg, South Carolina, US
South Carolina State University (SCSU)
Miller F. Whittaker Library
PO Box 7491
Orangeburg, South Carolina 29117
Location: 300 College Street NE **Phone:** +1(803) 536-
8640/42 **Fax:** +1(803) 536-8904, 536-8902 **WWW:** www.
scsu.edu **OPAC:** library.scsu.edu/catalog.html

Former Name: South Carolina State College (SCSC)
Founded: 1913 **Type:** Academic **Head:** Mary L. Smalls
Phone: +1(803) 536-8638 *Email:* smallsml@alpha1.scsu.
edu **Staff:** 8 Prof. 10 Other **Holdings:** 387,763 books 1,357
journals **Language of Collection/Services:** English / English **Subjects:** Comprehensive **Specializations:** Agribusiness, Agricultural Economics, Plants **Networks:** OCLC
Databases Used: Comprehensive **Loan:** Internationally
Service: Internationally **Photocopy:** Yes

South Dakota

3768   Brookings, South Dakota, US
South Dakota State University (SDSU)
Hilton M. Briggs Library
Box 2115
Brookings, South Dakota 57007-1098
Location: North Campus Drive **Phone:** +1(605) 688-5570
Fax: +1(605) 688-6133 **Email:** sdsu_blref@sdstate.edu
WWW: www.sdstate.edu/library **OPAC:** webpals.sdln.net/
webpals **Ariel IP:** 137.216.122.77

Former Name: Lincoln Memorial Library **Founded:** 1885
Type: Academic **Head:** Steve Marquardt *Phone:* +1(605)

688-5106 *Email:* steve_marquardt@sdstate.edu **Staff:** 13 Prof. 18 Other **Holdings:** 891,300 books 3,100 journals **Language of Collection/Services:** English / English **Subjects:** Agriculture (Tropics), Agribusiness, Agricultural Development, Agricultural Economics, Agricultural Engineering, Animal Husbandry, Biotechnology, Crops, Education/Extension, Entomology, Farming, Fisheries, Food Sciences, Forestry, Horticulture, Plant Pathology, Soil Science, Veterinary Medicine, Water Resources **Networks:** OCLC; South Dakota Library Network **Databases Developed:** Indian Country Today (newspaper) index - accessible via Internet at webpals.sdln.net/webpals/srchict.html **Databases Used:** Comprehensive **Loan:** Internationally **Photocopy:** Yes

3769   Brookings, South Dakota, US
South Dakota State University, College of
   Agriculture and Biological Sciences (SDSU)
Water Resources Institute (WRI)
Agricultural Engineering Bldg., Room 211
Brookings, South Dakota 57007-0650
Phone: +1(605) 688-4910 **Fax:** +1(605) 688-4917 **Email:** wrisdsu@mg.sdstate.edu **WWW:** web.sdstate.edu

Founded: 1965 **Type:** Academic **Head:** John Bischoff *Phone:* +1(605) 688-4910 *Email:* john_bischoff@sdstate.edu **Staff:** 7 Prof. 7 Other **Language of Collection/Services:** English **Subjects:** Agricultural Engineering, Crops, Fisheries, Water Resources **Loan:** Inhouse **Service:** Inhouse **Photocopy:** Yes

3770   Rapid City, South Dakota, US
South Dakota State University, College of
   Agriculture and Biological Sciences, West
   River Ag Center (SDSU, WRAC)
Library
1905 Plaza Blvd.
Rapid City, South Dakota 57702-9302
Phone: +1(605) 394-2236 **Fax:** +1(605) 394-6607

Founded: 1969 **Type:** Academic **Head:** Marty Buetler *Email:* beutlerm@ces.sdstate.edu **Staff:** 9 Prof. 3 Other **Holdings:** 400 books 6 journals **Language of Collection/Services:** English / English **Subjects:** Animal Husbandry, Crops, Farming, Plants, Soil Science, Water Resources **Loan:** Inhouse **Service:** Inhouse **Photocopy:** Yes

3771   Sioux Falls, South Dakota, US
United States Geological Survey, EROS Data
   Center
Don Lee Kulow Memorial Library
47914 252nd Street
Sioux Falls, South Dakota 57198
Phone: +1(605) 594-6565 **Fax:** +1(605) 594-6083 **WWW:** edcwww.cr.usgs.gov **OPAC:** edcwww.cr.usgs.gov/library.html

Founded: 1969 **Type:** Government **Head:** Laurie Ortega *Phone:* +1(605) 594-6565 *Email:* ortega@edcmail.cr.usgs.gov **Staff:** 1 Prof. **Holdings:** 8,000 books 100 journals **Language of Collection/Services:** English / English **Subjects:** Aerial Photography, Land Cover Mapping, Land Use, Landsat, Satellite Surveys **Specializations:** Geological Survey (USA) Documents, Landsat Satellite Data, National Air and

Space Administration (USA) Documents **Networks:** OCLC; SDLN **Databases Used:** Comprehensive **Loan:** Internationally **Service:** Internationally **Photocopy:** Yes

Tennessee

3772   Clarksville, Tennessee, US
Austin Peay State University
Felix G. Woodward Library
PO Box 4595
Clarksville, Tennessee 37044
Phone: +1(931) 221-7618 **Fax:** +1(931) 221-7296 **WWW:** www.apsu.edu **OPAC:** webpac.apsu.edu/webpac

Founded: 1927 **Type:** Academic **Head:** Dr. Donald Joyce *Phone:* +1(931) 221-7916 *Email:* joyced@apsu.edu **Staff:** 7 Prof. 16 Other **Holdings:** 1,221+ books 37 journals **Subjects:** Agricultural Education, Agricultural Engineering, Food Sciences, Forestry, Veterinary Medicine **Networks:** OCLC **Loan:** Internationally **Photocopy:** Yes

3773   Knoxville, Tennessee, US
University of Tennessee, Knoxville (UTK)
Agriculture-Veterinary Medicine Library
A-113 Vet Teach Hospital
2407 River Drive
Knoxville, Tennessee 37996-4500
Phone: +1(423) 974-7338 **Fax:** +1(423) 974-4732 **Email:** agvetlib@utk.edu **WWW:** www.utk.edu **OPAC:** gila.lib.utk.edu:8000

Founded: 1888 **Type:** Academic **Head:** Sandy Leach *Phone:* +1(423) 974-7922 *Email:* sandra-leach@utk.edu **Staff:** 2 Prof. 3 Other **Holdings:** 120,000 books 2,000 journals **Language of Collection/Services:** English / English **Subjects:** Agribusiness, Agricultural Economics, Agricultural Engineering, Animal Husbandry, Aquaculture, Crops, Entomology, Farming, Fisheries, Food Sciences, Forestry, Horticulture, Plant Pathology, Plants, Rural Sociology, Soil Science, Veterinary Medicine, Wildlife **Specializations:** Agriculture (USA - Southeast) **Networks:** OCLC; RLIN **Databases Used:** Agricola; CABCD; Medline **Loan:** In country **Service:** Internationally **Photocopy:** Yes

3774   Lewisburg, Tennessee, US
Tennessee Walking Horse Breeders' and
   Exhibitors' Association (TWHBEA)
Library
250 North Ellington Parkway
PO Box 286
Lewisburg, Tennessee 37091
Phone: +1(931) 359-1574 **Fax:** +1(931) 359-7530 **WWW:** www.twhbea.com

Type: Association **Head:** Mrs. Sharon Brandon, Secretary-Treasurer *Phone:* +1(931) 359-1574 **Subjects:** American Walking Pony, Horses **Loan:** Do not loan **Photocopy:** No

3775   Martin, Tennessee, US
University of Tennessee, Martin
Paul Meek Library
Martin, Tennessee 38238-5047

Phone: +1(901) 587-7065 **Fax:** +1(901) 587-7074 **WWW:** www.utm.edu **OPAC:** library.utm.edu/screens/opacmenu. html

Founded: 1900 **Type:** Academic **Head:** Steve Rogers, Interim Library Director *Phone:* +1(901) 587-7062 *Email:* srogers@utm.edu **Staff:** 10 Prof. 13 Other **Holdings:** 5,237 books 66 journals **Subjects:** Agricultural Economics, Animal Husbandry, Crops **Networks:** OCLC **Loan:** Internationally **Photocopy:** Yes

3776   Memphis, Tennessee, US
Memphis Botanic Garden Foundation Inc.,
    Goldsmith Civic Garden Center
Sybile Malloy Memorial Library
750 Cherry Road
Memphis, Tennessee 38117
Phone: +1(901) 585-1566 **Fax:** +1(901) 682-1561 **Email:** jamerbro@memphis.magibox.net **WWW:** www. memphisbotanicgarden.com

Founded: 1964 **Type:** Business **Head:** Yolande Welch *Phone:* +1(901) 685-1566 **Staff:** 1 Other **Holdings:** 2,050 books 15 journals **Language of Collection/Services:** English / English **Subjects:** Flowers, Horticulture, Plant Pathology, Plants, Soil **Loan:** Inhouse **Photocopy:** Yes

3777   Memphis, Tennessee, US
National Cotton Council of America
Library
PO Box 820285
Memphis, Tennessee 38182-0285
Location: 1918 North Parkway **Phone:** +1(901) 274-9030
Fax: +1(901) 725-0510 **WWW:** www.cotton.org

Founded: 1955 **Type:** Association **Staff:** 1 Prof. **Holdings:** 900 books 100 journals **Language of Collection/Services:** English **Subjects:** Agribusiness, Agricultural Economics, Agricultural Engineering, Biotechnology, Crops, Entomology, Farming, Plant Pathology, Water Resources **Specializations:** Cotton Industry **Databases Developed:** Beltwide Cotton Conferences Proceedings on COTNET - access by members only **Loan:** Do not loan **Service:** Internationally **Photocopy:** No

3778   Murfreesboro, Tennessee, US
National Spotted Saddle Horse Association, Inc.
    (NSSHA)
Information Center
PO Box 898
Murfreesboro, Tennessee 37133-0898
Location: 108 North Spring Street **Phone:** +1(615) 890-2864 **Email:** nssha898@aol.com **WWW:** www.dnj.com/ spothorse/index.html

Founded: 1979 **Type:** Business **Head:** Donna West **Staff:** 2 Prof. **Holdings:** 10 books 1,500 journals **Language of Collection/Services:** English **Subjects:** Horses, Spotted Saddle Horse **Loan:** In country **Photocopy:** Yes

3779   Nashville, Tennessee, US
Cheekwood, Tennessee, Botanical Gardens and
    Museum of Art
Botanical Gardens Library

1200 Forrest Park Drive
Nashville, Tennessee 37205-4242
Phone: +1(615) 356-8000 **Email:** info@cheekwood.org
WWW: www.cheekwood.org

Founded: 1971 **Type:** Association **Head:** Muriel H. Connell *Phone:* +1(615) 356-3306 **Staff:** 1 Prof. 2 Other **Holdings:** 4,300 books 61 journals **Language of Collection/ Services:** English / English **Subjects:** Gardening, Landscaping, Pest Control, Plants, Soil Science, Woody Plants **Specializations:** Botany, Ecology, Horticulture **Service:** Inhouse or members only **Photocopy:** Yes

3780   Nashville, Tennessee, US
Tennessee State Library and Archives (TSLA)
403 7th Avenue North
Nashville, Tennessee 37243-0312
Phone: +1(615) 741-2764 **Fax:** +1(615) 532-2472 **Email:** reference@mail.state.tn.us **WWW:** www.state.tn.us/sos/ statelib **OPAC:** www.auto-graphics.com/cgipac/mmx/tns

Founded: 1854 **Type:** Government **Head:** Edwin S. Gleaves *Email:* egleaves@mail.state.tn.us *Phone:* +1(615) 741-7996 **Staff:** 35 Prof. 62 Other **Holdings:** 540,741 books 1,620 journals **Language of Collection/Services:** English / English **Subjects:** Agricultural Development, Agricultural Economics, Agricultural Engineering, Crops, Education/Extension, Farming, Fisheries, Forestry, Horticulture, Water Resources **Specializations:** Government Documents (Tennessee), Government Documents (USA) **Loan:** Internationally **Service:** Internationally **Photocopy:** Yes

3781   Nashville, Tennessee, US
Tennessee State University, Libraries and Media
    Centers
Brown/Daniel Library
3500 Merritt Boulevard
Campus Box 9597
Nashville, Tennessee 37209
Phone: +1(615) 963-5211 **Fax:** +1(615) 963-5224 **WWW:** www.tnstate.edu/index.html **OPAC:** www.tnstate.edu/ library/Catalogs.html

Founded: 1912 **Type:** Academic **Head:** Mrs. Yildiz Barlas Binkley *Email:* ybinkley@tnstate.edu *Phone:* +1(615) 963-3682 **Staff:** 15.5 Prof. 19.5 Other **Holdings:** 3,594 books 34 journals **Subjects:** Animal Husbandry, Horticulture, Plants, Soil Science **Databases Used:** ABI/Inform; Agricola; Medline **Loan:** In country **Service:** In country **Photocopy:** Yes

3782   Nashville, Tennessee, US
U.S. Tobacco
Research and Development Library
800 Harrison Street
Nashville, Tennessee 37203
Fax: +1(615) 880-4692

Founded: 1980 **Type:** Business **Head:** Barbara Borrelli *Phone:* +1(615) 880-4647 *Email:* bborrelli@usthg.com **Staff:** 1 Prof. **Holdings:** 1,500 books 100 journals **Language of Collection/Services:** English **Subjects:** Tobacco

3783 Oak Ridge, Tennessee, US
Oak Ridge National Laboratory
Library
Box 2008
Oak Ridge, Tennessee 37831
WWW: www.ornl.gov **OPAC:** www.ornl.gov/~webworks
/tlp/tlp_web.htm

Founded: 1946 **Type:** Government **Holdings:** 1,090,000
books

Texas

3784 Austin, Texas, US
University of Texas at Austin, Bureau of Business
    Research
Natural Fibers Research and Information Center
    (NFRIC)
PO Box 7459
Austin, Texas 78713-7459
Location: 21st and Speedway, CBA South 6.400 **Phone:**
+1(512) 475-7817 **Fax:** +1(512) 471-1063 **Email:** natfiber
@uts.cc.utexas.edu **WWW:** www.utexas.edu/depts/bbr/
natfiber

Former Name: Natural Fibers Information Center, Natural
Fibers Economic Research, Cotton Economic Research
Founded: 1947 **Type:** Academic **Head:** Julia Kveton
Apodaca *Email:* natfiber@uts.cc.utexas.edu *Phone:* +1(512)
475-7817 **Staff:** 3 Other **Holdings:** 7,000 books 40 journals
Language of Collection/Services: English / English **Subjects:** Agricultural Development, Agricultural Economics,
Animal Husbandry, Crops, Farming **Specializations:** Cotton, Mohair, Wool **Databases Developed:** NatRes includes
CotRes, a searchable database of current and ongoing cotton
research in the U.S. (soon to expand to international) and
NatLinks, numerous links to other web sites related to natural
fibers research; NatStat - statistical database compiled from
government and industry sources on the natural fibers industry; NatNews - monthly online newsletter of current news
and information compiled from industry and government
sources; All are available on Internet at www.utexas.edu/
depts/bbr/natfiber **Loan:** Inhouse **Service:** Internationally
Photocopy: Yes

3785 College Station, Texas, US
Texas A & M University (TAMU)
Sterling C. Evans Library, Science/Engineering
    Services
College Station, Texas 77843-5000
Phone: +1(979) 845-5741 **Fax:** +1(979) 845-6238 **WWW:**
www.tamu.edu **OPAC:** voyager-am.tamu.edu **Ariel IP:**
165.91.220.14

Founded: 1876 **Type:** Academic **Head:** Dr. Fred Heath
Phone: +1(979) 845-8111 *Email:* fheath@tamu.edu **Staff:**
80 Prof. 167 Other **Holdings:** 2,300,000 books 19,000 jour-
nals **Language of Collection/Services:** English / English
Subjects: Agricultural Engineering, Biotechnology, Crops,
Forestry, Horticulture, Soil Science, Range Management
Specializations: Entomology, Rangelands **Networks:**
OCLC **Databases Used:** Comprehensive **Loan:** Internation-
ally **Service:** Internationally **Photocopy:** Yes

3786 College Station, Texas, US
Texas A & M University (TAMU)
West Campus Library
College Station, Texas 77843-5001
Phone: +1(979) 862-1066 **Fax:** +1(979) 862-2977 **WWW:**
www.tamu.edu **OPAC:** voyager-am.tamu.edu

Type: Academic **Head:** Dr. Rob McGeachin *Email:*
r-mcgeachin@tamu.edu **Subjects:** Animal Husbandry, Biochemistry, Biophysics, Crops, Entomology, Forestry, Horticulture, Poultry, Soil Science **Networks:** OCLC

3787 Dallas, Texas, US
Dallas Horticulture Center (DHC)
Horticulture Library
PO Box 152537
Dallas, Texas 75315
Location: 3601 Martin Luther King Blvd. **Phone:** +1(214)
428-7476 **Fax:** +1(214) 428-5338 **Email:** dhort@hotmail.
com **WWW:** www.startext.net/homes/dhc

Former Name: Dallas Civic Garden Center **Founded:** 1957
Type: Non-profit **Head:** Cheryl Stanco **Holdings:** 860
books 34 journals **Language of Collection/Services:** English **Subjects:** Horticulture **Loan:** Inhouse **Photocopy:** Yes

3788 Dallas, Texas, US
Environmental Protection Agency (EPA)
Region 6 Library
1445 Ross Avenue, Suite 1200
Dallas, Texas 75202-2733
Phone: +1(214) 665-6427 **Fax:** +1(214) 665-2714 **Email:**
library-reg6@epamail.epa.gov **WWW:** www.epa.gov/
earth1r6 **OPAC:** www.epa.gov/natlibra/ols.htm

Founded: 1971 **Type:** Government **Head:** Shari McAllister
Phone: +1(214) 665-6424 *Email:* mcallister.shari@epamail.
epa.gov **Staff:** 1 Prof. 1 Other **Holdings:** 71,894 books 20
journals **Language of Collection/Services:** English / Eng-
lish **Subjects:** Air Pollution, Code of Federal Regulations
(USA), Federal Register (USA), Hazardous Wastes, Noise,
Pesticides, Radiation, Soil Science, Solid Wastes, Toxic
Substances, Water Pollution, Water Quality **Specializations:** Environmental Protection Agency (USA) Documents,
Law (Arkansas), Law (Louisiana), Law (New Mexico), Law
(Oklahoma), Law (Texas), Law (USA), Office of Solid
Waste and Emergency Response (Environmental Protection
Agency, USA) Directives **Networks:** OCLC; OLS **Data-
bases Developed:** Hazardous Waste Superfund Collection
and Database - bibliographic database that provides access
by title, keyword, issuing office and date; includes summa-
ries.; Regional USDA Soil Surveys; ASTDR Toxicology
Profiles; EPA Health Effects Assessments **Databases Used:**
Comprehensive **Loan:** In country **Service:** Internationally
Photocopy: Yes

3789 Dallas, Texas, US
Frito-Lay Inc.
Frito-Lay Library
PO Box 650423
Dallas, Texas 75265-0423
Phone: +1(214) 334-4737 **WWW:** www.fritolay.com

Former Name: Technical Information Center **Founded:** 1980 **Type:** Business **Head:** Suzanne M. Ogden *Phone:* +1(214) 334-4732 *Email:* suzanne.ogden@fritolay.com **Staff:** 1 Prof. 1 Other **Holdings:** 2,500 books 450 journals **Language of Collection/Services:** English / English **Subjects:** Food Industry, Food Sciences **Specializations:** Snacks **Databases Used:** ABI/Inform **Loan:** Inhouse **Service:** Inhouse **Photocopy:** Yes

3790 Denton, Texas, US
American Donkey & Mule Society Inc. (ADMS)
Specialty Donkey and Mule Library
2901 North Elm Street
Denton, Texas 76201
Phone: +1(940) 382-6845 **Fax:** +1(940) 484-8417 **Email:** adms@juno.com **WWW:** www.fortunecity.com/business/gonda/118s

Founded: 1967 **Type:** Association **Head:** Mrs. Betsy Hutchins *Phone:* +1(940) 382-6845 *Email:* adms@juno.com **Staff:** 1 Other **Holdings:** 700 books 20 journals **Language of Collection/Services:** English **Subjects:** Animal Husbandry, Donkeys, Mules **Databases Developed:** Breeders Lists **Loan:** Do not loan **Service:** Inhouse **Photocopy:** Yes

3791 Fort Worth, Texas, US
American Paint Horse Association (APHA)
Library
PO Box 961023
Fort Worth, Texas 76161
Location: 99400 North I35 West **Phone:** +1(817) 834-2742 **Fax:** +1(817) 834-3152 **Email:** askapha@apha.com **WWW:** www.apha.com

Founded: 1962 **Type:** Association **Head:** Ed Roberts, Executive Secretary *Email:* eroberts@apha.com *Phone:* +1(817) 439-2742 ext 403 **Staff:** 12 Prof. 60 Other **Holdings:** 250 books 25 journals **Language of Collection/Services:** English **Subjects:** Horse Breeding **Specializations:** Equidae, Show Records, Studbooks **Photocopy:** Yes

3792 Galveston, Texas, US
National Marine Fisheries Service, Southeast
 Fisheries Science Center (NMFS)
Galveston Laboratory Library
4700 Avenue U
Galveston, Texas 77551-5997
Phone: +1(409) 766-3500 **Fax:** +1(409) 766-3508 **WWW:** www.nmfs.gov

Former Name: Bureau of Sport Fisheries, Bureau of Commercial Fisheries Library **Founded:** 1950 **Type:** Government **Head:** Mark Pattillo or Ms. Connie Thompson *Phone:* +1(409) 766-3509 *Email:* connie.thompson@noaa.gov **Staff:** 1 Prof. 2 Other **Holdings:** 5,226 books 80 journals **Language of Collection/Services:** English **Subjects:** Crabs, Fishes, Mollusca **Specializations:** Fisheries, Ichthyology, Marine Sciences, Oceanography, Zoology **Loan:** Inhouse **Photocopy:** Yes

3793 Kerrville, Texas, US
United States Department of Agriculture,
 Agricultural Research Service (USDA, ARS)

Knipling-Bushland U.S. Livestock Insects
 Laboratory
2700 Fredericksburg Road
Kerrville, Texas 78028-9184
WWW: www.ars.usda.gov

Founded: 1946 **Type:** Government **Head:** Sidney E. Kuntz *Phone:* +1(210) 257-3566 *Email:* sekunz@ktc.com **Holdings:** 3,000 books **Subjects:** Biological Control, Insect Control, Insect Pests, Integrated Pest Management, Livestock

3794 Lubbock, Texas, US
Texas Tech University (TTU)
Libraries
Box 40002
Lubbock, Texas 79409-0002
Location: Boston Avenue at 18th Street **Phone:** +1(806) 742-2236 **Fax:** +1(806) 742-1964 **WWW:** www.ttu.edu, www.texastech.edu **OPAC:** www.lib.ttu.edu/Default.htm

Former Name: Texas Technological College **Founded:** 1923 **Type:** Academic **Head:** Dr. E. Dale Cluff *Phone:* +1(806) 742-2261 *Email:* liedc@lib.ttu.edu **Staff:** 38 Prof. 50 Other **Holdings:** 1,200,000 books 14,000 journals **Language of Collection/Services:** English / English **Subjects:** Agriculture (Tropics), Agribusiness, Agricultural Development, Agricultural Economics, Agricultural Engineering, Animal Husbandry, Biotechnology, Crops, Education/Extension, Entomology, Farming, Fisheries, Food Sciences, Forestry, Horticulture, Plant Pathology, Soil Science, Veterinary Medicine, Water Resources **Specializations:** Cattle, Arid Lands, Cotton Industry, Feedlots, Irrigation **Networks:** OCLC **Loan:** Internationally **Service:** Internationally **Photocopy:** Yes

3795 Nacogdoches, Texas, US
Stephen F. Austin State University
Ralph W. Steen Library
PO Box 13055 SFA Station
Nacogdoches, Texas 75962-3055
Phone: +1(409) 468-4217, 468-1596 **Fax:** +1(409) 468-4117 **WWW:** www.sfasu.edu **OPAC:** libcat.sfasu.edu

Type: Academic **Head:** Alvin C. Cage *Phone:* +1(409) 468-4101 *Email:* acage@sfalib.sfasu.edu **Language of Collection/Services:** English

3796 Prairie View, Texas, US
Prairie View A & M University (PVAMU)
John B. Coleman Library
PO Box 519
Prairie View, Texas 77446
Phone: +1(409) 857-2612 **Fax:** +1(409) 857-2755 **WWW:** www.pvamu.edu/index.html **OPAC:** www.tamu.edu/pvamu/library/index.html

Former Name: W.R. Banks Library **Type:** Academic **Head:** Helen Yeh, Acting Director *Phone:* +1(409) 857-3192 *Email:* hyeh@coleman.pvam.edu **Staff:** 11 Prof. 15 Other **Holdings:** 284,500 books 1,189 journals **Language of Collection/Services:** English **Subjects:** Agribusiness, Agricultural Development, Agricultural Economics, Animal Husbandry, Crops, Education/Extension, Farming, Food

Sciences **Specializations:** Goats **Databases Used:** Agricola **Loan:** Inhouse **Service:** Internationally **Photocopy:** Yes

3797   Stephenville, Texas, US
         Tarleton State University (TSU)
         Dick Smith Library (DSLIB)
         Stephenville, Texas 76402
Phone: +1(254) 968-9249 **Fax:** +1(254) 968-9467 **Email:** reference@tarleton.edu **WWW:** www.tarleton.edu **OPAC:** www.tarleton.edu/~library **Ariel IP:** 165.95.24.115

Former Name: Tarleton State College, John Tarleton Agricultural College **Founded:** 1899 **Type:** Academic **Head:** Kenneth W. Jones *Phone:* +1(254) 968-9246 *Email:* kjones @tarleton.edu **Staff:** 11 Prof. 12 Other **Holdings:** 5,000 books 100 journals **Language of Collection/Services:** English **Subjects:** Agribusiness, Agricultural Economics, Agricultural Engineering, Animal Husbandry, Biotechnology, Crops, Education/Extension, Farming, Food Sciences, Forestry, Plant Pathology, Soil Science, Veterinary Medicine, Water Resources **Specializations:** Extension (USA) Documents (19th Century), Extension (USA) Documents (20th Century) **Networks:** OCLC **Databases Used:** Agricola **Loan:** In country **Photocopy:** Yes

3798   Weslaco, Texas, US
         United States Department of Agriculture,
         Agricultural Research Service, Kika de la
         Garza Subtropical Agricultural Research
         Laboratory, Beneficial Insects Research Unit
         (USDA, ARS, SARL)
         Library
         2413 East Highway 83
         Weslaco, Texas 78596
Phone: +1(956) 969-4870 **Fax:** +1(956) 969-5033 **WWW:** www.ars.usda.gov

Type: Government **Head:** Deena Brandenberger *Email:* dbrandenberger@weslaco.ars.usda.gov *Phone:*+1(956) 969-4852 **Holdings:** 480 books 12 journals **Subjects:** Honeybees **Loan:** Do not loan **Service:** Inhouse **Photocopy:** No

Utah

3799   Logan, Utah, US
         Utah State University (USU)
         USU Libraries, Merrill Library / Sci-Tech Library
         3000 Old Main Hill
         Logan, Utah 84322-3000
Phone: +1(435) 797-2917 (Sci-Tech Library) **Fax:** +1 (435) 797-2677 **Email:** annhed@cc.usu.edu **WWW:** www. usu.edu/~library **OPAC:** libcat.usu.edu **Ariel IP:** 129.123. 15.62

Former Name: Merrill Library **Founded:** 1888 **Type:** Academic **Head:** Max P. Peterson *Phone:* +1(435) 797-2631 *Email:* maxpet@cc.usu.edu **Staff:** 25 Prof. 52 Other **Holdings:** 1,417,185 books 14,863 journals **Language of Collection/Services:** English / English **Subjects:** Agricultural Economics, Agricultural Education, Agricultural Engineering, Animal Husbandry, Dairy Science, Food Sciences, Forestry, Irrigation, Meteorology, Nutrition, Plants, Soil Science, Veterinary Science **Networks:** OCLC **Databases**

Used: Comprehensive **Loan:** Internationally **Service:** Internationally **Photocopy:** Yes

3800   Newton, Utah, US
         United Suffolk Sheep Association
         Library
         PO Box 256
         17 West Main
         Newton, Utah 84327
Phone: +1(435) 563-6105 **Fax:** +1(435) 563-9357 **Email:** suffolksheep@pcu.net **WWW:** u-s-s-a.org

Former Name: American Suffolk Sheep Society **Type:** Association **Language of Collection/Services:** English **Subjects:** Sheep, Suffolk Sheep **Photocopy:** Yes

3801   Ogden, Utah, US
         United States Department of Agriculture, Forest
         Service, Rocky Mountain Research Station
         (USDA, FS, RMRS)
         Library
         324 25th Street
         Ogden, Utah 84401
Phone: +1(801) 625-5444 **Fax:** +1(801) 625-5129 **Email:** library@fs.fed.us **WWW:** www.fs.fed.us/rm

Former Name: Intermountain Research Station (INT), FS INFO-Intermountain, Westfornet **Founded:** 1964 **Type:** Government **Head:** Carol A. Ayer *Phone:* +1(801) 625-5445 *Email:* cayer@fs.fed.us **Staff:** 3 Prof. 9 Other **Holdings:** 50,000 books 250 journals **Language of Collection/Services:** English / English **Subjects:** Animal Husbandry, Entomology, Fisheries, Forestry, Natural Resources, Plant Pathology, Plants, Outdoor Recreation, Range Management, Soil Science, Water Resources, Wildfires, Wildlife **Networks:** FSLN, OCLC **Databases Used:** Agricola; TREE-CD; Water Resources Abstracts; Wildlife Worldwide **Loan:** Internationally **Service:** Inhouse **Photocopy:** No

3802   Provo, Utah, US
         Brigham Young University (BYU)
         Harold B. Lee Library (HBLL)
         Provo, Utah 84602
Phone: +1(801) 378-2987, 378-2987 (Science/Maps Reference Desk) **Fax:** +1(801) 378-6708 **WWW:** www.byu.edu **OPAC:** www.lib.byu.edu **Ariel IP:** 128.187.11.200 **Email:** julie_williamsen@byu.edu

Former Name: Brigham Young Academy, Heber J. Grant Library, J. Reuben Clark Jr. Library **Founded:** 1875 **Type:** Academic **Head:** Sterling Albrecht *Phone:* +1(801) 378-2905 *Email:* sterling_albrecht@byu.edu **Staff:** 6 Prof. 4 Other **Holdings:** 50,000 books 1,100 journals **Language of Collection/Services:** English / English **Subjects:** Agribusiness, Agricultural Development, Agricultural Economics, Agricultural Engineering, Animal Husbandry, Biotechnology, Crops, Education/Extension, Entomology, Farming, Fisheries, Food Sciences, Forestry, Horticulture, Plant Pathology, Plants, Soil Science, Veterinary Medicine, Water Resources **Networks:** OCLC; RLIN **Databases Developed:** Bibliography of Production Agriculture - 80,000 records on agricultural production from state and federal agricultural publications and also from Canadian provincial agricultural publications. **Databases Used:** Comprehensive **Loan:** Internationally **Service:** Internationally **Photocopy:** Yes

Vermont

3803   Burlington, Vermont, US
University of Vermont
Bailey/Howe Memorial Library
Burlington, Vermont 05405
Phone: +1(802) 656-2022 **WWW:** www.uvm.edu **OPAC:** voyager.uvm.edu

Type: Academic **Head:** Mara R. Saule, Acting Dean *Phone:* +1(802) 656-2003 *Email:* msaule@zoo.uvm.edu

3804   Burlington, Vermont, US
University of Vermont, Botany Department,
     Pringle Herbarium
Library
Burlington, Vermont 05405-0086
Phone: +1(802) 656-3221 **Fax:** +1(802) 656-0440 **WWW:** www.uvm.edu/~plantbio

Type: Academic **Head:** David S. Barrington *Phone:* +1(802) 656-3221 *Email:* dbarring@zoo.uvm.edu **Holdings:** 337,620 books **Subjects:** Plants

Virginia

3805   Alexandria, Virginia, US
American Horticultural Society (AHS)
Library
7931 East Boulevard Drive
Alexandria, Virginia 22308-1300
Phone: +1(703) 768-5700 **Fax:** +1(703) 768-8700 **WWW:** www.ahs.org

Type: Association **Head:** Alice Bagwill *Phone:* +1(703) 768-5700 ext 128 **Holdings:** 3,500 books **Language of Collection/Services:** English / English **Subjects:** Horticulture **Loan:** Inhouse **Service:** Inhouse and members **Photocopy:** Yes

3806   Arlington, Virginia, US
National Science Foundation (NSF)
Library
4201 Wilson Blvd., Room 225
Arlington, Virginia 22230
Phone: +1(703) 306-0658 **Fax:** +1(703) 306-0692 **Email:** library@nsf.gov **WWW:** www.nsf.gov

Founded: 1951 **Type:** Government **Head:** Mrs. Stephanie Bianchi *Email:* sbianchi@nsf.gov *Phone:* +1(703) 306-1125 ext 2058 **Staff:** 1 Prof. 1 Other **Holdings:** 15,000 books 200 journals **Language of Collection/Services:** English **Subjects:** Biotechnology, Plants, Water Resources **Networks:** OCLC **Loan:** Inhouse **Service:** Internationally **Photocopy:** Yes

3807   Blacksburg, Virginia, US
Virginia Polytechnic Institute and State University
     (VPI)

University Libraries, Carol M. Newman Library
PO Box 90001
Blacksburg, Virginia 24062-9001
Location: Drillfield Drive **Phone:** +1(540) 231-6170, 231-5532 (Science and Technology Reference Desk) **Fax:** +1(540) 231-7808 **WWW:** www.lib.vt.edu **OPAC:** www.lib.vt.edu/services/addison.html

Type: Academic **Head:** Dr. Eileen Hitchingham *Phone:* +1(540) 231-5593 *Email:* hitch@vt.edu **Staff:** 36.5 Prof. 102 Other **Holdings:** 2,405,290 books 13,024 journals **Language of Collection/Services:** English / English **Subjects:** Comprehensive **Specializations:** Agricultural Economics, Biotechnology, Horticulture, Veterinary Medicine **Networks:** OCLC **Databases Used:** Comprehensive **Loan:** Internationally **Service:** Internationally **Photocopy:** Yes

3808   Blacksburg, Virginia, US
Virginia Polytechnic Institute and State University
     (VPI)
University Libraries, Veterinary Medicine Library
Virginia-Maryland Regional College of Veterinary
     Medicine
Phase III, Duck Pond Drive
Blacksburg, Virginia 24061-0442
Location: Drillfield Drive **Phone:** +1(540) 231-6610 **Fax:** +1(540) 231-7367 **WWW:** www.lib.vt.edu **OPAC:** www.lib.vt.edu/services/addison.html

Type: Academic **Head:** Vicki Kok *Email:* vkok@vt.edu **Subjects:** Veterinary Medicine **Networks:** OCLC

3809   Boyce, Virginia, US
University of Virginia, Blandy Experimental Farm
Library
400 Blandy Farm Lane
Boyce, Virginia 22620
Phone: +1(540) 837-1758 **Fax:** +1(540) 837-1523 **Email:** blandy@virginia.edu **WWW:** www.virginia.edu/~blandy

Founded: 1929 **Type:** Academic **Head:** Michael A. Bowers *Phone:* +1(540) 837-1758 **Staff:** 4 Prof. **Holdings:** 1,500 books **Language of Collection/Services:** English / English **Subjects:** Ecology, Evolution, Horticulture **Loan:** Inhouse and through University of Virginia **Photocopy:** No

3810   Dunn Loring, Virginia, US
National Pest Management Association Inc,
     International
Library
8100 Oak Street
Dunn Loring, Virginia 22027
Phone: +1(703) 573-8330 **Fax:** +1(703) 573-4116 **WWW:** www.pestworld.org

Former Name: National Pest Control Association **Type:** Association **Head:** Greg Baumann *Phone:* +1(703) 573-8330 **Staff:** 12 Prof. 8 Other **Holdings:** 2,000 books **Language of Collection/Services:** English / English **Subjects:** Entomology, Toxicology **Loan:** Internationally **Service:** Internationally **Photocopy:** Yes

3811 Gloucester Point, Virginia, US

College of William and Mary, Virginia Institute of Marine Science, School of Marine Science (VIMS)
Library
PO Box 1346
Gloucester Point, Virginia 23062-1346

Phone: +1(804) 642-7116 **Fax:** +1(804) 642-7113 **Email:** dianeg@vims.edu **WWW:** www.vims.edu **OPAC:** www.vims.edu/library/#cat

Founded: 1947 **Type:** Academic **Head:** Charles A. McFadden *Phone:* +1(804) 642-7114 *Email:* chuck@vims.edu **Staff:** 3 Prof. **Holdings:** 35,000 books 521 journals **Language of Collection/Services:** English **Subjects:** Fisheries, Water Resources **Specializations:** Aquaculture **Databases Developed:** Chesapeake Bay Bibliography **Loan:** Internationally **Service:** Internationally **Photocopy:** Yes

3812 Manassas, Virginia, US

American Type Culture Collection (ATCC)
Library
10801 University Boulevard
Manassas, Virginia 20110-2209

Phone: +1(703) 365-2700 **Fax:** +1(703) 365-2740 **Email:** help@atcc.org **WWW:** www.atcc.org **OPAC:** phage.atcc.org/searchengine/all.html

Founded: 1965 **Type:** Non-profit, Research **Holdings:** 5,000 books 350 journals **Language of Collection/Services:** English **Subjects:** Biotechnology, Cell Culture, Microbiology, Plant Pathology **Loan:** Inhouse **Service:** Inhouse

3813 Norfolk, Virginia, US

Norfolk Botanical Garden Society (NBGS)
Heutte Horticultural Library
6700 Azalea Garden Road
Norfolk, Virginia 23518

Phone: +1(757) 441-5830 **Fax:** +1(757) 853-8294 **Email:** garden@norfolk.infi.net

Type: Non-profit **Head:** Lillian Eastman, volunteer coordinator **Staff:** 10 volunteers Other **Holdings:** 2,500 books **Language of Collection/Services:** English / English **Subjects:** Horticulture **Loan:** Inhouse and to members **Service:** Inhouse **Photocopy:** Yes

3814 Petersburg, Virginia, US

Virginia State University
Johnston Memorial Library
PO Box 9406
Petersburg, Virginia 23806

Phone: +1(804) 524-6946 **Fax:** +1(804) 524-5482 **Email:** mcwalker@vsu.edu **WWW:** www.vsu.edu **OPAC:** www.vsu.edu/library/Electronic%20Resources.htm

Type: Academic **Head:** Elsie Weatherington *Phone:* +1(804) 524-5040 *Email:* estephens@vsu.edu

3815 Richmond, Virginia, US

The Library of Virginia
General Library Division
800 East Broad Street
Richmond, Virginia 23219-8000

Phone: +1(804) 692-3777 **Fax:** +1(804) 692-3556 **WWW:** www.lva.lib.va.us **OPAC:** eagle.vsla.edu/catalog

Former Name: Virginia State Library and Archives (VSL&A) **Founded:** 1826 **Type:** Government, Research **Head:** Nolan T. Yelich *Phone:* +1(804) 692-3500 **Staff:** 16 Prof. 22 Other **Holdings:** 1,100,000 books 780 journals **Language of Collection/Services:** English / English **Specializations:** Tobacco, Government Documents (USA), Virginia **Networks:** OCLC **Loan:** In state **Service:** Internationally **Photocopy:** Yes

3816 Vienna, Virginia, US

American Resources Group, National Woodland Owners Association
Library
374 Maple Avenue East
Suite 210
Vienna, Virginia 22180-4718

Phone: +1(703) 255-2700 **Email:** nwoa@mindspring.com

Founded: 1981 **Type:** Association **Head:** Keith A. Argow *Phone:* +1(703) 255-2700 **Staff:** 2 Prof. **Holdings:** 2,300 books 27 journals **Language of Collection/Services:** English **Subjects:** Forestry, Woodlands **Specializations:** Private Forestry **Loan:** Do not loan **Photocopy:** Yes

3817 Vienna, Virginia, US

National Wildlife Federation (NWF)
Library Information Center
8925 Leesburg Pike
Vienna, Virginia 22814

Phone: +1(703) 790-4446 **Fax:** +1(703) 442-7332 **WWW:** www.nwf.org

Founded: 1960 **Type:** Government **Head:** Sharon Levy *Phone:* +1(703) 790-4446 **Staff:** 1 Prof. **Holdings:** 5,000 books 300 journals **Language of Collection/Services:** English **Specializations:** Conservation, Endangered Species, Natural History, Wildlife **Databases Used:** LEXIS-NEXIS **Loan:** In country **Photocopy:** Yes

3818 Winchester, Virginia, US

Welsh Pony and Cob Society of America, Inc. (WPCSA)
Library
PO Box 2977
Winchester, Virginia 22604

Location: 2222 Wilson Boulevard **Phone:** +1(540) 667-6195 **Fax:** +1(540) 667-3766 **Email:** wpcsa@crosslink.net **WWW:** scendtek.com/wpcsa/index.htm

Former Name: Welsh Pony Society of America **Founded:** 1906 **Type:** Association **Head:** Lisa L. Landis, Secretary **Staff:** 3 Other **Holdings:** 65 books 6 journals **Subjects:** Animal Husbandry **Loan:** Do not loan **Photocopy:** Yes

Washington

3819 Federal Way, Washington, US

Rhododendron Species Foundation
Lawrence J. Pierce Rhododendron Library
2525 South 336th Street

PO Box 3798
Federal Way, Washington 98063-3798
Phone: +1(253) 927-6960 **Fax:** +1(253) 838-4686 **Email:** rsf@halcyon.com **WWW:** www.halcyon.com/rsf

Holdings: 2,560 books 20 journals **Language of Collection/ Services:** English / English **Subjects:** Horticulture **Specializations:** Rhododendron **Loan:** Do not loan **Service:** Internationally **Photocopy:** Yes

3820   Port Townsend, Washington, US
Abundant Life Seed Foundation
Library
PO Box 772
Port Townsend, Washington 98368
Location: 930 Lawrence St. **Phone:** +1(360) 385-5660
Fax: +1(360) 385-7455 **Email:** abundant@olypen.com
WWW: csf.colorado.edu/perma/abundant

Founded: 1975 **Type:** Association **Head:** Aleta Anderson
Phone: +1(360) 385-5660 **Holdings:** 200 books **Language of Collection/Services:** English / English **Subjects:** Native Plants (USA - Pacific Northwest), Organic Gardening, Seed Production **Loan:** Do not loan **Photocopy:** No

3821   Pullman, Washington, US
Washington State University (WSU)
Owen Science and Engineering Library
Pullman, Washington 99164-3200
Phone: +1(509) 335-2674 **Fax:** +1(509) 335-2534 **Email:** owenref@mail.wsu.edu **WWW:** www.wsu.edu **OPAC:** griffin.wsu.edu

Founded: 1890 **Type:** Academic **Staff:** 6.44 Prof. 15.2 Other **Holdings:** 550,000 books 5,500 journals **Language of Collection/Services:** English / English **Subjects:** Comprehensive **Specializations:** Plant Pathology, Plant Physiology **Networks:** OCLC **Databases Used:** Comprehensive **Loan:** Internationally **Service:** Internationally **Photocopy:** Yes

3822   Pullman, Washington, US
Washington State University (WSU)
Veterinary Medical / Pharmacy Library
PO Box 646512
170 Wegner Hall
Pullman, Washington 99164-6512
Phone: +1(509) 335-9556 **Fax:** +1(509) 335-5158 **Email:** vetref@mail.wsu.edu **WWW:** www.wsulibs.wsu.edu/vet/vethmpag.htm **OPAC:** griffin.wsu.edu

Former Name: Veterinary Medical Library **Founded:** 1962 **Type:** Academic **Head:** Vicki F. Croft *Phone:* +1(509) 335-5544 *Email:* croft@wsu.edu **Staff:** 2 Prof. 2.5 Other **Holdings:** 23,500 books 800 journals **Language of Collection/Services:** English **Subjects:** Veterinary Medicine **Specializations:** Veterinary Medicine (History) **Databases Used:** Agricola; Biosis; CABCD; CAS; Medline **Loan:** Internationally **Service:** Internationally **Photocopy:** Yes

3823   Richland, Washington, US
Washington State University at Tri-Cities (WSU TRIC)
Consolidated Information Center, Max E. Benitz Memorial Library (CIC)

2770 University Drive
Richland, Washington 99352-1671
Phone: +1(509) 372-7430 **Fax:** +1(509) 372-7512 **WWW:** www2.tricity.wsu.edu/dis/consolid.htm **OPAC:** griffin.wsu.edu

Former Name: Joint University Center **Type:** Academic **Head:** Joseph R. Judy *Email:* jjudy@tricity.wsu.edu *Phone:* +1(509) 372-7449 **Staff:** 3 Prof. 6 Other **Holdings:** 10,000 books 85 journals **Language of Collection/Services:** English/English **Subjects:** Crops, Farming, Food Sciences, Plant Pathology, Plants, Soil Science **Networks:** OCLC **Loan:** Inhouse **Service:** Inhouse **Photocopy:** Yes

3824   Seattle, Washington, US
National Marine Fisheries Service, Northwest Fisheries Science Center and the Alaska Fisheries Science Center (NMFS, NWFSC/AFSC)
Library
2725 Montlake Boulevard E
Seattle, Washington 98112
Phone: +1(206) 860-3210 **Fax:** +1(206) 860-3217 **WWW:** www.nmfs.gov **OPAC:** research.fwfsc.noaa.gov/library/catalog.htm

Type: Government **Head:** Patricia Cook *Email:* patricia.a.cook@noaa.gov **Staff:** 1 Prof. 2 Other **Holdings:** 23,000 books **Language of Collection/Services:** English **Subjects:** Fisheries, Food Sciences **Networks:** OCLC **Loan:** In country **Service:** Inhouse **Photocopy:** Yes

3825   Seattle, Washington, US
University of Washington
Fisheries-Oceanography Library
151 Oceanography Teaching Building
Box 357952
Seattle, Washington 98195-7952
Phone: +1(206) 543-4279 **Fax:** +1(206) 543-4909 **Email:** fishlib@u.washington.edu **WWW:** www.lib.washington.edu **OPAC:** catalog.lib.washington.edu

Founded: 1951 **Type:** Academic **Head:** Pamela A. Mofjeld *Phone:* +1(206) 543-4279 *Email:* mofjeld@u.washington.edu **Staff:** 1.2 Prof. 2 Other **Holdings:** 35,500 books 650 journals **Language of Collection/Services:** English / English **Subjects:** Aquaculture, Fisheries, Food Sciences **Networks:** OCLC **Loan:** In country **Service:** Internationally **Photocopy:** Yes

3826   Seattle, Washington, US
University of Washington
Forest Resources Library
Box 352112
Seattle, Washington 98195-2112
Location: 60 Bloedel Hall **Fax:** +1(206) 543-8375 **Email:** forlib@u.washington.edu **WWW:** www.lib.washington.edu **OPAC:** catalog.lib.washington.edu

Founded: 1920's **Type:** Academic **Head:** Carol C. Green *Phone:* +1(206) 543-2758 *Email:* ccgreen@u.washington.edu **Staff:** 1 Prof. 1.5 Other **Holdings:** 50,000 books 1,100 journals **Language of Collection/Services:** English / English **Subjects:** Forestry, International Trade, Logging, Plant

Pathology, Pulp and Paper Industry, Soil Science, Wildlife Conservation, Wood **Networks:** OCLC **Databases Used:** Comprehensive **Loan:** Internationally **Service:** Internationally **Photocopy:** Yes

3827   Seattle, Washington, US
         University of Washington
         Natural Sciences Library (NSL)
         Box 352900
         Seattle, Washington 98195-2900

Location: Allen Library South, Ground and First Floors
Phone: +1(206) 543-1244 **Fax:** +1(206) 685-1665, 685-3892 **Email:** natsci@u.washington.edu **WWW:** www.lib.washington.edu **OPAC:** catalog.lib.washington.edu **Ariel IP:** 128.95.223.58

Type: Academic **Head:** Nancy Blase *Phone:* +1(206) 685-2132 *Email:* nblase@u.washington.edu **Staff:** 4 Prof. 4 Other **Holdings:** 247,000 books 2,110 journals **Language of Collection/Services:** English / English **Subjects:** Botany, Flora, Molecular Biology, Plant Ecology, Plant Physiology, Taxonomy **Specializations:** Botany (Pacific Northwest) **Databases Used:** Comprehensive **Photocopy:** Yes

3828   Seattle, Washington, US
         University of Washington, Center for Urban
              Horticulture
         Elisabeth C. Miller Library
         Box 354115
         Seattle, Washington 98195

Location: 3501 Northeast 41st Street **Phone:** +1(206) 543-0415 **Fax:** +1(206) 685-2692 **Email:** hortlib@u.washington.edu **WWW:** depts.washington.edu.hortlib

Founded: 1985 **Type:** Academic **Head:** Val Easton *Email:* veast@u.washington.edu **Staff:** 2 Prof. 2 Other **Holdings:** 5,000 books 200 journals **Subjects:** Forestry, Horticulture, Plant Pathology, Soil Science **Networks:** OCLC **Loan:** Inhouse **Service:** Inhouse **Photocopy:** Yes

West Virginia

3829   Morgantown, West Virginia, US
         West Virginia University
         Evansdale Library
         PO Box 6105
         Morgantown, West Virginia 26506-6105

Location: Evansdale Drive **Phone:** +1(304) 293-4696 ext 5113 **Fax:** +1(304) 293-7330 **Email:** illevan@wvu.edu **WWW:** www.wvu.edu **OPAC:** www.libraries.wvu.edu **Ariel IP:** 157.182.199.203

Founded: 1980 **Type:** Academic **Head:** Jo Ann Calzonetti *Phone:* +1(304) 293-4696 ext 5112 *Email:* jcalzone@wvu.edu **Staff:** 6 Prof. 11 Other **Holdings:** 25,000 books 428 journals **Language of Collection/Services:** English **Subjects:** Agriculture (Tropics), Agribusiness, Agricultural Development, Agricultural Economics, Agricultural Engineering, Animal Husbandry, Biotechnology, Crops, Education/ Extension, Entomology, Farming, Fisheries, Food Sciences, Forestry, Horticulture, Plant Pathology, Soil Science, Veterinary Medicine, Water Resources **Networks:**

OCLC **Databases Used:** Comprehensive **Loan:** Internationally **Service:** Internationally **Photocopy:** Yes

Wisconsin

3830   La Crosse, Wisconsin, US
         United States Geological Survey, Upper Midwest
              Environmental Sciences Center (USGS)
         Library
         2630 Fanta Reed Road
         La Crosse, Wisconsin 54603

Location: 2630 Fanta Reed Road **Phone:** +1(608) 783-6451 **WWW:** www.umesc.er.usgs.gov

Type: Government **Head:** Kathy Mannstedt *Phone:* +1(608) 781-6215 *Email:* kathy_mannstedt@usgs.gov **Language of Collection/Services:** English **Subjects:** Animal Husbandry, Fisheries, Veterinary Medicine, Water Resources **Specializations:** Chemicals **Loan:** Internationally **Service:** Internationally **Photocopy:** Yes

3831   Madison, Wisconsin, US
         American Society of Agronomy
         Information Center
         677 South Segoe Road
         Madison, Wisconsin 53711

Phone: +1(608) 273-8090 **Fax:** +1(608) 273-2021 **Email:** headquarters@agronomy.org **WWW:** www.agronomy.org

Type: Association **Head:** Keith R. Schlesinger *Phone:* +1 (608) 273-8090 ext 322 *Email:* kschlesinger@agronomy.org **Subjects:** Agronomy

3832   Madison, Wisconsin, US
         Crop Science Society of America
         Information Center
         677 South Segoe Road
         Madison, Wisconsin 53711

Phone: +1(608) 273-8080 **Fax:** +1(608) 273-2021 **Email:** headquarters@agronomy.org **WWW:** www.crops.org

Type: Association **Head:** Keith R. Schlesinger *Phone:* +1 (608) 273-8090 ext 322 *Email:* kschlesinger@agronomy.org **Subjects:** Crops

3833   Madison, Wisconsin, US
         Kraft Foods, Oscar Mayer Foods Division
         Technology Information Group
         Box 7188
         Madison, Wisconsin 53707-7188

Phone: +1(608) 241-3311 **Fax:** +1(608) 285-4025 **WWW:** www.oscar-mayer.com/om/index.html

Type: Business **Head:** Thomas R. Whitemarsh *Email:* twhitemarsh@kraft.com **Staff:** 1 Prof. 1 Other **Holdings:** 2,000 books 200 journals **Language of Collection/Services:** English **Subjects:** Food Sciences, Meat, Poultry

3834   Madison, Wisconsin, US
         Soil Science Society of America
         Information Center
         677 South Segoe Road
         Madison, Wisconsin 53711

Phone: +1(608) 273-8080 **Fax:** +1(608) 273-2021 **Email:** headquarters@agronomy.org **WWW:** www.soils.org

Type: Association **Head:** Keith R. Schlesinger *Phone:* +1 (608) 273-8090 ext 322 *Email:* kschlesinger@agronomy.org **Subjects:** Soil Science

3835   Madison, Wisconsin, US
United States Department of Agriculture, Forest Service, Forest Products Laboratory (USDA, FS, FPL)
FPL Library
One Gifford Pinchot Drive
Madison, Wisconsin 53705-2398
Phone: +1(608) 231-9441 **Fax:** +1(608) 231-9311 **Email:** library/fpl@fs.fed.us **WWW:** www.fpl.fs.fed.us

Founded: 1910 **Type:** Government **Head:** Julie Blankenburg *Email:* jblanken/fpl@fs.fed.us *Phone:* +1(608) 231-9491 **Staff:** 1 Prof. 2.25 Other **Holdings:** 112,600 books 500 journals **Language of Collection/Services:** English / English **Subjects:** Biotechnology, Forest Products, Pulping, Paper, Wood Preservation, Wood Properties **Specializations:** Mycology, Wood, Wood Anatomy **Networks:** OCLC **Databases Used:** Agricola **Loan:** In country and Canada **Service:** Internationally **Photocopy:** Yes

3836   Madison, Wisconsin, US
University of Wisconsin, Madison
Plant Pathology Memorial Library
584 Russell Labs
1630 Linden Drive
Madison, Wisconsin 53706
Fax: +1(608) 263-2626 **WWW:** www.plantpath.wisc.edu/library.pp **OPAC:** www.library.wisc.edu

Type: Academic **Head:** Patricia J. Herrling *Phone:* +1(608) 262-8698 *Email:* pjh@plantpath.wisc.edu **Staff:** 1 Prof. 2 Other **Holdings:** 70,347 books 83 journals **Language of Collection/Services:** English / English **Subjects:** Entomology, Plant Pathology **Networks:** OCLC **Databases Used:** Comprehensive **Loan:** Inhouse **Service:** Internationally **Photocopy:** Yes

3837   Madison, Wisconsin, US
University of Wisconsin, Madison
Steenbock Memorial Library
550 Babcock Drive
Madison, Wisconsin 53706
Phone: +1(608) 262-9635 **Fax:** +1(608) 263-3221 **Email:** asksteenbock@library.wisc.edu **WWW:** www.library.wisc.edu/libraries/Steenbock **OPAC:** www.library.wisc.edu

Founded: 1890 **Type:** Academic **Head:** Jean Gilbertson *Phone:* +1(608) 263-6864 *Email:* gilbert@doit.wisc.edu, jgilbertson@library.wisc.edu **Staff:** 9 Prof. 9.5 Other **Holdings:** 180,000 books 1,800 journals **Language of Collection /Services:** English / English **Subjects:** Agriculture (Tropics), Agribusiness, Agricultural Development, Agricultural Economics, Agricultural Engineering, Animal Husbandry, Biotechnology, Crops, Education/Extension, Entomology, Farming, Fisheries, Food Sciences, Forestry, Horticulture, Plant Pathology, Soil Science, Veterinary Medicine, Water

Resources **Databases Used:** Agricola; Agris; Biosis; FSTA; Medline **Loan:** In country **Photocopy:** Yes

3838   Madison, Wisconsin, US
University of Wisconsin, Madison, Botany Department
Herbarium Library
158 Birge Hall
430 Lincoln Dr
Madison, Wisconsin 53706-1381
Phone: +1(608) 262-2792 **Fax:** +1(608) 262-7509 **Email:** peberry@facstaff.wisc.edu **WWW:** www.wisc.edu/botany

Founded: 1849 **Type:** Academic **Head:** Dr. Paul E. Berry, Director *Email:* peberry@facstaff.wisc.edu *Phone:* +1(608) 265-9237 **Staff:** 3 Prof. **Holdings:** 123,000 books 30 journals **Language of Collection/Services:** English **Subjects:** Agriculture (Tropics), Classification, Crops, Ethnobotany **Specializations:** Evolution, Grasses, Solanaceae, Plant Succession, Zea Mays **Databases Developed:** WISCOMP - partial catalog of specimen holdings (label data for 47,000 herbarium sheets) **Databases Used:** Comprehensive **Loan:** Inhouse **Service:** Internationally **Photocopy:** Yes

3839   Madison, Wisconsin, US
University of Wisconsin, Madison, Land Tenure Center (LTC)
Information Specialist
1357 University Ave., Rm. 220
Madison, Wisconsin 53715
Phone: +1(608) 262-1240 **Fax:** +1(608) 262-2141 **Email:** ltc-uw@facstaff.wisc.edu **WWW:** www.wisc.edu **OPAC:** www.library.wisc.edu

Founded: 1962 **Type:** Academic **Head:** Beverly R. Phillips *Phone:* +1(608) 262-1240 *Email:* brphilli@facstaff.wisc.edu **Staff:** 1.5 Prof. 2 Other **Holdings:** 65,000 books 150 journals **Language of Collection/Services:** English, Spanish, French, Portuguese, German/English, Spanish **Subjects:** Agriculture (Tropics), Agrarian Reform, Agricultural Development, Agricultural Economics, Farming, Rural Development, Tenure Systems, Women in Agriculture, Women in Development **Networks:** OCLC **Loan:** Internationally **Service:** In country **Photocopy:** Yes

3840   Madison, Wisconsin, US
Wisconsin State Department of Natural Resources (DNR)
Library
Box 7921
Madison, Wisconsin 53707
Location: 101 S. Webster **Phone:** +1(608) 266-8933 **Fax:** +1(608) 264-8943 **Email:** librar@dnr.state.wi.us **WWW:** www.dnr.state.wi.us

Founded: 1978 **Type:** Government **Head:** Erin Baggot *Phone:* +1(608) 267-7479 *Email:* baggoe@dnr.state.wi.us **Staff:** 5 Prof. 4 Other **Holdings:** 30,500 books 380 journals **Language of Collection/Services:** English / English **Subjects:** Agricultural Engineering, Education/Extension, Fisheries, Forestry, Pollution, Soil Science, Water Resources, Wildlife **Specializations:** Environmental Protection, Resource Management **Networks:** OCLC; WISCAT **Data-**

bases Used: Comprehensive **Loan:** Inhouse **Service:** Inhouse **Photocopy:** Yes

3841   Milwaukee, Wisconsin, US
         Milwaukee Public Library, Science and Business
             Division
         Library
         814 West Wisconsin Avenue
         Milwaukee, Wisconsin 53233
Phone: +1(414) 278-3000, 286-3000 **Fax:** +1(414) 278-2137 **WWW:** www.mpl.org **OPAC:** www.mpl.org

Type: Government **Head:** Theodore Cebula *Phone:* +1(414) 278-3247 **Language of Collection/Services:** English **Subjects:** Agribusiness, Agricultural Economics, Agricultural Engineering, Crops, Education/Extension, Farming, Food Sciences, Forestry, Soil Science, Water Resources **Loan:** In country **Service:** In country **Photocopy:** Yes

3842   Milwaukee, Wisconsin, US
         Wisconsin State Department of Natural Resources,
             Southeast District
         Library
         2300 North Martin Luther King Jr. Drive
         Box 12436
         Milwaukee, Wisconsin 53212
Phone: +1(414) 263-8500, 263-8493 **Fax:** +1(414) 263-8606 **WWW:** www.dnr.state.wi.us

Founded: 1979 **Type:** Government **Head:** Kathleen Schultz *Phone:* +1(414) 562-9536 *Email:* schulk@dnr.state.wi.us **Staff:** 1 Prof. **Holdings:** 2,135 books 115 journals **Language of Collection/Services:** English **Subjects:** Air Pollution, Fisheries, Forestry, Solid Wastes, Water Pollution, Water Resources **Loan:** In country **Service:** Internationally **Photocopy:** Yes

3843   River Falls, Wisconsin, US
         University of Wisconsin, River Falls (UWRF)
         Chalmer Davee Library
         410 S. 3rd Street
         River Falls, Wisconsin 54022
Phone: +1(715) 425-3343 **Fax:** +1(715) 425-0609 **Email:** refdesk@uwrf.edu **WWW:** www.uwrf.edu **OPAC:** www.uwrf.edu/library

Founded: 1874 **Type:** Academic **Head:** Christina D. Baum *Phone:* +1(715) 425-3222 *Email:* christina.d.baum@uwrf.edu **Staff:** 8 Prof. 13 Other **Holdings:** 4,100 books 222 journals **Language of Collection/Services:** English **Subjects:** Agriculture (Tropics), Agribusiness, Agricultural Development, Agricultural Economics, Agricultural Engineering, Biotechnology, Crops, Education/Extension, Entomology, Farming, Fisheries, Food Sciences, Forestry, Horticulture, Plant Pathology, Plants, Soil Science, Veterinary Medicine, Water Resources **Specializations:** Animal Husbandry, Cheeses, Horse Diseases, Horse Riding, Horses, Milk Products **Networks:** OCLC **Databases Used:** Comprehensive **Loan:** Internationally **Service:** In country **Photocopy:** Yes

Wyoming

3844   Laramie, Wyoming, US
         United States Department of Agriculture,
             Agricultural Research Service,
             Arthropod-Borne Animal Diseases Research
             Laboratory (USDA, ARS, ABADRL)
         Library
         University Station
         Box 3965
         Laramie, Wyoming 82071-3965
Phone: +1(307) 766-3600 **Fax:** +1(307) 766-3500 **WWW:** www.ars.usda.gov

Founded: 1954 **Type:** Government **Staff:** 11 Prof. 19 Other **Holdings:** 2,000 books **Subjects:** Entomology, Veterinary Medicine **Photocopy:** No

3845   Laramie, Wyoming, US
         University of Wyoming
         Coe Library, Government Documents Division
         PO Box 3334
         Laramie, Wyoming 82071
Location: 13th & Ivinson **Phone:** +1(307) 766-3190 **Fax:** +1(307) 766-3062 **OPAC:** www-lib.uwyo.edu/uwcatplus **WWW:** www.uwyo.edu

Type: Academic **Head:** Keith Cottam *Phone:* +1(307) 766-2070 *Email:* kcottam@uwyo.edu **Staff:** 2 Prof. 3 Other **Holdings:** 70,000 books **Subjects:** Agribusiness, Agricultural Economics, Government Documents (USA) **Loan:** In country **Photocopy:** Yes

3846   Laramie, Wyoming, US
         University of Wyoming
         Science Library
         BioSciences Building
         University Station
         Box 3262
         Laramie, Wyoming 82071
Phone: +1(307) 766-6539 **Fax:** +1(307) 766-6757 **Email:** sciref@uwyo.edu **OPAC:** www-lib.uwyo.edu/uwcatplus **WWW:** www.uwyo.edu

Founded: 1970 **Type:** Academic **Head:** Lori Phillips *Phone:* +1(307) 766-3859 *Email:* lphil@uwyo.edu **Staff:** 4 Prof. 2 Other **Holdings:** 300,000 books 3,100 journals **Language of Collection/Services:** English / English **Subjects:** Agricultural Engineering, Animal Husbandry, Biotechnology, Crops, Fisheries, Food Sciences, Forestry, Horticulture, Plant Pathology, Soil Science, Veterinary Medicine, Water Resources **Databases Developed:** O.A. Beath Selenium Database; available via Internet at www-lib.uwyo.edu/db/BSD **Databases Used:** Comprehensive **Loan:** Internationally **Service:** Inhouse **Photocopy:** Yes

Uruguay

3847   Colonia, Uruguay
         National Institute of Agricultural Research, Albert
             Boerger Experiment Station

Central Library
Ruta 50, Km. 11
Colonia, Colonia
Location: Estación Experimental La Estanzuela **Phone:**
+598(522) 2005 **Fax:** +598(522) 4061 **Email:** bib_le@inia.
org.uy

Non-English Name: Instituto Nacional de Investigación
Agropecuaria, Estación Experimental "Albert Boerger"
(INIA-La Estanzuela), Biblioteca Central **Founded:** 1923
Type: Government **Head:** Lic. Graciela Vila *Phone:*
+598(522) 2005 **Staff:** 1 Prof. 2 Other **Holdings:** 7,000
books 200 journals **Subjects:** Nutrition, Veterinary Medicine **Loan:** In country **Photocopy:** Yes

3848   Montevideo, Uruguay
National Institute of Agricultural Research
Management of Extension and Information
Andes 1365, Piso 12
CP 11100
Montevideo
Fax: +598(2) 923633 **Email:** gabero@inia.org.uy **WWW:**
www.inia.org.uy

Non-English Name: Instituto Nacional de Investigación
Agropecuaria (INIA), Gerencia de Difusión e Información
Type: Government **Networks:** AGRIS

3849   Montevideo, Uruguay
National Institute of Fisheries
Library
CC 1612
Montevideo
Location: Constituyente 1497

Non-English Name: Instituto Nacional de Pesca (INAPE),
Biblioteca **Founded:** 1981 **Type:** Government **Head:** Fer-
nando Cerri *Phone:* +598(2) 43180, 43176 ext 26 **Staff:** 1
Prof. 1 Other **Holdings:** 4,000 books 90 journals **Subjects:**
Aquaculture, Farming, Fish Products, Fisheries, Fishing
Vessels, Food Sciences, Water Resources **Loan:** In country

3850   Montevideo, Uruguay
Rural Association of Uruguay
Library
Av. Uruguay, 872 p. 5 ap. 501
Montevideo
WWW: www.aru.com.uy

Non-English Name: Asociación Rural del Uruguay (ARU),
Biblioteca **Founded:** 1871 **Type:** Association **Head:** Luis
Pedro Sáenz *Phone:* +598(2) 920484 **Staff:** 1 Prof. **Hold-
ings:** 3,000 books 100 journals **Subjects:** Agricultural De-
velopment, Agricultural Economics, Animal Husbandry,
Crops, Farming, Forestry, Horticulture, Plant Pathology,
Soil Science, Veterinary Medicine **Loan:** In country **Photo-
copy:** No

3851   Montevideo, Uruguay
University of the Republic, Agronomy Faculty
Department of Documentation and Library
Av. Garzon, 780
Montevideo

Fax: +598(2) 307-8868 **Email:** biblio@fagro.edu.uy
WWW: www.rau.edu.uy/universidad/bibuni

Non-English Name: Universidad de la República, Facultad
de Agronomía, Departamento de Documentación y Biblioteca **Founded:** 1907 **Type:** Academic **Head:** Lic. María
Nilda García **Staff:** 12 Prof. **Holdings:** 40,000 books **Subjects:** Agriculture (Tropics), Agribusiness, Agricultural Development, Agricultural Economics, Crops, Agricultural
Engineering, Animal Husbandry, Biotechnology, Education/
Extension, Entomology, Farming, Fisheries, Food Sciences,
Forestry, Horticulture, Plant Pathology, Soil Science, Veterinary Medicine, Water Resources **Loan:** In country **Photocopy:** Yes

3852   Montevideo, Uruguay
University of the Republic, Veterinary Faculty
Department of Documentation and Library
Distrito 6 - Casilla No. 16.062
11600 Montevideo
Phone: +598(2) 622-6409 **Fax:** +598(2) 622-6408 **Email:**
postmaster@fvddb.edu.uy **WWW:** www.rau.edu.uy/
universidad **OPAC:** www.rau.edu.uy/universidad/bibuni

Non-English Name: Universidad de la República, Facultad
de Veterinaria, Departamento de Documentación y Biblioteca **Founded:** 1907 **Type:** Academic **Head:** Lic. Beatriz
Saráchaga *Phone:* +598(2) 622-6409 *Email:* bsara@fvddb.
edu.uy **Staff:** 7 Prof. 11 Other **Holdings:** 26,400 books 465
journals **Language of Collection/Services:** Spanish, Eng-
lish/Spanish **Subjects:** Animal Husbandry, Entomology,
Animal Production, Farming, Fisheries, Pastures **Specializations:** Animal Production, Food Sciences, Veterinary Medicine **Databases Developed:** SIBUR - Periodicals and books
in libraries/documentation centers of University of the Republic **Databases Used:** Agricola; Agris; BEASTCD; VET-
CD **Loan:** In country **Service:** In country **Photocopy:** Yes

Uzbekistan

♦3853   Chimlai, Uzbekistan
Sh. Nusaev Karakalpak Scientific Research
   Institute of Agriculture
Library
Karakalpak ASSR
Chimlai 743310
Founded: 1958 **Type:** Government **Holdings:** 36,000 books

3854   Karshy, Uzbekistan
Karshy Engineering Economic Institute (KEEI)
Institute Library
Mustakillic 225
Karshy, Kashkadarya 730000
Phone: +7(522) 35816 **Fax:** +7(522) 32758

Non-English Name: Qarshi muhandislik iqtisodiyot instituti, Institut kutubhonasi **Founded:** 1975 **Type:** Government
Head: Keldiyorova Nora Ravshanovna *Phone:* +7(522)
35514 **Staff:** 1 Prof. **Holdings:** 89,000 books 52 journals
Language of Collection/Services: Uzbek, Russian, English,
German / Uzbek, Russian, English, German **Subjects:** Agricultural Economics, Agricultural Engineering, Food Tech-

nology, Irrigation, Mechanization **Databases Used:** Comprehensive **Loan:** Internationally **Service:** Internationally **Photocopy:** Yes

♦**3855   Kuigan-yar, Uzbekistan**
Andizhan Institute of Cotton Growing
Library
Andizhan District
Andizhan Region
Kuigan-yar 711520

Founded: 1964 **Type:** Academic **Holdings:** 11,000 books **Subjects:** Cotton

♦**3856   Samarkand, Uzbekistan**
All-Union Scientific Research Institute of
Astrakhan Sheep Breeding
Library
K. Marx St., 47
Samarkand 703023

Founded: 1929 **Type:** Government **Holdings:** 111,800 books **Subjects:** Animal Breeding, Sheep

♦**3857   Samarkand, Uzbekistan**
V.V. Kuibyshev Samarkand Agriculture Institute
Library
K. Marx St., 77
Samarkand 703003

Founded: 1930 **Type:** Academic **Holdings:** 126,900 books

3858   Samarkand District, Uzbekistan
Uzbek Scientific Research Veterinary Institute
Library
Tailyak P/O
Samarkand District 704453
Phone: +7(36666) 65630 **Fax:** +7(36666) 65233

Non-English Name: Ozbekiston veterinariya ilmiy tadgigot instituti, kutubxona **Founded:** 1924 **Type:** Government **Head:** Xalikova Zebo **Staff:** 2 Prof. 3 Other **Holdings:** 195,000 books 25 journals **Language of Collection/Services:** Russian / Russian **Subjects:** Veterinary Science **Specializations:** Biology, Immunology, Medicine **Loan:** Do not loan **Photocopy:** Yes

♦**3859   Tashkent, Uzbekistan**
Central Asian Scientific Research Design Institute
of the Food Industry
Library
Navoi St., 9
Tashkent 700011

Founded: 1973 **Type:** Government **Holdings:** 5,000 books **Subjects:** Food Sciences

♦**3860   Tashkent, Uzbekistan**
R.R. Shredera Scientific Production Union of
Horticulture, Viticulture and Winemaking
Library
Glavpochtamt Main Post Office
ab/ya Subscriber Box
Tashkent 700000

Founded: 1898 **Type:** Government **Holdings:** 29,200 books **Subjects:** Horticulture, Vineyards, Winemaking

♦**3861   Tashkent, Uzbekistan**
Tashkent Agriculture Institute
Library
Selkhozinstitute
Tashkent 700183

Founded: 1932 **Type:** Academic **Holdings:** 66,000 books

3862   Tashkent, Uzbekistan
Tashkent Institute of Engineers of Irrigation and
Agricultural Mechanization
Library
Kary-Niyazova St., 39
Tashkent 700000

Founded: 1934 **Type:** Academic **Holdings:** 76,200 books **Subjects:** Agricultural Engineering, Irrigation, Mechanization

♦**3863   Tashkent, Uzbekistan**
Uzbek Scientific Research Institute of Plant
Protection
Scientific Technical Library
UzNIIZR
Tashkent 700140

Former Name: Central Asian Scientific Research Institute of Plant Protection **Founded:** 1958 **Type:** Academic **Holdings:** 7,702 books 130 journals **Language of Collection/Services:** Russian / Uzbek **Subjects:** Plant Protection **Service:** Inhouse **Photocopy:** No

♦**3864   Tashkent, Uzbekistan**
V.D. Shurin Central Asian Scientific Research
Institute of Irrigation
Scientific and Technical Library
Karasu 4
House 11
Tashkent 700187
Phone: +7(3712) 651256 ext 445 **Fax:** +7(3712) 442603

Founded: 1925 **Type:** Government **Staff:** 2 Prof. 1 Other **Holdings:** 105,000 books 30,000 journals **Language of Collection/Services:** Russian / Russian, Uzbek **Subjects:** Environment, Irrigation, Reclamation, Water Resources **Loan:** In country **Service:** In country **Photocopy:** Yes

♦**3865   Tashkent, Uzbekistan**
V.I. Lenin All-Union Academy of Agricultural
Sciences, Central Asian Branch (VASKnNIL)
Central Scientific Agricultural Library
Alley, Paradov 1
Tashkent District
Tashkent 700029
Phone: +7(3712) 394723

Founded: 1929 **Type:** Government **Staff:** 30 Prof. 19 Other **Holdings:** 463,550 books 465 journals **Subjects:** Agribusiness, Agricultural Development, Agricultural Economics, Agricultural Engineering, Animal Husbandry, Biotechnology, Crops, Education/Extension, Entomology, Farming, Food Sciences, Forestry, Horticulture, Plant Pathology, Soil

Science, Veterinary Medicine **Loan:** In country **Photocopy:** Yes

♦**3866   Tashkent District, Uzbekistan**
All-Union Scientific Research Institute of Cotton
Breeding and Seed Production
Library
Salarbes P/O
Ordzhonikidze Region
Tashkent District 702147

Founded: 1920 **Type:** Government **Holdings:** 8,400 books
Subjects: Cotton

♦**3867   Tashkent District, Uzbekistan**
All-Union Scientific Research Institute of Cotton
Growing
Library
Akkavak P/O
Ordzhonikidze Region
Tashkent District 702133

Founded: 1930 **Type:** Government **Holdings:** 20,200 books
Subjects: Cotton

♦**3868   Tashkent District, Uzbekistan**
Central Asian Scientific Research Institute of
Mechanization and Electrification of
Agriculture
Library
Gulbakhor
Yangiyul Region
Tashkent District 702841

Founded: 1927 **Type:** Government **Holdings:** 10,500 books
Subjects: Electrification, Mechanization

♦**3869   Tashkent District, Uzbekistan**
Uzbek Scientific Research Institute of Rice
Library
Avangard P/O
Sredne-Chizchik Region
Tashkent District 702310

Founded: 1930 **Type:** Government **Holdings:** 8,700 books
Subjects: Rice

♦**3870   Tashkent District, Uzbekistan**
Uzbek Scientific Research Institute of Stock
Breeding
Library
Krasnyi P/O
Vodopad
Tashkent District 702145

Founded: 1940 **Type:** Government **Holdings:** 13,200 books
Subjects: Animal Breeding, Livestock

♦**3871   Tashkent District, Uzbekistan**
Uzbek Scientific Research Institute of Vegetable,
Melon and Potato Growing
Library
Kok-Sarai P/O
Tashkent Region
Tashkent District 702015

Founded: 1935 **Type:** Government **Holdings:** 20,100 books
Subjects: Melons, Potatoes, Vegetables

Vanuatu

3872   Espiritu Santo, Vanuatu
Ministry of Agriculture, Livestock, Forestry and
Fisheries, Vanuatu Agricultural Research and
Training Centre
Library
PO Box 231
Espiritu Santo
Location: Saraoutou, Santo **Phone:** +678 36320 **Fax:**
+678 36355 **Email:** labouiss@cirad-vu.orstom.fr

Non-English Name: Centre Agronomique de Recherche et
de Formation du Vanuatu, Bibliothèque **Founded:** 1963
Type: Government

3873   Port Vila, Vanuatu
Department of Agriculture and Horticulture,
Information Section
Vanuatu National Agricultural Library (VNAL)
Private Mail Bag 040
Port Vila
Phone: +678 22432, 23130 **Fax:** +678 25265 **Email:**
agriculture@vanuatu.pactok.net

Founded: 1983 **Type:** Government **Staff:** 2 Prof. 3 Other
Holdings: 300 books 50 journals **Language of Collec-
tion/Services:** English **Subjects:** Agricultural Develop-
ment, Animal Production, Crop Production, Plants, Rural
Sociology, Training **Networks:** AGRIS **Loan:** In country
Photocopy: No

3874   Port Vila, Vanuatu
Department of Forestry, Information Section
Library
Private Mail Bag 064
Port Vila
Phone: +678 23171 **Fax:** +678 25051 **Email:** vdof@
pactok.peg.apc.org

Type: Government **Head:** Ms. Lesale Hamish **Subjects:**
Forestry

3875   Port Vila, Vanuatu
Department of Livestock
Library
Private Mail Bag 095
Port Vila
Location: Tagabe, Efate **Phone:** +678 23519 **Fax:** +678
23185 **Email:** laefstok@vanuatu.com.vu

Type: Government **Subjects:** Livestock

3876   Port Vila, Vanuatu
Foundation for the Peoples of the South Pacific
International (FSPI)
Library
PO Box 951
Port Vila

Phone: +678 22915 **Fax:** +678 24510 **Email:** fspi@wantok.org.vu

Type: Non-government

Venezuela

3877 Barinas, Venezuela
National Experimental University of Los Llanos
    Occidentales Ezequiel Zamora
Central Library
Avenida 23 de Enero UNELLEZ
Alto Barinas
Barinas

Email: mvalero@saman.unellez.edu.ve **WWW:** www.unellez.edu.ve

Non-English Name: Universidad Nacional Experimental de los Llanos Occidentales Ezequiel Zamora, Biblioteca Central **Founded:** 1975 **Type:** Academic **Staff:** 3 Prof. 17 Other **Holdings:** 8,000 books 2,000 journals **Loan:** Inhouse **Photocopy:** No

3878 Barquisimeto, Venezuela
Fundación para el Desarrollo de la Región Centro
    Occidental de Venezuela (FUDECO)
Biblioteca Técnica Científica Centralizada
Apdo 254
Barquisimeto, Lara

Location: Edificio Fudeco, Av. Liberatador Diagonal con el Complejo Ferial **Phone:** +58(51) 538022 ext 22 **Email:** fudeco@cantv.net

Founded: 1965 **Type:** Government **Head:** Cecilia Vega Febres *Phone:* +58(51) 538022 **Staff:** 2 Prof. 6 Other **Holdings:** 40,000 books 3,000 journals **Language of Collection/Services:** Spanish / Spanish **Subjects:** Agricultural Economics, Agricultural Planning **Networks:** CD Universidad de Colima (México) **Databases Developed:** Documents produced by FUDECO **Loan:** In country **Service:** Internationally **Photocopy:** Yes

3879 Caracas, Venezuela
Ministerio de Agricultura y Cría (MAC)
Biblioteca Central "Alberto Adriani"
Parque Central Torre Este Piso 1
Caracas, Distrito Federal

Phone: +58(2) 509-0281, 509-0522

Founded: 1936 **Type:** Government **Staff:** 2 Prof. 10 Other **Holdings:** 80,000 books **Subjects:** Fisheries **Loan:** In country **Photocopy:** Yes

3880 Caracas, Venezuela
Venezuelan Institute of Scientific Research
Marcel Roche Library
Apdo 21827
Caracas 1020-A

Location: Carretera Panamericana Km 11, Altos de Pipe, Estado Miranda **Phone:** +58(2) 504-1236/7, 504-1282 **Fax:** +58(2) 504-1423 **Email:** bibliotk@ivic.ivic.ve **WWW:** www.ivic.ve

Non-English Name: Instituto Venezolano de Investigaciones Científicas (IVIC), Biblioteca Marcel Roche **Founded:** 1959 **Type:** Government **Staff:** 10 Prof. 21 Other **Holdings:** 6,500 journals **Language of Collection/Services:** English **Subjects:** Biotechnology, Entomology, Food Sciences, Plant Pathology, Soil Science **Databases Used:** Comprehensive **Loan:** In country **Service:** In country **Photocopy:** Yes

3881 Los Guaritos, Venezuela
Universidad de Oriente
Biblioteca de Agronomía y Zootecnia
Campus Universitario
Los Guaritos, Monagas 6203

WWW: www.monagas.udo.edu.ve

Founded: 1962 **Type:** Academic **Staff:** 1 Prof. 7 Other **Holdings:** 13,008 books 429 journals **Subjects:** Biology, Agricultural Engineering, Rural Economy, Rural Sociology **Loan:** In country

3882 Maracaibo, Venezuela
Corporation of Development of the Zuliana
    Region
Information and Documentation Center
Av. 4 con calle 83, Edif. Corpozulia, P.B.
Maracaibo, Zulia

Fax: +58(61) 920663 **Email:** cid@corpozulia.org **WWW:** www.corpozulia.org

Non-English Name: Corporación de Desarrollo de la Región Zuliana (CORPOZULIA), Centro de Información y Documentación **Founded:** 1971 **Type:** Government **Head:** Leonardo Rafael Chavez Proaño *Phone:* +58(61) 921811, 921840 ext 2303/4 *Email:* cid@corpozulia.org **Staff:** 2 Prof. 5 Other **Holdings:** 12,645 books 12 journals **Language of Collection/Services:** Spanish **Subjects:** Animal Husbandry, Crops, Farming, Fisheries, Food Sciences **Databases Developed:** Citations to inhouse technical reports **Loan:** In country **Photocopy:** Yes

3883 Maracaibo, Venezuela
University of Zulia, Agronomy Faculty
Library
Apdo 526
Maracaibo, Zulia

Location: Av. 16 (Guajira) Núcleo Agropecuario **WWW:** www.luz.ve

Non-English Name: Universidad del Zulia, Facultad de Agronomía, Biblioteca **Founded:** 1960 **Type:** Academic **Staff:** 2 Prof. 5 Other **Holdings:** 15,500 books 110 journals **Subjects:** Agricultural Economics, Agricultural Engineering, Animal Production, Crop Production, Entomology **Loan:** In country **Photocopy:** Yes

3884 Maracay, Venezuela
Central University of Venezuela, Agronomy
    Faculty
Celestino Bonfanti Library
Apdo 4579
Maracay, Aragua 2101

Location: Avenida Universidad, Vía El Limón **Phone:** +58 (43) 22242 **Fax:** +58(43) 25204 **WWW:** www.sagi.ucv. edu.ve

Non-English Name: Universidad Central de Venezuela, Facultad de Agronomía (UCV), Biblioteca Celestino Bonfanti **Founded:** 1953 **Type:** Academic **Staff:** 1 Prof. 11 Other **Holdings:** 15,000 books 300 journals **Language of Collection/Services:** Spanish **Subjects:** Comprehensive **Specializations:** Agricultural Meteorology **Databases Developed:** MICROISIS - Staff publications **Loan:** In country **Photocopy:** No

3885   Maracay, Venezuela
         Central University of Venezuela, School of
              Veterinary Science
         Library
         Apdo 4563
         Maracay, Aragua
Location: Maracay 2 KO - Edo. Aragua **WWW:** bibliovet. veter.ucv.ve, www.sagi.ucv.edu.ve

Non-English Name: Universidad Central de Venezuela, Facultad de Ciencias Veterinarias (UCV, FCV), Biblioteca **Founded:** 1950 **Head:** Lic. Dora Nuñez de Castro *Phone:* +58(43) 20301/5 ext 223, 388 **Staff:** 1 Prof. 5 Other **Holdings:** 5,400 books 250 journals **Subjects:** Veterinary Science **Loan:** Do not loan **Photocopy:** Yes

3886   Maracay, Venezuela
         Centro Nacional de Investigaciones Agropecuarias
              (CENIAP)
         Servicios de Biblioteca y Documentación
         Apartado 4653
         Maracay 2101, Aragua
Location: Edificio 7, Zona Universitaria vía El Limón **Phone:** +58(43) 454108 **Fax:** +58(43) 454320 **Email:** uaid @reacciun.ve **OPAC:** bav.fonaiap.gov.ve

Type: Government **Head:** Lic. Aida Rivero A. **Networks:** AGRIS

3887   Merida, Venezuela
         University of Los Andes, Faculty of Forestry and
              Environmental Sciences
         Library
         Vía Chorros de Milla
         Merida, Merida 5101
Phone: +58(74) 401501 **Fax:** +58(74) 401503 **WWW:** www.serbi.ula.ve

Non-English Name: Universidad de Los Andes, Facultad de Ciencias Forestales y Ambientales, Biblioteca **Founded:** 1952 **Type:** Academic **Staff:** 1 Prof. 7 Other **Holdings:** 18 journals **Subjects:** Environment, Forestry, Plant Pathology, Plant Protection, Soil Science **Loan:** Do not loan **Photocopy:** Yes

3888   Rubio, Venezuela
         National Foundation of Agricultural Investigation,
              Agricultural Research Center of Tachira State
         Simon Bolivar Library
         Rubio, Tachira

Phone: +58(76) 66783, 66354 **WWW:** www.fonaiap.gov. ve

Non-English Name: Fondo Nacional de Investigaciones Agropecuarias, Centro de Investigaciones Agropecuarias del Estado Táchira (FONAIAP, CIAE Táchira), Biblioteca Simón Bolívar **Type:** Government **Staff:** 1 Prof. **Holdings:** 600 books 20 journals **Subjects:** Cereals, Coffee, Fruits, Legumes, Root Crops, Tubers, Vegetables **Loan:** Inhouse **Photocopy:** No

3889   Yaritagua, Venezuela
         National Foundation of Agricultural Investigation,
              Agricultural Research Center of Yaracuy
              State
         Library
         El Rodeo Km 3
         Yaritagua, Yaracuy
Fax: +58(51) 823591, 820679 **Email:** ciaey@reacciun.ve **WWW:** www.fonaiap.gov.ve

Non-English Name: Fondo Nacional de Investigaciones Agropecuarias, Centro de Investigaciones Agropecuarias del Estado Yaracuy (FONAIAP, CIAE Yaracuy), Biblioteca **Former Name:** Estación Experimental Yaracuy **Founded:** 1955 **Type:** Government **Head:** Ramona del C. Rivero Méndez *Email:* ciaey@reacciun.ve *Phone:* +58(51) 82359, 820679 **Staff:** 1 Prof. **Holdings:** 300 books 100 journals **Language of Collection/Services:** Spanish / Spanish **Subjects:** Legumes, Maize, Plantago, Root Crops, Soil, Sorghum **Specializations:** Sugarcane **Databases Used:** Agris **Loan:** Do not loan **Photocopy:** No

Vietnam

3890   Hanoi, Vietnam
         Ministry of Agriculture and Rural Development
              (MARD)
         Information Centre for Agriculture and Rural
              Development (ICARD)
         2 Ngoc Ha St. Ba Dinh Dist.
         Hanoi
Phone: +84(4) 823-0381 **Fax:** +84(4) 823-0381 **Email:** icard@hn.vnn.vn

Non-English Name: Bo Nong nghiep va Phat trien Nong thon (BoNN&PTNT), Trung tam Thong tin Nong nghiep va Phat trien Nong thon **Former Name:** Ministry of Agriculture and Food Industry (MAFI), Information Centre for Agriculture and Food Industry (ICAFI), Library of Agriculture and Food Industry (LAFI) **Type:** Academic **Head:** Mr. Nguyen Tien San *Phone:* +84(4) 823-0381 *Email:* icard@ hn.vnn.vn **Staff:** 4 Prof. 10 Other **Holdings:** 45,000 books 400 journals **Language of Collection/Services:** Vietnamese, English, Russian, French/Vietnamese, English, Russian, French **Subjects:** Agriculture (Tropics), Agricultural Engineering, Animal Husbandry, Biotechnology, Crops, Entomology, Farming, Fisheries, Food Sciences, Forestry, Horticulture, Plant Pathology, Plants, Soil Science, Veterinary Medicine, Water Resources **Networks:** AGRIS **Databases Developed:** Bibliographic and factual databases on Vietnamese agriculture and food industries **Databases**

Used: Agris; CABCD **Loan:** In country **Service:** Internationally **Photocopy:** Yes

Virgin Islands

3891 St. Thomas, Virgin Islands
University of the Virgin Islands
Ralph M. Paiewonsky Library
2 John Brewer's Bay
St. Thomas 00802-9990
Phone: +1(340) 692-1369 **Fax:** +1(340) 639-1365 **Email:** sbarnet@uvi.edu **WWW:** library.uvi.edu/index.htm
OPAC: telnet://bertha.uvi.edu (login: vtpac)

Former Name: College of the Virgin Islands **Founded:** 1962 **Type:** Academic **Head:** Jennifer Jackson *Phone:* +1 (340) 693-4131 *Email:* jjackso@uvi.edu **Staff:** 3.5 Prof. 4 Other **Holdings:** 750 books 12 journals **Language of Collection/Services:** English/English **Networks:** OCLC **Loan:** Internationally **Service:** In country **Photocopy:** Yes

3892 St. Croix, Virgin Islands
University of the Virgin Islands (UVI)
St. Croix Campus Library
RR 02, Box 10,000
Kingshill
St. Croix 00850
Fax: +1(340) 692-4135 **WWW:** www.uvi.edu **OPAC:** telnet://bertha.uvi.edu (login: xpac)

Former Name: College of the Virgin Islands **Founded:** 1962 **Type:** Academic **Head:** Jennifer Jackson *Phone:* +1 (340) 692-4130 *Email:* jjackso@uvi.edu **Staff:** 2 Prof. 3 Other **Holdings:** 31,000 books 320 journals **Language of Collection/Services:** English / English **Subjects:** Animal Husbandry, Crops, Education/Extension, Fish Culture, Hydroponics **Networks:** OCLC **Loan:** Internationally **Service:** Internationally **Photocopy:** Yes

Yemen

3893 Sana'a, Yemen
Ministry of Agriculture and Water Resources
Agricultural Research Documentation Centre
Al-Kuwait Street
PO Box 2805
Sana'a

Type: Government **Networks:** AGRIS

Zambia

3894 Chilanga, Zambia
Ministry of Agriculture, Food and Fisheries,
    Mount Makulu Central Agricultural Research
    Station
Library
Private Bag 7
Chilanga

Phone: +260(1) 278655, 278008 ext 111 **Fax:** +260(1) 278930

Founded: 1953 **Type:** Government **Staff:** 1 Prof. 4 Other **Holdings:** 35,000 books 200 journals **Language of Collection/Services:** English **Subjects:** Comprehensive **Networks:** AGRIS **Databases Developed:** Zambia--10,000 non-conventional research documents **Loan:** In country **Service:** Internationally **Photocopy:** Yes

♦**3895 Choma, Zambia**
Ministry of Agriculture, Food and Fisheries,
    Mochipapa Research Station
Library
PO Box 630090
Choma
Phone: +260() 21504

Type: Research **Staff:** 4 Prof. 12 Other **Language of Collection/Services:** English **Photocopy:** Yes

3896 Kabwe, Zambia
Pan African Institute for Development (PAID)
Library and Documentation Centre
Box 80448
Kabwe, Central Province
Location: Mukonchi Road, Buyantanshi Compound
Phone: +260(5) 223651 **Fax:** +260(5) 223451

Founded: 1980 **Type:** International **Staff:** 1 Prof. 3 Other **Holdings:** 600 books 10 journals **Language of Collection/Services:** English **Subjects:** Agribusiness, Agricultural Economics, Agricultural Engineering, Animal Husbandry, Crops **Specializations:** Economic Development, Social Development **Loan:** Inhouse **Photocopy:** Yes

♦**3897 Kalulushi, Zambia**
Kalulushi Farm College (KAFACO)
Library
PO Box 260005
Kalulushi
Phone: +260() 733306

Former Name: Mindolo Demonstration Farm **Type:** Academic **Staff:** 6 Prof. 9 Other **Holdings:** 153 books 97 journals **Language of Collection/Services:** English **Subjects:** Animal Husbandry, Animal Power, Crops, Farm Machinery, Farm Management, Soil Science **Photocopy:** No

3898 Kalulushi, Zambia
Zambia Centre for Horticultural Training, Chapula
    (ZCHT-Chapula)
Library
PO Box 260525
Kalulushi

Former Name: Chapula Irrigation Scheme **Type:** Government **Head:** D.F. Mwansasu *Phone:* +263(2) 733007 **Staff:** 5 Prof. 6 Other **Language of Collection/Services:** English / English **Subjects:** Floriculture, Fruits, Horticulture, Vegetables **Loan:** In country **Service:** In country **Photocopy:** Yes

◆**3899 Kapirimposhi, Zambia**
Department of Technical Education and
    Vocational Training, Nkumbi International
    College
Library
Private Bag 5
Kapirimposhi
Phone: +260(5) 362085

Founded: 1966 **Type:** Academic **Staff:** 30 Prof. 45 Other
Holdings: 5,000 books **Language of Collection/Services:**
English / English **Photocopy:** Yes

3900 Katete, Zambia
Katete Centre for Agricultural Marketing
    (KCAM)
Library
PO Box 550099
Katete

Former Name: Provincial Cooperative Training Centre
(PCTC) **Founded:** 1980 **Type:** Government **Staff:** 1 Other
Holdings: 700 books **Language of Collection/Services:**
English **Subjects:** Agribusiness, Animal Husbandry, Crops
Specializations: Business Law, Marketing, Management
Photocopy: No

3901 Lusaka, Zambia
Central Veterinary Research Institute (CVRI)
Library
Box 33980
Lusaka
Location: Balmoral Some 25KM south-west of Lusaka
Fax: +260(1) 233444 **Email:** cvri@zamnet.zm

Former Name: Central Veterinary Research Station **Found-
ed:** 1928 **Type:** Government **Head:** Mr. Jacob G. Chirwa
Phone: +260(1) 230622 *Email:* cvri@zamnet.zm **Staff:** 1
Prof. 2 Other **Holdings:** 9,000 books 3 journals **Language of
Collection/Services:** English **Subjects:** Agriculture (Trop-
ics), Animal Husbandry, Entomology **Specializations:** Vet-
erinary Medicine **Photocopy:** Yes **Service:** Inhouse **Loan:**
In country

◆**3902 Lusaka, Zambia**
Evelyn Hone College of Applied Arts and
    Commerce
Library
PO Box 30029
Lusaka
Location: Church Road

Founded: 1963 **Type:** Academic **Staff:** 1 Prof. 6 Other
Holdings: 100 books **Subjects:** Livestock **Loan:** In country
Photocopy: No

3903 Lusaka, Zambia
National Institute for Scientific and Industrial
    Research (NISIR)
Information Services Unit (ISU)
PB 310158
15302 Chelston
Lusaka

Location: International Airport Road **Fax:** +260(1) 283533
Email: unepzam@zamnet.zm

Former Name: National Council for Scientific Research
(NCSR), Documentation and Scientific Information Centre
(DSIC) **Founded:** 1968 **Head:** W.C. Mushipi *Phone:* +260
(1) 281081 **Staff:** 4 Prof. 15 Other **Holdings:** 10,000 books
50 journals **Language of Collection/Services:** English **Sub-
jects:** Animal Feeding, Animal Health, Animal Husbandry,
Entomology, Food Technology, Pesticides, Plant Breeding,
Plant Ecology, Plants, Silviculture, Water Resources **Loan:**
In country **Service:** In country **Photocopy:** Yes

3904 Lusaka, Zambia
Natural Resources Development College (NRDC)
Library
PO Box CH 310099
Chelston
Lusaka
Phone: +260(1) 224610, 283676

Founded: 1964 **Type:** Academic **Head:** Mrs. D.M. Sichula
Phone: +260(1) 224610 ext 33 **Staff:** 1 Prof. 4 Other **Hold-
ings:** 780,000 books 9 journals **Language of Collection/
Services:** English / English **Subjects:** Agribusiness, Agri-
cultural Engineering, Animal Husbandry, Crops, Entomol-
ogy, Extension, Fisheries, Food Sciences, Water Resources
Engineering **Loan:** Internationally **Service:** Internationally
Photocopy: Yes

3905 Lusaka, Zambia
University of Zambia
Library
PO Box 32379
Lusaka
Location: Great East Road **Phone:** +260(1) 250845 **Fax:**
+260(1) 250845 **Email:** library@unza.zm **WWW:** www.
unza.zm **OPAC:** www.unza.zm/library/library.htm

Founded: 1966 **Type:** Academic **Head:** Dr. Hudwell Mwa-
calimba *Email:* hmwacalimba@library.unza.zm **Staff:** 41
Prof. 56 Other **Holdings:** 5,000 books 70 journals **Subjects:**
Agricultural Economics, Agricultural Engineering, Animal
Husbandry, Crops, Soil Science **Loan:** Internationally **Pho-
tocopy:** Yes

3906 Lusaka, Zambia
University of Zambia
Veterinary Medicine Library
PO Box 32379
Lusaka
Phone: +260(1) 250845 **Fax:** +260(1) 250753, 253952
Email: library@unza.zm **WWW:** www.unza.zm **OPAC:**
www.unza.zm/library/library.htm

Founded: 1966 **Type:** Academic **Head:** Likukela Walusiku,
Acting Head *Email:* lwalusiku@library.unza.zm **Subjects:**
Veterinary Medicine

◆**3907 Masaiti, Zambia**
Masaiti Farm Institute (MFI)
Library
PO Box 90049
Masaiti, Luanshya

Phone: +260(2) 760026

Type: Training **Staff:** 12 Other **Holdings:** 2,000 books 500 journals **Language of Collection/Services:** English **Subjects:** Agricultural Economics, Agricultural Engineering, Animal Husbandry, Crops, Dairy Farming, Extension, Farm Management, Food Storage, Horticulture, Irrigation, Nutrition, Pests, Pigs, Poultry, Rabbits, Soil Science, Veterinary Medicine **Loan:** Inhouse **Service:** Inhouse **Photocopy:** No

♦**3908 Mazabuka, Zambia**
Zambia Institute of Animal Health
Library
PO Box 670237
Mazabuka

Location: Mazabuka Research Station **Phone:** +260() 30600, 30796

Type: Research **Staff:** 4 Prof. 6 Other **Language of Collection/Services:** English **Subjects:** Animal Husbandry **Photocopy:** No

3909 Monze, Zambia
Ministry of Agriculture, Food and Fisheries,
    Zambia College of Agriculture - Monze
Library
PO Box 660053
Monze

Phone: +260(32) 50544

Former Name: Ministry of Agriculture and Water Development (MAWD) **Founded:** 1947 **Type:** Government **Staff:** 8 Prof. 24 Other **Holdings:** 9,796 books 200 journals **Language of Collection/Services:** English / English **Subjects:** Agricultural Economics, Agricultural Engineering, Animal Husbandry, Botany, Crops, Extension, Zoology **Loan:** Inhouse **Service:** Inhouse **Photocopy:** Yes

3910 Ndola, Zambia
Northern Technical College (NORTEC)
Library
PO Box 250093
Ndola

Location: Chela Road **Fax:** +260(2) 680595

Founded: 1960 **Type:** Academic **Head:** P. Nabombe *Phone:* +260(2) 680141 **Staff:** 1 Prof. 3 Other **Holdings:** 18,000 books 10 journals **Language of Collection/Services:** English / English **Subjects:** Chemical Technology, Chemistry, Engineering, Mathematics, Physics **Loan:** Inhouse **Service:** Inhouse **Photocopy:** No

3911 Ndola, Zambia
Tropical Diseases Research Centre (TDRC)
Library and Information Services
PB 71769
Ndola

Phone: +260(2) 610961/4 **Fax:** +260(2) 612837, 614487 **Email:** tdrc@zamnet.zm

Founded: 1977 **Staff:** 2 Prof. 3 Other **Holdings:** 20,000 books 50 journals **Language of Collection/Services:** English **Subjects:** Animal Health, Human Nutrition, Malnutrition, Statistics, Trace Elements **Loan:** Inhouse **Service:** Internationally **Photocopy:** Yes

Zimbabwe

♦**3912 Bulawayo, Zimbabwe**
Ministry of Lands and Agriculture, Department of
    Research and Specialist Services, Matopos
    Research Station (DRSS)
Library
Private Bag K5137
Bulawayo

Phone: +263(83) 8212

Former Name: Ministry of Lands, Agriculture and Water Development **Founded:** 1935 **Type:** Government **Staff:** 11 Prof. 12 Other **Holdings:** 1,500 books 24 journals **Language of Collection/Services:** English / English, Ndebele **Subjects:** Animal Breeding, Animal Husbandry, Animal Nutrition, Range Management, Ruminants **Loan:** In country **Photocopy:** Yes

3913 Bulawayo, Zimbabwe
National Free Library of Zimbabwe (NFLZ)
PO Box 1773
Bulawayo

Location: 12th Avenue Ext. **Phone:** +263(9) 62359, 69827 **Fax:** +263(9) 77662

Former Name: National Free Library of Rhodesia **Founded:** 1945 **Type:** Academic **Staff:** 5 Prof. 20 Other **Holdings:** 95,000 books 132 journals **Language of Collection/Services:** English **Subjects:** Agriculture (Tropics), Agricultural Development, Agricultural Economics, Biotechnology, Entomology, Farming, Forestry, Horticulture, Veterinary Medicine **Loan:** Internationally **Photocopy:** Yes

3914 Chipinge, Zimbabwe
Ministry of Lands and Agriculture, Department of
    Research and Specialist Services, Chipinge
    Coffee Research Station (MOLA, DRSS)
Library
PO Box 61
Chipinge

Phone: +263(24) 127 2476 **Fax:** +263(27) 2442 **Email:** rsscoffee@mango.zw

Former Name: Ministry of Lands, Agriculture and Rural Resettlement **Founded:** 1964 **Type:** Government **Head:** Dumisani Kutywayo *Email:* rsscoffee@mango.zw *Phone:* +263(24) 127 2476 **Staff:** 3 Prof. **Holdings:** 132 books 20 journals **Language of Collection/Services:** English / English **Subjects:** Coffee, Insect Pests, Plant Diseases, Plants **Loan:** Inhouse **Service:** Inhouse **Photocopy:** Yes

3915 Chipinge, Zimbabwe
Ministry of Lands and Agriculture, Department of
    Research and Specialist Services, Save Valley
    Experiment Station (MOLA, DRSS)
Library
P Bag 2037
Chipinge

Phone: +263(24) 127-239129

Former Name: Ministry of Lands, Agriculture and Rural Resettlement **Type:** Research **Head:** *Phone:* +263(24) 221

Staff: 2 Prof. 38 Other **Language of Collection/Services:** English / English **Subjects:** Agricultural Economics, Crops, Entomology, Soil **Loan:** Inhouse **Service:** Inhouse **Photocopy:** Yes

♦**3916 Chiredzi, Zimbabwe**
     Ministry of Lands and Agriculture, Department of Research and Specialist Services, Chisumbanje Experiment Station (MOLA, DRSS)
     Library
     P Bag 7022
     Chiredzi
Phone: +263(31) 232924

Former Name: Ministry of Lands, Agriculture and Rural Resettlement **Type:** Government **Language of Collection/Services:** English **Subjects:** Agricultural Engineering, Crops, Horticulture, Plant Protection

3917 Chiredzi, Zimbabwe
     Ministry of Lands and Agriculture, Department of Research and Specialist Services, Chiredzi Research Station (MOLA, DRSS)
     Lowveld Research Stations Library (LRSL)
     PO Box 97
     Chiredzi
Phone: +263(31) 2397 **Email:** rsschiredzi@mango.zw

Former Name: Ministry of Lands, Agriculture and Rural Resettlement **Founded:** 1966 **Type:** Government **Head:** Mr. J. Bansa *Phone:* +263(31) 2397/8 **Staff:** 2 Other **Holdings:** 900 books 58 journals **Language of Collection/Services:** English **Subjects:** Agricultural Development, Agriculture (Tropics), Horticulture, Plant Protection, Water Resources, Soil **Specializations:** Agricultural Economics, Agricultural Engineering, Crops, Food Sciences, Nutrition **Databases Used:** Agris; CABCD **Loan:** In country **Photocopy:** Yes

♦**3918 Harare, Zimbabwe**
     Ministry of Information, Posts, and Telecommunications
     Library
     Linquenda House
     Box 8150, Causeway
     Harare
Location: 10th Floor Linquenda House, Baker Avenue cnr First Street, Rooms 1005 & 1006 **Phone:** +263(4) 703894

Former Name: Ministry of Information **Founded:** 1961 **Type:** Government **Staff:** 1 Prof. 1 Other **Holdings:** 100 books 15 journals **Language of Collection/Services:** English **Subjects:** Agribusiness, Agricultural Development, Agricultural Engineering, Beekeeping, Farm Management, Crops, Farming, Fisheries, Forestry, Horticulture, Irrigation, Pest Control, Pest Management, Plant Protection, Small Farms, Soil Conservation, Soil Science, Veterinary Medicine, Water Resources **Loan:** Do not loan **Service:** Inhouse **Photocopy:** Yes

3919 Harare, Zimbabwe
     Ministry of Lands and Agriculture (MOLA)
     Central Library (CL)
     Bag 7701

     Causeway
     Harare
Location: No. 1 Borrowdale Road **Phone:** +263(4) 706081 /9 **Fax:** +263(4) 734646 **Email:** nlccp@zamserv.zamtel.zm

Founded: 1906 **Type:** Government **Head:** Mr. Arthur Mangau (Acting) *Phone:* +263(4) 706081/9 ext185 **Staff:** 2 Prof. 4 Other **Holdings:** 8,470 books 500 journals **Language of Collection/Services:** English / English **Subjects:** Comprehensive **Specializations:** Agroforestry, Animal Production, Beef Production, Beekeeping, Crop Production, Dairy Farming, Floriculture, Marketing **Networks:** AGRIS **Databases Developed:** AGRIN - National Agricultural Information Database contains bibliographic information on all publications produced in Zimbabwe; CARIN - National Agricultural Information Database of on-going research projects in Zimbabwe; UNLIST - Periodical Index; PULIST - bibliographic information of photocopies of journal articles **Databases Used:** Agricola; CABCD; TROPAG & RURAL; Agris **Loan:** Internationally **Service:** Internationally **Photocopy:** Yes

3920 Harare, Zimbabwe
     Ministry of Lands and Agriculture, Department of Agricultural, Technical and Extension Services, Training Branch (MOLA, AGRITEX)
     Publications Bureau
     PO Box 8117, Causeway
     Harare
Location: Central House, Central Avenue **Phone:** +263(4) 794381

Former Name: Ministry of Lands, Agriculture and Rural Resettlement, CONEX Training Branch, Publications Bureau **Founded:** 1971 **Type:** Government **Staff:** 1 Prof. 3 Other **Holdings:** 5,800 books 52 journals **Language of Collection/Services:** English **Subjects:** Agriculture (Tropics), Animal Husbandry, Crops, Education/Extension, Farming, Fisheries, Food Sciences, Forestry, Water Resources, Land Use **Specializations:** Extension, Field Crops, Horticulture **Loan:** In country **Service:** Internationally **Photocopy:** Yes

3921 Harare, Zimbabwe
     Ministry of Lands and Agriculture, Department of Research and Specialist Services (MOLA, DRSS)
     Information Services
     Fifth Street Extension
     PB 8108
     Causeway
     Harare
Phone: +263(4) 704531

Former Name: Ministry of Lands, Agriculture and Rural Resettlement **Type:** Government **Staff:** 2 Prof. 4 Other **Holdings:** 2,520 books 13 journals **Subjects:** Animal Production, Crop Production, Plant Protection

3922 Harare, Zimbabwe
Ministry of Lands and Agriculture, Department of
Research and Specialist Services (DRSS)
SRGH Library
PO Box CY550, Causeway
Harare

Location: Downie Avenue, Alexandra Park **Phone:** +263
(4) 744170, 725313 **Fax:** +263(4) 708938 **Email:** srgh@
cst.co.zw

Founded: 1923 **Type:** Government **Head:** Maxwell Mah-
lunge *Phone:* +263(4) 725313, 708938 *Email:* srgh@cst.co.
zw **Staff:** 1 Other **Holdings:** 4,694 books 98 journals **Language of Collection/Services:** Latin / English **Subjects:**
Botany, Herbaria, Plant Ecology, Plants, Taxonomy **Specializations:** Flora Zambesiaca **Databases Developed:** Specimen Database; Species Database **Loan:** Internationally
Service: Internationally **Photocopy:** Yes

♦3923 Harare, Zimbabwe
Ministry of Lands and Agriculture, Department of
Research and Specialist Services, Plant
Protection Research Institute (MOLA, DRSS,
PPRI)
Library
5th Street Extension
PB 8100
Harare
Phone: +263(4) 704531

Former Name: Ministry of Lands, Agriculture and Rural
Resettlement **Founded:** 1909 **Holdings:** 3,500 books 25
journals **Subjects:** Entomology, Pest Control, Plant Protection, Plant Diseases, Stored Products

♦3924 Harare, Zimbabwe
Ministry of Lands and Agriculture (MOLA)
Pig Industry Board (PIB)
HG 297 Highlands
Harare

Location: Cromlet Road (Off Harare - Mutoko Road),
Arcturus **Phone:** +263(74) 394 **Fax:** +263(74) 395

Former Name: Ministry of Lands, Agriculture and Rural
Resettlement **Founded:** 1952 **Type:** Parastatal **Staff:** 3 Prof.
8 Other **Holdings:** 100 books 6 journals **Language of Col-
lection/Services:** English **Subjects:** Pigs **Photocopy:** Yes

3925 Harare, Zimbabwe
Ministry of Lands and Agriculture, Veterinary
Research Laboratory (MOLA)
Veterinary Research Library
PO Box 8101
Causeway
Harare
Phone: +263(4) 705885 ext 117 **Fax:** +263(4) 707952
Email: ncube@healthnet.zw

Former Name: Ministry of Lands, Agriculture and Rural
Resettlement, Veterinary Diagnostic Research Branch
Founded: 1977 **Type:** Government **Staff:** 1 Prof. 1 Other
Holdings: 1,877 books 28 journals **Language of Collection/**
Services: English **Subjects:** Animal Husbandry, Computer
Science, Entomology, Farming, Fisheries, Poultry, Veteri-

nary Medicine **Loan:** Internationally **Service:**
Internationally **Photocopy:** Yes

3926 Harare, Zimbabwe
Public Service Commission, Domboshawa
National Training Centre (DNTC)
Library
Private Bag 7746 Causeway
Harare, Mashonaland East
Phone: +263(4) 882245, 882960 **Fax:** +263(4) 882245

Founded: 1957 **Type:** Government **Head:** K.K. Muwonde
Phone: +263(4) 882245, 882960 ext 131 **Staff:** 2 Prof. **Hold-
ings:** 1,064 books 920 journals **Language of Collection/**
Services: English / English, Shona, Ndebele **Subjects:** Agri-
cultural Economics, Agricultural Education, Agricultural
Engineering, Animal Husbandry, Forestry, Social Sciences
Loan: In country **Service:** In country **Photocopy:** Yes

♦3927 Harare, Zimbabwe
Tobacco Research Board (TRB)
Library
PB 1909
Harare
Location: Airport Ring Road **Phone:** +263(4) 50411 **Fax:**
+263(4) 50402

Founded: 1954 **Staff:** 1 Prof. **Holdings:** 11,500 books 260
journals **Language of Collection/Services:** English **Subjects:** Agricultural Engineering, Biotechnology, Crop Production, Entomology, Plant Breeding, Plant Pathology, Plant
Protection, Plants, Soil Science, Stored Products **Specializations:** Tobacco **Databases Used:** CABCD **Loan:** In country
Photocopy: Yes

3928 Harare, Zimbabwe
University of Zimbabwe (UZ)
Library
PO Box MP45
Mount Pleasant
Harare
Location: Main campus **Phone:** +263(4) 303211 ext 1170
Fax: +263(4) 307773 **Email:** rsd@uzlib.uz.ac.zw **WWW:**
wwww.uz.ac.zw

Founded: 1953 **Type:** Academic **Head:** Stan M. Made
Phone: +263(4) 303211 ext 1164 *Email:* stan.made@uzlib.
uz.ac.zw **Staff:** 24 Prof. 116 Other **Holdings:** 500,000 books
Language of Collection/Services: English / English **Subjects:** Agricultural Education, Agricultural Economics, Animal Husbandry, Crops, Forestry, Veterinary Medicine
Loan: Internationally **Photocopy:** Yes

3929 Harare, Zimbabwe
University of Zimbabwe (UZ)
Veterinary Library
MP45, Mount Pleasant
Harare
Phone: +263(4) 303211 **Fax:** +263(4) 333407, 335249
WWW: www.uz.ac.zw

Head: Agnes Chikonzo *Email:* achi@uzlib.uz.zw **Subjects:**
Veterinary Science

3930   Harare, Zimbabwe
University of Zimbabwe, Institute of Development Studies (UZ, IDS)
Library
PO Box 880
Harare

Location: Mount Pleasant **Phone:** +263(4) 333341/3 ext 233, 307900/6 **Fax:** +263(4) 333345 **Email:** idslibrary@ idsl.uz.zw **WWW:** wwww.uz.ac.zw

Former Name: Zimbabwe Institute of Development Studies (ZIDS) **Founded:** 1983 **Type:** Academic, Government **Head:** Audrey Mhlanga *Phone:* +263(4) 333341/3 ext 233, 307900/6 *Email:* mhlanga@idsl.uz.zs **Staff:** 3 Prof. 2 Other **Holdings:** 30,000 books 150 journals **Language of Collection/Services:** English / English **Specializations:** Agricultural Development **Loan:** Inhouse **Service:** Internationally **Photocopy:** Yes

3931   Harare, Zimbabwe
Zimbabwe Forestry Commission (FC)
Forest Research Centre (FRC)
HG 595 Highlands
Harare

Location: 1 Orange Grove Drive, Highlands **Phone:** +263 (4) 496877, 496878 **Fax:** +263(4) 497070 **Email:** frchigh @harare.iafrica.com **WWW:** www.zimbabwe.net/business/ frc

Founded: 1969 **Type:** Parastatal **Head:** Mrs. Francisca Muringai *Email:* frchigh@harare.iafrica.com *Phone:* +263 (4) 46878, 46879 **Staff:** 1 Prof. **Holdings:** 4,000 books 7 journals **Language of Collection/Services:** English / English **Subjects:** Forestry **Specializations:** Biometry, Entomology, Statistics **Databases Used:** CABCD **Loan:** In country **Service:** Internationally **Photocopy:** Yes

♦**3932   Marondera, Zimbabwe**
Ministry of Lands and Agriculture, Department of Research and Specialist Services, Grasslands Research Station (MOLA, DRSS)
Library
Private Bag 3701
Marondera
Phone: +263(79) 3526/8

Former Name: Ministry of Lands, Agriculture and Rural Resettlement **Founded:** 1950 **Type:** Government **Staff:** 1 Other **Holdings:** 500 books 18 journals **Subjects:** Animal Nutrition, Grassland Management **Loan:** Do not loan **Photocopy:** No

3933   Marondera, Zimbabwe
Ministry of Lands and Agriculture, Department of Research and Specialist Services, Soil

Productivity Research Laboratory (MOLA, DRSS, SPRL)
Library
PB 3757
Marondera
Phone: +263(79) 23621, 24391 **Fax:** +263(79) 24391 **Email:** sprl@utande.co.zw

Former Name: Ministry of Lands, Agriculture and Rural Resettlement **Founded:** 1963 **Head:** D.K.C. Dhliwayo *Phone:* +263(79) 23621 *Email:* sprl@utande.co.zw **Staff:** 10 Prof. 20 Other **Holdings:** 300 books 9 journals **Language of Collection/Services:** English / English **Subjects:** Agriculture (Tropics), Cycling, Farming Systems, Nitrogen Fixation, Organic Matter, Soil Fertility, Soil Science **Loan:** Inhouse **Photocopy:** Yes

3934   Mazowe Village, Zimbabwe
Ministry of Lands and Agriculture, Department of Research and Specialist Services, Henderson Research Station (MOLA, DRSS)
Library
Private Bag 2004
Mazowe Village, Mashonaland Central

Former Name: Ministry of Lands, Agriculture and Rural Resettlement **Founded:** 1950 **Type:** Government **Head:** Mr. B. Mupeta *Phone:* +263(75) 2281-3 **Staff:** 1 Other **Holdings:** 1,100 books 30 journals **Language of Collection/Services:** English **Subjects:** Agricultural Economics, Animal Husbandry, Biotechnology, Crops, Range Management, Veterinary Medicine **Specializations:** Animal Breeding, Animal Husbandry, Animal Nutrition, Animal Physiology, Pastures, Weeds **Loan:** In country **Photocopy:** No

♦**3935   Rusape, Zimbabwe**
Ministry of Lands and Agriculture, Department of Research and Specialist Services, Nyanga Experiment Station (MOLA, DRSS)
Library
PB 8044
Rusape
Location: Nyanga District

Former Name: Ministry of Lands, Agriculture and Rural Resettlement, Rhodes Inyanga Experiment Station, Rhodes Nyanga Experiment Station **Founded:** 1963 **Type:** Government **Staff:** 2 Other **Holdings:** 500 books 9 journals **Language of Collection/Services:** English **Subjects:** Crops, Entomology, Farming, Horticulture, Plant Pathology **Specializations:** Farming (History - Zimbabwe - Eastern Districts), Soil Fauna, Temperate Fruits **Loan:** Internationally **Photocopy:** No

Acronyms and Abbreviations

Acronyms and abbreviations for databases, database vendors, institutions, and networks that appear in the directory are spelled out or described here to avoid repetition, save space, and assist the user to identify organizations. No verification was done and no attempt to be exhaustive was made. The country from which the acronym or abbreviation was obtained is noted in square brackets.
Country abbreviations: UK=United Kingdom; US = United States.

AACREA – Asociación Argentina de Consorcios Regionales de Experimentación Agrícola [Argentina]

AAF – Académie d'Agriculture de France [France]

AAFC – Agriculture and Agri-Food Canada [Canada]

AAFS – Academy of Agricultural and Forestry Sciences [Romania]

AAMU – Alabama A&M University [US]

AARD – Agency for Agricultural Research and Development [Indonesia]

AARI – Anadolu Agricultural Research Institute [Turkey]

AARI – Ayub Agricultural Research Institute [Pakistan]

AAU – Assam Agriculture University [India]

AB – Centrum voor Agrobiologisch Onderzoek [Netherlands]

ABAC – Abraham Baldwin Agricultural College [US]

ABAD – Agency for Barani Areas Development [Pakistan]

ABADRL – Arthropod-Borne Animal Diseases Research Laboratory [US]

ABARE – Australian Bureau of Agricultural and Resource Economics [Australia]

ABN – Australian Bibliographic Network [Australia]

ABOA – Australian Bibliography on Agriculture [Australia]

ABS – Archbold Biological Station [US]

ABU – Ahmadu Bello University [Nigeria]

ACA – Ambo College of Agriculture [Ethiopia]

ACADI – Arab Center for Agricultural Documentation and Information [Sudan]

ACARPA – Associação de Crédito e Assistência Rural do Paraná [Brazil]

ACC – Agriculture College of Coimbra [Portugal]

ACES Library – Agricultural, Consumer and Environmental Sciences Library [US]

ACFTSC – ASEAN - Canada Forest Tree Seed Centre [Thailand]

ACPC – Agricultural Credit Policy Council [Philippines]

ACSAD – Arab Center for the Studies of Arid Zones and Dry Lands [Syria]

ACTI – Agricultural Science and Technology Institute [Guatemala]

ADBP – Agricultural Development Bank of Pakistan [Pakistan]

ADI – Área de Documentação e Informação [Brazil]

AdL – Akademie der Landwirtschaftswissenschaften der DDR [Germany]

ADMS – American Donkey & Mule Society Inc. [US]

ADRI – Animal Diseases Research Institute [Canada]

ADRI – Animal Diseases Research Institute [Tanzania]

ADRON – Anne van Dijk Rijstonderzoekscentrum Nickerie [Suriname]

AERC – Agricultural Engineering Research Center [Taiwan]

AERDRI – Agricultural Extension and Rural Development Research Institute [Egypt]

AES – A.E. Staley Manufacturing Company [US]

AETIC – Agricultural Engineering Technical Information Center [Taiwan]

AFBF – American Farm Bureau Federation [US]

AFFA – Agriculture, Fisheries and Forestry, Australia [Australia]

AFISC – Australian Food Industry Science Centre [Australia]

AFOCEL – Association Forêt-Cellulose [France]

AFRC – Agricultural and Food Research Council [UK]

AFRC – Albion Fisheries Research Centre [Mauritius]

AFRI – Arid Forest Research Institute [India]

AFRISTAT – Observatoire Economique et Statistique pour l'Afrique Subsaharienne [Mali]

AFSIC – Alternative Farming Systems Information Center [US]

AFTSC – ASEAN Forest Tree Seed Centre [Thailand]

AgNIC – Agricultural Network Information Center [US]

AgResearch – New Zealand Pastoral Agriculture Research Institute [New Zealand]

AgriCensus – Agricultural Census Organization [Pakistan]

AGRIDOC – Agricultural Documentation Centre [Seychelles]

AGRIHORT – Agri-Horticultural Society of India [India]

AGRITEX – Department of Agricultural, Technical and Extension Services [Zimbabwe]

AGRIVARSITY – University of Agriculture [Pakistan]

AHKL – Akhter Hameed Khan Library [Bangladesh]

AHOF – Arabian Horse Owners Foundation [US]

AHS – American Horticultural Society [US]

AHSF – Abdul Hameed Shoman Public Library [Jordan]

AHT – Agrar- und Hydrotechnik GmbH [Germany]

AHT – Animal Health Trust [UK]

AI – Área de Informação [Brazil]

AI/SEDE – Área de Informação da Sede [Brazil]

AIB – American Institute of Baking [US]

AIC – Agricultural Information Centre [Bangladesh]

AIC – Agriculture Information Center [US]

AIC – Aquaculture Information Center [US]

AID – Área de Informação e Documentação [Brazil]

AIFM – ASEAN Institute of Forest Management [Malaysia]

AINFO – Área de Informação [Brazil]

AIT – Asian Institute of Technology [Thailand]

AJCA – Awassa Junior College of Agriculture [Ethiopia]

ALBC – American Livestock Breeds Conservancy [US]

ALIC – Agricultural Library and Information Centre [New Zealand]

ALIC – Arid Lands Information Center [US]

Allerton PVL – Allerton Provincial Veterinary Library [South Africa]

AMBC – American Minor Breeds Conservancy [US]

AMI – American Mushroom Institute [US]

AMNH – American Museum of Natural History [US]

AMU-X – Autonomous Metropolitan University, Xochimilco Campus [Mexico]

ANDI – Asociación Nacional de Industriales [Colombia]

ANM – Australian Newsprint Mills Ltd. [Australia]

AOAD – Arab Organization for Agricultural Development [Sudan]

APCom – Agricultural Prices Commission [Pakistan]

APD – Agricultural Planning Division [Trinidad and Tobago]

APHA – American Paint Horse Association [US]

APIRS – Aquatic, Wetland and Invasive Plant Information Retrieval System [US]

APRI – Animal Production Research Institute [Egypt]

APTLIN – Academia Sinica/Peking University/Tsinghua University Library and Information Network [China]

APU – Agricultural Policy Unit [Senegal]

AQD – Aquaculture Department [Philippines]

AQIMA – Ministry of Agriculture, National Animal Quarantine Institute [China]

AR – Akademia Rolnicza im. H. Kollataja w Krakowie [Poland]

AR-T – Akademia Rolniczo-Techniczna w Olsztynie [Poland]

ARARI – Aegean Regional Agricultural Research Institute [Turkey]

ARC – Agricultural Research Center [Egypt]

ARC – Agricultural Research Center [Philippines]

ARC – Agricultural Research Centre [Pakistan]

ARC – Agricultural Research Corporation [Sudan]

ARC – Agricultural Research Council [South Africa]

ARCT – African Regional Center of Technology [Senegal]

AREC – Agricultural Research and Education Center [US]

AREC – Agricultural Research and Extension Center [Turkey]

AREEO – Agricultural Research, Education and Extension Organization [Iran]

ARI – Agharkar Research Institute [India]

ARI – Animal Research Institute [Ghana]

ARIU – Agriculture Research Institute Ukiriguru [Tanzania]

ARL – Agriculture Reference Library [Ghana]

ARLIS – Alaska Resources Library and Information Services [US]

ARS – Agricultural Research Service [US]

ARSRILP – All-Russia Scientific Research Institute of Labor Protection [Russia]

ARTI – Agrarian Research and Training Institute [Sri Lanka]

ARU – Asociación Rural del Uruguay [Uruguay]

ASAS – Academia de Stiinte Agricole si Silvice [Romania]

ASCA – Aklan State College of Agriculture [Philippines]

ASCR – Academy of Science of Czech Republic [Czech Republic]

ASDC – Agricultural Scientific Documentation Center [Cambodia]

ASE – Agri Service Ethiopia [Ethiopia]

ASF – Agricultural Sciences Faculty [Argentina]

ASFA – Aquatic Science and Fisheries Abstracts [International]

ASG – Austrian Society for Surveying and Geoinformation [Austria]

ASHM – American Saddle Horse Museum [US]

ASIA – American Sheep Industry Association [US]

ASIC – Agricultural Science Information Center [Taiwan]

ASIDC – Agricultural Scientific Information and Documentation Center [Iran]

ASOCAÑA – Asociación de Cultivadores de Caña de Azúcar de Colombia [Colombia]

ASPC – American Sheep Producers Council [US]

ASPC – American Shetland Pony Club [US]

ASRCT – Applied Scientific Research Corporation of Thailand [Thailand]

ASTA – Administration des Services Techniques de l'Agriculture [Luxembourg]

ASTA – American Seed Trade Association [US]

ASU – Ain Shams University [Egypt]

ASU – Alcorn State University [US]

ASU – Arizona State University [US]

ATAE – Anadolu Tarimsal Arastirma Enstitüsü [Turkey]

ATBU – Abubakar Tafawa Balewa University [Nigeria]

ATCC – American Type Culture Collection [US]

ATE – Agrotiki Trapeza tis Ellados [Greece]

ATEK – Agrártudományi Egyetem Keszthely [Hungary]

ATI – Agricultural Technical Institute [US]

ATO – African Timber Organisation [Gabon]

ATO – Instituut voor Agrotechnologisch Onderzoek [Netherlands]

ATOL – ATOL studie & documentatie-centrum voor Aangepaste Technologie en Projectbeheer in Ontwikkelingslanden [Belgium]

ATOL – ATOL Study and Documentation Centre on Appropriate Technology and Project Management in Developing Countries [Belgium]

ATR – Akademia Techniczno-Rolnicza [Poland]

ATTRA Resource Center – Appropriate Technology Transfer for Rural Areas Resource Center [US]

ATU – Arkansas Tech University [US]

AU – Azabu University [Japan]

AUA – Alemaya University of Agriculture [Ethiopia]

AUGURA – Asociación de Bananeros de Colombia [Colombia]

AUN – Agricultural University of Norway [Norway]

AÜZF – Atatürk Universitesi, Ziraat Fakültesi [Turkey]

AVMA – American Veterinary Medical Association [US]

AVRDC – Asian Vegetable Research and Development Center [Taiwan]

AWC – Australian Wool Corporation [Australia]

AWIC – Animal Welfare Information Center [US]

AWRI – Australian Wine Research Institute [Australia]

AWRRC – Agriculture and Water Resources Research Center [Iraq]

AzETKTMEi – Azerbaycan Elmi Tedgigat Kend Tesarrufatinin Mekaniklesdirilmesi ve Elektriklesdirilmesi Institutu [Azerbaijan]

AZRI – Arid Zone Research Institute [Australia]

B. Nauk. – Biblioteka Naukowa [Poland]

BAAC – Bank for Agriculture and Agricultural Cooperatives [Thailand]

BAAFS – Beijing Academy of Agricultural and Forestry Sciences [China]

BABF – Bundesanstalt für Bergbauernfragen [Austria]

BAC – Biblioteca Agropecuaria de Colombia [Colombia]

BAC – Bukura Agricultural College [Kenya]

Badan Litbang Pertanian – Badan Penelitian dan Pengembangan Pertanian [Indonesia]

BADC – Bangladesh Agricultural Development Corporation [Bangladesh]

BADC – Brackishwater Aquaculture Development Centre [Indonesia]

BAEU – Beijing Agricultural Engineering University [China]

BafM – Bundesanstalt für Milchforschung [Germany]

BAGKF – Bundesanstalt für Getreide-, Kartoffel- und Fettforschung in Detmold and Münster [Germany]

BAI – Bangladesh Agricultural Institute [Bangladesh]

BAKT – Bundesanstalt für Kulturtechnik und Bodenwasserhaushalt [Austria]

BAL – Bundesanstalt für alpenländische Landwirtschaft Gumpenstein [Austria]

Balitjas – Balai Penelitian Tanaman Jagung dan Serealia Lain [Indonesia]

Balitkanlut – Balai Penelitian Perikanan Laut [Indonesia]

Balitpa – Balai Penelitian Tanaman Padi [Indonesia]

Balittan – Balai Penelitian Tanaman Pangan Banjarbaru [Indonesia]

Balittan Sukamandi – Balai Penelitian Tanaman Pangan Sukamandi [Indonesia]

Balittra – Balai Penelitian Tanaman Pangan Lahan Rawa [Indonesia]

BAN – Biblioteca Agrícola Nacional [Peru]

BAN – Bulgarska Akademia na Naukite [Bulgaria]

BANSDOC – Bangladesh Scientific Documentation Centre [Bangladesh]

BANSLINK – Bangladesh National Science Libraries Information Network [Bangladesh]

BARC – Bangladesh Agricultural Research Council [Bangladesh]

BARD – Bangladesh Academy for Rural Development [Bangladesh]

BARI – Bangladesh Agricultural Research Institute [Bangladesh]

BARI – Barani Agricultural Research Institute [Pakistan]

BARIF – Banjarbaru Research Institute for Food Crops [Indonesia]

BARS – Bvumbwe Agricultural Research Station [Malawi]

BAS – Bulgarian Academy of Sciences [Bulgaria]

BAS – Bureau of Agricultural Statistics [Philippines]

BASURI – Bangladesh Sugarcane Research Institute [Bangladesh]

BATU – Belarus Agrarian Technical University [Belarus]

BAU – Bangladesh Agricultural University [Bangladesh]

BAU – Beijing Agricultural University [China]

BAU – Birsa Agricultural University [India]

BAW – Bundesamt für Wasserwirtschaft [Austria]

BAZ – Bundesanstalt für Züchtungsforschung an Kulturpflanzen [Germany]

BBA – Biologische Bundesanstalt für Land- und Forstwirtschaft [Germany]

BBSRC – Biotechnology and Biological Sciences Research Council [UK]

BCA – Biblioteca de Ciencias Agrarias [Argentina]

BCA – Bibliothèque canadienne de l'agriculture [Canada]

BCA – Botswana College of Agriculture [Botswana]

BCCR – Banco Central de Costa Rica [Costa Rica]

BCDC – Biological Control Documentation Center [US]

BCL – Bunda College Library [Malawi]

BCO – Biblioteca Conmemorativa Orton [Costa Rica]

BCRI – B. C. Research Inc. [Canada]

BCRS – Biblioteca Centrale della Regione Siciliana [Italy]

BCSM – Spencer Entomological Museum [Canada]

BDA – Bureau de la Documentation et des Archives [Congo, Republic of the]

BDB – Bodemkundige Dienst van België [Belgium]

BDPA – Bureau pour le Développement de la Production Agricole [France]

BEAGRI/PR – Biblioteca Estadual de Agricultura [Brazil]

BELAL – Belarus Agricultural Library [Belarus]

BelNIIK – Belaruskaga navukovadasledchaga instytuta bul'bavodstva [Belarus]

BelSKHB – Belorusskaya sel'skokhozyajstvennaya biblioteka [Belarus]

BelSRIPP – Belarus Scientific Research Institute of Plant Protection [Belarus]

BES Library – Biological and Environmental Sciences Library [US]

BFAFi – Bundesforschungsanstalt für Fischerei [Germany]

BFAR – Bundesforschungsanstalt für Rebenzüchtung [Germany]

BFAR – Bureau of Fisheries and Aquatic Resources [Philippines]

BFAV – Bundesforschungsanstalt für Viruskrankheiten der Tiere [Germany]

BFE – Bundesforschungsanstalt für Ernährung [Germany]

BFH – Bundesforschungsanstalt für Forst- und Holzwirtschaft [Germany]

BFL – Bundesamt für Forstwesen und Landschaftsschutz [Switzerland]

BfN – Bundesamt für Naturschutz [Germany]

BFRI – Bangladesh Forest Research Institute [Bangladesh]

BG – Biblioteca Geral [Portugal]

BG – Biblioteka Główna [Poland]

Bhv – Bændaskólinn á Hvanneyri [Iceland]

BI – Bændasamtök Íslands [Iceland]

BIAHI – Boehringer Ingelheim Animal Health Inc. [US]

BIAS – Bashang Institute of Agricultural Sciences [China]

BIB – Bibliothèque Internationale de la Betterave [Belgium]

BIBA – Bibliografia Agrícola Chilena [Chile]

BIBSYS – Norwegian Union Catalogue [Norway]

BIC – Business Information Center [US]

BIDOC – Bibliothèque (Centre de Documentation) [Benin]

BIDS – Bangladesh Institute of Development Studies [Bangladesh]

BINA – Bangladesh Institute of Nuclear Agriculture [Bangladesh]

BINAF – Biblioteca Nacional Agropecuaria y Forestal [Cuba]

Biosis – Biological Abstracts, Inc. [US]

BIOTECH – National Institute of Molecular Biology and Biotechnology [Philippines]

BIRC – Bio-Integral Resource Center [US]

BIVB – Bureau Interprofessionnel des Vins de Bourgogne [France]

BL – British Library [UK]

BLDS – British Library for Development Studies [UK]

BLP – Bibliothèque Lecture Publique [Mali]

BLRI – Balaton Limnological Research Institute [Hungary]

BLRI – Bangladesh Livestock Research Institute [Bangladesh]

BLW – Bundesamt für Landwirtschaft [Switzerland]

BMBRI – Brewing and Malting Barley Research Institute [Canada]

BML – Bundesministerium für Ernährung, Landwirtschaft und Forsten [Germany]

BMLF – Bundesministerium für Land- und Forstwirtschaft [Austria]

BMNH – British Museum (Natural History) [UK]

BMS – Bamfield Marine Station [Canada]

BMS – Biblioteka Matice Srpske [Serbia and Montenegro]

BN – Bibliothèque Nationale [Madagascar]

BNLS – Botswana National Library Service [Botswana]

BOINT – Branzowy Osrodek Informacji Naukowo-Technicznej [Poland]

BOINTE – Branzowy Osrodek Informacji Naukowej, Technicznej i Ekonomicznej [Poland]

BOITE – Branzowy Osrodek Informacji Techniczno-Ekonomicznej [Poland]

BOKU – Universität für Bodenkultur Wien [Austria]

BoNN&PTNT – Bo Nong nghiep va Phat trien Nong thon [Vietnam]

BOPED – Bureau of Planning and Economic Development [Ethiopia]

BPBM – Bernice P. Bishop Museum [US]

BPI – Benaki Phytopathological Institute [Greece]

BPI – Bureau of Plant Industry [Philippines]

BR - Sevaré – Bibliothèque Rizière Sevaré [Mali]

BRACO – Bureau Régional pour l'Afrique Centrale et Occidentale [Senegal]

BRAIN – Bio-oriented Technology Research Advancement Institution [Japan]

BRC – Brandon Research Centre [Canada]

BRIP – Belarusian Research Institute of Potato Growing [Belarus]

BRR – Biblioteca "Rómulo Raggio" [Argentina]

BRRI – Bangladesh Rice Research Institute [Bangladesh]

BRSA – Biblioteca Republicana Stiintifica Agrara [Moldova]

BSE – Bibliothèque des Sciences Exactes [Belgium]

BSFIC – Bangladesh Sugar and Food Industries Corporation [Bangladesh]

BSH – Bundesamt für Seeschiffahrt und Hydrographie [Germany]

BSL – Biological Sciences Library [Australia]

BSMRAU – Bangabandhu Sheikh Mujibur Rahman Agricultural University [Bangladesh]

BSRTI – Bangladesh Sericulture Research and Training Institute [Bangladesh]

BSSRC – Biotechnology and Biological Sciences Research Council [UK]

BST – Bibliothèque des Sciences et Techniques [Belgium]

BST – Business, Science and Technology Department [US]

BSU – Benguet State University [Philippines]

BTC – Botswana Technology Centre [Botswana]

BTI – Bodentechnologisches Institut [Germany]

BTI – Boyce Thompson Institute for Plant Research [US]

BTIS – Botswana Technical Information Library [Botswana]

BTRI – Bangladesh Tea Research Institute [Bangladesh]

BU – Biblioteca Universitária [Brazil]

BUC – Bulolo University College [Papua New Guinea]

BUMP – Bibliothèque universitaire Moretus Plantin [Belgium]

BUU – Burapha University [Thailand]

BUWAL – Bundesamt für Umwelt, Wald und Landschaft [Switzerland]

BVBB – Bibliotheksverbund Berlin-Brandenburg [Germany]

BWP – Biblioteca Wilson Popenoe [Honduras]

BYU – Brigham Young University [US]

C&FR – New Zealand Institute for Crop and Food Research [New Zealand]

CAAFS – Cangzhou Academy of Agricultural and Forestry Sciences [China]

CAAM – Chinese Academy of Agricultural Mechanization [China]

CAAS – Chinese Academy of Agricultural Sciences [China]

CABCD – CAB International [UK]

CABI – CAB International [UK]

CAE – Centre for Agricultural Economics [Belgium]

CAER – Center for Agro Economic Research [Indonesia]

CAES – Chia-yi Agricultural Experiment Station [Taiwan]

CAF – Chinese Academy of Forestry [China]

CAFL – Central Agricultural and Forestry Library [Czech Republic]

CAFS – Chinese Academy of Fishery Science [China]

CAH – College of Agriculture, Hódmezővásárhely [Hungary]

CAIR – Centre for the Application of Isotopes and Radiation [Indonesia]

CAK – Centralna Agronomska Knjiznica [Croatia]

CAL – Canadian Agriculture Library [Canada]

CAL – Central Agricultural Library [Bulgaria]

CAL – Central Agricultural Library [Poland]

Cal Poly – California Polytechnic State University (San Luis Obispo) [US]

Cal Poly Pomona – California Polytechnic State University (Pomona) [US]

CALIS – College of Agriculture Library Information System [India]

CALM – Western Australia Department of Conservation and Land Management [Australia]

CALREC – Center for Agricultural Library and Research Communication [Indonesia]

CANR – College of Agriculture and Natural Resources [Iran]

CAR – Center of Academic Resources [Thailand]

CARD – Centre for Agricultural Research and Development [Bhutan]

CARDER-Atacora – Centre d'Action Régionale pour le Développement Rural de l'Atacora [Benin]

CARDER-Mono – Centre d'Action Régionale pour le Développement Rural du Mono [Benin]

CARDI – Cambodian Agricultural Research and Development Institute [Cambodia]

CARDI – Caribbean Agricultural Research and Development Institute [Trinidad and Tobago]

CARI – Central Agricultural Research Institute [Liberia]

CARI – Central Avian Research Institute [India]

CARIS – Current Agricultural Research Information System [FAO]

CARL UnCover – Colorado Alliance of Research Libraries [US]

CAS – California Academy of Sciences [US]

CAS – Chemical Abstracts Service [US]

CAS – Chinese Academy of Sciences [China]

CASER – Center for Agro-Socioeconomic Research [Indonesia]

CASurveyor – Chemical Abstracts Surveyor [US]

CATAS – China Academy of Tropical Agricultural Sciences [China]

CATIE – Centro Agronómico Tropical de Investigación y Enseñanza [Costa Rica]

CATNIP – Cataloguing Network in Pietermaritzburg [South Africa]

CAU – China Agricultural University [China]

CAWM Mweka – College of African Wildlife Management, Mweka [Tanzania]

CAZRI – Central Arid Zone Research Institute [India]

CBCA – Canadian Business and Current Affairs [Canada]

CBK – Centralna biotehniska knjiznica [Slovenia]

CBL – Central Biotechnical Library [Slovenia]

CBL – Chesapeake Biological Laboratory [US]

CBR – Centralna Biblioteka Rolnicza [Poland]

CCA-ONG – Comité de Coordination des Actions des O.N.G. [Mali]

CCAIAN – Chambre de Commerce, d'Agriculture, d'Industrie et d'Artisanat du Niger [Niger]

CCAIT – Chambre de Commerce d'Agriculture et d'Industrie du Togo [Togo]

CCFRA – Campden and Chorleywood Food Research Association [UK]

CCG – Commission Canadienne des Grains [Canada]

CCIA – Chamber of Commerce, Industry and Agriculture of Antananarivo [Madagascar]

CCIA – Chambre de Commerce, d'Industrie et d'Agriculture d'Antananarivo [Madagascar]

CCIA – Corporación Colombiana de Investigación Agropecuaria [Colombia]

CCL – Camden-Carroll Library [US]

CCMA – Centro de Ciencias Medioambientales [Spain]

CCMS – Centre for Coastal and Marine Studies [UK]

CCN – Catálogo Coletivo Nacional de Periódicos [Brazil]

CCPE – Catalogo Coletivo de Periodicos da EMBRAPA [Brazil]

CCPP – Catálogo Colectivo de Publicaciones Periodicas [Argentina]

CCPPAA – Catalogo Colectivo de Publicaciones Periódicas del INTA [Argentina]

CCPPPIP – Centrul de Cercetare Proiectare pentru Piscicultura, Pescuit si Industrializarea Pestelui Galati [Romania]

CCRI – Central Cotton Research Institute [Pakistan]

CCS HAU – Chaudhary Charan Singh Haryana Agricultural University [India]

CCUC – Catalog Collectiv de les Universitats Catalones [Spain]

CDA – Centre de Documentation Agricole [Congo, Democratic Republic of the]

CDA – Centre de Documentation Agricole [Djibouti]

CDA – Centre de Documentation Agricole [Morocco]

CDA – Centro de Documentação e Informação do Sector Agrário [Mozambique]

CDAS – Centre de Documentation des Archives du Sénégal [Senegal]

CDCU – Centro de Documentação Científica Ultramarina [Portugal]

CDD – Centre de Documentation [Cote d'Ivoire]

CDEDA – Centre de Documentation et de Divulgation Agricole [Guinea-Bissau]

CDI – Centraal Diergeneeskundig Instituut [Netherlands]

CDI – Centre de Documentation et d'Information [Burkina Faso]

CDI – Centre de Documentation et d'Information [France]

CDI – Centre de Documentation-Information [Morocco]

CDI – Centro de Documentação e Informação [Mozambique]

CDI – Centro de Documentação e Informação [Portugal]

CDIA – Centre de Documentation et d'Information Agricoles [Togo]

CDIA – Centre de Documentation et d'Informations Agricoles [Benin]

CDOC – Centre de Documentation et de Communication [Senegal]

CDRI – Cambodia Development Resource Institute [Cambodia]

CDT – Centre de Documentation Technique [Togo]

CEA – Central Environmental Authority [Sri Lanka]

CEA – Centre d'Economie Agricole [Belgium]

CECAT – China-EU Centre for Agricultural Technology [China]

CEDAF – Centre d'Etude et de Documentation Africaines [Belgium]

CEDASPE – Centro de Documentação de Agricultura, Silvicultura e Pesca [Mozambique]

CEDIA – Centro de Documentación e Información Agrícola [Guatemala]

CEDICTA – Centro de Documentación [Guatemala]

CEDIE – Centre for Environment Development Information Exchange [Kenya]

CEDIF – Centro de Información Forestal [Peru]

CEDIS – Centre de Documentation et d'Information Scientific [Congo, Republic of the]

CEDIS – Centre de Documentation et d'Information Scientifique [Lebanon]

CEDIT – Centro de Documentação e Informações Técnicas [Brazil]

CEDOC – Centro de Documentação [Brazil]

CEDUST – Centre de Documentation Universitaire Scientifique et Technique [Guinea]

CEES – Center for Environmental and Estuarine Studies [US]

CEFAS – Centre for Environment, Fisheries and Aquaculture Sciences [UK]

CEFOD – Centre d'Etudes et de Formation pour le Développement [Chad]

CEH – Centre for Ecology and Hydrology [UK]

CEI – Czech Environmental Institute [Czech Republic]

CELIB – Central Library [Thailand]

CEMAGREF – Centre National du Machinisme Agricole du Génie Rural des Eaux et des Forêts [France]

CENADORA – Centro Nacional de Documentación Agropecuaria [Dominican Republic]

CENAGRI – Coordenação Nacional de Informação Documental Agrícola [Brazil]

CENARGEN – Centro Nacional de Recursos Genéticos e Biotecnologia [Brazil]

CENCA – Centro de Consulta del Agua [Mexico]

CENCOA – Central de Cooperativas Agrarias [Colombia]

CENDID – Centre National de Documentation et d'Information pour le Développement Rural [Guinea]

CENDOC – Documentation Center [Peru]

CENIAP – Centro Nacional de Investigaciones Agropecuarias [Venezuela]

CENICAFE – Centro Nacional de Investigaciones de Café "Pedro Uribe Mejía" [Colombia]

CENICAÑA – Centro de Investigación de la Caña de Azúcar de Colombia [Colombia]

CENIDA – Centro Nacional de Información y Documentación Agraria [Equatorial Guinea]

CENIDA – Centro Nacional de Información y Documentación Agropecuaria [Nicaragua]

CENIDOC – Centro Nacional de Información y Documentación Científica [Spain]

CENRADERU – Centre National de la Recherche Appliquée au Développement Rural [Madagascar]

CENTA – Centro Nacional de Tecnología Agropecuaria [El Salvador]

CENTEC – Bibliotheek Centrum Techniek [Netherlands]

CERNET – China Education and Research Network [China]

CERPOD – Centre d'Etudes et de Recherche pour la Population et le Développement [Mali]

CES – Center for Environmental Science [US]

CES Library – Central Experiment Station Library [Trinidad and Tobago]

CEWRE – Centre of Excellence in Water Resources Engineering [Pakistan]

CFDRA – Campden Food and Drink Research Association [UK]

CFL – Central Food Library [Czech Republic]

CFNR – College of Forestry and Natural Resources [Philippines]

CFS – Canadian Forest Service [Canada]

CFSAN – Center for Food Safety and Applied Nutrition [US]

CGC – Canadian Grain Commission [Canada]

CGI – Cellule de Gestion de l'Information [Cote d'Ivoire]

CGPRDI – China Grain Products Research and Development Institute [Taiwan]

CGPRT – Regional Co-ordination Centre for Research and Development of Coarse Grains, Pulses, Roots and Tuber Crops in the Humid Tropics of Asia and the Pacific [Indonesia]

CHRC – Chanthaburi Horticultural Research Center [Thailand]

CIAE – Central Institute of Agricultural Engineering [India]

CIAE – Centro de Investigaciones Agropecuarias del Estado Táchira [Venezuela]

CIAM – Centro de Investigaciones Agrarias de Mabegondo [Spain]

CIAP – Cambodia-IRRI-Australia Project [Cambodia]

CIAS – Cangzhou Institute of Agricultural Sciences [China]

CIAT – Centro Internacional de Agricultura Tropical [Colombia]

CIB – Coconut Industry Board [Jamaica]

CIB – Comité Interprofessionnel des Vins de Bourgogne [France]

CIBA – Central Institute of Brackishwater Aquaculture [India]

CIBAGRI – Centro de Información Bioagrícola [Argentina]

CIBAGRO – Centro de Información Bioagropecuaria y Forestal [Argentina]

CIBC – CAB Institute of Biological Control [Trinidad and Tobago]

CIC – Cargill Information Center [US]

CIC – Coconut Information Centre [Sri Lanka]

CICA – Centro de Investigaciones en Ciencias Agropecuarias [Argentina]

CICB – Centre d'Information et de Conservation des Bibliothèques [Belgium]

CICR – Central Institute for Cotton Research [India]

CICV – Centro de Investigaciones en Ciencias Veterinarias [Argentina]

CID – Centro de Información y Documentación [Panama]

CID – Centro de Información y Documentación en el Estado de Guanajuato [Mexico]

CIDA – Centro de Información y Documentación de la Agricultura [Cuba]

CIDA – Centro de Investigación y Desarrollo Agroalimentario [Spain]

CIDAGRO – Centro de Información Documental Agropecuaria [Panama]

CIDARC – Centre d'Information et de Documentation en Agronomie des Régions Chaudes [France]

CIDAT – Centre d'Informatique Appliquée au Développement et à l'Agriculture Tropicale [Belgium]

CIDCAP – Centro de Información y Documentación en Ciencias Acuáticas y Pesqueras [Peru]

CIDH – Centro de Investigación y Desarrollo Hortícola [Spain]

CIDR – Centre d'Information et de Documentation pour le Développement Rural [Niger]

CIDRA – Centre de l'Information et de la Documentation des Régions Arides [Tunisia]

CIDST – Centre d'Information et de Documentation Scientifique et Technique [Madagascar]

CIDT – Compagnie Ivoirienne pour le Développement des Textiles [Cote d'Ivoire]

CIEFAP – Centro de Investigación Forestal Andino Patagónico [Argentina]

CIEH – Comité Interafricain d'Etudes Hydrauliques [Burkina Faso]

CIESM – Centro de Investigaciones sobre la Economía, la Sociedad y el Medio [Spain]

CIFA – Central Institute of Freshwater Aquaculture [India]

CIFC – Centro de Investigação das Ferrugens do Cafeeiro [Portugal]

CIFE – Central Institute of Fisheries Education [India]

CIFH – Centro de Investigación y Formación Hortícola [Spain]

CIFOR – Center for International Forestry Research [Indonesia]

CIFRI – Central Inland Capture Fisheries Research Institute [India]

CIFT – Central Institute of Fisheries Technology [India]

CIHEAM – Centre International de Hautes Etudes Agronomiques Méditerranéennes [France]

CIHNP – Central Institute of Horticulture for Northern Plains [India]

CIMMYT – Centro Internacional de Mejoramiento de Maíz y Trigo [Mexico]

CINDOC – Centro de Información y Documentación Científica [Spain]

CINU – Centre d'Information des Nations Unies [Madagascar]

CIP – Centro Internacional de la Papa [Peru]

CIP – Changli Institute of Pomology [China]

CIP – International Potato Center [Peru]

CIPI – Cotton and Industrial Plants Institute [Greece]

CIR – Center of Information and Reference [China]

CIRAD – Centre de Coopération Internationale en Recherche Agronomique pour le Développement [France]

CIRB – Central Institute for Research on Buffaloes [India]

CIRCOT – Central Institute of Research on Cotton Technology [India]

CIRES – Centre Ivoirien de Recherche Economique et Sociale [Cote d'Ivoire]

CIRG – Central Institute for Research on Goats [India]

CIRN – Centro de Investigaciones de Recursos Naturales [Argentina]

CISTH – Central Institute for Sub-Tropical Horticulture [India]

CISTID – Centre for Industrial, Scientific and Technological Information and Documentation [Seychelles]

CIT – Central Institute of Technology [New Zealand]

CL – Central Library [Zimbabwe]

CLA – Central Library and Archives [Hungary]

CLAIR – Center for Library and Information Resources [Thailand]

CLINES – CSIRO Library Network [Australia]

CLO – Centrum voor Landbouwkundig Onderzoek [Belgium]

CLPKS KONCLAB – Centralne Laboratorium Przemyslu Koncentratów Spozywczych "KONCLAB" [Poland]

CLPT – Centralne Laboratorium Przemyslu Tytoniowego [Poland]

CLPZ – Centralne Laboratorium Przemyslu Ziemniaczanego [Poland]

CLSU – Central Luzon State University [Philippines]

CLTPiPZ – Centralne Laboratorium Technologii Przetwórstwa i Przechowalnictwa Zbóz [Poland]

CMDT – Compagnie Malienne pour le Développement des Textiles [Mali]

CME – Chicago Mercantile Exchange [US]

CMFRI – Central Marine Fisheries Research Institute [India]

CML – College Main Library [Philippines]

CMSCH – Ceskomoravská spolecnost chovatelu [Czech Republic]

CMSU – Central Missouri State University [US]

CMU – Central Mindanao University [Philippines]

CMU – Chiang Mai University [Thailand]

CND – Centre National de Documentation [Congo, Republic of the]

CND – Centre National de Documentation [Morocco]

CNDA – Centre National de Documentation Agricole [Algeria]

CNDA – Centre National de Documentation Agricole [Benin]

CNDA – Centre National de Documentation Agricole [Burkina Faso]

CNDA – Centre National de Documentation Agricole [Central African Republic]

CNDA – Centre National de Documentation Agricole [Rwanda]

CNDA – Centre National de Documentation Agricole [Tunisia]

CNDES – Centre National de Documentation Economique et Sociales [Central African Republic]

CNDIA – Centre National de Documentation et d'Information Agricole [Benin]

CNDIST – Centre National de Documentation et d'Information Scientifique et Technique [Congo, Republic of the]

CNDST – Centre National de Documentation Scientifique et Technique [Belgium]

CNERV – Centre National d'Elevage et de Recherche Vétérinaire [Mauritania]

CNPA – Centro Nacional de Pesquisa do Algodão [Brazil]

CNPAB – Centro Nacional de Pesquisa de Agrobiologia [Brazil]

CNPAF – Centro Nacional de Pesquisa de Arroz e Feijão [Brazil]

CNPAI – Centro Nacional de Pesquisa de Agricultura Irrigada [Brazil]

CNPAT – Centro Nacional de Pesquisa de Agroindústria Tropical [Brazil]

CNPC – Centro Nacional de Pesquisa de Caprinos [Brazil]

CNPCa – Centro Nacional de Pesquisa de Caju [Brazil]

CNPCo – Centro Nacional de Pesquisa de Coco [Brazil]

CNPDA – Centro Nacional de Pesquisa de Defesa da Agricultura [Brazil]

CNPDIA – Centro Nacional de Pesquisa e Desenvolvimento de Instrumentação Agropecuária [Brazil]

CNPF – Centro Nacional de Pesquisa de Florestas [Brazil]

CNPFT – Centro Nacional de Pesquisa de Fruteiras de Clima Temperado [Brazil]

CNPGC – Centro Nacional de Pesquisa de Gado de Corte [Brazil]

CNPGL – Centro Nacional de Pesquisa de Gado de Leite [Brazil]

CNPH – Centro Nacional de Pesquisa de Hortaliças [Brazil]

CNPMA – Centro Nacional de Pesquisa de Monitoramento e Avaliação de Impacto Ambiental [Brazil]

CNPMFT – Centro Nacional de Pesquisa de Mandioca e Fruticultura Tropical [Brazil]

CNPMS – Centro Nacional de Pesquisa de Milho e Sorgo [Brazil]

CNPO – Centro Nacional de Pesquisa de Ovinos [Brazil]

CNPS – Centro Nacional de Pesquisa de Solos [Brazil]

CNPSA – Centro Nacional de Pesquisa de Suínos e Aves [Brazil]

CNPSo – Centro Nacional de Pesquisa de Soja [Brazil]

CNPT – Centro Nacional de Pesquisa de Trigo [Brazil]

CNPTIA – Centro Nacional de Pesquisa Tecnológica em Informática para Agricultura [Brazil]

CNPUV – Centro Nacional de Pesquisa de Uva e Vinho [Brazil]

CNR – Consiglio Nazionale delle Ricerche [Italy]

CNRA – Centre National de Recherches Agronomiques [Senegal]

CNRF – Centre National Recherches Forestières [Congo, Republic of the]

CNRO – Centre National de Recherches Océanographiques [Madagascar]

CNRRI – China National Rice Research Institute [China]

CNRS – Conseil National Recherche Scientifique [Lebanon]

CNRST – Centre National de la Recherche Scientifique et Technologique [Burkina Faso]

CNRST – Centre National de Recherche Scientifique et Technologique [Mali]

CNU – Chonnam National University [Korea, South]

COBORU – Centralny Osrodek Badania Odmian Roslin Uprawnych [Poland]

COBRO – Centralny Osrodek Badawezo-Roznojowy Ogrodnictwa [Poland]

CODA – Cotton Development Administration [Philippines]

CODESRIA – Council for the Development of Social Science Research in Africa [Senegal]

CODICE – CODESRIA Documentation and Information Center [Senegal]

Compendex – COMPuterized ENgineering InDEX [US]

CONIF – Corporación Nacional de Investigación y Fomento Forestal [Colombia]

CORD – Centre on Rural Documentation [India]

CORPOZULIA – Corporación de Desarrollo de la Región Zuliana [Venezuela]

COTA – Collectif d'Echange pour la Technologie Appropriée [Belgium]

CP – Colegio de Posgraduados [Mexico]

CPAC – Centro de Pesquisa Agropecuária dos Cerrados [Brazil]

CPACT – Centro de Pesquisa Agropecuária de Clima Temperado [Brazil]

CPAF – Centro de Pesquisa Agroflorestal [Brazil]

CPAMN – Centro de Pesquisa Agropecuária do Meio Norte [Brazil]

CPAO – Centro de Pesquisa Agropecuária do Oeste [Brazil]

CPAP – Centro de Pesquisa Agropecuária do Pantanal [Brazil]

CPATB – Centro de Pesquisas Agropecuárias de Terras Baixas de Clima Temperado [Brazil]

CPATC – Centro de Pesquisa Agropecuária dos Tabuleiros Costeiros [Brazil]

CPATSA – Centro de Pesquisa Agropecuária do Trópico Semi-Árido [Brazil]

CPATU – Centro de Pesquisa Agropecuária do Trópico Úmido [Brazil]

CPCRI – Central Plantation Crops Research Institute [India]

CPPNLCD – Cellule Provisoire du Programme National de Lutte contre la Désertification [Mali]

CPPSE – Centro de Pesquisa de Pecuária do Sudeste [Brazil]

CPPSUL – Centro de Pesquisa de Pecuária dos Campos Sul Brasileiros [Brazil]

CPRI – Central Potato Research Institute [India]

CPRO – Centre for Plant Breeding and Reproduction Research [Netherlands]

CPS – Cellule de Planification Statistique [Mali]

CPU – Central Philippine University [Philippines]

CRA-SH – Centre de Recherche Agronomique des Savanes Humides [Togo]

CRAF – Centre de Recherche Agronomique de Foulaya [Guinea]

CRAL – Centre de Recherches Agronomiques de Loudima [Congo, Republic of the]

CRAT – Centre Régional Africain de Technologie [Senegal]

CRDA – Centre de Recherche et de Développement sur les Aliments [Canada]

CRDH – Centre de Recherche et de Développement en Horticulture [Canada]

CRDI – Centre de Recherche pour le Développement International [Senegal]

CRDI – Cotton Research and Development Institute [Philippines]

CRDO – Centre de Documentation [Senegal]

CREC – Citrus Research and Education Center [US]

CREPA – Centre pour la Recherche, l'Economie at la Promotion Agricole [Belgium]

CRF – Coffee Research Foundation [Kenya]

CRI – Cereal Research Institute [Czech Republic]

CRI – Coconut Research Institute [Sri Lanka]

CRI – Cotton Research Institute [Egypt]

CRI – Crown Research Institutes [New Zealand]

CRIA – Central Research Institute for Food Crops, Sukamandi Branch [Indonesia]

CRIA – Centro Regional de Investigaciones Agrarias [Spain]

CRICYT – Centro Regional de Investigaciones Científicas y Tecnológicas [Argentina]

CRID – Centre pour la Recherche Interdisciplinaire sur le Développement [Belgium]

CRIDA – Central Research Institute for Dryland Agriculture [India]

538

CRIDA – Centro Regional de Investigación y Desarrollo Agrario [Spain]

CRIG – Cocoa Research Institute of Ghana [Ghana]

CRIJAF – Central Research Institute for Jute and Allied Fibres [India]

CRIN – Cocoa Research Institute of Nigeria [Nigeria]

CRJJ – Centre de Recherches de Jouy-en-Josas [France]

CRLS Biblioteca – Biblioteca da Coordenadoria Regional de Lagoa Seca [Brazil]

CRODT – Centre de Recherches Océanographiques de Dakar-Thiroye [Senegal]

CRRA – Centre Régional de Recherche Agronomique [Mali]

CRRI – Central Rice Research Institute [India]

CRRL – Central Reference and Research Library [Ghana]

CRTA – Centre de Recherche sur les Trypanosomoses Animales [Burkina Faso]

CRVZ – Centre de Recherche Vétérinaire et Zootechnique [Congo, Republic of the]

CRZ – Centre de Recherches Zootechniques de Dahra [Senegal]

CSAF – Centro di Sperimentazione Agricola e Forestale [Italy]

CSAL – Central Scientific Agricultural Library [Russia]

CSAL – Central Scientific Agricultural Library [Ukraine]

CSAS – Czechoslovak Academy of Sciences [Czech Republic]

CSAU – Agroengineering University of Chelyabinsk [Russia]

CSAV – Akademie ved Ceské republiky [Czech Republic]

CSC – Catanduanes State College [Philippines]

CSEL – Centennial Science and Engineering Library [US]

CSFER – Centre for Social Forestry and Eco-Rehabilitation [India]

CSHL – Cold Spring Harbor Laboratory [US]

CSIC – Consejo Superior de Investigaciones Científicas [Spain]

CSIR – Council for Scientific and Industrial Research [Ghana]

CSIR – Council for Scientific and Industrial Research [South Africa]

CSIR – Council of Scientific and Industrial Research [India]

CSIRO – Commonwealth Scientific and Industrial Research Organisation [Australia]

CSL – Central Science Library [US]

CSO – Central Statistics Office [Botswana]

CSSAC – Camarines Sur State Agricultural College [Philippines]

CSSRI – Central Soil Salinity Research Institute [India]

CSTDB – Chinese Scientific/Technical Database [China]

CSTEI – Centre for Scientific, Technical, and Economic Information [Bulgaria]

CSU – Colorado State University [US]

CSUC – California State University, Chico [US]

CSUS – California State University, Sacramento [US]

CSWCRTI – Central Soil and Water Conservation Research and Training Intitute [India]

CSWRI – Central Sheep and Wool Research Institute [India]

CTA – Centre Technique de Coopération Agricole et Rurale ACP-EU [Netherlands]

CTAA – Centro de Tecnologia Agrícola e Alimentar [Brazil]

CTAA – Centro Nacional de Pesquisa de Tecnologia Agroindustrial de Alimentos [Brazil]

CTBA – Centre Technique du Bois et de l'Ameublement [France]

CTCRI – Central Tuber Crops Research Institute [India]

CTFT – Centre Technique Forestier [Congo, Republic of the]

CTI – Central Técnica de Informações [Brazil]

CTRI – Central Tobacco Research Institute [India]

CTRL – Cotton Technological Research Laboratory [India]

CTVM – Centre for Tropical Veterinary Medicine [UK]

CU – Chulalongkorn University [Thailand]

CUA – Czech University of Agriculture Prague [Czech Republic]

CUC – Cuttington University College [Liberia]

CUNY – City University of New York [US]

CURDES – Centre Universitaire de Recherche pour le Développement Economique et Social [Burundi]

CVC – Corporación Autónoma Regional del Valle del Cauca [Colombia]

CVL – Central Veterinary Laboratory [Tanzania]

CVRI – Central Veterinary Research Institute [Zambia]

CWB – Canadian Wheat Board [Canada]

CYT – C.Y. Thompson Library [US]

CZU – Ceská zemedelská univerzita v Praze [Czech Republic]

DA – Department of Agriculture [Philippines]

DAF – Department of Agriculture and Forestry [Sierra Leone]

DAFF – Department of Agriculture, Food and Forestry [Ireland]

DAFS – Department of Agriculture and Fisheries for Scotland [UK]

DAL – Department of Agriculture and Livestock [Papua New Guinea]

DAMV – Delaware Agricultural Museum and Village [US]

DANI – Department of Agriculture for Northern Ireland [UK]

DANR – Department of Agriculture and Natural Resources [Philippines]

DAR – Department of Agricultural Research [Malawi]

DARA – Department of Agriculture and Rural Affairs [Australia]

DARD – Department of Agriculture and Rural Development [UK]

DAS – Department of Animal Science [China]

DAS – Direction des Archives du Sénégal [Senegal]

DAS – Dow Agrosciences [US]

DATE – Debreceni Agrártudományi Egyetem [Hungary]

DATEC – Dipartimento federale dell' Ambiente, dei Trasporti, dell' Energia e delle Comunicazioni [Switzerland]

DAV – Department of Agriculture, Victoria [Australia]

DCA – Dipartimento di Colture Arboree [Italy]

DCAH – Durham College of Agriculture and Horticulture [UK]

DCB – Development Center for Biotechnology [Taiwan]

DCIST – Direction de la Coopération et de l'Information Scientifique et Technique [Cote d'Ivoire]

DCRC – District of Columbia Reference Center [US]

DCRS – Dodo Creek Research Station [Solomon Islands]

DCSTP – Database of Chinese Scientific and Technical Periodicals [China]

DDI – Division de Documentation et d'Information [Morocco]

DEF – Direction des Eaux et Forêts [Madagascar]

DEFC – Direction des Eaux, Forêts, Chasses et de la Conservation des Sols [Senegal]

DEI – Deutsches Entomologisches Institut - Eberswalde [Germany]

DELNET – Delhi Library Network [India]

DENR – Department of Environment and Natural Resources [Philippines]

DEPAGRI – Département de l'Agriculture [Congo, Democratic Republic of the]

DES – Desert Botanical Garden [US]

DETEC – Département fédéral de l'Environnement, des Transports, de l'Energie et de la Communication [Switzerland]

DFE – Département fédéral de l'Economique [Switzerland]

DFI – Département fédéral de l'Interieur [Switzerland]

DFID – Department for International Development [UK]

DFLRI – Danish Forest and Landscape Research Institute [Denmark]

DFO – Department of Fisheries and Oceans [Canada]

DGA – Direction Générale des Archives Nationales [Gabon]

DGPD – Direction Générale du Plan et du Développement [Togo]

DGRST – Délégation Générale de la Recherche Scientifique et Technique [Congo, Republic of the]

DHC – Dallas Horticulture Center [US]

DHI – Deutsches Hydrographisches Institut [Germany]

DI – Department of Information [Czech Republic]

DIAF – Dipartimento Ingegneria Agraria e Forestale [Italy]

DIBD – Divisão de Biblioteca e Documentação [Brazil]

DID – Departamento de Documentação e Informação [Mozambique]

DID – Departamento de Informação e Documentação [Brazil]

DIDCT – Departamento de Informação e Documentação Cientifica e Técnica [Portugal]

DIFRES – Danish Institute for Fisheries Research [Denmark]

DIN – Departamento de Informação e Informática [Brazil]

DINiW – Dzial Informacji Naukowej i Wydawnictw [Poland]

DIR – Direction de l'Infrastructure Rurale [Madagascar]

DIRC – Documentation and Information Resource Center [Cambodia]

DIS – Documentation and Information Service [Senegal]

DIST – Direction de l'Information Scientifique et Technique [Cote d'Ivoire]

DIST – Division de la Documentation et Information Scientifique et Technique [Togo]

DITS – Documentation, Information and Training Service [Nepal]

DITSL – Deutsches Institut für Tropische und Subtropische Landwirtschaft GmbH [Germany]

DLD – Department of Livestock Development [Thailand]

DLD – Directorate of Lac Development [India]

DLIS – Department of Library and Information Services [UK]

DLO – Dienst Landbouwkundig Onderzoek [Netherlands]

DMRI – Danish Meat Research Institute [Denmark]

DNE – Direction Nationale de l'Elevage [Mali]

DNEF – Direction Nationale des Eaux et Forêts [Mali]

DNGR – Direction Nationale du Génie Rural [Mali]

DNPEA – Departamento Nacional de Pesquisa Agropecuária [Brazil]

DNR – Minnesota State Department of Natural Resources [US]

DNR – Wisconsin State Department of Natural Resources [US]

DNRA – Direction Nationale de la Recherche Agronomique [Togo]

DNRE – Department of Natural Resources and Environment [Australia]

DNTC – Domboshawa National Training Centre [Zimbabwe]

Do/Bi – Fachgebiet Dokumentation/Bibliothek [Germany]

DOA – Department of Agriculture [Thailand]

DOST – Department of Science and Technology [Philippines]

DOST-ESEP – Department of Science and Technology, Engineering and Science Education Project [Philippines]

DPF – Dirección de Producción Forestal [Argentina]

DPF – Direction de la Production Forestière [Togo]

DPI – Department of Primary Industry [Australia]

DPI – Division of Plant Industry [US]

DPIE – Department of Primary Industries and Energy [Australia]

DPIF – Northern Territory Department of Primary Industry and Fisheries [Australia]

DPPC – Development and Project Planning Centre [UK]

DRAER – Direction Régionale de l'Aménagement et Equipement Rural [Mali]

DRAiNnet – Drainage Information Network [Netherlands]

DRC – Davao Research Center [Philippines]

DRC – Development Resource Centre [New Zealand]

DRC – Drainage Research Centre [Pakistan]

DRDR/RC – Direction Regionale du Développement Rural - Région Centrale [Togo]

DREC – Delta Research and Extension Center [US]

DRI – Dairy Research Institute [Australia]

DRPF – Département des Recherches sur les Productions Forestières e l'Hydrobiologie [Senegal]

DRSS – Department of Research and Specialist Services [Zimbabwe]

DRV – Deutscher Raiffeisenverband e.V. [Germany]

DS – Direction de la Statistique [Morocco]

DSAC – Don Severino Agricultural College [Philippines]

DSC – Development Study Centre [Israel]

DSI – Directorate of Scientific Information [Pakistan]

DSIC – Documentation and Scientific Information Centre [Zambia]

DSII – Department of Scientific Information and Informatics [Belarus]

DSIR – Department of Scientific and Industrial Research [New Zealand]

DSLIB – Dick Smith Library [US]

DSTI – Department of Scientific-Technical Information [Slovakia]

DSU – Delaware State University [US]

DUPONT – E.I. du Pont de Nemours & Company, Inc. [US]

DUT – Delft University of Technology [Netherlands]

DVJB – Danmarks Veterinær- og Jordbrugsbibliotek [Denmark]

DVK – Departement van de Kwaliteit van Dierlijke Produkten en Transformatietechnologie [Belgium]

DVP – Departement Plantengenetica en -Veredeling [Belgium]

DVV – Departement Dierenvoeding en Veehouderij [Belgium]

DVZ – Departement Zeevisserij (CLO Ghent) [Belgium]

DWTC – Federale Diensten voor Wetenschappenlijke, Technische en Culturele Aangelegenheden [Belgium]

DWTI – Dienst voor Wetenschappelijke en Technische Informatie [Belgium]

EAAFRO – East African Agriculture and Forestry Research Organization [Kenya]

EAFV – Eidgenössische Anstalt für das forstliche Versuchswesen [Switzerland]

EAP – Escuela Agrícola Panamericana [Honduras]

EAS – Economic Affairs Secretariat [Antigua and Barbuda]

EAU – Estonian Agricultural University [Estonia]

EAVK – Ecole Agricole et Vétérinaire de Kabutaré [Rwanda]

EBDA – Empresa Baiana de Desenvolvimento Agrícola [Brazil]

ECAFE – United Nations Economic Commission for Asia and the Far East [Thailand]

ECAG – Escuela Centroamericana de Ganadería [Costa Rica]

ECCM – Eastern Caribbean Common Market [Antigua and Barbuda]

ECIAF – East Caribbean Institute of Agriculture and Forestry [Trinidad and Tobago]

ECODISC – Ecological Abstracts [UK]

EconLit – Economics Literature [US]

ECORC – Eastern Cereal and Oilseed Research Centre [Canada]

EDI – Eidgenössisches Departement des Inneren [Switzerland]

EDICA – Egyptian Documentation and Information Centre for Agriculture [Egypt]

EEA – Estación Experimental Agropecuaria [Argentina]

EEAD – Estación Experimental de Aula Dei [Spain]

EEI – Pesagro-Rio/Estação Experimental de Itaguaí [Brazil]

EEZ – Estación Experimental del Zaidín [Spain]

EEZA – Estación Experimental de Zonas Aridas [Spain]

EFE – Erdészeti és Faipari Egyetem [Hungary]

ÉFK – Élelmiszeripari Foiskolai Kar [Hungary]

EFN – Estação Florestal Nacional [Portugal]

EFW Library – Entomology, Fisheries and Wildlife Library [US]

EISMV – Ecole Inter-Etats des Sciences et Médecine Vétérinaires [Senegal]

ELCI – Environment Liaison Centre International [Kenya]

ELFIS – Die deutsche agrarwissenschaftliche Literaturdatenbank [Germany]

ELMS – Environment and Land Management Sector Coordination Unit [Lesotho]

ELVI TRK – Eisti Lsomakasvatuse je Veterinaaria Teadusliku Uurimise Instituut [Estonia]

EMATER – Empresa de Assistência Técnica e Extensão Rural [Brazil]

EMBRAPA – Brazilian Agricultural Research Corporation [Brazil]

EMBRAPA – Empresa Brasileira de Pesquisa Agropecuária [Brazil]

Embrapa Agrobiologia – Centro Nacional de Pesquisa de Agrobiologia [Brazil]

Embrapa Agroindústria de Alimentos – Centro Nacional de Pesquisa de Tecnologia Agroindustrial de Alimentos [Brazil]

Embrapa Agroindústrial Tropical – Centro Nacional de Pesquisa de Agroindústria Tropical [Brazil]

Embrapa Agropecuária Oeste – Centro de Pesquisa Agropecuária do Oeste [Brazil]

Embrapa Algodão – Centro Nacional de Pesquisa do Algodão [Brazil]

Embrapa Amapá – Centro de Pesquisa Agroflorestal do Amapá [Brazil]

Embrapa Amazônia Ocidental – Centro de Pesquisa Agroflorestal da Amazônia Ocidental [Brazil]

Embrapa Amazônia Oriental – Centro de Pesquisa Agroflorestal da Amazônia Oriental [Brazil]

Embrapa Arroz e Feijão – Centro Nacional de Pesquisa de Arroz e Feijão [Brazil]

Embrapa Caprinos – Centro Nacional de Pesquisa de Caprinos [Brazil]

Embrapa Cerrados – Centro de Pesquisa Agropecuária dos Cerrados [Brazil]

Embrapa Clima Temperado – Centro de Pesquisa Agropecuária de Clima Temperado [Brazil]

Embrapa Florestas – Centro Nacional de Pesquisa de Florestas [Brazil]

Embrapa Gado de Corte – Centro Nacional de Pesquisa de Gado de Corte [Brazil]

Embrapa Gado de Leite – Centro Nacional de Pesquisa de Gado de Leite [Brazil]

Embrapa Hortaliças – Centro Nacional de Pesquisa de Hortaliças [Brazil]

Embrapa Informática Agropecuária – Centro Nacional de Pesquisa Tecnológica em Informática para Agricultura [Brazil]

Embrapa Instrumentação Agropecuária – Centro Nacional de Pesquisa e Desenvolvimento de Instrumentação Agropecuária [Brazil]

Embrapa Mandioca e Fruticultura – Centro Nacional de Pesquisa de Mandioca e Fruticultura Tropical [Brazil]

Embrapa Meio Ambiente – Centro Nacional de Pesquisa de Monitoramento e Avaliação de Impacto Ambiental [Brazil]

Embrapa Meio-Norte – Centro de Pesquisa Agropecuária do Meio Norte [Brazil]

Embrapa Milho e Sorgo – Centro Nacional de Pesquisa de Milho e Sorgo [Brazil]

Embrapa Monitoramento por Satélite – Núcleo de Monitoramento Ambiental e de Recursos Naturais por Satélite [Brazil]

Embrapa Pantanal – Centro de Pesquisa Agropecuária do Pantanal [Brazil]

Embrapa Pecuária Sudeste – Centro de Pesquisa de Pecuária do Sudeste [Brazil]

Embrapa Pecuária Sul – Centro de Pesquisa de Pecuária dos Campos Sul Brasileiros [Brazil]

Embrapa Recursos Genéticos e Biotecnologia – Centro Nacional de Recursos Genéticos e Biotecnologia [Brazil]

Embrapa Rondônia – Centro de Pesquisa Agroflorestal de Rondônia [Brazil]

Embrapa Roraima – Centro de Pesquisa Agroflorestal de Roraima [Brazil]

Embrapa Sementes Básicas – Serviço de Produção de Sementes Básicas [Brazil]

Embrapa Semi-Árido – Centro de Pesquisa Agropecuária do Trópico Semi-Árido [Brazil]

Embrapa Soils – Brazilian Agricultural Research Corporation - Soils [Brazil]

Embrapa Soja – Centro Nacional de Pesquisa de Soja [Brazil]

Embrapa Solos – Empresa Brasileira de Pesquisa Agropecuária - Solos [Brazil]

Embrapa Tabuleiros Costeiros – Centro de Pesquisa Agropecuária dos Tabuleiros Costeiros [Brazil]

Embrapa Trigo – Centro Nacional de Pesquisa de Trigo [Brazil]

Embrapa Uva e Vinho – Centro Nacional de Pesquisa de Uva e Vinho [Brazil]

EMCAPA – Empresa Capixaba de Pesquisa Agropecuária [Brazil]

EMEPA-PB – Empresa Estadual de Pesquisa Agropecuária da Paraíba [Brazil]

EMETA No. 2 – Escuela Media Experimental Técnico Agropecuaria No. 2 [Argentina]

EMPASC – Empresa Catarinense de Pesquisa Agropecuária [Brazil]

EMU – Eduardo Mondlane University [Mozambique]

ENAL – Egyptian National Agriculture Library [Egypt]

ENAM – Ecole Nationale d'Agriculture de Meknès [Morocco]

ENCC – Ente Nazionale Cellulosa e Carta [Italy]

ENDA TM – Environment and Development in the Third World [Senegal]

ENGREF – Ecole Nationale du Génie Rural des Eaux et des Forêts [France]

ENMP – Estação Nacional de Melhoramento de Plantas [Portugal]

ENMU – Eastern New Mexico University [US]

ENSA – Ecole Nationale Supérieure d'Agriculture [Senegal]

ENSA – Ecole Supérieure d'Agronomie [Cote d'Ivoire]

ENSA.M – Ecole Nationale Supérieure Agronomique de Montpellier [France]

ENSAIA – Ecole Nationale Supérieure d'Agronomie et des Industries Alimentaires [France]

ENSAR – Ecole Nationale Supérieure Agronomique de Rennes [France]

EPA – Environmental Protection Agency [US]

EPABA – Empresa de Pesquisa Agropecuária da Bahia [Brazil]

EPAMIG – Empresa de Pesquisa Agropecuária de Minas Gerais [Brazil]

EPEA – Escuela Provincial de Educación Agrotécnica [Argentina]

EPMÜ – Eesti Pollumajandusülikool [Estonia]

ERC – Education Resource Centre [Australia]

ERDB – Ecosystems Research and Development Bureau [Philippines]

EREC/BG – Everglades Research and Education Center, Belle Glade [US]

ERIC – Educational Resources Information Center [US]

ERL – Environmental Research Laboratory [US]

ERTI – Erdészeti Tudományos Intézet [Hungary]

ESA – Ecole Supérieure d'Agriculture d'Angers [France]

ESAB – Escola Superior d'Agricultura de Barcelona [Spain]

ESAC – Escola Superior Agrária de Coimbra [Portugal]

ESALQ – Escola Superior de Agricultura "Luiz de Queiroz" [Brazil]

ESCAP – United Nations Economic and Social Commission for Asia and the Pacific [Thailand]

ESCI – Earth Sciences Library [Canada]

ESF – College of Environmental Science and Forestry [US]

ESPOCH – Escuela Superior Politécnica de Chimborazo [Ecuador]

ESSC – Eastern Samar State College [Philippines]

ETH – Eidgenössische Technische Hochschule Zürich [Switzerland]

ETSEA – Escola Tècnica Superior d'Enginyeria Agrària de Lleida [Spain]

ETSIA – Escuela Técnica Superior de Ingenieros Agrónomos [Spain]

ETSIAM – Escuela Técnica Superior de Ingenieros Agrónomos y Montes [Spain]

ETSIM – Escuela Técnica Superior de Ingenieros de Montes [Spain]

EÚ – Ceský ekologický ústav [Czech Republic]

EUITA – Escuela Universitaria de Ingeniería Técnica Agrícola [Spain]

EUL – Edinburgh University Library [UK]

EVD – Eidgenössisches Volkswirtschaftsdepartement [Switzerland]

EZN – Estação Zootécnica Nacional [Portugal]

FA – Faculty of Agriculture [Japan]

FAC – Eidgenössische Forschungsanstalt für Agrikulturchemie und Umwelthygiene [Switzerland]

FACA y FACV – Facultad de Ciencias Agrarias y Facultad de Ciencias Veterinarias [Argentina]

FADINAP – Fertilizer Advisory, Development and Information Network for Asia and the Pacific [Thailand]

FAEM – Faculdade de Agronomia Eliseu Maciel [Brazil]

FAES – Fukushima Prefecture Agricultural Experiment Station [Japan]

FAL – Bundesforschungsanstalt für Landwirtschaft [Germany]

FAL – Eidgenössische Forschungsanstalt für Agrarökologie und Landbau [Switzerland]

FAM – Eidgenössische Forschungsanstalt für Milchwirtschaft [Switzerland]

FAMV – Faculté d'Agronomie et de Médecine Vétérinaire [Haiti]

FAO – Food and Agriculture Organization [Italy]

FAOSTAT – Food and Agriculture Organization Statistics [International]

FARC – Food and Agricultural Research Council [Mauritius]

FAT – Eidgenössische Forschungsanstalt für Agrarwirtschaft und Landtechnik [Switzerland]

FAU – Fujian Agricultural University [China]

FAVE – Facultad de Agronomía y Veterinaria [Argentina]

FAW – Eidgenössische Forschungsanstalt für Obst-, Wein- und Gartenbau [Switzerland]

FB – Fundamentala Biblioteka [Latvia]

FBB – Fachbibliothek für Biologie [Austria]

FBC – Fourah Bay College [Sierra Leone]

FBN – Forschungsinstitut für die Biologie Landwirtschaftlicher Nutztiere [Germany]

FC – Zimbabwe Forestry Commission [Zimbabwe]

FCA – Faculdade de Ciências Agronômicas [Brazil]

FCA – Facultad de Ciencias Agrarias [Argentina]

FCA – Fiji College of Agriculture [Fiji]

FCF – Fujian College of Forestry [China]

FCPI – Fodder Crops and Pastures Institute [Greece]

FCRI – Fish Culture Research Institute [Hungary]

FCV – Facultad de Ciencias Veterinarias [Venezuela]

FDACS – Florida Department of Agriculture and Consumer Services [US]

FDAF – Fund for the Development of Agricultural and Fishery Activities in Mexico [Mexico]

FDAM – Fisheries Development Authority of Malaysia [Malaysia]

FDAR – Federal Department of Agricultural Research [Nigeria]

FDC – Federation of Danish Agricultural Cooperatives [Denmark]

FDC – Food Development Centre [Canada]

FDL – Frederick Douglass Library [US]

FECSU – Farmer Extension Communication Support Unit [Bhutan]

FEDERACAFE – Federación Nacional de Cafeteros de Colombia [Colombia]

FEI – Finnish Environment Institute [Finland]

FESRIA – Far Eastern Scientific Research Institute of Agriculture [Russia]

FF/SL – Family Farm/Stewardship Library [Canada]

FFL – Freshwater Fisheries Laboratory [UK]

FFPRI – Forestry and Forest Products Research Institute [Japan]

FGHRI – Forestry and Game Management Research Institute [Czech Republic]

FH Weihenstephan – Fachhochschule Weihenstephan [Germany]

FHIA – Fundación Hondureña de Investigación Agrícola [Honduras]

FIA – Fertilizer Industry Authority [Philippines]

FiBL – Forschungsinstitut für Biologischen Landbau [Switzerland]

FIRA – Fondo de Garantía y Fomento para la Agricultura, Ganadería y la Pesca [Mexico]

FK – Fakulteta za kmetijstvo [Slovenia]

FMCT – Federal Ministry of Commerce and Tourism [Nigeria]

FMEL – Florida Medical Entomology Laboratory [US]

FMRI – Finnish Meat Research Institute [Finland]

FMRI – Florida Marine Research Institute [US]

FMST – Federal Ministry of Science and Technology [Nigeria]

FMV – Faculdade de Medicina Veterinária [Portugal]

FMV – Faculté de la Médecine Vétérinaire [Belgium]

FMVZ – Faculdade de Medicina Veterinária e Zootecnia [Brazil]

FNIC – Food and Nutrition Information Center [US]

FNP – Institut fédéal de Recherches sur la Forêt, la Niege et le Paysage [Switzerland]

FNP – Instituto federale di Ricerca per la Foresta, la Neve e il Paesaggio [Switzerland]

FÖMI – Földmérési és Távérzékelési Intézet [Hungary]

FONAIAP – Fondo Nacional de Investigaciones Agropecuarias [Venezuela]

FORESC – Forest Research and Survey Centre [Nepal]

FORIG – Forestry Research Institute of Ghana [Ghana]

FORSEARCH – Forest Products Research Institute [Ghana]

FPA – Fertilizer and Pesticide Authority [Philippines]

FPL – Forest Products Laboratory [US]

FPRDI – Forest Products Research and Development Institute [Philippines]

FRC – Fisheries Research Centre [Ireland]

FRC – Forest Research Centre [Zimbabwe]

FRC – Forestry Research Center [Ethiopia]

FRDC – Food Research and Development Centre [Canada]

FRDC – Forest Research and Development Centre [Indonesia]

FRI – Fisheries Research Institute [Bangladesh]

FRI – Fisheries Research Institute [Malaysia]

FRI – Food Research Institute [Ghana]

FRI – Forest Research Institute [Bulgaria]

FRI – Forest Research Institute [Greece]

FRI – Forest Research Institute [India]

FRI – Forest Research Institute [Slovakia]

FRI – Forestry Research Institute [Korea, South]

FRIC – Central Forestry Library [Nepal]

FRIM – Forest Research Institute Malaysia [Malaysia]

FRIM – Forestry Research Institute of Malawi [Malawi]

FRIN – Forestry Research Institute of Nigeria [Nigeria]

FRS – Fisheries Research Services [UK]

FRU – Fisheries Research Station [Malawi]

FS – Forest Service [US]

FSA – Faculté des Sciences Agronomiques [Benin]

FSLN – Forest Service Library Network [US]

FSPI – Foundation for the Peoples of the South Pacific International [Vanuatu]

FSRO – Forest Survey and Research Office [Nepal]

FSTA – Food Science and Technology Abstracts [UK]

FSTM – Faculté des Sciences et Techniques - Mohammadia [Morocco]

FTG – Fairchild Tropical Garden [US]

FTI – Forestry Training Institute [Tanzania]

FTRS – Fruit Tree Research Station [Japan]

FUAU – Federal University of Agriculture, Umudike [Nigeria]

FUDECO – Fundación para el Desarrollo de la Región Centro Occidental de Venezuela [Venezuela]

FUL – Fondation Universitaire Luxenbourgeoise [Belgium]

FUNDP – Facultés Universitaires Notre-Dame de la Paix Namur [Belgium]

FUSAGx – Faculté Universitaire des Sciences Agronomiques de Gembloux [Belgium]

FUTO – Federal University of Technology, Owerri [Nigeria]

FVA – Forstliche Versuchs- und Forschungsanstalt Baden-Württemberg [Germany]

FVK – Fakultní vedecká knihovna [Czech Republic]

FVM – Faculty of Veterinary Medicine [Mozambique]

FVSU – Fort Valley State University [US]

FWS – United States Fish and Wildlife Service [US]

GAAS – Gansu Academy of Agricultural Sciences [China]

GAC – Guizhou Agricultural College [China]

GAMRI – Guangdong Agricultural Machinery Research Institute [China]

GATE – Gödölloi Agrártudományi Egyetem [Hungary]

GAU – Gansu Agricultural University [China]

Gb – Göteborgs Universitetsbibliotek [Sweden]

GBPU & AT – G.B. Pant University of Agriculture and Technology [India]

GBV – Gemeinsamet Bibliotheksverbund [Germany]

GC – Gambia College [Gambia]

GCREC – Gulf Coast Research and Education Center [US]

GCRL – Gulf Coast Research Laboratory [US]

GDAAS – Guangdong Academy of Agricultural Sciences [China]

GDFID – Guangdong Forestry Information Division [China]

GDFRI – Guangdong Forestry Research Institute [China]

GDRRI – Guangdong Rice Research Institute [China]

GED – Gulf Ecology Division [US]

GEGNIR – National and University Library Catalog [Iceland]

GeoRef – Bibliography and Index of Geology [US]

GHES – Gunma Horticultural Experiment Station [Japan]

GIAHVM – Guizhou Institute of Animal Husbandry and Veterinary Medicine [China]

GIS – Gozdarski inštitut Slovenije [Slovenia]

GLSC – Great Lakes Science Center [US]

GM – Gazdasagi Miniszterium [Hungary]

GMARI – Grassland and Mountain Agriculture Research Institute [Slovakia]

GMI – General Mills Inc. [US]

GPA – Georgiko Panepistimio Athinon [Greece]

GPIBFC – Guizhou Provincial Institute of Bast Fiber Crops [China]

GPIH – Guizhou Provincial Institute of Herbage [China]

GRI – Grassland Research Institute [China]

GRI – Grassland Research Institute [UK]

GSR – Groupement de la Science et de la Recherche [Switzerland]

GSR – Gruppo della Scienza e dell Ricerca [Switzerland]

GU – Gomal University [Pakistan]

GU – Guizhou University [China]

GUAS – Gödöllo University of Agricultural Sciences [Hungary]

GUASNR – Gorgan University of Agricultural Sciences and Natural Resources [Iran]

GWF – Gruppe für Wissenschaft und Forschung [Switzerland]

GXAAS – Guangxi Academy of Agricultural Sciences [China]

GXMRI – Guangxi Maize Research Institute [China]

GyDKF Kht – Erdi Gyümölcs- és Disznövénytermesztési Kutató-Fejlesztö Kht. [Hungary]

GYFK – Mezogazdasági Föiskolai Kar [Hungary]

HAAFS – Hebei Academy of Agricultural and Forestry Sciences [China]

HAGRES – Hokkaido Central Agricultural Experiment Station [Japan]

HAKI – Haltenyésztési Kutató Intézet [Hungary]

HAMKK Mustiala – Hämeen Ammattikorkeakoulu, Mustialanyksikkö [Finland]

HARC – Hawaii Agriculture Research Center [US]

HARSSC – Harbin Agricultural Remote Sensing Sub-Center [China]

HARTI – Hector Kobbekaduwa Agrarian Research and Training Institute [Sri Lanka]

HBLL – Harold B. Lee Library [US]

HBZ-Katalog – Union Catalog of North Rhine-Westfalia [Germany]

HCB – Hellenic Cotton Board [Greece]

HCL – Harvard College Libraries [US]

HCRL – Horticultural Crops Research Laboratory [US]

HDAAS – Handan Academy of Agricultural Sciences [China]

HEA – New Zealand Horticulture Export Authority [New Zealand]

HELIN – Higher Education Library Information Network [US]

HELÚ – Helmintologický ústavne [Slovakia]

HESA – Haute école suisse d'agronomie [Switzerland]

HET – Hevostutkimus [Finland]

HFRI – Hunan Fisheries Research Institute [China]

HIMAT – Instituto Colombiano de Hidrología, Meteorología y Adecuación de Tierras [Colombia]

HiNT – Høgskolen i Nord-Trøndelag [Norway]

HIOSH – Hawaii Occupational Safety and Health Division [US]

HLMRI – Huhhot Livestock Machinery Research Institute [China]

HMILFN – Hessisches Ministerium für Umwelt, Landwirtschaft, und Forsten [Germany]

HMSC – Hatfield Marine Science Center [US]

HNFRI – Hokkaido National Fisheries Research Institute [Japan]

HOL – Hezekiah Oluwasanmi Library [Nigeria]

HORTI – Tengeru Horticultural Research and Training Institute [Tanzania]

HortResearch – Horticulture and Food Research Institute of New Zealand [New Zealand]

HOS – Home Orchard Society [US]

HPGRC – Hokkaido Plant Genetic Resource Center [Japan]

HPI – Heifer Project International [US]

HPIFS – Hunan Provincial Institute of Fishery Science [China]

HPKV – Himachal Pradesh Krishi Vishwa Vidyalaya [India]

HRDC – Horticultural Research and Development Centre [Canada]

HRI – Hannah Research Institute [UK]

HRI – Horticulture Research Institute [Egypt]

HRIO – Horticultural Research Institute of Ontario [Canada]

HSNY – Horticultural Society of New York [US]

HSPA – Hawaiian Sugar Planters' Association [US]

HSRI – Hydraulics and Sediment Research Institute [Egypt]

HSU – Humboldt State University [US]

HSW – Hochschule Wädenswil [Switzerland]

HU – Hirosaki University [Japan]

HUL – Hiroshima University Library [Japan]

HUT – Helsinki University of Technology [Finland]

HY – Helsingin Yliopisto [Finland]

IA – Instytut Agrofizyki im. B. Dobrzanskiego [Poland]

IAAE – Institute for Application of Atomic Energy in Agriculture [China]

IAAS – Institute of Agriculture and Animal Science [Nepal]

IAC – Internationaal Agrarisch Centrum [Netherlands]

IAC – International Agricultural Centre [Netherlands]

IAC – Ishikawa Agricultural College [Japan]

IACR – Institute of Arable Crops Research [UK]

IAFI – Institute of Agricultural and Food Information [Czech Republic]

IAH – Institute for Animal Health [UK]

IAM – Institute of Agricultural Machinery [Japan]

IAMB – Institut Agronomique Méditerranéen de Bari [Italy]

IAMM – Institut Agronomique Méditerranéen de Montpellier [France]

IAMZ – Instituto Agronómico Mediterráneo de Zaragoza [Spain]

IAPAR – Fundação Instituto Agronômico do Paraná [Brazil]

IAPG – Institute of Animal Physiology and Genetics [Czech Republic]

IAPGR – Institute of Animal Physiology and Genetics Research [UK]

IAPH – Institut Agricole de la Province de Hainaut [Belgium]

IAR&T – Institute of Agricultural Research and Training [Nigeria]

IARI – Indian Agricultural Research Institute, Pusa [India]

IAS – Instituto Agronómico Salesiano [Dominican Republic]

IASA – International Alliance for Sustainable Agriculture [US]

IASRI – Indian Agricultural Statistics Research Institute [India]

IAT – Institute of Agronomy and Animal Hygiene in the Tropics [Germany]

IATA – Instituto Agroquímica Tecnología Alimentos [Spain]

IAVH II – Institut Agronomique et Vétérinaire Hassan II [Morocco]

IAVS – Institute of Animal and Veterinary Sciences [China]

IB – Instytut Botaniki im. Wladyslawa Szafera [Poland]

IB-SP – Instituto Biológico - São Paulo [Brazil]

IBA – Universidad de Buenos Aires [Argentina]

IBB – Institute of Biochemistry and Biophysics [Poland]

IBB – Instytut Biochemii i Biofizyki [Poland]

IBF – Institut für Bodenforschung [Austria]

IBFC – Institute of Bast Fibre Crops [China]

IBICT – Instituto Brasileiro de Informação em Ciência e Tecnologia [Brazil]

IBL – Instytut Badawczy Lesnictwa [Poland]

IBMARNR – Instituto Brasileiro de Meio Ambiente e Recursos Naturais Renováveis [Brazil]

IBMER – Instytut Budownicta, Mechanizacji i Elektryfikacji Rolnictwa [Poland]

IBODA – Instituto de Botánica Darwinion [Argentina]

IBPGR – International Board for Plant Genetic Resources [Italy]

IBPP – Institute of Biological Plant Protection [Moldova]

IBPRS – Instytut Biotechnologii Przemyslu Rolno-Spozywczego [Poland]

IBRA – International Bee Research Association [UK]

IBRCEC – Indonesian Biotechnology Research Institute for Estate Crops [Indonesia]

IBRD – International Bank for Reconstruction and Development [US]

IBSRAM – International Board for Soil Research and Management [Fiji]

IBSRAM – International Board for Soil Research and Management [Thailand]

IBt – Instituto de Botánico [Brazil]

IBTA – Instituto Boliviano de Tecnología Agropecuaria [Bolivia]

IBVL – Instituut voor Bewaring en Verwerking van Landbouwproducten [Netherlands]

IC – Imperial College [UK]

ICA – Instituto Colombiano Agropecuario [Colombia]

ICAFI – Information Centre for Agriculture and Food Industry [Vietnam]

ICAR – Indian Council of Agricultural Research [India]

ICARD – Information Centre for Agriculture and Rural Development [Vietnam]

ICARDA – International Center for Agricultural Research in the Dry Areas [Syria]

ICARNET – Indian Council for Agricultural Research Network [India]

ICCC – Institutul de cercetari pentry culturile de camp [Moldova]

ICFR – Institute for Commercial Forestry Research [South Africa]

ICFRE – Indian Council of Forestry Research and Education [India]

ICHS – Information Centre for Horticultural Sciences [India]

ICIMOD – International Centre for Integrated Mountain Development [Nepal]

ICIPE – International Centre of Insect Physiology and Ecology [Kenya]

ICITID – Institutul de Cercetare si Inginerie Tehnologica pentru Irigatii si Drenaje [Romania]

ICLARM – International Center for Living Aquatic Resources Management [Philippines]

ICM – Instituto de Ciencias del Mar [Spain]

ICO – International Coffee Organization [UK]

ICPA – Institutul de Cercetari pentru Pedologie si Agrochimie [Romania]

ICPC – Institutul de Cercetare si Productie a Cartofului [Romania]

ICPCB – Institutul de Cercetare si Productie pentru Cresteres Bovinelor [Romania]

ICPCP – Institutul de Cercetare si Productie pentry Cultura Pajistilor Brasov [Romania]

ICRAF – International Centre for Research in Agroforestry [Kenya]

ICRISAT – International Crops Research Institute for the Semi Arid Tropics [India]

ICTA – Instituto de Ciencia y Tecnología Agrícolas [Guatemala]

ICVV Valea Calugareasca – Institutului de Cercetari Pentru Viticultura si Vinificatie [Romania]

ICYT – Instituto de Información y Documentación en Ciencia y Tecnología [Spain]

ID – Instituut voor Dierhouderij en Diergezondheid [Netherlands]

ID – Instytut Dendrologi [Poland]

ID – Irrigation Department [Sri Lanka]

IDC – Information and Documentation Center [Brazil]

IDC – International Development Centre [UK]

IDD – Information and Data Division [China]

IDE – Informations- und Dokumentationsstelle für Ernährung [Germany]

IDEA – Centre for International Development Education and Action [New Zealand]

IDEAM – Instituto de Hidrología, Meteorología y Estudios Ambientales [Colombia]

IDIAP – Instituto de Investigación Agropecuaria de Panamá [Panama]

IDR – Institut du Développement Rural [Burkina Faso]

IDRC – International Development Research Centre [Canada]

IDS – Institute of Development Studies [UK]

IDS – Institute of Development Studies [Zimbabwe]

IDU – Information and Documentation Unit [India]

IE – Institute of Epizootology [Ukraine]

IE – Instytut Ekologii [Poland]

IEB – Institute of Experimental Botany [Czech Republic]

IECVM – Institute of Experimental and Clinical Veterinary Medicine [Ukraine]

IEG – Instituto de Economía y Geografía [Spain]

IEGA – Instituto de Economía y Geografía Aplicadas [Spain]

IELR – Institut efiromaslichnykh i lekarstvennykh rastenij [Ukraine]

IEO – Instituto Español de Oceanografía [Spain]

IEP – Institute of Environmental Protection [Poland]

IER – Institut d'Economie Rurale [Mali]

IERiGZ – Instytut Ekonomiki Rolnictwa i Gospodarki Zywnosciowej [Poland]

IESL – Informal Employment and Sustainable Livlihoods Project [Palau]

IETU – Instytut Ekologii Terenów Uprzemyslowionych [Poland]

IEW – International Environment Wallonie [Belgium]

IFAD – International Fund for Agricultural Development [Italy]

IFAS – Institute of Food and Agricultural Sciences [US]

IFB – Illinois Farm Bureau [US]

IFDC – International Fertilizer Development Center [US]

IFDC-A – International Fertilizer Development Center for Africa [Togo]

IFES – Ibaraki Prefectural Forest Experiment Station [Japan]

IFFIVE – Instituto de Fitopatología y Fisiología Vegetal [Argentina]

IFGB – Institut für Gärungsgewerbe und Biotechnologie [Germany]

IFGTB – Institute of Forest Genetics and Tree Breeding [India]

IFORD – Institut de Formation et de Recherche Démographiques [Cameroon]

IFP – Institute of Forest Productivity [India]

IFPRI – International Food Policy Research Institute [US]

IFR – Institute for Fisheries Research [US]

IFVC – Institute of Field and Vegetable Crops [Serbia and Montenegro]

IfW – Institut für Weltwirtschaft [Germany]

IG – Institut za Gorata [Bulgaria]

IGAP – Institute of Grassland and Animal Products [UK]

IGC – Institute of Genetics and Cytology [Belarus]

IGE – Institute of Genetic Ecology [Japan]

IGEAF – Instituto de Genética "Ewald A. Favret" [Argentina]

IGER – Institute of Grassland and Environmental Research [UK]

IGFA – International Game Fish Association [US]

IGFRI – Indian Grassland and Fodder Research Institute [India]

IGFS – Institut für Gewässerökologie, Fischereibiologie und Seenkunde [Austria]

IGiHZ – Instytut Genetyki i Hodowli Zwierzat [Poland]

IGR – Instytut Genetyki Roslin [Poland]

IGS – Instituut vir Groente en Sierplante [South Africa]

IGZ – Institut für Gemüse- und Zierpflanzenbau [Germany]

IHAR – Instytut Hodowli i Aklimatyzacji Roslin [Poland]

IHAR-Bonin – Instytut Hodowli i Aklimatyzacji Roslin - Oddzial Bonin [Poland]

IHD – Institute for Horticultural Development [Australia]

IHP Zalec – Institut za hmeljarstvo in pivovarstvo Zalec [Slovenia]

IHR – Institute of Horticultural Research [UK]

II – Information Institute [China]

IIA – Istituto di Ingegneria Agraria [Italy]

IIAG – Instituto de Investigaciones Agrobiológicas de Galicia [Spain]

IIBC – International Institute of Biological Control [Pakistan]

IICA – Instituto Interamericano de Cooperación para la Agricultura [Costa Rica]

IICA – Interamerican Institute of Co-operation in Agriculture [Costa Rica]

IICT – Instituto de Investigação Científica Tropical [Portugal]

IIF – Institut International du Froid [France]

IIFG – Institute of Irrigated Fruit Growing [Ukraine]

IIHR – Indian Institute of Horticultural Research [India]

IIM – Instituto de Investigaciones Marinas [Spain]

IIMI – International Irrigation Management Institute [Sri Lanka]

IIPGR – Institute for Introduction and Plant Genetic Resources [Bulgaria]

IIR – International Institute of Refrigeration [France]

IISR – Indian Institute of Spices Research [India]

IISR – Institute for Irrigation and Salinity Research [Australia]

IIT – Israel Institute of Technology [Israel]

IIT Kharagpur – Indian Institute of Technology Kharagpur [India]

IITA – International Institute of Tropical Agriculture [Nigeria]

IITF – International Institute of Tropical Forestry [Puerto Rico]

IKFB – Institouto Ktinotrophikon Phyton ke Boskon [Greece]

ILCA – International Livestock Centre for Africa [Ethiopia]

ILEIA – Centre for Research and Information on Low External Input and Sustainable Agriculture [Netherlands]

ILF – International Library of Fishes [US]

ILRAD – International Laboratory for Research on Animal Diseases [Kenya]

ILRI – Indian Lac Research Institute [India]

ILRI – International Institute for Land Reclamation and Improvement [Netherlands]

ILRI – International Livestock Research Institute [Ethiopia]

ILRI – International Livestock Research Institute [Kenya]

IMAAS – Inner Mongolia Academy of Agricultural Sciences [China]

IMAG – Instituut voor Mechanisatie, Arbeid en Gebouwen [Netherlands]

IMAG – Instituut voor Milieu- en Agritechniek [Netherlands]

IMARPE – Instituto del Mar del Perú [Peru]

IMC – Information Management Center [US]

IMERNAR – Instituto Mexicano de Recursos Naturales Renovables, A.C. [Mexico]

IMGW – Instytut Meteorologii i Gospodarki Wodnej [Poland]

IMH – International Museum of the Horse [US]

IML – Institut Maurice-Lamontagne [Canada]

IMS – Institute of Marine Sciences [US]

IMS – Instytut Maszyn Spozywczych [Poland]

IMTA – Instituto Mexicano de Tecnología del Agua [Mexico]

IMWM – Institute of Meteorology and Water Management [Poland]

INA P-G – Institut National Agronomique Paris-Grignon [France]

INADES – Institut Africain pour le Développement Economique et Social [Cote d'Ivoire]

INAPE – Instituto Nacional de Pesca [Uruguay]

INAT – Institut National Agronomique de Tunisie [Tunisia]

INCAE – Instituto Centroamericano de Administración de Empresas [Costa Rica]

INCAP – Instituto de Nutrición de Centro América y Panamá [Guatemala]

INCIVA – Instituto Vallecaucano de Investigaciones Científicas [Colombia]

INCV – Institut National des Cultures Vivrières [Togo]

INDOTEC – Instituto Dominicano de Tecnología Industrial [Dominican Republic]

INDR – Institut National de Développement Rural [Senegal]

INEA – Istituto Nazionale di Economia Agraria [Italy]

INEP – Instituto Nacional de Estudos e Pesquisas [Guinea-Bissau]

INF – Informationszentrum und Bibliothek [Germany]

INFODOC – Informatie-en Documentatiecentrum [Belgium]

Infopêche – Intergovernmental Organization for Marketing Information and Cooperation Service for Fishery Products in Africa [Cote d'Ivoire]

INFOR – Instituto Forestal [Chile]

Infruitec/Nietvoorbij – Fruit, Vine and Wine Research Institute [South Africa]

INFS – Istituto Nazionale per la Fauna Selvatica [Italy]

INIA – Instituto de Investigaciones Agropecuarias [Chile]

INIA – Instituto Nacional de Investigação Agraria [Cape Verde]

INIA – Instituto Nacional de Investigação Agrária [Portugal]

INIA – Instituto Nacional de Investigação Agronómica [Mozambique]

INIA – Instituto Nacional de Investigaciones Agrarias [Spain]

INIA – Instituto Nacional de Investigaciones Agrícolas [Mexico]

INIA – Instituto Nacional de Investigación Agropecuaria [Uruguay]

INIA – Instituto Nacional de Investigación y Tecnología Agraria y Alimentaria [Spain]

INIAP – Instituto Nacional de Investigaciones Agropecuarias [Ecuador]

INIDEP – Instituto Nacional de Investigación y Desarrollo Pesquero [Argentina]

INIFAP – Instituto Nacional de Investigaciones Forestales, Agrícolas y Pecuarias [Mexico]

INIP – Instituto Nacional de Investigação das Pescas [Portugal]

INIVE – Instituto Nacional de Investigação Veterinária [Mozambique]

INMV Pasteur – Institutul National de Medicina Veterinara Pasteur [Romania]

INPA – Instituto Nacional de Pesquisa da Amazônia [Brazil]

INPES – Instituto de Planejamento Econômico e Social [Brazil]

INRA – Institut National de la Recherche Agronomique [France]

INRA – Institut National de la Recherche Agronomique [Morocco]

INRAAG – INRA Centre Antilles-Guyane [Guadeloupe]

INRAN – Institut National de Recherche Agronomique du Niger [Niger]

INRAT – Institut National de la Recherche Agronomique de Tunisie [Tunisia]

INS – Institut National des Sols [Togo]

INS – Instytut Nawozow Sztucznych [Poland]

INSAH – Institut du Sahel [Mali]

INSDOC – Indian National Scientific Documentation Centre [India]

INSEA – Institut National des Statistiques et d'Economie Appliquée [Morocco]

Inspec – Institution of Electrical Engineers Database for Physics, Electronics and Computing [UK]

INTA – Institut de Nutrition et de Technologie Alimentaire [Togo]

INTA – Instituto Nacional de Tecnología Agropecuaria [Argentina]

INTROP – Informationszentrum für Tropischen Pflanzenschutz [Germany]

INVA – Institut National de la Vulgarisation Agricole [Algeria]

INZV – Institut National Zootechnique et Véterinaire [Togo]

IOB – Institut Ovochivnitstva e Bashtannictva [Ukraine]

IOC – Institute of Oil Crops [China]

IofAp – Institute of Apiculture [Slovakia]

IOLR – Israel Oceanographic and Limnological Research Ltd. [Israel]

IOPRI – Indonesian Oil Palm Research Institute [Indonesia]

IOR – Instytut Ochrony Roslin [Poland]

IOS – Instytut Ochrony Srodowiska [Poland]

IP – Resea Yching Institute of Pomology [China]

IPA – Empresa Pernambucana de Pesquisa Agropecuária [Brazil]

IPB – Institut Pasteur du Bruxelles [Belgium]

IPB – Institut Pertanian Bogor [Indonesia]

IPBP – Institutul de Protectie Biologica a Plantelor [Moldova]

IPC – Instytut Przemyslu Cukrowniczego [Poland]

IPD, AC – Institut Panafricain pour le Développement, Afrique Centrale Francophone [Cameroon]

IPD, AOS – Institut Panafricain pour le Développement, Afrique de l'Ouest Sahel [Burkina Faso]

IPDR – Institut Pratique de Développement Rural [Niger]

IPEA – Instituto de Pesquisa Econômica Aplicada [Brazil]

IPEAL – Instituto de Pesquisa Agropecuária do Leste [Brazil]

IPEF – Instituto de Pesquisas e Estudos Florestais [Brazil]

IPESAT – Institut Provincial d'Enseignement Supérieur Agricole et Technique [Belgium]

IPF – Institut für Pflanzenschutzforschung [Germany]

IPGFTC – Ibaraki Prefectural Government Forestry Technology Center [Japan]

IPGRI – International Plant Genetic Resources Institute [Italy]

IPIMAR – Instituto Português de Investigação Marítima [Portugal]

IPMiT – Instytut Przemyslu Miesnego i Tluszczowego [Poland]

IPP – Institut Penyelidikan Perikanan [Malaysia]

IPPC – Integrated Plant Protection Center [US]

IPPD – Institut po Pochvoznanie i Programirane na Dobivite [Bulgaria]

IPPP – Institute of Plant Pathology and Physiology [Argentina]

IPR – Institut Polytechnique Rural [Mali]

IPR/Katibougou – Institut Polytechnique Rural de Katibougou [Mali]

IPSA – Institute of Postgraduate Studies in Agriculture [Bangladesh]

IPT – Instituto de Pesquisa Tecnológica do Estado de São Paulo [Brazil]

IPV – Istituto di Pathologia Vegetale [Italy]

IPVDF – Instituto de Pesquisas Veterinárias "Desidério Finamor" [Brazil]

IPZ GÜ – Institut für Pflanzenzüchtung Gülzow-Güstrow [Germany]

IRA – Institut de la Recherche Agronomique [Cameroon]

IRA – Institut des Régions Arides [Tunisia]

IRAD – Institut de la Recherche Agricole pour le Développement [Cameroon]

IRAF – Institut de Recherches Agronomiques et Forestières [Gabon]

IRB – Institute of Radiation Breeding [Japan]

IRBAB – Institut Royal Belge pour l'Amélioration de la Betterave [Belgium]

IRBET – Institut de Recherche en Biologie et Ecologie Tropical [Burkina Faso]

IRC – Information Research Center [US]

IRC – Information Resource Centre [Kenya]

IRC – Instructional Resources Center [Thailand]

IRCC – Institut de Recherche Café-Cacao [Togo]

IRCT – Institut de Recherches du Coton et des Textiles Exotiques [Togo]

IRD – Institut de Recherche pour le Développement [Burkina Faso]

IRD – Institut de Recherche pour le Développement [Cameroon]

IRD – Institut de Recherche pour le Développement [Central African Republic]

IRD – Institut de Recherche pour le Développement [Congo, Republic of the]

IRD – Institut de Recherche pour le Développement [Cote d'Ivoire]

IRD – Institut de Recherche pour le Développement [Mali]

IRD – Institut de Recherche pour le Développement [New Caledonia]

IRD – Institut de Recherche pour le Développement [Niger]

IRD – Institut de Recherche pour le Développement [Senegal]

IRD – Institut de Recherche pour le Développement [Togo]

IRE – Institut für Rurale Entwicklung [Germany]

IRiPZ – Instytut Roslin i Przetworów Zielarskich [Poland]

IRL – Istituto per la Ricerca sul Legno [Italy]

IRMDFR – Institute of Rain and Moist Deciduous Forest Research [India]

IRNAS – Instituto de Recursos Naturales y Agrobiología de Sevilla [Spain]

IRNASA – Instituto de Recursos Naturales y Agrobiología de Salamanca [Spain]

IRPD – International Rural Projects Data Base and Rural Tourism Resource Center [Israel]

IRRI – International Rice Research Institute [Philippines]

IRS – Instytut Rybactwa Sródladowego [Poland]

IRScNB – Institut Royal des Sciences Naturelles de Belgique [Belgium]

IRSMLDC – Ian R. Smith Memorial Library and Documentation Center [Philippines]

IRTA – Institut de Recerca i Tecnologia Agroalimentàries [Spain]

IRWiR – Instytut Rozwoju Wsi i Rolnictwa [Poland]

IRZ – Institut für Rebenzüchtung Geilweilerhof [Germany]

IS – Information Service [Senegal]

IS/L – Management and Technical Information Services / Library [US]

ISA – Instituto Superior de Agronomia [Portugal]

ISA – Istituto Sperimentale Agronomico [Italy]

ISABU – Institut des Sciences Agronomiques du Burundi [Burundi]

ISAF – Institut de Sciences Agrozootechniques Foulaya [Guinea]

ISAR – Institut des Sciences Agronomiques du Rwanda [Rwanda]

ISAS – Institute of Southern African Studies [Lesotho]

ISB – Institute of Sugar Beet [Ukraine]

ISC – Istituto Sperimentale per la Cerealicoltura [Italy]

ISCA – Isabela State College of Agriculture [Philippines]

ISCAF – Ifugao State College of Agriculture and Forestry [Philippines]

ISCI – Istituto Sperimentale per le Colture Industriali [Italy]

ISDR – Institut Supérieur de Développement Rural [Central African Republic]

ISF-FO – Istituto Sperimentale per la Frutticoltura, Sezione di Forli [Italy]

ISI – Institut Supérieur Industriel [Belgium]

ISI – Institute for Scientific Information - Central Library [Czech Republic]

ISK – Instytut Sadownictwa i Kwiaciarstwa [Poland]

ISL – Information Services and Library [Czech Republic]

ISMEA – Istituto per Studi, Recerche, e Informazioni sul Mercato Agricolo [Italy]

ISNAR – International Service for National Agricultural Research [Netherlands]

ISNP – Istituto Sperimentale per la Nutrizione delle Piante [Italy]

ISOC – Instituto de Información y Documentación en Ciencias Sociales y Humanidades [Spain]

ISP – Istituto di Sperimentazione per la Pioppicoltura [Italy]

ISRA – Institut Sénégalais de Recherches Agricoles [Senegal]

ISRI – Indonesian Sugar Research Institute [Indonesia]

ISRIC – International Soil Reference and Information Centre [Netherlands]

ISS – Institute of Soil Science [China]

ISSA – Information Support Services for Agriculture [US]

ISSC – Institute of Southern Subtropical Crops [China]

ISSDS – Istituto Sperimentale per lo Studio e la Difesa del Suolo [Italy]

IST – Istituto Sperimentale per il Tabacco [Italy]

ISTI – Institute for Science and Technology Information [Korea, North]

ISTI – Institute of Scientific and Technical Information [China]

ISTIA – Institute of Scientific and Technical Information for Agriculture [Czech Republic]

ISTIA – Institute of Scientific and Technical Information for Agriculture [Slovakia]

ISTIC – Institute for Scientific and Technical Information of China [China]

ISU – Information Services Unit [Zambia]

ISU – Iowa State University [US]

ISV – Istituto Sperimentale per la Viticoltura [Italy]

ISW – Ingenieurschule Wädenswil [Switzerland]

ISZ – Istituto Sperimentale per la Zootecnia [Italy]

ITA – Institut de Technologie Agro-Alimentaire de Saint-Hyacinthe [Canada]

ITA – Institut de Technologie Alimentaire [Senegal]

ITCVM – Institute of Traditional Chinese Veterinary Medicine [China]

ITDG – Intermediate Technology Development Group [Peru]

ITE – Institute of Terrestrial Ecology [UK]

ITESM – Instituto Tecnológico de Estudios Superiores de Monterrey [Mexico]

ITF – Institute of Tropical Forestry [Puerto Rico]

ITG – Instituut voor Tropische Geneeskunde Prins Leopold [Belgium]

ITL – Istituto per la Tecnologia del Legno [Italy]

ITRA – Institut Togolais de Recherche Agricole [Togo]

ITSC – Institute for Tropical and Subtropical Crops [South Africa]

ITSG – Instituut vir Tropiese en Subtropiese Gewasse [South Africa]

ITSI – Institute of Technology and Science Information [China]

ITZ – Institut für Tierzuchtwissenschaft [Germany]

IuD – Information und Dokumentation [Germany]

IUFRO – International Union of Forestry Research Organizations [Austria]

IUL – Institut für Umweltschutz und Landwirtschaft [Switzerland]

IVIC – Instituto Venezolano de Investigaciones Científicas [Venezuela]

IVM – Institute of Vegetable and Melon Growing [Ukraine]

IVRI – Indian Veterinary Research Institute [India]

IWarz – Instytut Warzywnictwa [Poland]

IWASRI – International Waterlogging and Salinity Research Institute [Pakistan]

IWet – Instytut Weterynarii [Poland]

IWMI – International Water Management Institute [Sri Lanka]

IWN – Instytut Włókien Naturalnych [Poland]

IWST – Institute of Wood Science and Technology [India]

IZ – Informationszentrale (Forstliche) [Germany]

IZ – Instytut Zootechniki [Poland]

IZK Maritsa – Institut po zelenchukovi kulturi "Maritsa" [Bulgaria]

IZR – Institut za zastita na rasteniata [Bulgaria]

IZS – Instytut Zroshuvanoho Sadivnytstva [Ukraine]

JAAS – Jiangsu Academy of Agricultural Sciences [China]

JAC – Japan Agricultural Cooperatives [Japan]

JASI – Japan Agricultural Sciences Index [Japan]

JATE-SZÉF – JATE Szegedi Elelmiazeripari Föiskolai Kar [Hungary]

JAU – Jiangxi Agricultural University [China]

JBN – Jardín Botánico Nacional [Cuba]

JBNB – Jardin Botanique National de Belgique [Belgium]

JBT – Institutionen för Jordbrukets Biosystem och Teknologi [Sweden]

JCAAS – Jilin City Academy of Agricultural Sciences [China]

JCL – John Crerar Library [US]

JCU – James Cook University of North Queensland [Australia]

JFML – John Fornachon Memorial Library [Australia]

JIC – John Innes Centre [UK]

JICA – Japan International Cooperation Agency [Japan]

JICU – Junta de Investigações Científicas do Ultramar [Portugal]

JIRCAS – Japan International Research Center for Agricultural Sciences [Japan]

JLAU – Jilin Agricultural University [China]

Jõgeva PBI – Jõgeva Plant Breeding Institute [Estonia]

Jõgeva SAI – Jõgeva Sordiaretuse Instituut [Estonia]

JOIS – JICST [Japan Information Center of Science and Technology] Online Information Service [Japan]

JSNFRI – Japan Sea National Fisheries Research Institute [Japan]

JTRL – Jute Technological Research Laboratories [India]

JU – Jihoceske univerzita Ceské budejovice [Czech Republic]

JXAAS – Jiangxi Academy of Agricultural Sciences [China]

JXITCVM – Jiangxi Institute of Traditional Chinese Veterinary Medicine [China]

KAC – Kamphaengphet Agricultural College [Thailand]

KAC – Kearney Agricultural Center [US]

KADOC – Kenya Agricultural Documentation Center [Kenya]

KAFACO – Kalulushi Farm College [Zambia]

KANA – Komiti for the Advancement of Nutrition and Agriculture [Fiji]

KARI – Kenya Agricultural Research Institute [Kenya]

KATKI – Kisállattenyésztési és Takarmányozási Kutató Intézet [Hungary]

KazSRV – Kazakh Scientific Research Veterinary Institute [Kazakhstan]

KBIVB – Koninklijk Belgisch Instituut tot Verbetering van de Biet [Belgium]

KBS – W.K. Kellogg Biological Station [US]

KCAM – Katete Centre for Agricultural Marketing [Zambia]

KCAT – Kamphangphet College of Agriculture and Technology [Thailand]

KCDRRiOW – Krajowe Centrum Doradztwa Rozwoju Rolnictwa i Obszarów Wiejskich [Poland]

KCL – Oy Keskuslaboratorio, Centrallaboratorium Ab [Finland]

KDI – Kenneth Dike Library [Nigeria]

KÉE – Kertészeti és Élelmiszeripari Egyetem [Hungary]

KEEI – Karshy Engineering Economic Institute [Uzbekistan]

KENSIDOC – Kenya National Scientific Information, Documentation and Communication Center [Kenya]

KFC – Kenya Forestry College [Kenya]

KFRI – Kerala Forest Research Institute [India]

KHP – Kentucky Horse Park [US]

KI – Kutató Intézete [Hungary]

KIE – Kapnologiko Institouto Ellados [Greece]

KIRDI – Kenya Industrial Research and Development Institute [Kenya]

KIT – Koninklijk Instituut voor de Tropen [Netherlands]

KK – Központi Könyvtára [Hungary]

KKAC – Khon Kaen Agriculture College [Thailand]

KKL – Központi Könyvtár és Levéltár [Hungary]

KKU – Khon Kaen University [Thailand]

KMITL – King Mongkut's Institute of Technology Ladkrabang [Thailand]

KNAES – Kyushu National Agricultural Experiment Station [Japan]

KNLS – Kenya National Library Services [Kenya]

KNU – Kyungpook National University [Korea, South]

Korat Seri. Res. Cen. – Nakornratchasima Sericultural Research Center [Thailand]

KPKÖ – Központi Könyvtár [Hungary]

KPU – Kyoto Prefectural University [Japan]

KSISTI – Kazak State Research Institute of Scientific and Technical Information [Kazakhstan]

KSLA – Kungl. Skogs- och Lantbruksakademien [Sweden]

KSU – Kansas State University [US]

KU – Kasetsart University [Thailand]

KU – Kenyatta University [Kenya]

KU – Kyushu University [Japan]

KÚ – Kniznica ústavu [Slovakia]

KU Leuven – Katholieke Universiteit Leuven [Belgium]

Küt. Müd. – Kütüphane Müdürlügü [Turkey]

KVL – Den Kgl. Veterinær- og Landbohøjskole [Denmark]

KWF – Kuratorium für Waldarbeit und Forsttechnik E.V. [Germany]

KY – Kyorin University [Japan]

KYMEL – Kyorin University Medical Library [Japan]

L & DC – Library and Documentation Centre [India]

L&DU – Library and Documentation Unit [India]

L/RC – Library/Resource Center [US]

LAAS – Liaoning Academy of Agricultural Sciences [China]

LAEI – Lietuvos agrarines ekonomikos institutas [Lithuania]

LAES – Lowlands Agriculture Experiment Station [Papua New Guinea]

LAFI – Library of Agriculture and Food Industry [Vietnam]

LAPL – Los Angeles Public Library [US]

LARS – Long Ashton Research Station [UK]

LARTC – Lampang Agricultural Research and Training Center [Thailand]

LARTI – Lyamungu Agricultural Research and Training Institute [Tanzania]

LASRA – New Zealand Leather and Shoe Research Association [New Zealand]

LAVM – Lviv Academy of Veterinary Medicine [Ukraine]

LBA – Laboratório de Biologia Animal [Brazil]

LBN – Lembaga Biolgi Nasional [Indonesia]

LBT – Institutionen för Lantbrukets Byggnadsteknik [Sweden]

LCA – Library for the College of Agriculture [Japan]

LCC – Lethbridge Community College [Canada]

LCR – Lesy Ceské republiky s.p. [Czech Republic]

LCV – Laboratoire Central Vétérinaire [Mali]

LE – Vakgroep Landbouweconomie [Belgium]

LEI – Landbouw-Econonisch Instituut [Netherlands]

LES – Lowveld Experiment Station [Swaziland]

LFA – Landesforschungsanstalt für Landwirtschaft un Fischerei [Germany]

LGM – Lembaga Getah Malaysia [Malaysia]

LGNCRDC – La Granja National Crop Research and Development Center [Philippines]

LHDA – Lesotho Highlands Development Authority [Lesotho]

LHL – Linda Hall Library [US]

LHSL – Life and Health Sciences Library [US]

LIA – Lithuanian Institute of Agriculture [Lithuania]

LIAE – Lithuanian Institute of Agrarian Economics [Lithuania]

LIAgEng – Lithuanian Institute of Agricultural Engineering [Lithuania]

LIAS – Lishui Institute of Agricultural Sciences [China]

LIAS – Lithuanian Institute of Animal Science [Lithuania]

LIAVPS – Lanzhou Institute of Animal Veterinary Pharmaceutical Sciences [China]

LIBIS – Union Catalogue of Scientific Libraries of Lithuania [Lithuania]

LIBRIS – Library Information System [Sweden]

LIC – Library and Information Centre [UK]

LIC – Library and Information Service [Thailand]

LID – Library and Information Department [China]

LIDC – Library, Information and Documentation Centre [Nigeria]

LIH – Lithuanian Institute of Horticulture [Lithuania]

LIHRL – Long Island Horticultural Research Laboratory [US]

LIPI – Lembaga Ilmu Pengetahuan Indonesia [Indonesia]

LIS – Library and Information Services [Syria]

LIS – Library and Information Services [US]

LIS – Library and Information System [Botswana]

LIS – Library Information Services [Philippines]

LISI – Library and Institute of Scientific Information [Slovakia]

Litbang – Badan Penelitian dan Pengembangan Pertanian [Indonesia]

LITI – Livestock Training Institute [Tanzania]

LIU – Lincoln University [New Zealand]

LKIM – Lembaga Kemajuan Ikan Malaysia [Malaysia]

LLU – Latvijas Lauksaimniecibas Universitate [Latvia]

LMI – Lietuvos misku institutas [Lithuania]

LNERV – Laboratoire National de l'Elevage et de Recherches Vétérinaires [Senegal]

LNR – Landbounavorsingsraad [South Africa]

LNS – Library for Natural Sciences [Russia]

LPP – Lembaga Pendidikan Perkebunan [Indonesia]

LPRI – Livestock Production Research Institute [Tanzania]

LRC – Joseph F. Drake Memorial Learning Resources Center [US]

LRC – Lethbridge Research Centre [Canada]

LRDC – Library and Regional Documentation Center [Thailand]

LRM – Library and Records Management [Australia]

LRSL – Lowveld Research Stations Library [Zimbabwe]

LSDI – Lietuvos sodininkystes ir darzininkystes institutas [Lithuania]

LSU – Louisiana State University [US]

LTC – Land Tenure Center [US]

LTIT – Livestock Training Institute Tengeru [Tanzania]

LTK – Lihateollisuuden Tutkimuskeskus [Finland]

LTU – La Trobe University [Australia]

LU – Langston University [US]

LUA – Lithuanian University of Agriculture [Lithuania]

LUIS – Library User Information Service [US]

LVA – Lietuvos veterinarijos akademija [Lithuania]

LVI – Lietuvos veterinarijos institutas [Lithuania]

LVRI – Lanzhou Veterinary Research Institute [China]

LVÚ – Lesnícky výskumný ústav [Slovakia]

LVUI – Lietuvos vandens ukio institutas [Lithuania]

LVZZPI "Agra" – Latvian Scientific Research Institute of Agriculture [Latvia]

LWMI – Lithuanian Water Management Institute [Lithuania]

LZI – Lietuvos zemdirbystes institutas [Lithuania]

LZUII – Lietuvos zemes ukio inzinerijos institutas [Lithuania]

LZUU – Lietuvos zemès ukio universitetas [Lithuania]

MA – Ministère de l'Agriculture [Senegal]

MA – Ministry of Agriculture [Malawi]

MA – Ministry of Agriculture [Senegal]

MAAR – Ministry of Agriculture and Agrarian Reform [Syria]

MAARA – Ministério da Agricultura, do Abastecimento e da Reforma Agrária [Brazil]

MAC – Ministerio de Agricultura y Cría [Venezuela]

MAC – Ministry of Agriculture and Cooperatives [Tanzania]

MADRP – Ministère de l'Agriculture, du Développement Rural et des Pêches Maritimes [Morocco]

MADRP – Ministério da Agricultura, do Desenvolvimento Rural e das Pescas [Portugal]

MAEDR – Ministère de l'Agriculture, de l'Elevage et du Développement Rural [Gabon]

MAF – Ministry of Agriculture and Fisheries [New Zealand]

MAF – Ministry of Agriculture and Fisheries [Solomon Islands]

MAFF – Ministry of Agriculture, Fisheries and Food [UK]

MAFF – Ministry of Agriculture, Fisheries and Forests [Fiji]

MAFF – Ministry of Agriculture, Food and Fisheries [Barbados]

MAFF – Ministry of Agriculture, Forestry and Fisheries [Cambodia]

MAFF – Ministry of Agriculture, Forestry and Fisheries [Japan]

MAFF – Ministry of Agriculture, Forests and Fisheries [Samoa]

MAFFM – Ministry of Agriculture, Forests, Fisheries and Meteorology [Samoa]

MAFI – Ministry of Agriculture and Food Industry [Vietnam]

MaFRI – Marine and Freshwater Resources Institute [Australia]

MAG – Ministerio de Agricultura y Ganadería [Costa Rica]

MAI – Ministry of Agriculture and Irrigation [Malawi]

MAICH – Mesogeiako Agronomiko Institouto Chanion [Greece]

MAJUIKAN – Lembaga Kemajuan Ikan Malaysia [Malaysia]

MAL – Ministry of Agriculture and Lands [Jamaica]

MAL&MR – Ministry of Agriculture, Land and Marine Resources [Trinidad and Tobago]

MALD – Ministry of Agriculture and Livestock Development [Kenya]

MALD – Ministry of Agriculture and Livestock Development [Malawi]

MALD – Ministry of Agriculture and Livestock Development [Tanzania]

MALMD – Ministry of Agriculture, Livestock and Marketing Development [Kenya]

Malomkubato Kft. – Malomipari Kutató és Fejeesztö Kft. [Hungary]

MAMR – Ministry of Agriculture and Marine Resources [Seychelles]

MAP – Ministère de l'Agriculture [Algeria]

MAPA – Ministerio de Agricultura, Pesca y Alimentación [Spain]

MAPAQ – Ministère de l'Agriculture, des Pêcheries et de l'Alimentation, Québec [Canada]

MAPyA – Ministerio de Agricultura, Pesca y Alimentación [Spain]

MARA – Ministère de l'Agriculture et de la Réforme Agraire [Morocco]

MARC – Meat Animal Research Center [US]

MARC – Mount Albert Research Centre [New Zealand]

MARD – Ministry of Agriculture and Rural Development [Vietnam]

MARDF – Ministry of Agriculture, Rural Development and Fisheries [Portugal]

MARDI – Malaysian Agricultural Research and Development Institute [Malaysia]

MARM – Ministere l'Agrikiltir ek Resours Maren [Seychelles]

MATEC – Mambusao Agricultural and Technical College [Philippines]

MATFORSK – Norsk Institutt for Nøringsmiddel Forskning [Norway]

MATI – Ministry of Agriculture Training Institutes [Tanzania]

MAWD – Ministry of Agriculture and Water Development [Zambia]

MAWRD – Ministry of Agriculture, Water and Development [Namibia]

MBA – Marine Biological Association [UK]

MBG – Misión Biológica de Galicia [Spain]

MBL – Marine Biological Laboratory [US]

MCC – Museum of Czech Countryside [Czech Republic]

MCM – Marine and Coastal Management [South Africa]

MCV – Muzeum ceského venkova [Czech Republic]

MDR – Ministère du Développement Rural [Benin]

MDR – Ministère du Développement Rural [Congo, Republic of the]

MDR – Ministère du Développement Rural [Guinea]

MDR – Ministère du Développement Rural [Togo]

MEA – Ministry of Economic Affairs [Hungary]

MEADR – Ministère d'Etat à l'Agriculture et au Développement Rural [Madagascar]

MEG – Münchner Entomologische Gesellschaft e.V. [Germany]

MEN – Ministère de l'Education Nationale [Haiti]

MEN – Ministère de l'Education Nationale [Senegal]

MEPN – Ministère de l'Environnement et de la Protection de la Nature [Senegal]

MESRIT – Ministry of Higher Education, Research and Technological Innovation [Cote d'Ivoire]

METLA – Metsäntutkimuslaitos [Finland]

MFI – Masaiti Farm Institute [Zambia]

MFK – Mezogazdasági Foiskolai Kar, Hódmezovásárhely [Hungary]

MFPMEFE – Ministry of Food Production, Marine Exploitation, Forestry and the Environment [Trinidad and Tobago]

MGE – Minneapolis Grain Exchange [US]

MGFK – Mezögazdasági Gépészüzemmérnöki Föiskolai Kar [Hungary]

MIAT – Maejo Institute of Agricultural Technology [Thailand]

MICC – Ministère de l'Information, de la Culture et de la Communication [Madagascar]

MID – Marketing Information Department [US]

MILAI – Mie Library Advanced Information Network System [Japan]

MINAGRA – Ministère de l'Agriculture et des Ressources Animales [Cote d'Ivoire]

MINAGRI – Ministère de l'Agriculture [Cameroon]

MINAGRI – Ministère de l'Agriculture, de l'Elevage et des Forêts [Rwanda]

MINAGRI – Ministère de l'Agriculture et de l'Elevage [Burundi]

MINAGRI – Ministerio de Agricultura, Ganadería y Desarrollo Rural [Equatorial Guinea]

MINEDUC – Ministère de l'Education Nationale [Burundi]

MinRol – Ministerstwo Rolnictwa i Rozwoju Wsi [Poland]

MinSCAT – Mindoro State College of Agriculture and Technology [Philippines]

MIO – Monsanto Information Organization [US]

MIRS-Davis – Monsanto Information Resources and Services - Davis [US]

MKU – Minami Kyushu University [Japan]

MLURI – Macaulay Land Use Research Institute [UK]

MOA – Ministry of Agriculture [Bangladesh]

MoA – Ministry of Agriculture [China]

MOA – Ministry of Agriculture [Dominica]

MoA – Ministry of Agriculture [Ethiopia]

MOA – Ministry of Agriculture [Kenya]

MOAC – Ministry of Agriculture and Cooperatives [Swaziland]

MOAC – Ministry of Agriculture and Cooperatives [Thailand]

MOAL&M – Ministry of Agriculture, Livestock Development and Marketing [Kenya]

MOC – Ministry of Agriculture and Cooperatives [Tanzania]

MOFA – Ministry of Food and Agriculture [Ghana]

MOLA – Ministry of Lands and Agriculture [Zimbabwe]

Monterrey Tech – Monterrey Institute of Advanced Technological Studies [Mexico]

MORIF – Maros Research Institute for Food Crops [Indonesia]

MPAEF – Ministère de la Production Animale (Elevage et Pêche) et des Eaux et Forêts [Madagascar]

MPARA – Ministère de la Production Agricole et de la Réforme Agraire [Madagascar]

MPR – Ministère de la Promotion Rurale [Central African Republic]

MRB – Malaysian Rubber Board [Malaysia]

MRI – Moredun Research Institute [UK]

MRiGZ – Ministerstwo Rolnictwa i Gospodarki Zywnosciowej [Poland]

MRPRA – Malaysian Rubber Producers' Research Association [UK]

MRRDB – Malaysian Rubber Research and Development Board [Malaysia]

MRS – Ministère de la Recherche Scientifique [Cote d'Ivoire]

MRS – Ministère de la Recherche Scientifique [Madagascar]

MRSTD – Ministère de la Recherche Scientifique et Technologique pour le Développement [Madagascar]

MSC – Maryland State College [US]

MSIRI – Mauritius Sugar Industry Research Institute [Mauritius]

MSL – Marston Science Library [US]

MSL – Montana State Library [US]

MSU – Michigan State University [US]

MSU – Morehead State University [US]

MSU - Bottineau – Minot State University, Bottineau Branch [US]

MTA – Magyar Tudományos Akadémia [Hungary]

MTK – Maa- ja metsätaloustuottajain Keskusliitto [Finland]

MTT – Maatalouden Tutkimuskeskus [Finland]

MTU – Michigan Technological University [US]

MU – Meijo University [Japan]

MUVA – Milchwirtschaftliche Untersuchungs- und Versuchsanstalt Kempten [Germany]

MV – Museum Victoria [Australia]

MVC Library – Madras Veterinary College Library [India]

MVKK – Mezögazdasági Víz- és Környezeígazdálkodási Kar [Hungary]

MZLU – Mendelova zemedelaská a lesnická univerzita v Brne [Czech Republic]

MZLVA – Ústav védeckotechnickych informací pro zemedelství ÚVTIZ [Czech Republic]

NAARM – National Academy of Agricultural Research Management [India]

NAC – Ningxia Agricultural College [China]

NACAR – National Academic Centre of Agrarian Research of the Republic of Kazakhstan [Kazakhstan]

NACARD – National Advisory Centre for Agriculture and Rural Development [Poland]

NACIAD – National Centre for Information on Agrarian Development [Sri Lanka]

NACSIS – National Center for Science Information System [Japan]

NADC – National Animal Disease Center [US]

NADIC – National Agricultural Documentation and Information Centre [Uganda]

NADLIN – National Documentation Centre, Library and Information Network [Pakistan]

NADOC – National Agricultural Documentation Centre [Sierra Leone]

NAE – Narenciye Arastirma Enstitüsü [Turkey]

NAGREF – National Agricultural Research Foundation [Greece]

NAHRC – National Animal Husbandry Research Centre [Kenya]

NAIC – National Agricultural Information Center [Namibia]

NAL – National Agricultural Library [US]

NALDOC – National Agricultural Library and Documentation Centre [Bangladesh]

NAMRIA – National Mapping and Resource Information Authority [Philippines]

NAPRI – National Animal Production Research Institute [Nigeria]

NARA – National Aquatic Resources Research and Development Agency [Sri Lanka]

NARC – National Agricultural Research Centre [Kenya]

NARC – National Agricultural Research Centre [Pakistan]

NARC – National Agriculture Research Center [Japan]

NARC – Nepal Agricultural Research Council [Nepal]

NARI – National Agricultural Research Institute [Guyana]

NARI – National Agricultural Research Institute [Papua New Guinea]

NASTLIC – National Science and Technology Library and Information Centre [Ghana]

NAU – Northeast Agricultural University [China]

NAU – Northern Arizona University [US]

NAWIC – Namibian Agriculture and Water Information Centre [Namibia]

NB – Naukova Bibliteka [Ukraine]

NBAGR – National Bureau of Animal Genetic Resources [India]

NBFGR – National Bureau of Fish Genetic Resources [India]

NBG – National Botanical Garden [Cuba]

NBGB – National Botanical Garden of Belgium [Belgium]

NBGS – Norfolk Botanical Garden Society [US]

NBPGR – National Bureau of Plant Genetic Resources [India]

NBSS&LUP – National Bureau of Soil Survey and Land-Use Planning [India]

NC A&T – North Carolina Agricultural & Technical State University [US]

NCAID – National Center for Agricultural Information and Documentation [Syria]

NCARTT – National Center for Agricultural Research and Technology Transfer [Jordan]

NCAT – National Center for Appropriate Technology [US]

NCAUR – National Center for Agricultural Utilization Research [US]

NCC – Nature Conservancy Council [UK]

NCDSTI – National Center of Documentation and Scientific and Technical Information [Congo, Republic of the]

NCGA – National Corn Growers Association [US]

NCHU – National Chung Hsing University [Taiwan]

NCIT – National Chia-yi Institute of Technology [Taiwan]

NCMR – National Centre for Marine Research [Greece]

NCMRT – National Centre for Mushroom Research and Training [India]

NCPA – National Cattlemen's Beef Association [US]

NCRD – National Centre for Rural Development [Pakistan]

NCRI – National Cereals Research Institute [Nigeria]

NCSR – National Council for Scientific Research [Lebanon]

NCSR – National Council for Scientific Research [Zambia]

NCST – National Council for Science and Technology [Kenya]

NCSU – North Carolina State University [US]

NCT – Nakhonrajsrima College of Agriculture and Technology [Thailand]

NCWTD – National Centrum voor Wetenschappelijke en Technisch Documentrarie [Belgium]

NDC – Namibia Development Corporation [Namibia]

NDL – National Diet Library [Japan]

NDRI – National Dairy Research Institute [India]

NDSU – North Dakota State University [US]

NDUAT – Narendra Deva University of Agriculture and Technology [India]

NEIC – National Enforcement Investigations Center [US]

NEIC – National Environmental Information Center [Sri Lanka]

NEM – National Education Ministry [Haiti]

Nencki – Instytut Biologii Doswiadczalnej im. M. Nenckiego [Poland]

NERC – Natural Environment Research Council [UK]

NET – Network Information Center [Egypt]

NEWFS – New England Wild Flower Society Inc. [US]

NF – Samuel Roberts Noble Foundation [US]

NFDC – National Fertilizer Development Centre [Pakistan]

NFLIC – National Forest Library and Information Centre [India]

NFLZ – National Free Library of Zimbabwe [Zimbabwe]

NFNC – National Food and Nutrition Committee [Fiji]

NFRI – National Food Research Institute [Japan]

NFRI – NSW Fisheries Research Institute [Australia]

NFRIC – Natural Fibers Research and Information Center [US]

NFU – Nanjing Forestry University [China]

NGRI – National Grassland Research Institute [Japan]

NGWIC – National Ground Water Information Center [US]

NHM – Natural History Museum [UK]

NIA – National Irrigation Administration [Philippines]

NIAB – National Institute of Agricultural Botany [UK]

NIAB – Nuclear Institute for Agriculture and Biology [Pakistan]

NIAES – National Institute of Agro-Environmental Sciences [Japan]

NIAH – National Institute of Animal Health [Japan]

NIAH – National Institute of Animal Health [Thailand]

NIAI – National Institute of Animal Industry [Japan]

NIAID – National Institute of Allergy and Infectious Diseases [US]

NIAR – National Institute of Agrobiological Resources [Japan]

NIAS – Nanchong Institute of Agricultural Sciences [China]

NIAT – National Institute of Agricultural Technology [Argentina]

NIB – Nacionalni institut za biologijo [Slovenia]

NIBGE – National Institute for Biotechnology and Genetic Engineering [Pakistan]

NIC – Nutrition Information Center [Germany]

NICA – National Institute of Coastal Aquaculture [Thailand]

NIFA – Nuclear Institute for Food and Agriculture [Pakistan]

NIFTS – National Institute of Fruit Tree Science [Japan]

NIH – National Institutes of Health [US]

NIHORT – National Horticultural Research Institute [Nigeria]

NIIT – National I-Lan Institute of Technology [Taiwan]

NIOMR – Nigerian Institute for Oceanography and Marine Research [Nigeria]

NIPA "N. Poushkarov" – Nauchno-izsledovatelski institut po pochvoznanie i agroekologia "N. Poushkarov" [Bulgaria]

NIPB – Navorsingsinstituut vir Plantbeskerming [South Africa]

NIPM – National Institute of Plantation Management [Sri Lanka]

NIRD – National Institute of Rural Development [India]

NIRJAFT – National Institute of Research on Jute and Allied Fibres Technology [India]

NISES – National Institute of Sericultural and Entomological Science [Japan]

NISIR – National Institute for Scientific and Industrial Research [Zambia]

NISK – Norsk institutt for skogforskning [Norway]

NITK – Navorsingsinstituut vir Tabak en Katoen [South Africa]

NIVOT – National Research Institute of Vegetables, Ornamental Plants and Tea [Japan]

NIZO – Nederlands Instituut voor Zuivelonderzoek [Netherlands]

NIZO – NIZO Food Research [Netherlands]

NKI – Növényvédelmi Kutatóintézete [Hungary]

NLAS – National Library for Agricultural Sciences [Indonesia]

NLC – Nebraska Library Commission [US]

NLfB – Niedersächsisches Landesamt für Bodenforschung [Germany]

NLGEE – National Laboratory of Grassland Ecological Engineering [China]

NLH – Norges Landbrukshøgskole [Norway]

NLS – National Library of Scotland [UK]

NLSMB – National Livestock and Meat Board [US]

NLVS – National Library of Veterinary Science [India]

NMA – Núcleo de Monitoramento Ambiental e de Recursos Naturais por Satélite [Brazil]

NMBL – National Marine Biological Library [UK]

NMFS – National Marine Fisheries Service [US]

NMST – National Museum of Science and Technology [Canada]

NMSU – New Mexico State University [US]

NOAA – National Oceanic and Atmospheric Administration [US]

Nobel – Det Norske Nobelinstitutt [Norway]

Nobel – Norwegian Nobel Institute [Norway]

NORTEC – Northern Technical College [Zambia]

NPB – Nationale Plantentuin van Belgie [Belgium]

NPPI – National Pingtung Polytechnic Institute [Taiwan]

NPUST – National Pingtung University of Science and Technology [Taiwan]

NRC – Natural Resources Canada [Canada]

NRC – Natural Resources College [Malawi]

NRC (Camel) – National Research Centre for Camel [India]

NRC (Cashew) – National Research Centre for Cashew [India]

NRC (Citrus) – National Research Centre for Citrus [India]

NRC (Coldwater Fish) – National Research Centre on Coldwater Fisheries [India]

NRC (Equines) – National Research Centre for Equines [India]

NRC (Mithun) – National Research Centre for Mithun [India]

NRC (Soya) – National Research Centre on Soyabean [India]

NRC (Spices) – National Research Centre for Spices [India]

NRC (Yak) – National Research Centre on Yak [India]

NRCG – National Research Centre for Groundnut [India]

NRCM – National Research Center for Mushroom [India]

NRDC – Natural Resources Development College [Zambia]

NRIA – National Research Institute of Aquaculture [Japan]

NRIAE – National Research Institute of Agricultural Economics [Japan]

NRIAP – National Research Institute of Animal Production [Poland]

NRIFE – National Research Institute of Fisheries Engineering [Japan]

NRIFSF – National Research Institute of Far Seas Fisheries [Japan]

NRIS – Natural Resource Information System [US]

NRL – Natural Resources Library [US]

NRS – Naduruloulou Research Station [Fiji]

NS/S – Native Seeds/SEARCH [US]

NSAC – Nova Scotia Agricultural College [Canada]

NSF – National Science Foundation [US]

NSL – National Sedimentation Laboratory [US]

NSL – Natural Sciences Library [US]

NSLA – Nevada State Library and Archives [US]

NSPIC – National Sweetpotato Information Center [US]

NSPRI – Nigerian Stored Products Research Institute [Nigeria]

NSSHA – National Spotted Saddle Horse Association, Inc. [US]

NSU – Northwestern State University of Louisiana [US]

NSWA – NSW Agriculture [Australia]

NSWDA – New South Wales Department of Agriculture [Australia]

NTA – National Tobacco Administration [Philippines]

NTB – Naukovo-Technitchna Biblioteka [Ukraine]

NTB/ITs – Nauchno-tekhnicheskaja Biblioteka/Informatsionny Tsentr [Russia]

NTBG – National Tropical Botanical Garden [US]

NTCMST – National Taiwan College of Marine Science and Technology [Taiwan]

NTDH – Nord-Trøndelag distriktshøgskole [Norway]

NTI – Norsk Treteknisk Institutt [Norway]

NTIA – Núcleo Tecnológico de Informática para Agropecuária [Brazil]

NTICL – National Technical Information Centre and Library [Hungary]

NTOU – National Taiwan Ocean University [Taiwan]

NTU – National Taiwan University [Taiwan]

NU – Naresuan University [Thailand]

NU – University of Sydney [Australia]

NUBS – Nihon University, College of Bioresource Sciences [Japan]

NUC – National University of Comahue [Argentina]

NUCA – Camden Branch Library [Australia]

NUCSSI – National Union Catalog of Scientific Serials in India [India]

NUID – National University of Ireland - Dublin [Ireland]

NUL – National University of Lesotho [Lesotho]

NVGGA – Napa Valley Grape Growers Association [US]

NVH – Norges Veterinærhøgskole [Norway]

NVL – National Veterinary Laboratory [Botswana]

NVZC – Nippon Veterinary and Zootechnical College [Japan]

NWADI – North West Agricultural Development Institute [South Africa]

NWAU – Northwest Agricultural University [China]

NWF – National Wildlife Federation [US]

NWFP-AU – North West Frontier Province Agricultural University [Pakistan]

NWFSC/AFSC – Northwest Fisheries Science Center and the Alaska Fisheries Science Center [US]

NWRC – North Western Research Center [Russia]

NY SED – New York State Education Department [US]

NYBG – New York Botanical Garden [US]

NYCAMH – New York Center for Agricultural Medicine and Health [US]

NYSHA – New York State Historical Association [US]

NYSL – New York State Library [US]

NZBN – New Zealand Bibliographic Network [New Zealand]

NZDB – New Zealand Dairy Board [New Zealand]

NZDRI – New Zealand Dairy Research Institute [New Zealand]

OAB – Organisation Africaine du Bois [Gabon]

OAE – Ormancilik Arastirma Enstitüsü [Turkey]

OALS – Office of Arid Lands Studies [US]

OARDC – Ohio Agricultural Research and Development Center [US]

OAU – Obafemi Awolowo University [Nigeria]

OBD – Oddzial Badawczy Drobiarstwa w Zakrzewie k. Poznania [Poland]

OBIS – Oborové informacní stredisko [Slovakia]

OBIS VTEI – Odborové informacné stredisko pre vinohradníctvo a vinárstvo [Slovakia]

OBIS-VTEI – Odborové informacné stredisko vedeckotechnichych a ekonomickych informácií [Slovakia]

OBU – Ouachita Baptist University [US]

OCLC – Online Computer Library Center [US]

ODA – Overseas Development Administration [UK]

ODI – Overseas Development Institute [UK]

ODNR – Ohio Department of Natural Resources [US]

OECS – Organisation of Eastern Caribbean States [Antigua and Barbuda]

OFEFP – Office fédéral de l'Environnement, des Forêts et du Paysage [Switzerland]

OFI – Oxford Forestry Institute [UK]

OGI – Oregon Graduate Institute of Science and Technology [US]

OHVN – Opération Haute Vallée du Niger [Mali]

OI – Oddelení informatiky [Czech Republic]

OIE – Office International des Epizooties [France]

OIN – Osrodek Informacji Naukowej [Poland]

OMBEVI – Office Malien du Bétail et de la Viande [Mali]

OMgK – Országos Mezõgazdasági Könyvtár és Dokumentációs Központ [Hungary]

OMIKK – Orszagos Müszaki Informacios Központ es Könyvtar [Hungary]

ON – Office du Niger [Mali]

ONIC – Office National Interprofessionnel des Céréales [France]

ONTIPI – Otdel za nauchno-tehnicheska informatsiya [Bulgaria]

ONU – Organisation des Nations-Unies [International]

OPL – Omaha Public Library [US]

OPU – Osaka Prefecture University [Japan]

ORANA – Office de Recherches sur l'Alimentation et la Nutrition Africaines [Senegal]

ORM/Mopti – Office Riz Mopti [Mali]

ORMVAH – Office Régional de Mise en Valeur Agricole du Haouz [Morocco]

ORSTOM – Institut Français de Recherche Scientifique pour le Développement en Coopération [France]

ORSTOM – Office de la Recherche Scientifique et Technique d'Outre-Mer [France]

OSAFT – Odessa State Academy of Food Technology [Ukraine]

OSHA – Occupational Safety and Health Administration [US]

OSTC – Federal Office for Scientific, Technical and Cultural Affairs [Belgium]

OSU – Ohio State University [US]

OSU – Oklahoma State University [US]

OSU – Oregon State University [US]

OSU – Osh State University [Kyrgyzstan]

OTEI – Oddelení technickoekonomických informací [Czech Republic]

OTS – Office of Technical Service [Taiwan]

OUAT – Orissa University of Agriculture and Technology [India]

ÖVG – Österreichicher Gesellschaft für Vermessung und Geoinformation [Austria]

OVI – Onderstepoort Veeartsenykunde-instituut [South Africa]

OVI – Onderstepoort Veterinary Institute [South Africa]

OVTEI – Oddelenie vedecko-technických informácií [Slovakia]

P/SE – Pusat Penelitian Sosial Ekonomi Pertanian [Indonesia]

P3GI – Pusat Penelitian Perkebunan Gula Indonesia [Indonesia]

PAC – Pampanga Agricultural College [Philippines]

PAEC – Pakistan Atomic Energy Commission [Pakistan]

PAID – Pan African Institute for Development [Burkina Faso]

PAID – Pan African Institute for Development [Cameroon]

PAID – Pan African Institute for Development [Zambia]

PAIR – Pusat Aplikasi Isotop dan Radiasi [Indonesia]

PAIS – Public Affairs Information Service, Inc. [US]

PAMI – Prairie Agriculture Machinery Institute [Canada]

PAN – Polska Akademia Nauk [Poland]

Paprican – Pulp and Paper Research Institute of Canada [Canada]

PARC – Pakistan Agricultural Research Council [Pakistan]

PARC (Summerland) – Pacific Agriculture Research Centre (Summerland) [Canada]

PARD – Pakistan Academy for Rural Development [Pakistan]

PARI – Punjab Agricultural Research Institute [Pakistan]

PAS – Plottier Agritechnical School [Argentina]

PAS – Polish Academy of Sciences [Poland]

PASEGES – Panellinia Synomospondia Enoseon Georgikon Synetairismon [Greece]

PASTIC – Pakistan Scientific and Technological Information Centre [Pakistan]

PATE – Pannon Agrártudományi Egyetem [Hungary]

PATS – Ponape Agricultural Trade School [Micronesia]

PAU – Punjab Agricultural University [India]

PaÚ – Parazitologicky ústav [Slovakia]

PAV – Praktijkonderzoek voor de Akkerbouw en der Vollengrondsgroenteteelt [Netherlands]

PBG – Proefstation voor Bloemisterij en Glasgroente [Netherlands]

PBS – Pacific Biological Station [Canada]

PCA – Philippine Coconut Authority [Philippines]

PCAMRD – Philippine Council for Aquatic and Marine Resources Development [Philippines]

PCARRD – Philippine Council for Agriculture, Forestry and Natural Resources Research and Development [Philippines]

PCC – Palau Community College [Palau]

PCCF – Peninsula Conservation Center Foundation [US]

PCRC – Prachin Buri Rice Research Center [Thailand]

PCRWR – Pakistan Council of Research in Water Resources [Pakistan]

PCS – Potash Corporation of Saskatchewan Inc. [Canada]

PCTC – Provincial Cooperative Training Centre [Zambia]

PDI – Pacific Development Institute [Fiji]

PDII – Pusat Dokumentasi dan Informasi Ilmiah [Indonesia]

PERD – Policy and Economic Research Division [Canada]

PESAGRO-RIO – Empresa de Pesquisa Agropecuária do Estado do Rio de Janeiro [Brazil]

PFC – Pacific Forestry Centre [Canada]

PFRA – Prairie Farm Rehabilitation Administration [Canada]

PFT – Prehrambeno Tehnoloski Fakultet [Croatia]

PGDIC – Plant Genome Data and Information Center [US]

PGMSI – Dzhambul Hydro Land Reclamation Building Institute [Kazakhstan]

PGRC/E – Plant Genetic Resources Centre/Ethiopia [Ethiopia]

PGRFP – Pacific German Regional Forestry Programme [Fiji]

PGU – Persian Gulf University [Iran]

PHBA – Palomino Horse Breeders of America, Inc. [US]

PHDS – Post-Harvest Documentation Service [US]

PHILCOA – Philippine Coconut Administration [Philippines]

PHREC – Panhandle Research and Extension Center [US]

PHS – Pennsylvania Horticultural Society [US]

PIADC – Plum Island Animal Disease Center [US]

PIAGRO – Programa de Información Agropecuaria [Costa Rica]

PIB – Pig Industry Board [Zimbabwe]

PIDE – Pakistan Institute of Development Economics [Pakistan]

PIMR – Przemyslowy Instytut Maszyn Rolniczych [Poland]

PIWet – Panstwowy Instytut Weterynaryjny [Poland]

PKU – Peking University [China]

PLATAX – Plant Taxonomy Group [Netherlands]

PLAVER – Laboratorium voor Plantenveredeling [Netherlands]

PLC – Public Lands Council [US]

PMB – Potato Marketing Board [UK]

PMBC – Phuket Marine Biological Center [Thailand]

PML – Plymouth Marine Laboratory [UK]

PNAC – Palawan National Agricultural College [Philippines]

PolTox – Pollution and Toxicology [International]

PORIM – Palm Oil Research Institute of Malaysia [Malaysia]

PORLA – Palm Oil Registration and Licensing Authority [Malaysia]

PPAE – Pusat Penelitian Agro Ekonomi [Indonesia]

PPATHRI – Plant Pathology Research Institute [Egypt]

PPI – Plant Protection Institute [Poland]

PPKS – Pusat Penelitian Kelapa Sawit [Indonesia]

PPMU – Planning, Programming and Monitoring Unit [Gambia]

PPRI – Plant Protection Research Institute [Egypt]

PPRI – Plant Protection Research Institute [South Africa]

PPRI – Plant Protection Research Institute [Zimbabwe]

PPTK – Pusat Penelitian Teh dan Kina [Indonesia]

PPU – Perpustakaan Pusat Unsyiah [Indonesia]

PRB – Poultry Research Branch [Poland]

PRC – Potato Research Centre [Canada]

PRIT – Pig Research Institute Taiwan [Taiwan]

PRRC – Phrae Rice Research Center [Thailand]

PSBS – Pacific Southwest Biological Services, Inc. [US]

PSL RRC – Phitsanulok Rice Research Center [Thailand]

PSPC – Panay State Polytechnic College [Philippines]

PSU – Pennsylvania State University [US]

PSU – Prince of Songkla University [Thailand]

PTBG – Pacific Tropical Botanical Garden [US]

PTG – Proefstation voor Tuinbouw onder Glas [Netherlands]

PTS – Papiertechnische Stiftung [Germany]

PTT RRC – Pathum Thani Rice Research Center [Thailand]

PU – University of Pretoria [South Africa]

PUDOC – Centre for Agricultural Publishing and Documentation [Netherlands]

Puslitbang Biologi – Pusat Penelitian dan Pengembagan Biologi [Indonesia]

Puslitbang Hut – Pusat Penelitian dan Pengembangan Hutan dan Konservasi Alam [Indonesia]

Puslitbang Limnologi – Pusat Penelitian dan Pengembangan Limnologi [Indonesia]

PUSTAKA – Pusat Perpustakaan Pertanian dan Komunikasi Penelitian [Indonesia]

Pusvetma – Pusat Veterinaria Farma [Indonesia]

PVAMU – Prairie View A & M University [US]

QAAFS – Qinghai Academy of Agricultural and Forestry Sciences [China]

QAASVM – Qinghai Academy of Animal Science and Veterinary Medicine [China]

QAC – Queensland Agricultural College [Australia]

QC – Queens College [US]

QCGC – Queensland Cane Growers Council [Australia]

QDF – Queensland Forest Service [Australia]

QDNR – Queensland Department of Natural Resources [Australia]

QDPI – Queensland Department of Primary Industries [Australia]

QEH – Queen Elizabeth House [UK]

QFI Library – Queensland Fisheries Library [Australia]

QUB – Queen's University of Belfast [UK]

RAAS – Russian Academy of Agricultural Sciences [Russia]

RAAS SB – Russian Academy of Agricultural Sciences, Siberian Branch [Russia]

RAAW – Rural Agricultural and Allied Workers Trade Group [UK]

RAC – Station fédérale de Recherches Agronomiques de Changins [Switzerland]

RAF – Regional Office for Africa [Ghana]

RALA – Rannsóknastofnun Landbúnadarins [Iceland]

RAP – Federal Research Station for Animal Production [Switzerland]

RARI, Bahawalpur – Regional Agricultural Research Institute, Bahawalpur [Pakistan]

RAS – Russian Academy of Sciences [Russia]

RASE – Royal Agricultural Society of England [UK]

RASKHN – Rossyiskoi Akademii selskokhoziastvennykh nauk [Russia]

RASL – Republican Agrarian Scientific Library [Moldova]

RAU – Rajasthan Agricultural University [India]

RBD Library – Ralph Brown Draughon Library [US]

RBG Kew – Royal Botanic Gardens, Kew [UK]

RBGE – Royal Botanic Garden, Edinburgh [UK]

RCA – Rajasthan College of Agriculture [India]

RCA – Research Centre for Agrobotany [Hungary]

RCAFE – Research Center for Agricultural and Forest Environment [Poland]

RCAT – Ridgetown College of Agricultural Technology [Canada]

RCAT – Roi-Et College of Agriculture and Technology [Thailand]

RCNEHR – Research Complex for North Eastern Hilly Region [India]

RCVS – Royal College of Veterinary Surgeons [UK]

RDA – Rural Development Academy [Bangladesh]

RDS – Royal Dublin Society [Ireland]

REDABU – Réseau de Documentation et d'Information Agricole Burundais [Burundi]

REDACI – Réseau National de Documentation Agricole en Côte d'Ivoire [Cote d'Ivoire]

REDSO/ESA – Regional Economic Development Services Office for Eastern and Southern Africa [Kenya]

RENIB – Red Nacional de Información Bibliográfica [Chile]

RESADOC – Réseau Sahélien de Documentation et d'Information Scientifiques et Techniques [Mali]

RESINFRU – Research Institute for Fruit Growing and Ornamentals, Erd [Hungary]

RFD – Royal Forest Department [Thailand]

RGU – Rakuno Gakuen University [Japan]

RHS – Royal Horticultural Society [UK]

RI – Roslin Institute [UK]

RIAE – Research Institute of Agricultural Engineering [Czech Republic]

RIAFE – Research Institute of Agriculture and Food Economics [Slovakia]

RIAN – Research Institute of Animal Nutrition Ltd. [Czech Republic]

RIAP – Research Institute for Animal Production [Indonesia]

RIAP – Research Institute of Animal Production [Slovakia]

RIB – Research Institute for Bioresources [Japan]

RIBM PLC – Research Institute of Brewing and Malting PLC [Czech Republic]

RIC – Rural Information Center [US]

RIFP – Research Institute for Fodder Plants, Ltd. - Troubsko [Czech Republic]

RIFSA – Research Institute for Food Crops on Swampy Areas [Indonesia]

RIKEN – Institute of Physical and Chemical Research [Japan]

RIKILT – Rijkskwaliteitsinstituut voor Land- en Tuinbouwprodukten [Netherlands]

RIMC – Research Institute for Maize and Other Cereals [Indonesia]

RIMF – Research Institute for Marine Fisheries [Indonesia]

RIOG – Research and Breeding Institute of Ornamental Gardening [Czech Republic]

RIPP – Research Institute of Plant Production [Slovakia]

RIR – Research Institute for Rice [Indonesia]

RISPA – Research Institute of Sumatra Planters' Association [Indonesia]

RISSAC – Research Institute for Soil Science and Agricultural Chemistry [Hungary]

RIT – Rajamangala Institute of Technology [Thailand]

RITC – Research Institute for Tea and Cinchona [Indonesia]

RIUD – Research Information Utilization Division [Philippines]

RIV – Research Institute of Vegetables [Slovakia]

RIVM – Research Institute of Veterinary Medicine [Slovakia]

RIVO – Rijksinstituut voor Visserijonderzoek [Netherlands]

RIVS – Research Institute for Veterinary Science [Indonesia]

RJB – Real Jardín Botánico [Spain]

RL – Research Library [Czech Republic]

RL – Research Library [Ukraine]

RM-IC – Research Management Information Center [Philippines]

RMC – Research Management Center [Philippines]

RML Library – Rocky Mountain Laboratories Library [US]

RMRS – Rocky Mountain Research Station [US]

RNE – Near East Regional Office [Egypt]

RNR-RC – Renewable Natural Resources Research Centre [Bhutan]

RNSKHB – Republican Scientific Agricultural Library [Kazakhstan]

RPAC – Rhone-Poulenc Ag Company [US]

RPI – Division of Research Planning and Information [Japan]

RRC – Regional Research Centre [Kenya]

RRC – Regional Research Centre [Trinidad and Tobago]

RRI – Rice Research Institute [China]

RRI – Rice Research Institute [Pakistan]

RRI – Rubber Research Institute [Thailand]

RRIM – Rubber Research Institute of Malaysia [Malaysia]

RRIN – Rubber Research Institute of Nigeria [Nigeria]

RRIPPI – All-Russia Research Institute of Poultry Processing Industry [Russia]

RRISL – Rubber Research Institute of Sri Lanka [Sri Lanka]

RRL – Romulo Raggio Library [Argentina]

RRS – Rice Research Station, Rokupr [Sierra Leone]

RSC – Resource Sciences Centre Library [Australia]

RSC – Royal Society of Chemistry [UK]

RSEHN – Real Sociedad Española de Historia Natural [Spain]

RSMAS – Dorothy and Lewis Rosenstiel School of Marine and Atmospheric Sciences [US]

RTCD – Research and Training Center for Development [Chad]

RUCA – Rijksuniversitair Centrum Antwerpen [Belgium]

RUG – Rijksuniversiteit Gent [Belgium]

RuG – Rijksuniversiteit te Groningen [Netherlands]

RVC – Royal Veterinary College [UK]

RvL – Rijksstation voor Landbouwtechniek [Belgium]

RVV – Rijksstation voor Veevoeding [Belgium]

RZSSA – Royal Zoological Society of South Australia, Inc. [Australia]

SAAS – Shaanxi Academy of Agricultural Sciences [China]

SAASC – South Australian Aquatic Sciences Centre [Australia]

SABINET – South African Bibliographic Network [South Africa]

SAC – Scottish Agricultural College [UK]

SAC – Shanghai Agricultural College [China]

SAC – Sociedad de Agricultores de Colombia [Colombia]

SACCAR – Southern African Centre for Cooperation in Agricultural and Natural Resources Research and Training [Botswana]

SADC – Southern African Development Community [Lesotho]

SADCC – Southern African Development Coordination Conference [Lesotho]

SAF – Saskatchewan Agriculture and Food [Canada]

SAF – Società Agricola e Forestale per la Piante da Cellulosa e da Carta [Italy]

SAF – Society of American Foresters [US]

SAFICC – Structure Nationale d'Appui à la Filière Café-Cacao [Togo]

SAGAR – Secretaría de Agricultura, Ganadería y Desarrollo Rural [Mexico]

SAGPyA – Secretaría de Agricultura, Ganadería, Pesca y Alimentación [Argentina]

SARDI – South Australian Research and Development Institute [Australia]

SARH – Secretaría de Agricultura y Recursos Hidráulicos [Mexico]

SARL – Kika de la Garza Subtropical Agricultural Research Laboratory [US]

SARTC – Sakon Nakorn Agricultural Research and Training Center [Thailand]

SASA – Scottish Agricultural Science Agency [UK]

SASA – South African Sugar Association [South Africa]

SASU – Liaoning Institute of Saline and Alkali Soil Utilization [China]

SAU – Sichuan Agricultural University [China]

SAUM – State Agrarian University of Moldova [Moldova]

SAV – Slovenská akadémia vied [Slovakia]

SB RAS – Russian Academy of Sciences, Siberian Branch [Russia]

SBA – Scottish Beekeepers Association [UK]

SBAT – Service Botanique et Agronomique de Tunisie [Tunisia]

SBD – Serviço de Biblioteca e Documentação [Brazil]

SBDP – Service de la Bibliothèque, de la Documentation et des Publications [Cameroon]

SBI – Sugarcane Breeding Institute [India]

SBRI – Sugar Beet Research Institute [China]

SBS – Seychelles Bureau of Standards [Seychelles]

SBSI – Sugar Beet Seed Institute [Iran]

SBV – Schweizerischer Bauernverband [Switzerland]

SCA – Swiss College of Agriculture [Switzerland]

SCA Caracal – Statiunea de Cercetari Agricole Caracal [Romania]

SCA Livada – Statiunea de Cercetari Agricole Livada [Romania]

SCATC – South China Academy of Tropical Crops [China]

SCAU – South China Agricultural University [China]

SCCASS Braila – Statiunea Centrala de Cercetari pentru Ameliorarea Solurilor Saraturate Braila [Romania]

SCCCPN Dabuleni – Centrala de Cercetari pentru Cultura Plantelor pe Nisipuri Dabuleni [Romania]

SCCI Marculesti – Statiunea de Cercetari pentru Culturi Irigate Marculesti - Calarasi [Romania]

SCD – Service Commun de Documentation [France]

SCI – Science Citation Index [US]

SCRC – Shrimp Culture Research Centre [Indonesia]

SCRC – Sugarcane Research Centre [Fiji]

SCRI – Scottish Crop Research Institute [UK]

SCRI – Sugar Crops Research Institute [Egypt]

SCSC – South Carolina State College [US]

SCSU – South Carolina State University [US]

SCVV – Statiunea de Cercetare Viti-Vinicole [Romania]

SD – Service de Documentation [Senegal]

SD – Serviços de Documentação [Portugal]

SDA – Service de la Documentation et des Archives [Congo, Republic of the]

SDB – National Science Development Board [Philippines]

SDI – Service de Documentation et d'Information [Senegal]

SDI – Serviços de Documentação e Informação [Portugal]

SDIC – Scientech Documentation and Information Center [China]

SDLN – South Dakota Library Network [US]

SDoc – Service Documentation Générale [Madagascar]

SDSC – San Diego State College [US]

SDSU – San Diego State University [US]

SDSU – South Dakota State University [US]

SDVÚ – Statny drevarsky výzkumný ústav [Slovakia]

SEAB/PR – Secretaria de Estado da Agricultura e do Abastecimento [Brazil]

SEAFDEC – Southeast Asian Fisheries Development Center [Philippines]

SEAFDEC – Southeast Asian Fisheries Development Center [Thailand]

SEAFIS – Southeast Asian Fisheries Information System [Thailand]

SEAMEO – Southeast Asian Ministers of Education Organization [Philippines]

SEAMEO BIOTROP – Southeast Asia Regional Center for Tropical Biology [Indonesia]

SEARCA – Southeast Asian Regional Center for Graduate Study and Research in Agriculture [Philippines]

SECEDOC – Servicio Centralizado de Documentación [Argentina]

SEDAGRO – Comisión para el Desarrollo Agrícola y Ganadera del Estado de México [Mexico]

SEDI – Service de la Documentation et d'Information [Cote d'Ivoire]

SEDIP – Service Documentation Information Publication [Mali]

SEICA – Servicio de Información y Documentación [Colombia]

SEIDAL – Servicio Andino de Información y Documentación Forestal [Colombia]

SEL – Science-Engineering Library [US]

SENASA – Servicio Nacional de Sanidad y Calidad Agroalimentaria [Argentina]

SERAD – Scottish Executive Rural Affairs Department [UK]

SERBIDOC – Servicio de Biblioteca y Documentación [Peru]

SESAM – School of Environmental Science and Management [Philippines]

SEUR – Subregional Office for Central and Eastern Europe [Hungary]

SFA – Seychelles Fishing Authority [Seychelles]

SFD – Sea Fisheries Department (CLO Ghent) [Belgium]

SFI – Soils and Fertilizers Institute [China]

SFIC – Shandong Forestry Information Center [China]

SFRI – Sea Fisheries Research Institute [South Africa]

SFRI – Shandong Forestry Research Institute [China]

SFU – Shanghai Fisheries University [China]

SFU – Simon Fraser University [Canada]

SFW – Stellenbosch Farmers Winery [South Africa]

SGGW – Szkola Glówna Gospodarstwa Wiejskiego [Poland]

SHC – Sunraysia Horticultural Centre [Australia]

SHL – Schweizerische Hochschule für Landwirtschaft [Switzerland]

SIA – Sugar Industry Authority [Jamaica]

SIAAS – Sichuan Academy of Agricultural Sciences [China]

SIAM – Shijiazhuang Institute of Agricultural Modernization [China]

SIAS – Shaoxing Institute of Agricultural Sciences [China]

SIAST – Saskatchewan Institute of Applied Science and Technology [Canada]

SIBDI – Sistema de Bibliotecas, Documentación e Información [Costa Rica]

SIBL – Science, Industry and Business Library [US]

SIC – Studijni a informacní centrum [Czech Republic]

SICHE – Solomon Islands College of Higher Education [Solomon Islands]

SID – Setor de Informação e Documentação [Brazil]

SIDBAP – Servicio de Información y Documentación sobre Banano y Plátano [Colombia]

SIF – V.N. Sukachev Institute of Forestry [Russia]

SIG – Scientific Information Group [US]

SIGZ – System Informacji o Gospodarce Zywnosciowej [Poland]

SIL – Smithsonian Institution Libraries [US]

SIN – Setor de Informação [Brazil]

SIPPB – Siberian Institute of Plant Physiology and Biochemistry [Russia]

SIRI – Sugar Industry Research Institute [Jamaica]

SIST – Service d'Information Scientifique et Technique [Belgium]

SIU – Scientific Information Unit [Mexico]

SIU – Scientific Information Unit [Slovakia]

SIYE – Servicio de Información y Estadística [Argentina]

SJV – Statens jordbruksvsrk [Sweden]

SkogForsk – Stiftelsen Skogsbrukets Forskningsinstitut [Sweden]

SKUAST – Sher-e-Kashmir University of Agricultural Sciences and Technology [India]

SKZÚZ – Státní kontrolní a zkusební ústav zemedelsky [Czech Republic]

SL – Scientific Library [Ukraine]

SLDK – Slovenská lesnícka a drevárska kniznica [Slovakia]

SLDS – Scientific Library and Documentation Service [Philippines]

SLIC – Scientech Literature Information Centre [China]

SlPK – Slovenská pol'nohospodárska kniznica [Slovakia]

SLS – Scientific Literature Services Program [Philippines]

SLU – Sveriges Lantbruksuniversitet [Sweden]

SMRI – Sugar Milling Research Institute [South Africa]

SMSU – Southwest Missouri State University [US]

SMTIS – Service de Méthodologie et du Traitement des Informations Statistiques [Madagascar]

SNA – Sociedad Nacional de Agricultura [Chile]

SNAP – Solano County, Napa County and Partners [US]

SNLCS – Serviço Nacional de Levantamento e Conservação do Solo [Brazil]

SNLS – Swaziland National Library Service [Swaziland]

SNR – School of Natural Resources [Solomon Islands]

SNRI – Stichting Nationaal Rijstonderzoeks Instituut [Suriname]

SNU – South National University [Argentina]

SOA – School of Agriculture [Samoa]

SOAEFD – Scottish Office Agriculture, Environment and Fisheries Department [UK]

SONADER – Société Nationale pour le Développement Rural [Mauritania]

SORIH – Solok Research Institute for Horticulture [Indonesia]

SOTOCO – Société Togolaise du Coton [Togo]

SPB ZNSKHB – Sankt-Peterburgs-kaya Zentralnaya nauchnaya selskokhozaistvennaya biblioteka [Russia]

SPC – Secretariat of the Pacific Community [Fiji]

SPI – Shandong Pomology Institute [China]

SPIFS – Shaanxi Provincial Institute of Forestry Science [China]

SPII – Seed and Plant Improvement Institute [Iran]

SPP – Státní plemenárské podniky [Czech Republic]

SPRCTA – South Pacific Regional College of Tropical Agriculture [Samoa]

SPREP – South Pacific Regional Environment Programme [Samoa]

SPRI – Shandong Peanuts Research Institute [China]

SPRL – Soil Productivity Research Laboratory [Zimbabwe]

SPSB – Serviço de Produção de Sementes Básicas [Brazil]

SPU – Slovenská pol'nohospodárska univerzita [Slovakia]

SQU – Sultan Qaboos University [Oman]

SRA – Sugar Regulatory Administration [Philippines]

SRA/Cinzana – Station de Recherche Agronomique de Cinzana [Mali]

SRA N'Tarla – Station de Recherche Agronomique de N'Tarla [Mali]

SRBE – Société Royale Belge d'Entomologie [Belgium]

SRC – Saskatchewan Research Council [Canada]

SRC – Scientific Research Council [Iraq]

SRDI – Soil Resources Development Institute [Bangladesh]

SRI – Silsoe Research Institute [UK]

SRI – Soil Research Institute [Ghana]

SRI – Soybean Research Institute [China]

SRI – Sugar Research Institute [Australia]

SRI – Sugarcane Research Institute [Sri Lanka]

SRRC – Southern Regional Research Center [US]

SRS – Státní rostlinolékarská správa [Czech Republic]

SRTI – Sugarcane Research and Training Institute [Bangladesh]

SRZ – Station de Recherches Zootechniques [Mali]

SSB – Soils Service of Belgium [Belgium]

SSC – Settlement Study Centre [Israel]

SSL – Scottish Science Library [UK]

SSTC – Services Fédéraux de Affaires Scientifiques, Techniques et Culturelles [Belgium]

St.-Pet. Sci. Agr. Lib. – Saint Petersburg Central Scientific Agricultural Library [Russia]

STB – Science Technology and Business [UK]

StFX – St. Francis Xavier University [Canada]

STII – Scientific and Technological Information Institute [China]

STIS – National Centre for Scientific and Technical Information [Belgium]

STL – Scientific and Technical Library [Russia]

STL – Scientific Technical Library [Ukraine]

Stu RB Erfurt – Stadt- und Regionalbibliothek Stadtverwaltung Erfurt [Germany]

SU – Shimane University [Japan]

SU – Shinshu University [Japan]

SU – Silliman University [Philippines]

SUAS – Swedish University of Agricultural Sciences [Sweden]

SUB – Niedersächsische Staats- und Universitätsbibliothek [Germany]

SUH – State University of Haiti [Haiti]

SUNY – State University of New York [US]

SURIF – Sukamandi Research Institute for Food Crops [Indonesia]

SUT – Suranaree University of Technology [Thailand]

SVA – Statens Veterinärmedicinska Anstalt [Sweden]

SVIS – Stredisko verejných informacnich sluzeb pro zivotni prostredi [Czech Republic]

SVRDC – Southern Veterinary Research and Diagnostic Center [Thailand]

SVS – Statens Veterinære Serumlaboratorium [Denmark]

SWAB – Svalöf Weibull AB [Sweden]

SWCLU – Soil and Water Conservation and Land Utilization [Lesotho]

SWFSC – Southwest Fisheries Science Center [US]

SWIRI – Shanghai Wood Industry Research Institute [China]

SWIS – Swiss Wildlife Information Service [Switzerland]

SWP – Saskatchewan Wheat Pool [Canada]

SWRI – Soil and Water Research Institute [Egypt]

SZNIIMESK – Severo-Zapadny Nauchno-Issledovatelskij Institut Mekhanizatsii i Elektrifikatsii Selskogo Khoziajstva [Russia]

SZNZ – Severo-Zapadny Nauchny Zentr [Russia]

TAAS – Tianjin Academy of Agricultural Sciences [China]

TACTRI – Taiwan Agricultural Chemicals and Toxic Substances Research Institute [Taiwan]

TAESH – Takikawa Animal Experiment Station [Japan]

TAFORI – Tanzania Forestry Research Institute [Tanzania]

Tainan DAIS – Tainan District Agricultural Improvement Station [Taiwan]

TAKI – Talajtani és Agrokémiai Kutató Intézete [Hungary]

TALIRO – Tanzania Livestock Research Organization [Tanzania]

TAMU – Texas A & M University [US]

TANDOC – Tanzania National Documentation Centre [Tanzania]

TANUVAS – Tamil Nadu Veterinary and Animal Sciences University [India]

TAPPI – Technical Association of the Pulp and Paper Industry [US]

TARC – Trangie Agricultural Research Centre [Australia]

TARC – Tropical Agricultural Research Center [Japan]

TARI – Taiwan Agricultural Research Institute [Taiwan]

TARO – Tanzania Agriculture Research Organization [Tanzania]

TARRC – Tun Abdul Razak Research Centre [UK]

TASES – Taiwan Agricultural and Sericultural Experiment Station [Taiwan]

TAU – Tajik Agricultural University [Tajikistan]

TBIC – Tsukuba International Centre [Japan]

TBRI – Taiwan Banana Research Institute [Taiwan]

TCA – Tarlac College of Agriculture [Philippines]

TCC – Taveuni Coconut Centre [Fiji]

TCCI – Tamworth Centre for Crop Improvement [Australia]

TCRI – Tobacco and Cotton Research Institute [South Africa]

TCRIY – Tropical Crops Research Institute of Yunnan [China]

TDRC – Tropical Diseases Research Centre [Zambia]

TECHINFORMI – Georgian Research Institute for Scientific and Technical Information [Georgia]

TEEAL – The Essential Electronic Agricultural Library [US]

TEXTEK – Textile Technology [South Africa]

TFC – Tasmania Forestry Commission [Australia]

TFDA – Taiwan Floriculture Development Association [Taiwan]

TFRI – Taiwan Fisheries Research Institute [Taiwan]

TFRI – Tropical Forest Research Institute [India]

TFRI – Tropical Forestry Research Institute [China]

TFRIS – Temperate Forest Research Institute [India]

TGWU – Transport and General Workers Union [UK]

TIC – Thailand Information Center [Thailand]

TIG – Tobacco Institute of Greece [Greece]

TIL – Technical Information Library [Nigeria]

TIS – Technical Information Services [US]

TISTR – Thailand Institute of Scientific and Technological Research [Thailand]

TKK – Teknillinen Korkeakoulu [Finland]

TLRI – Taiwan Livestock Research Institute [Taiwan]

TLS – Tanzania Library Service [Tanzania]

TMDAIS – Taiwan Miaoli District Agricultural Improvement Station [Taiwan]

TNAES – Tohoku National Agricultural Experiment Station [Japan]

TNAU – Tamil Nadu Agricultural University [India]

TNDC – Thai National Documentation Center [Thailand]

TNFRI – Tohoku National Fisheries Research Institute [Japan]

TNO Voeding – TNO Hoofdgroep Voeding en Voedingsmiddelen [Netherlands]

TPRI – Tropical Pesticides Research Institute [Tanzania]

TPU – Toyama Prefectural University [Japan]

Trätek – Institutet för Träteknisk Forskning [Sweden]

TRB – Tobacco Research Board [Zimbabwe]

TREC – Tropical Research and Education Center [US]

TRFCA – Tea Research Foundation - Central Africa [Malawi]

TRFK – Tea Research Foundation of Kenya [Kenya]

TRI – Tea Research Institute [Sri Lanka]

TRPC – Natal Town and Regional Planning Commission [South Africa]

TSIPS – Taiwan Seed Improvement and Propagation Station [Taiwan]

TSLA – Tennessee State Library and Archives [US]

TsNSHB – Tsentral'na Naukova Sil'skohospodars'ka Biblioteka [Ukraine]

TSS – Taiwan Seed Service [Taiwan]

TSU – Tarleton State University [US]

TTES – Taiwan Tea Experiment Station [Taiwan]

TTIC – Technology Transfer Information Center [US]

TTRI – Tsetse and Trypanosomiasis Research Institute [Tanzania]

TTU – Texas Tech University [US]

TU – Technická univerzita [Slovakia]

TU – Thracian University [Bulgaria]

TU – Tohoku University [Japan]

TU – Trakiiski Universitet [Bulgaria]

TU – Tribhuvan University [Nepal]

TU – Tuskegee University [US]

TU Delft – Technische Universiteit Delft [Netherlands]

TUA – Tokyo University of Agriculture [Japan]

TUAM – Tarimsal Uygulama ve Araflorintirma Merkezi [Turkey]

TUAT – Tokyo University of Agriculture and Technology [Japan]

TUF – Tokyo University of Fisheries [Japan]

TUSVM – Tufts University School of Veterinary Medicine [US]

TWHBEA – Tennessee Walking Horse Breeders' and Exhibitors' Association [US]

U of K – University of Khartoum [Sudan]

UA – Universidad de Antioquía [Colombia]

UA – University of Agriculture [Poland]

UA – University of Arizona [US]

UA – University of Asmara [Eritrea]

UAAN – Ukraiin'ska Akademia Agrarnykh Nauk [Ukraine]

UAAS – Ukrainian Academy of Agricultural Sciences [Ukraine]

UAB – Universitat Autonoma de Barcelona [Spain]

UAC – Universidade dos Açores [Portugal]

UAC – Uyole Agricultural Centre [Tanzania]

UACH – Universidad Autónoma Chapingo [Mexico]

UAF – University of Alaska, Fairbanks [US]

UALG – Universidade do Algarve [Portugal]

UAM – University of Agriculture, Makurdi [Nigeria]

UAM-X – Universidad Autónoma Metropolitana, Unidad Xochimilco [Mexico]

UANL – Universidad Autónoma de Nuevo León [Mexico]

UAPB – University of Arkansas, Pine Bluff [US]

UAPDIA – Unidade de Apoio à Pesquisa e Desenvolvimento de Instrumentação Agropecuária [Brazil]

UAS – University of Agricultural Sciences [India]

UASM – Universitatea Agrare de Stat din Moldova [Moldova]

UB – Universitat de Barcelona [Spain]

UB – Universitätsbibliothek [Austria]

UB – Universitätsbibliothek [Germany]

UB – University of Botswana [Botswana]

UBFCRC – Ubonratchathani Field Crops Research Center [Thailand]

UBU – Ubonratchathani University [Thailand]

UBW – Universitätsbibliothek Wien [Austria]

UC – Universidade de Coimbra [Portugal]

UC – University of Chicago [US]

UCA – Universidad Católica Argentina [Argentina]

UCA – University of Central Arkansas [US]

UCB – University of California, Berkeley [US]

UCD – Unité Centrale de Documentation [France]

UCD – University College Dublin [Ireland]

UCD – University of California, Davis [US]

UCL – Université Catholique de Louvain [Belgium]

UCSB – University of California, Santa Barbara [US]

UCSC – University of California, Santa Cruz [US]

UCV – Universidad Católica de Valparaíso [Chile]

UCV – Universidad Central de Venezuela [Venezuela]

UD Géographie – Unité de Documentation de Géographie [Belgium]

UD Zoologie – Unité de Documentation de Zoologie [Belgium]

UDA – Unité de Documentation Agricole [Haiti]

UdL – Universitat de Lleida [Spain]

UDS – University for Development Studies [Ghana]

UDs – University of Dschang [Cameroon]

UDSKR – Ukraiinska Doslidna Stantsia karantynu roslin [Ukraine]

UEH – Université d'Etat d'Haïti [Haiti]

UEL – Universidade Estadual de Londrina [Brazil]

UEM – Universidade Eduardo Mondlane [Mozambique]

UEPAE – Unidade de Execução de Pesquisa de Âmbito Estadual [Brazil]

UEPAT – Unidade de Execução de Pesquisa de Âmbito Territorial [Brazil]

UESPQ – Ukrainian Experiment Station of Plant Quarantine [Ukraine]

UET – University of Engineering and Technology [Pakistan]

ÚEVM – Ústav experimentálnej veterinárnej medicíny [Slovakia]

UF – University of Florida [US]

UFAFP – Ufficio federale dell'Ambiente, delle Foreste e del Paesaggio [Switzerland]

UFC – Universidade Federal do Ceará [Brazil]

UFRRJ – Universidade Federal Rural do Rio de Janeiro [Brazil]

UG – University of Gezira [Sudan]

UG – University of Ghana [Ghana]

UGA – University of Georgia [US]

UGM – Universitas Gadjah Mada [Indonesia]

UHF – Dr. Yashwant Singh Parmar University of Horticulture and Forestry [India]

UHFI – University of Horticulture and Food Industry [Hungary]

UI – University of Ibadan [Nigeria]

UI – University of Idaho [US]

UIA – Universitaire Instelling Antwerpen [Belgium]

UIST – Unité d'Information Scientifique et Technique [Madagascar]

UISU – Universitas Islam Sumatera Utara [Indonesia]

UIUC – University of Illinois at Urbana-Champaign [US]

UK – United Kingdom

UK – University of Kentucky [US]

ÚKIS – Ústřední knihovna a informacní středisko [Czech Republic]

UkrISSAR – Ukrainian Institut for Soil Science and Agrochemistry Research "A.N. Sokolovsky" [Ukraine]

ÚKSUP – Ústredny kontrolny a skusobny ústav polnohospodársky [Slovakia]

UL – Université Laval [Canada]

ULB – Université Libre de Bruxelles [Belgium]

ULBES – Uladovo-Lylinetska Breeding Experiment Station [Ukraine]

ULDSS – Uladovo-Lylinetska Doslidno Selectsiyna Station [Ukraine]

ULg – Université de Liège [Belgium]

ULg – University of Liege [Belgium]

ULg-V – Université de Liège, Faculté de la Médecine Vétérinaire [Belgium]

ULM – University of Louisiana at Monroe [US]

ULS – Universidad de La Salle [Colombia]

ULS – University Library Services [Philippines]

UM – Universitario de Mayagüez [Puerto Rico]

UM – University of Maryland [US]

UM – University of Mauritius [Mauritius]

UMC – University of Missouri, Columbia [US]

UMES – University of Maryland, Eastern Shore [US]

UN – United Nations [Algeria]

UNAAB – Federal University of Agriculture, Abeokuta [Nigeria]

UNALM – Universidad Nacional Agraria La Molina [Peru]

UNAM – Universidad Nacional Autónoma de México [Mexico]

UNAM – University of Namibia [Namibia]

UNB – Université Nationale du Bénin [Benin]

UNB – University of New Brunswick [Canada]

UNC – Universidad Nacional del Comahue [Argentina]

Uncen – Universitas Cenderawasih [Indonesia]

UNEP – United Nations Environment Programme [Kenya]

Unesco – United Nations Educational, Scientific and Cultural Organization [Cameroon]

UNESP – Universidade Estadual Paulista [Brazil]

UNH – University of New Hampshire [US]

UNIBRAW – Universitas Brawijaya [Indonesia]

UNIGUY – University of Guyana [Guyana]

UNILLANOS – Universidad Tecnológica de los Llanos Orientales [Colombia]

Uniport – University of Port Harcourt [Nigeria]

UNISUCRE – Universidad de Sucre [Colombia]

UNISWA – University of Swaziland [Swaziland]

UNITECH – Papua New Guinea University of Technology [Papua New Guinea]

UNITRA – University of Transkei [South Africa]

UNL – Universidad Nacional del Litoral [Argentina]

UNL – University of Nebraska - Lincoln [US]

UNLAM – Universitas Lammbung Mangkurat [Indonesia]

UNLE – Universidad de Léon [Spain]

UNLP – Universidad Nacional de La Plata [Argentina]

UNLPam – Universidad Nacional de La Pampa [Argentina]

UNM – University of New Mexico [US]

UNN – University of Nigeria, Nsukka [Nigeria]

UNNE – Universidad Nacional del Nordeste [Argentina]

UNP – University of Natal, Pietermaritzburg [South Africa]

UNPAD – Universitas Padjadjaran [Indonesia]

Unpatti – Universitas Pattimura [Indonesia]

UNPHU – Universidad Nacional Pedro Henríquez Ureña [Dominican Republic]

UNR – University of Nevada Reno [US]

UNRAM – Universitas Mataram [Indonesia]

UNRC – Universidad Nacional Río Cuarto [Argentina]

UNS – Universidad Nacional del Sur [Argentina]

UNS – Universitas Sebelas Maret [Indonesia]

UNSE – Universidad Nacional de Santiago del Estero [Argentina]

UNSYIAH – Universitas Syiah Kuala [Indonesia]

UNTAD – Universitas Tadulako [Indonesia]

UNUD – Universitas Udayana [Indonesia]

UOG – University of Guam [Guam]

UOV – University of Vudal [Papua New Guinea]

UOVS – Universiteit van die Oranje Vrystaat [South Africa]

UPA – Unité de Politique Agricole [Senegal]

UPCA – University of the Philippines College of Agriculture [Philippines]

UPEB – Unión de Países Exportadores de Banano [Panama]

ÚPK – Ústrední potravinárská knihovna [Czech Republic]

UPLB – University of the Philippines Los Baños [Philippines]

UPM – Universidad Politecnica de Madrid [Spain]

UPM – Universiti Putra Malaysia [Malaysia]

UPNa – Universidad Pública de Navarra [Spain]

UPR – Universidad de Puerto Rico [Puerto Rico]

UPR – University of Puerto Rico [Puerto Rico]

UPV – Universidad Politécnica de Valencia [Spain]

UPV – Universitat Politècnica València [Spain]

UQ – University of Queensland [Australia]

UQAR – University of Quebec at Rimouski [Canada]

UQG – University of Queensland, Gatton College [Australia]

UR – University of Ruhuna [Sri Lanka]

URD – Unité Régionale de Documentation [Guadeloupe]

URL – Ukiriguru Research Library [Tanzania]

US – United States

US – Universiteit van Stellenbosch [South Africa]

US – University of Stellenbosch [South Africa]

US FDA – United States Food and Drug Administration [US]

USAID – United States Agency for International Development [US]

USDA – United States Department of Agriculture [US]

USFQ – Universidad San Francisco de Quito [Ecuador]

USGS – United States Geological Survey [US]

USL – University of Sierra Leone [Sierra Leone]

USM – Universiti Sains Malaysia [Malaysia]

USM – University of Science Malaysia [Malaysia]

USM – University of Southern Mindanao [Philippines]

USM – University of Southern Mississippi [US]

USP – Universidade de São Paulo [Brazil]

USP – University of the South Pacific [Fiji]

USP – University of the South Pacific [Samoa]

USP Centre Tonga – University of the South Pacific, Tonga Centre [Tonga]

UST – University of Science and Technology [Ghana]

USU – Utah State University [US]

UT – Universidad del Tolima [Colombia]

UTA – University of Technology and Agriculture [Poland]

UTAD – Universidade de Trás-os-Montes e Alto Douro [Portugal]

UTK – University of Tennessee, Knoxville [US]

UTL – Universidade Tecnica de Lisboa [Portugal]

UU – Universiteit Utrecht [Netherlands]

ÚVc – Ústav vcelárstva [Slovakia]

UVEK – Eidgenössisches Departement für Umwelt, Verkehr, Energie und Kommunikation [Switzerland]

UVI – University of the Virgin Islands [Virgin Islands]

UVic – University of Victoria [Canada]

ÚVIK – Ústav vedeckých informácií a kniznica [Slovakia]

ÚVIS – Ústav vedeckych informací - ústrední knihovna [Czech Republic]

UVL – Univerzita veterinárskeho lekárstva [Slovakia]

UVM – University of Veterinary Medicine [Slovakia]

ÚVTIP – Ústav vedecko-technických informácií pre pôdohospodárstvo [Slovakia]

ÚVTIZ – Ústav védeckotechnickych informací pro zemedelství [Czech Republic]

UWA – University of Western Australia [Australia]

UWB – University of Wales Bangor [UK]

UWI – University of the West Indies [Trinidad and Tobago]

UWM – Uniwersytet Warminsko-Mazurski w Olsztynie [Poland]

UWRF – University of Wisconsin, River Falls [US]

UWS,H – University of Western Sydney, Hawkesbury [Australia]

UZ – University of Zimbabwe [Zimbabwe]

ÚZLK – Ústrední zemedelská a lesnická knihovna [Czech Republic]

ÚZPI – Ústav zemedelskych a potravinárskych informací [Czech Republic]

VASKnNIL – V.I. Lenin All-Union Academy of Agricultural Sciences [Uzbekistan]

VBC – Veterinary Biology Centre [Indonesia]

VBGA – VanDusen Botanical Gardens Association [Canada]

VCAH – Victorian College of Agriculture and Horticulture [Australia]

VECOL – Empresa Colombiana de Productos Veterinarios [Colombia]

Vet-Labs – Veterinary Research Laboratory [Kenya]

VFU – Veterinární a farmaceutická univerzita [Czech Republic]

VIAS – Victorian Institute of Animal Sciences [Australia]

VIMS – Virginia Institute of Marine Science [US]

VINITI – All-Russian Scientific and Technical Information Institute [Russia]

VINITI – Vserossiisky Institutt Nauchnoi i Tekhnicheskoi Informatsii [Russia]

VIS-K – Vcelárske informacné stredisko - kniznica [Slovakia]

VISCA – Visayas State College of Agriculture [Philippines]

VLA – Veterinary Laboratories Agency [UK]

VMI – Veterinary Medicine Institute [Ukraine]

VNAL – Vanuatu National Agricultural Library [Vanuatu]

VNIIMS – Vserossiiskii Nauchno-Issledovatelskii Institut Maslodeliya Syrodeliya [Russia]

VNIIPP – Vserossiysky Nauchno-Issledovatelsky Institut Ptitseperqbqty vayustchey Promyshlennosty [Russia]

563

VOPI – Roodeplaat Vegetable and Ornamental Plant Institute [South
Africa]

VPI – Virginia Polytechnic Institute
and State University [US]

VPKAS – Vivekananda Parvatiya
Krishi Anusandhan Shala [India]

VRA – Volta River Authority [Ghana]

VRI – Veterinary Research Institute
[Czech Republic]

VRI – Veterinary Research Institute
[Malaysia]

VRI – Veterinary Research Institute
[Sri Lanka]

VRL – Veterinary Research Laboratory [Ireland]

VSAU – Voronezh State Agricultural
University [Russia]

VSCHK – Vyzkumná stanice pro chov
koní [Czech Republic]

VSL&A – Virginia State Library and
Archives [US]

VSLD – Vysoká skola lesnícka a
drevárska [Slovakia]

VSP – Vysoká skola pol'nohospodárska [Slovakia]

VŠÚOZ – Výzkumný a šlechtitelský
ústav okrasného zahradnictví
[Czech Republic]

VSÚP – Výzkumný a šlechtitelský ústav pícninársky [Czech Republic]

VSZ – Vysoká škola zemedelská
[Czech Republic]

VTEI – Stredisko vedeckych, technickhych a ekonomickych informácií [Slovakia]

VTEI – Vedecko-technické a ekonomické informace [Czech
Republic]

VTEI – Vedecko-technickych informacní [Czech Republic]

VTEI – Vedeckotechnické informace
a knihovna [Czech Republic]

VTHBL – Veterinary Teaching Hospital Branch Library [US]

VTI – Oddeleni vedecko-technických
informací [Czech Republic]

VTI – Vedecko-technické Informácie
[Slovakia]

VÚB – Výzkumný ústav bramborárský [Czech Republic]

VÚCHS – Výzkumný ústav pro chov
skotu, s.r.o. [Czech Republic]

VÚEPP – Výskumný ústav ekonomiky polnohospodárstva a potravinárstva [Slovakia]

VÚEZVZ – Výzkumný ústav ekonomiky zemedelství a vyzivy
[Czech Republic]

VÚK – Výskumný ústav krmivársky
[Slovakia]

VÚLH – Výskumný ústav lesného
hospodárstva [Slovakia]

VÚLHM – Výzkumný Ústav Lesního
Hospodáství a Myslivosti
[Czech Republic]

VÚLP – Výskumný ústav lúk a pasienkov [Slovakia]

VÚMPP – Výzkumný ústav mlynského a pekárenského prumyslu
[Czech Republic]

VÚO – Výskumný ústav ovciarsky
[Slovakia]

VÚP – Výzkumný ústav pícninársky,
spol. s.r.o. Troubsko [Czech
Republic]

VÚPS a.s. – Výzkumný ústav pivovarský a sladarský a.s. [Czech
Republic]

VÚRH – Výzkumný ústav rybársky a
hydrobiologicky [Czech
Republic]

VÚRV – Výskumný ústav rastlinnej
výroby [Slovakia]

VÚTP – Výzkumný ústav tukového
prumyslu [Czech Republic]

VÚTPHP – Výskumný ústav travnych
porastov a horskeho polnohospodarstva [Slovakia]

VÚV – Výzkumný ústav vodohospodársky [Czech Republic]

VÚVc – Výzkumný ústav vcelarsky v
Dole [Czech Republic]

VÚVH – Výskumný ústav vodného
hospodárstva [Slovakia]

VÚVM – Výskumný ústav veterinárnej medicíny [Slovakia]

VÚVV – Výskumný ústav vinohradnícky a vinársky [Slovakia]

VÚVZ – Výzkumný ústav vyzivy
zvírat, s.r.o. [Czech Republic]

VÚZ – Výskumný ústav zeleninársky
[Slovakia]

VÚZE – Výzkumný ústav zemedelské
ekonomiky [Czech Republic]

VÚZT – Výzkumný ústav zemedelské
techniky [Czech Republic]

VÚZV – Výskumný ústav zivocísnej
výroby [Slovakia]

VÚZV – Výzkumný ústav zivocisné
výroby [Czech Republic]

VZ – Facultad de Medicina Veterinaria y Zootecnia [Colombia]

WAB – Wissenschaftliche Allgemeinbibliothek der Stadt Erfurt
[Germany]

WACRI – West African Cocoa Research Institute [Nigeria]

Wageningen UR – Wageningen University and Research Centre
[Netherlands]

WAI – Wollongbar Agricultural Institute [Australia]

WAICENT – World Agricultural Information Centre [Italy]

WAPDA – Water and Power Development Authority [Pakistan]

WARDA – West Africa Rice Development Association [Cote d'Ivoire]

WASPRU – West African Stored
Products Research Unit [Nigeria]

WAU – Wageningen Agricultural
University [Netherlands]

WAU – Warsaw Agricultural University [Poland]

WCARO – West and Central Africa
Regional Office [Senegal]

WCVM – Western College of Veterinary Medicine [Canada]

WGCF – Wondo Genet College of
Forestry [Ethiopia]

WHATT – Worldwide Hospitality and
Tourism Trends [UK]

WHOI – Woods Hole Oceanographic
Institution [US]

WIBDECO – Windward Islands Banana Development and Exporting Co. Ltd [Saint Lucia]

WII – Wildlife Institute of India
[India]

WINBAN – Windward Islands Banana Growers Association [Saint
Lucia]

WIRS – Welsh Institute of Rural
Studies [UK]

WL – Waterloopkundig Laboratorium
[Netherlands]

WL – WL/delft hydraulics
[Netherlands]

WPBS – Welsh Plant Breeding Station
[UK]

WPCSA – Welsh Pony and Cob
Society of America, Inc. [US]

WPI – Worcester Polytechnic Institute
[US]

WQIC – Water Quality Information
Center [US]

WRAC – West River Ag Center [US]

WRI – Water Research Institute
[Slovakia]

WRI – Water Resources Institute [US]

WRI – Wattle Research Institute
[South Africa]

WRI – World Resources Institute [US]

WRRC – Water Resource Research
Center [US]

WRRC – Western Regional Research
Center [US]

WRRI – New Mexico Water Resources Research Institute [US]

WRRI – Water Resources Research
Institute [Ghana]

WRRU – Water Resources Research
Unit [Ghana]

WSL – Eidgenössische Forschungsanstalt für Wald, Schnee und Landschaft [Switzerland]

WSRP – Wyzsza Szkola Rolniczo-Pedagogiczna [Poland]

WSU – Washington State University [US]

WSU TRIC – Washington State University at Tri-Cities [US]

WWF – World Wildlife Fund [Central African Republic]

WWF – World Wildlife Fund-United States [US]

WWF-Pakistan – World Wildlife Fund for Nature Pakistan [Pakistan]

XAU – Xinjiang Agricultural University [China]

XRIAS – Xiamen Research Institute of Agricultural Sciences [China]

YAF – Yunnan Academy of Forestry [China]

YAI – Yanco Agricultural Institute [Australia]

YCRS – Yellow Cattle Research Section [China]

YSFRI – Yellow Sea Fisheries Research Institute [China]

YSRIA – Yakutsk Scientific Research Institute of Agriculture [Russia]

YU – Yamagata University [Japan]

YUPSI – V.Ya. Yuryev Institute of Plant Science [Ukraine]

ZAAS – Zhejiang Academy of Agricultural Sciences [China]

ZADI – Zentralstelle für Agrardokumentation und Information [Germany]

ZBL – Deutsche Zentralbibliothek für Landbauwissenschaft [Germany]

ZBS – Zaklad Badania Ssaków [Poland]

ZBSRiL – Zaklad Badan Srodowiska Rolniczego i Lesnego [Poland]

ZBW – Deutsche Zentralbibliothek für Wirtschaftswissenschaften [Germany]

ZCHT-Chapula – Zambia Centre for Horticultural Training, Chapula [Zambia]

ZIB – Zentrale Informationsstelle und Bibliothek [Germany]

ZIDS – Zimbabwe Institute of Development Studies [Zimbabwe]

ZIN – Zaklad Informacji Naukowej [Poland]

ZINT – Zaklad Informacji Naukowo-Technicznej [Poland]

ZIS – Základné informacné stredisko [Slovakia]

ZKI – Zöldségtermesztési Kutató Intézet [Hungary]

ZOBINT – Zaklad Organizacji Badan i Informacji Naukowo-Technicznej [Poland]

ZRTC – Zonal Research and Training Centre [Tanzania]

ZU – Zhejiang University [China]

City Index for Selected Countries

The directory is organized alphabetically by country and then by city except for Australia, Brazil, Canada, China, Japan, and the United States which are organized alphbetically first by state/province and then by city. To locate cities in these six countries, use the following city index to identify the name of the state or province.

Australia

Adelaide – South Australia
Alice Springs – Northern Territory
Armidale – New South Wales
Attwood – Victoria
Beecroft – New South Wales
Bentley Delivery Centre – Western
   Australia
Boyer – Tasmania
Brisbane – Queensland
Bundoora – Victoria
Camden – New South Wales
Canberra – Australian Capital
   Territory
Clayton – Victoria
Cronulla – New South Wales
Darwin – Northern Territory
Dookie College – Victoria
East Perth – Western Australia
Ellinbank – Victoria
Fairfield – Victoria
Floreat Park – Western Australia
Gatton College – Queensland
Geelong – Victoria
Glen Osmond – South Australia
Griffith – New South Wales
Hamilton – Victoria
Heidelberg – Victoria
Henley Beach – South Australia
Highett – Victoria
Hobart – Tasmania
Horsham – Victoria
Hurtsville – New South Wales
Indooroopilly – Queensland
Kyabram – Victoria
Mackay – Queensland
Manly Vale – New South Wales
Mareeba – Queensland
Melbourne – Victoria
Merbein – Victoria
Mildura – Victoria
Moorooka – Queensland
Nedlands – Western Australia
New Town – Tasmania
North Beach – Western Australia
North Ryde – New South Wales
Northam – Western Australia
Orange – New South Wales

Parkes – Australian Capital Territory
Parkville – Victoria
Perth – Western Australia
Queenscliff – Victoria
Richmond – New South Wales
Rockhampton – Queensland
Roseworthy – South Australia
South Brisbane – Queensland
South Yarra – Victoria
St. Lucia – Queensland
Sydney – New South Wales
Tamworth – New South Wales
Tatura – Victoria
Terang – Victoria
'TOCAL' Paterson – New South
   Wales
Toowoomba – Queensland
Townsville – Queensland
Trangie – New South Wales
Wagga Wagga – New South Wales
Wanneroo – Western Australia
Warragul – Victoria
Werribee – Victoria
Wollongbar – New South Wales
Yanco – New South Wales

Brazil

Alegre – Espírito Santo
Aracaju – Sergipe
Bagé – Rio Grande do Sul
Belém – Pará
Belo Horizonte – Minas Gerais
Bento Gonçalves – Rio Grande do
   Sul
Boa Vista – Roraima
Botucatu – São Paulo
Brasília – Distrito Federal
Campina Grande – Paraíba
Campinas – São Paulo
Campo Grande – Mato Grosso do Sul
Colombo – Paraná
Concórdia – Santa Catarina
Corumbá – Mato Grosso do Sul
Cruz das Almas – Bahia
Curitiba – Paraná
Dourados – Mato Grosso do Sul
Florianópolis – Santa Catarina
Fortaleza – Ceará

Guaíba – Rio Grande do Sul
Itaguaí – Rio de Janeiro
Jaguariúna – São Paulo
João Pessoa – Paraíba
Juiz de Fora – Minas Gerais
Londrina – Paraná
Macapá – Amapá
Manaus – Amazonas
Niteroí – Rio de Janeiro
Nova Odessa – São Paulo
Parnaíba – Piauí
Passo Fundo – Rio Grande do Sul
Pelotas – Rio Grande do Sul
Petrolina – Pernambuco
Piracicaba – São Paulo
Planaltina – Distrito Federal
Ponta Grossa – Paraná
Porto Alegre – Rio Grande do Sul
Porto Velho – Rondônia
Recife – Pernambuco
Rio Branco – Acre
Rio de Janeiro – Rio de Janeiro
Salvador – Bahia
Santo Antônio de Goiás – Goiás
São Carlos – São Paulo
São Paulo – São Paulo
Seropédica – Rio de Janeiro
Sete Lagoas – Minas Gerais
Sobral – Ceará
Teresina – Piauí
Visosa – Minas Gerais
Vitória – Espírito Santo

Canada

Agassiz – British Columbia
Antigonish – Nova Scotia
Bamfield – British Columbia
Bedford – Nova Scotia
Brandon – Manitoba
Burlington – Ontario
Burnaby – British Columbia
Charlesbourg – Québec
Charlottetown – Prince Edward
   Island
Cochrane – Alberta
Corner Brook – Newfoundland
Darthmouth – Nova Scotia
Delta – British Columbia

Downsview – Ontario
Edmonton – Alberta
Fairview – Alberta
Fredericton – New Brunswick
Gaspé – Québec
Guelph – Ontario
Hamilton – Ontario
Harrow – Ontario
Hull – Québec
Humboldt – Saskatchewan
Kamloops – British Columbia
Kemptville – Ontario
Kentville – Nova Scotia
La Pocatière – Québec
Lacombe – Alberta
Leduc – Alberta
Lennoxville – Québec
Lethbridge – Alberta
London – Ontario
Longueuil – Québec
Mont-Joli – Québec
Montréal – Québec
Nanaimo – British Columbia
Nepean – Ontario
Niagara Falls – Ontario
North Vancouver – British Columbia
North York – Ontario
Olds – Alberta
Ottawa – Ontario
Peterborough – Ontario
Pointe Claire – Québec
Portage la Prairie – Manitoba
Québec – Québec
Regina – Saskatchewan
Rez-de-chaussée – Québec
Ridgetown – Ontario
Rimouski – Québec
Rouyn-Noranda – Québec
Sackville – New Brunswick
Saint Andrews – New Brunswick
Saint-Hyacinthe – Québec
Saint-Jean-Sur-Richelieu – Québec
Saint John's – Newfoundland
Sainte Anne-de-Bellevue – Québec
Sainte-Foy – Québec
Saskatoon – Saskatchewan
Sault Sainte Marie – Ontario
Summerland – British Columbia
Swift Current – Saskatchewan
Thunder Bay – Ontario
Toronto – Ontario
Truro – Nova Scotia
Vancouver – British Columbia
Vegreville – Alberta
Vermilion – Alberta
Victoria – British Columbia
Vineland Station – Ontario
Whitehorse – Yukon Territory
Winnipeg – Manitoba
Wolfville – Nova Scotia
Yellowknife – Northwest Territories

China

Anyang – Henan
Baoding – Hebei
Beijing – Beijing
Cangzhou – Hebei
Changchun – Jilin
Changsha – Hunan
Chengdu – Sichuan
Chongqing – Chongqing
Dalian – Liaoning
Danxian – Hainan
Dushan – Guizhou
Fuzhou – Fujian
Gongzhuling – Jilin
Guangzhou – Guangdong
Guiyang – Guizhou
Handan – Hebei
Hangzhou – Zhejiang
Harbin – Heilongjiang
Hefei – Anhui
Hohhot – Inner Mongolia
Hongyuan – Sichuan
Hulan – Heilongjiang
Jiamusi – Heilongjiang
Jiangjin – Sichuan
Jilin – Jilin
Jinan – Shandong
Kunming – Yunnan
Lanzhou – Gansu
Lhasa – Xizang
Linfen – Shanxi
Linzhi – Xizang
Lishui – Zhejiang
Luoyang – Henan
Nanchang – Jiangxi
Nanchong – Sichuan
Nanjing – Jiangsu
Nanning – Guangxi
Nanping – Fujian
Panjin – Liaoning
Panzhihua – Sichuan
Qingdao – Shandong
Qingzhou – Shandong
Qinhuangdao – Hebei
Qiqihaer – Heilongjiang
Shanghai – Shanghai
Shaoxing – Zhejiang
Shenyang – Liaoning
Shihezi – Xinjiang
Shijiazhuang – Hebei
Tai'an – Shandong
Taigu – Shanxi
Taiyuan – Shanxi
Tianjin – Tianjin
Urumqi – Xinjiang
Wuhan – Hubei
Xiamen – Fujian
Xianyang – Shaanxi
Xingcheng – Liaoning
Xining – Qinghai

Xinzhou – Shanxi
Xishuangbanna – Yunnan
Ya'an – Sichuan
Yangling – Shaanxi
Yangling District – Shaanxi
Yangzhou – Jiangsu
Yantai – Shandong
Yinchuan – Ningxia
Yongning – Ningxia
Yuanjiang – Hunan
Yuncheng – Shanxi
Zhangbei – Hebei
Zhangzhou – Fujian
Zhanjiang – Guangdong
Zhengzhou – Henan
Zhenjiang – Jiangsu

Japan

Abashiri – Hokkaido
Aichi, *see* Nagakute, Aichi – Aichi
Akita – Akita
Ami, Inashiki – Ibaraki
Anou, Age – Mie
Azuma, Sawa – Gunma
Chiba – Chiba
Ebetsu – Hokkaido
Fuchu – Tokyo
Fujisawa – Kanagawa
Fukuoka – Fukuoka
Fukuyama – Hiroshima
Habikino – Osaka
Haibara – Shizuoka
Higashi-Hiroshima – Hiroshima
Higashi-Ibaraki, *see* Uchihara,
    Higashi-Ibaraki – Ibaraki
Hirosaki – Aomori
Hiroshima, *see* Higashi-Hiroshima –
    Hiroshima
Ibaraki, *see* Uchihara, Higashi-
    Ibaraki – Ibaraki
Imizu, *see* Kosugi, Imizu – Toyama
Inashiki – Ibaraki; See also Ami,
    Inashiki – Ibaraki
Ishikawa, *see* Nonoichi, Ishikawa –
    Ishikawa
Iwata – Shizuoka
Joetsu – Niigata
Kagoshima – Kagoshima
Kamikawa, *see* Shintoku, Kamikawa
    – Hokkaido
Kashima – Ibaraki
Kida, *see* Mikicho, Kida – Kagawa
Kikuchi, *see* Nishigoshi, Kikuchi –
    Kumamoto
Kobe – Hyogo
Koriyama – Fukushima
Kosugi, Imizu – Toyama
Koyu, *see* Takanabe, Koyu –
    Miyazaki
Kumamoto – Kumamoto

Kunneppu, Toro – Hokkaido
Kurashiki – Okayama
Kuroishi – Aomori
Kushiro – Hokkaido
Kyoto – Kyoto
Machida – Tokyo
Maebashi – Gunma
Maki, Nishikanbara – Niigata
Masuho, Minamikoma – Yamanashi
Matsudo – Chiba
Matsue – Shimane
Matsuyama – Ehime
Mikicho, Kida – Kagawa
Minamikoma, *see* Masuho,
    Minamikoma – Yamanashi
Mitaka – Tokyo
Miyazaki – Miyazaki
Morioka – Iwate
Musashino – Tokyo
Nagakute, Aichi – Aichi
Nagano – Nagano
Naganuma, Yuubari – Hokkaido
Nagoya – Aichi
Naka – Ibaraki; *See also* Ohmiya,
    Naka – Ibaraki
Nakagami, *see* Nishihara, Nakagami
    – Okinawa
Nankoku – Kochi
Nansei, Watarai – Mie
Nasu, *see* Nishinasuno, Nasu –
    Tochigi
Niigata – Niigata
Nishigoshi, Kikuchi – Kumamoto
Nishihara, Nakagami – Okinawa
Nishikanbara, *see* Maki,
    Nishikanbara – Niigata
Nishinasuno, Nasu – Tochigi
Nonoichi, Ishikawa – Ishikawa
Obihiro – Hokkaido
Ohmiya, Naka – Ibaraki
Oku, *see* Ushimado, Oku – Okayama
Omiya – Saitama
Osato – Saitama
Saga – Saga
Sagamihara – Kanagawa
Sakai – Osaka
Sapporo – Hokkaido
Sawa, *see* Azuma, Sawa – Gunma
Sendai – Miyagi
Shimizu – Shizuoka
Shintoku, Kamikawa – Hokkaido
Shiogama – Miyagi
Takamatsu – Kagawa
Takanabe, Koyu – Miyazaki
Takikawa – Hokkaido
Tokyo – Tokyo
Tsu – Mie
Tsukuba – Ibaraki
Tsuruoka – Yamagata
Uchihara, Higashi–Ibaraki – Ibaraki
Ushimado, Oku – Okayama
Utsunomiya – Tochigi

Wako – Saitama
Watarai, *see* Nansei, Watarai – Mie
Yamaguchi – Yamaguchi
Yokohama – Kanagawa
Yuubari, *see* Naganuma, Yuubari –
    Hokkaido
Zentsuji – Kagawa

United States

Ada – Oklahoma
Aiea – Hawaii
Akron – Colorado
Albany – California
Albany – New York
Albuquerque – New Mexico
Alcorn State – Mississippi
Alexandria – Virginia
Alfred – New York
Alva – Oklahoma
Ames – Iowa
Amherst – Massachusetts
Anchorage – Alaska
Ankeny – Iowa
Ann Arbor – Michigan
Anselmo – Nebraska
Arcata – California
Ardmore – Oklahoma
Arkadelphia – Arkansas
Arlington – Virginia
Athens – Georgia
Atlanta – Georgia
Auburn – Alabama
Austin – Texas
Avondale – Pennsylvania
Baton Rouge – Louisiana
Beaverton – Oregon
Belle Glade – Florida
Beltsville – Maryland
Bemidji – Minnesota
Berkeley – California
Bethesda – Maryland
Birmingham – Alabama
Bismarck – North Dakota
Blacksburg – Virginia
Bloomington – Illinois
Boston – Massachusetts
Bottineau – North Dakota
Boyce – Virginia
Boylston – Massachusetts
Bozeman – Montana
Bradenton – Florida
Bronx – New York
Brookings – South Dakota
Brooklyn – New York
Brooksville – Florida
Buffalo – New York
Burlington – Vermont
Cambridge – Maryland
Cambridge – Massachusetts
Carbondale – Illinois

Carson City – Nevada
Champaign – Illinois
Chanhassen – Minnesota
Chapel Hill – North Carolina
Chazy – New York
Chevy Chase – Maryland
Chicago – Illinois
Chico – California
Cincinnati – Ohio
Claremont – California
Clarksville – Tennessee
Clay Center – Nebraska
Clemson – South Carolina
Cleveland – Ohio
Clinton – Iowa
Cobleskill – New York
Cold Spring Harbor – New York
College Park – Maryland
College Station – Texas
Columbia – Missouri
Columbus – Ohio
Conway – Arkansas
Cooperstown – New York
Corvallis – Oregon
Cottage Grove – Oregon
Dallas – Texas
Dania Beach – Florida
Davis – California
Decatur – Illinois
Delaware – Ohio
Delhi – New York
Denton – Texas
Denver – Colorado
DeRuyter – New York
Des Moines – Iowa
Detroit – Michigan
Douglas – Alaska
Dover – Delaware
Downers Grove – Illinois
Doylestown – Pennsylvania
Dunn Loring – Virginia
Durham – New Hampshire
Durham – North Carolina
East Hanover – New Jersey
East Lansing – Michigan
Ely – Nevada
Englewood – Colorado
Eugene – Oregon
Fairbanks – Alaska
Falcon Heights – Minnesota
Fargo – North Dakota
Farmingdale – New York
Fayetteville – Arkansas
Federal Way – Washington
Fergus Falls – Minnesota
Finley – Oklahoma
Flagstaff – Arizona
Flushing – New York
Fort Collins – Colorado
Fort Lauderdale – Florida
Fort Pierce – Florida
Fort Valley – Georgia

City Index for Selected Countries

Fort Wayne – Indiana
Fort Worth – Texas
Framingham – Massachusetts
Frankfort – Kentucky
Fremont – Michigan
Fresno – California
Gainesville – Florida
Galveston – Texas
Geneva – New York
Glencoe – Illinois
Gloucester Point – Virginia
Greenfield – Indiana
Greenport – New York
Greensboro – North Carolina
Griffin – Georgia
Groton – Connecticut
Gulf Breeze – Florida
Hamilton – Illinois
Hamilton – Montana
Harrisburg – Pennsylvania
Healdsburg – California
Helena – Montana
Hickory Corners – Michigan
Highlands – New Jersey
Hillsboro – New Hampshire
Homestead – Florida
Honolulu – Hawaii
Houghton – Michigan
Indianapolis – Indiana
Iowa City – Iowa
Ithaca – New York
Jefferson City – Missouri
Johnston – Iowa
Juneau – Alaska
Kansas City – Kansas
Kansas City – Missouri
Kennett Square – Pennsylvania
Kerrville – Texas
Kimberly – Idaho
Kingston – Rhode Island
Kirtland – Ohio
Knoxville – Tennessee
Kodiak – Alaska
La Crosse – Wisconsin
La Jolla – California
Lafayette – California
Lake Alfred – Florida
Lake Placid – Florida
Langston – Oklahoma
Laramie – Wyoming
Las Cruces – New Mexico
Lawai – Hawaii
Lawrence – Kansas
Lewisburg – Tennessee
Lexington – Kentucky
Lincoln – Massachusetts
Lincoln – Nebraska
Lisle – Illinois
Little Rock – Arkansas
Logan – Utah
Longmont – Colorado
Los Angeles – California

Lubbock – Texas
Lucas – Ohio
Macomb – Illinois
Madison – Wisconsin
Magnolia – Arkansas
Manassas – Virginia
Manhattan – Kansas
Mansfield – Ohio
Martin – Tennessee
Marysville – Ohio
Maryville – Missouri
Memphis – Tennessee
Miami – Florida
Middlebury – Connecticut
Midland – Michigan
Millbrook – New York
Milo – Iowa
Milwaukee – Wisconsin
Minneapolis – Minnesota
Mississippi State – Mississippi
Missoula – Montana
Modesto – California
Moline – Illinois
Monroe – Louisiana
Morehead – Kentucky
Morgantown – West Virginia
Morrilton – Arkansas
Morrisville – New York
Morton – Illinois
Moscow – Idaho
Mossville – Illinois
Murfreesboro – Tennessee
Murray – Kentucky
Muscatine – Iowa
Muscle Shoals – Alabama
Nacogdoches – Texas
Napa – California
Nashville – Tennessee
Natchitoches – Louisiana
National City – California
New Brunswick – New Jersey
New Haven – Connecticut
New Orleans – Louisiana
New York – New York
Newark – Delaware
Newport – Oregon
Newton – Utah
Norfolk – Virginia
Normal – Alabama
Normal – Illinois
North Grafton – Massachusetts
Oak Ridge – Tennessee
Ocean Springs – Mississippi
Ogden – Utah
Omaha – Nebraska
Orangeburg – South Carolina
Orono – Maine
Oxford – Mississippi
Painesville – Ohio
Palo Alto – California
Panama City – Florida
Park Ridge – Illinois

Parlier – California
Paul Smiths – New York
Peoria – Illinois
Petersburg – Virginia
Petersham – Massachusetts
Philadelphia – Pennsylvania
Phoenix – Arizona
Pine Bluff – Arkansas
Piscataway – New Jersey
Pittsboro – North Carolina
Pittsburgh – Pennsylvania
Pomona – California
Port Townsend – Washington
Portales – New Mexico
Prairie View – Texas
Princess Anne – Maryland
Princeton – New Jersey
Providence – Rhode Island
Provo – Utah
Pullman – Washington
Put–In–Bay – Ohio
Raleigh – North Carolina
Rapid City – South Dakota
Reelsville – Indiana
Reno – Nevada
Research Triangle Park – North
  Carolina
Richland – Washington
Richmond – California
Richmond – Virginia
River Falls – Wisconsin
Riverhead – New York
Riverside – California
Rochester – New York
Russellville – Arkansas
Ruston – Louisiana
Sacramento – California
Saint Joseph – Missouri
Salem – Oregon
San Diego – California
San Francisco – California
San Luis Obispo – California
San Marino – California
Santa Barbara – California
Santa Cruz – California
Savannah – Georgia
Schaumburg – Illinois
Scottsbluff – Nebraska
Seattle – Washington
Sidney – Montana
Sioux Falls – South Dakota
Solomons – Maryland
Somerset – New Jersey
Springfield – Missouri
St. Helena – California
St. Louis – Missouri
St. Paul – Minnesota
St. Petersburg – Florida
Stamford – Connecticut
Stephenville – Texas
Stillwater – Oklahoma
Stoneville – Mississippi

City Index for Selected Countries

Storrs – Connecticut
Syracuse – New York
Tallahassee – Florida
Tempe – Arizona
Tiburon – California
Tifton – Georgia
Tigard – Oregon
Toledo – Ohio
Trenton – New Jersey
Tucson – Arizona
Tulsa – Oklahoma

Tuskegee – Alabama
University Park – Pennsylvania
Urbana – Illinois
Vero Beach – Florida
Vienna – Virginia
Warrensburg – Missouri
Washington – District of Columbia
Weslaco – Texas
West Boothbay Harbor – Maine
West Lafayette – Indiana
West Palm Beach – Florida

Westerville – Ohio
Westminster – Colorado
Westminster – Maryland
Willow Springs – Missouri
Wilmington – Delaware
Winchester – Virginia
Woods Hole – Massachusetts
Wooster – Ohio
Worcester – Massachusetts
Wyndmoor – Pennsylvania

Institution Index

The Institution Index includes current, former, and variant names in English and/or whatever language or transliteration was provided by the respondent. Some inconsistencies exist because of differences in what information people provided on the forms. References are to entry numbers.
Country abbreviations: UK=United Kingdom; US = United States.

Ministère de l'Agriculture (Algeria) – 3; (Belgium) – 299,
306; (Cameroon) – 502; (Chad) – 652; (Mali) – 1812;
(Senegal) – 2705; (Tunisia) – 3098

Ministère de l'Agriculture, de l'Elevage, des Eaux et Forêts
et de la Pêche (Congo, Republic of the) – 890

Ministère de l'Agriculture, de l'Elevage et des Forêts
(Rwanda) – 2686

Ministère de l'Agriculture, de l'Elevage et du
Développement Rural (Gabon) – 1124

Ministère de l'Agriculture, des Eaux et Forêts (Guinea) –
1259

Ministère de l'Agriculture, des Pêcheries et de
l'Alimentation, Québec (Canada) – 601, 603, 608,
612, 617, 626

Ministère de l'Agriculture, du Développement Rural et des
Pêches Maritimes (Morocco) – 1907, 1908, 1915,
1916

Ministère de l'Agriculture, Elevage et Mer (Djibouti) – 981

Ministère de l'Agriculture et de l'Elevage (Burkina Faso) –
474; (Burundi) – 481, 482; (Niger) – 2007

Ministère de l'Agriculture et de la Pêche (France) – 1103,
1104

Ministère de l'Agriculture et de la Réforme Agraire
(Morocco) – 1907, 1908, 1911

Ministère de l'Agriculture et des Ressources Animales
(Burkina Faso) – 474; (Cote d'Ivoire) – 908

Ministère de l'Agriculture et du Développement Rural
(Chad) – 652

Ministère de l'Education Nationale (Burundi) – 483; (Haiti)
– 1266; (Senegal) – 2703, 2715

Ministère de l'Elevage et des Ressources Naturelles (Mali)
– 1811

Ministère de l'Enseignement Supérieur, de la Recherche et
de l'Innovation Technologique (Cote d'Ivoire) – 909

Ministère de l'Enseignement supérieur et de la Recherche
Scientifique (Madagascar) – 1772

Ministère de l'Environnement (Mali) – 1813

Ministère de l'Environnement et de la Protection de la
Nature (Senegal) – 2704

Ministère de l'Environnement, Québec (Canada) – 613

Ministère de l'Information, de la Culture et de la
Communication (Madagascar) – 1766

Ministère de la Prévision Economique et du Plan
(Morocco) – 1913, 1914, 1917

Ministère de la Production Agricole et de la Réforme
Agraire (Madagascar) – 1767, 1769

Ministère de la Production Animale (Madagascar) – 1768

Ministère de la Promotion Rurale (Central African
Republic) – 646

Ministère de la Recherche Scientifique (Cote d'Ivoire) –
909; (Gabon) – 1125; (Madagascar) – 1770

Ministère de la Recherche Scientifique et Technique
(Cameroon) – 501

Ministère de la Recherche Scientifique et Technologique
pour le Développement (Madagascar) – 1772

Ministère de la Santé (Morocco) – 1904

Ministère de la Science et de la Technologie (Congo,
Republic of the) – 891

Ministère délégue a l'Economie au Plan (Central African
Republic) – 647

Ministère des Affaires Sociales et de la Promotion de la
Femme et de la Solidarité Nationale (Central African
Republic) – 648

Ministère des Classes moyennes et de l'Agriculture
(Belgium) – 299, 300, 306

Ministère des Finances et du Plan (Niger) – 2005

Ministère des Ressources Naturelles, Québec (Canada) –
600, 627

Ministère du Développement et de l'Agriculture
(Guinea-Bissau) – 1262

Ministère du Développement Rural (Benin) – 334; (Congo,
Republic of the) – 890; (Guinea) – 1259; (Niger) –
2006; (Togo) – 3066

Ministère du Développement Rural et de l'Hydraulique
Villageoise (Togo) – 3078

Ministère du Plan (Morocco) – 1917

Ministere l'Agrikiltir ek Resours Maren (Seychelles) –
2724

Ministerie van Landbouw (Belgium) – 299, 324

Ministerie van Middenstand en Landbouw (Belgium) –
299, 321, 324

Ministeriet for Fødevarer, Landbrug og Fisheri (Denmark)
– 968, 971, 976, 978

Ministério da Agricultura, do Abastecimento e da Reforma
Agrária (Brazil) – 379

Ministério da Agricultura, do Desenvolvimento Rural e das
Pescas (Portugal) – 2288, 2296

Ministério da Agricultura e Desenvolvimento Rural
(Angola) – 7

Ministério da Agricultura e Pescas (Mozambique) – 1923

Ministerio de Agricultura (Colombia) – 879

Ministerio de Agricultura, Ganadería, Industria y Comercio
(Argentina) – 72

Ministerio de Agricultura, Ganadería y Desarrollo Rural
(Equatorial Guinea) – 1013

Ministerio de Agricultura, Pesca y Alimentación (Spain) –
2841, 2848

Ministerio de Agricultura y Cría (Venezuela) – 3879

Ministerio de Agricultura y Ganadería (Argentina) – 72;
(Costa Rica) – 902, 903; (El Salvador) – 1011;
(Paraguay) – 2156

Ministerio de Desarrollo Económico (Bolivia) – 347

Ministerio de la Agricultura (Cuba) – 922

Ministerstvo podohospodárstva SR (Slovakia) – 2749

Ministerstvo zemedelství (Czech Republic) – 948

Ministerstwo Rolnictwa i Gospodarki Zywnosciowej
(Poland) – 2261, 2276

Ministerstwo Rolnictwa i Rozwoju Wsi (Poland) – 2258,
2261, 2276

Ministerul Educatiei Nationale (Romania) – 2309

Ministry for Industry (Hungary) – 1281

Ministry for Industry and Commerce (Hungary) – 1281

Ministry of Agriculture (Bangladesh) – 221; (Belgium) –
299, 300, 324; (Bhutan) – 339, 340, 341, 342, 343,
344; (Botswana) – 360; (Brazil) – 379; (Cameroon) –
502; (China) – 696, 764, 802; (Colombia) – 879;
(Cook Islands) – 897; (Cuba) – 922; (Czech Republic)
– 948; (Dominica) – 982; (Ethiopia) – 1025, 1035;
(Ghana) – 1226; (Greece) – 1240, 1241; (Iran) –
1459; (Jordan) – 1670; (Kenya) – 1682, 1686, 1696,
1697, 1698; (Lesotho) – 1736; (Liberia) – 1742, 1743;
(Malawi) – 1774, 1775, 1778; (Malaysia) – 1792;

Monash University (Australia) – 147

Mondlane, Eduardo, *see* Eduardo Mondlane University (Mozambique) – 1920, 1921, 1922

Mongkut, King, *see* King Mongkut's Institute of Technology (Thailand) – 2994

Mono-Hy Sugar Beet Seed Inc. (US) – 3409

Monsanto (US) – 3367

Monsanto Company (US) – 3626

Monsanto Information Center (US) – 3626

Monsanto Information Organization (US) – 3626

Monsanto Information Resources and Services - Davis (US) – 3367

Montana State College (US) – 3631

Montana State Library (US) – 3633

Montana State University (US) – 3631

Monterrey Institute of Advanced Technological Studies, Queretaro Campus (Mexico) – 1864

Montgomery Library (US) – 3452

Montpellier National High School of Agronomy (France) – 1095

Montreal Botanical Garden (Canada) – 609

Moon, F. Franklin, *see* F. Franklin Moon Library (US) – 3696

Moredun Research Institute (UK) – 3299

Morehead State University (US) – 3540

Moretus Plantin University Library (Belgium) – 325

Morgan Library (US) – 3406

Morofsky, Walter F., *see* Walter F. Morofsky Memorial Library (US) – 3587

Morrell, J.B., *see* J.B. Morrell Library (UK) – 3325

Morris Arboretum (US) – 3755

Morris, John A., *see* John A. Morris Memorial Library (US) – 3538

Morris Library (US) – 3481

Morton Arboretum (US) – 3494

Morton, Sterling, *see* Sterling Morton Library (US) – 3494

Moscow Agricultural Academy, Kaluga Branch (Russia) – 2385

Moscow Breeding Experiment Station (Russia) – 2507

Moscow Hydro Land Reclamation Institute (Russia) – 2465

Moscow Land Tenure System Engineers Institute (Russia) – 2476

Moscow Scientific Research and Project Technological Institute of Land Use (Russia) – 2505

Moscow State Agricultural Engineering University (Russia) – 2466

Moskovskiji gidromeliorativnij institut (Russia) – 2465

Mount Albert Research Centre (New Zealand) – 1975

Mount Makulu Central Agricultural Research Station (Zambia) – 3894

Mountain State Agricultural College (Philippines) – 2193

Mouseio Goulandri Fysikis Istorias (Greece) – 1247

Mullins Library (US) – 3353

Münchner Entomologische Gesellschaft e.V. (Germany) – 1208

Munda Forest Research Library (Solomon Islands) – 2773

Municipal Museum of Natural History (Italy) – 1546

Municipal Museum of Natural Sciences (Spain) – 2819

Muresk Institute of Agriculture (Australia) – 178

Murmansk State Reindeer Breeding Experiment Station (Russia) – 2514

Murphy, D.A., *see* D.A. Murphy Library (US) – 3646

Murray, *see* Riverina-Murray Institute of Higher Education (Australia) – 106

Murray, J.K., *see* J.K. Murray Library (Australia) – 118

Murray State University (US) – 3541

Musée Royal de l'Afrique Centrale (Belgium) – 331

Museo Civico di Storia Naturale (Italy) – 1546

Museo Municipal de Ciencias Naturales (Spain) – 2819

Museu Paraense Emílio Goeldi (Brazil) – 392

Museum Library (Czech Republic) – 937

Museum of Czech Countryside (Czech Republic) – 937

Museum of Natural History (Denmark) – 965

Museum Victoria (Australia) – 161

Mustiala Agricultural College (Finland) – 1075

Mustiala Agricultural Institute (Finland) – 1075

Mustialan Maatalousoppilaitos (Finland) – 1075

Mustialanyksikkö (Finland) – 1075

Muzeum ceského venkova (Czech Republic) – 937

Mycolaiv Experiment Station of Feedstuff Production (Ukraine) – 3193

Myerscough College (UK) – 3311

Mykolaiiv State Agricultural Institute (Ukraine) – 3194

Mykolaiivski Silskogospodarskii Instytyt (Ukraine) – 3194

Mykolaivska Doslidna Stantsia Kormovyrobnytstva (Ukraine) – 3193

N.I. Vavilov All-Russia Scientific Research Institute of Plant Growing (Russia) – 2587

N.I. Vavilov All-Union Scientific Research Institute of Plant Growing (Turkmenistan) – 3122

N. Poushkarov Institute of Soil Science and Yield Programming (Bulgaria) – 466

Nabisco Brands Inc. (US) – 3653

Nacionalni institut za biologijo (Slovenia) – 2758

Naduruloulou Research Station (Fiji) – 1042

Naesgaard Agricultural College (Denmark) – 979

Næsgaard Agerbrugsskole (Denmark) – 979

Nafarroako Unibertsitate Publikoa (Spain) – 2845

Nagoya University (Japan) – 1556

Nakhon Sithammarat Saiyai (Thailand) – 3032

Nakhonphanom Agricultural College (Thailand) – 3027

Nakhonphanom College of Agriculture and Technology (Thailand) – 3027

Nakhonrajsrima Agricultural College (Thailand) – 3028

Nakhonrajsrima College of Agriculture and Technology (Thailand) – 3028

Nakornratchasima Experiment Station (Thailand) – 3029

Nakornratchasima Sericultural Research Center (Thailand) – 3029

Namibia Development Corporation (Namibia) – 1927

Namibian Agriculture and Water Information Centre (Namibia) – 1926

Namulonge Research Station (Uganda) – 3125

Nanchong Institute of Agricultural Sciences (China) – 824

Nanjing Agricultural College (China) – 766

Nanjing Agricultural University (China) – 765, 766

Nanjing Forestry University (China) – 767

Nanjing Institute for Agricultural Mechanization (China) – 764

Nanjing Technological College of Forest Products (China) – 767

Napa Valley Grape Growers Association (US) – 3378

Napa Valley Wine Library (US) – 3399

Narathiwat Agricultural College (Thailand) – 3035

National Center for Research on Cotton (Brazil) – 393

National Center for Research on Dairy Cattle (Brazil) – 389

National Center for Research on Goats (Brazil) – 373

National Center for Research on Grapes and Wine (Brazil) – 421

National Center for Research on Monitoring and Evaluating Environmental Impact (Brazil) – 439

National Center for Research on Rice and Beans (Brazil) – 382

National Center for Research on Soil (Brazil) – 418

National Center for Research on Soil Biology (Brazil) – 416

National Center for Research on Soybean (Brazil) – 401

National Center for Research on Tropical Agroindustry (Brazil) – 371

National Center for Research on Wheat (Brazil) – 423

National Center for Rural Development (Pakistan) – 2072

National Center for Scientific and Technical Documentation (Belgium) – 297

National Center of Agricultural Technology (El Salvador) – 1011

National Center of Documentation and Scientific and Technical Information (Congo, Republic of the) – 888

National Center of Water Information (Mexico) – 1855

National Centre for Genetic and Biotechnology Resources (Brazil) – 377

National Centre for Information on Agrarian Development (Sri Lanka) – 2866

National Centre for Marine Research (Greece) – 1245

National Centre for Mushroom Research and Training (India) – 1404

National Centre for Research (Sudan) – 2881

National Centre for Rural Development (Pakistan) – 2073

National Centre for Scientific and Technical Information (Belgium) – 297

National Centrum voor Wetenschappelijke en Technisch Documentrarie (Belgium) – 297

National Cereals Research Institute (Nigeria) – 2017

National Chia-yi Institute of Technology (Taiwan) – 2930, 2930

National Chung Hsing University (Taiwan) – 2945

National Coconut Research Center (Brazil) – 453

National College of Viticulture and Winemaking, Stauceni (Moldova) – 1893

National Corn Growers Association (US) – 3627

National Corporation of Forest Research and Fomentation (Colombia) – 880

National Cotton Council of America (US) – 3777

National Council for Research (Sudan) – 2881

National Council for Science and Technology (Kenya) – 1702

National Council for Scientific Research (Lebanon) – 1733; (Zambia) – 3903

National Dairy Research Institute (India) – 1320, 1368

National Department of Agriculture (South Africa) – 2799

National Diet Library (Japan) – 1652

National Diet of Japan (Japan) – 1652

National Direction of Forests and Water (Mali) – 1813

National Documentation Centre (Morocco) – 1917; (Saint Vincent and the Grenadines) – 2688; (Sudan) – 2881

National Documentation Centre - Agricultural Library (Dominica) – 983

National Documentation Centre, Library and Information Network (Pakistan) – 2078

National Education Ministry (Haiti) – 1266

National Enforcement Investigations Center (US) – 3403

National Environmental Information Center (Sri Lanka) – 2865

National Experimental University of Los Llanos Occidentales Ezequiel Zamora (Venezuela) – 3877

National Federation of Coffee Growers of Colombia (Colombia) – 881

National Fertilizer Development Centre (Pakistan) – 2074

National Fisheries Research Center - Great Lakes (US) – 3578

National Food and Nutrition Committee (Fiji) – 1057

National Food Research Institute (Japan) – 1592

National Forest Institute (Argentina) – 18

National Forest Library and Information Centre (India) – 1342

National Forestry Library (New Zealand) – 1990

National Forestry Research Center (Laos) – 1725

National Forestry Station (Portugal) – 2289

National Forestry Training Institute (Solomon Islands) – 2769

National Foundation of Agricultural Investigation (Venezuela) – 3888, 3889

National Free Library of Rhodesia (Zimbabwe) – 3913

National Free Library of Zimbabwe (Zimbabwe) – 3913

National Grange (US) – 3427

National Grassland Research Institute (Japan) – 1647

National Ground Water Association (US) – 3726

National Ground Water Information Center (US) – 3726

National Horticultural Research Institute (Nigeria) – 2022

National Hydrology Research Centre (Canada) – 637

National I-Lan Institute of Agriculture and Technology (Taiwan) – 2936

National I-Lan Institute of Technology (Taiwan) – 2936

National Industrial Association (Colombia) – 862

National Inland Fisheries Institute (Thailand) – 2987

National Institute for Agricultural Economics (Italy) – 1539

National Institute for Agricultural Research (Ecuador) – 989; (France) – 1085, 1089, 1090, 1091

National Institute for Agricultural Technology (Argentina) – 44, 71

National Institute for Amazonian Research (Brazil) – 368

National Institute for Biotechnology and Genetic Engineering (Pakistan) – 2063

National Institute for Fisheries Research and Development (Argentina) – 51

National Institute for Research on Jute and Allied Fibres Technology (India) – 1332

National Institute for Rural Development (Senegal) – 2715

National Institute for Scientific and Industrial Research (Zambia) – 3903

National Institute of Agricultural and Nutrition Research (Spain) – 2841

National Institute of Agricultural Botany (UK) – 3244

National Institute of Agricultural Engineering (Belgium) – 324

National Institute of Agricultural Research (France) – 1115; (Mexico) – 1851; (Morocco) – 1918, 1919; (Mozambique) – 1924; (Spain) – 2841; (Uruguay) – 3847, 3848

Subject Index

The majority of terms are consistent with the *CAB Thesaurus*. References are to entry numbers. Country abbreviations: UK=United Kingdom; US = United States.

Comprehensive Collections

Many institutions maintain comprehensive collections on agricultural information subjects. Rather than listing numerous subjects individually, they are noted here as primary sources of agricultural information in all fields.

Argentina 17, 30, 36, 39, 68, 73; **Australia** *New South Wales* 84, 102; *Queensland* 127; *South Australia* 136, 138; *Victoria* 164; **Bangladesh** 229; **Belarus** 261; **Belgium** 297, 310; **Benin** 335; **Brazil** *Ceará* 372; *Paraná* 402; *São Paulo* 443; **Bulgaria** 458; **Canada** *Nova Scotia* 563; *Ontario* 581; **Chile** 663, 674; **China** *Beijing* 696, 697; *Fujian* 700; *Gansu* 709; *Guangdong* 716; *Hebei* 730; *Heilongjiang* 739; *Hubei* 750; *Hunan* 752; *Jiangsu* 762; *Jiangxi* 771; *Jilin* 773, 777, 780; *Liaoning* 784, 787; *Ningxia* 790; *Shaanxi* 793; *Shandong* 804; *Sichuan* 821, 826; *Tianjin* 829; *Xinjiang* 833, 836; *Yunnan* 839; *Zhejiang* 846; **Costa Rica** 905; **Cote d'Ivoire** 909; **Cuba** 922; **Czech Republic** 925, 946; **Dominican Republic** 987; **Ecuador** 990; **Fiji** 1041; **Finland** 1077; **France** 1110; **Georgia** 1132; **Germany** 1159, 1160, 1220; **Ghana** 1236; **Greece** 1252; **India** 1319, 1363, 1377, 1386, 1409; **Indonesia** 1437; **Ireland** 1482; **Italy** 1534, 1546; **Japan** *Aichi* 1555, 1556; *Ehime* 1562; *Hiroshima* 1568; *Hokkaido* 1575; *Ibaraki* 1591, 1601; *Ishikawa* 1602; *Iwate* 1603; *Kagoshima* 1609; *Kyoto* 1616, 1617; *Mie* 1620; *Miyazaki* 1625, 1626; *Nagano* 1627; *Okinawa* 1634; *Shimane* 1641; *Tokyo* 1649, 1652, 1654; *Yamaguchi* 1665; **Kenya** 1696; **Korea, South** 1717; **Latvia** 1727; **Lebanon** 1733; **Lithuania** 1760; **Malaysia** 1797; **Mauritius** 1845, 1849; **Mexico** 1850, 1852, 1856, 1863; **Namibia** 1926; **Netherlands** 1956, 1958; **Nigeria** 2039; **Oman** 2054; **Pakistan** 2077; **Papua New Guinea** 2141; **Philippines** 2179, 2194, 2208, 2222; **Poland** 2229, 2235, 2243, 2276, 2281, 2282; **Portugal** 2288; **Puerto Rico** 2301; **Romania** 2310; **Russia** 2395, 2467, 2559, 2577, 2588, 2591, 2606, 2650; **Slovenia** 2760; **Solomon Islands** 2772; **South Africa** 2799; **Spain** 2817; **Sri Lanka** 2872; **Sudan** 2883; **Suriname** 2886; **Sweden** 2893, 2897, 2906; **Switzerland** 2922; **Taiwan** 2930, 2947, 2950, 2951; **Tanzania** 2966; **Thailand** 2993, 3015, 3019, 3041, 3053; **Tonga** 3083; **Trinidad and Tobago** 3093; **Tunisia** 3098; **Turkey** 3102; **UK** 3229, 3238, 3239, 3313, 3323; **Ukraine** 3153, 3160, 3166, 3190; **US** *California* 3376, 3385; *Florida* 3446; *Illinois* 3503; *Kentucky* 3533; *Maryland* 3551, 3553, 3557; *Michigan* 3584; *Missouri* 3618, 3620; *New Jersey* 3655; *South Carolina* 3767; *Virginia* 3807; *Washington* 3821; **Venezuela** 3884; **Zambia** 3894; **Zimbabwe** 3919

Acarology – **Canada** 596; **China** 698

Accounting – **Swaziland** 2890; **Ukraine** 3135

Acid Rain – **Hungary** 1278; **Poland** 2240

Acupuncture – **China** 772; **US** 3326

Administration – **Brazil** 376; **Colombia** 859, 867; **Mexico** 1859, 1859; **Senegal** 2706; **Tanzania** 2968

Advertising – **US** 3595

Aerial Photography – **US** 3771

Afforestation – **India** 1315, 1402; **Latvia** 1730; **Senegal** 2704; **Tanzania** 2963

Africa (*See also* East Africa; Southern Africa) – **Kenya** 1694, 1704; **Swaziland** 2891

African Horse Sickness – **US** 3680

African Swine Fever – **US** 3680

Agrarian Reform – **Colombia** 873, 876; **Peru** 2159; **Portugal** 2295; **US** 3839

Agribusiness (*See also* Business) – **Argentina** 12, 30, 32, 48; **Armenia** 77; **Australia** *Australian Capital Territory* 80, 82; *New South Wales* 87, 94, 96, 97, 101, 104, 106; *Queensland* 112, 118; *Victoria* 146, 153, 159, 168, 171; *Western Australia* 173, 176, 178; **Austria** 188; **Belarus** 232, 244, 246, 247, 252, 265, 269, 270, 273, 276, 277, 283, 288; **Benin** 336; **Botswana** 357; **Brazil** *Amazonas* 367; *Ceará* 371; *Paraná* 402; *Rio de Janeiro* 417; *Rio Grande do Sul* 421, 426; *São Paulo* 435; **Burkina Faso** 478; **Cameroon** 496, 497, 502; **Canada** *Alberta* 507, 511, 512, 513, 520; *Manitoba* 542; *Ontario* 569, 577; *Québec* 603, 612, 625; *Saskatchewan* 632, 634, 639, 640; **Chile** 658, 668; **China** *Beijing* 683, 696; *Fujian* 699, 703; *Guangxi* 718; *Hainan* 727; *Hebei* 728, 729; *Heilongjiang* 741; *Hunan* 753; *Qinghai* 791; *Xinjiang* 832; *Yunnan* 843; *Zhejiang* 845, 848; **Colombia** 857, 860, 866, 867, 874; **Costa Rica** 898, 903; **Croatia** 917, 920; **Czech Republic** 944; **Denmark** 973; **Egypt** 993; **Ethiopia** 1028, 1031; **Fiji** 1057; **Finland** 1068; **France** 1084, 1091, 1093, 1099, 1101, 1103, 1104; **Germany** 1152, 1155, 1191, 1193, 1202, 1216; **Greece** 1241, 1243; **Guatemala** 1257, 1258; **Honduras** 1269; **Hungary** 1282, 1287, 1294, 1297, 1299, 1302, 1308; **India** 1318, 1320, 1322, 1333, 1353, 1384, 1391, 1400, 1405; **Indonesia** 1411, 1412, 1417, 1419, 1427, 1431, 1435, 1436, 1443, 1447, 1450, 1451, 1453; **Iran** 1463; **Ireland** 1477, 1485; **Israel** 1495, 1496, 1498; **Italy** 1503, 1507, 1525, 1527, 1539; **Japan** *Aomori* 1558; *Kagawa* 1606; *Kanagawa* 1610; *Shizuoka* 1643; *Tochigi* 1648; *Tokyo* 1661; **Jordan** 1668, 1670;

Dietetic Foods (*See also* Foods) – **Germany** 1175; **Poland** 2248

Dietetics – **Germany** 1175; **Israel** 1495

Disease Control – **Australia** 123; **China** 823, 825

Disease Prevention – **Brazil** 378, 422; **Mexico** 1860; **Nicaragua** 2000

Diseases (*See also* Animal Diseases; Aujeszky's Disease; Bacterial Diseases; Bird Diseases; Cattle Diseases; Dog Diseases; Fish Diseases; Foot and Mouth Disease; Horse Diseases; Infectious Diseases; Marek's Disease; Newcastle Disease; Plant Diseases; Poultry Diseases; Respiratory Diseases; Skin Diseases; Uterine Diseases; Venereal Diseases) – **Taiwan** 2931

Diversification – **Antigua and Barbuda** 9; **US** 3553e

Diversity (*See also* Biodiversity) – **Canada** 538; **Kenya** 1703; **Thailand** 3051; **US** 3391

Documentation – **India** 1382; **Netherlands** 1955; **Slovenia** 2760

Dog Diseases (*See also* Diseases) – **Mexico** 1860

Dolphins – **US** 3373

Domestic Animals – **Austria** 196; **Ireland** 1483

Domestic Gardens (*See also* Gardens; Home Gardens) – **Ireland** 1483

Donkeys – **US** 3790

Drainage – **Australia** 167; **Brazil** 404; **Canada** 516; **Chile** 655; **Egypt** 999; **Hungary** 1306; **India** 1327, 1366, 1382; **Ireland** 1483; **Israel** 1492; **Italy** 1542; **Madagascar** 1767; **Netherlands** 1953; **Pakistan** 2078, 2095, 2096, 2130; **Romania** 2314; **Serbia and Montenegro** 2719; **Sierra Leone** 2729; **Slovakia** 2738; **Sri Lanka** 2868; **UK** 3238

Drinking Water (*See also* Water) – **US** 3484

Drought – **Canada** 629

Drought Resistance – **US** 3366

Drug Research – **US** 3411

Drugs – **Taiwan** 2950

Dry Beans – **Turkey** 3109; **US** 3646

Dry Farming (*See also* Farming) – **Australia** 157, 175; **Canada** 643; **India** 1347, 1351; **Kenya** 1703; **Swaziland** 2891; **US** 3341, 3349

Dry Farming Crops (*See also* Crops) – **US** 3646

Dry Lands – **Syria** 2927

Drying – **France** 1108; **Norway** 2048

Dryland Farming *see* Dry Farming

Dusts – **US** 3594

Dwarf Cultivars – **US** 3415

Dyes – **India** 1398

Earth Sciences – **Hungary** 1278; **New Caledonia** 1970

East Africa – **Kenya** 1704

EC *see* European Communities

Echinococcosis – **China** 706

Eco-agriculture *see* Organic Farming

Ecology (*See also* Agroecology; Chemical Ecology; Economic Ecology; Forest Ecology; Human Ecology; Landscape Ecology; Marine Ecology; Plant Ecology) – **Argentina** 54; **Australia** *New South Wales* 90; *Western Australia* 175; **Austria** 188, 190; **Belgium** 304, 315, 329; **Benin** 335; **Brazil** *Distrito Federal* 375; *Pará* 392; *Paraná* 395; *São Paulo* 448, 449, 451; **Bulgaria** 462, 468; **Burundi** 484; **Canada** *British Columbia* 525; *Québec* 609; **China** *Jiangsu* 767; *Shanxi* 815; *Sichuan* 825; **Colombia** 861, 871; **Congo, Republic of**

the 890; **Denmark** 975; **Ethiopia** 1024, 1035; **Finland** 1077; **France** 1096, 1104, 1105; **Germany** 1178; **Greece** 1247; **Hungary** 1278, 1307; **India** 1315, 1338, 1339, 1343, 1364, 1402, 1406; **Indonesia** 1428; **Israel** 1492, 1493; **Italy** 1542; **Madagascar** 1768; **Malaysia** 1783, 1795; **Mali** 1805; **Nepal** 1930; **Netherlands** 1945, 1957; **New Zealand** 1980; **Pakistan** 2123; **Papua New Guinea** 2155; **Poland** 2225, 2236, 2239, 2240, 2245, 2252, 2254, 2264, 2282; **Russia** 2461; **Senegal** 2705, 2706; **Slovakia** 2750, 2756; **Slovenia** 2758, 2759, 2761; **South Africa** 2778, 2798; **Spain** 2823, 2837, 2843; **Switzerland** 2913, 2914, 2919; **Taiwan** 2948, 2952; **Tanzania** 2963; **Tunisia** 3096; **UK** 3243, 3262, 3268, 3296; **Ukraine** 3128, 3147, 3161, 3162, 3221; **US** *Alaska* 3337; *California* 3362; *District of Columbia* 3429; *Florida* 3451; *Maryland* 3559; *New York* 3670, 3682; *Ohio* 3725; *Oregon* 3739; *Tennessee* 3779; *Virginia* 3809

Econometrics – **Germany** 1181

Economic Botany – **Canada** 609; **Cuba** 923; **Germany** 1195; **India** 1316; **Japan** 1561; **UK** 3314; **US** 3711

Economic Development – **Belgium** 330; **Burundi** 480; **Cambodia** 485; **Cameroon** 497; **Ethiopia** 1032; **Fiji** 1059; **Guatemala** 1256; **Mali** 1804; **Niger** 2005; **Senegal** 2703, 2706; **Thailand** 2990; **US** 3551, 3553e, 3603; **Zambia** 3896

Economic Ecology (*See also* Ecology) – **Colombia** 875

Economic Sociology (*See also* Sociology) – **Germany** 1185

Economics (*See also* Agricultural Economics; Development Economics; Forest Economics; Home Economics; Natural Resource Economics) – **Belgium** 295, 304; **Brazil** 419; **Canada** 511, 538; **Hungary** 1305; **Indonesia** 1444; **Italy** 1536; **Lesotho** 1736; **Morocco** 1913; **Philippines** 2207; **Suriname** 2886; **Turkey** 3113; **Ukraine** 3134, 3154; **US** 3531

Economics (Austria) – **Austria** 186

Ecophysiology (*See also* Physiology) – **Germany** 1217

Ecosystems (*See also* Systems) – **Colombia** 875; **Philippines** 2176; **US** 3559

Ecotoxicity Tests – **Belgium** 307

Ecotoxicology – **Poland** 2239; **Switzerland** 2922

Edaphic Factors – **Mexico** 1853

Edible Fungi (*See also* Fungi) – **China** 703, 810; **New Zealand** 1981

Edible Species – **Japan** 1605

Education (*See also* Education/Extension) – **Belgium** 291, 295, 298, 316; **Czech Republic** 951; **Estonia** 1017; **Greece** 1247; **Hungary** 1280, 1281; **India** 1379; **Iran** 1464; **Mali** 1821; **Mauritius** 1846; **Poland** 2278; **Portugal** 2285; **Russia** 2355; **Slovakia** 2749; **US** 3392, 3720

Education/Extension (*See also* Agricultural Education; Education; Environmental Education; Nutrition Education; Safety Education) – **Argentina** 12, 32, 48, 50; **Australia** *Australian Capital Territory* 82; *New South Wales* 87, 94, 96, 97, 101, 104; *Queensland* 112, 117, 118, 122; *Victoria* 148, 154, 168; *Western Australia* 173, 176, 178; **Austria** 188; **Bangladesh** 210, 212, 214, 221, 222, 225, 227; **Belarus** 232, 244, 246, 247, 252, 265, 269, 270, 273, 276, 277, 283, 288; **Belgium** 291, 295, 296, 298, 316; **Benin** 337; **Bolivia** 346; **Botswana** 355, 357, 360, 362; **Brazil** *Bahia* 370; *Distrito Federal*

694

Rapeseed – **Brazil** 423

Rare Books (Herbals) – **US** 3718

Rare Breeds – **US** 3701

Rattan – **Malaysia** 1789

Raw Materials – **Georgia** 1128

Reafforestation *see* Afforestation

Real Estate *see* Property

Reclamation – **Belarus** 235, 256, 285; **Canada** 519, 520; **China** 742, 761; **Estonia** 1016; **Georgia** 1136; **India** 1371; **Ireland** 1475; **Kazakhstan** 1680; **Pakistan** 2096 **Russia** 2328, 2379, 2461, 2465, 2525, 2567, 2637, 2658; **Ukraine** 3162; **Uzbekistan** 3864

Recreation (*See also* Outdoor Recreation) – **Netherlands** 1959; **UK** 3236, 3258; **US** 3702

Red Sea – **Israel** 1491

Reforestation *see* Afforestation

Refrigeration – **France** 1102; **Russia** 2474

Regeneration – **US** 3375

Regional Development – **Ethiopia** 1032

Regional Planning (*See also* Planning) – **Austria** 188, 193; **Belgium** 295; **Ethiopia** 1032; **Netherlands** 1959

Regional Policy (*See also* Policy) – **Austria** 186

Reindeer – **Russia** 2435; **Sweden** 2900

Remote Sensing (*See also* Satellite Surveys) – **Canada** 538; **China** 737; **Hungary** 1280; **India** 1382; **Malaysia** 1790; **New Caledonia** 1970; **Russia** 2658; **US** 3342, 3606

Renewable Resources (*See also* Resources) – **Botswana** 358; **Canada** 620; **Greece** 1243; **New Zealand** 1986; **Russia** 2447

Reproduction – **Argentina** 21; **Australia** 124; **Brazil** 428; **Poland** 2231; **Slovakia** 2744, 2750; **South Africa** 2781; **UK** 3315; **US** 3609

Research (*See also* Agricultural Research; Drug Research; Farming Systems Research; Food Research; Government Research; Organization of Research; Resistance Research) – **Madagascar** 1764

Research and Development *see* Research

Research Institutes – **Netherlands** 1944

Research Management (*See also* Management) – **Philippines** 2180

Research Policy (*See also* Policy) – **India** 1352; **Netherlands** 1944; **US** 3553g

Reserved Areas – **Poland** 2240

Resettlement *see* Settlement

Residues (*See also* Pesticide Residues; Wood Residues) – **Canada** 596

Resins – **India** 1398

Resistance Research – **Germany** 1142

Resorcinols – **China** 706

Resource Conservation – **Brazil** 391; **South Africa** 2783

Resource Development – **Mali** 1813; **South Africa** 2812

Resource Management (*See also* Management) – **Colombia** 853; **India** 1403; **Netherlands** 1955; **Philippines** 2199; **US** 3738, 3840

Resources (*See also* Aquatic Resources; Forest Resources; Genetic Resources; Human Resources; Land Resources; Marine Resources; Natural Resources; Plant Genetic Resources; Renewable Resources; Soil Resources; Water Resources) – **Australia** 137

Respiratory Diseases (*See also* Diseases) – **Mexico** 1860; **US** 3673

Retail Food Industry (*See also* Industry) – **US** 3610

Rhododendron – **US** 3415, 3819

Rice – **Australia** 109; **Bangladesh** 223; **Brazil** 365, 366, 382, 407, 408; **Cambodia** 486; **China** 713, 753, 764, 777, 782, 828, 844, 848; **Colombia** 853, 865; **Cote d'Ivoire** 913; **Guatemala** 1257; **India** 1340; **Indonesia** 1447; **Italy** 1548; **Japan** 1557, 1587, 1588; **Mali** 1834; **Nigeria** 2017, 2021; **Pakistan** 2061, 2082; **Philippines** 2204; **Russia** 2415; **Sierra Leone** 2730; **Suriname** 2885; **Thailand** 2999, 3036, 3040, 3042, 3044, 3047; **Ukraine** 3160; **US** 3353, 3365, 3439, 3542; **Uzbekistan** 3869

River Buffaloes *see* Buffaloes

Rivers – **Egypt** 999

Root Crops – **Fiji** 1062; **Guadeloupe** 1254; **India** 1407; **Malawi** 1778; **Philippines** 2169; **Trinidad and Tobago** 3086; **US** 3333; **Venezuela** 3888, 3889

Root Crops (Andean Group) – **Peru** 2162

Rootstocks – **Romania** 2321

Rosin – **China** 715

Rotations – **Russia** 2628

Rubber – **China** 717, 727, 843; **India** 1333; **Malaysia** 1791; **Sri Lanka** 2862; **Thailand** 3001, 3003; **UK** 3275

Rubber Plants – **Brazil** 365, 366

Rubber Trees (*See also* Trees) – **Brazil** 367

Rumen – **Poland** 2231

Ruminant Feeding (*See also* Feeding) – **China** 705

Ruminants – **New Zealand** 1986; **Romania** 2305; **Trinidad and Tobago** 3086; **UK** 3299; **Zimbabwe** 3912

Rural Affairs *see* Rural Sociology

Rural Business Administration (*See also* Business) – **Australia** 168

Rural Communities – **UK** 3230

Rural Development – **Bangladesh** 210; **Belgium** 293; **Brazil** 396, 397, 404; **Cameroon** 497, 497; **Canada** 629; **Chad** 653; **Colombia** 876; **Ethiopia** 1019; **Fiji** 1059; **France** 1100; **India** 1327; **Italy** 1533; **Korea, South** 1716; **Madagascar** 1764, 1770; **Malawi** 1777; **Mali** 1802, 1812, 1817, 1834, 1835; **Mexico** 1853, 1866; **Mozambique** 1921; **Nepal** 1930; **Netherlands** 1935, 1937; **Pakistan** 2067, 2072, 2073, 2114; **Peru** 2159; **Portugal** 2295; **Senegal** 2702; **South Africa** 2789; **Sri Lanka** 2866, 2867; **Sudan** 2880, 2884; **Swaziland** 2890; **Tunisia** 3096; **US** 3360, 3553e, 3839

Rural Development (Africa) – **Germany** 1185

Rural Development (Asia) – **Germany** 1185

Rural Development Projects *see* Development Projects

Rural Economy – **Algeria** 2; **Australia** 168; **Brazil** 379, 399, 405; **Burundi** 484; **Cameroon** 496; **Canada** 614; **Central African Republic** 649, 650; **Congo, Republic of the** 889; **Cote d'Ivoire** 913; **France** 1114; **Guadeloupe** 1254; **Guinea** 1261; **Mali** 1802; **Morocco** 1908; **Niger** 2006; **Philippines** 2207; **Thailand** 2981; **Venezuela** 3881

Rural Industry (*See also* Industry) – **Finland** 1075

Rural Law (*See also* Law) – **Brazil** 397; **Germany** 1197; **Switzerland** 2913

Rural Life Photography – **US** 3511

Rural Planning (*See also* Planning) – **Cote d'Ivoire** 912; **Spain** 2860; **Switzerland** 2913; **UK** 3230

Rural Society – **US** 3417

Rural Society (History – 19th Century) – **US** 3560